"*Touched by Christ* is a monumental achievement. Lawrence Feingold provides a comprehensive study of Catholic sacramental theology and practice informed by Scripture, the Fathers, St. Thomas Aquinas, and the Magisterium of the Catholic Church. This volume touches on all the major areas of sacramental theology from the institution of the sacraments by Christ to topics such as sacramental causality, grace, matter, form, validity, liceity, and fruitfulness. I know of no other work on the sacraments that is so comprehensive, well-informed, and theologically sound as this one."

ROBERT FASTIGGI
Bishop Kevin M. Britt Chair of Dogmatic Theology and Christology,
Sacred Heart Major Seminary

"Feingold brings his talent for thoroughness and clarity to this brilliant treatment of the sacramental economy. In contradiction to modernity's general loss of the sacramental vision, this volume reestablishes the fittingness of sacraments on the grounds of Christology and anthropology. It brings us to a renewed spiritual understanding of the sacramental life by conjoining historical sources, theological questions, and pastoral concerns. Superb for the classroom or for personal theological study."

DAVID W. FAGERBERG
Professor of Theology, University of Notre Dame

"Larry Feingold has done it yet again! Accessible, erudite, and engaging, this book should be assigned in all colleges and seminaries as the go-to introduction to the sacraments of the Catholic Church. Everyone from parish study groups to expert scholars will benefit from its wide-ranging erudition, concise clarity, and profound faith. Instructive and inspiring!"

MATTHEW LEVERING
James N. and Mary D. Perry Jr. Chair of Theology,
Mundelein Seminary

"The Catholic Church has been waiting for this volume for over a generation. Professor Lawrence Feingold has distinguished himself—yet again—as one of the finest sapiential pedagogues among the guild of Catholic theologians today. In *Touched by Christ*, Feingold presents the totality of the Church's sacramental doctrine in one self-contained volume without decoupling the seven sacraments from their general foundation or offering a general theology of the sacraments without proper reference to each of the seven. There is no single-volume treatment of the sacraments in print today that accomplishes as much as *Touched by Christ*. With the level of erudition and fidelity that is manifest on every page, this volume is sure to be the standard-bearer and common point of reference for students and scholars of sacramental theology for years to come."

ROGER W. NUTT
Provost, Ave Maria University

TOUCHED
BY CHRIST

TOUCHED BY CHRIST

THE SACRAMENTAL ECONOMY

LAWRENCE FEINGOLD

EMMAUS
ACADEMIC

www.emmausacademic.com
Steubenville, Ohio

EMMAUS
A C A D E M I C

Steubenville, Ohio
www.emmausacademic.com
A Division of The St. Paul Center for Biblical Theology
Editor-in-Chief: Scott Hahn
1468 Parkview Circle
Steubenville, Ohio 43952

Library of Congress Cataloging-in-Publication Data applied for

ISBN: 978-1-64585-096-0 (hard cover) / 978-1-64585-097-7 (paperback) /
978-1-64585-098-4 (ebook)

Unless otherwise noted, Scripture quotations are taken from The Revised Standard Version
Second Catholic Edition (Ignatius Edition) Copyright © 2006 by the Division of Christian Education of the National Council of the Churches of Christ in the United States of
America. Used by permission. All rights reserved.

Excerpts from the Catechism of the Catholic Church, second edition, copyright © 2000,
Libreria Editrice Vaticana--United States Conference of Catholic Bishops, Washington,
D.C. Noted as *CCC* in the text.

Imprimatur: In accordance with CIC 827, permission to publish has been granted on June 9,
2020, by the Most Reverend Mark S. Rivituso, Auxiliary Bishop, Archdiocese of St. Louis.
Permission to publish is an indication that nothing contrary to Church teaching is contained
in this work. It does not imply any endorsement of the opinions expressed in the publication;
nor is any liability assumed by this permission.

Cover image: *Christ Healing the Blind Man* (ca. 1645), Eustache Le Sueur, Prussian Palaces
and Gardens Foundation Berlin-Brandenburg

Cover design and layout by Emily Demary

To Mary, Mother of the Church,
and to Marsha, my wife, who spent countless hours
editing and improving the text.

"What was to be seen of our Redeemer has passed over into
the Sacraments."
St. Leo the Great, *Sermon* 74.2

Contents

ABBREVIATIONS   XXVII

INTRODUCTION   XXXI

   THE INCARNATION AND THE SACRAMENTS   XXXI

    The Good Samaritan and the Sacraments   xxxiv

    *The Blood and Water Flowing from the Side of
     Christ Represent the Sacraments*   XXXV

   GOAL OF THE WORK   XXXVIII

    Principal Sources   xxxix

   PLAN OF THE WORK   XI

**PART I. FITTINGNESS AND INSTITUTION OF
THE SACRAMENTS**   1

CHAPTER 1. FITTINGNESS OF THE
SACRAMENTAL ECONOMY   3

   THE SACRAMENTAL ECONOMY   3

    Old Testament Prophecies of the Sacramental Economy   4

    Centrality of the Sacraments in the Life of the Church 7

   WHY DID CHRIST INSTITUTE A SACRAMENTAL
   ECONOMY USING SENSIBLE SIGNS?   9

    *Sanctification through Sensible Signs Mirrors Man's
     Place in Creation*   10

    *Sanctification through Sensible Signs Is Fitting for
     Man's Natural Way of Knowing*   12

     The Sacraments Mirror Human Culture   14

    The Sacraments Mirror the Incarnation   15

    The Trinitarian Movement of the Sacraments   17

    *The Sacraments Mirror the Church, Giving Her
     Visible Structure and Invisible Life*   17

    *Sanctification through Sensible Signs Heals Man
     Where He Is Frequently Tempted*   20

Fittingness of the Sacramentality of Penance   22

Faith and the Sacraments   26

Sacraments and Typology   28

*The Sacraments Represent Sanctification in the
Past, Present, and Future*   29

STUDY QUESTIONS   35

SUGGESTIONS FOR FURTHER READING   36

CHAPTER 2. WHAT ARE SACRAMENTS?
DEVELOPMENT OF THE DEFINITION OF SACRAMENT   37

SACRAMENT AND MYSTERY   38

The Pauline Concept of "Mystery"   38

Distinction between Sacrament and Mystery   40

PATRISTIC AND MEDIEVAL DEFINITIONS OF SACRAMENT   42

Augustinian Definition of Sacrament   44

*Definitions of Sacrament in the Latin Tradition
after Augustine*   46

*Aquinas's Definition of Sacrament: Signs of the
Sacred Realities That Sanctify Man*   49

*St. Thomas's Definition of Sacrament in His
Commentary on the* Sentences   49

St. Thomas's Definition of Sacrament in the
Summa theologiae   51

PROTESTANT DEFINITIONS OF SACRAMENT   59

DEFINITION OF SACRAMENT AFTER THE
COUNCIL OF TRENT   62

*Summary: Four Fundamental Elements in the
Definition of the Sacraments of the New Covenant*   63

STUDY QUESTIONS   66

SUGGESTIONS FOR FURTHER READING   66

CHAPTER 3. THE SEVEN SACRAMENTS   69

FITTINGNESS OF THE SEVEN SACRAMENTS AND
THEIR HARMONY   74

*The Seven Sacraments Are Analogous to Seven
Natural Necessities of Life*   74

On the Notion of Maturity in St. Thomas's Analogy   78

Why Can Some Sacraments Be Repeated and Not Others?   81

*The Seven Sacraments Align with the Seven Principal
Virtues and with Remedies for the Effects of Sin*   82

The Seven Sacraments and the Holiness of the Church   83

The Seven Sacraments and the Communion of the Church   85

The Sacraments and the New Covenant   87

The Sacraments and the Maternity of the Church   89

THE EUCHARIST IS THE SUMMIT OF THE SACRAMENTAL
ECONOMY   90

THE CHURCH HAS THE NATURE OF A SACRAMENT   94

STUDY QUESTIONS   98

SUGGESTIONS FOR FURTHER READING   98

CHAPTER 4. CHRIST INSTITUTED THE SACRAMENTS   99

SCRIPTURAL WITNESS OF JESUS'S INSTITUTION OF THE
SACRAMENTS   99

Institution of Baptism   100

Institution of the Eucharist   101

Institution of Holy Orders at the Last Supper   102

Institution of Penance   103

Promise of the Gift of the Spirit   103

Anointing of the Sick   104

Matrimony   105

IN HOW SPECIFIC A MANNER DID CHRIST INSTITUTE
THE SACRAMENTS?   106

Substance of the Sacraments   108

*Two Senses in Which Something Is Said to Be a Necessary
or Essential Element of a Sacrament*   111

*The Liturgy of Israel and the Matter and Form of the
Sacraments*   113

REASONS OF FITTINGNESS FOR THE INSTITUTION OF
THE SACRAMENTS BY CHRIST   114

The Sacraments Extend the Reach of Christ's Humanity   114

The Sacraments Are Instruments of the Divine Omnipotence   115

Christ Alone Merited the Grace Given by the Sacraments   116

The Sacraments Send the Holy Spirit   116

The Sacraments Give Birth to and Build the Church   117

Modernist View of the Institution of the Sacraments   121

Rahner's Theory on the Implicit Institution of the
Sacraments by Christ   122

STUDY QUESTIONS   128

SUGGESTIONS FOR FURTHER READING   128

PART II. THE OUTWARD SACRAMENTAL SIGN   **131**

CHAPTER 5. MATTER AND FORM OF THE SACRAMENTS   133

FOUR COMPONENTS OF THE SACRAMENTAL SIGN:
MATTER AND FORM, MINISTER AND SUBJECT   134

"MATTER" AND "FORM" APPLIED TO THE SACRAMENTS   135

SYMBOLISM OF THE MATTER OF THE SACRAMENTS   138

Complex Symbolism of the Baptismal Immersion   140

Confirmation/Chrismation   142

The Bread and Wine in the Eucharist   145

Why Oil for Anointing of the Sick?   147

Laying on of Hands in Ordination   148

What Is the Matter for Reconciliation?   151

Matter and Form in Matrimony   152

SACRAMENTAL FORM   154

Change and Development in Sacramental Form   155

The Form of Baptism   155

The Form of the Eucharist   159

The Form of Confirmation   162

The Form of Holy Orders   164

The Form of Penance   166

The Form of Anointing of the Sick   168

Invalidity of Sacramental Form Due to Substantial
Change of Meaning   169

STUDY QUESTIONS   172

SUGGESTIONS FOR FURTHER READING   172

CHAPTER 6. THE SUBJECT AND THE MINISTER OF
THE SACRAMENTS   175

1. INTENTION OF THE SACRAMENTAL SUBJECT AND
MINISTER   175

Actual, Virtual, and Habitual Intention   182

Mormon Baptism Lacks Proper Intention to
    Do What the Church Does   185

2. NECESSARY CONDITIONS IN THE RECIPIENT
    OF THE SACRAMENTS   187

Living and Baptized; Conditional Administration   187

Conditions Required in the Subject of the Sacraments
    of Healing   188

Why Gender Complementarity for the Sacrament
    of Matrimony?   189

Why Male Gender for the Sacrament of Holy Orders?   195

Infallible Status of This Teaching: Ordinatio Sacerdotalis   201

Marian and Petrine Dimensions of the Church   203

When Can Sacraments Be Administered to Non-Catholics?   204

3. NECESSARY CONDITIONS IN THE MINISTER OF
    THE SACRAMENTS   206

Holy Orders Configures the Minister to Christ   206

Minister of the Eucharist   208

Minister of Holy Orders   208

Minister of Confirmation   209

Minister of the Sacrament of Reconciliation   213

Minister of the Sacrament of Anointing of the Sick   215

Protestant Rejection of Holy Orders   217

CONCLUSION: THE PERSONAL DIMENSION OF THE
    SACRAMENTAL SIGN   219

STUDY QUESTIONS   220

SUGGESTIONS FOR FURTHER READING   221

PART III. THE EFFECTS OF THE SACRAMENTS   **223**

CHAPTER 7. SACRAMENTAL CHARACTER   225

DEVELOPMENT OF THE THEOLOGY OF SACRAMENTAL
    CHARACTER   225

St. Augustine's Distinction between the Sacrament,
    the Reality of the Sacrament, and the Abiding Character   225

Biblical Foundation of Sacramental Character   226

The Patristic Notion of Sacramental Seal   229

Analogy of the Royal Seal 229

Three Meanings of the Seal 232

The Rebaptism Controversy and Sacramental Character 235

St. Thomas Aquinas on the Nature of Sacramental Character 241

Distinguishing Mark of Christian Identity 242

Priestly Mission 244

Spiritual Power 245

Ontological Reality of Character 246

Indelible Character 249

Magisterial Teaching on Sacramental Character 252

HOW THE THREE CHARACTERS DIFFER 254

Baptismal Character 255

Character of Confirmation 256

Distinction between the Ministerial and Common
Priesthood: An Effect of Sacramental Character 260

Character of Holy Orders 262

Three Grades of Holy Orders 263

THE GRANDEUR OF SACRAMENTAL CHARACTER 268

The Trinitarian Dimension of Sacramental Character 268

Character: A Solemn and Consoling Doctrine 270

STUDY QUESTIONS 270

SUGGESTIONS FOR FURTHER READING 272

CHAPTER 8. RES ET SACRAMENTUM 273

RES ET SACRAMENTUM IN THE EUCHARIST 273

The Three Levels in the Eucharist 273

Is the Res et Sacramentum of the Eucharist Christ's
Body and Blood, or Deeper Incorporation into
the Church? 278

RES ET SACRAMENTUM APPLIED TO THE SACRAMENTS
THAT GIVE CHARACTER 279

RES ET SACRAMENTUM IN MATRIMONY 280

RES ET SACRAMENTUM IN ANOINTING OF THE SICK 283

RES ET SACRAMENTUM IN THE SACRAMENT OF PENANCE 287

Thesis of Peter Lombard and St. Thomas: Interior
Penance Is the Res et Sacramentum 288

Alternative Proposal: Reconciliation with the Church
  Is the Res et Sacramentum   291

Proposal: The Res et Sacramentum *of Penance Is a*
  Configuration to Christ Who Did Penance for Sin   295

  New Identity in Christ   295

  New Ecclesial Mission   297

  Spiritual Power to Bring Forth Fruits of Repentance
    in the Church   298

REFLECTIONS ON THE THREE LEVELS OF THE
SACRAMENTS AND THE IMPORTANCE OF THE
RES ET SACRAMENTUM   300

  Differing Durability of the Three Levels of the
    Sacraments   300

  Licitness, Validity, and Fruitfulness   301

  Christological and Ecclesial Dimensions of the
    Res et Sacramentum   302

STUDY QUESTIONS   304

SUGGESTIONS FOR FURTHER READING   304

CHAPTER 9. THE GIFTS OF GRACE COMMUNICATED
BY THE SACRAMENTS   307

  OUR SUPERNATURAL ENDOWMENT   308

    The Gratuitousness of Grace with Respect to Nature   308

    Obediential Potency Specific to the Rational Creature
      Made in the Image of God   310

    The Distinction between Sanctifying Grace and
      Actual Grace   312

    Actual Grace: Operative and Cooperative   314

  SANCTIFYING GRACE AND THE HABITUAL GIFTS
  THAT FLOW FROM IT   315

    Sanctifying Grace as a Sharing in the Divine Nature   315

    Distinction between Sanctifying Grace, Charity, and
      the Holy Spirit   317

      Threefold Distinction between Nature, Inclination,
        and Action   317

      Fittingness of Habitual Gifts That Enable Action
        to Proceed from an Intrinsic Principle   319

    The Theological Virtues   321

Faith	322
Hope	322
Charity	323
Infused Moral Virtues	326
The Indwelling of the Trinity	328
Divine Filiation	332
Gifts of the Holy Spirit	333
THE FORGIVENESS OF ORIGINAL AND MORTAL SIN IN THE ACT OF JUSTIFICATION	336
The Council of Trent on the Causes of Justification	339
STUDY QUESTIONS	341
SUGGESTIONS FOR FURTHER READING	342
CHAPTER 10. SACRAMENTAL GRACES PROPER TO EACH SACRAMENT	343
1. COMMON AND PROPER EFFECTS OF THE SEVEN SACRAMENTS	343
Communication of Sanctifying Grace: Initiating and Increasing Divine Life	343
Graces Proper to Each Sacrament according to Their Purpose	344
Interpretation of Cajetan: Sacramental Graces Are Actual Graces	347
Interpretation of John of St. Thomas: Sacramental Grace Adds a Special Modality to Habitual Grace	349
Sacramental Grace and Docility to God's Inspirations	352
Pius XI on the Sacramental Grace of Matrimony	354
Sacramental Grace and the Disposition of the Recipient	356
Connection between Sacramental Grace and the Res et Sacramentum	357
2. SACRAMENTAL GRACES OF THE SEVEN SACRAMENTS	359
Sacramental Grace of Baptism	359
Sacramental Grace of Confirmation	361
Sacrament of Fortitude and Magnanimity	363
Confirmation and the Gifts of Knowledge, Understanding, and Wisdom	364
Sacramental Grace of the Eucharist	366

Sacramental Grace of Penance   367

  Restoration of the Grace of Justification   367

  Actual Graces to Avoid the Sins Confessed and
    to Grow in the Opposing Virtues   368

  Actual Graces Aid the Penitent to Do Penance for Sin   368

  Spiritual Consolation   371

  Duration of the Sacramental Graces of Penance   372

Sacramental Grace of Anointing of the Sick   372

Sacramental Grace of Matrimony   375

Sacramental Grace of Holy Orders   377

  Sacramental Graces of Holy Orders and the
    Gifts of the Holy Spirit   378

3. CONDITIONS FOR FRUITFULNESS OF THE SACRAMENTS   381

Necessity of Faith   381

Necessity of Repentance   383

Degrees of Fruitfulness   386

STUDY QUESTIONS   386

SUGGESTIONS FOR FURTHER READING   387

**PART IV. THE INSTRUMENTAL CAUSALITY OF
THE SACRAMENTS**   **389**

CHAPTER 11. CAUSALITY OF THE SACRAMENTS
AS INSTRUMENTS OF CHRIST: THE THEOLOGICAL
TRADITION TO AQUINAS   391

THE NEW TESTAMENT ON THE EFFICACY OF THE
SACRAMENTS   392

SACRAMENTAL EFFICACY ACCORDING TO THE
FATHERS OF THE CHURCH   394

Tertullian   394

St. Ambrose   395

St. Cyril of Jerusalem   397

St. John Chrysostom   399

St. Augustine   400

St. Cyril of Alexandria   402

St. John Damascene   403

MEDIEVAL THEORIES OF SACRAMENTAL
    CAUSALITY TO AQUINAS 403

Sacraments as Causes of Grace: Hugh of St.
    Victor and Peter Lombard 406

The Sacraments as Necessary Occasions for the
    Reception of Grace 408

Alexander of Hales and St. Albert: The Sacraments
    Give a Disposition for Grace 413

STUDY QUESTIONS 416

SUGGESTIONS FOR FURTHER READING 416

CHAPTER 12. ST. THOMAS AQUINAS ON
SACRAMENTAL CAUSALITY 419

THE SACRAMENTS ARE NOT MERE SIGNS
    GUARANTEEING THE INFUSION OF GRACE
    BUT ARE TRUE CAUSES 419

ST. THOMAS'S SOLUTION: THE SACRAMENTS
    ARE INSTRUMENTAL EFFICIENT CAUSES 422

Instrumental Causality 422

Christ's Humanity Is the Instrument of His Divinity . 426

Conjoined and Separated Instruments 426

Analogy between Christ's Miracles and Sacramental
    Action 429

OBJECTION: CAN AN INSTRUMENT COOPERATE IN
    THE INFUSION OF GRACE? 431

The Difference between the Infusion of Grace and
    the Creation of the Human Soul 434

AQUINAS'S MATURE THEORY OF TWOFOLD
    INSTRUMENTAL CAUSALITY 437

Do the Sacraments Contain Grace? 438

ANALOGY OF HUMAN WORDS WITH THE
    WORDS OF GOD 442

The Sacramental Sign Cooperates by Its Own
    Proper Action 443

CHRIST'S HUMAN ACTS ARE PRIVILEGED
    INSTRUMENTS AT WORK THROUGH THE SACRAMENTS . 444

Christ's Passion Is the Universal Meritorious Cause . 445

*The Mysteries of Christ's Life Are Exemplar
Causes of the Christian Life*   446

*The Mysteries of Christ's Life Are Efficient
Causes Configuring Us to Him through the Sacraments*   447

*The Sacraments Apply the Causality of Christ's
Paschal Mystery to the Faithful*   450

SUMMARY OF ST. THOMAS'S CONTRIBUTION TO
SACRAMENTAL CAUSALITY   453

STUDY QUESTIONS   455

SUGGESTIONS FOR FURTHER READING   455

CHAPTER 13. CAUSALITY OF THE SACRAMENTS
EX OPERE OPERATO: THE REFORMATION AND
POST-TRIDENTINE THEORIES   457

MAGISTERIAL TEACHING ON SACRAMENTAL
EFFICACY BEFORE TRENT   457

*The Council of Florence: The Sacraments of the
New Covenant Compared with Those of the Old*   457

*The Sinful State of the Minister Does Not Affect
Sacramental Efficacy*   458

PROTESTANT REJECTION OF THE DOCTRINE
THAT SACRAMENTS OPERATE *EX OPERE OPERATO*   459

Luther's Views on Sacramental Efficacy   460

Calvin's Rejection of Sacramental Causality ex
opere operato   463

*Catholic Response to Protestant Views on
Sacramental Efficacy: The Sacraments Are
Living Divine Words*   466

THE DEFINITION OF SACRAMENTAL CAUSALITY
EX OPERE OPERATO   468

*Importance of Dispositions in the Minister
and Recipient*   474

POST-TRIDENTINE DEBATE ON SACRAMENTAL CAUSALITY   475

*Are the Sacraments Efficacious through Physical
or Moral Causality?*   475

Moral Causality and Melchior Cano   478

*Cajetan and the Thesis That the Sacraments
Exercise Efficient Causality*   481

Karl Rahner's Theory of Sacramental Causality   482

*How Does Rahner's Theory Account for the
Ontological Effects of the Sacraments?*   488

*Transignification: Denial of Efficient Causality
with Regard to the Eucharist*   489

Chauvet's Critique of the Category of Causality   491

Conclusion   493

Study Questions   496

Suggestions for Further Reading   497

PART V. GRACE GIVEN THROUGH DESIRE
FOR THE SACRAMENTS   **499**

CHAPTER 14. SANCTIFICATION THROUGH
THE SACRAMENTAL RITES OF THE OLD COVENANT   501

1. SACRAMENTS OF THE OLD COVENANT
BEFORE THE PROMULGATION OF THE GOSPEL   501

St. Thomas on the Sacraments of the Old Law   501

*The Sacraments of the Old Covenant Did Not
Function* ex opere operato   504

*St. Thomas Aquinas on the Difference between
the Sacraments of the Old and New Covenants*   506

*The Sacraments of the Old Covenant Were Occasions
for Imparting Grace*   509

2. THE RITES OF ISRAEL AFTER THE
PROMULGATION OF THE GOSPEL   515

The Old Covenant "Has Never Been Revoked"   515

*Christian Participation in the Sacramental Rites
of the Old Covenant*   521

Melito and the Analogy of the Model for a Statue   523

*St. Augustine and St. Jerome on the Observance of
Rites of the Old Covenant after Calvary*   524

*St. Thomas on Observance of the Sacraments of the
Old Covenant after the Promulgation of the Gospel*   526

*The Council of Florence on Observance of the Sacraments
of the Old Covenant after the Promulgation of the Gospel*   529

Objections to Aquinas's Argument That Observance
  of the Old Testament Sacraments after the
  Promulgation of the Gospel Implies Sin against Faith ... 533
Observance of Old Testament Sacraments Need
  Not Imply That Christ Has Not Yet Come ... 533
What Is Sufficient Promulgation of the Gospel? ... 537
St. Thomas's Principles Need Not Imply That the
  Sacraments of the Old Covenant Have Become Deadly ... 539
Reasons in Favor of the Devotional Observance of
  Elements of the Old Testament Ceremonial Law ... 540
Conditions for the Devotional Observance of Elements
  of the Old Testament Ceremonial Law ... 543
STUDY QUESTIONS ... 545
SUGGESTIONS FOR FURTHER READING ... 546

CHAPTER 15. SACRAMENTAL GRACE RECEIVED
THROUGH DESIRE ... 549
  THREE WAYS TO GAIN OR GROW IN GRACE ... 549
  NECESSITY OF THE SACRAMENTS ... 552
    Necessity of Means and Necessity of Precept ... 553
    Absolute Necessity of Means ... 553
    Relative Necessity of Means: Most Fitting Means ... 555
    Necessity of Precept: Ordinary Means ... 557
    The Necessity of Baptism ... 558
  DEVELOPMENT OF DOCTRINE ON BAPTISM OF DESIRE ... 561
    Baptism of Blood ... 561
    St. Cyprian ... 562
    St. Ambrose ... 562
    St. Augustine ... 564
    St. Fulgentius of Ruspe ... 566
    Gregory the Great and Venerable Bede on the
      Salvation of Righteous Gentiles ... 567
    Hugh of St. Victor ... 568
    Peter Lombard ... 570
    Innocent II ... 570
    Innocent III ... 571
    St. Thomas Aquinas ... 571

Advantages of Sacramental Baptism over Baptism of Desire   576

The Councils of Florence and Trent on Baptism of Desire   577

Sufficient Grace and the Condemnation of Calvinism and Jansenism   578

Development of Doctrine on Invincible Ignorance   580

Explicit and Implicit Desire for Baptism: The Letter of the Holy Office to Archbishop Cushing of 1949   583

Vatican II and Post-Conciliar Magisterium on Baptism of Desire and the Necessity of Baptism   585

SPIRITUAL COMMUNION   591

St. Augustine   591

St. Thomas Aquinas on Spiritual Communion   592

The Council of Trent to the Present   596

DESIRE FOR THE SACRAMENT OF PENANCE   599

Desire for Penance in the Practice of the Early Church   599

Theologians of the Twelfth and Thirteenth Centuries   601

The Council of Trent and Subsequent Magisterium on Desire for Penance   603

DESIRE FOR CONFIRMATION   605

DESIRE FOR ANOINTING OF THE SICK   608

Desire for the Graces to Sanctify Matrimony by Those with a Valid but Non-Sacramental Marriage   609

IMPORTANCE OF THE DOCTRINE OF SACRAMENTAL GRACE THROUGH DESIRE   609

Desire for the Sacraments among Protestants   611

Desire for the Sacraments among Non-Christians   612

STUDY QUESTIONS   614

SUGGESTIONS FOR FURTHER READING   615

CHAPTER 16. THE DESIRE OF THE CHURCH FOR THE SALVATION OF INFANTS WHO DIE WITHOUT BAPTISM   617

THE THOMISTIC DOCTRINE OF LIMBO   619

1. The Penalty of Original Sin Is the Loss of the Beatific Vision   620

2. Since Its Promulgation, Baptism Is the One and Only
Ordinary Means for the Forgiveness of Original Sin;
Its Lack Can Be Supplied by a Desire for Baptism or
Baptism of Blood   622

3. It Is Not Fitting That There Be Suffering after Death
for Those Who Die without Personal Sin   625

4. A Purely Natural Happiness Is Possible   626

    Opposition to the Thomistic Position   628

5. St. Thomas's Two Attempts to Explain How a Purely
Natural Happiness without Suffering Could Be
Possible in This Economy of Salvation   630

    Early Hypothesis in the Commentary on the Sentences:
Those in Limbo Know What They Are Missing   630

    Problems with Aquinas's Earlier Hypothesis: "Faith" in
Limbo without Hope and Charity?   633

    Later Hypothesis from De Malo: Those in Limbo Do
Not Know What They Are Missing   634

    Problems with the Later Hypothesis   635

REASONS FOR HOPE FOR THE SALVATION OF INFANTS
WHO DIE WITHOUT BAPTISM   638

God Is Not Bound by the Sacraments   638

Vatican II and Post-Conciliar Teaching on Hope for
Infants Who Die without Baptism   641

The Necessity of Baptism as the Sole Ordinary Means,
and God's Extraordinary Action   644

The Role of the Desire of Parents and the Church for
the Salvation of Infants Not Able to Receive Baptism   646

    Salvation of Babies through the Faith of Their Parents
before the Promulgation of Baptism   646

    Cardinal Cajetan's Proposal Concerning Parental
Desire for Baptism   649

    Extension of Cajetan's Proposal   653

ARGUMENTS OF FITTINGNESS FOR AND AGAINST THE
HOPE OF SALVATION FOR THOSE WHO DIE
UNBAPTIZED BEFORE THE AGE OF REASON   656

Maritain's Argument for Limbo Based on the
Hierarchy of Creation   656

Gratuitousness Argument   658

Is the Necessity of Baptism Undermined without Limbo?   *658*

God's Universal Salvific Will   *661*

STUDY QUESTIONS   664

SUGGESTIONS FOR FURTHER READING   665

CONCLUSION   667

   1. SACRAMENTS AND THE DEVELOPMENT OF DOCTRINE   667

   Definition and Number of the Sacraments   *669*

   The Three Levels of the Sacraments   *669*

   Sacramental Grace   *671*

   Sacramental Causality   *671*

   Sacraments of the Old Covenant   *673*

   Grace of the Sacraments Received through Desire   *675*

   Development of Doctrine on Hope for Those Who Die Unbaptized before the Age of Reason   *677*

   2. FOSTERING A SACRAMENTAL SPIRITUALITY   678

   Sacramental Spirituality   *679*

     Sacraments and Faith   *679*

     Sacraments and the Trinity   *681*

   Spirituality of Baptism and Confirmation   *682*

     The Baptismal Call to Holiness and to Consecrate Earthly Realities   *685*

     Eucharistic Focus of Baptism and Confirmation   *686*

   Spirituality of Penance   *687*

   Spirituality of Anointing   *688*

   Spirituality of Marriage   *689*

   Spirituality of Priestly Character   *690*

   Eucharistic Spirituality   *693*

     Mary, the Model of the Sacramental Life   *696*

   STUDY QUESTIONS   696

   SUGGESTIONS FOR FURTHER READING   697

SELECT BIBLIOGRAPHY   699

   MAGISTERIAL TEXTS   699

     Conciliar Documents   *699*

     Papal Documents   *700*

Other Magisterial Texts and Collections   702

PATRISTIC SOURCES   704

MEDIEVAL, REFORMATION, AND RENAISSANCE SOURCES   708

SECONDARY SOURCES   711

INDEX OF SUBJECTS AND NAMES   751

SCRIPTURE INDEX   793

Abbreviations

Magisterial (and Related) Sources:

AAS	*Acta Apostolicae Sedis*
CCC	*Catechism of the Catholic Church.* 2nd edition. Washington, DC: United States Catholic Conference, 2000.
CCT	*The Roman Catechism.* Translated by Robert I. Bradley and Eugene Kevane. Boston: St. Paul Editions, 1985. This work is also known as the *Catechism of the Council of Trent.*
CDF	Congregation for the Doctrine of the Faith
CIC	*Codex iuris canonici. Code of Canon Law: Latin-English Edition.* Washington, DC: Canon Law Society of America, 1998.
DS	Denzinger, Heinrich. *Enchiridion Symbolorum. Compendium of Creeds, Definitions, and Declarations on Matters of Faith and Morals.* 43rd edition. Edited by Peter Hünermann. English edition edited by Robert Fastiggi and Anne Englund Nash. San Francisco: Ignatius Press, 2012.
ITC	International Theological Commission
LG	Second Vatican Council. Dogmatic Constitution on the Church, *Lumen Gentium.* November 21, 1964.
Rites	International Commission on English in the Liturgy. *The Rites of the Catholic Church as Revised by the Second Vatican Ecumenical Council.* 2 vols. Collegeville, MN: Liturgical Press, 1990–1991.

English quotations from magisterial documents are taken from the Vatican website (http://w2.vatican.va/content/vatican/en.html) unless otherwise indicated.

Other Abbreviations:

ACW   Ancient Christian Writers series. Westminster, MD: Newman Press, 1946–.

ANF   *Ante-Nicene Fathers: Translations of the Writings of the Fathers down to A.D. 325.* Edinburgh: T&T Clark; Grand Rapids, MI: Wm. B. Eerdmanns, 1994–1997.

CCCM   *Corpus Christianorum, continuatio mediaevalis.* Turnhout, BE: Brepols, 1966–.

FC   Fathers of the Church series. New York: CIMA Publishing; Washington, DC: Catholic University of America Press, 1947–.

LW   *Luther's Works.* Edited by Jaroslav Pelikan. 55 vols. Philadelphia and St. Louis, MO: Fortress Press and Concordia, 1955–1986.

*NPNF*1   *Nicene and Post-Nicene Fathers*, First series. Peabody, MA: Hendrickson Publishers, 1994.

*NPNF*2   *Nicene and Post-Nicene Fathers.* Second series. Peabody, MA: Hendrickson Publishers, 1994.

OHST   *The Oxford Handbook of Sacramental Theology.* Edited by Hans Boersma and Matthew Levering. Oxford; New York: Oxford University Press, 2015.

PG   *Patrologiae Cursus Completus. Series Graeca.* Edited by J.P. Migne. Paris, 1856–1867.

PL   *Patrologiae Cursus Completus. Series Latina.* Edited by J.P. Migne. Paris, 1844–1865.

Sentences   Peter Lombard. *The Sentences. Book 4: On the Doctrine of Signs.* Translated by Giulio Silano. Mediaeval Sources in Translation 48. Toronto: Pontifical Institute of Mediaeval Studies, 2010.

ST   Thomas Aquinas. *Summa theologiae.* 2nd edition. Translated by Fathers of the English Dominican Province. London: Burns, Oates, & Washbourne, 1920–1932.

SCG   Thomas Aquinas, *Summa contra gentiles.* Translated by Anton Pegis, James Anderson, Vernon Bourke, and Charles O'Neil. 4 vols. Notre Dame, IN: University of Notre Dame Press, 1975.

In Sent.   Thomas Aquinas. *Scriptum super Sententiis.* English translations from *Commentary on the Sentences, Book IV.*

	Translated by Beth Mortensen. Vols. 7–10 of Latin/English Edition of the Works of St. Thomas Aquinas. Green Bay, WI: Aquinas Institute, 2017.
WSA	The Works of Saint Augustine: A Translation for the 21st Century series.
WTA	Latin/English Edition of the Works of St. Thomas Aquinas. Lander, WY: Aquinas Institute for the Study of Sacred Doctrine, 2012.

a.:	article
ad:	response to an objection
bk.:	book or *liber*
can.:	canon
ch.:	chapter or *capitulum*
d.:	*distinctio*
disp.:	*disputatio*
lect.:	*lectio* (a section in a commentary)
no.:	paragraph number
obj.:	objection
p.:	part
q.:	question
qla.:	*quaestiuncula* (little question; used in St. Thomas's commentary on the *Sentences*)

Introduction

The Incarnation and the Sacraments

The Incarnation is the center of all God's plans for mankind. Two millennia ago, the Word became flesh. He dwelt among us for thirty-three years, completed His Paschal mystery, rose from the dead, and forty days later left this earth in His Ascension. However, He still wished to remain among us so that we could encounter Him in His humanity with its life-giving and medicinal power, and therefore He established the sacraments of the Church to be the principal means of encounter with His humanity between His Ascension and His Second Coming. St. Leo the Great said: "What was to be seen of our Redeemer has passed over into the Sacraments," so that "faith might be more perfect and more firm."[1]

Two thousand years ago the Word Incarnate pronounced words

---

[1] Leo the Great, Sermon 74.2, in *Sermons*, trans. J. P. Freeland and A. J. Conway, FC 93 (Washington, DC: Catholic University of America Press, 1996), 326. Quoted in Odo Casel, *The Mystery of Christian Worship* (New York: Crossroad, 1999), 28. See E. Schillebeeckx, O.P. *Christ the Sacrament of the Encounter with God* (New York: Sheed & Ward, 1963), 41: "Christ's incarnation is, as it were, some paces ahead of our deification, so that for a time he has passed out of sight beyond the visible horizon. . . . This is not all: Christ makes his presence among us actively visible and tangible too, not directly through his own bodiliness, but by extending among us on earth in visible form the function of his bodily reality which is in heaven. This precisely is what the sacraments are: the earthly extension of the 'body of the Lord.'" See also David W. Fagerberg, "Liturgy, Signs, and Sacraments," in *The Oxford Handbook of Sacramental Theology* (*OHST*), ed. Hans Boersma and Matthew Levering (Oxford; New York: Oxford University Press, 2015), 455–65, at 464: "An eternal life enters the temporal realm. . . . Water and blood were released from Christ's side by the soldier's spear and thus poured forth baptism and Eucharist. The sacraments do not stand between us and Jesus, like a wall, they extend from Jesus to us, like a bridge, and the faithful can swim up as they flow to the very heart of Christ and put their lips to his blood."

of power in His public ministry. At His word, the wind and sea were calmed, lepers and paralytics were healed, the dead rose, and sins were forgiven. His words accomplished what they signified because the Son of man is also the Son of God by whose word all things are governed.

Christ's miracles differed from those worked by others because He did them in His own name. For example, in Mark 1:40–42, a leper comes to Jesus and says: "'If you will, you can make me clean.'" Jesus, moved with pity, responds: "'I will; be clean.' And immediately the leprosy left him, and he was made clean." A similar scenario takes place with a man possessed by an unclean spirit, to whom Jesus says: "'Be silent, and come out of him!' And the unclean spirit, convulsing him and crying with a loud voice, came out of him" (Mark 1:25–26). Jesus's words did what they said; they made the leper clean and expelled the demon. For this reason, the crowds said: "'What is this? A new teaching! With authority he commands even the unclean spirits, and they obey him'" (Mark 1:27).[2] We see this authority emphasized also in the miracle of the paralytic in Matthew 9:5–8:

> "Which is easier, to say, 'Your sins are forgiven,' or to say, 'Rise and walk'? But that you may know that the Son of man has authority on earth to forgive sins"—he then said to the paralytic—"Rise, take up your bed and go home." And he rose and went home. When the crowds saw it, they were afraid, and they glorified God, who had given such authority to men.

This miracle has a special interest from the point of view of sacramental theology because Jesus heals the paralytic through the power of His word in order to show that He has the authority not only to heal the body but also to forgive sins through His word.

This power can also be seen in Matthew 10:1, in which Christ gave to His Apostles a share in His authority to work through His word: "He called to him his twelve disciples and gave them authority over unclean spirits, to cast them out, and to heal every disease and every infirmity."[3] The centurion in Capernaum amazed Jesus because

---

[2] On the divine claim implicit in the fact that Jesus's words have this authority to do what they say, see Lawrence Feingold, *Faith Comes from What Is Heard: An Introduction to Fundamental Theology* (Steubenville, OH: Emmaus Academic, 2016), 377.

[3] It is reasonable to associate this text, parallel with Mark 6:13, with the institution of the sacrament of Anointing of the Sick. See the Council of Trent,

of his faith that Jesus could command nature with power, as a centurion can command his troops and "say to one, 'Go,' and he goes, and to another, 'Come,' and he comes" (Matt 8:9). If Jesus's word is one of authority over nature, it has no less power in the supernatural order with respect to the infusion of grace, the forgiveness of sins, and the building up of the Church.

Today His words and gestures of power continue to be heard and seen throughout the world at every moment in the sacramental liturgy of His Church. As they accomplished what they signified during His earthly life, they continue to do so today. Yet whereas in His miraculous words of healing there was sensible evidence of their efficacy, His sacramental words, although no less efficacious, must be believed in the darkness of faith. The sacraments of the New Covenant are sacraments of faith because they presuppose faith in Christ and in His Church, and they were instituted to nourish and exercise that faith and make it alive with hope and charity.

The sacraments are not something marginal in Christ's work. They are the privileged means of union between Christ and us. They build up the Church as nerves and arteries by which the grace of the Head comes to the members and the Father is glorified.[4] Without the sacraments there can be no Mystical Body of Christ on this earth, for the sacraments are the channels that convey the life of the Head to the members of His Body. For this reason, the *Catechism of the Catholic Church*, §1116 refers to the sacraments as "the masterworks of God."

The sacraments can also be understood as mystical gates by which the divine life that entered our world in the Incarnation still passes to us through Christ and His Spirit. In the Incarnation He forged a way between heaven and earth, of which Psalm 24:7 provides an image: "Lift up your heads, O gates! and be lifted up, O ancient doors! that the King of glory may come in." Also in His Resurrection, the "gates of righteousness" were opened for the crucified King: "Open to me the

---

Doctrine on the Sacrament of Extreme Unction (session 14, Nov 25, 1551), ch. 1 (DS, 1695).

4   See Matthias Joseph Scheeben, *The Mysteries of Christianity*, trans. Cyril Vollert (St. Louis, MO: B. Herder, 1951), 581: "The substantial sacrament of the Eucharist is the heart of the Church; but the sacramental functions are the arteries of the Church's life, and the organs by which the members of the body are formed and kept together in their manifold relations to the divine head." See also Louis Bouyer, "The Sacramental System," in *Sacraments: The Gestures of Christ*, ed. Denis O'Callaghan (New York: Sheed & Ward, 1964), 46.

gates of righteousness, that I may enter through them and give thanks to the LORD" (Ps 118:19). After His Ascension, He did not close those doors, but continues to pour out His Spirit and His Blood through sacramental gates.

This image of sacramental gates is marvelously developed by the fourteenth-century Byzantine theologian and mystic, Nicholas Cabasilas:

> He did not remove us from here, but He made us heavenly while yet remaining on earth and imparted to us the heavenly life without leading us up to heaven, but by bending heaven to us and bringing it down.... Accordingly, through these sacred Mysteries[5] as through windows the Sun of Righteousness enters this dark world. He puts to death the life which accords with this world, but raises up that which is above the world. ...This way the Lord traced by coming to us, this gate He opened by entering into the world. When He returned to the Father He suffered it not to be closed, but from Him He comes through it to sojourn among men, or rather, He is constantly present with us.... For this reason the most sacred Mysteries may fittingly be called "gates of righteousness,"[6] for it is God's supreme loving-kindness and goodness towards mankind ... which has provided us with these entrances into heaven.[7]

The Good Samaritan and the Sacraments

Many of the Fathers and Doctors of the Church interpret the parable of the Good Samaritan as an allegory of salvation history.[8] The man

---

[5] "Mysteries" is the Byzantine term for "sacraments."

[6] Ps 118:19.

[7] Nicholas Cabasilas, *The Life in Christ* 1.6, trans. Carmino J. deCatanzaro (Crestwood, NY: St. Vladimir's Seminary Press, 1974), 50–53. See Panayiotis Nellas, *Deification in Christ: Orthodox Perspectives on the Nature of the Human Person*, trans. Norman Russell (Crestwood, NY: St. Vladimir's Seminary Press, 1987), 144–45.

[8] See Irenaeus, *Against Heresies* 3.17.3, in *ANF* 1:445, in which he says that the Lord "Himself compassionated, and bound up his wounds, giving two royal denaria"; Clement of Alexandria, *Who Is the Rich Man That Shall Be Saved?* 29, PG 9:634; Origen, Homily 34 on Luke 10:25–37, in *Origen: Homilies on Luke; Fragments on Luke*, trans. Joseph Lienhard (Washington, DC: Catholic University of America Press, 1996), 138. See Bertrand De Margerie, S.J., *An*

who is robbed on the way from Jerusalem to Jericho represents Adam, who is stripped of the inheritance of original justice by his consent to Satan's temptation, and who is left wounded on the road down from the City of God. In Adam are included all his descendants. The priest and Levite represent the Old Covenant, which could not yet save wounded Adam and his descendants. The Good Samaritan represents Jesus Christ, whose saving work is indicated when the Samaritan anoints the wounds of the victim. The Church is the inn to which Jesus entrusts the wounded man until His return. Jesus is the ultimate good neighbor to every man. The sacraments have an important place in this allegory, for they are represented by the healing oil applied to the wounds of the victim. The great twelfth-century theologian, Peter Lombard (ca. 1100–1160), begins the fourth book of his influential *Sentences* with this analogy: "For the Samaritan, assuming responsibility for the wounded man, applied the bindings of the sacraments to care for him, because God instituted the remedies of the sacraments against the wounds of original and actual sin."[9]

The sacraments of the New Covenant, beginning with Baptism, provide a remedy for original and personal sin and their consequences. Neither Christ's work of redemption nor the sacramental system that He established can be rightly understood without understanding original sin, in consequence of which each man comes into this world expelled from Eden, deprived of sanctifying grace, and subject to death, both bodily and spiritual, as well as to concupiscence. Christ came to restore to us what had been lost through original and personal sin and to give us renewed access to the tree of life, which He is, as the Word, Author, and Bread of Life.

The Blood and Water Flowing from the Side of Christ Represent the Sacraments

A still more powerful image of the meaning and purpose of the sacraments is in John 19:34, which says that after Christ breathed His

---

Introduction to the History of Exegesis, vol. 1, *The Greek Fathers*, trans. Leonard Maluf (Petersham, MA: Saint Bede's Publications, 1993), 70–75; Feingold, *Faith Comes from What Is Heard*, 14–15.

[9] Peter Lombard, *Sentences*, bk. 4, d. 1, ch. 1, no. 1, in *The Sentences, Book 4: On the Doctrine of Signs*, trans. Giulio Silano, Mediaeval Sources in Translation 48 (Toronto: Pontifical Institute of Mediaeval Studies, 2010), 3. The final version of the *Sentences* was published between 1155 and 1157.

last on Calvary, "one of the soldiers pierced his side with a spear, and at once there came out blood and water." The Fathers see the water and blood as symbols of the principal sacraments—Baptism and the Eucharist—and thus of the sacramental system.[10] As Eve was made from the rib taken from Adam's side, so the New Eve,[11] the Church, is made from the sacraments that come forth from Christ's pierced side. Theodoret of Cyrus eloquently expresses the patristic view:

> His side was pierced as Adam's was; yet there came forth not a woman who, being beguiled, was to be the death-bearer, but a fountain of life that regenerates the world by its two streams: the one to renew us in the baptismal font and clothe us with the garment of immortality, the other to feed us, the reborn, at the table of God, just as babes are nourished with milk.[12]

Pius XII echoes the Fathers in his encyclical on the liturgy:

> Lifted up between heaven and earth, He offers the saving sacrifice of His life, and pours forth, as it were, from His pierced Heart, the sacraments destined to impart the treasures of redemption to the souls of men. All this He does for the glory of His Father and man's ever greater sanctification.[13]

The sacraments are the fruit of Christ's Passion. Christ's Passion

---

[10] See Quodvultdeus, bishop of Carthage at the time of St. Augustine, in *Quodvultdeus of Carthage: The Creedal Homilies*, trans. and ed. Thomas Macy Finn, ACW 60 (New York: The Newman Press, 2004), 37: "For his side was pierced, as the gospel says, and immediately there flowed out blood and water, which are the twin sacraments of the Church: the water, which became her bath, and the blood which became her dowry." See also John Damascene, *An Exact Exposition of the Orthodox Faith* 4.9, in *Writings*, trans. F. H. Chase, Jr., FC 37 (Washington, DC: Catholic University of America Press, 1958), 345: "He made a fountain of forgiveness gush out for us from His sacred and immaculate side, both water unto regeneration and the washing away of sin and destruction, and blood as drink productive of life everlasting."

[11] This title is applied by the Fathers both to Mary and to the Church. See Hugo Rahner, *Our Lady and the Church* (Bethesda, MD: Zaccheus Press, 2004), 5–13.

[12] Theodoret of Cyrus, *On the Incarnation of the Lord* 28 [27], in the *Office of Readings*, Monday in the 19th week of Ordinary Time; in Milton Walsh, *Witness of the Saints: Patristic Readings in the Liturgy of the Hours* (San Francisco: Ignatius Press, 2012), p. 305, no. 459.

[13] Pius XII, Encyclical on the Sacred Liturgy *Mediator Dei* (Nov 20, 1947), §17.

made superabundant satisfaction for all human sin, original and personal, and merited grace for all men. The sacramental system applies to mankind the graces that have been merited on Calvary, restoring, in a sensible way suitable to human nature, the supernatural justice and grace lost through sin.

This central importance of the sacraments, however, has increasingly been obscured for much of Christian culture since the eighteenth century. This culture born of the Reformation and the Enlightenment has become less and less sensitive to signs and symbols, increasingly suspicious of Tradition, prizing self-sufficiency and pragmatic reliance on the factual and functional, and tending to see all reality through a materialist and consumerist lens that excludes the possibility of any supernatural action in the world.[14] The rejection of most of the sacramental system by the Protestant Reformation, and especially the naturalistic view of liberal Protestantism of the last two centuries, has greatly undermined the modern Christian's ability to see the world sacramentally.[15] The modern secularized world has become "disenchanted,"[16] losing faith in the wondrous reality of direct contact with Christ and His grace offered through the sacraments.

The sacraments presuppose faith in Christ and in His grace, of which they are the conduits. They allow us to encounter Jesus in the darkness of faith. We know of them through Scripture and Tradition and they are clothed in liturgical prayers that have been continuously transmitted and organically developed for two thousand years. They

---

[14] See Joseph Ratzinger, "The Sacramental Foundation of Christian Existence," in *Theology of the Liturgy: The Sacramental Foundation of Christian Existence*, ed. Michael Miller, trans. Kenneth Baker and Michael Miller, *Collected Works*, vol. 11 (San Francisco: Ignatius Press, 2014), 153–55, 169.

[15] See Brad S. Gregory, *The Unintended Reformation: How a Religious Revolution Secularized Society* (Cambridge: Harvard University Press, 2012), 41–43, 45, 53, 57; James F. White, *The Sacraments in Protestant Practice and Faith* (Nashville: Abingdon Press, 1999), 22–23.

[16] This phrase was popularized by Max Weber in his essay, "Science as a Vocation," in *From Max Weber: Essays in Sociology*, trans. H.H. Gerth and C. Wright Mills (New York: Oxford University Press, 1946), 129–56, at 139: "It means that principally there are no mysterious incalculable forces that come into play, but rather that one can, in principle, master all things by calculation. This means that the world is disenchanted. One need no longer have recourse to magical means in order to master or implore the spirits, as did the savage, for whom such mysterious powers existed. Technical means and calculations perform the service." See David Brown, "A Sacramental World: Why It Matters," in *OHST*, 603.

make use of the humblest realities such as words, gestures, water, bread, wine, and olive oil, and yet we believe that they bestow immeasurable riches, infinitely disproportionate to the humble action that is seen, to those who believe and are properly disposed. The sacraments, finally, presuppose the intimate union of body and spirit, so that the spirit can be intimately touched by grace through bodily things empowered by the word of Christ. The sacraments sanctify us in a way marvelously fitted to human nature, to the Incarnation, and to the Trinitarian life.

GOAL OF THE WORK

This book was born as course notes for a class on the Sacraments in General that I have taught at Kenrick-Glennon Seminary for several years, and its principal purpose is to serve as a textbook for seminary formation, although I hope that it can also serve all those who seek a deeper understanding of the sacraments, which the *Catechism of the Catholic Church*, §1116 speaks of as "'the masterworks of God' in the new and everlasting covenant." Before studying the individual sacraments, it is helpful to study the nature of the sacraments in general and the sacramental system as a whole, in which the individual sacraments take their place as seven distinct means of sanctification. For this reason, St. Thomas Aquinas, before treating the individual sacraments in the third part of his *Summa theologiae*, dedicated six questions to the sacraments in general.[17]

As in a course on the Sacraments in General, this book studies the nature of the sacraments, their fittingness and purpose, their relationship with Christ and the New Covenant, their relationship with the Old Covenant that prefigured them, their levels of signification and content, their sensible nature, their necessity, the character and grace that they communicate, the nature of their causality, and the role of desire in anticipating some of their effects. A particular focus is on the arduous question of how the sacraments of the New Covenant cause the grace that they signify, and how their efficacy differs from that of the sacramental rites of the Old Covenant. The thesis of this book is that the sacraments of the New Covenant should be understood as instruments of Christ's humanity that are used as His words of power to accomplish the sanctification they signify, and thereby communi-

---

[17] *ST* III, qq. 60–65.

cate the Holy Spirit, infuse grace, and build up ecclesial communion in those who receive them with the right dispositions.

Principal Sources

Scripture does not explicitly contain a doctrine on the sacraments in general, although it touches on each sacrament. Likewise, none of the Fathers wrote a complete treatise on the sacraments in general, although they wrote on individual sacraments according to the needs of pastoral ministry. A particularly valuable source are the sermons of the Fathers given to neophytes after receiving Christian initiation.[18]

It is first in the twelfth century that we find two influential systematic treatises on the sacraments. The first is Hugh of St. Victor's *On the Sacraments of the Christian Faith*, written around 1134. The second, a generation later, is the fourth book of Peter Lombard's *Sentences*, the final version of which dates from 1155–1157.[19] The work of these twelfth-century theologians culminated in the following century in Aquinas's short treatise on the sacraments in general in the *Summa theologiae* III, qq. 60–65, and his earlier treatment of the sacraments in the fourth book of his Commentary on the *Sentences*.[20]

The Magisterium treated the sacraments in general in the Council of Florence in the Bull of Union with the Armenians *Exsultate Deo*.[21] The bull closely follows a short treatise by St. Thomas on

---

[18] See Edward Yarnold, ed., *The Awe-Inspiring Rites of Initiation: The Origins of the R.C.I.A.*, 2nd ed. (Collegeville, MN: Liturgical Press, 1994).

[19] See Thomas Finn, "The Sacramental World in the Sentences of Peter Lombard," *Theological Studies* 69 (2008): 557–82, at 560; Ignatius Brady, O.F.M., ed., *Prolegomena* to Peter Lombard, *Sententiae in IV libris distinctae*, 3rd ed., Spicilegium Bonaventurianum 4 and 5, (Grottaferrata [Rome]: Editiones Collegii S. Bonaventurae ad Claras Aquas, 1971), 117–18. On Peter Lombard's contribution to sacramental theology, see Elizabeth Frances Rogers, *Peter Lombard and the Sacramental System* (New York: Columbia University, 1917).

[20] Thomas Aquinas, *In IV Sent.*, d. 1, q. 1, aa. 1–5; d. 2, q. 1, aa. 1–4.

[21] Nov 22, 1439. The teaching on the sacraments in general are contained in DS, 1310–13. The sacraments in particular are covered in DS, 1314–27. The intention of this document can be inferred from the opening sentence of this section of the bull (DS, 1310): "In order to facilitate the instruction of the Armenians of today and in the future, we reduce the truth about the sacraments of the Church to the following very brief formula." Thus it seems that the intention of the document is to aid the instruction of the faithful of a particular church rather than to teach something definitively for the universal Church. Thus it does not seem to involve the charism of infallibility.

the sacraments entitled "On the Articles of Faith and the Sacraments of the Church."[22] The most important magisterial document on the sacraments in general is from the Council of Trent, session 7, which includes thirteen canons on the subject.[23] The Second Vatican Council treats the sacraments in *Lumen Gentium*, §11, and many other places. Other important sources are the *Catechism of the Council of Trent* (also known as the *Roman Catechism*),[24] and the *Catechism of the Catholic Church*, both of which have a rich treatment on the sacraments.

PLAN OF THE WORK

This work is divided into five parts. The first four chapters are an introduction to the theme of the sacraments, exploring their fittingness, definition, and institution by Christ. The first chapter on fittingness is crucial for our increasingly non-sacramental Western culture. Why did Christ will to sanctify us using sensible sacramental signs? A key philosophical principle that has great applications to many different branches of theology is that *everything is received according to the mode of the receiver*.[25] Since man is both a bodily and a spiritual being who communicates rational ideas through sensible signs, it is fitting that sanctification come to us in a mode appropriate to us, through sensible signs that convey what they represent. The sacraments give us a share in the divine life in a manner supremely adapted to the human recipient.

At the same time the sacraments manifest a complementary principle that is less familiar: gifts are given according to the mode of the giver. Since God's mode is superabundant generosity while respecting the freedom of the recipient, the sacraments give superabundantly while respecting the freedom of our dispositions. No less importantly,

---

[22] Thomas Aquinas, *De articulis fidei et ecclesiae sacramentis ad archiepiscopum Panormitanum*, in *Opuscula Theologica*, vol. 1, *De re dogmatica et morali*, ed. Raymund Verardo (Turin and Rome: Marietti, 1954), 147–51; English translation by J. B. Collins in St. Thomas Aquinas, *God's Greatest Gifts: Commentaries on the Commandments and the Sacraments* (Manchester, NH: Sophia Press, 1992), 83–100.

[23] Council of Trent, Decree on the Sacraments (session 7, Mar 3, 1547; DS, 1601–13).

[24] *The Roman Catechism*, trans. Robert I. Bradley and Eugene Kevane (Boston: St. Paul Editions, 1985), abbreviated as *CCT*.

[25] See, for example, *ST* I, q. 84, a. 1; III, q. 11, a. 5.

the giver here is Jesus Christ, true man and true God, and He gives to us according to His incarnational mode. Thus the sacraments communicate His divine life through sensible signs that reflect and signify the human life He has taken up for our sakes. Here the giver has taken on the mode of the recipient so that we may receive the divine gift more perfectly. Another aspect of giving according to the mode of the giver is that Christ gives us grace according to His divine-human (theandric) mode.[26] It belongs to Christ's words, as human, to signify, and as divine, to do what they say. Thus it is proper to the words of Christ to do what they signify, and He gives grace to us in that way, through words that speak with authority.

The second part treats the outward sacramental sign, which consists in the matter and form of the sacraments (chapter 5), and the subject and minister (chapter 6). Among other things, chapter 6 treats the controversial topics of the complementarity of man and woman for Matrimony, and of male gender for the priesthood so as to represent Christ the Bridegroom in His spousal relationship with His Bride, the Church.

The third part treats the effects of the sacraments, which are twofold. One of the great developments of sacramental theology was the recognition that the sacraments are composed not only of two "levels"—sign and reality of grace—but that there is a third intermediate level that mediates grace and remains present after the outward sacramental sign has ceased to exist. It is thus an intermediate effect or reality (*res*) of the sacrament and a further sign (*sacramentum*) and cause of the final effect that is grace, and is accordingly known as the *res et sacramentum*, which means "reality and sign." In Baptism, Confirmation, and Holy Orders, this intermediate level is sacramental character, which is treated in chapter 7. Character is imprinted indelibly by the outward sacramental sign, and gives Christian identity, an ecclesial mission, and the spiritual power to carry it out.

Something analogous to sacramental character exists in the other four sacraments, generally referred to by the Latin term, *res et sacramentum*, which is treated in chapter 8. In the Eucharist, this intermediate level is the Body and Blood of Christ, present by

---

[26] See *ST* III, q. 19, a. 1, ad 1: "Dionysius places in Christ a theandric—*i.e.*, a God-manlike or Divino-human operation—not by any confusion of the operations or powers of both natures, but inasmuch as His Divine operation employs the human, and His human operation shares in the power of the Divine."

transubstantiation under the sacramental species. It was with regard to the Eucharist, after the Berengarian heresy, that the three levels of the sacraments were formally distinguished and the three-fold distinction was applied to all the sacraments. The application of the category of *res et sacramentum* to Penance and Anointing of the Sick is more difficult to understand and is still debated. I propose that the *res et sacramentum* in these two sacraments should be understood in a way analogous to sacramental character, giving a new configuration to Christ in His Passion, and an ecclesial mission, respectively, to do penance and to exercise redemptive suffering on behalf of the Church and the world.

The principal effect of the sacraments is the grace they confer, which is treated in chapters 9–10. Chapter 9 treats the nature of grace itself and the gifts that accompany sanctifying grace, which are conferred by all the sacraments. These habitual gifts are faith, hope, charity, divine filiation, the indwelling of the Holy Spirit, His seven gifts mentioned in Isaiah 11:2–3, and the infused moral virtues. Chapter 10 examines the particular graces conferred by each sacrament. It would be redundant to have seven sacraments if they all conferred the same effect. Theologians therefore agree that in addition to this common effect of sanctifying grace and the gifts inseparable from it, each sacrament gives particular graces that aid the recipient to fulfill the mission of the sacrament. The nature of these particular graces, referred to as sacramental grace, has been debated through the centuries. St. Thomas held that they are divine aids to fulfill the purpose of the sacrament, and Thomas Cardinal Cajetan (Thomas de Vio, 1469–1534) interpreted this to refer to actual graces given over time, which has become the common view of theologians. It is debated whether the particular sacramental graces also involve a habitual gift.[27] I argue that it is reasonable to hold that since the sacraments each confer a particular ecclesial mission, they would also help the rightly disposed recipient to be habitually docile to the actual graces and inspirations that aid the recipient in carrying out that mission. Thus I hold that sacramental grace strengthens and focuses the seven gifts of the Holy Spirit to increase docility to His inspirations with regard to the particular ecclesial mission and configuration with Christ given by each sacrament.

---

[27] This view has been defended by John of St. Thomas in *Cursus Theologicus*, vol. 9, disp. 24, a. 2 (Paris: Vivès, 1886), 283–98.

The fourth part of the book on the causality of the sacraments is perhaps the most controversial and difficult. How can the sacraments, which consist of sensible signs, impart supernatural grace and give us a share in the divine nature? The New Testament and the Fathers affirm the power of the sacraments to work on the soul but do not pose the question of the kind of causality that is at work. The scholastics of the twelfth and thirteenth century pose this question and offer three different solutions: (a) the sacraments are necessary conditions or occasions for the infusing of grace according to a divine pact (St. Bernard, St. Bonaventure, Scotus, and the Nominalist tradition); (b) the sacraments bring about a necessary disposition for the infusion of grace, which is the *res et sacramentum* (Alexander of Hales, St. Albert, early St. Thomas); or (c) the sacraments are instrumental causes of grace in two steps, imprinting the *res et sacramentum*, which in turn is the instrumental cause of the infusion of grace (the mature position of St. Thomas), which I hold to be the best solution.

Chapter 12 focuses on St. Thomas's mature theory of the instrumental causality of the sacraments, which are understood as instruments used by Christ's humanity, our eternal High Priest, whose divine power works through them so that they cause what they represent. One of the great merits of this theory, as opposed to sacramental occasionalism, is the way in which the Incarnation is brought into the heart of sacramental efficacy.[28] Through the hypostatic union, Christ is the perfect Mediator and our eternal High Priest, whose priesthood is exercised through the sacraments, which He uses as "separated instruments" that serve to extend the reach of His humanity and make contact with us today.[29] Unfortunately, St. Thomas's theory was not widely known until the time of Cardinal Cajetan in the sixteenth century.[30]

Chapter 13 explores Protestant negations of sacramental efficacy

---

[28] See Reginald Lynch, *The Cleansing of the Heart: The Sacraments as Instrumental Causes in the Thomistic Tradition* (Washington, DC: Catholic University of America Press, 2017), 2–3.

[29] See François Taymans d'Eypernon, *The Blessed Trinity and the Sacraments* (Westminster, MD: Newman Press, 1961), 36–38: "Throughout the work of Redemption there operates a law which is verified in all domains; we may call it the law of salvation through contact. . . . If the world is to be saved by contact with Christ, it follows that this contact must be possible everywhere and at all times. . . . It is by the sacramental sign that God establishes contact with sinful man and by His grace transforms man into His own image."

[30] See Reginald Lynch, "The Sacraments as Causes of Sanctification," *Nova et Vetera* (English) 12, no. 3 (2014): 791–836, at 809–12.

and the response of Trent defining that the sacraments grant grace *ex opere operato*, given the proper dispositions in the recipient. This left room, however, for continued debate among Catholic theologians over the mode of causality by which the sacraments work *ex opere operato*. The views debated in the thirteenth century continued to be debated under the new names of moral and physical causality. In the mid-twentieth century, a quite different kind of theory was introduced by Karl Rahner, which does not ascribe efficient causality to the sacraments but sees them as "intrinsic symbols" that manifest what the Church already is.[31] Such a position, I will argue, fails to manifest the centrality of the Incarnation and how Christ builds up the Church, His Bride, from the sacraments, symbolized by the water and blood that comes forth from His pierced side on the Cross in John 19:34. Without the exercise of efficient causality, it is impossible to explain how the sacraments bring about a new infusion of grace, the forgiveness of sins, and new supernatural realities, such as sacramental character, the matrimonial bond, and, above all, the Body and Blood of Christ in the Eucharist.

Part five examines the difficult question of how the essential effects of the sacraments of the New Covenant can be received through desire for them without their actual reception. Chapter 14 poses this question with regard to the sacramental rites of the Mosaic Law. If the sacraments of the New Covenant exercise true causality in the granting of grace, what should we think about the causal efficacy of the sacramental rites of the Old Covenant? On the one hand, the

---

[31] See Karl Rahner, S.J., *The Church and the Sacraments*, 3rd ed., trans. W. J. O'Hara (New York: Herder and Herder, 1963), 34–40. The original German is *Kirche und Sakramente* (Freiburg in Breisgau: Herder, 1961). Some of its contents were anticipated by an article of 1955 by the same title: "Kirche und Sakramente," *Geist und Leben* 28 (1955): 434–53. Rahner's position denying that the sacraments exercise efficient causality in the order of grace has been developed by Louis-Marie Chauvet in *Symbol and Sacrament* (Collegeville, MN: Liturgical Press, 1995); *The Sacraments: The Word of God at the Mercy of the Body* (Collegeville, MN: Liturgical Press, 2001). For Chauvet's critique of St. Thomas's view of sacramental causality and a defense of the latter, see Liam Walsh, "The Divine and the Human in St. Thomas's Theology of Sacraments," in *Ordo sapientiae et amoris: Image et message de Saint Thomas D'Aquin à travers les récentes études historiques, herméneutiques et doctrinales*, ed. Carlos-Josaphat Pinto de Oliveira (Fribourg: Editions Universitaires Fribourg Suisse, 1993), 321–52, esp. 323–25; Bernard Blankenhorn, "The Instrumental Causality of the Sacraments: Thomas Aquinas and Louis-Marie Chauvet," *Nova et Vetera* (English) 4, no. 2 (2006): 255–94.

Council of Florence teaches that the sacraments of the Old Covenant did not cause grace as do those of the New, but only prefigure it.[32] On the other hand, the Fathers, the medieval theologians, and the Magisterium have affirmed that through circumcision, grace was given and original sin was forgiven. As will be seen, St. Thomas's theory of sacramental causality makes possible a coherent explanation of the difference between the Old and New Testament sacraments since it sees Christ's humanity as the central link of the causal chain between God and the sacraments of the Church. The sacraments are efficacious because Christ speaks words of divine power and authority through them. Before the Incarnation, however, Christ's humanity was not yet present to give causal efficacy to sacraments. Those of the Old Covenant, instituted before the Incarnation, could only be prefigurations of the New Testament sacraments that could serve as occasions for sanctification through the desire of the people of God working through faith, hope, and love. Another question regarding the sacraments of the Old Covenant is their status after Christ's Paschal mystery and the promulgation of the Gospel, which is discussed in the second part of chapter 14.

This leads to the broader question, addressed in chapter 15, of how the graces ordinarily given by the sacraments can be anticipated by desire for them. This question was first posed with regard to Baptism, and underwent a long and sustained development. The desire in question, which can be explicit or implicit, has to be moved by an impulse of actual grace and animated by faith, hope, charity, and perfect contrition. For an implicit desire, there also has to be invincible ignorance. The doctrine that grace is given by God not just through sacramental reception but also through a desire for the sacrament, can apply to all of the sacraments except Holy Orders, on account of its public nature.[33]

But what about those who die without Baptism before the age of reason and thus before they are able to make a personal act of desire for the sacraments? Can the desire of their parents and the Church be of avail to them? This question is posed in chapter 16, which examines the teaching of the *Catechism of the Catholic Church*, §1261 that "the

---

[32] Council of Florence, Bull of Union with the Armenians *Exsultate Deo* (Nov 22, 1439; DS, 1310).

[33] See Jean-Hervé Nicolas, *Synthèse dogmatique: de la Trinité à la Trinité* (Fribourg: Editions Universitaires, 1985), 789.

great mercy of God who desires that all men should be saved, and Jesus's tenderness toward children . . . allow us to hope that there is a way of salvation for children who have died without Baptism."

PART ONE

FITTINGNESS AND INSTITUTION OF THE SACRAMENTS

Chapter One

Fittingness of the Sacramental Economy

The Sacramental Economy

Every culture makes use of religious symbols to worship God and to represent His mysteries and the union with Him for which we yearn. A religion with no sacred signs would be incomprehensible for human beings. God instituted many different kinds of sacred signs in the Old Covenant. The New Covenant, however, is endowed with a system of sacred sensible signs for the worship of God and the sanctification of the faithful—the seven sacraments—which have a unique efficacy. In numerous places in the New Testament we can see that Jesus instituted sacred rites in the New Covenant that are not only signs of something sacred, as in the religions of the world and in the Old Covenant, but are also endowed with a singular power that comes from the Incarnation and Paschal mystery of Christ, who encounters, touches, and transforms us with His divine/human words in the sacraments.

Because of their unique efficacy in infusing God's grace, we speak not simply of a sacramental system of worship but also of a sacramental *economy*, taking the word "economy" to refer to a distribution of goods and an interchange of gifts. Christ is the center of the "economy of salvation" because He has taken on what is ours—human nature and the conditions of human life—so as to give us a share of what is His: the divine life and the sending of the Holy Spirit. The treasures of participation in the Trinitarian life come to us through the humanity of Christ, hypostatically joined to His divinity. After ascending into heaven, Christ's humanity continues to come to us and touch us through the humble means of the seven sacraments that build up and give life to the Church. The interchange of gifts between God and humanity is channeled through the sacraments. Through them, or through desire for them, human beings are sanctified and God is glorified. This culminates in the Eucharist, source and summit, in which the faithful are nourished by the Body and Blood of the Son of God, and in which all of creation, with the Incarnate Son, is offered back to the Father. The sacramental economy connects the members of the Mystical Body with their Head, and, at least as the object of desire, gives life to the world.

Old Testament Prophecies of the Sacramental Economy

The sacramental economy of the New Testament is given a central place in the messianic prophecies of the Old Testament.[1] Jeremiah 31:31–34 foretells a "new covenant," and characterizes it as the writing of the law of God on the heart:

> Behold, the days are coming, says the LORD, when I will make a new covenant with the house of Israel and the house of Judah, not like the covenant which I made with their fathers. . . . But this is the covenant which I will make with the house of Israel after those days, says the LORD: I will put my law within them, and I will write it upon their hearts; and I will be their God, and they shall be my people. And no longer shall each man teach his neighbor and each his brother, saying, "Know the LORD," for they shall all know me, from the least of them to the greatest, says the LORD; for I will forgive their iniquity, and I will remember their sin no more.

What does it mean for God to write the Law on the heart? Since God's Law essentially consists in the double commandment of charity, He writes His law on the heart by giving us the gift of charity, through which the faithful will to do the law not out of fear of punishment but out of love. The infusion of sanctifying grace and charity also brings about the forgiveness of sins, which is how the passage con-

---

[1] See Lawrence Feingold, *The Mystery of Israel and the Church*, vol. 3, *The Messianic Kingdom of Israel* (St. Louis, MO: Miriam Press, 2010), 23–25.

cludes. Grace and charity are also the principle of the gifts of the Holy
Spirit of wisdom, understanding, and knowledge, by which the Lord
is known not through study but by intimate friendship with Him.
Hence Jeremiah says of those in whose hearts God has put His law,
"they shall all know me." The prophecy does not say how the law will
be written on the heart. The New Testament reveals that the principal
means are sacramental.

A parallel prophecy is Ezekiel 36:25–27, which uses more direct
sacramental imagery:

> I will sprinkle clean water upon you, and you shall be clean
> from all your uncleannesses, and from all your idols I will
> cleanse you. A new heart I will give you, and a new spirit
> I will put within you; and I will take out of your flesh the
> heart of stone and give you a heart of flesh. And I will put my
> spirit within you, and cause you to walk in my statutes and be
> careful to observe my ordinances.

The cleansing with clean water announces the baptismal cleansing of
the New Covenant, and the giving of the Spirit refers to Confirmation
as well as the Eucharist and other sacraments.[2] Baptism is also alluded
to in Zechariah 13:1: "On that day there shall be a fountain opened for
the house of David and the inhabitants of Jerusalem to cleanse them
from sin and uncleanness."[3] The longing for the cleansing of Baptism
is powerfully expressed in the penitential Psalm 51:7: "Purge me with
hyssop, and I shall be clean; wash me, and I shall be whiter than snow."

Another key prophetic text is Joel 2:28–29, which speaks of the
promise of the pouring out of the Spirit in a universal way: "And it
shall come to pass afterward, that I will pour out my spirit on all flesh;
your sons and your daughters shall prophesy, your old men shall dream
dreams, and your young men shall see visions. Even upon the menservants and maidservants in those days, I will pour out my spirit." St.
Peter, in Acts 2:16, proclaimed this text as fulfilled in the miracle of

---

[2] As will be seen in chapter 9, the infusion of charity, the gift of the Holy Spirit,
and the forgiveness of original and mortal sin are inseparable.

[3] Other prophetic texts alluding to a future sacramental forgiveness of sins
include Mic 7:19: "You will cast all our sins into the depths of the sea"; and Isa
1:16–18: "Wash yourselves; make yourselves clean; . . . though your sins are like
scarlet, they shall be as white as snow; though they are red like crimson, they
shall become like wool."

Pentecost. The sacrament of Confirmation makes the event of Pentecost present throughout the life of the Church,[4] as St. Paul VI teaches in his Apostolic Constitution on Confirmation *Divinae Consortium Naturae*:

> Peter regarded the Spirit who had thus come down upon the apostles as the gift of the Messianic age (see Acts 2:17-18). Then those who believed the apostles' preaching were baptized and they too received "the gift of the Holy Spirit" (Acts 2:38). From that time on the apostles, in fulfillment of Christ's wish, imparted to the newly baptized by the laying on of hands the gift of the Spirit that completes the grace of Baptism. . . . This laying on of hands is rightly recognized by reason of Catholic tradition as the beginning of the sacrament of Confirmation, which in a certain way perpetuates the grace of Pentecost in the Church.[5]

The Eucharist is foretold in various prophecies[6] and figures. A suggestive image is in Isaiah 25:6–8:

> On this mountain the LORD of hosts will make for all peoples a feast of fat things, a feast of choice wines—of fat things full of marrow, of choice wines well refined. And he will destroy on this mountain the covering that is cast over all peoples, the veil that is spread over all nations. He will swallow up death for ever.

The combination of a supernatural sacrificial feast including choice wine, together with the promise of the destruction of death, foreshadows Jesus's Bread of Life discourse, in which He promises eternal life to those who partake of the feast of His Body and Blood:

---

[4] See *ST* III, q. 72, a. 2, ad 1; q. 72, a. 5.

[5] Paul VI, Apostolic Constitution on the Sacrament of Confirmation *Divinae Consortium Naturae* (Aug 15, 1971), in *Rites*, 1:473–74.

[6] See Mal 1:11: "For from the rising of the sun to its setting my name is great among the nations, and in every place incense is offered to my name, and a pure offering." The Fathers of the Church recognize the Eucharist as this pure offering made to God in every place among the nations. See Lawrence Feingold, *The Eucharist: Mystery of Presence, Sacrifice, and Communion* (Steubenville, OH: Emmaus Academic, 2018), 130, 139, 160.

"he who eats my flesh and drinks my blood has eternal life, and I will raise him up at the last day" (John 6:54).

Centrality of the Sacraments in the Life of the Church

As the life of Israel through the centuries was structured by the sacramental rites of the Old Covenant, so it was fitting that Jesus continue that sacramental structure[7] but transform those rites in accordance with the messianic expectations of an internalization of the Law and an abundant communication of the Holy Spirit to infuse charity and forgive sins. The New Covenant thus shows a combination of continuity and transformation with regard to the sacramental life of the Old Covenant.

Jesus made use of Jewish ritual immersion to manifest Himself to Israel, to institute Baptism, and to prefigure the effects of Confirmation. John the Baptist bears witness to this: "I saw the Spirit descend as a dove from heaven and remain on him. I myself did not know him; but he who sent me to baptize with water said to me, 'He on whom you see the Spirit descend and remain, this is he who baptizes with the Holy Spirit'" (John 1:32–33). Jesus continues to baptize with the Holy Spirit through the sacraments of Baptism and Confirmation. He took a rite with deep roots in Israel—ritual ablution or immersion[8]—and gives it a new efficacy by which the Spirit works through it.

The central sacrament of the New Covenant, the Eucharist, was instituted in the context of the celebration of the Passover, in which Jesus gave Himself to be our Paschal Lamb in the new Passover of the Church. Holy Orders was instituted at the same time, when Jesus said to His Apostles, "Do this in memory of me." Finally, He chose the Jewish feast of Pentecost to send His Spirit, giving the sacrament of Confirmation.

The Acts of the Apostles shows us the centrality of the sacraments in the life of the Church in her first two decades. At that time (as at every time in the Church), ecclesial life centered on the "breaking of

---

[7] See Frank Gavin, *The Jewish Antecedents of the Christian Sacraments* (New York: Ktav Publishing House, 1969), 1–25; Robert Hayward, "The Jewish Roots of Christian Liturgy," in *T&T Clark Companion to Liturgy*, ed. Alcuin Reid (London: Bloomsbury T&T Clark, 2016), 23–42.

[8] See Gavin, *Jewish Antecedents of the Christian Sacraments*, 26–58.

bread,"[9] which is the Eucharist, and on the apostolic ministry, which was aided by the institution of the order of deacons.[10] Three thousand were baptized on Pentecost, and we see Baptism and Confirmation administered when the faith spread to Samaria and the Greek world.[11] This centrality of the sacraments becomes still more evident in the writing of the Apostolic Fathers, such as St. Ignatius of Antioch[12] and St. Justin Martyr. In his *First Apology*, St. Justin gives a detailed description of the sacramental liturgy of Baptism and the Eucharist.[13]

The life of the Church as we see it in the New Testament and throughout the ages is marked by sensible rites, prefigured by those of the Old Covenant, by which the grace won for us by Christ, which is a share in His divine life, is both represented and effectively communicated. The sacraments are visible channels of this invisible grace gained by Christ for His Church. As will be shown more fully in the following chapter, a sacrament of the New Covenant can be defined as a sacred sign of our sanctification by Christ, instituted by Him, which efficaciously confers a participation in the paschal grace that it represents, unless it encounters the obstacle of unrepentance. This grace is both a remedy for sin and a share in Christ's life in the Church.

The sacraments continue the mystery of the Incarnate Son. Because Christ is God and man, His invisible divine power works through His visible humanity, and the sacraments continue to make present this mystery of the divine-human action of Christ. No longer visible to us after His Ascension, He now works through these sensible sacramental signs. St. Thomas explains that in order for our human weakness to be able to receive the immense power of God's word, it is supremely fitting that that power work through the mediation of the humanity of Christ and His sacraments:

> The word is the power of God, by which all things are upheld. ... But because "the word of God is living and effectual, and more piercing than any two-edged sword" (Heb 4:12), for a

---

9 Acts 2:42, 46.

10 See Acts 6:2–6.

11 For Samaria, see Acts 8:12–17; for Ephesus, see Acts 19:2–6.

12 See Ignatius of Antioch, *Letter to the Ephesians* 5, 20; *Letter to the Romans* 7; *Letter to the Smyrnaeans* 8, *Letter to the Philadelphians* 4.

13 Justin Martyr, *First Apology* 61, 65–67, trans. Leslie William Barnard, in *St. Justin Martyr: The First and Second Apologies* (New York; Mahwah, NJ: Paulist Press, 1997), 66–71.

treatment so violent to be effective for us it was necessary that the infirmity of our flesh might be joined to it, so that it might be more suited to us; therefore "he had to become like his brethren in all things, so that he could be a merciful and faithful high priest" (Heb 2:17). And for this reason, "the Word became flesh and dwelt among us" (Jn 1:14). But because this treatment is so powerful that it can cure all men ("for power went out from him and he cured all," as it says in Luke 6:19), therefore from this universal medicine come forth other particular medicines resembling the universal medicine, and by these intermediaries the power of the universal medicine reaches the sick: and these are the sacraments, "in which under the cover of visible things, divine power works our healing in a hidden way,"[14] as Augustine says.[15]

The humanity of the Word incarnate is the universal remedy for all the ills of the human race.[16] The sacraments are seven more particular remedies that have come forth from Him as intermediaries capable of reaching all the sick in all ages and regions.

St. Albert compares the seven sacraments to the seven pillars that support Wisdom's house in Proverbs 9:1: "Wisdom has built her house, she has set up her seven pillars." As a house rests on her pillars, so the Church rests on her sacraments. St. Albert concludes that the seven columns of the Church therefore "are seven sacramental graces."[17]

WHY DID CHRIST INSTITUTE A SACRAMENTAL ECONOMY USING SENSIBLE SIGNS?

Why did Christ choose to bring about the sanctification of man using visible sacraments? Since the grace they signify and truly confer is

---

[14] This quote is actually from Isidore, *Etymologies*, bk. 6, ch. 19, no. 40 (PL 82:255).

[15] Thomas Aquinas, *In IV Sent.*, prologue, trans. Beth Mortensen, WTA, vol. 7 (Green Bay, WI: Aquinas Institute, 2017), 1. This is his introduction to his first treatise on the sacraments in his commentary on the fourth book of the *Sentences*.

[16] See Theodoret of Cyrus, *On the Incarnation of the Lord* 29 [28], in István Pásztori-Kupán, *Theodoret of Cyrus* (London and New York: Routledge, 2006), 165: "Our medication, therefore, is the suffering of our Saviour."

[17] Albert, *Commentarii in libros Sententiarum*, bk. IV, prologus, ed. Borgnet, in *Opera omnia*, vol. 29, *In IV Sent., d. 1–22* (Paris: Vivès, 1894), 2.

something invisible and spiritual, we might think that that grace would best be conferred in a purely invisible and spiritual way.

The short answer is that Christ saved the world by assuming the concrete physical realities of human life in His Incarnation and Paschal mystery. It is fitting that the salvation He won for us through human realities be communicated to us through sensible signs of those human realities He assumed for our salvation.

Needless to say, God had other possibilities. He could have chosen to bring mankind to heaven through other means than those He actually chose. He could have saved man simply by teaching him a doctrine of salvation. This is a great temptation for the human mind, expressed both in the ancient Gnostic heresies and the Enlightenment and liberal Protestant understanding, according to which Christ is the great moral or philosophical teacher. In such a view, the sacraments would have no essential place. Alternatively, if God simply infused grace into us in a purely spiritual way without sensible signs, there would be no sacramental economy.

Sanctification through Sensible Signs Mirrors Man's Place in Creation

The key to understanding why Christ chose a sacramental economy to impart grace is that man is a rational animal whose place in the hierarchy of creation is at the intersection of the material and spiritual worlds.[18] Our bodies situate us firmly in the material world. Our rational and spiritual souls, however, place us in the spiritual world as the lowest level of spiritual creatures. Human beings are at the top of one half of creation, the physical, but at the bottom of the other invisible half of creation, the spiritual, populated by myriads of angels above us.

This understanding of man's place in the universe is the profound sense in which man is said to be a *microcosm*, meaning a cosmos in

---

[18] See Bonaventure, *In IV Sent.*, d. 1, p. 1, a. 1, q. 1, sed contra 3, in *Commentary on the Sentences: Sacraments*, trans. Wayne Hellmann et al. (St. Bonaventure, NY: The Franciscan Institute, 2016), 46: "Human nature had fallen in soul and in body. In order that human nature be fully restored it was fitting that God take on the totality of human nature. Therefore if medicines are to correspond with the effect of restoration, it was fitting that the medicine be comprised of something corporeal and spiritual. Such are the sacraments. Therefore the sacraments ought to have been instituted."

miniature, or "little universe."[19] Man is a little universe because he has in himself both orders of God's creation. We have in our bodies the perfection of the physical universe, summing it up, and we have in our souls a part of the spiritual universe, although in its lowest form. We unite in ourselves all the different levels of God's creation.[20]

Because he has lost an understanding of his place in the universe, modern man tends to fall into one of the two opposing heresies of materialism and angelism.[21] The more common error of materialism consists in denying the existence of the spiritual realm altogether. Man would simply be a highly organized body, and what we think of as our soul would just be our marvelous organization. Angelism, on the other hand, consists in thinking of ourselves as if we were angels in some way. This comes from the founder of modern philosophy, René Descartes, who thought of man as two things: a thinking thing (*res cogitans*), and an extended thing (*res extensa*), which means a body endowed with dimensionality. For Descartes, our soul would be a kind of angel that is somehow joined to a body.[22] The problem with this conception is that it fails to do justice to the profound union of body and soul in man. Our body as well as our soul is an essential part of who we are.

Both materialism and angelism make it impossible to understand

---

[19] See Norris Clarke, S.J., "Living on the Edge: The Human Person as 'Frontier Being' and Microcosm," in *The Creative Retrieval of Saint Thomas Aquinas: Essays in Thomistic Philosophy, New and Old* (New York: Fordham University Press, 2009), 132–51; G. Verbeke, "Man as a 'Frontier' according to Aquinas," in *Aquinas and Problems of His Time,* eds. G. Verbeke and D. Verhelst (Leuven: Leuven University Press, 1976), 195–223.

[20] See *ST* I, q. 96, a. 2: "Man in a certain sense contains all things; and so according as he is master of what is within himself, in the same way he can have mastership over other things. Now we may consider four things in man: his 'reason,' which makes him like to the angels; his 'sensitive powers,' whereby he is like the animals; his 'natural forces,' which liken him to the plants; and 'the body itself,' wherein he is like to inanimate things."

[21] See Peter Kreeft, *Christianity for Modern Pagans: Pascal's Pensées Edited, Outlined and Explained* (San Francisco: Ignatius Press, 1993), 52–53: "The two fundamental human heresies, the two banes of modern philosophy, are animalism and angelism. Man has lost his place in the cosmos, the place between angel and beast. . . . The angelist reduces the world to a projection of the self; the animalist reduces the self to a species in the animal world. . . . Modern philosophy has lost its sane anthropology because it has lost its cosmology. Man does not know himself because he does not know his place in the cosmos."

[22] See Jacques Maritain, *Three Reformers: Luther, Descartes, Rousseau* (New York: Scribner's, 1929), 59–89.

why God wanted to institute sacraments. The materialist will admit the outward sacramental sign but fail to acknowledge any supernatural effect. Angelism, on the other hand, prefers that invisible graces be given only through a purely spiritual means, such as faith. The sacraments will be recast as mere signs of the giving of grace in a purely spiritual way through faith. This is the tendency of Protestantism,[23] which is further radicalized in the liberal Protestantism of the last two centuries.[24]

But since human nature is situated at the intersection of the spiritual and the material realms, it is fitting that our salvation come to us through means in which the two realms also intersect. The sacraments are such means since they communicate invisible grace through physical and sensible signs belonging to the material world. The sacramental system manifests the philosophical principle that everything is received according to the mode of the recipient. Since we are not angels but human beings, sanctification fittingly comes to us through sensible signs that respect our bodily condition.

Sanctification through Sensible Signs Is Fitting for Man's Natural Way of Knowing

As a rational animal, all our natural knowledge comes from abstraction from sense experience. Therefore it is natural for man to grasp spiritual realities through abstraction from sense knowledge. Thus it is also natural for man to learn about and receive spiritual realities through some kind of sensible contact and to worship God through sensible signs. For this reason it is fitting that Christ give to His Church a means of worship and sanctification involving sensible signs

---

[23] See Phillip Cary, "Why Luther Is Not Quite Protestant: The Logic of Faith in a Sacramental Promise," *Pro Ecclesia* 14, no. 4 (Fall 2005): 447–86.

[24] See Joseph Ratzinger, "The Sacramental Foundation of Christian Existence," in *Theology of the Liturgy*, 165–66: "When Bultmann says that spirit cannot be nourished by material things and with that thinks he has dispensed with the sacramental principle, ultimately the same naïve notion about man's spiritual autonomy [as in the idealism of Fichte] is still at work. . . . If, however, there is no such thing as the autonomy of the human spirit, . . . then the question is fundamentally different. Then his relationship to God, if it is to be a human relationship to God, must be just as man is: corporeal, fraternal, and historical. Or there is no such thing. The error of anti-sacramental idealism consists in the fact that it wants to make man into a pure spirit in God's sight. Instead of a man, the only thing remaining is a ghost that does not exist, and any religiosity that tried to build on such foundations has built on shifting sand."

in accordance with our way of knowing, as St. Thomas explains:

> Divine wisdom provides for each thing according to its mode; hence it is written (Wisdom 8:1) that "she . . . ordereth all things sweetly": wherefore also we are told (Matthew 25:15) that she "gave to everyone according to his proper ability." Now it is part of man's nature to acquire knowledge of the intelligible from the sensible. But a sign is that by means of which one attains to the knowledge of something else. Consequently, since the sacred things which are signified by the sacraments, are the spiritual and intelligible goods by means of which man is sanctified, it follows that the sacramental signs consist in sensible things: just as in the Divine Scriptures spiritual things are set before us under the guise of things sensible. And hence it is that sensible things are required for the sacraments; as Dionysius also proves in his book on the heavenly hierarchy (*Celestial Hierarchy* 1).[25]

The *Catechism of the Council of Trent* developed the same idea:

> We are so constituted by nature that we can understand nothing intellectually unless it is first perceived through the senses. Out of his goodness, the Creator of all things wisely decreed that the mysterious effect of his infinite power should be made intelligible to us by means of certain signs evident to our senses. If man were not clothed, as it were, in a material body, St. John Chrysostom tells us, goodness would have been presented to him in a manner likewise unclothed; but since his soul is in fact embodied, it is absolutely necessary that certain sensory signs be used if he is to have any understanding of what goodness is.[26]

---

[25] *ST* III, q. 60, a. 4. See also *ST* III, q. 61, a. 1: "Sacraments are necessary unto man's salvation for three reasons. The first is taken from the condition of human nature which is such that it has to be led by things corporeal and sensible to things spiritual and intelligible. Now it belongs to Divine providence to provide for each one according as its condition requires. Divine wisdom, therefore, fittingly provides man with means of salvation, in the shape of corporeal and sensible signs that are called sacraments."

[26] *CCT*, part 2, intro., §14, p. 151.

The Sacraments Mirror Human Culture

By sanctifying us through sensible sacraments, Christ has chosen the instruments of our sanctification to be analogous to cultural and artistic works, such as art, literature, and music, as well as religious rites, which always involve both a sensible and a spiritual dimension, as well as a social one. Because man is a rational animal, the products of our labor and the fundamental events of our physical life symbolize our spiritual yearnings as well as satisfy the needs of our biological existence. As long as we are conscious, nothing in human life is purely biological or functional. The human meal, for example, has a communal and spiritual dimension that is intrinsic to it and distinguishes it from animal eating.[27] Likewise the human sexual act is not only a biological act, but also has an exceedingly profound unitive and fruitful meaning that is at the root of human sexual morality and the sacramentality of marriage. We find a symbolism written into nature (the typology of creation), and we put a symbolism—more or less profound—into the work of our hands and also into the key events of our national and family histories. This capacity of man's works and deeds to embody desires that transcend the physical world is the natural foundation of sacramentality. Because man is naturally a symbol-making creature, it is fitting that man's salvation be worked out through sacraments in which symbols of creation and religion are elevated to the order of grace. Joseph Ratzinger states this eloquently:

> Thus the sacraments are at the same time a Christian novelty and a primordially human thing. The newness of Christianity and the oneness of the human element do not contradict each other. In Jesus Christ, creation is taken up and purified, and in just this way he proves to be the One who gives man an answer and is his salvation. The symbols of creation are signs pointing to Christ, and Christ is the fulfillment not only of history but also of creation: In him who is the *mysterium* of God, everything attains its unity.[28]

---

[27] See Joseph Ratzinger, "The Sacramental Foundation of Christian Existence," in *Theology of the Liturgy*, 156–57; Leon R. Kass, *The Hungry Soul: Eating and the Perfecting of Our Nature* (Chicago; London: University of Chicago Press, 1999).

[28] Joseph Ratzinger, "On the Concept of Sacrament," in *Theology of the Liturgy*, 184.

The *Catechism of the Catholic Church*, §1152 summarizes this fittingness of the sacraments:

> The sacraments of the Church do not abolish but purify and integrate all the richness of the signs and symbols of the cosmos and of social life. Further, they fulfill the types and figures of the Old Covenant, signify and make actively present the salvation wrought by Christ, and prefigure and anticipate the glory of heaven.

The sacraments exemplify God's perfect pedagogy by which He speaks to man in a way appropriate to human nature. He comes down to our level by a marvelous condescension[29] so that we can encounter Him with our whole being, body and soul.

The Sacraments Mirror the Incarnation

The divine condescension that we see in the fact that God speaks to man in a manner appropriate to our nature reaches its summit in the Incarnation. That the Word has become flesh in the midst of history is the most important foundation for the fittingness of the sacraments. Since the Word has taken on flesh and conversed with mankind in a sensible fashion appropriate for men, it is fitting that He sanctify us through some kind of continued contact with His sacred humanity, which is accomplished in a mysterious way through the sensible signs of the sacraments. The sacramental economy is thus profoundly fitting for the Church founded by the Word Incarnate. If Christ did not institute sacraments to sanctify His Church but gave grace in a purely spiritual way, there would be no manifestation of the truth that the Incarnation is the source of all human sanctification.

The sacraments therefore reflect not only man's nature, but still more profoundly, they reflect the two natures of the Word Incarnate and serve as extensions of His touch and of His words after His Ascension into heaven. Just as Christ is sensible through His humanity but invisible in His divine power, so also the sacraments are sensible in their aspect as sign, but their sensible word is endowed with omnipotent power to sanctify and realize what they represent and divinize the

---

[29] On the "divine condescension" in Revelation, see Feingold, *Faith Comes from What Is Heard*, 3–7.

recipients by giving them a share in Christ's divine life. This idea is beautifully stated by Cyprian Vagaggini:

> There are two aspects to this law of incarnation. First of all it signifies that God communicates divine life to man through and under the veil of sensible things, which means in turn that man is obliged to pass through these sensible things in order to receive that divine life. In the second place, it signifies that what results from that communication is an elevation of man to a divine mode of being and acting.[30]

Just as the Eternal One entered history through the Incarnation and became visible to our senses, His transcendent grace enters history and becomes indirectly visible through the visible sacramental signs through which divinizing grace is communicated and the power of the Paschal mystery made present.

The sacramental economy of the New Covenant has its foundation in the fact that the Word has become flesh. As will be seen more fully below,[31] the Incarnation divides the prefigurative or typological rites of the Old Covenant from the sacraments of the New. Before the Incarnation, the sacred rites of the Old Covenant prefigured Christ and constituted a visible promise of His grace. Because of the Incarnation, the sacraments of the New Covenant can do immeasurably more. Because they are wielded by the humanity of Christ, our eternal High Priest, they give us a contact with Him and enable us to receive His words of power today throughout the life of the Church. The sacraments are like an extension of the humanity of Christ and His Paschal mystery suited to our pilgrimage of faith and capable of reaching and touching us throughout time and space since His Coming.

The sacraments, therefore, are profoundly Christological. They only exist and operate through the fact of His Incarnation. Their mysterious power to give grace through sensible signs is modeled on the union of the two natures in Christ. Their structure matches the Christological mystery at the heart of the New Covenant.[32]

---

[30] Cyprian Vagaggini, *Theological Dimensions of the Liturgy*, trans. Leonard Doyle and W. A. Jurgens (Collegeville, MN: Liturgical Press, 1976), 300.

[31] See chapter 14 below, pp. 506–9.

[32] For a profound treatment of the Incarnation as the model or archetype for the sacraments, see Scheeben, *The Mysteries of Christianity*, 564–66.

The Trinitarian Movement of the Sacraments

The sacraments are also profoundly Trinitarian in their structure and operation. The Son of God acts through the sacraments to give us the Holy Spirit to unite us with His Father. The Father is the goal of the sacramental action, and the Second and Third Persons are the invisible agents of its efficacy in reconciling us with the Father. The Son acts through the sacraments as the eternal High Priest and communicates the Spirit through them. The Spirit that is given through the sacraments is the Spirit of the Son, through whom we are configured more closely with the identity and sonship of Christ and united with the Father as sons in the Son. St. Paul describes this process in Romans 8:15–17: "you have received the spirit of sonship. When we cry, 'Abba! Father!' it is the Spirit himself bearing witness with our spirit that we are children of God, and if children, then heirs, heirs of God and fellow heirs with Christ."

Perhaps the clearest image of this Trinitarian structure of the sacraments can be seen in the Baptism of Christ. Matthew 3:16–17 tells us that after his baptism by John, "the heavens were opened and he saw the Spirit of God descending like a dove, and alighting on him; and behold, a voice from heaven, saying, 'This is my beloved Son, with whom I am well pleased.'" In all the sacraments the Son wins for us the descent of the Holy Spirit who communicates to us the spirit of sonship, uniting us with the Father as His sons and daughters.[33]

The Sacraments Mirror the Church, Giving Her Visible Structure and Invisible Life

The sacraments in their visible and invisible dimensions mirror not only Christ but also the Church, for the Church as Christ's Mystical Body is made in His image, and is therefore endowed with both a visible human and an invisible divine dimension.[34] The Church as the

---

[33] See Fagerberg's definition of liturgy in, "Liturgy, Signs, and Sacraments," in *OHST*, 456, 458: "Liturgy is the perichoresis of the Trinity kenotically extended to invite our synergistic ascent into deification. . . . The Trinity's circulation of love turns itself outward, and in humility the Son and Spirit work the Father's good pleasure for all creation, which is to invite our ascent to participate in the very life of God; however, this cannot be forced, it must be done with our cooperation."

[34] On the visible and invisible dimensions of the Church, see Scheeben, *Mysteries*

Mystical Body is a "society structured with hierarchical organs" with a "visible delineation" and a "visible social structure"[35] and she has an invisible dimension, which is the Holy Spirit who vivifies her. The visible sacramental structure of the Church is the sign and instrument of the invisible communion in grace effected by the Holy Spirit, as Christ's sacred humanity was the living and rational instrument and "sacrament" of His divinity.

Since Christ willed to institute a visible Church that would involve a participation in His divine life, it was fitting that He institute means of sharing in His divine life that are visible and sensible and are capable of building up a visible Church. If Christ simply infused grace in us without any sensible signs or sacraments, the Church would be essentially invisible as the collection of those who cooperate with invisible grace, and would not bear a resemblance to or have any visible connection with her Incarnate Lord.

Since the sacraments make the Church and enable her to share in the life of her Head, and if the Church is to have both a visible and an invisible dimension, the sacraments must likewise have what they give, and be sensible means of divinization. Thus the sacraments can be said to mirror the Church, and vice versa. It is for this reason that the Second Vatican Council in *Lumen Gentium*, §48 speaks of the Church as the "universal sacrament of salvation."[36] So just as the Church is simultaneously both visible and invisible, so it is appropriate that the sacraments that build up the Church and mold her life through the ages also be visible signs that communicate invisible divine grace.

Lumen Gentium, §8 explains the inseparable unity of these two dimensions in the Church:

> Christ, the one Mediator, established and continually sustains here on earth His holy Church, the community of faith, hope and charity, as an entity with visible delineation through which He communicated truth and grace to all. But, the society

---

of Christianity, 539–42.

[35] See *LG*, §8.

[36] See also *LG*, §1: "The Church is in Christ like a sacrament or as a sign and instrument both of a very closely knit union with God and of the unity of the whole human race." On the Church as having the nature of a sacrament, see below, chapter 3, pp. 94–97.

structured with hierarchical organs and the Mystical Body of Christ, are not to be considered as two realities, nor are the visible assembly and the spiritual community, nor the earthly Church and the Church enriched with heavenly things; rather they form one complex reality which coalesces from a divine and a human element. For this reason, by no weak analogy, it is compared to the mystery of the incarnate Word. As the assumed nature inseparably united to Him, serves the divine Word as a living organ of salvation, so, in a similar way, does the visible social structure of the Church serve the Spirit of Christ, who vivifies it, in the building up of the body.

The sacramental system is the divinely appointed means by which the Church is given both a *visible* social dimension and an *invisible* supernatural life. Through their visible nature as signs, the sacraments make visible the members of the Church, her hierarchy, her worship, and sanctification. Without Baptism the Church would not be visible in her members, and without Holy Orders she would have no visible supernatural structure or governance. The *Catechism of the Council of Trent*, drawing on St. Augustine,[37] explains:

> There have to be certain distinguishing marks and symbols to identify the faithful. According to St. Augustine, there is no human society—whether its religion is true or false makes no difference—which can become as it were one body, unless it is held together by some bond of visible signs. Both these purposes are met by the sacraments of the New Law; they distinguish Christians from unbelievers, and they bind together the faithful themselves by a kind of sacred bond.[38]

The sacraments make visible members of the Church with a visible bond. The sacraments also bring the Church together in a common worship, especially in the Eucharistic Sacrifice. In a similar way, Israel

---

[37] Augustine, *Reply to Faustus the Manichaean* 19.11, trans. Richard Stothert, in *NPNF*1, 4:243: "There can be no religious society, whether the religion be true or false, without some sacrament or visible symbol to serve as a bond of union. The importance of these sacraments cannot be overstated." St. Thomas quotes this text in the *sed contra* in his explanation of the fittingness of the sacraments in *ST* III, q. 61, a. 1.

[38] *CCT*, part 2, intro., §14, p. 152.

was formed as a visible and holy people by the common bond of circumcision and her common worship commanded in the Law through the sacraments and sacrifices of the Old Covenant. But at the same time, as will be studied in chapter 14 below, the sacraments of the Church efficaciously realize the invisible holiness of the Church in a way that the Old Testament sacraments could not, because Christ had not yet come. The sacraments thus mirror the Church and at the same time make her to be what she is, a Bride of Christ made like Him through a visible and invisible likeness.

The Protestant Reformation was in part an attack on the visible aspect of the Church and her hierarchy. Luther[39] and Calvin[40] tended to excessively distinguish the visible and the invisible Church and to conceive the Church as essentially hidden or invisible. Not surprisingly, such a conception of the Church had repercussions, although in differing degrees, on the comprehension of the sacramental system.

Sanctification through Sensible Signs Heals Man Where He Is Frequently Tempted

Another reason for the sensible nature of the sacraments is that it is fitting to apply a remedy where there is a wound. Before the Fall, Adam and Eve were naked and unashamed. As a result of original sin, however, we have suffered the loss of the preternatural gift of integrity by which our sense appetites were kept in conformity with reason. Our sensible appetite frequently seduces us into acting against reason, for we can be vehemently attracted by some sensible and disordered good. Since the senses, which in God's plan are meant to lead us to natural and spiritual goods, are now a frequent cause of sin, God has willed to cure us from concupiscence by means of something sensible. St. Thomas explains the fittingness of healing man through sensible sacraments:

> In sinning [man] subjected himself by his affections to corporeal things. Now the healing remedy should be given to a man so as to reach the part affected by disease. Consequently

---

[39] For Luther's complex thought on this topic, see Mark A. Noll, "Martin Luther and the Concept of a 'True' Church," *Evangelical Quarterly* 50 (1978): 79–85.

[40] See John Calvin, *Institutes of the Christian Religion*, 4.1.7–12, trans. Henry Beveridge (Peabody, MA: Hendrickson Publishers, 2008), 677–80.

it was fitting that God should provide man with a spiritual medicine by means of certain corporeal signs; for if man were offered spiritual things without a veil, his mind being taken up with the material world would be unable to apply itself to them. . . . Lest, therefore, it should be too hard for man to be drawn away entirely from bodily actions, bodily exercise was offered to him in the sacraments, by which he might be trained to avoid superstitious practices . . . and all manner of harmful action.[41]

By giving us spiritual medicine in sensible form, the sacraments also inculcate humility, reminding us that we are not angels but human beings wounded by disordered attachment to physical things and therefore in need of sensible as well as spiritual remedies.[42] The *Catechism of the Council of Trent* explains:

This thought is of great importance in the pursuit of the Christian life—the sacraments repress and subdue the pride of the human heart and encourage the practice of humility, by forcing us in this submission of ourselves to things of sense to obey God, from whom we had wickedly departed in order to serve the elements of this world.[43]

---

[41] *ST* III, q. 61, a. 1.

[42] St. Bonaventure develops this argument of fittingness in his *Breviloquium*, part 6, ch. 1, nos. 3–4, trans. Dominic V. Monti (St. Bonaventure, NY: The Franciscan Institute, 2005), 212–13; and *In IV Sent.*, d. 1, p. 1, a . 1, q. 1, in *Commentary on the Sentences: Sacraments*, trans. Hellmann, 47: "It is of the highest wisdom to find a remedy in the very things that were the occasion of the fall. . . . Thus, because humans had taken the occasion for the fall from visible things, it befitted divine wisdom to find the remedy in the same things. This was advantageous on the part of the sick people, because they were blind with respect to being able to consider things rightly. Therefore, visible sacraments were given to them for their education. Humans were also carried away by proneness to anger. Therefore, corporeal sacraments were given them for their humiliation. They were also despicable with respect to their lusts so that they had no taste for spiritual things. Therefore, sacraments were given to them for training, lest they give rise in themselves to contempt or boredom, and this by perceiving one thing only or by contemplating only spiritual things." See also Hugh of St. Victor, *On the Sacraments of the Christian Faith* 1.9.3, trans. Roy J. Deferrari (Cambridge, MA: Mediaeval Academy of America, 1951), 156; Peter Lombard, *Sentences*, bk. 4, d. 1, ch. 5, nos. 1–4, trans. Silano, 5.

[43] *CCT*, part 2, intro., §14, p. 153.

The sacraments make possible a concrete encounter with Christ that is perfectly fitting for our human nature and its limitations. Pope Francis speaks of the sacraments in this way: "The Sacraments, as we know, are the locus of the closeness and the tenderness of God for mankind; they are the concrete way that God thought and wanted to come and meet us, to embrace us, without being ashamed of us and of our limitations."[44]

Fittingness of the Sacramentality of Penance

The sacrament of Penance poses a particular problem with regard to the fittingness of its sensible dimension, for perhaps more than with the other sacraments many wonder why it would not be sufficient to simply ask God in prayer for the forgiveness of sins. Why must there be a sacramental encounter with a priest that includes a confession of mortal sins complete in number and kind?[45] The sacrament of Penance, precisely because of its special difficulty, manifests in a particular way the various aspects of the fittingness of the sacraments that is anthropological, Christological, ecclesiological, and humbling.

The anthropological aspect assumes a special relevance in Penance

---

[44] Pope Francis, Address to seminarians and priests taking the course on the internal forum organized by the Apostolic Penitentiary, Mar 12, 2015.

[45] Many have spoken of the crisis of the sacrament of Penance in recent decades, manifested by a decline in the reception of sacramental Confession among Catholics. See John Paul II, Post-Synodal Apostolic Exhortation on Reconciliation and Penance in the Mission of the Church Today *Reconciliatio et Paenitentia* (Dec 2, 1984), §28: "For the sacrament of confession is indeed being undermined, on the one hand by the obscuring of the mortal and religious conscience, the lessening of a sense of sin, the distortion of the concept of repentance and the lack of effort to live an authentically Christian life. And on the other hand, it is being undermined by the sometimes widespread idea that one can obtain forgiveness directly from God, even in a habitual way, without approaching the sacrament of reconciliation." See also Cardinal Walter Kasper, *Mercy: The Essence of the Gospel and the Key to Christian Life,* trans. William Madges (New York; Mahwah, NJ: Paulist Press, 2013), 164–65: "Presently, one must speak of a serious crisis concerning this sacrament. In most parishes, the sacrament has largely fallen out of use and many Christians, even those who regularly participate in the Sunday Eucharist, do so without the sacramental praxis of penance. This fact is one of the deep wounds of the present church; this must be an occasion for us to seriously examine our personal and our pastoral conscience. For the future of the church, it is essential to come to a reinvigorated penitential order and a renewal of the sacrament of reconciliation."

because guilt and shame, when kept locked up within us, tend to fester. There is a natural human benefit to unburdening the feeling of guilt and sorrow by expressing it outwardly to God through the sacramental mediation of another human being who listens and then outwardly pronounces the most comforting of words in absolution. Confession thus enables the sinner to unburden the intolerable weight that lies on his conscience, share it with another, humbly come to terms with his sin, and seek counsel with the certainty of confidentiality. St. John Henry Newman, a few years after his entrance into the Catholic Church and priestly ordination, defended the sacrament of Penance from the stereotyped attack of Protestants and explained its profound anthropological benefit:

> How many are the souls, in distress, anxiety or loneliness, whose one need is to find a being to whom they can pour out their feelings unheard by the world? Tell them out they must; they cannot tell them out to those whom they see every hour. They want to tell them and not to tell them; and they want to tell them out, yet be as if they be not told; they wish to tell them to one who is strong enough to bear them, yet not too strong to despise them; they wish to tell them to one who can at once advise and can sympathize with them; they wish to relieve themselves of a load, to gain a solace. . . . How many a Protestant's heart would leap at the news of such a benefit, putting aside all distinct ideas of a sacramental ordinance, or of a grant of pardon and the conveyance of grace! If there is a heavenly idea in the Catholic Church, looking at it simply as an idea, surely, next after the Blessed Sacrament, Confession is such. . . . Oh what piercing, heart-subduing tranquility, provoking tears of joy, is poured, almost substantially and physically upon the soul, the oil of gladness, as Scripture calls it, when the penitent at length rises, his God reconciled to him, his sins rolled away for ever! This is confession as it is in fact; as those bear witness to it who know it by experience.[46]

Secondly, the minister in the sacraments represents Jesus Christ, eternal High Priest who merited our reconciliation with God on

---

[46] John Henry Newman, *The Present Position of Catholics in England* (New York: The America Press, 1942), 268–69.

Calvary. Without confession to a priest there would be no sacramental representation of Christ's own forgiveness, nor of His role as the Mediator of all grace.[47] The sacrament of Penance with confession made to a priest impresses on the mind the centrality of Christ and His Passion as the meritorious source of all forgiveness of sins. If sins were simply confessed to God in the silence of our hearts, there would be no liturgical sign that Christ through His Passion is the one mediator for all forgiveness of sins, won with the price of His Blood. The *Catechism of the Council of Trent* emphasized this:

> No one can be saved but through Christ and the merits of his Passion. It was most fitting in itself and useful to us, therefore, to have a sacrament instituted, by the power and efficacy of which the Blood of Christ would flow into our soul and wash away all our sins committed after Baptism. Such a sacrament would remind us that it is to our Savior alone that we owe this gift of reconciliation with God.[48]

Third, man is a profoundly social being, and our sins affect other human beings.[49] Confessing our sins to a priest brings the sins out of the closet of our interior solitude and acknowledges their social dimension, enabling us to recognize them with a degree of objectivity. All sin wounds the Church and her unity. Thus it is profoundly fitting that sins be manifested to a priestly minister who represents both Christ and the Church and brings about reconciliation in both the vertical and horizontal dimensions. Pope Francis stresses the great

---

[47] See Thomas Aquinas, *In IV Sent.*, d. 17, q. 3, a. 3, qla. 1, trans. Mortensen, 8:332: "The grace that is given in the sacraments descends to the members from the head; and so he alone is the minister of the sacraments, in which grace is given, who has the ministry over the true body of Christ. And this belongs to the priest alone, who can consecrate the Eucharist. And thus, since grace is conferred in the sacrament of penance, only a priest is the minister of this sacrament. And so sacramental confession, which should be made to a minister of the Church, must be made to him alone."

[48] *CCT*, part 2, ch. 4, §10, p. 260.

[49] See Anthony Akinwale, "Reconciliation," in *OHST*, 545: "Individualism facilitates the conception of religion as a purely private affair. Religion then is between me and my God. By extension, sin is an offence against God, and reconciliation is between me and my God. Unable to understand that religion is not a private but a personal act, individualism finds it difficult to accommodate a ritual of reconciliation that involves confession of sins."

importance of the interpersonal dimension of Confession in *The Name of God Is Mercy*:

> If you are not capable of talking to your brother about your mistakes, you can be sure that you can't talk about them with God, either, and therefore you end up confessing into the mirror, to yourself. We are social beings, and forgiveness has a social implication; my sin wounds mankind, my brothers and sisters, and society as a whole. Confessing to a priest is a way of putting my life into the hands and heart of someone else, someone who in that moment acts in the name of Jesus. It's a way to be real and authentic: we face the facts by looking at another person and not in the mirror. . . . It is true that I can talk to the Lord and ask him for forgiveness, implore him. And the Lord will forgive me immediately.[50] But it is important that I go to confession, that I sit in front of a priest who embodies Jesus, that I kneel before Mother Church, called to dispense the mercy of Christ. There is objectivity in this gesture of genuflection before the priest; it becomes the vehicle through which grace reaches and heals me.[51]

Fourth, the fact that the priest speaks the words of absolution after he hears the confession gives a certainty to the penitent that indeed his sins are forgiven, enabling a fresh start. For the priest speaks with the authority of Jesus Christ, who said to the paralytic: "My son, your sins are forgiven" (Mark 2:5). The intervention of the priest in Confession thus makes possible the joy and consolation of having the certainty of forgiveness, through hearing efficacious words of power and consolation spoken in the person of Christ.[52]

---

[50] On the anticipation of the effects of the sacrament of Penance through an act of perfect contrition, see chapter 15 below, pp. 601–5.

[51] Pope Francis (Jorge Mario Bergoglio), *The Name of God Is Mercy: A Conversation with Andrea Tornielli*, trans. Oonagh Stransky (New York: Random House, 2016), 21–23.

[52] See *CCT*, part 2, ch. 4, §10, p. 260: "The faithful should be taught why it was that Christ our Lord willed to number penance among the sacraments. One reason must have been his intention to remove all uncertainty as to the remission of sin promised by God. . . . Everyone has good reason to distrust the accuracy of his judgment regarding his own actions; and so there could be some real anxiety as to the genuineness and adequacy of his interior penance. To remove this anxiety, our Lord instituted the sacrament of Penance, in which

Finally, like all the sacraments, the simplicity of Penance is humbling. What weighed on conscience, perhaps for years, is removed by a few simple words said in the person of Jesus Christ, to be followed by an act of penance—generally by a prayer or act of charity—that is quickly accomplished. Both the necessity of confession and the simplicity of absolution work to foster humility.

Faith and the Sacraments

The sacraments are an appropriate means of sanctification in an economy of salvation in which we walk by faith before receiving the reward of faith, which is the vision of God. The sacraments both presuppose and foster the virtue of faith, the foundation of human salvation, by which we firmly believe the unseen things that God has revealed. For although the sacraments are visible, what is seen of them is very different from what is believed! Only faith can grasp the promise and the transcendent reality of grace operating in every sacramental celebration. Without faith, the sacramental signs would not be recognized as glorious occasions of encountering the Word made flesh. Just as faith was necessary for those in Capernaum two thousand years ago to recognize Jesus as having words of eternal life (John 6:68), so it is necessary today for those who witness a sacramental celebration to believe that the Son of God is still at work through words of power to sanctify His faithful. Thus every sacramental celebration provides an extraordinary concrete occasion for practicing and growing in faith, without which the sacraments cannot be fruitful.[53] This culminates in the Eucharist in which, as St. Thomas says, "Sight, touch, and taste in Thee are each deceived; the ear alone most safely is believed."[54]

There is an interesting discussion of the relation between the

---

through the absolution of the priest we are assured that our sins are forgiven. Our conscience is given peace because of the faith we rightly repose in the power of the sacraments. The voice of the priest lawfully pardoning our sins in this sacrament is accepted as the very voice of Christ himself."

[53] For the distinction between validity and fruitfulness in the sacraments, see chapter 10 below, pp. 381–86. In the case of infants receiving the sacraments of initiation, faith is supplied by the Church.

[54] Thomas Aquinas, *Adoro Te Devote*, trans. E. Caswall, in Raniero Cantalamessa, *This Is My Body: Eucharistic Reflections Inspired by Adoro Te Devote and Ave Verum* (Boston: Pauline Books & Media, 2005), 13.

virtue of faith and the sacraments in Pope Francis's encyclical *Lumen Fidei*, §40:

> Faith, in fact, needs a setting in which it can be witnessed to and communicated, a means which is suitable and proportionate to what is communicated. For transmitting a purely doctrinal content, an idea might suffice, or perhaps a book, or the repetition of a spoken message. But what is communicated in the Church, what is handed down in her living Tradition, is the new light born of an encounter with the true God, a light which touches us at the core of our being and engages our minds, wills and emotions, opening us to relationships lived in communion. There is a special means for passing down this fullness, a means capable of engaging the entire person, body and spirit, interior life and relationships with others. It is the sacraments, celebrated in the Church's liturgy. The sacraments communicate an incarnate memory, linked to the times and places of our lives, linked to all our senses; in them the whole person is engaged as a member of a living subject and part of a network of communitarian relationships. While the sacraments are indeed sacraments of faith, it can also be said that faith itself possesses a sacramental structure. The awakening of faith is linked to the dawning of a new sacramental sense in our lives as human beings and as Christians, in which visible and material realities are seen to point beyond themselves to the mystery of the eternal.

The Christian life of faith has a sacramental structure because God's providence and hidden transformative power can be seen to work through the concrete and humble realities of everyday life. A classic work of spirituality speaks of the "sacrament of the present moment."[55] What happens most powerfully in the sacraments is also at work in the daily life of those whose life is animated by the grace of the sacraments, which is able to touch all human realities and elevate them into an encounter with Christ. The exercise of faith in the sacraments ought to nourish a habitual capacity to see God's providence at work

---

[55] Jean-Pierre de Caussade, S.J. (1675–1751), *The Sacrament of the Present Moment*. This work has also been published under the title, *Abandonment to Divine Providence*.

in the events of daily life, which, in the eyes of faith, become occasions for the reception of divine inspirations and cooperation with actual graces that have their root in Baptism and the other sacraments.[56]

Sacraments and Typology

There is a close parallel between the fittingness of the sacramental system and biblical typology, which is the capacity of an event or action to prefigure a future salvific reality.[57] In order to reveal Himself to mankind, God makes use not only of words and propositions but also of historical realities and sensible concrete events described by the words of Scripture, which themselves are signs of other realities in Christ and His plan of sanctification. Not only do the Old Testament realities have typological meaning in Christ, but Christ's own deeds, especially in His Paschal mystery, are the type of the Christian life. Christ's death is the model and cause of the Christian death to sin, and His Resurrection is the type and cause of our resurrection to new life in Him, now spiritually through the sacraments and at His Second Coming in the body as well.[58] In both typology and the sacraments, God makes use of sensible realities to signify transcendent realities. The difference is that typology prefigures, but the sacraments not only signify but also cause what they signify, applying it to the recipient. Both typology and sacramentality are fitting for man because our connatural way of knowing goes from the sensible to the spiritual.

This parallelism between sacraments and typology implies that if the notion of typology becomes lost to contemporary Christians, the sacramental system will also cease to be fully meaningful. Both have to be recovered together. Joseph Ratzinger developed this thesis in his essay, "On the Concept of Sacrament":

> The Catholic concept of *sacramentum* is based on the "typological" interpretation of Scripture—an interpretation in terms of parallels to Christ. . . . This central thesis of mine now clarifies the reason for the crisis of Catholicism in the modern era; for one of its intellectual components is the replacement of typological thinking—that is, an interpretation that reads the texts

---

[56] See chapter 10 below on sacramental grace.
[57] See Feingold, *Faith Comes from What Is Heard*, 493–564.
[58] See Rom 6:5–11; Feingold, *Faith Comes from What Is Heard*, 535–40.

from the perspective of their future and with a view to their future—by literary-historical thinking, that is, an interpretation that reads the texts by looking back in time and tries to pin them down to their oldest meaning.[59]

The recovery of an awareness of biblical typology can be a great aid in the strengthening of an appreciation for the sacramental system in the faithful. Both typology and sacramentality derive from the fact that God treats us according to our nature as rational animals who learn first through the senses, which give us some likeness of the spiritual realities that transcend the natural order.

The Sacraments Represent Sanctification in the Past, Present, and Future

The sacraments are fitting for human sanctification also because, like man, they are profoundly historical, while yet transcending history's limitations. As man's life is more than mere chronology, in that our conscious present includes elements of the past and future, so the sacraments transcend the limitations of time's inexorable advance. By making present the historical event of Christ's Paschal mystery, the sacraments, like Christ, are also "suprahistorical," for the Paschal mystery transcends and recapitulates all of history. The Paschal mystery recapitulates history by being prefigured by all that came before it, and by being the archetype of our current sanctification in the Church and in the heavenly realities to come.[60]

After defining sacraments as signs of man's sanctification, St.

---

[59] Ratzinger, "On the Concept of Sacrament," in *Theology of the Liturgy*, 177–78.

[60] See Eph 1:9–12, in which St. Paul speaks of Christ as recapitulating all things: "For he has made known to us in all wisdom and insight the mystery of his will, according to his purpose which he set forth in Christ as a plan for the fulness of time, to unite all things in him, things in heaven and things on earth. In him, according to the purpose of him who accomplishes all things according to the counsel of his will, we who first hoped in Christ have been destined and appointed to live for the praise of his glory." The Greek word in Ephesians 1:10 that the RSV translates as "unite" is literally "recapitulate" (ἀνακεφαλαιώσασθαι), which means "to bring things back to their head." Christ recapitulates all things in Himself by being the Antitype for all of salvation history. Everything before the Incarnation was a preparation for and prefiguration of Christ, and everything after Him is to be conformed to His image in the Church, which shall finally be brought into the splendor of His glory.

Thomas asks whether the sacraments are signs of man's sanctification in one sense only or in multiple senses. One might think that they are signs of one thing only, so as to avoid ambiguity. Most human signs are signs of one reality and not of multiple realities. It is of the essence of the sacraments of the New Covenant, however, that they are a special kind of sign that simultaneously signifies at least three different realities pertaining to past, present, and future. Man's sanctification is a complex reality because it had a beginning in God's past saving actions, it continues now when man receives grace, and it will be consummated in the heavenly kingdom at the end of time in glory. Thus the sacraments signify man's effective sanctification in this threefold sense, combining past, present, and future. The sacrament is a memorial of the past event of Christ's Paschal mystery and makes that mystery present in power, sanctifying the present. The present reality of the sacrament and its grace, in turn, is an anticipation and pledge of the future realization of the fullness of salvation. St. Thomas explains:

> A sacrament properly speaking is that which is ordained to signify our sanctification. In which three things may be considered: the very cause of our sanctification, which is Christ's passion; the form of our sanctification, which is grace and the virtues; and the ultimate end of our sanctification, which is eternal life. And all these are signified by the sacraments. Consequently a sacrament is a sign that is both a reminder of the past, i.e. the passion of Christ; and an indication of that which is effected in us by Christ's passion, i.e. grace; and a prognostic, that is, a foretelling of future glory.[61]

---

[61] *ST* III, q. 60, a. 3. See also his earlier statement of this idea in *IV Sent.*, d. 1, a. 1, qla. 1, ad 4, trans. Mortensen, 7:11: "Sacraments of the New Law signify three things. They signify the first sanctifying cause, as baptism signifies the death of Christ; and in this regard they are commemorative signs. They also signify the effect of sanctification that they cause, and this is their principal signification; and in this way they are demonstrative signs. Nor is it any obstacle if someone does not receive sanctity, since this is not due to anything lacking in the sacrament, which, considered in itself, is such as to confer grace. Finally, they signify the goal of sanctification, namely eternal glory, and in this regard they are prognostic signs. The sacraments of the Old Law, however, were completely prognostic signs."

With regard to the objection that a multiplicity of senses would introduce confusion and ambiguity, St. Thomas answers that this would be the case only if the multiple senses are not related to each other, as in a pun. Here, however, the three aspects of the sacraments are intimately related in forming a complete whole consisting of the original cause in the past (Christ's Paschal mystery), an effect which is present sanctification, and a final effect in beatitude, in which there will be the consummation of what has now been initiated.[62]

The entire liturgy,[63] and the sacraments in particular, have this threefold temporal dimension, which signifies and in some way makes present the past and the future. They refer to the past insofar as they are a memorial of the works of salvation history, and particularly of Christ's Passion, death, and Resurrection, the culminating event of salvation history. This past event is made present as the cause and archetype of the sanctification given by the sacrament. The supernatural effect is made present through the sacrament, which produces the grace that it signifies. The fruit of Christ's Passion is applied to the soul and to the Church here and now, through which we are brought into greater conformity with Christ through the power of His Spirit working in the sacrament. The future aspect is the dimension of heavenly glory to which the sacrament is ordered, and of which it gives a pledge, foretaste, and participation.[64]

St. Paul succinctly brings together these three dimensions in describing the Eucharist in 1 Corinthians 11:26: "For as often as you eat

---

[62] *ST* III, q. 60, a. 3, ad 1: "Then is a sign ambiguous and the occasion of deception, when it signifies many things not ordained to one another. But when it signifies many things inasmuch as, through being mutually ordained, they form one thing, then the sign is not ambiguous but certain: thus this word 'man' signifies the soul and body inasmuch as together they form the human nature. In this way a sacrament signifies the three things aforesaid, inasmuch as by being in a certain order they are one thing."

[63] For an excellent exposition of these three senses in the liturgy, see Vagaggini, *Theological Dimensions of the Liturgy*, 69–95. To these three senses of liturgical signs, Vagaggini adds a fourth, which is that they are moral or "obligating signs" of our interior commitment to act in conformity with the holiness they express. See also Herbert Vorgrimler, *Sacramental Theology*, trans. Linda Maloney (Collegeville, MN: Liturgical Press, 1992), 90: "Sacramental praxis easily overlooks this making-present of all history as salvation history in every individual sacrament."

[64] On this threefold temporal dimension of the sacraments, which thus transcend time, see Schillebeeckx, *Christ the Sacrament of the Encounter with God*, 56–63.

this bread and drink the chalice, you proclaim the Lord's death until he comes." In every Mass we commemorate the Last Supper and the sacrifice of Christ on Calvary. These past events become present by having their fruit applied to us in Holy Communion and the other sacraments, which gives us a pledge and foretaste of the future glory to be revealed in Christ's Second Coming, which serves to increase our yearning.

The *Catechism of the Council of Trent* explains this threefold temporal dimension of the seven sacraments of the Church, based on St. Paul's teaching in Romans 6:3–5:

> These mysterious, divinely instituted signs called sacraments properly signify, by the same divine ordinance, more than just one reality. Besides the reality already mentioned, viz., the divine grace and our sanctification, there are in each of the sacraments two other realities, both of which are most intimately connected with that grace and sanctification. These other realities are, first, the Passion of our Lord, and secondly, the life of the blessed in heaven. They are related to our sanctification as its source and as its culmination respectively. Thus each sacrament of its very nature, as the Doctors of the Church have taught us, has a threefold signification: it recalls something from the past, it indicates something in the present, and it anticipates something in the future.
>
> This teaching is more than a mere opinion, for it is solidly based on the authority of the Sacred Scriptures. When St. Paul says, "All of us who have been baptized into Christ Jesus were baptized into his death" (Rm 6:3), he shows that Baptism is a sign in that it reminds us of the Passion and Death of our Lord. When he goes on to say, "We were buried therefore with him by baptism into death, so that as Christ was raised from the dead by the glory of the Father, we too might walk in newness of life" (Rm 6:4), he also shows that Baptism signifies the infusion of divine grace into the soul, by which we are enabled to renew our lives and fulfill what is expected of us. Finally, when he says, "If we have been united with him in a death like his, we shall certainly be united with him in a resurrection like his" (Rm 6:5), he shows that Baptism also signifies the eternal life itself—the life which through Baptism we shall one day attain.[65]

---

[65] *CCT*, part 2, intro., §12, pp. 150–51.

The sacraments are designed to join together, more than in any other human reality, the past of salvation history, the present in which it is celebrated, and the future for which we hope. This is because they have the mysterious power to realize what they symbolize. Since they symbolize past, present, and future events—as salvific cause, present application, and future fulfillment—all of these dimensions are made present through the sacrament. The past is made present as an inexhaustible cause is present in its effect, and the future fulfillment is made present through the communication of the seed and participation of that future fulfillment. This is possible because the divine power that operated in Christ's Paschal mystery, and is made present in the sacraments, is infinite and transcends time.[66] The greatest example of this is the Eucharist, in which the sacrifice celebrated on the altar is truly one with the sacrifice of Calvary.[67] It thus enables the faithful who were not able to stand by the Cross with Mary and John to nevertheless be present at that event in the sacrament and to co-offer it with Christ to His Father.

The other sacraments also make Christ's Paschal mystery present through configuring us to it, bringing about our death to sin and rebirth to new life in Christ. Baptism begins this process, as St. Paul makes clear in Romans 6:3–4: "Do you not know that all of us who have been baptized into Christ Jesus were baptized into his death? We were buried therefore with him by baptism into death, so that as Christ was raised from the dead by the glory of the Father, we too might walk in newness of life." Penance likewise works a spiritual death and resurrection from post-baptismal sin, applying to us the mercy won in the Passion. Anointing of the Sick configures the sick member of the faithful to Christ's Passion and its redemptive power. Matrimony makes the couple an icon of Christ's love for His Bride,

---

[66] See *CCC*, §1085: "His Paschal mystery is a real event that occurred in our history, but it is unique: all other historical events happen once, and then they pass away, swallowed up in the past. The Paschal mystery of Christ, by contrast, cannot remain only in the past, because by his death he destroyed death, and all that Christ is—all that he did and suffered for all men—participates in the divine eternity, and so transcends all times while being made present in them all. The event of the Cross and Resurrection *abides* and draws everything toward life." See also Feingold, *The Eucharist*, 366.

[67] See Council of Trent, Doctrine on the Sacrifice of the Mass (session 22, Sept 17, 1562), ch. 2 (DS, 1743): "It is one and the same victim; the same person now offers it by the ministry of His priests, who then offered Himself on the cross, the manner of offering alone being different."

the Church, by which "he gave himself up for her" (Eph 5:25) on Calvary. Holy Orders at the level of the priesthood makes Calvary present by enabling the priest to act in the person of Christ who feeds His Church with His Body and Blood. Confirmation, on the other hand, makes continually present the event of Pentecost in the life of the Church.[68]

The threefold signification is preeminently true of the sacraments of the New Covenant. St. Thomas, however, observes that the sacraments of the Old Covenant also have this threefold meaning. They principally point to a reality understood as future, which is twofold, referring both to the salvation to be worked by the Messiah[69] and to the future glory of the world to come. Secondly, there is also a past aspect to the sacraments of the Old Covenant, for they commemorate the great acts of God on behalf of Israel, above all in the Exodus, which are types of the future salvation to be worked by the Messiah.[70] Thus the feast of Passover commemorates the first Passover before leaving Egypt. The feast of Pentecost (*Shavuot*) commemorates the giving of the Torah on Mt. Sinai and the sealing of the covenant.[71] The feast of Booths (*Sukkoth*) commemorates the wandering in the desert for forty years.[72] Third, the feasts of Israel make those events liturgically and spiritually present throughout the course of Israel's history. Through celebrating the Passover, all generations of Israel are brought into spiritual connection with the generation that left Egypt

---

[68] With regard to past events, the sacramental liturgy is not limited to the commemoration of Christ's Paschal mystery; it can commemorate all the events of sacred history that are celebrated in the liturgy, such as the Resurrection, Pentecost, the Nativity, the Annunciation, etc. Thus in the liturgical celebration of Christmas, the past event commemorated is the birth of Christ. The present event is the conferral of graces that conform us to Christ and His birth, by which Christ is born more fully in our hearts. The future event is our birth into glory. Something similar could be said of the celebration of all the other mysteries presented in the liturgy. All the mysteries of the life of Christ are instruments of our sanctification to produce in us, through the sacraments, the holiness that they represent.

[69] See Thomas Aquinas, *In IV Sent.*, d. 1, q. 1, a. 1, qla. 1, trans. Mortensen, 7:10: "The sacraments of the Old Law are called sacraments, inasmuch as they represent those things that were accomplished in Christ, including the sacraments of the New Law."

[70] See Feingold, *Faith Comes from What Is Heard*, 517–22.

[71] Lawrence Feingold, *The Mystery of Israel and the Church*, vol. 1, *Figure and Fulfillment* (St. Louis, MO: Miriam Press, 2010), 115–18.

[72] Lawrence Feingold, *The Mystery of Israel and the Church*, 1:120–25.

and witnessed God's great prodigies.

The sacramental liturgy of the Church takes this basic threefold framework but modifies it in a way fitting for the liturgy of the New Covenant. In the Church, the principal events of sacred history that are commemorated are no longer those of the first Exodus but those of the Paschal mystery of Christ, which is the new Exodus.[73] Secondly, the future events that are hoped for no longer include the first coming of the Messiah and His redemption but rather His Second Coming and the heavenly glory that will be the final fruit of the salvation He merited for us on Calvary.

The events of salvation history commemorated by the sacraments and sacred rites of the Old Covenant are not the principal causes of our salvation but are rather types of the Paschal mystery. It is proper to the sacraments of the New Covenant that the past events that they make present liturgically are the saving events that are the meritorious and efficient causes of our salvation.

STUDY QUESTIONS

1. Why do we speak of a sacramental economy?
2. Is the sacramental economy of the New Covenant the object of messianic prophecies and types of the Old Testament?
3. Why did Christ institute a sacramental economy using sensible signs? In other words, why is a sacramental economy fitting for applying to mankind the fruits of Christ's salvation? Give several reasons based on (a) human nature; (b) the human way of knowing; (c) the Incarnation; (d) the Church; and (e) the life of faith.
4. Explain the relationship between the sacramental economy and biblical typology.
5. Explain the threefold temporal dimension (past, present, and future) of the sacraments.

---

[73] The prophets, as in Isa 43:18–19 and Jer 23:5–8, had already foretold this shift. See Feingold, *Faith Comes from What Is Heard*, 517–21; Jean Daniélou, *From Shadows to Reality: Studies in the Biblical Typology of the Fathers*, trans. Dom Wulstan Hibberd (Westminster, MD: The Newman Press, 1960), 153–57.

Suggestions for Further Reading

ST III, q. 60, aa. 3–4; q. 61, aa. 1–4.

Leeming, Bernard. *Principles of Sacramental Theology.* 2nd edition. London: Longmans; Westminster, MD: Newman Press, 1960. Pp. 590–604.

Miralles, Antonio. *I sacramenti cristiani: trattato generale.* 2nd edition. Rome: Apollinare studi, 2008. Pp. 69–78.

Nutt, Roger. *General Principles of Sacramental Theology.* Washington, DC: Catholic University of America Press, 2017. Pp. 93–96.

Ratzinger, Joseph. "The Sacramental Foundation of Christian Existence," and "On the Concept of Sacrament." In *Theology of the Liturgy: The Sacramental Foundation of Christian Existence.* Edited by Michael Miller. Translated by John Saward, Kenneth Baker, et al. *Collected Works*, vol. 11. San Francisco: Ignatius Press, 2014. Pp. 153–84.

Scheeben, Matthias Joseph. *The Mysteries of Christianity.* Translated by Cyril Vollert. St. Louis, MO: B. Herder, 1951. Pp. 558–66.

Vagaggini, Cyprian. *Theological Dimensions of the Liturgy.* Translated by Leonard J. Doyle and W. A. Jurgens. Collegeville, MN: Liturgical Press, 1976. Pp. 61–68, 300–34.

CHAPTER TWO

What Are Sacraments?
Development of the Definition
of Sacrament

The Church came fully into being on Pentecost with a complete sacramental system. This does not mean, however, that the Church came into being with a clear understanding of the sacraments and a corresponding theory of their nature and efficacy. The theological doctrine of the sacraments provides an excellent example of the long process of development of doctrine in the Church. The sacraments are there from the start, and the Fathers of the Church give a rich pastoral catechesis on them, but a proper theory of the sacraments that explains their nature, number, and efficacy takes many centuries of contemplation by saints and theologians in order to develop.[1] This development reaches maturity only in the twelfth and thirteenth centuries and is further perfected by the Council of Trent and the following centuries. In this labor each generation builds on the preceding one. Part of the impetus for the development of doctrine is the need for the Church

---

[1] See Second Vatican Council, Dogmatic Constitution on Divine Revelation *Dei Verbum* (Nov 18, 1965), §8: "This tradition which comes from the Apostles develops in the Church with the help of the Holy Spirit. For there is a growth in the understanding of the realities and the words which have been handed down. This happens through the contemplation and study made by believers, who treasure these things in their hearts (see Luke 2:19, 51) through a penetrating understanding of the spiritual realities which they experience, and through the preaching of those who have received through Episcopal succession the sure gift of truth. For as the centuries succeed one another, the Church constantly moves forward toward the fullness of divine truth until the words of God reach their complete fulfillment in her."

to respond to heresies, such as the Berengarian heresy of the eleventh century, the Protestant Reformation, and modernity's general loss of a sacramental vision, all of which have spurred theologians to reflect more deeply on the sacraments.

In this chapter we shall examine the development of the definition of sacrament. One might have thought that the Church and her theologians should always have had a good working definition of the notion of sacrament, but surprisingly, as we shall see, this was not fully worked out until the twelfth century. As will be seen below, the full definition of the sacraments of the New Covenant includes several aspects. (a) They are *sacred signs* (b) *instituted by Christ* who uses them as His instruments (c) to *efficaciously realize the sanctification they represent* (d) and so to build up the visible and invisible life of His Church, to whom they are entrusted.

SACRAMENT AND MYSTERY

The Pauline Concept of "Mystery"

Our English word "sacrament" comes from the Latin *sacramentum*, which was used by the Old Latin Bible (*Vetus Latina*) and St. Jerome's Latin Vulgate to translate the Greek word μυστήριον (*mysterion*), which is the word used by Greek-speaking Christians to refer to the sacraments as well as to the mysteries of the faith.

In the New Testament, the Greek word *mysterion* is used above all to refer to the mystery of God's plan of salvation in Christ and the Church, which was hidden from earlier generations.[2] In Ephesians 1:9–10, St. Paul says: "He has made known to us in all wisdom and insight the mystery[3] of his will, according to his purpose which he set forth in Christ as a plan for the fulness of time, to unite all

---

[2] On the notion of "mystery" in relation to the Christian liturgy, see Odo Casel, *The Mystery of Christian Worship* (New York: Crossroad, 1999), 9–13; Marc Cardinal Ouellet, *Mystery and Sacrament of Love: A Theology of Marriage and the Family for the New Evangelization* (Grand Rapids: Eerdmans, 2015), 209–26; William A. Van Roo, *The Christian Sacrament* (Rome: Editrice Pontificia Università Gregoriana, 1992), 29–35; Ratzinger, "On the Concept of Sacrament," in *Theology of the Liturgy*, 169–84.

[3] In the Vulgate translation, St. Jerome used the Latin *sacramentum* to translate the Greek *mysterion*.

things in him, things in heaven and things on earth." Thus we can say that the fundamental mystery is God's sacramental plan of salvation to unite all things in the Word made flesh. This union takes place in the Church through the communication of the grace of Christ through the sacraments. This brief text, then, teaches us that the *mystery* is first the Incarnation of Christ, and especially His Paschal mystery; it is also the Church as the Body of Christ, which is the union of all the members with Christ and with each other in Christ, and the incorporation of the Gentiles into it; it is grace which communicates Christ's life to us, and it is the sacraments as the channels of grace that bind us to Christ in the Church.

In Ephesians 3:2–10, the connection of *mystery* and the Church is further developed:

> Assuming that you have heard of the stewardship of God's grace that was given to me for you, how the mystery[4] was made known to me by revelation, as I have written briefly. When you read this you can perceive my insight into the mystery of Christ, which was not made known to the sons of men in other generations as it has now been revealed to his holy apostles and prophets by the Spirit; that is, how the Gentiles are fellow heirs, members of the same body, and partakers of the promise in Christ Jesus through the gospel. . . . To me, though I am the very least of all the saints, this grace was given, to preach to the Gentiles the unsearchable riches of Christ, and to make all men see what is the plan of the mystery[5] hidden for ages in God who created all things; that through the church the manifold wisdom of God might now be made known.

The mystery hidden for ages is God's plan for the divinization of men and for their communion with Him and with each other in the divine life, and His plan to superabundantly realize this supernatural communion in Christ through the Church[6] by making the sharing in the

---

4 Here, too, St. Jerome translated this as *sacramentum*.
5 Again St. Jerome translated this as *sacramentum*.
6 See Casel, *The Mystery of Christian Worship*, 12–13: "The content of the mystery of Christ is, therefore, the person of the god-man and his saving deed for the church; the church, in turn, enters into the mystery through this deed. . . .

divine life available not only to Jews but to all Gentiles as well.

Vatican II uses the word *sacramentum* in this Pauline sense of *mystery* to refer to the Church as the place of salvific union with the Trinity in Christ. *Lumen Gentium*, §48 states: "Rising from the dead, He sent His life-giving Spirit upon His disciples and through Him has established His Body which is the Church as the universal sacrament of salvation."[7]

Distinction between Sacrament and Mystery

Sacramentum in classical Latin means "a hidden sacred thing," which could include an oath or act of religious initiation.[8] Thus it could be used to refer both to the Christian mysteries in general, such as the Incarnation and redemption, but more commonly it was used to refer to sacred rites that have a hidden power and efficacy to communicate that mystery.

In the language of the early Church, *sacrament* and *mystery* at first are used interchangeably, but *sacrament* gradually came to be used above all to signify a visible sacred sign that brings about a mysterious hidden reality. The Latin theological tradition thus came to have two words with different though intimately related nuances—sacrament and mystery—where the Greek theological tradition uses the one word, *mysterion*, to refer both to the seven sacraments and to the mysteries such as the Trinity and the Incarnation.[9] Matthias Scheeben explains:

The Christian thing, therefore, . . . is a *mysterium* as St Paul means the word, a revelation made by God to man through acts of god-manhood, full of life and power; it is mankind's way to God made possible by this revelation and the grace of it communicating the solemn entry of the redeemed church into the presence of the everlasting Father through sacrifice."

[7] For this broad sense of the word "sacramentum" as indicating the mystery of Christ and the Church, see Antonio Miralles, *I sacramenti cristiani: trattato generale*, 2nd ed. (Rome: Apollinare studi, 2008), 13–68.

[8] For non-Christian examples of *sacramentum* used both to refer to a military oath and a rite of religious initiation, see Livy, *Ab urbe condita*, 10.38.2; 39.15.13; Apuleius, *Metamorphoses* 11.15; Casel, *The Mystery of Christian Worship*, 56. For early Christian usage, see Christine Mohrmann, "*Sacramentum* chez les plus anciens textes chrétiens," *Harvard Theological Review* 47 (1954): 141–52. Mohrmann's findings are summarized by Joseph T. Lienhard, "Sacramentum and the Eucharist in St. Augustine," *The Thomist* 77 (2013): 175–79. See also Van Roo, *The Christian Sacrament*, 36–40.

[9] See Charles Journet, "Le mystère de la sacramentalité: Le Christ, l'Église, les sept sacrements," *Nova et Vetera* (French) 49 (1974): 161: "The Greeks have

In its original meaning, the term "sacrament" can be synonymous with "mystery." . . . The Latin Fathers regularly use the word *sacramentum* as equivalent to the Greek μυστήριον. The difference pointed out later, that *sacramentum* connotes something visible, μυστήριον something invisible or hidden, does not originally appear. The Latin Fathers call entirely invisible things, such as the Trinity, *sacramenta*, while the Greeks refer to visible things, for example, the seven sacraments, simply as μυστήριον, because of the mysterious element in them. But in the course of time *sacramentum* came to mean, for the most part, visible things which in some way or other involve a mystery in the narrower sense, and which therefore are mysterious despite their visibility.[10]

After a process of development, the Latin Christian tradition came to use the word *sacramentum* in a more precise theological sense to indicate the sacred rites of the Church by which we are joined to Christ and receive a mysterious share in His divine life. The word thus came to designate a key part of the broader Pauline notion of mystery, signifying the sensible means established by Christ to give us a share in His life, building up the Church.[11] The word "sacrament" thus came to mean the sacred sign of a hidden reality of grace, which it mysteriously contains and communicates.[12]

---

only one word, that of mystery, to designate the profound realities that have been announced to us through divine revelation and that are the object of our faith. The Trinity, the Incarnation, the Church, these are all mysteries. The seven liturgical dramas of baptism, confirmation, the Eucharist . . . are for them [i.e., the Greeks] seven mysteries. The Latins have two words. When the mystery, in order to accommodate itself to our fragility, goes so far as to wrap itself in veils . . . men will be able to designate it as a sacrament, a sacred thing, a sacred sign, in order to separate it from profane realities. We will not say of the Trinity that it is a sacrament" (translation in Benoit-Dominique de La Soujeole, "The Economy of Salvation: Entitative Sacramentality and Operative Sacramentality," *The Thomist* 75 [2011]: 538).

10 Scheeben, *The Mysteries of Christianity*, 558.

11 See Lienhard, "Sacramentum and the Eucharist in St. Augustine," 178: "Augustine uses *mysterium* to designate things that are doctrinal and *sacramentum* to refer to what is ritual." For an in-depth study, see C. Couturier, "'Sacramentum' et 'mysterium' dans l'œuvre de saint Augustin," in Études augustiniennes, ed. H. Rondet and others, Théologie 28 (Paris: Aubier, 1953), 161–332.

12 See Alger of Liège, *De sacramentis corporis et sanguinis dominici*, bk. 1, ch. 4, in PL 180:751D (my translation): "It should be understood that sacrament

A fine articulation of the distinction between the Pauline use of the word "mystery" and the Latin *sacramentum* is given by St. John Paul II in his catechesis on the Theology of the Body:

> "Sacrament" is not synonymous with "mystery." The mystery remains, in fact, "hidden"—concealed in God himself—in such a way that even after its proclamation (or revelation) it does not cease to be called "mystery," and it is also preached as a mystery. The sacrament presupposes the revelation of the mystery and presupposes that man also accepts it by faith. Still, it is at the same time something more than the proclamation of the mystery and the acceptance of the mystery by faith. The sacrament consists in *"manifesting"* that *mystery in a sign* that serves not only to proclaim the mystery but also *to accomplish it* in man. The sacrament is a visible and efficacious sign of grace. It is a means for accomplishing in man the mystery hidden from eternity in God . . . (see Eph 1:9)—the mystery of God calling man to holiness in Christ and the mystery of man's predestination to become an adoptive son. The mystery is accomplished in a mysterious way, under the veil of a sign; nevertheless, that sign always "makes visible" the supernatural mystery that is at work in man under its veil.[13]

Sacrament and mystery are intimately joined. The sacrament manifests the mystery of Christ and the Church "hidden in God" that remains invisible under the veil of the sacrament, through which it can touch and sanctify us, "accomplishing" the mystery.

PATRISTIC AND MEDIEVAL DEFINITIONS OF SACRAMENT

Tertullian (AD 155–220) is held to be the first theologian to use the word *sacramentum* as the Latin equivalent to the Greek *mysterion*

---

and mystery differ in that a sacrament is a visible sign signifying something; whereas a mystery is a hidden thing signified by it." In the Eastern tradition, on the contrary, the word *mysterion* was used to refer to the sacraments as well as to mysteries in general.

[13] John Paul II, *Man and Woman He Created Them: A Theology of the Body*, trans. Michael Waldstein (Boston, MA: Pauline Books & Media, 2006), 489–90.

(referring to the sacred Christian rites) and apply it to Baptism and the Eucharist. He speaks of Baptism as "the sacrament of water, the water that washed away sins contracted at the time of our former blindness, the water that freed us unto eternal life."[14] The Eucharist is spoken of as "the sacrament of the Eucharist"[15] and "the sacrament of the Bread and the Cup."[16] It is interesting that he uses the latter expression in the context of affirming the real presence of Christ's Body and Blood against the Gnostics who denied that Christ had a true human body: "I have . . . by the sacrament of the Bread and the Cup, given proof of the verity of our Lord's Body and Blood, as opposed to Marcion's phantasm."[17]

Tertullian does not give a definition of sacrament, but speaks of it as a sacred sign that is efficacious to accomplish what it signifies:

> For us also the anointing flows over the body, but it profits us spiritually: just as the baptismal rite is a physical action since we are immersed into water, so its effect is spiritual because it frees us from our sins. Then hands were laid upon us while a blessing invoked and invited the Holy Spirit to come.[18]

St. Cyprian, who follows Tertullian in North Africa in the middle of the third century, uses the term in a very similar way. He speaks of the "sacrament of Baptism,"[19] which he also refers to as the "sacrament of salvation."[20] Of the Eucharist he says: "From the sacrament of the

---

14 See Tertullian, *De Baptismo* 1, in Lawrence J. Johnson, ed., *Worship in the Early Church: An Anthology of Historical Sources* (Collegeville, MN: Liturgical Press, 2009), 1:119. On Tertullian's use of *"sacramentum,"* see Miralles, *I sacramenti cristiani*, 86–88.

15 Tertullian, *De Corona* 3, *ANF* 3:94: "We take also, in congregations before daybreak, and from the hand of none but the presidents, the sacrament of the Eucharist."

16 Tertullian, *Adversus Marcionem* 5.8.3, trans. Ernest Evans (Oxford: Clarendon Press, 1972), 2:557.

17 Tertullian, *Adversus Marcionem* 5.8.3, 2:557.

18 Tertullian, *De baptismo* 7–8, in Johnson, ed., *Worship in the Early Church*, 1:123. See also Tertullian, *De resurrectione carnis* 8.3 (CCL 2.931), trans. Ernest Evans, *Tertullian's Treatise on the Resurrection* (London: SPCK, 1960), 25.

19 Cyprian, Letter 73.22.2 to Iubaianus, in *The Letters of St. Cyprian of Carthage, Letters 67–82*, trans. G. W. Clarke (New York; Mahwah, NJ: Newman Press, 1989), 67. On Cyprian's use of *"sacramentum,"* see Miralles, *I sacramenti cristiani*, 88–89.

20 Cyprian, Letter 69.12.2 to Magnus, in *The Letters of St. Cyprian of Carthage,*

cross you receive both food and drink."[21] Sometimes it is difficult to determine whether he is referring to what we today would call the sacrament or the mystery it represents and makes present, as when he speaks, in a liturgical context, of the "*sacramentum* of the Lord's Passion and our redemption."[22]

Augustinian Definition of Sacrament

Among the Fathers, St. Augustine has a particular importance for his prolonged reflection on the nature of the sacraments; the balance with which he develops various aspects of sacramental theology including the sign value, efficacy, and ecclesial nature of the sacraments; and for his profound influence on later Western sacramental theology.

He defines "sacrament" in a very broad way as a "sacred sign." This can be seen when he defines sacrifice as "a sacrament or sacred sign of an invisible sacrifice."[23] Here the term *sacrament* is equivalent to "sacred sign." In a letter he explains that signs "are called sacraments when they are applied to divine things."[24] Another definition is in his letter to Ianuarius: "There is a sacrament in any celebration when the commemoration of the event is so made that it is understood to indicate something which must be reverently received."[25] This latter definition

---

Letters 67–82, p. 41: "For washing away the stains of our sins in the sacrament of salvation is quite different from washing our flesh in an ordinary bath. In the latter case, to clean off the filth on our skin and body we have need of cakes of washing soda and like aids . . . whereas the heart of the believer is washed and the soul of man is cleansed by quite different means—by the merits of faith. In the case of those who receive the sacrament of salvation as a matter of urgency, through God's indulgent generosity His ceremonial, though not the fullest, still confers His full benefits upon those who believe."

21 Cyprian, *Jealousy and Envy* 17, in *Treatises*, trans. Roy Deferrari (Washington, DC: Catholic University of America Press, 1958), 307.

22 Cyprian, Letter 63.14.3 to Caecilius, in *The Letters of St. Cyprian of Carthage, Letters 67–82*, p. 106.

23 Augustine, *City of God* 10.5, in *The City of God, Books VIII–XVI*, trans. G. G. Walsh and G. Monahan, FC 14 (Washington, DC: Catholic University of America Press, 1952), 123.

24 Augustine, Letter 138 to Marcellinus (AD 412), in *Letters: Volume III (131–164)*, trans. Wilfrid Parsons, FC 20 (Washington, DC: Catholic University of America Press, 1953), 40.

25 Augustine, Letter 55 to Januarius (ca. AD 400), in *Letters: Volume I (1–82)*, trans. Wilfrid Parsons, FC 12 (Washington, DC: Catholic University of America Press, 1951), 261. On the interpretation of this text, see Van Roo, *The Christian*

is more precise in that it specifies that a sacrament is a sacred sign of a divine gift to men. Furthermore, the sensible sign corresponds to the divine gift in that it represents what is invisibly received. For "if the sacraments had no resemblance to the things which they represent, they would not be sacraments."[26]

Sacraments therefore belong in the category of signs. A sign, in the classic definition of St. Augustine, is that which "over and above the impression it makes on the senses, causes something else to come into the mind as a consequence of itself."[27]

St. Augustine used the term sacrament also to apply to the rites of the Old Testament, such as circumcision, the Passover, the various sacrifices of the Law, anointing, and priestly consecration. In doing so he highlights the continuity of the sacraments of the Old and New Testament while also pointing out their difference with regard to Christ, who is prefigured in those of the Old and present working in those of the New. Commenting on 1 Corinthians 10:1–4, he writes:

> Beyond question, the mystery of the kingdom of heaven, which in the fullness of time was to be revealed in the New Testament, was present but veiled in the Old.... In a mysterious way their food and drink were the same as ours, but the same only with regard to their meaning, not the same in kind....

He then makes another distinction between outward sacrament

Sacrament, 40.

[26] Augustine, Letter 98.7 (my translation, modified from *Letters: Volume II (83–130)*, trans. Wilfrid Parsons, FC 18 (Washington, DC: Catholic University of America Press, 1953), 137. See also Sermon 272 (between AD 405 and 411), trans. in Johnson, *Worship in the Early Church*, 3:76–77: "And the cup—or its contents—how can this be his Blood? These, my brothers and sisters, are called mysteries [*sacramenta*] because in them one thing is seen, another is understood. What is seen has a material appearance; what is understood brings forth spiritual fruit."

[27] Augustine, *On Christian Doctrine*, 2.1.1, trans. J. F. Shaw, in *NPNF*1, 2:535. The word "symbol" can be used as a synonym for "sign." Often, however, the word "symbol" refers to a particular kind of sign in which the reality referred to is mysterious, ineffable, and invisible, on a level far above the sensible sign that represents it. A stop sign, for example, is a mere sign, but the crucifix is a symbol. Sacraments are not mere conventional signs but *symbols* in this sense of the word. See the discussion of the notion of symbol in Gustave Martelet, *The Risen Christ and the Eucharistic World*, trans. René Hague (New York: Seabury Press, 1976), 17–29.

from the grace hidden in it, which presupposes the right dispositions in the recipient. After quoting 1 Corinthians 10:5, "Nevertheless with most of them God was not pleased," he says:

> The sacramental mysteries were available to all alike, but grace, which is the power hidden in the sacraments, was not common to all the people. Today, when the promise then veiled is revealed, this is still true, for the laver of rebirth in the name of Father, Son and Holy Spirit is common to all alike; but grace itself, whereby the members of Christ's body are brought to new life with their head, the grace of which that rite is the sacred sign—that is not common to all. Heretics have the same baptism, and so do false brethren within the Catholic community.[28]

The sacraments are bearers and communicators of grace to those who receive them worthily, but not to those without repentance or faith.

St. Augustine's broad definition of sacrament, like that of most of the other Fathers and theologians generally until Peter Lombard in the twelfth century, also includes what we today would call sacramentals. His definition does not clearly distinguish the two notions because it does not specify that the sacred signs are *efficacious causes* of grace. For this reason it also does not distinguish the sacraments of the New Testament from the rites of the Old Covenant.

Definitions of Sacrament in the Latin Tradition after Augustine

St. Isidore of Seville (560–636) marks another step in the definition of the notion of sacrament. He highlights not so much the notion of sacred sign, but rather the *secret* sanctifying power that works through bodily signs. He says that Baptism, Chrism [Confirmation], and the Body and Blood are sacraments "because under the covering of bodily things a divine power secretly works the salvation contained in these sacraments."[29] He also underlines the role of the Holy Spirit in the

---

[28] Augustine, *On the Psalms* 77.2, in *Expositions of the Psalms 73–98*, trans. Maria Boulding (Hyde Park, NY: New City Press, 2002), 91–92.

[29] Isidore, *Etymologies*, bk. 6, ch. 19, no. 40 (PL 82:255, my translation). Isidore highlights the aspect of "secret," which was one of the classical meanings of the

sacraments, who "mystically makes them life-giving."[30] In this way the efficacy of the sacrament to cause grace and its hidden mystery are more strongly affirmed than in St. Augustine's definition.[31] This will help to distinguish the sacraments of the Church from the sacramentals and from the sacred rites of the Old Covenant. St. Isidore does not yet give the list of seven sacraments, but he expressly names the three sacraments of Christian initiation: "baptism, chrism, and the Body and Blood."[32] His definition falls short, however, in an opposite way to Augustine, in not specifying that a sacrament is a special kind of sign—a sacred sign that through the divine power secretly works the salvific reality it represents.

Something similar can be said of the definition of sacrament given by St. Paschasius Radbertus (785–865) in the Carolingian renaissance of the ninth century: "A sacrament therefore is what is given to us in a divine celebration as a kind of pledge of salvation, in which what is visibly enacted works something very different inwardly that is to be received as holy."[33] This definition highlights the dimension of supernatural causality by specifying that the visible sign "works" an inward sanctification. The definition, however, lacks explicit reference to the sacrament's sign value, according to which it produces the spiritual effects that it visibly represents.

It was only in the twelfth century, in the aftermath of the Beren-

---

word *sacramentum.*

[30] Isidore, *Etymologies*, bk. 6, ch. 19, no. 42. The role of the Holy Spirit is also emphasized by Paschasius Radbertus in the first half of the ninth century in *De corpore et sanguine Domini* 3, ed. D. Paulus, CCCM, 16:26–27.

[31] St. Thomas comments on this definition (which he attributed mistakenly to St. Augustine) in *IV Sent.*, d. 1, q. 1, a. 1, qla. 4, trans. Mortensen, 7:13, in which he says that it "considers a sacrament with regard to what is principal in its account, namely, to cause holiness. And since sacraments are not the proper causes of holiness but secondary and instrumental causes, as it were, therefore sacraments are defined as instruments of sanctification. But an action is not attributed to an instrument, but to a principal agent, by whose power the instruments are applied to their work inasmuch as they are moved by it. And thus he does not say that sacraments are 'things that sanctify,' but that the hidden divine power existing in them sanctifies."

[32] Isidore, *Etymologies*, bk. 6, ch. 19, no. 39 (PL 82:255, my translation).

[33] Paschasius Radbertus, *De Corpore et Sanguine Domini* 3.1 (ca. AD 833), in CCCM 16, pp. 23–24 (my translation). See also 3.2 (my translation): "The sacraments of Christ in the Church are baptism, chrism, and the body and blood of the Lord, which are called sacraments because under their visible appearance that is seen, the body is secretly consecrated by divine power."

garian heresy,[34] that theologians worked out a more perfect and precise definition of the sacraments of the New Covenant as both sign of grace and cause of the grace signified. On this basis, they came to the consensus that there are precisely seven sacraments that fit the definition.

An important step in this direction is the definition given by Hugh of St. Victor (ca. 1096–1141) in his work, *On the Sacraments of the Christian Faith*. Hugh begins with St. Augustine's definition of sacrament as a sign of a sacred thing but finds it too broad to be a proper definition because statues, pictures, and letters can be signs of sacred things but are not sacraments.[35] He then gives a definition that applies only to the sacraments in the proper sense: "A sacrament is a corporeal or material element set before the senses without, representing by similitude and signifying by institution and containing by sanctification some invisible and spiritual grace."[36] This definition adds three further qualifications to the broad Augustinian notion of sacred sign. First, a sacrament must bear some natural resemblance to the grace that it communicates; secondly, it must be instituted by God, through which it acquires a more precise meaning willed by Him and indicated by the words; and third, it must in some way "contain" and communicate the grace that it represents.[37]

Shortly after Hugh, the anonymous *Summa sententiarum*, usually dated to around 1140,[38] gave a similar definition of sacrament as an

---

[34] For the Berengarian heresy, see Feingold, *The Eucharist*, 238–57.

[35] Nevertheless, Hugh still uses the word "sacrament" in the broad sense by which it can refer to the rites of the Old Covenant. See Hugh of St. Victor, *On the Sacraments of the Christian Faith*, Prologue 2, trans. Deferrari, 3: "The work of restoration is the Incarnation of the Word with all its sacraments, both those which have gone before from the beginning of time, and those which come after, even to the end of the world."

[36] Hugh of St. Victor, *On the Sacraments of the Christian Faith* 1.9.2, trans. Deferrari, 155. St. Bonaventure quotes this in his own definition of sacrament in *Breviloquium* 6.1.2.

[37] Hugh held that this definition applied also to the sacraments of the Old Covenant, which he saw as prefiguring signs of those of the New, through which the grace-giving power of sanctification contained in the New Testament sacraments could be accessed. See *On the Sacraments of the Christian Faith* 1.11.1–5, trans. Deferrari, 182–84.

[38] For the dating and context of this work, see Marcia Colish, *Peter Lombard* (New York: E. J. Brill, 1994), 63; D. E. Luscombe, *The School of Peter Abelard: The Influence of Abelard's Thought in the Early Scholastic Period* (Cambridge: Cambridge University Press, 2008), 199–213.

efficacious sign of the invisible grace that it confers: "A sacrament is the visible form of the invisible grace that is conferred by the sacrament. It is not only the sign of a sacred thing, but also efficacious."[39]

In his influential *Sentences*, Peter Lombard defines sacraments in a similar way as sacred signs that are also causes of the grace they represent: "It is a sign of God's grace and a form of invisible grace in such manner that it bears its image and is its cause. And so the sacraments were not instituted only for the sake of signifying, but also to sanctify."[40] Peter Lombard sees sacraments as a special class of sign that were instituted both to *signify* sanctification and *cause* the sanctification they signify.

The theologians of the thirteenth century generally follow Peter Lombard in defining "sacrament" by bringing together the aspect of sign and cause; they are signs of grace that effect what they signify. The *Summa* of Alexander of Hales states this clearly: "Most strictly, the sacraments of the new Law are those that effect what they symbolize, those that are the signs and causes of invisible grace."[41]

Aquinas's Definition of Sacrament: Signs of the Sacred Realities That Sanctify Man

St. Thomas's Definition of Sacrament in His Commentary on the Sentences

St. Thomas treats the sacraments and their definition in a systematic way both at the beginning and at the end of his career. In his early commentary on the *Sentences*, St. Thomas goes through the classic definitions of his predecessors that are given above and explains how they should be understood. He takes Augustine's definition as the best definition of sacrament in the broad sense insofar as it includes both the sacraments of the Old and the New Covenant. He also approves Peter Lombard's definition as the most complete definition of sacrament with regard to the New Covenant[42] and finds Hugh of

---

[39] *Summa sententiarum*, PL 176:117 (my translation).

[40] Peter Lombard, *Sentences* 4, d. 1, ch. 4, no. 2, trans. Silano, 4.

[41] Alexander of Hales, *Glossa in quatuor libros Sententiarum Petri Lombardi* 4, d. 1, 1, vol. 4 (Quaracchi, Florence: Editiones Collegii S. Bonaventurae, 1957), 9. English translation in Benoit-Dominique de La Soujeole, "The Sacraments and the Development of Doctrine," trans. Dominic M. Langevin, in *OHST*, 591.

[42] Thomas Aquinas, *In IV Sent.*, d. 1, q. 1, a. 1, qla. 3, trans. Mortensen, 7:12:

St. Victor's definition to be equivalent to it.[43]

He begins his own explanation with the etymology of *sacramentum*, which means something that actively sanctifies. St. Thomas points out, however, that since we are speaking of sacraments for human beings, they should consecrate or sanctify human beings in a way appropriate to rational animals.[44] It is proper to human beings to be perfected through knowledge, because we cannot love what we do not know. But our knowledge begins with the senses. Thus it is proper to human beings that invisible sanctification comes through sensible signs of that sanctification, according to the Augustinian definition.

He then says that this definition of the sacraments as sensible signs of man's sanctification can be applied to the sacraments of the New and Old Covenant but in two different ways. It applies to the sacraments of the New Covenant in that sensible signs signify both the causes of our sanctification—Christ's Paschal mystery and His grace—and the concrete application of that sanctification to the subject. The definition applies to the Old Testament sacraments insofar as the sacred sign represents the cause of sanctification but not the application of sanctification to the subject.[45] Thus the Old Testament sacraments

---

"The Master's definition quite thoroughly conveys the notion of sacrament, as we are speaking about sacraments now. For that they effect holiness is referred to in 'exists as a cause' and the mode befitting man as to his understanding is indicated when he says, 'in the visible form of invisible grace,' and the mode of signification connatural to man where he says, 'as it bears an image.'"

[43] *In IV Sent.*, d. 1, q. 1, a. 1, qla. 5.

[44] See *In IV Sent.*, d. 1, q. 1, a. 1, qla. 1, trans. Mortensen, 7:10: "'Sacrament,' according to the proper meaning of the word, seems to convey 'sanctity' in an active sense, so that anything that renders something sacred is called a sacrament, just as whatever renders something ornate is called an ornament. But since the actions of the things acting should be proportionate to the condition of the things acted upon, for this reason in the sanctification of man there should be a mode of sanctification befitting man according as he is rational, for this is what makes him a man. But insofar as he is rational, his knowledge arises from his senses. Thus it is necessary that he be sanctified in such a way that his sanctification also becomes known to him through the likenesses of sensible things."

[45] *In IV Sent.*, d. 1, q. 1, a. 1, qla. 1: "But sometimes it includes the mode of consecration that befits a man according as both the sanctifying causes and his own sanctification are made known to him through sensible likenesses. And in this way the sacraments of the New Law are called sacraments, for they not only consecrate but also signify sanctity in the way mentioned and signify the first causes of sanctification as well: for example, baptism both sanctifies, and designates purity and is a sign of the death of Christ. However, sometimes it includes only the signification of the consecrations mentioned, as a sign of health is

are said to be sacraments by analogy, as a sign of health, like a good complexion, can be said to be healthy.[46] He makes this clearer in a subsequent text:

> "Sacrament" is not divided into sacraments of the Old Law and of the New Law as a genus is divided into species, but as an analogous term is divided into its parts, as healthy is divided into those things having health and those things signifying it. But a sacrament is, simply speaking, what causes sanctity, while something that merely signifies is a sacrament only in a certain respect.[47]

The principal notion of sacrament is a *sacred sign of man's sanctification that is also the cause of that sanctification.* The secondary sense of the Old Testament sacraments is to be a sacred sign of man's sanctification, without directly causing it.

St. Thomas's Definition of Sacrament in the Summa theologiae

What Kind of Thing Is a Sacrament?

St. Thomas modifies his definition of sacrament when he returns to the topic in the beginning of his treatment of the sacraments in

---

called healthy. And in this way the sacraments of the Old Law are called sacraments, inasmuch as they represent those things that were accomplished in Christ, including the sacraments of the New Law."

[46] "Health" is the classic example of an analogical relationship used by Aristotle (*Metaphysics* 4.2.1003a33–35) and frequently cited by St. Thomas, as in *ST* III, q. 60, a. 1. We say that a person, animal, or plant is healthy in the primary sense (prime analogate), but we also extend the notion of healthy to foods, climates, exercise, complexions, thoughts, occupations, books, television programs, and so forth. What is the unifying principle that enables us to apply the same term to such different things? It is clear that all the things which are said to be healthy bear a *relation* to the health of the human being (or animal). "Healthy" is predicated first and directly of the human or animal body, and then secondarily of the climate, complexion, exercise, and the like, which all are signs or causes of health. See Aristotle, *Metaphysics* 4.2.1003a33–35. "Sacrament" thus implies a relation to sanctification, which could be that of being either a sign or cause of sanctification, or both.

[47] Thomas Aquinas, *In IV Sent.*, d. 1, q. 1, a. 1, qla. 3, ad 5, trans. Mortensen, 7:13.

the third part of the *Summa theologiae*, at the end of his career. The modification consists in removing the reference to causality from the general definition of sacrament and clarifying that sacraments are in the genus of "sign." Here, like Augustine but unlike Peter Lombard, he defines sacrament in such a way as to properly include those of the Old Testament.[48]

In order to perfectly define something, one needs to find its genus, which is the larger class to which it belongs, and its specific difference, which is the trait that distinguishes it from all other species in that genus. So the first question with regard to the definition of sacrament is the determination of its genus. What is the larger class of which it is a specific type?

A common sense answer is that the sacraments are religious rites or liturgical actions, and liturgical actions or rites are *symbolic* actions. It follows that sacraments belong in the genus of signs or symbols and not in that of cause. This is Aquinas's conclusion, which he puts forward as self-evident,[49] and as his authority he cites St. Augustine's classic definition. This clarification that sacraments belong in the genus of sacred signs is a major contribution of his mature thought. It is important because it puts the signifying aspect of the sacraments as the first component of their essence, and it shows their kinship with the entire human world of sacred or religious signs.[50]

Sacrament's Specific Difference

The greater difficulty in every definition is determining the specific difference that distinguishes the notion being defined from everything else in the same genus. St. Augustine's definition suggests that the specific difference is "sacred." But not all signs of sacred realities are said to be sacraments. All of creation can be said to be a sign of God, for "The heavens are telling the glory of God; and the firmament proclaims his handiwork" (Ps 19:1). But all of nature is not a sacrament. Likewise works of art and literature depicting religious themes are

---

[48] See Nicolas, *Synthèse dogmatique: de la Trinité à la Trinité*, 733.

[49] See *ST* III, q. 60, a. 1: "But now we are speaking of sacraments in a special sense, as implying the relation of sign: and in this way a sacrament is a kind of sign."

[50] See the excellent article by Hyacinthe-François Dondaine, "La définition des sacrements dans la *Somme théologique*," *Revue des Sciences Philosophiques et Théologiques* 31 (1947): 214–28, esp. 224–28.

signs of sacred things but not sacraments. What makes a sacred sign a sacrament?

St. Thomas proposes that sacraments are distinguished from other sacred signs by the fact that they are signs of a particular kind of sacred reality: that which sanctifies human beings, as the etymology of the word *sacramentum* indicates. Thus the specific difference of sacrament is that it is a sign of a sacred reality that brings about the sanctification of human beings.

Sacraments are proper to human beings in a double sense. First, they are proper to us insofar as they are signs or symbols. Man is properly a symbol-making creature, having both senses and intellect. Thus it is natural for us to use sensible images to represent our abstract ideas. All of human culture and communication is made up of a tremendous variety of signs and symbols.

Secondly, sacraments are proper to men with regard to what they represent and realize, which is our being brought into union with God. For it belongs to the spiritual creature alone to be *capax Dei*: capable of (union with) God. The angel is capable of sanctification but not of using symbols to represent and effect it. Brute animals are neither capable of using symbols nor of being brought into union with God. As a rational animal, man is a creature capable of knowing and loving God and of being sanctified by Him, and to whose nature it is proper to sensibly represent the way to union with Him. St. Thomas explains:

> Signs are given to men, to whom it is proper to discover the unknown by means of the known. Consequently a sacrament properly so called is that which is the sign of some sacred thing pertaining to man; so that properly speaking a sacrament . . . is defined as being the "sign of a holy thing so far as it makes men holy."[51]

St. Thomas thus keeps St. Augustine's classic but very broad definition of sacrament as a sacred sign but adds to it by specifying that it is a particular kind of sacred sign, for it signifies a sacred reality *by which man is sanctified*. In other words, the sacraments are *sacred signs of the grace merited by Christ's Paschal mystery*. In this way St. Thomas distinguishes sacraments from other signs referring to God, such as words about God or images that represent Him, like a mountain peak,

---

[51] *ST* III, q. 60, a. 2.

a mighty storm, or the starry sky. A sacrament is a sign not simply of holy things but of holy things that sanctify us through the work of Christ and the application of the grace He merited for us.

As seen in the previous chapter, the sacred realities that sanctify man are threefold: (a) Christ's Paschal mystery which merited grace for us, (b) the present application of sanctifying grace to us and the forgiveness of sins, and (c) future glory by which we will be fully sanctified.[52] Of these three, the principal sense signified by the sacraments of the New Covenant is the application of sanctifying grace.[53]

St. Thomas also explains that his definition distinguishes sacraments from sacramentals. A sacrament is a sign of man's effective sanctification, and a sacramental is a sign of man's disposing himself to receive that sanctification:

> Names are given to things considered in reference to their end and state of completeness. Now a disposition is not an end, whereas perfection is. Consequently things that signify *disposition to holiness* are not called sacraments, and with regard to these the objection is verified: only those are called sacraments which signify the perfection of holiness in man.[54]

The receiving of ashes on Ash Wednesday, for example, is a sign not directly of our sanctification but of our humbling ourselves, remember-

---

[52] See *ST* III, q. 60, a. 3; *In IV Sent.*, d. 1, a. 1, qla. 1, ad 4

[53] Thomas Aquinas, *In IV Sent.*, d. 1, a. 1, qla. 1, ad 4: "They also signify the effect of sanctification that they cause, and this is their principal signification; and in this way they are demonstrative signs."

[54] *ST* III, q. 60, a. 2, ad 3 (my italics). St. Thomas uses the pre-baptismal exorcisms as an example of a sacramental because they do not give grace but remove an obstacle. See *ST* III, q. 71, a. 3, ad 2: "It is essential to a sacrament to produce its principal effect, which is grace that remits sin, or supplies some defect in man. But those things that are done in the exorcism do not effect this; they merely remove these impediments. Consequently, they are not sacraments but sacramentals." See also *In IV Sent.*, d. 23, q. 1, a. 1, qla. 1, trans. Mortensen, 8:553: "Some of those things that the Church works visibly are sacraments, like baptism, and some are sacramentals, like exorcism, as was said above in Distinction 6. And the difference between them is this, that a sacrament is the name for that action of the Church that attains its principally intended effect in the administering of the sacraments; but a sacramental is the name for that action that, although it does not attain to that effect, nevertheless is ordered somehow to that principal action. Now the intended effect in the administering of the sacraments is the healing of the disease of sin."

ing that we are dust so as to receive sanctification from the sacraments. Thus it is a sacramental rather than a sacrament. Sacramentals could be defined as sacred signs, instituted by the Church, that represent (and thus aid) our disposing ourselves to receive sanctification from Christ through His sacraments.

In order to define the sacraments of the New Covenant in particular, two other properties, explained elsewhere by St. Thomas, complete the definition of the seven sacraments. First, sacraments are instituted by God rather than man. This is because they are instituted to sanctify man by giving grace, and the power to bestow grace (as principal cause) belongs only to God: "Since, therefore, the power of the sacrament is from God alone, it follows that God alone can institute the sacraments."[55] This applies both to the sacraments of the Old and New Covenant, although in the New they are instituted directly by God incarnate, the Founder and Head of the Church.

The second property applies only to the sacraments of the New Covenant and is the specific difference that distinguishes them from those of the Old Covenant. As will be seen in chapter 12 below, St. Thomas holds that the sacraments of the Church are instrumental causes empowered by the Incarnation, the merits of the Passion, and Christ's institution, to give the grace that they signify; they are efficacious signs.[56] This property is expressed by saying that the sacraments of the Church are efficacious *ex opere operato* (from the work done, that is, from the valid realization of the sacramental sign).[57] It is precisely this claim of efficacy *ex opere operato* that would be a major point of contention in the Protestant Reformation.

In a subsequent question on the causality of the sacraments, St. Thomas asks how something can be both a sign and a cause at the same time. He answers that the action of an instrument, although it is

---

[55] *ST* III, q. 64, a. 2.

[56] See *ST* III, q. 62, aa. 1–5; *In IV Sent.*, d. 1, q. 1, a. 4, qla. 1, sed contra 1, trans. Mortensen, 7:26: "On the contrary, this difference is commonly drawn between the sacraments of the New Law and of the Old Law, that the sacraments of the New Law effect what they represent, which the sacraments of the Old Law are not capable of doing. But sacraments represent invisible grace. If, therefore, the sacraments of the New Law do not cause grace, then they are not different from the sacraments of the Old Law."

[57] See Thomas Aquinas, *In IV Sent.*, d. 1, q. 1, a. 5, qla. 1. On St. Thomas's use of this term in his commentary on the *Sentences*, see Schillebeeckx, *Christ the Sacrament of the Encounter with God*, 82–89.

a kind of cause, is also an effect of the principal cause and thus can be a sign of its activity. The activity of Michelangelo's chisel is a visible sign of the invisible artistry in the mind of the sculptor, as well as a cause of the statue. It is in this way that the sacraments of the Church are signs of Christ's activity sanctifying through them, as well as instrumental causes of man's sanctification, moved by Christ. He writes:

> But an instrumental cause, if manifest, can be called a sign of a hidden effect, for this reason, that it is not merely a cause but also in a measure an effect in so far as it is moved by the principal agent. And in this sense the sacraments of the New Law are both cause and signs. Hence, too, is it that, to use the common expression, "they effect what they signify." From this it is clear that they *perfectly fulfil the conditions of a sacrament; being ordained to something sacred, not only as a sign, but also as a cause.*[58]

The Church's sacraments thus fulfill the etymological notion of sacrament more perfectly than those of the Old Covenant because they have a double relation to human sanctification, that of sign and cause, for they both represent our sanctification and cause what they represent.[59] They also more perfectly signify human sanctification because they represent it as something present, being realized here and now in the subject through their own instrumental causality in the hands of Christ.[60]

SACRAMENTS OF THE OLD AND NEW COVENANTS

St. Thomas's challenge was to define sacrament in such a way that it

---

[58] *ST* III, q. 62, a. 1, ad 1, my emphasis. See Manuel J. Ordeig, "Significación y causalidad sacramental según Santo Tomás de Aquino," *Scripta Theologica* 13 (1981): 63–114, at 99–102.

[59] See Peter Garland, *The Definition of Sacrament According to Saint Thomas* (Ottawa: University of Ottawa Press, 1959), 98–99: "Now the sacraments of the New Law, as well as having this relationship of sign to that which is intrinsically sacred, also have the relationship of cause to it. . . . Then according to the analogical character of the word sacrament, the sacraments of the New Law may be said to be sacraments for two reasons as a result of their twofold relationship of sign and cause to that which is intrinsically sacred."

[60] See La Soujeole, "The Sacraments and the Development of Doctrine," in *OHST*, 591: "What is signified is a sacred reality in the act of sanctification, that is to say, the sign of a cause at work."

could still retain its patristic broad sense by which, although primarily referring to the seven sacraments of the New Covenant, it also applies to sacraments of the Old Covenant, such as circumcision, priestly consecration, and the Paschal lamb.[61] They too are signs of the sacred reality that sanctifies man, which is the grace merited by Christ's Paschal mystery, which they prefigure. Today few Catholics are inclined to use the word sacrament to refer to any of the sacred rites of Judaism. St. Thomas, on the contrary, thought that it was important to take the word *sacrament* in such a way that it could be used in two analogous senses so as to apply both to the sacraments of the Old and New Covenant, thus pointing to their essential continuity in the plan of salvation.[62] Even though, as will be seen below, St. Thomas argues that the sacraments of the Old Covenant did not give grace *ex opere operato*[63] as do those of the New, they nevertheless were signs of man's

---

[61] For St. Thomas on the sacraments of the Old Law, see *ST* I-II, q. 102, a. 5. It is interesting that St. Thomas, like several of the Fathers, also sometimes speaks of the Church in a broad sense that includes the patriarchs and the faithful of the Old Covenant. See *ST* III, q. 8, a. 3, ad 3: "The holy Fathers did not make use of the legal sacraments as realities, but as images and shadows of what was to come. Now it is the same motion to an image inasmuch as it is an image, and to the reality, as is clear from the Philosopher (*De Memor. and Remin.* ii.). Hence the ancient Fathers, by observing the legal sacraments, were borne to Christ by the same faith and love whereby we also are borne to Him, and hence the ancient Fathers belong to the same Church as we." See Colman O'Neill, "St. Thomas on the Membership of the Church," *The Thomist* 27 (1963): 88–140, esp. 93–112.

[62] See Benoit-Dominique de La Soujeole, "The Economy of Salvation: Entitative Sacramentality and Operative Sacramentality," *The Thomist* 75 (2011): 543: "The fact that for St. Thomas the Jewish sacraments are sacraments in the proper sense permits us to say that he regards the entire economy of salvation as sacramental. Assuredly this is a very patristic intuition." This aspect of continuity is less pronounced in other medieval scholastics, such as Peter Lombard, who defines *sacramentum* as properly referring only to the seven sacraments of the New Covenant, and only improperly to the Old Testament sacraments. See his *Sentences*, bk 4, d. 1, ch. 4, p. 5, where he speaks of the sacraments of the Old Law: "And so they were signs; and yet, although less than properly, they are often called sacraments in the Scriptures, because they were signs of a sacred thing, which they certainly did not confer."

[63] For the meaning and history of this expression, which will be explained in chapter 13 below, see John F. Gallagher, *Significando causant: A Study of Sacramental Efficiency* (Fribourg, CH: University Press, 1965), 51: "By the time of Thomas the expressions meant that the sacraments of the new law were acts of Christ, efficacious of themselves, independent of the evil dispositions of the minister, who acts only as an instrument of God; moreover the grace coming

effective sanctification through Christ and were occasions in which God applied grace to the people of Israel, sanctifying them.

St. Thomas's definition of sacrament, "the sign of a holy thing so far as it makes men holy," has not been widely used in catechesis, probably because it is not a definition specifically of the sacraments of the New Covenant, since St. Thomas wanted it to apply also to the Old Testament sacraments. For this reason he does not include in his mature definition the specific difference of the New Testament sacraments, which is their efficacy in realizing the sanctification they signify.[64] One could modify his definition to make it proper to the New Testament sacraments: The sacraments are (a) *sacred signs of man's sanctification by Christ,* (b) *instituted and used by Him to cause the sanctification they represent.* The first part of the definition is common to the sacraments of both covenants, and the second part applies only to those of the New. The Old Testament sacraments could be defined as *sacred signs, instituted by God, prefiguring man's sanctification by Christ.*

I am very sympathetic to St. Thomas's mature intention, in contrast with his own earlier commentary, with Peter Lombard, and with the great majority of modern theologians,[65] in defining sacrament in such a way that it includes those of the Old Testament. This high-

---

to one from the sacraments does not come due to one's own merits or faith, or from the merits of the minister, as was the case in the old law, but from God Himself using the sacrament as a means of sanctifying men."

[64] For a different explanation of St. Thomas's intention in his definition of sacrament in *ST* III, q. 60, a. 2, see Louis-Marie Chauvet, *Symbol and Sacrament* (Collegeville, MN: Liturgical Press, 1995), 11–15. A weakness in his account is that he does not mention St. Thomas's intention to include the Old Testament sacraments in the definition. For a fuller treatment of St. Thomas's definition in the *Summa,* see Dondaine, "La définition des sacrements dans la *Somme théologique,*" *Revue des Sciences Philosophiques et Théologiques* 31 (1947): 214–28.

[65] See Garland, *The Definition of Sacrament,* 65: "The Angelic Dominican Doctor, in exposing his doctrine on the sacraments, proceeds in a manner quite different to the authors of most modern manuals of theology, who dispose of the whole matter of the sacraments of the Old Testament by briefly enumerating the differences between the sacraments of the two Dispensations. For St. Thomas, desiring unity, the link between the sacraments of the Old and New Testament is the most fundamental point." See also Garland, *The Definition of Sacrament,* 3–5. Suárez follows St. Thomas in defining *sacramentum* so as to include also the Old Testament sacraments. See Franciscus Suárez, *Commentaria ac Disputationes in Tertiam Partem D. Thomae,* in *ST* III, q. 60, disp. 1, sectio 4, in *Opera omnia,* vol. 20 (Paris: Vivès, 1866), 23, translated in Van Roo, *The Christian Sacrament,* 59: "A sacrament is a sensibly perceptible sign instituted to give some sanctification and to signify true holiness of soul."

lights the continuity of God's plan in salvation history and manifests the dignity of the rites of Israel.

There are important pastoral reasons, however, for preferring a definition proper to the New Testament sacraments, as Peter Lombard gives. It is more useful to the faithful to have a definition proper to the seven sacraments of the Church, the masterpieces of God for their sanctification. This is especially true after the rejection of the distinction between the sacraments of the Old and New Covenants by Calvin and his corresponding rejection of the causal efficacy of those of the New, as will be seen in chapter 13 below.

If one includes in the basic definition of sacrament their efficacy in causing what they signify, according to St. Thomas's procedure in his earlier Commentary on the *Sentences*, following Peter Lombard, one can still speak of Old Testament sacraments in a secondary analogical sense, as St. Thomas does there. They are sacraments by way of a relation of prefigurement. This has both advantages and disadvantages. The advantage is the clear notion of New Testament sacrament, highlighting its glory of causing the sanctification it represents. For this reason it is preferred both by catechesis and the Magisterium. This procedure also brings out better the centrality of Christ, the Church, and her sacraments in the plan of salvation history, for God has to become incarnate before there can be a sacrament in the full and perfect sense both of signification and causality. Christ has to come and speak the words of power through which the sacraments are efficacious in realizing what they represent.

The disadvantage is that defining sacraments in terms of their causal efficacy, which marks Catholic sacramental catechesis and theology in the post-Tridentine period, has often failed to sufficiently manifest their symbolic value and the intimate link between the sacraments of the two Covenants, which St. Thomas and St. Augustine so emphasized. St. Thomas's broad definition of sacrament—divinely instituted signs of the sacred realities that sanctify man—could help to recover this link.

PROTESTANT DEFINITIONS OF SACRAMENT

The definition of sacrament became a key issue in the Reformation. Rather than being viewed as sacred signs that cause the sanctification they signify, the sacraments were seen by Luther and other leaders of the Reformation above all as divinely instituted signs attesting to the certain *promises* of God. Luther's focus was not on the causality of the sacraments but on the infallible certainty of God's promise that is sensibly proclaimed directly to the believer in the sacrament, to be received in faith.[66] In his work of 1520, *The Babylonian Captivity of the Church*, Luther defined sacraments as "those promises [of God] which have signs attached to them."[67] He concludes there that only Baptism and the Eucharist are sacraments because "only in these two do we find both the divinely instituted sign and the promise of forgiveness of sins."[68]

Zwingli defined the sacraments as "nothing else than an initiatory ceremony or a pledging,"[69] seeing them only as outwards signs that distinguish the Christian from the non-Christian and that provide an outward occasion for the exercise of faith.

John Calvin, synthesizing his predecessors, defined sacrament as "an external sign, by which the Lord seals on our consciences his promises of good-will toward us, in order to sustain the weakness of our faith, and we in our turn testify our piety toward him." A briefer definition is: "a testimony of the divine favor toward us, confirmed by an external sign, with a corresponding attestation of our faith toward

---

[66] On the connection between the central notions of promise and faith, see Martin Luther, *Babylonian Captivity of the Church*, in *LW*, vol. 36, *Word and Sacrament II* (Philadelphia and St. Louis, MO: Muhlenberg Press and Concordia Publishing House, 1959), 42: "For God does not deal, nor has he ever dealt, with man otherwise than through a word of promise. . . . We in turn cannot deal with God otherwise than through faith in the Word of his promise. . . . For anyone can easily see that these two, promise and faith, must necessarily go together. For without the promise there is nothing to be believed; while without faith the promise is useless, since it is established and fulfilled through faith." For sympathetic and insightful presentations of Luther's understanding of sacraments and justification, and the differences between Luther and Calvin on this point, see Cary, "Why Luther Is Not Quite Protestant," 447–86; and Michael Root, "Luther and Calvin on the Role of Faith in the Sacraments: A Catholic Analysis," *Nova et Vetera* (English) 15, no. 4 (2017): 1065–84.

[67] Luther, *Babylonian Captivity of the Church*, in *LW*, 36:124. On the importance of this work for Protestant sacramental theology, see James F. White, *The Sacraments in Protestant Practice and Faith* (Nashville: Abingdon Press, 1999), 17: "The *Babylonian Captivity* stands as the most important single treatise shaping all Protestant sacramental life."

[68] Luther, *Babylonian Captivity of the Church*, in *LW*, 36:124..

[69] Ulrich Zwingli, *Commentary on True and False Religion*, ed. Samuel Macauley Jackson and Clarence Nevin Heller (Durham, NC: Labyrinth Press, 1981), 181, cited in White, *The Sacraments in Protestant Practice*, 19.

him."[70] Calvin, in common with the Catholic tradition, sees the sacraments as a work of divine pedagogy taking into account the human dependence on sense experience.[71]

This conception of sacrament found in Luther, Zwingli, and Calvin does not include what is most proper to the sacraments of the New Covenant, which is their causal power to efficaciously communicate here and now the grace that they represent, as long as the recipient poses no obstacle, and it tends to equate the sacraments of the New Covenant with those of the Old. As signs of a divine promise in the Protestant conception, the sacraments are a kind of "visible word"[72] to be received in faith, and, though they strengthen faith, they attest more to a future reality of promise than apply to us already here and now the grace won for us on Calvary.

In this way the sacraments are conceived of as not essentially distinct from revelation, other than by being a *visible* word addressed to us personally that enables us to attest to our faith through receiving it.[73] In the Catholic conception, on the contrary, sacraments are divine visible words that communicate not only the promise of grace but also its effective application in the present by being words of power to effect what they signify, creating deeper faith and sanctification in the recipients, according to their disposition.[74] Calvin explicitly denies

---

[70] John Calvin, *Institutes of the Christian Religion*, bk. 4, ch. 14.1, trans. Henry Beveridge (Peabody, MA: Hendrickson Publishers, 2008), 843.

[71] Calvin, *Institutes of the Christian Religion*, bk. 4, ch. 14.3, in Beveridge, 844: "Our merciful Lord, with boundless condescension, so accommodates himself to our capacity, that seeing how from our animal nature we are always creeping on the ground, and cleaving to the flesh, having no thought of what is spiritual, and not even forming an idea of it, he declines not by means of these earthly elements to lead us to himself, and even in the flesh to exhibit a mirror of spiritual blessings."

[72] This expression is from Augustine, *Tractate* 80.3.1 on John 15.3, in *Tractates on the Gospel of John 55–111*, trans. J. W. Rettig, FC 90 (Washington, DC: Catholic University of America Press, 1994), 117: "Take away the word, and what is the water except water? The word is added to the elemental substance, and it becomes a sacrament, also itself, as it were, a visible word." Calvin takes up this expression in the *Institutes*, bk. 4, ch. 14.5, p. 845.

[73] See Calvin, *Institutes*, 4.14.12, p. 849: "He spiritually nourishes our faith by means of the sacraments, whose only office is to make his promises visible to our eye, or rather, to be pledges of his promises."

[74] For a reflection on the value of this expression, "*verbum visibile*," and the incompleteness of the Protestant understanding of it, see Louis Bouyer, "Word and Sacrament," in *Sacraments: The Gestures of Christ*, ed. O'Callaghan, 139–52, at

this causal efficacy of the sacraments,[75] saying instead that they are essentially means by which the faithful exercise their faith.[76]

The Council of Trent responded to the Protestant notion of sacrament, infallibly teaching that the sacraments *contain the grace they signify*:

> If anyone says that the sacraments of the New Law do not contain the grace they signify or that they do not confer that grace on those who do not place an obstacle in the way, as if they were only external signs of the grace or justice received through faith and marks of the Christian profession by which among men the faithful are distinguished from the unbelievers, let him be anathema.[77]

DEFINITION OF SACRAMENT
AFTER THE COUNCIL OF TRENT

After the Council of Trent, definitions of the sacraments generally apply only to those of the New Covenant and include the three properties of being sacred signs of our sanctification, instituted by Christ, and efficacious in giving the grace they represent.

The *Catechism of the Council of Trent* defines a sacrament of the New Covenant as "something perceptible to the senses which, by

---

151–52: "We can see how the Protestants were right in describing the sacrament as a *verbum visible* and how they were wrong. They were not wrong in that they went too far in their way, but in that they stopped only half-way. They saw in the word only the word announced, and therefore in the sacrament nothing else than a more material—thus easier to grasp but less satisfactory—transcription of its meaning. Accordingly, the efficacy of the sacrament as that of the word preached was only to create and sustain our faith in a purely psychological way. To faith alone, as through its own power, was committed the task of seizing upon God's gift of grace. The Catholic doctrine is rather that . . . faith in the sacrament does not seize grace by its own power, but is rather itself the first gift to be awakened by divine grace as the object and product of the word."

[75] See Calvin, *Institutes*, 4.14.9, p. 847; and 4.14.14, p. 850.

[76] *Institutes*, bk. 4, ch. 14.6, p. 845: "Sacraments, therefore, are exercises which confirm our faith in the word of God; and because we are carnal, they are exhibited under carnal objects, that thus they may train us in accommodation to our sluggish capacity."

[77] Council of Trent, Decree on the Sacraments (session 7), can. 6 on the Sacraments in General (DS, 1606). Trent does not give a definition of sacrament but limits itself to excluding inadequate notions in thirteen canons.

virtue of its divine institution, has the power both to signify and to effect holiness."[78]

Leo XIII, in his encyclical on Anglican Orders, defines the sacraments as follows: "All know that the sacraments of the New Law, inasmuch as they are sensible and efficacious signs of invisible grace, must both signify the grace that they effect and effect the grace that they signify."[79] This is taken up also by Pius XII, in his Apostolic Constitution *Sacramentum Ordinis*.[80] This definition emphasizes the intimate connection between the sign and effect of the sacraments, for they confer the grace they signify.

The *Catechism of the Catholic Church* gives two definitions of the sacraments. In §1084 sacraments are defined as "perceptible signs (words and actions) accessible to our human nature. By the action of Christ and the power of the Holy Spirit they make present efficaciously the grace that they signify." In §1131 the sacraments are defined as "efficacious signs of grace, instituted by Christ and entrusted to the Church, by which divine life is dispensed to us. The visible rites by which the sacraments are celebrated signify and make present the graces proper to each sacrament."[81] The first definition emphasizes the action of Christ and the power of the Holy Spirit in realizing what the sacraments signify. The second definition adds to the first by mentioning that they were instituted by Christ and entrusted to the Church, and that each sacrament signifies and produces a special effect of grace proper to that sacrament.

Summary: Four Fundamental Elements in the Definition of the Sacraments of the New Covenant

There are four parts to the definition of the sacraments of the New

---

[78] *CCT*, part 2, intro., §11, p. 149.

[79] Leo XIII, Apostolic Letter on the Nullity of Anglican Orders *Apostolicae Curae* (Sept 15, 1896), §24 (DS, 3315).

[80] Pius XII, Apostolic Constitution on the Sacrament of Orders *Sacramentum Ordinis* (Nov 30, 1947), §3 (DS, 3858).

[81] The *Compendium of the Catechism of the Catholic Church*, §224 defines the sacraments as "efficacious signs of grace perceptible to the senses" that were "instituted by Christ and entrusted to the Church. Through them divine life is bestowed upon us."

Covenant. First, all sacraments are sensible signs of the sacred realities by which man is sanctified, according to the definitions of St. Augustine and St. Thomas. This is equivalent to saying that they represent the infusion of sanctifying grace and sacramental graces, merited by Christ's Passion, that give life in the Spirit by which man is sanctified and configured to Christ in His Paschal mystery. This is common to the sacraments of the Old and the New Covenant.

Second, they are distinct from the Old Covenant sacraments in that they were instituted by Jesus Christ who uses them as His instruments to touch the members of His Mystical Body after His Ascension into heaven. In this way they are distinguished from all other religious signs.

Third, because they were instituted by the Word Incarnate they have the power to realize the effects of grace that they signify, which is another way they are distinguished from all other religious rites. They are instruments of Christ with a power to bring about man's sanctification that comes from the Paschal mystery and the action of the Holy Spirit. Here lies the unfathomable dignity of the sacramental economy of the New Covenant.

A fourth property of the sacraments that should be included in their definition is their ecclesial nature, as emphasized in *Lumen Gentium*, §11. Not only are the sacraments entrusted to the Church, but they are also the source both of her visible and invisible life. They build up her supernatural life by making those who worthily receive them into her living members, differentiated into different ecclesial states by Baptism, Confirmation, and Matrimony, and Holy Orders, all ordered to the celebration of the Eucharist, the sacrament of ecclesial communion.[82] The *Code of Canon Law* stresses the ecclesial dimension in its definition of the sacraments given in canon 840:

> The sacraments of the New Testament were instituted by Christ the Lord and entrusted to the Church. As actions of Christ and the Church, they are signs and means which

---

[82] See the suggestion by Bernard Leeming to include this ecclesial dimension into the definition of sacrament, in his *Principles of Sacramental Theology*, 2nd ed. (Westminster, MD: Newman Press, 1960), x: "Might not a sacrament be better defined as 'an effective sign of a particular form of union with the Mystical Body, the Church, instituted by Jesus Christ, which gives grace to those who receive it rightly'?" On this ecclesial dimension of the sacramental liturgy, see Vagaggini, *Theological Dimensions of the Liturgy*, 272–99.

express and strengthen the faith, render worship to God, and effect the sanctification of humanity and thus contribute in the greatest way to establish, strengthen, and manifest ecclesiastical communion.

The *Catechism of the Catholic Church*, §1116 describes the sacraments as the life-giving channels of the Church and "the masterworks" of the New Covenant: "Sacraments are 'powers that come forth' from the Body of Christ, which is ever-living and life-giving. They are actions of the Holy Spirit at work in his Body, the Church. They are 'the masterworks of God' in the new and everlasting covenant."

As signs, the seven sacraments have an outward and sensible dimension chosen by Christ for its natural capacity to signify what belongs to man's sanctification. As sacred signs, the sacraments belong in the context of the worship of God. They are divinely given means to worship God and sanctify men, immeasurably surpassing all other religious rites.

As religious rites, the sacraments are endowed with both an ascending and a descending movement. They sensibly express man's interior worship of God, and they bring down divine gifts to man that effect his sanctification. Thus there is a dual direction of gift in the sacraments: from man to God in worship and from God to man in sanctification.[83] St. Thomas explains succinctly: "In the use of the sacraments two things may be considered, namely, the worship of God, and the sanctification of man: the former of which pertains to man as referred to God, and the latter pertains to God in reference to man."[84] Man's worship of God in the Church is the ascending dimension, and God's sanctification of man is the descending dimension. Christ's mediation as eternal High Priest consists in perfectly realizing these two dimensions: He gives glory to the Father, and He sanctifies His Mystical Body that He won with the price of His Blood. A key task of pastoral ministry today is to reawaken a sense of the infinite drama of our participation in Christ's ascending and descending action in the sacraments.

---

[83] See Thomas Joseph White, "Sacraments and Philosophy," in *OHST*, 588: "Just as the sacraments are the loci of the 'descent' of grace, they are also the place of religious 'ascent' of human beings toward God under grace. Owing to the divine institution of the sacraments, human religious life can be redeemed under the grace-filled effects of the sacraments, and the sacraments engender a life-giving form of religious worship." See also Miralles, *I sacramenti cristiani*, 192.

[84] *ST* III, q. 60, a. 5.

STUDY QUESTIONS

1. What is the Pauline notion of "mystery"? How does it relate to the theological concept of sacrament?
2. What is the Augustinian definition of sacrament? How does the notion develop up to St. Thomas Aquinas? What are the contributions of Hugh of St. Victor and Peter Lombard?
3. Explain St. Thomas's definition of sacrament in the *Summa theologiae*, giving the genus and specific difference.
4. How do the sacraments of the New Covenant differ from those of the Old Covenant? Explain their analogical relationship.
5. How do the definitions of a sacrament given by Luther and Calvin differ from the Catholic understanding as defined at the Council of Trent? Explain the significance and consequences of this difference.
6. How does the *Catechism of the Catholic Church* define "sacrament"? Explain the elements of the definition.
7. What are the four key elements that should enter into a definition of the sacraments of the New Covenant? Explain.
8. Explain the "ascending" and "descending" aspects of the sacraments.

SUGGESTIONS FOR FURTHER READING

ST III, q. 60, aa. 1–2.

Garland, Peter. *The Definition of Sacrament According to Saint Thomas.* Ottawa: University of Ottawa Press, 1959.

La Soujeole, Benoit-Dominique de, O.P. "The Sacraments and the Development of Doctrine." Translated by Dominic M. Langevin. In *The Oxford Handbook of Sacramental Theology*, edited by Hans Boersma and Matthew Levering. Oxford; New York: Oxford University Press, 2015. Pp. 590–601.

Miralles, Antonio. *I sacramenti cristiani: trattato generale.* 2nd edition. Rome: Apollinare studi, 2008. Pp. 13–68, 79–144.

Nutt, Roger. *General Principles of Sacramental Theology.* Washington, DC: Catholic University of America Press, 2017. Pp. 49–65.

Ordeig, Manuel J. "Significación y causalidad sacramental según Santo Tomás de Aquino." *Scripta Theologica* 13 (1981): 63–114.

Ratzinger, Joseph. "On the Concept of Sacrament." In *Theology of the*

Liturgy: The Sacramental Foundation of Christian Existence. Edited by Michael Miller. Translated by John Saward, Kenneth Baker, et al. *Collected Works*, vol. 11. San Francisco: Ignatius Press, 2014. Pp. 169–84.

Scheeben, Matthias Joseph. *The Mysteries of Christianity*. Translated by Cyril Vollert. St. Louis, MO: B. Herder, 1951. Pp. 558–63.

Van Roo, William A., S.J. *The Christian Sacrament*. Rome: Editrice Pontificia Università Gregoriana, 1992. Pp. 27–97.

CHAPTER THREE

The Seven Sacraments

Today Catholics take it for granted that there are seven sacraments, and they are surprised to learn that it was only in the twelfth century that theologians began to teach that. This is a striking example of the development of doctrine with regard to the sacraments. As seen in the preceding chapter, it was due to the work of the theologians of the twelfth century, such as Peter Lombard, that the word "sacrament" acquired a sense precise enough to determine their exact number. The Augustinian usage was broader and thus could include many more rites. Similarly, Eastern Fathers such as Pseudo-Dionysius used the word *mysterion* in a very broad sense, including many liturgical rites that we speak of as sacramentals.[1] The precise determination of the number of sacraments of the New Covenant only came about by defining the sacraments as sacred signs that efficaciously *cause* what they signify through being instituted by Christ, who works invisibly through them.[2]

St. Augustine and other Fathers sometimes used the word sacrament in this more restricted sense, and then the problem is that they generally mention by name only two such sacraments: Baptism and the Eucharist, corresponding to the water and blood that came forth from Christ's side on the Cross. As we have seen, Tertullian coined the Latin word "sacramentum" from the Greek *mysterion*, and

---

[1] See Pseudo-Dionysius, "The Ecclesiastical Hierarchy," in *Pseudo-Dionysius: The Complete Works*, trans. Colm Luibhéid, Classics of Western Spirituality (New York; Mahwah, NJ: Paulist Press, 1987), 193–260. Pseudo-Dionysius, for example, speaks of the consecration of the chrism as a sacrament (p. 224), as well as the consecration of the altar (p. 231).

[2] See Lawrence P. Everett, *The Nature of Sacramental Grace* (Washington, DC: Catholic University of America Press, 1948), 10.

he applied it directly to Baptism[3] and the Eucharist.[4] St. Augustine likewise generally names Baptism and the Eucharist as sacraments, as in the following text, although he also implies that there are others:

> He has laid on the society of His new people the obligation of sacraments, very few in number, very easy of observance, most sublime in their meaning, as, for example, baptism, hallowed by the name of the Trinity, Communion of His Body and His Blood, and whatever else is commended in the canonical writings.[5]

On one occasion St. Augustine also refers to the post-baptismal anointing (which later began to be called Confirmation) as a sacrament: "the sacrament of anointing, its invisible power itself being the invisible anointing that is the Holy Spirit."[6] As the celebration of Confirmation began to be separated from Baptism in the West from the fifth century,[7] Confirmation began to be frequently mentioned together with Baptism and the Eucharist as a sacrament. St. Isidore of Seville[8] in the seventh century, and Paschasius Radbertus[9]

---

3   Tertullian, *De baptismo* 9. Earlier in this work (chs. 7–8), Tertullian also refers to the giving of the Holy Spirit through a post-baptismal anointing and laying on of hands. Although he does not use the word "sacrament" to refer to it, he describes it as efficacious in communicating the Spirit. Thus it fulfils the notion of sacrament.

4   Tertullian, *De corona* 3.

5   Augustine, Letter 54.1, in *Letters: Volume I (1–82)*, trans. Parsons, 252. See also *De doctrina christiana* 3.9.13.31, in *On Christian Teaching*, trans. R. P. H. Green (Oxford: Oxford University Press, 1997), 75.

6   Augustine, Third Homily on 1 John, no. 12, in *Homilies on the First Epistle of John*, 62.

7   See the fifth-century homily on Pentecost attributed to Faustus of Riez, in E. C. Whitaker, ed., *Documents of the Baptismal Liturgy*, 3rd ed. (Collegeville, MN: Pueblo, 2003), 257–58. On this influential homily, see L. A. Van Buchem, *L'homélie pseudo-eusébienne de Pentecôte. L'origine de la "confirmatio" en Gaule méridionale et l'interprétation de ce rite par Fauste de Riez* (Nijmegen: Drukkerij Janssen, 1967); Eugene Finnegan, *Confirmation at an Impasse: The Historical Origins of the Sacrament of Confirmation* (Linus Publications, 2008), 179–88.

8   See Isidore, *Etymologies*, bk. 6, ch. 19, no. 39.

9   See Paschasius Radbertus, *De Corpore et Sanguine Domini* 3.2 in CCCM 16, pp. 23–24: "The sacraments of Christ in the Church are baptism, chrism, and the body and blood of the Lord."

and Rabanus Maurus[10] in the ninth century speak of three sacraments, which correspond to the three sacraments of initiation.

St. Augustine also speaks of Matrimony as a sacrament, which is indissoluble so as to represent the fidelity of Christ to His Bride:

> The good, therefore, of marriage among all nations and all men is in the cause of generation and in the fidelity of chastity; in the case of the people of God, however, the good is also in the sanctity of the sacrament. Because of this sanctity it is wrong for a woman, leaving with a divorce, to marry another man while her husband still lives.[11]

Anointing of the Sick is said to be a sacrament by Innocent I in a letter of AD 416, in which he says that this anointing cannot be received by those who are doing public penance and thus are excommunicated, because it is a sacrament: "That cannot be administered to penitents, because it is a kind of sacrament. For, how is it supposed that one species [of sacrament] can be granted to those to whom the rest of the sacraments are denied?"[12]

In the first half of the twelfth century, Hugh of St. Victor still uses the broad Augustinian sense of sacrament that includes sacramentals. Thus in addition to the sacraments of Christian initiation, Matrimony[13] and Anointing of the Sick,[14] he also uses the word *sacrament* to refer to the sprinkling of holy water, the sign of the cross, the reception of ashes, "the blowing of exorcism," and many other liturgical gestures, which we refer to as sacramentals. Of these he says: "There are certain sacraments in the Church and, although salvation does not depend on them principally, yet salvation is increased from them according as

---

[10] See Rabanus Maurus, *De clericorum institutione* 1.24 in *De clericorum institutione libri tres*, ed. Aloisius Knoepfler (Munich: Lentner, 1900), 41.

[11] Augustine, *The Good of Marriage* 24.32, trans. C. T. Wilcox, in *Treatises on Marriage and Other Subjects*, FC 27 (Washington, DC: Catholic University of America Press, 1955), 47–48.

[12] Innocent I, Letter to Decentius, bishop of Gubbio, (Mar 19, 416; DS, 216). This terminology is rare before the ninth century. See Antoine Chavasse, *Etude sur l'onction des infirmes dans l'Église latine du IIIe au XIe siècle* (Lyon: Facultés Catholiques de Lyon, 1942), 167.

[13] Hugh of St. Victor, *On the Sacraments of the Christian Faith*, bk. 2, part 11, no. 1, trans. Deferrari, 324.

[14] Hugh of St. Victor, *On the Sacraments of the Christian Faith*, bk. 2, part 15, no. 2, p. 431.

devotion is exercised."[15]

Shortly after Hugh of St. Victor, Peter Lombard finally formulated a definition of sacrament that was precise enough to exclude sacramentals and the rites of the Old Testament. This enabled him to determine that there are exactly seven sacraments in the proper sense of the word.[16] He writes:

> Let us now proceed to the sacraments of the New Law, which are: baptism, confirmation, the bread of blessing [the Eucharist], penance, extreme unction, orders, marriage. Of these, some offer a remedy against sin and confer helping grace, like baptism; others are only a remedy, like marriage; others fortify us with grace and virtue, like the Eucharist and orders.[17]

The great influence and diffusion of Peter Lombard's *Sentences* spread and consolidated the thesis that there are seven sacraments of the New Covenant.

The existence of seven sacraments was defined in the Second Council of Lyons in 1274:

> The same Holy Roman Church also holds and teaches that there are seven sacraments of the Church: one is baptism . . . ; another is the sacrament of confirmation, which bishops confer by the laying on of hands while they anoint the reborn; then penance, the Eucharist, the sacrament of order, matrimony, and extreme unction which, according to the doctrine of the Blessed James, is administered to the sick.[18]

At the Council of Florence in 1439, this list of seven sacraments is again put forth as the common doctrine of the Church: "There are seven sacraments of the New Law: namely, baptism, confirmation, Eucharist, penance, extreme unction, orders, and matrimony, which

---

[15] Hugh of St. Victor, *On the Sacraments of the Christian Faith*, bk. 2, part 9, no. 1, p. 315.

[16] Shortly before Peter Lombard, Roland Bandinelli, who later became Pope Alexander III, also speaks of the seven sacraments in his *Summa magistri Rolandi*.

[17] Peter Lombard, *Sentences*, bk. 4, d. 2, ch. 1, no. 1, trans. Silano, p. 9.

[18] Second Council of Lyon, Profession of Faith of Emperor Michael Paleologus (session 4, July 6, 1274; DS, 860).

differ greatly from the sacraments of the Old Law."[19] This list is followed by an explanation of the specific difference of the sacraments
by which they differ from sacramentals and the sacraments of the Old
Covenant: "The latter, in fact, did not cause grace, but they only prefigured the grace to be given through the Passion of Christ. These
sacraments of ours, however, both contain grace and communicate it
to those who worthily receive them." The precise list of seven sacraments presupposes the definition of sacraments as sacred signs that
communicate the sanctification they symbolize. The Eastern Orthodox tradition also accepts this teaching on the sevenfold sacramental
system, which they regard as pertaining to revealed truth through the
Church's constant practice.[20]

As seen above, Martin Luther held that only Baptism and the
Lord's Supper (the Eucharist) were properly sacraments, although he
also accepted Penance as a sacrament in an improper sense.[21] This
position resulted from the way that Luther conceived and defined sacraments as "promises which have signs attached to them."[22] Calvin
likewise only recognized Baptism and the Lord's Supper.[23] The Council

---

[19] Council of Florence, *Exsultate Deo* (DS, 1310).

[20] See Theophilus Spacil, *Doctrina theologiae orientis separati: de sacramentis in
genere* (Rome: Pont. Institutum Orientalium Studiorum, 1937), 65–80. On the
spreading of Lombard's sevenfold list to the Eastern Orthodox theological tradition, see Christiaan Kappes, "A New Narrative for the Reception of Seven
Sacraments into Orthodoxy: Peter Lombard's *Sentences* in Nicholas Cabasilas
and Symeon of Thessalonica and the Utilization of John Duns Scotus by the
Holy *Synaxis*," *Nova et Vetera* (English) 15, no. 2 (2017): 465–501.

[21] Martin Luther, "The Babylonian Captivity of the Church," in *LW*, 36:124. In
1519 in *The Sacrament of Penance* (*LW* 35:11) Luther also regarded Penance as
a sacrament because of its words of promise of the forgiveness of sins, and its
institution by Christ. However, in 1520 in *The Babylonian Captivity* he denies
it the name of sacrament because he held that it lacks a sensible sign other than
the words of absolution and because he saw it essentially as a return to Baptism.
See Cary, "Why Luther Is Not Quite Protestant," 456; Karl-Hermann Kandler,
"Luther and Lutherans on Confession, the 'Forgotten Sacrament,'" *Lutheran
Quarterly* 31 (2017): 50–63.

[22] Luther, "The Babylonian Captivity of the Church," in *LW*, 36:124. For the connection between Luther's definition of sacrament focusing on a divine promise
received in faith, and his reduction of the number of sacraments to two, see
Root, "Luther and Calvin on the Role of Faith in the Sacraments," 1070.

[23] See Calvin, *Institutes*, bk 4, ch. 14, no. 20, p. 854: "After these were abrogated
[the sacraments of the Old Testament], the two sacraments of Baptism and
the Lord's Supper, which the Christian church now employs, were instituted. I
speak of those which were instituted for the use of the whole Church. For the

of Trent responded by giving a solemn definition of the sevenfold list of sacraments commonly accepted since the twelfth century:

> If anyone says that the sacraments of the New Law were not all instituted by Jesus Christ our Lord; or that there are more or fewer than seven, that is: baptism, confirmation, the Eucharist, penance, extreme unction, orders, and matrimony; or that any one of these seven is not truly and properly a sacrament, let him be anathema.[24]

Nevertheless, it should be acknowledged that the seven sacraments are not equal. The Protestant thesis that there are only two sacraments corresponds to the fact that Baptism and the Eucharist are in fact the two most fundamental sacraments symbolically indicated by the water and blood that came from the side of Christ as it was pierced on Calvary. They are the root and summit of the sacramental system.

FITTINGNESS OF THE SEVEN SACRAMENTS AND THEIR HARMONY

Why did Christ institute these particular seven sacraments? Theology would not be able to deduce in advance what God ought to do for our salvation, but after He has done it, we can reflect on God's action in order to better appreciate its beauty and marvel. This is the value of what theologians call "arguments of fittingness."

The Seven Sacraments Are Analogous to Seven Natural Necessities of Life

St. Thomas gives a classic answer to why there are these seven sacraments by creating an analogy between natural life and supernatural life. As certain elements are necessary for man's natural life, so analogous elements are necessary for man's supernatural life. St. Thomas divides these necessary elements into two groups: that which is neces-

---

laying on of hands, by which the ministers of the Church are initiated into their office . . . I do not number among ordinary sacraments."

[24] Council of Trent, Decree on the Sacraments (session 7), can. 1 on the Sacraments in General (DS, 1601).

sary for the life of each individual, and that which is necessary for man as a social creature.[25]

What is necessary for each individual is birth, growth to maturity, nourishment, healing in times of illness, and preparation for death. So likewise in the supernatural life, it is necessary to have spiritual rebirth through Baptism, growth to spiritual maturity through Confirmation, spiritual nourishment in the Eucharist, spiritual healing through Penance, and spiritual preparation for death through the Sacrament of Anointing of the Sick.[26]

With regard to man's social nature, two kinds of society are necessary: the family and civil society; the former is based on marriage, and the latter requires some social authority or headship to keep it unified. It is fitting that the principles of these two societies be elevated by the

---

[25] See *ST* III, q. 65, a. 1: "For spiritual life has a certain conformity with the life of the body: just as other corporeal things have a certain likeness to things spiritual. Now a man attains perfection in the corporeal life in two ways: first, in regard to his own person; secondly, in regard to the whole community of the society in which he lives, for man is by nature a social animal." This analogy between the seven sacraments and the seven needs of our natural life was first presented by St. Thomas in *SCG* IV, ch. 58; and *De ecclesiae sacramentis*, in *Opuscula Theologica*, vol. 1, *De re dogmatica et morali*, no. 613, pp. 147–48; in English in *God's Greatest Gifts*, 84–86.

[26] See *ST* III, q. 65, a. 1: "With regard to himself man is perfected in the life of the body, in two ways; first, directly [per se], i.e. by acquiring some vital perfection; secondly, indirectly [per accidens], i.e. by the removal of hindrances to life, such as ailments, or the like. Now the life of the body is perfected 'directly,' in three ways. First, by generation whereby a man begins to be and to live: and corresponding to this in the spiritual life there is Baptism, which is a spiritual regeneration, according to Titus 3:5. . . . Secondly, by growth whereby a man is brought to perfect size and strength: and corresponding to this in the spiritual life there is Confirmation, in which the Holy Ghost is given to strengthen us. Wherefore the disciples who were already baptized were bidden thus: 'Stay you in the city till you be endued with power from on high' (Luke 24:49). Thirdly, by nourishment, whereby life and strength are preserved to man; and corresponding to this in the spiritual life there is the Eucharist. Wherefore it is said (John 6:54): 'Except you eat of the flesh of the Son of Man, and drink His blood, you shall not have life in you.' And this would be enough for man if he had an impassible life, both corporally and spiritually; but since man is liable at times to both corporal and spiritual infirmity, i.e. sin, hence man needs a cure from his infirmity; which cure is twofold. One is the healing, that restores health: and corresponding to this in the spiritual life there is Penance. . . . The other is the restoration of former vigor by means of suitable diet and exercise: and corresponding to this in the spiritual life there is Extreme Unction, which removes the remainder of sin, and prepares man for final glory."

sacramental order. Thus we have the elevation of marriage to a sacrament, and likewise governance of ecclesial society is elevated to the supernatural order through the sacrament of Holy Orders.[27]

Aquinas's explanation of fittingness was taken up by the Council of Florence in its decree for the Armenians (1439):

> There are seven sacraments of the New Law. . . . The first five of these are ordained to the interior spiritual perfection of the person; the last two are ordained to the government and the increase of the whole Church. For by baptism we are spiritually reborn and by confirmation we grow in grace and are strengthened in the faith; being reborn and strengthened, we are nourished with the divine food of the Eucharist. If by sin we become sick in soul, we are healed spiritually by penance; we are also healed in spirit, and in body in so far as it is good for the soul, by extreme unction. Through Orders the Church is governed and receives spiritual growth; through matrimony she receives bodily growth.[28]

Pius XII restated this argument of fittingness in his encyclical *Mystici Corporis Christi*:

> Now we see that the human body is given the proper means to provide for its own life, health and growth, and for that of all its members. Similarly, the Savior of mankind out of His infinite goodness has provided in a wonderful way for His Mystical Body, endowing it with the Sacraments, so that, as though by an uninterrupted series of graces, its members should be sustained from birth to death, and that generous provision might be made for the social needs of the Church.[29]

---

[27] See *ST* III, q. 65, a. 1: "In regard to the whole community, man is perfected in two ways. First, by receiving power to rule the community and to exercise public acts: and corresponding to this in the spiritual life there is the sacrament of order, according to the saying of Hebrews 7:27, that priests offer sacrifices not for themselves only, but also for the people. Secondly in regard to natural propagation. This is accomplished by Matrimony both in the corporal and in the spiritual life: since it is not only a sacrament but also a function of nature."

[28] DS, 1311. This magisterial text is closely based on St. Thomas's short treatise, *De ecclesiae sacramentis*, in *God's Greatest Gifts*, 84–86.

[29] Pius XII, Encyclical on the Mystical Body of Christ *Mystici Corporis Christi*

St. Paul VI also took up this idea with regard to Baptism, Confirmation, and the Eucharist in his Apostolic Constitution on the sacrament of Confirmation *Divinae Consortium Naturae*:

> The sharing in the divine nature received through the grace of Christ bears a certain likeness to the origin, development, and nourishing of natural life. The faithful are born anew by Baptism, strengthened by the sacrament of Confirmation, and finally are sustained by the food of eternal life in the Eucharist.[30]

The *Catechism of the Catholic Church*, §1210 briefly summarizes this Thomistic analogy: "The seven sacraments touch all the stages and all the important moments of Christian life: they give birth and increase, healing and mission to the Christian's life of faith. There is

---

(June 29, 1943), §18. The Thomistic analogy continues in §§18–20: "Through the waters of Baptism those who are born into this world dead in sin are not only born again and made members of the Church.... By the chrism of Confirmation, the faithful are given added strength to protect and defend the Church, their Mother, and the faith she has given them. In the Sacrament of Penance a saving medicine is offered for the members of the Church who have fallen into sin, ... In the Holy Eucharist the faithful are nourished and strengthened at the same banquet and by a divine, ineffable bond are united with each other and with the Divine Head of the whole Body. Finally, like a devoted mother, the Church is at the bedside of those who are sick unto death; and if it be not always God's will that by the holy anointing she restore health to the mortal body, nevertheless she administers spiritual medicine.... For the social needs of the Church Christ has provided in a particular way by the institution of two other Sacraments. Through Matrimony, in which the contracting parties are ministers of grace to each other, provision is made for the external and duly regulated increase of Christian society, and, what is of greater importance, for the correct religious education of the children, without which this Mystical Body would be in grave danger. Through Holy Orders men are set aside and consecrated to God, to offer the Sacrifice of the Eucharistic Victim, to nourish the flock of the faithful with the Bread of Angels and the food of doctrine, to guide them in the way of God's commandments and counsels and to strengthen them with all other supernatural helps."

[30] Paul VI, *Divinae Consortium Naturae*, in *Rites*, 1:477. See also *ST* III, q. 73, a. 1: "Now it is clear that just as generation is required for corporeal life, since thereby man receives life; and growth, whereby man is brought to maturity: so likewise food is required for the preservation of life. Consequently, just as for the spiritual life there had to be Baptism, which is spiritual generation; and Confirmation, which is spiritual growth: so there needed to be the sacrament of the Eucharist, which is spiritual food."

thus a certain resemblance between the stages of natural life and the stages of the spiritual life."[31]

On the Notion of Maturity in St. Thomas's Analogy

St. Thomas's analogy of the seven needs of our natural life and the seven sacraments greatly clarifies the nature of the sacramental system. It is not without some difficulties, of course, for no analogy from nature can be perfectly applied to the supernatural order. One difficulty with Aquinas's analogy is the notion of growth to maturity that is connected with Confirmation. The difficulty lies in the fact that Baptism and Confirmation were traditionally administered together, and still are in the Eastern rites and in the RCIA in the Latin rite. It seems odd that two sacraments that are traditionally received simultaneously be compared with birth and maturity.[32] There is no doubt that Baptism should be regarded as spiritual conception or birth. The difficulty lies with understanding Confirmation as the sacrament of spiritual maturity.

One simple way to respond to this objection is that St. Thomas speaks of Confirmation here not as the sacrament of maturity, but of "*growth* whereby a man is brought to perfect size and strength."[33] There is nothing incongruous with receiving a principle of growth to maturity at the very moment of spiritual birth.

Another complementary way to resolve the difficulty and further clarify the purpose of Confirmation is to understand maturity to indicate possession of *principles of mature movement or action*. Every animal needs principles of movement to live his natural life, and growth to maturity consists in acquiring the ability to exercise this proper movement or activity. The notions of maturity and movement are inti-

---

[31] See Fagerberg, "Liturgy, Signs, and Sacraments," in *OHST*, 463: "The sacraments communicate divine life: they inaugurate it, nourish it, heal it, and order it. This is how the sacraments are categorized: sacraments of initiation (baptism, confirmation, Eucharist), sacraments of healing (anointing the sick and reconciliation), and sacraments in the service of communion (holy orders and marriage). These accompany the faithful from the cradle to the grave, giving a foretaste of the heavenly liturgy."

[32] In fact, it is probable that an improper understanding of this analogy has contributed to a practice in the West in the second millennium of separating the two sacraments of Baptism and Confirmation, as maturity is separated from birth.

[33] *ST* III, q. 65, a. 1 (my italics).

mately related, for maturity is the state in which one is perfected in self-movement.

In the supernatural life we likewise need a *principle of supernatural movement*, which is given by the Holy Spirit and His seven gifts mentioned in Isaiah 11:2–3. It is precisely through receiving a docility to be moved by the Spirit and act in Him that we grow to supernatural maturity. Maturity in the spiritual life, paradoxically, means ever-increasing docility to the movement and guidance of the Holy Spirit. By giving a spiritual principle of movement through docility to the Holy Spirit, Confirmation prepares for spiritual maturity and, with our cooperation, brings it about. Confirmation, understood in this way, "completes" or "perfects" Baptism,[34] as mature movement and activity perfect life.

The fourteenth-century Byzantine theologian Nicholas Cabasilas presents the purpose of the sacrament of Chrismation in this way as giving the principle of supernatural movement, taking Acts 17:28 as his basis:

> In the sacred mysteries, then, . . . we are begotten and formed and wondrously united to the Saviour, for they are the means by which, as Paul says, "in Him we live, and move, and have our being" (Acts 17:28). . . . It is therefore by this Bread that we live and *by the chrism that we are moved*, once we have received being from the baptismal washing.[35]

Through Baptism we come to have *being* in Christ, through Confirmation we are able to *move* in Him through His Spirit, and through the Eucharist we *live* in Him and He lives in us.

Understanding Confirmation as giving the principles of supernatural movement that lead to spiritual maturity makes clearer why this sacrament is especially associated with the gift of the Holy Spirit, for His inspirations are the sources of supernatural activity and movement. All the sacraments give the Spirit and His grace, but only

---

[34] See *CCC*, §1288.

[35] Nicholas Cabasilas, *The Life in Christ* 1.6, pp. 49–50 (my italics). See also *The Life in Christ* 3.1, p. 103: "It would be fitting, then, that those who are thus spiritually created and begotten should obtain an energy suitable to such a birth, and a corresponding animation. This the sacred rite of the most divine chrism accomplishes for us. It activates the spiritual energies, one in one man, another in another."

Confirmation was instituted to give us the gift of the Spirit as the abiding animating source of our spiritual activity.

This also better manifests why it is fitting to receive Baptism and Confirmation together, as was done in the early Church and has continued to be observed in the Eastern rites, and now also for adults in the RCIA in the Latin rite. If Baptism gives life, and life involves self-movement, clearly it is fitting that the gift of supernatural life and divine filiation be coupled with the gift of a supernatural source of movement, which can be nothing other than the Holy Spirit and His gifts.

It is also fitting that Confirmation be tied with the Eucharist, for supernatural activity requires supernatural nourishment, and union with Christ, present in the Eucharist as the bread of life, is the goal of all supernatural activity.[36] Benedict XVI makes this point in *Sacramentum Caritatis*:

> If the Eucharist is truly the source and summit of the Church's life and mission, it follows that the process of Christian initiation must constantly be directed to the reception of this sacrament. As the Synod Fathers said, we need to ask ourselves whether in our Christian communities the close link between Baptism, Confirmation and Eucharist is sufficiently recognized. It must never be forgotten that our reception of Baptism and Confirmation is ordered to the Eucharist. Accordingly, our pastoral practice should reflect a more

---

[36] See the discussion of this question in Liam G. Walsh, *Sacraments of Initiation: A Theology of Life, Word, and Rite*, 2nd ed. (Chicago: Hillenbrand Books, 2011), 210–11: "To delay the two sacraments [Confirmation and the Eucharist] is not to deprive the infant entirely of their grace.... However, there is a real loss of sacramentality involved in breaking up the unity of initiation. It is more than a matter of liturgical propriety. Baptism alone does not express sacramentally the full reality of Christian grace: it does not express its Pentecostal fullness. By separating it from confirmation one risks offering an inadequate sacramental statement about Christian life.... In putting all three sacraments of initiation at the beginning of the process the Eastern tradition strongly emphasizes the priority of God's action in it. The Western tradition does this, if a little less emphatically, by baptizing infants." See also the defense of the unity of the three sacraments of initiation from an Orthodox perspective in John D. Zizioulas, *The Eucharistic Communion and the World*, ed. Luke Ben Tallon (New York; London: T&T Clark, 2011), 113–22; and Alexander Schmemann, *Of Water and the Spirit: A Liturgical Study of Baptism* (Crestwood, NY: St. Vladimir's Seminary Press, 1974), 115–21.

unitary understanding of the process of Christian initiation.[37]

Similarly, this analogy of Confirmation with supernatural movement shows how it would be harmful to routinely postpone administration of this sacrament well past the age of reason, because one would be postponing the full sacramental gift of spiritual activity moved by the Spirit. It would seem that an excessive postponing of Confirmation could lead to an attitude of practical naturalism or semi-Pelagianism whereby we are insufficiently reliant on the inspirations of the Holy Spirit in the Christian life. Finally, it manifests clearly how Confirmation is not a kind of recognition of spiritual maturity, but its foundation.[38]

Why Can Some Sacraments Be Repeated and Not Others?

The analogy given by St. Thomas relating the sacraments to the things essential for natural human life also explains why certain sacraments cannot be repeated whereas others can. Since the Eucharist is the sacrament of spiritual nourishment, and we repeatedly take nourishment, it is fitting that the Eucharist be a sacrament that not only can be repeated but should be repeated frequently. Since medicine is something that we need to take whenever we are ill, the spiritual medicine of Penance should be taken at appropriately frequent intervals to combat our spiritual ills, consisting in venial as well as mortal sins.

---

[37] Benedict XVI, Post-Synodal Apostolic Exhortation, *Sacramentum Caritatis* (Feb 22, 2007), §17. In §18, Benedict invites bishops to consider reevaluating the order in which the sacraments of Christian initiation are received so that the Eucharist is perceived as the summit and culmination of initiation into the Christian life: "It needs to be seen which practice better enables the faithful to put the sacrament of the Eucharist at the centre, as the goal of the whole process of initiation."

[38] See Bishop Samuel J. Aquila, "The Sacrament of Confirmation," 2011 Hillenbrand Lecture at the Liturgical Institute in Mundelein, available online at http://www.catholicculture.org/culture/library/view.cfm?recnum=9670. Accessed on May 11, 2020: "Confirmation at times is spoken of by some, who advocate a later age, as a way for the young person to make a personal commitment to their faith. This view distorts the sacrament of confirmation. Confirmation is not marked by a choice to believe or not believe in the Catholic faith. Rather as disciples we are chosen by God to receive the fullness of the Holy Spirit, to be sealed with the gift of the Holy Spirit generously bestowed by God, and we are called to cooperate with that grace."

Preparation for death or serious illness is rare, but it also can happen more than once, and so the Anointing of the Sick can be taken more than once, although not in the same stage of a single illness. A second marriage can be entered into after the death of a spouse.

Birth, however, is something that happens only once, and thus Baptism is received but once. Reception of the *principle* of spiritual movement and growth to maturity, which is the Holy Spirit and His gifts, likewise can only happen once,[39] although we continue to grow in spiritual maturity and activity throughout our lives. Hence Confirmation cannot be repeated. Holy Orders also cannot be repeated—although there are three grades—because it conforms the recipient with Christ, eternal High Priest, so as to act in His Person. As Christ's priesthood cannot be lost, so neither can the priesthood of those who are conformed to Christ's priesthood through the sacrament of Holy Orders. A priest can lose the faculties to exercise the priesthood, but he cannot lose the priesthood itself.

Another reason the sacraments of Baptism, Confirmation, and Holy Orders cannot be repeated is because they initiate a permanent state in the Church and imprint an ecclesial character that is indelible, as will be seen in chapter 7 below, whereas the other sacraments do not.

The Seven Sacraments Align with the Seven Principal Virtues and with Remedies for the Effects of Sin

Another argument of fittingness connects each sacrament with one of the seven principal virtues.[40] In reality, all the sacraments give all the virtues, and all the virtues are interconnected and grow together. Nevertheless, the particular mission of each sacrament and the sacramental graces associated with it can each be connected with one of these seven virtues. St. Thomas reports this argument of fittingness as something already traditional in his time:

Some, again, gather the number of sacraments from a certain

---

[39] It is true that we can lose the Holy Spirit through mortal sin. Penance, however, restores the gift of the Spirit, if it was lost through mortal sin, by taking away that obstacle to the Spirit's presence.

[40] These are the three theological virtues (faith, hope, and charity) and the four cardinal virtues (prudence, justice, temperance, and fortitude).

adaptation to the virtues and to the defects and penal effects resulting from sin. They say that Baptism corresponds to Faith, and is ordained as a remedy against original sin; Extreme Unction, to Hope, being ordained against venial sin; the Eucharist, to Charity, being ordained against the penal effect which is malice; Order, to Prudence, being ordained against ignorance; Penance to Justice, being ordained against mortal sin; Matrimony, to Temperance, being ordained against concupiscence; Confirmation, to Fortitude, being ordained against infirmity.[41]

Still another argument of fittingness views the seven sacraments in their medicinal function for healing different aspects of sin. St. Thomas writes:

> We may likewise gather the number of the sacraments from their being instituted as a remedy against the defect caused by sin. For Baptism is intended as a remedy against the absence of spiritual life; Confirmation, against the infirmity of soul found in those of recent birth; the Eucharist, against the soul's proneness to sin; Penance, against actual sin committed after baptism; Extreme Unction, against the remainders of sins— of those sins, namely, which are not sufficiently removed by Penance, whether through negligence or through ignorance; Order, against divisions in the community; Matrimony, as a remedy against concupiscence in the individual, and against the decrease in numbers that results from death.[42]

Such reasoning would be insufficient to demonstrate that Christ established seven sacraments. However, once we know the seven sacraments through Tradition, theology can reflect on why it is fitting that Christ instituted them in this way.

The Seven Sacraments and the Holiness of the Church

The seven sacraments are the source of the holiness of the Church, which they generate, strengthen, nourish, and restore in seven differ-

---

[41] *ST* III, q. 65, a. 1.
[42] *ST* III, q. 65, a. 1.

ent ways. The Church is holy first of all through Baptism, by which her members are given a new birth into the life of grace, cancelling whatever stains of sin were incurred in their past life. The Church, therefore, is holy in that she is spiritually fecund: she gives birth into the life of grace to all who enter her life-giving waters with the right disposition.

Second, she is holy in strengthening that supernatural life through the sacrament of Confirmation, in which a fuller outpouring of the gifts of the Holy Spirit is given to advance the recipient toward spiritual maturity and to make possible life in the Spirit and Christian witness. This makes one capable of fighting the good fight of faith as a soldier of Christ and a sharer in Christ's prophetic, priestly, and kingly mission.

Third, she is holy in giving a spiritual nourishment that is no less efficacious for the spiritual life than healthy food is for the physical life. The Eucharist communicates a greater union with Christ through an increase of charity. The extent of the increase depends on the fervor of one's disposition. The Eucharist also makes the Church holy in that it makes her capable of offering an immaculate and infinitely pleasing sacrifice to God the Father, the very sacrifice of Calvary, made present on our altars in every valid Mass. Furthermore, this sacrament sanctifies the Church by making Christ substantially present on every altar so that He may reside with us in every tabernacle.

Fourth, the Church is holy through the sacrament of Penance by which she can restore the supernatural life of a person who has lost that life through grave sin. Fifth, the Anointing of the Sick gives added grace in times of grave physical illness and special virtue in the face of death, empowering the redemptive value of suffering on behalf of the whole Body. Sixth, the sacrament of Matrimony sanctifies the fundamental building block of society, the family, and gives the spouses a lifelong series of sacramental graces to sanctify their marriage, educate their children in the grace of God, and to be a sign of Christ's love for His Church and of her love for Him.

Finally, the sacrament of Holy Orders sanctifies the Church by enabling the recipients of the sacrament to act in the very person of Christ, the Head of the Church, in the consecration of the Eucharist and in absolution of sin, cleansing the lack of holiness in the members of the Church. Holy Orders makes possible the Eucharistic dimension of the Church, the source and summit of her holiness, and is the key to the royal priesthood of the baptized and confirmed. For without

Holy Orders, there could be no Eucharist in which the lay faithful supremely exercise their common priesthood, offering themselves and their Christian life with Christ.[43] Holy Orders also provides a sacramental foundation for the exercise of authority in the Church for teaching and governing, so as to maintain her unity and fidelity. That authority is not a mere exercise of human power but a sacramental sharing in the power of Christ for the building up of His Body. The recipients of Holy Orders, like those who receive the sacrament of Matrimony, are also given a series of sacramental graces to make them worthy ministers of the multiform grace of Christ.

The sacraments serve as the nerves and arteries of the Church through which her supernatural life flows from the Head into the members, who are thus nourished by sanctifying grace and sacramental graces. Without the sacraments, the members would not be properly connected with the Head so as to form one Body.

The Seven Sacraments and the Communion of the Church

The fittingness of the seven sacraments can also be understood as seven ways of building up the communion or unity of the Church. Since the sacraments communicate the Holy Spirit, who proceeds as the love of the Father and the Son, the sacraments can be understood as seven modes of configuring the recipient to the unifying power of love in the communion of the Church.

Ecclesial communion first needs to be established by entrance into the Church, which is brought about by Baptism, which also enables one to receive and be sanctified by the Church's other sacraments. The unity of Baptism, mentioned in the Creed, is the instrument of the unity of the Church.

This membership is strengthened through Confirmation, which empowers the recipient not simply to be a member of the Church and to receive her other sacraments, but also to actively build up that communion[44] by participating in the three offices of Christ and through

---

[43] See *LG*, §§10–11.

[44] See *LG*, §11: "They [the faithful] are more perfectly bound to the Church by the sacrament of Confirmation, and the Holy Spirit endows them with special strength so that they are more strictly obliged to spread and defend the faith, both by word and by deed, as true witnesses of Christ."

the ecclesial charisms given by the Spirit. By giving the Spirit of love, Confirmation gives the vital force to maintain the unity of the one Body formed by Baptism. The unity of the Church built up by Baptism and the gift of the Spirit is eloquently expressed in Ephesians 4:1–8:

> I therefore, a prisoner for the Lord, beg you to walk in a manner worthy of the calling to which you have been called, . . . eager to maintain the unity of the Spirit in the bond of peace. There is one body and one Spirit, just as you were called to the one hope that belongs to your call, one Lord, one faith, one baptism, one God and Father of us all, who is above all and through all and in all. But grace was given to each of us according to the measure of Christ's gift. Therefore it is said, "When he ascended on high he led a host of captives, and he gave gifts to men."

The supreme sacrament of communion is the Eucharist, which consummates the building of unity begun by Baptism and Confirmation.[45] St. Paul manifests this in 1 Corinthians 10:16–17: "The cup of blessing which we bless, is it not a participation in the blood of Christ? The bread which we break, is it not a participation in the body of Christ? Because there is one bread, we who are many are one body, for we all partake of the one bread."[46] The Eucharist, according to *Lumen Gentium*, §11, is the "fount and apex of the whole Christian life," in which the faithful "offer the Divine Victim to God, and offer themselves along with It." The whole life of the Church is thus offered to the Father with the offering of the Son. The Sacrifice of the Mass draws down graces of conversion to the world to strengthen and spread her visible and invisible communion.[47] Reception of Holy Communion then nourishes the faithful with the gift of increased charity to build up the Church in holiness and unity.[48]

The other sacraments build communion in more particular ways.

---

[45] On the ecclesial effect of the Eucharist, see Gilles Emery, "The Ecclesial Fruit of the Eucharist in St. Thomas Aquinas," trans. Therese C. Scarpelli, *Nova et Vetera* (English) 2, no. 1 (2004): 43–60.

[46] On this theme, see John Paul II, Encyclical Letter on the Eucharist in Its Relationship to the Church, *Ecclesia de Eucharistia*, Apr 17, 2003; Feingold, *The Eucharist*, 320–27.

[47] See Feingold, *The Eucharist*, 451–56, 462–69.

[48] Feingold, *The Eucharist*, 516–22.

Penance re-establishes ecclesial communion when it has been lost through grave sin and heals the various forms of disunity caused by sin.[49] Anointing of the Sick fosters the redemptive power of suffering so that the sick person can offer his or her suffering for the needs of the whole Body.[50] Marriage is the sacrament of communion in the domestic church and creates icons of the communion between Christ and the Church.[51] Holy Orders is the sacrament of ecclesial unity by establishing headship in the Church to prevent schism, division, and anarchy in the Body.[52]

The Sacraments and the New Covenant

Just as the sacraments create the Church and constitute her super-natural life of holiness in seven fitting ways, so they also constitute the essential content of the New Covenant, which is God's promise that we will be able to participate in the Trinitarian life as sons and daughters of the Father in the Son, empowered by the Holy Spirit. The sacraments should be understood as mysterious privileges of the New Covenant for sanctification and worship in a Trinitarian way. Each sacrament fittingly realizes an essential aspect of the Covenant.

Baptism, like circumcision in the Old Covenant, introduces new members into the covenantal community, which is the Church, and gives a right of inheritance in the Promised Land.[53] Baptism is thus

---

[49] See *LG*, §11: "Those who approach the sacrament of Penance obtain pardon from the mercy of God for the offence committed against Him and are at the same time reconciled with the Church, which they have wounded by their sins, and which by charity, example, and prayer seeks their conversion."

[50] See *LG*, §11: "By the sacred anointing of the sick and the prayer of her priests the whole Church commends the sick to the suffering and glorified Lord, asking that He may lighten their suffering and save them; she exhorts them, moreover, to contribute to the welfare of the whole people of God by associating themselves freely with the passion and death of Christ."

[51] See *LG*, §11: "Christian spouses, in virtue of the sacrament of Matrimony . . . signify and partake of the mystery of that unity and fruitful love which exists between Christ and His Church. . . . From the wedlock of Christians there comes the family, in which new citizens of human society are born, who by the grace of the Holy Spirit received in baptism are made children of God, thus perpetuating the people of God through the centuries. The family is, so to speak, the domestic church."

[52] See *ST* III, q. 65, a. 1, in which St. Thomas says that Holy Orders was instituted "against divisions in the community."

[53] See Dermot Ryan, "Sacraments Foreshadowed," in *Sacraments: The Gestures of*

the gateway into the covenant, establishing a new family relationship with God—that of sons and daughters of the Father in the Son, to whom the Spirit of love is also given. This divine filiation also establishes a new family relationship of brotherhood among the baptized.

Through Confirmation the sons and daughters of the Covenant are more fully empowered with the Spirit, by whom the Law of God is written on the heart, and come to share fully in Christ's mission of building up the Church. Jeremiah 31:33 speaks of the New Covenant in terms of the law being written on the heart; Ezekiel 36:26–27 speaks of the Spirit being put within us to give hearts of flesh that walk according to the Law; and Joel 2:28–29 describes the messianic age as the age in which the Spirit is poured out on all flesh. The gift of the Holy Spirit in Confirmation realizes these prophecies, as Peter declared on Pentecost (Acts 2:16).

Holy Matrimony is the privileged sign of the very nature of the New Covenant as a spousal union between Christ, the Bridegroom, and His Bride, the Church, according to Ephesians 5:25–32. The sacrament aids Christian spouses to be living icons of the union between Christ and His Church.

Since the New Covenant is the definitive remedy to sin and the establishment of a filial and spousal relationship with God, the new Covenant needs a sacramental means of forgiveness for post-baptismal sin, by which those who have violated the covenant can be reconciled. This is given in the sacrament of Penance. Anointing further perfects the remedy against sin in those who are seriously ill and in danger of death. It also consecrates human sickness as a participation in Christ's Cross and fosters the redemptive power of suffering.

The apex of the relationship of the sacraments with the New Covenant is the Eucharist. Jesus connects the Eucharist with the New Covenant. His words of institution over the chalice identify it as the "blood of the covenant" (Matt 26:28; Mark 14:24), or, in the version of Paul and Luke, the cup "is the new covenant in my blood" (Luke 22:20; 1 Cor 11:25).

Christ's blood, present in the Eucharist, is the blood of the cove-

---

Christ, ed. O'Callaghan, 18: "Baptism, like circumcision, makes one a member of the People of God and gives one a right to an inheritance in the Promised Land. It reminds one of how Israel became the chosen people by passing through the waters of the Red Sea and entered into its inheritance through the waters of the Jordan."

nant because it merited our redemption, made satisfaction for sin, was a sacrifice more pleasing than all sin is displeasing, merited all graces to be given to mankind, won our reconciliation with the Father, and makes present the very sacrifice by which the covenant was sealed. The Eucharist, however, not only contains the price of the New Covenant but it also contains its life, for the New Covenant essentially consists in sharing in the life of the Son, present in the Eucharist and communicated to the faithful in Holy Communion.

The New Covenant, finally, needs a sacramental priesthood by which the sacraments can be administered and the Sacrifice of the Mass offered in the person of Christ, the head of the Church. Since the New Covenant is endowed with a sacrifice of infinite value, it needs a priesthood worthy of the sacrifice, which can only be the priesthood of Christ Himself. Holy Orders is crucial to the New Covenant because it allows Christ's mediation—offering sacrifice and sanctifying—to become "incarnate" in the Church.

The Sacraments and the Maternity of the Church

Because the Church is Christ's Bride, she must be fruitful in engendering children for her Bridegroom. She is, in fact, the most fruitful of all mothers, as witnessed by her glorious title of *catholic*. Her children have spread to every land and culture and realize the prophecy given to Abraham about his progeny, who are numerous like the sand of the sea and the stars of the sky. We have seen that the Fathers compare the birth of the Church with the birth of Eve from Adam's rib. The Church is born from the blood and water that came from Christ's pierced side on the Cross, and the water and blood represent the sacraments of Baptism and the Eucharist. Like Eve, the Church can be called the "mother of all"[54] those living the supernatural life.[55]

The sacraments are the principal mode by which the Church exercises her maternity. New children are born for the Church through Baptism, brought into spiritual activity and growth to matu-

---

[54] Gen 3:20.

[55] For a beautiful prophetic prefigurement of the catholic maternity of the Church, see Ps 87:3–7: "Glorious things are spoken of you, O city of God. . . . Philistia and Tyre, with Ethiopia— 'This one was born there,' they say. And of Zion it shall be said, 'This one and that one were born in her'; for the Most High himself will establish her. The LORD records as he registers the peoples, 'This one was born there. . . . All my springs are in you.'"

rity through Confirmation, nourished through the Eucharist, healed through Penance, and prepared for the final trial through Anointing. Holy Orders is crucial for the Church's maternity, for it provides the ordinary ministers for the sacraments, through which her maternity is realized.[56] Matrimony, finally, is an image of the Church's faithful fecundity and a privileged source of children who are brought into the Church through Baptism.

THE EUCHARIST IS THE SUMMIT OF THE SACRAMENTAL ECONOMY

The sacramental system, like all the works of God, is marked by order and hierarchy, for the seven sacraments are not equal in importance, although all are necessary to the life of the Church.[57] In this hierarchy Baptism is the root and portal, and the Eucharist is the summit.[58] The preeminence of the Eucharist comes from the fact that the Eucharist alone substantially contains Christ Himself, making Him present, whole and entire, in the midst of every congregation of the faithful. The other sacraments impart His grace and configure their recipients to Him, but the Eucharist *is* Him.[59] Nicholas Cabasilas explains the

---

[56] See Charles Journet, *The Church of the Word Incarnate: An Essay in Speculative Theology*, trans. A. H. C. Downes, vol. 1: *The Apostolic Hierarchy* (London and New York: Sheed & Ward, 1955), 93–95.

[57] See *CCT*, part 2, intro., §22, pp. 156–57: "Although all the sacraments have a divine efficacy, it is nevertheless very important to note that they are quite unequal in terms of necessity and dignity. This inequality is based, of course, on the differences in their respective significations. Three of the sacraments are clearly more necessary than the others; but even among these three the nature of their necessity varies. The only sacrament which is universally and uniquely necessary is Baptism. . . . Secondly, there is a necessity for the sacrament of Penance, but only in a relative sense. . . . Thirdly, the sacrament of Holy Orders, although not for each one of the faithful, is absolutely necessary for the Church as a whole. If, on the other hand, we compare the sacraments in terms of dignity, we immediately recognize the Holy Eucharist as far and away superior to all the others. This is because of its substantial holiness, and the number and greatness of its mysteries."

[58] See Feingold, *The Eucharist*, 31–36.

[59] See Peter Lombard, *Sentences* 4, d. 8, ch. 1, trans. Silano, 41: "And so it is excellently called 'Eucharist,' that is, good grace, because in this sacrament not only is there an increase of virtue and grace, but he who is the fount and origin of all grace is wholly received."

priority of the Eucharist in this way, for in it alone we receive not only the gifts of God, but the Giver of the gifts, in His risen life:

> After the Chrismation we go to the table. This is the perfection of the life in Christ; for those who attain it there is nothing lacking for the blessedness which they seek. It is no longer death and the tomb and a participation in the better life which we receive, but the risen One Himself. Nor do we receive such gifts of the Spirit as we may, but the very Benefactor Himself, the very Temple whereon is founded the whole compass of graces.[60]

Secondly, the Eucharist supremely realizes the goal of the entire sacramental system, which is to nourish us with the divine life. The most fitting means for growing in the life of grace is to receive the Word Incarnate into our very bodies. By worthily receiving His humanity, we grow in sharing His divine life and are progressively divinized.[61]

Third, the other sacraments sanctify through the merits of Christ's Passion, but the Eucharist alone makes the sacrifice of Calvary substantially present in every Eucharistic celebration, in that the Victim of Calvary is made present on the altar, with Christ Himself as the high priest working through his sacred ministers, offering Himself through them to His Father, and enabling the faithful to offer Him together with the gift of their own lives.[62]

Fourth, although faith must be operative in every sacramental action, for what is believed in the sacraments transcends what is seen,

---

[60] Nicholas Cabasilas, *The Life in Christ* 4.1, p. 113.

[61] See Thomas Aquinas, *De veritate*, q. 27, a. 4, trans. Robert W. Schmidt, *Truth* (Chicago: Henry Regnery, 1954), 3:333: "Thus the humanity of Christ is the instrumental cause of justification. This cause is applied to us spiritually through faith and bodily through the sacraments, because Christ's humanity is both spirit and body. This is done to the end that we may receive within ourselves the effect of sanctification, which is had through Christ. As a consequence the most perfect sacrament is that in which the body of Christ is really contained, the Eucharist. . . . But the other sacraments also share some of the efficacy by which Christ's humanity works instrumentally for our justification."

[62] See the Council of Trent, Doctrine on the Sacrifice of the Mass (session 22), ch. 2 (DS, 1743): "It is one and the same victim; the same person now offers it by the ministry of His priests, who then offered Himself on the cross, the manner of offering alone being different."

the Eucharist is the sacrament in which faith is most meritorious. The faithful must believe that Christ is substantially present in all His human and personal reality and makes present His sacrifice, even though the senses grasp nothing other than the species of bread and wine, which undergo no outward change.

Fifth, the Eucharist is the sacrament of charity, instituted to nourish charity and communion in the faithful, and charity is the queen of the virtues.[63]

A sixth preeminence of the Eucharist is that the other sacraments are primarily for the sanctification of human beings whereas the Eucharist's first purpose is to glorify God through offering to the Father the sacrifice of the Son, coupled with that of His Church. The Eucharist, more than any other sacrament, is marked by having an ascending dimension of glorification as its first movement.[64]

It is not uncommon for theologians to compare the Mass to the beating heart of a living body. All the organs are important for the life of the organism, but the heart has a special place in pumping the lifeblood to the whole body. Louis Bouyer draws out this analogy eloquently:

> The sacraments are not so much, as is sometimes said, seven facets of a single crystal through which the same living light and warmth of the mystery is refracted, but they are rather the constituent elements of a circulatory system through which the same life-giving blood is constantly diffusing from and concentrating back on a central focus, which is the heart of the mystical body. This focus, this pulsing heart is the Mass. For the Mass is not only the source of the whole sacramental order, as St Thomas says, because it contains the passion of Christ, source of all graces, it is also that which draws back to itself the whole life diffused through the members, so that in them all and from them all it tends

---

[63] See Feingold, *The Eucharist*, 5–10.

[64] See John Paul II, *Ecclesia de Eucharistia*, §13: "Certainly it is a gift given for our sake, and indeed that of all humanity, yet it is first and foremost a gift to the Father." See also La Soujeole, "The Sacraments and the Development of Doctrine," in *OHST*, 597: "The Eucharist's *ordo* places the *theocentric* dimension first. The Eucharist is celebrated above all in order to glorify God, for it is really the sacrifice of Christ.... The *anthropological* dimension is a consequence.... For the other six sacraments, the *ordo* is inversed."

to unity no less than it proceeds from unity.[65]

The Eucharist is the source of the sacramental life because it makes Christ and His Passion present; it is the summit of the Church's life because, as the Sacrifice of Christ and the Church, all the holy activity of the Church's life and all human and created realities except sin are offered to the Father through the Son in the Mass. All the sanctification given through the sacraments has the purpose of bearing fruit in the Christian life, and that whole Christian life made possible by the grace of the sacraments is offered to the Father in the Mass.

The preeminence of the Eucharist can also be seen through the fact that the other sacraments are ordered to it as an end.[66] Baptism opens the door to the Eucharist, and Confirmation strengthens the ability of the faithful to offer their Christian lives with Christ in the Sacrifice of the Mass.[67] Penance and Anointing of the Sick perfect the disposition of the faithful to receive Christ worthily. Holy Orders is also ordered to the Eucharist, for a priest is ordained principally to offer the great Sacrifice. Matrimony, finally, is the privileged sign of the spousal union between Christ and His Bride that is realized in the Eucharist.[68]

The Second Vatican Council speaks of the ordering of the other sacraments to the Eucharist in *Presbyterorum Ordinis*, §5:

The other sacraments, as well as with every ministry of the Church and every work of the apostolate, are tied together with

---

[65] Louis Bouyer, "The Sacramental System," in *Sacraments: The Gestures of Christ*, ed. O'Callaghan, 46.

[66] For an Eastern perspective on this thesis, drawing on Nicholas Cabasilas, see the profound presentation of the Eucharist as the heart of the sacramental system in Robert F. Slesinski, *A Primer on Church and Eucharist: Eastern Perspectives* (Fairfax, VA: Eastern Christian Publications, 2007), 75–95.

[67] See Bouyer, "The Sacramental System," 50: "Baptism and confirmation, then, are nothing else than the immediate preparation to take part in the Eucharist, as was so clearly taught by the ancient practice of giving them together in the Paschal celebration as a preliminary to the Paschal Mass itself."

[68] This argument is drawn from *ST* III, q. 65, a. 3: "For all the other sacraments seem to be ordained to this one as to their end. For it is manifest that the sacrament of Order is ordained to the consecration of the Eucharist, and the sacrament of Baptism to the reception of the Eucharist: while a man is perfected by Confirmation, so as not to fear to abstain from this sacrament. By Penance and Extreme Unction man is prepared to receive the Body of Christ worthily. And Matrimony at least in its signification, touches this sacrament; in so far as it signifies the union of Christ with the Church, of which union the Eucharist is a figure."

the Eucharist and are directed toward it. The Most Blessed Eucharist contains the entire spiritual boon of the Church, that is, Christ himself, our Pasch and Living Bread, by the action of the Holy Spirit through his very flesh vital and vital-izing, giving life to men who are thus invited and encouraged to offer themselves, their labors and all created things, together with him. In this light, the Eucharist shows itself as the source and summit of the whole work of preaching the Gospel.[69]

The ordering of the other sacraments to the Eucharist, the source and summit of the Church's life, is also manifested in the fact that the other sacraments, except Penance, are fittingly celebrated within the celebration of the Eucharist, whereas Penance prepares for the Eucharist. Pseudo-Dionysius makes this argument:

> This [the Eucharist] is indeed the sacrament of sacraments. . . . I submit that the perfection of the other hierarchical symbols is only achieved by way of the divine and perfecting gifts of Communion. For scarcely any of the hierarchic sacraments can be performed without the divine Eucharist as the high point of each rite, divinely bringing about a spiritual gathering to the One for him who receives the sacrament. . . . Each of the hierarchic sacraments is incomplete to the extent that it does not perfect our communion and 'gather' to the One.[70]

THE CHURCH HAS THE NATURE OF A SACRAMENT

The Second Vatican Council teaches that the Church is not merely the possessor of sacraments by which her members are sanctified,

---

[69] Second Vatican Council, Decree on the Ministry and Life of Priests, *Presbyter-orum Ordinis* (Dec 7, 1965), §5.

[70] *Ecclesiastical Hierarchy* 3, in *Pseudo-Dionysius: The Complete Works*, 209. St. Thomas follows Dionysius on this point in *ST* III, q. 65, a. 3: "Thirdly, this is made clear by considering the rites of the sacraments. For nearly all the sacraments terminate in the Eucharist, as Dionysius says (*Ecclesiastical Hierarchy* 3): thus those who have been ordained receive Holy Communion, as also do those who have been baptized, if they be adults."

but, on that account, she herself has the nature of a sacrament, in that her visible catholic unity in the world is an efficacious sign of the greater eschatological unity to come. The Church militant is a visible and efficacious sign of the perfect vertical and horizontal communion of the Church triumphant with the Blessed Trinity and all of saved humanity. The Church is a sacred sign of this eschatological unity in her whole life of charitable service and prophetic witness (kingly and prophetic mission), by which she attracts others to share in her life and communion. But she manifests herself as an efficacious sign especially in her Eucharistic liturgy as priests and laity offer up the sacrifice of reconciliation and draw down graces upon the world, leading to greater unity and salvation. *Sacrosanctum Concilium*, §26 introduces the idea, quoting St. Cyprian: "Liturgical services are not private functions, but are celebrations of the Church, which is the 'sacrament of unity,'[71] namely, the holy people united and ordered under their bishops."

Lumen Gentium, §1 develops the idea more completely: "The Church is in Christ like a sacrament or as a sign and instrument both of a very closely knit union with God and of the unity of the whole human race." *Lumen Gentium*, §48 returns to this idea in the context of the Church as an eschatological sign: "Rising from the dead He sent His life-giving Spirit upon His disciples and through Him has established His Body which is the Church as the universal sacrament of salvation." Here the Church is said to be a "sacrament of salvation" because of Christ's gift of the Spirit on Easter and Pentecost, instituting the sacraments of Reconciliation and Confirmation and establishing her as His living Body through the life-giving power of her sacraments.

Ad Gentes quotes *Lumen Gentium*, §48 and applies it to the missionary nature of the Church: "Divinely sent to the nations of the world to be unto them 'a universal sacrament of salvation,' the Church, driven by the inner necessity of her own catholicity, and obeying the mandate of her Founder (cf. Mark 16:16), strives ever to proclaim the Gospel to all men."[72]

Gaudium et Spes, §42 quotes *Lumen Gentium*, §1 and further develops some of its implications in the realm of culture:

---

[71] Cyprian, *On the Unity of the Catholic Church*, 7; cf. *Letter 66.8.3*.
[72] Second Vatican Council, Decree on the Mission Activity of the Church *Ad Gentes* (Dec 7, 1965), §1.

The promotion of unity belongs to the innermost nature of the Church, for she is, "thanks to her relationship with Christ, a sacramental sign and an instrument of intimate union with God, and of the unity of the whole human race" [*LG* 1]. Thus she shows the world that an authentic union, social and external, results from a union of minds and hearts, namely from that faith and charity by which her own unity is unbreakably rooted in the Holy Spirit. For the force which the Church can inject into the modern society of man consists in that faith and charity put into vital practice, not in any external dominion exercised by merely human means.[73]

The Church is a sacramental sign of unity insofar as she lives the practice of faith and charity in all the paths of ordinary life. But the power to live out of faith and charity comes from the sacraments and is nourished especially by the Eucharist.

These texts from the Second Vatican Council do not mean to say that the Church is the eighth sacrament but rather that the Church, born from the seven sacraments, is an efficacious sign of union with God and all men and is a source of salvation precisely because she carries these seven life-giving sacraments in her bosom as her dowry.[74]

---

[73] Second Vatican Council, Pastoral Constitution on the Church in the Modern World *Gaudium et Spes* (Dec 7, 1965), §42.

[74] On the Church as the primordial "sacrament," see Otto Semmelroth, *Church and Sacrament*, trans. Emily Schossberger (Notre Dame, IN: Fides Publishers, 1965); Kevin McNamara, "The Church, Sacrament of Christ," in *Sacraments: The Gestures of Christ*, ed. O'Callaghan, 76–90; Cyril Vollert, "The Church and the Sacraments," in *Readings in Sacramental Theology*, ed. C. S. Sullivan (Englewood Cliffs, NJ: Prentice-Hall, 1964), 89–103; and Karl Rahner, *The Church and the Sacraments*, 18–24, 39–41. Rahner's interpretation of the thesis that the Church has the nature of a sacrament differs from that expressed in the documents of the Second Vatican Council in that Rahner conceives of the Church as "the primal and fundamental sacrament" (*The Church and the Sacraments*, 19), as if she were intrinsically endowed with grace in a way prior to the seven sacraments, which he conceives as intrinsic symbols that manifest her fullness of grace. Rahner's view is intimately connected with his view of sacramental causality, which will be examined below in chapter 13, pp. 482–89; and with his thesis that Christ's institution of the sacraments could be implicit in his institution of the Church, discussed in chapter 4, pp. 122–27. For Rahner's understanding of the priority of the Church with respect to the sacraments, see Karl Rahner, *Theology of Pastoral Action*, trans. W. J. O'Hara (New York: Herder and Herder, 1968),

Just as Eve was called the "mother of all the living" (Gen 3:20), so the Church is the new Eve, the mother of those living in the order of grace. The life-giving grace and sanctification she imparts is itself the efficacious sign and seed of future glory. Similarly, the unity of God and man in the Church on earth is the sign and seed of the ultimate union of God and man in the Church in heaven.

St. John Paul II, in his Apostolic Exhortation *Reconciliatio et Paenitentia*, §11, explains that the Church is said to be a sacrament because she is created by the seven sacraments which give her supernatural life and which make it possible for her to be an instrument of conversion and reconciliation between God and man, and among men. Thus she is the "sacrament of reconciliation" in both the vertical and horizontal dimensions:

> She is a sacrament by reason of the seven sacraments which, each in its own way, "make the church."[75] For since they commemorate and renew Christ's paschal mystery, all the sacraments are a source of life for the church and in the church's hands they are means of conversion to God and of reconciliation among people.[76]

It can be seen both from *Lumen Gentium*, §48 and *Reconciliatio et Paenitentia*, §11 that the sacramentality of the Church should not be conceived to be ontologically prior to the seven sacraments or to be their source. Rather it is the reverse. The Church is a sacrament of unity and salvation because she is endowed by her Founder with seven life-giving channels of grace through which she receives the Holy Spirit to be her soul or animating principle.

45, discussed on p. 124–25 below. On Rahner's understanding of the Church as the primordial sacrament, see George Vass, *The Sacrament of the Future: An Evaluation of Karl Rahner's Concept of the Sacraments and the End of Time* (Leominster, UK: Gracewing, 2005), 94–116.

[75] Cf. Augustine, *De Civitate Dei* 22.17; *ST* III, q. 64, a. 2, ad 3.

[76] All of the seven sacraments, each in its own way, enable the Church to be an efficacious sign of reconciliation, as John Paul II explains in *Reconciliatio et Paenitentia*, §27.

STUDY QUESTIONS

1. Why did it take over a thousand years for the Church to define that there are exactly seven sacraments?
2. Why is it fitting that Christ instituted these particular seven sacraments? Explain St. Thomas's arguments of fittingness.
3. Explain how all seven sacraments contribute in complementary ways to the communion of the Church and to her holiness.
4. Why is the Eucharist the summit of the sacramental economy?
5. In what sense does Vatican II speak of the Church as "like a sacrament" (*Lumen Gentium*, §1)? What is the relationship between the seven sacraments and the sacramentality of the Church?

SUGGESTIONS FOR FURTHER READING

Bouyer, Louis. "The Sacramental System." In *Sacraments: The Gestures of Christ*. Edited by Denis O'Callaghan. New York: Sheed & Ward, 1964. Pp. 45–55.

John Paul II. Apostolic Exhortation on Reconciliation and Penance in the Mission of the Church Today *Reconciliatio et Paenitentia*. December 2, 1984. See §§11, 27.

Leeming, Bernard. *Principles of Sacramental Theology*. 2nd edition. London: Longmans; Westminster, MD: Newman Press, 1960. Pp. 553–89.

Miralles, Antonio. *I sacramenti cristiani: trattato generale*. 2nd edition. Rome: Apollinare studi, 2008. Pp. 69–78, 145–78.

Scheeben, Matthias Joseph. *The Mysteries of Christianity*. Translated by Cyril Vollert. St. Louis, MO: B. Herder, 1951. Pp. 562–82.

Semmelroth, Otto. *Church and Sacrament*. Translated by Emily Schossberger. Notre Dame, IN: Fides Publishers, 1965.

Second Vatican Council, Dogmatic Constitution on the Church *Lumen Gentium*. November 21, 1964. See §§1, 11.

CHAPTER FOUR

Christ Instituted
the Sacraments

SCRIPTURAL WITNESS OF JESUS'S INSTITUTION OF THE SACRAMENTS

All seven sacraments by which the Church is formed, gathered, and sanctified were instituted by Christ and promulgated either by Christ in person or by the Apostles, as witnessed in Scripture and Tradition. That Christ Himself instituted the sacraments is a dogma of faith defined in the Council of Trent: "If any one says that the sacraments of the New Law were not all instituted by Jesus Christ our Lord . . . let him be anathema."[1] The *Catechism of the Catholic Church*, §1114 cites this fundamental text: "'Adhering to the teaching of the Holy Scriptures, to the apostolic traditions, and to the consensus . . . of the Fathers,' we profess that 'the sacraments of the new law were . . . all instituted by Jesus Christ our Lord.'"

The Church's certainty about Christ's institution of the sacraments does not come from Scripture alone but also from her living Tradition, in the light of which she interprets her Scriptures in a process of development of doctrine.[2] Thus we should not seek from Scripture a sufficient historical demonstration of this dogma with regard to all

---

[1] Council of Trent, Decree on the Sacraments (session 7), can. 1 on the Sacraments in General (DS, 1601). See Pius XII, *Sacramentum Ordinis*, §1 (DS, 3857).

[2] See Second Vatican Council, *Dei Verbum*, §§8–9: "This tradition which comes from the Apostles develops in the Church with the help of the Holy Spirit. . . . Consequently it is not from Sacred Scripture alone that the Church draws her certainty about everything which has been revealed."

seven sacraments, but rather a manifestation of the general principle of Christ's institution. Scripture enables us to trace Christ's institution of most of the sacraments, although not with the same degree of specificity and clarity. As seen above, the sacraments are not equal in their importance in the life of the Church. It is not surprising that the Gospels indicate Jesus's institution of the sacraments most clearly with regard to Baptism and the Eucharist, which are the sacraments most central and necessary in the life of the Church.

Institution of Baptism

There are various moments in the institution of Baptism. The first and most decisive moment was Jesus's reception of John's baptism of repentance at the start of His public ministry. The Fathers and Doctors frequently state that Christ did so not to receive anything from the rite but in order to sanctify the waters for the sacrament of Baptism and give them the power to serve as His instrument in the washing away of sins and in the new creation of sons and daughters of God in His Church. St. Gregory Nazianzen says: "He comes to sanctify the Jordan for our sake and in readiness for us; he who is spirit and flesh comes to begin a new creation through the Spirit and water."[3] St. John Damascene writes: "He, however, was baptized not that He Himself stood in any need of purification but that by making my purification His own He might 'crush the heads of the dragons in the waters,'[4] wash away the sin and bury all of the old Adam in the water."[5] St. Thomas summarizes this view: "Owing to Christ's infinite power . . . through contact with His flesh the regenerative power entered not only into the waters which came into contact with Christ, but into all waters throughout the whole world and during all future ages."[6] For this reason St. Thomas identifies Jesus's baptism by John as the institution of the sacrament, although its promulgation came later:

> As stated above [q. 62, a. 1], sacraments derive from their

---

[3] St. Gregory Nazianzen, *Oration* 39.15, in *Liturgy of the Hours*, Office of Readings for the feast of the Baptism of Christ, 2nd reading.

[4] See Ps 74:13.

[5] John Damascene, *An Exact Exposition of the Orthodox Faith* 4.9, in *Writings*, 347.

[6] *ST* III, q. 78, a. 5.

institution the power of conferring grace. Wherefore it seems that a sacrament is then instituted, when it receives the power of producing its effect. Now Baptism received this power when Christ was baptized. Consequently Baptism was truly instituted then, if we consider it as a sacrament. But the obligation of receiving this sacrament was proclaimed to mankind after the Passion and Resurrection.[7]

Jesus explained the necessity of Baptism to Nicodemus in John 3:1–6.[8] In John 3:22–4:3,[9] we are told that the disciples of Jesus were already administering the Baptism of Jesus even as John the Baptist was baptizing nearby before his imprisonment. John 4:1–3 states: "When the Lord knew that the Pharisees had heard that Jesus was making and baptizing more disciples than John (although Jesus himself did not baptize, but only his disciples), he left Judea and departed again to Galilee." This passage indicates that early in His public ministry, Jesus's disciples were baptized with Jesus's Baptism, which was understood to be distinct from that of John. It is also interesting that Jesus Himself was not baptizing, but His disciples were, clearly in His name. Finally, Jesus promulgated Baptism before His Ascension, as recounted in Matthew 28:19: "Go therefore and make disciples of all nations, baptizing them in the name of the Father and of the Son and of the Holy Spirit."

Institution of the Eucharist

Since the Eucharist is the most central sacrament and the heart of the New Covenant, it is appropriate that Jesus's institution of the Eucharist is shown in the clearest and most determinate way in Scripture.

---

[7] *ST* III, q. 66, a. 2.

[8] Since Nicodemus came at night, he was presumably a secret disciple—not publicly identified as a follower and thus not yet baptized. Hence Jesus speaks to him about the necessity of Baptism.

[9] John 3:22–26: "After this Jesus and his disciples went into the land of Judea; there he remained with them and baptized. John also was baptizing at Aenon near Salim, because there was much water there; and people came and were baptized. For John had not yet been put in prison. Now a discussion arose between John's disciples and a Jew over purifying. And they came to John, and said to him, "Rabbi, he who was with you beyond the Jordan, to whom you bore witness, here he is, baptizing, and all are going to him."

Jesus explained the Eucharist in the synagogue of Capernaum after the miracle of the multiplication of the loaves and fish (John 6), and He formally instituted it in the Last Supper, as manifested in the four parallel accounts of the institution.[10] But, as in the other sacraments, Jesus left to His Church great discretion and flexibility in the organic unfolding of the Eucharistic liturgy over time and space.

Institution of Holy Orders at the Last Supper

Holy Orders and the Eucharist are intimately associated, for the offering of sacrifice implies a priesthood to offer it. For this reason, the Church sees the institution of the priesthood in the words of Jesus during the Last Supper, when Jesus said, "Do this in remembrance of me" (Luke 22:19). The Council of Trent states this conviction:

> Sacrifice and priesthood are by the ordinance of God so united that both have existed under every law. Since, therefore, in the New Testament the Catholic Church has received from the institution of Christ the holy, visible sacrifice of the Eucharist, it must also be acknowledged that there exists in the Church a new, visible, and external priesthood into which the old one was changed. Moreover, the Sacred Scriptures make it clear and the tradition of the Catholic Church has always taught that this priesthood was instituted by the same Lord our Savior and that the power of consecrating, offering, and administering his Body and Blood, and likewise of remitting and retaining sins, was given to the apostles and to their successors in the priesthood.[11]

We do not see that Jesus directly instituted the three grades of Holy Orders. The Apostles and their successors, presumably following an intention of Christ, adapted this distinction of grades of priestly service from that already present in Israel: the high priest who was the type of the bishop, the priests, and the Levites who were the types of the deacons instituted by the Apostles in Acts 6.

---

[10] Matt 26:20–29; Mark 14:17–25; Luke 22:14–20; 1 Cor 11:23–25.

[11] Council of Trent, Doctrine and Canons on the Sacrament of Orders (session 23, July 15, 1563), ch. 1 (DS, 1764).

Institution of Penance

Jesus instituted Penance principally on Easter Sunday, as we read in John 20:21–23:

> Jesus said to them again, "Peace be with you. As the Father has sent me, even so I send you." And when he had said this, he breathed on them, and said to them, "Receive the Holy Spirit. If you forgive the sins of any, they are forgiven; if you retain the sins of any, they are retained."

Penance is an Easter gift. The Council of Trent cites this text to establish Jesus's institution of the sacrament, and goes on to state:

> The universal consensus of the Fathers has always acknowledged that by so sublime an action and such clear words the power of forgiving and retaining sins was given to the apostles and their lawful successors for reconciling the faithful who have fallen after baptism.[12]

The way Penance has been administered has varied greatly in its practice, from the public penance of the early centuries to the private and frequent confession of later centuries. These differences, however, do not affect the essential substance of the sacrament, composed of contrition, confession, satisfaction, and absolution, and its proper effect of obtaining the forgiveness of post-baptismal sins and reconciliation with God and the Church.[13]

Promise of the Gift of the Spirit

Confirmation was first given—in an extraordinary way—on Pentecost, according to the promise of the gift of the Spirit made by Jesus to the Apostles in the discourse after the Last Supper, and in Acts 1:4–8. We can say that Jesus instituted the sacrament in John 14–16[14] when He

---

[12] Council of Trent, Doctrine on the Sacrament of Penance (session 14, Nov 25, 1551), ch. 1 (DS, 1670).

[13] See *CCC*, §§1447–48, and see below, pp. 151–52.

[14] Jesus made this promise three times during His discourse after the Last Supper. It is first found in John 14:16–17, 26, and then again in 15:26–27; and then in

promised to send the Spirit after His Ascension. St. Thomas writes:

> Therefore we must say that Christ instituted this sacrament
> not by bestowing, but by promising it, according to John 16:7:
> "If I go not, the Paraclete will not come to you, but if I go, I
> will send Him to you." And this was because in this sacrament
> the fulness of the Holy Spirit is bestowed, which was not to be
> given before Christ's Resurrection and Ascension; according
> to John 7:39: "As yet the Spirit was not given, because Jesus
> was not yet glorified."[15]

Since Confirmation involves the sending of the Holy Spirit as His
final gift to His disciples, Jesus wanted to first ascend into heaven so
that the Spirit could be sent from above by the Father and Son together.
Furthermore, in ascending into heaven and sending the Spirit from
there, Christ was fulfilling the figure of Moses, who ascended Mount
Sinai to receive the Law. Christ ascended higher than Moses to send a
better Law: the Holy Spirit who writes the Law on the heart, fulfilling
the prophecies of Jeremiah 31:33, Ezekiel 36:26–27, and Joel 2:28–29.

We see Confirmation—spoken of as the giving of the Spirit
through the laying on of hands—administered by the Apostles Peter
and John in Acts 8:14–17 and by St. Paul in Acts 19:6. In the case of
Confirmation, we do not see that Jesus determined either the matter or
the form of the sacrament. The Apostles and their successors made use
of two Jewish elements associated with the communication of the Holy
Spirit and His power: the laying on of hands and anointing with oil.
Jesus, however, clearly determined the proper effect of this sacrament,
which is the giving of the promised Holy Spirit to make the recipients
His witnesses in all nations with the Spirit's power to build up the
Church, as Jesus told the disciples in Acts 1:8: "You shall receive power
when the Holy Spirit has come upon you; and you shall be my witnesses
in Jerusalem and in all Judea and Samaria and to the end of the earth."

Anointing of the Sick

It seems that Anointing of the Sick was instituted by Christ when He
sent out the Twelve, for in Mark 6:13 we read that "they cast out many

---

a fuller form in John 16:7–15.

[15] *ST* III, q. 72, a. 1, ad 1.

demons, and anointed with oil many that were sick and healed them." Anointing of the Sick is promulgated in James 5:14–15: "Is any among you sick? Let him call for the elders of the church, and let them pray over him, anointing him with oil in the name of the Lord; and the prayer of faith will save the sick man, and the Lord will raise him up; and if he has committed sins, he will be forgiven." The Council of Trent defined that this sacrament "was instituted by Christ our Lord as a true and proper sacrament of the New Testament. It is alluded to indeed by Mark [6:13], but it is recommended to the faithful and promulgated by James the apostle and brother of the Lord."[16] The *Catechism of the Council of Trent* explains the implication of Mark 6:13 at greater length:

> There is possible evidence of its immediate institution by our Savior when he sent out his disciples in pairs on a missionary journey, for we are told by the Evangelist that "they went out and preached that men should repent. And they cast out many demons, and anointed with oil many that were sick and healed them" (Mk 6:12–13). This anointing of the sick could not have been invented by the apostles; it must have been prescribed by our Lord. And its purpose must have been a supernatural one, curing souls, rather than a merely natural one, using oil to cure bodies. This is the unanimous teaching of St. Denis, St. Ambrose, St. John Chrysostom, St. Gregory the Great.[17]

St. Paul VI, in the Apostolic Constitution *Sacram Unctionem Infirmorum* of November 30, 1972, reaffirmed the definitive teaching of the Council of Trent on this sacrament. The *Catechism of the Catholic Church*, §1511 repeats the same teaching: "This sacred anointing of the sick was instituted by Christ our Lord as a true and proper sacrament of the New Testament. It is alluded to indeed by Mark..."

Matrimony

Matrimony was raised to a sacrament by Christ through realizing the nuptial mystery with His Bride, the Church, in giving Himself for her through the shedding of His Blood, as explained by St. Paul in

---

[16] Council of Trent, Doctrine on the Sacrament of Extreme Unction (session 14, Nov 25, 1551), ch. 1 (DS, 1695); see also DS, 1716.

[17] *CCT*, part 2, ch. 5, §8, p. 301.

Ephesians 5:31–32. He also restored Matrimony to its original holiness in His teaching on marriage and its indissolubility (Matt 19:3–9; Mark 10:2–12), and sanctified it by working His first miracle at the wedding of Cana. Marriage itself was instituted by God at the creation of Adam and Eve,[18] but Christ instituted its sacramentality by realizing His Paschal mystery on behalf of His Bride to sanctify her and unite Himself with her, of which union Matrimony is a sacred sign.[19]

As Christ instituted Baptism by receiving it from John the Baptist, so He instituted marriage as a sacrament of His spousal union with the Church by realizing that spousal union with His Bride, and especially by dying for her, so "that he might sanctify her, having cleansed her by the washing of water with the word, that he might present the Church to himself in splendor, without spot or wrinkle or any such thing, that she might be holy and without blemish" (Eph 5:26–27). Because Christ has elevated a pre-existing natural institution in this sacrament, the Gospels do not show us a particular moment of institution in which a new sacramental sign is established, as is the case for the Eucharist and Baptism.

The entire life of the Church has been structured by the seven sacraments since Pentecost. While it is clear that the modes by which the sacraments have been administered have varied considerably, the fundamental purpose of each sacrament has remained the same throughout the centuries.

In How Specific a Manner Did Christ Institute the Sacraments?

While the Council of Trent defined that Christ instituted the seven

---

[18] See Gen 2:24; Council of Trent, Doctrine on the Sacrament of Matrimony (session 24, Nov 11, 1563; DS, 1797).

[19] See Council of Trent, Doctrine on the Sacrament of Matrimony (session 24, Nov 11, 1563; DS, 1799–1800): "Christ himself, who instituted the holy sacraments and brought them to perfection, merited for us by his Passion the grace that perfects that natural love, confirms the indissoluble union, and sanctifies the spouses. St. Paul suggests this [Eph 5:25, 32]. . . . Since, through Christ, matrimony in the evangelical law surpasses marital unions of the Old Law in grace, our holy Fathers, the councils, and the tradition of the universal Church have with good reason always taught that it is to be numbered among the sacraments of the New Law."

sacraments of the New Covenant, it did not determine the precise way in which He did this. There is room for theological discussion, therefore, on the degree of specificity of Christ's institution. What does it mean to say that Christ instituted a sacrament? It does not have to mean that He completely determined all the elements of its sacramental sign, as will be seen below. It must mean, however, that He structured the life of His Church by assigning to each sacrament a specific function of granting grace through sacramental signs that would represent that grace.

The Council of Trent left open the question of whether Christ instituted some of the sacraments in a *generic* way with the determination of the matter and form[20] of the sacramental sign left to the Church or in a *specific* way with fully determined matter and form. This was a question disputed by theologians of the period,[21] and in general the Council of Trent did not seek to settle questions disputed among Catholic theologians and limited its doctrinal pronouncements to excluding Protestant errors. Thus although Trent definitively teaches that Christ instituted all seven sacraments, it does not require Catholics to hold that Jesus instituted them in such a way that He Himself specifically determined each sacramental sign in its matter and form.

In fact, the history of the liturgy shows that there has been considerable variation with regard to many specific elements of matter and form. For example, Acts 8:17–19 and 19:6 speak of the giving of the Spirit (Confirmation) being conferred by the laying on of hands without mention of any anointing with oil, which soon became essential in the administration of this sacrament.[22] More examples of such

---

[20] For a discussion of the matter and form of the sacraments, see the following chapter.

[21] See the discussion of this question of generic or specific institution in Leeming, *Principles of Sacramental Theology*, 408–31, esp. 412–16 outlining the positions of various theologians from the time of the Council of Trent. See also Gulielmo (William) Van Roo, *De Sacramentis in genere* (Rome: Apud Aedes Universitatis Gregorianae, 1957), 95–128; Roger Nutt, *General Principles of Sacramental Theology* (Washington, DC: Catholic University of America Press, 2017), 180–83; Miralles, *I sacramenti cristiani*, 154–64; Clarence McAuliffe defends the thesis of specific institution in *De sacramentis in genere* (St. Louis, MO: B. Herder, 1960), 135–52 and in *Sacramental Theology: A Textbook for Advanced Students* (St. Louis, MO: B. Herder, 1961), 43–47.

[22] See *CCC*, §1289: "Very early, the better to signify the gift of the Holy Spirit, an anointing with perfumed oil (chrism) was added to the laying on of hands." For

variation will be given below and in the following chapter.

Substance of the Sacraments

The Council of Trent's teaching on Christ's institution of the sacraments is illuminated by an important clarification made in the decree on Communion under both species. To explain how it is possible that the Church modified the way that Holy Communion was received by the faithful (under both species or only under one), the Council laid down the crucial principle that the Church has a certain power to modify aspects of the matter and form of the sacraments, except with regard to their *substance*:

> [The holy Council] declares that, in the administration of the sacraments—provided their substance is preserved [*salva eorum substantia*]—there has always been in the Church that power to determine or modify what she judged more expedient for the benefit of those receiving the sacraments or for the reverence due to the sacraments themselves—according to the diversity of circumstances, times, and places. This, moreover, is what the apostle seems to have indicated rather clearly when he said: This is how one should regard us, as servants of Christ and stewards of the mysteries of God" [1 Cor 4:1].[23]

Therefore in the sacraments there is a nucleus or essence that is of divine law and origin, corresponding to the institution by Christ, which cannot be changed by the Church. This essential nucleus is to be distinguished from other (accidental) aspects of the matter, form, and administration of the sacraments that pertain to ecclesiastical law and can be modified according to the needs of diverse times, places,

---

a defense of the thesis that Christ left the sacramental sign of Confirmation to the Church to determine, see Cyprian Vagaggini, "'Per unctionem chrismatis in fronte, quae fit manus impositione': Una curiosa affermazione dell'*Ordo Confirmationis* del 1971 sulla materia prossima essenziale della Confermazione," in *Mysterion: nella celebrazione del Mistero di Cristo la vita della Chiesa: Miscellanea liturgica in occasione dei 70 anni dell'Abate Salvatore Marsili* (Turin: Elle di Ci, 1981), 417–28.

[23] The Council of Trent, Doctrine of Communion under Both Kinds and the Communion of Little Children (session 21, July 16, 1562), ch. 2 (DS, 1728).

cultures, and historical circumstances.

Pius XII refers to this nucleus or substance of the sacraments that comes from Christ's institution in his Apostolic Constitution *Sacramentum Ordinis*:

> In the course of the ages, the Church has not and could not substitute other sacraments for these sacraments instituted by Christ the Lord, since, as the Council of Trent teaches, the seven sacraments of the New Law have all been instituted by Jesus Christ, our Lord, and the Church has no power over the "substance of the sacraments," that is, over those things that, with the sources of divine revelation as witnesses, Christ the Lord himself decreed to be preserved in a sacramental sign.[24]

But whatever has been added to the substance of the sacraments by ecclesiastical law can also be taken away by her, according to the needs of the times, as Pius XII states in the same document.[25]

If an element that belongs to the essential nucleus of a sacrament as instituted by Christ is lacking, then the sacrament will be invalid. This means that the sacrament, intended by Christ as an efficacious sign of grace, does not exist as such and will not produce its proper effects. For example, if the Eucharist were celebrated without bread or wine,[26] it would be invalid, for these pertain to its essential matter instituted by Christ. Similarly, if Baptism were administered without water or without a Trinitarian form, it would be invalid.

It is not always easy, however, to distinguish what is of divine law in the sacraments and what is of ecclesiastical law. The problem is made more difficult by the fact that the Church may make the validity of a sacrament in a given liturgical rite at a given time depend on some of these elements that she herself has introduced, which thus pertain to ecclesiastical rather than divine law. A prominent example of such an addition now required for the validity of the sacrament is

---

[24] Pius XII, *Sacramentum Ordinis*, §1 (DS, 3857).

[25] Pius XII, *Sacramentum Ordinis*, §3 (DS, 3858): "But if, by the will and prescription of the Church, the same [handing over of the instruments] was at some time held as necessary even for validity, all know that the Church can also change and abrogate what she has established."

[26] See CIC, can. 924; Council of Florence, *Exsultate Deo* (DS, 1320); *ST* III, q. 74, aa. 3, 5.

the requirement imposed by the Council of Trent that marriage be celebrated according to the canonical form with the priest as witness. The purpose of this decree was to put an end to the abusive practice of clandestine marriages by rendering them invalid:

> There is no doubt that secret marriages, entered by free consent of the parties, are true and valid marriages as long as the Church has not made them null. . . . Nevertheless, the holy Church has always detested and prohibited such marriages for the best of reasons. . . . The holy council now renders incapable of marriage any who may attempt to contract marriage otherwise than in the presence of the parish priest or another priest, with the permission of the parish priest or the Ordinary, and two or three witnesses; and it decrees that such contracts are null and invalid and renders them so by this decree.[27]

Another example concerns the sacrament of Confirmation. In the current Latin rite, St. Paul VI established that it is necessary for the validity of the sacrament of Confirmation to anoint the recipient with chrism on the forehead accompanied by the words of the form, "N., be sealed with the Gift of the Holy Spirit."[28] This new form, drawn from the Byzantine rite, significantly changed the form necessary for validity in the Latin rite, which, in the previous seven centuries, had been: "I sign you with the sign of the cross and confirm you with the chrism of salvation. In the name of the Father and of the Son and of the Holy Spirit." We have seen that the Acts of the Apostles speaks only of a "laying on of hands" accompanied by an unspecified prayer for the gift of the Spirit. As in the case of Orders and Anointing of the Sick, no one essential prayer has been universally used to confer Confirmation.[29]

Two prominent examples of elements that belong to the substance of the sacrament and cannot be changed by ecclesiastical law are the fact that male gender is required for valid reception of priestly

---

[27] Council of Trent, Canons on a Reform of Marriage, Decree *Tametsi* (session 24, Nov 11, 1563), ch. 1 (DS, 1813, 1816). The current *Code of Canon of Law* maintains this requirement in CIC, can. 1108, §1.

[28] See Paul VI, Apostolic Constitution *Divinae Consortium Naturae*, in *Rites*, 1:477.

[29] For other examples of changes in the matter or form of the sacraments that pertain to ecclesiastical law, see the following chapter, pp. 149–51, 155–69.

ordination,[30] and that holy Matrimony must be between a man and a woman.[31]

Two Senses in Which Something Is Said to Be a Necessary or Essential Element of a Sacrament

It is important, therefore, to distinguish two different senses in which something is said to be necessary or essential to a sacramental rite. (1) Some elements are essential because they belong to the substance or essence of a sacrament always and everywhere by divine institution. (2) Other elements can be said, less properly, to be essential in that they are necessary for validity in a given rite in a given time and place through the determination of the Church, but have varied and thus are intrinsically changeable. The former elements are what Christ Himself instituted in a specific way and pertain to divine law and therefore can never be changed, such as bread and wine as the matter of the Eucharist. Such elements belong to the *substance or essence of the sacrament itself.* The latter sense refers to what is required for the validity of a sacrament according to ecclesiastical law in a given time or place, as in the requirement for canonical form in Matrimony. One might think of such elements as pertaining to the essence *of a rite* at a given time but not to the *substance of the sacrament itself* as instituted by Christ.[32]

The doctrine that Christ personally instituted the sacraments should be understood only according to their substance or nucleus

---

[30] See John Paul II, Apostolic Letter on Priestly Ordination *Ordinatio Sacerdotalis* (May 22, 1994), §4 (DS, 4983), discussed in ch. 6 below, pp. 201–3.

[31] See CIC, can. 1055, §1: "The matrimonial covenant, by which a man and a woman establish between themselves a partnership of the whole of life and which is ordered by its nature to the good of the spouses and the procreation and education of offspring, has been raised by Christ the Lord to the dignity of a sacrament between the baptized." See chapter 6 below for a discussion of the necessity of male gender to receive priestly ordination and gender complementarity for marriage.

[32] See Van Roo, *De Sacramentis in genere*, 119–25; Journet, *The Church of the Word Incarnate*, 1:117–19; H. Lennerz, *De sacramentis novae legis in genere*, 3rd ed. (Rome: Gregorian University, 1950), 294–99; Francis Hürth, "Constitutio Apostolica de Sacris Ordinibus, Textus et Commentarius cum Appendice," *Periodica de re morali, canonica, liturgica* 37 (1948): 1–56; Leeming, *Principles of Sacramental Theology*, 416; Peter Fransen, "Erwägungen über das Firmalter," *Zeitschrift Für Katholische Theologie* 84, no. 4 (1962): 401–26, at 403–05.

that pertains to divine law, and which does not preclude significant development in the way in which the sacraments are celebrated over the centuries.[33] Although the principle is clear, at times it can be quite difficult to concretely distinguish what pertains to the unchangeable substance of a sacrament established by Christ and what is a further specification given by the Church in the course of history. What the Church has introduced is potentially subject to modification even if she has made it necessary for the validity of the rite at a given time. This discernment requires accurate knowledge of the history of the liturgy under the guidance of the Magisterium of the Church, to whom this discernment ultimately belongs.[34]

Some medieval scholastics, such as Hugh of St. Victor[35] and St. Bonaventure,[36] held that some sacraments, like Confirmation and Anointing of the Sick, were instituted by the Apostles or by a Church council, contrary to the dogma later defined at Trent that Christ personally instituted all seven sacraments. This view does not actually imply a substantive difference with what was later defined at Trent. It seems to come principally from the fact that these theologi-

---

[33] See William A. Van Roo, "Reflections on Karl Rahner's *Kirche und Sakramente,*" *Gregorianum* 44 (1963): 465–500, at 495: "What is the minimum meaning of the proposition: Christ instituted a sacrament? Christ ordered the performance in His Church of a rite apt to signify and to confer a sanctification which He himself specified. He did not have to specify the details of the rite in all cases, though He did determine some details of the rites of some sacraments. But He did have to indicate a distinct effect of grace to be signified and produced, and He did have to indicate that it was to be signified and produced by a suitable rite. This is the minimum dogmatic notion of institution, involved in the defined truth itself."

[34] See Bernard Leeming, *Principles of Sacramental Theology* (Westminster, MD: Newman Press, 1963), xi: "The Church has always been convinced that the sacraments are the gifts of God, and, consequently, are inviolable and beyond her power to change. Accessory ceremonies, as everyone agrees, fall within the Church's competence to introduce, vary, or abolish; but the substance of the sacraments is part of the essential constitution of the Church. What, however, in the concrete makes up this 'substance' of a sacrament is a problem which perplexes the wisest of theologians, who can only speak tentatively." See also pp. 408–31.

[35] See Hugh of St. Victor, *On the Sacraments of the Christian Faith*, 2.15.2, trans. Deferrari, 431: "The sacrament of the anointing of the sick is read to have been established by the Apostles." See Leeming, *Principles of Sacramental Theology*, 409.

[36] See J. A. Wayne, "Bonaventure: On the Institution of the Sacraments," in *A Companion to Bonaventure*, ed. Jay M. Hammond, J. A. Wayne, and Jared Goff (Leiden; Boston: Brill, 2014), 333–57.

ans did not make a clear distinction between the substantial nucleus that is from Christ, and elements, such as anointing with chrism in Confirmation, that have been added by the Church and made necessary for validity. What they are affirming is that the current form of the sacrament with the elements currently necessary for validity has its origin not in Christ but in an action of the Church, which is true. This ecclesiastical action, however, presupposes Christ's prior institution of the sacrament and further specifies a particular mode of celebration.

The Liturgy of Israel and the Matter and Form of the Sacraments

We have seen that in instituting the sacraments of the New Covenant, Christ left important elements of the rite to be further determined by the Apostles and their successors. This power was not left to them in a vacuum, however, for Jesus would have expected them to interpret His institutional will in the context of the life and worship of Israel and the rich sacramental culture instituted by God in the Mosaic Law, and the Holy Spirit would have guided them in this process of discernment.

For example, although the Gospels do not show that Christ specified the laying on of hands or anointing with olive oil to be part of the matter for the sacramental sign that gives the Holy Spirit, which is our sacrament of Confirmation/Chrismation, it would be natural for the Apostles and their successors to make use of the Jewish rite of anointing to impart the Holy Spirit, as the Old Testament had done for kings, priests, and prophets. In the same way it would have been natural to make use of the gesture of the laying on of hands to indicate the transmission of spiritual gifts.

With regard to Holy Orders, we do not see that Jesus instituted the distinction of the three grades of bishop, priest, and deacon. Nevertheless, this distinction existed in the Aaronic priesthood of Israel, in which there was one High Priest, under whom there was a college of priests, and many Levites who served the liturgy in different ways. This threefold distinction in Israel surely influenced the Apostles and their successors in the early Church to distinguish three grades of ordained ministry in the Church (deacons, presbyters, and bishops) even if it took time for the distinction to become universal and the terminology to become precise.

Reasons of Fittingness for the Institution of the Sacraments by Christ

Why is it fitting that Christ Himself instituted the sacraments? The Church cannot institute sacraments for at least five reasons.

The Sacraments Extend the Reach of Christ's Humanity

First, the sacraments are instruments that effect a mysterious extension of Christ's humanity and the merit of His Paschal mystery, enabling Him, His words of power, His Passion and Resurrection, and His Spirit to touch us today. They are external instruments that have their power by being moved by the hands of Christ. Christ thus needed to personally institute the sacraments to give them this mysterious instrumental power to perform supernatural effects when moved by Him.[37] The principal agent has to choose or design the essential instruments through which he will work, and so Christ had to design and institute His sacramental instruments and their essential elements through which He would sanctify and build up His Church through the ages. In doing so He could leave the forms of celebration that clothe, shape, and enrich the liturgy to the discernment of His Body, the Church, but He Himself had to determine what is essential in His own instruments. No merely human authority could tell God what means to use to extend the reach of His humanity.

St. Thomas explains that Christ Himself through the Incarnation and Paschal mystery is the first and universal remedy for man's need for salvation, and the sacraments are more particular remedies that flow from the universal remedy that is Christ:

> But because this treatment [the Incarnation] is so powerful that it can cure all men ("for power went out from him and he cured all," as it says in Luke 6:19), therefore from this universal medicine come forth other particular medicines

---

[37] See Peter Lombard, *Sentences*, bk. 3, d. 19, ch. 5, in PL 192:797 (my translation), in which he says that Christ "is usually called the Redeemer according to His humanity, since according to it and in it He took up and fulfilled those sacraments which are the cause of our redemption."

resembling the universal medicine, and by these intermediaries the power of the universal medicine reaches the sick: and these are the sacraments, "in which, under the cover of visible things, divine power works our healing in a hidden way."[38]

The divine/human physician had to order and institute the particular medicines by which His saving power would come in contact with those who are to be members of His Body through the centuries. Or to use another metaphor, Christ, who is the fountain of the living waters of grace, had to establish stable and fitting channels by which the living waters would reach us, which channels are the seven sacraments. Without those channels the fountain would be unable to water those who thirst.

The Sacraments Are Instruments of the Divine Omnipotence

Second, Christ had to institute the sacraments because they are instruments of the divine omnipotence, and the only man who personally possesses divine omnipotence is the Word Incarnate. St. Thomas argues succinctly: "The institutor of anything is he who gives it strength and power: as in the case of those who institute laws. But the power of a sacrament is from God alone, as we have shown above. Therefore God alone can institute a sacrament."[39]

Every celebration of the sacraments involves a supernatural power to sanctify man that is proper to God alone. In other words, every sacrament involves a divine power greater than that displayed in any miracle of physical healing or in the suspension of the laws of nature. It is greater for it gives to the creature something infinitely dispro-

---

[38] Thomas Aquinas, *In IV Sent.*, proemium, trans. Mortensen, 7:1. The last quote is from St. Isidore of Seville, *Etymologies*, bk. 6, ch. 19, no. 40 (PL 82:255). See also *SCG* IV, ch. 56, nos. 1–2, 4:247: "The death of Christ is, so to say, the universal cause of human salvation, and since a universal cause must be applied singly to each of its effects, it was necessary to show men some remedies through which the benefit of Christ's death could somehow be conjoined to them. It is of this sort, of course, that the sacraments of the Church are said to be. Now, remedies of this kind had to be handed on with some visible signs."

[39] *ST* III, q. 64, a. 2, sed contra.

portionate to him: sanctifying grace, which is a participation in the divine nature. After the Incarnation it is fitting that this divine power work through Christ's humanity. The *Catechism of the Council of Trent* comments:

> If God alone can make us holy, then the sacraments by which we obtain holiness are simply the instruments of his action. Obviously, then, it is the same one God in Christ who must be recognized as the author no less of the sacraments than of holiness itself. . . . If the efficacy of the sacraments reaches, as it does, the inmost depths of the soul, then God is manifestly involved here, since he alone can enter into the ultimate sanctuary of man's heart.[40]

Christ Alone Merited the Grace Given by the Sacraments

Third, it is fitting that Christ institute the sacraments because He alone, through His Passion, merited their efficacy. It is just that He who merited all graces for humanity should also be the one to institute the ordinary means by which those merits are *applied* to humanity throughout the life of the Church. These ordinary means are the sacraments. In other words, Christ (in His divinity) is not only the efficient cause of all the grace given by the sacraments, but in His humanity He is also the meritorious cause of that same grace. Thus it is doubly fitting that He who works through the sacraments and merited the grace that they communicate should institute the sacraments and determine their essential nucleus and effects.

The Sacraments Send the Holy Spirit

Fourth, the sacraments give the Holy Spirit. John the Baptist, in instituting his baptism of repentance, said that he "came baptizing with water" (John 1:31), but the one coming after him is "he who baptizes with the Holy Spirit" (John 1:33). In the parallel text in Matthew 3:11, John the Baptist says, "I baptize you with water for repentance, but he who is coming after me is mightier than I, whose sandals I am not worthy to carry; he will baptize you with the Holy Spirit and with

---

[40] *CCT*, part 2, intro., §23, p. 157.

fire."[41] The implication is that John, as a mere man, even though he was the greatest prophet of Israel,[42] lacked the authority and power to communicate the divine Person of the Holy Spirit and His fire of charity through the baptism that he introduced.

The communication of the Holy Spirit is most direct and explicit in Confirmation, but every sacrament gives the Holy Spirit in a new way to deepen the life of the Spirit in us according to the mission of that sacrament. As seen above, Jesus instituted the sacrament of Penance in John 20:22–23 by breathing on the disciples in the upper room on Easter Sunday and saying to them: "Receive the Holy Spirit. If you forgive the sins of any, they are forgiven; if you retain the sins of any, they are retained." St. Peter Damian states that in the upper room Jesus "poured forth the sacraments through the in-breathing of the Holy Spirit."[43] The institution of Penance, like every other sacrament, implies a permanent gift of the Holy Spirit to the Church to be received for a given purpose of sanctification. This gift can only be given by Christ Himself. It belongs to Christ as the Second Person of the Trinity (together with the Father) to send the Third Person, the Paraclete, who proceeds as the mutual love of the Father and the Son. Among men, only Christ has authority over the Holy Spirit, and thus only He can institute a sacrament that will infallibly send the Spirit (as long as the recipient does not pose the obstacle of unrepentance).

The Sacraments Give Birth to and Build the Church

Fifth, the sacraments are what give rise to the Church; she is born from the sacraments, and not the reverse. The Church is the mother of

---

[41] See also Titus 3:4–7: "When the goodness and loving kindness of God our Savior appeared, he saved us, not because of deeds done by us in righteousness, but in virtue of his own mercy, by the washing of regeneration and renewal in the Holy Spirit, which he poured out upon us richly through Jesus Christ our Savior"; 1 Cor 12:13: "By one Spirit we were all baptized into one body—Jews or Greeks, slaves or free—and all were made to drink of one Spirit."

[42] See Luke 7:28, in which Jesus says: "I tell you, among those born of women none is greater than John."

[43] Peter Damian, opusculum 18, *Contra intemperantes clericos*, dissertatio 3, ch. 3 (PL 145:421B), in Boyd Taylor Coolman, "The Christo-Pneumatic-Ecclesial Character of Twelfth-Century Sacramental Theology," in *OHST*, 207.

all the faithful because she has been endowed with life-giving fruitfulness through her sacraments. The Church cannot institute sacraments because she cannot exist at all apart from the sacraments that give her supernatural life. Outside of their channels she has no life and thus no life-giving powers. Without Baptism, for example, the Church would have no members. Without Holy Orders, there would be no divinely established government in the Church, and there would be no Eucharist. Without the Eucharist, the Church would have no sacrifice to offer to God and no way to be nourished progressively in Christ's life. Only the Founder of the Church, who is Christ, can give her supernatural life by endowing her with sacraments.

That the Church is born from the sacraments is indicated in the patristic typological understanding of the Church as the New Eve born from the pierced side of Christ. A classic exposition of the typology of the blood and water from the side of Christ is found in St. John Chrysostom:

> Moreover, in addition to this, an ineffable mystery was also accomplished, for "There came out blood and water." It was not accidentally or by chance that these streams came forth, but because the Church has been established from both of these. Her members know this, since they have come to birth by water and are nourished by Flesh and Blood. The Mysteries have their source from there, so that when you approach the awesome chalice you may come as if you were about to drink from His very side.[44]

Another beautiful explanation of this idea is given by Quodvultdeus, bishop of Carthage at the time of St. Augustine:

> Let our Bridegroom ascend the wood of his bridal-chamber; let our Bridegroom ascend the wood of his marriage bed. Let him sleep by dying. Let his side be opened, and let the virgin Church come forth. Just as when Eve was made from the side of a sleeping Adam, so the Church was formed from the side of Christ, hanging on the cross. For his side was pierced, as the

---

[44] John Chrysostom, Homily 85 on John 19:34, in *Commentary on Saint John the Apostle and Evangelist: Homilies 48–88*, trans. Sister Thomas Aquinas Goggin (Washington, DC: Catholic University of America Press, 1959), 435.

gospel says, and immediately there flowed out blood and water, which are the twin sacraments of the Church: the water, which became her bath, and the blood which became her dowry.[45]

In the early third century, Tertullian presents the typology of the creation of Eve as something well-known:

> For as Adam was a figure of Christ, Adam's sleep shadowed out the death of Christ, who was to sleep a mortal slumber, that from the wound inflicted on His side might, in like manner (as Eve was formed), be typified the church, the true mother of the living.[46]

That the Church is born from the sacraments is also implied in Ephesians 5:25–27:

> Husbands, love your wives, as Christ loved the Church and gave himself up for her, that he might sanctify her, having cleansed her by the washing of water with the word, that he might present the Church to himself in splendor, without spot or wrinkle or any such thing, that she might be holy and without blemish.

The Church is sanctified and grace-filled not from herself, but from having been cleansed by the "washing of water with the word," which is an apt description of Baptism. She is kept "holy and without blemish" not by Baptism alone but also by the other sacraments, which all contribute in complementary ways to her holiness, as argued in chapter 3 above.[47]

The sacraments, as the dowry the Church has received from her Lord, are "of the Church" in the sense that she is their home and she exercises her supernatural life through them. The *Catechism of the Catholic Church*, §1118 explains:

> The sacraments are "of the Church" in the double sense that they are "by her" and "for her." They are "by the Church," for

---

[45] *Quodvultdeus of Carthage, The Creedal Homilies*, 37.
[46] Tertullian, *Treatise on the Soul* 43, in *ANF* 3:308.
[47] See pp. 83–90 above.

she is the sacrament of Christ's action at work in her through the mission of the Holy Spirit. They are "for the Church" in the sense that "the sacraments make the Church,"[48] since they manifest and communicate to men, above all in the Eucharist, the mystery of communion with the God who is love, One in three persons.

Sacramental actions are actions *by* the Church and *for* the Church. The glory of the Church is that she can do *supernatural actions with infinite value* by celebrating the sacraments through which Christ Himself works. Although they are also for her and make her to be what she is, they are not *from* her in that the Church does not give them to herself but receives them from her Bridegroom.

It is for this reason that the Church is spoken of as a bride and as a mother. She receives the active and life-giving principle of sanctifying grace and other divine gifts from her Bridegroom through receiving the sacraments, and she participates in transmitting this life-giving grace to new children through those same sacraments that she has received.[49] In other words, the Church is pregnant with new children through the sacraments that make her fecund. Just as a mother cannot make herself pregnant, but requires a spouse, so the Church as mother cannot institute new sacraments by which she could make herself pregnant with supernatural life, but she must receive them from her Bridegroom.

St. Thomas poses the question of whether the Apostles or their successors could institute other sacraments, and he responds:

> The apostles and their successors are God's vicars in governing the Church which is built on faith and the sacraments of faith. Wherefore, just as they may not institute another Church, so neither may they deliver another faith, nor institute other sacraments: on the contrary, the Church is said to be built up with the sacraments "which flowed from the side

---

[48] Augustine, *De civitate Dei* 22.17, PL 41:779.

[49] See Ratzinger, "On the Concept of Sacrament," in *Theology of the Liturgy*, 184: "Sacraments are liturgical acts of the Church in which the Church is involved as Church, that is, in which she not only functions as an association but takes action on the basis of that which she herself has not made and in which she gives more than she herself can give: the inclusion of man in the gift that she herself receives."

of Christ while hanging on the Cross."[50]

The Church therefore cannot institute any sacraments or even fundamentally change the essential matter or form of the sacraments as instituted by Christ. The Church is not master of the sacraments, but rather she is born from them and draws her entire supernatural life from them. Nevertheless, as seen above, she has the power to modify non-essential aspects of the sacraments according to her prudential judgment.[51]

Modernist View of the Institution of the Sacraments

One of the errors of Modernism, condemned by St. Pius X in 1907, was the thesis that the sacraments were not instituted directly by Christ but were gradually instituted by the Church in the first centuries as a development of some seeds latent in the teaching of Christ. This is equivalent to holding that Jesus only implicitly instituted the sacraments. Although the Council of Trent clearly teaches the determinate institution of the sacraments by Christ, Modernists, following the views of liberal Protestant scholars in the late nineteenth century, tended to hold that this teaching was incompatible with the findings of ecclesiastical history and needed to be radically reinterpreted.[52] Alfred Loisy, the most important Catholic Modernist, held that Jesus did not intend to found an institutional church but expected the imminent birth of the eschatological kingdom of God, and for this reason He could not have intended to institute sacraments that would structure and build up a Church that He did not foresee. Nevertheless, according to Loisy, the Church that arose after His death needed a sacramental worship, which it developed from the Last Supper and Jewish elements such as "baptism, anointing with oil, and laying on of hands."[53] The decree *Lamentabili* of the Holy Office, issued in 1907,

---

[50] *ST* III, q. 64, a. 2, ad 3.

[51] See Council of Trent, Doctrine of Communion under Both Kinds and the Communion of Little Children (session 21, July 16, 1562), ch. 2 (DS, 1728).

[52] See Leeming, *Principles of Sacramental Theology*, 385–91; Miralles, *I sacramenti cristiani*, 146–47; L. Allevi, "I misteri pagani e i sacramenti cristiani," in *Problemi e orientamenti di teologia dommatica*, ed. Pontificia Facoltà Teologica di Milano (Milan: C. Marzorati, 1957), 2:751–74.

[53] Alfred Loisy, *The Gospel and the Church*, trans. Christopher Home (New York:

condemned various errors of the Modernists regarding the institution of the sacraments. Three condemned propositions concern the sacraments in general:

> 39. The opinions on the origin of the sacraments with which the Fathers of Trent were imbued and that no doubt influenced their dogmatic canons are far different from those that now rightly prevail among historians of Christianity.

> 40. The sacraments had their origin in the fact that the apostles and their successors, swayed and moved by circumstances and events, interpreted some idea and intention of Christ.

> 41. The sacraments are intended merely to recall to man's mind the ever-beneficent presence of the Creator.[54]

Rahner's Theory on the Implicit Institution of the Sacraments by Christ

In *The Church and the Sacraments*, Karl Rahner defends the thesis that it is possible that Christ instituted the sacraments only in an *implicit* way through instituting the Church as the universal sacrament of God's victorious grace. He writes: "The institution of a sacrament can (it is not necessarily implied that it must always) follow simply from

---

Charles Scribner's Sons, 1909), 230–31: "The gospel, as such, was only a religious movement within the bosom of Judaism, an attempt to realize perfectly its principles and hopes. It would therefore be inconceivable that Jesus should have formulated a ritual before His final hour. He could only have begun to think of it at that supreme moment. . . . The supper of the Eucharist, then, stands out as the symbol of the kingdom, that the sacrifice of Jesus is to bring, . . . rather than the institution of a new ritual, as the thought of Jesus was bent, as always, on the idea of realizing the kingdom of Heaven rather than the direct idea of founding a new religion and a Church. However, it was the Church that came to the world. . . . As a religion it needed a ritual, and obtained it, of such a nature as its origin permitted or compelled. At first the worship was imitated from that of the Jews, so far as concerned the external forms of prayer, and also certain important rites, such as baptism, anointing with oil, and laying on of hands."

[54] Holy Office, Decree *Lamentabili* (1907), condemned propositions 39–41 (DS, 3439–41). See also DS, 3442–51, in which propositions that deny Christ's institution of individual sacraments are condemned.

the fact that Christ founded the Church with its sacramental nature."[55] Thus he says that one can speak of Christ's "implicit institution of a sacrament in the explicit instituting of the Church as the historically visible form of eschatologically victorious grace."[56]

We have seen that it is necessary to hold that Christ Himself instituted the sacraments, at least in a generic way, albeit with a considerable degree of specification left to the Church. Rahner's thesis does not directly depart from this dogma but reinterprets the way in which we can understand this generic institution by Christ. His proposal is that the sacraments were instituted implicitly by Christ when He founded the Church as the "primal and fundamental sacrament."[57] How should we evaluate this proposal?

The key to this question is the distinction between the notions of *implicit* and *generic* institution. Something is said to be implicit when it is contained in something else that is deliberately affirmed or established, even if there is no conscious awareness of its being thus contained. Generic institution implies that something is deliberately and consciously established, even though details of its functioning are left as yet undetermined. Generic institution involves both knowledge of what is being instituted and the deliberate will to do so, even though particular aspects of the sacramental sign are left to be determined by the Church. Implicit institution, on the other hand, does not necessarily imply either determinate knowledge of what is being instituted nor the deliberate will to do so.

If by the implicit institution of the sacraments one means only that *accidental* elements of the sacramental sign were implicit and left to the Church in her historical development, whereas their essential core and specific purpose was given by Christ, then this thesis is clearly true, and is equivalent to holding a generic institution of the sacraments, as held by many scholastic theologians, and would not involve any theological innovation.

Rahner, on the other hand, does not seem to understand implicit institution to mean that Christ left important elements of the sac-

---

[55] Rahner, *The Church and the Sacraments*, 41.

[56] Rahner, *The Church and the Sacraments*, 50. Rahner's position is similar to the Modernist view condemned by *Lamentabili*, but he seeks to give a stronger foundation to it through using the principle that Christ instituted the Church as the proto-sacrament.

[57] Rahner, *The Church and the Sacraments*, 19.

ramental sign indeterminate to be further specified by the Church.[58] Rather, he is putting forth the hypothesis that Christ did not directly intend to institute the essential elements, purpose, and effects of at least some of the sacraments. This would mean that the very substance of these sacraments, and not just the determination of their outward sign, has its origin from a development in the life of the Church, not contrary to Christ's general intentions but going beyond what He was explicitly aware of or deliberately willed to establish. If implicit institution is interpreted in this second way, then this is very problematic for the various reasons given above that show the supreme fittingness of the institution of the essential elements of the sacraments by Christ Himself.[59]

First, Rahner's theory, understood in the second sense, seems to invert the proper order between the Church and her sacraments. As we have seen, the Fathers see the blood and water coming from the side of Christ as symbolizing the birth of the Church through the sacraments, represented here by Baptism and the Eucharist. The Church derives her supernatural life from her sacraments and not the other way around. The Church does not sanctify the sacraments but is born from them and is sanctified by them and cannot properly exist without all of them, even though they are not equal in importance. As seen above, St. Thomas, in answering an objection suggesting that the Apostles could have instituted sacraments, replies: "Just as they may not institute another Church, so neither may they deliver another faith, nor institute other sacraments: on the contrary, the Church is said to be built up with the sacraments."[60]

Rahner maintains the ontological priority of the Church with respect to the sacraments, which is a necessary premise in order to maintain his thesis of the implicit institution of at least some of the sacraments. He makes this clear in his *Theology of Pastoral Action*: "The Church's own nature is ontologically prior to the seven sacra-

---

[58] Such an interpretation is clearly contrary to Rahner's intention, for generic institution was defended by numerous neo-scholastic theologians in the post-Tridentine period.

[59] For a brief summary and critique of Rahner's thesis, see William Van Roo, "Reflections on Karl Rahner's *Kirche und Sakramente*," *Gregorianum* 44 (1963): 465–500, esp. 493–500; Miralles, *I sacramenti cristiani*, 151–53; Ramón Arnau-García, *Tratado general de los sacramentos* (Madrid: Biblioteca de autores cristianos, 2001), 234–50.

[60] *ST* III, q. 64, a. 1, ad 3.

ments; they are partial realizations of the Church itself."[61] It is true that the Church is ontologically prior to the sacraments in terms of finality, because the sacraments are for the sake of the Church. However, the sacraments also have an ontological priority in terms of generation or efficient causality with respect to grace, for the Church as Christ's Bride is born and built up through the sacraments.

Using the analogy of the sacraments to the seven needs of our natural life given in the preceding chapter, it can be seen by analogy that the sacraments do not *derive* from the Church (even though she administers them), but the reverse. The fulfilment of the seven needs of our natural life mentioned by St. Thomas do not derive from civil society but from God and nature, and civil society is built up from them. Without the birth, growth, and nourishment of the members, there would be no civil society at all. Similarly there would be no fitting form of civil society without means of healing, marriage, and governance. Thus as civil society is built from the satisfaction of these fundamental needs, so the supernatural society of the Church is built up through spiritual birth, a supernatural principle of growth to maturity, nourishment, healing, the sanctification of marriage, and a supernatural headship or governance. Baptism, Confirmation, and Holy Orders configure the Church into head and members. Without those sacraments she simply could not exist and be constituted.

Secondly, Rahner's thesis presupposes that Christ and His grace are already present in the Church prior to the institution of the sacraments. He puts forth a model of the sacraments according to which they "are not properly to be understood as successive individual incursions of God into a secular world, but as 'outbursts' . . . of the innermost, ever present gracious endowment of the world with God himself into history."[62] Although Christ is present to His Church in different ways, in His Word and through prayer, the most important way that Christ and His grace are intimately present to the Church

---

[61] Karl Rahner, *Theology of Pastoral Action*, trans. W. J. O'Hara (New York: Herder and Herder, 1968), 45.

[62] Karl Rahner, "On the Theology of Worship," in *Theological Investigations*, vol. 19, *Faith and Ministry*, trans. Edward Quinn (New York: Crossroad, 1983), 143. For an earlier presentation of this idea, presented as a "Copernican revolution," see Karl Rahner, "Secular Life and the Sacraments: A Copernican Revolution," *The Tablet* (Mar 6, 1971): 236–38, and (Mar 13, 1971): 267–68. On this aspect of Rahner's sacramental theology, see Vass, *The Sacrament of the Future*, 6–13.

in all times and places is through the sacraments, through which He is present as the divine Physician, the Victim of Calvary, the giver of the Spirit, and the Life of the world. Through the Eucharist alone Christ is substantially present in His humanity, whole and entire, in our midst.[63]

Third, to hypothesize that the Church could institute sacraments is to assume that the Church has a certain dominion over grace and over the giving of the Holy Spirit. For the sacraments are sacred signs that confer grace and the indwelling of the Trinity. To institute a sacrament, therefore, is to institute a stable way in which grace is communicated throughout the life of the Church. But this can only be done by Him who has dominion over the giving of grace and of the Spirit. This is proper to Christ, as the one who is both the efficient and meritorious cause of grace and the Person from whom the Spirit proceeds. It can be seen from this that Rahner's theory on the relationship between the Church and the sacraments also presupposes a view of sacramental causality very different from that of St. Thomas Aquinas.[64] As will be seen in chapters 11–13 below, Christ's humanity acts in all the sacraments, making use of them as His separated instruments and continuations of His humanity to encounter us. For this reason, Christ Himself had to institute them and give them the power to be His instruments that He would work through.

Finally, there is a problem of Revelation. The Church comes to know supernatural mysteries only from Revelation. The seven sac-

---

[63] It is not because Christ is substantially present in the Church that He becomes present in the sacrament of the Eucharist as a kind of consequence, but rather the reverse. On Christ's substantial presence in the Eucharist, see Paul VI, Encyclical On the Holy Eucharist *Mysterium Fidei* (Sept 3, 1965), §39. After speaking in §§35–38 of Christ's presence in the Church in multiple ways, in §39 he speaks of the unique way that He is present to the Church in the Eucharist: "This presence is called 'real' not to exclude the idea that the others are 'real' too, but rather to indicate presence par excellence, because it is substantial and through it Christ becomes present whole and entire, God and man. And so it would be wrong for anyone to try to explain this manner of presence by dreaming up a so-called 'pneumatic' nature of the glorious body of Christ that would be present everywhere; or for anyone to limit it to symbolism, as if this most sacred Sacrament were to consist in nothing more than an efficacious sign 'of the spiritual presence of Christ and of His intimate union with the faithful, the members of His Mystical Body.'"

[64] For Rahner's view of sacramental causality, see chapter 13 below, pp. 482–89.

raments are an integral part of the mystery of the Church and of her supernatural life. How did the Church come to know about her sacraments if Christ did not reveal to the Apostles that the Church was to do a particular rite with a fixed nucleus through which grace would be given for a specific purpose? According to the theory of implicit institution, the revelation would not go from Christ to the Church, but the Church would come to know them from coming to know and manifest her own life. It is true that the Church knows what is of ecclesiastical law from knowing her own historical life. But what is of divine law and the foundation of her own life she must both learn and receive from the Lord.[65]

---

[65] See Van Roo, "Reflections on Rahner's *Kirche und Sakramente*," 494–95: "Why did the Church begin to perform these functions [the seven sacraments]? Because Christ told her to. The essence of the Church, and the essential functions of the Church, are known to her by revelation. It would be a misconception of revelation or of the essence of the Church or of both to suppose that just part of the essential functions of the Church had to be revealed, and that, knowing her own essence, she would just spontaneously perform all of her essential actions, as the tree flowers and puts forth fruit, and man begins to reason. The seven sacraments of the New Law are part of Christ's revelation, and the Apostles had to be given some sign, even though obscure, that they were to exercise these functions. . . . He did not have to specify the details of the rite in all cases, though He did determine some details of the rites of some sacraments. But He did have to indicate a distinct effect of grace to be signified and produced, and He did have to indicate that it was to be signified and produced by a suitable rite. This is the minimum dogmatic notion of institution involved in the defined truth itself." See also Cornelius Ernst, "Acts of Christ: Signs of Faith," in *Sacraments: The Gestures of Christ*, ed. O'Callaghan, 56–75, at 74: "It seems extremely odd that when we already have a *de fide* principle of interpretation of the scriptural texts, namely that Jesus instituted the seven sacraments, we should have recourse to yet another principle, not yet, at any rate, defined authoritatively by the Church [Rahner's theory of the Church as the primordial sacrament], in order to interpret the *de fide* principle and the scriptural texts. Thus while entirely (and gratefully) granting Father Rahner's case for maintaining that historically Jesus only instituted most of the sacraments *in genere tantum*, it would seem sufficient to say that the *a priori* principle which governed the increasing insight of the Church into the nature of the sacraments was precisely the principle that Jesus instituted them: that is to say, that in those pregnant engagements of her faith which we call the sacraments, the Church became increasingly aware that she was both doing and encountering Jesus's human will as the human expression of the *mysterion* of God's eternal saving will."

Study Questions

1. (a) What does the Council of Trent teach about Christ's institution of the sacraments? (b) Is it necessary to hold that Jesus instituted the sacraments by personally specifying all the elements of their matter and form now required for validity? (c) Explain the difference between specific and generic institution of the sacraments by Christ.
2. Does the New Testament manifest the teaching of Trent on the institution of the seven sacraments by Jesus? Explain.
3. Why should we hold that Christ personally instituted the sacraments? Give various reasons of fittingness.
4. (a) Can the Church institute new sacraments or essentially modify the sacraments? Explain the limits of the Church's power over the sacraments. (b) What is the difference between what pertains to divine law and what is of ecclesiastical law with regard to the sacraments? What does the Council of Trent imply about this question?
5. Can an aspect of a sacramental celebration that belongs only to ecclesiastical law be sometimes required by the Church for the valid celebration of a sacrament? (b) Explain the difference between belonging to the *substance or essence of the sacrament itself* and pertaining to the valid celebration of a rite at a given time.
6. Does the Church make the sacraments, or do the sacraments make the Church? Explain.
7. Explain Karl Rahner's theory about Christ's institution of the sacraments and evaluate it. How does it differ from holding that Christ instituted the sacraments in a generic as opposed to specific way?

Suggestions for Further Reading

ST III, q. 64, aa. 2–4.

Leeming, Bernard. *Principles of Sacramental Theology*. Westminster, MD: Newman Press, 1963. Pp. 385–431.

Miralles, Antonio. *I sacramenti cristiani: trattato generale*. 2nd edition. Rome: Apollinare studi, 2008. Pp. 145–64.

Nutt, Roger. General Principles of Sacramental Theology. Washington, DC: Catholic University of America Press, 2017. Pp. 175–183.

Pius XII. Apostolic Constitution, *Sacramentum Ordinis*. November 30, 1947.

Rahner, Karl. *The Church and the Sacraments*. 3rd edition. Translated by W. J. O'Hara. New York: Herder and Herder, 1963.

Van Roo, Gulielmo (William). *De Sacramentis in genere*. Rome: Apud Aedes Universitatis Gregorianae, 1957. Pp. 95–128.

_____. "Reflections on Karl Rahner's *Kirche und Sakramente*." *Gregorianum* 44 (1963): 465–500.

PART TWO

THE OUTWARD
SACRAMENTAL SIGN

CHAPTER FIVE

Matter and Form
of the Sacraments

The sacraments, according to St. Augustine's famous definition, are "sacred signs." Although their sanctifying power transcends their nature as signs, this power is intimately connected to their symbolism because the sacraments are efficacious signs that cause precisely what they signify. The words and signs are endowed with divine power because they are words and signs of Christ that are obeyed by creation. For this reason, the sanctifying power of the sacraments does not devalue their symbolic nature,[1] but presupposes it, elevates it, and gives it supernatural efficacy. The symbolic aspect of the sacraments has a certain logical primacy because the sacraments must first be endowed with meaning before they can be words or signs of power. The most humble aspect of the sacraments is the outward sign, but it is the foundation on which their power to communicate grace is based.

The sign value of the sacraments draws on three fundamental sources: creation and general human culture, the history of Israel and particularly the Exodus, and the Paschal mystery of Christ. The sacramental signs make reference to these three sources to represent the invisible grace that they confer.

---

[1] Karl Rahner criticizes theories of sacramental causality (such as the Thomist account) that stress the efficient causality of the sacraments because he thinks that it devalues their symbolic aspect. See Rahner, *The Church and the Sacraments*, 36: "In all these theories it is noteworthy that the fact that the sacraments are signs plays no part in explaining their causality. Their function as signs and their function as causes are juxtaposed without connection."

133

Four Components of the Sacramental Sign: Matter and Form, Minister and Subject

The outward sacramental sign involves four essential components. The sacramental sign is composed of (a) sensible elements and/or gestures and (b) a formula of words that further determines the meaning of the sensible elements. Theologians refer to these two aspects of the outward sign as the matter and form of the sacrament, by analogy with the hylomorphic composition of bodies. As the form determines the indeterminate matter of physical bodies and makes a thing to be what it is, so likewise in the sacraments the formula of words gives a particular meaning to the material elements or gesture.

In addition to the matter and form, there are two other visible elements that have an important sign value. These are the minister who uses the sign and pronounces the sacramental form, representing Christ,[2] and the subject who receives the sacrament. Thus the sacramental sign, understood in this broad sense, has four essential sensible components: matter, form, minister, and subject. The sensible conjunction of the matter and form, together with the proper minister and subject, realizes the visible sacramental sign.

In addition to these four essential components, the sacraments are clothed in rich liturgical prayers and gestures that embellish the sacrament and make its meaning clearer, more expressive, solemn, and memorable, but do not belong to its essential nucleus instituted by Christ. Thus they are mutable and develop organically throughout the life of the Church. In this chapter we shall examine the sacramental sign in its nucleus of matter and form, and in the following chapter treat of the subject and minister.

---

[2] See *CCT*, part 2, intro., §24, pp. 157–58: "Although God himself is the source and principal minister of the sacraments, he willed to confer them in his Church through instruments—instruments who would be, not angels, but men (see 1 Cor 4:1; Heb 5:1). In line with the constant tradition of the Church, having an official minister for the sacraments is no less necessary for their coming into being than are the matter and the form of the sacraments themselves."

"MATTER" AND "FORM" APPLIED
TO THE SACRAMENTS

The matter of the sacraments includes material elements and sensible gestures. Material elements include such things as bread, wine, water, and oil. The sensible gestures include pouring or immersing in water, anointing with oil, and the imposition of hands. The form is given by words that make explicit the meaning of the sensible elements and gestures according to the faith of the Church.

The classical expression of this understanding of matter and form as potency and act in the sacraments comes from St. Augustine, who, speaking of Baptism, says:

> Take away the word, and what is the water except water? The word is added to the elemental substance, and it becomes a sacrament, also itself, as it were, a visible word. . . . Whence is this power of water of such magnitude that it touches the body and yet washes clean the heart, except from the word's effecting it, not because it is said, but because it is believed?[3]

An example of this distinction of matter and form is implied by St. Paul in Ephesians 5:26 when he says that Christ gave Himself up for the Church, His bride, "that he might sanctify her, having cleansed her by the washing of water with the word." The washing of water is the matter of the sacrament, and the form is the word. This word would be the baptismal formula in the name of the Trinity given by Christ in Matthew 28:19. This idea is also present in St. Irenaeus, who speaks of the Eucharist being made when "the mingled cup and the manufactured bread receives the Word of God."[4] The bread and wine are the matter, and the Word of God refers to the prayer of consecration (institution narrative), which is the form.

The distinction of matter and form is evident in five sacraments, but is less clear in the sacraments of Matrimony and Penance, in which there is no external physical element or gesture that functions as the matter.[5] In place of sensible matter in these two sacraments we

---

[3]   Augustine, Tractate 80.3.1–2 on John 15.3, in *Tractates on the Gospel of John 55–111*, 117.

[4]   St. Irenaeus, *Against Heresies* 5.2.3, in *ANF* 1:528.

[5]   For the development of this doctrine on the composition of matter and form

find human spiritual actions—marital consent and repentance—and their sensible expression through words. St. Thomas explains this by making an analogy to two kinds of remedies that a doctor might prescribe. Some remedies are material elements applied to the patient by a doctor, such as a pill, ointment, bandage, surgery, or a special diet. Other remedies are acts of the patient himself, such as various kinds of exercise. Five of the sacraments make use of an exterior matter that is applied to or received by the recipient, as water is applied in Baptism and oil in Confirmation and Anointing of the Sick, or the laying on of hands in ordination and Confirmation. But Matrimony and Penance are sacraments of the second type that make use of the human acts of the recipient to be its matter, for in these two cases Christ has elevated a pre-existing human reality—marriage and the virtue of penance—to the dignity of a sacrament.[6]

This distinction between matter and form is taught by the Council of Florence in the Bull *Exsultate Deo* (1439), which also mentions the proper minister as a third component: "All these sacraments are accomplished by three elements: namely, by things as the matter, by words as the form, and by the person of the minister who confers the sacrament with the intention of doing what the Church does. If any of these is absent the sacrament is not accomplished."[7]

---

in the sacraments, see P. Pourrat, *Theology of the Sacraments: A Study in Positive Theology* (St. Louis, MO: B. Herder, 1910), 51–92.

[6] See Thomas Aquinas, *In IV Sent.*, d. 14, q. 1, a. 1, qla. 1, ad 1, trans. Mortensen, 8:9–10: "Among bodily medicines, some consist in the patient's only enduring or receiving something, like surgery on a wound or the application of a bandage, while others consist in the patient's active exertion, like exercises and things like that. In just the same way, among the sacraments some do not require any act from the one who is sanctified for the sacrament's substance, except incidentally, like removing anything that prevents it, as is seen in baptism and confirmation and the others like them. But some sacraments do require the act of the one who receives the sacrament, essentially and per se, for the essence of the sacrament, as is seen in penance and marriage. Therefore, in those sacraments that are completed without our act, it is the matter that causes and signifies, like a medicine applied from without. But among those sacraments that require our act, there is no matter of this kind, but the acts themselves appearing outwardly do here what the matter does in the other sacraments. Now, how those things that are outwardly performed are the cause of sanctification in penance will be clear from what follows. To be sure, in this definition 'material element' must be taken in a general way for the sensible cause, whether it is a certain corporeal matter, or a certain sensible act."

[7] Council of Florence, *Exsultate Deo* (DS, 1312). In addition to the matter, form,

The *Catechism of the Council of Trent* gives a good explanation of the matter and form of the sacraments:

> Actually, there are two things which, in combination, make up every sacrament. The first has the nature of matter and is called the "element." The second has the nature of form and is commonly called the "word." This language we have inherited from tradition, and the famous dictum of St. Augustine summarizes it well: "The word comes to the element, and it becomes a sacrament." By a "thing sensed," therefore, the Fathers understood not only the matter or element, such as water in Baptism, chrism in Confirmation, and oil in the anointing of the Sick—all of which fall under the eye—but also the words which constitute the form, and which are addressed to the ears. . . . These, then, are the parts which belong to the nature and substance of the sacraments, and of which every sacrament is necessarily composed.[8]

The *Catechism of the Council of Trent* also explains that the words of the form are necessary to properly determine the meaning of the sign, which would be ambiguous if the sacraments were only composed of elements without a particular form of words:

> Of all signs, words are evidently the most significant. Without them it would be very difficult to know just what the matter of the sacrament was supposed to designate. For instance, water can be used to cool as well as to cleanse; it can therefore signify either of these things. If in Baptism no words were added, one could only guess . . . as to what was signified. But when the words are added, we immediately recognize that Baptism possesses and signifies the power of cleansing. . . . The verbal form is so important that its omission—even if accidental—renders the sacrament null.[9]

---

and proper minister with the intention of realizing the sacrament, there must also be a proper subject who, if of the age of reason, intends to receive the sacrament.

[8]   *CCT*, part 2, intro., §15, 153–54.
[9]   *CCT*, part 2, intro., §16, 154.

Leo XIII made use of this principle in explaining his declaration of the nullity of the Anglican sacrament of Orders:

> In the rite of confecting and administering any sacrament, one rightly distinguishes between the ceremonial part and the essential part, usually called matter and form. All know that the sacraments of the New Law, inasmuch as they are sensible and efficacious signs of invisible grace, must both signify the grace that they effect and effect the grace that they signify. Even if this signification must be found in the whole essential rite, namely, in the matter and form, nevertheless, it pertains in a special way to the form, since the matter is the part not determined by itself but determined by the form. And this appears even more clearly in the sacrament of orders, the matter of which, as far as it can be considered in this case, is the imposition of hands, which, indeed, by itself signifies nothing definite, and it is used equally for certain orders and also for confirmation.[10]

Theologians further distinguish the matter of the sacraments into proximate and remote. The remote matter is the material element in itself, as in the water of Baptism, and the proximate matter is the use that is made of it, as in the action of washing or immersion of the subject by the minister, or in the act of confessing sins by the penitent, or the laying on of hands. The form is the formula of prayer that is applied to the proximate matter.

SYMBOLISM OF THE MATTER OF THE SACRAMENTS

Since the sacraments are sacred signs that communicate the grace that they represent, it is obvious that their symbolism is crucial and rich. They are not mere conventional signs (like a stop sign), but natural and historical signs, elevated by Christ, that signify by their very nature and through salvation history.[11] A first dimension of the symbolism of the

---

[10] Leo XIII, *Apostolicae Curae*, §24 (DS, 3315).

[11] See the Sacred Congregation for the Doctrine of the Faith, Declaration on the Question of Admission of Women to the Ministerial Priesthood, *Inter*

sacramental sign comes from creation. Water naturally washes and is associated with life and death. Bread and wine nourish. Oil comforts, heals, and beautifies. The laying on of hands is a natural expression of the transferring of power and gifts from one person to another.

The sacramental signs also have three other levels of signification tied to the history of salvation. We have seen above that the sacraments are complex signs that refer back to the past event of Christ's Paschal mystery and to the Jewish rites and events that prefigured it. They also signify our present reception of grace and sanctification and our future glorification. The sacramental signs signify all three of these temporal dimensions.

The symbolism of the sacraments makes use of a particular kind of analogy, sometimes referred to by philosophers as the "analogy of proportionality," in which the similarity lies between two relations. As A is to B, so A1 is to B1. For example, as natural washing with water (A) brings about physical cleansing (B), so baptismal washing (A1) brings about spiritual cleansing (B1). Or, as Jesus explained to Nicodemus, as natural birth is the entrance into natural life, so Baptism in water and the Spirit is the entrance into the divine life of Christ. With regard to the Eucharist, as bread and wine (A) are to physical nourishment (B), so the Eucharist (A1) is to spiritual nourishment (B1).[12] Jesus made this comparison in John 6, in which He contrasted the manna that nourished the physical life of the Israelites wandering in the desert with the Eucharist that nourishes with spiritual and divine life those who wander in the desert of this earthly life.

We have seen that St. Thomas used this kind of analogy in giving an argument of fittingness for the seven sacraments, in that he established a correspondence between the fundamental needs of our natural

---

Insigniores (1976), §4: "Moreover, it must not be forgotten that the sacramental signs are not conventional ones. Not only is it true that, in many respects, they are natural signs because they respond to the deep symbolism of actions and things, but they are more than this: they are principally meant to link the person of every period to the supreme Event of the history of salvation, in order to enable that person to understand, through all the Bible's wealth of pedagogy and symbolism, what grace they signify and produce."

[12] See Thomas Aquinas, *In IV Sent.*, d. 1, q. 1, a. 1, qla. 5, ad 3, trans. Mortensen, 7:14: "Between corporeal and spiritual things we do not look for a likeness by participation in the same quality, but for a likeness by proportion, which is a likeness of proportionate things; for example, just as water is for removing corporeal stains, so grace is for cleansing spiritual ones. According to this mode of likeness, even corporeal things are applied to spiritual things."

life with those of our supernatural life. The foundation of this kind of analogy is the relation between the natural and the supernatural orders. The sacraments serve as bridges between the two orders. Their symbolism comes from the natural order of creation, which represents the sanctification worked by Christ in granting us a share in His divine life. The natural qualities of the sacraments thus represent and cause the supernatural reality that can only be known and represented to us by analogy through their natural symbolism.[13]

Complex Symbolism of the Baptismal Immersion

The matter for Baptism is the washing with water, which can be done by immersion or by pouring, although immersion provides a more adequate representation. The physical washing with water is a natural symbol of spiritual washing from sin. As water washes the body, so the water of Baptism washes the repentant soul clean from the stains of sin, original or personal.

The symbolism of washing also was prefigured in the Jewish precept concerning ceremonial washing from ritual impurity. Baptism or ritual immersion (*tevilah*) in a ritual bath (*mikveh*) is part of the Mosaic Law,[14] and was prescribed for obtaining ritual purity after contact with something ritually unclean, and particularly for entering the Temple.[15] Archeologists have found numerous ritual immersion pools in ancient Israel as well as in the Diaspora.[16] They were generally about six or seven feet deep, with one stair for descending and another for ascending to mark that one goes down impure and comes up pure.[17]

A second aspect of the symbolism of the baptismal immersion is to represent death and resurrection, bringing about a participation in Christ's Paschal mystery, as St. Paul explains in Romans 6:3–11. The entrance into the water signifies death, and rising out of the water signifies new and supernatural life modeled on Christ's Resurrection.

---

[13] See Bertrand-Marie Perrin, *L'institution des Sacrements dans le Commentaire des Sentences de Saint Thomas* (Paris: Parole et silence, 2008), 86–89.

[14] Num 19:11–22 and Lev 15:1–33 summarize the laws of ritual cleansing.

[15] See Everett Ferguson, *Baptism in the Early Church: History, Theology, and Liturgy in the First Five Centuries* (Grand Rapids, MI: William B. Eerdmans, 2009), 60–82; E. P. Sanders, *Judaism: Practice and Belief 63BCE–66CE* (London: SCM Press, 1992), 222–30.

[16] See Sanders, *Judaism: Practice and Belief*, 223–29.

[17] See Sanders, *Judaism: Practice and Belief*, 224–25.

This second meaning of baptismal immersion was also implicit in the Jewish *tevilah*. Converts to Judaism around the time of Jesus were required to be baptized or immersed in the ritual bath[18] that was also understood to symbolize death and rebirth. Male converts have to be circumcised as well as immersed in the ritual bath,[19] whereas female proselytes only have the latter obligation. The proselyte who is washed in the *mikveh* is considered to be "in the status of a new born child."[20]

The water of Baptism is prefigured by various events in the Old Testament, such as the Flood, the crossing of the Red Sea, and the crossing of the Jordan River. These figures in salvation history are solemnly recalled in the blessing of the water for baptism at the Easter vigil liturgy:

> O God, whose Spirit in the first moments of the world's creation hovered over the waters, so that the very substance of water would even then take to itself the power to sanctify; O God, who by the outpouring of the flood foreshadowed regeneration, so that from the mystery of one and the same element of water would come an end to vice and a beginning of virtue; O God, who caused the children of Abraham to pass dry-shod through the Red Sea, so that the chosen people, set free from slavery to Pharaoh, would prefigure the people of the baptized. . .[21]

---

[18] The Babylonian Talmud, tractate *Yebamot*, ch. 4, speaks of immersion as essential to the rite of conversion, and as a long-received tradition. For a description of the rite of immersion for the proselyte, see Yebamot, ch. 4, 47a–b, in Jacob Neusner, ed., *The Babylonian Talmud: A Translation and Commentary* (Peabody, MA: Hendrickson Publishers, 2011), 8:241–42. See Gavin, *Jewish Antecedents of the Christian Sacraments*, 26–58. For a cautious approach to the dating of the origin of this Jewish practice, see Ferguson, *Baptism in the Early Church*, 76–79.

[19] See Babylonian Talmud, tractate *Yebamot*, ch. 4, in Neusner, 8:235: "A person is not deemed a proselyte until he is circumcised and immersed, and if he has not immersed, he remains a gentile."

[20] Babylonian Talmud, tractate Yebamot, ch. 2.4, V.13 D, trans. Neusner, 8:106. See also Yebamot 48b: R. Yosi rules that when "a convert is immersed [in a mikveh] he is comparable to a newborn child." See Rabbi J. Simcha Cohen, *Intermarriage and Conversion: A Halakhic Solution* (Hoboken, NJ: Ktav Publishing House, 1987), 67.

[21] *The Roman Missal*, 3rd typ. ed. (Washington, DC: United States Conference of Catholic Bishops, 2011), 377.

The cleansing signified by Baptism does not yet have its entire effect, and thus the waters of Baptism also prefigure the future state of glory in which we shall be rendered wholly immaculate and free from all the consequences of original sin, such as death, suffering, and concupiscence, that still plague us here on earth.[22] The triple immersion represents the Trinitarian life to which Baptism orders us and which will be the substance of the life of heaven.

Confirmation/Chrismation

The matter for Confirmation is a complex sign involving the laying on of the hand, anointing the forehead with chrism (olive oil with balsam), and tracing the sign of the cross. On the level of creation, olive oil is a sign of healing, beauty, strengthening, and combat, all of which are pertinent to the spiritual effect of the sacrament. The balsam gives to the chrism a perfumed smell, indicating that the recipient has received the "sweet odor of Christ." St. John Chrysostom explains the symbolism of the mixture of olive oil and balsam: "The unguent is for the bride, the oil is for the athlete."[23]

The rich meanings of anointing, especially in the sense of rendering beautiful, is given by a second-century Apologist, Theophilus of Antioch, in a work written to defend the Christian faith against the accusations of pagans:

And about your laughing at me and calling me "Christian," you know not what you are saying. First, because that which is anointed is sweet and serviceable, and far from contemptible. For ... what man, when he enters into this life or into the gymnasium, is not anointed with oil? And what work has either ornament or beauty unless it be anointed and burnished? Then the air and all that is under heaven is in a certain sort anointed by light and spirit; and are you unwilling to be anointed with the oil of God? Wherefore we are called Christians on this

---

[22] See *ST* III, q. 69, a. 3: "Baptism has the power to take away the penalties of the present life yet it does not take them away during the present life, but by its power they will be taken away from the just in the resurrection."

[23] John Chrysostom, Baptismal Instruction, translation in Whitaker, *Documents of the Baptismal Liturgy*, 43. This discourse is dated 388 and given in Antioch.

account, because we are anointed with the oil of God.[24]

David Lang explains the fittingness of oil for the purpose of Confirmation with regard to its natural qualities of richness and as a muscle relaxant:

> Oil has deep relevance for Confirmation. Oil signifies a certain richness or abundance, which is appropriate because Confirmation bestows a greater fullness of the gifts of the Holy Spirit. Moreover, since oil loosens or limbers the muscles and joints, a crucial state of fitness for athletes in contest and soldiers in battle, it symbolizes the readiness for spiritual combat that must mark mature Christians as soldiers of Christ (see *CCC*, §1293).[25]

The blessing of the oil in the ancient rite of Antioch beautifully expresses the spiritual meaning of chrism. As presented in the *Catechism of the Catholic Church*, §1297:

> The liturgy of Antioch expresses the epiclesis for the consecration of the sacred chrism (myron) in this way: "[Father . . . send your Holy Spirit] on us and on this oil which is before us and consecrate it, so that it may be for all who are anointed and marked with it holy myron, priestly myron, royal myron, anointing with gladness, clothing with light, a cloak of salvation, a spiritual gift, the sanctification of souls and bodies, imperishable happiness, the indelible seal, a buckler of faith, and a fearsome helmet against all the works of the adversary."

On the level of salvation history, the anointing represents our participation in Christ's anointing by the Holy Spirit, present from His conception and manifested at His Baptism when the Spirit descended on Him in the form of a dove (see Luke 3:22). Christ's anointing, and our participation in it through Confirmation, was richly prefigured by the anointing of priests, kings, and prophets in the Old Testament.[26]

---

[24] Theophilus of Antioch, Theophilus to Autolycus, in *ANF* 2:92.

[25] David Lang, *Why Matter Matters: Philosophical and Scriptural Reflections on the Sacraments* (Huntington, IN: Our Sunday Visitor, 2002), 97.

[26] See St. Cyril of Jerusalem, *Mystagogic Catecheses*, Sermon 3.6, in Yarnold,

St. Augustine, speaking of King David, highlights how the anointing at Confirmation configures us to Christ, priest and king:

> At that time, the anointing was reserved for the king and the priest; in those days only these two persons received the holy oil. In these two persons was prefigured one to come who should be both King and Priest, the one Christ holding both offices, and called the Christ by reason of His anointing. Not only has our Head, however, been anointed, but we ourselves also who are His Body.... We all share in the anointing and in Him we are all both Christ's and Christ, since in a certain way the whole Christ consists in both Head and Body.[27]

Louis Bouyer gives a good account of the Christological and pneumatological meaning of the anointing in Confirmation:

> It is a consecration of our whole being, body and soul, to be now and forever a temple, the temple of the Spirit. It means that the presence of the Spirit in us is no longer to be something accidental or transient but that he is to dwell in us permanently. This "Temple of the Spirit" is not just a picturesque figure for any kind of receptacle; it signifies, as the Fathers have it, a vessel which will take to itself forever the fragrance of the anointment. That is to say we are to be now

---

Awe-Inspiring Rites of Initiation, 84: "It is important for you to know that this anointing is foreshadowed in the Old Testament. When Moses entrusted to his brother the command of God and made him High Priest, after washing him with water he anointed him [Exod 40:12–13]. . . . Likewise when the High Priest raised Solomon to the kingship, he anointed him after washing him in the waters of Gihon [1 Kings 1:38–39]. This happened to Aaron and Solomon by way of figure, but to you not in figure but in truth, for you were truly anointed by the Holy Spirit. Christ is the beginning of your salvation, for he is truly the firstfruit while you are the whole lump. If the firstfruit is holy, clearly the holiness will pass to the whole lump." This typology is also pointed out by St. John Chrysostom in his third homily on 2 Corinthians (1:22), in *Saint Chrysostom: Homilies on the Epistles of Paul to the Corinthians NPNF*1, 12: 290–91.

27 Augustine, "Second Discourse on Psalm 26," no. 2, in *St. Augustine on the Psalms*, vol. 1, trans. Dame Scholastica Hebgin and Dame Felicitas Corrigan, ACW 29 (New York; Mahwah, NJ: Paulist Press, 1960), 261–62. See Jean-Pierre Torrell, *A Priestly People: Baptismal Priesthood and Priestly Ministry*, trans. Peter Heinegg (New York; Mahwah, NJ: Paulist Press, 2013), 49–50.

for the Spirit an animated temple of which he himself will be the soul. . . . Thus it is that we are to be anointed just like Christ the Anointed One, so that we are in actual reality associated with this royal priesthood.[28]

The laying on of hands, similarly, expresses the communication of a share in the power of the Holy Spirit, possessed fully by Christ. The gesture of laying hands on the head of another is a natural symbol of the communication of headship, authority, and the power that goes with it. Here the power is that of the Spirit who enables the recipient to give mature witness to Christ, to order created realities in His name, and participate in the task of building up His Church and offering all things to the Father.

Tracing the sign of the cross in oil on the forehead manifests the configuration of the faithful through the power of the Holy Spirit with the mystery of Christ's Passion. This also was prefigured in Ezekiel's prophetic vision of the sign of the Tau marking the foreheads of those "who sigh and groan over all the abominations" committed in Jerusalem (Ezek 9:4). The word for "mark" is *tau*, the last letter of the Hebrew alphabet (equivalent to our T), which in the ancient and middle Hebrew script was written in the form of a cross or x.[29] The theme of the marking of the elect on the forehead is taken up in the book of Revelation (7:3; 9:4; 14:1).

Our present participation in the power and indwelling of the Spirit is partial, and thus Confirmation points forward to the fullness of the anointing of the Spirit that will belong to the faithful in heavenly glory.

The Bread and Wine in the Eucharist

The matter of the Eucharist, wheat bread and wine from the grape, are apt symbols of three supernatural realities that the Eucharist makes

---

[28] Bouyer, "The Sacramental System," 51.

[29] See Tertullian, *Adversus Marcionem* 3.22, trans. Evans, 1:241: "For this same letter TAU of the Greeks, which is our T, has the appearance of the cross, which he foresaw we should have on our foreheads in the true and catholic Jerusalem. . . . And since all these are found in use with you also, the sign on the foreheads, and the sacraments of the churches, and the pureness of the sacrifices, you ought at once to break forth and affirm that it was for your Christ that the Creator's Spirit prophesied."

present: spiritual nourishment, Christ's sacrifice on Calvary in which His blood was separated from His body, and the communion of the Church which the Eucharist nourishes.[30]

Bread and wine, as universal forms of food and drink, naturally represent all nourishment.[31] Wheat bread as the "staff of life" was fittingly chosen by Christ to be the means to give us a participation in His divine Life. Wine, which "gladdens the heart of man" (Ps 104:15), also fittingly represents the spiritual intoxication given by the sharing in the divine life through Holy Communion.

Secondly, bread and wine have a fitting appearance to represent Christ's body and blood. By being separately consecrated, they represent the actual physical separation of Christ's body and blood, as the latter was poured out in His Passion.[32] The matter of the Eucharist was thus chosen not only for its natural symbolism of nourishment but also to represent the central event of salvation history. For this reason it is never permissible, "even in extreme urgent necessity, to consecrate one matter without the other."[33] The dual consecration of bread and wine into Christ's Body and Blood is necessary to realize the sacramental sign of Christ's sacrifice.

In addition, the bread and wine of the Eucharistic species are prefigured in a great variety of ways by the sacrificial and cultic use of bread and wine in the Old Covenant, such as in the Passover, the bread of the presence, other sacrifices of bread and wine, and the manna in the wilderness.[34]

The choice of bread and wine as matter for the Eucharist also

---

[30] For a fuller treatment of the symbolism of the bread and wine in the Eucharist, see Feingold, *The Eucharist*, 192–98.

[31] See *ST* III, q. 74, a. 1: "The reasonableness of this is seen first, in the use of this sacrament, which is eating: for, as water is used in the sacrament of Baptism for the purpose of spiritual cleansing, since bodily cleansing is commonly done with water; so bread and wine, wherewith men are commonly fed, are employed in this sacrament for the use of spiritual eating."

[32] *ST* III, q. 74, a. 1; Pius XII, *Mediator Dei*, §70: "The eucharistic species under which He is present symbolize the actual separation of His body and blood. Thus the commemorative representation of His death, which actually took place on Calvary, is repeated in every sacrifice of the altar, seeing that Jesus Christ is symbolically shown by separate symbols to be in a state of victimhood."

[33] CIC, can. 927.

[34] See Feingold, *The Eucharist*, 39–69; Brant Pitre, *Jesus and the Jewish Roots of the Eucharist: Unlocking the Secrets of the Last Supper* (New York: Doubleday Religion, 2011).

symbolizes the ecclesial effect of the Eucharist. Both bread and wine involve many individual grains and grapes being made into one loaf or drink. This symbolizes the ultimate effect of the Eucharist, which is the unity of the Church composed of many members that are bound together in charity in the communion of one Body. St. Augustine expresses this ecclesial symbolism of the Eucharistic elements:

> For it [the Eucharist] makes those by whom it is taken immortal and incorruptible, that is, the very society of saints, where there will be peace and full and perfect unity. For this reason . . . our Lord, Jesus Christ, manifested his body and blood in those things which are reduced from many to some one thing. For the one is made into one thing from many grains, the other flows together into one thing from many grapes.[35]

This sense is indicated by St. Paul in 1 Corinthians 10:17: "Because there is one bread, we who are many are one body, for we all partake of the one bread."[36] As Augustine indicates, this communion signified by bread and wine also prefigures the heavenly communion of the Church triumphant in which union with God and other human beings will be made perfect.

Why Oil for Anointing of the Sick?

The matter of the sacrament of Anointing is, as defined by the Council of Trent, "oil blessed by the bishop, because the anointing very aptly represents the grace of the Holy Spirit with which the soul of the sick is invisibly anointed."[37] The oil is preferably olive oil, but when this cannot be easily obtained, any vegetable oil can be used. The oil is ordinarily blessed at the Chrism Mass. In an emergency when oil

---

[35] Augustine, Tractate 26.17 on John 6:56, in *Tractates on the Gospel of John 11–27*, trans. J. W. Rettig, FC 79 (Washington, DC: Catholic University of America Press, 1988), 274, quoted in Emery, "The Ecclesial Fruit of the Eucharist," 44–45.

[36] See *ST* III, q. 74, a. 1: "Bread and wine are the proper matter of this sacrament. . . . Fourthly, as to the effect with regard to the whole Church, which is made up of many believers, just 'as bread is composed of many grains, and wine flows from many grapes,' as the gloss observes on 1 Cor. 10:17."

[37] Council of Trent, Doctrine on the Sacrament of Extreme Unction (session 14), ch. 1 (DS, 1695).

blessed by the bishop cannot be obtained, canon 999, §2 of the *Code of Canon Law* states that the priest himself may perform the blessing according to the liturgical rite, but only during the actual celebration of the sacrament.

The fittingness of olive oil for this sacrament comes from its medicinal qualities, because of which it is used in many cultures both for healing and consolation. The anointing is reminiscent of the gesture of the Good Samaritan in Luke 10:34, who poured oil on the wounds of the man left half dead. The *Catechism of the Catholic Church*, §1293 explains that "oil is a sign of healing, since it is soothing to bruises and wounds;[38] and it makes radiant with beauty, health, and strength." David Lang writes:

> It is appropriate for the seriously ill to be spiritually treated with a substance that represents healing of the sores of sin, soothing of its residual abrasions, comforting in bitter sorrow, imparting a pure glow of grace to the soul, endowing with flexible strength to resist diabolical onslaught in the final combat, and promising the overflowing happiness of eternal life.[39]

The application of the matter has been simplified in the Latin rite by St. Paul VI in his Apostolic Constitution *Sacram Unctionem Infirmorum* of 1972. The number of anointings is now two: one on the forehead and the other on the hands. It is appropriate to say the first part of the form while anointing the forehead and the second part while anointing the hands.[40]

Laying on of Hands in Ordination

In the sacrament of Holy Orders, the matter for all three grades is the laying on of hands on the head of the candidate by the bishop (CIC, can. 1009, §2). This is a natural sign of the transmission of headship,

---

[38] Cf. Isa 1:6; Lk 10:34.

[39] Lang, *Why Matter Matters*, 125–26.

[40] See *Pastoral Care of the Sick: Rites of Anointing and Viaticum*, §23, in *Rites*, 1:783. In a case of necessity, only one anointing is necessary for validity, preferably on the forehead (CIC, can. 1000). The anointing is ordinarily done with the right thumb of the priest, but an instrument could be used in case of necessity (CIC, can. 1000, §2).

and it was used in the Old Covenant where we see Moses laying his hands on Joshua to pass on leadership over Israel and a spirit of wisdom for that mission.[41] The laying on of hands was also used in rabbinical ordination at least in the first centuries after Christ.[42] Because it denotes a transmission of headship, the laying on of hands occurs on the head and not on another part of the body. This sign is mentioned in Acts 13:3 when Paul and Barnabas receive the laying on of hands before being sent out on their first missionary voyage. St. Paul likewise speaks of the communication of a gift of grace to Timothy through the laying on of hands, by himself (2 Tim 1:6) and by the council of presbyters (1 Tim 4:14).

Pius XII defined the essential matter and form of Holy Orders in his Apostolic Constitution *Sacramentum Ordinis* of 1947:

> Everyone knows, however, that the sacraments of the New Law, as sensible and efficient signs of invisible grace, owe and signify the grace that they effect and effect the grace that they signify. Now, the effects that should be produced and thus signified by the sacred ordination of the diaconate, presbyterate, and episcopate, namely, power and grace, are found to have been sufficiently signified in all the rites of the universal Church of different times and regions by the imposition of hands and by the words that determine this.[43]

Pius XII then clarifies which imposition of hands is the essential matter: "In the ordination of priests, the matter is the first imposition of the bishop's hands, which is done in silence."[44] He also clarified that the "handing over of the instruments" (*traditio instrumentorum*),

---

[41] See Num 27:20–23; Deut 34:9: "Joshua the son of Nun was full of the spirit of wisdom, for Moses had laid his hands upon him."

[42] See J. Ysebaert, *Greek Baptismal Terminology: Its Origins and Early Development* (Nijmegen: Dekker & Van de Vegt, 1962), 231: "In rabbinic literature the leaning on of hands is mentioned as the principal rite at the ordination of a rabbi and this custom is traced back to the appointment of Joshua. . . . The earliest reference would be the report from the Talmud Yerushalmi that R. Johanan b. Zakkai ordained his pupils R. Eliezer and R. Joshua, Sanh. 1.19a. This R. Johanan died around 80 AD and the ordination probably took place before 70 AD. From this it appears that the rite was known in the latter half of the first century AD. It fell into disuse in the course of the third century."

[43] Pius XII, *Sacramentum Ordinis*, §3 (DS, 3858).

[44] Pius XII, *Sacramentum Ordinis*, §5 (DS, 3860).

by which the presbyter is given the chalice and paten and the deacon is given the book of the Gospels, are *not* part of the essential matter of the sacrament of Holy Orders, despite the words of the Council of Florence which, following St. Thomas, speak of them as the matter of the sacrament.[45] The Council of Florence states: "The sixth sacrament is that of order. Its matter is that by the handing over of which order is conferred: thus the priesthood is conferred by handing over the chalice with wine and the paten with the bread; the diaconate by giving the book of the Gospels."[46]

Pius XII points out that the Council of Florence was aware that the Greek rite of ordination did not include the *traditio instrumentorum*, while still recognizing it as a valid rite of ordination. Thus the intention of the Council of Florence clearly was *not* to define that the *traditio instrumentorum* was the essential matter pertaining to the *substance* of the sacrament by divine law and being necessary always and everywhere.[47] The question is left open whether the Council of Florence understood it to be necessary for validity in the Latin rite by ecclesiastical law at that time. If so, Pius XII, in *Sacramentum Ordinis*, authoritatively declares that this is no longer the case:

> There is no one who does not know that the Roman Church always considered valid the ordinations conferred in the Greek

---

[45] The text of the Council of Florence is based on a short work by Thomas Aquinas, *De articulis fidei et Ecclesiae sacramentis*, in *Opuscula theologica*, vol. 1, *De re dogmatica et morali*, no. 626, p. 151; English translation in *God's Greatest Gifts*, 97: "The matter of Holy Orders is that matter which is handed over to the candidate at the conferring of the order. Thus, for example, priesthood is conferred by the handing over of the chalice. Likewise, each order is conferred by the handing over of that matter which in a special way pertains to the ministry of that particular order."

[46] Council of Florence, *Exsultate Deo* (DS, 1326).

[47] Some theologians hold, not without reason, that the Council of Florence did not intend to determine this question but only to put forward a common theological teaching for the instruction of the Armenians. At the Council of Trent, this question of the essential matter of Holy Orders was left undetermined as an open question. See H. Lennerz, *De Sacramento Ordinis*, 2nd ed. (Rome: Apud aedes universitatis Gregorianae, 1953), 135–37 (§§226–27). See the discussion of this point by Charles Journet, *The Church of the Word Incarnate*, 1:117–19, who holds, rightly I think, that the Council of Florence was not teaching an erroneous doctrine here but stating, unfortunately without clarification, that the handing over of the instruments was regarded as necessary matter in the Latin rite at that time, which pertains only to ecclesiastical and not to divine law.

rite, without the handing over of the instruments, so that at the Council of Florence, in which the union of the Greeks with the Church of Rome was accomplished, it was not imposed on the Greeks that they change the rite of ordination, or that they insert in it the handing over of the instruments. . . . From all this it is gathered that according to the mind of the same Council of Florence, the handing over of the instruments is not required for the substance and validity of this sacrament, according to the will of our Lord Jesus Christ himself. But if, by the will and prescription of the Church, the same [handing over of the instruments] was at some time held as necessary even for validity, all know that the Church can also change and abrogate what she has established. . . . By virtue of Our supreme apostolic authority . . . we determine and ordain: the matter of the holy orders of the diaconate, priesthood, and episcopate is the laying on of hands alone.[48]

What Is the Matter for Reconciliation?

As mentioned above, the distinction between matter and form in the sacraments is clear when use is made of some exterior material element in the sacramental sign, such as water, oil, bread and wine, and the laying on of hands. The distinction is less clear in the sacraments of Penance and Matrimony in which there is no exterior element in the sacramental sign. Medieval theologians, however, applied this distinction to these two sacraments by analogy.

In the sacrament of Reconciliation, Christ elevated the virtue of penance, with its proper acts, to be the matter of the sacrament of Penance. The virtue of penance essentially consists in interior contrition for sin, but also manifests itself in outward acts of confession and satisfaction. It is fitting, therefore, that these three acts of the virtue of penance be elevated into the matter of the sacrament. The Council of Florence, following St. Thomas Aquinas, briefly summarizes the matter and form of Penance:

> The fourth sacrament is penance. Its quasi-matter consists in the actions of the penitent, which are divided into three parts. The first of these is contrition of the heart, which requires

---

[48] Pius XII, *Sacramentum Ordinis*, §§3–4 (DS, 3858–59).

that one be sorry for the sin committed with the resolve not to sin in the future. The second is oral confession, which requires that the sinner confess to his priest in their integrity all the sins he remembers. The third is satisfaction for the sins according to the judgment of the priest, which is mainly achieved by prayer, fasting, and almsgiving. The form of this sacrament is the words of absolution which the priest pronounces when he says: "I absolve you."[49]

The matter of the sacrament of Penance is not an external element, as in Baptism, Confirmation, or Anointing, but the acts of the penitent, outwardly manifested in confession. As mentioned above, theologians sometimes divide the matter of a sacrament into remote and proximate.[50] The remote matter of the sacrament of Penance is personal post-baptismal sin. A person who has no personal sin (such as the Blessed Virgin or a person before the age of reason) cannot receive this sacrament, for there would be no matter for it. The proximate matter for Penance is comprised of three acts of the penitent with regard to sin: contrition, confession, and satisfaction. Contrition and confession presuppose a prior act of the penitent, which is an examination of conscience.

Matter and Form in Matrimony

In Matrimony, as in Penance, Christ elevated something natural that has existed from the beginning. In the case of Matrimony, Christ elevated marriage, the most fundamental social bond, into a sacred sign of His covenant with His Bride, the Church. As with Penance, there is no external matter in the sacrament of Matrimony. Instead,

---

[49] Council of Florence, *Exsultate Deo* (DS, 1323). This teaching was taken up by the Council of Trent, Doctrine on the Sacrament of Penance (session 14), ch. 3 (DS, 1673).

[50] See *ST* III, q. 84, a. 2: "Matter is twofold: proximate and remote. . . . The proximate matter of this sacrament consists in the acts of the penitent, the matter of which acts are the sins over which he grieves, which he confesses, and for which he satisfies. Hence it follows that sins are the remote matter of Penance, as a matter, not for approval, but for detestation, and destruction." See also *ST* III, q. 90, a. 1, ad 3: "Sins are the remote matter of Penance, insofar as they are the matter or object of the human acts, which are the proper matter of Penance as a sacrament."

the substance of the sacramental sign is composed of the human acts expressing consent that bring the marital covenant into being.

St. Thomas identifies the words of the spouses expressing their matrimonial consent as both the matter and the form of the sacrament. He states that "the words in which the matrimonial consent is expressed are the form of this sacrament, not the blessing of the priest, which is a kind of sacramental."[51] He also says that the matter is that same expression of marital consent: "The sacrament of Matrimony is completed by the act of the person who avails himself of this sacrament, just like penance. And thus, just as penance does not have any matter other than those sensible acts themselves which are in place of a material element, so it is with marriage."[52]

St. Thomas does not specify in what respect the words expressing interior consent are considered matter and in what sense they are considered form. The common view of theologians after the Council of Trent is that the words expressing interior consent of the spouses can be considered to be both matter and form because matrimonial consent involves two complementary aspects of giving oneself and receiving the gift of the other. The words of consent can be considered as the matter insofar as they express the mutual self-gift of the spouses, and they can be considered to be the form insofar as they express the mutual acceptance of the other's self-gift.[53] This was taught by Benedict XIV in the Constitution *Paucis abhinc* from 1758.[54] In this way the

---

[51] Thomas Aquinas, *In IV Sent.*, d. 26, q. 2, a. 1, ad 1, trans. Mortensen, 9:14.

[52] *In IV Sent.*, d. 26, q. 2, a. 1, ad 2, trans. Mortensen, 9:14. See also *ST* III, q. 84, a. 1, ad 1: "In those sacraments whose effect corresponds to that of some human act, the sensible human act itself takes the place of matter, as in the case of Penance and Matrimony, even as in bodily medicines, some are applied externally, such as plasters and drugs, while others are acts of the person who seeks to be cured, such as certain exercises."

[53] See Felix Cappello, *Tractatus Canonico-Moralis de Sacramentis*, vol. 5, *De Matrimonio*, 6th ed. (Taurini: Marietti, 1950), 27–29; Charles A. Schleck, *The Sacrament of Matrimony: A Dogmatic Study* (Milwaukee, WI: Bruce, 1964), 94–96. This view was taught by St. Robert Bellarmine, *De controversiis christianae fidei, De sacramento Matrimonii*, ch. 6, in *Opera omnia* (Paris: Vivès, 1873), 5:56–59. Suárez more clearly distinguished the active and passive aspects of marital consent as the form and matter of the sacrament in *Commentaria ac Disputationes in Tertiam Partem*, in *ST* III, q. 60, disp. 2, sectio 1, in *Opera omnia*, 20:32–33.

[54] Benedict XIV, Constitution *Paucis abhinc* (Mar 19, 1758): "The legitimate contract is both the matter and the form of the sacrament of Matrimony, for the matter is the mutual and legitimate giving of their bodies signified by words

spouses are mutually both the subjects and ministers of this sacrament to each other.[55]

SACRAMENTAL FORM

As seen above, sacramental form is composed of the words that give a more precise meaning to the gestures that make use of the sacramental matter. It is above all the sacramental form that manifests the purpose, meaning, and effects of the sacrament, for words are more precise than other signs. The actual words used in the sacramental form have varied over the centuries and in different liturgical rites, but the substantial meaning remains.

St. Thomas lays down the principle that the causality of the sacraments follows on their signification: "The aforesaid words, which work the consecration, operate sacramentally [that is, as sacred signs]. Consequently, the converting power latent under the forms of these sacraments follows the meaning, which is terminated in the uttering of the last word."[56] Since the sacraments cause what they signify, if the essential signification is fundamentally changed, the sacrament would not be valid.

The *Code of Canon Law* states: "In celebrating the sacraments the liturgical books approved by competent authority are to be observed faithfully; accordingly, no one is to add, omit, or alter anything in them on one's own authority."[57] If a minister of the sacrament on his own initiative, or an ecclesial community in schism or heresy, alters the words such that the meaning is substantially changed or a central content omitted, then the form would no longer be valid, for it would no longer signify what Jesus instituted it for. If he deliberately alters the words, but in such a way that the meaning is not changed, it will be valid but illicit. The 1962 *Missale Romanum* explained that a deliberate

---

and gestures that express the interior consent of the soul, and the form is the mutual and legitimate acceptance of their bodies" (my translation from the Latin quoted in Cappello, *De Matrimonio*, 29).

[55] See Pius XII, *Mystici Corporis Christi*, §20, where he teaches that in Matrimony, "the contracting parties are ministers of grace to each other."

[56] *ST* III, q. 78, a. 4, ad 3.

[57] CIC, can. 846, §1. See Second Vatican Council, *Sacrosanctum Concilium*, §22: "Therefore no other person, even if he be a priest, may add, remove, or change anything in the liturgy on his own authority."

change in the essential form that does not affect the meaning would be gravely illicit, but if the meaning were substantially altered, the sacrament would not be realized (and thus would be invalid).[58]

Change and Development in Sacramental Form

As seen in the previous chapter, the Church has the power to modify the form of the words as long as they continue to express this purpose and meaning of the sacrament, for the substantial meaning of the sacramental form indicating the purpose and effects of the sacrament can be expressed in many ways that differ only accidentally, and can be more or less fitting according to the needs of different times and places. For this reason there can be both development and reform in the sacramental liturgy. The Second Vatican Council, in *Sacrosanctum Concilium*, §21, states this principle with regard to reform of the liturgy:

> For the liturgy is made up of immutable elements divinely instituted, and of elements subject to change. These not only may but ought to be changed with the passage of time if they have suffered from the intrusion of anything out of harmony with the inner nature of the liturgy or have become unsuited to it.

The Form of Baptism

Christ's missionary mandate in Matthew 28:19 gives the essential form of Baptism: "Go therefore and make disciples of all nations, baptizing them in the name of the Father and of the Son and of the Holy Spirit." The Trinitarian form manifests the essential effect of Baptism, which is to introduce the baptized faithful into communion with the Triune God. The communion of the divine Persons is the archetype

---

[58] *Missale Romanum: Ex Decreto SS. Concilii Tridentini Restitutum Summorum Pontificum Cura Recognitum* (Vatican City: Typis Polyglottis Vaticanis, 1962), 1:lxvii (my translation): "If anyone leaves out or changes any part of the form of the consecration of the Body and Blood, and if the changed words do not signify the same thing, he would not realize the sacrament. But if he adds or omits something that does not change the sense, the sacrament would be realized but he would gravely sin."

for the supernatural communion of the Church[59] into which Baptism serves as the portal.

The combination of simplicity and unthinkable grandeur, which marks all of Christian Revelation, stands out especially in the form of Baptism. A short sentence works an immeasurable change of identity. From a mere creature one becomes a sharer in the divine nature, brought into the communion of Father, Son, and Holy Spirit. Being baptized in the name of the Trinity brings about a new relationship with each of the divine Persons. We are made beloved sons or daughters of the Father, in the Son, and given the "spirit of sonship" (Rom 8:15). St. Paul summarizes this new relationship in Galatians 4:6–7: "Because you are sons, God has sent the Spirit of his Son into our hearts, crying, 'Abba! Father!' So through God you are no longer a slave but a son, and if a son then an heir." This Trinitarian effect was manifested in Christ's baptism when the heavens were opened, the Spirit of God descended on Him "like a dove," and the voice of the Father was heard: "This is my beloved Son, with whom I am well pleased" (Matt 3:16–17).

An objection with regard to the Trinitarian form is given by the fact that several texts of the Acts of the Apostles speak of Baptism "in the name of Jesus"[60] rather than in the Trinitarian formula given in Matthew 28:19. It is not impossible that valid Baptism was administered by the Apostles in the first decades of the Church simply "in the name of Jesus." The *Catechism of the Council of Trent* has an interesting commentary on this question.[61] It concedes the possibility that the

---

[59] See *Gaudium et Spes*, §24: "Indeed, the Lord Jesus, when He prayed to the Father, 'that all may be one . . . as we are one' (John 17:21–22) opened up vistas closed to human reason, for He implied a certain likeness between the union of the divine Persons, and the unity of God's sons in truth and charity."

[60] Acts 2:38; 8:16; 10:48; 19:4.

[61] See *CCT*, part 2, ch. 1, §§15–16, pp. 170–71: "If the Apostles ever baptized exclusively in the one Name of our Lord Jesus Christ, they undoubtedly did so under the inspiration of the Holy Spirit. This practice would have made more manifest in the very beginning of the Church the greatness of the Name of Jesus Christ and the immensity of his divine power. As we reflect on it, we can easily enough conclude that this formula implicitly contains all that the Savior himself prescribed. For whoever says 'Jesus Christ' certainly implies the Person of the Father who anointed him, and also the Person of the Holy Spirit who was his anointing. That the apostles actually used this formula [in the name of the Lord Jesus alone] in baptizing is very doubtful, according to St. Ambrose and St. Basil. . . . They interpret the phrase 'Baptism in the Name

Apostles, through the inspiration of the Holy Spirit, initially did not use the Trinitarian formula but baptized in the name of Jesus alone to highlight the greatness of His name, in whom the other persons of the Trinity are implied.[62] Nevertheless, it seems more likely that Baptism "in the name of Jesus" was a shorthand way of describing Baptism that actually involved a Trinitarian form,[63] given the explicit reference to the Trinitarian formula in Matthew 28:19 and the universality of the Trinitarian form in all liturgical rites.

Our first extra-biblical testimony on the rite of Baptism is from the *Didache*, dated to around the end of the first century,[64] which gives the Trinitarian formula in a brief catechesis on Baptism:

> Now concerning baptism, baptize as follows: after you have reviewed all these things, baptize "in the name of the Father and of the Son and of the Holy Spirit" in running water. But if you have no running water, then baptize in some other water; and if you are not able to baptize in cold water, then do so in warm. But if you have neither, then pour water on the head three times "in the name of Father and Son and Holy Spirit."[65]

---

of Jesus Christ' as being simply a descriptive phrase, i.e., as a convenient and obvious way of distinguishing between the Baptism that came from John and the Baptism that came from Christ. We need not say, therefore, that the Apostles ever departed from the formula which was clearly the original one, viz., the one in which each of the divine Persons is distinctly named. It seems, moreover, that this is also the explanation of the Pauline phrase: 'as many of you as were baptized into Christ have put on Christ' (Gal 3:27). That is to say, they were baptized in the faith of Christ, and with no other form than what that same Christ had commanded to be used."

[62] This is the view of St. Thomas in *ST* III, q. 66, a. 6, ad 1: "It was by a special revelation from Christ that in the primitive Church the apostles baptized in the name of Christ; in order that the name of Christ, which was hateful to Jews and Gentiles, might become an object of veneration, in that the Holy Ghost was given in Baptism at the invocation of that Name."

[63] See John Damascene, *An Exact Exposition of the Orthodox Faith* 4.9, in *Writings*, trans. F. H. Chase Jr., FC 37 (Washington, DC: Catholic University of America Press, 1958), 344: "All those, however, who have not been baptized in the Holy Trinity must be baptized again. For, even though the divine Apostle says that 'we have been baptized in Christ and in his death' [Rom 6:3], he does not mean that the baptismal invocation should be made thus, but that baptism is a figure of Christ's death. . . . Therefore, being 'baptized in Christ' merely means believing in Him and being baptized."

[64] See Ferguson, *Baptism in the Early Church*, 201.

[65] *Didache* 7, in *The Apostolic Fathers: Greek Texts and English Translations*, trans.

It is interesting that the *Didache* also speaks of Baptism "into the name of the Lord" as a requirement for the Eucharist.[66] This seems to imply that "baptism into the name of the Lord" at this time was understood as a shorthand or equivalent term to denote baptism in the name of the Trinity.

In the baptismal rite contained in the *Apostolic Tradition*,[67] usually dated to the beginning of the third century, as well as that used by St. Ambrose in Milan[68] and St. Cyril of Jerusalem[69] in the later fourth century, the baptismal formula is given not in the literal way it appears in Matthew 28:19 or in the current Latin rite ("I baptize you in the name of the Father, and the Son, and the Holy Spirit") but in a credal dialogue in question and answer form about faith in the three Persons of the Trinity. The minister asked the person being baptized, "Do you believe in God the Father almighty?"[70] "Do you believe in our Lord Jesus Christ and in his cross?"[71] and "Do you believe also in the Holy Spirit?"[72] The person being baptized would answer, "I believe," after each question and was then immersed after each answer. This is still a Trinitarian formula, but it shows that the substantial nucleus for the baptismal formula is more flexible than one might have thought.

The Trinitarian formula of Baptism differs in the Eastern and Latin rite with regard to grammatical form. The Eastern rite uses a passive construction whereas the Latin rite uses an active construction, but the meaning is the same.[73] St. John Chrysostom describes

---

Michael W. Holmes, 3rd ed. (Grand Rapids, MI: Baker Books, 2007), 355.

[66] *Didache* 9.5, in Holmes, 359. See Ferguson, *Baptism in the Early Church*, 203.

[67] See Hippolytus, *On the Apostolic Tradition* 21.12–18, trans. Alistair Stewart-Sykes (Crestwood, NY: St. Vladimir's Seminary Press, 2001), 111–12.

[68] See Ambrose, *Sermons on the Sacraments* (*De sacramentis*) 2.20, in Yarnold, *The Awe-Inspiring Rites of Initiation*, 118.

[69] See Cyril of Jerusalem, *Mystagogic Catecheses*, Sermon 2.4, in Yarnold, *Awe-Inspiring Rites of Initiation*, 77–78.

[70] Ambrose, *Sermons on the Sacraments* 2.20, in Yarnold, *The Awe-Inspiring Rites of Initiation*, 118; Hippolytus, *On the Apostolic Tradition* 21.12, p. 111.

[71] Ambrose, *Sermons on the Sacraments* 2.20, in Yarnold, *The Awe-Inspiring Rites of Initiation*, 118. *On the Apostolic Tradition* 21.15 gives a longer version of this question regarding the second Person of the Trinity.

[72] Ambrose, *Sermons on the Sacraments* 2.20, in Yarnold, *The Awe-Inspiring Rites of Initiation*, 118. See the longer version of this question in *On the Apostolic Tradition* 21.17, p. 112: "Do you believe in the Holy Spirit and the holy church and the resurrection of the flesh?"

[73] See *CCC*, §1240.

the passive form in his homily to the neophytes and interprets it as emphasizing that the principal agent of Baptism is the Triune God:

> As the priest pronounced the words, *N. is baptized in the name of the Father and of the Son and of the Holy Spirit*, he plunges your head into the water and lifts it up again three times, by this sacred rite preparing you to receive the descent of the Holy Spirit. For the priest is not the only one who touches your head; Christ also touches it with his right hand. This is shown by the actual words of the one who baptizes you. He does not say, "I baptize N.," but rather, "N. is baptized." This shows that he is only the minister of the grace and merely lends his hand since he has been ordained for this by the Spirit. It is the Father, Son and Holy Spirit, the indivisible Trinity, who bring the whole rite to completion.[74]

The Form of the Eucharist

In the Eucharist the essential sacramental form was given by Jesus when He instituted it at the Last Supper, saying over the bread, "This is my body which is given for you" (Luke 22:19). And then over the chalice He said, "This chalice which is poured out for you is the new covenant in my blood" (Luke 22:20).[75] These words succinctly state what is realized by the sacrament. Christ's Body and Blood is made present as a sacrifice given and poured out for us, sealing the New Covenant which establishes communion with God and all those who enter into the covenant. This effect is complex. The immediate effect is the Real Presence of Christ's Body and Blood through transubstantiation. His Body and Blood, however, are made present as a sacrifice, as can be seen through the sacrificial connotations of Jesus's words of institution.[76] The sacrifice is offered for the same intentions for which Christ poured out His Blood on Calvary: forgiveness of sins and sealing of the New Covenant. And this sacrifice is to be received by the faithful

---

[74] John Chrysostom, Baptismal Homily 2.26, in Yarnold, *The Awe-Inspiring Rites of Initiation*, 162.

[75] For a synopsis of the four New Testament accounts of the institution narrative, see Feingold, *The Eucharist*, 83–86.

[76] See Feingold, *The Eucharist*, 106–16; Joachim Jeremias, *The Eucharistic Words of Jesus*, trans. Norman Perrin, 3rd ed. (Philadelphia: Fortress Press, 1977), 220–55; Raymond Moloney, *The Eucharist* (Collegeville: Liturgical Press, 1995), 40–46.

in Holy Communion, for we are told to "take" and "eat" (Matt 26:26) so as to be brought into unity with Christ and one another.

The Church, in her various liturgical rites, kept the substance of these words in the institution narrative (with accidental modifications) as a direct quotation pronounced by the priest in the person of Christ. This makes clear that Christ Himself is the High Priest who speaks through the lips of his ordained ministers. These words, present in almost all Eucharistic prayers, have been described as the beating heart of the Eucharistic liturgy.[77]

Various Fathers of the Church ascribe the power to convert the bread and wine into Christ's Body and Blood to the words of Christ, as words of creative power.[78] The Council of Florence, in the Decree for the Armenians, states that the essential form of the Eucharist "is the words of the Saviour with which he effected this sacrament; for the priest effects the sacrament by speaking in the person of Christ. It is by the power of these words that the substance of bread is changed into the body of Christ, and the substance of wine into his blood."[79]

These words are surrounded, however, by a rich tapestry of prayer in which the effects of the Eucharist are implored. This is especially true of the twofold epiclesis in which the Holy Spirit is asked to come down to convert the elements into Christ's Body and Blood, as well as to transform the hearts of the faithful into a worthy offering and a deeper communion.[80] As will be seen in chapter 8 below, these two

---

[77] Giraudo, "La genesi anaforica del racconto istituzionale alla luce dell'anafora di Addai e Mari: tra storia delle forme e liturgia comparata," in *The Anaphoral Genesis of the Institution Narrative in Light of the Anaphora of Addai and Mari: Acts of the International Liturgy Congress, Rome 25-26 Oct 2011* (Rome: Edizioni Orientalia Christiana, 2013), 429.

[78] See Ambrose, *Sermons on the Sacraments* (*De sacramentis*) 2.14, in Yarnold, *Awe-Inspiring Rites of Initiation*, 114–15, quoted below on p. 396; John Chrysostom, *De proditione Judae* [On the Betrayal of Judas], homily 1, trans. in Johannes Quasten, *Patrology*, vol. 3 (Westminster, MD: Newman Press, 1960), 481: "The priest is the representative when he pronounces those words, but the power and the grace are those of the Lord. 'This is my Body,' he says. This word changes the things that lie before us." See Feingold, *The Eucharist*, 201–03.

[79] Council of Florence, *Exsultate Deo* (DS, 1321).

[80] These two purposes for which the Holy Spirit is invoked are explained by the *Catechism of the Catholic Church*, §1353: "In the epiclesis, the Church asks the Father to send his Holy Spirit (or the power of his blessing) on the bread and wine, so that by his power they may become the body and blood of Jesus Christ and so that those who take part in the Eucharist may be one body and one spirit (some liturgical traditions put the epiclesis after the anamnesis)."

petitions of the epiclesis correspond to the *res et sacramentum*, which is the Real Presence of Christ, and the *res tantum*, the effect of grace of the sacrament, which is the communion of the Mystical Body.

Because the epiclesis in the Byzantine rite, with both of its petitions, comes after the institution narrative, beginning in the fourteenth and fifteenth centuries Eastern Orthodox theologians have attributed to the epiclesis the power to work the conversion of the elements.[81] In fact, we should think that transubstantiation is worked both by the words of Christ, as instrumental cause, and by the Holy Spirit working through them as the principal cause,[82] as is implied by the *Catechism of the Catholic Church*, §1353: "In the institution narrative, the power of the words and the action of Christ, and the power of the Holy Spirit, make sacramentally present under the species of bread and wine Christ's body and blood, his sacrifice offered on the cross once for all."

Although the substantial nucleus of the sacramental form was given by the words of Jesus at the Last Supper, certain modifications on the part of the Church are possible because our Gospel sources do not give only one formula but express the substance in different words, and the history of the Eucharistic liturgy shows a diversity of accents and development in the expression of the essential sacramental form. The most striking example of this is the primitive Anaphora of Addai and Mari, used by the Assyrian Church of the East, in which the Eucharistic Prayer lacks an explicit institution narrative. The Pontifical Council for Promoting Christian Unity in a document of 2001 judged that this Anaphora is a valid Eucharistic Prayer despite the absence of the institution narrative, because it is an ancient Eucharistic prayer of a church with apostolic succession, and because "the

---

[81] For a discussion of the development and nuances of the Orthodox position, see Michael Zheltov, "The Moment of Eucharistic Consecration in Byzantine Thought," in *Issues in Eucharistic Praying in East and West: Essays in Liturgical and Theological Analysis*, ed. Maxwell Johnson (Collegeville, MN: Liturgical Press, 2010), 263–306. For a detailed discussion of this controversy, see Theophilus Spacil, *Doctrina Theologiae orientis separati De SS. Eucharistia*, 2 vols. (Rome: Pont. Institutum Orientalium Studiorum, 1929), 2:6–114; S. Salaville, "Épiclèse eucharistique," in *Dictionnaire de théologie catholique*, vol. 5, ed. A. Vacant and E. Mangenot (Paris: Letouzey et Ané, 1913), 247–65. See also Ansgar Santogrossi, "Anaphoras without Institution Narrative: Historical and Dogmatic Considerations," *Nova et Vetera* (English) 10, no. 1 (2012): 27–59; Avvakumon, Yury P. "Sacramental Ritual in Middle and Later Byzantine Theology: Ninth-Fifteenth Centuries," in *OHST*, 260–61.

[82] See the discussion of this issue in Feingold, *The Eucharist*, 205–12.

words of Eucharistic Institution are indeed present in the Anaphora of Addai and Mari, not in a coherent narrative way and *ad litteram*, but rather in a dispersed euchological way, that is, integrated in successive prayers of thanksgiving, praise and intercession. All these elements constitute a 'quasi-narrative' of the Eucharistic Institution."[83]

The Form of Confirmation

The history of Confirmation shows a variety of sacramental formulas that accompanied the anointing and imposition of hands and specified its meaning.[84] Our earliest form is from the *Apostolic Tradition*, in which a prayer for the coming of the Holy Spirit was followed by an anointing in the name of the Trinity.[85] Towards the end of the fourth century, Theodore of Mopsuestia gives a similar Trinitarian formula: "So-and-so is sealed in the name of the Father and of the Son and of the Holy Spirit."[86] St. John Chrysostom gives a similar form for the pre-baptismal anointing with chrism: "N. is anointed in the name of the Father, the Son and the Holy Spirit."[87] St. Cyril of Jerusalem does

---

[83] Pontifical Council for Promoting Christian Unity, Guidelines for Admission to the Eucharist between the Chaldean Church and the Assyrian Church of the East (July 20, 2001), §3. For a discussion of the Anaphora of Addai and Mari with references to the abundant literature on this topic, see Feingold, *The Eucharist*, 212–25.

[84] See the variety of medieval forms in Finnegan, *Confirmation at an Impasse*, 313.

[85] Hippolytus, *On the Apostolic Tradition* 21.21–22, trans. Stewart-Sykes, 112: "The bishop, laying his hand on them invokes, saying: 'Lord God, you have made them worthy to deserve the remission of sins through the laver of regeneration: make them worthy to be filled with the Holy Spirit, send your grace upon them that they may serve you in accordance with your will...' After this, pouring the sanctified oil from his hand and putting it on his head he shall say: 'I anoint you with holy oil in God the Father Almighty and Christ Jesus and the Holy Spirit.'"

[86] In Hugh Riley, *Christian Initiation: A Comparative Study of the Interpretation of the Baptismal Liturgy in the Mystagogical Writings of Cyril of Jerusalem, John Chrysostom, Theodore of Mopsuestia, and Ambrose of Milan* (Washington, DC: Catholic University of America Press, 1974), 381.

[87] John Chrysostom, Baptismal Homily 2.22, in Yarnold, *The Awe-Inspiring Rites of Initiation*, 160. St. John Chrysostom's liturgy in Antioch, reflecting the early Syrian practice, does not have a post-baptismal anointing, as later became universal, but included a laying on of hands during the Baptism itself. A post-baptismal anointing began to be added in Syria in the late fourth and fifth centuries, as can be seen in the post-baptismal anointing given by Theodore of Mopsuestia. See Finnegan, *Confirmation at an Impasse*,

not directly give the form of words accompanying Chrismation, but he uses an expression close to what we later find in the Byzantine rite. He says that in a later homily he will explain "how like priests you have become partakers of the name of Christ; and how the *seal of the fellowship of the Holy Spirit has been given* to you."[88] In the Byzantine rite, the essential form is: "The seal of the gift of the Holy Spirit."[89]

In the twelfth century the Roman Pontifical gave the formula which then became common in the Latin rite: "I sign you with the sign of the cross and confirm you with the chrism of salvation. In the name of the Father and of the Son and of the Holy Spirit."[90] St. Paul VI, in his Apostolic Constitution on Confirmation decreed a new form for the Latin rite, bringing it into harmony with the Byzantine rite: "N., be sealed with the Gift of the Holy Spirit." Paul VI explained the change by saying that the new form modeled on the Byzantine rite better "expresses the Gift of the Holy Spirit himself and calls to mind the outpouring of the Spirit on the day of Pentecost."[91]

97–114. A third-century Syrian baptismal liturgy without a post-baptismal anointing is found in the *Didascalia Apostolorum* 3.12, in which the anointing is explained as the antitype prefigured by the anointing of the kings and priests of Israel. The bishop's action (whether in anointing and sealing, or in laying on his hand during the baptism) is associated with the giving of the Holy Spirit (*Didascalia Apostolorum* 2.32). See J.D.C. Fisher, *Confirmation: Then and Now* (London: SPCK, 1978), 89–93; Thomas Finn, *Early Christian Baptism and the Catechumenate: West and East Syria* (Collegeville, MN: Liturgical Press, 1992), 41. This raises the question of how the sacrament of Confirmation can be present in a pre-baptismal anointing, since Baptism is the gateway to the other sacraments and thus should be received first. I would answer that the sacramental sign of the giving of the Spirit would have been constituted here both by the pre-baptismal anointing by the bishop and the laying on of his hand in the baptism itself. The fact that these are not simultaneous does not seem to be a problem because non-simultaneous liturgical signs may form a complex sign spread out over time which has a unity of meaning that refers to a single reality of the giving of grace, which here would be the grace of Baptism and the communication of the Spirit (Confirmation) received together.

88 Cyril of Jerusalem, Lenten Catechesis 18.33, in *The Works of Saint Cyril of Jerusalem*, vol. 2, trans. L. P. McCauley and A. A. Stephenson, FC 61 (Washington, DC: Catholic University of America Press, 1969), 138.

89 See Finnegan, *Confirmation at an Impasse*, 107. The earliest liturgical text preserving this rite is the *Barberini Euchologion* from the ninth century.

90 See Paul VI, *Divinae Consortium Naturae*, in *Rites*, 1:477; Finnegan, *Confirmation at an Impasse*, 313.

91 Paul VI, *Divinae Consortium Naturae*, in *Rites*, 1:477: "As regards the words pro-

The Form of Holy Orders

No form of words was given by Jesus and recorded in the New Testament for the sacrament of Holy Orders. The liturgical rites in the Church specify with various prayers the precise meaning of the laying on of hands, which is the matter of the sacrament, in each of the three grades of Holy Orders.

The *Apostolic Tradition*, ascribed to Hippolytus, preserves a liturgy of episcopal consecration from about the beginning of the third century, in which the consecrating bishop prays:

> Even now pour out from yourself the power of the Spirit of governance, which you gave to your beloved child Jesus Christ, which he gave to the holy apostles, who set up the church in every place as your sanctuary, for the unceasing glory and praise of your name. Father, you know the heart; grant that your servant, whom you have chosen for oversight, should shepherd your flock and should serve before you as high priest without blame, serving by night and day.[92]

After the Second Vatican Council, St. Paul VI modified the sacramental form for episcopal consecration so as to follow the ancient prayer of the *Apostolic Tradition*, which, as he points out, is also still maintained "in large part, in the Ordination Rites of the Coptic and West Syrian liturgies. Thus in the very act of Ordination there is a witness to the harmony of tradition in East and West concerning the apostolic office of Bishops."[93] The current essential form in the

---

nounced in confirmation, we have examined with the consideration it deserves the dignity of the respected formulary used in the Latin Church, but we judge preferable the very ancient formulary belonging to the Byzantine Rite. This expresses the Gift of the Holy Spirit himself and calls to mind the outpouring of the Spirit on the day of Pentecost (see Acts 2:1–4, 38). We therefore adopt this formulary, rendering it almost word for word."

[92] Hippolytus, *On the Apostolic Tradition* 3.3–4, trans. Stewart-Sykes, 61.

[93] Paul VI, Apostolic Constitution Approving New Rites for the Ordination of Deacons, Priests, and Bishops *Pontificalis Romani Recognitio* (June 18, 1968), in Congregation for Divine Worship and the Discipline of the Sacraments, *The Roman Pontifical* (Vatican City: Vox Clara Committee, 2012), 14. The previous essential form, mandated by Pius XII in *Sacramentum Ordinis*, §6 (DS, 3861), was: "Fulfill in Thy priest the perfection of Thy ministry, and sanctify with the dew of heavenly ointment him who is adorned with the ornaments of

Latin rite mandated by Paul VI is:

> Pour out now upon this chosen one that power which is from you, the governing Spirit, whom you gave to your beloved Son, Jesus Christ, the Spirit whom he bestowed upon the holy Apostles, who established the Church in each place as your sanctuary for the glory and unceasing praise of your name.[94]

This ancient consecratory prayer has a Trinitarian form and is like an epiclesis. The consecrating bishop asks the Father to pour out the power of the Holy Spirit who was given in fullness to the humanity of His Son. The Son bestowed this "Spirit of governance" upon the Apostles who established the Church and appointed successors to receive the same governing Spirit through the laying on of their hands.

The essential form for priestly ordination is similar in structure. It implores the Father to grant "the Spirit of holiness" for the dignity of the priesthood:

> Grant, we pray, Almighty Father, to these your servants the dignity of the Priesthood; renew deep within them the Spirit of holiness; may they henceforth possess this office, which comes from you, O God, and is next in rank to the office of Bishop; and by the example of their manner of life, may they instill right conduct.[95]

The essential form for the ordination of deacons implores the sevenfold gift of the Spirit not for the priesthood, but for "carrying out the work of the ministry."[96]

---

all glorification." On the history of the form of Holy Orders in the Latin and Eastern rites, see P. Jounel, "Ordinations," in *The Church at Prayer*, vol. 3, *The Sacraments*, ed. A. G. Martimort, trans. Matthew J. O'Connell (Collegeville, MN: Liturgical Press, 1988), 139–79.

[94] *The Roman Pontifical*, 34.

[95] *The Roman Pontifical*, 79.

[96] *The Roman Pontifical*, 133: "Send forth upon him, Lord, we pray, the Holy Spirit, that he may be strengthened by the gift of your sevenfold grace for the faithful carrying out of the work of the ministry."

The Form of Penance

The essential form of Penance is the form of absolution pronounced by the priest: "I absolve you from your sins in the name of the Father and of the Son and of the Holy Spirit."[97] It is preceded, in the current form of the Latin rite, by a prayer which further develops its Trinitarian and ecclesial dimension: "God, the Father of mercies, through the death and resurrection of his Son has reconciled the world to himself and sent the Holy Spirit among us for the forgiveness of sins; through the ministry of the Church may God give you pardon and peace."[98]

The principal variation with regard to the form of absolution lies in the fact that in the first millennium in both East and West it was expressed as a prayer that the God of mercy absolve the sinner;[99] whereas in the Latin rite in the second millennium it began to be expressed in the indicative: "*I* absolve you..."[100]

The administration of Penance has undergone major developments with far-reaching consequences in the life of the Church, but these do not directly concern the matter and form of the sacrament composed of the three acts of the penitent and the priestly absolution, which have remained substantially the same. The practice of the

---

[97] *Order of Penance*, §19, *Rites*, 1:535. See the Council of Trent, Doctrine on the Sacrament of Penance (session 14), ch. 3 (DS, 1673): "The holy council teaches, moreover, that the form of the sacrament of penance, in which its power principally resides, consists in these words of the minister: I absolve you, etc. In accordance with a custom of the holy Church, certain prayers are laudably added to these; they do not, however, in any way belong to the essence of the form." See also the Council of Florence, *Exsultate Deo* (DS, 1323): "The form of this sacrament is the words of absolution, which the priest pronounces when he says: 'I absolve you.'"

[98] *Order of Penance*, §46, in *Rites*, 1:546–47. See the explanation in §19, in *Rites*, 1:535.

[99] An example of absolution in the form of prayer is found in the Gelasian Sacramentary from around 700, in Paul F. Palmer, *Sources of Christian Theology*, vol. 2, *Sacraments and Forgiveness; History and Doctrinal Development of Penance, Extreme Unction and Indulgences* (Westminster, MD: Newman Press, 1960), 162: "Almighty, everlasting God, in Thy fatherly kindness release the sins of this Thy servant who makes confession to Thee, that guilt of conscience may no longer harm him unto punishment; rather may Thy indulgent love [admit him] unto pardon. Through our Lord Jesus Christ." For other examples, see Palmer, *Sources of Christian Theology*, 2:167, 171.

[100] See John M. T. Barton, *Penance and Absolution* (London: Burns & Oates, 1961), 93–95; P. M. Gy, "Penance and Reconciliation," in *The Church at Prayer*, vol. 3, *The Sacraments*, ed. Martimort, 112.

early Church involved public penance, which could only be received once in a lifetime, for very serious sins, such as adultery, idolatry, and homicide.[101] This involved a private confession of sins and expression of contrition, followed by a generally lengthy period in which the penitent did public satisfaction as a member of the order of penitents, and was finally publicly reconciled, usually on Holy Thursday or Good Friday, and readmitted to Holy Communion.[102]

The beginning of the spread of the practice of "private" penance in the sixth century through the influence of the Irish missionaries consisted in taking away the public nature of the satisfaction imposed. It did not introduce private confession itself, for that already existed.[103] Rather, it introduced private satisfaction (the amount of which, still severe, was stipulated by penitential books) and, most importantly, the possibility of repeated reception of the sacrament by all members of the faithful who attained the age of reason. The spread of the practice of "private" penance (also called tariff-penance) in the early Middle Ages met a great need in the Church,[104] but it was not introduced without resistance.[105]

---

[101] For the practice of public penance and its evolution, see Gy, "Penance and Reconciliation," 102–12; Poschmann, *Penance and the Anointing of the Sick*, 6–134; Paul F. Palmer, *Sources of Christian Theology*, vol. 2, *Sacraments and Forgiveness; History and Doctrinal Development of Penance, Extreme Unction and Indulgences* (Westminster, MD: Newman Press, 1960), 10–184; *CCC*, §1447.

[102] See Gy, "Penance and Reconciliation," 107; Palmer, *Sacraments and Forgiveness*, 113.

[103] That the confession of sins was private can be seen from Leo the Great, who regarded this as an apostolic tradition, as can be seen from Letter 168, *Magna indignatione*, to all the Bishops of Campania, (Mar 6, 459; DS, 323): "I also decree that that presumption against the apostolic regulation, which I recently learned is being committed by some through unlawful usurpation, be banished by all means. With regard to penance, what is demanded of the faithful is clearly not that an acknowledgment of the nature of individual sins . . . be read publicly, since it suffices that the states of consciences be made known to the priests alone in secret confession. . . . For then, indeed, more will be able to be incited to penance if the conscience of the one confessing is not exposed to the ears of the people." See also the Council of Trent, Doctrine on the Sacrament of Penance (session 14), ch. 5 (DS, 1683); and can. 6 on Penance (DS, 1706).

[104] On the spread of the practice of private penance that could be repeated, see Poschmann, *Penance and the Anointing of the Sick*, 123–39; Gy, "Penance and Reconciliation," 108–10.

[105] See the Third Council of Toledo, can. 11, in *The Christian Faith*, ed. J. Dupuis and J. Neuner, 7th ed. (New York: Alba House, 2001) §1607, p. 661: "It came to our knowledge that in some Churches in Spain people go through the dis-

A further step in the evolution of the sacrament of Penance was the introduction of the practice of granting absolution right after the confession and before the completion of the works of satisfaction. Prior to the end of the first millennium, confession and absolution were separated by an often lengthy period in which the works of penance were accomplished. This change occurred gradually between the ninth and eleventh centuries.[106] After the year 1000, the combination of confession and absolution began to become the general practice.[107] By the twelfth century the practice of Penance achieved the same basic structure that has endured until today.

This gradual change in the practice of reconciliation, eliminating public or solemn penance and joining together confession and absolution, has had important implications for the theology of Penance and for the Christian life. First of all, it made the grace of the sacrament far more available in the life of the faithful, and made frequent Confession a key means in the pursuit of holiness. Secondly, it highlights the unlimited mercy of God. Third, it puts greater importance on the interior contrition expressed in the confession than on the completion of the exterior works of satisfaction. Fourth, the new practice also helped theologians to clearly distinguish between the forgiveness of the *guilt* of sin that involves conversion of heart, and expiation of the *temporal punishment* that remained for sins whose guilt was already forgiven.[108] In the earlier practice, absolution was often understood to mark the complete expiation of temporal punishment through outward works of penance. By giving absolution before the completion of the works of satisfaction, it becomes clear that the priestly absolution is for the forgiveness of the guilt of sin but does not yet signify the termination of the debt of temporal punishment.

The Form of Anointing of the Sick

The sacrament of Anointing also shows non-essential changes in sacramental form over the centuries. The sacramental form in use in the

---

cipline of penance for their sins, not according to the canons, but in a most shameful manner, that is, as often as they happen to fall into sin they ask for reconciliation from the priest."

[106] See Palmer, *Sacraments and Forgiveness*, 171–73.

[107] See Poschmann, *Penance and the Anointing of the Sick*, 145.

[108] On the notion of temporal punishment for sin, see chapter 10 below, pp. 368–70.

Latin rite for most of the second millennium was as follows: "Through this holy unction and His most pious mercy, may the Lord pardon you for whatever offenses you have committed."[109] The new form for the Latin rite introduced by Paul VI in 1972 is: "Through this holy anointing may the Lord in his love and mercy help you with the grace of the Holy Spirit. May the Lord who frees you from sin save you and raise you up."[110] In both cases the essential meaning is the same. Paul VI explains that the change was made so that "the effects of the sacrament might be better expressed,"[111] in accordance with James 5:14–15: "Is any among you sick? Let him call for the elders of the Church, and let them pray over him, anointing him with oil in the name of the Lord; and the prayer of faith will save the sick man, and the Lord will raise him up; and if he has committed sins, he will be forgiven."

Invalidity of Sacramental Form due to Substantial Change of Meaning

As mentioned above, if a sacramental form is so changed that it no longer signifies the substantial meaning, purpose, or effects of the sacrament, then it will cease to be valid.[112] A tragic example of the invalidity of a sacrament due to the omission of essential content of the sacramental form occurred with regard to the sacrament of Holy Orders in the Anglican Church in the mid-sixteenth century. Leo XIII judged that Anglican Orders were invalid because at the time of the Reformation, a substantial change was made in the form of

---

[109] See Council of Florence, *Exsultate Deo* (DS, 1325); Paul VI, Apostolic Constitution on the Sacrament of the Anointing of the Sick *Sacram Unctionem Infirmorum* (Nov 30, 1972), in *Rites*, 1:772.

[110] Paul VI, *Sacram Unctionem Infirmorum*, in *Rites*, 1:774.

[111] Paul VI, *Sacram Unctionem Infirmorum*, in *Rites* 1:773. For the effects of this sacrament, see chapter 10 below, pp. 372–75.

[112] See CDF, Doctrinal Note on the Modification of the Sacramental Formula of Baptism (Aug 6, 2020): "Modifying on one's own initiative the form of the celebration of a Sacrament does not constitute simply a liturgical abuse, like the transgression of a positive norm, but a *vulnus* inflicted upon the ecclesial communion and the identifiability of Christ's action, and in the most grave cases rendering invalid the Sacrament itself, because the nature of the ministerial action requires the transmission with fidelity of that which has been received.... The intention therefore cannot remain only at the interior level, with the risk of subjective distractions, but must be expressed in the exterior action constituted by the use of the matter and form of the Sacrament."

the rite of priestly ordination. The Edwardine formula for ordination was simply: "Receive the Holy Spirit." This formula was judged to be essentially different from that in use in the Catholic Church, for the Edwardine formula contained no reference whatever to the specific role of a priest, which is principally to offer the holy Sacrifice of the Mass. Leo XIII explains:

> All know that the Sacraments of the New Law, inasmuch as they are sensible and efficacious signs of invisible grace, must both signify the grace that they effect and effect the grace that they signify. . . . The words that, until quite recent times, have been generally held by Anglicans to be the proper form of priestly ordination: "Receive the Holy Spirit," certainly do not signify definitely the order of the priesthood or its grace and power, which is preeminently the power "to consecrate and offer the true Body and Blood of the Lord."[113] . . . It is true that this form was subsequently amplified by the addition of the words: "for the office and work of a priest"; but this proves, rather than anything else, that the Anglicans themselves had recognized that the first form had been defective and inadequate. Even if this addition could have lent the form a legitimate signification, it was made too late, when a century had already elapsed since the adoption of the Edwardine Ordinal, and when, consequently, with the hierarchy now extinct, the power of ordaining no longer existed.[114]

Another example of an essential change in sacramental form is the practice, inspired by a feminist ideology that considers the titles "Father" and "Son" to be sexist, of baptizing "in the name of the Creator, and of the Redeemer, and of the Sanctifier" or "in the name of the Creator, and of the Liberator, and of the Sustainer." The Congregation for the Doctrine of the Faith has determined that the Trinitarian form is not sufficiently manifested by these formulas, which would render Baptism invalid.[115]

---

[113] Council of Trent, Doctrine and Canons on the Sacrament of Order (session 23), can. 1 (DS, 1771).

[114] Leo XIII, *Apostolicae Curae*, §§24–26 (DS, 3315).

[115] CDF, Responses to Questions Proposed on the Validity of Baptism, (Feb 1, 2008). See the commentary on this document by Antonio Miralles posted on the

Another change in form that invalidates the sacrament of Baptism is the substitution of the pronoun "we" for "I" in the baptismal form: "We baptize you in the name of the Father and of the Son and of the Holy Spirit." The Congregation for the Doctrine of the Faith has pronounced that this baptismal form is invalid[116] because it implies that the minister is baptizing as the representative of the community rather than as representing Christ. On the contrary, it is Christ and not the community who baptizes through the minister, as taught by the Second Vatican Council in *Sacrosanctum Concilium*, §7: "By His power He is present in the sacraments, so that when a man baptizes it is really Christ Himself who baptizes."

The Doctrinal Note that accompanied this Response of the CDF explained the doctrinal issue that is at stake in the change of pronoun from "I" to "we":

> It is therefore fundamental that the sacramental action may not be achieved in its own name, but in the person of Christ who acts in his Church, and in the name of the Church. Therefore, in the specific case of the Sacrament of Baptism, not only does the minister not have the authority to modify the sacramental formula to his own liking, for the reasons of a christological and ecclesiological nature already articulated, but neither can he even declare that he is acting on behalf of the parents, godparents, relatives or friends, nor in the name of the assembly gathered for the celebration, because he acts insofar as he is the sign-presence of the same Christ.[117]

Vatican website, at http://www.vatican.va/roman_curia/congregations/cfaith/documents/rc_con_cfaith_doc_20080201_validity-baptism-miralles_en.html: "The Church has no right to change what Christ himself has instituted. Therefore, any Baptism is invalid when it does not contain the invocation of the Most Holy Trinity, with the distinct expression of the three Persons with their respective names. Throughout the ages, the Magisterium of the Church has repeatedly taught that Christian Baptism is administered in the name of the Father and of the Son and of the Holy Spirit.... The liturgical documents on the Rite of Baptism do not offer alternatives to the terms Father, Son and Holy Spirit."

[116] See CDF, Responses to Questions Proposed on the Validity of Baptism Conferred with the Formula "We baptize you in the name of the Father and of the Son and of the Holy Spirit" (Aug 6, 2020).

[117] CDF, Doctrinal Note on the Modification of the Sacramental Formula of Baptism (Aug 6, 2020).

STUDY QUESTIONS

1. Explain the distinction between matter and form in the sacraments, and why both are necessary.
2. How does the matter of the sacraments represent the spiritual effects caused by the sacrament? Explain the role of analogy in sacramental symbolism.
3. Explain the fittingness of immersion or pouring of water as the matter for Baptism.
4. Explain the fittingness of the matter for the sacrament of Confirmation and for Anointing of the Sick.
5. Explain the fittingness of (wheat) bread and wine from the grape for the Eucharist.
6. Why do the sacraments of Penance and Matrimony not make use of a sensible material element (such as water, oil, bread and wine, or the laying on of hands) like the other sacraments? What takes the place of matter in these two sacraments? How should we understand matter and form in the sacrament of Matrimony?
7. What is the remote and proximate matter for the sacrament of Penance?
8. What is the essential matter for Holy Orders?
9. Explain how the Church can change the form of words required for the validity of a sacrament. Give some examples.
10. Explain the major changes in the celebration of the sacrament of Penance in the history of the Church, and explain why they do not affect the substance of the matter and form.
11. What kind of change in sacramental form would render a sacrament invalid? Give examples.
12. Why did Leo XII judge that Anglican Orders were invalid?

SUGGESTIONS FOR FURTHER READING

Congregation for the Doctrine of the Faith. Responses to Questions Proposed on the Validity of Baptism Conferred with the Formula "We baptize you in the name of the Father and of the Son and of the Holy Spirit." August 6, 2020.

_____. Doctrinal Note on the Modification of the Sacramental Formula of Baptism. August 6, 2020.

Council of Florence. Bull of Union with the Armenians *Exsultate Deo*.

November 22, 1439.

Lang, David P. *Why Matter Matters: Philosophical and Scriptural Reflections on the Sacraments.* Huntington, IN: Our Sunday Visitor, 2002.

Leo XIII. Apostolic Letter on the Nullity of Anglican Orders *Apostolicae Curae.* September 13, 1896. DS, 3315–19.

Martimort, Aimé Georges, editor. *The Church at Prayer.* Vol. 3, *The Sacraments.* New edition. Translated by Matthew J. O'Connell. Collegeville, MN: Liturgical Press, 1988. Pp. 1–207.

Miralles, Antonio. *I sacramenti cristiani: trattato generale.* 2nd edition. Rome: Apollinare studi, 2008. Pp. 179–96.

Paul VI. Apostolic Constitution on the Sacrament of Confirmation *Divinae Consortium Naturae.* August 15, 1971.

———. Apostolic Constitution *Sacram Unctionem Infirmorum.* November 30, 1972.

Pius XII. Apostolic Constitution *Sacramentum Ordinis.* November 30, 1947.

Roza, Devin. *Fulfilled in Christ: The Sacraments: A Guide to Symbols and Types in the Bible and Tradition.* Steubenville, OH: Emmaus Academic, 2015.

Vagaggini, Cyprian. *Theological Dimensions of the Liturgy.* Translated by Leonard J. Doyle and W. A. Jurgens. Collegeville, MN: Liturgical Press, 1976. Pp. 69–85.

CHAPTER SIX

The Subject and the Minister
of the Sacraments

The symbolism of the sacraments is not limited to their matter and
form, but also extends to the minister and subject, who represent
Christ and His Bride, the Church, united in a nuptial mystery, as St.
Paul explains in Ephesians 5:25–32. This text also shows Christ as the
minister with respect to His Bride, who is the subject sacramentally
cleansed by Him "by the washing of water with the word, that he might
present the Church to himself in splendor, without spot or wrinkle or
any such thing, that she might be holy and without blemish" (Eph
5:26–27). In order to represent Christ and the Church, certain conditions are required in the minister and subject, which thus pertain to
the outward sensible sign. This aspect requires a fuller treatment today
than in earlier centuries because of the controversy regarding gender
as a requirement for the subject in the sacraments of Holy Orders and
Matrimony.

1. Intention of the Sacramental
Subject and Minister

The sacraments are administered and received by human beings
through human acts, which, in order to be properly human, must be
intentional. Therefore, in all the sacraments the minister must have
an intention to administer the sacrament[1] and a subject must have an
intention to receive it if the subject is capable of intention.

---

[1] See the Council of Trent, Decree on the Sacraments (session 7), can. 11 (DS,
    1611).

Children below the age of reason and the mentally handicapped who have never had the use of reason do not need to have an intention to receive the sacraments of initiation, since they are incapable of it. It becomes necessary only when they are capable of it. The reason for this is that God respects our nature, of which He is the author. It belongs to human nature that we come into this world totally dependent on the direction of our parents and society, and that while we lack the use of moral reason (until about seven years), those to whom we are entrusted make decisions for us. Since God wishes to save us socially and not simply as isolated individuals, He respects this condition of entrustment in which we come into the world and wills children to be brought to the baptismal font by their parents and to be baptized into the faith of the Church. But for those who have sufficient use of reason, it would violate our nature if God were to allow Himself to be forced on adults against their will (as in the forced baptism of adults, which would be invalid).[2] Hence the sacraments require the consent of adults, expressed through their intention to receive the sacrament.

A very general and basic intention to do what the Church does in administering a sacrament is always necessary in the minister of a sacrament for two reasons. First, the sacraments are signs that are proper to rational agents who use them intentionally. The celebration of a sacrament would not be a properly *human* act[3] if it were not animated by the intention to perform it. Secondly, the minister is acting as an instrument of Christ and the Church, and thus he must intend to act in an instrumental manner. This is only the case if he is *intending to do what the Church does* in confecting a sacrament.[4]

---

[2] See *ST* I-II, q. 113, a. 3, ad 1; III, q. 68, a. 9, ad 1, which quotes Augustine, *The Punishment and Forgiveness of Sins and the Baptism of Little Ones* 1.19.25.

[3] A *human* act, in the proper sense, is one that involves intellect and free choice. See *ST* I-II, q. 1, a. 1: "Of actions done by man those alone are properly called *human*, which are proper to man as man. Now man differs from irrational animals in this, that he is master of his actions. Wherefore those actions alone are properly called human, of which man is master. Now man is master of his actions through his reason and will; whence, too, the free-will is defined as 'the faculty and will of reason.' Therefore those actions are properly called human which proceed from a deliberate will. And if any other actions are found in man, they can be called actions *of a man*, but not properly *human* actions, since they are not proper to man as man."

[4] St. Bonaventure explains that intention is necessary in the minister because sacraments have their power not from their nature but from their institution. Thus one must intend that for which they were instituted. See Bonaventure, *In IV*

The practice of the patristic age generally presupposes this principle. In his *History of the Church*, Eusebius quotes from a letter by Pope Cornelius in which he describes the invalid ceremony in which Novatian, an anti-pope, had tried to induce three bishops to "consecrate" him as bishop by getting them drunk: "When they were hopelessly drunk, he forcibly compelled them to make him a bishop, by a counterfeit and invalid consecration."[5] Nevertheless, St. Augustine was uncertain about the question of the validity of sacraments done in jest, although in such cases there would clearly be a lack of intentionality.[6]

We find the necessity of intention expressed clearly in the sacramental treatises of the twelfth century by Hugh of St. Victor and Peter Lombard. Hugh of St. Victor writes:

> But it is quite ridiculous that where no intention of acting exists, the work be said to exist on account of a certain appearance made similar to the work, not assumed for this purpose but coming forth from something else whatsoever. Thus it is that certain ignorant persons think that those words which were instituted to perform the Eucharist, when proclaimed . . . with whatever intention over bread and wine, have the effect of consecration and sanctification, as if the sacraments of God were so instituted that they admit no reason for operating but . . . proceed to their effect without any intention or will on the part of those operating.[7]

Sent., d. 3, p. 1, a. 2, q. 1, ad 2, in *Commentary on the Sentences: Sacraments*, trans. Hellmann, 116–17.

[5] Eusebius, *History of the Church* 6.43, trans. G. A. Williamson (Minneapolis, MN: Augsburg, 1965), 282.

[6] Augustine, *On Baptism, against the Donatists*, 7.53.102, in *NPNF*1, 4:513: "When the man who received it did not himself hold such belief, but the whole thing was done as a farce, or a comedy, or a jest—if I were asked whether the baptism which was thus conferred should be approved, I should declare my opinion that we ought to pray for the declaration of God's judgment through the medium of some revelation seeking it with united prayer . . . humbly deferring all the time to the decision of those who were to give their judgment after me, in case they should set forth anything as already known and determined." This text is quoted in Peter Lombard's *Sentences*, bk 4, d. 6, ch. 5, no. 1, p. 36, who adds that it "seems to the wise that there was no baptism" here.

[7] Hugh of St. Victor, *On the Sacraments of the Christian Faith* 2.6.13, trans. Deferrari, 301.

Peter Lombard says: "In this [Baptism] and in other sacraments, just as the form is to be preserved, so also the intention of celebrating it is to be held."[8]

To make this act of intention, it is not necessary for the minister or recipient to understand exactly what the sacrament is, or to have a right faith concerning the sacrament, although obviously that is extremely desirable. It is sufficient for the minister simply to intend to do what the Church does in celebrating the sacrament, and for the subject to intend to receive what is given in the Church. In other words, it is enough for the minister to intend to perform the outward sacramental sign in accordance with the mind of the Church.[9] It is not necessary for the valid administration of the sacrament that the minister or recipient directly intend or even know the proper effects of the sacrament. We find this teaching clearly formulated by theologians in the thirteenth century.[10] St. Albert the Great writes:

> An intention on the part of the minister is required for Baptism; . . . but only of doing what the Church does, and this is expressed by the word of Baptism. . . . Hence, if this word is pronounced, with the intention of doing what the Church does, over one not baptized and not objecting then or afterwards, it is true Baptism. . . . But if it was mimicry, and the

---

[8] Peter Lombard, *Sentences*, bk 4, d. 6, ch. 5, no. 1, trans. Silano, p. 36.

[9] See Bernard Piault, *What Is a Sacrament?* trans. A. Manson (New York: Hawthorn Books, 1963), 166: "He [the minister] must intend to carry out some particular activity of the Church, to conform to her regulations but not necessarily to believe in the supernatural result. Hence any man, even though an unbeliever, may truly baptize if he carries out what the Church has laid down. Judas may perform the ceremonies; it is Christ who baptizes."

[10] See William of Auxerre (d. 1231), *Summa aurea*, bk. 4, q. 7: "If a minister uses the right form of words and has the intention of doing what the Church does, taking the expression in a broad way, for instance, if he intends to do what the Church is accustomed to do, it would be Baptism" (quoted in Lennerz, *De sacramentis novae legis*, 70, and translated in Leeming, *Principles of Sacramental Theology*, 439). Similarly, Sinibaldo Fieschi, who later became Pope Innocent IV (d. 1254), wrote: "Observe that for someone to be baptized, it is necessary that the minister intend to baptize and not merely to bathe or to wash away dirt; but it does not seem necessary, as regards the effect of Baptism, that he should know what Baptism is, or that in it grace is given, or that it is a sacrament" (*Commentarium super Libros quinque Decretalium*, in ch. 2, X, III, 42, trans. in Leeming, *Principles of Sacramental Theology*, 439).

subject objects, then he obtains nothing.[11]

He also specifies that even if the minister does not think that "it is good for anything," but still intends to "do what the Church does," then it is valid.[12]

St. Thomas poses the objection that if the intention of the minister is necessary for validity of the sacrament, then an element of uncertainty is brought into the sacramental system.[13] He answers that its certainty is not endangered by the necessity of the minister's intention, because the intention is manifested in the words, and the words express the intention of the Church, and it is presupposed that the minister is acting with this intention unless he makes a change in the words that indicates otherwise:

> Others with better reason hold that the minister of a sacrament acts in the person of the whole Church, whose minister he is; while in the words uttered by him, the intention of the Church is expressed; and that this suffices for the validity of the sacrament, except the contrary be expressed on the part either of the minister or of the recipient of the sacrament.[14]

This principle is used by Leo XIII in his encyclical on the validity of Anglican Orders from 1896:

> The Church does not judge about the mind or intention insofar as it is something by its nature internal; but insofar as it is manifested externally, she is bound to judge concerning it. When anyone has rightly and seriously made use of the due form and the matter requisite for effecting or conferring the sacrament, he is considered by the very fact to do what the Church does. On this principle rests the doctrine that a sacrament is truly conferred by the ministry of one who is a heretic or unbaptized, provided the Catholic rite be employed. On the other hand, if the rite be changed, with the manifest

---

[11] Albert, *In IV Sent.*, d. 5, a. 3, translated in Leeming, *Principles of Sacramental Theology*, 441.

[12] Albert, *In IV Sent.*, d. 5, a. 3, in Leeming, 441.

[13] *ST* III, q. 64, a. 8, obj. 2.

[14] *ST* III, q. 64, a. 8, ad 2.

intention of introducing another rite not approved by the Church and of rejecting what the Church does and what by the institution of Christ belongs to the nature of the sacrament, then it is clear that not only is the necessary intention wanting to the sacrament, but that the intention is adverse to and destructive of the sacrament.[15]

The necessity of a minimum intention in the minister was taught by the Council of Florence in the decree for the Armenians.[16] Luther denied the necessity of intention in the minister on the basis of the principle of justification by faith alone.[17] For this reason, it was infallibly defined at the Council of Trent, which teaches: "If anyone says that the intention at least of doing what the Church does is not required in the ministers when they are effecting and conferring the sacraments, let him be anathema."[18]

---

[15] Leo XIII, *Apostolicae Curae*, §33 (DS, 3318).

[16] Council of Florence, *Exsultate Deo* (DS, 1312): "All these sacraments are accomplished by three elements: namely, by things as the matter, by words as the form, and by the person of the minister who confers the sacrament with the intention of doing what the Church does. If any of these is absent, the sacrament is not accomplished." See also the Council of Constance, Bull *Inter cunctas* (1418; DS, 1262).

[17] See Luther, *Babylonian Captivity of the Church*, in *LW*, 36:63–64: "I have no doubt that if anyone receives baptism in the name of the Lord, even if the wicked minister should not give it in the name of the Lord, he would yet be truly baptized in the name of the Lord. For the power of baptism depends not so much on the faith or use of the one who confers it as on the faith or use of the one who receives it. We have an example of this in the story of a certain actor who was baptized in jest. These and similar perplexing disputes and questions are raised for us by those who ascribe nothing to faith and everything to works and rituals, whereas we owe everything to faith alone and nothing to rituals. Faith makes us free in spirit from all those scruples and fancies." See also the 12th condemned proposition attributed to Martin Luther in the Bull of Leo X, *Exsurge Domine* (1520; DS, 1462): "In the impossible supposition that one who confesses would not be sorry, or that the priest would give absolution not seriously but in jest, yet, if one believes that one is absolved, the penitent is in very truth absolved." This condemnation refers to Luther's *Explanations of the Ninety-five Theses*, in *LW* 31:105.

[18] Council of Trent, Decree on the Sacraments (session 7), can. 11 (DS, 1611). For an in-depth study of the meaning of Trent's teaching that the minister must intend to do what the Church does, see Giuseppe Rambaldi, *L'oggetto dell'intenzione sacramentale nei teologi dei secoli XVI e XVII* (Rome: Apud Aedes Universitatis Gregorianae, 1944). See also the condemnation of the proposition (taught by F. Farvacques) by Alexander VIII, Decree of the Holy Office, (Dec 7,

The intention to "do what the Church does" should be understood in a very general way. This is seen most clearly in the traditional practice of the Church that allows any person to baptize when there is danger of death, including an unbeliever, as long as he intends to do what the Church does in realizing the sacramental sign.[19] The *Catechism of the Catholic Church*, §1284 explains: "In case of necessity, any person can baptize provided that he have the intention of doing that which the Church does and provided that he pours water on the candidate's head while saying: 'I baptize you in the name of the Father, and of the Son, and of the Holy Spirit.'"

Since the minister of Baptism in extraordinary cases may be an unbeliever, it can be seen that it is possible to have the intention to administer a sacrament without personally having Catholic faith, as long as one intends to do what the Church does. In the case of Baptism, this means that the minister would understand Baptism in a very generic way as a rite of entrance into the Church. Similarly, in the sacrament of Matrimony, the spouses, who are the ministers of the sacrament, may have the intention to consent to the sacrament of Matrimony without personally having Catholic faith in the sacrament (as in the case of the baptized who have fallen away from the faith), for sacramental intention and the habit of divine faith are two distinct things, the former of which can be present without the latter.[20]

1690; DS, 2328): "Baptism is valid when conferred by a minister who observes all the external rite and form of baptizing, but within his heart resolves, I do not intend what the Church does." See Joseph de Aldama, S.J., "The General Theory of the Sacraments," in *Sacrae Theologiae Summa*, vol. 4A, *On the Sacraments in General; On Baptism, Confirmation, Eucharist, Penance and Anointing*, 3rd ed., trans. Kenneth Baker (Saddle River, NJ: Keep the Faith, 2015), 86.

[19] See CIC, can. 861, §2.

[20] On the question of the validity of the marriage of baptized non-believers, see John Paul II, Apostolic Exhortation on the Role of the Christian Family in the Modern World *Familiaris Consortio* (Nov 22, 1981), §68; ITC, "The Reciprocity between Faith and Sacraments in the Sacramental Economy," Mar 3, 2020, part 4, §§132–88; Benedict XVI, Address to the Tribunal of the Roman Rota on Jan 26, 2013, AAS 105 (2013): 168: "The indissoluble pact between a man and a woman does not, for the purposes of the sacrament, require of those engaged to be married, their personal faith; what it does require, as a necessary minimal condition, is the intention to do what the Church does. However, if it is important not to confuse the problem of the intention with that of the personal faith of those contracting marriage, it is nonetheless impossible to separate them completely." See also John Paul II, Address to the Prelate, Auditors, Officials, and Advocates of the Tribunal of the Roman Rota, Jan 30, 2003,

If this intention to administer or receive a sacrament is truly lacking in someone who has reached the age of reason,[21] the sacrament is invalid, which means that the sacrament is not received. No character is imprinted, and no grace is given. Thus if an adult is baptized against his will, that "Baptism" is invalid (non-existent) because the intention is clearly lacking. However, if someone intends to receive a sacrament merely for social reasons and without proper faith in the sacrament, but still intends to receive what the Church gives, whatever they think that is, such an intention is sufficient for validity although not for fruitfulness.

Actual, Virtual, and Habitual Intention

Theologians distinguish three kinds of intention for receiving or administering a sacrament: actual, virtual, and habitual. Actual intention is a conscious and deliberate act of willing to do something, such as to baptize or be baptized, confirm or be confirmed, to marry, etc. Normally, the intention to confer or receive a sacrament should be an actual intention at the moment of reception.

It can happen, however, that actual intention is lacking because of distraction or mental weakness. If a person has consciously chosen to receive a sacrament but in the act of reception is distracted and thinking about other things, did he lack the intention to receive the sacrament? No, for it is clear that he has not changed his mind if he continues to be there of his own free will, which reveals that the actual intention to receive the sacrament was present at a prior moment, was not repudiated, and is now producing the effect of the continued action. This is an example of a virtual intention which—although less than optimal—would be sufficient for the validity of the sacrament.

---

§8: "It is crucial to keep in mind that an attitude on the part of those getting married that does not take into account the supernatural dimension of marriage can render it null and void only if it undermines its validity on the natural level on which the sacramental sign itself takes place." See also the discussion on this point by Cormac Burke, *The Theology of Marriage: Personalism, Doctrine, and Canon Law* (Washington, DC: Catholic University of America Press, 2015), 10–25.

[21] The age of reason, for the purposes of sacramental theology, refers to the age in which someone can grasp first moral principles, like the golden rule, and is therefore capable of simple moral reasoning, which culminates in a judgment of conscience. This also involves the capacity to order oneself and one's acts to God (or at least to the good). See *ST* I-II, q. 89, a. 6.

Such intention is said to be virtual (which comes from the Latin word *virtus*, which means "power") because the power of the intention is manifested in the continuing action of receiving the sacrament. The power of the initial actual intention is still operative in motivating one's current action. The same consideration would apply to the minister of a sacrament.[22]

Habitual intention includes virtual intention but is broader because it does not presuppose that one has begun an action that is still continuing. Like a virtual intention, a habitual intention occurs when one has actually intended something and does not subsequently repudiate that intention. However, it is called (merely) habitual rather than virtual if it is not manifested in any continuing action. This can occur when someone has lost the capacity for actual intention, such as a person in a coma. Can one baptize a catechumen who has lost the use of reason due to an accident? Yes, for the catechumen demonstrated a prior actual intention preparing for entrance into the Church. As long as there are no clear signs that that actual intention was repudiated, one can assume that the person now has a habitual intention to receive the sacrament, and that would be sufficient.

St. Augustine recounts an episode of this type in book 4 of his *Confessions*. He had a very dear friend who, like him, was a catechumen, and whom he had inculcated with Manichean ideas. This friend fell into a coma that his family thought was irreversible and had him baptized in that state. He did, however, regain his senses, and, after Augustine expressed scorn for a sacrament received unconsciously, he forbade Augustine to disparage it:

> When he was sick with fever, for a long time he lay unconscious in a mortal sweat, and when his life was despaired of, he was baptized without his knowing it. To me this was a

---

[22] St. Thomas addresses such a case in *ST* III, q. 64, a. 8, ad 3: "Although he who thinks of something else, has no actual intention, yet he has habitual intention, which suffices for the validity of the sacrament; for instance if, when a priest goes to baptize someone, he intends to do to him what the Church does. Wherefore if subsequently during the exercise of the act his mind be distracted by other matters, the sacrament is valid in virtue of his original intention. Nevertheless, the minister of a sacrament should take great care to have actual intention. But this is not entirely in man's power, because when a man wishes to be very intent on something, he begins unintentionally to think of other things, according to Ps. 39:13: 'My heart hath forsaken me.'"

matter of no interest. I assumed that his soul would retain what it had received from me, not what had happened to his body while he was unconscious. But it turned out quite differently. For he recovered and was restored to health, and at once, as soon as I could speak with him . . . I attempted to joke with him, imagining that he too would laugh with me about the baptism which he had received when far away in mind and sense. But he had already learnt that he had received the sacrament. He was horrified at me as if I were an enemy, and with amazing and immediate frankness advised me that, if I wished to be his friend, I must stop saying this kind of thing to him. I was dumbfounded and perturbed; but I deferred telling him of all my feelings until he should get better and recover his health and strength. Then I would be able to do what I wished with him. But he was snatched away from my lunacy, so that he might be preserved with you for my consolation. After a few days, while I was absent, the fever returned, and he died.[23]

Similar considerations apply to the sacrament of Anointing of the Sick and Confirmation as for Baptism. With regard to those members of the faithful who have attained the age of reason and have lost consciousness, the *Code of Canon Law* states: "This sacrament [Anointing] is to be conferred on the sick who at least implicitly requested it when they were in control of their faculties."[24] When the subject is unconscious, a habitual intention continues and is sufficient for reception of the sacrament. A habitual intention is implicitly contained in the desire to do whatever is necessary for salvation. This can be assumed in all who practice the Catholic faith. Thus it is not necessary that one have explicitly expressed the desire to receive the sacrament of Anointing. Similarly, if baptized Catholics who have not been confirmed are in a coma and in danger of death, they should also be confirmed; their implicit consent is presumed, as with regard to Anointing.[25]

---

[23] Augustine, *Confessions* 4.4.8, trans. Henry Chadwick (Oxford: Oxford University Press, 1991), 57.

[24] CIC, can. 1006.

[25] Habitual intention can also come into play with regard to Matrimony in cases of radical sanation or convalidation. See CIC, canons 1156–64.

Mormon Baptism Lacks Proper Intention to Do What the Church Does

A decision of the Congregation for the Doctrine of the Faith of 2001[26] confirmed the invalidity of Mormon baptism. This invalidity is not because the form is literally different from the Catholic form (as in the case of Baptism "in the name of the Creator, and of the Redeemer, and of the Sanctifier"), but because the Mormon understanding of what is meant by Father, Son, and Holy Spirit is *radically* different from the Catholic understanding. This indicates that the intention to baptize in the name of the Trinity in the sense instituted by Christ and understood by the Catholic Church is lacking. Furthermore, Mormons do not understand Baptism as a sacrament instituted by Christ but as instituted at the beginning with Adam. Thus Baptism is not understood as the initiation into the New Covenant as willed by Christ.

This decision is explained in an article published in the *L'Osservatore Romano* by Luis Ladaria. He explains the radical difference between the Christian and the Mormon understanding of the terms, "Father," "Son," and "Holy Spirit," which he regards as not properly a Christian "heresy" which would arise from misunderstanding Christian doctrine.[27] The radically different understanding of the meaning of the Trinity and of the institution of Baptism shows that the baptismal

---

[26] CDF, Response to a Dubium on the Validity of Baptism Conferred by the Church of Jesus Christ of Latter-day Saints, called Mormons, June 5, 2001: "Question: Whether the baptism conferred by the community 'The Church of Jesus Christ of Latter-day Saints,' called 'Mormons' in the vernacular, is valid. Response: Negative."

[27] Luis Ladaria, S.J., "The Question of the Validity of Baptism Conferred in the Church of Jesus Christ of Latter-Day Saints," *L'Osservatore Romano* English Edition, Aug 1, 2001, p. 4: "There is not a true invocation of the Trinity because the Father, the Son and the Holy Spirit, according to the *Church of Jesus Christ of Latter-day Saints,* are not the three persons in which subsists the one Godhead, but three gods who form one divinity. . . . As is easily seen, to the similarity of titles there does not correspond in any way a doctrinal content which can lead to the Christian doctrine of the Trinity. The words Father, Son and Holy Spirit, have for the Mormons a meaning totally different from the Christian meaning. The differences are so great that one cannot even consider that this doctrine is a heresy which emerged out of a false understanding of the Christian doctrine. The teaching of the Mormons has a completely different matrix. We do not find ourselves, therefore, before the case of the validity of Baptism administered by heretics, affirmed already from the first Christian centuries, nor of Baptism conferred in non-Catholic ecclesial communities, as noted in Canon 869 §2."

formula is not said by Mormons with the intention of doing what the Christian church does in pronouncing the words:

> Such doctrinal diversity, regarding the very notion of God, prevents the minister of the *Church of Jesus Christ of Latter-day Saints* from having the intention of doing what the Catholic Church does when she confers Baptism, that is, doing what Christ willed her to do when he instituted and mandated the sacrament of Baptism. This becomes even more evident when we consider that in their understanding Baptism was not instituted by Christ but by God and began with Adam (cf. Book of Moses 6:64). Christ simply commanded the practice of this rite; but this was not an innovation. It is clear that the intention of the Church in conferring Baptism is certainly to follow the mandate of Christ (cf. Mt 28,19) but at the same time to confer the sacrament that Christ had instituted. According to the New Testament, there is an essential difference between the Baptism of John and Christian Baptism. The Baptism of the *Church of Jesus Christ of Latter-day Saints*, which originated not in Christ but already at the beginning of creation, is not Christian Baptism; indeed, it denies its newness. The Mormon minister, who must necessarily be the "priest," therefore radically formed in their own doctrine, cannot have any other intention than that of doing what the *Church of Jesus Christ of Latter-day Saints* does, which is quite different in respect to what the Catholic Church intends to do when it baptizes, that is, the conferral of the sacrament of Baptism instituted by Christ, which means participation in his death and resurrection (cf. Rom 6,3–11; Col 2,12–13).[28]

If, however, a Mormon were asked to baptize a Catholic or Protestant child in an emergency baptism, as may occur in a hospital, there would be no reason to question its validity, for in such a case one would assume that the Mormon was intending to do what the Catholic Church does.

---

[28] Ladaria, "The Question of the Validity of Baptism Conferred in the Church of Jesus Christ of Latter-Day Saints."

2. Necessary Conditions in the Recipient of the Sacraments

Living and Baptized; Conditional Administration

All of the sacraments require that the subject be a living human being. The sacraments are instituted for the human person only in this time of trial prior to death. If there is doubt about whether the recipient is alive, the sacraments are to be administered conditionally with regard to that doubt. For example, in administering Baptism, the minister would say: "If you are still alive, I baptize you . . ." The same condition can be made for the sacraments of Anointing and Confirmation. For reasons of pastoral prudence, the condition need not be audibly expressed.

Every sacrament except Baptism requires that the subject be validly baptized. The valid recipient of Baptism must be unbaptized. The three sacraments that imprint character (Baptism, Confirmation, and Holy Orders) are validly received only if the person has not already received that sacrament. With regard to the three levels of Holy Orders, the condition is that the subject not have received Holy Orders at the particular grade to which he is being ordained (diaconate, presbyterate, episcopate).

When there is reasonable doubt about a condition in the subject necessary for validity, sacraments can sometimes be administered conditionally. In such a case, if the subject is capable of receiving the sacrament, it is conferred; if not, it is not. The *Code of Canon Law*, canon 845, §2 provides for this in the case of the sacraments that imprint character when there is a doubt whether the sacraments were already received: "If after completing a diligent inquiry a prudent doubt still exists whether the sacraments mentioned in §1 [Baptism, Confirmation, and Holy Orders] were actually or validly conferred, they are to be conferred conditionally."

When a sacrament is conferred conditionally with regard to some doubt, the minister makes a verbal (or at least a mental) condition to address that uncertainty, such as the phrase: "if you are capable (of receiving this sacrament)." This condition should be expressed audibly when reasons for doubt about the condition of the subject are public. The purpose of the condition is to avoid scandal or confusion in the faithful and, out of reverence for the sacraments, to avoid subjecting them to the possibility of invalidity.

Conditions Required in the Subject
of the Sacraments of Healing

Since both the sacrament of Penance and Anointing of the Sick are instituted as sacraments of healing from sin and its effects, neither sacrament can be received before the age of reason, for such a child has no personal sins that need forgiveness or healing.

With regard to the sacrament of Penance, it is not enough that there be sins to confess, which is the remote matter. In addition, the penitent must be truly contrite, with at least imperfect contrition, for all mortal sins not yet sacramentally forgiven of which he is aware. Canon 987 gives this condition: "To receive the salvific remedy of the sacrament of penance, a member of the Christian faithful must be disposed in such a way that, rejecting sins committed and having a purpose of amendment, the person is turned back to God." This condition is necessary for the validity of the confession. Contrition forms an essential part of the matter of the sacrament, and thus it cannot ever be lacking.

The sacrament of Anointing requires two conditions in the subject: that there be a serious illness that entails a danger of death, and that one be at the age of reason, because the purpose of the sacrament is to further heal the wounds and remnants of sin. Canon 1004 gives the necessary conditions in the subject:

> The anointing of the sick can be administered to a member of the faithful who, having reached the use of reason, begins to be in danger due to sickness or old age.
>
> §2.† This sacrament can be repeated if the sick person, having recovered, again becomes gravely ill or if the condition becomes more grave during the same illness.

In a case of doubt "whether the sick person has attained the use of reason, is dangerously ill, or is dead," the sacrament is to be administered, as stipulated by canon 1005.

The *Ordo Unctionis Infirmorum* specifies the following:

> Great care and concern should be taken to see that those of the faithful whose health is seriously impaired by sickness or old age receive this sacrament. A prudent or reasonably sure judgment, without scruple, is sufficient for deciding on the

seriousness of an illness; if necessary a doctor may be consulted. . . . A sick person may be anointed before surgery whenever a serious illness is the reason for the surgery.

Elderly people may be anointed if they have become notably weakened even though no serious illness is present.

Sick children are to be anointed if they have sufficient use of reason to be strengthened by this sacrament. In case of doubt whether a child has reached the use of reason, the sacrament is to be conferred.[29]

Light sickness that does not pose any danger—such as a cold or other minor ailments or injuries—would not be sufficient for valid reception of the sacrament. However, when in doubt about whether the illness is serious or dangerous, the sacrament should be administered. It is enough that the illness seem serious and dangerous to the patient or doctor.

Those in danger of death without being sick, as in the case of soldiers before battle or a criminal before execution, cannot receive the sacrament of anointing because the subject must be actually and seriously infirm to receive the sacrament.[30]

Why Gender Complementarity for the Sacrament of Matrimony?

The subjects and ministers of Matrimony are a *man and woman* not bound by a prior marital bond or other impediment, having sufficient use of reason and discretion so as to give marital consent to one another and undertake the duties of marriage. Canon 1055, §1 gives a theological definition of marriage:

The matrimonial covenant, by which a man and a woman

---

[29] *Ordo Unctionis Infirmorum*, §§8–12, in *Rites*, 1:780–81.

[30] See *CCT*, part 2, ch. 5, §9, p. 302: "Extreme Unction, therefore, may be administered only to those who are seriously ill. It may not be given to anyone else, even those otherwise in danger of death—such as those undertaking a perilous journey, or going into battle, or even facing certain death by execution. Persons who are insane may not be anointed, especially those who are so from birth; nor may children who have not yet attained the use of reason, and therefore the capability of committing sin. For the purpose of this sacrament is to heal the vestiges of sin."

establish between themselves a partnership of the whole of life and which is ordered by its nature to the good of the spouses and the procreation and education of offspring, has been raised by Christ the Lord to the dignity of a sacrament between the baptized.

It is clear from this canon that the complementarity of gender, which makes possible a natural openness to the transmission of life, is an essential element of marriage. The sexual complementarity of man and woman is necessary for the sacramental sign of Matrimony in two ways: (a) to sacramentally represent God's fruitful love, and (b) to sacramentally represent the complementarity of Christ and the Church.[31]

The necessity of gender complementarity in marriage can also be inferred from the totality of the marital self-gift. St. Thomas speaks of marriage as a "maximum friendship,"[32] because in this friendship, as St. Paul VI and St. John Paul II have emphasized, each spouse offers to the other a *total* gift of self. The gift of self must be total because marriage is a sign and sacrament of God's love. St. Paul VI, in his encyclical *Humanae Vitae*, §9, describes the total nature of marital love as a sharing of all that one has for the sake of the beloved:

> It is a love which is total—that very special form of personal friendship in which husband and wife generously share everything, allowing no unreasonable exceptions and not thinking solely of their own convenience. Whoever really loves his partner loves not only for what he receives, but loves that partner for the partner's own sake, content to be able to enrich the other with the gift of himself.

---

[31] See Gerhard Ludwig Müller, *Priesthood and Diaconate: The Recipient of the Sacrament of Holy Orders from the Perspective of Creation Theology and Christology*, trans. Michael J. Miller (San Francisco: Ignatius Press, 2002), 93–94.

[32] St. Thomas Aquinas uses this expression to refer to marriage in *SCG* III, ch. 123, no. 6 (trans. Vernon J. Bourke), 3/2:148: "Furthermore, the greater that friendship is, the more solid and long-lasting will it be. Now, there seems to be the greatest friendship between husband and wife, for they are united not only in the act of fleshly union, which produces a certain gentle association even among beasts, but also in the partnership of the whole range of domestic activity. Consequently, as an indication of this, man must even 'leave his father and mother' for the sake of his wife, as is said in Genesis (2:24). Therefore, it is fitting for matrimony to be completely indissoluble." See Pieper, *The Four Cardinal Virtues*, 154.

The indissolubility and monogamous nature of marriage follow from this totality of self-gift. Another aspect of this totality, however, is that husband and wife mutually give their potential paternity and maternity to one another. Only a woman who is a potential mother can receive the gift of a man's paternity, and only a man who is a potential father can receive the gift of a woman's maternity. If paternity and maternity were not given to the other, then the gift of self would lack an important dimension of the human person and thus would lack a key element of total self-giving.

This consideration helps show how the unitive and the procreative dimension of the conjugal act are intrinsically tied together. The totality of the gift of self is expressed by being intrinsically open to life, such that the maternal and paternal dimension can be given, potentially giving rise to a common mission of the nurturing and education of children that may last throughout their lives. A sexual union whose potential gift of paternity and maternity is naturally impossible because it is not between a man and a woman cannot signify a total self-gift that potentially involves the mutual parental mission.[33]

The beauty of gender complementarity is that in the total self-gift of the spouses, each one gives something that the other does not and cannot have of himself. This is true both on the biological and the psychological/emotional level. On the biological level, the husband gives potential paternity and the wife gives potential maternity. Something analogous happens on the psychological and emotional level. The spouses give to each other, throughout their union, emotional and psychological gifts of paternity and maternity. This complementarity of the spouses makes their mutual gift of self much more significant, enabling it to be something marvelous, mysterious, and completing,

---

[33] Similarly, a sexual act whose fruitfulness is deliberately blocked by contraception cannot represent the total spousal self-gift that has to include one's potential maternity or paternity. See Paul VI, Encyclical *Humanae Vitae* (July 25, 1968), §§11–13; John Paul II, *Familiaris Consortio*, §32: "When couples, by means of recourse to contraception, separate these two meanings that God the Creator has inscribed in the being of man and woman and in the dynamism of their sexual communion, they act as 'arbiters' of the divine plan and they 'manipulate' and degrade human sexuality . . . by altering its value of 'total' self-giving. Thus the innate language that expresses the total reciprocal self-giving of husband and wife is overlaid, through contraception, by an objectively contradictory language, namely, that of not giving oneself totally to the other. This leads not only to a positive refusal to be open to life but also to a falsification of the inner truth of conjugal love, which is called upon to give itself in personal totality."

precisely because one does not already have what one receives.

It follows that a complementary union, formed of the union of two who are different and give themselves to each other in their diversity, is a far stronger and richer union than one formed of two who are fundamentally the same. Metaphysics offers analogies of this. The two complementary principles, matter and substantial form, unite to form a substance. Two pieces of matter or two substantial forms could not unite in that way. Similarly, act and potency unite in every created being. The composition of essence and *esse* is also a composition of complementary co-principles.

Two that are the same joined together simply make a larger amount of the same. Two cups of water simply make a larger cup. Two who are complementary make possible a new whole with new powers composed of the union of complementary gifts, in which each member of the union is enriched by gifts that he cannot possess of himself. On the biological level this is obvious. The union of husband and wife by nature has a possible fruitfulness that two males or females cannot have. But it is equally true on the psychological/emotional level. There are maternal and paternal gifts that fundamentally differ even though they can take on countless forms through our individual maternity and paternity.

God created human beings male and female so that each sex might better manifest different aspects of God and of our common humanity. This complementary character is summarized in the distinction between paternity and maternity to which man and woman are called.[34] God has endowed woman with a special aptitude for the particular virtues most intimately connected with her mission of maternity, and man with those more particularly connected with his mission of paternity.

The mission of maternity requires a special attentiveness to the

---

[34] See Dietrich von Hildebrand, *Man and Woman: Love and the Meaning of Intimacy* (Manchester, NH: Sophia Institute Press, 1992), 37: "What matters in our context is to understand, first, that man and woman differ not merely in a biological and physiological direction, but that they are *two different expressions of human nature;* and second, that the existence of this duality of human nature possesses a great value. Even if we prescind for the moment from all biological reasons as well as from procreation, we must see how much richer the world is because this difference exists, and that it is in no way desirable to efface as much as possible this difference in the spiritual realm, a trend which is unfortunately very widespread today."

life that grows and matures in her womb and is then nursed at her breasts. For this reason it is fitting that women tend to be wired in such a way that their attention is turned spontaneously to the personal sphere and to the concrete person in his or her totality. This requires a special gift of empathy, intuition, and sensitivity to the other, to affectivity and the sphere of the heart, in which mothers and potential mothers are gifted. The gift of paternity, on the other hand, leads the male sex to be generally more oriented towards governance, production, and abstract thought.[35] Since the father does not bear the child within his body, he does not have the same connatural intimacy with the growing life, but he naturally has the complementary task of providing for and defending his family. Men tend to be more attracted to the technological sphere that is connected with providing for the necessities of life.

In the Apostolic Letter On the Dignity and Vocation of Woman

---

[35] See Edith Stein, "Ethos of Women's Professions," in *Essays on Woman*, trans. Freda Mary Oben (Washington, DC: ICS Publications, 1987), 43–44 (this lecture was originally given in 1930). See also 248–49: "1. Man appears more *objective:* it is natural for him to dedicate his faculties to a discipline (be it mathematics or technology, a trade or business management) and thereby to subject himself to the precepts of this *discipline. Woman's attitude is personal*; and this has several meanings: in one instance she is happily involved with her total being in what she does; then, she has particular interest for the living, concrete person, and, indeed, as much for her own personal life and personal affairs as for those of other persons. 2. Through submission to a discipline, man easily experiences a *one-sided development.* In woman, there lives a natural drive towards *totality* and *self-containment.* And, again, this drive has a twofold direction: she herself would like to become a *complete human being*, one who is fully developed in every way; and she would like to help others to become so, and by all means, she would like to do justice to the complete human being whenever she has to deal with persons."

See also Alice von Hildebrand, *The Privilege of Being a Woman* (Ann Arbor, MI: Sapientia Press, 2002), 59–63; D. von Hildebrand, *Man and Woman*, 36: "If we try to delineate these specifically feminine and masculine features, we find in women a unity of personality by the fact that heart, intellect, and temperament are much more interwoven, whereas in man there is a specific capacity to emancipate himself with his intellect from the affective sphere. This unity of the feminine type of human person displays itself also in a greater unity of inner and exterior life, in a unity of style embracing the soul as well as the exterior demeanor. In a woman, the personality itself is more in the foreground than objective accomplishments; whereas man, who has a specific creativity, is more called than she is to objective accomplishments." See also John Paul II, *The Way to Christ: Spiritual Exercises* (New York: Harper & Row, 1984), 35–36; 51–53 (Exercises preached in 1962).

Mulieris Dignitatem, John Paul II draws out the particular characteristics of woman from her vocation to participate with God through the gift of *maternity*:

> Motherhood involves a special communion with the mystery of life, as it develops in the woman's womb. The mother is filled with wonder at this mystery of life, and "understands" with unique intuition what is happening inside her. In the light of the "beginning," the mother accepts and loves as a person the child she is carrying in her womb. This unique contact with the new human being developing within her gives rise to an attitude towards human beings—not only towards her own child, but every human being—which profoundly marks the woman's personality. It is commonly thought that women are more capable than men of paying attention to another person, and that motherhood develops this predisposition even more. The man—even with all his sharing in parenthood—always remains "outside" the process of pregnancy and the baby's birth; in many ways he has to learn his own "fatherhood" from the mother.[36]

Complementarity between the sexes, which is as much spiritual as physical, is a source of great richness to humanity as a whole and to the family in particular. This natural complementarity makes possible the specifically spousal form of love that is realized in marriage, in which man and woman give to each other what the other lacks, both as persons through their spiritual union and as potential mothers and fathers through their bodily gift to each other. Indeed, their complementary maternity and paternity is realized only through each other, through their bodily union that manifests and is called to enrich their spiritual union of love.[37]

---

[36] John Paul II, Apostolic Letter On the Dignity and Vocation of Woman *Mulieris Dignitatem* (Aug 15, 1988), §18. See also *Mulieris Dignitatem*, §30: "The moral and spiritual strength of a woman is joined to her awareness that God entrusts the human being to her in a special way. Of course, God entrusts every human being to each and every other human being. But this entrusting concerns women in a special way—precisely by reason of their femininity—and this in a particular way determines their vocation."

[37] This complementarity of man and woman as ordered to marriage has been well expressed by D. von Hildebrand, *Man and Woman: Love and the Meaning of Inti-*

This complementarity of male and female in marriage, in addition to being a great good for the family, is also a reality that serves as a sacred sign of the union of Christ, the Bridegroom, with the Church, His Bride. The union of Christ and His Church is a union that is supremely complementary. Although Christ unites Himself intimately with His Church, this communion does not take away the complementary differences between the Head and the members. Christ died for His Bride and sanctifies her with His Body and Blood. He, who is from above, gives the divine life to His members who receive it from Him in Baptism and the other sacraments. Without Christ, the Church would have no supernatural life, no sanctifying grace, no forgiveness of sins, no Head. But the Church supplies complementary gifts, such as receptivity, docility, and maternity. Christ contributes the active part and the source of grace, but the Church contributes the receptive and participatory part. Together they make up a union through mutual and complementary self-gift.

It can be seen from the complementarity between Christ and the Church that only a complementary union can properly represent Christ's union with His Bride. Neither two men nor two women can form a union that is maximally complementary in both the biological and the psychological dimensions. Only a union between a man and a woman that is by nature open to the gift of life can represent the supremely life-giving union between Christ and His Church. Gender complementarity, therefore, as established by God in the beginning, enters into the essence of the sacramental sign of marriage in virtue of the divine plan. Neither the Church nor the State can validly modify or annul what belongs to divine law.

Why Male Gender for the Sacrament of Holy Orders?

Closely related to the sacramental importance of gender complementarity in marriage is the essential requirement that priests in the New

---

macy, 37: "Man and woman are spiritually oriented toward each other; they are created for each other. First, they have a mission for each other; second, because of their complementary difference, a much closer communion and more ultimate love is possible between them than between persons of the same sex. Their mutual mission manifests itself in a wholesome mutual enrichment as well as in the mitigation of the dangers to which the masculine and the feminine type of human beings are exposed when they are deprived of this influence."

Covenant be male.[38] The fact that priests in the New Covenant are ordained to act in the *person of Christ* and so continue *His* priesthood during the time of the Church is the key to understanding why Christ instituted a male priesthood. The Catholic priesthood is essentially ordered to the Eucharist, to the offering of the Sacrifice of the Mass in the person of Christ, Head of the Church, which is His Bride. The necessity of male gender in the sacrament of Holy Orders has to be understood in this context.

Through the reception of the sacrament of Holy Orders, priests receive priestly character,[39] which gives them the spiritual power to act in the person of Christ[40] so as to consecrate the Eucharist and offer the Sacrifice of the Mass, forgive sins, and govern the Mystical Body of Christ. The sacramental sign, therefore, must reflect this spiritual power given by the sacrament to represent and act in the person of Christ, the Head and Bridegroom of His Church.[41]

The sacrament of Orders enables the priest to "lend to Christ his own voice and hands"[42] so that Christ Himself may pronounce

---

[38] On this topic, see Gerhard Ludwig Müller, *Priesthood and Diaconate: The Recipient of the Sacrament of Holy Orders from the Perspective of Creation Theology and Christology*, trans. Michael J. Miller (San Francisco: Ignatius Press, 2002).

[39] This will be explained in chapter 7 below.

[40] The Church expresses this in the phrase: *in persona Christi Capitis*. See *CCC*, §1548. See also *LG*, §28: "They [the priests] exercise their sacred function especially in the Eucharistic worship or the celebration of the Mass by which acting in the person of Christ and proclaiming His Mystery they unite the prayers of the faithful with the sacrifice of their Head"; *Presbyterorum Ordinis*, §2: "Priests, by the anointing of the Holy Spirit, are signed with a special character and are conformed to Christ the Priest in such a way that they can act in the person of Christ the Head."

[41] See CDF, *Inter Insigniores*, §4: "Moreover, it must not be forgotten that the sacramental signs are not conventional ones. Not only is it true that, in many respects, they are natural signs because they respond to the deep symbolism of actions and things, but they are more than this: they are principally meant to link the person of every period to the supreme Event of the history of salvation, in order to enable that person to understand, through all the Bible's wealth of pedagogy and symbolism, what grace they signify and produce. . . . Again the priestly ministry is not just a pastoral service; it ensures the continuity of the functions entrusted by Christ to the Apostles and the continuity of the powers related to those functions. Adaptations to civilizations and times therefore cannot abolish on essential points, the sacramental reference to constitutive events of Christianity and to Christ himself."

[42] Pius XII, *Mediator Dei*, §69, which is quoting St. John Chrysostom, Homily 86 on John 20:23.

the words of consecration in the Eucharist and effect transubstantiation through him. Likewise, Christ forgives sins through the words of absolution of the priest in the sacrament of Penance. So when we hear the words of consecration or absolution, the faithful must think that it is Christ in person who is speaking through His ordained minister and bringing into effect what has been spoken.

To show that the priest is ordained to act in *persona Christi*, the sacramental sign for the conferral of the priesthood, in addition to the laying on of hands (which is the matter of the sacrament), requires that the subject of ordination be *male* to symbolically represent Christ precisely in His role as Head of His Church. This aspect of the sacramental sign was chosen by Christ on account of its natural symbolism to represent the specific effect that it was instituted to realize. The Sacred Congregation for the Doctrine of the Faith explained this in a profound Declaration of 1976, *Inter Insigniores*:

> The Christian priesthood is therefore of a sacramental nature: the priest is a sign, the supernatural effectiveness of which comes from the ordination received, but a sign that must be perceptible and which the faithful must be able to recognize with ease. The whole sacramental economy is in fact based upon natural signs, on symbols imprinted upon the human psychology: "Sacramental signs," says St. Thomas, "represent what they signify by natural resemblance."
>
> The same natural resemblance is required for persons as for things: when Christ's role in the Eucharist is to be expressed sacramentally, there would not be this "natural resemblance" which must exist between Christ and his minister if the role of Christ were not taken by a man: in such a case it would be difficult to see in the minister the image of Christ. For Christ himself was and remains a man.[43]

Some may object that the gender of Christ is purely accidental and thus of no importance in symbolically representing Him in the sacrament of Holy Orders. However, this does not sufficiently acknowledge the role of Christ as Bridegroom. The most profound reason for the importance of Christ's male gender is that He has come into the world to bring men and women into union with God, a union which has the

---

[43] CDF, *Inter Insigniores*, §5 (DS, 4600).

sacred character of a *mystical marriage*. In this mystical marriage, all the faithful comprise the receptive and fruitful bride, and Christ is the Bridegroom, the new head of the human family, the new Adam, the Mediator between man and God. As seen above, gender is not irrelevant when it comes to marriage.

The Bridegroom takes the initiative in instituting this mystical marriage. The Church is necessarily *receptive* in this regard: she *receives* the Bridegroom who has loved her first, and without whom she can do nothing.[44] Christ is the active partner, the good shepherd of His flock, the vine to which we branches must be attached, the founder and wooer of His Church. That Christ is the Bridegroom who loved us first, before we were made loveable, is beautifully portrayed by St. Paul in Ephesians 5:25–32:

> Husbands, love your wives, as Christ loved the Church and gave himself up for her, that he might sanctify her, having cleansed her by the washing of water with the word, that he might present the Church to himself in splendor, without spot or wrinkle or any such thing, that she might be holy and without blemish. . . . "For this reason a man shall leave his father and mother and be joined to his wife, and the two shall become one flesh." This is a great mystery, and I mean in reference to Christ and the Church.

Christ left His Father in the Incarnation to become one flesh with His Church, His bride. It follows from the spousal relationship between Christ and His Church that the priests called to act in the person of Christ must symbolically represent Christ as Bridegroom. For this simple reason, they must be male as Christ was.

The nuptials between Christ and the Church, to be fully consummated in the beatific vision in heaven, are anticipated in the Holy Eucharist, which is both the sacrifice of our redemption and the wedding banquet of communion with the King of kings, in which the New Covenant is ratified in the Blood of the Lamb and mystically poured out for us on the altar.[45] Therefore, it is necessary that the priest, who acts in the person of Christ in bringing about this mystical

---

[44] See 1 John 4:10: "In this is love, not that we loved God but that he loved us and sent his Son to be the expiation for our sins." See also John 3:16; Eph 5:25–27.
[45] See Feingold, *The Eucharist*, xxx, 6–10, 22–23, 27–28.

marriage *especially in the celebration of the Eucharist*, be capable of sacramentally representing Christ precisely in His role as Bridegroom of the Church. This doctrine is explained in *Inter Insigniores*, §5:

> Nevertheless, the Incarnation of the Word took place according to the male sex: this is indeed a question of fact, and this fact, while not implying an alleged natural superiority of man over woman, cannot be disassociated from the economy of salvation. . . . For the salvation offered by God to men and women . . . took on, from the Old Testament Prophets onwards, the privileged form of a nuptial mystery: for God the Chosen People is seen as his ardently loved spouse. . . . From his pierced side will be born the Church, as Eve was born from Adam's side. At that time there is fully and eternally accomplished the nuptial mystery proclaimed . . . in the Old Testament: Christ is the Bridegroom; the Church is his bride, whom he loves because he has gained her by his blood and made her glorious, holy and without blemish, and henceforth he is inseparable from her. . . .
>
> That is why we can never ignore the fact that Christ is a man. And therefore, unless one is to disregard the importance of this symbolism for the economy of Revelation, it must be admitted that, in actions which demand the character of ordination and in which Christ himself, the author of the Covenant, the Bridegroom and Head of the Church, is represented, exercising his ministry of salvation—which is in the highest degree the case of the Eucharist—his role (this is the original sense of the word "persona") must be taken by a man.

The necessity that the priest be male has nothing to do with "any personal superiority of the latter in the order of values,"[46] but derives from the fact that Holy Orders is a sacrament, or *efficacious sacred sign*, a sign chosen by Christ to represent Himself as the bridegroom and head of the Church.

How do we know that Christ instituted a male priesthood? The twelve Apostles ordained at the Last Supper were all men. A woman who was infinitely more "qualified" was passed over: Mary the Mother of God and the Queen of heaven and earth. Likewise, Mary Magdalene,

---

[46] CDF, *Inter Insigniores*, §5 (DS, 4600).

who exceeded the Apostles in faith and love and who merited to see the risen Christ before the Apostles, was passed over. And then the Apostles in their turn only ordained men to be their successors, as did their successors up until our own time. The entire practice of the Church for two millennia confirms this Tradition. It is impossible that such a unanimous practice of the Church for two millennia not stem from apostolic Tradition.

St. John Paul II confirmed this teaching of *Inter Insigniores* in his Apostolic Letter *Mulieris Dignitatem* of 1988. Against the objection that Jesus called only men to be Apostles because of the patriarchal assumptions of his culture, he responds:

> *In calling only men as his Apostles,* Christ acted *in a completely free and sovereign manner.* In doing so, he exercised the same freedom with which, in all his behaviour, he emphasized the dignity and the vocation of women, without conforming to the prevailing customs and to the traditions sanctioned by the legislation of the time. Consequently, the assumption that he called men to be apostles in order to conform with the widespread mentality of his times, does not at all correspond to Christ's way of acting.[47]

John Paul II then goes on to explain the spousal meaning of the Eucharist, and consequently of the priest who offers the Eucharistic Sacrifice, confirming the teaching of *Inter Insigniores*:

> The "sincere gift" contained in the Sacrifice of the Cross gives definitive prominence to the spousal meaning of God's love. As the Redeemer of the world, Christ is the Bridegroom of the Church. *The Eucharist is the Sacrament of our Redemption.* It is *the Sacrament of the Bridegroom and of the Bride.* . . . Since Christ, in instituting the Eucharist, linked it in such an explicit way to the priestly service of the Apostles, it is legitimate to conclude that he thereby wished to express the relationship between man and woman, between what is "feminine" and what is "masculine." It is a relationship willed by God both in the mystery of creation and in the mystery of Redemption. It is *the Eucharist* above all that

---

[47] John Paul II, *Mulieris Dignitatem*, §26 (italics original).

expresses *the redemptive act of Christ the Bridegroom towards the Church the Bride.* This is clear and unambiguous when the sacramental ministry of the Eucharist, in which the priest acts "in *persona Christi,*" is performed by a man. This explanation confirms the teaching of the Declaration *Inter Insigniores,* published at the behest of Paul VI in response to the question concerning the admission of women to the ministerial priesthood.[48]

Infallible Status of This Teaching: Ordinatio Sacerdotalis

Six years later St. John Paul II returned to the subject to determine the question in a definitive way because of increased pressure by some for the ordination of women as priests. In his Apostolic Letter of 1994, *Ordinatio Sacerdotalis,* St. John Paul II has definitively and infallibly confirmed the constant universal Tradition of the Church that she has not received the authority from Jesus Christ to ordain women priests because the male priesthood of the New Covenant is of divine institution. The purpose of this very brief document was not to explain the reasons Christ instituted a male priesthood, reasons already cogently expressed in *Inter Insigniores* and *Mulieris Dignitatem,* §26. The purpose was rather to remove all doubt concerning the irrevocable nature of this teaching, already infallibly taught by the constant Tradition and practice of twenty centuries in the universal Church,[49] both East and West:

> In order that all doubt may be removed regarding a matter of great importance, a matter which pertains to the Church's divine constitution itself, in virtue of my ministry of confirming the brethren (cf. Lk 22:32) I declare that the Church has no authority whatsoever to confer priestly ordination on

---

[48] John Paul II, *Mulieris Dignitatem,* §26 (italics original).

[49] See John Paul II, *Ordinatio Sacerdotalis,* §4, DS, 4983: "Although the teaching that priestly ordination is to be reserved to men alone has been preserved by the constant and universal Tradition of the Church and firmly taught by the Magisterium in its more recent documents, at the present time in some places it is nonetheless considered still open to debate, or the Church's judgment that women are not to be admitted to ordination is considered to have a merely disciplinary force."

women and that this judgment is to be definitively held by all
the Church's faithful.[50]

John Paul II expressed himself very precisely to make it very clear
that this pronouncement is definitive and therefore *infallible*.[51] The
First and Second Vatican Councils have determined the conditions
necessary for a papal teaching to be infallible. The Pope must speak
(1) as universal Pastor exercising his apostolic charge over the universal Church, (2) with the intention of determining a question in
a definitive manner, and (3) in a matter concerning faith or morals.[52]
All of these requirements are realized in §4 of *Ordinatio Sacerdotalis*.
First, the Pope speaks as supreme pastor, "in virtue of my ministry of
confirming the brethren (cf. Lk 22:32)." Secondly, he clearly intends
to make a definitive act, for he says: "this judgment is to be *definitively*
held by all the Church's faithful." Finally, he makes it clear that this
question pertains to faith and morals, for it is "a matter which pertains to the Church's divine constitution itself." The Church's *divine*
constitution pertains to the Church's nature as a sacramental body
constituted by God, and thus it belongs in the realm of faith and not
merely ecclesiastical discipline.

John Paul II does not say that this truth is revealed by God
and therefore should be firmly *believed*, as in the definition of the
Immaculate Conception or Mary's Assumption into heaven,[53] but
rather states that it is to be "definitively *held*." This means that he is
not teaching it as a revealed dogma, but as a doctrine that is necessarily connected to revealed truth, and hence included in the deposit
of faith. The Church can teach a doctrine infallibly in two ways: as
directly revealed by God, for which reason it is to be firmly believed,
or as at least *necessarily connected* with revealed doctrine, on account

---

[50] John Paul II, *Ordinatio Sacerdotalis*, §4, DS, 4983.

[51] See Feingold, *Faith Comes from What Is Heard*, 264–66.

[52] See Vatican I, *Pastor Aeternus*; *LG*, §25; *CCC*, §891: "The Roman Pontiff, head
of the college of bishops, enjoys this infallibility in virtue of his office, when,
as supreme pastor and teacher of all the faithful—who confirms his brethren
in the faith—he proclaims by a definitive act a doctrine pertaining to faith or
morals."

[53] See Pius IX, *Ineffabilis Deus* (1854; DS, 2803); and Pius XII, *Munificentissimus
Deus* (1950), §44 (DS, 3903). Another example of a dogma defined as divinely
revealed is the definition of papal infallibility by the First Vatican Council in
the Dogmatic Constitution *Pastor Aeternus*, DS, 3073–74.

of which it is to be firmly *held* by the faithful. The teaching of this paragraph of *Ordinatio Sacerdotalis* falls into this second category. However, it is not unreasonable to think that this doctrine has in fact been revealed by God through the apostolic Tradition, and that the Church could declare it as such in the future.[54]

Marian and Petrine Dimensions of the Church

Many think that the impossibility for women to be ordained priests diminishes the role of women in the Church. This would be a misunderstanding that fails to see the fundamental Marian dimension of the Church. Whereas Christ became man to be the Bridegroom of the Church, the Church herself is always spoken of in the feminine gender to symbolize her receptive nature with respect to Christ and the Trinity and her fruitfulness through her sacraments. The Church is both Bride of Christ and Mother of the faithful. All of the faithful share in this dignity of being members of the Bride of Christ. Women are privileged in this role of bride, for they can more naturally internalize and express this spiritual relationship between the Church and her Bridegroom.

Furthermore, the holiest member of the Body of Christ is a woman, Mary, the Mother of Jesus, the Woman *par excellence*, whom Jesus refers to precisely as "woman." Just as Jesus is the "Son of man," the man for all men, so Mary is "the woman," the new mother of all the living, spoken of at the dawn of history in Genesis 3:15 and again at the end of the Bible in Revelation 12:1. The Church is essentially Marian because she is marked by the fact that Mary is the Mother of the Church and the quintessential model of her holiness. Mary is the model for every member of the Church and for every state of life. She is the perfect response to the Word of God.

At the same time, the Church is also essentially Petrine in that she is built on Peter and on the hierarchical structure given to her by the sacrament of Holy Orders. The Petrine function stands in service of the Marian dimension. The ordained priests enable the entire Church,

---

[54] See CDF, Doctrinal Commentary on the Concluding Formula of the *Professio Fidei* (June 29, 1998), §11, in *Origins* 28, no. 8 (July 16, 1998): 118, which expressly speaks of this possibility: "This does not foreclose the possibility that, in the future, the consciousness of the Church might progress to the point where this teaching could be defined as a doctrine to be believed as divinely revealed."

the Bride of Christ, to be sanctified in grace and truth in a mystical marriage with Christ.

When Can Sacraments Be Administered to Non-Catholics?

Another controversial topic with regard to the recipient of the sacraments is the question of reception of Holy Communion, Penance, and Anointing of the Sick by non-Catholics. The general legislation on sacramental intercommunion with non-Catholics is given in canon 844 of the *Code of Canon Law*.[55] Sections 3 and 4 of canon 844 distinguish between recipients who are Eastern Orthodox or equivalent and those who are Protestants, because the Orthodox have the same Catholic faith in the sacraments whereas Protestants generally do not. Two conditions are given to the Eastern Orthodox for receiving these sacraments from a Catholic minister: that they freely seek the sacrament on their own initiative and are properly disposed.[56]

Since the sacrament must be freely requested by the person, it would not be licit to administer Anointing of the Sick to a non-Catholic who is already unconscious and has not explicitly requested the sacrament prior to losing consciousness. It is also not licit for chaplains to ask non-Catholics, whether Orthodox or Protestant, if they wish to receive the sacrament, for the person must request it of his own accord.

For Protestants, four conditions are required for licit administration of these sacraments.[57] There must be danger of death; the person must freely and spontaneously request the sacrament himself; he must manifest Catholic faith with regard to the sacrament; and it must

---

[55] This corresponds to can. 671 in the *Code of Canons of the Eastern Churches*.

[56] See CIC, can. 844, §3: "Catholic ministers may licitly administer the sacraments of penance, Eucharist and anointing of the sick to members of the oriental churches which do not have full communion with the Catholic Church, if they ask on their own for the sacraments and are properly disposed. This holds also for members of other churches, which in the judgment of the Apostolic See are in the same condition as the oriental churches as far as these sacraments are concerned."

[57] See CIC, can. 844, §4: "If the danger of death is present or other grave necessity, in the judgment of the diocesan bishop or the conference of bishops, Catholic ministers may licitly administer these sacraments to other Christians who do not have full communion with the Catholic Church, who cannot approach a minister of their own community and on their own ask for it, provided they manifest Catholic faith in these sacraments and are properly disposed."

be impossible to receive the sacrament from a minister of his own denomination.

John Paul II comments on canon 844 in *Ecclesia de Eucharistia*, §46:

> In my Encyclical *Ut Unum Sint* I expressed my own appreciation of these norms, which make it possible to provide for the salvation of souls with proper discernment: "It is a source of joy to note that Catholic ministers are able, in certain particular cases, to administer the sacraments of the Eucharist, Penance and Anointing of the Sick to Christians who are not in full communion with the Catholic Church but who greatly desire to receive these sacraments, freely request them and manifest the faith which the Catholic Church professes with regard to these sacraments. Conversely, in specific cases and in particular circumstances, Catholics too can request these same sacraments from ministers of Churches in which these sacraments are valid."
>
> These conditions, from which no dispensation can be given, must be carefully respected, even though they deal with specific individual cases, because the denial of one or more truths of the faith regarding these sacraments and, among these, the truth regarding the need of the ministerial priesthood for their validity, renders the person asking improperly disposed to legitimately receiving them. And the opposite is also true: Catholics may not receive communion in those communities which lack a valid sacrament of Orders.
>
> The faithful observance of the body of norms established in this area is a manifestation and, at the same time, a guarantee of our love for Jesus Christ in the Blessed Sacrament, for our brothers and sisters of different Christian confessions—who have a right to our witness to the truth—and for the cause itself of the promotion of unity.

Concelebration of the Eucharist with priests or ministers of churches or ecclesial communities not in full communion with the Catholic Church is prohibited by canon 908.

3. Necessary Conditions in the Minister of the Sacraments

Holy Orders Configures the Minister to Christ

The sacramental system of the New Covenant is made possible by the Incarnation. Christ in His humanity acts in every sacramental action through His ministers, who are His living instruments.[58] Christ thus extends His humanity through the priest so as to encounter all the faithful throughout the life of the Church. He acts by a double instrumentality, making use of living ministers who represent Him and act in His name, and of external things (words and material elements) used by those ministers.

It is supremely fitting that these living instruments of sacramental action be made into sacramental ministers by another sacrament, which is Holy Orders. Christ instituted this sacrament of Orders at the Last Supper when He said: "Do this in remembrance of me" (Luke 22:19). Pius XII explains:

> Only to the apostles, and thenceforth to those on whom their successors have imposed hands, is granted the power of the priesthood, in virtue of which they represent the person of Jesus Christ before their people, acting at the same time as representatives of their people before God. This priesthood is not transmitted by heredity or human descent. It does not emanate from the Christian community. It is not a delegation from the people. Prior to acting as representative of the community before the throne of God, the priest is the ambassador of the divine Redeemer. He is God's vice-gerent in the midst of his flock precisely because Jesus Christ is Head of that body of which Christians are the members. The power entrusted to him, therefore, bears no natural resemblance to

---

[58] See chapter 12 below, pp. 422–29, for a discussion on the instrumental causality of the sacraments. St. Thomas explains this instrumental causality of the minister with regard to the sacrament of Penance, in his commentary on Matt 16:19, no. 1390, trans. Jeremy Holmes, *Commentary on the Gospel of Matthew: Chapters 13–28* (Lander, WY: Aquinas Institute for the Study of Sacred Doctrine, 2013), 38:102: "Thus I say that in a priest there is a certain spiritual, instrumental strength, from which he is called a 'minister,' and thus he works the remission of sins ministerially, just as water works baptism."

anything human. It is entirely supernatural. It comes from God. "As the Father hath sent me, I also send you [Jn 20:21]. . . he that heareth you heareth me [Lk 10:16]. . . go ye into the whole world and preach the gospel to every creature; he that believeth and is baptized shall be saved [Mk 16:15–16]."

That is why the visible, external priesthood of Jesus Christ is not handed down indiscriminately to all members of the Church in general, but is conferred on designated men, through what may be called the spiritual generation of holy orders.[59]

The priest is able to make Christ's Sacrifice present on the altar because Holy Orders configures him to Christ and enables Christ to be the principal priest in every priestly action:

It is the same priest, Christ Jesus, whose sacred Person his minister truly represents. Now the minister, by reason of the sacerdotal consecration which he has received, is truly made like to the High Priest and possesses the authority to act in the power and place of the person of Christ himself (*virtute ac persona ipsius Christi*).[60]

Although it is necessary that the sacramental minister be empowered with the character[61] of Holy Orders at an appropriate grade so as to link the sacramental action with Christ the High Priest, there are two exceptions to this rule. Because of the necessity of Baptism, in an emergency it can be done by anyone who intends to do what the Church does (CIC, can. 861; *CCC*, §1284). The second exception is Matrimony, in which the ministers are the spouses themselves in their formal expression of consent. They make their consent before the Church, who is represented ordinarily by a deacon, priest, or bishop, who serves as the canonical witness and gives the nuptial blessing. All the other sacraments require for validity a minister with Holy Orders at the level of priest or bishop.

---

[59] Pius XII, *Mediator Dei*, §§40–41.
[60] Pius XII, *Mediator Dei*, §69, quoted in *CCC*, §1548.
[61] See chapter 7 below, pp. 260–68.

Minister of the Eucharist

Canon 900 of the *Code of Canon Law* stipulates that "the minister who is able to confect the sacrament of the Eucharist in the person of Christ is a validly ordained priest alone."[62] The Eucharist is first and foremost a sacrifice offered to God the Father,[63] and the priesthood is ordered to the offering of sacrifice, as stated in Hebrews 5:1: "Every high priest chosen from among men is appointed to act on behalf of men in relation to God, to offer gifts and sacrifices for sins." It follows that the Eucharist can only be offered by one constituted as a priest of the New Covenant by sacramental configuration with Christ, the eternal High Priest.

Furthermore, the Mass is essentially the same sacrifice as that of Calvary, because the Victim and the Priest are the same in the Mass and on Calvary. The priest is the same because the Mass is offered principally by Christ, eternal High Priest, through the lips and hands of those who are ordained to act *in persona Christi*. As will be seen in the next chapter, priestly character configures the priest to Christ and confers the spiritual power to act sacramentally in His Person, above all in the celebration of the Eucharistic Sacrifice. Any validly ordained priest can validly confect the Eucharist. It is licitly celebrated by any priest who is not canonically impeded.[64]

Minister of Holy Orders

Canon 1012 of the *Code of Canon Law* states that "the minister of sacred ordination is a consecrated bishop." Ordination, especially at the grade of priesthood or episcopacy, gives the recipient a share in the headship of Christ over His Church. It is necessary that the sacramental transmission of headship be given only by a minister who has the fullness of that headship in the Church through episcopal consecration. Since Holy Orders at the level of the episcopacy makes the recipient a successor of the Apostles, this can be transmitted validly

---

[62] CIC, can. 900, §1.

[63] See John Paul II, Letter to Priests on Holy Thursday *Dominicae Cenae* (Feb 24, 1980), §9: "The Eucharist is above all else a sacrifice. It is the sacrifice of the Redemption and also the sacrifice of the New Covenant, as we believe and as the Eastern Churches clearly profess."

[64] See CIC, can. 900, §2.

only by one who is already a successor of the Apostles.

Furthermore, since the Apostles were constituted as a college under the headship of St. Peter, it is necessary that the choice of bishop to be ordained not be contrary to communion with the successor of Peter. Hence the person to be ordained to the episcopate requires a mandate from the Holy Father for licitness (but not for validity).[65] Ordaining a bishop against the will of the Holy Father is an extremely grave offense against the unity of the Church and incurs a *latae sententiae* excommunication, both on the part of the consecrating bishop and the one so consecrated.[66]

Minister of Confirmation

The Eastern and Latin rites have different practices with regard to the usual minister of Confirmation, or Chrismation as it is referred to in the East.[67] Originally, in both East and West, Baptism and Confirmation were administered together by the bishop. In the Acts of the Apostles, we see the sacramental gift of the Holy Spirit administered only by Apostles. In Acts 8, the deacon Philip evangelized Samaria and baptized the people, but was not able to give the Holy Spirit in Confirmation because he was only a deacon. For this reason two of the Apostles, Peter and John, went to Samaria to confirm them and thus confer the fuller gift of the Holy Spirit.[68] We see the sacrament of Confirmation again in Acts 19:2–7. When St. Paul arrived in Ephesus,

---

[65] See CIC, can. 1013: "No bishop is permitted to consecrate anyone a bishop unless it is first evident that there is a pontifical mandate."

[66] See CIC, can. 1382.

[67] A brief historical summary on this subject is given in *CCC*, §1290.

[68] See Acts 8:14–18. See Michael O'Dwyer, *Confirmation: A Study in the Development of Sacramental Theology* (New York: Benziger Brothers, 1915), 2–3: "We are told pointedly in the text that the Samaritans had *only* been baptised; clearly implying that something more was required for their full initiation, something which was distinct from baptism, but yet its complement. . . . Between the imposition of hands and the gift of the Holy Spirit there is a most intimate causal relation. The gift is the effect of the imposition. This is borne out also by the fact that Simon saw it was by the imposition of hands that the Holy Spirit was imparted, and sought to purchase the power of bestowing the same gift in the same manner. From all of which we conclude that the imposition of hands which bestowed the Holy Spirit is a rite distinct from baptism, and that the power to perform the ceremony is not implied in the power to baptize. In the minister, in the rite itself, and in the effect, the two ceremonies are different."

he found some disciples there and asked them if they had received the gift of the Holy Spirit when they were initiated into the faith. They replied that they did not even know of the existence of the Holy Spirit. Acts 19:5 does not specify the minister of their Christian Baptism, but Acts 19:6 expressly states that the Apostle Paul was the minister of their Confirmation, laying hands on them through which "the Holy Spirit came on them."

The bishops, successors of the Apostles, continued to be the ministers of the giving of the Spirit. But as the Church expanded and rural parishes multiplied, a bishop could not be present for every child's Baptism. This led to a pastoral dilemma in which the Eastern and Western traditions responded differently. If Baptism and Confirmation were to be kept together, it was necessary for the baptizing priest also to be able to confirm. This was how it was resolved in the East. If, on the other hand, Confirmation was to be reserved to the bishop, then the administration of the two sacraments generally had to be separated in practice, as occurred in the West.

Lumen Gentium, §26 states that bishops "are the original ministers of confirmation." The *Catechism of the Catholic Church*, §1312 follows *Lumen Gentium*, stating: "The *original minister* of Confirmation is the bishop." The *Code of Canon Law* for the Latin rite, however, speaks of the bishop as the "ordinary minister."[69] This is also the language of the Council of Trent: "If any one says that the ordinary minister of holy confirmation is not the bishop alone, but any simple priest whatsoever; let him be anathema."[70]

The term "original" was chosen by *Lumen Gentium* and the *Catechism of the Catholic Church* to accommodate the canonical practice in the Eastern churches in which every presbyter is granted the faculty to confer Chrismation by the universal law,[71] and thus the presbyter is the usual minister of the sacrament, which is normally conferred immediately after baptism. Nevertheless, the bishop remains the *orig-*

---

[69] See CIC, can. 882: "The ordinary minister of confirmation is a bishop; a presbyter provided with this faculty in virtue of universal law or the special grant of the competent authority also confers this sacrament validly."

[70] Council of Trent, Decree on the Sacraments (session 7), can. 3 on Confirmation (DS, 1630).

[71] See *Code of Canons of the Eastern Churches*, can. 696, §1: "All presbyters of the Eastern Churches can validly administer this sacrament either along with baptism or separately to all the Christian faithful of any Church *sui iuris* including the Latin Church."

inal minister from whom this power to confirm is granted to priests, although in different ways in the Latin rite and the Eastern churches. In the Eastern churches, the original bond of this sacrament with the office of bishop is expressed by the fact that the presbyter administers the sacrament with myron consecrated by the bishop.[72]

In the Latin rite, however, the bishop is not only the *original* but also the *ordinary* minister of the sacrament. This means that the bishop alone, through his office, always has the power to validly confirm in the Latin rite. Contrary to the practice in the Eastern churches, priests in the Latin rite do not automatically have this power to validly confirm. In the Latin rite, a priest can be delegated as minister in the place of the bishop for certain circumstances, and the universal law of the Church gives the power to validly confirm to any priest who "by virtue of office [e.g., pastor] or mandate of the diocesan bishop baptizes one who is no longer an infant or admits one already baptized into the full communion of the Catholic Church" in the Rite of Christian Initiation of Adults.[73] Since the bishop cannot be present in all the parishes of the diocese on the Easter vigil, the pastor who baptizes or receives the candidates into full communion with the Church has the power by universal law to confirm them. In addition, any priest can administer Confirmation in danger of death.[74] The *Catechism of the Catholic Church*, §1314 says that "the Church desires that none of her children, even the youngest, should depart this world without having been perfected by the Holy Spirit with the gift of Christ's fullness." Confirmation of children (not in danger of death) is reserved to the bishop (although, as stated in canon 884, it can be delegated to certain presbyters in case of need), and it is conferred on those who have reached the age of reason, which thus separates the Baptism and Confirmation of children both in time and with regard to the ordinary minister.

Both the Eastern and the Latin practice have advantages and disadvantages. The great advantage of the Eastern practice, faithful to that of the early Church, is that it emphasizes the unity of the three

---

[72] See *CCC*, §1312: "In the East, ordinarily the priest who baptizes also immediately confers Confirmation in one and the same celebration. But he does so with sacred chrism consecrated by the patriarch or the bishop, thus expressing the apostolic unity of the Church whose bonds are strengthened by the sacrament of Confirmation."

[73] CIC, can. 883, §2.

[74] CIC, can. 883, §3.

sacraments of Christian initiation, whether for babies or adults.[75] As seen above,[76] Baptism, Confirmation, and the Eucharist give Christian being, movement, and life,[77] and it is fitting that the Christian never be without the sacramental gift of the Spirit, who is the source of supernatural activity. The celebration of Confirmation immediately after Baptism visibly manifests the intimate connection between insertion into Christ through Baptism, and reception of the Holy Spirit, who is the Spirit of the Son. It is for this reason that, also in the Latin Rite, Confirmation immediately follows upon Baptism for adult catechumens in the *Rite of Christian Initiation of Adults*:

> In accord with the ancient practice followed in the Roman liturgy, adults are not to be baptized without receiving confirmation immediately afterward, unless some serious reason stands in the way. The conjunction of the two celebrations signifies the unity of the paschal mystery, the close link between the mission of the Son and the outpouring of the Holy Spirit, and the connection between the two sacraments through which the Son and the Holy Spirit come with the Father to those who are baptized.[78]

For this reason, the *Code of Canon Law* for the Latin Church requires that adults who are baptized "be confirmed immediately after Baptism and participate in the celebration of the Eucharist, also receiving Communion."[79]

The disadvantage of the Eastern practice is that the association of Confirmation with the bishop and apostolic succession, as maintained in the Latin practice, is less clearly manifested in the Eastern rite. It is still maintained there, however, through the use of the oil of Chrismation blessed by the bishop.[80]

---

[75] On the importance of the unity of the sacraments of initiation, see Zizioulas, *The Eucharistic Communion and the World*, 113–22.

[76] See above, chapter 3, pp. 78–81.

[77] See Cabasilas, *The Life in Christ* 1.6, pp. 49–50; and 3.1, p. 103.

[78] *Rite of Christian Initiation of Adults*, §215, in *Rites*, 146–47. See Paul Turner, *Confirmation: The Baby in Solomon's Court*, rev. ed. (Chicago: Hillenbrand Books, 2006), 2: "Placing Confirmation immediately after Baptism thus joins the gift of the Spirit to the mission of Jesus."

[79] CIC, can. 866.

[80] See *CCC*, §1312, §1292: "The practice of the Eastern Churches gives greater

The fittingness of the practice of the Latin rite lies in the fact that Confirmation effects in the recipients a deeper configuration with the Church, giving them the mission to actively build up the Church through participation in Christ's prophetic, priestly, and kingly offices. Thus it is fitting that this deeper configuration be realized by the head of the local church, the bishop, who is the source of unity in the Church. The *Catechism of the Catholic Church*, §1313 explains that the bishop is the ordinary minister in the Latin rite to manifest that Confirmation binds the recipient "more closely to the Church, to her apostolic origins, and to her mission of bearing witness to Christ."[81] The fittingness of the bishop as the minister of Confirmation is explained by St. Thomas through an analogy to a master craftsman in a workshop. Apprentices may do the rough work at the beginning, but the master craftsman puts the final touches on his masterpieces. Likewise, a CEO approves and implements the important works of his corporation. Similarly, the bishop, who possesses the highest power in the Church, is the one who sacramentally brings forth the mature Christian as a divine work.[82]

Minister of the Sacrament of Reconciliation

The minister of the sacrament of Penance is "the priest alone" (CIC, can. 965). Priestly character gives the priest the power "of the keys" to

---

emphasis to the unity of Christian initiation. That of the Latin Church more clearly expresses the communion of the new Christian with the bishop as guarantor and servant of the unity, catholicity and apostolicity of his Church, and hence the connection with the apostolic origins of Christ's Church."

[81] *CCC*, §1313.

[82] *ST* III, q. 72, a. 11: "In every work the final completion is reserved to the supreme act or power; thus the preparation of the matter belongs to the lower craftsmen, the higher gives the form, but the highest of all is he to whom pertains the use, which is the end of things made by art; thus also the letter which is written by the clerk, is signed by his employer. Now the faithful of Christ are a Divine work, according to 1 Corinthians 3:9: 'You are God's building'; and they are also 'an epistle,' as it were, 'written with the Spirit of God,' according to 2 Corinthians 3:2–3. And this sacrament of Confirmation is, as it were, the final completion of the sacrament of Baptism; in the sense that by Baptism man is built up into a spiritual dwelling, and is written like a spiritual letter; whereas by the sacrament of Confirmation, like a house already built, he is consecrated as a temple of the Holy Spirit, and as a letter already written, is signed with the sign of the cross. Therefore the conferring of this sacrament is reserved to bishops, who possess supreme power in the Church: just as in the primitive Church, the fullness of the Holy Spirit was given by the apostles, in whose place the bishops stand (Acts 8)."

absolve all sins as a minister of Christ. To validly exercise this power over particular subjects, however, in addition to the sacramental power to absolve from sin, the priest also needs the faculty of jurisdiction, which is a juridical competence or power over particular penitents in order to validly absolve them from their sins. This is necessary because the sacrament of Penance has a judicial aspect in which the priest acts as judge and has the power of the keys to bind—imposing works of satisfaction—as well as to loose from the bonds of sin, and, if necessary, from ecclesiastical censures. In order to act as judge over members of the faithful, one must have received jurisdiction over them. No one can validly command another unless he have jurisdiction over him.[83] The Council of Trent declares:

> It is in the nature and meaning of a judgment that the sentence be pronounced only over one's subjects. Hence the Church of God has always been convinced, and this council confirms as fully true, that absolution is of no value if it is pronounced by a priest on one over whom he has neither ordinary nor delegated jurisdiction.[84]

Canon 966, §1 of the *Code of Canon Law* states: "The valid absolution of sins requires that the minister have, in addition to the power of orders, the faculty of exercising it for the faithful to whom he imparts absolution." This faculty can arise through the universal law of the Church by fact of holding a particular office, such as pastor, or through the grant from the competent authority, such as one's local ordinary (§2).

Any priest who has received the faculty of hearing confessions,

---

[83] Thomas Aquinas, *In IV Sent.*, d. 17, q. 3, a. 3, qla. 4, trans. Mortensen, 8:335: "It is necessary that the person who is established as minister of this sacrament be such that he can command something to be done. Now, someone does not have command over another unless he has jurisdiction over him; and so it belongs to this sacrament of necessity not only that the minister have holy orders, as in the other sacraments, but also that he have jurisdiction; and so just as someone who is not a priest cannot confer this sacrament, so neither can someone who does not have jurisdiction. And because of this a confession must be made not just to a priest, but to one's own priest. For since a priest does not absolve except by binding someone to do something, the only one who can absolve is one who can bind someone to do something by his command."

[84] Council of Trent, Doctrine on the Sacrament of Penance (session 14), ch. 7 (DS, 1686).

either by virtue of the law or through a grant from his local ordinary, can validly hear confessions everywhere unless a local ordinary denies it in a particular case, as stipulated in canon 967, §2. Canon 976 states that in danger of death any validly ordained priest can absolve any penitent from all sins and censures. This is true even if another priest is present who has faculties. St. Thomas explains that this is because the end of the law is the salvation of souls, and urgent necessity warrants exemption from ordinary discipline.[85]

Minister of the Sacrament of Anointing of the Sick

The minister of the sacrament of Anointing of the Sick is a priest. Since Anointing of the Sick completes the work of the sacrament of Penance[86] in further purifying the soul from sin and its wounds, it is fitting that its minister be a priest or bishop who has the sacred power to act in the person of Christ.[87] This was defined in the Council of Trent, in the fourth canon on Anointing:

> If anyone says that the presbyters of the Church who, as blessed James exhorts, should be brought to anoint the sick are not priests ordained by a bishop but the senior members of each community and that, for this reason, the proper minister of extreme unction is not only the priest, let him be anathema.[88]

---

[85] Thomas Aquinas, *In IV Sent.*, d. 20, q. 1, a. 1, qla. 2, trans. Mortensen, 8:448: "Any priest, as someone with the power of the keys, has that power indifferently for all people and with regard to all sins. But the fact that he cannot absolve all people from all sins is because by the order of the Church he has limited jurisdiction, or none at all. But because necessity knows no law, in an emergency he is not prevented by the order of the Church from giving absolution by the fact that he also holds the keys sacramentally; and a person obtains as much from another's absolution as if he were absolved by his own priest. Nor at that moment can he be absolved only from sin by any priest, but also from the excommunication imposed by anyone."

[86] See *CCC*, §§1523, 1525.

[87] See John C. Kasza, "Anointing of the Sick," in *OHST*, 566: "Deacons may not anoint because they lack the capacity to act as an instrument of sacramental absolution. Because the sacrament is linked to the forgiveness of sin, only those having priestly ordination may confer sacramental anointing."

[88] Council of Trent, Doctrine on the Sacrament of Extreme Unction (session 14), can. 4 (DS, 1719).

Canon 1003, §1 of the *Code of Canon Law* states: "Every priest and a priest alone validly administers the anointing of the sick." The canon further explains that the priest should have jurisdiction over the recipient of the sacrament, such as a pastor, but that any priest may offer this sacrament for a reasonable cause and with the presumed consent of the pastor, or in the case of necessity.[89] The canon also specifies that "any priest is permitted to carry blessed oil with him so that he is able to administer the sacrament of the anointing of the sick in a case of necessity."[90]

In the patristic period, there is evidence that the oil of Anointing of the Sick, blessed by the bishop, was sometimes applied to the sick by the lay faithful when no priest was available.[91] This raises the question of whether the minister must always be a priest, in accordance with the practice and teaching of the second millennium, especially the definitive teaching of Trent. The best answer is that an anointing of oil blessed by the bishop but not administered by a priest, as was apparently a common practice in certain regions in the first millennium, should be regarded as a *sacramental*, but not as the *sacrament* of Anointing, in accordance with the interpretation of St. Thomas.[92] As a sacramental it could sometimes be the occasion of physical healing,

---

[89] See CIC, can. 1003, §2: "All priests to whom the care of souls has been entrusted have the duty and right of administering the anointing of the sick for the faithful entrusted to their pastoral office. For a reasonable cause, any other priest can administer this sacrament with at least the presumed consent of the priest mentioned above.

[90] CIC, can. 1003, §3.

[91] See Antoine Chavasse, *Etude sur l'onction des infirmes dans l'Église latine du IIIe au XIe siècle* (Lyon: Facultés Catholiques de Lyon, 1942), especially 168–75. See also Pope Innocent I, letter to Decentius, bishop of Gubbio, (DS, 216): which, as seen above, is also the earliest magisterial affirmation of Anointing as a sacrament: "There is no doubt that this anointing ought to be interpreted or understood of the sick faithful, who can be anointed with the holy oil of chrism, which prepared by a bishop, is permitted not only to priests, but also to all as Christians for anointing in their own necessity or in the necessity of their (people)."

[92] See Thomas Aquinas, *In IV Sent.*, d. 23, q. 2, a. 1, qla. 1, ad 2, trans. Mortensen, 8:570: "Those anointings [administered by lay people] were not sacramental, but from a certain devotion of those receiving this anointing and the merits of those anointing them or sending the oil, the effect of physical healing was obtained through the grace of healings, not through sacramental grace." See also Francisco A. P. Sola, S.J., "On Extreme Unction," in *Sacrae Theologiae Summa*, 4A:609–10.

but not the instrumental cause of the spiritual effects of the forgiveness of sins and the giving of grace, except through desire for the sacrament (as in Baptism of desire or spiritual communion).

The Congregation for the Doctrine of the Faith published an important "Note on the Minister of the Sacrament of Anointing of the Sick," which clarifies that it is to be firmly held by the faithful (*definitive tenendum*)[93] that only the priest can confer this sacrament. This recognizes that this doctrine has been infallibly taught by the Church through her ordinary universal Magisterium and requires the second grade of assent from the faithful. The principal reason that the minister of Anointing must be a priest is because

> in the administration of the sacraments, he acts *in persona Christi Capitis* and *in persona Ecclesiae.* The person who acts in this Sacrament is Jesus Christ; the priest is the living and visible instrument. He represents and makes Christ present in a special way, which is why the Sacrament has special dignity and efficacy in comparison with a sacramental.[94]

Protestant Rejection of Holy Orders

It could be argued that the gravest aspect of the Protestant Reformation was the rejection of Holy Orders, because this affects the divine constitution of the Church in its structuring principle and makes the Eucharist impossible.[95] In 1520, Luther denied the ecclesiastical hierarchy in *On the Babylonian Captivity of the Church*[96] and in his

---

[93] On the meaning of "*definitive tenendum,*" and CIC, can. 750, §2, see the Motu proprio of John Paul II, *Ad Tuendam Fidem* (June 29, 1998), issued with the CDF, Doctrinal Commentary on the Concluding Formula of the *Professio Fidei.*

[94] CDF, Note On the Minister of the Sacrament of Anointing of the Sick, with Commentary (Feb 11, 2005).

[95] See Bouyer, "Word and Sacrament," in *Sacraments: The Gestures of Christ*, ed. O'Callaghan, 151, speaking of the seven sacraments: "If the Eucharist is central among them . . . we can say with St Thomas that the most fundamental, from the point of view of the Church and its being is ordination. The intimate association which this sacrament realizes between those who are to bring the word to all mankind and this same word made flesh can be named the foundation stone of the whole sacramental order."

[96] Luther, *On the Babylonian Captivity of the Church*, in *LW*, 36:116: "Let everyone, therefore, who knows himself to be a Christian, be assured of this, that

Address to the Christian Nobility of the German Nation.[97] In its place he recognized only a priesthood of the faithful. In this view, the priest or pastor is not ontologically marked by priestly character but is simply one who fulfills the functions in the Church of preaching and presiding. This function of preaching is not essentially different, in this view, from other ecclesial vocations for which no special hierarchical mission is needed. Calvin recognized Holy Orders in a partial sense as a rite of the laying on of hands to impart ecclesial office, but he did not hold it to be a sacrament in the proper sense.[98]

The Lutheran and Calvinist rejection of the sacrament of Holy Orders led to the almost entire abolition of the sacramental system, leaving only those sacraments for which Holy Orders is not a necessary requirement for the minister. Thus they still have Baptism and Matrimony, although the latter is not generally recognized as a sacrament. This is so grave because the sacraments are the divinely appointed means by which the Church is given both a *visible* dimension and an *invisible* and supernatural life. Thus the rejection of the sacrament of Holy Orders and the consequent loss of the Church's full sacramental system was not only an attack on her visible life and hierarchical structuring but also, even if unintended, a tragic loss to her supernatural life, which is nourished directly through her visible means of sanctification—the sacraments, her ordinary means of purification and divinization. Dismantling key parts of the sacramental system has led Protestant ecclesial communities, contrary to their intention, to lose vital visible and invisible dimensions of the Church.

---

we are all equally priests, that is to say, we have the same power in respect to the Word and the sacraments." See also Luther, *The Misuse of the Mass* (1522), in *LW*, 36:138: "Every true Christian really ought to know that in the New Testament there is no outward, visible priest, except those whom the devil has exalted and set up through human lies. We have only one single priest, Christ."

[97] In *LW*, vol. 44, *The Christian in Society I*, ed. James Atkinson (Philadelphia: Fortress Press, 1966), 127–30. See also Luther, *The Freedom of a Christian*, in *LW* 31:329–77.

[98] See Calvin, *Institutes*, bk. 4, ch. 14.20, p. 854: "After these [sacraments of the Old Covenant] were abrogated, the two sacraments of Baptism and the Lord's Supper, which the Christian church now employs, were instituted. I speak of those which were instituted for the use of the whole church. For the laying on of hands, by which the ministers of the church are initiated into their office, though I have no objection to its being called a sacrament, I do not number among ordinary sacraments."

CONCLUSION: THE PERSONAL DIMENSION OF THE SACRAMENTAL SIGN

We have seen that the subject and minister enter into the constitution of the sacramental sign, broadly understood, because they represent Christ and the Church united in a spousal covenant. This is most apparent in Matrimony and Holy Orders. For this reason male gender in Holy Orders and the complementarity of male and female gender in Matrimony enter into the sacramental representation and are necessary conditions in the subjects of those sacraments. In a similar way male gender, to represent Christ the Bridegroom, is necessary in the minister of the sacraments except Baptism and Matrimony. This is not sexism but a level of symbolism that God has built into human nature and made use of in the economy of redemption, which has a profound nuptial dimension in that our God has come to us as our Bridegroom.

Through the fact that the subjects enter into the sacramental sign, there is a sense in which they give their bodies to Christ so that He can act through them. This is most apparent in Holy Orders at the level of priest or bishop, where the person ordained receives the power to act in *persona Christi*. The newly ordained priest's hands are consecrated with chrism to show that he is lending them to Christ to act through them, especially in the consecration of the Eucharist.[99] In Matrimony the spouses are abiding signs of Christ in His union with the Church. Their very bodies and their married lives as spouses and parents point beyond themselves to Christ and the Church.

Baptism and Confirmation also involve a representation of Christ, as will be seen in the following chapter, for the baptized and confirmed members of the faithful are permanently configured to Christ and the Church through sacramental character, and the Church is made visible to the world through them. By Confirmation one is made

---

[99] See Pius XII, *Mediator Dei*, §69: "Now the minister, by reason of the sacerdotal consecration which he has received, is made like to the High Priest and possesses the power of performing actions in virtue of Christ's very person. Wherefore in his priestly activity he in a certain manner 'lends his tongue, and gives his hand' to Christ." Pius XII is quoting St. John Chrysostom, Homily 86 on John 20:23, in *Commentary on Saint John the Apostle and Evangelist: Homilies 48–88*, 457: "Not even an angel, or an archangel, can effect anything with regard to what is given by God, but Father and Son and Holy Spirit direct everything. The priest simply lends his tongue and furnishes his hand."

an active and visible witness to Christ,[100] and given a priestly office of offering spiritual sacrifices to Christ, which are presented to the Father with Christ in the Sacrifice of the Mass. In Romans 12:1, St. Paul exhorts the faithful "to present your bodies as a living sacrifice, holy and acceptable to God, which is your spiritual worship."

In the sacrament of Anointing of the Sick, the serious illness of the subject makes possible a sacramental configuration with Christ's redemptive suffering. Christ makes use of our state of infirmity to manifest His redemptive mercy. Similarly in the sacrament of Penance, He makes use of our acts of contrition, confession, and satisfaction to be the matter of the sacrament and to make us configured to His satisfaction that reconciled the world.

While in the other sacraments, the faithful give their bodies in some sense to Christ so that He can act through them, in the Eucharist it is the reverse. Here Christ gives Himself in His whole being—Body, Blood, soul, and divinity—to the faithful, entering into our bodies so that we become literally the temple and tabernacle in which the Lord dwells. As He made use of the dwelling of Martha and Mary to dwell during His earthly life, so He now makes use of our very bodies to be His tabernacles when He comes to us bodily in Communion.

Study Questions

1. Explain the three kinds of intention: actual, habitual, and virtual. What kind of intention is necessary to administer or receive a sacrament?
2. When should sacraments be administered conditionally?
3. What are the necessary conditions in the subject for each of the seven sacraments?
4. Why is gender complementarity necessary for the sacrament of Matrimony?
5. Why is male gender necessary for the priesthood? What does the Church teach about this? Is this teaching infallible?

---

[100] See Chad C. Pecknold, and Lucas Laborde, "Confirmation," in *OHST*, 497: "The sacramental character that the confirmed Christian receives is a power that deputizes him or her to bear public witness to Christ. . . . It is a commissioning, and therefore it elevates the life of the confirmed Christian to a certain degree of sacramentality—they receive the power to become the 'good odor of Christ.'"

6. What are the necessary conditions in the minister for each of the seven sacraments? (b) Why is Holy Orders at the level of the priesthood necessary to be the minister for certain sacraments? (c) Why is episcopal character necessary to be the ordinary minister for certain sacraments? (d) Why does *Lumen Gentium*, §26 state that bishops "are the *original* ministers of confirmation"? (e) What grade of Holy Orders is required for administration of Anointing of the Sick?

Suggestions for Further Reading

Ashley, Benedict. "Gender and the Priesthood of Christ: A Theological Reflection." *The Thomist* 57 (1993): 343–79.

Congregation for the Doctrine of the Faith. "Note On the Minister of the Sacrament of Anointing of the Sick, with Commentary." February 11, 2005.

De Aldama, Joseph A. *Sacrae Theologiae Summa*. Vol. 4A, *On the Sacraments in General; On Baptism, Confirmation, Eucharist, Penance and Anointing*. 3rd edition. Translated by Kenneth Baker. Saddle River, NJ: Keep the Faith, 2015. Pp. 84–95.

John Paul II. Apostolic Letter On the Dignity and Vocation of Women, *Mulieris Dignitatem*. August 15, 1988. §26.

_____. Apostolic Letter *Ordinatio Sacerdotalis*. May 22, 1994.

Leeming, Bernard. *Principles of Sacramental Theology*. Westminster, MD: Newman Press, 1963. Pp. 435–96.

Little, Joyce A. "The New Evangelization and Gender: The Remystification of the Body." *Communio* 21 (Winter, 1994): 776–99.

Miller, Monica Migliorino. *Sexuality and Authority in the Catholic Church*. London; Toronto: Associated University Presses; Scranton, PA: University of Scranton Press, 1995.

Müller, Gerhard Ludwig. *Priesthood and Diaconate: The Recipient of the Sacrament of Holy Orders from the Perspective of Creation Theology and Christology*. Translated by Michael J. Miller. San Francisco: Ignatius Press, 2002.

Nutt, Roger. *General Principles of Sacramental Theology*. Washington, DC: Catholic University of America Press, 2017. Pp. 74–87.

Sacred Congregation for the Doctrine of the Faith. Declaration on the Question of Admission of Women to the Ministerial Priesthood, *Inter Insigniores*. October 15, 1976.

PART THREE

THE EFFECTS OF THE SACRAMENTS

CHAPTER SEVEN

Sacramental Character

DEVELOPMENT OF THE THEOLOGY OF SACRAMENTAL CHARACTER

St. Augustine's Distinction between the Sacrament, the Reality of the Sacrament, and the Abiding Character

Since the sacraments are sensible signs of our sanctification and confer what they signify, it follows that all the sacraments must have at least two levels: the outward sensible sign and the inward grace that they communicate, which is their principal effect. St. Augustine thus distinguished between the sacrament and the reality of grace communicated by it. In explaining why some people do not seem to benefit from receiving the sacraments, he stresses the importance of the disposition of the recipient who can pose an obstacle to the power of the sacrament, for "the sacrament is one thing, the efficacy of the sacrament another."[1] The former refers to the validity of the sacrament, and the latter to its fruitfulness, for St. Augustine emphasized that the sacraments can be valid without being fruitful. With regard to the Eucharist, he wrote that the reason the species of bread and wine "are called sacraments is that in them one thing is seen, another is to be understood. What can be seen has a bodily appearance, what is to be understood provides spiritual fruit."[2] Often he formulates this dis-

---

[1] Augustine, Tractate 26.11.2 on John 6:41–59, in *Tractates on the Gospel of John 11–27*, 268.

[2] Augustine, Sermon 272, in *Sermons (230–272B) on the Liturgical Seasons*, trans. Edmund Hill, WSA III/7 (New Rochelle: New City Press, 1993), 300.

tinction as between the *sacramentum* and the *res sacramenti*.[3] The latter term, which means "the thing (or reality) of the sacrament," refers to the supernatural effect imparted by the sacrament, which is the infusion of grace and charity. The two levels distinguished by Augustine can thus be called *sacramentum* and *res*: sign and reality.

This bipartite division, however, proved to be inadequate as a framework to think about the sacraments, which have a greater richness than this twofold division allows for. St. Augustine himself, in his theology of sacramental character that he worked out in controversy with the Donatists, as will be seen below, was one of the first to reflect deeply on an enduring sacramental reality distinct both from the outward sign and from the fruitfulness of the sacrament in giving grace, which is the *character* imprinted by the sacrament.[4]

Biblical Foundation of Sacramental Character

The term "character" in sacramental theology comes from the notion of a seal that imprints an image as a sign of possession, identity, authority, or mission, as on an official document, a coin, an animal, slave, or legionary. It comes from the Greek word χαρακτήρ, which signifies a seal in both an active sense, as an instrument for marking or impressing a seal, and a passive sense, as the seal, stamp, or distinctive mark that is impressed.[5] This sense of the word exists in English to indicate a letter stamped on a page.[6]

This Greek word is not used in a sacramental sense in the New Testament, but it is found in Hebrews 1:3 to refer to Christ as the "very stamp" (χαρακτήρ) of the Father: "He reflects the glory of God and bears the very stamp of his nature, upholding the universe by his word of power." This Christological usage of the term suggests its sac-

---

[3] See, for example, *ST* III, q. 80, a. 1, ad 1.
[4] See Leeming, *Principles of Sacramental Theology*, 154; see 146–57. As will be seen below, although St. Augustine spoke of the notion of sacramental character, he did not have a technical term for it and generally referred to it simply as the "*sacramentum*." See Nicholas Haring, "St. Augustine's Use of the Word *Character*," *Mediaeval Studies* 14 (1952): 79–97, at 85–86.
[5] See *The Compact Edition of the Oxford English Dictionary* (Oxford/New York: Oxford University Press, 1971), s.v. "Character," Def. I, 1: "A distinctive mark impressed, engraved, or otherwise formed; a brand, stamp."
[6] The more common use of the word "character" in English to denote personality is related in that our personal character or personality is distinctive and imprints itself on what we do.

ramental application. As Christ is the perfect imprint of the Father, so the faithful have been imprinted with the stamp of the Son by the agency of the Holy Spirit in Baptism.

The term "character" in sacramental theology is practically synonymous with the term "seal" (in Greek, σφραγίς),[7] which is used several times in the New Testament in connection with Baptism and its accompanying Chrismation. Nevertheless, this New Testament use of the notion of seal does not have the precise sense later given to the notion of sacramental character, for it may also refer to the grace of the Holy Spirit given through the sacrament.

In the Bread of Life discourse, Jesus uses the verb "to seal"[8] in a Christological context with sacramental implications. In John 6:27 He says that the people should seek not "for the food which perishes, but for the food which endures to eternal life, which the Son of man will give to you; for on him has God the Father set his seal." The implication is that Christ can give us the food of eternal life because through the mystery of the Incarnation He has been sealed by the Father with that same eternal life possessed by the Father.[9]

St. Paul alludes to a sacramental sealing in 2 Corinthians 1:21–22: "It is God who establishes us with you in Christ, and has commissioned

---

[7]   See Ysebaert, *Greek Baptismal Terminology*, 390–426.

[8]   The Greek is ἐσφράγισεν.

[9]   See St. Cyril of Alexandria's commentary on this text in his *Commentary on John*, trans. David R. Maxwell, ACT (Downers Grove, IL: InterVarsity Press, 2013), 1:197–98: "It is as though he said, I will not be unable to give you food that remains. . . . Even if I look like one of you, that is, as a human being with flesh, I have nevertheless been anointed and sealed by God the Father to an exact likeness with him. . . . So the Word from the substance of the Father is sealed by the Father not as bare Word or without flesh. Rather, through him those things are sealed that are brought up to likeness with God, as far as possible. . . . We receive from him, as through a seal, our being conformed to the Son, who is the image of the Father." See also Thomas Aquinas, Commentary on John 6:27, no. 898, trans. Fabian R. Larcher, WTA, 35:341: "Hilary explains it this way. God sealed, i.e., impressed with a seal. For when a seal is impressed on wax, the wax retains the entire figure of the seal, just as the Son has received the entire figure of the Father. Now the Son receives from the Father in two ways. One of these ways is eternal, and 'sealed' does not refer to this way, because when something is sealed the nature receiving the seal is not the same as the nature impressing the seal. Rather, these words should be understood as referring to the mystery of the incarnation, because God the Father has impressed his Word on human nature; this Word who is the 'brightness of his glory, and the figure of his substance' (Heb 1:3)."

[anointed][10] us; he has put his seal upon us and given us his Spirit in our hearts as a guarantee."[11] The terms in this passage are used in the liturgy of the sacrament of Confirmation: to anoint, to seal, and to give the Spirit. These last three verbs seem to indicate a past action—the Baptism and anointing of the Corinthians—that continues to operate in the present. The context of this passage is Jesus's own fidelity, "For all the promises of God find their Yes in him" (2 Cor 1:20). Thus the pledge of the Spirit that Christ seals in the faithful remains indelibly firm.

The action of "sealing" is also mentioned in two texts from Ephesians. In Ephesians 1:13–14 St. Paul speaks of three steps of Christian initiation: "In him you also, who have heard the word of truth, the gospel of your salvation, and have believed in him, were sealed with the promised Holy Spirit, who is the guarantee of our inheritance." The word of the Gospel was preached to the Ephesians, they believed it, and then they received the sacraments of initiation by which they were sealed with the Spirit, which is a pledge of the heavenly inheritance to come. In Ephesians 4:30, Paul refers back to the seal mentioned in 1:13 in order to exhort the Ephesians to persevere in the Christian life: "Do not grieve the Holy Spirit of God, in whom you were sealed for the day of redemption." All three of these Pauline texts refer to the twin sacraments of Christian initiation, Baptism and Confirmation, by which the Christian has been permanently "sealed" with the mystery of the divine Persons.[12]

The Old Testament parallel that underlies these texts is circumcision, which seals the body of the recipient with a physical mark that abides as a constant sign of belonging to the covenant. Although the outward signs of Baptism and Chrismation pass away like the act of circumcising, the mark remains as in circumcision, but as a spiritual rather than a physical mark.

---

[10] The Greek verb here is χρίσας, an aorist participle of the verb χρίω, which means to anoint; here it seems to refer to the anointing through the Spirit of the faithful at Baptism. See "χρίω" in W. Arndt, F. W. Danker, and W. Bauer, *A Greek-English Lexicon of the New Testament and Other Early Christian Literature*, 3rd ed. (Chicago: University of Chicago Press, 2000), 1091.

[11] The Douay-Rheims version better manifests the liturgical implications, using terms reminiscent of Baptism and Chrismation: "Now he that confirmeth us with you in Christ, and that hath anointed us, is God; Who also hath sealed us, and given the pledge of the Spirit in our hearts."

[12] On the implications of these three Pauline texts for sacramental character and its Trinitarian dimension, see Crescenzo Sepe, *La Dimensione trinitaria del carattere sacramentale* (Rome: Lateran University, 1969), 16–18.

Colossians 2:11–12 connects the symbolism of circumcision and Baptism and says that through the latter we have come to share in the spiritual circumcision of Christ:

> In him also you were circumcised with a circumcision made without hands, by putting off the body of flesh in the circumcision of Christ; and you were buried with him in baptism, in which you were also raised with him through faith in the working of God, who raised him from the dead.

St. Cyril of Jerusalem points out the parallel and difference between the two seals, citing Colossians 2:11:

> By the likeness of our faith, therefore, we become the adopted sons of Abraham; and consequent upon our faith, like him we receive the spiritual seal, being circumcised by the Holy Spirit through the laver of baptism, not in the foreskin of the body, but in the heart, according to the words of Jeremiah: "For the sake of the Lord, be circumcised, remove the foreskins of your hearts" [Jer 4:4], and according to the Apostle: In the "circumcision which is of Christ, buried together with him in baptism" [Col 2:11].[13]

Circumcision as a type of Christian initiation has the merit of clearly manifesting the abiding effect of the sacrament, which continues to mark the baptized, even if their lives no longer conform to the demands of the covenant with which they have been sealed.

The Patristic Notion of Sacramental Seal

Analogy of the Royal Seal

In order to speak about an abiding effect of the sacraments in imparting Christian identity even if the recipient later loses the state of grace or enters a heretical or schismatic sect, the Fathers and medieval theologians developed the analogy of the seal. Seals were used in ancient

---

[13] Cyril of Jerusalem, Lenten Catechesis 5.6, in *The Works of Saint Cyril of Jerusalem*, vol. 1, trans. L. P. McCauley and A. A. Stephenson, FC 61 (Washington, DC: Catholic University of America Press, 1969), 142–43.

cultures for various purposes. The king's letter or decree was stamped with the king's seal to show that the message had the authority or power of the king. A seal can also be put in a book to show its owner. A brand, which is a kind of seal, was also used in military service to visibly show one's membership in the legion and thus one's military identity and mission. If a soldier deserted his army, his seal became a sign of his betrayal.

St. Irenaeus expresses this idea using the example of a coin sealed with an inscription and the head of the ruler. Speaking in the context of his allegorical interpretation of the parable of the Good Samaritan, he says that Christ bound man's wounds through sacramental medications, so that, entrusting us to His Spirit, we receive "by the Spirit the image and superscription of the Father and the Son."[14] The comparison is suggested by the two coins given by the Good Samaritan to the victim. The implication is that Baptism and Chrismation (Confirmation) seal the Christian faithful with the image and inscription of the Trinity, and that this seal is the work of the Holy Spirit.

Clement of Alexandria also uses the analogy of the coin with its inscription and image:

> For he [the Christian] has through Christ the name of God written on him and the Spirit as an image. Even brute beasts through their branding show whose is the flock, and the branding-mark establishes a claim to them. Thus the soul of the believer, which has received the seal of truth, bears the marks of Christ upon it.[15]

The "seal of truth" is a reference to Baptism (and Confirmation) and its abiding mark of the name of God and the image of the Spirit, which here is compared to the seal imprinted on a coin. Thus Clement teaches that Baptism works a configuration to the Trinity. According to the analogy, this mark has two effects: (a) it gives Christian identity in the "name of God," which is sacramental character, and (b) it gives the Spirit Himself as living image, which also refers to the effect of grace. Although Clement does not specify, the latter can be lost but not the former.

---

[14] St. Irenaeus, *Against Heresies* 3.17.3, in *ANF* 1:445.

[15] Clement of Alexandria, *Ecloga* 86, trans. in Leeming, *Principles of Sacramental Theology*, 165.

St. Athanasius speaks of the seal received by the faithful in Christian initiation as having the "form of Christ who seals, and those who are sealed partake of it, being conformed to it."[16] The seal thus imprints identity in Christ and configuration to Him. This understanding of the seal, however, is not as precise as the later notion of sacramental character, for St. Athanasius does not distinguish the seal and its effect of grace,[17] and he identifies the seal with the Holy Spirit[18] who configures the faithful to Christ. He does not explain how the seal can remain if one loses the Holy Spirit through grave sin.

The military aspect of baptismal character was developed especially by St. Augustine in the context of the Donatist controversy.[19] Regarding those whom he exhorted to return to Catholic unity from the Donatist schism, he wrote:

> Similarly with those who possess the baptism of Christ; if they return to unity, we do not change or destroy their title, but we acknowledge the title of our King, the title of our Commander. What are we to say? O wretched patrimony, let Him whose title you bear own you; you bear the title of Christ, do not be the property of Donatus.[20]

He also develops this military analogy in another polemical work against the Donatists, imagining a scenario in which someone discovers that he has a military brand on his body, even though he never served in the army:

---

[16] St. Athanasius, Epistle 1.23 to Serapion, in *The Letters of Saint Athanasius Concerning the Holy Spirit*, trans. C. R. B. Shapland (London: The Epworth Press, 1951), 124.

[17] St. Athanasius, Epistle 1.23 to Serapion, in Shapland, 124: "Being thus sealed, we are duly made, as Peter put it 'sharers in the divine nature' [2 Pet 1:4]."

[18] St. Athanasius, Epistle 1.23 to Serapion, in Shapland, 123–24: "The Spirit is called unction and he is seal. . . . But if the Spirit is the unction and seal with which the Word anoints and seals all things, what likeness or propriety could the unction and the seal have to the things that are anointed and sealed?"

[19] On Augustine's use of the analogy of the military brand, see Nicholas Haring, "St. Augustine's Use of the Word *Character*," *Mediaeval Studies* 14 (1952): 79–97, at 81–83.

[20] Augustine, Second Discourse on Psalm 21.31, in *St. Augustine On the Psalms*, 1:228. See Jean Galot, *La nature du caractère sacramentel: étude de théologie médiévale* (Bruges: Desclée de Brouwer, 1956), 36–41.

> If perhaps the man . . . is shaken and horrified at the army's mark on his body and appeals to the emperor's clemency and, when his plea has been made and pardon granted, he now begins to serve in the army, is that mark repeated or is it not rather acknowledged with approval now that the man has been absolved and corrected?

Augustine then asks: "Is it possible that the Christian sacraments adhere less strongly than this bodily tattoo?"[21] He develops the same analogy in a sermon on Baptism:

> From the fact that the sacrament is not readministered to a deserter when he returns, it is clear that he could not have lost it when he withdrew. A military deserter is deprived of membership in the army, but he is still marked as a soldier of the king. And, if he signs another man with the same seal as his own, he does not give him participation in the life of the army; rather, he makes him—like the deserter himself—a soldier deprived of that membership. However, if the one would return to the army and if the other would join it, . . . to each of them peace would be restored, but in neither of them would the character be repeated which had once been sealed.[22]

Three Meanings of the Seal

A seal thus has three principal purposes: to show permanent identity, to give an abiding mission to a person (as to a soldier or minister), and to confer delegated power to someone to be able to carry out his mission. Sacramental character is an invisible word or seal that has all three of these meanings, in an analogous way.

First of all, it identifies the soul as belonging to Jesus Christ and to His Mystical Body. This hidden sacramental sign thus denotes and confers the glory of Christ's ownership and Christian identity.

Secondly, sacramental character is the sign of a mission given by

---

21 Augustine, *Answer to the Letter of Parmenian* 2.13.29, in *The Donatist Controversy I*, trans. Maureen Tilley and Boniface Ramsey (Hyde Park, NY: New City Press, 2019), 325–26.

22 Augustine, Sermon 8 (Denis), "Baptism," in *Commentary on the Lord's Sermon on the Mount with Seventeen Related Sermons*, trans. Denis J. Kavanagh, FC 11 (Washington, DC: Catholic University of America Press, 1951), 334.

the One whose image is imprinted on the soul, who is Jesus Christ. Sacramental character is the permanent sign of a mission received. It is an invisible and indelible word signifying the calling or vocation to share in the mission of Jesus Christ. As St. Augustine emphasizes, it is a mission that abides indelibly even in those who betray it. The mission is to participate, in three distinct ways, in the mission of Christ the High Priest, Prophet, and King. The Fathers of the Church[23] speak of the three offices of Christ through a reflection on the Old Testament rite of anointing priests, prophets, and kings with olive oil, which represented the spiritual anointing of the grace of the Holy Spirit. Christ, as the Anointed One, recapitulates all three roles. The Christian faithful are anointed and sealed in Confirmation to share in Christ's anointing, and are thus given to share in His priestly, prophetic, and kingly mission.[24]

St. John Chrysostom eloquently brings out these three aspects of the mission given to the faithful through being sealed in Christian initiation. In his commentary on 2 Corinthians 1:22 he writes:

> And what is, "anointed," and "sealed?" Gave the Spirit by Whom He did both these things, making at once prophets and priests and kings, for in old times these three sorts were anointed. But we have now not one of these dignities, but all three preeminently. For we are both to enjoy a kingdom and are made priests by offering our bodies for a sacrifice [Rom 12:1], . . . and we are constituted prophets too: for what things "eye hath not seen, nor ear heard," [1 Cor. 2:9] these have been revealed unto us. And in another way too we become kings: if we have the mind to get dominion over our unruly thoughts, for that such an one is a king and more than he who weareth the diadem.[25]

---

23 See Cyril of Jerusalem, *Mystagogic Catecheses*, Sermon 3.6, in Yarnold, *Awe-Inspiring Rites of Initiation*, 84. In his catechesis to the newly baptized and confirmed, he explains the typology of the Old Testament anointings that foreshadow Confirmation.

24 For the Old Testament anointings, see Exod 29:1–7 and Lev 8:6–12 for the anointing of Aaron and his sons as priests; 1 Sam 16:12–13 for the anointing of David as king; and 1 Kings 19:16, in which God commands Elijah to anoint Elisha to be a prophet after him.

25 John Chrysostom, commentary on 2 Cor 1:22 in Homily 3.4–5 in 2 Corinthians, *NPNF*1: 12:290.

After a digression illustrating the meaning of kingship over oneself, St. John Chrysostom summarizes:

> So also art thou thyself made king and priest and prophet in the Laver;[26] a king, having dashed to earth all the deeds of wickedness and slain thy sins; a priest, in that thou offerest thyself to God, having sacrificed thy body and being thyself slain also, "for if we died with Him," saith he, "we shall also live with Him;" (2 Tim 2:11) a prophet, knowing what shall be, and being inspired of God, and sealed. For as upon soldiers a seal, so is also the Spirit put upon the faithful. And if thou desert, thou art manifest [by it] to all. For the Jews had circumcision for a seal, but we, the earnest of the Spirit. Knowing then all this, and considering our high estate, let us exhibit a life worthy of the grace, that we may obtain also the kingdom to come.[27]

A third meaning of the seal is the reception of delegated power. In the Fathers this aspect of power associated with the seal is generally understood to be grace, which gives the power to accomplish the mission, as in the passage above. However, there is an aspect of spiritual power that pertains properly to character and is distinct from grace, which is the power to receive and administer other sacraments, which will be highlighted later by Thomas Aquinas, as will be seen below.[28]

The *Catechism of the Catholic Church*, §§1295–96 summarizes the meaning of the "seal" given in Confirmation, as explained by the Fathers:

> By this anointing the confirmand receives the "mark," the *seal* of the Holy Spirit. A seal is a symbol of a person, a sign of personal authority, or ownership of an object. Hence soldiers were marked with their leader's seal and slaves with their

---

[26] "Laver" is a reference to Baptism. In the liturgy of St. John Chrysostom, Baptism and Confirmation were celebrated together except in an emergency Baptism.

[27] John Chrysostom, commentary on 2 Cor 1:22 in Homily 3.7 in 2 Corinthians, *NPNF*1: 12:293.

[28] See *ST* III, q. 63, a. 2.

master's. A seal authenticates a juridical act or document and occasionally makes it secret.

Christ himself declared that he was marked with his Father's seal [Jn 6:27]. Christians are also marked with a seal: "It is God who establishes us with you in Christ and has commissioned us; he has put his seal on us and given us his Spirit in our hearts as a guarantee."[29] This seal of the Holy Spirit marks our total belonging to Christ, our enrollment in his service for ever, as well as the promise of divine protection in the great eschatological trial.

The Rebaptism Controversy and Sacramental Character

Although the patristic notion of the sacramental seal lays the foundation for the theological doctrine of sacramental character, the term is used in such a way that it is often not clear whether it refers to grace or something distinct from grace.[30] This point was clarified by St. Augustine in the course of the Donatist controversy.

In the third and fourth centuries, a fierce controversy arose in North Africa over whether Baptism imparted by heretics or schismatics is valid, and thus whether or not those baptized by heretics or schismatics should be baptized when they return to the unity of the Church. St. Cyprian, bishop of Carthage from AD 249–257,

---

[29] 2 Cor 1:21–22; cf. Eph 1:13; 4:30.

[30] See the summary of the patristic teaching on the seal by Thomas Marsh, "The Sacramental Character," in *Sacraments: The Gestures of Christ*, ed. O'Callaghan, 109–38, at 117: "In summing up the patristic teaching relevant to the theology of the character, one notes that this teaching is built around the biblical metaphor of the seal. In patristic writing this term covers a wider area than the reality later known as the sacramental character. But when the Fathers speak of the seal in a sacramental context, and this is the usual context, they are generally referring to what we call the sacramental character. The sacraments with which the seal is usually associated are first baptism and then, from the middle of the third century on, baptism and confirmation. Sometimes the term refers to the external rite but more usually it refers to a spiritual effect produced by the rite. In explaining the meaning of this effect, the Fathers speak of it as a sign that one belongs to God and the Church. They also see it as a transforming mark in that it consecrates and configures the Christian to Christ and to the Trinity. They do not, however, treat explicitly of the relation between grace and the seal but tend to consider the seal in its normal context as united to and involving the presence of grace."

vigorously argued for the invalidity of heretical and schismatic sacraments.[31] This meant that those baptized in a heretical or schismatic sect who returned to Catholic unity needed to be baptized. Pope Stephen I and later St. Augustine argued for the opposite position, holding with Tradition that Baptism is valid even when the minister is a heretic, schismatic, or lapsed in persecution, provided the essential elements of the sacramental sign are conserved. Stephen based himself on the ancient practice of Rome,[32] and St. Augustine saw this practice as belonging to apostolic Tradition on account of its universality:

> This custom, which I believe comes from apostolic tradition, like the many things that are not found in the [apostles'] writings or in the councils of those who followed them, and yet, because they are preserved by the universal Church, are believed to have been handed down and commended by none but them.[33]

St. Cyprian also based himself on a tradition, but of a much more recent origin. St. Augustine shows that St. Cyprian based his mistaken position on the authority of an earlier bishop of Carthage, Agrippinus, from whom he inherited this practice. He did not realize that Agrippinus's practice of rebaptizing those who were baptized in a schismatic or heretical sect was itself an innovation introduced by the first council of Carthage, a local synod presided over by Agrippinus in AD 217,

---

[31] Cyprian's position is expressed in letters 69–75, in *The Letters of St. Cyprian of Carthage, Letters 67–82*, pp. 32–94. See, for example, Letter 70.1.2–3, p. 46: "It is, however, no novel judgment but one determined long ago by our predecessors [Agrippinus and a council of Carthage over which he presided] and which we have followed . . . holding it as certain that no one can be baptized outside and away from the Church, on the grounds that there is only one baptism that has been appointed and that is in the holy Church. . . . How, we ask, can a man possibly cleanse and sanctify water when he is himself unclean and when the Holy Spirit is not within him? Whereas the Lord says in the book of Numbers: 'And everything which the unclean touches shall be unclean.' And how can a man who administers baptism possibly grant forgiveness of sins to another when he is himself unable to put aside his own sins, being outside the Church?"

[32] See the account of Stephen I's position in a letter of Bishop Firmilian of Caesarea to St. Cyprian, ch. 5 (DS, 111): "Stephen said that the apostles had prohibited the baptism of those who came from heresy and had handed this down to be observed by posterity."

[33] Augustine, *Baptism* 2.7.12, trans. Boniface Ramsey, in *The Donatist Controversy I* (Hyde Park, NY: New City Press, 2019), 431.

roughly forty years earlier.[34]

Scripture does not directly address the issue, although the New Testament implies that Baptism is only received once. Only those who received the Baptism of John were rebaptized, as in Acts 19:5, because they never received Christian baptism. In Ephesians 4:4–6, St. Paul strongly emphasizes the unity of Baptism which is bound up with the unity of the Church, her faith, and her Lord: "There is one body and one Spirit, just as you were called to the one hope that belongs to your call, one Lord, one faith, one baptism, one God and Father of us all." This suggests that the Church is one because she is built on one foundation, which is Christ and our insertion into Him through faith and Baptism.[35]

In 1 Corinthians 1:13–15, St. Paul speaks about the unity of Baptism in the one name of Jesus: "Was Paul crucified for you? Or were you baptized in the name of Paul? I am thankful that I baptized none of you except Crispus and Gaius; lest any one should say that you were baptized in my name." What this implies is that the efficacy and unity of Baptism stems not from the holiness of any minister,[36] but from the incorporation into the one Christ who died for all.

Nevertheless, the Scriptures do not clearly state the theological principles on which the practice of one Baptism rests. What was needed was a deeper understanding of the effects of the sacraments, and a distinction between licitness, validity, and fruitfulness, as well as a corresponding distinction between three levels of the sacraments (as will be seen more fully in the following chapter).

St. Cyprian argued that Baptism outside the unity of the Church, which is illicit, could not give grace, because grace and charity go together, and there cannot be charity outside of communion with the Church. This meant that heretical or schismatic Baptism would be both illicit and unfruitful, a position on which Cyprian and Pope Stephen were in agreement. St. Cyprian also took it to mean that it could not be valid, which is where his position departed from that of

---

[34] See Augustine, *Baptism* 2.7.12–9.14, trans. Ramsey, in *The Donatist Controversy I*, 431–34.

[35] St. John Damascene explains the unicity of Baptism by connecting it to the death of the Lord, according to Romans 6:2–11. See *An Exact Exposition of the Orthodox Faith* 4.9, in *Writings*, 343: "Therefore, just as the death of the Lord happened but once, so is it necessary to be baptized but once."

[36] See chapter 13, pp. 458, 469–72 below, on the meaning of sacramental efficacy *ex opere operato*.

Pope Stephen and the universal tradition of the Church. His position presupposes that if the effect of grace is not produced, nothing is effected. What he did not consider is that Baptism could be valid, producing an abiding and indelible effect, while still being unfruitful with regard to grace and salvation as long as the baptized remains culpably[37] outside of the Church.

Pope Stephen's position, on the other hand, based on tradition, makes sense only if in addition to the effect of grace, which is dependent on the disposition of the recipient, there is another abiding effect that does not depend on the charity or faith of the recipient.[38] This other abiding effect precludes rebaptism and provides the foundation for the grace of baptism to come to life and fruitfulness once the obstacle to the unity of the Church is removed by penance. This abiding effect later came to be called the character of the sacrament, or its seal.

The controversy was put on hold by persecution and the martyrdom of the protagonists, only to resurface later in the Donatist controversy, in which the Donatists continued some of the positions of St. Cyprian, regarding Baptism as invalid when conferred by those they regarded as unworthy ministers (that is, some who were said to have lapsed during the persecution and those they ordained and baptized). In his work *On Baptism*, written against the Donatists in 400–401, St. Augustine worked out some of the theological principles of sacramental character both with regard to Baptism and Holy Orders.

In this work, St. Augustine establishes from the practice of the Church that celebration of the sacraments outside of Catholic unity is both unlawful and unfruitful, but is not void, for its seal abides indelibly, even if not for the profit of one who is not in Catholic unity. St. Augustine argues that it abides simply from the fact that neither the Catholic Church nor the Donatists rebaptized those who fell into apostasy and then returned to the Church in penance. Even though grace would have been lost in apostasy, Baptism clearly was not lost, for it was not administered again. St. Augustine applied the same principle to Holy Orders. If a cleric apostatizes and then returns to Catholic unity, he is not re-ordained:

---

[37] St. Cyprian and his contemporaries presupposed the culpability of being in a schismatic or heretical Christian body. See chapter 15 below, pp. 580–90 for the notion of invincible ignorance and its development.

[38] See Leeming, *Principles of Sacramental Theology*, 130–31.

For, just as those who return to the Church, who were baptized before they left, are not rebaptized, neither by any means
are those who return, who were ordained before they left,
re-ordained, but they either confer what they used to confer,
if the Church's wellbeing demands it, or, if they do not confer
it, they nonetheless retain the sacrament of their ordination.[39]

St. Augustine deduces from this practice of the Church that the
sacrament must somehow abide, even when unfruitful, precisely so that
it can come back to life again through repentance. This applies both
(a) when Baptism or Holy Orders are received unfruitfully outside of
the Church in a heretical or schismatic sect or in a state of mortal sin;
and (b) when they are received fruitfully within the Church but the
person later (culpably) falls into heresy, schism, or apostasy, losing the
fruit of grace, and then returns to the Church.[40] This coming to life
(or back to life) of the sacrament is sometimes referred to as *reviviscence*. For example, those who receive Baptism without repentance are
truly baptized, but their sins are not forgiven and they do not receive
sanctifying grace because of the lack of repentance.[41] But a subsequent
repentance enables the forgiveness of sins and the infusion of grace to
take place, thus enabling Baptism to become fruitful.

What does it mean that the sacrament abides even when unfruitful? St. Augustine says: "Hence it is clear that baptism is in the
baptized person even when the baptized person is separated from the
Church; the baptism that is in him is, to be sure, separated along with

---

[39] Augustine, *Baptism* 1.1.2, trans. Ramsey, 392.

[40] Augustine, Baptism 1.1.2, trans. Ramsey, 392: "Just as what is possessed
without benefit outside of unity begins to be of benefit through reconciliation to unity, in the same way what has been conferred without benefit outside
begins to be of benefit through that same reconciliation." Like St. Cyprian,
St. Augustine presupposed the culpability of being in a schismatic or heretical
Christian body. Thus he assumes that the grace of the sacrament will not be
given until the heretic or schismatic actually returns to the unity of the visible
Church. See Gallagher, *Significando causant*, 35: "For Augustine charity and
grace are identified with the bond of charity and grace among the members of
the church. Outside the church, these do not exist, even though true sacraments
are received."

[41] Augustine, *Baptism* 1.12.18, trans. Ramsey, 408: "A person can truly be baptized
with Christ's baptism and yet ... his heart, persisting in malice or sacrilege, does
not allow the abolition of his sins to be accomplished."

him."[42] How is Baptism in the baptized person when it is separated from its effect of grace by the sin of schism or heresy or other mortal sin, and separated from the outward sacramental sign which has long since passed away?

Baptism abides through an effect of the outward sign that marks the recipient in an indelible way after the outward sign has ceased. This effect of the outward sign is an *abiding invisible sign* of having been baptized. St. Augustine thus speaks about it as an abiding effect of the outward sign, and an abiding cause for the effect of grace that can be given through it once the obstacle is removed. This abiding effect came to be called "sacramental character," and it mediates between the outward sign and the grace of the sacrament.

This is an interesting case of the theological concept being worked out before the existence of a precise theological term to express it. St. Augustine generally speaks about this abiding effect of Baptism simply as Baptism, or as the "sacrament"[43] that cannot be effaced. This way of referring to the abiding effect of Baptism and ordination, of course, is ambiguous, for no terminological distinction is made between the visible sacramental sign and the abiding invisible effect of sacramental character. Nevertheless, his meaning is easily grasped from the context. Even though the outward celebration of the sacrament has passed away, the sacrament itself has not passed away, for it abides, being the work of Christ that cannot be effaced by man. Hence to re-baptize, as the Donatists did, is to commit a crime against Baptism and against Christ's abiding work in it. From the twelfth century, this abiding effect of Baptism, Confirmation, and Holy Orders is referred to as "sacramental character." This later technical usage was probably taken from the fact that St. Augustine referred to this abiding effect using the analogy of military *character*, even though he did not generally use the term in the technical sense.[44]

---

[42] Augustine, *Baptism* 5.16.20, trans. Ramsey, 514.

[43] See Haring, "St. Augustine's Use of the Word *Character*," *Mediaeval Studies* 14 (1952): 79–97, at 85–86. See also Lynch, "The Sacraments as Causes of Sanctification," 795n7.

[44] See Haring, "St. Augustine's Use of the Word *Character*," 95–96: "This Augustinian usage of *sacramentum* designating a permanent and lasting element in Baptism and Holy Orders is one and, strictly speaking, the only reason why the Christian writers up to the second half of the twelfth century did not use the word *character* as we use it today. . . . In other words, Christian writers did not speak of character in the modern sense of the word for some seven centuries,

This is also a classic example of how sacramental theology is based on the liturgical and sacramental practice of the Church and develops from it. St. Augustine argued from the practice of the universal Church in accepting the validity of Baptism conferred by heretical and schismatic ministers, which he understood to be an apostolic tradition, and then he gave a theological justification for this practice that he already considered binding. In doing so he formulated the theological principles for the doctrine of sacramental character and what would later be referred to as the "reality and sign" (*res et sacramentum*) of the sacraments.

Nevertheless, neither St. Augustine nor other Fathers worked out a general theory of the sacraments articulated in three levels, in which the intermediate level is a combination of the other two. The bipartite distinction between *sacrament* and the *reality* (*res*) *of grace* remained the dominant conceptual framework for thinking about the sacraments until the twelfth century.

After St. Augustine, the theology of character remained relatively dormant until the late twelfth century, when reflection was renewed by the scholastics. In his *Sentences*, Peter Lombard simply states that Baptism, Confirmation, and Holy Orders are not to be repeated[45] and that Holy Orders involves the imprinting of a "spiritual character."[46] Sacramental character became a topic of rich theological reflection in the century and a half after Peter Lombard.[47]

St. Thomas Aquinas on the Nature of Sacramental Character

St. Thomas dedicates a question to sacramental character in his *Summa theologiae*, synthesizing the theological reflection of the previous generations. His reflection centers on the three aspects, seen above, of

---

because St. Augustine had not used the term in the modern sense."

[45] Peter Lombard, *Sentences*, bk. 4, d. 7, ch. 5, trans. Silano, 40.

[46] Lombard, *Sentences*, bk. 4, d. 24, ch. 13, trans. Silano, 148: "But if it were asked what it is that here is called an order, it may truly be said that it is some mark, that is, something sacred, by which spiritual power and office are granted to the one ordained. And so the spiritual character, when a promotion of power is made, is called an order or degree."

[47] For the development of the theological concept of character from the later twelfth century to St. Thomas, see the classic work by Jean Galot, *La nature du caractère sacramentel*, 41–171.

Christian identity, priestly mission, and spiritual power.[48]

Distinguishing Mark of Christian Identity

St. Thomas begins by taking up the patristic reflection on the seal and its principal meanings, and uses the example of the legionary who bears the sign of his military service to the emperor on his body. As the soldier or slave was marked by a seal on the body to show that he has been deputed for bodily service, so the Christian is marked by a spiritual seal to show that he has been deputed to spiritual service, which is the worship of God through Christ in His Church. Aquinas explains that the mark is of Christ:

> It is a sign conferring on a man a likeness to some principal person in whom is vested the authority over that to which he is assigned: thus soldiers who are assigned to military service, are marked with their leader's sign, by which they are, in a fashion, likened to him. And in this way those who are deputed to the Christian worship, of which Christ is the author, receive a character by which they are likened to Christ. Consequently, properly speaking, this is Christ's character.[49]

Character serves first to distinguish those who have been inserted into Christ's Body and consecrated to the worship of God in the Church:

> Now whenever anyone is deputed to some definite purpose he is wont to receive some outward sign thereof; thus in olden times soldiers who enlisted in the ranks used to be marked with certain characters on the body, through being deputed

---

[48] St. Thomas treats these three themes in *ST* III, q. 63. aa. 1–3, but in a different order: Christian identity (a. 1), spiritual power (a. 2), and participation in Christ's priesthood (a. 3).

[49] *ST* III, q. 63, a. 3, ad 2. See also ad 3: "A character distinguishes one from another, in relation to some particular end, to which he, who receives the character is ordained: as has been stated concerning the military character by which a soldier of the king is distinguished from the enemy's soldier in relation to the battle. In like manner the character of the faithful is that by which the faithful of Christ are distinguished from the servants of the devil, either in relation to eternal life, or in relation to the worship of the Church that now is. Of these the former is the result of charity and grace, as the objection runs; while the latter results from the sacramental character."

to a bodily service. Since, therefore, by the sacraments men are deputed to a spiritual service pertaining to the worship of God, it follows that by their means the faithful receive a certain spiritual character.[50]

Here St. Thomas has given an argument of fittingness for the existence of sacramental character.[51] Its primary purpose is to distinguish the members of the Church from the rest of mankind by a permanent distinguishing sign, as circumcision permanently distinguished Israelites from other peoples as a "kingdom of priests and a holy nation" (Exod 19:6). It is through baptismal character that the Church is a visible body made up of the baptized. If sacramental character were not an abiding reality stamped on the baptized, there would be no permanent mark distinguishing Christians from non-Christians and the Church would not be a truly visible society, but more like a club or voluntary association that one could join or leave at one's own pleasure. Secondly, the sacramental character of Holy Orders serves to distinguish ecclesial states within the Church and in particular to distinguish the hierarchy from the laity. This again pertains to the visibility of the Church; she is an organic body with a visible and abiding hierarchy.

St. Thomas poses an obvious objection here. How can something spiritual and invisible be a sign that distinguishes Christians from non-Christians? Is not visibility of the essence of a sign? He answers that even though sacramental character is invisible, it is imprinted through a visible rite, which is the outward sacramental sign, by which we know the existence of this abiding invisible sign:

> The character imprinted on the soul is a kind of sign in so far as it is imprinted by a sensible sacrament: since we know that a certain one has received the baptismal character, through his being cleansed by the sensible water. Nevertheless from a kind of likeness, anything that assimilates one thing to another, or

---

[50] *ST* III, q. 63, a. 1.

[51] The same argument appears in St. Thomas's earlier commentary, *In IV Sent.*, d. 4, q. 1, a. 1, sed contra 2, trans. Mortensen, 7:154: "Anywhere there is a certain distinction, it is appropriate that there be a certain character distinguishing it. But through the sacraments the faithful are distinguished from unbelievers, and the faithful from each other. Therefore, it is appropriate that a character be given in the sacraments."

discriminates one thing from another, even though it be not sensible, can be called a character or a seal; thus the Apostle calls Christ the figure or *character* "of the substance of the Father" (Heb 1:3).[52]

Character can be understood as an *intelligible* sign, even though it is not a *sensible* sign, for it is known by the intellect that infers its existence from the outward visible sign.[53]

Priestly Mission

Granted that character is a distinctive sign that stamps man with Christ, to what end are the faithful stamped? What is the end or mission of the Christian life? The ultimate end, of course, is the "enjoyment of glory," and it is for this end that sacraments give grace, for grace is the seed of glory. But the Christian life is also ordained to give glory to God during our Christian exile, and that is done through participating in Christ's priesthood, and it is for this end, according to St. Thomas, that sacramental character is given:

> Character is properly a kind of seal, whereby something is marked, as being ordained to some particular end: thus a coin is marked for use in exchange of goods, and soldiers are marked with a character as being deputed to military service. Now the faithful are deputed to a twofold end. First and principally to the enjoyment of glory. And for this purpose they are marked with the seal of grace according to Ezech. 9:4. . . . Second, each of the faithful is deputed to receive, or to bestow on others, things pertaining to the worship of God. And this, properly speaking, is the purpose of the sacramental character. Now the whole rite of the Christian religion is derived from Christ's priesthood. Consequently, it is clear that the sacramental character is specially the character of Christ, to Whose character the faithful are likened by reason of the sacramental

---

[52] *ST* III, q. 63, a. 1, ad 2.

[53] It seems that William of Auxerre was the first to give the answer to the objection, which then became commonly accepted and was taken up by St. Thomas. See Leeming, *Principles of Sacramental Theology*, 245–46; P. F. Palmer, "The Theology of the *Res et Sacramentum*," in *Readings in Sacramental Theology*, ed. C. S. Sullivan, (Englewood Cliffs, NJ: Prentice-Hall, 1964), 107–08.

characters, which are nothing else than certain participations of Christ's Priesthood, flowing from Christ Himself.[54]

The baptized, confirmed, and ordained faithful are inserted into Christ's priesthood in different ways, as will be seen below. This priesthood mediates between man and God, offering sacrifice to God and obtaining gifts of grace for men. Although St. Thomas only speaks of a participation in Christ's priesthood here, His kingly and prophetic offices are intimately related to it.[55]

Spiritual Power

Third, the recipient of the mission of sharing in the priesthood of Jesus Christ must receive a *spiritual power* to perform that mission. This mission carries with it the authority of Jesus Christ, who is the one sending and who gives a power to carry out the mission. Sacramental character provides a permanent spiritual power to participate with Christ in His priestly office. It is a supernatural participatory power by which members of the Church can act as instruments of Jesus Christ in His mission to glorify the Father and sanctify men, through receiving and bestowing divine gifts. St. Thomas writes:

> Now the worship of God consists either in receiving Divine gifts, or in bestowing them on others. And for both these purposes some power is needed; for to bestow something on others, active power is necessary; and in order to receive, we need a passive power. Consequently, a character signifies a certain spiritual power ordained unto things pertaining to the Divine worship. But it must be observed that this spiritual power is instrumental: as we have stated above (q. 62, a. 4) of the virtue which is in the sacraments. For to have a sacramental character belongs to God's ministers: and a

---

[54] *ST* III, q. 63, a. 3.

[55] For a comparison of St. Thomas's early teaching on sacramental character in the *Sentences* (in which all three offices seem to be implied) and his mature treatment in the *Summa*, in which he highlights participation in Christ's priesthood, see Marsh, "Sacramental Character," 122–31. On the theological importance of the connection of sacramental character with participation in the priesthood of Christ, see Yves M.-J. Congar, *Lay People in the Church: A Study for a Theology of Laity* (Westminster: Newman Press, 1965), 140–45.

minister is a kind of instrument.[56]

This spiritual power given by sacramental character confers both the power to receive sanctification and, in Holy Orders, to impart it to others. Baptismal character gives the passive power to receive other sacraments, and the character of Holy Orders gives the active power to administer sacraments in the name of Christ. As will be seen below, the character of Confirmation strengthens the passive power of receiving sanctification first conferred by Baptism, and also gives an active power to participate in the common priesthood of Christ and to participate in the exercise of His prophetic and kingly office in the Church.

Ontological Reality of Character

Given that sacramental character is both an invisible sign and a hidden reality effected by the outward sign (*res et sacramentum*), the thirteenth-century theologians posed the question of what kind of reality it has in the soul. Since it is not only a *sign*,[57] but also an abiding *reality* effected by the outward sign, it must also be something ontological in us by which we are marked and configured to Christ in a new and indelible way. Every sign signifying something else has to have a reality of its own that is the foundation of its ability to represent something else.[58] In what does this reality consist in the case of sacramental character? This proved to be a difficult theological question that perplexed and exercised the minds of the great thirteenth-century scholastics.

It would seem that the answer lies in speaking of it as an enduring instrumental spiritual power through which Christ can work to effect

---

[56] *ST* III, q. 63, a. 2.

[57] See *ST* III, q. 63, a. 3, ad 2: "The sacramental character is a thing [*res*] as regards the exterior sacrament, and a sacrament in regard to the ultimate effect. Consequently, something can be attributed to a character in two ways. First, if the character be considered as a sacrament: and thus it is a sign of the invisible grace which is conferred in the sacrament. Secondly, if it be considered as a character. . . . And in this way those who are deputed to the Christian worship, of which Christ is the author, receive a character by which they are likened to Christ."

[58] See *ST* III, q. 63, a. 2, ad 3: "The relation signified by the word *sign* must needs have some foundation. Now the relation signified by this sign which is a character, cannot be founded immediately on the essence of the soul: because then it would belong to every soul naturally. Consequently, there must be something in the soul on which such a relation is founded. And it is in this that a character essentially consists. Therefore it need not be in the genus *relation* as some have held."

sanctification. Sacramental character signifies Christ's priesthood precisely because it is a spiritual power through which Christ's priesthood can operate. This is the answer of St. Thomas;[59] nevertheless, the scholastic theologians of the thirteenth century gave various answers to this vexing question.

St. Albert proposed that it was a relation to God, as a consecration. It is reasonable to hold that character gives the recipient a new relation to the Trinity, as the invocation of the Trinity in Baptism and the sealing with the Spirit in Confirmation imply. However, a real relation requires a foundation.[60] What is the reality in the soul posited by sacramental character that is the foundation of a new relation to God? Various theologians therefore held that the foundation of this new relation is the fact that character is a supernatural *quality* of the soul by which the soul is consecrated and set apart from those who have not received the sacrament. This makes sense because sacramental character intrinsically distinguishes those who have received it from those who have not, marking them as members of the Church. This distinction, it would seem, is a kind of quality making them, as Aristotle says of qualities, to be *in a certain way*.[61] It is reasonable, therefore, to hold that sacramental character is a kind of spiritual quality.

But there are several different kinds of qualities. In his *Categories*, Aristotle distinguished four kinds of qualities: (a) habit or disposition, (b) power, (c) sensible qualities (such as red or high-pitched), and (d) sensible figures (such as circular or triangular).[62] Since sacramental character is an invisible and spiritual sign and reality, it cannot be a sensible quality or figure. This leaves three possibilities. It is either a supernatural habit or a supernatural power, or else it is a new kind of quality not analyzed by Aristotle.

Some great theologians, such as St. Albert[63] and St. Bonaventure,[64]

---

[59] St. Thomas argues that sacramental character is a spiritual power both in his early commentary *In IV Sent.*, d. 4, q. 1, a. 1 and in his mature treatment in *ST* III, q. 63, a. 2.

[60] See *ST* III, q. 63, a. 2, ad 3.

[61] See Aristotle, *Categories* 8, 8b25.

[62] See Aristotle, *Categories* 8.

[63] For St. Albert's and St. Bonaventure's theology of character, see Galot, *La nature du caractère sacramentel*, 147–71.

[64] See Bonaventure, *In IV Sent.*, d. 6, a. 1, q. 1, in *Commentary on the Sentences: Sacraments*, trans. Hellmann, 133: "Again, it is a given that character is a 'spiritual quality' of the soul. . . . Since therefore 'spiritual quality' is the first species of

held it to be a kind of habit or durable disposition that disposes the recipient in a stable way to the exercise of faith. They discarded the idea that character is a power because they thought that a power must belong to the nature of a thing, and thus would be a merely natural power present in all human beings.[65] St. Bonaventure writes:

> Hence in reality character is a certain quality that does not entirely perfect the soul, but which disposes the soul to further perfection, namely to grace. Therefore it is possible that character is a certain incomplete spiritual light and certain warmth freely given. Furthermore that light is called the seal of the soul, or to be sealed in the soul, according to what is read in the fourth Psalm: "The light of thy countenance, O LORD is sealed upon us" [Ps 4:6].[66]

The problem with this solution is that it fails to distinguish sacramental character from the ultimate effect of the sacrament, which is grace and spiritual illumination. Sanctifying grace is a supernatural habit by which the soul shares in the divine nature and is disposed to glory. Likewise the theological and supernatural virtues are habits. But sacramental character remains also in those who lack grace and interior illumination because of unrepented mortal sin. For this reason sacramental character cannot be identified with a virtuous quality of the soul or with sanctifying grace or its effects. Unlike habits, which are either good or evil, a power is open both to a good or bad use. The baptized or those who have received Holy Orders, for example, can use their ecclesial identity and priestly power, received through sacramental character, for great good or for enormous evil, as when they give scandal or commit sacrilege in celebrating the sacraments.

St. Thomas Aquinas, therefore, rejected the idea that character is a *habitus*,[67] and instead seems to be the first to defend that it is a spiritual

---

'quality,' and since, 'spiritual quality' is either a *habitus* or a *dispositio*, then character is either a *habitus* or a *dispositio*. However because character is not easily changed it is not a *dispositio* but a *habitus*."

[65] See Bonaventure, *In IV Sent.*, d. 6, a. 1, q. 1, in Hellmann, 133: "Character is not a potency, because it is not in all souls."

[66] Bonaventure, *In IV Sent.*, d. 6, a. 1, q. 1, in Hellmann, 137.

[67] See *ST* III, q. 63, a. 2, sed contra: "The Philosopher says (Ethic. 2): There are three things in the soul, power, habit, and passion. Now a character is not a passion: since a passion passes quickly, whereas a character is indelible, as will

power ordered to Christian worship, and to the reception and administration of the sacraments.[68] Since it is supernatural, this power is not intrinsic to human nature but must be received from above. It enables one to be moved by Christ and His Spirit, and so it is an instrumental[69] power subordinated to Christ and His priesthood. Character thus is a supernatural instrumental power of the soul that enables the soul to be configured to Christ and used and elevated by Him so as to participate in Christian worship and consecrate the world to Christ.[70]

In summary, it could be said that sacramental character is an efficacious sign written indelibly on the soul that configures and consecrates the soul to Christ and thus gives Christian identity according to a certain state in the Church, a corresponding ecclesial mission to share in Christ's priesthood in that ecclesial state, and it is an instrumental spiritual power to participate with Christ's priestly mission through receiving sacraments (Baptism), actively building up the Church and giving public witness to the faith (Confirmation),[71] and administering the sacraments (Holy Orders).

Indelible Character

Sacramental character has both the passive and the active aspects of a seal in the sense that it is both a passive imprint and an active impress. It is imprinted on the soul in a passive sense by the outward sacramental sign. Once imprinted, however, the seal remains indelibly present to be an active sacramental cause. As we have seen, although

---

be made clear further on (a. 5). In like manner it is not a habit: because no habit is indifferent to acting well or ill: whereas a character is indifferent to either, since some use it well, some ill. Now this cannot occur with a habit: because no one abuses a habit of virtue, or uses well an evil habit. It remains, therefore, that a character is a power."

[68] See *ST* III, q. 63, a. 2, quoted above.

[69] For a discussion of the sacraments as instrumental causes of grace, see chapter 12 below.

[70] For St. Thomas's doctrine on sacramental character and its relationship with the teaching of his predecessors and contemporaries, see Galot, *La nature du caractère sacramentel*, 171–97; Miralles, *I sacramenti cristiani*, 282–85; Nutt, *General Principles of Sacramental Theology*, 156–57; and Roger Nutt, "Configuration to Christ the Priest: Aquinas on Sacramental Character," *Angelicum* 85 (2008): 697–713.

[71] See *ST* III, q. 72, a. 5: "In Confirmation he receives power to do those things which pertain to the spiritual combat with the enemies of the Faith."

the outward sacramental sign is transient, character is a durable sign. Although it is distinct from grace, it continues to be present as an invisible sacramental "word" so as to be the active instrumental cause of sanctification throughout the life of the person sealed by Christ.[72] Character has the power to be an abiding instrumental cause of grace through the power of God "speaking" through it, not just when the sacrament was first received but also throughout life. This power of sanctification is twofold. First, character, as seen above, gives a power to receive and, in the case of Holy Orders, administer sacraments. Secondly, as will be explained more fully in chapter 10 below, sacramental character also has a mysterious power to communicate to the subject a continuing series of sacramental graces proper to the sanctification offered by that sacrament, through the power of God, as long as there is no obstacle, such as obstinate lack of repentance.

Sacramental character is indelible, first of all, because it is a participation in Christ's eternal priesthood. Through sacramental character first received in Baptism, a person is consecrated to share in the priesthood of Christ, and this consecration lasts as long as the consecrated soul itself and Christ's priesthood, neither of which will come to an end:

> In a sacramental character Christ's faithful have a share in His Priesthood. . . . Now Christ's Priesthood is eternal, according to Psalm 109:4: 'Thou art a priest for ever, according to the order of Melchisedech.' Consequently, every sanctification wrought by His Priesthood, is perpetual, enduring as long as the thing sanctified endures. This is clear even in inanimate things; for the consecration of a church or an altar lasts for ever unless they be destroyed. Since, therefore, the subject of a character is the soul as to its intellective part, where faith resides, as stated above (a. 4, ad 3); it is clear that, the intellect being perpetual and incorruptible, a character cannot be blotted out from the soul.[73]

---

[72] See *ST* III, q. 63, a. 3, ad 2: "The sacramental character is a thing [*res*: reality] as regards the exterior sacrament, and a sacrament in regard to the ultimate effect. Consequently, something can be attributed to a character in two ways. First, if the character be considered as a sacrament: and thus it is a sign of the invisible grace which is conferred in the sacrament."

[73] *ST* III, q. 63, a. 5.

Sanctifying grace is not indelible because its continuing presence depends on our free will to cooperate with it and not expel it through mortal sin. But sacramental character is like an image of Christ imprinted on the soul so that He can make use of us for the sanctification of the world. Since it is His instrument and image, it does not depend on our free will for its continued existence, but on His fidelity and power.[74]

Secondly, the indelible nature of character explains why the three sacraments that imprint character can be received only once, as St. Augustine explained. After the outward words and gestures have passed away, the sacramental character remains, which is the reason why it would be superfluous and irreverent to receive it again.

Third, the indelibility of sacramental character explains how the sacrament can come back to life if it was received validly but unworthily, in that it was received without true repentance or faith. If an adult receives Baptism, Confirmation, Holy Orders, Anointing of the Sick, or Matrimony without either true repentance for mortal sin or faith, then no grace will be received in that state of unrepentance. But if one subsequently repents, that repentance will take away the obstacle to efficacy, and the sacramental grace will be unleashed. This is referred to as the *reviviscence*, or *coming back to life*, of the sacrament.[75] Without the permanence of character, this would be very hard to explain. If the sacrament causes grace, how could that grace be given later if its cause—the sacramental sign—no longer exists? The answer is that even though the outward sacramental sign is transient, a character is also given—even when the sacrament is received unworthily—that remains in the soul as an efficacious sign of grace, such that it can cause the infusion of grace as soon as the obstacle of unrepentance is taken away.

---

[74] See *ST* III, q. 63, a. 5, ad 1: "Both grace and character are in the soul, but in different ways. For grace is in the soul, as a form having complete existence therein: whereas a character is in the soul, as an instrumental power, as stated above (a. 2). Now a complete form is in its subject according to the condition of the subject. And since the soul as long as it is a wayfarer is changeable in respect of the free-will, it results that grace is in the soul in a changeable manner. But an instrumental power follows rather the condition of the principal agent: and consequently a character exists in the soul in an indelible manner, not from any perfection of its own, but from the perfection of Christ's Priesthood, from which the character flows like an instrumental power."

[75] See P. A. Haynal, "De Reviviscentia Sacramentorum fictione recedente," *Angelicum* (1927): 51–80; 203–23; 382–405.

Fourth, the indelible nature of character explains how the sacrament, received once, can be the source of a long series of actual graces that last throughout one's Christian life. Even though the outward sacramental sign has long since passed away, the ever-present character continues to cause the granting of actual graces in accordance with the purpose of each sacrament, as will be seen in chapter 10 below. Since the mission conferred by sacramental character is supernatural, it requires grace to be realized. One of the axioms of theology is that when God gives a mission, He gives the grace to accomplish it. The mission conferred by sacramental character is supported by sacramental grace, which is the *res tantum*, or invisible reality signified by the character and by the outward sign. Character therefore is an invisible efficacious sign of the giving of the graces necessary for the mission, provided that the recipient places no obstacle of unrepented mortal sin.

Finally, the indelible nature of sacramental character gives a visibility and definition to the Church as composed of members and a hierarchy who are marked by an indelible seal. If membership in the Church or her hierarchy depended on an effect of the sacraments that is not indelible and could be lost, like sanctifying grace or charity, then it would always be very uncertain who her true members and hierarchy are, which would be catastrophic for her social and institutional life.

Magisterial Teaching on Sacramental Character

The term "sacramental character" first appears in the papal Magisterium at the beginning of the thirteenth century in a letter of Innocent III, in which he says that adults who are forcibly baptized do not receive the sacrament nor its interior character, but those who willingly receive Baptism, even if out of fear or in bad faith, "receive the imprint of the Christian character." He concludes: "The act of the sacrament impresses the character when it does not encounter the obstacle of an opposing will resisting it."[76]

That Baptism, Confirmation, and Holy Orders imprint character was taught by the Council of Florence:

Among these sacraments, there are three, namely, baptism, confirmation, and orders, that imprint an indelible character

---

[76] Innocent III, Letter to Archbishop Humbert of Arles *Maiores Ecclesiae causas*, (1201; DS, 781). I slightly modified the translation.

on the soul, which is a type of spiritual sign distinguishing [the recipient] from others. As a consequence, they may not be repeated in the same person. The other four, however, do not imprint a character and allow for repetition.[77]

At the Reformation, Luther denied sacramental character especially with regard to Holy Orders in his *Babylonian Captivity of the Church* of 1520:

According to what the Scriptures teach us, what we call the priesthood is a ministry. So I cannot understand at all why one who has once been made a priest cannot again become a layman; for the sole difference between him and a layman is his ministry. But to depose a man from the priesthood is by no means impossible, because even now it is the usual penalty imposed upon guilty priests. . . . For that fiction of an "indelible character" has long since become a laughingstock. I admit that the pope imparts this "character," but Christ knows nothing of it; and a priest who is consecrated with it becomes the life-long servant and captive, not of Christ, but of the pope. . . . Moreover, unless I am greatly mistaken, if this sacrament and this fiction ever fall to the ground, the papacy with its "characters" will scarcely survive.[78]

Zwingli[79] and Calvin[80] likewise rejected the character impressed by Holy Orders. Sacramental character in general was denied by Protestant theologians as lacking a biblical foundation. Nevertheless, they continued the practice of baptizing only once, which implies recognition of an abiding aspect to Baptism that is baptismal character, even if they rejected the term.

To counter the denial of Martin Luther and those who followed him, the Council of Trent infallibly defined the existence of sacramental character in Baptism, Confirmation, and Holy Orders:

---

[77] Council of Florence, *Exsultate Deo* (DS, 1313). I have slightly modified the translation.

[78] Luther, *Babylonian Captivity of the Church*, in *LW*, 36:117. See also pp. 110–11; and *The Misuse of the Mass*, in *LW*, 36:160, 201.

[79] Leeming, *Principles of Sacramental Theology*, 138.

[80] See Calvin, *Institutes*, bk, 4, ch. 19.28–31.

If anyone says that in the three sacraments, namely, baptism, confirmation, and orders, a character is not imprinted on the soul, that is, a kind of indelible spiritual sign by reason of which these sacraments cannot be repeated, let him be anathema.[81]

When treating Holy Orders, the Council of Trent reiterated the definition:

But since in the sacrament of orders, as also in baptism and confirmation, a character is imprinted that can be neither erased nor taken away, the holy council justly condemns the opinion of those who say that priests of the New Testament have only a temporary power and that those who have once been rightly ordained can again become lay persons if they do not exercise the ministry of the word of God.[82]

The *Catechism of the Catholic Church*, §1121, in addition to the indelible quality of character defined at Trent, explains other aspects of character. It states that it is by character that one is "made a member of the Church according to different states and functions." Character structures the visible Church. Secondly, it takes up the thesis of St. Thomas that character is that by which the "Christian shares in Christ's priesthood." Thus it is a "vocation to divine worship and to the service of the Church." Third, it highlights the fact that character is an abiding "positive disposition for grace." In this way the sacrament, given at a particular point in time, continues to operate over time in giving sacramental graces, and therefore it is a "promise and guarantee of divine protection."

How the Three Characters Differ

How do the three characters differ from one another if all are participations in Christ's three offices of priest, prophet, and king? Since

---

[81] Council of Trent, Decree on the Sacraments (session 7), can. 9 on the Sacraments in General (DS, 1609).

[82] Council of Trent, Doctrine and Canons on the Sacrament of Orders (session 23), ch. 4 (DS, 1767). See also can. 4 (DS, 1774): "If anyone says that . . . no character is imprinted by ordination; or that he who has once been a priest can again become a layman, let him be anathema."

character gives identity, mission, and spiritual power, we should expect these three characters to differ with regard to each.

The *Catechism of the Council of Trent*, following St. Thomas Aquinas,[83] explains sacramental character as a sacred power and as a distinguishing mark of those who have received that power in the Church, and it distinguishes the three characters as follows:

> The character has a twofold effect: it enables us to receive or perform something sacred; and it distinguishes those who have received it from those who have not. By virtue of the character of Baptism both effects are evident: by it we are qualified to receive the other sacraments, and by it the Christian is distinguished from those who do not profess the faith. The same is true of the characters of the other two sacraments. By the character of Confirmation we are armed and trained as soldiers of Christ, publicly to profess and defend his name against our enemies—whether the enemy within, or the spiritual powers of wickedness in high places (see Eph 6:11–12), and by it we are distinguished from those who are only baptized and thus, as it were, but newborn infants (see 1 Pt 2:2). By the character of Holy Orders the power of consecrating and administering the sacraments is conferred; as is also the distinction of those who possess it from all the rest of the faithful.[84]

Baptismal Character

Baptismal character gives the foundational Christian identity of being a member of the Body of Christ and the corresponding mission of adhering to the Body, receiving the other sacraments, and giving worship to God above all in the Eucharistic Sacrifice. It gives an initial spiritual power to receive the other sacraments, to participate in the worship of the Eternal High Priest in His Mystical Body, and thus to live the supernatural life of that Body in faith and as a witness to faith. *Lumen Gentium*, §11 states: "Incorporated in the Church through baptism, the faithful are destined by the baptismal character for the worship of the Christian religion; reborn as sons of God they must confess before men the faith which they have received from God

---

[83] See *ST* III, q. 63, aa. 1–3.

[84] *CCT*, part 2, intro., §31, p. 162.

through the Church." Pius XII speaks of baptismal character in his encyclical on the Liturgy *Mediator Dei*, §88:

> By the waters of baptism, as by common right, Christians are made members of the Mystical Body of Christ the Priest, and by the "character" which is imprinted on their souls, they are appointed to give worship to God. Thus they participate, according to their condition, in the priesthood of Christ.

To carry out this glorious mission of Baptism, character is, of course, not sufficient. The faithful need the aid of sanctifying and actual graces, which are the ultimate effect of the sacrament.

Character of Confirmation

What does Confirmation add to the character of Baptism? *Lumen Gentium*, §11 speaks of a more perfect bond with the Church and of an ecclesial mission to give witness: "They are more perfectly bound to the Church by the sacrament of Confirmation, and the Holy Spirit endows them with special strength so that they are more strictly obliged to spread and defend the faith, both by word and by deed, as true witnesses of Christ." The "special strength" of the Holy Spirit is the effect of grace, but being more "perfectly bound to the Church" pertains also to sacramental character, by which the confirmed receive an ecclesial mission of giving witness to Christ "by word and deed." Again, the ability to give mature witness will depend on their cooperation with grace, but the mission of being called to Christian witness is rooted in their indelible character.

The footnote in this text of *Lumen Gentium*, §11 refers, among other authors, to St. Thomas Aquinas. For St. Thomas the difference between the two characters is that Confirmation, whose purpose is to bring the recipient to spiritual maturity, gives the recipient an *active ecclesial mission* to build up the Church, to profess and live the faith socially before the world, and to engage in spiritual combat against the enemies of the faith and against what is contrary to the Christian life. The transformation of the Apostles after Pentecost manifests the new spiritual identity, mission, and power they received through having been anointed by the Holy Spirit. The character of Confirmation thus gives the identity of a Christian called to be moved by the Holy Spirit to actively build up the Church and give public witness to her faith.[85] St. Thomas explains the difference as follows, highlighting the aspects of spiritual combat and ecclesial witness in the character of Confirmation:

> By the sacrament of Confirmation man is given a spiritual power in respect of sacred actions other than those in respect of which he receives power in Baptism. For in Baptism he receives power to do those things which pertain to his own salvation, forasmuch as he lives to himself: whereas in Confirmation he receives power to do those things which pertain to the spiritual combat with the enemies of the Faith. This is evident from the example of the apostles, who, before they received the fulness of the Holy Ghost, were in the "upper room . . . persevering . . . in prayer" (Acts 1:13, 14); whereas afterwards they went out and feared not to confess their faith in public, even in the face of the enemies of the Christian Faith. And therefore it is evident that a character is imprinted in the sacrament of Confirmation.[86]

Lumen Gentium, §34 describes the mission of the laity as a supernatural participation in Christ's priestly office. Because of their participation in Christ's priestly mission through having been "anointed by the Holy Spirit" in Confirmation, they are called to consecrate the world to God:

> For besides intimately linking them to His life and His mission, He also gives them a sharing in His priestly function of offering spiritual worship for the glory of God and the salvation of men. For this reason the laity, dedicated to Christ and *anointed by the Holy Spirit*, are marvelously called and wonderfully prepared so that ever more abundant fruits of the Spirit may be produced in them. For all their works, prayers and apostolic endeavors, their ordinary married and family life, their daily occupations, their physical and mental relaxation, if carried

---

[85] On the ecclesial dimension of Confirmation and its relation to Pentecost, see Yves M.-J. Congar, *I Believe in the Holy Spirit*, trans. David Smith (New York: Crossroad, 1997), 218–22; Isaac Kizhakkeparampil, *The Invocation of the Holy Spirit as Constitutive of the Sacraments according to Cardinal Yves Congar* (Rome: Pontificia Università Gregoriana, 1995), 97–103.

[86] *ST* III, q. 72, a. 5, referred to in footnote 5 of *LG*, §11.

out in the Spirit, and even the hardships of life, if patiently borne—all these become "spiritual sacrifices acceptable to God through Jesus Christ." Together with the offering of the Lord's body, they are most fittingly offered in the celebration of the Eucharist. Thus, as those everywhere who adore in holy activity, the laity consecrate the world itself to God.[87]

The character of Confirmation gives the ecclesial mission to the sanctification of daily life. In order to accomplish it, however, character is insufficient and grace is necessary so that the activities of the Christian life may be carried out "in the Spirit."

It can be seen from *Lumen Gentium*, §34 that the three offices of Christ are intimately united, for the priestly offering of the faithful is portrayed here as the offering to God of all the ordinary activities of the Christian life, which include work, family life, prayer, apostolic activity, relaxation, and suffering. These works of the Christian are the content of the kingly office, by which the faithful are called to rightly order human realities in charity and service. By fulfilling their kingly office, the lay faithful also give prophetic witness through example. Thus the priestly office consists in offering, above all in the Eucharist, the content of the work of one's kingly service and prophetic witness. The prophetic and the kingly missions provide the matter for the priestly offering, and in this way the faithful participate in consecrating the world to Christ.[88]

The Apostolic Exhortation *Christifideles Laici* of St. John Paul II eloquently develops this theme of the participation of the lay faithful in the three offices of Christ, putting it forth as one of the principal fruits of the Second Vatican Council.[89] The baptized share in the

---

[87] *LG*, §34 (my italics). The laity's participation in the prophetic and kingly offices of Christ are treated in §§35 and 36, respectively.

[88] On the mission of the lay faithful to participate in the threefold mission of Christ, see Congar, *Lay People in the Church*, 121–323.

[89] See John Paul II, *Christifideles Laici* (Dec 30, 1988), §14: "In the wake of the Second Vatican Council, at the beginning of my pastoral ministry, my aim was to emphasize forcefully the priestly, prophetic and kingly dignity of the entire People of God." He then quotes from his homily at the beginning of his pastoral ministry as supreme shepherd of the Church, on Oct 22, 1978, in AAS 70 (1978), 946: "The Second Vatican Council has reminded us of the mystery of this power and of the fact that the mission of Christ—Priest, Prophet-Teacher, King—continues in the Church. Everyone, the whole People of God, shares in this threefold mission."

priestly office by being "united to him and to his sacrifice in the offering they make of themselves and their daily activities (cf. Rom 12:1, 2)." The lay faithful accomplish the prophetic mission when they "allow the newness and the power of the gospel to shine out everyday in their family and social life, as well as to express patiently and courageously in the contradictions of the present age their hope of future glory even 'through the framework of their secular life.'" Their kingship is exercised

> above all in the spiritual combat in which they seek to overcome in themselves the kingdom of sin (cf. Rom 6:12), and then to make a gift of themselves so as to serve, in justice and in charity, Jesus who is himself present in all his brothers and sisters. . . . But in particular the lay faithful are called to restore to creation all its original value. In ordering creation to the authentic well-being of humanity in an activity governed by the life of grace, they share in the exercise of the power with which the Risen Christ draws all things to himself.

The threefold participation of the laity in the mission of Christ "finds its source in the anointing of Baptism, its further development in Confirmation and its realization and dynamic sustenance in the Holy Eucharist."[90]

The Eastern Orthodox tradition likewise emphasizes that Chrismation (received together with Baptism) makes one a participant in Christ's threefold mission, which is symbolized by the anointing with chrism. John McGuckin explains the Orthodox understanding of this royal priesthood:

> This consecration is a fundamental reorientation; an abiding consecration that is 'sealed' into our flesh and soul, and our spirit's very structure, by the sacred chrism. It cannot be lost. . . . The anointing with the sacred chrism is the gift of grace that initiates the kingly, prophetic, and priestly charism of the individual Christian's knowledge of God. . . . This royal and priestly charism shared by all the faithful after chrismation demands its exercise in all members of Christ's Church. . . . Much effort, and energy, and interest is expended by most

---

[90] John Paul II, *Christifideles Laici*, §14.

of us in the prosecution of our ordinary careers. The care for the development of the priestly vocation that is committed to all the faithful in chrismation is something that is far more important, and requires an even higher level of energy and commitment. It is the vocation of vocations. This is the knowledge of God communicated to believers to make them prophets and priests after the chrismation. This knowledge could be described as a 'new instinct' for the will of God among us. It is a spiritual capacity for insight into the Scriptures, and into the very syntax of prayer, that must now be carefully nurtured.[91]

This participation in the priesthood of Christ through Confirmation fulfills the prophecy of Joel, by which God declared that He will "pour out" His "spirit on all flesh" (Joel 2:28), as confirmed by St. Peter on Pentecost in Acts 2:16. This gift is eloquently described by the twentieth-century Orthodox theologian, Nicholas Afanasiev:

We believe that in the Church the Old Testament prophecy has been fulfilled. . . . God pours out his Spirit not upon just a certain number but upon all His people. All are charismatics since all have received the Spirit as a "pledge" of the new age to which the Church belongs while still abiding in this old age. . . . Upon entering, the believer is set apart for ministry in the Church through the sending down of the Spirit. . . . The gift of the Spirit that every member of the faithful receives in the sacrament of initiation is the charism of the royal priesthood. . . . We are not aware of how extraordinary and audacious the idea of the priestly ministry of all members of the Church is.[92]

Distinction between the Ministerial and Common Priesthood: An Effect of Sacramental Character

Although all of the Christian faithful share in the priesthood of Christ

---

[91] John Anthony McGuckin, *The Orthodox Church: An Introduction to Its History, Doctrine, and Spiritual Culture* (Malden, MA; Oxford: Blackwell, 2008), 286–87.

[92] Nicholas Afanasiev, *The Church of the Holy Spirit*, trans. Vitaly Permiakov (Notre Dame, IN: University of Notre Dame Press, 2007), 3.

through the characters of Baptism and Confirmation, their participation in the priesthood of Christ is essentially distinct from the higher participation through priestly character imparted by Holy Orders. As *Lumen Gentium*, §10 states, this distinction is not just a matter of degree, but of essence:

> Though they differ from one another in essence and not only in degree, the common priesthood of the faithful and the ministerial or hierarchical priesthood are nonetheless interrelated: each of them in its own special way is a participation in the one priesthood of Christ. The ministerial priest, by the sacred power he enjoys, teaches and rules the priestly people; acting in the person of Christ, he makes present the Eucharistic sacrifice, and offers it to God in the name of all the people. But the faithful, in virtue of their royal priesthood, join in the offering of the Eucharist. They likewise exercise that priesthood in receiving the sacraments, in prayer and thanksgiving, in the witness of a holy life, and by self-denial and active charity.

Priestly character enables the priest to act in the person of Christ the Head of the Church (*in persona Christi capitis*), especially to make present the Eucharistic Sacrifice. The characters of Baptism and Confirmation, on the other hand, make the baptized faithful members of Christ's Body, which enables them to join in the offering of the Sacrifice of the Head. The character of Confirmation is the means by which the members are further empowered by the Spirit of Christ and called to actively offer the Sacrifice and join to it their own Christian lives of witness and service. It follows that all three sacramental characters have a Eucharistic focus,[93] which is the heart of Christ's priesthood. It also follows that the characters of Baptism and Confirmation, on the one hand, and of Holy Orders at the grade of priesthood, on the other, have a complementary relationship in that each needs the other to fulfill its mission. Without the ministerial priesthood, the royal or common

---

[93] See Matthew Levering, *Christ and the Catholic Priesthood: Ecclesial Hierarchy and the Pattern of the Trinity* (Chicago: Hillenbrand Books, 2010), 56. See also Benedict XVI, *Sacramentum Caritatis*, §17: "It must never be forgotten that our reception of Baptism and Confirmation is ordered to the Eucharist. . . . The Holy Eucharist, then, brings Christian initiation to completion and represents the centre and goal of all sacramental life."

priesthood would not be able to offer the works of the Christian life in the Mass, for there would be no Mass without the ministerial priesthood to realize transubstantiation and offer the Sacrifice in the person of Christ. But the mission of the ministerial priesthood is also to communicate spiritual goods to the faithful in the sacraments. No one is a priest for himself, but for the good of the whole Body.

Although the ministerial priesthood is essentially distinct from the common priesthood of the faithful, each successive character and corresponding sacred power presupposes the one that came before and builds on it, adding a deeper mission and a fuller sacred power. Thus the character of Confirmation, deputing one to mature service and witness, requires the character of Baptism, by which one is made a newborn member of Christ capable of receiving the other sacraments. Similarly, the character of Holy Orders requires that of Confirmation. One must first be empowered to be a mature witness of Christ before one can fittingly be deputed to act in His Person.

Character of Holy Orders

The Second Vatican Council, in the Decree on the Ministry and Life of Priests, *Presbyterorum Ordinis*, §2, defines priestly character in terms of the power to act in the person of Christ the Head of the Church: "The priesthood, while indeed it presupposes the sacraments of Christian initiation, is conferred by that special sacrament; through it priests, by the anointing of the Holy Spirit, are signed with a special character and are conformed to Christ the Priest in such a way that they can act in the person of Christ the Head." [94]

Holy Orders gives the further mission of enabling the recipient to participate in Christ's priestly office by acting in His person (*in persona Christi*) and sharing in His headship. The priest acts in the person of Christ, the Head of the Church, above all when he celebrates the sacraments, acting as an instrument through whom Christ's divine power works[95] to impart grace and forgive sins. This participation in Christ's

---

[94] See also *CCC*, §1551: "The sacrament of Holy Orders communicates a 'sacred power' which is none other than that of Christ."

[95] See Levering, *Christ and the Catholic Priesthood*, 166–67. See also *SCG* IV, ch. 74, no. 2, 4:286: "The instrument must be proportionate to the agent. Hence, the ministers of Christ must be in conformity with Him. But Christ ... wrought our salvation, in that He was God and man. . . . Therefore, the ministers of Christ must not only be men, but must participate somehow in His divinity

headship also elevates the prophetic and kingly offices of teaching and governance that are shared by the baptized and confirmed. Nevertheless, the holy exercise of this threefold mission requires not just priestly character, but the aid of sacramental grace and human and supernatural virtues.

In his sacramental role of participating in Christ's headship, the priest, through priestly character, "has the task not only of representing Christ—Head of the Church—before the assembly of the faithful, but also of acting in the name of the whole Church when presenting to God the prayer of the Church, and above all when offering the Eucharistic Sacrifice."[96]

Pius XII speaks about priestly character in *Mediator Dei*, §43:

> In the same way, actually that baptism is the distinctive mark of all Christians, and serves to differentiate them from those who have not been cleansed in this purifying stream and consequently are not members of Christ, the sacrament of holy orders sets the priest apart from the rest of the faithful who have not received this consecration. For they alone, in answer to an inward supernatural call, have entered the august ministry, where they are assigned to service in the sanctuary and become, as it were, the instruments God uses to communicate supernatural life from on high to the Mystical Body of Jesus Christ. Add to this . . . the fact that they alone have been marked with the indelible sign "conforming" them to Christ the Priest, and that their hands alone have been consecrated "in order that whatever they bless may be blessed, whatever they consecrate may become sacred and holy, in the name of our Lord Jesus Christ."

Three Grades of Holy Orders

The sacrament of Holy Orders differs from Baptism and Confirmation in that it imprints character in three hierarchical grades: diaconate, priesthood, and episcopate.[97] Of these three, the episcopate

---

through some spiritual power, for an instrument shares in the power of its principal agent. Now, it is this power that the Apostle calls 'the power which the Lord hath given me unto edification and not unto destruction' (2 Cor. 13:10)."

[96] *CCC*, §1552.

[97] See *LG*, §28: "The divinely established ecclesiastical ministry is exercised on

is the fullness of Holy Orders,[98] and the other two grades participate unequally in it.[99] Priests are "united with the bishops in sacerdotal dignity,"[100] whereas deacons, "at a lower level of the hierarchy"[101] participate in the service of the altar and charity, and cooperate with the ministry of the bishop and priests. Thus the character imprinted in the deacon is amplified and modified by priestly ordination, which in turn is brought to its fullness by episcopal consecration.

It is absolutely clear that the character of the priesthood is distinct from that of the diaconate, for the priest gains a sacred power to act in the person of Christ not possessed by the deacon.[102] This is manifested most clearly in the power to consecrate the Eucharist, give sacramental absolution, administer Anointing of the Sick, and receive

---

different levels by those who from antiquity have been called bishops, priests and deacons."

[98] See *LG*, §21.

[99] St. Thomas compares the grades of Holy Orders to the way the power of a king may be participated in by his ministers. Although St. Thomas does not distinguish between the sacramental character of the priest and the bishop, his analogy works better if one makes that distinction. In this comparison the fullness resides in the bishop and is participated in by the priests such that they can also act in the person of Christ the Head and consecrate the Eucharist. The deacon participates in a lower way, aiding the bishop in liturgical and charitable service. See Thomas Aquinas, *In IV Sent.*, d. 24, q. 2, a. 1, qla. 1, ad 3, trans. Mortensen, 8:612: "Although in a kingdom the whole fullness of power resides with the king, nevertheless the powers of the ministers do not prevent that they are certain participations of royal power; and it is similar in holy orders." See also ad 2 (611–12): "The distinction of orders is not a distinction of an integral whole into parts, nor of a universal whole, but of a potestative whole. The nature of a potestative whole is that the whole is in one thing according to its complete notion, but it is in others as a certain participation of it. And this is how it is here, for all the plenitude of this sacrament is in one order, namely, the priesthood. But in the others there is a certain participation of orders, and this is signified in what the Lord says to Moses: 'I will take some of your spirit and put it on them, so that they may bear the burden of the people along with you' (Num 11:17). And thus all orders are one sacrament." In the light of the teaching of *LG*, §21, we should say rather that the fullness of the sacrament is given through episcopal consecration and episcopal character and that a participation in its mission and spiritual power is given through priestly and diaconal character.

[100] *LG*, §28.

[101] *LG*, §29.

[102] See Second Vatican Council, Decree on the Ministry and Life of Priests, *Presbyterorum Ordinis*, §2: "Priests, by the anointing of the Holy Spirit, are signed with a special character and are conformed to Christ the Priest in such a way that they can act in the person of Christ the Head."

by delegation the power to administer Confirmation.

Although the order of diaconate does not confer the sacred powers just mentioned, the ordination of deacons imprints a character distinct from Baptism and Confirmation and from the two grades of Orders above it. This is taught by the *Catechism of the Catholic Church*, §1570: "The sacrament of Holy Orders marks them with an *imprint* ('character') which cannot be removed and which configures them to Christ, who made himself the 'deacon' or servant of all."[103] St. Paul VI, in the Apostolic Letter in which he gave norms for restoring the permanent diaconate, speaks of the diaconate as "adorned with its own indelible character and its own special grace."[104]

As seen above, character gives a new configuration to Christ, which is also a consecration. This configuration imparts a new stable ecclesial mission and is a durable instrumental cause of the graces to carry out the mission. The deacon receives a new configuration to Christ the servant (*diakonos*) and the mission to carry out the diaconal service in the Church, which requires a series of sacramental graces that have their foundation in diaconal character.[105] *Lumen Gentium*, §29 speaks

---

[103] *CCC*, §1570. St. Thomas held as probable that a character was imprinted in diaconate ordination. See *In IV Sent.*, d. 24, q. 1, a. 2, qla. 2. This is no longer to be regarded as merely probable, but implied by the teaching of the Second Vatican Council, and taught by St. Paul VI and the *Catechism of the Catholic Church*. St. Thomas also held it as probable that the five minor orders leading up to the diaconate were part of the sacrament of Holy Orders and imprinted a distinct character. This is clearly not the case, and the minor orders should be regarded as sacramentals, which do not imprint character. For St. Thomas's view on the sacramentality of the diaconate, see ITC, *From the Diakonia of Christ to the Diakonia of the Apostles: Historico-Theological Research Document* (Chicago; Mundelein, IL: Hillenbrand Books, 2003), 46–47.

[104] Paul VI, Apostolic Letter motu proprio *Sacrum Diaconatus Ordinem*, June 18, 1967.

[105] Sacramental character can be understood to be an instrumental spiritual power in two distinct senses. On the one hand, it is a power to receive other sacraments, as in the case of Baptism, or to administer sacraments in the person of Christ, as in the case of Holy Orders. In this sense, however, Confirmation and diaconal ordination would not add a power to receive or administer sacraments that is not already included in Baptism. On the other hand, as will be seen more fully in chapter 12, St. Thomas sees sacramental character as an abiding instrumental cause to impart the sacramental graces proper to that sacrament, as long as the recipient does not pose an obstacle. In this second sense, it is clear that the sacramental character of Confirmation and the diaconate differ from that of Baptism not only in the difference in the configuration with Christ that they establish but also because both the ecclesial mission and the sacramental graces given by the three characters are distinct, and therefore the power of

about the diaconate as follows:

> At a lower level of the hierarchy are deacons, upon whom hands are imposed "not unto the priesthood, but unto a ministry of service." For strengthened by sacramental grace, in communion with the bishop and his group of priests they serve in the diaconate of the liturgy, of the word, and of charity to the people of God.[106]

Whether episcopal consecration imprints a sacramental character distinct from that of the priest was debated for centuries. Many great theologians, such as St. Jerome,[107] Peter Lombard,[108] St. Bonaventure,[109] and St. Thomas,[110] denied this. Nevertheless, the position asserting

---

the different sacramental characters to mediate those sacramental graces must likewise be distinct.

[106] See also *LG*, §41: "Ministers of lesser rank are also sharers in the mission and grace of the Supreme Priest. In the first place among these ministers are deacons, who . . . are dispensers of Christ's mysteries and servants of the Church."

[107] See St. Jerome, Commentary on Titus 1:5 (PL 26:562–63), in *St. Jerome's Commentaries on Galatians, Titus, and Philemon*, trans. Thomas P. Scheck (Notre Dame, IN: University of Notre Dame Press, 2010), 289–90: "It is therefore the very same priest, who is a bishop, and before there existed . . . factions in the religion . . . the churches were governed by a common council of the priests. But after each one began to think that those whom he had baptized were his own and not Christ's, it was decreed for the whole world that one of the priests should be elected to preside over the others, to whom the entire care of the church should pertain, and the seeds of schism would be removed. . . . Therefore, just as the priests know that by the custom of the church they are subject to the one who was previously appointed over them, so the bishops know that they, more by custom than by the truth of the Lord's arrangement, are greater than the priests."

[108] See Peter Lombard, *Sentences*, bk. 4, dist. 24. See ITC, *From the Diakonia of Christ to the Diakonia of the Apostles*, 45.

[109] Bonaventure, *In IV Sent.*, dist. 24, p. 2, a. 2, q. 3, in *Commentary on the Sentences: Sacraments*, trans. Hellmann, 434. See Emmanuel Doronzo, *De Ordine*, vol. 2, *De Institutione* (Milwaukee, WI: Bruce, 1959), 128.

[110] The reason given by St. Thomas (as well as St. Bonaventure and St. Albert) for denying the sacramentality of episcopal consecration is very interesting and concerns the centrality of the Eucharist; they argue that since the bishop has no greater power than the priest for consecrating the Eucharist, episcopal consecration does not add to the power of the sacrament of Orders, but adds only a superiority in the power of jurisdiction and governance over the Mystical Body, which includes the power to ordain. See *In IV Sent.*, d. 24, q. 2, a. 1, qla. 2, trans. Mortensen, 8:613: "The distinction of orders should be taken according to their

a distinct episcopal character came to dominate increasingly in the centuries after the Council of Trent, and was defended by St. Robert Bellarmine[111] and many others.[112]

Without directly alluding to the controversy, the Second Vatican Council, in *Lumen Gentium*, §21, teaches that episcopal consecration confers "the fullness of the sacrament of Orders . . . , that fullness of power, namely, which . . . is called the high priesthood, the supreme power of the sacred ministry."[113] *Lumen Gentium*, §21 goes on to state that a distinct character is imprinted in the bishop:

> For from the tradition, which is expressed especially in liturgical rites and in the practice of both the Church of the East and of the West, it is clear that, by means of the imposition

---

relation to the Eucharist; for the power of orders is either for the consecration of the Eucharist itself, or for some ministry to be directed to this." Although St. Thomas is aware that Pseudo-Dionysius considers the bishop to be a distinct order superior to the priest, in response to the first objection in the same article (ibid., ad 1, p. 614) he interprets this as follows: "Dionysius is speaking of holy orders not according as they are sacraments, but according as they are directed to hierarchical actions. . . . But the orders are sacraments only by their relation to the greatest of sacraments; and this is why the number of orders should be gathered in accord with this." See also *In IV Sent.*, d. 24, q. 3, a. 2, qla. 2; ibid., ad 2, trans. Mortensen, 8:630: "Orders, according as it is a sacrament imprinting a character, is specially directed to the sacrament of the Eucharist, in which Christ himself is contained, for by the character we are configured to Christ himself. And therefore although a certain spiritual power is given to the bishop in his promotion with regard to the other sacraments, nevertheless that power does not have the nature of a character. And because of this the episcopate is not an order, according as orders are a certain sacrament." See Michael G. Sirilla, *The Ideal Bishop: St. Thomas Aquinas's Commentaries on the Pastoral Epistles* (Washington, DC: Catholic University of America Press, 2017), 25, 37; Joseph Lécuyer, "Les étapes de l'enseignement thomiste sur l'épiscopat," *Revue Thomiste* 57 (1957): 29–52, esp. 51–52, in which Lécuyer gives a good summary of St. Thomas's mature doctrine on the episcopate; ITC, *From the Diakonia of Christ to the Diakonia of the Apostles*, 46.

[111] See Robert Card. Bellarmine, *De controversiis christianae fidei, De sacramento Ordinis*, ch. 5, in *Opera omnia*, 5:26–28. See ITC, *From the Diakonia of Christ to the Diakonia of the Apostles*, 51.

[112] See Doronzo, *De Ordine*, 2:114–312, esp. 196–224; Felix Cappello, *Tractatus Canonico-Moralis de Sacramentis*, vol. 4, *De Sacra Ordinatione*, 2nd ed. (Taurini: Marietti, 1947), 21–47. For a good defense of the sacramentality of episcopal ordination, see Charles Journet, *The Church of the Word Incarnate*, 1:85, 98–120.

[113] See Jean Galot, *Theology of the Priesthood*, trans. Roger Balducelli (San Francisco: Ignatius Press, 1984), 183–84.

of hands and the words of consecration, the grace of the Holy
Spirit is so conferred, and the sacred character so impressed,
that bishops in an eminent and visible way sustain the roles
of Christ Himself as Teacher, Shepherd and High Priest,
and that they act in His person. Therefore it pertains to the
bishops to admit newly elected members into the Episcopal
body by means of the sacrament of Orders.[114]

The principal reason for this doctrine is that since episcopal consecration confers the fullness of Holy Orders, it must also confer a
corresponding fullness to the *character* of Holy Orders. This character gives to the bishop a new configuration to Christ, the Head and
Bridegroom of the Church, and a new ecclesial mission of headship
with regard to the local church over which he is to preside in charity.
For this exalted mission he will need many sacramental graces that
have their foundation in episcopal character.[115]

The existence of episcopal character, like that of the diaconate
and the priesthood, is also witnessed by the fact that one can only be
ordained to the episcopate once. This implies an indelible mark.[116]

The Grandeur of Sacramental Character

The Trinitarian Dimension of Sacramental Character

As witnessed at the Baptism of Christ, baptismal character gives a new
relation to the three divine Persons. Sacramental character directly

---

[114] See also CIC, canons 1008–09.

[115] For a discussion of episcopal character and the three munera of sanctifying,
teaching, and governing, see Guy Mansini, "Episcopal Munera and the Character of Episcopal Orders," *The Thomist* 66 (2002): 369–94; and his "Sacerdotal
Character at the Second Vatican Council," *The Thomist* 66 (2003): 539–77.

[116] See Gregory the Great, Letter to John, Bishop of Ravenna, in *NPNF*2, 12b:114:
"But as to what you say about one who has been ordained being ordained again,
it is exceedingly ridiculous. . . . For, as one who has been once baptized ought
not to be baptized again, so one who has been once consecrated cannot be
consecrated again to the same order." This argument is used by St. Robert Bellarmine to demonstrate that episcopal ordination imprints a character distinct
from that of priestly ordination, because it is for this reason that neither can be
repeated. The same argument also applies to the diaconate. See Bellarmine, *De
sacramento Ordinis*, ch. 5, in *Opera omnia*, 5:27, 29.

configures the faithful to Christ, making them sharers in His mission in the Church. This brings about a relation to the Father, of whom Christ is the perfect Image. Furthermore, it gives one a relation also to the Holy Spirit as the Love proceeding from the Father and the Son.

Although baptismal character already has a Trinitarian aspect, there is a further enrichment of the Trinitarian relations with the successive characters of Confirmation and Holy Orders. Baptismal character makes one a member of the Son and of His Church (animated by the Holy Spirit), called to give ecclesial worship to the Father through the Son and the Spirit.

The character of Confirmation deepens that Christological image, making it an imprint of Christ in His public mission of building up His Church, and thus it gives the confirmed faithful the ecclesial mission to be public witnesses or icons of Christ before the world, and active sharers in His threefold mission. This active participation in the threefold mission of Christ involves a new relation to the Father, who is the source and goal of all Revelation, kingship, and priesthood. This participation requires a special relation to the Holy Spirit, for the task of active and public sharing in the mission of the Son cannot be done by human prudence but requires increasing docility to the movements of the Holy Spirit, which is the purpose of the seven gifts of the Holy Spirit, who is Himself also given as the promised Paraclete. This relation to the Holy Spirit is clear in the current sacramental form of Confirmation: "Be sealed with the Gift of the Holy Spirit."

Holy Orders, especially at the level of the priesthood and episcopate, imprints an additional relation to all three divine Persons. The priest is uniquely configured to the Son so as to act sacramentally in His person. This engenders a new relation with the Person of the Father, for Holy Orders gives the mission to administer the sacraments and thus to give supernatural life as a parent in the order of grace, for which reason the priest is fittingly addressed as "father." This bears a natural analogy to what is proper to the Father: to beget the Son and be the font of the Trinitarian life. Holy Orders also bears a new relation to the Holy Spirit, the giver of life. Holy Orders gives the spiritual power to communicate the Holy Spirit and a sharing in the divine life through the administration of the sacraments, for the priest is enabled to act in the person of the Son who sends the Spirit. And to accomplish his sublime mission, the priest, and still more the bishop, must be supremely docile to the inspirations of the Spirit. The

Holy Spirit is thus fittingly invoked in the essential form of ordination in its three grades.

Character: A Solemn and Consoling Doctrine

The doctrine of sacramental character—as it developed from the liturgical practice of one Baptism, Chrismation, and ordination, and from the reflection on the New Testament notion of "seal"—has fundamental implications for the Christian life. The baptized and confirmed have been sealed with the imprint of Christ the King, who is the image of the Father. That image is a mark of Christ's headship over the baptized person, who is not his own. It is also a call to a glorious mission to bring one's life and activity into conformity with the image impressed by way of headship. By that conformity we will be judged. The very fact that the seal cannot be removed heightens its solemn aspect of ownership by Christ.

This seal, however, differs from all other seals by being dynamic. Other seals imprint a completed image into a receptive material. We should not imagine sacramental character in the same way. Although it is an indelible mark, it does not imprint a fixed and completed image in us as other seals do, but is a spiritual power that is the abiding instrument for granting the graces of the Holy Spirit so that the image of the King can be progressively realized in our lives day by day through our cooperation with those graces. It is like a blueprint of what we are called to be in Christ—a seal of identity and mission—endowed with a power to progressively impart the graces to realize the image over time according to the degree of our cooperation and desire. As will be made clearer in the chapter on sacramental grace, this means that sacramental character can always be "called upon" by the faithful in every need and circumstance of the Christian life. Sacramental character is a kind of image impressed upon us of the fidelity of the Triune God Himself. It testifies to Christ's proximity to us, for He has been stamped on our souls and has given us His Spirit, and thus it testifies to the readiness of His graces so that we can become ever more like to the image received.

The *Catechism of the Catholic Church*, §1121 highlights this solemn and consoling aspect of sacramental character: "This configuration to Christ and to the Church, brought about by the Spirit, is indelible; it remains for ever in the Christian as a positive disposition for grace, a promise and guarantee of divine protection, and as a vocation to divine worship and to the service of the Church."

STUDY QUESTIONS

1. How did the controversy over rebaptism that arose with St. Cyprian and the Donatists contribute to the recognition of an abiding effect of Baptism distinct from grace? How did St. Augustine respond to the Donatists? How did the Church's liturgical practice of Baptism and Holy Orders aid theological reflection on sacramental character?
2. What are the scriptural and patristic foundations for affirming sacramental character?
3. What is sacramental character, and what does it give to the recipient in the three sacraments that imprint character?
4. What kind of reality in the soul is engendered by reception of sacramental character?
5. What is the difference between the characters imprinted by Baptism and Confirmation?
6. What is the essential difference between the ministerial priesthood, brought about by priestly character, and the royal priesthood of the lay faithful, brought about by the characters of Baptism and Confirmation?
7. Is a distinct character imprinted by each of the three grades of Holy Orders? Explain.
8. How does sacramental character have a Trinitarian dimension?
9. What are some of the pastoral and spiritual implications of the Church's teaching on sacramental character?

SUGGESTIONS FOR FURTHER READING

Congar, Yves M.-J. *Lay People in the Church: A Study for a Theology of Laity*. Westminster: Newman Press, 1965. Pp. 121–294.

Donahue, John M. "Sacramental Character: The State of the Question." *The Thomist* 31 (1967): 445–64.

Galot, Jean. S.J. *La nature du caractère sacramentel: étude de théologie médievale*. Bruges: Desclée de Brouwer, 1956.

Leeming, Bernard. *Principles of Sacramental Theology*. Westminster,

MD: Newman Press, 1963. Pp. 129–83, 226–50.

Marsh, Thomas. "The Sacramental Character." In *Sacraments: The Gestures of Christ*. Edited by Denis O'Callaghan. New York: Sheed & Ward, 1964. Pp. 109–38.

Nutt, Roger. "Configuration to Christ the Priest: Aquinas on Sacramental Character." *Angelicum* 85 (2008): 697–713.

_____. *General Principles of Sacramental Theology*. Washington, DC: Catholic University of America Press, 2017. Pp. 151–65.

O'Neill, Colman E., O.P. "The Instrumentality of the Sacramental Character. An Interpretation of Summa Theologiae, III, q. 63, a. 2." *Irish Theological Quarterly* 25 (1958): 262–68.

Scheeben, Matthias Joseph. *The Mysteries of Christianity*. Translated by Cyril Vollert. St. Louis, MO: B. Herder, 1951. Pp. 582–92.

Sepe, Crescenzo. *La Dimensione trinitaria del carattere sacramentale*. Rome: Lateran University, 1969.

Torrell, Jean-Pierre. *A Priestly People: Baptismal Priesthood and Priestly Ministry*. Translated by Peter Heinegg. New York; Mahwah, NJ: Paulist Press, 2013.

CHAPTER EIGHT

Res et Sacramentum

We have seen in the previous chapter that in Baptism, Confirmation, and Holy Orders, there is an abiding intermediate level that is distinct both from the outward sacramental sign and from the inward effect of grace and sanctification. This became evident through two key facts. First, there was the universal tradition that these three sacraments could be received only once (in Holy Orders, only once at each grade) and could not be given again if someone lapsed from the faith and then returned to it in repentance. This implies that the sacrament has an abiding aspect distinct from grace, for the outward sign passes away and sanctifying grace can also be lost. Secondly, a minister who is not in a state of grace continues to administer valid sacraments. This also shows that there is an abiding effect in the person with Holy Orders, a spiritual power, distinct from and not dependent on the state of grace.

What about the other four sacraments? Is there something abiding in them that is distinct from the reality of grace conferred? The sacrament in which this is easiest to identify is the Eucharist, and it was with regard to the Eucharist that the scholastic theologians of the twelfth century developed a coherent theory of the three levels of the sacraments.

RES ET SACRAMENTUM IN THE EUCHARIST

The Three Levels in the Eucharist

The Berengarian controversy on the Eucharist in the middle of the eleventh century was the result of a deficient understanding of sacramental theology on the part of Berengarius of Tours (ca. 999–1088), who sought to apply the two Augustinian categories of *sacramentum* (sacramental sign) and *res* (reality of grace) to the Eucharist.[1] As in the Donatist understanding of Baptism, he acknowledged only these two levels of (a) the outward sign and (b) the mystery of grace communicated by it, and failed to recognize the existence of another effect distinct from grace, which is the Real Presence of Christ's Body and Blood.

Christ's Body and Blood in the Eucharist are not outward signs, for they are visible only to the eyes of faith. But neither are they a spiritual grace communicated by the sacrament, for Christ's Body and Blood are bodily realities, despite the mysterious mode of their presence. They mediate between the outward sacramental sign of the appearances of bread and wine, and the grace that they communicate. Christ's Body and Blood are invisible realities signified by the outward and sensible signs, but they are also mysterious signs and causes of the grace given by the sacrament and of the unity of the Church that is built up by grace and charity. The Body and Blood are therefore distinct both from the outward sacramental signs and from the realities of grace received, and constitute something intermediate composed of both aspects of sacred reality and sacred sign. For this reason the medieval theologians began to refer to this intermediate level as both *reality and sign—res et sacramentum*—to signify that it is both a supernatural invisible reality in itself and a sacred but now invisible sign and cause of the grace that is given.[2]

In other words, the dogma of faith regarding the Real Presence of Christ in the Eucharist made it clear to theologians that between the sacramental sign and the grace communicated, there is another mysterious reality signified by the outward sign, but which is itself a *hidden sign and instrumental cause* of the effects of grace that are the final fruit of the sacrament. The real but invisible presence of Christ's Body and Blood is the immediate instrumental cause of the grace communicated. Thus we have three levels: (a) the outward sacramental sign, which causes (b) the mysterious reality signified by the outward sign

---

[1] See Feingold, *The Eucharist*, 254–57.

[2] For the development of these categories with respect to the sacraments and the relation of that development to the controversy with Berengarius over the presence of Christ in the Eucharist, see R. F. King, "The Origin and Evolution of a Sacramental Formula: *Sacramentum Tantum, Res et Sacramentum, Res Tantum*," *The Thomist* 31 (1967): 21–82; Boyd Taylor Coolman, "The Christo-Pneumatic-Ecclesial Character of Twelfth-Century Sacramental Theology," in *OHST*, 201–17.

that is itself also a sign and cause of grace, and (c) the interior grace represented and instrumentally caused by the two dimensions of signs. Hugh of St. Victor formulated this distinction in the first half of the twelfth century:

> For although the sacrament is one, three distinct things are set forth there, namely, visible appearance, truth of body, and virtue of spiritual grace. For the visible species which is perceived visibly is one thing, the truth of body and blood which under visible appearance is believed invisibly another thing, and the spiritual grace which with body and blood is received invisibly and spiritually another.[3]

In Latin, the technical terms to designate these three levels are, respectively: *sacramentum tantum*, *res et sacramentum*, and *res tantum*. The first level is only a sign (*sacramentum tantum*), the second level is both a sign and a reality (*res et sacramentum*), and the third level is not a sign but only a reality (*res tantum*). These terms were popularized by appearing in the *Sentences* of Peter Lombard, which became the standard scholastic textbook for the following centuries, and was commented on by other theologians such as St. Bonaventure, St. Albert, St. Thomas, Bl. Duns Scotus, and their peers. Peter Lombard writes:

> And so there are three things to distinguish here: one, which is the sacrament alone [*sacramentum tantum*]; another, which is sacrament and thing [*res et sacramentum*]; a third, which is thing and not sacrament [*res et non sacramentum*]. The sacrament and not thing [*sacramentum et non res*] is the visible species of bread and wine; the sacrament and thing [*res et sacramentum*] is Christ's own flesh and blood; the thing and not sacrament [*res et non sacramentum*] is his mystical flesh.[4]

By the expression, "mystical flesh," Lombard is referring to the grace of the unity of Christ's Mystical Body, which is the ultimate effect of the Eucharist.

Half a century later, Pope Innocent III speaks of the three levels

---

[3] Hugh of St. Victor, *On the Sacraments of the Christian Faith* 2.8.7, trans. Deferrari, 308–09.

[4] Peter Lombard, *Sentences*, bk. 4, d. 8, ch. 7, nos. 1–2, trans. Silano, 44–45.

with regard to the Eucharist in a doctrinal letter:

> We must, however, distinguish accurately between three [elements] that in this sacrament are distinct; namely, the visible form, the reality of the body, and the spiritual power. The form is of bread and wine; the reality is the flesh and blood; the power is for unity and of charity. The first is "sacrament and not reality"; the second is "sacrament and reality"; the third is "reality and not the sacrament." But, the first is the sacrament of a twofold reality; the second is the sacrament of one [element] and the reality of the other; the third is the reality of a twofold sacrament.[5]

The following diagram shows the three levels of the Eucharist:

(sensible) sacramental sign (*sacramentum tantum*)	bread and wine
(hidden) reality and sign (*res et sacramentum*)	Body and Blood
(invisible) reality alone (*res tantum* or *res et non sacramentum*)	grace and charity, which build up the unity of the Church

Although the Latin terms can be translated literally, it is not easy to translate them into English in such a way that their meaning is understandable. The first term can be stated as the "sensible or outward sacramental sign." The third term can be referred to in English as the "reality of grace" communicated by the sacrament. The greatest difficulty is with the second term, *res et sacramentum*, for the literal translation, "reality and sign," is ambiguous. The meaning could be rendered by speaking of a "hidden reality and sign." It is a hidden supernatural *reality* of Christ or Christian identity, caused by the outward sacramental sign. At the same time it is an efficacious although hidden

---

[5] Letter to John, Archbishop of Lyons *Cum Marthae circa*, (Nov 29, 1202; DS, 783).

sign that instrumentally causes the grace it represents.

In His Bread of Life discourse, Jesus gives a succinct formulation of these three levels: "The bread which I shall give for the life of the world is my flesh" (John 6:51). The bread is the outward sacramental sign; Christ's flesh truly present under the form of bread is the grace-giving mystery (reality and sign); and the "life of the world" is the grace communicated (reality of grace).

These three levels are also distinguished in the rite of Benediction, taken from the office composed by St. Thomas Aquinas for the feast of Corpus Christi: "(1) O God, who in this wonderful Sacrament have left us a memorial of your Passion, grant us, we pray, (2) so to revere the sacred mysteries of your Body and Blood (3) that we may always experience in ourselves the fruits of your redemption."[6] The outward sacrament is the species of bread and wine, which have become the mystery of Christ's Body and Blood, which is the hidden *reality and sign*. This in turn is the sacramental cause of the application of the fruits of Christ's redemption to us, which is the *reality of grace*.

In summary, the *reality and sign* (*res et sacramentum*) in the Eucharist is the substantial reality of Christ's Body and Blood present under the visible appearances of bread and wine. It is a hidden reality produced by the outward sign, but is itself also a sign of spiritual realities that it efficaciously produces, which are grace and charity in the soul.

One might be tempted to think of the Real Presence as the *res tantum*: the reality alone. What reality could be more important than the very substance of Christ's humanity made invisibly present? As inconceivably great as it is, however, making present Christ's Body and Blood is not the ultimate finality of the Eucharist, for it is the sacrament of spiritual nourishment and charity. Thus Christ's Body and Blood is made invisibly present in order to nourish us with an increased participation in the divine life of Christ and in the charity of His Sacred Heart, which in turn brings the recipient deeper into the communion of the Mystical Body. That increased participation in Christ and the supernatural life and communion of His Church is the reality of grace (*res tantum*) of the Eucharist.[7]

---

[6] *The Roman Missal*, 3rd typ. ed., 499.

[7] For the communion and unity of the Church as an ultimate effect of the Eucharist, see Feingold, *The Eucharist*, 516–22.

Is the Res et Sacramentum of the Eucharist Christ's Body and Blood, or Deeper Incorporation into the Church?

Karl Rahner, in *The Church and the Sacraments*, proposes an ecclesial understanding of the *res et sacramentum* of the Eucharist according to which it would not be the Real Presence of Christ's Body and Blood, but rather the "more profound incorporation into the unity of the Body of Christ" brought about by Holy Communion.[8] This is part of a larger project of Rahner's to understand the *res et sacramentum* in all the sacraments as an ecclesial effect, as will be seen below with regard to Penance.[9] To support this position he refers to St. Augustine and St. Thomas who stress the ecclesial dimension of the Eucharist. Augustine and Aquinas, however, bring out the ecclesial dimension precisely as the ultimate fruit (*res tantum*)[10] produced by our being nourished with Christ's charity, which is effected by receiving the invisible *reality and sign* that is Christ's Body and Blood. Rahner's proposal should be rejected for failing to assign an adequate place to the Real Presence in the complex structure of the sacrament.[11]

---

[8] Rahner, *The Church and the Sacraments*, 83: "Participation in the physical Body of Christ by the reception of this sacrament imparts the grace of Christ to us in so far as this partaking of one bread is an efficacious sign of the renewed, deeper, and personally ratified participation and incorporation in that Body of Christ in which one can share in his Holy Spirit, that is to say, the Church. In other words *res et sacramentum*, first effect and intermediary cause of the other effects in this sacrament is the more profound incorporation into the unity of the Body of Christ."

[9] See Gilles Emery, "Reconciliation with the Church and Interior Penance: The Contribution of Thomas Aquinas on the Question of the *Res et Sacramentum* of Penance," trans. Robert E. Williams, *Nova et Vetera* (English) 1, no. 2 (2003): 283–302, at 291–92.

[10] See *ST* III, q. 79, a. 1: "Fourthly, the effect of this sacrament is considered from the species under which it is given. Hence Augustine says (Tract. 26 on John): 'Our Lord betokened His body and blood in things which out of many units are made into some one whole: for out of many grains is one thing made,' that is, bread; 'and many grapes flow into one thing,' that is, wine. And therefore he observes elsewhere (Tract. 26 on John): 'O sacrament of piety, O sign of unity, O bond of charity!'"

[11] Although Rahner does not indicate this and speaks here in a tentative way, his proposed rejection of Christ's Real Presence as the *res et sacramentum* of the Eucharist is probably linked with his rejection of efficient instrumental causality in sacramental action. As will be seen in chapter 13 below, 485–89, he proposes instead that the sacraments function as intrinsic symbols that manifest what the Church already is. If no efficient causality is in play, transubstantiation

Christ's humanity, present whole and entire in the Blessed Sacrament, is an abiding hidden sign and reality that is the very foundation and cornerstone of the Church. Christ's abiding presence with His Church under the sacramental species is the heart of the Church's entire life. Rahner's proposal fails to assign a proper place to the Real Presence in the architecture of Eucharistic theology. Furthermore, as seen above and as Rahner acknowledges, Innocent III clearly taught that the "reality of the Body" is the *res et sacramentum* of the Eucharist.[12]

Probably contrary to Rahner's intention, positing the ecclesial effect as the *res et sacramentum* ends up not only highlighting the ecclesial dimension at the expense of the more fundamental Christological reality, but also in fact undervalues the ecclesial dimension as the ultimate purpose of the sacrament. The Eucharist builds up the Church because the Eucharist *is* Christ, the Head and Bridegroom of the Church, present in all His human and personal reality to sanctify His Bride and unite her to Himself. In the traditional view exemplified by Aquinas, Christ's Body and Blood is the efficacious sign both of the divinizing effect for the recipient and of deeper ecclesial unity, which together and indivisibly make up the ultimate fruit of the sacrament. The deeper unity of the Mystical Body is not a means to other ends as the *res et sacramentum* is, but the most final effect of the sacrament (*res tantum*). The inherent order of the Eucharist moves from Christ's sacramental Body to His Mystical Body.[13]

RES ET SACRAMENTUM APPLIED TO THE SACRAMENTS THAT GIVE CHARACTER

The three levels worked out with regard to the Eucharist were applied also to the other sacraments. The easiest application is to the three sacraments that imprint character, for the sacramental character is the

---

tends to become reinterpreted as transignification, and the Real Presence tends to be reinterpreted in an ecclesial way.

[12] DS, 783, quoted above.

[13] See Henri de Lubac, *Corpus Mysticum: The Eucharist and the Church in the Middle Ages*, trans. Gemma Simmonds (Notre Dame, IN: University of Notre Dame Press, 2007); Joseph Ratzinger, *The Spirit of the Liturgy*, trans. John Saward (San Francisco: Ignatius Press, 2000), 86–88; Joseph Ratzinger, *Behold the Pierced One: An Approach to a Spiritual Christology*, trans. Graham Harrison (San Francisco: Ignatius Press, 1986), 89; Feingold, *The Eucharist*, 520–22.

res et sacramentum. St. Thomas applies this threefold distinction to Baptism in the first article on this sacrament in the *Summa theologiae*:

> In the sacrament of Baptism, three things may be considered: namely, that which is "sacrament only" [*sacramentum tantum*]; that which is "reality and sacrament" [*res et sacramentum*]; and that which is "reality only" [*res tantum*]. That which is *sacrament only*, is something visible and outward; the sign, namely, of the inward effect: for such is the very nature of a sacrament. . . . The Baptismal character is *both reality and sacrament*: because it is something real signified by the outward washing; and a sacramental sign of the inward justification: and this last is the *reality only*, in this sacrament—namely, the reality signified and not signifying.[14]

RES ET SACRAMENTUM IN MATRIMONY

In the sacrament of Matrimony, it is also easy to see that there is an intermediate effect distinct both from the outward sign that is transient, and the effect of grace, which may be blocked by mortal sin. This abiding effect is the sacramental covenant or bond that lasts until the death of one of the spouses, and this constitutes the *res et sacramentum* of Matrimony. This bond is produced by the outward sacramental sign, which is the mutual consent of the spouses given before witnesses.[15] The sacramental bond is an invisible reality and sacred sign in each of the spouses, uniting them to one another in a communion that symbolizes the indissoluble union between Christ and the Church.[16] It is a con-

---

[14] *ST* III, q. 66, a. 1 (my italics). See also *ST* III, q. 63, a. 6, ad 3: "Although a character is a reality and a sacrament [*res et sacramentum*], it does not follow that whatever is a reality and a sacrament, is also a character."

[15] See the Council of Florence, *Exsultate Deo* (DS, 1327): "The efficient cause of matrimony is the mutual consent duly expressed in words relating to the present."

[16] See John Paul II, *Familiaris Consortio*, §13: "Their belonging to each other is the real representation, by means of the sacramental sign, of the very relationship of Christ with the Church. Spouses are therefore the permanent reminder to the Church of what happened on the Cross; they are for one another and for the children witnesses to the salvation in which the sacrament makes them sharers. Of this salvation event marriage, like every sacrament, is a memorial, actuation and prophecy."

stant efficacious sign of the sacramental graces needed by the spouses to sanctify their conjugal union and parenthood.

The sacramental bond, like sacramental character,[17] gives the spouses a new relationship with Christ the Bridegroom of His Church, a new ecclesial mission to sanctify marriage and the family and form a domestic church,[18] and it is the stable foundation that signifies and instrumentally causes the graces that the spouses need to accomplish their spousal and parental mission. It consecrates the spouses to one another and to the mystery of Christ and the Church, and it abides until the death of one of the spouses.

The Second Vatican Council speaks of the sacrament of Matrimony as a *consecration* and elevation of the natural marriage bond:

> Authentic married love is caught up into divine love and is governed and enriched by Christ's redeeming power and the saving activity of the Church. . . . For this reason Christian spouses have a special sacrament by which they are fortified and receive a kind of consecration in the duties and dignity of their state.[19]

In *Humanae Vitae*, St. Paul VI also speaks of the sacrament of Matrimony as a consecration of the spouses to the vocation or mission proper to this sacrament to be witnesses before the world of Christ and the "holiness and joy" of His plan for married love:

> In humble obedience then to her voice, let Christian husbands and wives be mindful of their vocation to the Christian life, a vocation which, deriving from their Baptism, has been confirmed anew and made more explicit by the Sacrament of

---

[17] See Mark A. Pilon, *Magnum Mysterium: The Sacrament of Matrimony* (Staten Island, NY: St. Pauls, 2010), 74: "In its essential indissolubility, the bond created by the Sacrament of Matrimony at least partially resembles the permanent character received in Baptism or Confirmation, except that these latter 'marks' or 'seals' do not dissolve at death, but remain imprinted on the soul as everlasting 'likenesses' of Christ."

[18] See *CCC*, §1631: "Marriage introduces one into an ecclesial *order*, and creates rights and duties in the Church between the spouses and towards their children."

[19] Pastoral Constitution on the Church in the Modern World *Gaudium et Spes*, §48.

Matrimony. For *by this sacrament they are strengthened and, one might almost say, consecrated to the faithful fulfillment of their duties.* Thus will they realize to the full their calling and bear witness as becomes them, to Christ before the world. For the Lord has entrusted to them the task of making visible to men and women the holiness and joy of the law which united inseparably their love for one another and the cooperation they give to God's love, God who is the Author of human life.[20]

Paul VI does not explicitly identify this consecration with the *res et sacramentum* of Matrimony, but it is reasonable to make this identification, for the consecration, together with the mission it confers, is an abiding reality that lasts throughout their married life.

St. John Paul II speaks more specifically about the *reality and sign* of Matrimony in his Apostolic Exhortation *Familiaris Consortio,* §13:

> The spouses participate in it as spouses, together, as a couple, so that the first and immediate effect of marriage (*res et sacramentum*) is not supernatural grace itself, but the Christian conjugal bond, a typically Christian communion of two persons because it represents the mystery of Christ's incarnation and the mystery of His covenant. The content of participation in Christ's life is also specific: conjugal love involves a totality, in which all the elements of the person enter—appeal of the body and instinct, power of feeling and affectivity, aspiration of the spirit and of will. It aims at a deeply personal unity, the unity that, beyond union in one flesh, leads to forming one heart and soul; it demands indissolubility and faithfulness in definitive mutual giving; and it is open to fertility (cf. *Humanae vitae* 9). In a word it is a question of the normal characteristics of all natural conjugal love, but with a new significance which not only purifies and strengthens them, but raises them to the extent of making them the expression of specifically Christian values.

It is significant that John Paul II does not speak about the *res et sac-*

---

[20] Paul VI, *Humanae Vitae*, §25 (my italics).

ramentum here as a purely juridical bond, as some theologians do, but as a "typically Christian communion of two persons" that "represents the mystery of Christ's incarnation and the mystery of His covenant."

RES ET SACRAMENTUM IN ANOINTING OF THE SICK

Scholastic theologians have relatively little to say about the *res et sacramentum* in Anointing of the Sick. St. Thomas explains that Anointing does not imprint a character because it does not impart a stable status in the Church. However, he holds that the *res et sacramentum* of this sacrament is an interior anointing, which is the interior devotion of the penitent caused by the sacrament that works the healing of the remnants[21] of sin: "In this sacrament the reality-and-sacrament is not a character, but a kind of interior devotion which is a spiritual anointing."[22]

Other theologians speak of the *res et sacramentum* as a "relief and strengthening" of the sick person.[23] The problem with this kind of proposal is that this inward strengthening, relief, or devotion is properly an effect of grace that belongs to the *res tantum* and not to the *res et sacramentum*. The *res et sacramentum* should be a durable interior reality that is a sign and cause of this inner strengthening and healing, and a reality that remains throughout the illness even if the recipient

---

[21] The term "remnants (or remains) of sin" refers to the disordered dispositions that remain in the sinnner even after his sin is repented of and forgiven by God. St. Thomas explains this in *ST* III, q. 86, a. 5: "Mortal sin, in so far as it turns inordinately to a mutable good, produces in the soul a certain disposition, or even a habit, if the acts be repeated frequently. Now it has been said above (a. 4) that the guilt of mortal sin is pardoned through grace removing the aversion of the mind from God. Nevertheless when that which is on the part of the aversion has been taken away by grace, that which is on the part of the inordinate turning to a mutable good can remain, since this may happen to be without the other, as stated above (a. 4). Consequently, there is no reason why, after the guilt has been forgiven, the dispositions caused by preceding acts should not remain, which are called the remnants of sin. Yet they remain weakened and diminished, so as not to domineer over man, and they are after the manner of dispositions rather than of habits, like the *fomes* which remains after Baptism."

[22] Thomas Aquinas, *In IV Sent.*, d. 23, q. 1, a. 2, qla. 3, trans. Mortensen, 8:560 (*Supplement*, q. 30, a. 3, ad 3).

[23] See Felix M. Cappello, S.J., *Tractatus Canonico-Moralis de Sacramentis*, vol. 3, *De Extrema Unctione*, 3rd ed. (Taurini: Marietti, 1949), 145.

is not rightly disposed because of lack of repentance or faith to receive its effects of grace.

A better interpretation of the *res et sacramentum* of Anointing of the Sick, I propose, is to see it as a state of *consecration* of the seriously ill person that *configures* him to Christ who suffered in His Passion on behalf of His Body. This consecration sacramentally unites the illness of a member of Christ to the suffering of his Head throughout the time of the illness, so as to unleash its redemptive value both on behalf of the sick person and on behalf of the entire Church.[24] This interpretation is supported by the outward sacramental sign of Anointing, for an anointing with olive oil is frequently used to consecrate persons and objects in the liturgy, as in the consecration of an altar or the consecration of the hands of the priest in priestly ordination.[25]

Indeed, it seems that the *res et sacramentum* of each sacrament generally has the aspect of a consecration. This is clearest in the Eucharist, in which the *res et sacramentum* is the infinitely holy Body and Blood of Christ, which is the fruit of the consecration of the matter.[26] Sac-

---

[24] See *CCC*, §1521, quoted below. See also Miralles, *I sacramenti cristiani*, 207; Augustine DiNoia and Joseph Fox, "Priestly Dimensions of the Sacrament of the Anointing of the Sick," *The Priest* 62 (Aug 2006): 10–13, at 12: "While . . . Anointing of the Sick does not confer a permanent ontological character, it can nonetheless be said to confer an enduring eschatological configuration to Christ." P. F. Palmer suggests that the *res et sacramentum* of Anointing of the Sick configures the recipient with Christ's Passion also in the aspect of the consolation He received from an angel in Gethsemane. See Palmer, "The Theology of the *Res et Sacramentum*," 113.

[25] Anointing also has the meaning of medicinal relief and strengthening, but this would refer to the effect of grace of the sacrament.

[26] The Eucharist is unique in that what is directly consecrated is not the recipient but the matter of the sacrament, which becomes the holiest reality on earth, Christ's Body and Blood. See *ST* III, q. 73, a. 1, ad 3: "The difference between the Eucharist and other sacraments having sensible matter, is that whereas the Eucharist contains something which is sacred absolutely, namely, Christ's own body; the baptismal water contains something which is sacred in relation to something else, namely, the sanctifying power: and the same holds good of chrism and suchlike. Consequently, the sacrament of the Eucharist is completed in the very consecration of the matter, whereas the other sacraments are completed in the application of the matter for the sanctifying of the individual. And from this follows another difference. For, in the sacrament of the Eucharist, what is both reality and sacrament is in the matter itself; but what is reality only, namely, the grace bestowed, is in the recipient; whereas in Baptism both are in the recipient, namely, the character, which is both reality and sacrament, and the grace of pardon of sins, which is reality only. And the same holds good

ramental character consecrates not the matter of the sacrament but those who receive it, configuring them to Christ. Matrimony also consecrates the spouses to be the living image of the union of Christ and His Bride, as stated by *Gaudium et Spes*.[27]

Interpreted in this way, the *res et sacramentum* of Anointing would be analogous to sacramental character. Although Anointing does not imprint character, because it can be received more than once and does not confer a stable ecclesial mission, it is reasonable to suppose that it performs an analogous function, which we have analyzed in terms of *configuration* to Christ (Christian identity), ecclesial *mission*, and spiritual *power* in an illness. Although the seriously ill person does not receive a permanent ecclesial status, illness does give a particular ecclesial mission of redemptive suffering on behalf of the Church, a mission that lasts as long as the illness. The *invisible reality and sign* of Anointing thus could be understood as the imprinting of a new identification of the sick member of the faithful with Christ who suffered in His Passion. The sacramental anointing marks the suffering member of Christ with a spiritual consecration to His Passion.[28]

The mission of the sick member of the faithful is to make use of the suffering permitted by God for the redemptive purposes of growth in merit, growth in the spiritual life, satisfaction for the temporal punishment of sin, purification from sin and its remnants (such as worldly attitudes, disordered inclinations, wounds, and spiritual weakness resulting from sin), and for intercession on behalf of the whole Church through offering up one's suffering in union with Christ's redemptive suffering. The spiritual power given by the sacrament would be a series of actual graces to accomplish this mission throughout the time of the illness and an enhanced disposition to receive those graces.

This interpretation has two important advantages in that it emphasizes both the Christological and ecclesiological aspects of the *res et sacramentum*. Through the power of the sacrament, the person afflicted with illness is consecrated so as to be an efficacious sign of the redemptive suffering of Christ. Through this configuration with Christ,

---

of the other sacraments."

[27] *Gaudium et Spes*, §48 speaks of the sacrament of Matrimony as conferring "a kind of consecration in the duties and dignity of their state."

[28] See Scheeben, *Mysteries of Christianity*, 577, in which he holds that the *res et sacramentum* of Anointing is "found in the consecration imparted with a view to this conquest" over sin and death.

solidarity with the Church in this illness is efficaciously represented. Understanding the *res et sacramentum* of Anointing as a consecration of the sick person configured to the suffering Christ also explains why Anointing can only be received once during a given illness, or stage of an illness. A consecration lasts as long as the thing consecrated retains its identity. Thus the consecration given by Anointing, its *res et sacramentum*, lasts as long as the person remains gravely ill with that illness.

The *Catechism of the Catholic Church*, §1521 speaks of the sacrament of Anointing as a consecration, although without specifying that this consecration is the *res et sacramentum*:

> By the grace of this sacrament the sick person receives the strength and the gift of uniting himself more closely to Christ's Passion: in a certain way he is consecrated to bear fruit by configuration to the Savior's redemptive Passion. Suffering, a consequence of original sin, acquires a new meaning; it becomes a participation in the saving work of Jesus.

In §1523 the *Catechism of the Catholic Church* speaks of the sacrament of Anointing as completing our "conformity to the death and Resurrection of Christ."[29] The sacrament establishes an "eschatological configuration"[30] with the suffering and death of Christ and thus with the power of His Resurrection to overcome sin and its consequences. It is reasonable to see this consecration/configuration of the suffering member of Christ's Body to the sufferings of his or her Head as the *res et sacramentum* of the sacrament.

The explanation of the *res et sacramentum* of Anointing as a consecration of the sick person and of the redemptive power of his or her illness also explains its durable aspect. Although the sacramental sign of Anointing is transient, the sacrament must have a hidden durable sign that lasts as long as the illness lasts. During this time of illness, the *res et sacramentum*, like character, gives identity, mission, and power, and should be understood as an abiding instrumental cause of the sacramental graces to spiritually profit from the suffering for

---

[29] *CCC*, §1523: "The Anointing of the Sick completes our conformity to the death and Resurrection of Christ, just as Baptism began it. It completes the holy anointings that mark the whole Christian life."

[30] DiNoia and Fox, "Priestly Dimensions of the Sacrament of the Anointing of the Sick," 12.

one's own good and that of others, and for combatting the remnants of sin. It is like an abiding word of Christ written on the sick member of the faithful through the sacramental sign of the anointing, calling for the graces needed to sanctify the illness.

This interpretation of the *res et sacramentum* as a consecration of the illness to unleash its redemptive power is compatible with the position of St. Thomas, and can be seen as a development of it, adding to it the aspects of configuration to Christ's suffering and its corresponding ecclesial mission. The interior devotion of which he speaks can be connected with the spiritual power to offer the sufferings of illness as a penance that can have a special redemptive power with regard to the person's sins and also on behalf of the whole Church.[31]

RES ET SACRAMENTUM IN THE SACRAMENT OF PENANCE

The sacrament in which it is most difficult to identify the *res et sacramentum* is Penance. One reason for this difficulty is that one of the most important arguments for positing an intermediate and abiding effect of the sacrament, distinct from grace, is to explain how sacraments can come back to life when an obstacle blocking its fruitfulness—lack of repentance—is taken away. The sacrament of Penance, however, like the Eucharist, is unusual in that this sacrament cannot come back to life later if it was received without true repentance. This is because contrition is part of the matter of the sacrament, without which it cannot be valid. Thus it is harder in this sacrament to identify an abiding effect distinct from grace.

---

[31] We have seen in the previous chapter that St. Thomas, in *ST* III, a. 63, a. 2, analyzed sacramental character as a power and not a moral habit, because one can possess the power given by character independently of one's moral character. It seems that an analogous reasoning should apply to the *res et sacramentum* of Anointing and Matrimony. But interior devotion seems to be a virtuous habit—part of the virtue of religion—rather than a power. For this reason, it seems more in harmony with St. Thomas's principles to view the *res et sacramentum* of Anointing as a sacramental power to exercise redemptive power on behalf of the Church that objectively configures the seriously sick person to Christ in His redemptive suffering.

Thesis of Peter Lombard and St. Thomas: Interior Penance Is the *Res et Sacramentum*

Oddly enough, Penance was actually among the first sacraments for which the theologians of the twelfth century proposed a solution, identifying its *res et sacramentum* with "interior penance." This theory appears in Peter Lombard's *Sentences* as a position already held by others:

> And as in the sacrament of the body [Eucharist], so also in this sacrament they say that the sacrament alone is one thing, namely outward penance; another is sacrament and thing, namely inward penance; another is thing and not sacrament, namely the remission of sins. For inward penance is both the thing of the sacrament, that is, of outward penance, and the sacrament of the remission of sin, which it both signifies and brings about. Outward penance is also a sign of both inward penance and the remission of sins.[32]

St. Thomas Aquinas further developed this theory. He holds that the outward sacramental sign is composed of the three acts of the penitent—contrition, confession, and satisfaction—and the form of absolution said by the priest. The outward sign signifies and instrumentally brings about an inward repentance that is the *res et sacramentum*. This inward repentance, together with the outward sign, brings about the effect of grace, which is the forgiveness of sins and the infusion of sanctifying grace:

> In Penance also, there is something which is sacrament only [*sacramentum tantum*], that is, the acts performed outwardly both by the repentant sinner, and by the priest in giving absolution. That which is reality and sacrament [*res et sacramentum*] is the sinner's inward repentance; while that which is reality, and not sacrament, is the forgiveness of sin. The first of these taken altogether is the cause of the second; and the first and second together are the cause of the third.[33]

---

[32] *Sentences*, bk. 4, d. 22, ch. 2, no. 5, trans. Silano, p. 135.
[33] *ST* III, q. 84, a. 1, ad 3.

In other words, St. Thomas holds that the valid completion of the outward sign, composed of the matter consisting in the three acts of the penitent and the form given by the words of absolution, has the power to instrumentally produce or, if it is already present, to strengthen an interior effect of inward repentance in the heart of the penitent. This inward effect, however, is not the final fruit of the sacrament, for it is the sign and instrument of the ultimate effect of God's forgiving the sin confessed and infusing sanctifying and sacramental grace. This position is reasonable in that the forgiveness of sins and justification presupposes interior repentance that results from cooperation with actual grace.[34]

This chain of sacramental causality is similar to that in the Eucharist, in which the sacramental sign brings about the transubstantiation of the bread and wine into the Body and Blood of Christ, the *res et sacramentum*, which is the cause of the effects of grace through communion. Analogously in Penance St. Thomas thinks that the outward sign is the cause of the *res et sacramentum*, and the two together are the cause of the grace granted.

An important merit of this theory is that it emphasizes the role of the interior repentance of the penitent. This interior penance is an effect of the sacramental sign, and also a contributing instrumental cause in its ultimate effect of forgiveness.[35]

The difficulty with this solution is that interior penance, which is viewed as an effect of the sacramental sign, should already be possessed by the penitent before his confession, for contrition is one of the three parts of the matter of the sacrament, which is manifested in

---

[34] See *ST* III, q. 85, a. 5; III, q. 86, a. 2; q. 86, a. 6, ad 1–2; the Council of Trent, Decree on Justification (session 6, Jan 13, 1547), ch. 6 (DS, 1526).

[35] See Emery, "Reconciliation with the Church and Interior Penance," 294n38: "Thomas's originality lies in the efficacy he sees in this contrition and its place within the process of sacramental penance." See *ST* III, q. 86, a. 6: "Hence in Baptism forgiveness of sin is effected, in virtue not only of the form (but also of the matter, viz. water, albeit chiefly in virtue of the form) from which the water receives its power—and, similarly, the forgiveness of sin is the effect of Penance, chiefly by the power of the keys, which is vested in the ministers, who furnish the formal part of the sacrament . . . and secondarily by the instrumentality of those acts of the penitent which pertain to the virtue of penance, but only in so far as such acts are, in some way, subordinate to the keys of the Church. Accordingly it is evident that the forgiveness of sin is the effect of penance as a virtue, but still more of Penance as a sacrament."

the act of contrition before receiving absolution. How can something that is part of the outward sign also be an effect of it so as to constitute the *res et sacramentum*?

One way to explain this is as follows. Interior repentance is indeed a prerequisite for the sacrament, and it is brought about through God's inspiration in the heart of the penitent, drawing him to repent and desire the sacrament.[36] Nevertheless, this interior penance that is part of the matter of penance is supernaturally and efficaciously changed and strengthened by the efficacy of the sacramental absolution. Peter Lombard writes: "God himself absolves the penitent from the debt of punishment; and he so absolves him when he enlightens him within, inspiring true contrition of heart."[37] This can be understood in that interior contrition, if it was only imperfect (motivated only by fear of divine punishment), will be transformed into perfect contrition (motivated also by love for God) by the grace of the sacrament that restores charity, even if the penitent is not necessarily conscious of this effect.

This transformation of contrition, however, seems to pertain to the effect of grace (*res tantum*) rather than to the *res et sacramentum*.[38] Similarly, if the penitent already had perfect contrition, it would be strengthened by the grace gained by priestly absolution. This also, however, belongs to the effect of grace or *res tantum*. The Thomistic theory of interior penance does not seem to fully articulate how interior penance becomes a *res et sacramentum*, which is something intermediate that is an effect of the outward sign and logically precedes the effect of grace (even if they are simultaneous). Interior penance, on the other hand, seems to be either something expressed by the outward sign, and thus logically prior to the *res et sacramentum*, or a reality enriched by the grace of the sacrament, in which case it is part of the *res tantum* and thus logically posterior

---

[36] See *ST* III, q. 84, a. 1, ad 2: "In the sacrament of Penance . . . human actions take the place of matter, and these actions proceed from internal inspiration, wherefore the matter is not applied by the minister, but by God working inwardly." See also *ST* III, q. 90, a. 2, ad 1: "Contrition, as to its essence, is in the heart, and belongs to interior penance; yet, virtually, it belongs to exterior penance, inasmuch as it implies the purpose of confessing and making satisfaction."

[37] Peter Lombard, *Sentences*, bk. 4, d. 18, ch. 4, no. 5, trans. Silano, p. 108.

[38] This difficulty is pointed out by Jean-Hervé Nicolas, *Synthèse dogmatique: de la Trinité à la Trinité*, 1050.

to the *res et sacramentum*.[39] It needs to be clarified or more fully explained, as I will attempt to do below, how it is also simultaneously an abiding and efficacious interior sacramental *sign*, which is central to the notion of *res et sacramentum*.

Alternative Proposal: Reconciliation with the Church Is the *Res et Sacramentum*

Twentieth-century theologians have put forward a different interpretation of the *res et sacramentum*, seeing it as reconciliation with the Church. The words of absolution symbolize and produce reconciliation with the Church, and reconciliation with the Church then symbolizes and produces reconciliation with God.[40] This theory was defended in a celebrated doctoral dissertation from 1921 by Bartolomé Xiberta,[41] a Carmelite theologian, and it has been defended from a historical perspective by Bernhard Poschmann[42] and from a more theological and systematic perspective by Karl Rahner[43] and others.[44]

---

[39] See Emery's attempt to clarify this point in "Reconciliation with the Church and Interior Penance," 294: "Thus understood, inner penance is at once signified and obtained by the actions of the penitent and the minister. Inner penance may be considered under two aspects. On the one hand, in as much as it is an act of virtue it is the origin ("cause") of the outward penitential action, and is signified by it. On the other hand, in as much as it falls within a sacramental ecclesial gesture, inner penance acts efficaciously for the healing of sin; as such, it is obtained by the outward action."

[40] See Emery, "Reconciliation with the Church and Interior Penance," 283–302.

[41] Bartomeu M. Xiberta, *Clavis ecclesiae: de ordine absolutionis sacramentalis ad reconciliationem cum Ecclesia* (Barcelona: Apud Sectionem Sancti Paciani Facultatis Theologiae, 1974).

[42] See Bernhard Poschmann, "Die innere Struktur des Bußsakraments," *Münchener Theologische Zeitschrift* 1/3 (1950): 12–30; Emery, "Reconciliation with the Church and Interior Penance," 286–87

[43] See Karl Rahner, "Forgotten Truths Concerning the Sacrament of Penance," in *Theological Investigations*, vol. 2, trans. Karl-H. Kruger (Baltimore: Helicon, 1963), 135–74, esp. 168–72;Rahner, *The Church and the Sacraments*, 93–94. For a good brief analysis of Rahner's position, see Emery, "Reconciliation with the Church," 289–92.

[44] Other theologians who defend reconciliation with the Church as the *res et sacramentum* of Penance include Palmer, "The Theology of the *Res et Sacramentum*," in *Readings in Sacramental Theology*, 104–23; Vollert, "The Church and the Sacraments," in *Readings in Sacramental Theology*, 99; Leeming, *Principles of Sacramental Theology*, 361–66, C. Dumont, "La réconciliation avec l'Église et la nécessité de l'aveu sacramentel," *Nouvelle Revue Théologique* 81 (1959): 577–97;

This thesis has important merits. First, it is based on a rediscovery of the patristic understanding and practice of the sacrament. For the Fathers, the solemn termination of public penance through the imposition of the hands of the bishop dramatically readmitted the penitent into full ecclesial communion and thereby opened the way to the reception of Holy Communion.[45] It also seems to accord with Christ's words in Matthew 16:19: "whatever you bind on earth shall be bound in heaven, and whatever you loose on earth shall be loosed in heaven."[46]

Secondly, this thesis brings out the ecclesial dimension of this sacrament which can too easily be viewed in a merely individualistic way. Karl Rahner, Henri de Lubac, and other theologians in the mid-twentieth century stressed this ecclesial dimension of Penance, as of the sacramental system as a whole. De Lubac wrote:

> In St. Cyprian's view, for instance, the priest's intervention has for its immediate effect this "return" of the sinner, this return of one who has been "cut off" (excommunicated) to the assembly of the faithful; the cleansing of the soul is a natural consequence of this reimmersion in the stream of grace, and it should be defined as a return to the "communion" of saints. It is precisely because there can be no return to the grace of God without a return to the communion of the Church that the intervention of a minister of that Church is normally required.[47]

A third merit of this proposal is the intimate link it highlights

---

Schillebeeckx, *Christ the Sacrament of the Encounter with God*, 175; Nicolas, *Synthèse dogmatique: de la Trinité à la Trinité*, 1050–52.

[45] See Poschmann, *Penance and the Anointing of the Sick*, 25.

[46] However, it is likely that Matthew 16:19; 18:18, and John 20:22–23, do not intend to distinguish two different debts to be forgiven—one against the Church and one against God—but are better understood with regard to the ultimate effect of Penance, which is the freeing of a sinner from the bondage of sin (*res tantum*). What the Church's minister declares on earth—the forgiveness of sins—is accomplished by the Holy Spirit, working through the words of the priest. See Clarence McAuliffe, "Penance and Reconciliation with the Church," *Theological Studies* 26.1 (1965): 1–39, at 4.

[47] Henri de Lubac, *Catholicism: Christ and the Common Destiny of Man*, trans. Lancelot Sheppard and Sr. Elizabeth Englund (San Francisco: Ignatius Press, 1988), 88.

between the sacraments of Penance and the Eucharist, for according to this proposal, at least as articulated by its original proponents, the *res et sacramentum* is the full right to be admitted to the Eucharist.[48]

The Second Vatican Council, in *Lumen Gentium*, §11 also stressed the ecclesial dimension of Penance although without affirming that this is the *res et sacramentum*: "Those who approach the sacrament of Penance obtain pardon from the mercy of God for the offence committed against Him and are at the same time reconciled with the Church, which they have wounded by their sins, and which by charity, example, and prayer seeks their conversion."[49] This text, however, does not settle the question of whether reconciliation with the Church is the *res et sacramentum* or simply part of the *res tantum*. In other words, is the reconciliation with the Church an effect of reconciliation with God through the sacrament, or is justification the effect of reconciliation with the Church?[50] The thesis that reconciliation with the Church is the *res et sacramentum* would demand the latter response. *Lumen Gentium* does not pose this question and does not suggest that reconciliation with the Church is the sacramental cause of reconciliation with God.

There are, however, some important difficulties with this thesis. It works well for understanding the public penance of the early Church and today for the lifting of excommunication and other ecclesiastical censures, but it is more difficult to apply to the way the sacrament of Penance has been practiced in the second millennium, in which reconciliation with the Church is much less visible and dramatic. Furthermore, it seems to be overly juridical in character, for it appears to equate the *res et sacramentum* of Penance with the lifting of ecclesiastical censures, which are not involved in the great majority of sacramental confessions.

---

[48] See Maurice de la Taille, review of Xiberta in *Gregorianum* 4 (1923): 591–99, at 592.

[49] The ecclesial dimension of the sacrament of Penance is also emphasized by John Paul II in *Reconciliatio et Paenitentia*, §31, no. 4, but without suggesting that reconciliation with the Church is the *res et sacramentum* of Penance. The same is true of *CCC*, §1469, which quotes *Reconciliatio et Paenitentia*, §31, no. 4.

[50] See Paul Galtier, *De paenitentia: Tractatus dogmatico-historicus* (Rome: Apud Aedes Universitatis Gregorianae, 1956), 340, who holds that justification in the sacrament of Penance is not caused by reconciliation with the Church, but the reverse: "restoration to the Church . . . does not precede justification, but follows it."

Furthermore, it is an explanation that does not seem to apply well to the confession of venial sins alone, for venial sins do not break a Catholic's communion with the Church nor pose a canonical obstacle to the reception of the Eucharist. But if one has only committed venial sins, one can validly confess them. In such a case, what would be the *res et sacramentum* of Penance?

Then there is the deeper question of cause and effect. Do the words of absolution signify reconciliation first with God and consequently with the Church, or the other way around? If reconciliation with the Church is the *res et sacramentum*, it would have to be both the sign and cause of reconciliation with God. However, it seems that reconciliation with God and the reception of the graces of forgiveness, justification, and the actual graces that aid one to make satisfaction and persevere are what lead to deeper reconciliation with the Church. In other words, if one views reconciliation with the Church not merely in a juridical sense (like the lifting of excommunication) but also in the moral sense of mutual forgiveness between members of the Church and the gradual healing of divisions caused by sin, this ecclesial dimension is clearly an *effect* of God's grace and not the cause of it. This is taught by St. John Paul II in *Reconciliatio et Paenitentia*:

> It must be emphasized that the most precious result of the forgiveness obtained in the sacrament of penance consists in reconciliation with God, which takes place in the inmost heart of the son who was lost and found again, which every penitent is. But it has to be added that this reconciliation with God leads, as it were, to other reconciliations which repair the breaches caused by sin. The forgiven penitent is reconciled with himself in his inmost being, where he regains his own true identity. He is reconciled with his brethren whom he has in some way attacked and wounded. He is reconciled with the church. He is reconciled with all creation.[51]

The reconciliation with God "leads . . . to other reconciliations," including that with the Church. Thus it does not seem that reconciliation with the Church can be the *res et sacramentum* of Penance, for it is the effect and not the cause of reconciliation with God.

For this reason reconciliation with the Church and the healing of

---

[51] John Paul II, *Reconciliatio et Paenitentia*, §31, no. 5.

ecclesial wounds caused by sin would seem to be an ultimate effect of the sacrament of Penance, in a way similar to how ecclesial unity is an ultimate effect of the Eucharist and its ultimate *res tantum*, according to the consensus of scholastic theologians. The proponents of this thesis are right to emphasize that it is crucial for the new evangelization that we recover the ecclesial dimension of the sacrament of Penance. But this can be done by emphasizing that deeper communion with the Church and the interior strengthening of her unity and purity is an ultimate fruit of the sacrament of Penance that is to be desired for its own sake and not as an efficacious sign of something else. Ecclesial communion is not a merely instrumental reality that belongs to this world only, but also a fruit that will last into eternal life.

Proposal: The *Res et Sacramentum* of Penance Is a Configuration to Christ Who Did Penance for Sin

Since both of the dominant proposals for understanding the *res et sacramentum* of Penance are not without problems, I propose a clarification or development of St. Thomas's position that more explicitly develops its ecclesial dimension and stands in greater continuity with the analysis of sacramental character given above, as well as with the sacramental marital bond and the *res et sacramentum* of Anointing of the Sick. If we leave the Eucharist aside as a special case (whose *res et sacramentum* is the Body and Blood of Christ) and analyze the other six sacraments, then the three sacraments that imprint character can be used as the prime analogate to understand analogically the *res et sacramentum* of the other three sacraments: Penance, Matrimony, and Anointing of the Sick. St. Thomas's thesis that interior penance is the *res et sacramentum* can be reformulated in a way that responds to the objections made against it, highlights both its Christological and ecclesial dimensions,[52] and also highlights the three aspects of sacramental character analyzed above, which are *identity* in Christ, *ecclesial mission*, and *spiritual power*.

New Identity in Christ

Applying these three aspects by analogy to Penance, it would seem

---

[52] See the explanation of the Thomistic "interior penance" by Emery, "Reconciliation with the Church and Interior Penance," 292–96.

that the *res et sacramentum* consists in a new sacramental identity or configuration with Christ, whose mission included His supremely sorrowing over sin and doing penance for it. The Council of Trent states that through the Sacrament of Penance, "we conform ourselves to Christ Jesus, who made satisfaction for our sins."[53] This configuration is expressed by the matter of the sacrament, in which the penitent manifests contrition for his sins and his willingness to do the assigned work of penance. As the outward acts of the penitent establish this conformity with Christ, so the continuing inward penance continues the conformity as long as one remains in a state of grace. Although Christ is without sin, and thus He could not experience repentance for any personal sins, nevertheless His whole life, expressed especially in His agony in Gethsemane and His Passion, involved a supreme sorrow and work of satisfaction for the sins of the world. Because He is the new Adam, the new Head of humanity, Christ is the vicarious Penitent for the sins of the whole world, winning reconciliation for them.[54] The sacrament of Penance involves a renewed identification with this fundamental aspect of Christ's identity. The sacramental penitent is brought into sacramental conformity with the Penance of Christ.[55]

---

[53] Council of Trent, Doctrine on the Sacrament of Penance (session 14), ch. 8 (DS, 1690).

[54] See *ST* III, q. 8, a. 3, sed contra: "It is written (1 Tim. 4:10): 'Who is the Saviour of all men, especially of the faithful,' and (1 John 2:2): 'He is the propitiation for our sins, and not for ours only, but for those of the whole world.' Now to save men and to be a propitiation for their sins belongs to Christ as Head. Therefore Christ is the Head of all men."

[55] See Palmer, "The Theology of the *Res et Sacramentum*," 120: "We feel that Albert the Great is correct in likening the penitent to Christ in His expiatory suffering. True, all the faithful have the obligation 'to fill up what is wanting of the sufferings of Christ . . . for his body which is the Church' (Col 1, 24). Since, however, the reconciled penitent differs from one who has never severed or strained the bond of charity which unites the members of Christ's Mystical Body, it is understandable why the reconciled penitent is deputed in a special way to atone for the injury which he has done to that Body. And it is precisely in submitting to the penances imposed by the Church through the ministry of her priests that we are, as the Council of Trent asserts, 'made like to Christ Jesus who satisfied for our sins' [session 14, ch. 8, DS, 1690]." Although earlier in this essay Palmer defended the thesis that the *res et sacramentum* of Penance is reconciliation with the Church, in this concluding passage he seems to be in agreement with the interpretation that I am putting forward here, which is that the *res et sacramentum* of Penance is first a configuration with Christ "who satisfied for our sins," through which one receives

Thus we can think of the *res et sacramentum* of Penance, in the footsteps of St. Thomas, as *interior penance that has been sacramentally configured to the penance of Christ* for the sins of the whole world. Here the analogy with the sacrament of Matrimony is helpful. For, as seen above, the sacrament of Penance, like Matrimony, is the elevation of a pre-existing reality. As marriage existed from the beginning, so the virtue of penance has existed as a human reality since the Fall. In the sacrament of Matrimony, the marital covenant between members of the baptized faithful, created by the mutual marital consent of the spouses, is inserted into Christ and thereby becomes an abiding sacramental sign of the union between Christ and His Bride. Marriage from the beginning has always been a natural sign of God, but the marital union inside the New Covenant receives a new capacity to be a sacred and efficacious sign of Christ's union with His Church. Likewise, we have seen that serious illness receives a new sacramental configuration with Christ's redemptive suffering through Anointing. In a similar way, interior penance over sin, which has existed since the repentance of our first parents, when brought into sacramental union with Christ, becomes an efficacious sign of Christ's penance for sin and the reconciliation He worked for us. Just as Christ elevated marriage to a sacrament of His union with His Church by giving His life for His Bride, so in suffering and dying for our sins He has given a new configuration to the virtue of penance by elevating it into a sacrament of His satisfaction for sin, by which sin has been conquered and forgiven.

New Ecclesial Mission

From this sacramental identification with Christ sorrowing over sin and satisfying for it, the recipient of the sacrament of Penance receives a penitential *mission* to turn away from sin, sorrow over it, and do penance for it in order to help heal the wounds and divisions that sin has caused in oneself, in the Church, and in the world in many ways that we cannot fully see. Reception of the sacrament of Penance, today as in the early Church, imposes on the penitent the task of making satisfaction for sin in an ecclesial way through prayer, fasting, and almsgiving. In the early Church, this was formalized by

---

an ecclesial mission of satisfaction on behalf of the Body of Christ and in solidarity with her.

putting the penitent in a new public status as a member of the order of penitents. Although this no longer is manifested outwardly in the way that characterized the public penance especially of the third and fourth centuries, reception of the sacrament gives the penitent an invisible new "status" or mission as penitent, configured invisibly to Christ's own penance for the sins of the world.

Spiritual Power to Bring Forth Fruits
of Repentance in the Church

Since God does not give a mission without conferring a corresponding *power* to accomplish it, it is reasonable to think that this sacramental configuration of the penitent and his interior penance to the penance of Christ, which I hold to be the *res et sacramentum* of Penance, is the instrumental source of the series of graces needed by the penitent to persevere in his repentance and in the effort to make satisfaction for sin. As in the case of sacramental character, this explanation shows how the sacrament of Penance, even though its outward sign has passed away with the words of confession and absolution, can continue to remain the source of sacramental graces to combat sin, sorrow over it, and make satisfaction for it.

This configuration with Christ's penance will remain, it seems, until the penitent withdraws himself from it by falling into mortal sin, in which case it needs to be received again. The commission of venial sin does not contradict this identification with Christ's penance for sin but allows room for a fuller identification, which would be received progressively in the practice of frequent confession of venial sin.

This proposal has the advantage of showing how the *res et sacramentum* of Penance involves the three dimensions of identity in Christ, ecclesial mission, and spiritual power that we have analyzed in sacramental character, and it manifests the fact that the *res et sacramentum* gives a configuration with Christ, through which one becomes incorporated or related to the Church in a new way. It also highlights the aspect of greater durability of the invisible sign, which serves as a foundation for the giving of actual graces over time.

In reality, this proposal does not differ substantially from St. Thomas's thesis of interior penance as the *res et sacramentum*, but seeks to clarify how interior penance can be understood to be an invisible *reality and sign.* The interior penance that the penitent brings to the sacrament and expresses in the outward sign receives from the celebration of the sacrament a new sacramental configuration to Christ's satisfaction. Being joined to Christ by being submitted to the tribunal of His mercy and receiving absolution, it becomes an efficacious sign of that mercy that Christ can use as His instrument to draw down the graces needed by the penitent to do satisfaction for sin. Thus it is both an effect of the outward celebration of the sacrament and an abiding interior sign and instrument of its effect of grace.

The ecclesial dimension of Penance is a consequence of its Christological dimension. This ecclesial and Eucharistic dimension of the *res et sacramentum* of Penance is more than a canonical or juridical right to readmission to the Eucharist. It is first and foremost a configuration to Christ's sorrow over sin in His Body and His work of satisfaction for it, and the resulting mission to offer satisfaction for sin with Christ and cooperate in bringing about reconciliation in His Body, wounded by sin.

It is through this configuration to Christ's sorrow and satisfaction for sin that Penance is most profoundly tied to the Eucharist, for one can only fully and properly participate in the Eucharistic Sacrifice if one shares the interior dispositions of Christ who sorrows over sin and offers Himself in satisfaction for the sins of the world.[56] In other words, the ecclesial and Eucharistic dimension of Penance is not only or primarily a juridical reality, but above all a spiritual power to cooperate with Christ more deeply in sorrowing over and making satisfaction for one's own sins and the sins that wound the Church and the world.

---

[56] See Pius XII, *Mediator Dei*, §§80–81: "It is, therefore, desirable, Venerable Brethren, that all the faithful should be aware that to participate in the eucharistic sacrifice is their chief duty and supreme dignity. . . . Now the exhortation of the Apostle, 'Let this mind be in you which was also in Christ Jesus,' requires that all Christians should possess, as far as is humanly possible, the same dispositions as those which the divine Redeemer had when He offered Himself in sacrifice. . . . Moreover, it means that they must assume to some extent the character of a victim, that they deny themselves as the Gospel commands, that freely and of their own accord they do penance and that each detests and satisfies for his sins. It means, in a word, that we must all undergo with Christ a mystical death on the cross so that we can apply to ourselves the words of St. Paul, 'With Christ I am nailed to the cross.'" See also *LG*, §11: "Taking part in the Eucharistic Sacrifice, which is the source and summit of the whole Christian life, they offer the divine Victim to God, and offer themselves along with it."

REFLECTIONS ON THE THREE LEVELS OF THE SACRAMENTS AND THE IMPORTANCE OF THE *RES ET SACRAMENTUM*

Differing Durability of the Three Levels of the Sacraments

The identification of an intermediate level of reality and sign in the seven sacraments is a theological development based on prolonged reflection on the Church's sacramental practice, beginning with Baptism and then centering on the Eucharist. The distinction between the three levels of the sacraments is apparent first of all because they differ in their duration. The outward sacramental sign, by its very nature, is transient. It passes with the words and actions that comprise it. In the Eucharist, the sacramental signs of the bread and wine endure until their corruption, but the words of the sacramental form pass away immediately.

The intermediate level of non-sensible *reality and sign* (*res et sacramentum*), on the contrary, has a durable nature, although the extent of the duration varies in the different sacraments. In Baptism, Confirmation, and Holy Orders, the intermediate level lasts forever, for sacramental character is an indelible mark on the soul. In Matrimony, the intermediate reality is the marriage bond, which lasts until the death of one of the spouses. In the Eucharist, the intermediate level is the Body and Blood of Christ, which is present until the corruption of the sacramental species (the appearances of bread and wine). The *res et sacramentum* of Anointing lasts throughout the illness, during which time the sacrament is not repeated.

The interior grace is also durable. Sanctifying grace, which is the principal effect of the sacraments, is possessed in a habitual way but can be lost by mortal sin. Sacramental grace also includes a series of actual graces that help the recipient to accomplish the ends of that particular sacrament. Actual graces are transient, but their hidden foundation, the reality and sign (*res et sacramentum*), endures, according to the nature of the sacrament.

The three levels also differ in that only one level, the reality of grace, admits different degrees of fruitfulness, for it is dependent on the dispositions of the recipient. To the person who is better disposed by faith, hope, and love, more sacramental grace will be received.[57] The valid outward sign and the hidden reality and sign, on the other hand, are objective and do not depend on the degree of subjective dispositions. In validly administered sacraments, sacramental character is always equally imprinted, the Body and Blood of Christ are always equally made present, and the matrimonial bond is always established.

Licitness, Validity, and Fruitfulness

The three levels of the sacraments are connected with three notions crucial to the sacraments: licitness, validity, and fruitfulness. Licitness concerns only the outward sacramental sign and means that the sign, both in its essential and non-essential elements,[58] accords with the canonical regulations and rubrics established by the Church.

Validity concerns both the sacramental sign and the intermediate effect of the reality and sign. We say that a sacrament is valid when the sacramental sign has all its *essential* elements analyzed above in terms of matter and form (ch. 5), on the one hand, and subject and minister, with their proper intention (ch. 6), on the other. When this is the case, the *res et sacramentum* is infallibly realized. A sacrament is invalid when it is lacking at least one of these essential elements. The lack of an essential element blocks the realization of the intermediate level of *res et sacramentum*. A valid sacrament thus is one in which the *res et sacramentum* is realized. If Baptism, Confirmation, and Holy Orders are celebrated in a valid way, then their indelible character is always imprinted. Similarly, if the Eucharist is celebrated in a valid way, the Real Presence is necessarily brought about.

If a sacrament is licit, then it will also be valid, but the converse is not always true. Sacraments can be illicit and still valid, when the violation of the canonical order falls short of taking away any of the essential elements.

Fruitfulness concerns the effect of grace (*res tantum*). A sacrament is said to be fruitful when the effect of grace is realized. It is possible for sacraments to be valid but unfruitful. This occurs when the *res et*

---

[57] See Mark 4:25: "For to him who has will more be given."

[58] For essential elements, see chapter 4, pp. 108–13, and chapter 5, pp. 155–71 above. For licitness see CIC, can. 846, §1: "In celebrating the sacraments the liturgical books approved by competent authority are to be observed faithfully; accordingly, no one is to add, omit, or alter anything in them on one's own authority."

sacramentum is validly produced but the lack of proper dispositions in the recipient block the reception of sacramental grace, as when someone receives Baptism without repentance.[59] These dispositions required in those at the age of reason are essentially faith and repentance for mortal sins of which they are aware, as will be seen below.[60] The one sacrament that cannot be received validly but unfruitfully is Penance. This is because the disposition of the subject is part of the essential matter of the sacrament. The penitent must have at least imperfect contrition for the absolution to be valid. Penance can never be validly received without repentance.

As will be seen in chapter 15 below, it is also possible to receive the essential effect of the sacraments (except Holy Orders) through holy desire, without actually receiving a valid sacrament, and thus without receiving the *res et sacramentum*.

Christological and Ecclesial Dimensions of the *Res et Sacramentum*

The *res et sacramentum* always has a Christological and ecclesial focus, in that order.[61] In each case except for the Eucharist, the *res et sacramentum* involves a configuration of the recipient with Christ in a new way, giving a new mission that entails spiritual power. In the Eucharist, the *res et sacramentum* is not a configuration with Christ, but Christ Himself in the objective reality of His Body and Blood.[62] For this reason, as seen above, the Eucharist is the queen of the sacramental system. The remaining six sacraments configure the recipient

---

[59] See Augustine, *Baptism* 1.12.18, trans. Ramsey, 408: "A person can truly be baptized with Christ's baptism and yet . . . his heart, persisting in malice or sacrilege, does not allow the abolition of his sins to be accomplished."

[60] See chapter 10 below, pp. 381–86.

[61] See Scheeben, *Mysteries of Christianity*, 575, in which he defines the *res et sacramentum* as "a special union with the God-man as head of His mystical body by which participation in the spirit, that is, in the divinity and the divine life of the God-man, is granted to us on the basis of a special supernatural title, and for a special supernatural end."

[62] See *ST* III, q. 73, a. 1, ad 3: "In the sacrament of the Eucharist, what is both reality and sacrament is in the matter itself; but what is reality only, namely, the grace bestowed, is in the recipient; whereas in Baptism both are in the recipient, namely, the character, which is both reality and sacrament, and the grace of pardon of sins, which is reality only. And the same holds good of the other sacraments."

to Christ present in our midst in the Eucharist.

In Baptism, Confirmation, and Holy Orders, the *res et sacramentum* is sacramental character, by which the recipient receives a new quality of configuration with Christ, a new ecclesial mission, and a corresponding spiritual power. The foundational configuration is given by Baptism, through which the baptized are incorporated into Christ and His Body. Confirmation configures the Christian to Christ's activity impelled by the Spirit, building up His Body in a prophetic, kingly, and priestly way. Holy Orders configures its recipients to act in the person of Christ, the Head and Bridegroom of the Church.

In the three remaining sacraments—Matrimony, Penance, and Anointing of the Sick—the *res et sacramentum* should be understood in a way analogous to sacramental character, as configuring the recipient to Christ in a new way, although not in the form of a permanent status within the Church. Matrimony configures the spouses to Christ the Bridegroom in that the spousal love of husband and wife is a sacred efficacious sign of Christ's spousal love for His Bride. The sacramental marital bond, which is the *res et sacramentum*, is an elevation in Christ and configuration to Him of the natural marital bond. This sacramental bond, inhering in the spouses, is the enduring foundation for the countless actual graces needed by the spouses to sanctify marriage and parenthood in the image of Christ the Bridegroom. Anointing of the Sick gives the gravely ill and physically weakened members of the Body a new configuration with the suffering of Christ in His Passion. As we have seen this has an ecclesial mission and calls forth special gifts of grace. Penance, finally, establishes in the penitent a new configuration to Christ who sorrowed and did penance for sin in His Passion and death.[63] This gives the penitent an ecclesial mission and the corresponding spiritual power to share in Christ's work of penance and reconciliation on behalf of His Body injured by sin.

---

[63] See the Council of Trent, Doctrine on the Sacrament of Penance (session 14), ch. 8 (DS, 1690).

Study Questions

1. Why did it prove insufficient to posit only two levels in the sacraments: the outward sign and the effect of grace? In other words, why is it necessary to hold a third intermediate level in the sacraments? How are the three levels distinguished in the Eucharist?
2. Why is this intermediate level referred to as *res et sacramentum*? Explain the meaning of this term.
3. Does the *res et sacramentum* have a greater permanence than the outward sacramental sign? Explain. Why is this important?
4. (a) What is the *res et sacramentum* in the Eucharist? (b) What is the *res et sacramentum* in the sacrament of Matrimony?
5. What is the *res et sacramentum* in Anointing of the Sick?
6. What is the *res et sacramentum* in the sacrament of Penance? What are the two theories in this regard? Explain the difficulties and merits of each position.
7. What is the difference between validity, licitness, and fruitfulness of the sacraments? How are these terms related to the three levels of the sacraments?
8. Explain the difference in durability of the three levels of the sacraments.
9. Does the *res et sacramentum* always have a Christological and ecclesial meaning? Explain.

Suggestions for Further Reading

Emery, Gilles. "Reconciliation with the Church and Interior Penance: The Contribution of Thomas Aquinas on the Question of the *Res et Sacramentum* of Penance." Translated by Robert E. Williams. *Nova et Vetera* (English) 1, no. 2 (2003): 283–302.

Leeming, Bernard. *Principles of Sacramental Theology*. Westminster, MD: Newman Press, 1963. Pp. 251–79.

Miyakawa, Toshiyuki. "The Ecclesial Meaning of the 'Res et Sacramentum.'" *The Thomist* 31 (1967): 381–444.

Nutt, Roger. *General Principles of Sacramental Theology*. Washington, DC: Catholic University of America Press, 2017. Pp. 166–74.

Palmer, P. F. "The Theology of the *Res et Sacramentum*." In *Readings in Sacramental Theology*, 104–23. Edited by C. S. Sullivan. Englewood Cliffs, NJ: Prentice-Hall, 1964.

Scheeben, Matthias Joseph. *The Mysteries of Christianity*. Translated by Cyril Vollert. St. Louis, MO: B. Herder, 1951. Pp. 582–92.

CHAPTER NINE

The Gifts of Grace Communicated by the Sacraments

The most important thing to consider with regard to the sacraments is the end for which God instituted them. God has graciously elevated man to a supernatural end, which is a sharing in His own beatitude. He wills us to receive that end through a real sharing in His life already here on earth in His Church, so that by leading a supernatural life in this world, we can merit our supernatural end and thus participate in attaining it. The sacraments are the ordinary means chosen by God to infuse in us a mysterious participation in God's own inner life.

Grace and the other supernatural gifts that accompany it comprise the sacraments' ultimate effect, that which is the *reality alone* (*res tantum*) and not a sign of anything else. This invisible reality sanctifying man is signified by the outward sacramental sign and by the invisible *reality and sign* (*res et sacramentum*), and is infused into the soul by the instrumental power of those sacramental signs. The grace given by the sacraments is first and foremost sanctifying grace, which is a participation in the divine nature or divine life (see 2 Pet 1:4). As powers or faculties flow from a nature, so from sanctifying grace flow the three theological virtues of faith, hope, and charity. Together with charity, the faithful receive the seven gifts of the Holy Spirit, the infused moral virtues, the indwelling of the Blessed Trinity, and divine filiation.

In addition to sanctifying grace and all that accompanies it, each sacrament also offers more specific actual graces that are tied to its purpose. The sacraments give a particular mission, especially those that imprint character, and thus also impart a series of actual graces that enable the recipient to worthily fulfill that mission in a dynamic and unfolding manner. These graces depend on our correspondence with the actual graces already received. The more we cooperate with grace, the more grace we shall receive.

In other words, the sacraments confer sanctifying grace, the other habitual supernatural gifts that flow from it, justification and the forgiveness of sins, and a series of actual graces to accomplish the purpose of each sacrament. In order to understand the action of the sacraments in infusing grace, as will be treated in the following chapter, it is helpful to review Catholic teaching on actual grace, sanctifying grace, and the other supernatural gifts that flow from sanctifying grace, which is the object of this chapter.

OUR SUPERNATURAL ENDOWMENT

The Gratuitousness of Grace with Respect to Nature

Grace in the proper sense of the word refers to a special gift that is entirely above the nature of a creature, by which the creature is ordered to God's own beatitude and made a participant in God's own inner life. This gift receives the technical name of *grace* for it is *doubly gratuitous*. All God's gifts of nature are ultimately gratuitous. The gift of supernatural grace, however, is gratuitous in a double or special sense, because it presupposes the prior free gift of creation and nature, to which it is added as a *free supernatural gift*.[1] It is a gift over and above

---

[1] See *ST* I-II, q. 111, a. 1, ad 2: "Grace, inasmuch as it is gratuitously given, excludes the notion of debt. Now debt may be taken in two ways:—first, as arising from merit; and this regards the person whose it is to do meritorious works, according to Romans 4:4: 'Now to him that worketh, the reward is not reckoned according to grace, but according to debt.' The second debt regards the condition of nature. Thus we say it is due to a man to have reason, and whatever else belongs to human nature. Yet in neither way is debt taken to mean that God is under an obligation to His creature, but rather that the creature ought to be subject to God, that the Divine ordination may be fulfilled in it, which is that a certain nature should have certain conditions or properties, and that by doing certain works it should attain to something further. And hence natural endowments are not a debt in the first sense but in the second. But supernatural gifts are due in neither sense. Hence they especially merit the name of grace." See also Lawrence Feingold, *The Natural Desire to See God According to St. Thomas Aquinas and His Interpreters* (Ave Maria, FL: Sapientia

the free gift of creation, and a gift over and above anything *due* to the natural order that has been freely created.

Everything that God creates has its source in the divine love. God's love is the cause of His gifts of being and goodness to the creature. However, there are two distinct types of being and goodness that God can give. First of all, God gives the gift of being and nature to a thing in creation. This first gift establishes the natural order. On the basis of this first gift, God maintains the natural order and the natural being of things, making it possible for them to reach their natural end.

Over and above this first gift of natural being and goodness, by which everything is established in its own nature and order, God can give another gift whereby He raises the creature above the order of its own nature to make it share mysteriously in God's own nature, life, and beatitude. This gift is thus very aptly called "supernatural." It is also properly called grace (in the sense of an especially gratuitous gift), for it is absolutely gratuitous with respect to the natural order itself. Creation is gratuitous with respect to the nothingness out of which the creature was drawn. Supernatural grace is gratuitous not only with respect to nothingness, but also with respect to the natural order of the creature. Nothingness can do nothing to merit creation. Thus creation is gratuitous. Likewise, the natural order, once created, can do nothing to merit being elevated to participate in God's own inner life, for that life is infinitely above the level of any creature. Therefore, the supernatural elevation of the rational creature to participate in the beatitude of God is *doubly gratuitous*, for it is a gift so good that it cannot belong to the nature of any creature. The beatitude of God is proper and natural to God alone. To participate by nature in God's own inner life and beatitude would imply that a creature is divine by nature, and thus would not be distinct from God, and therefore not a creature.

God loves everything He creates, but He is said to love things more or less according to the good that He freely grants them, for love is the willing of good to another. Thus He loves man more than beasts because He grants men a higher gift, a rational nature by which we can know and love God. Similarly, His gift of grace manifests a greater love by which He bestows on us the greater good of sharing in His own nature, enabling us to know and love Him in an immeasurably higher way. All of creation manifests God's love, but the gift of grace manifests a higher and more amazing love, for through it God

Press of Ave Maria University, 2010), 224–29.

communicates to us a share in His own life. St. Thomas explains:

> According to this difference of good the love of God to the
> creature is looked at differently. For one is common, whereby
> He loves "all things that are" (Wisdom 11:24), and thereby
> gives things their natural being. But the second is a special
> love, whereby He draws the rational creature above the con-
> dition of its nature to a participation of the Divine good; and
> according to this love He is said to love anyone simply, since it
> is by this love that God simply wishes the eternal good, which
> is Himself, for the creature.[2]

Just as God's love is the source of grace, so it is the source of the
sacraments, which are the ever-flowing channels of grace. Although
supernatural gifts are totally gratuitous, God has willed to give them
through ordinary channels that are intrinsically efficacious and infallible. These ordinary channels are the sacraments of the New Covenant.

Obediential Potency Specific to the Rational Creature Made in the Image of God

If grace transcends natural power and is gratuitous with respect to
nature, what kind of capacity do we have to receive it? We cannot call
it simply a "natural potency," for this would make it seem that grace
and glory are natural to man, which would imply the Pelagian heresy.
But if we call it a "supernatural potency," the same confusion could
result because it would imply that our nature is naturally endowed
with supernatural potencies.

The medieval scholastics answered with the notion of obediential
potency.[3] Although human nature has no natural power to produce
or receive grace, it has the power to obey God if He wishes to elevate
the human person to share in His nature and beatitude. This term is
appropriate for it manages to avoid the implication that our soul has
natural potencies for the supernatural.

Obediential potency is used as a technical term to indicate a capac-

---

[2] *ST* I-II, q. 110, a. 1.

[3] For the notion of obediential potency in relation to supernatural gifts, see Feingold, *The Natural Desire to See God*, 101–65, 443–47, from which this section is
adapted.

ity or openness in the creature to obey God by receiving from Him a gift or perfection above the order of natural causes whenever He wills to work above nature. Because of God's sovereign power over created being, all creation has the innate capacity to "obey" the will of the Creator and to be caused to do whatever He wills.[4] The specific nature of the creature and the natural laws that govern it do not bind the hands of the Creator and make Him incapable of intervening in His work beyond the limits of the natural order that He has established. In the words of the centurion in the Gospel (Matt 8:8–9): "Only say the word, and my servant will be healed. For I am a man under authority, with soldiers under me; and I say to one, 'Go,' and he goes, and to another, 'Come,' and he comes." And after the miraculous calming of the sea, the Apostles exclaim: "What sort of man is this, that even winds and sea obey him?" (Matt 8:27). Obediential potency is a biblical idea.[5] This potency is as wide as God's omnipotence itself, which extends to all being. All creatures are open to receive, above their nature, whatever is not intrinsically contradictory.

This capacity to obey God above nature is used in contrast with *natural passive potency*, which is the capacity to receive a perfection through natural active powers, *in accordance with the laws of nature.* Thus natural passive potency and obediential potency are two different kinds of passive potencies, corresponding to two different kinds of agents: natural and divine.

St. Thomas gives a definition of obediential potency in *ST* III, q. 11, a. 1:

> It must be borne in mind that in the human soul, as in every creature, there is a twofold passive power. One is in comparison with a natural agent; the other in comparison with the First Agent, which can bring any creature to a higher act than a natural agent can bring it, and this is usually called the *obediential potency* of a creature.[6]

---

[4] Thomas Aquinas, *De virtutibus*, q. un., a. 10, ad 13: "In every creature there is a certain *obediential* potency, according to which every creature *obeys* God so as to receive in itself whatever He wills."

[5] See also Ps 104:30: "When you send forth your Spirit, they are created."

[6] In this article, St. Thomas brings in this distinction in order to determine the particular kind of potency that existed in Christ's human soul for receiving infused knowledge of all Revelation. See also *ST* III, q. 1, a. 3, ad 3; *De veritate*, q. 8, a. 12, ad 4; q. 29, a. 3, ad 3; q. 8, a. 4, ad 13; *De virtutibus*, q. un., a. 10, ad

Rational creatures have obediential potencies that are specific to them. St. Thomas uses the category of obediential potency to refer to the capacity of a spiritual nature to be elevated above its natural powers by the intervention of God, who works in and above that nature, infusing sanctifying grace, faith, hope, charity, the gifts of the Holy Spirit, and the light of glory.[7] Only a creature created in the image of God has the specific obediential potency to be perfected further in that image, by being carried from a natural to a supernatural likeness without losing its nature or personal identity. This capacity of human beings and angels for elevation is mysterious and can only be known by revelation. This capacity for the supernatural is based on the natural power of a spiritual nature to attain to God in some way (although imperfectly), which can then be extended and elevated by grace. The imperfection of the natural image of God in man, intrinsic to our creaturely status and aggravated by sin, is healed and elevated by grace and glory.

The Distinction between Sanctifying Grace and Actual Grace

In the natural order, God's creative Word is the source of all being and natures, and also the source of all movement. Both being and movement are indicated in the words: "Let there be light!" God gives to every creature the act of being in a certain nature, and He also gives to them the first impulse by which they begin to move and act on other things.

The same can be said, analogously, of the supernatural order. God is the source of *supernatural being or life* and also the source of *supernatural movement* by which creatures move toward salvation. Both supernatural being and supernatural movement are indicated in Jesus's words when He says: "I came that they may have life, and have it abundantly" (John 10:10) and "Apart from me you can do nothing" (John 15:5).

The supernatural being or life that God gives to a rational creature is an abiding and thus habitual principle in the creature, unless it is lost through mortal sin. The supernatural movement that God gives is a transient and temporary impulse to aid us at a given moment to *act*

13; III *Sent.*, d. 1, q. 1, a. 3, ad 4.
[7] See Feingold, *The Natural Desire to See God*, 111–12.

above our nature. Both of these aids are gratuitous and supernatural, and thus they both receive the name of grace. However, they are two different types of gifts: one an abiding form of being (supernatural life) and the other a transitory movement (supernatural illumination or attraction). These two types of grace are referred to as *sanctifying grace* (also called *habitual grace*), which is the habitual and abiding principle of supernatural life, and *actual grace*, which is a transient divine aid, a divine impulse or movement enabling us to accomplish an action leading to salvation or sanctification.

St. Thomas explains the difference between actual and sanctifying grace (although he does not use these terms) as that between a movement coming from without and a habit that is possessed within.[8] The gratuitous effect of God's love in man's soul that manifests itself as a movement in man's mind and will by which he sees the moral good and seeks to put it in practice, is *actual grace*. The gratuitous effect of God's love that is infused in the soul as a supernatural quality, giving it a participation in the divine nature and abiding in the soul in a habitual way, is *sanctifying grace*.

The *Catechism of the Catholic Church*, §2000 defines the two types of grace as follows:

> Sanctifying grace is an habitual gift, a stable and supernatural disposition that perfects the soul itself to enable it to live with God, to act by his love. *Habitual grace*, the permanent disposition to live and act in keeping with God's call, is distinguished from *actual graces* which refer to God's interventions, whether at the beginning of conversion or in the course of the work of sanctification.

This distinction between actual grace and sanctifying grace—corresponding to supernatural movement and supernatural being—can also be explained by distinguishing two different kinds of causes: the efficient and the formal cause. An efficient cause is that which brings something into being or motion, whereas a formal cause is an

---

[8] See *ST* I-II, q. 110, a. 2 (my italics): "Man is aided by God's gratuitous will in two ways: first, inasmuch as man's soul is moved by God to know or will or do something, and in this way the gratuitous effect in man is not a quality, but a *movement* of the soul [actual grace]; for 'motion is the act of the mover in the moved.' Secondly, man is helped by God's gratuitous will, inasmuch as a *habitual* gift is infused by God into the soul."

intrinsic principle that makes something to be what it is. For example, the efficient cause of a statue is the sculptor and the strokes of his chisel, whereas the formal cause of the sculpture is its particular form imprinted by the chisel, by which it is precisely that statue. Similarly, a house painter and his paintbrush are the efficient causes of the painting of a wall, whereas whiteness is the formal cause of the white wall. Or again, the violinist and the strokes of the bow are the efficient causes of the beauty of a piece of music, whereas the formal cause is the pleasing proportion and harmony of the sounds themselves.

According to this analogy, actual grace is a supernatural movement from God that is a kind of efficient cause that moves, prompts, and aids the soul to do supernaturally good acts. It does this in a properly human way not by moving us like a puppet, but through moving our spiritual faculties by illuminating our intellect and attracting our will so that we can then respond freely. Actual graces are like the strokes of a divine bow or chisel, whereas sanctifying grace is the supernatural "harmony" or "divine proportionality" that is produced in the soul itself. Sanctifying grace is thus a formal cause that makes the soul pleasing to God by giving it a share in the divine nature.[9]

Actual Grace: Operative and Cooperative

As a sculptor may work upon a statue with the blows of the chisel before the formal cause of harmony is produced, so God may work upon the soul with actual grace before a person comes to receive sanctifying grace. The efficient cause (the sculptor and his chisel) needs to work on the statue both before its beauty has begun to appear and all the while that it grows in the form of beauty. Likewise, God makes use of actual graces as efficient causes to bring about conversion in us and to continue the work of our sanctification.

There are two kinds of actual grace, called operative and cooperative grace. Operative grace infallibly causes a first movement in the soul towards the good desired by God.[10] These operative graces consist

---

[9] See *ST* I-II, q. 110, a. 2, ad 1 (speaking of sanctifying grace): "Grace, as a quality, is said to act upon the soul, not after the manner of an efficient cause, but after the manner of a formal cause, as whiteness makes a thing white, and justice, just."

[10] See *ST* I-II, q. 111, a. 2: "The operation of an effect is not attributed to the thing moved but to the mover. Hence in that effect in which our mind is moved and does not move [itself], but in which God is the sole mover, the operation

in illuminations of our mind to understand something that we had not previously understood, and attractions in our will to God and His plan. This grace gives us the power to choose to cooperate with it by acting in accordance with this supernatural illumination and attraction, while leaving us the freedom not to. When we choose to act in accordance with this divine impulse, God continues His aid through cooperative grace to support our free movement. These further aids are sufficient to enable us to act well, but they do not infallibly move our will in its free choice to follow or not to follow the impulse of grace, and so we have the possibility of freely resisting them at any point in the course of our voluntary action.[11]

Sanctifying Grace and the Habitual Gifts That Flow from It

Sanctifying Grace as a Sharing in the Divine Nature

To act well on the supernatural level, not only do we need actual grace—both operative and cooperative—to be the first efficient cause of the good act that sets it in motion, but we also need sanctifying grace to be the first formal cause out of which that act proceeds, as

---

is attributed to God, and it is with reference to this that we speak of *operating grace*. But in that effect in which our mind both moves [itself] and is moved, the operation is not only attributed to God, but also to the soul; and it is with reference to this that we speak of *co-operating grace*." St. Thomas takes this distinction from Augustine, *Grace and Free Will* 17.33, trans. Robert Russell, in *St. Augustine: The Teacher, The Free Choice of the Will, Grace and Free Will* (Washington, DC: Catholic University of America Press, 1968), 288–89 (my italics): "For He who first works in us the power to will is the same who cooperates in bringing this work to perfection in those who will it. Accordingly, the Apostle says: 'I am convinced of this, that he who has begun a good work in you will bring it to perfection until the day of Christ Jesus' (Phil 1:6). *God, then, works in us, without our cooperation, the power to will, but once we begin to will, and do so in a way that brings us to act, then it is that He cooperates with us.* But if He does not work in us the power to will or does not cooperate in our act of willing, we are powerless to perform good works of a salutary nature."

11 See Lawrence Feingold, "God's Movement of the Soul through Operative and Cooperative Grace," in *Thomism and Predestination: Principles and Disputations*, ed. Steven A. Long, Roger W. Nutt, and Thomas Joseph White (Washington, DC: Catholic University of America Press, 2017), 166–91.

out of a new abiding supernatural principle. Sanctifying grace and the theological virtues are an intrinsic principle, like a second nature, by which our supernatural acts moved by actual grace have a connatural quality, come forth with a certain facility and joy, and have a foundation in our soul itself.[12]

Natural things get to their natural ends because they have been equipped from the very start with an interior principle of movement and action leading them on a natural path to their natural end. We call this interior principle the nature of a thing. Natural things have natural means built into them that correspond to their natural ends. In order for an oak tree to grow to its proper stature, it has to be equipped from the start, already in the seed, with an inner principle of growth proportionate to its final state and with organs or faculties to realize that end. In order for an eagle to realize its eagle nature, it must have wings to soar. For a man to make use of his rational nature, it is fitting that he have a head set high for seeing and hearing and thinking, and hands for building.

The same thing must be true analogously in the supernatural order. In order to journey effectively to a supernatural end, we have to be equipped with a supernatural gift that is already a seed or germ of that end, to make us proportionate to it and capable of arriving. This seed or germ of the supernatural end must be an interior principle of supernatural movement and action, a kind of second nature. But this interior principle cannot simply be our human nature, for our nature is not proportionate to our supernatural end. Thus this interior principle must be supernatural. It is called sanctifying grace. A biblical source for this notion is 2 Peter 1:3–4:

> His divine power has granted to us all things that pertain to life and godliness, through the knowledge of him who called us to his own glory and excellence, by which he has granted to us his precious and very great promises, that through these you may escape from the corruption that is in the world because of passion, and become partakers of the divine nature.

Sanctifying grace, by making us "partakers of the divine nature," makes us mysteriously "proportioned" or fitted to share in God's own beatitude.

---

[12] See *ST* I-II, q. 62, a. 1.

Distinction between Sanctifying Grace, Charity, and the Holy Spirit

A difficult problem in the theology of grace with which the medieval theologians wrestled concerns the distinction between three inseparable gifts: sanctifying grace, charity, and the indwelling of the Holy Spirit. Are they merely different terms designating the same reality, or are they distinct realities? Both sanctifying grace and charity are habitual gifts that abide in the soul in a state of grace. Furthermore, everyone who has sanctifying grace has charity and the indwelling. Nevertheless, St. Thomas argues that sanctifying grace and charity are really distinct from each other and from the Holy Spirit indwelling in the soul.[13] In this he opposed the view of some earlier medieval theologians, such as Peter Lombard, who said that "the very same Holy Spirit is the love or charity by which we love God and neighbour."[14] Neither sanctifying grace nor charity can be simply identified with the Holy Spirit because grace and charity are infused and grow in us through the work of the Holy Spirit, as St. Paul teaches in Romans 5:5: "God's love has been poured into our hearts through the Holy Spirit who has been given to us." Grace and charity are spoken of as qualities we possess through Him, as when we speak of a charitable or grace-filled person. But the Holy Spirit is a divine Person who in Himself cannot change or be a quality of the soul.

Threefold Distinction between Nature, Inclination, and Action

St. Thomas addresses the difference between sanctifying grace and charity in a masterful way in *De veritate*, q. 27, a. 2. To show the dif-

---

[13] See *ST* II-II, q. 24, a. 2: "Charity can be in us neither naturally, nor through acquisition by the natural powers, but by the infusion of the Holy Spirit, Who is the love of the Father and the Son, and the participation of Whom in us is created charity."

[14] Peter Lombard, *Sentences*, bk. 1, d. 17, ch. 1, no. 2, trans. Silano, p. 88. St. Thomas argues against this position in his commentary on the *Sentences*, *In I Sent.*, d. 17, q. 1, a. 1. English translation in *On Love and Charity: Readings from the Commentary on the Sentences of Peter Lombard*, trans. Peter A. Kwasniewski, Thomas Bolin, and Joseph Bolin (Washington, DC: Catholic University of America Press, 2008), 7–15.

ference between them he makes reference to a threefold distinction found in natural things between *nature*, *inclination*, and *action*.[15] He gives the example of a rock that has a certain *nature*, from which there results an *inclination* towards the center. If there is nothing to obstruct it, it naturally *moves* towards the center to which it is inclined.[16] If we apply this scheme to man, then man has a rational *nature* that is naturally ordered to a natural end, for which he has a natural *inclination*, and which "he *can work to achieve* by his natural powers."[17] This end consists in a certain contemplation of God such as is possible to man according to the capabilities of his nature, and which even philosophers such as Aristotle saw to be the final happiness of man.

However, by faith we know that God has destined man for an end that infinitely exceeds the principles and even aspirations of human nature or any nature which has been or could be created, and which is proportionate only to God Himself.[18] In order for man to

---

[15] This same distinction can be found in *De malo*, q. 6, in which these three factors as they exist in creatures without knowledge are compared with the way they exist in men: "As in irrational creatures there is found form, which is the principle of action, and inclination following form, which is called natural appetite, from which action follows; likewise in man there is found an intelligible form, and an inclination of the will following on the form that is known, from which exterior action follows." See Feingold, *The Natural Desire to See God*, 86–88.

[16] *De veritate*, q. 27, a. 2 (my translation and italics): "Since different natures have different ends, three things are necessary in natural things for the attainment of some end: namely, a *nature proportioned to that end*; an *inclination to that end*, which is the *natural appetite* for the end; and *movement to that end*. This can be seen in the earth [or in a rock], for example, which has a *certain nature* by which it is fitting for it to be in the center [of a gravitational field], and there follows on this nature an *inclination* to that center insofar as it naturally desires that place, even when it has been removed from the center by a violent motion, and when the violence is removed it *moves* downwards."

[17] See *De veritate*, q. 27, a. 2 (my italics): "Man by his nature is proportioned to a *certain end*, for which he has a *natural appetite*, and which he *can work to achieve by his natural powers*. This end is a certain contemplation of the divine attributes, in the measure in which this is possible for man through his natural powers; and in this end even the philosophers placed the final happiness of man."

[18] *De veritate*, q. 27, a. 2: "But God has prepared man for another end that exceeds the proportionality of human nature. This end is eternal life which consists in the vision of God in His essence, an end which exceeds the proportionality of any created nature, being connatural to God alone."

achieve this end, it is not enough for God simply to give man the means for attaining it by moving him directly to supernatural acts, as through operative actual grace. This would correspond only to the third element of the threefold scheme that St. Thomas has analyzed. Each of the three elements needs to be re-proportioned to the supernatural level, so to speak, so that man's movement towards his supernatural end can have the same perfection found in nature with regard to natural ends.

A new proportionality or supernatural dimension needs to be given to man's nature, by which he will be proportioned to the end of eternal life. This can only come about through sharing in the divine nature, according to 2 Peter 1:4, which is aptly referred to as divinization or *theosis*. From this elevation of man's nature to share in the divine, there must flow a new inclination to the supernatural end. Finally, the acts by which that end is acquired must be proportioned to the elevation of that end. The new proportionality is given by sanctifying grace; the new inclination by the theological virtues of faith, hope, and charity; and the acquisition or meriting of the end is given by means of the other infused moral virtues and gifts of the Holy Spirit, which are directed by charity, and through which one cooperates with actual grace.

In this way one can clearly see the distinction between sanctifying grace and charity, for the former corresponds on the supernatural order to our rational nature while the latter corresponds to the inclination flowing from that nature. Sanctifying grace perfects nature by giving the creature a share in the divine nature, and charity perfects the natural inclination of the will by giving it a new orientation so that it is directed not merely to God as the author of nature but also to God as the author of grace, who invites the creature to share in His intimate life. Actual grace, the infused moral virtues, and the gifts of the Holy Spirit, as will be seen below, are the principles of supernatural and meritorious moral action.

Fittingness of Habitual Gifts That Enable Action to Proceed from an Intrinsic Principle

This analogy established by St. Thomas in *De veritate*, q. 27, a. 2 between nature, natural inclination, and movement on the natural and supernatural orders is intended to show that it is profoundly fitting that God, in ordering us to a supernatural end, give us not only principles of movement to that end, as we would expect, but also give us something like a new nature—sanctifying grace—and a new inclination to that end, which is charity. This argument is based on the principle that God, in establishing a supernatural order for us, will endow the supernatural order with the same kinds of principles that he has instilled in all natural things. The supernatural order should not be less fittingly provided for than the natural order.

Natural things are ordered to an end not just by being moved to it by God, but also through the fact that God has given each thing a nature, understood in the Aristotelian sense of an intrinsic principle of movement ordered to an end in which the substance comes to rest. From each nature there flow natural inclinations to the ends to which that nature is ordered. The fact that each thing has a nature endowed with natural inclinations makes it possible for movement to flow from within. For this reason nature is not like a puppet show. The fact that movement flows from nature and from natural inclination makes movement *connatural*, giving it an ease and readiness. We see this also in natural virtues, which make it possible for virtuous action to be accomplished in a connatural way with ease, readiness, and joy.[19] Without the habit of virtue, we find good acts to be far more difficult and laborious. Sanctifying grace and charity provide something analogous on the supernatural order. Their presence makes supernatural movements mysteriously "connatural" to the creature elevated to the supernatural order, so that supernatural movements can be directed to our supernatural end with ease, readiness, and joy.[20]

---

[19] See *CCC*, § 1804: "*Human virtues* are firm attitudes, stable dispositions, habitual perfections of intellect and will that govern our actions, order our passions, and guide our conduct according to reason and faith. They make possible ease, self-mastery, and joy in leading a morally good life."

[20] St. Thomas explains this fittingness that grace be an intrinsic principle in us in *ST* I–II, q. 110, a. 2, in which he distinguishes actual and sanctifying grace. With regard to the latter, he says: "Secondly, man is helped by God's gratuitous will, inasmuch as a habitual gift is infused by God into the soul; and for this reason, that it is not fitting that God should provide less for those He loves, that they may acquire supernatural good, than for creatures, whom He loves that they may acquire natural good. Now He so provides for natural creatures, that not merely does He move them to their natural acts, but He bestows upon them certain forms and powers, which are the principles of acts, in order that they may of themselves be inclined to these movements, and thus the movements whereby they are moved by God become natural and easy to creatures, according to Wisdom 8:1: 'she . . . orders all things sweetly.' Much more therefore does He infuse into such as He moves towards the acquisition

The Theological Virtues

Sanctifying grace enriches the soul with other magnificent supernatural gifts that flow from sharing in the divine life. The most important of these are the theological virtues. They are called "theological" for three reasons: they have God as their object, they have God as their cause, and they can only be known through divine Revelation.[21]

Since God is their object, the theological virtues rightly order and incline us to our *supernatural* end, to which we are not sufficiently ordered by our natural spiritual faculties.[22] To show this, St. Thomas frequently cites 1 Corinthians 2:9: "What no eye has seen, nor ear heard, nor the heart of man conceived, what God has prepared for those who love Him."[23] Therefore, with regard both to the intellect (the "eye") and to the will (the "heart"), "something needs to be supernaturally added to man to order him to a supernatural end."[24]

Thus we see that in addition to sanctifying grace, we also need the three theological virtues of faith, hope, and charity to more closely unite us with God. Faith perfects the intellect, and hope and charity perfect the will. As intellect and will flow from human nature, so analogously faith, hope, and charity flow from sanctifying grace. Every soul that has sanctifying grace possesses faith, hope, and charity, all of

---

of supernatural good, certain forms or supernatural qualities, whereby they may be moved by Him sweetly and promptly to acquire eternal good; and thus the gift of grace is a quality."

[21] See *ST* I-II, q. 62, a. 1: "Such like principles are called 'theological virtues': first, because their object is God, inasmuch as they rightly order us to God: secondly, because they are infused in us by God alone; thirdly, because these virtues are not made known to us, save by Divine revelation, contained in Holy Scripture." See also *CCC*, §§1812–13: "They have the One and Triune God for their origin, motive, and object. The theological virtues are the foundation of Christian moral activity; they animate it and give it its special character. They inform and give life to all the moral virtues. They are infused by God into the souls of the faithful to make them capable of acting as his children and of meriting eternal life. They are the pledge of the presence and action of the Holy Spirit in the faculties of the human being."

[22] See *ST* I-II, q. 62, a. 3: "It is necessary that certain divine principles [the theological virtues] be super-added by God, by which a man may be ordered to supernatural beatitude just as he is ordered to his connatural end by means of his natural principles, although not without divine assistance."

[23] See Feingold, *The Natural Desire to See God*, 44–45, 411–12.

[24] *ST* I-II, q. 62, a. 3.

which grow together like the fingers of a hand.[25]

Faith

The intellect needs to be perfected by the habit of faith to adhere to God's Revelation, to know the end to which we are ordered and the means by which to arrive. The virtue of faith is the "supernatural virtue whereby, inspired and assisted by the grace of God, we believe that what he has revealed is true, not because the intrinsic truth of things is recognized by the natural light of reason, but because of the authority of God himself who reveals them, who can neither err nor deceive."[26] Faith has God as its object insofar as He is the living Truth to whom we must conform our minds and give the "obedience of faith,"[27] "an obedience by which man commits his whole self freely to God, offering 'the full submission of intellect and will to God who reveals,'[28] and freely assenting to the truth revealed by Him."[29]

Hope

The will or heart needs to be ordered to our final end in two ways: through hope and charity.[30] These two theological virtues cor-

---

[25] There is an interesting difference between the theological and the moral virtues. Whereas the moral virtues such as temperance and fortitude realize their perfection in a golden mean between the extremes of excess and deficiency, the theological virtues of faith, hope, and charity can never be excessive. One can never love God for His own sake in an excessive way, nor can one hope in Him too much, nor believe too much in His word of truth. See *ST* I-II, q. 64, a. 4: "The measure and rule of theological virtue is God Himself: because our faith is ruled according to Divine truth; charity, according to His goodness; hope, according to the immensity of His omnipotence and loving kindness. This measure surpasses all human power: so that never can we love God as much as He ought to be loved, nor believe and hope in Him as much as we should. Much less therefore can there be excess in such things. Accordingly the good of such virtues does not consist in a mean, but increases the more we approach to the summit."

[26] Vatican I, Dogmatic Constitution on the Catholic Faith, *Dei Filius*, ch. 3 (DS, 3008).

[27] Rom 16:26

[28] See Vatican I, *Dei Filius*, ch. 3 (DS, 3008).

[29] Second Vatican Council, *Dei Verbum*, §5.

[30] See *ST* I-II, q. 62, a. 3, ad 1: "The very nature of the will suffices to give it a natural order to the [natural] end, both with regard to intending the

respond to two different forms of love: love of desire and love of friendship. Love of desire is that by which we desire *goods* (for ourselves or others). Love of friendship is that by which we desire the good *for a person*.[31] Hope elevates the will's love of desire by which we love God as the supreme good (for ourselves), and charity elevates the love of friendship, lifting it up to God so as to desire His glory for His sake.[32]

First, the will must tend to that end as to something possible to attain, for no one can intend to reach an end thought to be impossible. Ordered activity towards an end presupposes the intention to gain that end, and an effective intention presupposes a judgment of real possibility. In the case of our supernatural end, this effective intention is given by the virtue of hope, which is the habit of firmly desiring God as the object of our beatitude.

With theological hope we desire heavenly beatitude not through our own power but through God's gracious aid. The *Catechism of the Catholic Church*, §1817 defines it as "the theological virtue by which we desire the kingdom of heaven and eternal life as our happiness, placing our trust in Christ's promises and relying not on our own strength, but on the help of the grace of the Holy Spirit." God is the object of hope insofar as He is the source and content of the beatitude we long for and the provider of the grace we need to obtain that beatitude.

Charity

This intention of hope in itself, however, is insufficient to fully order the will to heavenly beatitude, because our supernatural end does not consist merely in receiving a gift that is hoped for but also in giving ourselves back to God in an intimate union[33] of filial and spousal

---

end and to its conformity with the end. But for the will to be ordered to things above its nature, the nature of the power is insufficient in both of these respects. Consequently there is need for an additional supernatural habit in both respects."

[31] See *ST* I-II q. 26, a. 4.

[32] See Lawrence Feingold, "The Word Breathes Forth Love: The Psychological Analogy for the Trinity," *Nova et Vetera* (English) 17, no. 2 (Spring 2019): 501–32.

[33] See *ST* I-II, q. 62, a. 3: "The will is directed to this end, both as to that end as something attainable—and this pertains to hope—and as to a certain spiritual

friendship. We need charity to love Him back in this way, for love is a unitive power.[34]

Charity is the virtue "by which we love God above all things for His own sake" as our Father, "and our neighbor as ourselves for the love of God."[35] Charity's two personal objects—God and neighbor—are united because God is the proper motive for charity's love of neighbor created in God's image and redeemed by the blood of the Word incarnate.

Charity is the most important gift that we receive with sanctifying grace. It is the only theological virtue that remains after death, and it is the form and animator of all the other supernatural virtues.[36] The theological virtue of charity corresponds to the love of friendship or *agape*. This can be seen from Scripture, for when speaking of the theological virtue of love for God (charity), the writers of the New Testament do not use the word "*eros*" (love of desire) but rather the word "*agape*" (love of benevolence).[37] In a similar way, the English word "charity" is used to indicate the theological virtue of supernatural love and the acts of fraternal love that flow from it, to distinguish it from other kinds of love.

In common English today, we normally use the word "charity" only in the secondary sense of good works of disinterested love for our neighbor. Nevertheless, the principal theological meaning of the word is the love for God above all things, which is the theological virtue of charity. "Charity" is our English equivalent of *agape*, and it means a love of friendship with God and, for His sake, a love of benevolence for the children of God.

This is a teaching that is very profound although very simple. The supernatural love that God commands us to have for Him, this benevolent love, is also a love of *friendship*. Friendship consists in a

---

union, whereby the will is, so to speak, transformed into that end—and this belongs to charity."

[34] See *ST* I-II, q. 28, a. 1 and *In III Sent.*, d. 27, q. 1, a. 1, ad 1; and Feingold, "The Word Breathes Forth Love," 525–26.

[35] *CCC*, §1822.

[36] See *ST* II-II, q. 23, aa. 7 and 8.

[37] Following *ST* I-II q. 26, a. 4, I take *eros* to indicate a desire for something for the good of oneself or another (*amor concupiscentiae*). For example, I can desire a house for myself or for another. I take *agape* to refer to the love for that person for whom the good is desired (*amor amicitiae*). So I have *agape*, or friendship love, for the person for whom the house is loved.

mutual benevolent love between persons and includes a sharing of life. God has loved us first, enabling us to love Him in return and to rejoice in the fact that He is who He is, and in His infinite goodness; and it includes the desire to give ourselves to Him and belong to Him entirely in a spousal and filial way. Furthermore, there is a sharing of life between God and the soul in a state of grace, although this is a great mystery. By giving us sanctifying grace, God has given us a certain sharing in his own inner inter-Trinitarian life. It follows that the virtue of supernatural charity can only exist in those who are made adopted children of God by sanctifying grace. Charity flows directly from sanctifying grace and is inseparable from it.

Charity, therefore, is entirely supernatural and given to us directly by God.[38] The ordinary means for its infusion are the sacraments of the Church. Although in everyday language we may speak of charity as if it were something natural—the natural virtue of generosity or friendliness—true fraternal charity differs greatly from natural generosity in its motive, because charity is always motivated by filial love of God above all and directed to our neighbor as a beloved child of God. Someone who fails to see his neighbor as a creature loved immensely by God cannot love him with supernatural charity although he can be very generous to him. Charity in the proper sense of the word thus presupposes faith and grace. Charity elevates natural generosity and directs it, as grace elevates nature.

Since charity is a love of friendship with God, it is clear that it is incompatible with mortal sin, which always involves freely preferring a gravely disordered creaturely satisfaction to the fulfillment of God's Law as known in conscience, and thus despising God in comparison with the satisfaction that one desires. Charity, therefore, must always include contrition for grave sin of which one is aware in conscience. In fact, it will include *perfect contrition*[39] for sin, which is sorrow for

---

[38] See *ST* II-II, q. 24, a. 2: "Charity is a friendship of man for God, founded upon the fellowship of everlasting happiness. Now this fellowship is in respect, not of natural, but of gratuitous gifts . . . on account of which charity itself surpasses our natural facilities. Now that which surpasses the faculty of nature, cannot be natural or acquired by the natural powers, since a natural effect does not transcend its cause. Therefore charity can be in us neither naturally, nor through acquisition by the natural powers, but by the infusion of the Holy Spirit, Who is the love of the Father and the Son, and the participation of Whom in us is created charity."

[39] The "perfect" in perfect contrition refers to the motive for the sorrow, which is

offending God not only because one will be punished or go to hell, but principally because it offends God, whom one loves above all things. Without perfect contrition for sin, there can be no communion of life with God.

Infused Moral Virtues

In addition to the theological virtues, there also exist supernatural moral virtues that God infuses into the soul together with sanctifying grace. These supernatural moral virtues are parallel with the naturally acquired ones, but distinct in that they are supernatural and ordered to our supernatural end.

The ultimate reason for the distinction of the supernatural moral virtues from the natural ones is that a habit or virtue must be proportioned to its end. To reach a supernatural end, we need virtues directed specifically to that end. If a habit has a supernatural end, it must have a supernatural mode of being as well, which will be different from a natural habit ordered to a natural end.[40]

Furthermore, the genesis of a supernatural habit must be distinct from that of a natural habit, for natural habits can be acquired through our own acts whereas supernatural habits must have a supernatural source, which is grace. It follows that natural habits (virtues and vices) are acquired through practice whereas supernatural virtues can only be received by being infused from God. This ordinarily occurs through the sacraments.

St. Thomas explains the necessity of infused supernatural virtues in *ST* I-II, q. 63, a. 3:

> Effects must needs be proportionate to their causes and principles. Now all virtues, intellectual and moral, that are acquired by our actions, arise from certain natural principles pre-existing in us. . . . Instead of these natural principles, God bestows on us the theological virtues, whereby we are directed

---

love for God, and not to the fact that one is doing it perfectly. Perfect contrition is possessed not only by the most perfect saints but also by all who are in a state of grace and have charity.

[40] On the infused moral virtues and their distinction from the natural virtues, see Reginald Garrigou-Lagrange, *The Three Ages of the Interior Life: Prelude of Eternal Life*, trans. Timothea Doyle (Rockford, IL: TAN Books, 1989), 1:59–64.

to a supernatural end, as stated above [q. 62, a. 1]. Therefore, we need to receive from God other habits corresponding, in due proportion, to the theological virtues, which habits are to the theological virtues, what the moral and intellectual virtues are to the natural principles of virtue.

The theological virtues are the principles of all the other infused virtues, as the habit of first moral principles (by which we know the golden rule, the primacy of the common good, the double commandment of love, etc.) is the cause of the acquired moral virtues. These supernatural moral virtues are infused into the soul at Baptism together with sanctifying grace, and they increase in the soul together with every increase in sanctifying grace.

This means that a person in the state of grace has the moral virtues in a twofold form: natural and supernatural. There is a natural prudence, justice, temperance, and courage, and a supernatural prudence, justice, temperance, and courage. The natural and the supernatural virtues are distinguished by the end to which they are ordered: man's natural or supernatural end.

The classical philosophers wrote about the natural virtues, whereas Scripture is principally concerned with the supernatural moral virtues. St. Thomas writes: "It is obvious that the acquired virtues, of which the philosophers spoke, are ordered only to perfecting men in civil life, not as they are ordered to achieving celestial glory. . . . But the cardinal virtues, insofar as they are gratuitous and infused, as we speak of them now, perfect man in the present life as ordered to celestial glory."[41]

Natural prudence, for example, is the virtue of right reasoning about things to be done so as to reach man's natural end. Supernatural prudence is the same virtue but ordered to attaining heaven. Certain things—such as the renunciations involved in the evangelical counsels of poverty, chastity, and obedience—can be prudent for the sake of gaining glory, which might not seem prudent from the point of view of attaining natural happiness.

Similarly, natural temperance is moderation of the pleasures

---

[41] Thomas Aquinas, *Disputed Questions on the Cardinal Virtues*, a. 4, in *Disputed Questions on Virtue: Quaestio disputata de virtutibus in communi and Quaestio disputata de virtutibus cardinalibus*, trans. Ralph McInerny (South Bend, IN: St. Augustine's Press, 1999), 137.

of food, drink, and sexuality for the purpose of natural happiness whereas supernatural temperance moderates those pleasures for the higher end of attaining heaven. Supernatural temperance goes beyond natural temperance because sometimes it is supernaturally fitting to mortify our desires beyond what health would require, as in the penances of Lent.[42] Natural temperance can lead one to fast for health reasons whereas supernatural temperance leads one to fast as an act of penance. Similarly, supernatural patience and humility sometimes lead us to cheerfully tolerate and put up with harsh or abusive treatment and language that natural virtue would not require us to endure. Likewise, supernatural fortitude requires making sacrifices and enduring hardships and persecution for the sake of the Kingdom of God that go far beyond what would generally be required merely to attain temporal peace.

The Indwelling of the Trinity

In addition to the gifts of grace and the theological and infused moral virtues, the Holy Spirit Himself is given to the baptized and confirmed. As charity is infused into our hearts by the Spirit, the gift of the Spirit Himself is given to us, as St. Paul teaches in Romans 5:5. Although sanctifying grace and charity are created realities in the soul, they truly cause God to be present in the soul in a new and special way as the *Beloved* of our soul.

Jesus revealed this magnificent truth of the indwelling to the Apostles in His discourse after the Last Supper in John's Gospel, after instituting the Eucharist and as He was about to die for them and for us. Jesus chose this moment to tell them and us about the indwelling of the three divine Persons. In John 14:15–26 He begins by promising the gift of the Holy Spirit, but then adds that He and His Father will also come to dwell in us if we love Him:

> "If you love me, you will keep my commandments. And I will ask the Father, and he will give you another Counselor, to be with you for ever, even the Spirit of truth, whom the world cannot receive, because it neither sees him nor knows him; you know him, for *he dwells with you*, and *will be in you*.
> "I will not leave you desolate; *I will come to you*. . . . In that

---

[42] See *ST* I-II, q. 63, a. 4.

day you will know that *I am in my Father, and you in me, and I in you.* He who has my commandments and keeps them, he it is who loves me; and *he who loves me will be loved by my Father, and I will love him and manifest myself to him."* Judas (not Iscariot) said to him, "Lord, how is it that you will manifest yourself to us, and not to the world?" Jesus answered him, "If a man loves me, he will keep my word, and my Father will love him, and *we will come to him and make our home with him. . . .* These things I have spoken to you, while I am still with you. But the Counselor, the Holy Spirit, whom the Father will send in my name, he will teach you all things, and bring to your remembrance all that I have said to you."

The indwelling is of all three divine Persons together, as we see in John 14, but it is often attributed in a special way to the Holy Spirit,[43] because He is the divine Person who proceeds as the fruit of the mutual love of the Father and Son.[44]

This truth of the divine indwelling is the heart and soul of the spiritual life. St. Teresa of Avila puts it at the center of her great classic, *Interior Castle*: "Sisters, we realize that the soul of the just person is nothing else but a paradise where the Lord says He finds His delight. So then, what do you think that abode will be like where a King so powerful, so wise, so pure, so full of all good things takes His delight?"[45]

The indwelling of the blessed Trinity in the soul of the justified is a mystery of faith that can only be known by Revelation. Nevertheless, theology seeks to penetrate into the mystery in order to render it more intelligible through analogy with the things of our experience.

---

[43] For texts attributing the indwelling to the Holy Spirit in particular, see 1 Cor 3:16-17: "Do you not know that you are God's temple and that God's Spirit dwells in you?"; 1 Cor 6:19: "Do you not know that your body is a temple of the Holy Spirit within you, which you have from God? You are not your own"; 2 Tim 1:14: "Guard the truth that has been entrusted to you by the Holy Spirit who dwells within us." For texts attributing the indwelling simply to God, see 1 John 4:16: "God is love, and he who abides in love abides in God, and God abides in him"; 2 Cor 6:16: "What agreement has the temple of God with idols? For we are the temple of the living God."

[44] See *ST* I, q. 38, a. 2; q. 43, a. 5 and ad 1–2.

[45] *Interior Castle*, bk. 1, ch. 1, trans. Kieran Kavanaugh and Otilio Rodriguez, *The Collected Works of St. Teresa of Avila*, vol. 2 (Washington, DC: ICS Publications, 1980), 283.

How is it that the Trinity dwells in the just soul? Is not God already present in all His creatures? How then does He come to the soul in justification so as to make His abode in it? What kind of presence is this? For clearly it is different from the way in which God is present in all things.

In order to answer this question, one must first analyze how God is present in all His creatures, and then differentiate that omnipresence from the special presence caused by the divine indwelling. This is the way that St. Thomas Aquinas treats this question in *ST* I, q. 43, a. 3. He begins by distinguishing three ways in which God is present in all things: by imparting being, by power, and by knowledge.

First of all, God is present in all things by giving them being and continually sustaining them in being. If God did not continually sustain created being, it would sink back into nothingness and be annihilated, for created being is caused by God and utterly dependent on Him. Secondly, God is present in all things through His omnipotent power by which He can work in them whatever He wills. Third, He is present to all things in that they are perfectly present to Him through His omniscience.

However, the divine indwelling transcends all of these modes of presence because they are common to all things, whereas the indwelling is reserved to those who are in a state of grace. St. Thomas reasons therefore that the indwelling is a fourth kind of presence that is not just due to power but is *affective* and involves the intimate union of love. The indwelling is a presence through the love of charity by which God begins to exist in the soul not simply by holding the soul in being but also as the soul's *beloved*. Since charity flows immediately from sanctifying grace, all those who are in a state of grace have charity and thus possess God interiorly as the object of their love who dwells in the temple of the heart.[46]

---

[46] *ST* I, q. 43, a. 3: "The divine person is fittingly sent in the sense that He exists newly in any one; and He is given as possessed by anyone; and neither of these is otherwise than by sanctifying grace. For God is in all things by His essence, power and presence, according to His one common mode, as the cause existing in the effects which participate in His goodness. Above and beyond this common mode, however, there is one special mode belonging to the rational nature wherein God is said to be present as the object known is in the knower, and the beloved in the lover. And since the rational creature by its operation of knowledge and love attains to God Himself, according to this special mode God is said not only to exist in the rational creature but also to dwell therein

Whenever we love someone, the movement of love makes the beloved present interiorly in our heart as the object of our love. All lovers bear witness to this anthropological truth when they say that they carry the beloved in their hearts. If love of a created person makes that person present in the heart, how much more that is true of God. For God is present in the hearts of those who love Him not simply as the object of the love but also as the Lover of the soul who can make His presence felt interiorly through His secret movements of grace and consolation.

The only condition for the indwelling is that we love Him back and try to keep His commandments, as Jesus makes clear in John 14:15 and 21. The only way to lose the indwelling therefore is by unrepented mortal sin. If we sin gravely, we expel Him as the Beloved because grave sin puts ourselves as the beloved of our soul in His place. But when we repent from the heart (with perfect contrition) and resolve to make a good confession, He returns immediately as the Beloved.

The indwelling of the Trinity in the soul begins at the moment of justification. This occurs in Baptism (or through Baptism of desire), and it is restored in the sacrament of Penance (or an act of perfect contrition) if it was lost through mortal sin. The other sacraments, by increasing sanctifying grace and charity, also give an increase of the indwelling. At first sight it might appear that the indwelling would not admit of grades of more or less. But since it is a special presence of God as the Beloved of the soul present in His temple, it follows that an increase of love for God enables Him to become the soul's Beloved in an increasingly profound way.[47]

---

as in His own temple. So no other effect can be put down as the reason why the divine person is in the rational creature in a new mode, except sanctifying grace. Hence, the divine person is sent, and proceeds temporally only according to sanctifying grace. Again, we are said to possess only what we can freely use or enjoy: and to have the power of enjoying the divine person can only be according to sanctifying grace. And thus the Holy Spirit is possessed by man, and dwells within him, in the very gift itself of sanctifying grace. Hence the Holy Spirit Himself is given and sent." See also *ST* I, q. 8, a. 3, ad 4.

[47] See Hugh of St. Victor, *On the Sacraments of the Christian Faith* 2.1.13, trans. Deferrari, 251–52: "Therefore, although He who is everywhere does not live in all, even in those in whom He dwells He does not dwell equally.... How is it that among all the saints some are more saintly, unless it is that they have God as a dweller more abundantly.... He Himself of eternal stability remaining in Himself can be present wholly to all things and wholly to each, although those

Divine Filiation

Because we are made sharers in the divine nature through sanctifying grace, we are thereby made to be God's adopted sons and daughters. To be a son or daughter, properly speaking, one must share in the nature of the parent. When we create products of technology or craft, they cannot be said to be our children except by metaphor, for they do not share our nature although they bear its imprint. Similarly, the works of God in natural creation bear His imprint, but they cannot be said to be His sons or daughters because they do not share in the divine nature.

Grace, therefore, by giving us a share in the divine nature, truly makes us sons and daughters of God, not just through a metaphorical way of speaking. This sonship, however, is not natural because we are not constituted that way through our nature. Only the Second Person of the Trinity is a natural son, properly speaking. Our sonship is received as a gift superadded to the initial gift of being created with a rational nature. Thus we are fittingly said to be *adopted* sons and daughters of God. And we are adopted through the grace merited for us by the natural Son, Jesus Christ, in His Passion.

It follows that every human being who has been justified and is in a state of grace is a son or daughter of God. This gift is associated with the sacrament of Baptism because that is the ordinary way sanctifying grace is first received.[48]

As adopted sons and daughters, it is fitting that we be given a special filial love for God as our Father. This is the virtue of charity that flows from sanctifying grace, as seen above. Since the Holy Spirit is the divine Person who proceeds as the mutual love of the Father and the Son, it is fitting that the gift of this filial love is attributed to the Holy Spirit, who assimilates us to the Son. In Galatians 4:6–7, St. Paul writes: "Because you are sons, God has sent the Spirit of his Son into our hearts, crying, 'Abba! Father!' So through God you are no longer

---

in whom He dwells have Him according to the diversity of their capacity, some more, others less."

[48] See the Council of Trent, Decree on Justification (session 6), ch. 4 (DS, 1524), which speaks of justification as "a transition from the state in which man is born a son of the first Adam to the state of grace and adoption as sons of God through the second Adam, Jesus Christ our Savior. After the promulgation of the gospel, this transition cannot take place without the bath of regeneration, or the desire for it."

a slave but a son, and if a son then an heir." And again in Romans 8:14–17:

> All who are led by the Spirit of God are sons of God. For you did not receive the spirit of slavery to fall back into fear, but you have received the spirit of sonship. When we cry, "Abba! Father!" it is the Spirit himself bearing witness with our spirit that we are children of God, and if children, then heirs, heirs of God and fellow heirs with Christ, provided we suffer with him in order that we may also be glorified with him.

Gifts of the Holy Spirit

Together with sanctifying grace, the supernatural virtues, the indwelling, and divine filiation, the faithful also receive the seven gifts of the Holy Spirit, which help us to cooperate with His secret inspirations of actual grace. How do we know God's secret plans for us and the hidden desires of His Spirit? We can only know them by being attentive and docile to these inspirations. This is the sublime function of the gifts of the Holy Spirit.

The *Catechism of the Catholic Church*, §1830 defines the gifts of the Holy Spirit as "permanent dispositions which make man docile in following the promptings of the Holy Spirit." These dispositions are like the sails of a ship that catch the movements of actual grace breathed forth by the Holy Spirit. The gifts are necessary for salvation because even the theological virtues and the supernatural infused moral virtues are not enough to lead man safely and with ease to his supernatural end. The faithful need a special docility to the particular insights and inspirations that God sends to lead them directly and securely to do God's will.

The seven gifts of the Holy Spirit are wisdom, understanding, counsel, fortitude, knowledge, piety, and fear of the Lord, as revealed in Isaiah 11:2–3.[49] These gifts aid the theological and the super-

---

[49] Isaiah 11:2–3: "The Spirit of the LORD shall rest upon him, the spirit of wisdom and understanding, the spirit of counsel and might, the spirit of knowledge and the fear of the LORD. And his delight shall be in the fear of the LORD." The original Hebrew text gives only six gifts of the Holy Spirit, since fear of the

natural moral virtues to operate by making us *habitually docile to the movements of actual grace in our soul*. St. Thomas Aquinas has given a classical explanation of the necessity and general function of the gifts of the Holy Spirit,[50] and their distinction from the supernatural virtues that they aid and perfect:

> In order to differentiate the gifts from the virtues, we must be guided by the way in which Scripture expresses itself, for we find there that the term employed is "spirit" rather than "gift." For thus it is written (Isaiah 11:2–3): "The spirit . . . of wisdom and of understanding . . . shall rest upon him," etc.: from which words we are clearly given to understand that these seven are there set down as being in us by divine inspiration. Now inspiration denotes motion from without. For it must be noted that in man there is a twofold principle of movement, one within him, viz. the reason; the other extrinsic to him, that is, God. . . . Now it is evident that whatever is moved must be proportionate to its mover: and the perfection of the mobile as such, consists in a disposition whereby it is disposed to be well moved by its mover. Hence the more exalted the mover, the more perfect must be the disposition whereby the mobile is made proportionate to its mover: thus we see that a disciple needs a more perfect disposition in order to receive a higher teaching from his master. Now it is manifest that human virtues perfect man according as it is natural for him to be moved by his reason in his interior and exterior actions. Consequently man needs yet higher perfections, whereby to be disposed to be moved by God. These

---

Lord is given twice. In the Septuagint and the Vulgate translations, instead of repeating "fear of the Lord," piety (*eusebeia, pietas*) is introduced, bringing the gifts to seven. Through the Septuagint and Vulgate, the sevenfold enumeration of the gifts has entered deeply into the Catholic tradition in both East and West, and they are listed as seven in *CCC*, §1830.

[50] For St. Thomas's doctrine on the gifts of the Holy Spirit, see Luis M. Martinez, *The Sanctifier*, trans. Sr. M. Aquinas (Boston: Pauline Books & Media, 2003); Reginald Garrigou-Lagrange, *Christian Perfection and Contemplation: According to St. Thomas Aquinas and St. John of the Cross*, trans. Timothea Doyle (Rockford, IL: TAN Books, 2003), 271–310; Garrigou-Lagrange, *The Three Ages of the Interior Life*, 1:66–88; Robert Edward Brennan, *The Seven Horns of the Lamb: A Study of the Gifts Based on Saint Thomas Aquinas* (Milwaukee, WI: Bruce, 1966).

perfections are called gifts, not only because they are infused by God, but also because by them man is disposed to become amenable to the Divine inspiration, according to Isaiah 50:5: "The Lord ... hath opened my ear, and I do not resist; I have not gone back." Even the Philosopher says in the chapter "On Good Fortune" (*Ethica Eudemica* 7.8) that for those who are moved by Divine instinct, there is no need to take counsel according to human reason, but only to follow their inner promptings, since they are moved by a principle higher than human reason.[51]

The gifts are necessary for salvation because even the help of the theological virtues and the supernatural infused moral virtues (supernatural prudence, justice, temperance, and fortitude) are not enough to lead man safely and with ease to his supernatural end. Reason illuminated by faith is not always sufficient to show us God's particular will for us. The faithful need special insights and strengths that lead them directly and securely to do God's will and to be docile to His supernatural movements. St. Thomas explains:

> In matters directed to the supernatural end, to which man's reason moves him, according as it is, in a manner, and imperfectly, informed by the theological virtues, the motion of reason does not suffice, unless it receive in addition the prompting or motion of the Holy Spirit, according to Romans 8:14–17: "Whosoever are led by the Spirit of God, they are sons of God ... and if sons, heirs also": and Psalm 143:10: "Thy good Spirit shall lead me into the right land," because none can receive the inheritance of that land of the Blessed except he be moved and led to it by the Holy Spirit. Therefore, in order to accomplish this end, it is necessary for man to have the gift of the Holy Spirit.[52]

The gifts of the Holy Spirit are likened to sails of a ship by which it can be easily and promptly moved by a higher mover, the wind of the Holy Spirit, through the impulses of actual grace.[53] Thus the gifts of

---

[51] *ST* I-II, q. 68, a. 1.

[52] *ST* I-II, q. 68. a. 2.

[53] See Garrigou-Lagrange, *The Three Ages of the Interior Life*, 1:72–73.

the Holy Spirit lead us to act in a supernatural way through discernment of and docility to God's directing aid.

How often it happens that we are perplexed as to what course of action is God's will for us, or what would be the best way to exercise charity in a given situation. In cases like this, we need the gift of counsel to make us docile to God's promptings, showing the way to the fulfillment of God's plan, which He knows perfectly and of which we are ignorant.

In matters of faith, when a subtle new heresy is introduced, the saints are immediately aware of its heretical nature by the gift of understanding, which gives them greater penetration into the mysteries of faith by way of "connaturality." The saints and those more advanced in the spiritual life gain a "Catholic nose" to sniff out what departs from Catholic truth.

Likewise when we pray, we need to be attentive to God's inspirations through the gifts of piety, knowledge, counsel, and wisdom so as to praise God in a more worthy manner and to request what is truly good for us. For this reason, St. Paul in Romans 8:26–27 says that "the Spirit helps us in our weakness; for we do not know how to pray as we ought, but the Spirit himself intercedes for us with sighs too deep for words. And he who searches the hearts of men knows what is the mind of the Spirit, because the Spirit intercedes for the saints according to the will of God."

The gifts of the Holy Spirit are present in all who are in a state of grace because docility is a consequence of love. If we lack charity, we will lack docility to divine inspirations. Because docility is a fruit of love, these gifts will grow in the soul together with the increase of sanctifying grace and charity. Their activity becomes more marked as sanctifying grace increases. As with sanctifying grace, the sacraments are the ordinary channels by which the gifts of the Holy Spirit are given to us.

The Forgiveness of Original and Mortal Sin in the Act of Justification

The sacraments not only infuse sanctifying grace but also forgive sins. This could be considered the other side of the same coin. It is impossible for sanctifying grace to be infused while original and mortal sin remain, for they are contrary to it, and likewise it is impossible for original or mortal sin to be forgiven without the infusion of sanctifying grace[54] and of the habits of faith, hope, and charity.[55]

The essence of the punishment of original sin is the deprivation of sanctifying grace. If Adam and Eve had not sinned, their offspring would have been conceived in original justice. But because of original sin, their offspring, except for Mary and Jesus, are conceived without sanctifying grace, without which we cannot be saved. It is thus absolutely necessary for salvation that original sin be forgiven, which means nothing other than the infusion of sanctifying grace.

In a similar way, personal mortal sin for those at the age of reason is forgiven through the infusion of sanctifying grace, which occurs through Baptism or a holy desire for it, or the sacrament of Penance, or an act of perfect contrition that anticipates the effect of the sacrament, as will be seen in chapter 15 below. Many actual graces are given to lead an adult to justification. The Council of Trent, in its celebrated decree on justification, describes the process:

---

[54] See *ST* I-II, q. 113, a. 2: "Now an offense is remitted to anyone, only when the soul of the offender is at peace with the offended. Hence sin is remitted to us, when God is at peace with us, and this peace consists in the love whereby God loves us. Now God's love, considered on the part of the Divine act, is eternal and unchangeable; whereas, as regards the effect it imprints on us, it is sometimes interrupted, inasmuch as we sometimes fall short of it and once more require it. Now the effect of the Divine love in us, which is taken away by sin, is grace, whereby a man is made worthy of eternal life, from which sin shuts him out. Hence we could not conceive the remission of guilt, without the infusion of grace." On the relationship between the simultaneous infusion of grace and the forgiveness of sins, see La Soujeole, "The Sacraments and the Development of Doctrine," *OHST*, 593: "From the point of view of God—he who bestows grace—baptismal grace is the communicated divine life that drives away sin, as the sun drives away the night. But from the point of view of this action's effect in man, what we have here is a movement from death toward life, that is to say, a movement by which the subject separates himself from one extremity (*a quo*: spiritual death) in order to move to the opposite extremity (*ad quem*: spiritual life). From this point of view, the abandonment of the state of sin possesses a priority over the acquisition of life, even though both take place at the same time (one sole movement)."

[55] On justification and the infusion of charity, see Rom 5:5: "Hope does not disappoint us, because God's love has been poured into our hearts through the Holy Spirit who has been given to us." That we are saved through hope, see Rom 8:24. On the infusion of faith, hope, and charity in justification, see the Council of Trent, Decree on Justification (DS, 1530), quoted below.

Adults are disposed for that justice when, awakened and assisted by divine grace, they conceive faith from hearing and are freely led to God, believing to be true what has been divinely revealed and promised, especially that the sinner is justified by God's grace "through the redemption which is in Christ Jesus" [Rom 3:24]; when, understanding that they are sinners and turning from the fear of divine justice—which gives them a salutary shock—to the consideration of God's mercy, they are raised up in hope, confident that God will be merciful to them because of Christ; and they begin to love God as the source of all justice and are thereby moved by a certain hatred and detestation for sin, that is, by that repentance which must be practiced before baptism when, finally, they determine to receive baptism, to begin a new life, and to keep the divine commandments.[56]

The justification of an adult cannot take place without the act of the supernatural virtue of penance by which one repents, for love for God, of all grave sins committed of which one is aware. St. Thomas says: "It is impossible for a mortal actual sin to be pardoned without penance, if we speak of penance as a virtue."[57] St. Thomas outlines the steps by which the act of perfect contrition is generated, resulting in justification:

We may speak of penance, with regard to the acts whereby in penance we co-operate with God operating, the first principle [Cf. I-II, 113] of which acts is the operation of God in turning the heart, according to Lamentations 5:21: "Convert us, O Lord, to Thee, and we shall be converted"; the second, an act of faith; the third, a movement of servile fear, whereby a man is withdrawn from sin through fear of punishment; the fourth, a movement of hope, whereby a man makes a purpose of amendment, in the hope of obtaining pardon; the fifth, a movement of charity, whereby sin is displeasing to man for its own sake and no longer for the sake of the punishment; the sixth, a movement of filial fear whereby a man,

---

[56] Council of Trent, Decree on Justification (session 6, Jan 13, 1547), ch. 6, (DS, 1526).

[57] *ST* III, q. 86, a. 2.

of his own accord, offers to make amends to God through fear of Him.[58]

In summary, then, the act of supernatural repentance generally issues forth, through cooperation with actual grace, from prior supernatural acts of unformed faith (not yet accompanied by charity), fear of hell (servile fear), and hope of salvation. If the act of penance is only based on these motives, it will be an act of imperfect contrition, which does not accomplish justification but disposes one for seeking the sacraments of Baptism or Penance. If the motive of charity is added, also by cooperation with actual grace, then servile fear becomes filial fear, and the act of penance becomes perfect contrition, resulting in justification, which is the passing from the state of mortal sin into the state of grace.

The Council of Trent on the Causes of Justification

After speaking about the preparation for justification, the Council of Trent lists various causes of justification. The Council distinguishes (1) the principal efficient cause that brings it about, which is the power of God; (2) the purpose (final cause), which is the glory of God and giving of eternal life; (3) the meritorious cause that won justification for us, which is the Passion of Christ; (4) the instrumental efficient cause by which it is applied to us, which is Baptism; and (5) the formal or interior cause by which we are made interiorly just, which is sanctifying grace and supernatural charity (which flows from sanctifying grace).[59] To these we should add (6) the preparatory cause, which is faith, by which one seeks Baptism and without which "it is impossible to please Him" (Heb 11:6).

Justification is the result of all of these causes working together. It is produced in our souls by the power of God through the instrumentality of Baptism, which we seek through faith. It was merited by

---

[58] *ST* III, q. 85, a. 5.

[59] The *CCC*, §1992 summarizes this doctrine as follows: "Justification has been *merited for us by the Passion of Christ* who offered himself on the cross as a living victim, holy and pleasing to God, and whose blood has become the instrument of atonement for the sins of all men. Justification is conferred in Baptism, the sacrament of faith. It conforms us to the righteousness of God, who makes us inwardly just by the power of his mercy. Its purpose is the glory of God and of Christ, and the gift of eternal life."

Christ's Passion. It consists interiorly or formally in the infusion of sanctifying grace and charity in our souls, conforming us interiorly to Christ. Its purpose is the communication of eternal life for the glory of God.[60]

Of these various causes of justification, Catholics and Protestants disagree principally on the interior or formal cause. A "formal cause" is an interior cause by which a thing is what it is. It may be easier to understand by referring to this as the "interior cause." The Decree on Justification stresses that this justice is not something merely imputed, but that it inheres in those who are justified:

> Finally, the *single formal cause* is "the justice of God, not that by which He Himself is just, but that by which He makes us just," namely, the justice that we have as a gift from him and by which we are spiritually renewed [cf. Eph 4:23]. Thus, not only are we considered just, but we are truly called and are just [cf. 1 Jn 3:1], each one receiving within himself his own justice, according to the measure that "the Holy Spirit apportions to each one individually as he wills" [cf. 1 Cor 12:11], and according to each one's personal disposition and cooperation.[61]

The Decree goes on to state that justice is applied to those who are made just by the infusion of the habits of faith, hope, and charity, citing Romans 5:5 to show that justification consists in receiving the gift of charity infused into the heart:

---

[60] Council of Trent, Decree on Justification (session 6, Jan 13, 1547), ch. 7 (DS, 1529) My italics: "The causes of this justification are the following: the *final cause* is the glory of God and of Christ and life everlasting. The *efficient cause* is the merciful God who gratuitously washes and sanctifies [cf. 1 Cor 6:11], sealing and anointing [cf. 2 Cor 1:21] "with the promised Holy Spirit, who is the guarantee of our inheritance" [Eph 1:13–14]. The *meritorious cause* is the most beloved only begotten Son of God, our Lord Jesus Christ, who, "while we were enemies" [Rom 5:10], "out of the great love with which he loved us" [Eph 2:4], merited for us justification by His most holy Passion on the wood of the Cross and made satisfaction for us to God the Father. The *instrumental cause* is the sacrament of baptism, which is the "sacrament of faith," without which no man was ever justified."

[61] Council of Trent, Decree on Justification (session 6), ch. 7 (DS, 1529). My italics.

For although no one can be just unless the merits of the Passion of our Lord Jesus Christ are imparted to him, still this communication takes place in the justification of the sinner, when by the merit of the same most holy Passion, "God's love is poured through the Holy Spirit into the hearts" [Rom 5:5] of those who are being justified and inheres in them. Hence, in the very act of justification, together with the remission of sins, man receives through Jesus Christ, into whom he is inserted, the gifts of faith, hope, and charity, all infused at the same time.[62]

STUDY QUESTIONS

1. Explain the gratuitousness of grace. Why can it be said that grace is doubly gratuitous?
2. Explain the distinction between sanctifying grace and actual grace.
3. What is meant by the distinction between operative and cooperative grace?
4. Explain the analogy used by St. Thomas between nature, inclination, and movement to an end, and its application to the supernatural order.
5. What is the relationship between sanctifying grace and divine sonship?
6. What is the relationship between sanctifying grace and charity?
7. What is the relationship between sanctifying grace, charity, and the indwelling of the Holy Spirit?
8. What is the relationship between sanctifying grace, charity, and the gifts of the Holy Spirit?
9. What is the relationship between charity and the forgiveness of sins?
10. What are the steps leading up to the justification of an adult, according to the Council of Trent?
11. What are the causes of justification mentioned by the Council of Trent in the Decree on Justification? What is the formal cause of justification? Why is this important? Explain.

---

[62] Council of Trent, Decree on Justification (session 6), ch. 7 (DS, 1530).

SUGGESTIONS FOR FURTHER READING

Aumann, Jordan. *Spiritual Theology*. London; New York: Continuum, 2006. Pp. 66–101; 247–315.

Brennan, Robert Edward, O.P. *The Seven Horns of the Lamb: A Study of the Gifts Based on Saint Thomas Aquinas*. Milwaukee: Bruce Publishing, 1966.

Council of Trent. Decree on Justification. Session 6, January 13, 1547.

Gardeil, Ambroise, O.P. *The Holy Spirit in Christian Life*. St. Louis, MO: Herder, 1954.

Garrigou-Lagrange, Reginald. *The Three Ages of the Interior Life*. Vol. 1. Translated by Timothea Doyle. Rockford IL: Tan Books, 1989. Pp. 48–118.

Martinez, Luis M. *The Sanctifier*. Translated by Sr. M. Aquinas. Boston: Pauline Books & Media, 2003.

CHAPTER TEN

Sacramental Graces Proper
to Each Sacrament

1. COMMON AND PROPER EFFECTS
OF THE SEVEN SACRAMENTS

Communication of Sanctifying Grace:
Initiating and Increasing Divine Life

The principal mission of the sacraments is to communicate sanctifying grace as the foundation of the supernatural life. All of the sacraments communicate sanctifying grace, *ex opere operato*, to all those who validly receive them without posing an obstacle such as lack of repentance or faith. It is proper to Baptism to communicate sanctifying grace for the first time, giving birth to the supernatural life and washing the soul from original and mortal sin. Penance restores sanctifying grace if it was lost through mortal sin. Penance also can give an increase of sanctifying grace to those who have no mortal sins and thus confess only venial sins. The other sacraments communicate an increase of sanctifying grace. Together with sanctifying grace, the sacraments also communicate everything that is inseparable from it: faith, hope, charity, the infused moral virtues, the gifts of the Holy Spirit, and the indwelling of the Holy Trinity.

Theologians distinguish "sacraments of the *living*" from "sacraments of the *dead*," taking "living" and "dead" in the supernatural sense of being in a state of grace or being in a state of mortal sin. Sacraments of the dead are Baptism and Penance. They are ordered respectively to the initial gift and to the restoration of sanctifying grace, which spiritually raises to life those dead through original or mortal sin.

Sacraments of the living, which are Confirmation, Eucharist, Matrimony, Anointing of the Sick, and Holy Orders, presuppose that the recipient is spiritually alive and are ordered to giving an increase of sanctifying grace. Anointing of the Sick may, in exceptional cases, also restore sanctifying grace when someone is unable to receive the sacrament of Penance before Anointing (as in those who are unconscious) but has at least imperfect contrition for unconfessed mortal sins.[1]

Graces Proper to Each Sacrament according to Their Purpose

In addition to giving sanctifying grace and the gifts that flow from it, each sacrament also gives graces that are proper to its specific purpose and which are represented by its sacramental sign. This proper effect is generally referred to as "sacramental grace," although the term can also be used in the broader sense of all the graces given by the sacrament, including the common effect of sanctifying grace and all that flows from it.[2] One could think of the proper effect of the sacraments (sacramental grace) as individualizing characteristics that differentiate the graces given by the different sacraments according to their particular purpose.

The existence of graces proper to each sacrament can be seen in two ways. First, it would be redundant to have seven sacraments if they all gave the same effect. We have shown above that it is fitting that there are seven sacraments by a comparison with seven fundamental needs of our natural life, to which there correspond seven different needs of our supernatural life. The seven sacraments therefore must differ in the particular graces they give to meet these different spiritual needs.[3] Secondly, we have seen that the sacraments give precisely the

---

[1] See *CCC*, §1532, which states that Anointing grants "the forgiveness of sins, if the sick person was not able to obtain it through the sacrament of Penance." See also Thomas Aquinas, *In IV Sent.*, d. 23, q. 1, a. 2, qla. 1 (*Supplement*, q. 29, a. 4); Francisco A. P. Sola, "On Extreme Unction," in *Sacrae Theologiae Summa*, 4A:612.

[2] See J.-H. Nicolas, " La grâce sacramentelle," *Revue thomiste* 61 (1961): 171.

[3] See *ST* III, q. 65, a. 1. The first objection in this article asks why we need seven sacraments if Christ's Passion and the divine power cause our salvation. He responds (ad 1): "The same principal agent uses various instruments unto various effects, in accordance with the thing to be done. In the same way the Divine power and the Passion of Christ work in us through the various sacraments as through various instruments."

grace that they represent. Since the symbolism of each sacrament differs from the others, it follows that the graces given should likewise differ. The difference in the sacramental sign should manifest a different aspect of grace suited to a different spiritual need.

The *Catechism of the Catholic Church*, §1129 teaches: "'Sacramental grace' is the grace of the Holy Spirit, given by Christ and proper to each sacrament. The Spirit heals and transforms those who receive him by conforming them to the Son of God." Since the sacraments conform us to Christ in different ways, the graces they give ought to differ according to the specific purpose and symbolism of each sacrament.

St. Thomas speaks about sacramental graces in various articles in which he asks whether the individual sacraments give a grace distinct from the common effect of sanctifying grace, the infused virtues, and the gifts of the Holy Spirit. He consistently answers that sacramental graces flow from sanctifying grace and the infused virtues, but differ from them by being a special effect of a particular sacrament that fulfills the purpose of that sacrament.

In his early work, *De veritate*, in harmony with St. Bonaventure and St. Albert,[4] St. Thomas says the different sacramental graces have different ways of providing a remedy to sin and its consequences:

> Just as different virtues and different gifts of the Holy Spirit are directed to different actions, so too the different effects of the sacraments are like different medicines for sin and different shares in the efficacy of our Lord's passion, which depend upon sanctifying grace, as do the virtues and gifts.
>
> The virtues and gifts have a special name, however, because the acts to which they are directed are evident. They are accordingly distinguished from grace in name also. But the defects of sin, against which the sacraments are instituted, are hidden. Hence the effects of the sacraments do not have a proper name but go by the name of grace, for they are called sacramental graces, and the sacraments are distinguished on the basis of these graces as their proper effects. Those effects, moreover, belong to sanctifying grace, which also is joined to those effects. Thus along with their proper effects they have a common effect, sanctifying grace, which is given by means of the sacraments to

---

4   See J.-H. Nicolas, "La grâce sacramentelle," 167–70.

one who does not have it and increased by them in one who does.[5]

The general defects caused by sin are a certain complacency with sin in the will, ignorance in the practical intellect, weakness in the irascible appetite, and disordered inclinations in the concupiscible appetite.[6] Thus sacramental graces would strengthen the soul against these four fundamental consequences of sin.

In his later treatment of this topic in *ST* III, q. 62, a. 2, St. Thomas does not limit the aid of sacramental grace only to the medicinal function of remedying the defects caused by sin, but states that sacramental graces also give a positive divine assistance to living that aspect of the Christian life to which that sacrament is ordered.[7] As we have seen, the purpose of the sacraments is not only remedying sin but also imparting a share in the divine life and aiding the recipient to live that supernatural life in the world according to his state of life, and according to the configuration with Christ and the corresponding mission imparted by each sacrament.[8] In this article, St. Thomas writes:

> Grace, considered in itself, perfects the essence of the soul, in so far as it is a certain participated likeness of the Divine Nature. And just as the soul's powers flow from its essence, so from grace there flow certain perfections into the powers of the soul, which are called virtues and gifts, whereby the powers are perfected in reference to their actions. Now the *sacraments are ordained unto certain special effects which are necessary in the Christian life*: thus Baptism is ordained unto a certain spiritual regeneration, by which man dies to vice and becomes a member of Christ: which effect is something

---

[5] Thomas Aquinas, *De veritate*, q. 27, a. 5, ad 12, trans. Schmidt, *Truth*, 3:343–44 (my italics). See also his earlier article from his early commentary on the *Sentences*, *In IV Sent.*, d. 1, q. 1, a. 4, qla. 5.

[6] See *ST* I-II, q. 85, a. 3.

[7] On this change in St. Thomas's mature view, see George Shea, "A Survey of the Theology of Sacramental Grace," *Proceedings of the CTSA* (1953): 81–130, at 91–93; Nicolas, "La grâce sacramentelle," 169–70.

[8] See *ST* III, q. 65, a. 1: "The sacraments of the Church were instituted for a twofold purpose: namely, in order to perfect man in things pertaining to the worship of God according to the religion of Christian life, and to be a remedy against the defects caused by sin. And in either way it is becoming that there should be seven sacraments."

special in addition to the actions of the soul's powers: and the same holds true of the other sacraments. Consequently just as the virtues and gifts confer, in addition to grace commonly so called, a certain special perfection ordained to the powers' proper actions, so does sacramental grace confer, over and above grace commonly so called, and in addition to the virtues and gifts, *a certain Divine assistance in obtaining the end of the sacrament.* It is thus that sacramental grace confers something in addition to the grace of the virtues and gifts.[9]

St. Thomas does not specify the precise nature of the "divine assistance" given by sacramental grace, other than that it is something added to sanctifying grace and the supernatural virtues, and adds to them by being ordered precisely to the purpose of each sacrament. This has given rise to different ways of interpreting the nature of sacramental grace on the part of Thomists.[10]

Interpretation of Cajetan: Sacramental Graces Are Actual Graces

As we have seen, in addition to sanctifying grace and the habitual supernatural gifts that flow from it, we also need *actual grace*,[11] which is a divine impulse that moves our spiritual faculties, *illuminating* our intellect to grasp supernatural truths and *attracting* our will to desire and choose supernatural goods. Every act ordered to our supernatural end begins with actual grace. To act well on the supernatural order we need both actual grace and habitual (sanctifying) grace. The actual grace illuminates and attracts, giving a supernatural impulse, and the habitual grace gives the recipient a predisposition and a connatural principle to make good use of the actual grace received. As seen in the previous chapter, sanctifying grace perfects us in the order of being and is a stable supernatural disposition, whereas actual grace is a divine impulse or inspiration that aids us in the order of movement to act for our supernatural end. It makes sense, therefore, to think that the sacraments would be intended by Christ to perfect us in both ways.

---

[9] *ST* III, q. 62, a. 2, my italics.

[10] See Everett, *The Nature of Sacramental Grace*, 60–62, for the exposition of the three principal positions of Capreolus, Cajetan, and John of St. Thomas.

[11] For the distinction of sanctifying grace and actual graces, see *CCC*, §2000.

Since sanctifying grace is one habit, and since the other gifts that flow from it are tied to it, it seems to follow that the seven sacraments do not differ with regard to the effect of sanctifying grace except insofar as Baptism (or Baptism of desire) gives it for the first time, Penance restores it if it was lost, and the other sacraments increase it. Thus it seems that the effect of grace proper to each sacrament cannot principally be sanctifying grace and the gifts insofar as they are tied to it, for this is the common effect of all the sacraments.

Since the seven sacraments give different effects of grace, it seems to follow that the difference of graces must lie principally on the level of actual grace. For actual graces are not a habit but particular impulses (such as illuminations or attractions) directly ordered to action, and these impulses differ from one another. It is reasonable, therefore, to think that each sacrament gives particular actual graces ordered to its particular purpose.

It seems that the first theologian to explicitly identify sacramental grace with actual graces was Cardinal Cajetan (Thomas de Vio, 1469–1534), in his influential commentary on Aquinas's *Summa theologiae*,[12] for he interprets the "divine aid" spoken of by St. Thomas to mean actual grace. This has gradually become the dominant view of theologians.[13] Each sacrament, as an instrumental cause, brings about a series of actual graces ordered to the specific purpose of that sacra-

---

[12] See Card. Cajetan, commentary on *ST* III, q. 62, a. 2, no. 2, in *Sancti Thomae Aquinatis Opera omnia*, Leonine ed., vol. 12 (Rome: Typographia poliglotta S. C. de Propaganda Fide, 1906), 23: "Since in this place (III, q. 62, a. 2, c.) St. Thomas expressly says that sacramental grace adds a divine aid, the latter is not to be diverted to the opposite genus of grace, namely, habitual; rather, faithfully following the sense of the text, one should understand that sacramental grace is specifically distinguished from the grace of the virtues and gifts, not as one habit from another, but rather as a gratuitous divine aid from a gratuitous habitual gift." Translation in Shea, "A Survey of the Theology of Sacramental Grace," 105. For Cajetan's theology of sacramental grace, see pp. 104–08; Everett, *The Nature of Sacramental Grace*, 64–70, 134–35. Everett (134–35) argues that Cajetan was the first to clearly propose this thesis.

[13] See Shea, "A Survey of the Theology of Sacramental Grace," 120: "There is almost universal agreement that sacramental grace involves a right to obtain special actual graces when needed to further the proper end of a sacrament"; Adolphe Tanquerey, *The Spiritual Life: A Treatise on Ascetical and Mystical Theology*, 2nd ed., trans. Herman Branderis (Rockford, IL: TAN Books, 2000), 130. That the sacramental grace of Matrimony includes actual graces is taught by Pius XI in his Encyclical on Christian Marriage, *Casti Connubii* (1930), §40.

ment as long as no obstacle, such as unrepented mortal sin, blocks the divine action.[14]

Francisco Suárez (1548–1617) developed this line of thought by holding that sacramental grace adds to sanctifying grace by giving the recipient, as long as he remains in a state of grace, a habitual right to the reception of those actual graces ordered to accomplishing the purpose of the sacrament.[15] Baptism, for example, in addition to infusing sanctifying grace and forgiving original and personal sin and their temporal punishment, grants to the subject "a special aid to be configured to Christ, with whom he is buried in Baptism, and to keep the divine commandments, and to worthily receive the other sacraments, because it is the door of the sacraments."[16] Confirmation, in addition to an increase in sanctifying grace, gives the recipient special aids of actual grace to bear firm and intrepid witness to the faith.[17]

Interpretation of John of St. Thomas: Sacramental Grace Adds a Special Modality to Habitual Grace

Another complementary interpretation of sacramental graces is to see them as particular modifications of habitual grace ordered to the mission of each sacrament. This view has been put forth by St. Bonaventure, St. Albert the Great, and in a more developed form by

---

[14] Many theologians explain this by saying that each sacrament gives a kind of covenantal "right" to the graces ordered to its purpose. See Joseph A. de Aldama, "On the Sacraments in General," in *Sacrae Theologiae Summa*, 4A:43–45, esp. 43: "These *helps* will be given at the opportune time, that is, when they are demanded by the end of the sacrament. However, the *right* to them is permanent, according as it is rooted in habitual grace, and so it is also lost with it." I have argued above, however, that it is better to see the *res et sacramentum* of each sacrament as an abiding instrumental cause of these actual graces. Rather than simply giving a covenantal right to graces, the *res et sacramentum* is better understood as an abiding instrumental cause of graces, working in the soul as a persevering divine word of power signifying and bringing about configuration with Christ.

[15] See Everett, *The Nature of Sacramental Grace*, 81–84.

[16] Franciscus Suárez, *Commentaria ac Disputationes in Tertiam Partem D. Thomae*, in *ST* III, q. 62, a. 4, disp. 7, sectio 3, no. 5, in *Opera omnia*, vol. 20 (Paris: Vivès, 1866), 112. Suárez prefaces this view by saying "it is likely and may be piously believed."

[17] See Suárez, Commentaria ac Disputationes in Tertiam Partem D. Thomae, in ST III, q. 62, a. 4, disp. 7, sectio 3, no. 5.

John of St. Thomas (1589–1644).[18]

St. Bonaventure holds that the sacramental graces proper to each sacrament are special habits ordered to overcoming the various defects caused by sin. He writes:

> Thus *gratia gratum faciens* [sanctifying grace] is one, but the underlying habits differ one from another. Similarly, when I say sacramental grace, I mean not only grace, but also the effect of its healing. That grace is indeed one, but the effects of its healing are many. Therefore grace in the sacraments is distinguished from that in gifts and virtues by distinguishing their effects and underlying habits. Hence, sacramental grace on account of sin adds some effect beyond the grace of virtues.[19]

It is not clear from St. Bonaventure's explanation, however, precisely what habits sacramental grace adds to the common effect of sanctifying grace and all that flows from it, and how they differ from one another.

St. Albert's view is similar to St. Bonaventure's, for he also holds sacramental graces to be habitual graces, added to sanctifying grace and the virtues and gifts, which strengthen the soul in different ways against sin and its effects. For example, St. Albert holds that the grace of Confirmation differs from that of Baptism in that the former "cures a sickness which baptismal grace does not cure."[20] Both sacraments give a habitual grace that makes one pleasing to God, but they differ in that each one also gives its own distinct kind of grace that combats the effects of sin relating to that particular sacrament.

Several centuries later, John of St. Thomas interpreted St.

---

[18] John of St. Thomas defends his position in *Cursus Theologicus*, vol. 9, disp. 24, a. 2 (Paris: Vivès, 1886), 283–98. For John of St. Thomas's view of sacramental grace, see Everett, *The Nature of Sacramental Grace*, 96–118, and the summary on pp. 138–39.

[19] Bonaventure, *In IV Sent.*, d. 1, p. 1, a. 1, q. 6, resp., in *Commentary on the Sentences: Sacraments*, trans. Hellmann, 81. See Everett, *The Nature of Sacramental Grace*, 37–40; Nicolas, "La grâce sacramentelle," 168–69.

[20] Albert, *In IV Sent.*, d. 7, a. 5, in *Opera omnia*, vol. 29 (Paris: Vivès, 1895), 162, trans. Everett, *The Nature of Sacramental Grace*, 47. See also Albert, *In IV Sent.*, d. 1, a. 4, sol., p. 12; Everett, *The Nature of Sacramental Grace*, 44–48; Nicolas, "La grâce sacramentelle," 167–68.

Thomas in a way similar to the opinion of St. Bonaventure and St. Albert, for he also understands sacramental grace to refer to habitual grace rather than actual. He differs from his predecessors and improves upon them, however, in that he denies that sacramental graces are habits different in kind from the common grace. They differ not in species but in *modality*.[21] He interprets the "divine aid" mentioned by St. Thomas to mean a particular *modality* of sanctifying grace, of the gifts, and of virtues, which is oriented to the proper purpose of each sacrament. The purpose of this modality of grace is to enable the acts proper to that sacrament to come from a connatural principle[22] and to bring about a new configuration with Christ.[23] Sacramental grace differs from common grace not by being a different kind of grace but by corresponding to a new configuration with Christ in each sacrament. He writes: "And if you should ask in what this mode and formality consists, I answer that it consists in a certain derivation and imitation of the grace of Christ, or of the perfection which is in Christ, in so far as we are his members."[24] Being sacramentally configured to Christ through Confirmation, for example, enables one to confess Him publicly with a new connatural power lacking to the person who is not confirmed.[25]

---

[21] See Everett, *The Nature of Sacramental Grace*, 107; John of St. Thomas, *Cursus Theologicus*, vol. 9, disp. 24, a. 2, nn. 16–18, p. 288.

[22] Although all grace is supernatural, it can be called "connatural" insofar as it comes from an habitual supernatural principle, which here is a new configuration with Christ established by the *res et sacramentum*.

[23] See John of St. Thomas, *Cursus Theologicus*, vol. 9, disp. 24, a. 2, nn. 13–14, 23, pp. 287, 290; Everett, *The Nature of Sacramental Grace*, 106.

[24] John of St. Thomas, *Cursus Theologicus*, vol. 9, disp. 24, a. 2, no. 20, p. 289, translated in Everett, *The Nature of Sacramental Grace*, 108.

[25] See John of St. Thomas, *Cursus Theologicus*, vol. 9, disp. 24, a. 2, nn. 23, 30 pp. 290, 291, translated in Everett, *The Nature of Sacramental Grace*, 109–10: "And just as wisdom which is a gift, and wisdom which is a discipline are distinguished because the gift perceives from its connaturality and taste for divine things, but the discipline from reasoning about these divine things, as also, in its own way, to confess [faith in Christ] from connaturality and union with Christ through the sacrament of confirmation differs from the mode of confessing the faith from the intensity of the faith, even though substantially it is the same act." On the difference between acquired and infused wisdom, see *ST* I, q. 1, a. 6, ad 3; II-II, q. 45, a. 2; Feingold, *Faith Comes from What Is Heard*, 140–41.

Sacramental Grace and Docility to God's Inspirations

As so often happens in Catholic theology, it seems that the correct position here is a both/and. Sacramental grace adds to sanctifying grace a series of actual graces ordered to the purpose of the sacrament, according to the line of interpretation initiated by Cajetan, which has gained a theological consensus.[26] However, it seems that John of St. Thomas, and St. Bonaventure and St. Albert before him, were not wrong in holding that the sacramental graces proper to each sacrament are not limited only to a series of actual graces that are given as we need them but also include an abiding gift proper to the purpose of the sacrament. I hold that this abiding gift should be understood as a *habitual gift of greater docility to those actual graces ordered to the particular purpose of that sacrament.* Although the gifts of the Holy Spirit are part of the common effect of grace, I am arguing that the individual sacraments focus and enhance the gifts of the Holy Spirit according to their particular ecclesial mission.

The principal reason for this is that, since actual graces require our cooperation so that they can result in free and meritorious action,[27] it would be fitting for the sacraments to give not only the actual graces that are ordered to the purpose of each sacrament but also a habitual docility to be receptive to and cooperate with those graces. Since everything is received according to the mode of the receiver, no less important than the actual graces received are the interior dispositions that incline the recipient to be docile to those graces and act on them through active cooperation.

As we have seen in the preceding chapter, St. Thomas understands the gifts of the Holy Spirit as habits of docility to the inspirations of actual grace.[28] This docility or receptivity to movements of actual grace depends on sanctifying grace and charity.[29] We are docile to

---

[26] See above, p. 228n790.

[27] See *ST* I-II, q. 111, a. 2; Feingold, "God's Movement of the Soul," 166–91.

[28] See *ST* I-II, q. 68, a. 1.

[29] See *ST* I-II, q. 68, a. 5: "Now the Holy Spirit dwells in us by charity, according to Rom. 5:5: 'The charity of God is poured forth in our hearts by the Holy Ghost, Who is given to us,' even as our reason is perfected by prudence. Wherefore, just as the moral virtues are united together in prudence, so the gifts of the Holy Ghost are connected together in charity: so that whoever has charity, has all the gifts of the Holy Ghost, none of which can one possess without charity."

those whom we love. The more we love our teachers, the more we are capable of being instructed by them. If this is true of human teachers, it is still more true of the inward Teacher, the Paraclete.[30] Thus the common effect of the sacraments—an increase in sanctifying grace and charity—brings about, as part of that common effect, a corresponding increase in the gifts of the Holy Spirit, which are gifts of docility to the Holy Spirit's movements.

In addition to this common effect of increasing the gifts of the Holy Spirit, I propose that the sacramental grace of each sacrament strengthens the docility that comes from grace and charity by *focusing it according to the mission proper to that sacrament*. It is part of human experience that our docility is not always uniform, even to those whom we love. We are more docile to advice when it corresponds to our inward identity and sense of mission. Thus since we have shown above that the sacramental characters and the analogous *reality and sign* of Matrimony, Anointing of the Sick, and Penance, give a new configuration with Christ and a new ecclesial mission, it is reasonable to think that the sacramental grace of the sacrament would serve to strengthen docility to the Holy Spirit precisely according to the particular configuration with Christ and mission that has been received. In other words, sacramental grace differs according to the different signification of the *reality and sign* of each sacrament, which acts as an abiding interior instrument to bring about the particular graces, actual and habitual, that it signifies. In the case of the Eucharist, Christ Himself in His Body and Blood is the *reality and sign*. Reception of Holy Communion thus gives the particular mission to love Christ in Himself and in our neighbor more perfectly and a corresponding docility to the inspirations of the Holy Spirit in this regard.

Thus it seems reasonable to hold that, in addition to giving a series of actual graces, the sacraments also give *gifts of docility to the Holy Spirit in a way proper to the particular purpose of each sacrament* to help the recipients to be habitually docile to the actual graces sent by God to aid them in carrying out the ecclesial mission given by that sacrament. This would seem to involve the enhancing or focusing of the gifts of the Holy Spirit *in a particular way* so as to further con-

---

[30] See John 14:26: "The Counselor, the Holy Spirit, whom the Father will send in my name, he will teach you all things, and bring to your remembrance all that I have said to you."

figure the soul in docility to Jesus Christ, according to the purpose of the sacrament.

Pius XI on the Sacramental Grace of Matrimony

The conclusion that sacramental grace gives both actual graces and habitual gifts of docility to cooperate with them is implied by the teaching of Pius XI on the sacramental grace of Matrimony. In his encyclical *Casti Connubii*, he explains that the grace given by the sacrament of Matrimony includes both the right to actual graces and "particular gifts" and dispositions:

> By the very fact, therefore, that the faithful with sincere mind give such consent, they open up for themselves a treasure of sacramental grace from which they draw supernatural power for the fulfilling of their rights and duties faithfully, holily, perseveringly even unto death. Hence this sacrament not only increases sanctifying grace, the permanent principle of the supernatural life, in those who, as the expression is, place no obstacle (*obex*) in its way, but also adds particular gifts, dispositions, seeds of grace, by elevating and perfecting the natural powers. By these gifts the parties are assisted not only in understanding, but in knowing intimately, in adhering to firmly, in willing effectively, and in successfully putting into practice, those things which pertain to the marriage state, its aims and duties, giving them in fine right to the actual assistance of grace, whensoever they need it for fulfilling the duties of their state.[31]

In this profound text, Pius XI gives three different effects of the sacrament, which together make up the reality of grace (*res tantum*) conferred by the sacrament. (a) There is an increase of sanctifying grace. With this we can add the other effects that are inseparable from it, such as the theological and infused moral virtues and gifts of the Holy Spirit. This is the common effect of all the sacraments. Pius XI then mentions two different kinds of particular effects proper to this sacrament. (b) One of these is the aid of actual graces whenever the spouses need them in the course of their marriage "for fulfilling the

---

[31] Pius XI, *Casti Connubii*, §40.

duties of their state," which Pius XI mentions at the end of the text quoted above. (c) The other kind of sacramental graces are various habitual gifts ordered to the end of the sacrament. These are referred to here as "particular gifts, dispositions, seeds of grace" that enable the spouses to intimately know and will the goods proper to the married state in a connatural way. This is a good description of the purpose of the gifts of the Holy Spirit—which involve connatural knowledge and affectivity in harmony with the inspirations of the Holy Spirit—but here applied in a particular way to the mission given by the married state. Thus the three kinds of grace given by the sacrament of Matrimony are: (a) increase of the common effects of grace, (b) actual graces ordered to sanctifying marriage, and (c) particular habitual gifts and dispositions, which we can associate with gifts of the Holy Spirit further oriented to sanctifying marriage.

It seems reasonable to think that this threefold distinction of the graces given by the sacrament of Matrimony applies to all seven sacraments. Sacramental grace thus adds two different kinds of grace to the common effect of grace. One is a series of actual graces throughout the duration of the *res et sacramentum*, which is the abiding sacramental foundation of these transient sacramental graces. Sacramental grace also gives particular dispositions of docility, which are gifts of the Holy Spirit further ordered to the mission of the sacrament. All three of these effects are appropriated to the Holy Spirit.[32] Many texts in the liturgy, such as the epiclesis for the sanctification of the faithful, refer to this manifold action of the Holy Spirit.[33]

This thesis that sacramental grace adds both a series of actual graces and gifts of habitual docility to them is in harmony with St. Thomas's assertion that sacramental grace flows from sanctifying grace and presupposes it.[34] The particular strengthening of docility to the Holy Spirit presupposes that one already has sanctifying grace, charity, and the gifts of the Holy Spirit. If someone falls into a state of mortal sin, this effect of sacramental grace will be lost together with sanctifying grace and all that flows from it.

---

[32] For the action of the Holy Spirit through the sacraments, see Miralles, *I sacramenti cristiani*, 226–49.

[33] See, for example, Eucharistic Prayer III, in *The Roman Missal*, 3rd typ. ed., 653: "Grant that we, who are nourished by the Body and Blood of your Son and filled with his Holy Spirit, may become one body, one spirit in Christ. May he make of us an eternal offering to you."

[34] See *De veritate*, q. 27, a. 5, ad 12.

Sacramental Grace and the
Disposition of the Recipient

Great pastoral consequences follow from this teaching. In order to be receptive to the sacramental graces of each sacrament one must remain in a state of grace. When this is lost, the mission remains, but the means to accomplish the mission are tragically lacking. Thus if bishops, priests, married, or confirmed members of the faithful fall into a state of mortal sin, they lose the docility to the actual graces that they need to accomplish the exalted mission to which they have been called through reception of sacramental character or the matrimonial bond. This teaching sheds light on the tragic fact that sacramental reception does not always correspond to an increase of holiness. If the sacraments are as powerful as the Catholic faith teaches that they are, why do the fruits not always follow?[35] Indeed, the sacraments are far more powerful than we can conceive, but they presuppose the human freedom to want, or not to want, to be docile to them. If we *will* to remain faithful, God Himself grants supernatural gifts of docility tailored to the mission of each sacrament and strengthened according to the degree of one's charity. Pius XI makes this point forcefully with regard to the sacramental graces of Matrimony in *Casti Connubii*:

> Nevertheless, since it is a law of divine Providence in the supernatural order that men do not reap the full fruit of the Sacraments which they receive after acquiring the use of reason unless they cooperate with grace, the grace of matrimony will remain for the most part an unused talent hidden in the field

---

[35] See Ralph Martin, "The Post-Christendom Sacramental Crisis: The Wisdom of Thomas Aquinas," *Nova et Vetera* (English) 11, no. 1 (2013): 57–75. Martin identifies a partial cause of the contemporary phenonenon of widespread sacramental unfruitfulness on a lack of emphasis in catechesis and preaching on the importance of interior dispositions in receiving sacramental grace. See 64–65: "The reaction to the theology of the Protestant reformers produced in the Catholic Church what could be regarded as an overemphasis on the *ex opere operato* (by the fact of the action being performed) aspect of the sacraments working, to the neglect of the practical importance of the *ex opere operantis* (from the action of the doer) aspect. . . . In the very heart of our theological tradition resides a great wisdom—that of St. Thomas Aquinas—about the importance of preparation and subjective disposition on the part of those receiving the sacraments in order for them to actually bear fruit in the lives of their recipients."

unless the parties exercise these supernatural powers and cultivate and develop the seeds of grace they have received. If, however, doing all that lies with their power, they cooperate diligently, they will be able with ease to bear the burdens of their state and to fulfill their duties. By such a sacrament they will be strengthened, sanctified and in a manner consecrated.[36]

All sacramental graces are received according to the mode of the recipient. God gives us supernatural gifts in accordance with our mode of being that is free, historical, progressive, and although supremely needy, unable to receive everything at once. It follows that the actual graces given by the sacraments, and especially by those sacraments that imprint character, are received progressively. Cooperation with a particular operative grace—illumination of the intellect or attraction of the will—opens us up to receive additional graces and so forth without limit.

Sacramental grace, although efficaciously imparted *ex opere operato*, is not given by God mechanically but in a uniquely personal way that intimately respects our desires to receive His grace. Both the intensity of the sanctifying grace and the number and intensity of actual graces are related to our dispositions of hunger and thirst. The law governing this process is given in the beatitude: "Blessed are those who hunger and thirst for righteousness, for they shall be satisfied" (Matt 5:6).

It is reasonable to hold that sacramental graces are tied both to our actual desires for them and to the degree of charity we possess, according to Jesus's words in Matthew 25:29: "For to every one who has will more be given, and he will have abundance." In order to receive sacramental graces, one must first of all be brought into and remain in a state of grace. Everyone who receives the sacraments without the obstacle of unrepented mortal sin will receive more grace, but the degree of increase depends on the strength of the desire for growing in union.[37]

Connection between Sacramental Grace and the *Res et Sacramentum*

There is a most intimate connection between the *reality and sign* (*res*

---

[36] Pius XI, *Casti Connubii*, §41.
[37] See Garrigou-Lagrange, *The Three Ages of the Interior Life*, 1:141–43.

et sacramentum) in each sacrament and the sacramental graces proper to it. The key principle governing the sacraments is that they efficaciously produce the grace they signify. Since the *reality and sign* is itself an invisible and durable sacramental sign, it efficaciously produces what it signifies, as will be argued in the following chapters, as long as no obstacle blocks it from achieving its effect. It follows that sacramental grace in the different sacraments will differ in accordance with the difference in the abiding *reality and sign* and the particular ecclesial mission and configuration with Christ that it imprints.[38]

The role of the *reality and sign* as instrumental cause is most evident in the Eucharist, where the *reality and sign* is Christ's own Body and Blood received in Holy Communion. It is extremely fitting that the substantial presence of Jesus's Body and Blood, given and shed for us and received into the bodies of the faithful, be the instrumental cause for nourishing our supernatural organism with sanctifying and actual grace, charity, and the other gifts that accompany charity. Christ's life, substantially present in the Eucharist, most fittingly nourishes the growth of His life in us. Furthermore, since the Eucharist is instituted to foster love, it must impart a special docility to be moved by particular inspirations of the Holy Spirit that excite concrete movements of love for God and neighbor.[39]

After the Eucharist, the role of the *res et sacramentum* in giving grace is most evident in the three sacraments that imprint character. We have seen that sacramental character gives a new identity in Christ and a new mission to participate in Christ's offices of priest, prophet, and king. This new identity and mission, imprinted on the soul as an invisible word representing Christ's priestly mission, should be understood as an efficacious word of Christ that continues to speak, calling down in a progressive way the graces that empower the recipients to accomplish the mission that flows from their sacramental identity.

The indelible character imprinted in Baptism, Confirmation, and Holy Orders acts as a perpetual instrumental cause and an efficacious indelible sign of the actual graces, and the corresponding gifts of

---

[38] See Nicolas, *Synthèse dogmatique: de la Trinité à la Trinité*, 788, in which he argues that sacramental grace is "sanctifying grace (habitual and actual) *in relation* to the *res et sacramentum*" (my translation; italics original).

[39] See *ST* III, q. 79, a. 1, ad 2: "Through this sacrament [the Eucharist], as far as its power is concerned, not only is the habit of grace and of virtue bestowed, but it is furthermore aroused to act, according to 2 Cor. 5:14: 'The charity of Christ presseth us.'"

docility, suitable for carrying out the mission proper to that sacrament. These graces to live out the mission conferred by the sacrament build on one another, and thus one's personal cooperation with the graces received enables one to receive new graces.

The sacramental marital bond, which is an abiding sign of Christ's self-giving love for His Bride, acts like a sacramental character. As an efficacious sign, it calls down actual graces to aid the spouses in their sublime mission of being an icon of the love between Christ and His Church. As stated above, it seems that something analogous should be said of the reality and sign of Penance and Anointing of the Sick. As abiding and invisible sacramental signs, they efficaciously call down the specific actual graces proper to the penitential and healing mission of these sacraments.

2. SACRAMENTAL GRACES OF THE SEVEN SACRAMENTS

As in the analysis of Pius XI with regard to the grace of Matrimony, in each of the sacraments we can distinguish three aspects of the grace that they impart: (a) the common effect of sanctifying grace and of what flows from it, which are the theological and infused moral virtues and the gifts of the Holy Spirit; (b) actual graces ordered to fulfilling the mission conferred by the sacrament; and (c) particular gifts and dispositions that give a habitual docility to cooperate with those actual graces. In each sacrament these graces are represented by the outward sacramental sign and called for by the ecclesial mission given by the reality and sign of the sacrament.

Sacramental Grace of Baptism

It is proper to Baptism above all to impart the initial gift of sanctifying grace and all the gifts that flow from it. This has the effect of forgiving original sin and, for adults, personal mortal sin.

Baptism is also the source of countless actual graces needed in the Christian life. Since Baptism makes us members of Christ and of His Church called to die to sin and live a life of holiness, this sacrament gives a series of graces throughout our life to make us capable of the glorious mission to live a Christ-like life to the glory of the Father. The scope of these graces is unlimited, embracing the entire Christian life.[40] As seen above, St. Thomas succinctly explains the graces of Baptism as "ordained unto a certain spiritual regeneration, by which man dies to vice and becomes a member of Christ."[41] This effect is symbolized by the sacramental sign of Baptism, as seen in chapter 5 above. The washing with water signifies washing from sin so as to live in holiness, and the immersion into the water and rising up from it symbolizes participation in Christ's death and Resurrection, in accordance with Romans 6:3–4.

Baptism is the source not only of the actual graces but also of the habitual dispositions, such as filial fear of the Lord, needed to die to vice and live in Christ throughout one's life. Furthermore, since Baptism makes one an adopted son or daughter of God, the mission of Baptism is to live in accordance with that sublime dignity, for which one needs a special gift of piety or reverence for God as one's Father and for Christ as Head of the Mystical Body. St. Leo the Great, in a Christmas sermon, has admirably expressed the dignity, mission, and responsibility of the baptized:

> Christian, recognize your dignity and, now that you share in God's own nature, do not return to your former base condition by sinning. Remember who is your head and of whose body you are a member. Never forget that you have been rescued from the power of darkness and brought into the light of the Kingdom of God.[42]

The baptized are continually to call to mind that they have died to sin and have been made members of such a glorious head, and they should therefore call upon the graces of Baptism to live this "upward

---

[40] See Bl. Columba Marmion, *Christ, the Life of the Soul*, trans. Alan Bancroft (Bethesda, MD: Zaccheus Press, 2005), 211 (emphasis original): "The whole of Christian asceticism derives from baptismal grace. . . . *The Christian life is nothing other than the progressive and continued development, the application in practice, throughout the whole of our human existence, of the twofold initial act put into us in seed form at baptism, of the twofold super-natural result of 'death' and of 'life' produced by this sacrament.* In that is to be found the whole program of Christianity."

[41] *ST* III, q. 62, a. 2.

[42] St. Leo the Great, Sermon 21 *in Nativitate Domini*, 3: PL 54, 192C, quoted in *CCC*, §1691, at the beginning of part III on the Christian life.

call of God in Christ Jesus" (Phil 3:14).[43]

Sacramental Grace of Confirmation

Confirmation extends the mission of Baptism to the level of mature action through the inspirations of the Holy Spirit. Those confirmed are called to the glorious mission of actively building up the Church in the world through Christian witness in the face of trials and spiritual combat. *Lumen Gentium*, §11 speaks of the purpose of Confirmation as completing what was begun in Baptism by reception of a fuller gift of the Spirit by which the faithful are enriched with a special strength to be true and active witnesses of Christ. Spiritual maturity and supernatural activity through cooperation with the inspirations of the Holy Spirit are required to be a true and active witness of Christ in the world and to share in the Church's mission to spread the Gospel by example, words, and prayer.

Protestants often object to Catholic doctrine on Confirmation because the idea that Confirmation "completes" or "perfects" Baptism seems to imply that Baptism by itself is insufficient or imperfect, which would seem to denigrate Baptism. Can we say that Confirmation is the completion of Baptism? It is the completion of Baptism in a way similar to how Pentecost is a fulfillment of the Paschal mystery.[44] Pentecost completes Easter by giving the full fruit of the Spirit won on Calvary and thus empowering a grace-filled human participation in

---

[43] Didymus of Alexandria, a Father of the fourth century, describes the grace of Baptism in *De Trinitate* 2.12, in Quasten, *Patrology*, 3:98: "The Holy Spirit as God renovates us in baptism, and in union with the Father and the Son, brings us back from a state of deformity to our pristine beauty and so fills us with His grace that we can no longer make room for anything that is unworthy of our love; He frees us from sin and death and from the things of the earth; makes us spiritual men, sharers in the divine glory, sons and heirs of God and of the Father. He conforms us to the image of the Son of God, makes us co-heirs and His brothers."

[44] See Karl Joseph Becker, "Le don de la confirmation," *La Maison-Dieu* 168 (1986): 15–32, at 32: "Perhaps it would be better to ask: Does the meaning of Baptism call for another participation in the glorified Lord? Certainly yes." See also Cabasilas, *The Life in Christ* 4.1, 114: "Now then, when we were baptized the Mystery achieved for us all that belonged to it, but we were not yet perfect. We were without the gifts of the Spirit which depend on the most holy chrism. For those who had been baptized by Philip (Acts 8:12) the Holy Spirit was not yet present to bestow these graces, but in addition to Baptism the hands of John and Peter were needed."

the Lord's missionary mandate. Baptism gives the full common effect of grace, including the indwelling of the Holy Spirit and the seven gifts of the Spirit. Nevertheless, Baptism gives those gifts of grace as to one newly born, and Confirmation gives them so as to bring the confirmed faithful to be instruments of the Holy Spirit in building up the Church as mature witnesses, like the disciples on Pentecost.

Confirmation is the sacramental continuation of Pentecost, through which the bishops hand on to the baptized the same gift of the Holy Spirit that was poured out on the apostles at Pentecost.[45] Paul VI in his Apostolic Constitution on Confirmation says that "through the sacrament of confirmation those who have been born anew in baptism receive the inexpressible Gift, the Holy Spirit himself, by whom 'they are endowed . . . with special strength.'"[46] Confirmation gives the Gift of the Holy Spirit not as an entirely new gift, but as a deepening proper to the movement of growth to spiritual maturity and to "life in the Spirit." The indwelling Spirit brings with Him an increase of His seven gifts of wisdom, understanding, counsel, knowledge, fortitude, piety, and fear of the Lord, ordered to Christian witness, service, the common priesthood of the faithful, and a deepening of communion in the Body of Christ.[47] Confirmation sacramentally enables the faith-

---

[45] See the decree of the Congregation for Divine Worship of Aug 22, 1971, in *Rites*, 1:471, which institutes the new rite of Confirmation: "In the sacrament of confirmation the apostles and the bishops, who are their successors, hand on to the baptized the special gift of the Holy Spirit, promised by Christ the Lord and poured out upon the apostles at Pentecost. Thus the initiation in the Christian life is completed so that believers are strengthened by power from heaven, made true witnesses of Christ in word and deed, and bound more closely to the Church."

[46] Paul VI, *Divinae Consortium Naturae*, in *Rites*, 1:474, citing *LG*, §11.

[47] See Paul VI, *Divinae Consortium Naturae*, in *Rites*, 1:474: "Having been signed with the character of this sacrament, they are 'more closely bound to the Church' and 'they are more strictly obliged to spread and defend the faith, both by word and by deed, as true witnesses of Christ.'" See also *CCC*, §1303: "It [Confirmation] roots us more deeply in the divine filiation which makes us cry, 'Abba! Father!'; it unites us more firmly to Christ; it increases the gifts of the Holy Spirit in us; it renders our bond with the Church more perfect; it gives us a special strength of the Holy Spirit to spread and defend the faith by word and action as true witnesses of Christ, to confess the name of Christ boldly, and never to be ashamed of the Cross." These effects are expressed by the prayer of the celebrant before Confirmation in the current Latin Rite in *Rites*, 1:162–63: "My dear newly baptized, born again in Christ by baptism, you have become members of Christ and of his priestly people. Now you are to share in the outpouring of the Holy Spirit among us, the Spirit sent by the Lord upon his

ful, through the power of the Spirit they have received, to participate more actively and interiorly in the Church's liturgy, especially in the Sacrifice of the Mass, offering their Christian life to the Father with Christ.[48]

Sacrament of Fortitude and Magnanimity

Although Confirmation gives all the gifts of the Holy Spirit, which is part of the common effect of all the sacraments, the gift of fortitude has a special role in the mission of Confirmation. As seen above, medieval theologians explained the fittingness of the seven sacraments with regard to their connection with the seven fundamental virtues, and the sacrament of Confirmation was connected with the cardinal virtue of fortitude,[49] which strengthens against obstacles, weakness, fear, human respect,[50] and discouragement. The gift of fortitude is a supernatural disposition of docility to the inspirations of the Holy Spirit that lead the faithful to courageous witness and heroic service, despite obstacles and human weakness.

Cyril of Jerusalem speaks of this strengthening by relating it to the gift of the Spirit received by Christ after His Baptism:

> For as Christ after His Baptism and the visitation of the Holy Spirit went forth and overthrew the adversary, so must you after holy Baptism and the mystical Chrism, clad in the armor of the Holy Spirit, stand firm against the forces of the Enemy

---

apostles at Pentecost and given by them and their successors to the baptized. The promised strength of the Holy Spirit, which you are to receive, will make you more like Christ and help you to witness to his suffering, death, and resurrection. It will strengthen you to be active members of the Church and to build up the Body of Christ in faith and love."

[48] See Bishop Samuel Aquila, "The Sacrament of Confirmation," 2011 Hillenbrand Lecture: "In the teaching of Aquinas one could venture to say that confirmation plays a role in enabling one to actively participate in the Eucharistic liturgy, as we become true worshippers of the Father, united to Jesus in his own worship of the Father."

[49] See *ST* III, q. 65, a. 1: "Confirmation [corresponds] to Fortitude, being ordained against infirmity."

[50] See *ST* III, q. 72, a. 9: "Man is hindered from freely confessing Christ's name, by two things,—by fear and by shame. . . . And therefore man is signed with chrism, that neither fear nor shame may hinder him from confessing the name of Christ."

and overthrow them, saying: "I can do all things in the Christ who strengthens me" [Phil 4:13].[51]

The reference to Philippians 4:13, in addition to fortitude, also ties Confirmation to the closely related virtue of magnanimity, which means "greatness of soul." Confirmation configures the faithful to Christ in this aspect of magnanimous spiritual combat for the good of the Church and society, which is a sharing in Christ's kingly mission. Confirmation serves not only to fortify the soul in giving witness but also to attract the Christian to the glorious and noble mission of being a co-redeemer with Christ, of building up His Church, and of doing everything "for the greater glory of God." The sacramental graces of Confirmation are ordered to the progressive awareness and realization of this sublime calling of sharing in the three offices of Christ— prophet, priest, and king.

Confirmation and the Gifts of Knowledge, Understanding, and Wisdom

Since Confirmation gives the mission of sharing in Christ's prophetic mission, the confirmed faithful need special graces to complete this mission. No one can give effective witness to a faith that is not understood, and thus continued intellectual formation is necessary to accomplish this mission. Learning acquired by study is not enough, however, for two reasons. First, this knowledge is supernatural, and we can neither understand it nor pass it on effectively without the aid of an interior Teacher, the Holy Spirit, whose inspirations illuminate the intellect to understand, aid the imagination in forming helpful analogies, and stir the will to desire to study and share the faith. Thus part of the sacramental grace of Confirmation will be a continual series of illuminations of our minds to progressively understand the faith and transmit it in a living and attractive manner.

Actual graces are not enough, however, to perfectly accomplish this task. For knowledge, understanding, and wisdom to be truly possessed and internalized, they have to exist as a stable disposition that has a connatural quality that comes from having an abiding relationship with the interior Teacher. Connatural knowledge is drawn not

---

[51] Cyril of Jerusalem, *Mystagogical Catechesis* 3.4, in *The Works of Saint Cyril of Jerusalem*, trans. Stephenson, 2:172.

simply from intellectual inference but also is seen intuitively and can be touched and tasted, as it were. This kind of connatural knowledge of the faith is given by the gifts of the Holy Spirit of understanding, knowledge, and wisdom. The gift of understanding gives the faithful a "Catholic nose" to recognize truth and error in matters of faith, and to penetrate the truths in a habitual way through analogy with their human experience.[52] The gift of knowledge involves a supernatural understanding of created realities,[53] and the gift of wisdom allows the faithful to rightly judge and order things in the light of the Cross of Christ and the love of the Triune God.[54]

These gifts are spoken of in 1 John 2:27: "The anointing which you received from him abides in you, and you have no need that any one should teach you; as his anointing teaches you about everything, and is true, and is no lie, just as it has taught you, abide in him." Here John is speaking about a supernatural anointing that abides in the Christian and is an interior teacher who teaches the Christian all things. It is reasonable to think that this abiding gift of interior anointing refers to the sacramental grace of Confirmation, promised by Jesus at the Last Supper in John 14:16–17: "I will ask the Father, and he will give you another Counselor, to be with you for ever, even the Spirit of truth." This gift, given in Pentecost and in every Confirmation, was prophesied by Jeremiah 31:34: "No longer shall each man teach his neighbor and each his brother, saying, 'Know the LORD,' for they shall all know me, from the least of them to the greatest, says the LORD." This obviously does not mean that sacramental grace gives all Christians the acquired knowledge of the faith that comes from catechesis and study. Sacramental grace does not substitute for human effort but empowers the faithful for the superhuman task of carrying out the missionary mandate, and thus He gives knowledge, understanding, and wisdom from above, which we receive according to our disposition of love and desire. St. Augustine, in his commentary on 1 John 2:27, highlights the role of the Interior Teacher and our need for docility through the power of the interior

---

[52] See Martinez, *The Sanctifier*, 197–207; Feingold, *The Mystery of Israel and the Church*, vol. 2, *Things New and Old* (St. Louis, MO: Miriam Press, 2010), 196–97.

[53] See Martinez, *The Sanctifier*, 187–96; Feingold, *The Mystery of Israel and the Church*, 2:193–94.

[54] See Martinez, *The Sanctifier*, 209–19; Feingold, *The Mystery of Israel and the Church*, 2:197–99.

anointing that has been sacramentally received:

> For my part, I have spoken to all. But those to whom that anointing does not speak within, whom the Holy Spirit does not teach within, go back untaught. Instructions from outside are kinds of aids and suggestions. He who teaches hearts has his chair in heaven. . . . There is, therefore, an Interior Master who teaches. Christ teaches, his inspiration teaches. Where his inspiration and his anointing are not, words from outside make useless sounds.[55]

Sacramental Grace of the Eucharist

The sacramental grace proper to the purpose of the Eucharist is to nourish the soul with the ardor of charity for God and neighbor so as to foster union in its vertical and horizontal dimensions.[56] The grace of the Eucharist is like Confirmation in that both perfect the soul, but whereas Confirmation aims at supernatural action and Christian witness through docility, the Eucharist aims directly at union with Christ and the Church, which is the goal of all ecclesial action.[57] The Eucharist, as a marriage feast with the Son, is directly ordered to spousal union with God. The sacramental grace of the Eucharist attracts and stimulates the soul to make interior acts of affective love for God and neighbor that ought to overflow into firm resolutions and acts of charity, resulting in increased communion. St. Thomas explains:

> This sacrament confers grace spiritually together with the virtue of charity. Hence Damascene (*De Fide Orthod.* 4) compares this sacrament to the burning coal which Isaias saw (6:6). . . . But as Gregory observes in a Homily for Pente-

---

[55] Augustine, Tractate 3.13.2 on 1 John 2:27, in *Tractates on the Gospel of John 112–24; Tractates on the First Epistle of John*, trans. J. W. Rettig, FC 92 (Washington, DC: Catholic University of America Press, 1995), 171–72.

[56] For a fuller discussion of the sacramental graces of the Eucharist, see Feingold, *The Eucharist*, 498–526.

[57] See *ST* III, q. 79, a. 1, ad 1, in which St. Thomas states that in Confirmation, "grace is increased and perfected for resisting the outward assaults of Christ's enemies" whereas in the Eucharist "grace receives increase, and the spiritual life is perfected, so that man may stand perfect in himself by union with God."

cost, "God's love is never idle; for, wherever it is, it does great works." And consequently through this sacrament, as far as its power is concerned, not only is the habit of grace and of virtue bestowed, but it is furthermore aroused to act, according to 2 Cor. 5:14: "The charity of Christ presseth us."[58]

By nourishing charity with one's neighbor, the Eucharist has the proper effect of strengthening the bond of unity in the Church, giving graces that lead to mutual reconciliation and enhanced communion, and overcoming divisions caused by sin. In a particular way the Eucharist nourishes the capacity of the soul to forgive injuries and love one's enemies. And because it causes us to grow in the love of God, the Eucharist also aids the soul to grow in deeper contrition and interior conversion. It thus indirectly but powerfully nourishes the proper effect of the sacrament of Penance to forgive sins and ward off future ones.

Since the *res et sacramentum* of the Eucharist, Christ's Body and Blood,[59] is in the faithful after Communion for only a short time, a period of thanksgiving after Communion is an especially fruitful time for receiving actual graces and inspirations that tend to the increase and practice of charity.[60]

Sacramental Grace of Penance

Restoration of the Grace of Justification

It is proper to the sacrament of Penance to restore sanctifying grace and charity if they were lost through mortal sin, enabling the penitent to "recover the grace of justification."[61] Together with sanctifying grace, all the supernatural gifts that flow from it are also restored. This effect is simultaneous with and inseparable from the forgiveness of mortal sin and the cancelling of the debt of eternal punishment. If the penitent is already in a state of grace, either because he only has

---

[58] *ST* III, q. 79, a. 1, ad 2.

[59] By concomitance, the whole of Christ's humanity is present under either species. See the Council of Trent, Decree on the Sacrament of the Eucharist (session 13, Oct. 11, 1551), can. 3 (DS, 1653).

[60] See Pius XII, *Mediator Dei*, §126; Feingold, *The Eucharist*, 583–84.

[61] *CCC*, §1446.

venial sins to confess or because he has done an act of perfect contrition after a mortal sin, then valid reception of the sacrament increases sanctifying grace, from which flows a corresponding strengthening of the theological virtues, the infused moral virtues, the gifts of the Holy Spirit, and of the divine indwelling.

Actual Graces to Avoid the Sins Confessed and to Grow in the Opposing Virtues

According to our analysis above, the sacramental grace of Penance will consist in a series of actual graces necessary to fulfill the purpose of the sacrament and an increase in the habitual gifts of docility to cooperate with them. That purpose here is to strengthen the penitent in repentance for the sins he has confessed, to deepen his desire to make reparation for them, to better sanctify those areas of his life, and to avoid falling again into sin. Penance configures the penitent to Christ crucified for sin and risen to new life, and so the sacramental graces of Penance are ordered "to crucify the 'old man' so that the 'new' can be born by the power of Christ."[62] These graces both strengthen the desire of the will to turn from sin and illuminate practical reason to act with prudence. They also lead to a deepening of the sense of sin and interior contrition. It is reasonable to think that these actual graces of ongoing repentance will be accompanied by a deepening of the gifts of fear of the Lord, fortitude, knowledge, and counsel, to augment docility to divine inspirations calling one to avoid sin and be attentive to its deceitful allure. These graces will not come all at once but as they are needed and sought. As with the sacramental graces of the other sacraments, they are a dynamic series that increase insofar as one cooperates actively with the ones already received.

Actual Graces Aid the Penitent to Do Penance for Sin

The sacramental grace of Penance is also ordered to help the penitent make satisfaction for the temporal punishment for sin. Every mortal sin, by its very nature, brings about the debt of two kinds of punishments: eternal and temporal.[63] This is because every mortal

---

[62] John Paul II, *Reconciliatio et Paenitentia*, §26.
[63] Venial sin, on the other hand, only causes a debt of temporal punishment. The

sin involves a movement of the will away from God and toward some created object that the person loves more than God because he is willing to break God's law so as to obtain that created good. In other words, mortal sin carries with it both an aversion from God and a "conversion" to some creature. On account of these two aspects, there is a twofold disorder. First, there is a turning away from the infinite Good. Second, there is a turning toward some finite object deemed to be good, although in fact it is contrary to first moral principles. In turning to the creature in this disordered way, there is always some abuse of the creature and its natural finality by the fact that it has been ordered to one's own satisfaction instead of to the glory of God. This introduces a disorder into creation for which reparation has to be made.

Each of these disorders naturally incurs its proper penalty. The proper penalty for turning away from the infinite Good is to lose that infinite Good. Thus if the will remains turned away from God until the moment of death, one incurs the eternal punishment of loss of God (pain of loss; *poena damni*).

The disordered turning to creatures against first moral principles and conscience naturally incurs a second penalty, which is the loss of those creaturely satisfactions that one sought in a disordered way.[64]

---

distinction between eternal and temporal punishment is explained in *CCC*, §§1472–73: "To understand this doctrine and practice of the Church, it is necessary to understand that sin has a double consequence. Grave sin deprives us of communion with God and therefore makes us incapable of eternal life, the privation of which is called the 'eternal punishment' of sin. On the other hand every sin, even venial, entails an unhealthy attachment to creatures, which must be purified either here on earth, or after death in the state called Purgatory. This purification frees one from what is called the 'temporal punishment' of sin. . . . The forgiveness of sin and restoration of communion with God entail the remission of the eternal punishment of sin, but temporal punishment of sin remains. While patiently bearing sufferings and trials of all kinds and, when the day comes, serenely facing death, the Christian must strive to accept this temporal punishment of sin as a grace."

64 St. Thomas explains these consequences of sin in *ST* III, q. 86, a. 4: "In mortal sin there are two things, namely, a turning from the immutable Good, and an inordinate turning to mutable good. Accordingly, in so far as mortal sin turns away from the immutable Good, it induces a debt of eternal punishment, so that whosoever sins against the eternal Good should be punished eternally. Again, in so far as mortal sin turns inordinately to a mutable good, it gives rise to a debt of some punishment, because the disorder of guilt is not brought back to the order of justice, except by punishment: since it is just that he who has

The Council of Trent infallibly defined that the forgiveness of the eternal punishment for sin does not necessarily mean the forgiveness of the temporal punishment, which will have to be satisfied by works of penance on earth or in purgatory.[65] This penalty is finite by nature, and varies in degree according to the degree of the disorder and abuse of the creature. This temporal punishment for sins whose guilt is forgiven is either suffered during this life or, if it is not yet completed, in purgatory. Works of penance done during this life not only pay the temporal penalty but also are capable of restoring some of the good in the world that was injured by one's sin.

Venial sin only incurs a temporal punishment for sin because, by its nature, it does not involve a direct turning away from God but only a "detour," as it were, from His will. Since it involves a disordered attachment to some created satisfactions, it incurs temporal punishment for sin.[66]

Given that the purpose of the sacrament of Penance is to undo the effects of post-baptismal sin, it makes sense that the graces of the sacrament are ordered to aiding the recipient to live a life of penance through works of almsgiving, prayer, and different kinds of self-denial, such as fasting, to remove the debt of the temporal penalty for sin. Furthermore, since the sacrament configures the penitent to Christ, who did satisfaction for the sins of His Body, the sacramental graces can also help the penitent to do penance for the sins of the ecclesial Body and to heal the wounds and divisions caused by sin.

It is reasonable to think that the sacramental grace of Penance also

---

been too indulgent to his will, should suffer something against his will, for thus will equality be restored. Hence it is written (Apocalypse 18:7): 'As much as she hath glorified herself, and lived in delicacies, so much torment and sorrow give ye to her.'"

[65] See Council of Trent, Doctrine on the Sacrament of Penance (session 14), ch. 8 (DS, 1689): "The holy Synod declares that it is absolutely false and contrary to the word of God that the guilt is never forgiven by the Lord without the entire punishment also being remitted." See also canons 12 and 15, (DS, 1712 and 1715).

[66] See *ST* III, q. 86, a. 4: "If man turns inordinately to a mutable good, without turning from God, as happens in venial sins, he incurs a debt, not of eternal but of temporal punishment. Consequently when guilt is pardoned through grace, the soul ceases to be turned away from God, through being united to God by grace: so that at the same time, the debt of punishment is taken away, albeit a debt of some temporal punishment may yet remain." See also *ST* I-II, q. 87, a. 4.

strengthens habitual dispositions to cooperate with the actual graces mentioned above. These dispositions would include a strengthening of the supernatural virtue of penance to make satisfaction with Christ,[67] the gift of fear of the Lord, and the gift of knowledge, which makes one intimately and connaturally aware of the vanity of created things if they are sought as a final end.[68] Together these gifts of the Holy Spirit give a supernatural sense of sin,[69] the fostering of which is a particular mission of the sacrament of Penance.

Spiritual Consolation

Another effect of the grace proper to the sacrament of Penance is the habitual supernatural interior peace of a conscience that is reconciled with God and no longer accusing. This effect gives a taste of the "peace of God, which passes all understanding" (Phil 4:7). Pope Francis spoke about this peace in his General Audience on the sacrament of Penance of February 19, 2014:

> Forgiveness is not the fruit of our own efforts but rather a gift, it is a gift of the Holy Spirit who fills us with the wellspring of mercy and of grace that flows unceasingly from the open heart of the Crucified and Risen Christ. Secondly, it reminds us that we can truly be at peace only if we allow ourselves to be reconciled, in the Lord Jesus, with the Father and with the brethren. And we have all felt this in our hearts, when we

---

[67] See Reginald Masterson, "The Sacramental Grace of Penance," in *Proceedings of the XIII Annual Convention of the Catholic Theological Society of America*, (St. Paul, MN: 1958), 17–47, available online at https://ejournals.bc.edu/index.php/ctsa/article/view/2457/2086, accessed May 12, 2020; and Palmer, who refers to Masteron's work in "The Theology of the *Res et Sacramentum*," 120.

[68] On the gifts of fear of the Lord and knowledge, see Martinez, *The Sanctifier*, 149–54, 188–96. These gifts are part of the common effect of grace insofar as they stem from sanctifying grace and charity. However, I am proposing that the sacramental grace of the sacrament of Penance gives a special focus to them, ordering them to the strengthening of interior penance and to a new configuration with Christ who supremely satisfied for sin.

[69] John Paul II speaks about the "sense of sin" in *Reconciliatio et Paenitentia*, §18, in which he defines it as "a fine sensitivity and an acute perception of the seeds of death contained in sin, as well as a sensitivity and an acuteness of perception for identifying them in the thousand guises under which sin shows itself." See below, p. 687.

have gone to confession with a soul weighed down and with a little sadness; and when we receive Jesus' forgiveness we feel at peace, with that peace of soul which is so beautiful, and which only Jesus can give, only Him.[70]

Duration of the Sacramental Graces of Penance

How long do the sacramental graces of Penance remain active in the penitent? This is intimately related to the question posed above regarding the duration of the *res et sacramentum* of this sacrament. It is reasonable to hold that both the *res et sacramentum* of Penance and the series of actual graces that stem from that sacrament will remain alive as long as the penitent remains in a state of grace.

There is one effect of the sacrament, however, which is not ever lost. This is the forgiveness of the sins presented in confession for which one has true contrition. Past sins once forgiven are blotted out permanently, although we can fall back into sin again through new ones. If the person falls again into sin, they are only guilty of the new sin and never of the old one that was forgiven.[71]

Sacramental Grace of Anointing of the Sick

In order to specify the sacramental graces of Anointing, we have to understand the purpose for which it was instituted. Anointing of the Sick can be considered to be the completion of Penance (which it normally presupposes) in a way analogous to the way Confirmation is a completion of Baptism.[72]

The sacrament of Anointing of the Sick was instituted for the seriously ill to aid them in three closely interrelated ways. First of all,

---

[70] Pope Francis, General Audience on the Sacrament of Penance, Feb 19, 2014.

[71] See *ST* III, q. 89, a. 5, ad 1: "The very works themselves of sin are removed by Penance, so that, by God's mercy, no further stain or debt of punishment is incurred on their account."

[72] See Council of Trent, Doctrine on the Sacrament of Extreme Unction (session 14, July 15, 1563), ch. 9 (DS, 1694), which speaks of Extreme Unction as "the consummation not only of penance but also of the whole Christian life which ought to be a continual penance." See also *SCG* IV, ch. 73, no. 3, 4:284: "It is clear that this sacrament is the last, that it somehow tends to consummate the entire spiritual healing, and that in it a man is, as it were, prepared for the perception of glory. For this reason also it is named *extreme unction*."

to help prepare the seriously ill for death and entrance into glory, the sacrament serves as a further remedy against sin and its wounds or "remnants," which include the temporal penalty for sin and the disordered inclinations that sin leaves even after it has been repented of and forgiven by Penance. If Penance could not be received first, Anointing also has the effect of forgiving sins for which the person has at least imperfect contrition.[73] Since the healing of sin and its wounds is its principal purpose, Anointing of the Sick can only be received (in the Latin rite) by those who have attained the age of reason and have remnants or remains of sin that need to be purged.[74]

Secondly, they are anointed to receive spiritual (and sometimes bodily) strengthening and comfort in their trial.[75] The virtue of hope is associated in a particular way with this sacrament, for the sacrament strengthens the recipient against despair and depression caused by physical weakness, the proximity of death, and the temptations of

---

[73] When Penance could not be received first and grave sins are forgiven by Anointing of the Sick, those sins, even though forgiven, should still be confessed at the person's next confession in accordance with CIC, can. 988, §1. See Thomas Aquinas, *In IV Sent.*, d. 23, q. 1, a. 2, qla.1, trans. Mortensen, 8:557–58: "A sacrament's principal effect must be gathered from its very signification. But this sacrament is applied according to the mode of a certain medication, just as baptism is by the mode of cleansing. Now medicine is for dispelling illness; and so this sacrament is principally instituted for healing the illness of sins: so that as baptism is a certain spiritual regeneration and penance a certain spiritual revival, so also extreme unction is a certain spiritual healing or medication. Now just as physical medication presupposes physical life in the one medicated, so spiritual medication presupposes spiritual life; and so this sacrament is not given against defects by which the spiritual life is destroyed, namely, original and mortal sin, but against those defects by which a person is spiritually ill and does not have the complete strength for acts of grace or glory. And this defect is nothing other than a certain weakness and unsuitability that is left in us from actual or original sin; and against this weakness a person is strengthened by this sacrament. But because grace causes this strength, which is not compatible with sin, therefore as a result if it encounters any sin, whether mortal or venial in guilt, it takes it away, as long as no obstacle is placed on the part of the recipient, as was also said above about Eucharist and confirmation."

[74] See CIC, can. 1004: "The anointing of the sick can be administered to a member of the faithful who, having reached the use of reason, begins to be in danger due to sickness or old age."

[75] See *ST* III, q. 65, a. 1: "Extreme Unction . . . removes the remainder of sin, and prepares man for final glory."

Satan.[76] The Council of Trent explains these effects of grace:

> For the reality is the grace of the Holy Spirit, whose anointing takes away the sins, if there be any still to be expiated, and also the remains of sin; it comforts and strengthens the soul of the sick person by awakening in him great confidence in the divine mercy; supported by this, the sick bears more lightly the inconveniences and trials of his illness and resists more easily the temptations of the devil, who lies in wait for his heel [cf. Gen 3:15]; at times it also restores bodily health when it is expedient for the salvation of the soul.[77]

Third, in addition to healing the remnants of sin and aiding the faithful in the trial of illness, the sacramental graces of Anointing are also ordered to unleashing the redemptive power of the suffering endured by the recipient, so that it can be offered for the good of the Church as well as for the purification of the suffering member.[78]

In *Reconciliatio et Paenitentia*, §27, St. John Paul II speaks of the sacramental grace of Anointing as leading to a complete reconciliation with the Father, accepting suffering and eventual death as a self-offering:

> The anointing of the sick in the trial of illness and old age and especially at the Christian's final hour is a sign of definitive conversion to the Lord and of total acceptance of suffering and death as a penance for sins. And in this is accomplished supreme reconciliation with the Father.

---

[76] See *ST* III, q. 65, a. 1: "Extreme Unction [corresponds] to Hope, being ordained against venial sin."

[77] Council of Trent, Doctrine of the Sacrament of Extreme Unction (session 14, Nov 25, 1551), ch. 2 (DS, 1696).

[78] See *CCC*, §1521: "By the grace of this sacrament the sick person receives the strength and the gift of uniting himself more closely to Christ's Passion: in a certain way he is consecrated to bear fruit by configuration to the Savior's redemptive Passion. Suffering, a consequence of original sin, acquires a new meaning; it becomes a participation in the saving work of Jesus." See also *CCC*, §1532: "The special grace of the sacrament of the Anointing of the Sick has as its effects: the uniting of the sick person to the passion of Christ, for his own good and that of the whole Church; the strengthening, peace, and courage to endure in a Christian manner the sufferings of illness or old age."

The sacramental graces of Anointing are ordered to fostering this attitude modelled on Christ's interior self-offering in satisfaction for sin. This profound text explains how the sacrament of Anointing can thus "complete" the healing for sin that is worked by the sacrament of Penance. It also clarifies the sense in which Anointing can eliminate the "remnants of sin," which would be those attitudes that oppose and weaken this total self-offering to the Father.

To bring about this complete self-offering, the recipient will need to receive both actual graces, to illuminate the mind and attract the will to it, and a special strengthening of certain gifts of the Holy Spirit, such as piety, fortitude, and above all the wisdom of the Cross,[79] to be configured to Christ's self-emptying in love and abandonment.

Sacramental Grace of Matrimony

By elevating natural marriage to the supernatural level, the sacrament of Matrimony gives to the spouses the exalted mission of living their spousal and parental love as concrete and sensible signs of Christ's love for His Church. The sacramental graces of Matrimony are therefore ordered to the realization of this daunting and noble mission that exceeds human power. We can see the need of the sacramental graces of Matrimony from the disciples' comment after Jesus explained the indissolubility of marriage in Matthew 19:10: "If such is the case of a man with his wife, it is not expedient to marry." Jesus goes on to explain, after the encounter with the rich young man, "With men this is impossible, but with God all things are possible" (Matt 19:26). Although this saying directly refers to His teaching on evangelical poverty, it applies well to the previous scene of the discussion on the indissolubility of marriage.

A more direct reference to the graces of Matrimony is in Ephesians 5:25–33, in which St. Paul exhorts husbands to love their wives "as Christ loved the church and gave himself up for her" (Eph 5:25). He goes on to say that Christian marriage "is a great mystery, and I mean in reference to Christ and the church" (Eph 5:32). In order for spouses to love one another with Christ's own love, they need, in addition to an increase of the virtue of charity, particular graces to aid the exercise of charity in their concrete circumstances.

---

[79] On the relationship between wisdom and the Cross, see 1 Cor 1:18–2:2; Feingold, *The Mystery of Israel and the Church*, 2:197–99.

Many magisterial texts speak of the graces given to the spouses through Holy Matrimony. The Council of Trent demonstrates that Matrimony is a sacrament by pointing to the grace that it confers on the spouses to love one another as Christ has loved His Bride, according to Ephesians 5:25–32:

> But the grace which was to perfect that natural love, and confirm the indissoluble union, and sanctify those united in marriage, Christ Himself, institutor and perfector of the venerable sacraments, merited for us by His passion. The Apostle Paul intimates this, when he says: "Men, love your wives as Christ loved the Church, and delivered himself up for it" [Eph. 5:25], directly adding: "This is a great Sacrament; but I speak in Christ and in the Church" [Eph. 5:32].[80]

Matrimony thus strengthens the ability of the spouses to love one another and their children with a supernatural love of charity, of which Christ is the supreme model as well as the meritorious and efficient cause. The Council of Trent does not distinguish between sanctifying and actual grace here, but it is reasonable to infer that the sacrament would confer both kinds of grace to perfect the spouses in sacrificial love both habitually and in their concrete circumstances.

In his encyclical on this sacrament, *Casti Connubii* from 1930, Pius XI explains the sacramental graces of Matrimony in greater depth, as seen earlier in this chapter. He makes it clear that the graces of Matrimony last throughout the life of the marriage and include not only sanctifying grace but also particular gifts of the Holy Spirit tailored to the sanctification of the married state, and the assistance of actual graces for all the particular needs of that state.[81]

The Second Vatican Council, in *Gaudium et Spes*, §48, speaks of the sacramental marital bond as a consecration of the spouses that calls forth graces to "strengthen them in their sublime office of being a father or a mother." This strengthening enables them to practice faith, hope, and charity in the circumstances of ordinary family life; it helps them to make their family into an authentic domestic church in which all the members of the family live their faith; and it also aids

---

[80] Council of Trent, Doctrine Concerning the Sacrament of Matrimony (session 24, Nov 11, 1563; DS, 1799).
[81] Pius XI, *Casti Connubii* (1930), §40.

the parents to accomplish their mission as the primary educators of their children.[82]

Among the various gifts of the Holy Spirit pertinent to the needs of the married, St. John Paul emphasizes the importance of the gift of piety for sanctifying the conjugal life of spouses. This gives them a supernatural attentiveness and reverence for the mystery of God's plan for human sexuality rooted in creation and redemption.[83]

The sacramental graces of marriage will be tailored to the identity, needs, difficulties, and mission of the spouses in their concrete situation. Sacramental grace should not be thought of as something abstract and generic. On the contrary, it enables the individuality and particular mission of the recipient to blossom and flourish. The sacramental graces of Matrimony will give to each couple an ability to live out a particular charism of marriage proper to them and different from others, which will be a particular way of manifesting the union of Christ and His Bride.

Sacramental Grace of Holy Orders

Those who receive Holy Orders are given a sacramental character that is the foundation or invisible stamp that calls forth a long chain of actual graces necessary to adequately fulfill the mission of deacon, priest, or bishop through the course of their lives. These actual graces,

---

[82] See *Gaudium et Spes*, §48: "By virtue of this sacrament, as spouses fulfil their conjugal and family obligation, they are penetrated with the spirit of Christ, which suffuses their whole lives with faith, hope and charity. Thus they increasingly advance the perfection of their own personalities, as well as their mutual sanctification, and hence contribute jointly to the glory of God. As a result, with their parents leading the way by example and family prayer, children and indeed everyone gathered around the family hearth will find a readier path to human maturity, salvation and holiness. Graced with the dignity and office of fatherhood and motherhood, parents will energetically acquit themselves of a duty which devolves primarily on them, namely education and especially religious education."

[83] See John Paul II, *Man and Woman He Created Them*, 54:4–57:6, pp. 344–55. See esp. 57:2, pp. 352–53: "Among these gifts, known . . . as the seven gifts of the Holy Spirit (see Isa 11:2), the one most congenial to the virtue of purity seems to be *the gift of 'piety.'* . . . If purity disposes man to 'keep his own body with holiness and reverence,' as we read in 1 Thessalonians 4:3–5, piety as a gift of the Holy Spirit seems to serve purity in a particular way by making the human subject sensitive to the dignity that belongs to the human body in virtue of the mystery of creation and of redemption."

however, also depend on the cooperation of the subject, and thus they can be lost through infidelity, or they can increase through prayer, fidelity, and zeal. These actual graces foster and stimulate the exercise of heroic pastoral charity and prudence by which the deacon, priest, or bishop is made to conform more and more closely to Christ, the Good Shepherd, to whom he is configured by the sacramental character of Holy Orders.[84]

The Second Vatican Council, in its Decree on the Ministry and Life of Priests *Presbyterorum Ordinis*, §12 refers to the sacramental grace of the priesthood:

> Since, therefore, every priest in his own fashion acts in place of Christ himself, he is enriched by a special grace, so that, as he serves the flock committed to him and the entire People of God, he may the better grow in the grace of him whose tasks he performs, because to the weakness of our flesh there is brought the holiness of him who for us was made a High Priest.

This special grace received at ordination is a dynamic gift meant to grow continually. It is ordered to service of the local and universal Church, and configures him in his weakness with Christ, "whose tasks he performs."

Sacramental Graces of Holy Orders and the Gifts of the Holy Spirit

The sacramental graces of Holy Orders can be seen to orient the seven gifts of the Holy Spirit in a particular way to act in sacrificial service to the Body of Christ by administering the sacraments, offering the Sacrifice of the Mass, and leading the local church or parish in the pursuit of holiness, charity, and the teaching of the faith. Because of its connection with the mission of governance and spiritual direction, the sacramental graces of Holy Orders are particularly connected with

---

[84] See R. Garrigou-Lagrange, *The Priest in Union with Christ*, trans. G. W. Shelton (Westminster, MD: Newman Press, 1952), 22: "The grace of Holy Orders is conferred that the priest may fulfill his sacred duties—the act of consecration, sacramental absolution, preaching, spiritual direction—with ever-increasing holiness: and so we speak of priestly love and priestly prudence."

the Spirit's gift of counsel that strengthens the virtue of prudence by discernment of divine guidance.[85]

The sacramental grace of Holy Orders also strengthens spiritual paternity and fosters the spiritual bond with those entrusted to their headship. This can be understood in connection with the gift of piety, which strengthens the intimate sense of divine filiation in the recipient. The gifts of piety and fear of the Lord are ordered to helping the priest to administer the sacraments with a filial reverence from the Holy Spirit. This intimate and supernatural filial reverence also is ordered to exercising a spiritual paternity with regard to the faithful entrusted to their headship and ministry. The gifts of wisdom, understanding, and knowledge are also supremely needed to teach the mysteries of the Gospel.

Above all, the graces of Holy Orders concern the habit and exercise of pastoral charity and the fostering of unity in the Body of Christ under the guidance of the gift of wisdom.[86] In *Pastores Dabo Vobis*, St. John Paul II underlines the relational aspect of the sacramental grace of the priesthood:

> In this way the fundamentally "relational" dimension of priestly identity can be understood. Through the priesthood which arises from the depths of the ineffable mystery of God, that is, from the love of the Father, the grace of Jesus Christ and the Holy Spirit's gift of unity, the priest sacramentally enters into communion with the bishop and with other priests in order to serve the People of God who are the Church and to draw all mankind to Christ in accordance with the Lord's prayer: "Holy Father, keep them in your

---

[85] See *Presbyterorum Ordinis*, §15: "Among the virtues that priests must possess for their sacred ministry none is so important as a frame of mind and soul whereby they are always ready to know and do the will of him who sent them and not their own will. The divine task that they are called by the Holy Spirit to fulfill surpasses all human wisdom and human ability. 'God chooses the weak things of the world to confound the strong' (1 Cor 1:27). . . . Filled with the Holy Spirit, he is guided by him who desires the salvation of all men. He understands this desire of God and follows it in the ordinary circumstances of his everyday life. With humble disposition he waits upon all whom God has sent him to serve in the work assigned to him and in the multiple experiences of his life."

[86] See *ST* III, q. 65, a. 1, in which St. Thomas says that Holy Orders was instituted as a remedy "against divisions in the community" caused by sin.

name, which you have given me, that they may be one, even as we are one . . . so that the world may believe that you have sent me" (Jn. 17:11, 21).[87]

The bishop, who has been given the fullness of the priesthood, will receive, if he cooperates with grace, special gifts of the Holy Spirit to teach, sanctify, and govern the local church. In particular the sacrament will impart the gift of wisdom for preaching, teaching, and guiding his flock.[88] St. Paul refers to the grace proper to the episcopate in 1 Timothy 4:14 and 2 Timothy 1:6. In 1 Timothy 4:14–16, Timothy is exhorted:

> Do not neglect the gift you have, which was given you by prophetic utterance when the elders laid their hands upon you. Practice these duties, devote yourself to them, so that all may see your progress. Take heed to yourself and to your teaching; hold to that, for by so doing you will save both yourself and your hearers.

The gift received through the laying on of hands most probably refers to the sacramental grace of Holy Orders to be a successor of the Apostles. This gift of grace is particularly connected with teaching and the ministry of the Word.

The sacramental graces of the order of deacons flow from the special configuration of the deacon with Christ the servant, who "came not to be served but to serve." As Joseph Lécuyer states: "If the sacrament of Order in its higher degrees makes men representatives, signs or sacraments of Christ the priest, the diaconate will be ordained to represent Christ vividly in the Church in the mission which he attributes to himself of serving His Father and serving men."[89]

---

[87] John Paul II, Post-Synodal Apostolic Exhortation on the Formation of Priests in the Circumstances of the Present Day *Pastores Dabo Vobis* (Mar 15, 1992) , §12.

[88] For St. Thomas on the sacramental graces of the episcopal state, which he treated above all in his commentary on the Pastoral Epistles, see Michael G. Sirilla, *The Ideal Bishop: St. Thomas Aquinas's Commentaries on the Pastoral Epistles* (Washington, DC: Catholic University of America Press, 2017).

[89] Joseph Lécuyer, *What Is a Priest?*, trans. Lancelot Sheppard (New York: Hawthorn Books, 1959), 58.

3. CONDITIONS FOR FRUITFULNESS OF THE SACRAMENTS

We have seen that not every valid reception of a sacrament is fruitful in conferring the sacramental graces of the sacrament. It was partly for this reason that theologians such as St. Augustine distinguished sacramental character from sacramental grace. For the reception of sacraments by adults to be fruitful in producing both the common and proper effects of grace, the recipients must have two other conditions in addition to the conditions for validity mentioned in chapters 5–6 above. If they are at the age of reason, they must make an act of faith and contrition for past grave sins of which they are aware, which includes the firm purpose of amendment to avoid grave sin in the future. Both the act of faith and repentance are included in the rite of Baptism: faith is expressed in the profession of the Creed, and contrition and a resolution to avoid sin is expressed in the renunciation of sin and the snares of the devil.[90]

Necessity of Faith

Faith is necessary for the recipient at the age of reason because the sacraments are signs that are received and grasped only by faith.[91] One must trust the divine physician and desire healing before one can rightly receive the medicine he prescribes. Faith is the foundation of hope and love, through which contrition is made perfect. We can see the necessity of faith by analogy with the miracles of Christ, in which He asked for faith and healed those who manifested it.[92]

Jesus strongly emphasizes the need for faith in order to receive

---

[90] On the role of faith and repentance in Baptism, see Van Roo, *The Christian Sacrament*, 4–5, 12–13; on the testimony of the early Church, see Ferguson, "Sacraments in the Pre-Nicene Period," in *OHST*, 127.

[91] See Sean Fagan, "Sacramental Spirituality," in *Sacraments: The Gestures of Christ*, ed. O'Callaghan, 161: "The sacraments are first and foremost sacraments of the faith. . . . Each sacrament invokes faith, is defined and measured by faith. . . . The sacraments properly received with full awareness of their import are the most outstanding acts of faith of which we are capable. . . . This is because each sacrament in its own way sums up the whole supernatural economy of God's dealing with his children."

[92] See, for example, Matt 8:13: "To the centurion Jesus said, 'Go; let it be done for you as you have believed'"; and Matt 15:28: "O woman, great is your faith! Let it be done for you as you desire."

the sacramental gift of the Eucharist in the Bread of Life discourse. He begins the discourse in John 6:29 by saying that "This is the work of God, that you believe in him whom he has sent." The theme of faith continues to build as Jesus increases the difficulty of what the disciples are to believe by speaking of eating His flesh and drinking His blood. The climax comes as many leave for lack of faith, whereas Simon Peter says: "You have the words of eternal life; and we have believed, and have come to know, that you are the Holy One of God" (John 6:68–69).

To receive supernatural gifts, it is necessary for those who are at the age of reason to have supernatural faith in the Giver of the gifts and in the immensity of what He gives us in the sacraments above the limits of nature.[93] Hebrews 11:6 states this principle: "Without faith it is impossible to please him. For whoever would draw near to God must believe that he exists and that he rewards those who seek him." An act of divine faith therefore is a necessary condition for adults to receive sanctifying grace through Baptism[94] and the other sacraments. St. Augustine eloquently states: "Whence is this power of water of such magnitude that it touches the body and yet washes clean the heart, except from the word's effecting it, not because it is said, but because it is believed?"[95]

---

[93] The Protestant tradition has the merit of highlighting the fundamental importance of faith in receiving the sacraments. See Root, "Luther and Calvin on the Role of Faith in the Sacraments," 1065–84. For the difference between Luther and Calvin with regard to faith in the sacramental promise, see Cary, "Why Luther Is Not Quite Protestant," 447–86.

[94] See *ST* III, q. 68, a. 8: "Baptism produces a twofold effect in the soul, viz., the character and grace. Therefore in two ways may a thing be necessary for Baptism. First, as something without which grace, which is the ultimate effect of the sacrament, cannot be had. And thus right faith is necessary for Baptism, because, as it appears from Rom. 3:22, 'the justice of God is by faith of Jesus Christ.' Secondly, something is required of necessity for Baptism, because without it the baptismal character cannot be imprinted. And thus right faith is not necessary in the one baptized any more than in the one who baptizes: provided the other conditions are fulfilled which are essential to the sacrament. For the sacrament is not perfected by the righteousness of the minister or of the recipient of Baptism, but by the power of God."

[95] Augustine, Tractate 80.11.2 on John 15.3, in *Tractates on the Gospel of John 55–111*, 117.

Necessity of Repentance

In addition to requiring faith, Jesus also exhorted his listeners to repentance. Mark 1:15 summarizes Jesus's preaching with the phrase: "Repent, and believe in the gospel." On Pentecost, Peter exhorted his listeners to "repent, and be baptized" (Acts 2:38).

The *Catechism of the Council of Trent* speaks very strongly on the need for repentance before Baptism:

> Another requisite is repentance for past sins, together with a firm purpose of amendment for the future. If anyone deliberately indulging some sinful habit should dare to approach the baptismal font, he should definitely be refused; for what can more obstruct the grace of Baptism than an obdurate impenitence? Baptism should be sought in order to put on Christ and to be united to him (see Gal 3:27). It is therefore obvious that he who intends to remain in sin should be denied access to it. If we recall that nothing pertaining to Christ and his Church is meant to be in vain, then that Baptism which can produce no sanctifying grace, because the recipient chooses to live in sin, is indeed in vain and must not be allowed to take place.[96]

If an adult receives Baptism in a state of mortal sin, without contrition or a firm resolution to avoid such sin in the future, then the grace of Baptism will be blocked.[97] Character will be imprinted and the sacrament will be valid, however, as long as the person intends to receive the sacrament. The same applies to a case in which Baptism is received without faith (but with the intention to receive the sacrament). It will be valid but unfruitful.

What is a person to do in such a case? Baptism cannot be

---

[96] *CCT*, part 2, ch. 1, §40, pp. 182–83.

[97] See Augustine, *Baptism* 1.12.18, trans. Boniface Ramsey, 408: "A person can truly be baptized with Christ's baptism and yet . . . his heart, persisting in malice or sacrilege, does not allow the abolition of his sins to be accomplished." See also *ST* III, q. 69, a. 9: "As Damascene says (*De Fide Orthod.* 2), 'God does not compel man to be righteous.' Consequently in order that a man be justified by Baptism, his will must needs embrace both Baptism and the baptismal effect. Now, a man is said to be insincere by reason of his will being in contradiction with either Baptism or its effect."

repeated, nor is there any need for that. Baptismal character makes it possible for the subject to receive the sacrament of Penance. If a person received Baptism unfruitfully because of a lack of contrition or firm resolution to avoid sin and later repents and receives the sacrament of Penance, then the grace of Baptism will be received at that time through the abiding character of Baptism. The instrumental power of baptismal character to infuse grace, which had been blocked by the presence of grave sin, produces its effect once the obstacle is removed by Penance. As seen in chapter 7 above, St. Augustine held, against the Donatists, that there could be valid but unfruitful reception of Baptism by adults in a heretical or schismatic sect.[98]

St. Thomas discusses the case of Baptism of unrepentant sinners in *ST* III, q. 68, a. 4. He asks whether sinners should be baptized. It is necessary to make a distinction, he replies, between two types of sinners: repentant and unrepentant. Repentant sinners, obviously, should be baptized, for the sacrament was instituted to save sinners. But what about unrepentant sinners? They should not be baptized until they manifest a resolution to remove themselves from a state of mortal sin. No one can be washed from the guilt of sin unless they interiorly renounce the sin itself. Otherwise there will be a contradiction between the sacramental sign and the reality of the heart.

The case is similar with regard to other sacraments. The sacrament of Anointing is not to be conferred, according to canon 1007, to those "who persevere obstinately in manifest grave sin." However, in those who have lost consciousness, if there was any probable indication of repentance, Anointing can be given, as long as scandal is avoided.[99] For the valid and fruitful reception of the sacrament of Penance, an act of (at least imperfect) contrition must be made that extends to all mortal sin not yet absolved of which the person is

---

[98] Augustine, Sermon 8 (Denis), "Baptism," in *Commentary on the Lord's Sermon on the Mount*, 333–34: "See, then, how it can come to pass that a man may have the baptism of Christ and still not have the faith or the love of Christ; how it is that he may have the sacrament of holiness and still not be reckoned in the lot of the holy. With regard to the mere sacrament itself, it makes no difference whether someone receives the baptism of Christ where the unity of Christ is not. For, in the case of desertion from the Church by someone who had been baptized in the Church, the deserter will be deprived of the holiness of the life, but he will not lose the sacramental character."

[99] See William H. Woestman, *Sacraments: Initiation, Penance, Anointing of the Sick: Commentary on Canons 840–1007* (Ottawa: Faculty of Canon Law, Saint Paul University, 1992), 320.

aware. The absence of such contrition renders the sacrament not only unfruitful but also invalid.[100] This is because at least imperfect interior contrition is necessary matter for the sacrament, without which it cannot exist.[101] Penance, therefore, is the one sacrament that can never be valid but unfruitful.

To receive the Eucharist fruitfully, one must be in a state of grace. Furthermore, one must also have received sacramental absolution for mortal sins of which one is aware, unless there is no opportunity to confess and there is a grave reason for receiving, in which case "the person is to remember the obligation to make an act of perfect contrition which includes the resolution of confessing as soon as possible."[102] As will be seen in chapter 15 below, the act of perfect contrition with the intention of sacramentally confessing anticipates the principal effect of Penance, which is the forgiveness of mortal sin and the restoration of the state of grace. Grave reason to celebrate Mass (and thus to receive Communion as celebrant) would be the duty of pastors to their faithful. The lay faithful do not ordinarily have grave reason to receive Communion, because its principal effect can be gained by a spiritual communion after an act of perfect contrition.[103]

The presence of venial sin to which one is still attached does not completely block the increase of sanctifying grace and charity, but, insofar as the mind is distracted from devotion by the venial sin, it may block another effect of the Eucharist, which is an infusion of spiritual

---

[100] See CIC, can. 987: "To receive the salvific remedy of the sacrament of penance, a member of the Christian faithful must be disposed in such a way that, rejecting sins committed and having a purpose of amendment, the person is turned back to God."

[101] See Severino González Rivas, S.J., "On Penance," in *Sacrae Theologiae Summa*, 4A:510.

[102] CIC, can. 916: "A person who is conscious of grave sin is not to celebrate Mass or receive the body of the Lord without previous sacramental confession unless there is a grave reason and there is no opportunity to confess; in this case the person is to remember the obligation to make an act of perfect contrition which includes the resolution of confessing as soon as possible."

[103] See the commentary on can. 916 by Davide Mussone in *L'Eucaristia nel Codice di Diritto Canonico: Commento ai cann. 897–958* (Città del Vaticano: Libreria Editrice Vaticana, 2002), 84–87. The content of can. 916 is based on the Council of Trent, Decree on the Sacrament of the Eucharist (session 13, Oct 11, 1551), ch. 7 (DS, 1646–47).

joy and interior consolation.[104]

To ensure the fruitful reception of the sacrament of Matrimony, canon 1065, §2 states that "spouses are urged especially to approach the sacraments of Penance and of the Most Holy Eucharist."

Degrees of Fruitfulness

The dispositions of faith and repentance are necessary not only as minimum conditions for the fruitfulness of the sacraments. The intensity of repentance, faith, hope, and especially charity in the recipient determines the degree of grace given by the sacraments. This is an important consequence of the principle that everything is received according to the mode of the receiver. Thus we should think that no two adults receiving the same sacrament receive the same graces, for each will have a different disposition of desire, contrition, faith, hope, and charity.

This principle applies to the disposition of the recipient not only at the moment of the reception of the sacrament but also as long as one possesses the *res et sacramentum*, which is the foundation of the series of sacramental graces given over time. Thus the sacramental graces of Baptism, Confirmation, Matrimony, and Holy Orders will be given in accordance with the variation of the dispositions of the subjects over time. The sacraments are dynamic seeds of growth whose degree of fruitfulness continually depends on the soil of personal disposition and desire. This accords with Jesus's parable of the sower and His words in Matthew 25:29: "To every one who has will more be given, and he will have abundance."

STUDY QUESTIONS

1. What is meant by "sacraments of the living" and "sacraments of the dead"?
2. Why is it fitting that there be a sacramental grace proper to each sacrament, distinct from the common effect of sanctifying grace and the other gifts that always accompany it?
3. What does the sacramental grace proper to a particular sacrament consist in?

---

[104] See *ST* III, q. 79, a. 8.

4. How can a sacrament give sacramental graces long after the sacrament has been received, as in the cases of Baptism, Confirmation, Holy Orders, and Matrimony? Can this also happen with Anointing of the Sick?
5. What is the relation between sacramental grace and the *res et sacramentum* of a particular sacrament?
6. Explain what sacramental graces are proper to each of the seven sacraments. Connect these sacramental graces with the purpose of each sacrament, its sacramental sign, and its *res et sacramentum*.
7. How does the disposition of the recipient affect the reception of sacramental graces?
8. What are the conditions for an adult to receive a sacrament fruitfully?

Suggestions for Further Reading

Everett, Lawrence P. *The Nature of Sacramental Grace*. Washington, DC: Catholic University of America Press, 1948.

Feingold, Lawrence. *The Eucharist: Mystery of Presence, Sacrifice, and Communion*. Steubenville, OH: Emmaus Academic, 2018. Pp. 487–522.

Masterson, Robert Reginald. "Sacramental Graces: Modes of Sanctifying Grace." *The Thomist* 18 (1955): 311–72.

Miralles, Antonio. *I sacramenti cristiani: trattato generale*. 2nd edition. Rome: Apollinare studi, 2008. Pp. 250–61.

Nicolas, J.-H. "La grâce sacramentelle." *Revue thomiste* 61 (1961): 165–92; 522–38.

Nutt, Roger. *General Principles of Sacramental Theology*. Washington, DC: Catholic University of America Press, 2017. Pp. 138–50.

Shea, George. "A Survey of the Theology of Sacramental Grace." *Proceedings of the CTSA* (1953): 81–130.

Schleck, Charles A. "St. Thomas on the Nature of Sacramental Grace." *The Thomist* 18 (1955): 1–30; 242–78.

Tanquerey, Adolphe. *The Spiritual Life: A Treatise on Ascetical and Mystical Theology*. 2nd edition. Translated by Herman Branderis. Rockford, IL: TAN Books, 2000. Pp. 130–50.

PART FOUR

THE INSTRUMENTAL CAUSALITY OF THE SACRAMENTS

CHAPTER ELEVEN

Causality of the Sacraments as Instruments of Christ: The Theological Tradition to Aquinas

The Word became flesh in order to use His humanity for the salvation of all men of all times and places. However, since Jesus lived as a man on this earth for a short time in one tiny part of the world, He desired to devise some way to make Himself present as man to succeeding ages throughout the world. Even though He has ascended into Heaven and left us here below in the darkness of faith, with the corresponding possibility of merit, He still wishes us to encounter His glorious humanity and its salvific power to communicate the Holy Spirit. The sacraments are the divinely appointed means for this encounter with Christ and His Spirit in faith. They sanctify us by providing a mysterious—that is, sacramental—contact with Christ's humanity even after He has physically ascended into heaven. The sacraments allow us today to hear and be transformed by Christ's words of power, as when He said to the paralytic in Capernaum, "Child, your sins are forgiven" (Mark 2:5), or as He said to the Apostles on Easter Sunday: "Receive the Holy Spirit" (John 20:22). The sacraments are extensions or channels of Christ's efficacious words, capable of bridging the gaps of time and space to make contact with the faithful throughout the life of the Church.

We have seen that the sacraments of the New Covenant have a mysterious capacity to cause the grace they signify. But how can sensible signs cause grace? Since sanctifying grace is a participation in the divine nature, grace can only be produced in a creature through the omnipotence of God. How then are the sacraments true causes of grace? This problem has vexed theologians through the ages, and a variety of conflicting solutions have been offered, which, I will argue, are not equally successful in maintaining the robust sense of sacramental causality that we find in the sources of Revelation.

THE NEW TESTAMENT ON THE EFFICACY OF THE SACRAMENTS

Sacramental efficacy is proclaimed very clearly in the Gospels with regard to Baptism, the Eucharist, and Penance. At the beginning of the Gospel of Mark, John the Baptist distinguishes his baptism from that of Jesus by the fact that he baptizes in water but Jesus will baptize with the Holy Spirit.[1] The interior efficacy of the sacraments is similarly expressed by John the Baptist in John 1:33: "He who sent me to baptize with water said to me, 'He on whom you see the Spirit descend and remain, this is he who baptizes with the Holy Spirit.'" Christ, who baptizes with the Holy Spirit, is the principal minister in every Christian Baptism, and the same is true of the other sacraments. In his dialogue with Nicodemus in John 3:5–6, Jesus clearly reveals the spiritual power of Baptism and the gift of the Spirit to accomplish a spiritual rebirth: "Truly, truly, I say to you, unless one is born of water and the Spirit, he cannot enter the kingdom of God. That which is born of the flesh is flesh, and that which is born of the Spirit is spirit."

The most powerful witness to sacramental efficacy is in the Bread of Life discourse, where Jesus says: "I am the living bread which came down from heaven; if any one eats of this bread, he will live for ever; and the bread which I shall give for the life of the world is my flesh" (John 6:51). The Eucharist, unlike the manna received by the Israelites in the desert, has the power to give eternal life because it feeds us with the flesh and blood of the Word Incarnate.

With regard to Penance, Jesus's words to the Eleven on Easter Sunday in John 20:22–23 show the efficacy of priestly absolution: "Receive the Holy Spirit. If you forgive the sins of any, they are forgiven; if you retain the sins of any, they are retained."

Sacramental efficacy is also clear in the rest of the New Testament. For example, in Romans 6:3–4, St. Paul says that baptismal immersion symbolically represents Christ's death and Resurrection, and also

---

[1] Mark 1:8: "I have baptized you with water; but he will baptize you with the Holy Spirit."

accomplishes a real participation in what it symbolizes, which is that the baptized die to sin and rise to new life in Christ: "Do you not know that all of us who have been baptized into Christ Jesus were baptized into his death? We were buried therefore with him by baptism into death, so that as Christ was raised from the dead by the glory of the Father, we too might walk in newness of life." Here Paul indicates that Baptism effects a real participation in the Paschal mystery.

The efficacy of Baptism is also indicated in Ephesians 5:25–26: "Christ loved the church and gave himself up for her, that he might sanctify her, having cleansed her by the washing of water with the word." The "washing of water with the word" is an apt description of Baptism, which works a real spiritual cleansing of Christ's Bride, the Church. Christ cleanses the soul through the sacrament, composed of the matter of water and the word of the baptismal formula. A few verses later, in Ephesians 5:32, St. Paul speaks of marriage as a "great mystery" insofar as it is a sacred sign of "Christ and the church."

With regard to the Eucharist, St. Paul says that it represents the unity of the body of Christ and also brings about that unity: "The bread which we break, is it not a participation in the body of Christ? Because there is one bread, we who are many are one body, for we all partake of the one bread" (1 Cor 10:16–17).

The power of the laying on of hands to communicate grace in priestly ordination is indicated in 2 Timothy 1:6, where St. Paul exhorts Timothy: "I remind you to rekindle the gift of God that is within you through the laying on of my hands."

The power of the laying on of hands to communicate the Holy Spirit in Confirmation is indicated in Acts 8:17 when Peter and John go to the Samaritans baptized by Philip: "Then they laid their hands on them and they received the Holy Spirit." The implication is that the sacramental laying on of hands causes the communication of the Spirit. We see this again in Acts 19:6: "When Paul had laid his hands upon them, the Holy Spirit came on them."

The salvific power of Anointing of the Sick is indicated in James 5:14–15: "Is any among you sick? Let him call for the elders of the church, and let them pray over him, anointing him with oil in the name of the Lord; and the prayer of faith will save the sick man, and the Lord will raise him up; and if he has committed sins, he will be forgiven." The sacramental "prayer of faith" is put forward as the cause of the salvation and forgiveness that comes to the recipient.

The common thread in all these texts is the power of the sacramental word to communicate a share in the salvific life of Christ and the power of His Spirit. As Jesus's word was efficacious in working miracles, so His sacramental word is efficacious in communicating a share in His life and His Spirit, in forgiving and overcoming sin, and thereby in building up the unity of the Church.

SACRAMENTAL EFFICACY ACCORDING TO THE FATHERS OF THE CHURCH

The Fathers of the Church received this doctrine on the salvific efficacy of the sacraments from the New Testament and the oral Tradition. They manifest their faith in this efficacy, marveling at it and pointing to the divine power that works through the sacraments.

The Eucharist and Baptism are the principal subjects of their reflections on sacramental power. There are many testimonies on the efficacy of Christ's words in the Mass to produce both His Body and Blood, and to make us sharers in His eternal life.[2] St. Ignatius of Antioch, around AD 107, speaks of the Eucharist as the "medicine of immortality,"[3] which implies that it is an instrumental cause of eternal life, as medicine is of health.

St. Justin Martyr, in the middle of the second century, writes: "We have been taught that the food eucharistized through the word of prayer that is from Him, from which our blood and flesh are nourished by transformation, is the flesh and blood of that Jesus who became incarnate."[4] St. Justin speaks of the "word of prayer"—the sacramental word—as having power to transform the elements.

Tertullian

At the beginning of the third century, Tertullian speaks in a similar way of the efficacy of the sacraments of Christian initiation. What is done to the flesh—sacramental washing, anointing and feeding—

---

[2] See Feingold, *The Eucharist*, 129–75.

[3] *Letter to the Ephesians* 20, in *The Apostolic Fathers: Greek Texts and English Translations*, trans. Michael W. Holmes, 3rd ed. (Grand Rapids, MI: Baker Academic, 2007), 199: "Gather together . . . breaking one bread, which is the medicine of immortality, the antidote we take in order not to die but to live forever in Jesus Christ."

[4] *First Apology* 66, trans. Barnard, pp. 70–71.

works a spiritual effect on the soul:

> The flesh is washed that the soul may be made spotless: the flesh is anointed that the soul may be consecrated: the flesh is signed [with the cross] that the soul too may be protected: the flesh is overshadowed by the imposition of the hand that the soul may be illumined by the Spirit: the flesh feeds on the Body and Blood of Christ so that the soul also may be replete with God.[5]

To help illustrate their efficacy, Tertullian compares the action of sacraments to the production of music from the mechanical action of an ancient water organ (hydraulis). As a musician uses the passage of air over water to produce musical notes and the spiritual effect of music, the divine artist makes use of physical things such as water and oil to produce the spiritual effect of sanctification, the forgiveness of sins, and the giving of the Spirit: "If human ingenuity can make a stream of air descend upon the water, and if the hands of an artist can animate these two associated elements with another stream of such beauty, then why cannot God modulate with holy hands the sublime melody of the Spirit upon the human person?"[6]

St. Ambrose

In his *Sermons on the Sacraments* addressed to the neophytes, St. Ambrose gives a magnificent explanation of the power of Christ's words in the sacraments to effect what they represent. With regard to Baptism he says:

---

[5] Tertullian, *De resurrectione carnis* 8.3 (CCL 2.931), trans. Ernest Evans, *Tertullian's Treatise on the Resurrection* (London: SPCK, 1960), 25. This text is quoted by Paul VI in his Apostolic Constitution *Divinae Consortium Naturae*, in *Rites*, 1:472. See also Tertullian, *De baptismo* 7–8, trans. Ernest Evans (London: SPCK, 1964), 17–19: "The unction flows upon the flesh, but turns to spiritual profit, just as in the baptism itself there is an act that touches the flesh, that we are immersed in water, but a spiritual effect, that we are set free from sins. Next follows the imposition of the hand in benediction, inviting and welcoming the Holy Spirit. . . . At this point that most holy Spirit willingly comes down from the Father upon bodies cleansed and blessed."

[6] Tertullian, *De baptismo* 7–8, in *Worship in the Early Church*, L. J. Johnson, ed., 1:123. Tertullian here is referring to a hydraulic organ, invented in the third century BC.

The priest comes, he says a prayer at the font, he invokes the name of the Father, the presence of the Son and the Holy Spirit; he uses heavenly words. They are heavenly words, because they are the words of Christ which say that we must baptize in the name of the Father and of the Son and of the Holy Spirit. If at a word of men, at the invocation by one of the saints, the Trinity was present [symbolized by the fire from heaven brought down by the prayer of Elijah in 1 Kings 18:36–38], how much more efficacious this presence is where the eternal word is working![7]

With regard to the Eucharist, he explains:

Perhaps you say: "The bread I have here is ordinary bread." Yes, before the sacramental words are uttered this bread is nothing but bread. But at the consecration this bread becomes the body of Christ. Let us reason this out. How can something which is bread be the body of Christ? Well, by what words is the consecration effected, and whose words are they? The words of the Lord Jesus. All that is said before are the words of the priest: praise is offered to God, the prayer is offered up, petitions are made for the people, for kings, for all others. But when the moment comes for bringing the most holy sacrament into being, the priest does not use his own words any longer: he uses the words of Christ. Therefore, it is Christ's word that brings this sacrament into being.[8]

He then emphasizes the omnipotent power of Christ's words through which the world was made: "What is this word of Christ? It is the word by which all things were made. . . . Before the consecration it was not the body of Christ, but after the consecration I tell you that it is now the body of Christ. He spoke and it was made."[9]

---

[7] Ambrose, *Sermons on the Sacraments* (*De sacramentis*) 2.14, in Yarnold, *Awe-Inspiring Rites of Initiation*, 114–15.

[8] Ambrose, *Sermons on the Sacraments*, 4.14, in Yarnold, *Awe-Inspiring Rites of Initiation*, 132–33.

[9] Ambrose, *Sermons on the Sacraments*, 4.15–16, in Yarnold, *Awe-Inspiring Rites of Initiation*, 133.

He then goes on to reiterate the same point, quoting the institution narrative:

> The day before he suffered, it says, he took bread in his holy hands. Before it is consecrated, it is bread; but when the words of Christ have been uttered over it, it is the body of Christ. Listen to what he says then: "Take and eat of this, all of you, for this is my body." And the chalice, before the words of Christ, is full of wine and water. But when the words of Christ have done their work, it becomes the blood of Christ which has redeemed the people.[10]

St. Ambrose's phrase, "when the words of Christ have *done their work*"[11] is a marvelous expression of sacramental efficacy. This expression stands at the root of the later scholastic phrase, *ex opere operato*. The words of institution in the Eucharist realize what they represent because the words are Christ's and are said by the priest in the person of Christ, and thus Christ gives them the power as His instruments to effect what He wishes. Something analogous happens in the other sacraments. The words spoken by the minister are given instrumental power by Christ, who is the principal agent in all sacramental action.

St. Cyril of Jerusalem

In his sermons to the neophytes of Jerusalem, St. Cyril, like St. Ambrose who was his contemporary, also stresses the power of the sacramental words. While explaining the rite of Chrismation (Confirmation as celebrated in the Eastern rite), he compares the consecrated oil to the consecrated bread and wine in the Eucharist:

> Be sure not to regard the chrism merely as ointment. Just as the bread of the Eucharist after the invocation of the Holy Spirit is no longer just bread, but the body of Christ, so the holy chrism after the invocation is no longer ordinary oint-

---

[10] Ambrose, *Sermons on the Sacraments*, 4.23, in Yarnold, *Awe-Inspiring Rites of Initiation*, 137.

[11] See *Sancti Ambrosii Opera*, pars septima, ed. Otto Faller, CSEL 73 (Vienna: Hoelder–Pichler-Tempsky, 1955), 56, lines 22–23 for the original Latin phrase: "ubi verba Christi operata fuerint, ibi sanguis efficitur."

ment but Christ's grace, which through the presence of the Holy Spirit instills his divinity into us. It is applied to your forehead and organs of sense with a symbolic meaning; the body is anointed with visible ointment, and the soul is sanctified by the holy, hidden Spirit.[12]

St. Cyril thus says that the words of the priestly prayer over the chrism, as over the bread and wine, have a power to sanctify both the external elements and the human soul who receives them. The visible anointing both represents and efficaciously realizes an invisible anointing of the Holy Spirit, on the pattern and exemplar of Christ's own invisible anointing by the Holy Spirit. Here we see the fundamental principle of sacramental causality, which is that the words and elements efficaciously realize the sanctification they represent.

In the following sermon on the Eucharist, St. Cyril speaks with still greater emphasis on the power of the words to transform the elements of bread and wine:

> Since, then, Christ himself clearly described the bread to us in the words "This is my body," who will dare henceforward to dispute it? And since he has emphatically said, "This is my blood," who will waver in the slightest and say it is not his blood?
>
> By his own power on a previous occasion he turned the water into wine at Cana in Galilee; so it is surely credible that he has changed wine into blood. If he performed that wonderful miracle just because he had been invited to a human marriage, we shall certainly be much more willing to admit that he has conferred on the wedding-guests[13] the savouring of his body and blood.[14]

Thus the faithful should believe that the words of Christ said in His name by the minister, as words of power, are able to accomplish what they say.

---

[12] Cyril of Jerusalem, *Mystagogic Catecheses* 3.3, in Yarnold, *Awe-Inspiring Rites of Initiation*, 80–81.

[13] See Mark 2:19.

[14] Cyril of Jerusalem, *Mystagogic Catecheses* 4.1–2, in Yarnold, *Awe-Inspiring Rites of Initiation*, 86.

St. John Chrysostom

In his instructions to those about to be baptized, St. John Chrysostom vigorously exhorts the catechumens to believe in the power of the sacraments of Christian initiation to accomplish spiritually what they visibly represent:

> When you come to the sacred initiation, the eyes of the flesh see water; the eyes of the faith behold the Spirit. Those eyes see the body being baptized; these see the old man being buried. The eyes of the flesh see the flesh being washed; the eyes of the spirit see the soul being cleansed. The eyes of the body see the body emerging from the water; the eyes of faith see the new man come forth brightly shining from that sacred purification. Our bodily eyes see the priest as, from above, he lays his right hand on the head and touches; our spiritual eyes see the great High Priest as he stretches forth his invisible hand to touch his head. For, at that moment, the one who baptizes is not a man but the only-begotten Son of God.[15]

Thus Christ is the principal agent in every Baptism, working through the sacred minister and the sacramental sign.

St. John Chrysostom also shows the efficacy of Baptism by comparison with circumcision: "Whatever in the former case circumcision achieved by way of putting off the flesh, in this case baptism achieves by way of putting off sins."[16] As circumcision cuts away the foreskin, so Baptism removes sins.

Baptismal efficacy is also manifested in a homily on John 3:5:

> When we immerse our heads in the water, just as if in a grave, the old man is buried, and, having sunk down, is entirely

---

[15] Baptismal Homily, Papadopoulos-Kerameus no. 3.12, translation in Whitaker, *Documents of the Baptismal Liturgy*, 41. This discourse is dated 388 and given in Antioch. See also his Baptismal Homily, Stavronikita series 2.10, in Yarnold, *Awe-Inspiring Rites of Initiation*, 155: "It is not a man who performs the rites but the gracious presence of the Spirit who sanctifies the natural properties of the water and who touches your head along with the hand of the priest."

[16] John Chrysostom, Homily 39.19 on Genesis, in *Homilies on Genesis 18–45*, trans. R. C. Hill, FC 82 (Washington, DC: Catholic University of America Press, 1990), 388.

hidden once for all; then, when we emerge, the new man rises again. Just as it is easy for us to be immersed and to emerge [from the water], so it is easy for God to bury the old man and raise up the new.[17]

Chrysostom is no less forceful in his expression of the power of the words of Jesus in the Eucharist:

The priest is the representative when he pronounces those words, but the power and the grace are those of the Lord. "This is my Body," he says. This word changes the things that lie before us; and as that sentence "increase and multiply," once spoken, extends through all time and gives to our nature the power to reproduce itself; even so that saying "This is my Body," once uttered, does at every table in the Churches from that time to the present day, and even till Christ's coming, make the sacrifice complete.[18]

As Jesus gave to the water of Baptism and the Trinitarian form the power to "bury the old man and raise up the new," so He gave to the words that He spoke at the Last Supper the power to work in every Eucharistic celebration until the end of time, provided that a priestly minister speaks them with the intention of acting in His Person.

St. Augustine

Sacramental efficacy is well captured in St. Augustine's much quoted phrase from a baptismal homily: "Whence is this power of water of such magnitude that it touches the body and yet washes clean the heart, except from the word's effecting it, not because it is said, but because it is believed?"[19]

---

[17] John Chrysostom, Homily 25.2 on John 3:5, in *Commentary on Saint John the Apostle and Evangelist: Homilies 1–47*, trans. T. A. Goggin (Washington, DC: Catholic University of America Press, 1957), 247.

[18] John Chrysostom, *De proditione Judae* [On the Betrayal of Judas], homily 1, in Quasten, *Patrology*, 3:481.

[19] Augustine, Tractate 80.3.2 on John 15:3, in *Tractates on the Gospel of John 55–111*, 117. For an interpretation of this text, see E. Hocedez, "La conception augustinienne du sacrement dans le tractatus 80 in Ioannem," *Recherches de science religieuse* 10 (1919): 1–29; M.-F. Berrouard, "Le Tractatus 80, 3 in Iohan-

In his commentary on John 1:33, St. Augustine forcefully teaches that the intrinsic efficacy of the sacrament of Baptism in no way depends on the moral worthiness of the minister who celebrates it:

> And what was given by Paul, and what was given by Peter, is Christ's; and if it was given by Judas, it was Christ's. Judas gave it, and baptism was not administered after Judas. John [the Baptist] gave it, and baptism was administered after John [Acts 19:3–5]. For, if baptism was given by Judas, it was Christ's; but that which was given by John was John's. We do not prefer Judas to John; but we do rightly prefer Christ's baptism, even when given through Judas' hands, to John's baptism, even when given through John's hands.[20]

With regard to the giving of the Holy Spirit through the laying on of hands in Confirmation, St. Augustine stresses both the efficacy and the fact that the ministers (the Apostles and their successors) are not the principal agent but are acting on behalf of Christ:

> After that (Pentecost), the Holy Spirit started being given through the ministry of the apostles. They would lay hands on people, and he would come. But this wasn't something that came from men; the minister must not lay claim to more than what he does as minister. The benefactor is one person, the administrator of the grant another.[21]

In both of these texts St. Augustine is stressing, against the Donatists and others, that validity of the sacraments does not depend on the holiness of the minister but on the fact that he is acting as ecclesial minister on behalf of Christ. This doctrine will later be referred to using the phrase *ex opere operato*. The sacraments have power not from the holiness of the minister (or recipient) but from the holiness of

---

nis Evangelium de saint Augustin: La parole, le sacrement et la foi," *Revues des études augustiniennes* 33 (1987): 235–54. The reference to the faith of the recipient should not be understood as the cause of sacramental efficacy, but rather as a necessary condition in the recipient for fruitful reception, as seen above.

[20] Augustine, Tractate 5.18.2–3 on John 1:33, in *Tractates on the Gospel of John 1–10*, trans. J. W. Rettig, FC 78 (Washington, DC: Catholic University of America Press, 1988), 126.

[21] Augustine, Sermon 266.3, in *Sermons (230–272B)*, trans. Hill, 268.

Christ working through the minister and the sacramental sign.

Augustine likewise stresses the efficacy of the power of the words of Christ in the Eucharist to convert the bread and wine into His Body and Blood:

> And from there we come now to what is done in the holy prayers which you are going to hear, that with the application of the word we may have the body and blood of Christ. Take away the word, I mean, it's just bread and wine; add the word, and it's now something else. And what is that something else? The body of Christ, and the blood of Christ. So take away the word, it's bread and wine; add the word and it will become the sacrament. To this you say, *Amen.*[22]

St. Cyril of Alexandria

In interpreting John 3:5, St. Cyril of Alexandria speaks of the water of Baptism as receiving a power from the Holy Spirit, which he compares to the power of water to heat when touched by a flame:

> Just as water that is poured into a kettle receives an impression of the fire's power by association with the tips of the flame, so also through the activity of the Spirit, perceptible water is transformed into a divine and ineffable power and sanctifies those with whom it comes into contact.[23]

According to this analogy, the baptismal water works sanctification not through its own power but through the power of the Holy Spirit working through it, like the heat of fire working through boiling water. This is a striking image of the causal power of Baptism and of its participated or instrumental nature.

In his commentary on the Bread of Life discourse, St. Cyril of Alexandria highlights the efficacy of the Body and Blood of Christ

---

[22] Augustine, *Sermon* 229.3, *Sermons (184–229Z) on the Liturgical Seasons*, trans. Edmund Hill, WSA III/6 (New Rochelle, NY: New City Press, 1993), 266.

[23] Cyril of Alexandria, Commentary on John 3:5, in *Commentary on John*, trans. David R. Maxwell, ed. Joel C. Elowsky, vol. 1, Ancient Christian Texts (Downers Grove, IL: InterVarsity Press, 2013), 98.

to give supernatural life and dispel death: "But the precious blood of Christ is found to be truly 'true drink,' uprooting all decay from the foundations and dislodging death, which had taken up residence in human flesh. That is because it is the blood of not just anyone but of the one who is by nature life itself."[24]

St. John Damascene

St. John Damascene, treating the nature of Baptism, describes its causal efficacy in sanctifying the soul:

> For, since man is twofold, being of body and soul, the puri-fication He gave us is also twofold, through water and the Spirit, with the Spirit renewing in us what is to His image and likeness and the water by the grace of the Spirit purifying the body from sin and delivering it from destruction—the water completing the figure of the death and the Spirit producing the guarantee of life.[25]

All of these texts show us that the Fathers assert the awesome fact that the sacraments confer the grace they signify. They do not, however, pose more detailed questions as to what kind of causality is involved in sacramental action. This problem was taken up by scholastic theologians of the twelfth and thirteenth centuries.

MEDIEVAL THEORIES OF SACRAMENTAL CAUSALITY TO AQUINAS

In the twelfth and thirteenth centuries in Western Europe, scholastic theologians sought to formulate Catholic doctrine on the sacraments in a more precise way proper to the university setting of the study of theology. Spurred by the Berengarian controversy over the Eucha-rist, scholastic theologians had to defend sacramental efficacy against Berengarius. This development coincided providentially in the Latin West with a renewed contact with Aristotle's thought on causality.

---

[24] Cyril of Alexandria, Commentary on John 3:5, in *Commentary on John*, 1:238.

[25] John Damascene, *An Exact Exposition of the Orthodox Faith* 4.9, in *Writings*, 345.

Although all the scholastics of this period defended the efficacy of the sacraments, there was no consensus on how to theologically explain that efficacy. Their explanations can be divided into two broad camps according to how they answer the following question: Are the sacraments (a) necessary conditions, occasions, or dispositions, for receiving grace directly from God, as is the case with the sacraments of the Old Covenant, or are they (b) true efficient causes of grace?

In order to understand the question and its importance, one must grasp the difference between an efficient cause and an occasion or necessary condition (*sine qua non*). A cause is a real principle on which something else depends in its being or in its becoming.[26] St. Thomas says that the term principle implies only "an order or sequence, whereas the term cause implies some influence on the being of the thing caused."[27] Aristotle famously distinguished four kinds of causes: material, formal, efficient, and final. The material and formal causes are intrinsic to a thing and are its co-principles, whereas the efficient and final causes are extrinsic. The final cause is the purpose or goal that motivates an agent to produce an effect. This agent is the efficient cause. Necessary conditions or occasions are not any of these four causes, nor a fifth kind of cause, but rather they are circumstances presupposed to the causal action of the four causes as necessary conditions for them.

When we speak of the causality of the sacraments in infusing grace, we are clearly not referring either to a material cause, for grace, being a spiritual reality, does not have a material cause out of which it is composed.[28] Nor are we referring to a formal cause, because the form of grace, which is a participation in the divine life, infinitely transcends the natural world, and thus could not belong to a sensible sign. Nor, finally, are we seeking the final cause because that is the sanctification of man and the glory of God. If the sacraments are truly causes with respect to grace, then they must be efficient causes of some

---

[26] See Thomas Aquinas, *Commentary on Aristotle's Physics.*, bk. 1, lect. 1, no. 5, trans. Richard J. Blackwell, Richard J. Spath, and W. Edmund Thirkel (Notre Dame, IN: Dumb Ox Books, 1999), 3: "Those things are called causes upon which things depend for their existence or their coming to be."

[27] *Commentary on Aristotle's Metaphysics.*, bk. 5, lect. 1, no. 751, trans. John P. Rowan (Notre Dame, IN: Dumb Ox Books, 1995), 277.

[28] A disposition of the subject can be considered to be a kind of material cause, taken in a broad sense. A disposition, like a certain kind of matter, makes a subject disposed to receive certain forms.

kind that operate in producing sanctification.

A necessary condition or occasion, on the other hand, is not properly an efficient cause on which something else directly depends, or by which it is directly influenced, in its being or becoming. An efficient cause directly produces the effect, which depends for its very being on its efficient cause. A necessary condition or occasion, on the contrary, is not an *agent* that brings about a change but a particular circumstance that enables an agent to operate as efficient cause. An occasion does not properly do work but is a condition that enables work to be done. For example, the occasion of having the bases loaded in a baseball game is a necessary condition for a grand slam, but it is not its efficient cause, which is the swing of the batter that hits the ball out of the park. Having the bases loaded does not of itself do or cause anything, but it enables the efficient cause—the batter—to bring in four runs through his action of hitting a home run. Similarly, a signal for a race to begin or for soldiers to shoot is not an efficient cause of the running or the shooting. It is the legs of the runners that cause the running and the hands and guns of the soldiers that cause the shooting. But the signal is the sign and occasion for the start of the race or the attack. It is the cause of the knowledge in the runners or soldiers of when to begin. Another example of an occasion would be a winning lottery ticket. The lottery ticket is not the efficient cause of the wealth that comes to the winner, but it designates the recipient of that wealth.

Using these analogies, are the sacraments (a) like the occasion of having the bases loaded, or the winning lottery ticket, or the signal for a race or an attack? Or are they (b) like the bat that hits the ball out of the ballpark, the legs that do the running, or the guns that do the shooting? Both positions—regarding the sacraments as *occasions* of grace or *causes* of grace—have difficulties. If one holds that sacraments are efficient causes, then one must give some account of how a material element can be an efficient cause of spiritual grace, which seems impossible, for nothing can give what it does not have.[29] But if one holds that the sacraments are mere signs that provide the occasions or necessary conditions in which another agent—God—infuses grace into the designated recipients, how does this accord with the strong words of the New Testament and the Fathers on the power of the sacraments?

---

[29] For a good statement of this difficulty, see Leeming, *Principles of Sacramental Theology*, 284.

The view that sees the sacraments as necessary conditions, occasions, or signals rather than efficient causes of grace was defended by St. Bernard, St. Bonaventure, and the Franciscan school, followed by the Nominalists of the fourteenth and fifteenth centuries. The opposing position regarding the sacraments as efficient causes of grace (in some mysterious manner) was given prominence by the authority of Peter Lombard. We have seen in chapter 2 above that his definition of the sacraments contains a reference to their causality in producing grace.[30] The mature St. Thomas was the greatest defender of the causal efficiency of the sacraments, which he explained by introducing the notion of instrumental causality, as will be seen in the following chapter.

Sacraments as Causes of Grace: Hugh of St. Victor and Peter Lombard

Like that given by St. Isidore, the definition of a sacrament by Hugh of St. Victor in the mid-twelfth century, as seen above, has the merit of highlighting the causal efficacy of the sacraments, which are spoken of as if they were vials for medicine, "containing by sanctification some invisible and spiritual grace."[31] This formulation does not specify, however, how the sacraments contain and communicate this grace. On the one hand, this phrase of Hugh of St. Victor seems to exclude a view of the sacraments as mere signs of grace or occasions for receiving grace, for the medicine vial is more than an occasion for healing. It falls short, however, in seeing the sacraments as a proper cause. For although the medicine is a cause of health, the medicine container is not. The analogy is ambiguous. Are the sacraments more like medicines or their containers? Hugh of St. Victor highlights the problem himself, saying: "If, therefore, vases are the sacraments of spiritual grace, they do not heal from their own, since vases do not cure the sick but medicine does."[32]

---

[30] Peter Lombard, *Sentences*, bk. 4, d. 1, ch. 4, no. 2. See p. 49 above.

[31] Hugh of St. Victor, *On the Sacraments of the Christian Faith* 1.9.2, trans. Deferrari, 155.

[32] Hugh of St. Victor, *On the Sacraments of the Christian Faith* 1.9.4, trans. Deferrari, 160. St. Bonaventure draws the same conclusion from this analogy. See *In IV Sent.*, d. 1, p. 1, a. 1, q. 3, resp., in *Commentary on the Sentences: Sacraments*, trans. Hellmann, 58 (my italics): "Sacraments are able to be called vases for another reason. This is because just as that which is in a vase is not of it

Peter Lombard, who studied under Hugh of St. Victor, resolves the ambiguity of Hugh's analogy in favor of true causality, and asserts that a sacrament is "a sign of God's grace and a form of invisible grace in such manner that it bears its image and is its cause. And so the sacraments were not instituted only for the sake of signifying, but also to sanctify."[33] The sacraments do not merely signify the promise of sanctification, but are said to be its "cause." The particular kind of causality, however, is not specified.

Peter Lombard, developing an insight of Hugh of St. Victor,[34] anticipates the later solution of Thomas Aquinas in implying that the sacraments are instrumental or "ministerial causes." He made use of the concept of instrumentality to explain how the words uttered by a merely human minister can work the forgiveness of sins in Baptism or Penance:

He [God] was able to give them the power to remit sins: not the same power by which he himself is powerful, but a created power, by which a servant may be able to remit sins, and yet not as the author of the remission, but as its minister, and yet not without God as author: just as the minister has it as

---

nor from it, but nevertheless grace is drawn up with it, so *grace is neither from the sacraments nor of the sacraments*. Grace originates from the eternal fountain. From this is grace drawn up by the soul in these sacraments. Therefore just as one who returns to a vase when he requires liquid, so in searching for the liquor of grace and not having it, one ought to hasten back to these sacraments."

[33] Peter Lombard, *Sentences* 4, d. 1, ch. 4, no. 2, trans. Silano, 4. Another definition of sacrament that influenced Peter Lombard was that of the anonymous author of the *Summa sententiarum*, PL 176:117 (my translation): "A sacrament is the visible form of the invisible grace that is conferred by the sacrament. It is not only the sign of a sacred thing, but also efficacious."

[34] See Hugh of St. Victor, *On the Sacraments of the Christian Faith* 1.9.4, trans. Deferrari, 159–60: "For he himself [the Savior] cooperates with the one who ministers, by whose virtue through the ministry of the one ministering what is to be sanctified is sanctified, that there may be truly one virtue through one work to one effect; this virtue, indeed, in the two operating simultaneously is so distinguished, since it is given by the one, ministered by the other. There is one by whom it is given, the other through whom it is sent. . . . Thus God alone sanctifies and blesses, because from Him Himself is all sanctification and benediction; yet the priest, as a minister of God, sanctifies and blesses, since through him is a certain sanctification and benediction which even itself is also from God who is author in the gift and through God who is a cooperator in the ministry."

part of his ministry that he sanctify outwardly, so he might have it in his ministry to cleanse inwardly; and just as he does the former with God as author, who with him and in him works that outwardly, so he might cleanse interiorly, with God as author, who would make use of his word as if of some ministry.[35]

The Sacraments as Necessary Occasions for the Reception of Grace

Many medieval theologians sought to explain the efficacy of the sacraments by seeing the sacramental rite as marking out the recipient of God's action in granting grace. The sacraments thus would be conditions or occasions, established by Christ, for the application of the grace that He merited for us on Calvary, like markers designating who should be given grace. In technical terms, the sacraments would not be causes of grace in the proper sense, but necessary conditions for receiving grace on account of a covenant established in the blood of Christ. This type of position, which could be referred to as sacramental occasionalism, sacramental extrinsicism,[36] or covenantal causality,[37] was

---

[35] Peter Lombard, *Sentences*, bk. 4, d. 5, ch. 3, no. 3, trans. Silano, 31.

[36] This kind of position could also be described as sacramental extrinsicism because it holds that the grace is not intrinsically contained in any proper sense by the sacrament but is extrinsic to the sacrament and given infallibly by God to those receiving a valid sacrament with the right dispositions. As the lead coin or seal in St. Bonaventure's analogy has no significant intrinsic value but enables one to receive things of value from a third party, so the sacrament with respect to grace. See Gallagher, *Significando causant*, 262–63: "In that [scholastic] period we found two trends of thought: the one which we have called the extrinsic approach to the problem, which denied any real power in the sacramental rite to cause. God directly causes the effect symbolized by the rite, on the occasion of the sacraments being given; or on condition of their being given; or because of some agreement or pact so to act. The latter was the Franciscan opinion, destined to continue to our own times. The other trend of thought was that which we have called the intrinsic approach. The sacramental rite has power as used by God to effect a spiritual reality in the soul, the very reality it symbolizes."

[37] This name is appropriate because this thesis holds that God, on account of His New Covenant, infallibly grants grace in the case of valid sacraments received with the right dispositions. For an analysis and defense of this position, see William Courtenay, "The King and the Leaden Coin: The Economic Background of 'sine qua non' Causality," *Traditio* 29 (1972): 185–209, esp. 187.

implied by St. Bernard[38] and defended by St. Bonaventure as probable,[39] and continued to be maintained into the fourteenth century by Duns Scotus, Durandus,[40] and Gabriel Biel, and in general by the followers of the Scotist and nominalist schools.

St. Bonaventure illustrates this theory through the example of a lead coin or seal, which would be a monetary instrument similar to our paper currency. He attributes this analogy to great theologians who preceded him:

> To this they offer this example: a king decreed that anyone who had a certain seal would receive a hundred pounds. After his decree the seal does not have any absolute property that it did not previously have. However, it is ordered to something to which it was not previously. Thus because it possesses an effective ordering, it is said to have the power to cause someone to have a hundred pounds. Therefore that seal is said to be worth one hundred pounds, and nevertheless it does not have more value now than previously. So if you should ask what is the power in that seal, the response is that it is not something absolute, but it is power for something.[41]

St. Bonaventure says that these theologians draw the conclusion that the sacraments are "causes" of grace in a way analogous to our

---

[38] Bernard, *In Coena Domini sermo de baptismo, sacramento altaris et ablutione pedum* 2, PL 183:271–72. St. Bernard does not explicitly formulate the view that the sacraments are occasions rather than causes of grace, but the example he uses of the investiture of abbots and bishops seems to imply this view. See William Courtenay, "Sacrament, Symbol and Causality in Bernard of Clairvaux," in *Bernard of Clairvaux: Studies Presented to Dom Jean Leclercq*, ed. Basil Pennington (Washington, DC: Cistercian Publications, 1973), 111–22.

[39] For a summary presentation of St. Bonaventure's position, see Reginald Lynch, "The Sacraments as Causes of Sanctification," 805–07. Prior to St. Bonaventure, a position of this type was defended by William of Auvergne (d. 1249) in *De Legibus*, ch. 27. See Reginald Lynch, "Domingo Bañez on Moral and Physical Causality: Christic Merit and Sacramental Realism," *Angelicum* 91 (2014): 105–25, at 110; Irène Rosier-Catach, "Signes sacramentels et signes magiques; Guillaume d'Auvergne et la théorie du pacte," in *Autour de Guillaume d'Auvergne (1249)*, ed. F. Morenzoni and Jean-Yves Tilliette (Turnhout, BE: Brepols, 2005), 101–02.

[40] See Gallagher, *Significando causant*, 153.

[41] Bonaventure, *In IV Sent.*, d. 1, p. 1, a. 1, q. 4, in *Commentary on the Sentences: Sacraments*, trans. Hellmann, 71–72.

dollar bill. It is a sign lacking intrinsic value—for it is not itself made of gold—but it enables one to receive a certain amount of gold. Similarly the sacraments would not contain grace but would be tokens which, when properly received in sacramental worship, cause the rightly disposed recipient to receive grace directly from God.

> Thus they say that the sacraments are similar seals decreed by God, so that when one receives them in the proper manner they should have a measure of grace or have grace for this act. Such effective ordering, I say, is according to them the power of the sacrament, and by reason of it, it disposes the human being to have grace, because it effectively orders to having and receiving grace.
>
> Again they say that on the basis of this covenant the Lord binds himself in some way to giving grace to the receiver of a sacrament.[42]

The sacraments, according to this position, would be indispensable conditions established by divine decree, but not properly causes of grace.[43] What they directly cause is the designation of the recipient of a sacramental action in which God alone grants the grace directly. It seems that St. Bonaventure views them as having a sanctifying power only by way of a relation to God's power at work on the occasion of their celebration.

In his commentary on the *Sentences*, St. Bonaventure does not put forth this theory in his own name, and, although he thinks that this position is easier to defend, he leaves the debate open between this theory and another, defended by the *Summa* of Alexander of Hales and St. Albert, that sees the *res et sacramentum* of the sacraments as a dispositive cause of grace, which will be explained below.[44] In his *Bre-*

---

[42] Bonaventure, In IV Sent., d. 1, p. 1, a. 1, q. 4, in *Commentary on the Sentences: Sacraments*, trans. Hellmann, 71–72.

[43] See also Bonaventure, *In IV Sent.*, q. 2, ad 2, in *Commentary on the Sentences: Sacraments*, trans. Hellmann, 53: "A sacrament does not truly have the character of a cause, nor grace the character of an effect."

[44] See Bonaventure, *In IV Sent.*, d. 1, p. 1, a. 1, q. 4, in *Commentary on the Sentences: Sacraments*, trans. Hellmann, 73: "Either of these positions seems probable enough; but the latter seems to me easier to defend. But I do not know which is more true, because, when we speak of things miraculous, reason is not so much to be relied on. We concede therefore that the sacraments of

viloquium, St. Bonaventure briefly summarizes his position. Although the sacraments can be said to be "vessels" or "causes" of grace, as maintained respectively by Hugh of St. Victor and Peter Lombard, they are not properly efficient causes. The reason for this is that grace cannot be infused into the soul by any other than God, who is the sole efficient cause:

> Finally, it is in and through these divinely instituted sensible signs that the grace of the Holy Spirit is encountered and received by those who approach them. Therefore, these sacraments are called "vessels of grace" and the "cause" of grace. This is not because grace is substantially contained in them or causally effected by them, for grace dwells only within the soul and is infused by none but God. Rather, it is because God has decreed that we are to draw the grace of our healing from Christ, the supreme Physician in and through these sensible signs, "although God has not restricted his power to the sacraments."[45]

Bl. Duns Scotus further developed St. Bonaventure's position.[46]

---

the New Law are a cause, and that they effect and dispose, by extension of the meaning of these words, as was said, and this is safe to say. Whether they contain more, I choose neither to affirm nor deny." Earlier in his commentary, *In IV Sent.,* d. 1, p. 1, a. 1, q. 1, ad 1, St. Bonaventure seems also to affirm that the sacraments give a disposition to grace. He states that sacramental action is different from God's act of creating out of nothing because in the latter case there is no pre-existing subject to dispose, but in sacramental action there is: "To the objection that he did not communicate the power to create, it must be said that creation is from non-being. Therefore in it neither the power to dispose nor the power to inform is necessary, but only the power to effect. . . . However, because justification is the bettering of some being, it can be informative and dispositive and effective. It does not befit God to inform; therefore he gave this to the creature as grace. To dispose is ours with God's help, but to effect is God's alone. Therefore he does not share effective power with anything, but he gives informative power to grace, and dispositive power in the sacraments" (Hellmann, 48).

45 Bonaventure, *Breviloquium* 6.1.5, trans. Monti, 213–14.

46 For Scotus's position on sacramental causality, see *Ox. In IV Sent.,* d. 1, q. 5, in *Opera omnia,* vol. 16 (Paris: Vivès, 1894), 167; Gallagher, *Significando causant,* 149–51; A. O'Neil, "La Causalité sacramentelle d'après le Docteur subtil," *Etudes franciscaines* 30 (1913): 141–55; Lynch, "The Sacraments as Causes of Sanctification," 815; Lynch, *Cleansing of the Heart,* 35–36; Richard Cross, *Duns Scotus* (Oxford: Oxford University Press, 1999), 136–37.

Scotus gave various arguments against St. Thomas's theory of instrumental efficient causality, objections repeated over the centuries,[47] and held that the sacramental sign was a necessary disposition or condition for God to create both the *res et sacramentum* and the effect of grace. Although he used a different terminology, his position seems to be that sacraments are necessary conditions according to a divine pact or covenant for God to infallibly produce the *res et sacramentum* and to infuse grace.

A fourteenth-century follower of Scotus, Peter of Aquila (d. 1370), gives a good summary of this kind of position that continued to be maintained by Scotists and nominalists up to the Council of Trent:

> Because a cause is that upon whose existence something else follows, there are two ways of speaking of a cause. The first, in the strict sense, when upon the presence of one being, by its power and from the nature of things, there follows the being of the other, and thus fire is the cause of heat. But the other way of speaking of a cause is less strict, when at the presence of one being the other being follows, but not through the power of the first, nor by the nature of things, but merely from the will of someone; and in this sense a condition, or a *causa sine qua non*, is called a cause. . . . The sacraments of the New Law in the first sense are not effective causes of grace, but they are causes in the second and less strict sense. Whence, when the Master [Peter Lombard] and the saints say that the sacraments effect what they signify, they must not be understood as if sacraments in the strict sense effected grace, but that God effects grace at their presence, and this is sufficient to justify the Master and others in fixing a difference between

---

[47] For Scotus's objections to St. Thomas's position, see Gallagher, *Significando causant*, 151: "Scotus goes on to marshal arguments against physical causality. How can a rite that is successive produce an effect *in instanti*? Where can that instrumental power be, in the matter, or in the words, or in both? . . . For Scotus the supernatural so exceeds the natural that the sacrament, composed of words and things, cannot touch it even instrumentally. Grace and character are both created and supernatural; hence, no instrument can be employed in causing them." For a good critique of Scotus's position from a Thomistic perspective, see Gallagher, *Significando causant*, 152.

412

the sacraments of the Old and of the New Law.[48]

The greatest problem with this theory is that the sacraments of the New Covenant would simply be sacred signs of God's action, which does not seem to correspond to the strong view of sacramental efficacy found in the New Testament and the writings of the Fathers of the Church, which, as seen above, speak of the sacraments as possessing causal efficacy to impart the Spirit, forgive sins, and give supernatural life. Furthermore, according to this explanation they would not differ essentially from circumcision in the Old Covenant except through their institution by Christ,[49] for, as will be seen in chapter 14 below, we should hold that the sacraments of the Old Covenant were occasions on which God infallibly gave grace to those who were properly disposed and did not pose an obstacle.[50]

Alexander of Hales and St. Albert: The Sacraments Give a Disposition for Grace

The thirteenth-century theologians who attempted to defend true efficient sacramental causality had to give some answer to the principal objection against sacramental causality, which is that God alone can give grace. How can the sacraments participate in something that belongs to God alone? Two solutions were proposed: (a) the sacra-

---

[48] Peter of Aquila, *In 4 Sent.*, q. 1, c. 1, translated in Leeming, *Principles of Sacramental Theology*, 11.

[49] See Bonaventure, *In IV Sent.*, d. 1, p. 1, a. 1, q. 5, resp., in *Commentary on the Sentences: Sacraments*, trans. Hellmann, 79 (my italics): "Thus by reason of conjoined faith, which was in the old sacraments first, there is through them justification *per accidens*. In this there is a difference between the old and the new. In the sacraments of the New Law, with regard to works worked, there is justification not only *per accidens*, but also *per se*. An evident sign of this difference is made clear in the way the old and new sacraments signify. And if the reason for this is asked, the response is taken from what has been said above, that the causality of the sacraments is nothing other than a certain efficacious ordering toward the reception of grace by divine covenant. This was only in the sacraments of the New Law, and not the Old, *except in circumcision, because there was a covenant*. This is why in the latter there is an agreement and ordering, and not in the former, because then was the time of figures and of overcoming hardness. Now is the time of grace." See White, "Sacraments and Philosophy," in *OHST*, 585.

[50] See the critique of theories of sacramental occasionalism by White, "Sacraments and Philosophy," in *OHST*, 583–85.

ments efficiently produce a proximate disposition for grace, and (b) the sacraments function as instruments of God. As we shall see in the following chapter, St. Thomas adopted both of these solutions in his early commentary on the *Sentences* of Peter Lombard, but in his later works, especially the *Summa theologiae*, he abandoned the first solution in favor of an exclusive embrace of the second.

The first of these solutions to be proposed was that of dispositive causality. Several great thirteenth-century theologians, such as Alexander of Hales and St. Albert, understood sacramental causality not as the direct infusion of grace into the soul, which would be an action reserved to God alone, but as the creation of a necessary disposition in the subject for the reception of grace. The kind of cause that creates a disposition that enables another agent to act, by taking away an obstacle or preparing the recipient to receive an action, is called by the technical name of dispositive cause.[51]

The *Summa theologica* of Alexander of Hales and collaborators (the Parisian Franciscan school of the 1250s) proposes the theory that the sacraments are efficient causes, not directly of grace, but of the *res et sacramentum* (character in the three sacraments which imprint it, and an adornment of the soul [*ornatus*] in the other sacraments).[52] Sacramental character is understood, according to this theory, as a dispositive cause of grace because it gives to the soul a necessary disposition to grace as long as no obstacle is present. The *res et sacramentum* would thus be like a material-dispositive cause somehow disposing the recipient to receive grace:

> I say, putting forth an opinion and not asserting, that the sacraments are the causes of some effect in the soul. I say not only by "disposing," but also "effecting." Simply speaking, they cause by realizing the character and adorning the soul. Therefore, I say that each sacrament in some way adorns the soul or imprints character or in some other way imprints or seals it,

---

[51] See the analysis of dispositive causes according to Aquinas and Scotus in Jean-Luc Solère, "Scotus versus Aquinas on Instrumental Causality," in *Oxford Studies in Medieval Philosophy*, vol. 7, ed. Robert Pasnau (Oxford: Oxford University Press, 2019), 147–85, at 163–67; 171–72. St. Thomas distinguishes instrumental causes into dispositive and perfective.

[52] One problem with this solution is that it is not clear how it would apply to the Eucharist since there the *res et sacramentum* is the Body and Blood of Christ, and these would not just give the recipient a disposition for grace.

and that it is of this adornment or seal that the sacraments are efficient causes. It is proper to a spiritual sacrament to put a seal in some way on the soul itself, as it was proper to carnal sacraments, such as circumcision, to put a seal on the flesh. Thus the carnal law, that is, circumcision, was in itself efficacious in producing a carnal sign in the flesh, so the sacrament of the spiritual Law is efficacious in producing a seal on the soul.[53]

St. Albert also defends this view that the sacramental sign is an efficient cause, not directly of grace, but of the *res et sacramentum*. He understands the *res et sacramentum* as giving a proximate and necessary disposition for the reception of grace and forgiveness. The sacrament functions, therefore, by creating a disposition in the soul for the reception of grace.[54] According to this view, the outward sacramental sign is an efficient cause of the *res et sacramentum*, which is a dispositive cause (a kind of material cause in the broad sense), disposing the subject for the reception of grace. God alone, in this view, and not the sacrament, would be the efficient cause of the infusing of grace.

St. Thomas receives this position that the sacraments cause grace by creating a disposition for it in the soul from St. Albert and defends it in his early commentary on the *Sentences*.[55] At the same time, he enriches and transforms St. Albert's position by introducing the notion of instrumental causality. In the works of his maturity, such as *ST* III, q. 62, St. Thomas no longer speaks of the sacraments as creating a disposition for grace but directly states that the sacraments are instrumental causes of grace itself.

---

[53] Alexander of Hales and collaborators, *Summa theologica*, p. 4, q. 5, a. 5, my translation of the Latin text quoted in M. Gierens, *De causalitate sacramentorum: seu de modo explicandi efficientiam sacramentorum novae legis. Textus scholasticorum principaliorum* (Rome: Apud aedes Pont. Universitatis Gregorianae, 1935), 30.

[54] See Albert, *Summa de sacramentis*, q. 1, a. 1, and *In IV Sent.*, d. 1b, a. 5, in H. D. Simonin and G. Meersseman, eds., *De sacramentorum efficientia apud theologos Ord. Praed.* Fasc. 1, 1229-1276 (Rome: Pont. Institutum Internationale Angelicum, 1936), 44–45 and 53–55.

[55] Thomas Aquinas, *In IV Sent.*, d. 1, q. 1, a. 4, qla. 1, 4.

STUDY QUESTIONS

1. How does the New Testament manifest the causal efficacy of the sacraments?
2. In what ways do the Fathers of the Church assert the causal efficacy of the sacraments? Give some examples from Tertullian, St. Ambrose, St. Cyril of Jerusalem, and St. Augustine.
3. What is the position of Hugh of St. Victor and Peter Lombard on sacramental causality?
4. Explain the difference between a necessary condition or occasion, on the one hand, and an efficient cause, on the other. How is this relevant for understanding the sacraments? What are the difficulties with each approach to sacramental causality?
5. Explain St. Bonaventure's theory of sacramental efficacy. What analogy does he use?
6. Explain the theory of Alexander of Hales and St. Albert on sacramental causality.

SUGGESTIONS FOR FURTHER READING

Bonaventure. *In IV Sent.*, d. 1, p. 1, a. 1, qq. 1–5. In *Commentary on the Sentences: Sacraments*. Translated by Wayne Hellmann, Timothy R. Lecroy, and Luke Davis Townsend. St. Bonaventure, NY: The Franciscan Institute, 2016. Pp. 46–79.

Courtenay, William. "The King and the Leaden Coin: The Economic Background of 'sine qua non' Causality." *Traditio* 29 (1972): 185–209.

Gallagher, John F. *Significando causant: A Study of Sacramental Efficiency*. Fribourg, CH: University Press, 1965. Pp. 1–33; 55–81.

Lynch, Reginald M., O.P. *The Cleansing of the Heart: The Sacraments as Instrumental Causes in the Thomistic Tradition*. Washington, DC: Catholic University of America Press, 2017. Pp. 10–36

———. "The Sacraments as Causes of Sanctification." *Nova et Vetera* (English) 12, no. 3 (2014): 791–807.

White, Thomas Joseph, O.P. "Sacraments and Philosophy." In *The Oxford Handbook of Sacramental Theology*. Edited by Hans Boersma and Matthew Levering. Oxford; New York: Oxford University Press, 2015. Pp. 582–85.

Yarnold, Edward, S.J. *The Awe-Inspiring Rites of Initiation: The Origins of the R.C.I.A.* 2nd edition. Collegeville, MN: Liturgical Press, 1994.

Chapter Twelve

St. Thomas Aquinas on Sacramental Causality

S t. Thomas's profound account of sacramental causality centers on the notion that the sacraments are instruments of Christ through which, after His Ascension, He continues to touch and transform us through His saving words and deeds to make us into His living images.

THE SACRAMENTS ARE NOT MERE SIGNS GUARANTEEING THE INFUSION OF GRACE BUT ARE TRUE CAUSES

The starting point of St. Thomas's account of sacramental causality is the recognition that the sources of Revelation speak of the sacraments of the New Covenant as *true causes* of the sanctification they represent. It is the task of theology to elucidate how this can be.

When he considers the question of the causality of the sacraments in both his early and his mature works, he contrasts his position with the thesis held or defended as probable by some of his predecessors and contemporaries, such as St. Bonaventure. According to that theory the sacraments are causes of grace only in the sense that they are guaranteed conditions that designate those to whom God has committed Himself to infallibly infuse grace (unless there is an obstacle), but without cooperating as agents of that infusion. The reason for that position, as seen above, is that these theologians were unable to explain how sensible and physical signs could be a true cause of grace. St. Thomas characterizes their position as follows:

For certain people say that they [the sacraments] are not causes as though they did anything in the soul, but are causes in the manner of guaranteed conditions, for the uncreated power—that is, God's—which alone causes the effects pertaining to grace in the soul, assists the sacraments through a certain ordination and agreement, as it were, from God. For thus he has ordained and agreed, as it were, that whoever receives the sacraments will receive grace from them at the same time, not as though the sacraments did anything for that. And it is the same with someone who receives a lead nickel made according to an ordination such that whoever had one of those nickels would have one hundred pounds from the king: for indeed, the nickel itself does not give those hundred pounds, but only the king accepting it. And since no such agreement was made in the sacraments of the Old Law that those approaching them would receive graces, for this reason they are said not to confer grace, but only to promise it.[1]

This view is rejected by St. Thomas, who holds that then the sacraments would only be *signs* or *occasions* of grace, as were the sacraments of the Old Covenant, whereas the New Testament and the Fathers state that they are also *causes* of grace, as has been seen above. St. Thomas says:

> But if we examine the question properly, we shall see that according to the above mode the sacraments are mere signs. For the leaden coin is nothing but a sign of the king's command that this man should receive money. In like manner the book is a sign of the conferring of a canonry. Hence, according to this opinion the sacraments of the New Law would be mere signs of grace; whereas we have it on the authority of many saints that the sacraments of the New

---

[1] Thomas Aquinas, *In IV Sent.*, d. 1, q. 1, a. 4, qla. 1, trans. Mortensen, 7:29–30. See also the parallel text in *ST* III, q. 62, a. 1: "Some, however, say that they [the sacraments] are the cause of grace not by their own operation, but in so far as God causes grace in the soul when the sacraments are employed. And they give as an example a man who on presenting a leaden coin, receives, by the king's command, a hundred pounds: not as though the leaden coin, by any operation of its own, caused him to be given that sum of money; this being the effect of the mere will of the king." See also *De veritate*, q. 27, a. 4.

Law not only signify, but also cause grace.[2]

In other words, if the sacraments simply serve to designate who should receive grace, as the lead coin designates who should receive stipulated goods, then the sacraments themselves would not be contributing to the effect of sanctification.[3] They would only be signs marking those whom God has covenantally stipulated that He would sanctify. But Christ spoke of the sacraments of the Eucharist and Baptism in a stronger way than that. In John 6:55–57, He did not say that eating His flesh would simply designate who should receive sanctification directly from God. He speaks of His Body and Blood as true food for the soul: "For my flesh is food indeed, and my blood is drink indeed. He who eats my flesh and drinks my blood abides in me, and I in him. As the living Father sent me, and I live because of the Father, so he who eats me will live because of me."[4] Similarly Christ's words about Baptism in John 3:5–6 imply that water and the Spirit bring about spiritual rebirth. St. Augustine also speaks in that way when he says that the water of Baptism "touches the body and yet washes clean the heart."[5]

---

[2] *ST* III, q. 62, a. 1.

[3] See Thomas Aquinas, *In IV Sent.*, d. 1, q. 1, a. 4, qla. 1, trans. Mortensen, 7:30 (my italics): "But this does not seem sufficient to do justice to the sayings of the saints. For causes in the manner of guaranteed conditions, *if nothing whatsoever were done to bring about the effect either by disposing or improving*, will have, as to the nature of causing, no more effect than accidental causes have, as white is the cause of a house if the builder is white; and according to this, the sacraments were only accidental causes of sanctification. For that ordination or agreement which they speak of gives them nothing of the nature of a cause, but only of the nature of a sign, as also a lead nickel is only a sign indicating who should receive it. But what is accidental is ignored by art nor is it included in a definition; hence in the definition of a sacrament no causality would be included, nor would holy men have taken the trouble to say much about it."

[4] Theories of sacramental occasionalism or covenantal causality are especially inadequate with regard to the Eucharist.

[5] Augustine, Tractate 80.3.2 on John 15:3, in *Tractates on the Gospel of John 55–111*, 117. See Reginald Lynch on the importance of this text of St. Augustine for the theologians of the twelfth and thirteenth century, in "The Sacraments as Causes of Sanctification," 799: "Augustine's teaching on the efficacy of the Word in relation to the waters of baptism became an interpretive locus for sacramental causality. In his tractates on John, Augustine taught that the water of baptism, made a sacrament by the presence of the Word, not only touches the body but cleanses the heart as well: *corpus tangat et cor abluat*. Because Augustine says unambiguously that the waters of baptism cleanse the heart, it seems

St. Thomas's Solution: The Sacraments Are Instrumental Efficient Causes

Another solution, therefore, must be found to explain how material elements can be efficient causes of grace. To this difficult problem that his predecessors had not resolved in a satisfactory way, St. Thomas offers a simple and brilliant solution by introducing the idea of instrumental causality.[6] Although Tertullian and Peter Lombard alluded to this notion by way of analogy, St. Thomas seems to be the first theologian to apply this category in an explicit and well-developed way to explain sacramental causality, and it should be counted among his key contributions to sacramental theology.[7]

Instrumental Causality

Instrumental causality occurs when a cause produces its effect by

---

that something causal is being said of the water itself, albeit with obvious and necessary reference to the power and presence of the Word. The interpretation of this phrase, broadly circulated by Peter Lombard, occupied the best minds of the scholastic period." Tertullian also implies that the sacraments are more than necessary conditions and are true causes, in *De resurrectione carnis* 8.3 (CCL 2.931), trans. Evans, *Tertullian's Treatise on the Resurrection*, 25, quoted in the previous chapter.

[6] See Perrin, *L'institution des Sacrements*, 44–48.

[7] This doctrine is already present in St. Thomas's commentary on the *Sentences*, *In IV Sent.*, d. 1, q. 1, a. 4, qla. 1–3. In *IV Sent.*, d. 8, q. 2, a. 3, and ad 1 and ad 4, he uses instrumental causality to explain the power of the words of the Eucharistic consecration to produce transubstantiation. In his early works, such as the commentary on the *Sentences*, St. Thomas tries to combine the notion of instrumental causality with St. Albert's theory of dispositive causality, whereas in his mature works, such as the *Summa theologiae*, the emphasis on dispositive causality disappears. On the originality of St. Thomas on this issue, see D. van Meegeren, *De causalitate instrumentali humanitatis Christi iuxta D. Thomae doctrinam expositio exegetica* (Venlo: NVN Venlosche Courant, 1940), 13–40. Immediate predecessors to St. Thomas in an approach to the use of the category of instrumental causality include Card. Stephen Langton (d. 1228), Hugh of St. Cher (second Dominican Master at the University of Paris from 1230–36), and Peter of Tarantasia. See Damien Van den Eynde, "Stephen Langton und Hugh of St. Cher on the Causality of the Sacraments," *Franciscan Studies* 11 (1951): 141–55. For Peter of Tarantasia, see H. D. Simonin, and G. Meersseman, eds., *De sacramentorum efficientia apud theologos Ord. Praed*, fasc. 1, 1229–1276 (Rome: Pont. Institutum Internationale Angelicum, 1936), 108–17.

making use of the mediation of a subordinate agent.[8] This subordinate agent is called an instrument or instrumental cause, which is an efficient cause that produces an effect higher than itself. This is possible because the instrument is being moved and used by a higher cause, referred to as the *principal* cause, which moves the instrument directly or indirectly to execute a plan proper to or intended by the principal cause.

Instrumental causes are omnipresent in living things and in all human arts and technology. Every living body makes use of organs, which are instruments of the organism for its different functions. The eye is a natural instrument for seeing whose power can be amplified by other man-made instruments such as a telescope or microscope. Likewise the hand is a privileged instrument of the body that is marvelously adapted to make use of other instruments to extend our power and control.

An instrument acts in accordance with its own nature while being moved by the principal cause in accordance with its higher plan. The instrument thus *serves* the principal cause by lending its own activity to a higher direction. The effect is produced through the cooperation of the instrumental cause with the principal cause that is directing it, such that the principal cause achieves its end through the activity of the instrument. For example, the proper effect of the paintbrush is to apply paint and of the chisel to cut, but this action of the paintbrush or chisel is under the control of the hand, whose power it extends. The hand, likewise, is under the control of the eye, mind, and will of the artist. In this way, the paintbrush or chisel, while doing its own proper act of applying paint or cutting, produces an effect that vastly transcends the unaided power of the instrument.

The instrument seems to violate a first principle of reason: nothing can give what it does not possess. The paintbrush or chisel produces an intelligible and beautiful design, which it does not have by nature. This first principle is not really violated, however, for the true cause is the combination of the principal and the instrumental cause. The effect transcends the instrument taken by itself, which lacks reason and a sense of beauty, but does not transcend the principal cause, which is the trained mind and imagination of the artist. The effect thus manifests the superior plan intended by the principal cause, and for this

---

[8] This section on instrumental causality is adapted from the corresponding section in Feingold, *The Eucharist*, 184–90.

reason the effect is attributed more to the principal cause than to the instrument, even though both are true causes of the effect.[9]

Instrumental causality thus explains how a lower level of being, such as a sensible sign, can be the instrumental agent of an effect belonging to the spiritual and supernatural order, for the effect will be on the level of the principal cause. Aquinas writes:

> An efficient cause is twofold: principal and instrumental. The principal cause works by the power of its form, to which form the effect is likened; just as fire by its own heat makes some-thing hot. In this way none but God can cause grace. . . . But the instrumental cause works not by the power of its form, but only by the motion whereby it is moved by the principal agent: so that the effect is not likened to the instrument but to the principal agent: for instance, the couch is not like the axe, but like the art which is in the craftsman's mind. [10]

Instrumental causality explains how something can be a true cause of an effect higher than itself. There are many examples of this in theology, for it occurs whenever a created reality acts as an instrument of God's salvific plan. The prophets, for example, were instruments of divine Revelation in communicating through human words what had been revealed to them by divine illumination. In a similar way, the authors of Holy Scripture, acting as instruments of God through His inspiration, wrote books that are not only their work but also the Word of God.[11] The sacred authors worked on their own level through historical research, gathering the testimony of witnesses, ordering and synthesizing the material, and finally writing it down with suitable metaphors and figures of speech. But while working on their own level, they were guided by a higher agent—the Holy Spirit—who directed their efforts to a higher goal: God's Revelation to mankind which shares in God's own infallible truth.[12]

---

[9] See *ST* I-II, q. 16, a. 1: "An action is not properly attributed to the instrument, but to the principal agent." See also *In IV Sent.*, d. 47, q. 2, a. 1, sol. 3, ad 2.

[10] *ST* III, q. 62, a. 1.

[11] See Feingold, *Faith Comes from What Is Heard*, 289–95.

[12] On inspiration, see Second Vatican Council, *Dei Verbum*, §11: "In composing the sacred books, God chose men and while employed by Him they made use of their powers and abilities, so that with Him acting in them and through them, they, as true authors, consigned to writing everything and only those things which

Another broader example of instrumentality can be seen in the doctrine of divine providence. Ultimately all creatures and their operations are instruments, each in their own way, of God's providential plan, which directs all things to their ends for the realization of God's plan in the universe. Secondary causes act according to their own nature, unaware of the direction of Providence, but a higher plan is realized through their action.

The application of this category of instrumental causality explains how realities on a lower level of being—sensible signs and words—can be instruments of a divine plan of sanctification, and can be agents in the infusion of supernatural grace. This answers the most obvious objection against the Catholic doctrine that the sacraments are true causes of supernatural gifts. The sacraments can give something that they do not possess in themselves and which transcends their nature as sensible signs, insofar as they are moved by a higher agent, which is ultimately the divine omnipotence working through the humanity of Christ, who instituted them and merited their efficacy.[13] The sacraments cannot be a principal cause of grace just as the sacred authors could not be a principal cause of divine Revelation. But as the sacred authors could write the Word of God moved by the divine Spirit, so the sacraments can sanctify in that they are moved by the Holy Spirit, the Sanctifier, and Christ's humanity, who work through them.

He wanted." On the truth of Scripture, see *Dei Verbum*, §11: "Therefore, since everything asserted by the inspired authors or sacred writers must be held to be asserted by the Holy Spirit, it follows that the books of Scripture must be acknowledged as teaching solidly, faithfully and without error that truth which God wanted put into sacred writings for the sake of salvation." On the human activity of the four evangelists, see *Dei Verbum*, §19: "The sacred authors wrote the four Gospels, selecting some things from the many which had been handed on by word of mouth or in writing, reducing some of them to a synthesis, explaining some things in view of the situation of their churches and preserving the form of proclamation."

[13] See *SCG* IV, ch. 56, no. 7, 4:247–48: "Nor is it unsuitable that by things visible and bodily a spiritual salvation is served. For visible things of this kind are the instruments, so to say, of a God who was made flesh and suffered. Now, an instrument does not operate by the power of its nature, but by the power of its principal agent who puts it into operation. Thus, also, then, do visible things of this kind work out a spiritual salvation—not by a property of their own nature, but by Christ's institution, and from the latter they receive their instrumental power."

Christ's Humanity Is the Instrument of His Divinity

The highest example of instrumentality is the Incarnation, through which all of Christ's human actions serve as supreme instruments of our salvation. St. Thomas received this idea from St. John Damascene and the Greek patristic tradition, and applied it to Christ's miracles, the actions or mysteries of His human life, and His sacramental action. In treating the hypostatic union, St. John Damascene explained that while the divine and human natures of Christ preserved their own properties, the divine power worked through the actions of the human nature: "The divinity acted through the flesh, because the flesh served as an instrument of the divinity."[14]

St. Thomas develops this idea in the question on the hypostatic union in the *Summa theologiae*: "Nothing prevents what is assumed into the unity of the hypostasis from being as an instrument, even as the body of man or his members."[15] As the human body is a magnificent living and conjoined instrument of the soul, so Christ's humanity is a living and conjoined instrument of His divinity.

Conjoined and Separated Instruments

At first sight it may seem strange to speak of the human body, or

---

[14] John Damascene, *An Exact Exposition of the Orthodox Faith* 3.15, in *Writings*, 311: "Therefore, the divinity communicates its excellences to the flesh while remaining with no part of the sufferings of the flesh. For His flesh did not suffer through the divinity in the same way that the divinity acted through the flesh, because the flesh served as an instrument of the divinity." For the influence of St. John Damascene on St. Thomas's Christology and his doctrine of sacramental causality, see Blankenhorn, "The Instrumental Causality of the Sacraments," 262–63, 268–78.

[15] *ST* III, q. 2, a. 6, ad 4. St. Thomas develops this idea in *ST* III, q. 7, a. 1, ad 3; q. 8, a. 1, ad 1: "To give grace or the Holy Ghost belongs to Christ as He is God, authoritatively; but instrumentally it belongs also to Him as man, inasmuch as His manhood is the instrument of His Godhead. And hence by the power of the Godhead His actions were beneficial—*i.e.*, by causing grace in us, both meritoriously and efficiently." A good brief explanation of this doctrine is given by Charles Journet, *Theology of the Church*, trans. Victor Szczurek (San Francisco: Ignatius Press, 2004), 52: "The holy humanity of Christ is, in the hands of God, as an instrument, an organ destined to transmit to the world the graces of salvation. But the words, 'instrument' and 'organ' must be given an absolutely unique sense here. First of all, the humanity of Christ is a free instrument, the most free, the most loving, the most sensible that has ever been created."

Christ's humanity, as a kind of instrument, for we tend to think of instruments as separated from us. But as St. Thomas explains, there are two kinds of instruments: conjoined and separated. Our own bodies are marvelous living and personal instruments of our souls by which we accomplish our vital actions. Indeed, every living organ is a particular kind of instrument for realizing that vital activity, as the eye is the instrument of sight.

Many human arts make use primarily of the instrumentality of our body, as in singing, acting, teaching, etc. The physical members of an artist, such as his hands, eyes, ears, and voice, are instruments of the mind of the artist, which is the principal cause. We can call these organs "conjoined instruments." Other arts use extrinsic instruments to extend the reach and power of our bodily instruments, as in a telescope or microscope. Similarly, chisels, paintbrushes, trumpets, flutes, spoken or written words or signs, are extrinsic or "separated instruments." Normally we make use of separated instruments by means of the conjoined instruments of our hands, as when we write.[16]

These two levels of instrumental causes that operate in all human arts also combine in the sacraments. The humanity of Christ is the conjoined instrument of His divine power and mercy, united by the hypostatic union. His human acts of self-offering, immolation, death, and Resurrection are acts of the conjoined instrument. The sacred ministers and sacramental signs are used by Him as separated instruments that extend the reach of His humanity and apply the merits of Calvary to this earth after His glorious Ascension to realize in us a likeness of His Paschal mystery.[17] For this reason, as seen above, they could only be instituted directly by Him. St. Thomas explains:

> A sacrament works to cause grace in the manner of an instrument, of which there are two kinds. One kind is separate, as in the case of a stick; the other is united, as a hand. Now the separate instrument is moved by means of the united instrument, as a stick by the hand. The principal efficient cause of grace

---

[16] See *ST* III, q. 64, a. 4: "For a united instrument, the more powerful it is, is all the more able to lend its power to the separated instrument; as the hand can to a stick."

[17] As will be seen below, through desire motivated by faith, hope, charity, and repentance, the essential effect of the sacraments is able to reach all men of all time, even those who lived before their institution or who, through no grave fault of their own, have never come to believe in them.

is God Himself, in comparison with whom Christ's humanity is a united instrument, whereas the sacrament is a separate instrument. It is necessary, therefore, that the saving power in the sacraments be derived from Christ's divinity through His humanity.[18]

Because the Word Incarnate merited all grace for mankind in His Passion, God has willed to use the humanity of Christ when He infuses that grace into our souls. For this reason He instituted a sacramental economy. God infuses grace in the world through Christ's humanity, the great conjoined instrument of our sanctification, and makes use of the sacraments as His extrinsic instruments that apply that sanctification to us individually. The Church is created by contact with Christ's humanity through the instruments by which His humanity and His Passion are able to touch us after His Ascension: the seven sacraments.

As we have seen above, Christ makes use of two different kinds of separated instruments. The minister who administers the sacrament is a living instrument of Christ, and the matter and form of the sacraments—composed of words, gestures, and things—are inanimate separated instruments of the minister. Thus the divine power makes use of Christ's humanity, which makes use of the minister as a living but separated instrument, who makes use of words, gestures, and things. The sacrament of Holy Orders, by imprinting priestly character, enables the ordained priest or bishop to act as a living instrument of the humanity of Christ so as to administer the sacraments *in persona Christi capitis* (in the person of Christ, the head of the Church). The sacrament of Holy Orders is thus crucial to the sacramental economy because the priest is a sacramental link between the conjoined instrument—the humanity of Christ—and the other extrinsic instruments of the Godhead in the application of grace to souls.[19] The priest, when he acts in the person of Christ, enables Christ to work in the sacra-

---

[18] *ST* III, q. 62, a. 5 (my translation). St. Thomas introduces this distinction of conjoined and separated instruments in *SCG* IV, ch. 41, and applies it explicitly to the sacraments in the third part of the *Summa theologiae*. See Meegeren, *De causalitate instrumentali humanitatis Christi*, 110–80.

[19] See La Soujeole, "The Sacraments and the Development of Doctrine," in *OHST*, 599 [italics original]: "It [priestly ordination] makes the minister a *separated* sign and instrument of Christ and the Church, a *sacramental link* between Christ and men (*CCC*, §1120)."

ments through him and apply grace to souls.[20]

It follows that Christ's glorious humanity is at work now in every sacramental action. In a chain of instrumental causes, the higher conjoined instrument moves the lower extrinsic instruments to their effect, as the soul moves the arm to move the hammer to move the chisel to carve the statue. The highest instrument in sacramental action is Christ's humanity, which is the conjoined instrument using the separated sacramental signs. Christ's glorious humanity thus is active throughout the life of the Church in all sacramental action. This is suggested by Hebrews 7:23–26:

> The former priests were many in number, because they were prevented by death from continuing in office; but he holds his priesthood permanently, because he continues for ever. Consequently he is able for all time to save those who draw near to God through him, since he always lives to make intercession for them. For it was fitting that we should have such a high priest, holy, blameless, unstained, separated from sinners, exalted above the heavens.

Analogy between Christ's Miracles and Sacramental Action

There is a very close analogy between Christ's use of instruments in His sacramental action and in His miracles. This analogy is suggested by Christ Himself in Matthew 9:5–8 when He forgave the sins of the paralytic. To demonstrate His divine authority to forgive sins, He told the paralytic: "Rise, take up your bed and go home." His human words were the agents both of the miraculous healing that could be seen and of the forgiveness that continues in the sacrament of Penance, which is to be believed.

In his miracles, His human words and gestures were the instruments of His divine power that worked through them.[21] When Christ

---

[20] There are two exceptions to this. Because of the necessity of Baptism, Christ willed that in extraordinary circumstances, such as danger of death, any person can serve as the minister that makes Christ's voice present. Nevertheless, the ordinary minister is the bishop, priest, or deacon, as prescribed in CIC, can. 861. The other exception is Matrimony in which the ministers are the spouses.

[21] See Leo the Great, Letter 28 to Bishop Flavian of Constantinople "Lectis dilectionis tuae" (Tome of Leo), ch. 4 (DS, 294): "For each nature does what

spoke with authority, the divine power worked through His words so that they did what they said: devils were expelled, winds were calmed, lepers healed, the blind were given sight, the sick healed, the dead were raised, and sinners were forgiven and reconciled.[22] Theologians refer to these actions as "theandric," which means divine-human.[23] It is a term applied to actions of Christ that manifest the complementary operation of both natures, divine and human, at the same time, each acting in the way proper to it.

In Christ's use of words and gestures in working miracles, we find a chain of instrumental causes. Christ's divinity used His humanity, which used words and gestures, which were received with faith by the beneficiary, in order to work miracles. In sacramental action, we find the same chain of instrumental causes being used by the divine power. Drawing on St. John Damascene, Aquinas writes:

> We must therefore say that neither a sacrament nor any other creature can give grace as a principal agent, because this is proper to the divine power exclusively. . . . But the sacraments work instrumentally toward the production of grace. This is explained as follows. Damascene says that in Christ His human nature was like a tool of His divinity, and thus His human nature shared somewhat in the working of the divine power.[24] By touching a leper, for instance, Christ made him clean. The very touch of Christ thus caused the health of the leper instrumentally. It was not merely in corporeal effects

---

is proper to each in communion with the other: the Word does what pertains to the Word, and the flesh to what pertains to the flesh. One shines forth with miracles; the other succumbs to injuries."

[22] See *ST* III, q. 13, a. 2: "If we speak of the soul of Christ as it is the instrument of the Word united to Him, it had an instrumental power to effect all the miraculous transmutations ordainable to the end of the Incarnation, which is to 're-establish all things that are in heaven and on earth.'"

[23] See *ST* III, q. 19, a. 1, ad 1: "Dionysius places in Christ a theandric—*i.e.*, a God-manlike or Divino-human operation—not by any confusion of the operations or powers of both natures, but inasmuch as His Divine operation employs the human, and His human operation shares in the power of the Divine." See Ruggero Biagi, *La causalità dell'umanità di Cristo e dei Sacramenti nella "Summa theologiae" di san Tommaso d'Aquino* (Bologna: Edizioni Studio Domenicano, 1985), 65–66.

[24] See John Damascene, *An Exact Exposition of the Orthodox Faith* 3.15, in *Writings*, 311.

that Christ's human nature shared instrumentally in the effect of the divine power but also in spiritual effects. Thus Christ's blood poured out for us had the ability to wash away sins. . . . Thus the humanity of Christ is the instrumental cause of justification. This cause is applied to us spiritually through faith and bodily through the sacraments, because Christ's humanity is both spirit and body. This is done to the end that we may receive within ourselves the effect of sanctification, which is had through Christ. As a consequence the most perfect sacrament is that in which the body of Christ is really contained, the Eucharist. . . . But the other sacraments also share some of the efficacy by which Christ's humanity works instrumentally for our justification.[25]

The sacraments instituted by Christ can be instruments in justification and the infusion of grace because Christ's humanity is a first and privileged instrument of His divinity in infusing grace, as in working miracles. That very humanity is present in the Eucharist substantially, directly working its effect of sanctification. In the other sacraments, Christ works through the sacramental sign and the *res et sacramentum*, by which the soul is configured to Christ.[26]

OBJECTION: CAN AN INSTRUMENT COOPERATE IN THE INFUSION OF GRACE?

To understand how the sacraments can be instruments of the infusion of grace, it is necessary to pose a broader question. Is it possible for any instrument to cooperate in the infusion of grace? This question arises

---

[25] *De veritate*, q. 27, a. 4, trans. Schmidt, *Truth*, 3:332–33.

[26] See Blankenhorn, commenting on this text from *De veritate*, q. 27, a. 4, in "The Instrumental Causality of the Sacraments," 273–74: "Jesus operates physically and spiritually, and so does the Eucharist. The perfect sacrament thus demonstrates an intimate ontological connection between Christ and the sacraments. . . . The Eucharist is the model sacrament whose efficacy is found in the other six sacraments to a lesser degree, mainly because Christ's presence is not as intense. The doctrine of the Real Presence entails the principle that the whole sacramental order continues the causal efficacy of Christ's humanity. The Real Presence is thus a kind of bridge between sacramental efficacy and Christ's humanity."

because St. Thomas, in harmony with other scholastic theologians, held that no instrument could cooperate with God in the work of creation,[27] which refers to the creation of subsisting beings *ex nihilo*.[28] Even in human generation, the parents only cooperate in the creation of the body of the offspring, but God creates the soul out of nothing and infuses it into the body. Is the transmission of grace an act of creation, in which no created agent can participate? It may seem that it is, for grace—the participation in the divine nature—is not educed from any natural potency of human nature, since it is an utterly supernatural reality. How can created realities be instruments in producing a participation in the divine nature?

It seems that this consideration is the principal reason why most scholastic theologians, except St. Thomas and his later disciples starting with Cajetan, have denied that the sacraments are instrumental efficient causes of grace, and held that the sacraments are merely conditions *sine qua non*, or occasions, or at most dispositive or moral causes[29] for the infusion of grace.

---

[27] See *ST* I, q. 45, a. 5: "It happens, however, that something participates the proper action of another, not by its own power, but instrumentally, inasmuch as it acts by the power of another; as air can heat and ignite by the power of fire. And so some have supposed that although creation is the proper act of the universal cause, still some inferior cause acting by the power of the first cause, can create. . . . But such a thing cannot be, because the secondary instrumental cause does not participate the action of the superior cause, except inasmuch as by something proper to itself it acts dispositively to the effect of the principal agent. If therefore it effects nothing, according to what is proper to itself, it is used to no purpose; nor would there be any need of certain instruments for certain actions. Thus we see that a saw, in cutting wood, which it does by the property of its own form, produces the form of a bench, which is the proper effect of the principal agent. Now the proper effect of God creating is what is presupposed to all other effects, and that is absolute being. Hence nothing else can act dispositively and instrumentally to this effect, since creation is not from anything presupposed, which can be disposed by the action of the instrumental agent. So therefore it is impossible for any creature to create, either by its own power or instrumentally—that is, ministerially. And above all it is absurd to suppose that a body can create, for no body acts except by touching or moving; and thus it requires in its action some pre-existing thing, which can be touched or moved, which is contrary to the very idea of creation."

[28] See *ST* I, q. 45, a. 4.

[29] Theologians defending forms of dispositive causality include Alexander of Hales, St. Albert, the early St. Thomas, most Thomists before Cajetan, such as Capreolus and Sylvester of Ferrara, and many defenders of moral causality after the Council of Trent, as will be seen in the following chapter.

In other words, St. Thomas's introduction of instrumental causality did not completely solve the problem of how the sacraments can be true efficient causes of grace. In reality there are two problems that needed to be solved. The first problem is: How can the sacraments, being sensible realities, produce a spiritual and supernatural effect? St. Thomas brilliantly answered this problem through introducing instrumental causality, already in his earliest work on the topic, the Commentary on the *Sentences*.[30] There he held that the outward sacramental sign was an instrumental efficient cause used by Christ in producing the supernatural effect of the *res et sacramentum*.

The second problem proved to be more difficult. Even if an instrument can be the cause of a supernatural effect, such as the *res et sacramentum*, can an instrument participate in the infusion of sanctifying grace? The reason for this second question is that the infusion of grace seems to be a kind of creation *ex nihilo*, and only God can create from nothing. Even though an instrument can work above its own level, can any instrument be a tool directly in the infusion of grace?

St. Thomas answered this second question negatively in his Commentary on the *Sentences*, and for this reason his early teaching on sacramental causality was similar to St. Albert and the *Summa* of Alexander of Hales in positing that the sacramental sign, working as instrumental cause, creates a *disposition* for grace—which is the *res et sacramentum*—but is not a true instrumental cause of grace. Thus the early St. Thomas limited the instrumental causality of the sacraments to the production of the *res et sacramentum*, which disposes for the reception of grace but does not instrumentally cause it. Like his contemporaries he held that God was the sole efficient cause of the infusion of grace. In that early work he held a view that he would later rightly abandon, which is that the role of the outward sacramental sign in the infusion of grace was analogous to the role of the parents in the infusion of the soul into their offspring.[31]

In human procreation, the parents bring about, through the union of egg and sperm, the formation of a new human body with its own genetic code. This provides the proximate disposition of the matter for the creation and infusion of the human soul by God. The parents cannot create the soul, nor even cooperate as instrumental causes in its creation, for the human soul is a subsistent spiritual form that transcends the

---

[30] See Thomas Aquinas, *In IV Sent.*, d. 1, q. 1, a. 4, qla. 1–4.
[31] Thomas Aquinas, *In IV Sent.*, d. 1, q. 1, a. 4, qla. 1.

potency of matter and thus cannot be educed from the potency of the egg and sperm.[32] What the parents do is cooperate to form the ultimate disposition that is the necessary prerequisite for God to create and infuse the soul into that new body.

Applying this analogy to the sacraments, the sacramental sign would be like the action of the parents; the sacraments would cause the proximate disposition for grace, but their instrumental action would not attain to grace itself, but only to the disposition (the *res et sacramentum*) for the grace to be created directly by God alone. As we have seen above, St. Thomas developed this view from St. Albert and the *Summa* of Alexander of Hales.[33]

The Difference between the Infusion of Grace and the Creation of the Human Soul

Shortly after his commentary on the *Sentences*, in *De veritate*, St. Thomas changed his view on this question and came to see that this analogy between the creation of the human soul and the infusion of grace was inadequate. This led to an important transformation of his teaching on sacramental causality.[34] The reason for Aquinas's change

---

[32] See *ST* I, q. 90, a. 2; q. 118, a. 2.

[33] See Thomas Aquinas, *In IV Sent.*, d. 1, q. 1, a. 4, qla. 1, trans. Mortensen, 7:30: "And thus other men say that two things result in the soul from the sacraments. The first is a sacrament-and-reality, like a character, or some adornment of the soul in sacraments in which no character is imprinted; the other is a reality alone, like grace. Therefore, with respect to the first the sacraments are causes bringing about effects in some way; but with respect to the second they are causes disposing with such a disposition that it is a necessity, unless there were an impediment on the part of the person receiving; and this seems more consistent with the theologians and sayings of the saints." St. Thomas goes on to explain this position using instrumental causality (Mortensen, 31): "Now a certain action befits material instruments like this by their own nature, as water cleanses and oil makes the body sleek; but furthermore, as they are instruments of divine mercy justifying us, they attain instrumentally to a certain effect in the soul itself, which corresponds first to the sacraments, like a character or something of that sort. But to the final effect, which is grace, they do not attain even instrumentally, except dispositively, inasmuch as what they attain to as efficacious instruments is a disposition, which is necessary in itself for the reception of grace."

[34] Three careful and detailed studies of the evolution of St. Thomas's thought on sacramental causality are Gallagher, *Significando causant*, 82–134; Lynch, *Cleansing of the Heart*, 67–143; and Blankenhorn, "The Instrumental Causality of the Sacraments," 260–91. See also Chauvet, *Symbol and Sacrament*, 11–21.

of view comes from a more accurate analysis of the difference between the creation of the human soul and the infusion of grace.[35] In both cases—the infusion of the soul into the body at conception and the infusion of grace into the soul at Baptism—there is no natural potency in matter. But there is a difference. The human soul has being in itself. In philosophical terms, it subsists. Sanctifying grace, on the contrary, is a supernatural quality of the soul, which in philosophical terms is an accident, something that does not have being in itself but in another. The infusion of grace does not imply the creation of a new subject, but the supernatural modification of a human subject. Sanctifying grace is not properly said to be created *ex nihilo* precisely because it is a supernatural *quality* of the soul and not a subsisting thing, like the human soul or an angel. Only subsisting realities that have being in themselves are said to be created.[36]

Because sanctifying grace is a participation in the divine nature, only God can be the principal cause of the infusion of grace, since nothing can give what it does not have. However, since grace is not properly created, there is no intrinsic reason why God cannot use a creature as an instrument in educing grace from the obediential potency of the soul, although it is extremely surprising and marvelous. An obediential potency is the power to obey God when He wills to work something in the creature above its nature.[37] Creatures have an obediential power for miracles to be done in them by the power of God, and rational creatures made in the image of God have a specific

---

[35] See Lynch, *Cleansing of the Heart*, 100–102; 116–20.

[36] See *De veritate*, q. 27, a. 3, ad 9, trans. Schmidt, *Truth*, 3:323: "To be created properly applies to subsistent beings, to which it properly belongs to be and to become; but forms that are not subsistent, whether accidental or substantial forms, are properly not created but co-created, just as they do not have being of themselves but in another. Even though they do not have as one of their constituents any matter *from which* they come, yet they do have matter *in which* they are, upon which they depend and by whose change they are brought forth into existence. Consequently their becoming is properly the transformation of their subjects. Hence by reason of the matter *in which* they are, creation is not properly ascribed to them. The case is different, however, for a rational soul, which is a subsistent form; and so being created properly applies to it."

[37] St. Thomas discusses the notion of obediential potency in *ST* III, q. 11, a. 1 (my italics): "It must be borne in mind that in the human soul, *as in every creature*, there is a twofold passive power. One is in comparison with a natural agent; the other in comparison with the First Agent, which can bring any creature to a higher act than a natural agent can bring it, and this is usually called the *obediential potency* of a creature."

obediential power to receive grace.[38] And just as created agents can be instrumental causes in miracles, so there is no reason why created agents, such as the humanity of Christ and the sacraments, cannot be instrumental causes in the infusion of grace.

No creature can serve as an instrument in the creation of a subsistent being *ex nihilo*. This is because "nothing"—the absence of any thing—by definition has no reality that a created instrument can act upon to dispose it in some way to bring something else into being. Nothing can act on *nothing*. However, in the case of the infusion of grace, there is an existing subject, which is the human being. There is no reason why an instrument cannot be used to act on an existing human being in such a way that the instrument cooperates in God's principal causality as a conduit of His power.[39] Insofar as they are moved by God as principal agent, the sacraments bring forth a supernatural quality from the specific obediential potency of the human soul, which is *capax Dei*, capable of divinization.[40] The sacraments should not be thought of as vessels that contain a supernatural substance (grace) but as instruments which, through the principal causality of God working through the humanity of Christ, bring forth grace and other supernatural qualities from a mysterious capacity for divinization in us, open to obeying the word of God.

Something similar happened in Jesus's miracles. His words had power to serve as instruments in multiplying bread, in turning water

---

[38] For the notion of an obediential potency specific to the rational creature, see Feingold, *The Natural Desire to See God*, 112–20, 153–54, 165, 175–77, 413–14, 443–47.

[39] See *De veritate*, q. 27, a. 4, ad. 15, trans. Schmidt, *Truth*, 3:336: "Creation does not presuppose anything in which the action of an instrumental agent could terminate, but re-creation does. There is accordingly no parallel."

[40] See Lynch, *Cleansing of the Heart*, 143: "By extension, the sacramental elements themselves exhibit a similar obedience when employed by God as efficacious signs to effect the obediential elevation of the person in grace"; Gallagher, *Significando Causant*, 101: "The created power in the sacrament to cause spiritual effects, then, is due to its obediential potency." See Thomas Aquinas, *In IV Sent.*, d. 8, q. 2, a. 3, ad 4, trans. Mortensen, 7:369: "No creature can do those things that are above nature as principal agent; however, it can cause a motion by uncreated power as instrumental agent: for as there is an obediential potency in creation, so that whatever the Creator has disposed happens in it, thus also so that it happens by means of it, which is the definition of an instrument." On the role of obediential potency in sacramental action, see also Bellarmine, *De Controversiis, De Sacramentis in genere*, bk. 2, ch. 11, in *Opera omnia* 3:450; Suárez, *Opera omnia*, vol. 20, on *ST* III, q. 62, a. 4, disp. 9, sectio 2, p. 147.

into wine, in restoring life to corpses. In all of these cases His words were applied to pre-existing realities to change them in ways that could only be accomplished by the omnipotence of God acting as principal cause through Jesus's words of power.

AQUINAS'S MATURE THEORY OF TWOFOLD INSTRUMENTAL CAUSALITY

This insight that the infusion of sanctifying grace does not involve a creation *ex nihilo* (as in the creation of the human soul) opened the way for St. Thomas's mature theory that extends the instrumental causality of the sacrament directly to the effect of grace. Starting with his *Disputed Questions On Truth* (*De veritate*) and, above all, in the third part of the *Summa theologiae*, St. Thomas continues to maintain the first part of his early position, which is that the sacramental sign instrumentally produces the *res et sacramentum*, but, in opposition to his earlier view, he comes to hold that the *res et sacramentum* in turn is an instrumental cause, and not just a disposition, for the infusion of grace. Christ, the principal agent, works both through the outward sign and the *res et sacramentum*—which can be understood as the abiding "continuation" of the sacramental sign, like a printed word—to infuse grace into the recipient.[41]

This thesis is clearest with regard to the Eucharist. Here the sacramental sign consisting in the matter of the bread and wine and the words of the sacramental form ("This is my body...") is the instrumental cause of transubstantiation by which Christ becomes present in His Body and Blood, which is the *res et sacramentum*. The Body and Blood received in Holy Communion, in turn, is the instrumental cause of the grace received by the faithful, which is the *res tantum*. Christ's Body

---

[41] St. Thomas states this principle most clearly with regard to the sacrament of Penance in *ST* III, q. 84, a. 1, ad 3: "In Penance also, there is something which is sacrament only, viz. the acts performed outwardly both by the repentant sinner, and by the priest in giving absolution; that which is reality and sacrament [*res et sacramentum*] is the sinner's inward repentance; while that which is reality, and not sacrament, is the forgiveness of sin. The first of these taken altogether is the cause of the second; and the first and second together are the cause of the third." This thesis is implied also in St. Thomas's understanding of sacramental character as an instrumental power with regard to grace, as explained in *ST* III, q. 63, a. 2.

and Blood can cause grace in us because Christ's humanity is the con-joined instrument of His Godhead who divinizes the faithful through reception of His humanity. St. Thomas holds that in the other sacra-ments, something analogous happens through the *res et sacramentum*, which, by configuring the soul to Christ, serves as an instrumental cause in the imparting of grace.

In *De veritate*, q. 27, written only a few years after his commen-tary on the *Sentences*, it seems that St. Thomas had already modified and simplified his view.[42] He abandoned the analogy of the parents in the act of procreation who bring about the proximate disposition for the infusion of the soul. Instead, he teaches simply that the sac-rament is an instrumental cause of grace, by being an instrument of Christ's humanity, which is an instrument of his divinity. There is a chain of instrumental causes. Christ as eternal high priest makes use of the sacramental minister, who makes use of the matter and form of the sacrament, which imprints the *res et sacramentum*, through which grace is given to the subject who is rightly disposed by faith and repentance. Each link in this chain is an instrumental cause of the following effects.

In the *Summa contra Gentiles* St. Thomas speaks of the priestly minister as participating in the power of the divinity through priestly character so that he can be an instrumental cause of the effect of grace:

> The ministers of Christ must not only be men, but must participate somehow in His divinity through some spiritual power, for an instrument shares in the power of its principal agent. Now, it is this power that the Apostle calls "the power which the Lord hath given me unto edification and not unto destruction" (2 Cor 13:10).[43]

Do the Sacraments Contain Grace?

St. Thomas, like other medieval theologians, poses the question of whether the sacraments contain grace. At first sight it would seem that they do not, for how can a sensible phenomenon, such as material

---

[42] See Blankenhorn, "The Instrumental Causality of the Sacraments," 269–75, on the transitional nature of St. Thomas's teaching on sacramental causality in *De veritate*.

[43] *SCG* IV, ch. 74, no. 2, 4:286.

things, words, or gestures, contain grace? Opponents of St. Thomas's understanding of sacramental causality frequently make this kind of argument. It seems absurd to hold that the sensible sacramental signs, such as water, oil, or words, contain a supernatural quality of participation in the divine nature.

St. Thomas answers that the sacraments contain grace in the way proper to an instrumental cause. The grace is not contained in the sacramental sign substantially or as a permanent intrinsic quality, but in the way that the power of a principal cause is possessed by an instrument in the act of being used.

When a paintbrush lies on Raphael's table, it is merely a stick with some bristles, deprived of actual artistic power. When the paintbrush is used by Raphael to paint a masterpiece, the brush, as it is being moved by the artist, contains in a certain incomplete and passive way the conception of the artist. Similarly, a violin on the table does not contain music. But when it is played by a master, it carries the art of music in a temporal and transient way through the movement of the bow by the musician.

In an analogous way, the sacraments are instruments of grace in a temporal and transient manner.[44] The outward sacramental sign is realized in time and exercises its sacramental effect as soon as it is complete. The power of giving grace is in the sacramental sign in a transient way as the sacramental gesture is realized.[45] St. Thomas explains:

> Those who hold that the sacraments do not cause grace save by a certain coincidence, deny the sacraments any power that is itself productive of the sacramental effect, and hold that the Divine power assists the sacraments and produces their effect. But if we hold that a sacrament is an instrumental cause of grace, we must needs allow that there is in the sac-

---

[44] *ST* III, q. 62, a. 3, ad 3: "In a sacrament, grace has a passing and incomplete mode of being: and consequently it is not unfitting to say that the sacraments contain grace." See *De veritate*, q. 27 a. 4 ad 4; *De unione Verbi incarnati*, a. 5, ad 12 (my translation): "An instrument, insofar as it moved by an agent, receives a certain intentional power from the input of the agent, which, through the instrument, is transmitted to the effect."

[45] As seen above, the *res et sacramentum* is also a sign and instrument of grace that has a greater duration of being, and thus it can exercise its sacramental power after the outward sacramental sign has passed away.

raments a certain instrumental power of bringing about the sacramental effects. Now such power is proportionate to the instrument: and consequently it stands in comparison to the complete and perfect power of anything, as the instrument to the principal agent. For an instrument . . . does not work save as moved by the principal agent, which works of itself. And therefore the power of the principal agent exists in nature completely and perfectly: whereas the instrumental power has a being that passes from one thing into another, and is incomplete; just as motion is an imperfect act passing from agent to patient.[46]

Is grace contained in the sacramental sign as a kind of transient quality? St. Thomas answers that grace is in the sacramental sign in an "incomplete" way through an instrumental *movement* by which the sacramental sign is used by Christ to transmit a supernatural quality to the recipient.[47] St. Thomas describes this transient instrumental power at work in Baptism:

> Now, the sanctification is not completed in water; but a certain sanctifying instrumental virtue [power], not permanent but transient, passes from the water, in which it is, into man who is the subject of true sanctification. Consequently the sacrament is not completed in the very water, but in applying the water to man—*i.e.*, in the washing.[48]

Thus, when we say that the sacraments "contain" grace, we should not think of the sacraments as containing supernatural qualities in some stable way as a kind of vessel containing medicine or paint. Rather they are said to contain grace only imperfectly insofar as they are used and moved by Christ to be instruments to infuse supernatural qualities *in us*. Similarly, the paintbrush does not have the virtue of art in itself but receives from the painter a transient instrumental power to create

---

[46] *ST* III, q. 62, a. 4.

[47] See *ST* III, q. 62, a. 4, ad 2: "Just as motion, through being an imperfect act, is not properly in a genus, but is reducible to a genus of perfect act, for instance, alteration to the genus of quality: so, instrumental power, properly speaking, is not in any genus, but is reducible to a genus and species of perfect act."

[48] *ST* III, q. 66, a. 1.

beauty in the work of art in the moment of use. Likewise, when Christ worked miracles through his words, He gave them a transient instrumental power to be the instrument of His all-powerful divine will in healing the sick or raising the dead.

As the outward sacramental sign receives from Christ a transient instrumental power in the communication of grace, so analogously the *res et sacramentum*, imprinted by the outward sign, is also used by Christ as an abiding instrumental power to continue to give grace.[49] The difference between them is that the *res et sacramentum* abides—permanently in the case of sacramental character—whereas the sacramental sign passes away with the cessation of the words. A human analogy for the abiding nature of the instrumental power of the *res et sacramentum* is the printed word, which abides as an instrument of communication long after the spoken word has passed away. We can say that the printed word, as long as it lasts, contains a meaning. In a similar way, the *res et sacramentum* can be said to "contain" grace in that it is likewise an abiding instrumental word of power. In the Eucharist, the *res et sacramentum*—Christ's Body and Blood—has an abiding sanctifying power by virtue of the hypostatic union through which it is the humanity of the Word. In the other sacraments, the sanctifying power of the *res et sacramentum* would come through the fact that it is a configuration to Christ's humanity, who can work through it as His abiding efficacious word printed not on paper but on the soul. This imprinting is clearest in the three sacraments that give indelible character, but I have argued that the *res et sacramentum* of the other three sacraments also gives a distinct configuration to Christ. In Matrimony this configuration is to Christ the Bridegroom in His spousal union with the Church. In Penance the configuration is with Christ who satisfied for sin, and in Anointing of the Sick, it is with Christ's redemptive suffering.

---

[49] See *ST* III, q. 63, a. 2: "A character signifies a certain spiritual power ordained unto things pertaining to the Divine worship. But it must be observed that this spiritual power is instrumental: as we have stated above [q. 62, a. 4] of the virtue which is in the sacraments. For to have a sacramental character belongs to God's ministers: and a minister is a kind of instrument.... Consequently, just as the virtue which is in the sacraments is not of itself in a genus, but is reducible to a genus, for the reason that it is of a transitory and incomplete nature: so also a character is not properly in a genus or species, but is reducible to the second species of quality."

Analogy of Human Words
with the Words of God

It is helpful to compare the instrumental causality of ordinary human signs with sacramental signs.[50] Ordinary human words, oral or written, are sounds or shapes that accomplish something immensely greater than themselves. The sounds or shapes themselves have no understanding, but transmit a rational understanding to the listener. This is because they are being used by rational beings who are the principal agents. The instrument, while doing what is proper to its own nature (existing as a collection of sounds or shapes), accomplishes an instrumental effect that is above the nature of the instrument and is on the level of the principal agent. Mindless shapes and sounds produce rational communication because they are being used by rational beings.

We should expect something analogous to be the case for sacramental signs. What they accomplish should be on the level not of the minister or recipient but of the principal agent of sacramental action, who is God, making use of the humanity of Christ, which makes use of the sacramental signs. Thus it is fitting that sacramental signs transcend the action of communication, which is proper to human words, and partake of the creative power of the Word Incarnate. It is proper to the Word of God to be an omnipotent cause that infallibly brings about its effect. The words used in sacramental action, therefore, because they are instruments of the Word, are capable of bringing about a divine effect, which is a participation in His nature through the infusion of grace. If mindless shapes and sounds can produce rational communication when used by rational animals, it is not unreasonable to think that sounds and gestures can produce a supernatural effect when used by a supernatural agent.

Christ, as the principal agent of sacramental action, can use words and gestures to refer to supernatural realities, and at the same time,

---

[50] See *ST* III, q. 62, a. 4, ad 1: "A spiritual power cannot be in a corporeal subject, after the manner of a permanent and complete power, as the argument proves. But there is nothing to hinder an instrumental spiritual power from being in a body; in so far as a body can be moved by a particular spiritual substance so as to produce a particular spiritual effect; thus in the very voice which is perceived by the senses there is a certain spiritual power, inasmuch as it proceeds from a mental concept, of arousing the mind of the hearer. It is in this way that a spiritual power is in the sacraments, inasmuch as they are ordained by God unto the production of a spiritual effect."

because of His omnipotence, He can bring into being those super-natural realities that are represented by His words and gestures. St. Thomas explains the instrumentality exercised by the Word Incarnate:

> The sacraments have an instrumental power to produce a spiritual effect. Since the sacrament is realized with a divine invocation, it realizes this effect. And this is fitting because the Word, through which all the sacraments have power, took on flesh and was the Word of God. And since the flesh of Christ had the instrumental power to do miracles because of its union with the Word, so the sacraments have it through their union with Christ who was crucified and suffered.[51]

Perhaps this can be grasped best by keeping in mind the distinction between the divine and the human intellect. The divine intellect is the cause of reality; the human intellect receives knowledge of reality. God creates through His Word; we understand through our words. Thus it is fitting that the divine Word uses words in a divine creative way, whereas we use words in a human way to signify what we have understood and to arouse that knowledge in another. God alone can use words not merely to signify and arouse understanding but also to *cause* the being that is signified. The sacraments of the New Covenant *use words in this divine way*. They can do so because sacramental words and signs are being used by Christ who has the power, through His divinity, to make His words and signs cause what they signify.

The Sacramental Sign Cooperates by Its Own Proper Action

The objection is often made against St. Thomas's theory of sacramental causality that the sacramental instrument does not seem to be able to contribute anything by its proper action to the conferring of grace.[52] This objection presupposes St. Thomas's teaching that in order for something to be an instrumental cause, its own proper action must

---

[51] *Quodlibet* 12, q. 9, a. 1, my translation from the Latin text in *Questioni su argomenti vari—Quaestiones quodlibetales*, ed. Roberto Coggi (Bologna: Edizioni Studio Domenicano, 2003), 2:718.

[52] See, for example, Karl Rahner in *The Church and the Sacraments*, 36–37, which will be discussed in the following chapter.

contribute something to the effect, even though its proper action is elevated by the principal cause. Thus a chisel contributes by cutting, which is its proper effect, while the cutting is directed by the mind of the artist in a way that transcends the chisel.

How does this happen in the sacraments? The proper effect of the sacramental signs, like all signs, is to signify. The sacramental signs signify the different ways in which Christ sanctifies us through them: washing us from sin, anointing us with grace and power, and nourishing us with His Body. St. Thomas poses this objection in *De veritate*.[53] He responds: "The natural action of a material instrument helps toward the effect of the sacrament insofar as the sacrament is applied by it to the recipient and insofar as the signification of the sacrament is completed by the said action, as the signification of baptism by washing."[54] In other words, the sacramental sign contributes in two crucial ways to the realization of the effect of grace: it makes present Christ's words and gestures that are omnipotent signs of sanctification, and applies them to a particular subject. The omnipotent power of the principal agent elevates the sacramental signs by working through them to realize the sanctification they signify.

CHRIST'S HUMAN ACTS ARE PRIVILEGED INSTRUMENTS AT WORK THROUGH THE SACRAMENTS

In his earliest work on sacramental causality in his commentary on the *Sentences*, St. Thomas introduces the notion of instrumental causality but does not yet directly link it to the instrumentality of Christ's human actions. Beginning with *De veritate* and continuing to part III of the *Summa theologiae*, where it is especially prominent,

---

[53] *De veritate*, q. 27, a. 4, obj. 17, trans. Schmidt, *Truth*, 3:329: "In every instrument its natural action, which contributes something to the effect intended by the principal agent, is required. But the natural action of a material element does not seem to have anything to do with the effect of grace which God intends to produce in the soul. . . . Such sacraments therefore do not work toward the conferring of grace as instruments."

[54] *De veritate*, q. 27, a. 4, ad 17, trans. Schmidt, *Truth*, 3:336. See also ad 13, p. 335: "In keeping with its own form a sacrament signifies or is such as to signify the effect to which it is divinely ordained. In this respect it is a suitable instrument, because the sacraments cause by signifying."

St. Thomas developed the idea that Christ's human actions, through the hypostatic union, have the power to serve as instrumental efficient causes of our salvation, which are applied to us through the sacraments and faith.[55]

St. Thomas argues that all the mysteries of Christ's earthly life—His birth, Passion, death, burial, Resurrection, and Ascension—worked instrumentally, through their union with the divinity, and serve as instrumental causes of our salvation. In explaining how the sacraments derive their power from Christ's Passion, whose power in turn comes from the hypostatic union, St. Thomas writes: "His flesh, and the mysteries accomplished therein, are as instrumental causes in the process of giving life to the soul."[56]

The mysteries of the life of Christ, especially His Passion, are instrumental causes of our salvation at work in the sacraments in three ways: (1) meriting all human salvation, (2) being the model of the sanctification worked by the sacraments, and (3) being an instrumental efficient cause of that sanctification that is applied to us through the sacraments. Of these three, the first two are easier to understand than the third.

Christ's Passion Is the Universal Meritorious Cause

Christ's Passion is the fundamental meritorious cause of all human salvation. A meritorious cause makes something *due* to someone.[57] It can be understood as a special type of efficient cause that produces a particular kind of immaterial effect, which is a disposition or right in a subject by which something is justly or mercifully due to him from

---

[55] See *De veritate*, q. 27, a. 4, quoted above on pp. 430–31. St. Thomas announces this idea at the beginning of his treatment of the sacraments in *ST* III, q. 60, prologue: "After considering those things that concern the mystery of the incarnate Word, we must consider the sacraments of the Church which derive their efficacy from the Word incarnate Himself."

[56] *ST* III, q. 62, a. 5, ad 1.

[57] See Thomas Aquinas, *De veritate*, q. 29, a. 6, trans. Schmidt, *Truth*, 3:427: "Merit is the cause of reward, not as a final cause (for in this sense the reward is rather the cause of the merit), but rather by reduction to efficient causality, inasmuch as merit makes a man worthy of a reward and in this way disposes him for it." From merit a *right* is derived, which in turn is a cause for the sake of which other agents ought to act in the line of final causality. This right specifies their act of justice.

another. A meritorious cause is not an efficient cause of grace or other gifts, but of a kind of "right" for them to be given.

Because He is Head of His mystical body and of humanity, Christ could freely merit not only for Himself but also for all His actual and potential members, mercifully making it due to them to receive graces from God. As St. Thomas says,

> Grace was in Christ not merely as in an individual, but also as in the Head of the whole Church, to Whom all are united, as members to a head, who constitute one mystical person. And hence it is that Christ's merit extends to others inasmuch as they are His members; even as in a man the action of the head reaches in a manner to all his members, since it perceives not merely for itself alone, but for all the members.[58]

All sacramental action applies this universal merit of the Passion to grant grace to the faithful throughout the life of the Church.

The Mysteries of Christ's Life Are Exemplar Causes of the Christian Life

In addition to meriting all grace, the mysteries of Christ's life are also exemplar causes of our salvation. An exemplar cause serves as a model for an effect, as the blueprint is the model for a house, a score for a piece of music, or a script for a play. It is a kind of formal cause, but it differs from the usual sense of formal cause in being extrinsic and prior to the effect.

All of Christ's human actions are exemplar causes of the Christian life.[59] His self-emptying, as described in Philippians 2:5–9, is the model for all Christian humility. His sacrificial love is the model for all Christian spouses, as St. Paul makes clear in Ephesians 5:25–33. His generosity in becoming poor for our sakes is the model for Christian almsgiving.[60] His redemptive suffering is the model for all Christians

---

[58] *ST* III, q. 19, a. 4.

[59] In other words, the events or mysteries of Christ's life serve as moral types of the Christian life. See *CCC*, §117, and Feingold, *Faith Comes from What Is Heard*, 497–99; 535–36.

[60] In exhorting the Corinthians to generosity in 2 Cor 8:9, St. Paul says: "You know the grace of our Lord Jesus Christ, that though he was rich, yet for your sake he became poor, so that by his poverty you might become rich."

to "complete what is lacking in Christ's afflictions for the sake of his body" (Col 1:24).

The Mysteries of Christ's Life Are Efficient Causes Configuring Us to Him through the Sacraments

An exemplar cause as such does not directly produce its likeness in another, and therefore an exemplar cause, such as a blueprint or musical score, needs an efficient cause, such as a builder or an orchestra, to realize it.

Now we, through our natural actions and free will, are not capable of being efficient causes for realizing in ourselves a true image of Christ's life. To think otherwise would be the Pelagian heresy. Therefore, in addition to being an exemplar cause, Christ also needs to be the efficient cause by which the model given by His life gets reproduced in us. How does He do this?

In a marvelous way, Christ's human acts are simultaneously exemplar and efficient causes that both model what we are to be and are mysteriously at work to realize the likeness of that model in us. Christ's human acts are *efficacious models* wielded by the divine power to realize in us a *configuration* with Christ in His Paschal mystery by imprinting on us, through the sacraments, spiritual effects represented by bodily actions of Christ.

A fundamental principle of efficient causality is that causes produce effects similar to themselves. Like begets like, for the form possessed by the agent gets communicated to the effect. A hot object makes other things hot, and light illuminates. Something similar happens in spiritual things, although not mechanically. A teacher who has deep knowledge is able to communicate that knowledge to others, and a virtuous person can lead others to virtue. In the supernatural order we see that God has made supreme use of this principle. One of the reasons that the Word was made flesh is so that the key events of His life could become the causes, by way of likeness and power, of similar effects in us. Thus He assumed death so that we might die to sin.

In this way the mysteries of Christ's life serve both as the exemplar and efficient causes of similar effects in mankind. The divine plan uses Christ's human actions as instrumental efficient *causes to bring about in us what they represent*. The human actions of Christ throughout the Paschal mystery—His Passion, death, Resurrection, and Ascension—are the conjoined instruments that work through the sacraments, which represent them, to bring about in us an *effect similar to themselves*. Christ's death is thus the exemplar and efficient instrumental cause of our death to sin and to the old man. His Resurrection and Ascension are the exemplar and efficient causes of our rising to new life.

When St. Thomas treats the mysteries of Christ's life in the third part of the *Summa theologiae*, he distinguishes between the way in which Christ's Passion causes our redemption through merit, which is easier to understand, and through being an instrumental efficient cause of our death to sin. With regard to the latter, he writes:

> There is a twofold efficient agency—namely, the principal and the instrumental. Now the principal efficient cause of man's salvation is God. But since Christ's humanity is the "instrument of the Godhead," as stated above (q. 43, a. 2), therefore all Christ's actions and sufferings operate instrumentally in virtue of His Godhead for the salvation of men. Consequently, then, Christ's Passion accomplishes man's salvation efficiently.[61]

The same reasoning is applied to Christ's experiencing of death. Unlike the Passion, the fact of Christ's death during the three days in which His soul was separated from His body could not be meritorious in itself, for no one merits simply by being dead. Nevertheless, Christ's experience of death is an instrumental cause of our death to sin and corruption. St. Thomas writes:

> Christ's death cannot be the cause of our salvation by way of merit, but only by way of causality, that is to say, inasmuch as the Godhead was not separated from Christ's flesh by death; and therefore, whatever befell Christ's flesh, even when the soul was departed, was conducive to salvation in virtue of the Godhead united. But the *effect of any cause is properly estimated according to its resemblance to the cause*. Consequently, since death is a kind of privation of one's own life, the effect of Christ's death is considered in relation to the removal of the obstacles to our salvation: and these are the death of the soul

---

[61] *ST* III, q. 48, a. 6.

and of the body. Hence Christ's death is said to have destroyed in us both the death of the soul, caused by sin . . . and the death of the body, consisting in the separation of the soul, according to 1 Cor 15:54: "Death is swallowed up in victory."[62]

Christ's Resurrection similarly could not be a meritorious cause, for it is after the end of His earthly life and does not involve any difficulty, but it is used by God to be an exemplar and instrumental efficient cause of our rising to new supernatural life through the forgiveness of sin and the infusion of sanctifying grace.

> Christ's Resurrection works in virtue of the Godhead; now this virtue extends not only to the Resurrection of bodies, but also to that of souls: for it comes of God that the soul lives by grace, and that the body lives by the soul. Consequently, Christ's Resurrection has instrumentally an effective power not only with regard to the resurrection of bodies, but also with respect to the resurrection of souls. In like fashion it is an exemplar cause with regard to the resurrection of souls, because even in our souls we must be conformed with the rising Christ as the Apostle says (Rom 6:4–11): "Christ is risen from the dead by the glory of the Father, so we also may walk in newness of life."[63]

Christ's Ascension similarly works as an exemplar and instrumental efficient cause in realizing our spiritual ascension to heaven,[64] in accordance with Colossians 3:1–3: "If then you have been raised with Christ, seek the things that are above, where Christ is, seated at the right hand of God. Set your minds on things that are above, not on things that are on earth. For you have died, and your life is hidden with Christ in God."

---

[62] *ST* III, q. 50, a. 6 (my italics).

[63] *ST* III, q. 56, a. 2. See Jean-Pierre Torrell, "La causalité salvifique de la résurrection du Christ selon saint Thomas," *Revue Thomiste* 96 (1996): 179–208.

[64] See *ST* III, q. 57, a. 6, ad 2: "Christ's Passion is the cause of our ascending to heaven, properly speaking, by removing the hindrance which is sin, and also by way of merit: whereas Christ's Ascension is the direct cause of our ascension, as by beginning it in Him Who is our Head, with Whom the members must be united."

The Sacraments Apply the Causality of
Christ's Paschal Mystery to the Faithful

If Christ's Passion, death, Resurrection, and Ascension are instrumental efficient causes of our salvation, we may wonder why we need the sacraments at all. Why did not Christ's Passion and Resurrection simply cause all human salvation once and for all, such that nothing more would now be necessary? St. Thomas poses this objection,[65] and answers that the Paschal mystery of Christ is a universal cause of the salvation of all men of all times and places, but this universal cause needs to be applied to all men personally and on various occasions to be a remedy for sins. This personal application occurs through the sacraments: "Since Christ's Passion preceded, as a kind of universal cause of the forgiveness of sins, it needs to be applied to each individual for the cleansing of personal sins. Now this is done by baptism and penance and the other sacraments, which derive their power from Christ's Passion."[66] Thus the sacraments are instruments of Christ's Paschal mystery,[67] which is an instrument of His divinity. St. Thomas's teaching here is firmly grounded in the teaching of St. Paul in Romans 6:3–4 with regard to Baptism, through which Christ's Paschal mystery

---

[65] *ST* III, q. 49, a. 1, obj. 4: "Given an efficient cause, nothing else is required for producing the effect. But other things besides are required for the forgiveness of sins, such as baptism and penance. Consequently it seems that Christ's Passion is not the sufficient cause of the forgiveness of sins."

[66] *ST* III, q. 49, a. 1, ad 4. A similar objection is posed in *ST* III, q. 61, a. 1, obj. 3, to which St. Thomas responds (ad 3): "Christ's Passion is a sufficient cause of man's salvation. But it does not follow that the sacraments are not also necessary for that purpose: because they obtain their effect through the power of Christ's Passion; and Christ's Passion is, so to say, applied to man through the sacraments according to the Apostle (Rom 6:3): 'All we who are baptized in Christ Jesus, are baptized in His death.'" See van Meegeren, *De causalitate instrumentali humanitatis Christi*, 160–61. Nevertheless, as will be seen in chapters 14 and 15, the effect can also be realized spiritually through devout desire for it, as in Baptism of desire. See *ST* III, q. 62, a. 6: "Now nothing hinders that which is subsequent in point of time, from causing movement, even before it exists in reality, in so far as it pre-exists in an act of the soul: thus the end, which is subsequent in point of time, moves the agent in so far as it is apprehended and desired by him."

[67] See *ST* III, q. 65, a. 1, ad 1: "The same principal agent uses various instruments unto various effects, in accordance with the thing to be done. In the same way the Divine power and the Passion of Christ work in us through the various sacraments as through various instruments."

is reproduced in the lives of the faithful, who die to sin and rise to new life in Him:

> Do you not know that all of us who have been baptized into Christ Jesus were baptized into his death? We were buried therefore with him by baptism into death, so that as Christ was raised from the dead by the glory of the Father, we too might walk in newness of life.

In other words, Christ's death and Resurrection is the model of the transformation that takes place in the baptized, by which they are made dead to the sins of their past life and are resurrected into life in Christ in His Church. Through the sacrament of Baptism, His death and Resurrection come into contact with the baptized so as to be the instrumental efficient causes of that transformation in His image.

Christ's death and Resurrection are at work in the faithful through all three levels of the sacrament of Baptism. In the outward sacramental sign of Baptism, the immersion represents Christ's death, and the rising from the baptismal font represents Christ's Resurrection, as seen in chapter 5 above. The faithful are configured to Christ's death and Resurrection by receiving an efficacious sign of participation in His death and Resurrection. Furthermore, the likeness in the outward sacramental sign is indelibly stamped on the faithful through the inward sign, which is baptismal character, creating an abiding configuration with the crucified and risen Christ. This character continues to resound as the word of Christ, calling down the grace that conforms us to the mission of the sacrament.[68] Therefore, as long as the faithful do not pose an obstacle, the configuration to Christ through character also produces a *spiritual* likeness through the effect of grace, by which we truly share in death to sin (through justification) and His risen life (through sanctifying grace).

Similarly, Christ's Passion, death, and Resurrection are at work in the Eucharist, for the faithful are assimilated to Christ's sacrifice through receiving His Body given for us and Blood poured out in His Passion, and which are now glorified so as to be the seed of eternal life and the "medicine of immortality."[69]

The sacraments enable Christ's past salvific actions to be applied

---

[68] See Isa 55:10–11.

[69] Ignatius, *Letter to the Ephesians* 20, in *The Apostolic Fathers*, trans. Holmes, 199.

to the faithful throughout the centuries in the Church, transforming us in their likeness. Although the mysteries of Christ's life are in the past, He continues to touch us with their instrumental power that endures and continues to operate through the sacraments until the end of time. Christ can do this because the actions of His humanity are the actions of an infinite divine Person, and thus transcend the limits of finitude and time, and can be applied by the divine power throughout the time of the Church.[70] Just as Christ's Passion merited grace for all men of all times and places, so the exemplar and efficient causality of the mysteries of Christ's life are unlimited and capable of working in all subsequent[71] times and places until the end of time. The sacraments put us mysteriously into real contact with the infinite power of Christ's Paschal mystery, which remains ever operative. Through the sacraments, the faithful in every age of the Church are truly touched and transformed by Christ's Passion and Resurrection so as to receive the imprint of His death and rising in the destruction of sin and the reception of a share in His divine life.

---

[70] See *ST* III, q. 52, a. 8: "Now Christ's Passion had a virtue which was neither temporal nor transitory, but everlasting, according to Heb. 10:14: 'For by one oblation He hath perfected for ever them that are sanctified.' And so it is evident that Christ's Passion had no greater efficacy then than it has now." St. Thomas applies this doctrine to the Resurrection of Christ in *ST* III, q. 56, a. 1, ad 3: "And therefore, just as all other things which Christ did and endured in His humanity are profitable to our salvation through the power of the Godhead, as already stated [q. 48, a. 6], so also is Christ's Resurrection the efficient cause of ours, through the Divine power whose office it is to quicken the dead; and this power by its presence is in touch with all places and times; and such virtual contact suffices for its efficiency." See Torrell, "La causalité salvifique de la résurrection," 201.

[71] See Torrell, "La causalité salvifique de la résurrection," 202. The conjoined instrument must first exist through the Incarnation before it can be fittingly applied to human beings through sacraments (separated instruments). For this reason the sacraments of the Old and New Covenant differ in kind in that only the latter can be efficient instrumental causes applying to mankind the efficient causality of the mysteries of Christ's life (once they have occurred in history). The grace merited by Christ was applied retroactively by God to sanctify men living before the Incarnation (as in the Immaculate Conception and the sanctification of all the just before Christ), but the efficient causality of the mysteries of Christ's life, as it works through the sacraments of the New Covenant, presupposes that the Incarnation has already occurred.

SUMMARY OF ST. THOMAS'S CONTRIBUTION TO SACRAMENTAL CAUSALITY

1. The sacraments are true efficient causes of grace and not just necessary conditions or occasions in which God infallibly gives grace. An efficient cause has a greater dignity than an occasion or condition because the cause directly imprints a form into the recipient. St. Thomas holds it to be a truth revealed in Scripture and Tradition that the sacraments have the dignity of causes. By washing, anointing, or nourishing the body, they work mysteriously to wash, anoint, and nourish the soul.

2. The sacraments are *instrumental* efficient causes of grace, which explains how they can give something spiritual and supernatural that is immeasurably above their own level. This thesis is the principal merit of St. Thomas's doctrine.

3. St. Thomas distinguishes two kinds of instruments: conjoined and separated. The humanity of Christ is the great conjoined instrument of His divinity. The sacraments should be conceived as separated instruments in the hands of Christ, the conjoined instrument. This doctrine has the great merit of showing the most intimate connection between Christ and the sacraments. This connection is highlighted in the very plan of the third part of the *Summa theologiae*, which begins with the Incarnation and the mysteries of Christ's life and then passes on to the sacraments, which enable us to come into contact with Christ in the Church. There is a marvelous chain of instrumental causes at work in the sacraments, and the central link of this chain is the humanity of Christ, the "conjoined instrument" of our salvation.

4. Although no creature can be used as an instrument in God's work of creation *ex nihilo*, there is no inherent reason why an instrument cannot be used in God's work of infusing grace into our souls. The sacramental instrument here is doing something on its own level, which is to signify an invisible effect and come into sensible contact with a recipient.[72]

    Sacramental causality does not consist in creating grace out of nothing but of educing it from a real capacity of the human person made in the image of God. By being created in the image of God, we are *capax Dei*, capable of being raised to a higher

---

[72] *De veritate*, q. 27, a. 4, ad 17, trans. Schmidt, *Truth*, 3:336.

likeness with God. St. Thomas's theology refers to this mysterious capacity to receive grace and glory as an obediential potency specific to the rational creature.

5. The instrumental causality of the sacraments operates in two steps: the sacramental sign is the instrumental cause of the *res et sacramentum*, which in turn instrumentally causes the effect of grace, according to St. Thomas's mature teaching, beginning with *De veritate*. This marks a great improvement over his theory in the commentary on the *Sentences*.

6. Therefore, both the outward sacramental sign and the *res et sacramentum* can be understood as words of power which do what they say, like the words of Christ which worked physical miracles. The *res et sacramentum* is like an invisible and abiding word of power.

7. The effect of an instrumental cause includes something proper to the instrument and something proper to the principal cause. In the celebration of the sacraments, what is proper to the instrument (the sacramental sign) is to signify human sanctification and come into contact with the recipient,[73] whereas the infusion of grace is proper to the principal cause. Christ thus fittingly chose the sacramental signs for their ability to do these two things: to signify the graces He wishes to give us and to come into contact with the faithful in the Church through the centuries. The divine power, to whom it is proper to speak omnipotent words and to infuse grace, elevates the sacramental instrument by making it capable of not only signifying grace but also of causing it to exist in the recipient. This explanation does equal justice to the sign value of the sacraments and to their instrumental causal efficacy, which comes from their being used by Christ.

8. In this way of understanding the sacraments, the humanity of Christ (rather than the Church) could be seen as the "super-sacrament" that is the foundation of the sacramental system, at work in every celebration of the sacraments through which the Church is built up.[74] Christ makes use of the culminating acts of His earthly life as instruments in His work of salvation that serve as merito-

---

[73] *De veritate*, q. 27, a. 4, ad 17, trans. Schmidt, Truth, 3:336.

[74] This seems much more satisfactory than the thesis of Karl Rahner, expounded in *The Church and the Sacraments*, 18–24, 39–41, according to which the Church, after Christ, would be "the primal and fundamental sacrament" (p. 19), "in as much as the Church's whole reality is to be the real presence of God's grace" (p. 39).

rious, exemplar, and efficient causes.

The Passion and Resurrection are types of death to sin and of rising to supernatural life. They are efficacious signs that signify and have power to realize what they signify. The sacraments represent Christ's Passion and Resurrection and apply the inexhaustible power of these acts to the recipient. The Paschal mystery, although belonging to past time, transcends time as the action of a divine Person, and continues to operate and touch us today through the sacraments, molding us into its likeness according to the docility of our dispositions.

Study Questions

1. In what sense can the sacraments be understood as instruments of Christ? Explain the notion of instrumental causality and how it applies to the sacraments.
2. How does St. Thomas answer the objection that it seems impossible for a sensible agent to be a cause of the infusion of grace?
3. How does St. Thomas's theory of sacramental causality differ from those of his contemporaries?
4. How does St. Thomas simplify his theory of sacramental causality in his mature works (after his commentary on the *Sentences*)? Explain the twofold causality at work in the sacraments in St. Thomas's mature theory, and relate it to the three levels of the sacraments.
5. How does the distinction between conjoined and extrinsic instruments apply to the sacraments? Describe the chain of instrumental causes at work in the sacraments.
6. How do the mysteries of Christ's life serve as causes of our salvation? Distinguish meritorious, exemplar, and efficient causality. (b) How are the mysteries of Christ's life able to act throughout history? (c) How are the mysteries of Christ's life active in sacramental causality?

Suggestions for Further Reading

Biagi, Ruggero. *La causalità dell'umanità di Cristo e dei Sacramenti nella "Summa theologiae" di san Tommaso d'Aquino.* Bologna: Edizioni

Studio Domenicano, 1985.

Blankenhorn, Bernard. "The Instrumental Causality of the Sacraments: Thomas Aquinas and Louis-Marie Chauvet." *Nova et Vetera* (English) 4, no. 2 (2006): 255–94.

Gallagher, John F. *Significando causant: A Study of Sacramental Efficiency*. Fribourg, CH: University Press, 1965. Pp. 82–134.

Lynch, Reginald M., O.P. "Cajetan's Harp: Sacraments and the Life of Grace in Light of Perfective Instrumentality." *The Thomist* 78 (2014): 65–106.

_____. *The Cleansing of the Heart: The Sacraments as Instrumental Causes in the Thomistic Tradition*. Washington, DC: Catholic University of America Press, 2017. Pp. 67–153.

_____. "The Sacraments as Causes of Sanctification." *Nova et Vetera* (English) 12, no. 3 (2014): 791–836, especially 807–11.

Nutt, Roger. *General Principles of Sacramental Theology*. Washington, DC: Catholic University of America Press, 2017. Pp. 99–137.

O'Neill, Colman E. *Meeting Christ in the Sacraments*. Revised edition, revised by Romanus Cessario. Staten Island, NY: St. Paul's, 1991. Pp. 23–76.

Walsh, Liam G., O.P. "The Divine and the Human in St. Thomas's Theology of Sacraments." In *Ordo sapientiae et amoris: Image et message de Saint Thomas D'Aquin à travers les récentes études historiques, herméneutiques et doctrinales*, 321–52. Edited by Carlos-Josaphat Pinto de Oliveira, O.P. Fribourg, CH: Editions Universitaires Fribourg Suisse, 1993.

CHAPTER THIRTEEN

Causality of the Sacraments *ex opere operato*: The Reformation and Post-Tridentine Theories

MAGISTERIAL TEACHING ON SACRAMENTAL EFFICACY BEFORE TRENT

The Council of Florence: The Sacraments of the New Covenant Compared with Those of the Old

Prior to the Reformation, the Church defended the efficacy of the sacraments to confer grace against two heretical views. One was a tendency to equate the sacraments of the new Law with those of the Old, as can be seen in the Judaizers combatted by St. Paul in Galatians. The Council of Florence condemned this view. In its Decree for the Armenians, it affirmed the causal efficacy of the sacraments of the New Covenant, stating that the seven sacraments of the New Covenant "differ greatly from the sacraments of the Old Law. The latter, in fact, did not cause grace, but they only prefigured the grace to be given through the Passion of Christ. These sacraments of ours, however, both contain grace and communicate it to those who worthily receive them."[1]

This text does not enter into how the sacraments contain and communicate grace, leaving wide latitude to different theological schools. The key point is that the sacraments of the New Covenant have an

---

[1] Council of Florence, *Exsultate Deo* (DS, 1310).

efficacy essentially different from those of the Old in that the latter are not true causes of grace, but prefigure it; whereas the sacraments of the Church are causes of grace in that they both *contain* and *communicate* it to those who do not pose an obstacle. A deeper exploration of this difference will be given in the following chapter.

The Council of Trent confirmed this teaching on the essential difference between the Old and New Testament sacraments, but in a more general way: "If anyone says that these same sacraments of the New Law do not differ from the sacraments of the Old Law, except that the ceremonies and external rites are different, let him be anathema."[2]

The Sinful State of the Minister Does Not Affect Sacramental Efficacy

Another heretical view concerning sacramental efficacy is thinking that a minister in mortal sin is unable to validly confer the sacraments and give grace. This was an error of the Donatists in the fourth century, combatted by St. Augustine, and it reappeared in the Albigensians and Waldensians of the Middle Ages. It was against this type of error that the expression *ex opere operato* was first used to signify that the sanctification imparted by the sacrament did not come from the minister or his personal holiness but from the sacramental rite itself, as long as there was no obstacle on the part of the recipient. Thus it was taught that the sacraments are efficacious through the "work done" (*opus operatum*) and not from the "work of the minister" (*opus operantis*).

In 1208, Innocent III taught this in a profession of faith for the Waldensians:

> We do not reject the sacraments that are conferred in the Church, in cooperation with the inestimable and invisible power of the Holy Spirit, even though these sacraments be administered by a sinful priest, as long as he is recognized by the Church. . . . For the evil life of a bishop or a priest has no harmful effect on either the baptism of an infant or the consecration of the Eucharist or other ecclesiastical duties performed for the faithful.[3]

---

[2] Council of Trent, Decree on the Sacraments (session 7), can. 2 on the Sacraments in General (DS, 1602).

[3] Innocent III, Letter to the Archbishop of Tarragona *Eius exemplo*, (Dec 18,

The Council of Trent repeated this teaching: "If anyone says that a minister in the state of mortal sin, though he observes all the essentials that belong to the effecting or conferring of the sacrament, does not effect or confer the sacrament, let him be anathema."[4]

PROTESTANT REJECTION OF THE DOCTRINE THAT SACRAMENTS OPERATE *EX OPERE OPERATO*

One of the principal issues dividing the original Protestants from the Catholic Church was how the sacraments contribute to man's justification and whether they are efficacious *ex opere operato*. Indeed, over half of the dogmatic canons of the Council of Trent concern the sacraments. It is not hard to understand how the power of the sacraments to work *ex opere operato* would be a sign of contradiction, for it is a sublime mystery intimately related to the Incarnation. The *Catechism of the Council of Trent* draws attention to this:

> How so great and marvelous an effect is produced by the sacraments—how, to use St. Augustine's expression, "water cleanses the body and reaches the heart"—is indeed something that man's mind by reason alone is unable to comprehend. For it is self-evident that nothing of a purely sense nature can reach the soul. Yet, by the light of faith, we know that in the sacraments exists the power of the omnipotent God, effecting that which natural elements of themselves can never accomplish.[5]

One thing uniting practically all Protestants is their rejection of the efficacy of the sacraments *ex opere operato*. This rejection, however, is partly based on a misunderstanding of the meaning of the term. It was, and still is, erroneously understood to mean that the disposition

---

1208; DS, 793). In his theological treatise, *De sacro altaris mysterio* 3.5 (PL 217:844), Innocent III wrote: "Although the work of the minister [*opus operans*] may sometimes be unclean, the [sacramental] work done [*opus operatum*] is always clean." See Emmanuel Doronzo, *De Sacramentis in genere* (Milwaukee, WI: Bruce, 1946), 146.

4   Council of Trent, Decree on the Sacraments (session 7), can. 12 on the Sacraments in General (DS, 1612).

5   *CCT*, part 2, intro., §27, p. 160.

of the recipient is irrelevant to the efficacy of the sacrament. This would make the sacraments seem like "magic." In reality, the phrase is principally intended to signify that the lack of holiness in the sacramental *minister* does not impede the sacramental action because the principal minister of the sacramental work (*opus operatum*) is Christ. A second Protestant misunderstanding of the term is to take it to mean that the recipient of the sacrament is doing a "good work" which thus would be meritorious, implying a Pelagian attitude of self-justification.[6] This totally misses the meaning of the term. The "work done" (*opus operatum*) refers to the valid realization of the outward sacramental sign (which brings about the *res et sacramentum*) and not to any meritorious activity of the recipient or minister. Nevertheless, in addition to misunderstandings of the meaning of the phrase, there is a substantial difference between the Catholic and Protestant views on sacramental causality.

Luther's Views on Sacramental Efficacy

Although Luther ardently defended certain aspects of sacramental efficacy (when received in faith) against more radical Reformers like Zwingli,[7] his doctrine of justification by faith alone shaped his interpretation of sacramental efficacy. If faith is the decisive element in justification, what is done by the sacrament? As seen above, Luther understands the sacraments as divinely instituted signs of a divine

---

[6] See Calvin, *Institutes*, bk. 4, ch. 14.26, p. 857: "It is here proper to remind the reader, that all the trifling talk of the sophists concerning the *opus operatum*, is not only false, but repugnant to the very nature of sacraments, which God appointed in order that believers, who are void and in want of all good, might bring nothing of their own, but simply beg. Hence it follows, that in receiving them they do nothing which deserves praise, and that in this action (which in respect of them is merely passive) no work can be ascribed to them."

[7] See Jonathan Trigg, "Luther on Baptism and Penance," in *The Oxford Handbook of Martin Luther's Theology*, ed. Robert Kolb, Irene Dingel, and L'ubomír Batka (Oxford: Oxford University Press, 2014), 311: "In the 1520s, especially from about 1527, Luther is increasingly aware of his need to contend with new sets of opponents. He sees opponents like Zwingli, and various elements of the 'Radical Reformation,' as in varying ways undermining the efficacy and objectivity of the sacraments, even if they do so in the name of faith and the Word. In their magnification of faith and the inward, they despise the commonplace outward—mere water, such as a maid washes with or a cow drinks—and they ignore the fact that God has bound his word of promise and command to that despised outward thing."

promise that are to be received in faith. The sacraments thus would be supreme and divinely mandated occasions for the exercise of faith in a sacramental word spoken by Christ directly to the believing recipient. Luther speaks of them as "sacraments of justifying faith."[8]

Luther rightly stresses the necessity for the recipient to have faith. This is a crucial condition for the fruitfulness of the sacrament. Nevertheless, he so puts the emphasis on the faith of the recipient that one could see faith as the *cause* of the sacramental efficacy and deny that the sacraments have a power to grant grace intrinsic to the sacrament, as long as the recipient does not pose an obstacle. Luther does not quite go so far, especially when he defends sacramental efficacy against Zwingli and his followers in the mid-1520s,[9] but this could be concluded from his line of reasoning and became the tendency of the later Protestant tradition. In *The Babylonian Captivity of the Church* he writes:

> A great majority have supposed that there is some hidden spiritual power in the word and water, which works the grace of God in the soul of the recipient. Others deny this and hold that there is no power in the sacraments, but that grace is given by God alone, who according to his covenant is present in the sacraments which he has instituted. Yet all are agreed that the sacraments are "effective signs" of grace, and they reach this conclusion by this one argument: if the sacraments of the New Law were mere signs, there would be no apparent reason why they should surpass those of the Old Law. . . .
>
> Such views, however, must be carefully avoided and shunned, because they are godless and infidel, contrary to

---

[8] Luther, *The Babylonian Captivity of the Church*, in *LW* 36:65. The Council of Trent, Sacraments in General (session 7, Mar 3, 1547), can. 8 (DS, 1608) refers to this view in condemning those who hold that "faith alone in the divine promise is sufficient to obtain grace."

[9] See, for example, Luther's *Greater Catechism* on the subject of infant Baptism: "For my faith does not make the baptism, but receives baptism. . . . We bring the child in the belief and hope that it has faith, and pray God to give it faith." In J.D.C. Fisher, *Christian Initiation: The Reformation Period: Some Early Reformed Rites of Baptism and Confirmation and Other Contemporary Documents* (Chicago: Hillenbrand Books, 2007), 5. See Root, "Luther and Calvin on the Role of Faith in the Sacraments," 1073: "For Luther after the early 1520s, sacraments are both signs and means of grace, oriented to faith as receptive, but having effects in the individual beyond faith."

faith and inconsistent with the nature of the sacraments. For it is an error to hold that the sacraments of the New Law differ from those of the Old Law in the effectiveness of their signs. For in this they are the same. The same God who now saves us by baptism and the bread, saved Abel by his sacrifice, Noah by the rainbow, Abraham by circumcision, and all the others by their respective signs. . . .

But our signs or sacraments, as well as those of the fathers, have attached to them a word of promise which requires faith. . . . Hence they are signs or sacraments of justification, for they are sacraments of justifying faith and not of works. Their whole efficacy, therefore, consists in faith itself, not in the doing of a work. . . . It cannot be true, therefore, that there is contained in the sacraments a power efficacious for justification, or that they are "effective signs" of grace. All such things are said to the detriment of faith, and out of ignorance of the divine promise. Unless you should call them "effective" in the sense that they certainly and effectively impart grace where faith is unmistakably present.[10]

As can be seen from this passage, Luther's view of sacramental efficacy through faith led him to equate the efficacy of the sacraments of the Old and New Covenant, thus breaking decisively from the whole scholastic tradition. Despite their different views of the causality of the sacraments in the infusion of grace, scholastics like St. Bonaventure and St. Thomas agreed that the New Testament sacraments had a causal efficacy distinct from those of the Old Covenant. Luther's position was also incompatible with the teaching of the Council of Florence on this matter. Nevertheless, the last sentence quoted above shows that Luther still held on to some form of sacramental efficacy where faith grasps Christ's infallible promise offered in the sacrament, and in this he differed from the dominant forms of Protestantism that followed him.[11]

---

[10] Luther, *The Babylonian Captivity of the Church*, in *LW* 36:64–67.

[11] This is the thesis of Cary's profound article, "Why Luther Is Not Quite Protestant," *Pro Ecclesia* 14/4 (Fall 2005): 447–86.

Calvin's Rejection of Sacramental Causality *ex opere operato*

Like Luther before him, Calvin rejected the Catholic understanding of sacramental efficacy, denying that the sacraments work *ex opere operato*. In fact, he saw this to be a "fatal and pestilential" invention of the devil:

> For the schools of the sophists have taught with general consent that the sacraments of the new law, in other words, those now in use in the Christian church, justify, and confer grace, provided only that we do not interpose the obstacle of mortal sin. It is impossible to describe how fatal and pestilential this sentiment is, and the more so, that for many ages it has, to the great loss of the church, prevailed over a considerable part of the world. It is plainly of the devil.[12]

For Calvin the sacraments are "a testimony of the divine favor toward us, confirmed by an external sign, with a corresponding attestation of our faith toward him."[13] Sacraments thus are a privileged and divinely mandated means for us to attest our faith in God's promise of favor, sensibly manifested. As such, their efficacy consists in nourishing faith. He writes:

> Wherefore, with regard to the increase and confirmation of faith, I would remind the reader . . . that in assigning this office to the sacraments, it is not as if I thought there is a kind of secret efficacy perpetually inherent in them, by which they can of themselves promote or strengthen faith, but because our Lord has instituted them for the express purpose of helping to establish and increase our faith. The sacraments duly perform their office only when accompanied by the Spirit, the internal Master, whose energy alone penetrates the heart, stirs up the affections. . . . If He is wanting, the sacraments can avail us no

---

[12] Calvin, *Institutes*, bk. 4, ch. 14.14, p. 850. For Calvin's rejection of sacramental efficacy *ex opere operato* and its coherence with his rejection of the category of *res et sacramentum*, see Root, "Luther and Calvin on the Role of Faith in the Sacraments," 1080–81.

[13] Calvin, *Institutes*, bk. 4, ch. 14.1, p. 843.

more than the sun shining on the eyeballs of the blind.[14]

To illustrate his meaning, Calvin compares the sacraments with bread and other foods by which He gives us physical nourishment: "So in like manner he spiritually nourishes our faith by means of the sacraments, whose only office is to make his promises visible to our eye, or rather, to be pledges of his promises."[15] The comparison of physical and spiritual nourishment is traditional, and was used by Jesus in John 6 as well as by St. Thomas, as seen above.[16] Calvin, however, changes and weakens the comparison by stipulating that the sacraments nourish faith only by being pledges of God's promises. Food nourishes our bodies by being an efficient cause of nourishment. Calvin's understanding of the sacraments as sensible pledges leaves no room for them to exercise any kind of efficient causality. If the sacraments' "only office is to make his promises visible to our eye," then they are being understood only as signs, and not as true causes of what they represent. As such the sacraments do not have an efficacy distinct from God's other words of promise contained in the Scriptures: "It is an error to suppose that anything more is conferred by the sacraments than is offered by the word of God, and obtained by true faith. From this another thing follows—i.e., that assurance of salvation does not depend on participation in the sacraments, as if justification consisted in it."[17]

The Council of Trent condemned this kind of view in the fifth canon on the Sacraments: "If anyone says that these sacraments are instituted only for the sake of nourishing the faith, let him be anathema."[18]

Since Calvin rejected the notion that the sacraments have an

---

[14] Calvin, *Institutes*, bk. 4, ch. 14.9, p. 847.

[15] Calvin, *Institutes*, bk. 4, ch. 14.12, p. 849.

[16] *ST* III, q. 65, a. 1.

[17] Calvin, *Institutes*, bk. 4, ch. 14.14, p. 850. See also ch. 14.17, p. 851: "Let it be a fixed point that the office of the sacraments differs not from the word of God. . . . We must beware of being led into a kindred error by the terms, somewhat too extravagant, which ancient Christian writers have employed in extolling the dignity of the sacraments. We must not suppose that there is some latent virtue inherent in the sacraments by which they, in themselves, confer the gifts of the Holy Spirit upon us. . . . They do not of themselves bestow any grace, but they announce and manifest it, and, like earnests and badges, give a ratification of the gifts which the divine liberality has bestowed upon us."

[18] Council of Trent, Decree on the Sacraments (session 7), can. 5 on the Sacraments in General (DS, 1605).

intrinsic power to realize the sanctification they signify, like Luther, he equated the efficacy of the sacraments of the New Covenant with those of the Old.[19] The only difference between circumcision and Baptism would be the rite. He explains:

> The Scholastic dogma . . . by which the difference between the sacraments of the old and the new dispensation is made so great that the former did nothing but shadow forth the grace of God, while the latter actually confer that, must be altogether exploded. . . . [The apostle] first makes them [Jews] equal to us in the sacraments, and leaves us not one iota of privilege which could give us hopes of impunity. Nor can we justly attribute more to our baptism than he elsewhere attributes to circumcision, when he terms it a seal of the righteousness of faith (Rom 4:11). Whatever, therefore, is now exhibited to us in the sacraments, the Jews formerly received in theirs. . . . The same efficacy which ours possess they experienced in theirs—i.e., that they were seals of the divine favor toward them in regard to the hope of eternal salvation.[20]

Calvin is correct when he says that the sacraments do not give us "hopes of impunity." The purpose of the sacraments is not to make us free from blame, but to be channels of God's grace with which we can cooperate. But to whom more is given, more is expected.

Finally, Calvin rejects the "fiction by which the cause of justification and the power of the Holy Spirit are included in elements as vessels and vehicles."[21] Calvin is alluding here to the sacramental doctrine of Hugh of St. Victor, also adopted by the Council of Florence and Trent. Nevertheless, as we have seen, he is rejecting a distorted view of Catholic teaching. Grace is not in the sacraments as water is in a cup or medicine in a vial, but as the design in the mind of the artist is present in the paintbrush executing that design, or as the

---

[19] As seen above, this thesis of Luther and Calvin equating the sacraments of the New Covenant with those of the Old was condemned by the Council of Trent in the Decree on the Sacraments (session 7), can. 2 on the Sacraments in General (DS, 1602): "If anyone says that these same sacraments of the New Law do not differ from the sacraments of the Old Law, except that the ceremonies and external rites are different, let him be anathema."

[20] Calvin, *Institutes*, bk. 4, ch. 14.23, p. 855.

[21] Calvin, *Institutes*, bk. 4, ch. 14.17, p. 852.

divine omnipotence was in the words of Christ saying to the leper: "Be clean!" (Matt 8:3). In other words, God's grace is present in the sacraments not as a *thing* is present in a larger thing (water in a cup) but as the *power* or *movement* of the principal agent is present in a transitory way in the instrument as it is being used.

Catholic Response to Protestant Views on Sacramental Efficacy: The Sacraments Are Living Divine Words

In order to present the Catholic understanding of sacramental efficacy to Protestants, Louis Bouyer has proposed that we should focus on the category of the Word of God, which is so dear to the Protestant tradition.[22] Luther and Calvin conceived of the sacraments as *Verbum Dei visibile*, a visible Word of God. Bouyer points out, however, that neither Luther nor Calvin realized the full implications of this profound idea.[23] If the sacraments as visible words of God are thought of as mere visible instruction, then this would be a reduction of the sacraments to their aspect of visible representation of the faith. Very often the Protestant tradition tended to view the sacraments in this light as visible or sensible proclamations of the promises of God. The twentieth-century Reformed theologian, Karl Barth, says: "This is the essence of baptism: to be this picture, this witness and sign."[24] For him it is a *witness* and sign of God's gift of the grace of regeneration, but only that, and not properly the *cause* of that new life in Christ.

As Scripture notes, however, God's Word has the property not only of communication and proclamation but also of creation and *transformation*. It is powerful to accomplish what it signifies. "For the word of God is living and active, sharper than any two-edged sword, piercing to the division of soul and spirit."[25] It is, as St. Paul says in 1 Thessalonians 2:13, "at work in you believers." Isaiah 55:10–11 states this principle most clearly:

---

22 Louis Bouyer, *The Word, Church and Sacraments in Protestantism and Catholicism*, trans. A. V. Littledale, (San Francisco: Ignatius Press, 2004), 80–92.

23 Bouyer, *The Word, Church and Sacraments*, 71. See also Bouyer, "Word and Sacrament," in *Sacraments: The Gestures of Christ*, ed. O'Callaghan, 151–52.

24 Karl Barth, *The Teaching of the Church Regarding Baptism*, trans. Ernest A. Payne (London: SCM Press, 1948), 15. On Barth's sacramental theology, see Miralles, *I sacramenti cristiani*, 128–30.

25 Heb 4:12.

As the rain and the snow come down from heaven, and do not return there but water the earth, making it bring forth and sprout, giving seed to the sower and bread to the eater, so shall my word be that goes forth from my mouth; it shall not return to me empty, but it shall accomplish that which I intend, and prosper in the thing for which I sent it.

The Protestant tradition is deeply attentive to this efficacious aspect of God's Word. If we apply this idea to the sacraments, these visible words of God should have a creative and transformative power of themselves. They are living words that have divine instrumental power, being said by Christ Himself through the minister. But that is precisely the essential meaning of the efficacy of sacramental action *ex opere operato*. The sacraments produce the effect that they represent by the intrinsic power of God's faithful Word, as long as there is no obstacle to block their efficacy. Bouyer writes:

What, then, is it which works this wonderful thing, the reality of which remains veiled under signs and is perceptible only to the faith which takes hold of the divine Word? Precisely the power of the divine Word, proclaimed by those he sent for the purpose as if he himself were speaking again in them; and it is, indeed, he who in them speaks to us by them, but always factually and directly. It is not our merits or prayers, nor even our faith, in so far as all these are from us—nor those of the faithful or the officiating priest—that is able to bring about such an effect. God alone can do so, God who spoke once and for all in Christ, in Christ who continues to speak in his apostles and the apostolic Church, their continuation. In this way, the sacrament derives all its virtue from the divine Word, the Word which instituted it during Christ's life on earth, the Word which Christ handed on to his apostles, and after them to the ministers who succeeded them; so that when they speak in his name, repeating what he said, it is always, to the eye of faith, he who is speaking and who, speaking as he did in time past, does again what he did then by his words.[26]

This is a magnificent explanation of the Catholic understanding of

---

[26] Bouyer, *The Word, Church and Sacraments*, 85–86.

sacramental efficacy *ex opere operato*. Christ works through the sacraments because he is speaking through them today with power, as He did during His public ministry two thousand years ago. And this is true not only of the sacramental sign, but also of sacramental character and the *res et sacramentum* in the other sacraments, which are abiding sacramental words of power through which Christ continues to speak. Bouyer goes on to emphasize the living nature of Christ's Word, as active today as ever:

> All this is comprehensible and possible only if it is fully understood that the Word of God cannot consist merely in something written, but is primarily a living Word. It is a living Word of which it is not enough to say that it is entrusted to the Church; its presence, ever active through the ages, being the presence of Christ himself, is what constitutes the Church. This presence is perpetuated in and through those he has chosen as his ministers precisely so that they will speak in his name in every place and through all generations, promising to give His Word as spoken by them the same virtue as it had when uttered by him.[27]

Protestants tend to oppose the Catholic understanding of the sacraments because they fear that it is a superstitious ascribing of semi-magical powers to human words. There is no doubt that the sacraments can be received and administered in a merely mechanical way that is not attentive to the power of the sacramental Word. It is not superstitious, however, to believe in the power and glory of these visible words of God that accomplish what they represent in a way proper to the theandric power of the incarnate Word.

The Definition of Sacramental Causality *ex opere operato*

By far the most important magisterial pronouncement on sacramental efficacy is that of the Council of Trent in its decree on the sacraments in general, in session 7, promulgated in 1547. The Council sought to defend sacramental efficacy in such a way as to exclude Protestant

---

[27] Bouyer, *The Word, Church and Sacraments*, 87.

errors while not entering into more technical issues debated among Catholic theological schools.[28] The key notion that Trent defines is that the sacraments are efficacious *ex opere operato*.

Because the sacraments are instruments wielded by the humanity of Christ, they are *intrinsically efficacious*. As long as the priest validly celebrates the sacramental sign with the intention of doing what the Church does,[29] and as long as the recipient poses no obstacle, the sacraments will impart grace. Catholic theology expresses this intrinsic efficacy of the sacraments of the Church through the phrase *ex opere operato*, which literally means "by the work worked," or "by the work that has been realized."[30] This means that grace is produced through the sacramental action, or in the words of the *Catechism of the Catholic Church*, §1128: "by the very fact of the action's being performed." The "work" here refers to the valid realization of the sacramental sign. Thus the sacraments achieve their effect not from the sanctity of the minister but by the performance of "all the essentials which belong to the effecting or conferring of the sacrament,"[31] with the intention of doing what the Church does. The *Catechism* continues: "From the moment that a sacrament is celebrated in accordance with the intention of the Church, the power of Christ and his Spirit acts in and through it, independently of the personal holiness of the minister."[32]

That the sacraments are efficacious *ex opere operato*, as long as there is no obstacle in the recipient, is a dogma of faith defined in the Council of Trent in the Decree on the Sacraments. Canon 6 defines

---

[28] See Lynch, *Cleansing of the Heart*, 49–54; Lynch, "The Sacraments as Causes of Sanctification," 820–22.

[29] See Council of Trent, Decree on the Sacraments (session 7), can. 11 on the Sacraments in General (DS, 1611).

[30] For the meaning of "*ex opere operato*" as used by the Council of Trent, see Gallagher, *Significando causant*, 51: "When the council of Trent uses the expression, it uses it mainly in reference to the subjective side, that is, to show that the merits or faith of the recipient are not the basis for the efficacy of the sacraments. The sacraments are not intended merely to increase faith, which in turn brings grace. Rather, the sacraments confer grace *ex opere operato*, by force of the rite itself as used by God." For a fuller discussion of the meaning of the expression at the Council of Trent and the various Protestant positions that it was excluding, see Leeming, *Principles of Sacramental Theology*, 5–27.

[31] Council of Trent, Decree on the Sacraments (session 7), can. 12 on the Sacraments in General (DS, 1612).

[32] *CCC*, §1128.

the teaching already given by the Council of Florence[33] that the sacraments 'contain' and confer the grace that they signify on all those who do not pose an obstacle:

> If anyone says that the sacraments of the New Law do not contain the grace they signify or that they do not confer that grace on those who do not place an obstacle in the way, as if they were only external signs of the grace or justice received through faith and marks of the Christian profession by which among men the faithful are distinguished from the unbelievers, let him be anathema.[34]

The Council of Trent does not define how the sacraments contain and confer grace on those who do not pose an obstacle. This is left open for theological discussion. This definition, although not meant to exclude positions debated by Catholic theologians, is hard to reconcile with theories of sacramental occasionalism, discussed in chapter 11 above, which therefore were no longer proposed by Catholic theologians in the same way after Trent.

The seventh canon defines the universal and infallible efficacy of valid sacraments for those who receive with the proper dispositions:

> If anyone says that, as far as God's part is concerned, grace is not given through these sacraments always and to all men, even if they receive them rightly, but only sometimes and to some, let him be anathema.[35]

The Protestant view that ascribes the efficacy of the sacraments to the faith exercised in its reception, rather than to the intrinsic power of the sacrament (*ex opere operato*), is condemned in the eighth canon:

> If anyone says that through the sacraments of the New Law

---

[33] Council of Florence, *Exsultate Deo* (DS, 1310).

[34] Council of Trent, Decree on the Sacraments (session 7), can. 6 on the Sacraments in General (DS, 1606).

[35] Council of Trent, Decree on the Sacraments (session 7), can. 7 (DS, 1607). This canon excludes the idea that on the occasion of the valid reception of the sacraments with the right dispositions, the Holy Spirit may communicate His gifts of grace to some and not to others. The opposite view is implied by Calvin in *Institutes of the Christian Religion*, bk. 4, ch. 14.9, p. 847, quoted above.

grace is not conferred by the performance of the rite itself [*ex opere operato*] but that faith alone in the divine promise is sufficient to obtain grace, let him be anathema.[36]

The intrinsic efficacy of the sacraments comes from the fact that Christ is the principal minister, who, through His omnipotence, moves the instrumental cause—the sacramental sign—to enable it to imprint character and infuse grace. St. Thomas explains that "the sacrament is not wrought by the righteousness of either the celebrant or the recipient, but by the power of God."[37] This is implied by St. Paul in 1 Corinthians 3:6–7: "I planted, Apollos watered, but God gave the growth. So neither he who plants nor he who waters is anything, but only God who gives the growth."

The *Catechism of the Council of Trent* expresses this point with clarity:

> Because in the performance of their sacred functions they represent not their own but the person of Christ, these instrumental ministers validly effect and confer the sacraments—no matter how good or evil they may be in their persons. The only conditions for this validity are that they use the matter and the form instituted by Christ and preserved in the Catholic Church, and that they intend to do what the Church does. Therefore, unless the recipients on their own part deliberately resist the Holy Spirit, nothing can prevent them from receiving the sacramental grace. This explicit teaching of the church was first established beyond all doubt by St. Augustine's arguments against the Donatists. . . . Just as in planting trees, the vices of the planter do not impede the growth of the tree, so too—the comparison is obvious—those who were planted in Christ by the ministry of bad men sustain no injury from a guilt which is not their own. Thus, as some Fathers of the Church have noted, Judas Iscariot must have baptized many people; yet none of them was ever known to have been rebaptized.[38]

---

[36] Council of Trent, Decree on the Sacraments (session 7), can. 8 (DS, 1608).
[37] *ST* III, q. 68, a. 8, cited in *CCC*, §1128.
[38] *CCT*, part 2, intro., §25, p. 158.

The teaching of the Council of Trent on the causal efficacy of the sacraments is explained by the *Catechism of the Catholic Church*, §1127:

> Celebrated worthily in faith, the sacraments confer the grace that they signify. They are efficacious because in them Christ himself is at work: it is he who baptizes, he who acts in his sacraments in order to communicate the grace that each sacrament signifies. . . . As fire transforms into itself everything it touches, so the Holy Spirit transforms into the divine life whatever is subjected to his power.

The *Catechism* (§1128) goes on to clarify that the phrase "*ex opere operato*" refers to the work of Christ: "This is the meaning of the Church's affirmation that the sacraments act *ex opere operato* (literally: 'by the very fact of the action's being performed'), i.e., by virtue of the saving work of Christ, accomplished once for all."[39]

Prayers in general, on the contrary, are not fruitful merely from the fact that the action is performed (*ex opere operato*), but from the personal contribution of the one praying.[40] Theology expresses this with the phrase, *ex opere operantis*: "from the work of the person who is acting." This refers to the moral quality and merit of the one who does the action.

The intrinsic efficacy of the sacraments—*ex opere operato*—comes from the fact that the principal agent is Christ, and the minister is merely His instrument, like a living paintbrush or chisel in His hands. In other words, the efficacy of the sacraments comes not from the holiness of the instrumental minister, but from Christ.[41] Only the prin-

---

[39] See Ratzinger, "On the Concept of Sacrament," in *Theology of the Liturgy*, 180. See also Paul VI, *Mysterium Fidei*, §38: "No one is unaware that the sacraments are the actions of Christ who administers them through men. And so the sacraments are holy in themselves and they pour grace into the soul by the power of Christ, when they touch the body."

[40] See John 9:31: "We know that God does not listen to sinners, but if any one is a worshiper of God and does his will, God listens to him."

[41] See Semmelroth, *Church and Sacrament*, 96: "The concept *ex opere operato* stands in opposition to another way in which the operation of grace through the sacraments can be presented. *Ex opere operato* means primarily NOT *ex opere operantis*, that is, not depending on the merit of the human performance. One wonders if the reformers of the sixteenth century, as well as Protestant Christians today who so often fear the magic in the Catholic teaching on the sacraments, have realized actually how much their own basic demands are

cipal agent, by His divine power acting through the instrumentality of the sacramental sign, can work inwardly in the soul of the recipient, imprinting character and imparting grace. As long as the minister intends to do what the Church does, his personal unworthiness or even lack of faith does not block Christ and His Spirit from acting inwardly in the soul of the recipient. In an emergency, a non-baptized person can baptize if he intends to do what the Church does. But how can he give what he does not possess? St. Thomas responds:

> The man who baptizes offers but his outward ministration; whereas Christ it is who baptizes inwardly, who can use all men to whatever purpose He wills. Consequently, the unbaptized can baptize: because, as Pope Nicolas I says, "the Baptism is not theirs," i.e., the baptizers', "but His," i.e. Christ's.[42]

Similarly, a wicked minister can give grace through the sacraments because he is not transmitting his own holiness, as if he were the principal agent, but is like a conduit through which Christ's grace passes. St. Thomas writes:

> The ministers of the Church work instrumentally in the sacraments, because, in a way, a minister is of the nature of an instrument. But ... an instrument acts not by reason of its own form, but by the power of the one who moves it. Consequently, whatever form or power an instrument has in addition to that which it has as an instrument, is accidental to it: for instance, that a physician's body, which is the instrument of his soul, wherein is his medical art, be healthy or sickly; or that a pipe, through which water passes, be of silver or lead. Therefore the ministers of the Church can confer the sacraments, though they be wicked.[43]

---

fulfilled here. The stress on the sacraments imparting grace *ex opere operato* prevents the misconception, such as that found in the Pelagian heresy in the early days of the Church, that man could obtain grace through the merits of his own works, that is, *ex opere operantis*. In opposition to this, the sacrament stresses that grace is not obtained as a result of human action on God, but through the operation of a sign of God's promise instituted by him."

[42] *ST* III, q. 67, a. 5, ad 1.

[43] *ST* III, q. 64, a. 5.

In those sacraments that require the minister to be a priest, it is priestly character received in ordination, not holiness, that enables the minister to be Christ's instrument. However, it is holiness that enables him to be a *good* and inspiring minister of Christ. St. Thomas states that "Christ works in the sacraments, both by wicked men as lifeless instruments, and by good men as living instruments."[44]

Importance of Dispositions in the Minister and Recipient

Since the sacraments are efficacious *ex opere operato*, does this mean that it makes no difference whether the minister of a sacrament is a great saint or sinner? Or that it makes no difference whether it is celebrated with reverence or irreverence? Not at all. Directly and per se, the holiness of the minister and the reverence of the celebration do not determine the validity or fruitfulness of the sacrament. Indirectly, however, a holy priest and a reverent celebration can have a powerful effect on the fruitfulness of the sacrament, for they can arouse greater devotion, contrition, reverence, and faith in the recipients, by which they will be more receptive to the grace of the sacrament. This is a key principle of pastoral theology.

The fact that the sacraments work *ex opere operato* does not mean that they always give the same amount of grace, for they do not operate in a mechanical or automatic way. Although the sacramental graces are given through the power of Christ and the merits of His Passion, which do not vary, their fruitfulness, or the amount of grace received by the subjects, will vary, for this depends also on the disposition of the recipient, according to Jesus's saying in Mark 4:25: "For to him who has will more be given."[45] The philosophical principle that everything is received according to the mode of the receiver can be applied here. In other words, the personal disposition of the recipient, but not that of the minister, directly affects the fruitfulness of the sacrament. A reverent and holy minister, however, can contribute greatly to the dispositions of the recipient.

The Second Vatican Council speaks about the great pastoral importance of the holiness of the sacramental minister in the Decree on the Ministry and Life of Priests *Presbyterorum Ordinis*, §12:

---

[44] *ST* III, q. 64, a. 5, ad 2.

[45] See *CCC*, §1128: "Nevertheless, the fruits of the sacraments also depend on the disposition of the one who receives them."

The very holiness of priests is of the greatest benefit for the fruitful fulfillment of their ministry. While it is possible for God's grace to carry out the work of salvation through unworthy ministers, yet God ordinarily prefers to show his wonders through those men who are more submissive to the impulse and guidance of the Holy Spirit and who, because of their intimate union with Christ and their holiness of life, are able to say with St. Paul: "It is no longer I who live, but Christ who lives in me" (Gal. 2:20).

St. John Paul II also emphasizes this in his Apostolic Exhortation *Pastores Dabo Vobis*, §25:

> There can be no doubt that the exercise of the priestly ministry, especially in the celebration of the sacraments, receives its saving effects from the action of Christ himself who becomes present in the sacraments. But ... God's plan has ordained that the efficacy of the exercise of the ministry is also conditioned by a greater or lesser human receptivity and participation. In particular, the greater or lesser degree of the holiness of the minister has a real effect on the proclamation of the word, the celebration of the sacraments and the leadership of the community in charity.

Another reason the reverent celebration of the sacrament contributes to the fruitfulness of the effect is that the sacramental liturgy includes many prayers that do not belong to the essence of the sacrament itself. These prayers, instituted by the Church, are not efficacious *ex opere operato*, but through the faith and devotion of the participants, *ex opere operantis*. As mentioned above, the power of prayer is conditioned by the faith and devotion of the heart that prays.

POST-TRIDENTINE DEBATE ON SACRAMENTAL CAUSALITY

Are the Sacraments Efficacious through Physical or Moral Causality?

We have seen that the Council of Trent defined that the sacraments contain and confer grace *ex opere operato*, and that Baptism is the instrumental cause of justification,[46] but it left open *how* they confer grace. As we have seen, the precise way in which the sacraments participate in causing the effects of grace had been debated from the twelfth through the fifteenth centuries, and it continued to be debated in the centuries after the Council of Trent. In the post-Tridentine period, this debate was posed as a question of whether the sacraments are efficacious *ex opere operato* through *physical* or *moral* causality.[47] In other words, do the sacraments work as instrumental *efficient* causes in the infusion of grace, according to the view of St. Thomas and his followers, or as *meritorious* causes infallibly inducing God to act in infusing grace, according to the view of many post-Tridentine theologians, beginning with Melchior Cano?

In scholastic terminology, a physical cause is an efficient cause on which the *being* of an effect, whether material or spiritual, depends.[48] This term is unfortunate because it is easily misunderstood to mean a natural or a material cause while the intention of those who introduced the term was to indicate an efficient cause. For this reason, it would be better to refer to this position as *instrumental efficient causality*.

A moral cause is one that acts only indirectly by *motivating* a rational agent to act.[49] Merit, which makes it due for another agent to

---

[46] Council of Trent, Decree on Justification (session 6, Jan 13, 1547), ch. 7 (DS, 1529): "The instrumental cause is the sacrament of baptism, which is the 'sacrament of faith,' without which no man was ever justified."

[47] For this debate, see Edouard Hugon, *La causalité instrumentale en théologie* (Paris: Pierre Téqui, 1907), 73–172; Gallagher, *Significando causant*, 154–61, 189–202; Lynch, *Cleansing of the Heart*, 154–200; Lynch, "Domingo Bañez on Moral and Physical Causality: Christic Merit and Sacramental Realism," *Angelicum* 91 (2014): 105–25; Johann Auer, *A General Doctrine of the Sacraments and the Mystery of the Eucharist*, trans. Erasmo Leiva-Merikakis, vol. 6 of *Dogmatic Theology*, ed. Johann Auer and Joseph Ratzinger (Washington, DC: Catholic University of America Press, 1995), 78–80; Miralles, *I sacramenti christiani*, 341–42.

[48] See Gallagher, *Significando causant*, 190.

[49] See Johannes Baptist Franzelin, *Tractatus de sacramentis in genere* (Rome: S.C. de Propaganda Fide; Taurini: Marietti, 1868), 109, English trans. by White, "Sacraments and Philosophy," in *OHST*, 585: "A moral cause properly speaking differs from a mere condition without which the effect does not occur, in that a moral cause is accompanied by some power, dignity, and excellence which—although it does not physically influence and work toward the very being of the effect produced—does nevertheless present a reason to the physical cause. By contrast, in that which is a mere condition *sine qua non*, there is no such dignity or power." Franzelin was perhaps the most eminent nineteenth-century defender of the theory of the moral causality of the sacraments.

act, is a kind moral cause. For example, the work of a bricklayer is the efficient instrumental cause of the building of the house but is a moral or meritorious cause of his being paid. His work makes it due for his employer to pay him a just wage, which should motivate the employer to pay the wage. The moral cause motivates a rational agent to act whereas an efficient cause produces its effect directly.

Moral causality occurs when something produces an effect through being known as desirable or *due* by a rational agent, who then directly produces the effect. A moral cause thus is in the line of final causality, and is a kind of subordinate final cause because it serves to motivate the action (efficient causality) of a rational agent. Christ's Passion causes our salvation as a meritorious cause in this way, by making it fitting and due for God to offer to the whole human race the grace for salvation.

This post-Tridentine debate on sacramental causality was unnecessarily complicated by the terminology of "physical" or "moral" causes. To refer to the sacraments as "physical" causes seems strange since they are signs that have supernatural effects.[50] The debate is clarified if we focus on the kind of causality that is involved. Are the sacraments meritorious causes *moving God to act*, or are they instrumental efficient causes *moved by God* in the infusion of grace?

This debate is really about the following question. Are the sacraments efficacious because they infallibly *move God to act* in fidelity to His covenant, or because they are infallibly *moved by God* to produce the effect of grace?[51] The thesis of moral causality, like that of the earlier theory of sacramental occasionalism, holds the former position. The opposing Thomistic thesis (referred to as physical causality) maintains the latter, and postulates a chain of instrumental causes by which the divine power uses Christ's humanity, who uses the sacrament to cause

---

[50] See Gallagher, *Significando causant*, 190: "The word 'physical' is particularly unsuitable in this context, for it connotes corporeal or material. It leads to the impression that this theory holds that the sacrament is a grossly materialistic reality that somehow causes grace due to corporeal contact. That impression is false. And so we prefer not to use this term. The term 'physical' is used here in contradistinction to the term 'moral' used by moral causality. . . . What the word means is that the sacraments are truly efficient causes, instrumental causes, of grace. The effect of grace flows from the sacraments as from true instrumental causes. Hence we shall refer to this opinion as that of 'efficient' causality."

[51] See Hugon, *La causalité instrumentale en théologie*, 130; See Alexandre Ganoczy, *An Introduction to Catholic Sacramental Theology*, trans. William Thomas (New York; Ramsey, NJ: Paulist Press, 1984), 33–34.

the *res et sacramentum*, which is an instrument in the infusion of grace. The chain of agents could be represented as follows:

- God → humanity of Christ and the Paschal mystery → sacred minister → sacramental sign → *res et sacramentum* → infusion of grace.[53]

Moral Causality and Melchior Cano

The principal argument used in favor of the theory of moral causality is that the alternative explanation, physical causality, is held to be impossible.[52] Moral causality is defended therefore to preserve sacramental causality while denying that the sacraments are efficient causes of grace. It is very similar to the earlier theories of sacramental occasionalism in denying that the sacraments exercise efficient causality, but it differs terminologically from those earlier theories because after the Councils of Florence and Trent it was necessary to hold that the sacraments confer or cause grace. This theory therefore emphasizes a type of causality, which is held to be moral rather than physical.[53]

This thesis that the sacraments cause grace by a *moral or meritorious causality* was introduced by two sixteenth-century Spanish Dominicans, Francisco de Vitoria (1483–1546) and his famous pupil Melchior Cano (1509–1560).[54] Cano illustrates the theory with the example of someone who is taken captive by the Turks and is ransomed by someone who offers a large sum of money to redeem him. In such a case we would rightly regard both the person of the benefactor and the purse of money that was given to redeem him as true causes of his release. He argues that something analogous happens in the administration of the sacraments. Christ takes the place of the benefactor, and the sacraments are like the purse offered to redeem us. He

---

[52] See, for example, Joseph de Aldama, S.J., "The General Theory of the Sacraments," in *Sacrae Theologiae Summa*, 4A:74: "Sacraments are not physical causes of grace. This theory has incurable difficulties, without any positive reason whatsoever that can persuade us to admit them. Therefore this theory is not to be held."

[53] See Lynch, "Domingo Bañez on Moral and Physical Causality, 111–13.

[54] Other well-known theologians who followed this position include the Jesuits Gabriel Vázquez (1549–1604), Cardinal de Lugo (1583–1660), and Johann Baptist Franzelin (1816–1886). On Cano's position and its close relationship to the earlier theory of sacramental occasionalism, see Lynch, "Domingo Bañez on Moral and Physical Causality," 105–25.

holds that they contain the merit of the blood of Christ, which acts as a meritorious cause to induce God to give us the grace merited by His sacrifice.[55]

There are several problems with this explanation. First, it conflates the way the Passion of Christ is the meritorious cause of our salvation and the way the sacraments participate in the work of salvation.[56] The Passion is undoubtedly a meritorious cause that has merited all human salvation. Every grace given in human history since the Fall has been merited by Christ's Passion. The grace given to the Israelites in their worship according to the Mosaic Law, as well as the grace received by righteous Gentiles, came through the merits of Christ on the Cross.

A meritorious cause can have effects that are chronologically prior to it because God knows it eternally and can apply it throughout history. Thus God applied the merits of Calvary to give graces to inspire the repentance of Adam and Eve, the meritorious offering of Abel, the justice of Enoch and Noah, the faith of Abraham, Sarah, and the patriarchs, and so forth. Thus the sacraments and sacrifices of the Old Covenant that prefigure the Paschal mystery of Christ could also be occasions for receiving grace merited by the Passion that they prefigure. The model proposed by Melchior Cano to explain the efficacy of the sacraments of the New Covenant, like that of St. Bonaventure and Scotus, works well for those of the Old Covenant. But, as seen above, the Councils of Florence and Trent both teach that the efficacy of the sacraments of the New Covenant differs from those of the Old, which prefigure but do not themselves contain and confer grace.[57]

The sacraments of the New Covenant, on the other hand, work what they signify, and what they signify is effective sanctification. For example, in Baptism and Confirmation, the washing and anointing

---

[55] Cano, *Relectio de sacramentis*, pars IV (Venice, 1759, first published in 1550), 489, quoted in Gallagher, *Significando causant*, 156–57. A twentieth-century variant of the moral causality theory is that of Louis Cardinal Billot, who speaks of "intentional causality" to explain sacramental efficacy. See Billot, *De Ecclesiae Sacramentis: Commentarius in Tertiam Partem S. Thomae*, vol. 1, 7th ed. (Rome: Apud aedes universitatis Gregorianae, 1931). The theory holds that the sacraments serve as infallible designations of the subjects who are to receive grace from God. This seems to be very similar to the views of St. Bonaventure, the Scotists, and the proponents of moral causality. See Leeming, *Principles of Sacramental Theology*, 337–39; Miralles, *I sacramenti christiani*, 343.

[56] This point is made by White, "Sacraments and Philosophy," in *OHST*, 586.

[57] Council of Florence, *Exsultate Deo* (DS, 1310); Council of Trent, Decree on the Sacraments (session 7), can. on the Sacraments in General 2 (DS, 1602).

of the body signify and cause the washing and anointing of the soul. Furthermore, we have seen above that Christ is active in the sacraments through His humanity, which is the instrument conjoined to the divinity, giving to the words and gestures of the sacramental sign the divine power to realize what they signify.

It is true that Cano's thesis can be applied to the Eucharist, but only insofar as it is a sacrifice. In the Mass, the Church offers to God the Father the sacrifice of the Son and pleads that graces be showered down on the world.[58] In Holy Communion, however, and the other six sacraments, this explanation is insufficient. The sacramental liturgy does not present the sacraments as pleading for grace before God, but as efficacious in imparting the grace that is represented, such as washing the soul, giving the Holy Spirit, forgiving sin, and nourishing our life with the Body of Christ.

Matthias Scheeben offers a good critique of this theory:

> Regarded as moral causes, the sacraments would hardly be real instruments of the grace-producing power of Christ and the Holy Spirit; they would rather be instruments employed by Christ to make us worthy of the grace to be received. We could not with any appropriateness say that the Holy Spirit works through the sacraments; strictly speaking, we should have to avow that the sacraments work upon the Holy Spirit to induce Him to exercise His sanctifying power. But the first of these two alternatives, that the Holy Spirit works through the sacraments is too strongly emphasized in the language of Holy Scripture and the Fathers to permit of our overlooking it or explaining it in a moral sense. Moreover, the relation of the God-man to us . . . supplies a weighty argument for such causality, and at the same time seems to furnish a satisfactory explanation of the matter.[59]

In the last sentence quoted above, Scheeben is referring to St. Thomas's theory that Christ's human actions, because of the hypostatic union, are endowed with the power to be instrumental efficient causes that serve to realize the salvific effects that they represent.[60] Thus

---

[58] See Feingold, *The Eucharist*, 367–68, 451–69.
[59] Scheeben, *The Mysteries of Christianity*, 570.
[60] For Scheeben's profound account of St. Thomas's theory of the instrumen-

Christ's death and Resurrection are efficient causes of our death to sin and rising to supernatural life.[61] This efficient power in Christ's actions has been transmitted by Him to His sacraments, through which it is transmitted to us in His Mystical Body.

Cajetan and the Thesis That the Sacraments Exercise Efficient Causality

We have seen that the thesis that the sacraments are instrumental *efficient* causes of grace was taught by St. Thomas in *ST* III, q. 62, and other works after his early commentary on the *Sentences*. However, it represented a significant innovation with respect to his earlier teaching and with respect to all his contemporaries. Thus it is not surprising that St. Thomas's later position was not received by his earlier followers.[62] This was due also to the fact that St. Thomas's commentary on the *Sentences* was his most widely known work for two centuries, until Cajetan completed his great commentary on the *Summa theologiae*. St. Thomas's mature position on sacramental causality was not properly received by other theologians until Cajetan's commentary on the *Tertia pars*, in the early sixteenth century.[63]

The position of the mature St. Thomas, championed by Cajetan,[64] was then taken up in the later sixteenth century by Bánez[65] and, under the name of "physical causality," became the standard position of the Dominican commentators on St. Thomas, such as John of St.

---

tal efficient causality of Christ's humanity and its role in the sacraments, see Scheeben, *The Mysteries of Christianity*, 456–64.

[61] See *ST* III, q. 48, a. 6; q. 49, a. 1; q. 56, a. 2.

[62] In the fifteenth century, John Capreolus (ca. 1380–1444) taught the earlier position of St. Thomas. See Capreolus, *Defensiones Theologiae Divi Thomae Aquinatis*, ed. Ceslai Paban and Thomae Pègues, vol. 6 (Tours: Alfred Cattier, 1906), 4. In the early sixteenth century, Sylvester of Ferrara (ca. 1474–1528) also favored the early position of St. Thomas. See Gallagher, *Significando causant*, 135–41.

[63] See Lynch, "The Sacraments as Causes of Sanctification," 809–12.

[64] Cajetan, commentary on the *Summa theologiae*, III, q. 62. a. 1, in *Sancti Thomae Aquinatis Opera omnia*, Leonine ed., vol. 12 (Rome, 1906), 21 (my translation): "The sacrament instrumentally attains to [the realization of] sacramental grace; and it is not necessary to have recourse to a prior disposition to grace."

[65] See Domingo Bánez, *Comentarios Inéditos a la Tercera Parte de Santo Tomas*, vol. 2, *De Sacramentis: QQ. 60–90*, ed. Vincente Beltran de Heredia, Biblioteca de Teólogos Españoles 19 (Salamanca: Consejo Superior de Investigaciones Cientificas, Inst. Francisco Suarez, 1953), 43–51.

Thomas.[66] It has also been defended by many eminent theologians of other religious orders, including Jesuits such as St. Robert Bellarmine[67] and Suárez,[68] the Carmelites of Salamanca (Salmanticenses),[69] and many others, such as Scheeben.

Karl Rahner's Theory of Sacramental Causality

In his work *The Church and the Sacraments* (1961), Karl Rahner critiqued both of the dominant views on sacramental causality outlined above (physical and moral causality) and then proposed a new explanation. He holds that previous attempts to explain sacramental causality fail because they seek to understand it along the lines of efficient transitive action.[70] He claims that this inevitably tends to separate the sign aspect of the sacraments from their causality.[71] He rejects the Thomistic theory of "physical" or efficient causal efficacy as follows:

> "Physical" causality inevitably does most to push the symbolic character of the sacraments into the background. It explains the possibility of reviviscence of the sacraments only with the help of very intricate supplementary hypotheses. It can give no real meaning to the instrumentality of the sacraments, cannot explain what the instrument itself can contribute to the effect,

---

[66] See John of St. Thomas, *Cursus Theologicus*, vol. 9, disp. 24, a. 1, dubium 9 (Paris: Vivès, 1886), 268–83.

[67] Bellarmine, *De Controversiis, De Sacramentis in genere*, bk. 2, ch. 11, in *Opera omnia*, 4:448–49. After presenting the theory of moral causality, he writes (448): "Nevertheless I hold that thesis which assigns to the sacraments true efficient causality to be far more probable and secure."

[68] Suárez, *Opera omnia*, vol. 20, in *ST* III, q. 62, a. 4, disp. 9, sectio 2 pp. 154–59. In pp. 149–54, Suárez gives a good overview of the arguments of those who defend the moral causality of the sacraments, after which he defends the thesis of efficient instrumental causality.

[69] Salmanticenses, *Cursus Theologicus*, vol. 17, *De sacramentis in communi*, disp. 4, dubium 4 (Paris, Palmé, 1881), 319–39.

[70] Rahner, *The Church and the Sacraments*, 35: "Usually the question of the kind of causality at work in the sacraments is envisaged unconsciously, as though as a matter of course, in terms of the concept of transitive efficient cause borrowed from the philosophic doctrine of the categories. God, sacramental sign and grace are envisaged from the start as quite distinct factors, almost as though they were physical things."

[71] A similar critique is made by J. A. Appleyard, "How Does a Sacrament 'Cause by Signifying'?" *Science et Esprit* 23 [1971]: 167–200.

grace, nor make it intelligible how precisely a "symbol" can be the physical instrument of supernatural grace. That theory overlooks that a sign itself is not a "physical" thing, especially as in the sacraments it is composed of words and ritual gestures which themselves are separated in time.[72]

Rahner has given many arguments here against the Thomistic position, but they are not hard to refute from the Thomistic perspective. The first and most important critique is that the Thomistic position undermines the symbolic dimension of the sacraments. As we have seen, the sacraments, because they are instruments of Christ, have a "theandric" power—like the words and gestures used in Christ's miracles—to effect what they signify. Therefore the symbolic aspect of the sacraments is in no way diminished by regarding them as instrumental efficient causes that realize what they represent. On the contrary, the Thomistic understanding of sacramental causality greatly emphasizes the symbolic dimension of the sacraments of the New Covenant by clarifying that their causality, as words of power, works through their symbolism. They are signs that cause what they signify, and therefore St. Thomas, following St. Augustine, puts the sacraments in the genus of sacred signs, and sees their efficacy in realizing what they signify as the specific difference of the sacraments of the New Covenant. They physically or efficiently cause grace only through first being fully constituted as signs instituted and given power by Christ.

A second criticism given by Rahner is that the Thomistic position is unable to clearly explain the reviviscence of the sacraments. Reviviscence refers to the fact that sacraments—Baptism, Confirmation, Anointing of the Sick, Matrimony, or Holy Orders—that were received validly but unfruitfully because of lack of repentance in the subject can come back to life when the obstacle is removed by repentance and a good confession (or perfect contrition and the

---

[72] Rahner, *The Church and the Sacraments*, 36–37. As noted above, I agree with Rahner that the term "physical" is misleading and can be misinterpreted along the lines of his criticism here. Rahner's purpose, however, is to conclude that the explanations given by previous theological schools have been insufficient. Therefore, his criticism has to be applied against the best form of Thomistic sacramental theory and not against a possible misinterpretation of it or an unfortunate choice of terms to express it. In other words, it seems that Rahner has set up a straw man, which he takes down with a few sentences.

intention to confess).[73] Rahner's objection here is that it does not seem possible that the sacramental sign, which has long since ceased to exist, can serve as an efficient cause of grace when the sacrament later "comes back to life." The response is simple from the Thomistic perspective. As we have seen, it is precisely for this reason that theologians hold that there is a hidden sacramental *reality and sign* that endures, called the *res et sacramentum*.[74] In the case of Baptism, Confirmation, and Holy Orders, this abiding effect is sacramental character. Even though the outward sacramental sign has passed away, sacramental character or the *res et sacramentum* in Matrimony or Anointing of the Sick remains present in the soul as an invisible sign that is still efficacious to give the grace that it signifies as soon as the obstacle is removed.[75]

Rahner's third criticism is that the Thomistic position cannot account for how a symbol, as symbol, can be a cause of grace. This is the most difficult question for the Thomistic position, and also its greatest strength. If a symbol were used by a mere man as the principal agent, it would only be able to signify grace, and not to cause it. But the principal agent here is Christ, the Word Incarnate, who acts through it with His divine power so that the matter and form of the

---

[73] See P. A. Haynal, "De Reviviscentia Sacramentorum fictione recedente," *Angelicum* (1927): 51–80; 203–23; 382–405.

[74] See chapters 7–8 above, and Scheeben, *Mysteries of Christianity*, 579–80. See the explanation by Gallagher in *Significando causant*, 254: "For the case of distance in time, 'reviviscence,' as it is called, . . . the numerically distinct action of God causing grace when the *obex* is removed uses the humanity of Christ as instrument and also the sacramental character. . . . The action, however, is one as sacramental with the former action of the sacramental rite, which extended only to causing the character due to the presence of the *obex*. That first action is now extended to cause grace. Character is the link that connects the two actions, making them one sacramentally."

[75] With regard to Baptism, see *ST* III, q. 69, a. 10: "Baptism is a spiritual regeneration. Now when a thing is generated, it receives together with the form, the form's effect, unless there be an obstacle; and when this is removed, the form of the thing generated produces its effect: thus at the same time as a weighty body is generated, it has a downward movement, unless something prevent this; and when the obstacle is removed, it begins forthwith to move downwards. In like manner when a man is baptized, he receives the character, which is like a form; and he receives in consequence its proper effect, which is grace whereby all his sins are remitted. But this effect is sometimes hindered by insincerity. Wherefore, when this obstacle is removed by Penance, Baptism forthwith produces its effect."

sacraments, as *words of power*, accomplish what they represent.[76] It is in answering this kind of objection from a Christological perspective that the Thomistic position is most profound.

Finally, repeating an objection already made by Scotus,[77] Rahner implies that the fact that the sacramental sign is realized over a span of time poses a problem for regarding it as an efficient cause of an instantaneous infusion of grace. The answer to this objection is that the causality of the sacraments works through their symbolism so that their efficacy is realized at the moment when their sign value is fully manifested.

Rahner summarizes his critique of the previous dominant theories of sacramental causality (whether defending physical or moral causality) by faulting them for using the category of transitive efficient causality, which he holds to be more suited to the production of material things: "The fundamental defect that leads all these theories into conceptual difficulties, consists . . . in tacitly laying down the pattern of transitive efficient causality, in which one factor adequately distinct from another must produce the latter."[78]

After rejecting the principal theories of sacramental efficacy advanced by Catholic theologians,[79] Rahner proposes to understand sacramental causality under the category of "intrinsic symbol," which is a sign that manifests the deeper identity of a thing.[80] According to this theory, the sacraments function as signs that manifest what the

---

[76] See chapter 12 above, pp. 442–44.

[77] See Gallagher, *Significando causant*, 151.

[78] Rahner, *The Church and the Sacraments*, 37. See also p. 35.

[79] For Rahner's critique of the theory of moral causality and of Card. Billot's theory of intentional causality, see *The Church and the Sacraments*, 37.

[80] See Rahner, *The Church and the Sacraments*, 37–38: "With the approach we have been using, it can become clear that the sacraments precisely as signs are causes of grace, that it is a case here of causation by symbols, of the kind that belongs to what by its very nature is a symbol. By such 'natural symbols' or intrinsically real symbols, we mean . . . the visible and tangible form in which something that appears, notifies its presence, and by so doing, makes itself present. . . . An example of this relationship is available for the scholastic philosopher in the relation between soul and body. The body is the manifestation of the soul, through which and in which the soul realizes its own essence. The sign is therefore a cause of what it signifies by being the way in which what is signified effects itself. The kind of causality expressed in such a conception of symbolism occurs on various levels of human reality. In substantial being (body as the sign or symbol of the soul); in the sphere of activity (bodily gesture through which the inner attitude itself which is expressed by it first attains its own full depth)."

Church (and the world) already is—the presence of Christ's victorious grace. This theory of sacramental causality presupposes a particular understanding of the Incarnation, the Church, grace, and what Rahner has referred to as the "supernatural existential,"[81] a gratuitous habitual ordering to our supernatural end intrinsically affecting every concrete human being from conception, "always and everywhere present at the very heart of human existence."[82] Rahner holds that the Church, because of the Incarnation, *is* the presence of Christ's grace. Thus he sees the Church as the ultimate sacrament, filled with grace and conferring grace by manifesting it through the sacraments that express her inner life. He writes:

> The Church in her visible historical form is herself an intrinsic symbol of the eschatologically triumphant grace of God; in that spatio-temporal visible form, this grace is made present. And because the sacraments are the actual fulfillment, the actualization of the Church's very nature, in regard to indi-

---

[81] See Karl Rahner, "Concerning the Relationship Between Nature and Grace," *Theological Investigations*, vol. 1, trans. Cornelius Ernst (Baltimore: Helicon Press, 1961), 297–317, an expanded version of an article that appeared first in *Orientierung*, 14 (1950): 141–45. See especially 312–13: "The capacity for the God of self-bestowing personal Love is the central and abiding existential of man as he really is. . . . But that means that this central, abiding existential, consisting in the ordination to the threefold God of grace and eternal life, is itself to be characterized as unexacted, as 'supernatural.'" See also "Nature and Grace," *Theological Investigations*, vol. 4, trans. Kevin Smyth (Baltimore: Helicon Press, 1966), 165–88; Feingold, *The Natural Desire to See God*, 329–39. The notion of the supernatural existential is applied by Rahner to the sacraments (although without using that term) in Rahner, "Secular Life and the Sacraments: A Copernican Revolution," *The Tablet* (Mar 13, 1971): 267–68; and "On the Theology of Worship," in *Theological Investigations*, vol. 19, *Faith and Ministry*, 142–43: "The *second* way of considering the operation of grace starts out from the assumption that the secular world from the outset is always encompassed and permeated with the grace of the divine self-communication. This grace is always and everywhere present in the world. . . . Its unmeritedness does not prevent it from being the existential always and everywhere present at the very heart of human existence." On the importance of the notion of the supernatural existential for Rahner's understanding of the efficacy of the sacraments as intrinsic symbols, see Vass, *The Sacrament of the Future*, 7–12, 102–3. On the development of Rahner's thought on the supernatural existential, see David Coffey, "The Whole Rahner on the Supernatural Existential," *Theological Studies* 65 (2004): 95–118.

[82] Rahner, "On the Theology of Worship," in *Theological Investigations*, 19:143.

vidual men, precisely in as much as the Church's whole reality is to be the real presence of God's grace, as the new covenant, these sacramental signs are efficacious. Their efficacy is that of the intrinsic symbol. . . . The sign effects grace, by grace producing the sacrament as sign of the sanctification effected. This, of course, can only be said if the Church as an entity is truly and inseparably connected with grace.[83]

One problem with Rahner's thesis is apparent in the last sentence quoted above. How is the Church "truly and inseparably connected with grace"? Is this inseparable connection considered to be prior to the sacraments, which merely manifest what she is; or is the Church "truly and inseparably connected with grace" primarily through the causality of her sacraments in infusing grace to her members in marvelous ways? If we answer in the second way, then Rahner's thesis fails. But if one answers in the first way, this position leaves unexplained how the Church becomes the place of God's "eschatologically triumphant grace" in the first place. It seems that Rahner is conceiving the Church along the lines of Christ's capital grace,[84] which is a fulness of grace received into Christ's humanity in order to overflow into the Mystical Body. But how does Christ's capital grace overflow into the Church? This is precisely why the sacraments exist, in order to be the channels of grace connecting the Head and the members, like supernatural arteries flowing throughout the Mystical Body so that the Church can share in the life of her Head.

In other words, Rahner's position should be rejected for the same reasons indicated in chapter four above with regard to his thesis that Christ instituted the sacraments only implicitly through instituting the Church. According to Rahner's theory, the Church is filled with grace, as it were, logically prior to the institution of the sacraments, and grace flows from Christ into the Church and from the Church into the sacraments, which manifest through their symbolism the grace that already pervades the Church.[85] For the traditional Catholic view, on the contrary, Christ is the source of the grace communicated to the Church through the sacraments, which are real conduits of grace endowed with causal efficacy to touch the members of the Church in

---

[83] Rahner, *The Church and the Sacraments*, 39–40.

[84] See *ST* III, q. 8.

[85] See Rahner, *Theology of Pastoral Action*, 45, discussed on pp. 124–25 above.

various ways and make grace present in them. This sanctification of the members is what builds up the Church and fills her with supernatural life.

Rahner's position is untenable because it reduces the causality of the sacraments to their symbolic value in manifesting the grace-filled reality of the Church. It is true, of course, that the sacraments function as symbols, but they are elevated by Christ to produce an effect through that sign value that other symbols cannot do. Rahner denies this elevation by saying that sacramental causality involves "causation by symbols, of the kind that belongs to what by its very nature is a symbol"[86] and by excluding "the concept of transitive efficient cause."[87]

How Does Rahner's Theory Account for the Ontological Effects of the Sacraments?

Rahner's theory has an insurmountable difficulty accounting for an ontological change that occurs through the sacraments. As we have seen, there are two distinct kinds of effects of the sacraments: the reality and sign (*res et sacramentum*), and the conferring of sanctifying grace and the other supernatural gifts that go with it. In both cases, an effect begins to exist that previously did not exist, or at least not in the same degree. Thus there is an actualization of an obediential potency, which requires an efficient cause.

If the instrumental efficient causality of the sacraments is denied, how can one account for the fact that a sacramental character or *res et sacramentum* is in fact produced by the sacrament, bringing about an ontological change?[88] If the sacraments are intrinsic symbols that manifest what one already is, how can such a theory explain the fact that a baptized or ordained person receives a new identity, mission, and spiritual power that he did not previously have, which indelibly imprinted on his soul? Priestly ordination cannot just be a manifestation of what the Church is or what her members already are, but a real conferral of a spiritual power to administer the sacraments not previously possessed. In order for priestly character, for example, to begin to exist through ordination where it had not previously existed, this

---

[86] Rahner, *The Church and the Sacraments*, 37.
[87] Rahner, *The Church and the Sacraments*, 35.
[88] See Council of Trent, Decree on the Sacraments (session 7), can. 9 on the Sacraments in General (DS, 1609).

spiritual power must be brought from potency into act. An efficient cause is required to do that.

The same problem exists still more acutely with regard to the grace given by the sacraments. How can Baptism work an infusion of sanctifying grace that forgives original sin if no efficient causality takes place? A most momentous ontological change occurs when a baby is baptized or when a sinner previously in mortal sin is absolved. In both cases, sanctifying grace, which previously was absent, is infused. The obediential potency to receive the life of God is actualized in an instant through the power of the sacrament. This requires a supreme exercise of divine power working through the sacrament as an efficient cause bringing about a momentous supernatural effect. Indeed, St. Thomas saw the justification of the sinner as the greatest work of God, greater even than the act of the creation of heaven and earth.[89] But creation surely involves God's efficient causality. Justification does so no less.

Transignification: Denial of Efficient Causality with Regard to the Eucharist

Rahner's theory about sacramental causation is most problematic with regard to the Eucharist, for it implies the notion of transignification rather than transubstantiation. If the sacramental sign does not work by way of instrumental efficient causality but only by intrinsic symbolism, then the words of consecration would not effect a change of substance, in the Aristotelian sense of the word, from bread into Christ's Body and Blood, but only a change of meaning or finality.

This idea of transignification, which is an application to the Eucharist of an understanding of the sacraments as "intrinsic symbols," was developed by various theologians in the late 1950s and 1960s, such as Piet Schoonenberg, S.J. and Edward Schillebeeckx, O.P.[90] Schoonen-

---

[89] See *ST* I-II, q. 113, a. 9: "A work may be called great on account of what is made, and thus the justification of the ungodly, which terminates at the eternal good of a share in the Godhead, is greater than the creation of heaven and earth."

[90] See E. Schillebeeckx, *The Eucharist*, trans. N. D. Smith (New York: Sheed & Ward, 1968); Charles Davis, "Understanding the Real Presence," in *The Word in History: The St. Xavier Symposium*, ed. T. Patrick Burke (New York: Sheed & Ward, 1966), 154–78; P. Schoonenberg, "Christus' tegenwoordigheid voor ons," *Verbum* 31 (1964): 393–415; J. De Baciocchi, "Présence eucharistique et transsubstantiation," *Irénikon* 32 (1959): 139–61. See the review of the German

berg writes: "Through this consecration, Christ is not dragged out of heaven, in a spatial way, nor is there a physical or chemical change in the bread and wine. What happens is a change of signs; the transubstantiation is a transfinalization or a transignification, but this takes place in the depths which only Christ, in his most real self-giving, reaches."[91] Schillebeeckx writes:

> The Eucharist . . . takes the form of a commemorative meal in which the usual secular significance of the bread and wine is withdrawn and these become bearers of Christ's gift of himself. . . . In this commemorative meal, bread and wine become the subject of a new *establishment of meaning*, not by men, but by the living Lord *in* the Church, through which they become the *sign* of the real presence of Christ giving himself to us.[92]

In his encyclical *Mysterium Fidei* of 1965, St. Paul VI condemned this theory of transignification as insufficient to express the mystery of the Eucharistic conversion:

> It is not permissible . . . to concentrate on the notion of sacramental sign as if the symbolism—which no one will deny is certainly present in the Most Blessed Eucharist—fully expressed and exhausted the manner of Christ's presence in

---

edition of Schillebeeckx's book by Joseph Ratzinger in *Theology of the Liturgy*, 243–48. The section on the Eucharist in the Dutch Catechism, *De Nieuwe Katechismus: geloofsverkondiging voor volswassenen* (*The New Catechism: Proclamation of the Faith for Adults*) (Hilversum: Brand, 1966), 391–408, shows the influence of this theological position. For an excellent overview of this general position, its development, proponents, philosophical presuppositions, and theological weaknesses, see Ibáñez, *L'Eucaristia, Dono e Mistero*, 390–409; see also the insightful critique of trans-signification theories by Roch Kereszty, "Real Presence, Manifold Presence: Christ and the Church's Eucharist," *Antiphon* 6, no. 3 (2001): 23–36. See also Feingold, *The Eucharist*, 314–19.

[91] Piet Schoonenberg, "Presence and Eucharistic Presence," *Cross Currents* 17 (Winter 1967): 39–54, at 54. It should be observed that Schoonenberg has set up a strawman opponent. Reputable theologians do not understand transubstantiation either as dragging Christ out of heaven in a spatial way or as causing an empirical change in the accidents or chemical properties of the bread and wine. See Feingold, *The Eucharist*, 259–91.

[92] Schillebeeckx, *The Eucharist*, 137.

this Sacrament; or to discuss the mystery of transubstantiation without mentioning what the Council of Trent had to say about the marvelous conversion of the whole substance of the bread into the Body and the whole substance of the wine into the Blood of Christ, as if they involve nothing more than "transignification," or "transfinalization" as they call it. . . . Everyone can see that the spread of these and similar opinions does great harm to belief in and devotion to the Eucharist.[93]

There is no doubt that there is a change of meaning of the Eucharistic species after the consecration. This transignification, however, comes about because the substance of the bread and wine have been converted into the substance of Christ's body and blood. This conversion requires an efficient cause in which the divine omnipotence works through the words of the priestly minister. A change in symbolism alone cannot account for the Church's faith in the Real Presence. Paul VI explains:

> As a result of transubstantiation, the species of bread and wine undoubtedly take on a new signification and a new finality, for they are no longer ordinary bread and wine but instead a sign of something sacred and a sign of spiritual food; but they take on this new signification, this new finality, precisely because they contain a new "reality" which we can rightly call *ontological*. For what now lies beneath the aforementioned species is not what was there before, but something completely different; and not just in the estimation of Church belief but in reality, since once the substance or nature of the bread and wine has been changed into the body and blood of Christ, nothing remains of the bread and the wine except for the species.[94]

Chauvet's Critique of the Category of Causality

Rahner's symbolic approach to sacramental efficacy had great influence in the decades following the publication of *The Church and the Sacraments*, and was developed, among others, by Louis-Marie

---

[93] Paul VI, *Mysterium Fidei*, §§11–12.
[94] Paul VI, *Mysterium Fidei*, §46 (DS, 4413; italics original).

Chauvet.[95] Building on a Heideggerian foundation, Chauvet sees the foundational flaw of the Thomistic approach to the sacraments to lie in its focus on efficient causality. He claims that posing the question of efficient causality necessarily leads one to think erroneously of grace as a kind of "product."[96] He asks:

> *How did it come about that, when attempting to comprehend the-*
> *ologically the sacramental relation with God expressed most fully*
> *under the term "grace," the Scholastics (and here we will consider*
> *only Thomas Aquinas) singled out for privileged consideration the*
> *category of "cause"?* . . . On the one hand, *grace* can in no way
> be considered as an object or a value. It is the paradigmatic
> case of something that is a non-object, a non-value; otherwise
> it runs the risk of being regated in the very graciousness and
> gratuitousness which in fact constitute it. On the other hand,
> in Scholastic discourse, the category of *causality* is always tied

---

[95] See Louis-Marie Chauvet, *Symbol and Sacrament* (Collegeville, MN: Liturgical Press, 1995); *The Sacraments: The Word of God at the Mercy of the Body* (Collegeville, MN: Liturgical Press, 2001). For Chauvet's critique of St. Thomas's view of sacramental causality and a defense of the latter, see Liam Walsh, "The Divine and the Human in St. Thomas's Theology of Sacraments," in *Ordo sapientiae et amoris: Image et message de Saint Thomas D'Aquin à travers les récentes études historiques, herméneutiques et doctrinales*, ed. Carlos-Josaphat Pinto de Oliveira (Fribourg: Editions Universitaires Fribourg Suisse, 1993), 321–52, esp. 323–25; Bernard Blankenhorn, "The Instrumental Causality of the Sacraments: Thomas Aquinas and Louis-Marie Chauvet," *Nova et Vetera* (English) 4, no. 2 (2006): 255–94. See also Glenn P. Ambrose, *The Theology of Louis-Marie Chauvet: Overcoming Onto-Theology with the Sacramental Tradition* (Burlington, VT: Ashgate, 2012); Joseph C. Mudd, *Eucharist as Meaning: Critical Metaphysics and Contemporary Sacramental Theology* (Collegeville, MN: Liturgical Press, 2014), 1–37.

[96] See Chauvet, *The Sacraments*, xiv, in which he criticizes conceiving the sacraments as instruments: "This image has the disadvantage of suggesting the idea of a quasi automatic production, as long as the instrument is properly utilized by the minister. Besides, grace thus 'produced' risks being seen precisely as a product, a product-which-is-an-object." See also Walsh, "The Divine and the Human in St. Thomas's Theology of Sacraments," 324: "For Chauvet the pervasive flaw in the sacramental theology of Thomas is its appeal to causality to explain the reality of sacraments as moments of grace. He sees the appeal to divine causality as an instance of the kind of 'ontotheology' that Heidegger finds inevitable but unacceptable in Greek metaphysics. . . . The concept of causality being employed is, according to Chauvet, one of technical 'production': to cause is to make a product." See also Ambrose, *The Theology of Louis-Marie Chauvet*, 46–49.

to the idea of production or augmentation; thus, it always pre-supposes an explanatory model implying production. . . . Our initial question must then be why the Scholastics chose this idea, apparently so inadequate and poorly suited to expressing the modality of relation between God and humankind in the sacraments.[97]

His answer is essentially the Heideggerian view that Western metaphysics is at fault: "Western thought is unable to represent to itself the relations between subjects or of subjects with God in any way other than one according to a technical model of cause and effect."[98]

In response, I would say that in order to shed light on the data of Revelation, which speak of the sacraments as bringing about momentous changes in the supernatural order, it is necessary to make use of the notion of "cause" to make this change intelligible. All theology involves the use of analogy by taking a phenomenon of human experience—such as the notion of efficient causality—and elevating it to the supernatural level, purifying the analogous concept of that which belongs to the material sphere. The identification of a chain of causes of a new infusion of grace does not reduce grace to the level of a material thing but seeks to elevate our understanding of the way that the sacraments participate in bringing about the most momentous of changes: justification and sanctification, which involve a new or increased sharing in the divine life. The sources of Revelation and the Magisterium require the theologian to give an account of how the sacraments contain and communicate the grace that they represent and how they bring about this new participation in the divine life. This requires a theory of sacramental causality. To deny the category of causality is to evade the theologian's task to "account for the hope that is in" us (1 Pet 3:15).[99]

CONCLUSION

After this review of over eight centuries of debate about the causal efficacy of the sacraments, it might be useful, at the risk of oversim-

---

[97] Chauvet, *Symbol and Sacrament*, 7 (italics original).

[98] Chauvet, *Symbol and Sacrament*, 22.

[99] See Miralles, *I sacramenti christiani*, 350–51.

plification, to put the various theories into four broad categories. Although the sources of Revelation in Scripture and the Fathers do not present a theory of the causal efficacy of the sacraments, the fact of their marvelous efficacy is affirmed in various ways, and it is the task of systematic theology to attempt to give the most faithful account of it. The Magisterium of the Church has set a minimal limit to the debate by affirming that the sacraments truly contain and confer the grace that they represent.[100] We have seen four principal ways of understanding the causal efficacy of the sacraments. All four positions wrestle with the principal difficulty, which is how sensible signs can contain and confer the grace they represent.

One way is the line taken by St. Bernard, St. Bonaventure, Duns Scotus, and the nominalist tradition, which was slightly modified by Melchior Cano and those who took up his theory of moral causality. This position could be referred to as covenantal causality, or sacramental extrinsicism.[101] This type of position answers the principal difficulty by affirming that God alone is the efficient cause of the infusion of grace, and that the sacrament is properly a kind of necessary condition for the exercise of God's causality, by virtue of His Covenant. In other words, this thesis denies to the sacrament a real participation in the efficient causality of infusing grace, leaving that to God alone. This position fails to fully distinguish the mode of efficacy of the sacraments of the Old and New Covenant.

A second position is that of St. Thomas Aquinas, which sees the sacraments as instrumental causes used by the humanity of Christ.[102] His mature position is that the outward sacramental sign is the instru-

---

[100] Council of Trent, Decree on the Sacraments (session 7), can. 6 on the Sacraments in General (DS, 1606): "If anyone says that the sacraments of the New Law do not contain the grace they signify or that they do not confer that grace on those who do not place an obstacle in the way, . . . let him be anathema."

[101] A modification of this position has been given in the twentieth century in the theory of Cardinal Billot, often referred to as "intentional causality."

[102] This position has two variants. The early St. Thomas held that the sacrament is only an instrumental cause of the *res et sacramentum*, which is the proximate disposition for the reception of grace. This position could be called "dispositive causality." Although his earlier position was followed for some centuries, the great majority of Thomists since Cajetan follow his mature position. The theory of dispositive causality is similar to theories of moral causality in that both positions hold that the sacraments are not properly instrumental efficient causes of grace, and only give a proximate disposition of some kind for receiving grace.

mental cause of the *res et sacramentum*, which, as *sacramentum*, is itself an efficacious sign of the grace that is infused as long as there is no obstacle. Thus there is a double sacramental causality involved: from the outward sign to the interior sign to the infusion of grace.

This position seeks to meet the major difficulty by the analogy of instrumental causality. An instrument always acts above its own level because it is elevated by the principal cause that utilizes it. Thus the effect transcends the level of the instrumental cause while truly being produced by it.

This raises a second difficulty. In instrumental causality, the instrument, by doing its own proper action, cooperates in realizing the higher effect. How does that happen here? In the sacraments, the proper effect of the sacrament is to signify, and the higher effect that it realizes by being used by a higher agent—Christ—is to bring about what it signifies. This occurs because the sacrament is being used by Christ, to whom it is proper to use words with "authority," words that do what they say. The sacramental words and signs are instruments that can do this only insofar as they are words and signs of Christ, who alone can use them in that way.

Both the first and second positions affirm God's efficient causality in infusing grace through reception of the sacrament, but they differ in the role that the sacramental sign and the *res et sacramentum* play in that efficient causality. The second position gives greater dignity to the words and signs used by Christ as participating in His power to speak through them.

Two other positions deny the exercise of efficient causality in the reception of the sacraments, although in different ways. The third position is represented by various Protestant views, which, although with different accents, deny any causality *ex opere operato* of the sacraments and view them as sensible signs of God's infallible promises, instituted to arouse and invigorate faith and its public exercise. The Council of Trent, by defining the *ex opere causality* of the sacraments, put theories of this kind out of the bounds of orthodoxy.

A fourth position that sees the sacraments as intrinsic symbols also denies that the sacraments should be viewed as exercising efficient causality. It differs from Protestant views by emphasizing that the sacraments are manifesting a present action of grace, to be understood presumably along the lines of Rahner's understanding of the "supernatural existential." They are not merely sensible and public divine promises of future transformation but also manifestations of what the

Church already is as the primordial sacrament, and in this sense they can be said to contain and confer grace.

The problem with a view of this kind is that it tends to reduce the role of the sacraments to manifesting a divine action that would always and everywhere be at work independently of the sacramental action. Such a position does not fit with the analogy of Christ's miracles, which were not always at work, but which only occurred through His action in speaking words of power, words which did what they said. Nor does it fit with the New Testament account of the change brought about by being born anew from water and the Spirit, and having life from receiving Christ's Body and drinking His Blood. This position attempts to meet the major difficulty of how sensible signs can give the grace that they signify by blurring the distinction between potency and act with respect to grace, and diminishing the drama of the passage from spiritual death into life and the subsequent passage from grace unto grace. With regard to the Eucharist, the exclusion of efficient causality can no longer coherently account for transubstantiation from bread and wine to Christ's Body and Blood. Similarly, without the exercise of efficient causality in the reception of the sacraments, one cannot understand how one begins to have sacramental character and the new spiritual power that it implies.

Of the four positions, I hold that Thomas's mature position is by far the most faithful to the sources of Revelation and manifests a great fittingness. But at the same time, it has greater difficulties precisely because it takes seriously a participation of the sacrament in the infusion of grace, as an instrument of Christ. It meets those difficulties in a profound way by looking to Christ and taking His theandric miraculous actions manifested in the Gospels as the model of His sacramental action that extends His reach to touch us today with grace and power.

STUDY QUESTIONS

1. Does the efficacy of the sacraments depend on the holiness of the minister? Explain.
2. (a) Do Protestants, such as Calvin, generally hold that the sacraments function *ex opere operato*? (b) Briefly explain Calvin's position on the efficacy of the sacraments. (c) How can the Catholic position on sacramental efficacy be presented in a way

that could help Protestants to understand it?

3. What is meant by the doctrine that the sacraments work *ex opere operato*?

4. Respond to the following objection: No one can give what one does not possess, and a minister in a state of mortal sin does not possess sanctifying grace. How can he give it to another through the celebration of a sacrament?

5. Explain the post-Tridentine debate over two opposing views of sacramental causality: moral vs. physical causality.

6. Explain Karl Rahner's theory of sacramental causality, and compare his position to that of St. Thomas, the theory of moral causality, and the Lutheran and Calvinist understanding.

Suggestions for Further Reading

Bouyer, Louis. "Word and Sacrament." In *Sacraments: The Gestures of Christ*. Edited by Denis O'Callaghan. New York: Sheed & Ward, 1964. Pp. 139–52.

_____. *The Word, Church and Sacraments in Protestantism and Catholicism*. Translated by A. V. Littledale. San Francisco: Ignatius Press, 2004. Pp. 67–92.

Cessario, Romanus, O.P. "Sacramental Causality: Da capo!" *Nova et Vetera* (English) 11, no. 2 (2013): 307–16.

Council of Trent. Decree on the Sacraments. Session 7, March 3, 1547. DS, 1600–1613.

Gallagher, John F. *Significando causant: A Study of Sacramental Efficiency*. Fribourg, CH: University Press, 1965. Pp. 37–54; 154–264.

Lynch, Reginald M., O.P. "Cajetan's Harp: Sacraments and the Life of Grace in Light of Perfective Instrumentality." *The Thomist* 78 (2014): 65-106.

_____. *The Cleansing of the Heart: The Sacraments as Instrumental Causes in the Thomistic Tradition*. Washington, DC: Catholic University of America Press, 2017. Pp. 154–205.

_____. "The Sacraments as Causes of Sanctification." *Nova et Vetera* (English) 12, no. 3 (2014): 791–836, especially 811–36.

Miralles, Antonio. *I sacramenti cristiani: trattato generale*. 2nd edition. Rome: Apollinare studi, 2008. Pp. 331–51.

Rahner, Karl. *The Church and the Sacraments*. 3rd edition. Translated by W. J. O'Hara. New York: Herder and Herder, 1963.

Scheeben, Matthias Joseph. *The Mysteries of Christianity*. Translated by Cyril Vollert. St. Louis, MO: B. Herder, 1951. Pp. 452–65; 567–572.

White, Thomas Joseph, O.P. "Sacraments and Philosophy." In *The Oxford Handbook of Sacramental Theology*. Edited by Hans Boersma and Matthew Levering. Oxford; New York: Oxford University Press, 2015. Pp. 585–89.

PART FIVE

GRACE GIVEN THROUGH DESIRE FOR THE SACRAMENTS

CHAPTER FOURTEEN

Sanctification through the Sacramental Rites of the Old Covenant

We have seen above that the councils of Florence and Trent both taught that the sacraments of the Old and New Covenant differ in their causal efficacy. In this chapter we shall examine the sacramental rites of the Old Covenant, their role in the sanctification of Israel, their essential difference from the sacraments of the New Covenant in causal power, and the Christological reason for this difference. We shall also take up the difficult question of whether, as prefiguring signs, they continue to have a religious value and serve as occasions of sanctification after the institution and promulgation of the New Covenant.

1. SACRAMENTS OF THE OLD COVENANT BEFORE THE PROMULGATION OF THE GOSPEL

St. Thomas on the Sacraments of the Old Law

It was common for the Fathers and Doctors to treat of the "sacraments" of the Old Covenant in a general way as rites that prefigure those of the New Covenant. St. Thomas, in his treatise on the Old Law, gives a more detailed analysis. He makes an important distinction between three types of precepts in the Law of Moses: moral, ceremonial, and judicial.[1] The moral precepts, such as the Ten Com-

---

[1] *ST* I-II, q. 99, aa. 2–4.

mandments, pertain to the natural moral law. Ceremonial precepts, such as those regarding the feasts of Israel, sacrificial offerings, and dietary prescriptions, pertain to liturgical law. Judicial precepts were a form of divinely sanctioned civil law that determined particular ways of enforcing the moral law in ancient Israel. The Old Testament sacraments belong among the ceremonial precepts, which are divided into "sacrifices, sacred things, sacraments, and observances."[2] "Sacraments" are defined as "things applied to the worshippers of God for their consecration so as, in some way, to depute them to the worship of God."[3] Thus they were consecrations that made the people of Israel, as God said on Mt. Sinai, His "own possession among all peoples," and "a kingdom of priests and a holy nation" (Exod 19:5–6).

Like the other aspects of the ceremonial law, the Old Testament sacraments have two purposes.[4] First, they are a divinely given means of worship, sanctifying the people through their exercise of faith and devotion and setting them apart as a people consecrated to the Lord. This is the literal sense of these precepts. Secondly, they prefigure the sacraments of the New Covenant, which is their typological meaning.[5]

According to St. Thomas, most of the sacraments of the New Covenant are directly prefigured by a sacramental rite of the Old Covenant. The Old Covenant sacrament that first consecrates a person to God is circumcision, which prefigures Baptism. The solemn sacrifice and feast of the Paschal Lamb on Passover prefigured the Eucharist in

---

[2] *ST* I-II, q. 101, a. 4.

[3] *ST* I-II, q. 102, a. 5.

[4] See *ST* I-II, q. 102, a. 2: "The reason for whatever conduces to an end must be taken from that end. Now the end of the ceremonial precepts was twofold: for they were ordained to the Divine worship, for that particular time, and to the foreshadowing of Christ. . . . Accordingly the reasons for the ceremonial precepts of the Old Law can be taken in two ways. First, in respect of the Divine worship which was to be observed for that particular time: and these reasons are literal: whether they refer to the shunning of idolatry; or recall certain Divine benefits; or remind men of the Divine excellence; or point out the disposition of mind which was then required in those who worshipped God. Secondly, their reasons can be gathered from the point of view of their being ordained to foreshadow Christ: and thus their reasons are figurative and mystical: whether they be taken from Christ Himself and the Church, which pertains to the allegorical sense; or to the morals of the Christian people, which pertains to the moral sense; or to the state of future glory, in as much as we are brought thereto by Christ, which refers to the anagogical sense."

[5] For the senses of Scripture, see *CCC*, §117, and Feingold, *Faith Comes from What Is Heard*, 493–514.

numerous ways.[6] The consecration of priests, and of the High Priest in particular,[7] prefigures Holy Orders. Ritual purifications prefigure the sacrament of Penance.[8]

Matrimony existed under the Old Law, but "not as the sacrament of the union of Christ with the Church, for that union was not as yet brought about. Hence under the Old Law it was allowable to give a bill of divorce, which is contrary to the nature of a sacrament."[9] Matrimony in the Old Covenant certainly was a prefiguration of the spousal union of Christ and the Church and an occasion of grace, and thus it could be counted as a sacrament of the Old Covenant, although St. Thomas does not seem to do so because of the provision for divorce.

St. Thomas holds that Confirmation and Anointing of the Sick lack a corresponding Old Testament sacrament because their purpose is to bring to completion, for Confirmation "completes" Baptism[10] and Anointing "completes" Penance.[11] But the Old Covenant was not yet meant to be the completion, for that was reserved to Christ to institute for His Bride:

> To the sacrament of Confirmation, which is the sacrament of the fulness of grace, there would be no corresponding sacrament of the Old Law, because the time of fulness had not yet

---

[6] See *ST* III, q. 73, a. 6.

[7] See Exod 29:1–7; Lev 8:6–12

[8] See *ST* I-II, q. 102, a. 5, ad 3: "Some of the sacraments of the New Law had corresponding figurative sacraments in the Old Law. For Baptism, which is the sacrament of Faith, corresponds to circumcision. Hence it is written (Col 2:11–12): 'You are circumcised ... in the circumcision of Our Lord Jesus Christ; buried with Him in Baptism.' In the New Law the sacrament of the Eucharist corresponds to the banquet of the paschal lamb. The sacrament of Penance in the New Law corresponds to all the purifications of the Old Law. The sacrament of Orders corresponds to the consecration of the pontiff and of the priests."

[9] *ST* I-II, q. 102, a. 5, ad 3.

[10] See Paul VI, *Divinae Consortium Naturae*: "From that time on the apostles, in fulfillment of Christ's will, imparted to the newly baptized by the laying on of hands the gift of the Spirit that completes the grace of Baptism." This is cited in *CCC*, §1288.

[11] See *CCC*, §1523: "The Anointing of the Sick completes our conformity to the death and Resurrection of Christ, just as Baptism began it. It completes the holy anointings that mark the whole Christian life." An interesting prefiguration of Anointing of the Sick is the rite of the Mosaic law for the purification of a leper who has already been cured of his leprosy, given in Lev 14:1–32.

come, since "the Law brought no man to perfection" (Heb. 7:19). The same applies to the sacrament of Extreme Unction, which is an immediate preparation for entrance into glory, to which the way was not yet opened out in the Old Law, since the price had not yet been paid.[12]

Although the Old Covenant lacked a sacrament of spiritual maturity, Confirmation was nevertheless prefigured by the three anointings given in the Old Testament for priests, prophets, and kings, although they differ from Confirmation in being restricted to very few individuals. Confirmation is prefigured in a particular way by the anointing of Saul, David, and the kings who are descendants of the Davidic line. The anointing of David by Samuel, as related in 1 Samuel 16:13, shows the effect of the rite: "Samuel took the horn of oil, and anointed him in the midst of his brothers; and the Spirit of the LORD came mightily upon David from that day forward." The special outpouring of the Holy Spirit that was reserved for the kings of Israel in the Old Covenant is poured out in the New Testament on all the members of Christ, the Anointed Son of David. This fuller outpouring was foretold by Joel 2:28–29: "It shall come to pass afterward, that I will pour out my spirit on all flesh; your sons and your daughters shall prophesy, your old men shall dream dreams, and your young men shall see visions. Even upon the menservants and maidservants in those days, I will pour out my spirit." St. Peter applies this text to the Christian sacramental gift of the Holy Spirit in Acts 2:15–21.

The Sacraments of the Old Covenant Did Not Function *ex opere operato*

We have seen that the intrinsic efficacy of the sacraments that function *ex opere operato* is a property unique to the seven sacraments of the New Covenant. They are signs that represent the sanctification of the people of God, and efficacious instruments for imparting the grace they symbolize. The sacraments of the Old Covenant could accomplish the first of these purposes but not the second. They are divinely instituted means for the worship of God, public signs and manifestations of faith in God's redemption and human sanctification that would come through the Messiah, but they were not yet instru-

---

[12] *ST* I-II, q. 102, a. 5, ad 3.

ments in the hands of the Messiah to directly impart the grace of His redemption. Nevertheless, through this manifestation of their faith in His Covenant, God conferred grace on Israel. In Romans 4:9–11, St. Paul implies that circumcision was not intrinsically efficacious but was rather a sign of the faith that justified:

> We say that faith was reckoned to Abraham as righteousness. How then was it reckoned to him? Was it before or after he had been circumcised? It was not after, but before he was circumcised. He received circumcision as a sign or seal of the righteousness which he had by faith while he was still uncircumcised.

Furthermore, St. Paul speaks of the rites of the Old Law, in comparison with those of the New, as "weak and beggarly" elements (Gal 4:9). Hebrews 9:13–14 brings out the contrast between the sacraments of the Old and the New Covenants:

> If the sprinkling of defiled persons with the blood of goats and bulls and with the ashes of a heifer sanctifies for the purification of the flesh, how much more shall the blood of Christ, who through the eternal Spirit offered himself without blemish to God, purify your conscience from dead works to serve the living God.

We see from this that the rites of the Old Testament do not have the intrinsic power to purify man's interior, for they are outward signs "pointing to what would be effected by our sacraments of the New Law."[13] They are not instruments applying to the faithful the merits gained from the Blood of Christ, but rather signs of the salvation to come and occasions to exercise faith and so merit grace.

As seen above, both the Council of Florence and Trent declared that the sacraments of the New Law differ essentially from those of the Old, and not merely in their outward forms. The Council of Florence teaches that the "seven sacraments of the New Law . . . differ greatly from the sacraments of the Old Law. The latter, in fact, did not cause grace, but they only prefigured the grace to be given through the Passion of Christ. These sacraments of ours, however, both contain

---

[13] *CCT*, part 2, intro., §29, p. 161.

grace and communicate it to those who worthily receive them."[14] Although Trent does not specify how they differ essentially, it implies that the sacraments of the Mosaic Law do not have the same property of being efficacious *ex opere operato*.[15]

St. Thomas Aquinas on the Difference between the Sacraments of the Old and New Covenants

St. Thomas gives a profound reason for this difference between the sacraments of the Old and New Covenants. The sacraments of the Old Covenant could not fittingly work *ex opere operato* simply because Christ had not yet become incarnate.[16] Using the distinction between extrinsic instruments (such as a chisel) and a conjoined instrument (such as one's own hand or body), it is not hard to see the difference between the causality of the rites of the Old and the New Covenant. When the sacraments of the Old Covenant were instituted through Moses, the Word had not yet become flesh. There was no living instru-

---

[14] Council of Florence, *Exsultate Deo* (DS, 1310).

[15] Council of Trent, Decree on the Sacraments (session 7), can. 2 on the Sacraments in General (DS, 1602): "If anyone says that these same sacraments of the New Law do not differ from the sacraments of the Old Law, except that the ceremonies and external rites are different, let him be anathema."

[16] See *SCG* IV, ch. 57, no. 1, 4:248: "This salvation was promised, indeed, before Christ's Incarnation and death but not displayed; it was the incarnate and suffering Word who brought about this kind of salvation. Therefore, the sacraments which preceded Christ's Incarnation had to be such as signified and somehow promised salvation. But the sacraments which follow the suffering of Christ ought to be such as deliver this salvation to men, not merely such as point to it by signs." See also Ratzinger, "On the Concept of Sacrament," in *Theology of the Liturgy*, 179–80: "The Old Testament *sacramenta* are, from beginning to end, a movement toward what is as yet undisclosed; they are an invitation to a way. . . . But as of that moment when Christ suffered and, having come from the Father, remains now with us forever, something new happened: the reality to which everything was still pending is now here. Therefore a sacrament now is the representation of the given, a transfer to what has already happened. Medieval theology later explained this by the contrast—since then so often misunderstood—between *ex opere operato* and *ex opere operantis*. Originally this distinction pertained to the contrast between the Old and the New Testament, between promise and fulfillment. Originally the formula was not just *ex opere operato*, but *ex opere operato Christi*. This means: the sacraments now no longer work by foreshadowing and asking; rather, they are effective as a result of what has already happened, and therein is manifest the act of liberation accomplished by Christ."

ment belonging to our world that was *joined* to the divinity as His humanity.

Without this conjoined instrument, which is the humanity of Christ, separated or extrinsic instruments could not be wielded and directed by the principal agent in a fitting manner. Thus we can say that the sacramental rites of the Old Covenant were signs instituted by God, pointing to the conjoined instrument, Jesus Christ, who was to come, and to the future separated instruments that He would use. But since the Messiah had not yet come in the flesh, they were not yet instruments that could be wielded by His hand. Christ's humanity, as the humanity of a divine Person, is the fitting link between the divine power and the extrinsic sacraments that would be used by our High Priest to extend the reach of His humanity so as to touch us here with His incarnate power. Thus the Incarnation was necessary for the sacraments to be perfected as the instruments of His humanity.[17]

The faithful of Israel were justified by their faith in the coming of the Messiah. St. Thomas explains that a future event can achieve its effect in advance of its actual occurrence insofar as it is somehow known, desired, and loved, and thus already active interiorly in a person's spiritual life.[18] The future salvific events in God's plan of salvation were believed and hoped for in the celebration of the rites of Israel, which are signs of these future salvific events and also memorials of God's saving action in Israel's history that typologically prefigure Christ and the Church.

An instrumental efficient cause, on the other hand, can operate

---

[17] See Schillebeeckx, *Christ the Sacrament of the Encounter with God*, 85.

[18] See *ST* III, q. 62, a. 6: "Now nothing hinders that which is subsequent in point of time, from causing movement, even before it exists in reality, in so far as it pre-exists in an act of the soul: thus the end, which is subsequent in point of time, moves the agent in so far as it is apprehended and desired by him. On the other hand, what does not yet actually exist, does not cause movement if we consider the use of exterior things. Consequently, the efficient cause cannot in point of time come into existence after causing movement, as does the final cause. It is therefore clear that the sacraments of the New Law do reasonably derive the power of justification from Christ's Passion, which is the cause of man's righteousness; whereas the sacraments of the Old Law did not. Nevertheless the Fathers of old were justified by faith in Christ's Passion, just as we are. And the sacraments of the Old Law were a kind of protestation of that faith, inasmuch as they signified Christ's Passion and its effects. It is therefore manifest that the sacraments of the Old Law were not endowed with any power by which they conduced to the bestowal of justifying grace: and they merely signified faith by which men were justified."

only when the principal cause is at work in it. For example, a chisel can function as an efficient cause only when the sculptor is present and holding the chisel in his hand. Before that time the chisel cannot carve the statue. However, an *image* of the chisel at work in the hand of the artist can produce some effect in the mind of an observer. It can be a sign that the statue will be made when the sculptor arrives. The image can give hope to a client that the statue he has commissioned will one day be completed. The rites of Israel were like images or tools without the sculptor physically present to use them. They were signs, instituted by God, manifesting faith and hope in future salvific events, and their pious use drew down God's grace upon Israel.

The sacraments of the New Covenant, on the other hand, are instruments in the hand of Christ who has come and merited through His Passion the successful completion of the entire work of salvation. Although His human body, the conjoined instrument, has ascended into heaven, He can still work on earth through separated instruments and sacred ministers whose words and gestures are realized in His Person through the sacrament of Holy Orders.

St. Thomas's reasoning presupposes first the universal efficacy of Christ's Passion as the meritorious source of all grace. Secondly, his argument distinguishes two different ways by which Christ's Passion can be operative in or applied to human beings. The Passion can be operative (a) through spiritual acts of desire working through faith, hope, and love, as well as (b) through sensible instrumental efficient causes that apply the grace won on Calvary to the soul *ex opere operato*. Spiritual acts of desire, faith, hope, and love, are the result of actual grace and human cooperation. In this sense they can be said to work *ex opere operantis*, from the activity of the acting person who is aided by actual grace. Instrumental causes applying the sanctifying grace merited by the Passion, on the other hand, function *ex opere operato*, from the work worked.

The former way (*ex opere operantis*) could be operative before the Incarnation, insofar as the redemption to be worked by the Messiah was the object of Israel's hope. The use of instrumental efficient causes (*ex opere operato*), however, presupposes the actual occurrence of the Incarnation, so that the extrinsic instruments can be instituted and used by the conjoined instrument of Christ's humanity, like a chisel in the hand of a sculptor. Before the Incarnation there could be an efficacious desire in the souls of the Israelites for the sacraments of the Messiah, working through faith and hope on the occasion of the rites of Israel, but the sacraments of the New Covenant require that the Incarnation already be present so that Christ's humanity can serve as the conjoined instrument that uses extrinsic instruments—the Church's sacraments—to touch and heal us.

This need for the Incarnation especially applies to the Eucharist, which is the heart of the New Covenant. Here the sacrament is not only wielded by the Incarnate Word through a priestly minister, but it also makes His sacred humanity present among us as the new *shekinah*, the Victim of Calvary who is offered in sacrifice and received in Holy Communion. The rites of the Old Covenant and the Eucharist, although in typological continuity, differ infinitely in what they make present. The Eucharist alone makes present the humanity of the Word.

The Sacraments of the Old Covenant Were Occasions for Imparting Grace

Even though the rites of Israel did not cause grace *ex opere operato*, they were still occasions for the infusion of grace. Pope Innocent III, in a letter of 1201 to Humbert, Archbishop of Arles, teaches that "original sin was remitted by the mystery of circumcision and the danger of damnation avoided."[19] This was the general view in the West since St. Augustine, who wrote:

> The removal of this sin [original sin] in the infant was signified by the circumcision on the eighth day, that is, by the sacrament of the mediator who was to come in the flesh. For the righteous people of old were also saved through the same faith in Christ who was to come in the flesh and die for us and rise.[20] . . . At that time circumcision was a sign of the righteousness coming from faith, and from the time that circumcision was instituted in the people of God, it had the power to signify the purification from the original and ancient sin even in the little ones.[21]

---

[19] DS, 780.

[20] St. Augustine sees the eighth day on which circumcision was to be performed as a prefiguring sign of Christ's Resurrection on the day after the Sabbath, which the Fathers speak of as the eighth day.

[21] Augustine, *Marriage and Desire* 2.11.24, in *Answer to the Pelagians II*, trans. Roland J. Teske, WSA, I/24 (Hyde Park, NY: New City Press, 1998), 67–68. See Leeming, *Principles of Sacramental Theology*, 609: "In the Western Church,

St. Augustine's view that original sin was taken away on the occasion of circumcision was taught by Gregory the Great,[22] Venerable Bede,[23] Hugh of St. Victor,[24] and Peter Lombard in his *Sentences*.[25] St. Thomas Aquinas likewise held that sanctifying grace was conferred on the faithful of Israel on the occasion of receiving the sacraments of the Old Covenant, such as circumcision. He quotes Romans 2:25 in which St. Paul says that "circumcision indeed is of value," and explains: "inasmuch as it remits original sin."[26] Commenting on Romans 4:11–12, however, he distinguishes it from Baptism and specifies that "*ex opere operato* circumcision did not have effective power either to remove guilt

---

since the time of St. Augustine, it had been universally held that original sin was remitted in circumcision."

[22] See Gregory the Great, *Morals on the Book of Job* 4.3, trans. John Henry Parker, vol. 1 (London, 1844), 179: "For every man that is not absolved by the water of regeneration, is tied and bound by the guilt of the original bond. But that which the water of Baptism avails for with us, this either faith alone did of old in behalf of infants, or, for those of riper years, the virtue of sacrifice, or, for all that came of the stock of Abraham, the mystery of circumcision."

[23] See Bede, Homily 11, bk. 1, *On the Octave Day of Christmas*, in *Homilies on the Gospels Book One: Advent to Lent*, trans. Lawrence T. Martin (Collegeville, MN: Cistercian Publications, 2008), 104–05: "Under the law, circumcision offered the same help of a health-giving treatment against the wound of original sin that now, in the time of revealed grace, baptism is wont to do, except that they [who were under the law] could not yet enter the gate of the heavenly kingdom, . . . and so, consoled in the bosom of Abraham by a blessed rest after death, they awaited with blissful hope their entry into heavenly peace. . . . Both purifications, namely that of circumcision under the law and that of baptism under the gospel, were provided as graces for taking away the first transgression." Peter Lombard cites this text in his *Sentences*, bk. 4, d. 1, ch. 7, trans. Silano, p. 6, and then comments: "By these words, it is plainly asserted that through circumcision, from the moment of its institution, remission of original and actual sin was granted by God to children and adults, just as it is now granted through baptism."

[24] See Hugh of St. Victor, *On the Sacraments of the Christian Faith*, 1.12.2, trans. Deferrari, 190: "The sacrament of circumcision was given to the seed of Abraham alike for sanctifying and for marking, for sanctifying that it might be justified, for marking that it might be distinguished from the rest of nations."

[25] See Peter Lombard, *Sentences*, bk. 4, d. 1, ch. 7, trans. Silano, p. 6: "And yet there was one among those sacraments, namely circumcision, which conferred the same remedy against sin as baptism does now." On the teaching of the early scholastics on the granting of grace through the ceremonial law, see Artur Michael Landgraf, *Dogmengeschichte der Frühscholastik*, vol. 3/1, *Die Lehre von den Sakramenten* (Regensburg: Friedrich Pustet, 1954), 19–60.

[26] Thomas Aquinas, *Commentary on the Letter of Saint Paul to the Romans* 2:25, lectio 4, no. 238, trans. Larcher, WTA, 37:82.

or to produce justice. It was merely a sign of justice, as the Apostle says here. But through faith in Christ, of which circumcision was a sign, it removed original sin and conferred the help of grace to act righteously."[27]

Although circumcision did not work *ex opere operato*, Aquinas held that the same gifts of grace were given on the occasion of circumcision as through Baptism (although not necessarily in the same degree), and in this he differed from his contemporaries. He explains how grace was conferred with circumcision in *ST* III, q. 70, a. 4.[28] All theologians, he states, agreed that original sin was remitted by the rite of circumcision. They differed, however, with regard to the effects of grace bestowed. Some theologians, such as Peter Lombard, held that circumcision remitted original sin, but bestowed no grace.[29] This is impossible, however, because original sin essentially consists in the privation of sanctifying grace. Thus the remission of original sin necessarily implies the giving of sanctifying grace.[30]

A second position on this issue held that grace was imparted at circumcision in order to bring about the forgiveness of original sin but without bringing about the other positive effects of grace. St. Thomas responds that it is impossible that grace not bring about its positive effects, for they flow from the very nature of grace.[31] These effects

---

[27] Aquinas, *Commentary on the Letter of Saint Paul to the Romans*, commentary on Romans 4:11–12, lectio 2, no. 349, 37:119.

[28] See also *ST* III, q. 62, a. 6, ad 3.

[29] See Peter Lombard, *Sentences*, bk. 4, d. 1, ch. 9, no. 5, trans. Silano, 8: "For in circumcision sins only were remitted, but neither the grace which assists in good works, nor the possession or increase of the virtues was granted by it, as happens in baptism, where not only are sins abolished, but also helping grace is conferred and the virtues are increased."

[30] See *ST* III, q. 70, a. 4: "All are agreed in saying that original sin was remitted in circumcision. But some said that no grace was conferred, and that the only effect was to remit sin. The Master [Peter Lombard] holds this opinion in *Sentences*, bk. 4, d. 1, and in a gloss on Romans 4:11. But this is impossible, since guilt is not remitted except by grace, according to Romans 3:2: 'Being justified freely by His grace,' etc." On this view, see Landgraf, *Dogmengeschichte der Frühscholastik*, 3/1:61–86.

[31] See *ST* III, q. 70, a. 4: "Wherefore others said that grace was bestowed by circumcision, as to that effect which is the remission of guilt, but not as to its positive effects; lest they should be compelled to say that the grace bestowed in circumcision sufficed for the fulfilling of the precepts of the Law, and that, consequently, the coming of Christ was unnecessary. But neither can this opinion stand. First, because by circumcision children received the power of obtaining

include making the soul pleasing to God, transforming the recipient into a son of God and an heir of heaven, giving the theological virtues, the gifts of the Holy Spirit, and the indwelling of the Holy Spirit. Grace removes original sin and its deformity precisely by bringing about these effects in the soul.

The reason some theologians held that grace could not give its positive effects, as St. Thomas observes, was because they thought that otherwise "they should be compelled to say that the grace bestowed in circumcision sufficed for the fulfilling of the precepts of the Law, and that, consequently, the coming of Christ was unnecessary."[32] It is true that the grace sufficed, but it does not follow that Christ's coming was unnecessary, since Christ on Calvary merited the grace given in circumcision, like every other grace.

A third position is that the grace that was conferred at circumcision both brought about the forgiveness of original sin and also made the recipient an heir of heaven, but was not sufficient to enable the recipient to accomplish the Law of God and prevail against concupiscence.[33] St. Thomas himself held this position in his early commentary on the *Sentences*.[34] In the *Summa theologiae*, however, St. Thomas repudiates his earlier defense of this position because sanctifying grace and charity, given in circumcision, immeasurably transcend concupiscence.[35]

St. Thomas concludes therefore that the grace given in circumcision accomplishes the same effects as the grace given through the

---

glory at the allotted time, which is the last positive effect of grace. Secondly, because, in the order of the formal cause, positive effects naturally precede those that denote privation, although it is the reverse in the order of the material cause: since a form does not remove a privation save by informing the subject." On this view, see Landgraf, *Dogmengeschichte der Frühscholastik*, 3/1:86–92.

[32] *ST* III, q. 70, a. 4.

[33] See *ST* III, q. 70, a. 4: "Consequently, others said that grace was conferred in circumcision, also as a particular positive effect consisting in being made worthy of eternal life; but not as to all its effects, for it did not suffice for the repression of the concupiscence of the *fomes*, nor again for the fulfilment of the precepts of the Law. And this was my opinion at one time (*In IV Sent.*, d. 1, q. 2, a. 4)." The Latin word *fomes* literally means "tinder" but is used by theologians to signify the spontaneous inclination of the sense appetite that can lead to sin.

[34] See Thomas Aquinas, *In IV Sent.*, d. 1, q. 2, a. 4.

[35] See *ST* III, q. 70, a. 4: "But if one consider the matter carefully, it is clear that this is not true. Because the least grace can resist any degree of concupiscence, and avoid every mortal sin, that is committed in transgressing the precepts of the Law; for the smallest degree of charity loves God more than cupidity loves 'thousands of gold and silver pieces' (Ps 118:72)."

sacraments of the New Covenant. This does not mean, however, that circumcision has the same efficacy as Baptism, which would be contrary to the teaching of Scripture. St. Thomas therefore puts the key distinction between Baptism and circumcision not principally *in their effects but in the kind of causality* they exercise. Baptism works as an instrumental cause of grace in the hand of Christ, like a chisel in the hand of the sculptor, whereas circumcision is not an efficient instrumental cause but a manifestation of Israel's faith and an occasion for God to bestow grace, as a sign pointing to the coming of the divine sculptor.[36]

Circumcision was an occasion of sanctification in a way similar to the other sacraments of the Old Law with one important difference, which is that the subject is normally a person not yet at the age of reason. Sacred rites that do not work *ex opere operato* but through the spiritual acts of the worshippers ordinarily directly benefit only those who make the spiritual acts of faith, hope, and charity. They can benefit others only indirectly by way of intercession. In circumcision, the circumcised babies are incapable of making personal acts of faith, hope, and charity, but these acts are made on their behalf by the parents and the community. Since babies are naturally entrusted to parents and the community, it is fitting that God respect this dependence also in the supernatural order by allowing the parents to act on behalf of the children in their faithful realization of the rite, which is a kind of intercession commanded by God Himself.

If original sin was remitted on the occasion of circumcision, which was received only by boys, what about the girls of Israel? Peter Lombard

---

[36] See *ST* III, q. 70, a. 4 (my italics): "We must say, therefore, that grace was bestowed in circumcision as to all the effects of grace, but not as in Baptism. Because in Baptism grace is bestowed by the very power of Baptism itself, which power Baptism has as the instrument of Christ's Passion already consummated. Whereas circumcision bestowed grace, inasmuch as it was a sign of faith in Christ's future Passion: so that the man who was circumcised, professed to embrace that faith; whether, being an adult, he made profession for himself, or, being a child, someone else made profession for him. Hence, too, the Apostle says (Rom 4:11), that Abraham 'received the sign of circumcision, a seal of the justice of the faith': because, to wit, justice was of faith signified: not of circumcision signifying. And since *Baptism operates instrumentally by the power of Christ's Passion, whereas circumcision does not*, therefore Baptism imprints a character that incorporates man in Christ, and bestows grace more copiously than does circumcision; since greater is the effect of a thing already present, than of the hope thereof."

suggests the girls in Israel would be sanctified through the faith of their parents, as in the nations outside of Israel.[37] The fact that the rites of Israel did not function *ex opere operato* is helpful here. Reception of the rite of circumcision was *the occasion* of God's remitting original sin, but the salvific effect did not come through circumcision as through a uniquely efficacious instrument, and thus the salvific effect was not limited to the act of circumcision. It seems that the best way to explain how the giving of grace in the Old Covenant is tied to circumcision is that circumcision is the visible sign by which males become members of the people of Israel, and justification is given by God to the members of Israel on the occasion of their incorporation into the people of God (unless, in the case of adults, they pose the obstacle of unrepentance).[38] Girls likewise would be participants of this grace when they are incorporated into the people of Israel, as on the celebration of their naming (*Simchat bat*).[39]

St. Thomas also holds that the grace of God would have been given to remit original sin prior to the institution of circumcision and to the nations outside of Israel. He hypothesizes that this gift would have been given on the occasion of the prayers of parents for the sanctification of their children, according to the rites of their culture:

---

[37] See Peter Lombard, *Sentences*, bk. 4, d. 1, ch. 8, trans. Silano, 7: "Regarding the men who lived before circumcision, and the women who lived before and after, it is asked what remedy they had against sin. Some say that sacrifices and oblations were helpful to them for the remission of sin. But it is better to say that the men who issued from Abraham were justified by circumcision, and the women by faith and good work, either their own, if they were adults, or their parents', if they were little. As for those who lived before circumcision, children were justified by the faith of their parents." A similar view was held by Gandulphus of Bologna (died ca. 1185) in his commentary on bk. 4 of the *Sentences*, in which he argues that girls in the Old Covenant were saved simply by the faith of the parents or some offering not directly stipulated by the Law. See Richard Weberberger, O.S.B., "Limbus puerorum. Zur Entstehung eines theologischen Begriffes," *Recherches de théologie ancienne et médiévale* 35 (1968): 115.

[38] See Christianus Pesch, *De Sacramentis*, pars 1: *De Sacramentis in genere. De Baptismo. De Confirmatione. De Eucharistia* (Freiburg im Breisgau, GE: B. Herder, 1914), 76 (my translation): "Being incorporated into the People of God was the condition of sanctification for Israelites. Circumcision was the instrument of incorporation into the People of God. Thus man attained to justification by way of circumcision."

[39] See Ronald L. Eisenberg, *The JPS Guide to Jewish Traditions* (Philadelphia: The Jewish Publication Society, 2004), 13–14.

Just as before the institution of circumcision, faith in Christ to come justified both children and adults, so, too, after its institution. But before, there was no need of a sign expressive of this faith; because as yet believers had not begun to be united together apart from unbelievers for the worship of one God. It is probable, however, that parents who were believers offered up some prayers to God for their children, especially if these were in any danger. Or bestowed some blessing on them, as a "seal of faith"; just as the adults offered prayers and sacrifices for themselves.[40]

Although the celebration of the sacraments of the Old Covenant were occasions of sanctification, St. Thomas holds that they did not imprint sacramental character or have a *res et sacramentum*, which are proper to the sacraments of the New Covenant.[41] Nevertheless, the outward visible seal of circumcision prefigures the interior seal of the character of Baptism and Confirmation.

2. THE RITES OF ISRAEL AFTER THE PROMULGATION OF THE GOSPEL

The Old Covenant "Has Never Been Revoked"

If the sacramental rites of Israel before Christ were the occasions of an infusion of grace, we may ask whether that continues to be the case after the Passion of Christ when celebrated by Jews who are invincibly ignorant of the truth of the New Covenant. This is a special case of the more general topic of sacramental grace received through desire, which will be treated in the next chapter. An answer to this question requires an understanding of invincible (or inculpable) ignorance, on the one hand, and of God's fidelity to His own promises, which include His election of the Jewish people and His covenant with them, on the other. The notion of invincible ignorance was one that evolved slowly

---

[40] *ST* III, q. 70, a. 4, ad 2. See also *ST* III, q. 61, a. 3.

[41] See Thomas Aquinas, *In IV Sent.*, d. 4, q. 1, a. 4, qla. 1, ad 2, trans. Mortensen, 7:169: "Sacraments of the Old Law conferred nothing by the work performed [*ex opere operato*], and thus those actions did not require any spiritual power; and therefore neither from them nor for them was a character imprinted." See Schillebeeckx, *Christ the Sacrament of the Encounter with God*, 85–86.

in the Church, as will be seen in the following chapter. It appears in magisterial documents for the first time in the nineteenth century.[42]

Although this depends on the divine mercy, it seems theologically certain that God continues to give grace on the occasion of the rites of the Old Covenant when they are celebrated by Jews with invincible ignorance of the truth of Christianity and with the disposition of faith, hope, and charity. Worship done in faith, hope, and charity is meritorious, and thus, like other acts of charity, it merits an increase of grace.[43]

This is also based on the principle that the election of the Jewish people has not been revoked, according to Romans 11:29: "For the gifts and the call of God are irrevocable." This conclusion also follows from the principle that God remains faithful even when men are unfaithful in different respects. In Romans 3:3, speaking of the Jewish people, St. Paul says: "What if some were unfaithful? Does their faithlessness nullify the faithfulness of God?"[44] Similarly in 2 Timothy 2:13: "If we are faithless, he remains faithful—for he cannot deny himself."

The Second Vatican Council cited Romans 11:29 in *Nostra Aetate*, §4: "God holds the Jews most dear for the sake of their Fathers; He does not repent of the gifts He makes or of the calls He issues—such is the witness of the Apostle."[45] This teaching of *Nostra Aetate* was clarified by St. John Paul II in a discourse to representatives of the

---

[42] See Pius IX, On Promotion of False Doctrines *Quanto Conficiamur Moerore* (Aug 10, 1863; DS, 2866), and his earlier encyclical, *Singulari Quadam* (Dec 9, 1854) in Denzinger, *Sources of Catholic Dogma*, trans. Roy Deferrari, 13th ed., §1647. Invincible ignorance is discussed in chapter 15 below, pp. 580–90.

[43] See Council of Trent, Decree on Justification (session 6, Jan 13, 1547), chs. 10, 16, canons 24, 32 (DS, 1535, 1545, 1574, 1582); *CCC*, §2010.

[44] See Aquinas's commentary on Romans 3:3, lectio 1, nos. 253–55, trans. Larcher, 37:87–88: "For if the Jews' prerogative were taken away on account of the unbelief of some, it would follow that man's unbelief would nullify God's faithfulness—which is an unacceptable conclusion. . . . This faithfulness would be nullified, if it happened that the Jews had no advantage, just because some have not believed. For God promised to multiply that people and make it great. . . . The reason is based on the fact that God in Himself is true."

[45] Second Vatican Council, Declaration on the Relation of the Church to Non-Christian Religions *Nostra Aetate*. (Oct 28, 1965). On this teaching, see Gavin D'Costa, *Vatican II: Catholic Doctrines on Jews and Muslims* (Oxford: Oxford University Press, 2016), 113–59; Feingold, *The Mystery of Israel and the Church*, 3:229–31. For postconciliar teaching on this issue, see D'Costa, *Catholic Doctrines on Jews After the Second Vatican Council* (Oxford: Oxford University Press, 2019).

Jewish people in 1980. Speaking of Jewish-Christian dialogue, he said: "This dialogue, that is, the meeting between the people of God of the Old Covenant, never revoked by God [cf. Rom 11:29], and that of the New Covenant, is at the same time a dialogue within our Church, that is to say, between the first and the second part of her Bible."[46] This teaching was taken up by the *Catechism of the Catholic Church*, §121, which ties the permanent value of the books of the Old Testament with the fact that "the Old Covenant has never been revoked." It has also been reaffirmed by Pope Francis in *Evangelii Gaudium (The Joy of the Gospel)*: "We hold the Jewish people in special regard because their covenant with God has never been revoked, for 'the gifts and the call of God are irrevocable' (Rom 11:29)."[47] This repeated teaching, although not definitive, pertains to the ordinary Magisterium of the Church. Because of this development, Catholics can no longer hold the "supersessionist" view that the Jewish people have lost their

---

[46] John Paul II, Discourse to Representatives of the Jewish People in Mainz (Nov 17, 1980) §2. See the Commission for Religious Relations with the Jews, Notes on the Correct Way to Present the Jews and Judaism in Preaching and Catechesis in the Roman Catholic Church (June 24, 1985), §4: "The Holy Father has stated this permanent reality of the Jewish people in a remarkable theological formula, in his allocution to the Jewish community of West Germany at Mainz, on Nov 17th, 1980: 'the people of God of the Old Covenant, which has never been revoked.'" On the development this statement marks with respect to *Nostra Aetate*, see the Commission for Religious Relations with the Jews, "The Gifts and the Calling of God Are Irrevocable" (Rom 11:29): A Reflection on Theological Questions Pertaining to Catholic–Jewish Relations on the Occasion of the 50th Anniversary of *Nostra Aetate* (Dec 10 2015), §39.

[47] Pope Francis, Apostolic Exhortation on the Proclamation of the Gospel in Today's World *Evangelii Gaudium* (Nov 24, 2013), §247. See the Pontifical Biblical Commission, *The Jewish People and Their Sacred Scriptures in the Christian Bible*, §65c (Vatican City: Libreria Editrice Vaticana, 2002), 161: "The New Testament takes for granted that the election of Israel, the people of the covenant, is irrevocable: it preserves intact its prerogatives (Rm 9:4) and its priority status in history, in the offer of salvation (Ac 13:23) and in the Word of God (13:46). But God has also offered to Israel a 'new covenant' (Jr 31:31); this is now established through the blood of Jesus. The Church is composed of Israelites who have accepted the new covenant, and of other believers who have joined them. As a people of the new covenant, the Church is conscious of existing only in virtue of belonging to Christ Jesus, the Messiah of Israel, and because of its link with the apostles, who were all Israelites. Far from being a substitution for Israel, the Church is in solidarity with it." See also the Commission for Religious Relations with the Jews, "The Gifts and the Calling of God Are Irrevocable" §27: "The New Covenant does not revoke the earlier covenants, but it brings them to fulfilment."

covenant relationship with God, together with its promises and obligations, as some theologians assumed in the past.[48]

This conclusion is also supported by St. Thomas's theory of the causality of sacraments of the Old and New Covenants, as seen above. One great strength of St. Thomas's sacramental theology is that it distinguishes the efficacy of the sacraments of the Old and New Covenants because of their relation to the Incarnation, and not based on an extrinsic factor such as a divine abrogation or divine decree.

In the Protestant context, because of the denial of sacramental efficacy *ex opere operato*, the intrinsic difference between the sacraments of the New Covenant and those of the Old is not so clearly seen. Often, as in Calvin[49] and Zwingli, they are put on the same level, differing only according to the dispensation they belong to. This is also true, although to a lesser extent, in Catholic theories of sacramental causality that view the sacraments of the New Covenant, like those of the Old, as necessary occasions or conditions of grace rather than instrumental efficient causes empowered by Christ working through them.

This lack of distinction between the causal power of the sacraments of the Old and New Covenants, such as is often found in Protestant theology or Catholic theology influenced by nominalist and voluntarist currents, can foster an overly simplistic supersessionist view of the worship of Israel according to which the ceremonial law of the Old Testament has simply been replaced by that of the Church, as the Church has replaced Israel as the new people of God. The problem with such a view is that it puts the two covenants on the same plane, as it were, such that a new sacramental system can go into effect only by extrinsically replacing the other.[50] That is, priority can be given to

---

[48] For Aquinas's view on the continued election of the Jewish people, in accordance with Rom 11:29, see Bruce D. Marshall, "Christ and Israel: An Unsolved Problem in Catholic Theology," in *The Call of Abraham: Essays on the Election of Israel in Honor of Jon D. Levenson*, ed. Gary A. Anderson and Jon D. Levenson (Notre Dame, IN: University of Notre Dame Press, 2013), 330–50, at 336–40; Marshall, "Religion and Election: Aquinas on Natural Law, Judaism, and Salvation in Christ." *Nova et Vetera* (English) 14, no. 1 (2016): 104–25; Matthew A. Tapie, *Aquinas on Israel and the Church: The Question of Supersessionism in the Theology of Thomas Aquinas* (Eugene, OR: Pickwick Publications, 2016).

[49] See Calvin, *Institutes*, bk. 4, ch. 14.

[50] On the theological position of supersessionism, see Gavin D'Costa, "The Mystery of Israel: Jews, Hebrew Catholics, Messianic Judaism, the Catholic Church, and the Mosaic Ceremonial Laws," *Nova et Vetera* (English) 16, no.

the covenant that is from Christ only if the Old Covenant has been abrogated. Instead of replacement, we should think of the relationship between the two covenants as that between type and fulfilment. The Old Testament sacraments have been "superseded"[51] in the sense that

---

3 (2018): 939–77; Douglas Farrow, "Jew and Gentile in the Church Today," *Nova et Vetera* (English) 16, no. 3 (2018): 979–93; Douglas Farrow, *Theological Negotiations: Proposals in Soteriology and Anthropology* (Grand Rapids, MI: Baker Academic, 2018), 209–50; Emmanuel Perrier, "The Election of Israel Today: Supersessionism, Post-supersessionism, and Fulfillment," *Nova et Vetera* (English) 7, no. 2 (2009): 485–504; R. Kendall Soulen, *The God of Israel and Christian Theology* (Minneapolis: Fortress Press, 1996); R. Kendall Soulen, "Replacement Theology," in *A Dictionary of Jewish-Christian Relations*, ed. Edward Kessler and Neil Wenborn (Cambridge: Cambridge University Press, 2008), 375–76; R. Kendall Soulen, "'They Are Israelites: The Priority of the Present Tense for Jewish-Christian Relations," in *Between Gospel and Election: Explorations in the Interpretation of Romans 9-11*, ed. Florian Wilk (Tübingen: Mohr Siebeck, 2010), 497–504; Matthew Levering, *Jewish-Christian Dialogue and the Life of Wisdom: Engagements with the Theology of Michael Novak* (New York: Continuum, 2010), 12–46; David Novak, *Talking with Christians: Musings of a Jewish Theologian* (Grand Rapids, MI: Eerdmans, 2005), 8–25.

[51] Since the sacraments of the New Covenant "supersede" those of the Old Covenant by *transcending* them and *fulfilling* their typology and ultimate purpose, one can speak in this way of the New Covenant and its sacraments as "superseding" the Old, and thus it is not incorrect to speak of "supersessionism" with regard to the covenants and sacraments if interpreted in this sense of fulfillment. Douglas Farrow uses the term "supersessionism" in this broad way in *Theological Negotiations*, 220–22, in which he contrasts two forms of supersessionism: hard and soft. Hard supersessionism would be a position that sees the Old Covenant as abrogated by the New and the people of the Old Covenant disinherited. Such a position is incompatible with the teaching of the recent Magisterium that the Old Covenant has not been revoked. "Soft supersessionism," in Farrow's terminology, "regards the new covenant as a continuation of the old, if in thoroughgoing transformation" (p. 222). He then distinguishes two forms of soft supersessionism. The view that I am defending in this chapter coincides with the second form of soft supersessionism that Farrow characterizes as follows: "Because God wills to preserve the Jewish people as such, and because Jewish Christians continue to belong to that people—to Israel according to the flesh as well as to Israel according to the Spirit—the Mosaic form of the covenant should continue to shape even baptized Jews in a manner distinct from baptized Gentiles, albeit not in any fashion that effectively divides them from the latter" (p. 222). Although I am in agreement with Farrow's profound analysis, I think it is better to refer to a position of this kind by the term "fulfilment" rather than "soft supersessionism" so as to avoid confusion with unacceptable or hard forms of supersessionism and to highlight that Christ is the fulfillment of all things, and of Israel in a particular way. See Levering, *Jewish-Christian Dialogue*, 21; Perrier, "The Election of Israel Today," 487: "Supersessionism is incapable of

they have been *fulfilled* by new sacraments that immeasurably transcend them, as Christ immeasurably transcends and fulfills but does not replace Moses.

Paradoxically, the failure to distinguish between the causal powers of the two sacramental systems could also be used to justify a "dual covenant" approach. Although there can be different nuances of dual covenant theories,[52] a simplistic form of it would hold two equal paths to God: the worship of the Old Covenant would remain God's intention for Israel whereas the worship of the New Covenant would be for Gentile Christians.[53] In other words, both radical supersessionism and dual covenant theories presuppose that the sacramental systems of the Old and New Covenants operate in more or less the same way.

St. Thomas's theory of sacramental causality, on the other hand, enables us to see how the sacraments of the Old Covenant, by their very nature as typological prefigurements, could not have the efficacy of those of the New Covenant. Therefore, no recourse to an extrinsic abrogation of the rites of the Old Covenant is necessary in order to explain their lack of intrinsic salvific power. Even though Christ has come and initiated a New Covenant, the rites of the Old Covenant can continue to do what they were divinely intended to do, which is to prefigure and point to the Paschal mystery of the Messiah; to provide a communal means of giving worship to God and expressing justifying faith, hope, and love; and to serve as occasions for the sanctification of Israel. In other words, even though they could never

---

integrating the perspective of fulfillment, which consists neither in a pure and simple substitution, nor in a pure and simple juxtaposition."

[52] See the critique of different forms of dual covenant theories in Farrow, *Theological Negotiations*, 213–44. Farrow engages especially with the far more nuanced form that this approach takes in Mark Kinzer's *Post-Missionary Messianic Judaism: Redefining Christian Engagement with the Jewish People* (Grand Rapids, MI: Brazos Press, 2005); and *Searching Her Own Mystery:* Nostra Aetate, *the Jewish People, and the Identity of the Church* (Eugene, OR: Cascade Books, 2015).

[53] See, for example, Rosemary Radford Ruether, *Faith and Fratricide* (Eugene, OR: Wipf & Stock, 1996), 251–57. For a critique of dual covenant theories, see the Commission for Religious Relations with the Jews, "The Gifts and the Calling of God Are Irrevocable," §35: "Since God has never revoked his covenant with his people Israel, there cannot be different paths or approaches to God's salvation. The theory that there may be two different paths to salvation, the Jewish path without Christ and the path with the Christ, whom Christians believe is Jesus of Nazareth, would in fact endanger the foundations of Christian faith. Confessing the universal and therefore also exclusive mediation of salvation through Jesus Christ belongs to the core of Christian faith."

give grace in the manner proper to the sacraments of the Church, they can fulfill functions similar to those of sacramentals in the New Covenant, which are occasions for devotion and for the exercise of the theological virtues, disposing for the sacraments and, if one is in the state of grace, meriting the reception of further graces.

We should not think that the coming of Christ and His institution of the Church and the sacraments have directly *devalued* the sacraments of Israel. Nor should we think that the sacraments of the New Covenant could coexist on the same level with them. On the contrary, because of the Incarnation, the seven sacraments of the Church are able to do something—give us a living contact with the Word Incarnate—which the rites of Israel could never do. They are not devalued or simply replaced, but something immeasurably greater has come. In a similar way, Christ has not devalued Moses, but someone greater than Moses is here. According to the Thomistic view of sacramental causality, therefore, we do not have to think that Christ has simply revoked the Old Covenant to initiate the New. As Jesus said in Matthew 5:17: "Do not think that I have come to abolish the law and the prophets; I have come not to abolish them but to fulfil them."

Thus the observance of the ceremonial Law of Moses by Jews today, who may very often be inculpably ignorant of the Catholic faith for lack of an appropriate evangelization, should be seen not as something sinful but as something still pleasing to God and meritorious.[54] Christians therefore should have a reverent attitude towards Jewish worship. Such an attitude is also crucial for dialogue with the Jewish community.

Christian Participation in the Sacramental Rites of the Old Covenant

A second and more difficult question concerns Christian participation in the sacramental rites of the Old Covenant, such as circumcision or the Passover meal, as well as other practices of the Jewish ceremonial law. This question comes up especially with regard to Christians of Jewish heritage. As seen above, Christians cannot consider the sacramental rites of the Old Covenant to be on the same level as the sacramental liturgy of the New Covenant,[55] for which they are a typo-

---

[54] Nevertheless, invincible ignorance of Christ is something tragic in itself, for it is the lack of the most important and beautiful truths.

[55] See the Council of Trent, Canons on the Sacraments in General (session 7, Mar

logical preparation, nor can they hold such rites to be necessary for salvation.[56]

The Council of Jerusalem determined that Gentiles were not to be pressured to practice the Jewish ceremonial law in general, but instructed them to refrain from consumption of animal blood.[57] It did not determine, however, that Christians of Jewish heritage were to refrain from practicing elements of the Jewish ceremonial law.[58]

Some Christians of Jewish origin in the early Church continued to follow the Jewish ceremonial law until the fourth century.[59] The general practice of the Church from the early second century onwards, however, was not to permit Jewish converts to continue to practice the rites of the Jewish ceremonial law.[60]

3, 1547), can. 2 (DS, 1602).

[56] See the Council of Florence, Bull of Union with the Copts and the Ethiopians, *Cantate Domino*, Decree for the Jacobites (Feb 4, 1442; DS, 1348).

[57] See Acts 15:1–29. On the Jerusalem Council's prohibition of animal blood, see *ST* I-II, q. 103, a. 4, ad 3: "These foods were forbidden literally, not with the purpose of enforcing compliance with the legal ceremonies, but in order to further the union of Gentiles and Jews living side by side. Because blood and things strangled were loathsome to the Jews by ancient custom; while the Jews might have suspected the Gentiles of relapse into idolatry if the latter had partaken of things offered to idols. Hence these things were prohibited for the time being, during which the Gentiles and Jews were to become united together. But as time went on, with the lapse of the cause, the effect lapsed also, when the truth of the Gospel teaching was divulged, wherein Our Lord taught that 'not that which entereth into the mouth defileth a man' (Mt 15:11); and that 'nothing is to be rejected that is received with thanksgiving' (1 Tim 4:4)."

[58] See Augustine, Letter 82 to St. Jerome (AD 405), in Saint Augustine, *Letters*, vol. 1 (1–82), trans. Sr. Wilfrid Parson, FC 12 (Washington, DC: Catholic University of America Press, 1951), 397–98: "The Apostles had just decreed in Jerusalem itself that no one was to compel the Gentiles to live like the Jews, but they had not decreed that no one was to prevent the Jews from living like Jews, although the Christian teaching did not oblige them to do so."

[59] See Jean Daniélou, *The Theology of Jewish Christianity*, trans. John Baker (London: Darton, Longman & Todd, 1964); Feingold, *The Mystery of Israel and the Church*, 1:180–82.

[60] See Ignatius of Antioch, Letter to the Magnesians 8–10, in *The Apostolic Fathers*, trans. Holmes, 207–09. For a study of the historical development and consequences of this view, see Ronald E. Diprose, *Israel and the Church: The Origin and Effects of Replacement Theology* (Waynesboro, GA: Authentic Media, 2004). For the patristic period, see 69–136. See also Mark Kinzer, *Post-Missionary Messianic Judaism: Redefining Christian Engagement with the Jewish People* (Grand Rapids, MI: Brazos Press, 2005), 181–209.

Melito and the Analogy of the Model for a Statue

An interesting justification for the prohibition on the observance of the elements of the ceremonial Law of Moses by Jewish Christians is given by Melito of Sardis, in his Sermon *"On the Passover,"* in which he uses the analogy of a plaster model for a statue. When an artist wants to make a precious statue or painting, he generally begins with a model or sketch that guides the execution of the final work. The more important the work, the more care is spent on the model, which is the fundamental reference point as long as the work is in progress. Once the final work is completed, however, the model is no longer necessary and can be discarded.

Since the Paschal mystery of Christ is the center of human history and the sacraments of the New Covenant are God's masterworks, He made a kind of "model" or type of them in the world beforehand, to be a preparation for the Incarnation of God. This preparation was nothing less than the entire history of Israel, the chosen people, and the worship that He gave them through the Torah. Now God did not make a model of the Redemption as a guide for His own artistry but rather as a preparation for mankind—a preparation realized in one people gratuitously chosen to be the one in which God would become man. Melito writes:

> This happens with any advance preparation. A work does not just spring up as intended, but through what may be seen in a working model, which is made of wax, or clay, or wood, as a pattern of the intention, so that which is to be built, lofty in magnitude, and mighty in power, and beautiful in form, and rich in embellishment, can be visualized in a small, expendable pattern. But when that to which the type pointed has come to pass, then what once bore the image of the future work is destroyed, yielding up its image to the reality. For what was once precious becomes valueless when the truly precious appears. . . . Now if it is thus for the corruptible, so also for the incorruptible: if thus for the terrestrial, so also for the celestial. Indeed, the salvation and truth of the Lord were foreshadowed in the people, and the ordinances of the gospel were proclaimed beforehand in the law. . . . The type was

valued before the reality. . . But when the Church arose, and
the Gospel was shed abroad, the type was rendered useless,
yielding its power to the reality; and the law came to its end,
yielding its power to the gospel. Just as a pattern is left empty
when its image is surrendered to reality, and a parable is made
useless, when its interpretation is made known, so also, the law
was finished when the gospel was revealed.[61]

Melito thought that the types of the Old Testament had entirely
lost their value when their fulfillment was revealed, for they were a
provisional preparation pointing to the New. It seems to me, however,
that his analogy suggests a more moderate conclusion. The type or
model conserves its value even after the fulfillment, although in a different way than before, precisely by continuing to serve as a pointer or
arrow to the finished work. After Gian Lorenzo Bernini has finished a
statue, the clay model and the sketches are no longer necessary for the
construction of the marble statue. However, they still have great value
in demonstrating the remarkable preparation that went into the finished work, and through their own intrinsic beauty they help to enrich
our appreciation for the finished work. Christ's fulfilment of the typological dimension of the ceremonies of the Old Covenant does not
take away their value and beauty but rather reveals their intrinsic connection with Him and with the sacraments of His Church. If we still
admire the models of Bernini or the sketches of Leonardo, Raphael,
or Rubens, may we not still revere the models used by God Himself,
even while we distinguish the models from their immeasurably greater
fulfillment?

St. Augustine and St. Jerome on the Observance of Rites of the Old Covenant after Calvary

There is an interesting exchange of letters on the subject of Christian participation in the ceremonies of the Old Covenant between St.
Augustine and St. Jerome.[62] They both agreed that Jewish converts of

---

[61] Melito of Sardis, *Sermon "On the Passover,"* §§36–42, trans. Richard C. White
(Lexington, KY: Lexington Theological Seminary Library, 1976), 26–28.

[62] See Augustine, Letter 82 to St. Jerome of AD 405, in *Saint Augustine, Letters*,
vol. 1 (1–82), 390–420. For St. Jerome, see his Letter 75 to Augustine of AD
404, in *Saint Augustine, Letters*, vol. 1 (1–82), 342–67. For an overview of this
correspondence between St. Augustine and St. Jerome, see Robert J. O'Connell,

their time were not to continue to practice the ceremonial law of the Old Covenant. They disagreed, however, on the time in which such worship ceased to be lawfully offered by Christians. St. Jerome maintained that the Passion of Christ marked the end of the time in which the ceremonial rites of Israel were pleasing to God. But what about the fact that the Apostles continue to follow the liturgy of the Old Covenant and other aspects of the ceremonial law?[63] St. Jerome argued that the Apostles continued to observe only by a kind of simulation. They only appeared to be celebrating so as to avoid giving scandal to Jews. St. Augustine, on the contrary, forcefully rejected the idea of an apostolic simulation. Instead, he argued that during the apostolic age, the rites of Israel continued to be lawfully practiced by Jewish believers in Christ, but that this was no longer the case after the sufficient promulgation of the Gospel at the end of the apostolic age. He compared continued practice of ceremonial rites of the Old Law to the honor given to the bodies of the faithful departed before they are buried.[64]

According to St. Augustine, if the rites of the Old Covenant were

---

S.J., "When Saintly Fathers Feuded: The Correspondence between Augustine and Jerome," *Thought* 54 (1979): 344–64. For a Messianic Jewish perspective on this correspondence, see Kinzer, *Post-Missionary Messianic Judaism*, 202–09.

[63] See Acts 3:1; 10:14; 21:24–27.

[64] See Augustine, Letter 82 to St. Jerome, in *Letters*, vol. 1 (1–82), 401–03: "I say, therefore, that circumcision and the other ordinances of this sort were divinely revealed to the former people through the Testament which we call Old, as types of future things, which were to be fulfilled by Christ. When this fulfillment had come, those obligations remained for the instruction of Christians, to be read simply for the understanding of the previous prophecy, but not to be performed through necessity, as if men had still to await the coming revelation of the faith which was foreshadowed by these things. However, although they were not to be imposed on the Gentiles, they were not thereby to be removed from the customary life of the Jews, as if they were worthy of scorn and condemnation. Gradually, therefore, and by degrees . . . through the conversion of those Jews whom the presence of the Lord in the flesh and the times of the Apostles found living thus, all that activity of the shadows was to be ended. . . . Now, however, with the coming of faith, foreshadowed as it was by those early mysteries, . . . those former things have lost the life of their binding force. So, then, they are to be treated in such a manner as are the dead bodies of our kindred: they are to be carried out for burial, not as a matter of form, but as a religious duty; they are not immediately to be abandoned or exposed to the attacks of enemies, as to the teeth of dogs. From now on, if any Christian, though he be a converted Jew, should wish to keep these observances in such a way, he will not be a devout funeral attendant or bearer of the body, but an impious violator of a tomb, digging up dead ashes."

simply prohibited after the Passion of Christ, the impression would be that they were not actually from God and were no different from the rites of pagan religions. St. Paul in particular was suspected by Jewish Christians of his time of holding such a teaching, for which reason James asked Paul to join himself to four other Jewish Christians fulfilling a Nazirite vow and offering sacrifice in the Temple (Acts 21:21–26).[65] Thus the ceremonial rites of the Old Covenant continued to be celebrated by the Apostles, including St. Paul,[66] to manifest faith in the continuity of the Covenants and the fact that rites of the Mosaic Law were truly from God. However, Augustine thought that after the Gospel was sufficiently promulgated, it was no longer fitting that the rites of the Old Covenant be practiced by Christians because it could easily cause confusion by blurring the distinction between what is necessary for salvation—the sacraments of the New Covenant—and what was merely the typological preparation for those sacraments.

St. Thomas on Observance of the Sacraments of the Old Covenant after the Promulgation of the Gospel

St. Thomas, in his treatise on the Old Law, takes the position of St. Augustine in this controversy[67] and gives a theological justification for

---

[65] See Augustine's commentary on Acts 21:21–26 in his Letter 82 to St. Jerome, 396–97: "It is quite clear, I think, that James gave this advice in order to show the falsity of the views supposed to be Paul's, which certain Jews who had come to believe in Christ, but who were still 'zealous for the law,' had heard about him, namely, that through the teaching of Christ the commandments, written by the direction of God and transmitted by Moses to the fathers, were to be thought sacrilegious and worthy of rejection.... There was no more fitting way for him to repel the injustice of this false charge than by performing personally the ceremonies which he was supposed to condemn as sacrilegious. In this way he would prove two things: that the Jews were not to be prevented from observing these obligations as if they were wrong and that the Gentiles were not to be forced to observe them as if they were necessary."

[66] See Acts 16:3; 18:18; 21:21–26. See Augustine, Letter 82 to St. Jerome, 395–96, which says that St. Paul's purpose in participating in these ceremonial rites of the Old Covenant "was to avoid the appearance of condemning those ceremonies which God had ordered to be performed in earlier times, to which they were appropriate, as foreshadowings of things to come, while condemnation was to be made of the idolatry of the Gentiles."

[67] See *ST* I-II, q. 103, a. 4, ad 1: "On this point there seems to have been a difference of opinion between Jerome and Augustine. For Jerome distinguished two periods of time. One was the time previous to Christ's Passion, during

the practice of the Church in his time prohibiting observance of the ceremonial law of the Old Covenant. He argues that the rites of Israel not only ceased to be the occasions of the giving of grace but, in fact, became gravely sinful for anyone to practice after the promulgation of the Gospel.

St. Thomas's reasoning is that liturgical rites are expressions of faith. In the expression of faith the time element is significant. Since the rites of the Old Covenant are typological prefigurations of the Passion of Christ and of the sacraments of the New Covenant as something still to come, he reasons that to continue to celebrate such rites would be liturgically to profess Christ's First Coming as still in the future and thus to signify something contrary to Christian faith:

> All ceremonies are professions of faith, in which the interior worship of God consists. Now man can make profession of his inward faith, by deeds as well as by words: and in either pro-

---

which the legal ceremonies were neither dead, since they were obligatory, and did expiate in their own fashion; nor deadly, because it was not sinful to observe them. But immediately after Christ's Passion they began to be not only dead, so as no longer to be either effectual or binding; but also deadly, so that whoever observed them was guilty of mortal sin. Hence he maintained that after the Passion the apostles never observed the legal ceremonies in real earnest; but only by a kind of pious pretense, lest . . . they should scandalize the Jews and hinder their conversion. . . . But since it seems unbecoming that the apostles . . . should have made use of pretense, in things pertaining to the salvation of the faithful; therefore Augustine [*Epist.* 82] more fittingly distinguished three periods of time. One was the time that preceded the Passion of Christ, during which the legal ceremonies were neither deadly nor dead: another period was after the publication of the Gospel, during which the legal ceremonies are both dead and deadly. The third is a middle period, viz., from the Passion of Christ until the publication of the Gospel, during which the legal ceremonies were dead indeed, because they had neither effect nor binding force; but were not deadly, because it was lawful for the Jewish converts to Christianity to observe them, provided they did not put their trust in them so as to hold them to be necessary unto salvation, as though faith in Christ could not justify without the legal observances. . . . The reason why the Holy Ghost did not wish the converted Jews to be debarred at once from observing the legal ceremonies, while converted heathens were forbidden to observe the rites of heathendom, was in order to show that there is a difference between these rites. For heathenish ceremonial was rejected as absolutely unlawful, and as prohibited by God for all time; whereas the legal ceremonial ceased as being fulfilled through Christ's Passion, being instituted by God as a figure of Christ."

fession, if he make a false declaration, he sins mortally. Now, though our faith in Christ is the same as that of the fathers of old; yet, since they came before Christ, whereas we come after Him, the same faith is expressed in different words, by us and by them. For by them was it said: "Behold a virgin shall conceive and bear a son," where the verbs are in the future tense: whereas we express the same by means of verbs in the past tense, and say that she "conceived and bore." In like manner the ceremonies of the Old Law betokened Christ as having yet to be born and to suffer: whereas our sacraments signify Him as already born and having suffered. Consequently, just as it would be a mortal sin now for anyone, in making a profession of faith, to say that Christ is yet to be born, which the fathers of old said devoutly and truthfully; so too it would be a mortal sin now to observe those ceremonies which the fathers of old fulfilled with devotion and fidelity. Such is the teaching of Augustine (*Contra Faustum* 19.16), who says: "It is no longer promised that He shall be born, shall suffer and rise again, truths of which their sacraments were a kind of image: but it is declared that He is already born, has suffered and risen again; of which our sacraments, in which Christians share, are the actual representation."[68]

St. Thomas's reasoning presupposes that participation in an Old Testament rite effectively communicates, through liturgical actions, that Christ is still expected and has not yet come.[69] Participation in the sacraments of the Church, on the contrary, liturgically signifies the faith that Christ has already come.

---

[68] *ST* I-II, q. 103, a. 4. This doctrine is repeated in Aquinas's biblical commentaries. See, for example, *Commentary on the Epistle to the Hebrews* 7:5, lectio 2, no. 339, trans. Larcher (Lander, WY: Aquinas Institute for the Study of Sacred Doctrine, 2012), 149–50: "There were in the law some precepts purely ceremonial, such as circumcision, the offering of the lamb, and so on. Such laws, since they were only figurative, it is no longer licit to observe, for they were a figure of something to come; hence, anyone who observes them now would be signifying that Christ is still to come." For a good overview of the different nuances of St. Thomas's biblical commentaries relating to this topic, see Tapie, *Aquinas on Israel and the Church.*

[69] Objections to St. Thomas's reasoning in this article (*ST* I-II, q. 103, a. 4) will be examined later in this chapter.

The Council of Florence on Observance of the Sacraments of the Old Covenant after the Promulgation of the Gospel

In harmony with the reasoning of this article of St. Thomas, the Council of Florence, in the Bull of Union with the Copts and the Ethiopians, *Cantate Domino*, severely prohibited any continued celebration of the ceremonial law of the Old Testament by Christians. First the conciliar text states that Christians may not base their hope for salvation on the rites of the Old Law and regard them as necessary for salvation, for they only prefigure and do not contain and apply the fruits of Christ's Passion:

> She (the holy Roman Church) firmly believes, professes, and teaches that the legal prescriptions of the Old Testament or the Mosaic law, which are divided into ceremonies, holy sacrifices, and sacraments, because they were instituted to signify something in the future, although they were adequate for the divine cult of that age, once our Lord Jesus Christ who was signified by them had come, came to an end and the sacraments of the New Testament had their beginning. Whoever, even after the Passion, places his hope in the legal prescriptions and submits himself to them as necessary for salvation, as if faith in Christ without them could not save, sins mortally. She does not deny that from Christ's Passion until the promulgation of the gospel they could have been retained, provided they were in no way believed to be necessary for salvation. But she asserts that after the promulgation of the gospel they cannot be observed without loss of eternal salvation.[70]

A number of doctrinal affirmations are contained in this paragraph. First, the ceremonial rites of the Law of Moses were instituted to prefigure Christ.[71] Secondly, these legal prescriptions came to an end "once our Lord Jesus Christ who was signified by them had come"

---

[70] Council of Florence, *Cantate Domino* (DS, 1348).

[71] This does not exclude that there may also have been other reasons as well for these precepts, such as giving a suitable means of divine worship to Israel. See *ST* I-II, q. 102, a. 2: "The end of the ceremonial precepts was twofold: for they were ordained to the Divine worship, for that particular time, and to the foreshadowing of Christ."

and instituted the sacraments of the New Covenant. What exactly the Council meant by this "coming to an end" is not specified, but the context indicates that their obligatory status as "legal prescriptions" came to an end in order to make way for the sacramental economy of the New Covenant. Third, because Christ has redeemed mankind and applies that redemption through the sacraments of the New Covenant, the faithful must put their hope in Christ and the sacraments instituted by Him and not in the sacraments and other liturgical rites of the Old Covenant. This is the principal dogmatic teaching in this text, and it is clearly a dogma of faith requiring firm belief by the faithful.[72] Fourth, the rites of the Old Covenant could have been retained until the time of the promulgation of the Gospel as long as one did not put hope of salvation in them. Here *Cantate* is following the thesis of St. Augustine in his Letter 82 to St. Jerome. Fifth, after the promulgation of the Gospel, the old rites should no longer be observed even if one does not place one's hope in them. Here the reasoning seems to be that given by St. Thomas in *ST* I-II, q. 103, a. 4. The notion of "promulgation of the Gospel" is not defined, and this point will be examined below.

After this doctrinal paragraph, the document gives a strongly worded disciplinary prohibition on the observance of circumcision or any other ceremonial rite of the Old Covenant after the promulgation of the Gospel, even if they are not done as if necessary for salvation.

> Therefore, she denounces all who after that time observe circumcision, the Sabbath, and other legal prescriptions as strangers to the faith of Christ and unable to share in eternal salvation, unless they recoil at some time from these errors. Therefore, she strictly *orders* all who glory in the name of Christian not to practice circumcision either before or after

---

[72] This teaching is based on many New Testament texts, and is reaffirmed by the Council of Trent, Decree on Justification (session 6, Jan 13, 1547) ch. 1 (DS, 1521), as well as by the CDF, Declaration *Dominus Jesus* on the Unicity and Salvific Universality of Jesus Christ and the Church (2000), §§14 and 20 (DS, 5087, 5089). See Farrow, *Theological Negotiations*, 239: "It is the settled mind of the Church that Jesus Christ has fulfilled and transcended the Mosaic form of the covenant and that he has introduced through his death and resurrection a genuinely new form of covenantal life. This the Council of Florence, in *Cantate Domino*, reaffirmed and made perfectly clear, though that document was not directed at the problem of messianic Judaism."

baptism, since whether or not they place their hope in it, it cannot possibly be observed without loss of eternal salvation.[73]

The reason for this prohibition is not directly stated, but we can suppose it to be what is stated in the previous paragraph, which is that the rites of the Old Covenant signify Christ's coming as still future, like the Old Testament prophecies.

The use of the word "orders" (*praecipit*) in the last sentence quoted above from the Bull *Cantate Domino* indicates that this is a disciplinary precept prohibiting circumcision and other practices of the ceremonial law of the Old Covenant. A disciplinary precept orders or prohibits a certain behavior and requires obedience only as long as it is in force. This Bull is directed to the particular situation of the Egyptian Coptic Church, called Jacobite, in which at this time certain practices from the Jewish ceremonial law were being observed by Gentile Christians, such as circumcision, the Sabbath, and certain dietary restrictions.[74] This prohibition on the observance of all rites pertaining to the ceremonial Law of Moses should be seen as a disciplinary decree for that particular church at that particular time, which is no longer in effect.[75] The 1983 Code of Canon Law contains no prohibition of circumcision or other ceremonial rites of the Old Covenant.

Benedict XIV, in the encyclical *Ex quo primum* in the mid-eighteenth century, declared that elements of the Jewish ceremonial law could be observed for a "just and serious reason,"[76] as was done by the Council of Jerusalem. *Ex quo primum* presupposes the teaching of the Council of Florence but clarifies and gives further nuance to it. In this document, Pope Benedict XIV approved a book of liturgical prayers (*Euchologion*) used in the Eastern rite by the Greek Uniates. The liturgical prayers contained certain elements of the ceremonial Law of Moses that were still customary in parts of Eastern Christianity although no longer in the West. Some theologians wanted those

---

[73] Council of Florence, *Cantate Domino* (DS, 1348; my italics).

[74] See D'Costa, *Catholic Doctrines on Jews*, 37. On the disciplinary nature of this prohibition, see Farrow, *Theological Negotiations*, 228–30, 245.

[75] On the interpretation of this teaching of the Bull *Cantate Domino* of the Council of Florence, see D'Costa, "The Mystery of Israel," 955–66; *Catholic Doctrines on Jews*, 44–54.

[76] Benedict XIV, On the Euchologian *Ex quo primum* (Mar 1, 1756), §63, in *The Papal Encyclicals 1740–1878*, ed. Claudia Carlen (Wilmington, NC: McGrath Publishing, 1981), 99.

elements eliminated. Benedict XIV decided not to modify the prayer book, reasoning that elements of the ceremonial law of the Mosaic Law could be observed *as long as there was some pastoral utility in their observance*. He notes that some elements of the ceremonial law were imposed on the early Christians by the Council of Jerusalem (Acts 15) for the purpose of establishing peace between Jews and Gentiles in the Church. Those laws were retained longer in the Eastern churches than in the West. Hence Benedict XIV judged that some elements of the ceremonial precepts could be retained or observed subject to the mind of the Church. He wrote:

> Although the ceremonial precepts of the old Law have come to an end with the promulgation of the Gospel, and the new Law does not contain any precept which distinguishes between clean and unclean foods, nevertheless the Church of Christ has the power of renewing the obligation to observe some of the old precepts for just and serious reasons, despite their abrogation by the new Law.[77]

It is clear from this magisterial text that observance of elements from the ceremonial law of Moses is not always sinful nor need it liturgically imply that Christ has not yet come. The Church can even require the observance of some of them for Gentile Christians if the needs of the time suggest it, as was the case in the Council of Jerusalem and in certain prayers of the *Euchologion*. The key principle therefore is that the Church can regulate their use according to her prudential judgment to serve pastoral needs.

The Bull *Cantate Domino* of the Council of Florence stated this same principle with regard to the dietary laws of the Old Covenant:

> She [the Holy Roman Church] declares that no type of food accepted by human society should be condemned, ... although for the health of the body, for the practice of virtue, or for the sake of regular and ecclesiastical discipline many things that are not proscribed can and should be omitted.[78]

---

[77] Benedict XIV, On the Euchologian *Ex quo primum*, §63, in Carlen, *The Papal Encyclicals 1740–1878*, 99. On *Ex quo primum*, see D'Costa, "The Mystery of Israel," 960–66; D'Costa, *Catholic Doctrines on Jews*, 49–54.

[78] Council of Florence, *Cantate Domino* (DS, 1350).

Thus despite its severe prohibition, the Council of Florence recognized that the Church could permit or require elements of the ceremonial Law of Moses, as was done by the Council of Jerusalem, for the sake of "ecclesiastical discipline." It follows that the prohibition given by this Council cannot be taken as a dogmatic teaching that such observance is always and everywhere contrary to faith and sinful, but rather should be seen as a disciplinary measure according to the prudential judgment of the Church for that time and place, which could be reversed by the same authority of the Church according to a different prudential judgment in different circumstances.[79]

Objections to Aquinas's Argument That Observance of the Old Testament Sacraments after the Promulgation of the Gospel Implies Sin against Faith

The reasoning of St. Thomas, implied also in the teaching of the Council of Florence in the Bull *Cantate Domino*, needs to be qualified by a more realistic understanding of the complexity of liturgical intention and of the notion of "promulgation of the Gospel."

Observance of Old Testament Sacraments Need Not Imply That Christ Has Not Yet Come

The fact that the rites of the Old Covenant prefigure the sacrifice of Christ and the sacraments of the Church does not necessarily imply that a present participation in such rites (as in the celebration of a Passover seder) has to be understood as a liturgical intention to proclaim that Christ's coming is expected *as future*, and thus that He has not yet come. We see from the New Testament that the Apostles themselves

---

[79] See Farrow, *Theological Negotiations*, 228–30: "The documents in question [*Cantate Domino* and *Ex quo primum*] did have Gentile practices in view primarily; though their logic certainly applies to Jews, it is worked out in a context in which Christian Jews are almost out of mind. And when they return to mind—as they do today, thanks be to God—they require of the Church a new and different awareness of their needs, which have changed, as have those of Gentiles.... It is a matter of the Gentile learning again, in this neo-Marcionite and all too gnostic age of ours, to respect the earthiness of his salvation and to embrace the Jew as Jew; and of the Jew learning once again how to be both Jew and Christian, while glorying ... in the very freedom of which Paul spoke."

and the whole first generation of Christians from the circumcision continued to observe much of the ceremonial Law of Moses. Christ Himself observed the ceremonial Law, not signifying thereby that He had not yet come, but transforming it as He transformed all that He assumed in His humanity. His liturgical intention would have been to obey the precepts out of reverence for the covenant and for His Father, who was honored by it, in solidarity with all of Israel, and to fulfill the figures in His Person.

In a similar way, the intention of a Christian lector in reading from the Old Testament prophecies in the liturgy of the Word is not to proclaim the Messiah's coming as future, as it would be understood when read in a synagogue, but to proclaim it as fulfilled in Christ. The meaning of liturgical ceremonies is determined in part by the faith and intention of the participants. It is also clear that when the messianic prophecies of the Old Testament are proclaimed in the liturgy, they do not lose their importance from the fact that they have been fulfilled in Christ but, on the contrary, are confirmed and magnified by that fulfillment. In the same way, the ceremonial rites of Israel can retain a prophetic or typological value that is not annulled by their being fulfilled in Christ[80] but instead fills us with admiration and wonder at the beauty and depth of God's plan of salvation. The obligatory quality of those rites has passed away, but their prophetic, typological, and revelatory value remains.

Acts 21:20–24 gives a vivid picture of the early Church in Jerusalem continuing to observe the ceremonial Law. When St. Paul arrived in Jerusalem after his third missionary voyage, James and the elders encouraged him to participate in the fulfilment of a Nazirite vow:

> You see, brother, how many thousands there are among the Jews of those who have believed; they are all zealous for the law, and they have been told about you that you teach all the Jews who are among the Gentiles to forsake Moses, telling

---

[80] See *ST* II-II, q. 10, a. 11, in which St. Thomas argues that although pagan rites should be prohibited in a Christian state, Jewish ceremonies should be permitted: "Thus from the fact that the Jews observe their rites, which, of old, foreshadowed the truth of the faith which we hold, there follows this good— that our very enemies bear witness to our faith, and that our faith is represented in a figure, so to speak." See the discussion of this text by Bruce D. Marshall in "*Quasi in Figura*: A Brief Reflection on Jewish Election, after Thomas Aquinas," *Nova et Vetera* (English) 7, no. 2 (2009): 477–84, at 482–84.

them not to circumcise their children or observe the customs. What then is to be done? They will certainly hear that you have come. Do therefore what we tell you. We have four men who are under a vow; take these men and purify yourself along with them and pay their expenses, so that they may shave their heads. Thus all will know that there is nothing in what they have been told about you but that you yourself live in observance of the law.

Clearly the Christian community in Jerusalem under James, and St. Paul himself, were not signifying by their observance that Christ had not yet come. On the contrary, they observed the Old Testament rites with the new realization of their deepest meaning, as signs prefiguring Christ who had already come and fulfilled the Law and made all things new. It follows that these rites can be celebrated with faith in Christ's fulfillment of the Old Testament types.[81] Such re-enactments can help the faithful to grasp God's plan of salvation through which events in the Old Testament, commemorated in the liturgy of Israel, prefigure the Paschal mystery of Christ, the Church, and her sacraments.

Furthermore, St. Thomas teaches that the ceremonial precepts of the Old Covenant, in addition to prefiguring Christ's coming, also have the value of giving fitting worship to God according to His command and of serving as a memorial of the foundational events of the life of Israel.[82] In addition, observance of the ceremonial precepts puts one in a continuity of worship stretching back to Moses and Abraham. St. Thomas's argument that continued celebration of ceremonial rites of the Old Covenant implies a sin against faith would be valid if the *only* reason for observing such a rite would be to profess faith in Christ as *still to come*, and if it were understood precisely in this way by those who observed such a rite, so that it would cause scandal to others by signifying disbelief in the Incarnation.[83] But if there are other reasons

---

[81] See Michael Wyschogrod, "A Jewish Reading of St. Thomas Aquinas," in *Understanding Scripture: Explorations of Jewish and Christian Traditions of Interpretation*, ed. Clemens Thoma and Michael Wyschogrod. (New York; Mahwah, NJ: Paulist Press, 1987), 136: "If the commandments before Christ predicted him, could they not after Christ celebrate the prediction that came true?"

[82] See *ST* I-II, q. 102, a. 2.

[83] Indeed, in the context of medieval society, such scandal may have been likely to follow from Jewish Christian observance of elements of the ceremonial law.

for observing such a rite that would edify rather than cause scandal, as can be seen in the practice of the apostolic generation, then the argument would fail. The Jewish theologian Michael Wyschogrod articulates this objection eloquently:

> For even if there is, from the point of view of Christian faith, a large element of prefigurement of Christ in the Old Testament, does it have to follow that someone who refrains from eating pork or who fasts on the Day of Atonement is committing a mortal sin? Must his action be interpreted as saying that 'Christ was to be born' (q. 103, a. 4) rather than that he had been born, thereby denying Christ? Could adherence to the Mosaic Law not be interpreted much more benevolently, as love of God and his commandments, as fidelity to a holy way of life out of which—for Christian faith—the Redeemer was born? If the commandments before Christ predicted him, could they not after Christ celebrate the prediction that came true and point to the final fulfillment that both Jews and Christians await? In short, the argument that the Mosaic commandments predict Christ and that to adhere to them after Christ is a mortal sin because one is denying that he has come by so doing is a rather thin reed on which to hang the case for the ceremonial commandments turning into mortal sin after Christ. It is almost as if Thomas starts with that conviction and then looks around for some justification of it which he achieves by the ingenious argument of the prediction that turns into denial.[84]

Wyschogrod makes two important points in this text. First, he holds that St. Thomas seems to have insufficiently taken into consideration something that he himself emphasized earlier in his treatise on the Old Law, and that is that the ceremonial precepts had other purposes beside prefiguration, the most important of which is simply to be a divinely mandated form of worship connecting Jews today to their foundations in Revelation and to their whole people throughout the centuries.

---

[84] Wyschogrod, "A Jewish Reading of St. Thomas Aquinas," 136. See also 138: "The teaching that obedience to the Mosaic ceremonial law after Christ is mortal sin not only strains Christianity's contemporary relationship with Judaism but needlessly weakens Christianity's bond with the Old Testament."

Secondly, he charges St. Thomas with starting with a conclusion and seeking an ingenious justification for it. I do not think that Wyschogrod is wrong in thinking that St. Thomas started with the conviction supplied by his cultural and ecclesial context, in which Christian observance of the ceremonial law of Moses had been banned for centuries in a disciplinary way, and then set out to justify it theologically.[85] St. Thomas's habitual way of doing theology was to take the mind and life of the Church of his day as the starting point of theological reasoning.[86] Our cultural and ecclesial context, however, has greatly changed, and doctrine has developed in various ways that affect this problem.

What Is Sufficient Promulgation of the Gospel?

One of the ways that our ecclesial context has changed is that we have gained a far greater appreciation of the extent of invincible ignorance and the insufficiency of the "promulgation of the Gospel" in our world. Both St. Thomas and the Council of Florence hold that observance of the ceremonial Law of Moses would constitute a sin against faith only in a time after the full promulgation of the Gospel. The reasoning seems to be that before the full promulgation of the Gospel, participation in such rites could serve positive functions such as indicating that Jewish worship was from God and pointing to continuity between the covenants, which would be less necessary in a completely Christian society. Thus in our cultural context of significant pluralism and ongoing evangelization, as in the apostolic age, Christian participation in aspects of the ceremonial law of Moses could signify reverence for the liturgical practices proper to the Old Covenant in their worship of God and prefiguring of the Messiah.[87]

The Council of Florence implies this in its discussion of the decree of the Council of Jerusalem in Acts 15:29 that required Gentile

---

[85] See Kinzer, *Post-Missionary Messianic Judaism*, 207.

[86] See, for example, *ST* II-II, q. 10, a. 12: "The custom of the Church has very great authority and ought to be jealously observed in all things, since the very doctrine of catholic doctors derives its authority from the Church. Hence we ought to abide by the authority of the Church rather than by that of an Augustine or a Jerome or of any doctor whatever. Now it was never the custom of the Church to baptize the children of Jews against the will of their parents..."

[87] See the insightful analysis of this issue by D'Costa in *Catholic Doctrines on Jews*, 38–57.

Christians to observe some ceremonial precepts of Moses, such as abstaining "from blood and from what is strangled." *Cantate Domino* explains that "as soon as the Christian religion was promulgated to the point that no Jew according to the flesh appeared within it, . . . since the cause of this apostolic prohibition ceased, so its effect also ceased."[88] In other words, the observance of elements of the ceremonial Law of Moses served important pastoral functions in the apostolic age in which many Christians were "from among the circumcision,"[89] that is, Jewish. These functions would cease to be pressing in a cultural context in which there were practically no Christians aware of having a Jewish heritage. We, however, live in a context that is more akin to the apostolic age than to the medieval Christendom that formed the outlook of Aquinas and the Council of Florence, for today there are many Christians (including this writer) proud to have a Jewish heritage.[90]

Medieval Christians tended to assume that the promulgation of the Gospel was something definitively completed by the close of the apostolic age. This assumption has long ceased to be convincing, especially after the discovery of the Americas some decades after the Council of Florence.[91] For centuries we have increasingly become aware that the Gospel has been communicated adequately to only a limited portion of humanity, and that even in Western society, increasing numbers have not been properly exposed to the motives of credibility for the Catholic faith. Wherever there is invincible ignorance in significant numbers, the promulgation of the Gospel has not been fully achieved. This promulgation exists in varying degrees in different times and places and continues to be accomplished throughout the life of the Church.

If the Gospel is not fully promulgated in a given cultural context,

---

[88] Council of Florence, *Cantate Domino* (DS, 1350).

[89] See Acts 10:45; 11:2; Rom 4:12; Gal 2:12; Col 4:11.

[90] See D'Costa, *Catholic Doctrines on Jews*, 45: "In fact, and this is most significant, *Cantate* lends credence to a different practice within the Church were there to be Jews of the flesh within the Church. It recognizes that the teaching of Acts 15:29 served to unify the church by accepting that Jews would follow certain practices that were not required of gentiles, while ensuring common table fellowship. This only ended, in its historical narrating, when there were no more 'carnal Jews' within the Church. . . . However, now that there are 'carnal Jews' or better, 'Jews of the flesh,' within the Church, the question is reopened. The narrative sequence assumed by *Cantate* is disrupted."

[91] See *LG*, §16; Pius IX, *Quanto Conficiamur Moerore* (DS, 2866).

as, for example, in most Western societies today, then, according to the reasoning of St. Augustine and St. Thomas, assumed also by the Council of Florence, it would follow that in that cultural context, it should still be licit for Hebrew Catholics to freely continue to observe certain ceremonial rites of the Old Covenant as in the apostolic age.[92]

St. Thomas's Principles Need Not Imply That the Sacraments of the Old Covenant Have Become Deadly

It seems therefore that St. Thomas's theory of sacramental causality can support a view of the sacramental rites of the Old Covenant during the time of the Church that is more positive than he himself held. What certainly follows from his principles is that in the time of the New Covenant, the principal means of worshipping God are the seven sacraments instituted by the Messiah. The sacraments of the Old Covenant can no longer occupy the center-stage in divine worship but must give way to those instituted by Christ through which He Himself acts with His words and gestures of power. In this sense the Old Covenant sacraments have been "superseded" by the seven sacraments of the Church that fulfill their typology and realize what they point to but cannot themselves accomplish.[93] It does not seem necessary, however, according to St. Thomas's principles, that participation in the Old Testament sacraments now be regarded as "deadly," even though he comes to this conclusion. For example, after distinguishing three states of salvation history—the Old Covenant, the New Cove-

---

[92] See the comments on the Council of Florence and how it should be interpreted in the light of more recent magisterial teachings by Gavin D'Costa, "Israel, Jewish Christians, Messianic Christians, and the Catholic Church," *The Hebrew Catholic* 103 (Spring 2018): 14–15; further developed in his "The Mystery of Israel," 945–70; and *Catholic Doctrines on Jews*, 27–63, esp. 38–43.

[93] See Marshall, "*Quasi in Figura*: A Brief Reflection on Jewish Election," 477–84, at 481: "Thomas himself seems quite clear on this score, and so has no trouble viewing the Church's rites and sacraments as straightforward replacements for the old ones: 'the ceremonies of the law are taken away (*tolluntur*) when they are fulfilled' (*ST* I-II, q. 107, a. 2, ad 1). Thus baptism 'succeeds' circumcision, and the celebration of the Easter Triduum 'succeeds' the Passover (*ST* I-II, q. 103, a. 3, ad 4). Thomas says 'succedit' here, but he might as well have said 'supersedet.'" See also Marshall, "Christ and Israel: An Unsolved Problem in Catholic Theology," 339: "Baptism, for example, does not compete with circumcision as a sacramental rite by which God joins his people to himself. It *replaces* circumcision as the appropriate sacramental means for union with Christ."

nant, and the heavenly Church—St. Thomas states:

> The ceremonies of the first-mentioned state which fore-shad-
> owed the second and third states, had need to *cease* at the
> advent of the second state; and other ceremonies had to be
> introduced which would be in keeping with the state of divine
> worship for that particular time, wherein heavenly goods are a
> thing of the future, but the Divine favors whereby we obtain
> the heavenly boons are a thing of the present.[94]

I hold that St. Thomas's reasoning shows that the ceremonies
proper to the Old Covenant must *cease to be central* in the New Covenant and *cease to be obligatory* so as to make room for the "masterworks
of God," the seven sacraments of the Church.[95] But it does not follow
that they must *cease altogether* after the promulgation of the Gospel
or be regarded as sins against faith. Something can cease to be central
without being prohibited or considered harmful. (Moses, for example,
ceases to be central after Christ without becoming anathema.) The
prohibition of such rites seems to have been a prudential and disciplinary way of ensuring that the sacraments of the New Covenant
remain central in the life of the Church, but that purpose could be
accomplished in other ways, such as catechesis.

Reasons in Favor of the Devotional Observance of Elements of the Old Testament Ceremonial Law

We have seen above that St. Thomas argued against continued Christian
observance of the Old Testament sacraments after the promulgation
of the Gospel on the grounds that such observance would liturgically
signify that the Messiah has not yet come, and would thus amount
to a false profession of faith. This argument would fail if Christian
observance of such rites could have other pastoral purposes and be
animated by other liturgical intentions without intending to signify
Christ's coming as future.

I hold that free devotional or catechetical observance of some of
these typological figures in the current context could serve at least

---

[94] *ST* I-II, q. 103, a. 3 (my italics).
[95] See the profound reflections on this point in Farrow, *Theological Negotiations*,
217–46.

five important pastoral purposes. First of all, such observances, if they are understood to prefigure Christ who has already come, would help Christians be more aware of the typology of Israel and the vital connection between Israel and the Church. It would help Christians recognize their roots in the history of the chosen people, of which most people are unaware. Seeing these types helps provide motives of credibility for faith and to show the vital and intrinsic connection between Israel and the Church.

Secondly, a devotional and catechetical observance by Christians of certain elements of the Old Testament ceremonial law, such as the Passover seder, shows reverence for the worship and prayer of the Old Covenant, which would be helpful in reducing anti-Semitic attitudes among Christians. This is in harmony with St. Augustine's view on why the apostolic generation continued to observe elements of the Mosaic ceremonial Law as seen in Acts 21:20–24.[96] In the wake of the Holocaust, this is not of small importance.

Third, it would be a way for Jewish Christians to remain connected in some measure with the glorious heritage, worship, and messianic longing of their people. Without any shared liturgical practice, it is difficult for Jewish Christians to retain a living connection with this heritage that is so central to salvation history.[97] Thus it could help prevent the complete loss of Jewish identity in Jewish Christians

---

[96] See Augustine, Letter 82 to St. Jerome, in *Letters: Volume 1 (1–82)*, trans. Parsons, 395–96: "His [St. Paul's] purpose was to avoid the appearance of condemning those ceremonies which God had ordered to be performed in earlier times, to which they were appropriate, as foreshadowings of things to come, while condemnation was to be made of the idolatry of the Gentiles."

[97] See Farrow, *Theological Negotiations*, 233–34: "The distinction between Jew and Gentile is not thereby eliminated [by the New Covenant], any more than the distinction between man and woman is eliminated, though the relation between the two has fundamentally changed due to their common access to the grace of God. In this new relation Jews have the responsibility to teach messianic Gentiles how to appropriate the Old Testament and to show non-messianic Jews how to receive the New Testament. To this end, they may and (with the encouragement of the Church) ordinarily should maintain their identity as Jews by circumcision and by perpetuating inherited patterns of prayer and devotion and learning and living, insofar as these are conducive to maturity and to effective mission through Christian refashioning, though never in such a way as to impinge on their common sacramental and liturgical life with Gentiles. It must always be clear, as Matthew Levering has argued, that the Jewishness of Jews is fulfilled via their sacramental union with Jesus, in whom the demands of Torah have already been met and reconfigured in the Spirit for the whole Church."

through assimilation. Otherwise, it is typical that the children and grandchildren of Hebrew Catholics easily lose the sense of belonging to the Jewish people.[98]

Fourth, such observance could help Jews outside the Church come to understand that belief in Christ on the part of Jews does not have to lead to the disappearance of the people of Israel.[99] Insofar as such observance is prohibited, leading to the loss of Jewish identity in Jewish Christians mentioned above, large-scale conversion of Jews to Christianity is seen by the Jewish community, not unreasonably, as a dire threat to their continued existence.[100]

Fifth, such observances can serve as a devotion to the humanity of Christ and to the Holy Family, for Christ was "born of a woman, born under the Law" (Gal 4:4). The salvific mysteries of Christ's life include His practice of the rites of the Old Covenant. His circumcision, for example, has been liturgically commemorated from the first millennium in East and West on the Octave of Christmas and is a

---

[98] See Elias Friedman, *Jewish Identity* (New York: Miriam Press, 1987), 64: "Daniélou maintained that even if all Israel had embraced Christianity the continuity of Israel would not have been threatened. How could he know? The history of Judaeo-Christianity belies his facile optimism. . . . In the personal experience of the author of these pages, to guarantee the continuity of Jewry's history, in the hypothesis of an entry en masse of Jews into the faith, steps would have to be taken and obstacles overcome."

[99] See Friedman, *Jewish Identity*, 94: "The impression made on the Jew by the regime of assimilation was disastrous. It outraged him in the deepest fibres of his self-understanding. Secularists and religious Jews closed ranks in defense against the menace of the Christian Mission." To overcome this, Fr. Friedman worked for the realization of a Hebrew-Catholic community in the Church (the Association of Hebrew Catholics) in which Jewish identity would be maintained, as he states on p. 172: "If the existence of a Hebrew-Catholic community demonstrates to the Jews that the official Church does not intend to bring about the destruction of Jewry by assimilation, that would be a great gain for the Church."

[100] See the paradox articulated by Bruce Marshall in "Christ and Israel: An Unsolved Problem in Catholic Theology," in 339–40: "We arrive, then, at what seems to be the basic theological problem about Christ and Israel. Aquinas is a striking witness to this problem. . . . God wills the election of Israel irrevocably, up to and including the end-time salvation of the descendants of Abraham, Isaac, and Jacob according to the flesh. But God no longer wills the practice of Judaism, indeed he apparently wills that it not be practiced. How, though, are the Jewish people going to make it to the eschaton without Judaism? The practice of Judaism is, it seems, indispensable for the Jewish people to remain, over time, distinct from the gentiles. Without it they would soon vanish, like the Hittites, into the sea of nations."

rich theme of Christian art. It was the first blood that He shed for the human race and a magnificent type of the divine condescension and humility by which the Lord of the Covenant is marked with its sign, and the Pure One is marked as cleansed from sin.

Like other sacramentals and devotions[101] in the life of the Church, Christians, including Jewish Christians, ought to have freedom to practice them or not, insofar as they find them conducive to piety and growth in intimacy with Jesus. The use of certain ceremonial rites of the Old Covenant, practiced as devotions to Christ and the life of the Holy Family, could be considered to function as sacramentals, which work to better dispose the faithful for the fruitful reception of the sacraments and to exercise faith, hope, and charity.

Conditions for the Devotional Observance of Elements of the Old Testament Ceremonial Law

In order to avoid falling into the kind of liturgical error spoken of by St. Thomas or giving scandal in that way, and for bringing out the typological value of such observances, certain principles should animate their use. First of all, like other forms of Christian public devotion, their celebration is subject to the Magisterium of the Church and episcopal authority.

Secondly, it should somehow be made clear in such observances that one's intention is to celebrate them as prefigurations of a reality that one believes is already present. Hebrew Catholic observance of rituals such as the Passover seder, therefore, should not be equated with Jewish liturgy, as if we thought we were doing exactly the same thing. That will not be the case insofar as it involves types of the Messiah, for the intention of the Christian participant in observing such rites will be to point to Christ who has already come and fulfilled the figure. Such elements of the Old Covenant will be made new by the faith of

---

[101] On the role and value of special devotions in the Christian life, see *CCC*, §§1674–76; Jacques Leclercq, *The Interior Life*, trans. Fergus Murphy (New York: P. J. Kenedy & Sons, 1961), 94–114. For a description of special devotions, see 97: "A devotion may be special because of its object, when it is concerned with a person, a saint, for instance, or an aspect of a person, such as the devotion to the name of Jesus or to the Immaculate Conception; and the devotion may be special in respect of its form, as the rosary in the general devotion to the Blessed Virgin. A devotion cannot lay claim to this name of special devotion unless it is not of itself necessary for Catholic life."

the New Covenant in the Christians who participate. For this purpose it would be helpful that the typology in the rite be explained catechetically within the celebration as prefiguring Christ. For example, in the Hebrew Catholic celebration of the Passover seder, various elements could be pointed out as prefiguring Christ's Paschal mystery and the institution of the Eucharist.[102] It may be objected that such catechetical additions would make such a Christian "seder" different from authentic Jewish worship. That is indeed true, but even without any catechetical addition, Christian participation in such a rite must be different than that of Jews without Christian faith precisely because of this difference in faith.[103] Christians will understand the types as prefiguring Christ who has already come and transformed the Passover seder, the memorial of the Exodus, into the Eucharist, the sacramental memorial of Christ's "exodus"[104] and the New Covenant in His Blood.

Third, it is very important that the faithful clearly understand the difference between such prefiguring rites and the seven sacraments of the New Covenant.[105] Observances of ceremonies from the Mosaic Law, therefore, cannot be principal and foundational in the worship of Hebrew Catholics as they are for Jews who have not come to faith in Christ. The principal elements of worship of Hebrew Catholics, as for all Christians, must be the sacraments of the New Covenant, especially the Eucharist. This also implies that the liturgical calendar of Hebrew

---

[102] See http://www.hebrewcatholic.net/the-ahc-passover-haggadah/.

[103] See Raymond Card. Burke, "An Interview with Archbishop Raymond L. Burke for the Occasion of the AHC Conference of Oct 1–3, 2010," by David Moss, in *You Shall Be My Witnesses: Hebrew Catholics and the Mission of the Church* (St. Louis, MO: Association of Hebrew Catholics, 2010), 36–37 in which Archbishop Burke was asked "about Hebrew Catholics observing their traditions in the light of Christ." He responded: "I think the key is, . . . that these celebrations are all carried out in the light of Christ, in other words, fully informed by the Christian faith, but not losing that preparation for Christ which was in the Seder meal and in other prayers and rituals of the Jewish people. So, as long as those prayers—let's take, for instance, the Passover Seder—are celebrated with full Christian faith in which they take on their fullest meaning, this, I think, is a wonderful devotion, and I would think a particular devotion for Hebrew Catholics, but also for non-Hebrew Catholics who would understand fully the meaning of these celebrations." See https://www.hebrewcatholic.net/you-shall-be-my-witnesses-fb/.

[104] See Luke 9:31.

[105] See Council of Florence, *Exsultate Deo* (DS, 1310); *Cantate Domino* (DS, 1348); Council of Trent, Decree on Justification (session 6), ch. 1 (DS, 1521); Decree on the Sacraments (session 7), can. 2 on the Sacraments in General (DS, 1602).

Catholics, like all other Catholics, must revolve around the Paschal mystery and thus around Easter. This distinguishes Hebrew Catholic worship from that of Messianic Jewish congregations,[106] which in practice tend to adopt the Jewish liturgical cycle as the foundation of their worship,[107] adding Christian elements to it such as readings from the New Testament.

Finally, such observances involving Old Testament types should be voluntary for Hebrew Catholics as they are for other Catholics. The obligation of the ceremonial law of the Old Covenant has been taken away by the establishment of a New Covenant with its own liturgical life and corresponding law.[108] Such observances of elements of the Old Covenant on the part of Catholics should be understood as voluntary devotions that are not in competition with the Church's sacraments but, like sacramentals, may help dispose one for the sacramental life instituted by the Word Incarnate.

Study Questions

1. (a) Did the rites of the Old Covenant function *ex opere operato*? (b) What is the position of St. Thomas on the sanctification worked by circumcision?
2. (a) Explain the difference between the causal efficacy of the sacraments of the New Covenant and those of the Old. (b) How is this difference related to the Incarnation? (c) How does the

---

[106] On Messianic Judaism, see David Rudolph and Joel Willitts, eds., *Introduction to Messianic Judaism: Its Ecclesial Context and Biblical Foundations* (Grand Rapids, MI: Zondervan, 2013).

[107] Rudolph and Willetts, *Introduction to Messianic Judaism*, 29–31, 37–43.

[108] Messianic Jews, on the contrary, tend to hold that continued observance of the Mosaic law, also with regard to worship and the ceremonial precepts in general, is incumbent on Jewish believers in Christ out of fidelity to the Old Covenant, although not for salvation. This position is argued forcefully by Mark Kinzer in *Post-Missionary Messianic Judaism*, and *Searching Her Own Mystery: Nostra Aetate, the Jewish People, and the Identity of the Church*. Such a view, obviously, requires a radically revisionist interpretation of many texts of St. Paul that assert that the Christian, whether Jew or Gentile, is freed from the obligation of the ceremonial law of Moses, which St. Paul often speaks of as "works of the Law." For two excellent responses to Kinzer's position, see Levering, *Jewish-Christian Dialogue and the Life of Wisdom*, 32–53, and Douglas Farrow, *Theological Negotiations*, 235–50.

distinction between conjoined and extrinsic instruments apply to the sacraments of the Old Covenant?

3. What should be held concerning the sanctifying power of the sacramental rites of the Old Covenant after Christ when celebrated by Jews inculpably ignorant of the New Covenant?

4. What is the current teaching of the Church on the question of whether the Old Covenant has been revoked? What is the scriptural foundation for this teaching?

5. What was at issue in the dispute between St. Jerome and St. Augustine on the observance of the ceremonial Law of Moses by the Apostles? How does St. Augustine reconcile the apostolic observance with the discipline of his time in which such observance was forbidden?

6. (a) Why does St. Thomas argue that the continued observance of the rites of the ceremonial Law (by Hebrew Catholics) would be gravely sinful? (b) What does the Council of Florence teach in this regard? (c) What does Benedict XIV teach about the power of the Church to permit observances from the ceremonial Law of the Old Covenant?

7. What arguments can be made in favor of the licitness of the devotional observance of some rites of the ceremonial Law of the Old Covenant (as in participation in a Passover seder) if done not as obligatory for salvation but as a kind of sacramental or devotional practice?

Suggestions for Further Reading

Aquinas, Thomas. *ST* III, q. 62, a. 6; *ST* I-II q. 103, a. 4.

Augustine. Letter 82 to St. Jerome. In Saint Augustine, *Letters*, vol. 1 (1–82). Translated by Sr. Wilfrid Parson. Washington, DC: The Catholic University of America Press, 1951. Pp. 390–420.

D'Costa, Gavin. *Catholic Doctrines on Jews After the Second Vatican Council*. Oxford: Oxford University Press, 2019.

_____. "The Mystery of Israel: Jews, Hebrew Catholics, Messianic Judaism, the Catholic Church, and the Mosaic Ceremonial Laws." *Nova et Vetera* (English) 16, no. 3 (2018): 939–77.

_____. *Vatican II: Catholic Doctrines on Jews and Muslims*. Oxford: Oxford University Press, 2016. Pp.113–59.

Farrow, Douglas. "Jew and Gentile in the Church Today." *Nova et*

Vetera (English) 16, no. 3 (2018): 979–93.

_____. *Theological Negotiations: Proposals in Soteriology and Anthropology*. Grand Rapids, MI: Baker Academic, 2018. Pp. 209–50.

Leeming, Bernard. *Principles of Sacramental Theology*. Westminster, MD: Newman Press, 1963. Pp. 604–14.

Levering, Matthew. *Jewish-Christian Dialogue and the Life of Wisdom: Engagements with the Theology of Michael Novak*. New York: Continuum, 2010. Pp. 12–46.

Marshall, Bruce D. "Christ and Israel: An Unsolved Problem in Catholic Theology." In *The Call of Abraham: Essays on the Election of Israel in Honor of Jon D. Levenson*. Edited by Gary A. Anderson and Jon D. Levenson. Notre Dame, IN: University of Notre Dame Press, 2013. Pp. 330–50.

_____. "Quasi in Figura: A Brief Reflection on Jewish Election, after Thomas Aquinas." *Nova et Vetera* (English) 7, no. 2 (2009): 477–84.

_____. "Religion and Election: Aquinas on Natural Law, Judaism, and Salvation in Christ." *Nova et Vetera* (English) 14, no. 1 (2016): 104–25.

Tapie, Matthew A. *Aquinas on Israel and the Church: The Question of Supersessionism in the Theology of Thomas Aquinas*. Eugene, OR: Pickwick Publications, 2016.

Wyschogrod, Michael. "A Jewish Reading of St. Thomas Aquinas." In *Understanding Scripture: Explorations of Jewish and Christian Traditions of Interpretation*. Edited by Clemens Thoma and Michael Wyschogrod. New York; Mahwah, NJ: Paulist Press, 1987. Pp. 125–40.

CHAPTER FIFTEEN

Sacramental Grace
Received through Desire

THREE WAYS TO GAIN OR GROW IN GRACE

How do we gain or grow in grace? Since it is absolutely indispensable for salvation to die in a state of grace, and since grace is the seed of glory, this is among the most important questions of theology. Scripture and the Catholic theological Tradition speak of three ways to gain or grow in grace: sacraments, desire or prayer, and merit.[1] The ordinary way to gain or grow in grace is the subject of this book: the seven sacraments of the Church.

Jesus clearly expresses the necessity of the sacraments for receiving grace with regard to the two most important sacraments of Baptism and the Eucharist. In His nocturnal conversation with Nicodemus in John 3:3–6, Jesus proclaims the necessity of Baptism for salvation:

"Truly, truly, I say to you, unless one is born anew, he cannot

---

[1] See, for example, Garrigou-Lagrange, *Three Ages of the Interior Life*, 1:132–43; Aumann, *Spiritual Theology*, 208–09: "To put on Christ and to grow in his likeness require the use of positive means by which grace and charity can reach their full expansion and intensity. These positive means can be divided into the three principal ones that are necessary for all Christians—the sacraments, meritorious good works, and the prayer of petition.... The sacraments are the most efficacious, for they produce their effects *ex opere operato*, that is, they infallibly produce grace in those who receive the sacraments with the proper dispositions. The other two means ... produce their effects *ex opere operantis*, that is, their efficacy depends on the dispositions of the human agent, working under the impetus of grace."

see the kingdom of God." Nicodemus said to him, "How can a man be born when he is old? Can he enter a second time into his mother's womb and be born?" Jesus answered, "Truly, truly, I say to you, unless one is born of water and the Spirit, he cannot enter the kingdom of God. That which is born of the flesh is flesh, and that which is born of the Spirit is spirit.

The necessity of the Eucharist for salvation is proclaimed in an equally solemn way in the Bread of Life discourse in John 6:53–54: "Truly, truly, I say to you, unless you eat the flesh of the Son of man and drink his blood, you have no life in you; he who eats my flesh and drinks my blood has eternal life, and I will raise him up at the last day." As Jesus's words imply, God binds Himself to give the grace of a share in His divine and eternal life through the sacraments, provided they are received with the necessary dispositions.

If, however, grace were given exclusively through the sacraments of Church, this would imply that no one could be saved outside the visible Church even if they were outside through no grave fault of their own. This would be incompatible with God's universal salvific will proclaimed in 1 Timothy 2:3–4: "God our Savior, who desires all men to be saved and to come to the knowledge of the truth." It would also be incompatible with strong affirmations in Scripture that assert that "every one who calls upon the name of the Lord will be saved,"[2] whether Jew or Greek. For many have called upon the name of the Lord, even if imperfectly known, who have not had access to or knowledge of the Church's sacraments.

A second way to gain or grow in grace, therefore, is through prayer, which is the expression of desire for God. Prayer appeals to God's mercy that can also work outside the sacramental system. A powerful example of the efficacy of such prayer is that of the good thief on the Cross, who prayed "Jesus, remember me when you come into your kingly power" (Luke 23:42). Although unable to receive Baptism, these words nevertheless merited the response: "Truly, I say to you, today you will be with me in Paradise" (Luke 23:43).

Jesus frequently alludes to the power of desire or prayer for the reception of grace. In the Sermon on the Mount, He teaches:

Ask, and it will be given you; seek, and you will find; knock,

---

2 Rom 10:13, quoting Joel 2:32.

and it will be opened to you. For every one who asks receives, and he who seeks finds, and to him who knocks it will be opened. Or what man of you, if his son asks him for bread, will give him a stone? Or if he asks for a fish, will give him a serpent? If you then, who are evil, know how to give good gifts to your children, how much more will your Father who is in heaven give good things to those who ask him![3]

All prayer for grace and salvation involves at least an implicit desire for the sacraments as the ordinary means for receiving grace.

Merit is a third means of growing in grace for those who already possess sanctifying grace gained through the sacraments or desire for them. All works of charity done in a state of grace merit an increase of grace.[4] Jesus speaks of merit in Matthew 10:42 when He says that "whoever gives to one of these little ones even a cup of cold water because he is a disciple, truly, I say to you, he shall not lose his reward." St. Paul likewise refers to merit in 2 Timothy 4:8: "There is laid up for me the crown of righteousness, which the Lord, the righteous judge, will award to me on that Day, and not only to me but also to all who have loved his appearing."[5]

Merit as a means of growth in grace, however, always presupposes

---

[3] Matt 7:7–11. Other New Testament texts asserting the efficacious power of prayer include Matt 21:22: "Whatever you ask in prayer, you will receive, if you have faith"; John 14:13: "Whatever you ask in my name, I will do it, that the Father may be glorified in the Son"; John 15:7: " If you abide in me, and my words abide in you, ask whatever you will, and it shall be done for you"; John 16:24: "Ask, and you will receive, that your joy may be full"; 1 John 5:14–15: "This is the confidence which we have in him, that if we ask anything according to his will he hears us. And if we know that he hears us in whatever we ask, we know that we have obtained the requests made of him." See Aumann, *Spiritual Theology*, 234–35.

[4] See the Council of Trent, Decree on Justification (session 6), can. 32 (DS, 1582), "If anyone says that the good works of the justified man are the gifts of God in such a way that they are not also the good merits of the justified man himself; or that by the good works he performs through the grace of God and the merits of Jesus Christ (of whom he is a living member), the justified man does not truly merit an increase of grace, eternal life, and (provided he dies in the state of grace) the attainment of this eternal life, as well as an increase of glory, let him be anathema."

[5] Both Matt 10:42 and 2 Tim 4:8, together with many other New Testament texts, are quoted by the Council of Trent in the Decree on Justification, ch. 16 (DS, 1545–48).

that one has already received grace and the virtue of charity through the sacraments or through a salutary desire for them by which the effects of the sacraments can be anticipated. For we cannot merit for ourselves the grace of our own justification. It follows that all grace is tied to the sacraments or desire for them.[6]

Necessity of the Sacraments

Are the sacraments necessary for salvation? In order to answer this question, one must first distinguish between different kinds of necessity and also between the three levels of the sacraments. The habitual grace given by the sacraments, the *res tantum*, is absolutely necessary for salvation, but it is possible to receive the grace of the sacraments through a salutary desire for that grace, without receiving the sacramental sign when it is not possible to receive it, or when a person is invincibly ignorant of it.

Such a desire for grace is made possible by actual grace and presupposes, at least implicitly, acts of faith, hope, and charity, which also are made possible by the aid of actual grace. This is not a vicious circle—needing grace in order to receive grace—because actual and sanctifying grace are distinct, as seen in chapter 9 above. God gives actual graces to lead us to desire the forgiveness of sins and an abiding communion with God. This very desire, as a fruit of grace, has, through God's mercy, a power to call down and anticipate the grace of the sacraments. In the Sermon on the Mount Jesus stresses the power of desire: "Ask, and it will be given you" (Matt 7:7).

Reception of the grace of the sacraments through desire has been most discussed with regard to Baptism, but it also applies to the other sacraments with the exception of Holy Orders, which involves a public

---

[6] See Nicolas, "La grâce sacramentelle," 525–38; Nicolas, *Synthèse dogmatique: de la Trinité à la Trinité*, 789 (my translation): "If all grace given in this economy of salvation established by God is sacramental, this is because, in this economy, the Church is the universal mediatrix." See also Fagan, "Sacramental Spirituality," in *Sacraments: The Gestures of Christ*, ed. O'Callaghan, 157: "It is not an exaggeration to claim that in the present economy all grace is sacramental because given in virtue of a sacrament received either actually or in desire"; Colman E. O'Neill, *Meeting Christ in the Sacraments*, revised by Romanus Cessario (Staten Island, NY: St. Paul's, 1991), 299.

and visible status in the Church that cannot be received by desire.[7] We shall focus primarily on Baptism, but the same principles apply also to the other sacraments whose grace can be received through desire. Baptism is necessary because it is the ordinary means instituted by Christ for His disciples to receive the life of the Spirit, which is supernatural grace. The *Catechism of the Catholic Church*, §1257 explains: "The Lord himself affirms that Baptism is necessary for salvation. He also commands his disciples to proclaim the Gospel to all nations and to baptize them." However, in the next sentence, it qualifies this necessity to allow for invincible ignorance and for the fact that God does not require what is impossible, stating: "Baptism is necessary for salvation for those to whom the Gospel has been proclaimed and who have had the possibility of asking for this sacrament."[8]

Necessity of Means and Necessity of Precept

The sacraments are necessary as a means to attain the end of salvation and sanctification. Something is said to be necessary as a means to an end according to various degrees of necessity.

Absolute Necessity of Means

A means is *absolutely* necessary for an end when it is the *only means* to that end, without exception. This would be an indispensable or unique means, which is absolutely necessary to obtain an end. For example, in order to live, I must first be conceived, by an indispensable necessity of means.

Is there anything necessary for salvation by an indispensable necessity of means? Yes, sanctifying grace and the theological virtues

---

[7] See Jean-Hervé Nicolas, *Synthèse dogmatique: de la Trinité à la Trinité*, 789 (my translation): "If the sacramental grace of Holy Orders cannot be received in this way, that is without the *res et sacramentum*, it is because for this sacrament the ecclesial finality takes precedence over its personal finality. . . . One is a priest for the Church." With regard to Matrimony, one cannot contract the matrimonial bond by desire, for it requires the public exchange of consent. Nevertheless, it seems reasonable to think that some sacramental graces of Matrimony could be received through desire by couples who have a valid but non-sacramental marriage in that one or both are not baptized, and yet they have desire for Baptism (implicit or explicit) and a desire to sanctify their marriage so that they could love with a participation of the divine love.

[8] See *LG*, §14.

are necessary for salvation in this way.[9] Sanctifying grace is the seed
of glory. No one can be born to heavenly glory who dies without the
seed of glory, which is grace. This necessity for the seed of glory is
similar to the physical necessity according to which no oak tree can
grow without first having been an acorn. Although it is true that God's
omnipotence is not bound by this law, no exception is to be expected
because this necessity of grace pertains to the order universally willed
by God. Therefore, the *res tantum* of the sacraments—the reality of
sanctifying grace that they give—is absolutely necessary for salvation
and sanctification.

Another thing necessary for salvation by an indispensable necessity
of means is the forgiveness of original sin and of personal mortal sin.
This is the other side of the coin of the necessity of sanctifying grace,
for the forgiveness of original and mortal sin implies the infusion of
sanctifying grace. With regard to the necessity for the forgiveness of
original sin or actual mortal sin, Innocent III declared:

> We say that two kinds of sin must be distinguished, origi-
> nal and actual: original, which is contracted without consent;
> and actual, which is committed with consent. Thus original
> sin, which is contracted without consent is remitted without
> consent through the power of the sacrament [of baptism]; but
> actual sin, which is committed with consent, is by no means
> remitted without consent. . . . The punishment of original sin
> is the deprivation of the vision of God, but the punishment of
> actual sin is the torment of eternal hell.[10]

As Innocent III implies, if a person is aware that he has committed a
mortal sin, then an act of contrition is also necessary for salvation by
an indispensable necessity of means.[11]

---

[9] See the Council of Trent, Decree on Justification (session 6), chs. 7–8 (DS, 1530–32) and canons 1 and 11 (DS, 1551 and 1561). On the necessity of the virtue of faith, see also Riccardo Lombardi, *The Salvation of the Unbeliever* (London: Burns & Oates, 1956), 26–30, esp. 29: "To begin with habitual faith, this is certainly of absolute necessity as a means of salvation, a necessity which can admit of no exception, which we have called by the theological name of 'necessity of means.' To put it simply: nobody has ever been saved, or will ever be saved, without infused faith."

[10] Innocent III, *Maiores Ecclesiae causas* (DS, 780).

[11] See *ST* III, q. 86, a. 2: "It is impossible that God pardon a man for an offence,

Since the forgiveness of sins was merited by Christ's sacrifice on Calvary, the accomplishment of that sacrifice and the application of its merit to us are also necessary for salvation by an indispensable necessity of means.

For those with use of reason, prayer and acts of faith,[12] hope,[13] and charity[14] are also necessary by an indispensable necessity of means. Prayer is necessary because it is the means by which we freely order ourselves to God and ask for the graces we need. In summary, sanctifying grace (which implies the forgiveness of original and mortal sin) and the theological virtues—merited by Christ's Passion—have always been necessary for salvation by an indispensable necessity of means.

Relative Necessity of Means: Most Fitting Means

Another kind of necessity of means is when something is not the only possible means, but it is the most fitting means of those that are possible. This could be called a relative rather than an absolute necessity. The Incarnation is said to be necessary in this manner. God could have saved us in many ways, for He is omnipotent, but the Incarnation and the Passion of Christ are the most fitting and wise means for our sal-

---

without his will being changed. Now the offence of mortal sin is due to man's will being turned away from God, through being turned to some mutable good. Consequently, for the pardon of this offence against God, it is necessary for man's will to be so changed as to turn to God and to renounce having turned to something else in the aforesaid manner, together with a purpose of amendment; all of which belongs to the nature of penance as a virtue. Therefore it is impossible for a sin to be pardoned anyone without penance as a virtue."

[12] The necessity of faith is given in Heb 11:6: "Without faith it is impossible to please him. For whoever would draw near to God must believe that he exists and that he rewards those who seek him." See the Council of Trent, Decree on Justification (session 6), ch. 6 (DS, 1526–27); *ST* II-II, q. 2, a. 3: "In order that a man arrive at the perfect vision of heavenly happiness, he must first of all believe God, as a disciple believes the master who is teaching him." See also Lombardi, *The Salvation of the Unbeliever*, 30–34.

[13] See Rom 8:24: "For in this hope we were saved." See also *ST* II-II, q. 22, a. 1, in which St. Thomas argues that faith and hope are the foundations or preambles of the entire divine law and are necessary to order oneself to God: "The preambles to the Law are those without which no law is possible: such are the precepts relating to the act of faith and the act of hope, because the act of faith inclines man's mind so that he believes the Author of the Law to be One to Whom he owes submission, while, by the hope of a reward, he is induced to observe the precepts."

[14] See Matt 25:34–46.

vation, which thus can be said to be necessary. St. Thomas makes this argument to show the fittingness of the Incarnation:

> A thing is said to be necessary for a certain end in two ways. First, when the end cannot be without it; as food is necessary for the preservation of human life. Secondly, when the end is attained better and more conveniently, as a horse is necessary for a journey. In the first way it was not necessary that God should become incarnate for the restoration of human nature. For God of His omnipotent power could have restored human nature in many other ways. But in the second way it was necessary that God should become incarnate for the restoration of human nature.[15]

As seen in the first chapter, there are many reasons why the sacraments are the most fitting means for God to use to sanctify us. The sacraments are most fitting because they are a means of sanctification proportionate to our nature, being sensible signs that make use of the symbolism built into nature and salvation history. Secondly, they are means by which Christ's humanity can act on us and touch us sensibly, making possible an encounter with Him and His Spirit in a visible, concrete, and certain way. Third, the sacraments are ecclesial events that sanctify human beings in the Church and imprint an ecclesial mission through the *res et sacramentum*. Thus we can speak of a relative necessity for God to give us salvation through sacraments.

Therefore, even though it is possible to receive the grace ordinarily communicated by the sacraments through desire without actually receiving the sacraments, as will be seen below, this is not as fitting a way for human beings to receive sanctification, for it does not manifest Christ's role in sanctification, nor incorporate them into the Church, nor give the *res et sacramentum*. This lack of fittingness is even more true when the desire is only implicit because one is ignorant of the truth about Christ and the Church.

Desiring the sacraments, however, is not actually *another* means of salvation—a less fitting or extraordinary means—for it is not properly an independent means at all. It is simply desiring the one means that

---

[15] *ST* III, q. 1, a. 2. The fittingness of Christ's Passion is argued by Aquinas in *ST* III, q. 46, aa. 1–3.

God has appointed for mankind. For although God could have chosen other means to sanctify us, there are *no human means at all* by which we can give ourselves sanctifying grace, for it is infinitely above us, being a sharing in the life of God. Only God can give us a means to salvation, and He has given us one: the sacramental system of which Baptism is the one and only entrance.

Necessity of Precept: Ordinary Means

Another way that a means may be necessary is when a particular means, judged by the legitimate authority to be the most fitting, is made obligatory by a positive law that is commanded and promulgated. A law of this kind is binding only after its promulgation and only on those who ought to know about it. Examples of this kind of necessity are the ceremonial precepts of the Mosaic Law, such as circumcision, the feasts of Israel, the dietary laws, and laws of ritual purification. These laws were obligatory only on the children of Israel, only after they were promulgated on Mt. Sinai, only until they have received the proclamation of the Gospel, and only on those who ought to know about them. In a similar way, entrance into the Church is necessary only after its promulgation by the Apostles and their successors, and again only on those who ought to know about it.[16] Something commanded in this way can be said to be the *ordinary* means.

The International Theological Commission speaks of this kind of necessity as of a "second order," as opposed to the absolute necessity of the saving work of Christ applied to each person.[17] If something is necessary as the only *ordinary, fitting, or legally mandated* means

---

[16] See *LG*, §14: "In explicit terms He Himself affirmed the necessity of faith and baptism and thereby affirmed also the necessity of the Church, for through baptism as through a door men enter the Church. Whosoever, therefore, knowing that the Catholic Church was made necessary by Christ, would refuse to enter or to remain in it, could not be saved."

[17] International Theological Commission (ITC), "The Hope of Salvation for Infants Who Die without Being Baptised," 2007, §10, in ITC, *Texts and Documents, 1986–2007* (San Francisco: Ignatius Press, 2009), 360: "The necessity of sacramental baptism is a necessity of the second order compared to the absolute necessity of God's saving act through Jesus Christ for the final salvation of every human being. Sacramental baptism is necessary because it is the ordinary means through which a person shares the beneficial effects of Jesus' death and resurrection."

to an end, one might also attain it through other *extraordinary* or *less fitting* means if the legally mandated means are not possible or if one is ignorant of them. The indispensable necessity of means differs from a necessity of ordinary means or precept because in the latter case, if the ordinary means are not possible, one might be dispensed from them and still obtain the end.

The Necessity of Baptism

Is the sacrament of Baptism intrinsically necessary in the same way as sanctifying grace and the theological virtues? No, for if it were, it would have been necessary from the beginning of the human race, as dying in a state of grace has always been necessary. Christ instituted the sacraments to be the *sole ordinary channels* mandated by divine law by which we obtain and grow in sanctifying grace in the New Covenant. In other words, Baptism and the other sacraments are necessary by a necessity of divine precept as the only ordinary means to sanctifying grace, whereas sanctifying grace and charity are necessary for salvation as indispensable means.[18] We could say that the sacrament of Baptism is the unique ordinary and divinely prescribed (but not indispensable) means to receive the indispensable means. Or to put it another way, *the effect* of Baptism is indispensable for salvation but not the *sacrament itself*, for God can supply that indispensable effect while bypassing the ordinary means that He has mandated, which are the sacraments.

There are no other human means that could take the place of Baptism, for we cannot give ourselves a share in the divine life. The *Catechism of the Catholic Church*, §1257 makes this clear: "The Church does not know of any means other than Baptism that assures

---

[18] A similar distinction is made by Francis Sullivan in *Salvation Outside the Church?: Tracing the History of the Catholic Response* (Eugene, OR: Wipf & Stock, 2002), 138 (italics original): "The necessity of belonging to the Catholic Church for salvation is a necessity both of divine precept and of means. There are two kinds of necessity of means. Some means are intrinsically necessary for salvation: such are faith in God and repentance for personal sin. For such means as these, in the case of adults, there is no possible substitute. Other things, however, have been established as means necessary for salvation by a positive decree. This is not the same as simple necessity of precept, since what has been established by divine decree *as a necessary means* must always, in some sense, enter into the obtaining of the intended effect."

entry into eternal beatitude; this is why she takes care not to neglect the mission she has received from the Lord to see that all who can be baptized are 'reborn of water and the Spirit.'" We are not free, therefore, to choose some other means of salvation, for there are no human means to choose from. God, however, has other means at His disposal, although none so fitting, for He can sanctify us directly by giving us the essential effects of the sacraments—the *res tantum*—without actual reception of the sacramental sign or the *res et sacramentum*.

That God is not bound by His sacraments is theologically certain. In the mid-twelfth century, the *Summa sententiarum* stated: "God did not bind His power to the sacraments, and although He has decreed to give salvation through the sacraments, He nonetheless can and does give it without these."[19] Shortly before, Hugh of St. Victor explained the same thesis at greater length:

> It is within God's power to save man without these but it is not within man's power to attain to salvation without these. For God could have saved man, even if he had not instituted these, but man could not by any means be saved if he contemned these. . . . Now God can save man without these, who can bestow upon man His virtue and sanctification and salvation in whatever way He wills. For by that spirit with which He teaches man without word, He can also justify without sacrament if He wills, since the virtue of God is not subject to elements from necessity.[20]

As examples of extra-sacramental salvation, he cites the prophet Jeremiah, John the Baptist, and those who "under the natural law pleased God."[21]

Shortly afterwards, Peter Lombard wrote: "Although God could have given grace to man without the sacraments, by which he did not

---

[19] *Summa sententiarum*, tract. 5, ch. 6, (PL 176: 133D), English translation in Ilaria Morali, "Religions and Salvation," in *Catholic Engagement with World Religions: A Comprehensive Study*, ed. Karl Joseph Becker and Ilaria Morali (Maryknoll, NY: Orbis Books, 2010), 62.

[20] Hugh of St. Victor, *On the Sacraments of the Christian Faith* 1.9.5, trans. Deferrari, 161.

[21] Hugh of St. Victor, *On the Sacraments of the Christian Faith* 1.9.5, trans. Deferrari, 161.

bind his own power, he nevertheless instituted the sacraments."[22] St. Bonaventure echoes this teaching a century later: "God has decreed that we are to draw the grace of our healing from Christ, the supreme Physician in and through these sensible signs, 'although God has not restricted his power to the sacraments.'"[23] St. Thomas has the same doctrine[24] and it is emphasized in the *Catechism of the Catholic Church*, §1257: "*God has bound salvation to the sacrament of Baptism, but he himself is not bound by his sacraments.*"[25]

As the ordinary channels of His grace, the sacraments are binding on us by a grave necessity of precept and as the most fitting means for God to use. God's power to infuse grace, however, is not limited to these ordinary channels. The grace given by Baptism is absolutely necessary for salvation, but that same grace could be received in an extraordinary way without receiving the sacrament. Thus grace was received extra-sacramentally by the good thief on the cross through his contrition and faith, by the centurion Cornelius through his faith and charity, by John the Baptist in the womb at the Visitation, by Mary in her Immaculate Conception, by the Holy Innocents, by all the saints of the Old Testament, and by all those who lived before Christ who sought to do God's will above all else.

In an analogous way, the Christian Tradition recognizes that the grace of Baptism can be received prior to the reception of the sacrament by Baptism of blood and desire for Baptism. The *Catechism of the Catholic Church*, §1258 states this ancient doctrine: "This *Baptism of blood*, like the *desire for Baptism*, brings about the fruits of Baptism without being a sacrament."

This doctrine on reception of grace through desire for a sacrament, moved by faith, hope, and charity, applies not only to Baptism, but also to Confirmation,[26] the Eucharist, Penance, and probably to Anointing of the Sick, as will be seen below. The application of sacramental grace through desire is developed by theologians most fully with regard to Baptism, the Eucharist, and Penance.

---

[22] Peter Lombard, *Sentences*, bk. 4, d. 1, ch. 5, trans. Silano, p. 6.

[23] Bonaventure, *Breviloquium* 6.1.5, trans. Monti, 213–14.

[24] See *ST* III, q. 68, a. 2; a. 11, ad 1.

[25] Italics original. See also John Paul II, *Reconciliatio et Paenitentia*, §31, no. 1.

[26] *ST* III, q. 72, a. 6, ad 1.

Development of Doctrine on Baptism of Desire

Baptism of Blood

The beginnings of the Church's doctrine on how the effect of Baptism might be supplied without actually receiving the sacrament came with regard to martyrs who died for the faith as catechumens without the sacrament of Baptism. Their salvation without sacramental Baptism came to be known as Baptism of blood, in that the shedding of their blood for the faith was a sign that they were made participants in the fruits of the Cross of Christ, to which they were configured not by water but by blood and suffering for his name.[27] As the *Catechism of the Catholic Church*, §1258 states: "The Church has always held the firm conviction that those who suffer death for the sake of the faith without having received Baptism are baptized by their death for and with Christ." St. Augustine gave a classic statement of the common patristic doctrine on Baptism of blood in *The City of God*:

> I have in mind those unbaptized persons who die confessing the name of Christ. They receive the forgiveness of their sins as completely as if they had been cleansed by the waters of baptism. For, He who said: "Unless a man be born again of water and the Spirit, he cannot enter into the kingdom of God," made exceptions in other decisions which are no less universal: "Everyone who acknowledges me before men, I also will acknowledge him before my Father in heaven"; and again: "He who loses his life for my sake will find it."[28]

---

[27] See *ST* III, q. 66, a. 11. On the development of this doctrine, see John Henry Newman, *An Essay on the Development of Christian Doctrine*, 6th ed. (Notre Dame, IN: University of Notre Dame Press, 1989), 406: "It was the doctrine of the Church that Martyrdom was meritorious, that it had a certain supernatural efficacy in it, and that the blood of the Saints received from the grace of the One Redeemer a certain expiatory power. Martyrdom stood in the place of Baptism, where the Sacrament had not been administered. It exempted the soul from all preparatory waiting, and gained its immediate admittance into glory. 'All crimes are pardoned for the sake of this work,' says Tertullian."

[28] *The City of God* 13.7, in *The City of God, Books VIII–XVI*, trans. Walsh and Monahan, 307.

St. Cyprian

St. Cyprian was among the first theologians to explain the theology of Baptism of blood. In response to a question regarding the salvation of a catechumen who was martyred for the faith, he also marks the beginnings of a doctrine on Baptism of desire:

> In the first place, such catechumens do hold the faith and truth of the Church complete, they march forth from the camp of God to do battle with the devil possessed of a full and sincere knowledge of God the Father and of Christ and the Holy Spirit; and in the second place, they are not in fact deprived of the sacrament of baptism, inasmuch as they are baptized with the greatest and most glorious baptism of all, that of blood. It was of this that the Lord Himself said that He had another baptism with which to be baptized. And the Lord further declared in the Gospel that those baptized in their own blood and sanctified with a martyr's suffering are made perfect and obtain the grace which God has promised; for when, in the midst of His own sufferings, He spoke to the thief who believed and confessed, He promised that he would be with Him in paradise.[29]

The example of the good thief is not actually to the point, as St. Augustine would later point out, because he was not a martyr. His case suggests Baptism of desire, although St. Cyprian does not distinguish between the two.

St. Ambrose

St. Ambrose asserts the existence both of Baptism of blood and of desire in his *Funeral Oration for the Emperor Valentinian II*, who died as a catechumen in the year 392 after he had asked Ambrose to come to Gaul to baptize him. In his funeral oration, St. Ambrose holds that he received the grace of Baptism through his desire for the sacrament:

> He frequently addressed me when I was far from him, and

---

[29] Cyprian, Letter 73.22.2 to Iubaianus, in *The Letters of St. Cyprian of Carthage, Letters 67–82*, p. 67.

let it be known that he wished to be initiated into the sacred mysteries, preferably by me. . . . I was already crossing the ridges of the Alps when, lo and behold, there came news, bitter for myself and everybody, of the death of so great an emperor. . . . I have lost him whose father in the Gospel I was about to become. But he did not lose the grace which he had demanded.[30] . . . His state is now such that you have no need to fear for him. . . .[31]

Grant therefore, O holy Father, to your servant the gift that Moses received because he saw in spirit. . . . Grant, I say, to your servant Valentinian, the gift that he desired, the gift for which he asked, when he was healthy, strong and safe. If because of illness, he had postponed his request, he would surely have not been totally beyond your mercy, as he would have been deprived by the speedy passing of time, not by his own decision. Grant therefore to your servant the gift of your grace, which he never rejected. . . . How could this man, who had Your spirit, not receive Your grace?[32]

But if it really is a cause for worry that the mysteries have not been celebrated, it follows that not even martyrs receive crowns, if they are catechumens; for (on that assumption) they cannot be crowned unless they have been initiated. But if the martyrs have in fact been baptized in their own blood, then Valentinian's piety and intention have in effect baptized him too.[33]

St. Ambrose uses the doctrine of Baptism of blood as a well-established doctrine and argues from that to Baptism of desire. It is interesting that Ambrose uses Moses as an example of someone justified by Baptism of desire. This would clearly apply also to the other holy men and women of Israel who lived in the grace of God.

---

[30] Ambrose, *De obitu Valentiniani* 23, 26, 29–30, in *Ambrose of Milan: Political Letters and Speeches*, trans. J. H. W. G. Liebeschuetz (Liverpool: Liverpool University Press, 2005), 374–78.

[31] Ambrose, *De obitu Valentiniani* 41, in Liebeschuetz, 383.

[32] Ambrose, *De obitu Valentiniani* 52, in Liebeschuetz, 387–88.

[33] Ambrose, *De obitu Valentiniani* 53, in Liebeschuetz, 388.

St. Augustine

St. Augustine speaks about Baptism of desire in his treatise *On Baptism against the Donatists*. Reflecting on the salvation of the good thief, he writes:

> That the place of baptism is sometimes supplied by martyr-dom is supported by an argument by no means trivial, which the blessed Cyprian adduces from the thief, to whom, though he was not baptized, it was yet said, "Today shalt thou be with me in paradise." On considering which again and again, I find that not only martyrdom for the sake of Christ may supply what was wanting of baptism, but also faith and conversion of heart, if recourse may not be had to the celebration of the mystery of baptism for want of time. For neither was that thief crucified for the name of Christ, but as the reward of his own deeds; nor did he suffer because he believed, but he believed while suffering. It was shown, therefore, in the case of that thief, how great is the power, even without the visible sacra-ment of baptism, of what the apostle says, "With the heart man believeth unto righteousness, and with the mouth confes-sion is made unto salvation." But the want is supplied invisibly only when the administration of baptism is prevented, not by contempt for religion, but by the necessity of the moment.[34]

Later he summarizes: "In the thief the gracious goodness of the Almighty supplied what had been wanting in the sacrament of baptism, because it had been missing not from pride or contempt, but from want of opportunity."[35]

Although St. Augustine admitted in the case of the good thief the

---

[34] Augustine, *On Baptism, against the Donatists* 4.22.29, trans. J. R. King, in *NPNF*1, 4:460. (I prefer this translation to that given by Tilley and Ramsey in *The Donatist Controversy I*, p. 494, which gives Augustine's words a different sense.) St. Augustine gives the same interpretation of the good thief in *Quaes-tionum in Heptateuchum Libri Septem* 3.84 (on Lev 21:15), in PL 34:713, and *A Miscellany of 83 Questions*, question 62. But see Augustine's caution regarding this interpretation in *Revisions* II.18(45), and I.26.2.qu.62, because it is uncer-tain that the thief was unbaptized.

[35] Augustine, *On Baptism, against the Donatists* 4.24.31, trans. King, in *NPNF*1, 4:462.

possibility of an explicit Baptism of desire that enabled him to attain salvation, he did not regard catechumens who died without Baptism as able to attain salvation, especially if they were negligent through delaying reception of the sacrament. Hence he urges them to hurry to the baptismal font.[36]

Another aspect of Augustine's teaching on Baptism of desire concerns the doctrine that the just who lived before the promulgation of the Gospel were saved through the grace of Christ, now applied through the sacraments, which they desired at least implicitly. He writes: "The saving grace of this religion, the only true one, through which alone true salvation is truly promised, has never been refused to anyone who was worthy of it, and whoever lacked it was unworthy of it."[37] This gives the principle underlying the doctrine of implicit desire

---

[36] See Augustine, *Punishment and Forgiveness of Sins*, 2.26.42, in *Answer to the Pelagians*, trans. Roland Teske, WSA I/23 (Hyde Park, NY: New City Press, 1997), 108: "If catechumens are not baptized, their sanctification is useless for entering the kingdom of heaven or for the forgiveness of sins." See also Sermon 97A.3, in *Sermons on the New Testament*, trans. Edmund Hill, WSA III/4 (Brooklyn, NY: New City Press, 1992), 41: "So in short I say to your holinesses; any Christians, who are still catechumens, should take pains to get their sins forgiven. After all, they already bear the sign of Christ on their foreheads, they already enter the church, they already call upon this name that is above every name and yet they are still carrying the burden of their sins. They haven't yet been forgiven, because they are only forgiven in holy baptism." This teaching is also implied in his Sermon 142, Appendix, "On the Burial of Catechumens," in *Newly Discovered Sermons*, trans. Edmund Hill, WSA III/11 (Hyde Park, NY: New City Press, 1997), 131–33. Here St. Augustine is addressing catechumens who are putting off Baptism, warning them that they are in danger of forfeiting eternal life, and that catechumens who die unbaptized, according to the Church's discipline, "ought not to be buried among the bodies of the faithful" (p. 131). See also Sermon 27.6 (III/2:107–08). At this time many catechumens, like Augustine himself, remained for many years as catechumens without proximate desire and preparation for Baptism.

[37] Augustine, Letter 102 to Deogratias, in *Letters: Volume II (83–130)*, trans. Parsons, 159. See also an earlier passage in the same letter, pp. 155–56: "Therefore, from the beginning of the human race, all those who believed in Him and knew Him and lived a good and devout life according to His commands, whenever and wherever they lived, undoubtedly were saved by Him. Just as we believe in Him, both as remaining with the Father and as having come in the flesh, so the ancients believed in Him, both remaining with the Father and about to come in the flesh. We should not think that there are different kinds of faith, or more than one kind of salvation, because what is now spoken of in the course of time as something accomplished was then foretold as something to come; and, because one and the same thing is foretold or preached by diverse

for Baptism. Nevertheless, St. Augustine did not apply this principle to people of his own day, in which he presupposed that the Gospel was already promulgated. After this general promulgation he held that even if some had not yet heard the Gospel, they would not be saved on account of original or personal sin.[38]

St. Fulgentius of Ruspe

After St. Augustine, a less nuanced position is found in some of his Latin followers, who recognized Baptism of blood but not of desire. St. Fulgentius of Ruspe (ca. 462–533) admitted a Baptism of desire before Christ for those who had faith in his coming, but denied this could grant salvation after Christ's institution of Baptism:

> Throughout history, by the mysteries Christ has instituted through the faith of his Incarnation, they have arrived at that kingdom, those whom God has freely saved with no merits of good will or good works preceding. Just as from that time onward when our Savior said, "If anyone is not reborn from water and the Spirit, he cannot enter the Kingdom of God" [John 3:5], without the Sacrament of Baptism, apart from those who poured out their blood for Christ in the Catholic Church but without Baptism, no one can receive either the kingdom of heaven or eternal life.[39]

Nevertheless, the practice of the patristic Church of baptizing children shortly after birth but delaying the Baptism of adults until the Easter vigil, and only after the completion of a lengthy catechumenate, shows that adults were not considered to require Baptism with the same urgency as infants. This implies recognition that the grace of Baptism could have been supplied in case of sudden death

---

rites or ceremonies, we are not to think that they are different things or that there are different kinds of salvation."

[38] See Sullivan, in *Salvation Outside the Church?*, 36–37, where he argues that in his mature anti-Pelagian period St. Augustine modified his earlier position affirming the possibility of implicit Baptism of desire.

[39] Fulgentius, *To Peter on the Faith* 3.43, in *Fulgentius: Selected Works*, trans. R. B. Eno, FC 95 (Washington, DC: Catholic University of America Press, 1997), 88. This work was attributed to St. Augustine during the Middle Ages, and is cited as such by Peter Lombard.

by the very desire of the catechumen for Baptism.

Gregory the Great and Venerable Bede on the Salvation of Righteous Gentiles

St. Gregory the Great and Venerable Bede taught that the righteous who lived before the promulgation of the Gospel, such as Job, had original sin forgiven through their faith. Gregory writes: "But that which the water of Baptism avails for with us, this either faith alone did of old in behalf of infants, or, for those of riper years, the virtue of sacrifice, or, for all that came of the stock of Abraham, the mystery of circumcision."[40] Bede's teaching is very similar:

> And so that the favors of heavenly condescension might not be lacking to any period of this transitory world, those who [lived] from the inception of the world up to the time of the giving of circumcision, and those from other countries who [lived] after the giving of circumcision, also pleased God, either by the offering of sacrificial offerings, or alternatively by the virtue of faith alone, since they committed their souls and those of their own to the Creator, [and so] took care to free [themselves] from the bonds of the original guilt. For "without faith it is impossible to please God."[41]

This teaching, which became common among the scholastics,[42] implies a doctrine of Baptism of desire at least for the people who lived before the promulgation of the Gospel. In this justifying faith spoken of by Gregory and Bede, there would be an implicit desire for salvation and thus for Baptism, although neither Gregory nor Bede make this clear.

---

[40] Gregory the Great, *Morals on the Book of Job* 4.3, trans. Parker, 1:179.

[41] Bede, Homily 11, bk. 1, *On the Octave Day of Christmas*, in *Homilies on the Gospels Book One: Advent to Lent*, trans. Lawrence T. Martin, (Collegeville, MN: Cistercian Publications, 2008), 105.

[42] See St. Bernard, *Ad Hugonem de sancto Victore, Epistula seu Tractatus de Baptismo* (Letter to Hugh of St. Victor on Baptism), PL 182:1033–34; Hugh of St. Victor, *On the Sacraments of the Christian Faith* 1.12.2; Peter Lombard, *Sentences*, bk. 4, d. 1, ch. 8, trans. Silano, p. 7: "As for those who lived before circumcision, children were justified by the faith of their parents, and parents by the power of sacrifices, namely, the power which they perceived spiritually in those sacrifices."

Hugh of St. Victor

Hugh of St. Victor (1096–1141) poses the question of whether, after the promulgation of the Gospel, it is possible to be saved without receiving the sacrament of Baptism. He argues vigorously that an unbaptized person can be saved not only by Baptism of blood but also by a desire for the sacrament, inspired by faith and love, when actual reception of the sacrament is not possible. He writes:

> Yet where faith is with love, just as merit is not diminished, even if the work which is in a proposed good of devotion is not accomplished externally, so the effect of salvation is not impeded, even if the sacrament which is in true will and desire is prevented at the moment of necessity.[43]

If someone were to deny the possibility of Baptism of desire by citing John 3:5, Hugh responds that this text must be understood in harmony with other texts that speak of salvation for all who confess Christ before men and believe in Him:

> For He who said: "Unless a man be born again of the water and the Holy Ghost, he cannot enter into the kingdom of God," the same also said elsewhere: "He who shall confess me before men, I will also confess him before my Father" [Mt 10:32]. . . . Likewise He who said: "Unless a man be born again of the water and the Holy Ghost, he cannot enter into the kingdom of God," He himself said: "He who believeth in me, shall not die for ever."[44]

His conclusion, therefore, is that "to be baptized can be in the will, even when it is not in possibility, and on this account justly is good will with the devotion of its faith not despised, although in a moment of necessity he is prevented from receiving that sacrament of water which is external."[45]

---

[43] Hugh of St. Victor, *On the Sacraments of the Christian Faith* 1.9.8, trans. Deferrari, 165.

[44] Hugh of St. Victor, *On the Sacraments of the Christian Faith* 2.6.7, in Deferrari, 294.

[45] Hugh of St. Victor, *On the Sacraments of the Christian Faith* 2.6.7, in Deferrari, 294.

Hugh, however, is referring here only to those who have an explicit Baptism of desire. This he holds to be necessary after the promulgation of the Gospel, which he regards as having been fully accomplished in his time.[46] Before the full promulgation of the Gospel, however, he holds that an implicit desire would have been sufficient, as could be had by "faith operating through love" in Israel or in the just among the gentiles.[47] Hugh's view that the Gospel had been fully promulgated in the world of his time was the shared presupposition of his age (the age of Christendom).[48] It required the discovery of the New World for theologians to see the error of this presupposition, as will be seen below. His reasoning, however, leaves room for a broader application of the doctrine of an implicit Baptism of desire among those to whom the gospel has not been fully and credibly promulgated.

---

[46] See Hugh of St. Victor, *On the Sacraments of the Christian Faith* 2.6.5, in Deferrari, 292: "Now then regarding those who, situated afar off or placed nearby in hiding, were taken away from this life by chance without knowledge of the divine institution, it seems to me that we should have the same opinion as regarding those who, before the institution itself, were either in the prepuce or in the law, since what the times did for the one, absence performed for the other. Now if anyone wishes to be stubborn and contends that some of this kind still live in unknown regions and in remote seats of the world, who perhaps have not heard the divine mandate of receiving the sacrament of baptism, I affirm that either there is no such person or, should there be someone, if his sin had not prevented, he could have heard and known and was obligated without delay, especially when the Scripture clearly proclaims: 'Their sound hath gone forth unto all the earth: and their words unto the ends of the world' (Ps 18:5). If then their sound has gone forth unto all the earth, in all the earth either they have been heard and their contemners are condemned or they have not been heard according to their sin, and being ignorant they are ignored and are not saved. Such is my opinion regarding the time of the institution of baptism and regarding the obligation of receiving baptism."

[47] With regard to the just among the nations, see Hugh of St. Victor, *On the Sacraments of the Christian Faith* 1.12.2, p. 188: "Surely meanwhile whoever of the faithful were not of the seed of Abraham were not . . . held by any obligation to receive circumcision which had been imposed on the seed of Abraham only, but by faith operating through love just as formerly under the natural law, before circumcision was instituted, the just who were without circumcision were saved."

[48] This attitude begins to be manifested in the Fathers of the late fourth century after the large-scale christianization of the Roman Empire. See Sullivan, *Salvation Outside the Church?*, 23–27.

Peter Lombard

Peter Lombard takes basically the same position on this matter as Hugh. He introduces the question by making the Augustinian distinction between the outward sacramental sign and the reality of the sacrament, which is grace. He holds, with Augustine, that it is possible to receive the sacramental sign without receiving the reality of grace, because of the obstacle of lack of faith or repentance. Similarly, it is possible to receive the reality of grace without having received the sacramental sign, as long as that is not due to contempt for the sacrament. The first case of this is Baptism of blood. He then goes on to say, paraphrasing Augustine, that it is not "suffering alone which fills the role of baptism, but also faith and contrition, where necessity precludes the sacrament."[49] Peter makes an argument from the power and nobility of faith to support this: "And reason itself proves the same point. For if baptism suffices for children who are incapable of believing, much more does faith suffice for adults who are willing, but unable, to be baptized."

Peter also addresses the more rigorous text from St. Fulgentius (which he thought was by Augustine) denying Baptism of desire, by saying that what is written there must be interpreted as applying only to those who have the opportunity of receiving sacramental Baptism and are not prevented by death. He then gives a crucial principle: "For so long as he is able to satisfy the requirement [for sacramental Baptism], he is bound if he does not satisfy it; but when he is unable and yet willing, God, who did not constrain his power by [establishing] the sacraments, does not hold it against him."[50]

Innocent II

In the twelfth and thirteenth centuries, the doctrine of Baptism of desire is asserted not only in theological treatises but also in papal letters. In a letter to the bishop of Cremonia, Pope Innocent II (d. 1143) affirms that Baptism of desire remits original sin:

> The presbyter who, you said, ended his final days without the
> water of baptism we declare without hesitation to have been

---

[49] Peter Lombard, *Sentences*, bk. 4, dist. 4, ch. 4.3, trans. Silano, p. 21.
[50] Lombard, *Sentences*, bk. 4, dist. 4, ch. 4.10, p. 24.

freed from original sin and to have attained the joy of the heavenly fatherland since he persevered in the faith of Holy Mother Church and in the confession of Christ's name. In addition, read in the eighth book of Augustine's *The City of God* where, among other things, it says: "Baptism is administered invisibly when it is impeded, not by the contempt of religion, but by the barrier of necessity."[51] Likewise, go back to the book of blessed Ambrose *On the Death of Valentianus* which affirms the same doctrine.[52]

Innocent III

Pope Innocent III addressed the question of Baptism of desire in a letter to the Bishop of Metz of 1206 in which he discusses the case of a Jew who, in danger of death and living only among Jews, baptized himself in the name of the Father, the Son, and the Holy Spirit. Innocent III replied that that Baptism was invalid because no one can baptize himself. There must be a distinction of person between the minister and the recipient. This serves to sacramentally represent the fact that we receive salvation not from ourselves but from Christ. Thus the man, if he survived, would still have had to be baptized unconditionally. However, if he did not survive, the Pope said that one should not doubt about his salvation: "If, however, such a person had died immediately, he would have entered into his heavenly home without delay because of his faith in the sacrament, even if not because of the sacrament of faith."[53]

St. Thomas Aquinas

In his treatment of Baptism of blood and Baptism of desire, St. Thomas clarifies that there is only one sacrament of Baptism, administered with water and the Trinitarian form. Baptism of blood and desire are

---

[51] The correct reference is to Augustine's *On Baptism, against the Donatists* 4.22.29, as given above. Innocent II may also have been thinking of *The City of God* 13.7, which affirms Baptism of blood.

[52] Innocent II, Letter to the Bishop of Cremona *Apostolicam sedem* (DS, 741).

[53] Innocent III, Letter to Bishop Berthold of Metz *Debitum pastoralis officii*, , of (Aug 28, 1206; DS, 788).

not sacraments[54] but ways by which one can gain the primary effect of the sacrament—forgiveness of original and personal sin and the infusion of sanctifying grace, which is the *res tantum*—without receiving either the outward sign or sacramental character.[55]

St. Thomas gives a theological foundation to Baptism of blood and Baptism of desire by connecting them respectively with the Passion of Christ and the Holy Spirit. In Baptism, the Holy Spirit is the principal cause who works through the sacramental representation of Christ's death and resurrection to imprint on the soul a spiritual likeness: death to sin and rising to new supernatural life in Christ, as St. Paul explains in Romans 6:3–4. Both the Holy Spirit and the Passion of Christ are at work in the sacrament of Baptism, but of course their infinite power is not limited to the sacramental instrument and can also work outside of it.

An unbaptized person who gives his life for Christ is configured to Christ's death not sacramentally but in reality. St. Thomas writes:

> A man may, without Baptism of Water, receive the sacramental effect from Christ's Passion, in so far as he is conformed to Christ by suffering for Him. Hence it is written (Rev 7:14): "These are they who are come out of great tribulation, and have washed their robes and have made them white in the blood of the Lamb."[56]

Christ's Passion can work through the physical configuration to Christ of the unbaptized martyr to bring about the same spiritual effects in the martyr as sacramental Baptism: forgiveness of original sin (if it was not yet forgiven by Baptism of desire), the infusion of sanctifying grace (or if already possessed, an increase), and the forgiveness of the temporal punishment for sin. As mentioned above, one effect of Baptism is not given: since this configuration is not sacramental but

---

[54] See *ST* III, q. 66, a. 11, ad 2: "A sacrament is a kind of sign. The other two, however, are like the Baptism of Water, not, indeed, in the nature of sign, but in the baptismal effect. Consequently they are not sacraments." See also *In IV Sent.*, d. 4, q. 3, a. 3, qla. 1, trans. Mortensen, 7:200: "Properly speaking, there is only one baptism, which is celebrated in water under a determinate form of words. . . . The other kinds are called baptisms by their order to this baptism."

[55] See Thomas Aquinas, *In IV Sent.*, d. 4, q. 3, a. 3, qla. 1, ad 3, trans. Mortensen, 7:201.

[56] *ST* III, q. 66, a. 11.

real, it does not imprint sacramental character.

In the case of a person who has a desire for Baptism but dies without it and does not give his life for Christ, then there is neither a sacramental configuration to Christ's death and resurrection nor a configuration through the shedding of blood, but there is an inward configuration through desire and repentance. This inward configuration is the work of the Holy Spirit and configures one to Him, as the divine Person who proceeds by love. When through His actual grace one is disposed and conformed to the Holy Spirit so as to desire Baptism explicitly or implicitly, repent of one's sins, and make an act of faith, hope, and love, the Holy Spirit will work the effect of Baptism outside of the sacrament:

> In like manner a man receives the effect of Baptism by the power of the Holy Spirit, not only without Baptism of Water, but also without Baptism of Blood: forasmuch as his heart is moved by the Holy Spirit to believe in and love God and to repent of his sins: wherefore this is also called Baptism of Repentance. Of this it is written (Isaiah 4:4): "If the Lord shall wash away the filth of the daughters of Zion, and shall wash away the blood of Jerusalem out of the midst thereof, by the spirit of judgment, and by the spirit of burning." Thus, therefore, each of these other Baptisms is called Baptism, forasmuch as it takes the place of Baptism.[57]

Of the three forms of Baptism, each has an excellence proper to itself:

> As stated above [a. 11], the shedding of blood for Christ's sake, and the inward operation of the Holy Spirit, are called baptisms, in so far as they produce the effect of the Baptism of Water. Now the Baptism of Water derives its efficacy from Christ's Passion and from the Holy Spirit, as already stated. These two causes act in each of these three Baptisms; most excellently, however, in the Baptism of Blood. For Christ's Passion acts in the Baptism of Water by way of a figurative representation; in the Baptism of the Spirit or of Repentance,

---

[57] *ST* III, q. 66, a. 11. St. Thomas goes on to quote Augustine, *On Baptism, against the Donatists* 4.22.29, quoted above.

by way of desire, but in the Baptism of Blood, by way of imitating the act. In like manner, too, the power of the Holy Spirit acts in the Baptism of Water through a certain hidden power; in the Baptism of Repentance by moving the heart; but in the Baptism of Blood by the highest degree of fervor of dilection and love, according to John 15:13: "Greater love than this no man hath that a man lay down his life for his friends."[58]

St. Thomas also addresses Baptism of desire in *ST* III, q. 68, a. 2, in which he asks whether anyone can be saved without Baptism. The answer is affirmative. For his authority he cites St. Augustine's commentary on Leviticus 21:15, in which Augustine says: "Some have received the invisible sanctification without visible sacraments, and to their profit; but though it is possible to have the visible sanctification, consisting in a visible sacrament, without the invisible sanctification, it will be to no profit."[59] The good thief and the centurion Cornelius (Acts 10:44–48) are examples of receiving the invisible sanctification without (or prior to) receiving the visible sacrament, and Simon Magus is an example of the reverse. St. Thomas then comments: "Since, therefore, the sacrament of Baptism pertains to the visible sanctification, it seems that a man can obtain salvation without the sacrament of Baptism, by means of the invisible sanctification."[60] In the body of the article St. Thomas argues as follows:

> The sacrament of Baptism may be wanting to anyone in reality but not in desire: for instance, when a man wishes to be baptized, but by some ill-chance he is forestalled by death before receiving Baptism. And such a man can obtain salvation without being actually baptized, on account of his desire for Baptism, which desire is the outcome of "faith that worketh by charity," whereby God, Whose power is not tied to visible sacraments, sanctifies man inwardly. Hence Ambrose says of Valentinian, who died while yet a catechumen: "I lost him whom I was to regenerate: but he did not

---

[58] *ST* III, q. 66, a. 12.
[59] Augustine, *Questionum in Heptateuchum Libri Septem* 3.84 (on Lev 21:15), in PL 34:713.
[60] *ST* III, q. 68, a. 2, sed contra.

lose the grace he prayed for."[61]

In the reply to the third objection, St. Thomas writes that "the sacrament of Baptism is said to be necessary for salvation in so far as man cannot be saved without, at least, Baptism of desire; 'which, with God, counts for the deed.'"[62]

In the next article, St. Thomas mentions Baptism of desire as the reason why Baptism is not deferred for infants, but generally is for adults, so that they can have a fuller catechesis and receive the sacraments of Christian initiation in solemn fashion on the Easter vigil.

> For if they be children, Baptism should not be deferred. First, because in them we do not look for better instruction or fuller conversion. Secondly, because of the danger of death, for no other remedy is available for them besides the sacrament of Baptism. On the other hand, *adults have a remedy in the mere desire for Baptism*, as stated above. And therefore Baptism should not be conferred on adults as soon as they are converted, but it should be deferred until some fixed time.... This is needful as being useful for those who are baptized; for they require a certain space of time in order to be fully instructed in the faith, and to be drilled in those things that pertain to the Christian mode of life. Thirdly, a certain reverence for the sacrament demands a delay whereby men are admitted to Baptism at the principal festivities, that is, of Easter and Pentecost, the result being that they receive the sacrament with greater devotion.[63]

In other words, the existence of Baptism of desire is implied in the very practice of the Church from the first centuries by which infant Baptism is administered shortly after birth, whereas adults were baptized generally only on solemn occasions unless there was danger of death.

St. Thomas also specifies that the desire for Baptism that anticipates its effect need not be explicit, as in the catechumen, but can also

---

[61] *ST* III, q. 68, a. 2.

[62] *ST* III, q. 68, a. 2, ad 3, in which he is quoting Augustine, *Ennarationes in Psalmos*, 57.3.4 (PL 36:677).

[63] *ST* III, q. 68, a. 3.

be *implicit*, as in just pagans who do not yet know about Baptism, like the centurion Cornelius:

> Man receives the forgiveness of sins before Baptism in so far as he has Baptism of desire, explicitly or implicitly. . . . So also before Baptism Cornelius and others like him receive grace and virtues through their faith in Christ and their desire for Baptism, implicit or explicit: but afterwards when baptized, they receive a yet greater fulness of grace and virtues.[64]

Advantages of Sacramental Baptism over Baptism of Desire

If Baptism of desire already obtains the effect of justification, what is the utility of the sacrament of Baptism? St. Thomas answers that, in addition to giving a "greater fullness of grace," it is only the sacrament of Baptism that makes the baptized visible members of Christ's Body, the Church:

> Adults who already believe in Christ are incorporated in Him mentally [*mentaliter*]. But afterwards, when they are baptized, they are incorporated in Him, corporally, as it were, i.e. by the visible sacrament; without the desire of which they could not have been incorporated in Him even mentally.[65]

The sacrament of Baptism adds to desire for Baptism in five ways. First, one could not have Baptism of desire without desiring to actually receive the sacrament of Baptism, either implicitly or explicitly. Second, the sacrament adds baptismal character which makes one a visible member of the Church, configured to Christ, called to share in His mission, and capable of receiving the other sacraments. Third, baptismal character gives an abiding foundation for the sacramental graces of Baptism, which are the actual graces that help us live out the mission given by the sacrament. Fourth, actual reception of the sacrament gives a further increase of sanctifying grace and all that flows from it. Fifth, the sacrament of Baptism also removes all debt of temporal punishment for sin that would need to be expiated

---

[64] *ST* III, q. 69, a. 4, ad 2.
[65] *ST* III, q. 69, a. 5, ad 1.

in purgatory. St. Thomas explains the last point:

> The Passion of Christ is communicated to every baptized person, so that he is healed just as if he himself had suffered and died. Now Christ's Passion, as stated above (Question 68, Article 5), is a sufficient satisfaction for all the sins of all men. Consequently he who is baptized, is freed from the debt of all punishment due to him for his sins, just as if he himself had offered sufficient satisfaction for all his sins.[66]

The Councils of Florence and Trent on Baptism of Desire

The Council of Florence does not contain a teaching on Baptism of desire, such as appears in the scholastic theologians of the preceding centuries. On the contrary, it seems to exclude it on account of a vigorous affirmation of the dogma "*extra ecclesiam nulla salus*," quoting St. Fulgentius:

> She firmly believes, professes, and preaches that "none of those who are outside of the Catholic Church, not only pagans,"[67] but also Jews, heretics, and schismatics, can become sharers of eternal life, but they will go into the eternal fire . . . unless, before the end of their life, they are joined to her.[68]

However, the Council implicitly holds the notion of Baptism of desire with regard to catechumens, for in the same Bull it says that Baptism for infants should never be deferred,[69] although it is deferred for adults. As mentioned above, this implies that the catechumen is not *extra ecclesiam* in the sense that would exclude him from salvation. This implies the doctrine of Baptism of desire.[70]

Unlike Florence, the Council of Trent explicitly speaks of Baptism

---

[66] *ST* III, q. 69, a. 2.

[67] The text quotes Fulgentius, *To Peter on the Faith* 38.81, in *Fulgentius: Selected Works*, trans. Eno, 104.

[68] Council of Florence, *Cantate Domino* (DS, 1351).

[69] Council of Florence, *Cantate Domino* (DS, 1349).

[70] See the analysis by Brian Harrison in "Father Feeney and the *implicitum votum ecclesiae*," in *Living Tradition: Organ of the Roman Theological Forum* 149 (Nov 2011).

of desire in the Decree on Justification, in which it states that after the promulgation of the Gospel, one cannot be justified and adopted as a son of God "without the bath of regeneration, *or the desire for it.*"[71] Thus those who die without Baptism outside of the visible Church can still be saved through a holy desire for it. This qualification must be borne in mind to rightly understand the teaching of *Cantate Domino* in the hermeneutic of continuity.

The *Catechism of the Council of Trent* refers to Baptism of desire when speaking about the preparation of adults for Baptism. Unlike infants, adults are not to be baptized immediately (except in danger of death), but only after a fitting preparation. The *Catechism* explains: "This delay does not carry with it the same danger that we saw in the case of infants, for if any unforeseen accident should deprive adults of Baptism, their intention to receive it and their repentance for past sins will compensate for it."[72]

Sufficient Grace and the Condemnation of Calvinism and Jansenism

Further light on the possibility of Baptism of desire comes from the condemnation of a tenet of Calvinism and Jansenism that held that God does not give sufficient grace for salvation to all men but only to the predestined.[73] It is theologically certain that God makes salvation concretely possible even to those who, having attained the age of reason, are invincibly ignorant of the necessity of Baptism and entrance into the Church.[74] This possibility of salvation implies that

---

[71] Council of Trent, Decree on Justification (session 6), ch. 4 (DS, 1524).

[72] *CCT*, part 2, ch. 1, §36, p. 181.

[73] See Innocent X, Constitution *Cum occasione*, (May 31, 1653; DS, 2001), which condemns the following proposition of Cornelius Jansen: "Some of God's commandments cannot be observed by just men with the strength they have in the present state, even if they wish and strive to observe them; nor do they have the grace that would make their observance possible." See also Pius V, Bull *Ex omnibus afflictionibus*, (Oct 1, 1567; DS, 1954), which condemns the following proposition of Michael Baius (a forerunner of Jansenism): "The proposition that God has not commanded man to do the impossible is falsely attributed to Augustine, since it belongs to Pelagius."

[74] See Second Vatican Council, *LG*, §16; *Gaudium et Spes*, §22: "All this holds true not only for Christians, but for all men of good will in whose hearts grace works in an unseen way. For, since Christ died for all men, and since the ultimate vocation of man is in fact one, and divine, we ought to believe that the Holy

the essential effect of Baptism, which is the infusion of sanctifying grace and justification, can be gained by cooperation with God's grace even without reception of the sacrament of Baptism.

Catholic doctrine on this point is expressed in the axiom that God does not command the impossible but is ready to aid us with his grace if we seek His help through prayer. The Council of Trent quotes St. Augustine who says: "For God does not command the impossible, but when He commands He admonishes you to do what you can and to pray for what you cannot do,"[75] and then the Council adds, "and he helps you to be able to do it."[76] Sufficient grace is given to all, and therefore every person who attains the age of reason has the real possibility of salvation through cooperation with that grace. It could not be truly said that God desires the salvation of all if He did not give sufficient grace to all.

This raises the question of how this sufficient grace makes salvation possible for those who were never given a sufficient opportunity to know Christ, the Church, and the sacraments, so as to explicitly desire Baptism. In other words, how is salvation possible for those outside the visible Church through no fault of their own, and how is this compatible with the principle of *no salvation outside the Church*?

In response to this question theologians distinguish explicit and implicit desire for Baptism. An explicit desire to enter the Church presupposes knowledge of revelation and faith in the Church as the ark of salvation willed by God. This is the condition of catechumens. However, there can be a true *implicit* desire to enter the Church and receive Baptism even among those who are not aware that God has instituted the Catholic Church as the ark of salvation. Pius XII makes this clear in his encyclical of 1943, *Mystici Corporis Christi*, in which he speaks of "an unconscious desire and longing" by which some of those who are outside the visible Church "have a certain relationship with the Mystical Body of the Redeemer."[77]

The difference between explicit and implicit desire is that in the former case, the object of the desire is known, while in the latter

---

Spirit in a manner known only to God offers to every man the possibility of being associated with this paschal mystery."
[75] Augustine, *De natura et gratia*, ch. 43.50, PL 44:271.
[76] Council of Trent, Decree on Justification (session 6), ch. 11 (DS, 1536).
[77] Pius XII, *Mystici Corporis Christi*, §103 (DS, 3821.

the object is not directly known or intended, but is included under a broader object that is explicitly desired. For example, if one sincerely desires to do God's will in religious matters, not knowing that this entails Baptism, one would be implicitly desiring Baptism through explicitly desiring to do His will. The object of implicit desire is "folded up"[78] within the object of explicit desire.

Development of Doctrine on Invincible Ignorance

Ignorance is said to be invincible when it is not brought about by gravely culpable negligence or prejudice. When ignorance is inculpable, a person has no reason to doubt the rectitude of the judgment of his conscience, which errs only through ignorance that was not willed or self-inflicted. Ignorance is culpable or vincible, on the other hand, when it is the result of culpable negligence or prejudice, or is positively willed to avoid the suspected consequences of coming to know the truth.[79]

The notion of invincible ignorance is clearly developed in the works of St. Thomas and his contemporaries.[80] But like his contemporaries, St. Thomas thought that it was not possible to be invincibly ignorant of the Gospel in the world of his time because he thought

---

[78] The word "implicit" comes from the Latin *implico*, from *in-plico*: to fold into.

[79] See *ST* I-II, q. 6, a. 8: "Ignorance is *consequent* to the act of the will, in so far as ignorance itself is voluntary: and this happens in two ways. . . . First, because the act of the will is brought to bear on the ignorance: as when a man wishes not to know, that he may have an excuse for sin, or that he may not be withheld from sin; according to Job 21:14: 'We desire not the knowledge of Thy ways.' And this is called *affected ignorance.*—Secondly, ignorance is said to be voluntary, when it regards that which one can and ought to know: for in this sense *not to act* and *not to will* are said to be voluntary. . . . And ignorance of this kind happens, either when one does not actually consider what one can and ought to consider;—this is called *ignorance of evil choice*, and arises from some passion or habit: or when one does not take the trouble to acquire the knowledge which one ought to have; in which sense, ignorance of the general principles of law, which one ought to know, is voluntary, as being due to negligence."

[80] See *ST* I-II, q. 6, a. 8: "Ignorance is *antecedent* to the act of the will, when it is not voluntary, and yet is the cause of man's willing what he would not will otherwise. Thus a man may be ignorant of some circumstance of his act, which he was not bound to know, the result being that he does that which he would not do, if he knew of that circumstance; for instance, a man, after taking proper precaution, may not know that someone is coming along the road, so that he shoots an arrow and slays a passer-by. Such ignorance causes involuntariness simply."

that the Gospel had been sufficiently promulgated in the whole world.[81] The discovery of the New World, however, which made it obvious that millions of human beings then living had never heard the Gospel, led the theologians of the sixteenth century to reevaluate that unreasonable assumption. Among the first to do so was a Flemish anti-Calvinist controversialist, Albert Pigge (1490–1542), who wrote:

> This is altogether certain: that it is impossible to establish the same time by which it can be said, or could ever be said, that the Gospel was sufficiently promulgated to everyone. For God has not determined the same time for the calling of all nations. For even now, in many regions of the world, there are many nations on whom the light of the Savior has not shone, and a greatly increasing number to whom this light is only now beginning to shine through our missionaries. There can be no doubt that such peoples are in the same condition that Cornelius was in before he was instructed in the faith by Peter.[82]

This idea that invincible ignorance with regard to Christianity could still exist in many parts of the world was accepted and developed by theologians such as the Dominicans Francisco de Vitoria (1493–1546)[83] and Domingo Soto (1494–1560),[84] and the Jesuits Francisco Suárez (1548–1619)[85] and Juan de Lugo (1583–1660),[86] and gradually became a common teaching.

Francisco de Vitoria, in his work, *On the American Indians*, stressed that people could remain invincibly ignorant even if the Gospel were announced to them, but without sufficient motives of credibility: "The barbarians are not bound to believe from the first moment that the Christian faith is announced to them, in the sense of committing a mortal sin merely by not believing a simple announcement, unaccompanied by miracles or any other kind of proof or persuasion."[87] Indeed,

---

[81] See Sullivan, *Salvation Outside the Church?*, 52–58; Thomas Aquinas, *De veritate*, q. 14, a. 11, ad 1; *In III Sent.*, d. 25. q. 2, a. 1, qla. 1, ad 1.

[82] Albert Pigge, *De libero hominis arbitrio*, bk. 10, fol. 180c–181r, in Sullivan, *Salvation Outside the Church?*, 78–79.

[83] See Sullivan, *Salvation Outside the Church?*, 70–73.

[84] See Sullivan, *Salvation Outside the Church?*, 75–76.

[85] See Sullivan, *Salvation Outside the Church?*, 91–94.

[86] See Sullivan, *Salvation Outside the Church?*, 94–98.

[87] Francisco de Vitoria, *On the American Indians* 2.3–4, in *Vitoria: Political Writ-*

he holds, reasonably, that the scandalous acts of Christians can be responsible for continued invincible ignorance.

> It is not sufficiently clear to me that the Christian faith has up to now been announced and set before the barbarians in such a way as to oblige them to believe it under pain of fresh sin. By this I mean that . . . they are not bound to believe unless the faith has been set before them with persuasive probability. But I have not heard of any miracles or signs, nor of any exemplary saintliness of life sufficient to convert them. On the contrary, I hear only of provocations, savage crimes, and multitudes of unholy acts. From this, it does not appear that the Christian religion has been preached to them in a sufficiently pious way to oblige their acquiescence.[88]

The reasoning used by Vitoria with regard to the American Indians can also be applied to Jews faced with the scandal of anti-semitism, and many other groups.

Juan de Lugo added an important consideration. He argued that a first contact with the proclamation of the Gospel normally does not immediately provide a moral obligation to assent to the faith, but an obligation to look into it more fully and seek its motives of credibility. Inculpable ignorance implies that one is not culpable of the ignorance through negligence but has taken due diligence to remove it.

> Thus, while a first preaching of the faith might not suffice to impose a proximate obligation of believing, it could suffice for a remote obligation. People in this situation, of whom there are a great many nowadays, among the heretics, the pagans, and especially among the Turks and other Moslems, if they do not exercise the required diligence [in inquiring further], will no longer have an ignorance that is invincible and inculpable. However, if they do exercise the required diligence, but still are not able to find sufficient knowledge for a prudent decision to embrace the Christian faith, their ignorance will still

---

ings, ed. Anthony Pagden and Jeremy Lawrance (Cambridge: Cambridge University Press, 2010), 269.

[88] De Vitoria, *On the American Indians* 2.3–4, in Pagden and Lawrance, 271.

remain invincible.[89]

The existence of invincible ignorance with regard to Christian faith first enters papal Magisterium in the nineteenth century with Bl. Pius IX in an encyclical of 1854, *Singulari Quadam*. He warns, however, that only God knows how far invincible ignorance extends:

> It is necessary to hold for certain that they who labor in ignorance of the true religion, if this ignorance is invincible, are not stained by any guilt in this matter in the eyes of God. Now, in truth, who would arrogate so much to himself as to mark the limits of such an ignorance, because of the nature and variety of peoples, regions, innate dispositions, and of so many other things?[90]

He returned to this subject in an encyclical of 1863:

> We know as well as you that those who suffer from invincible ignorance with regard to our most holy religion, by carefully keeping the natural law and its precepts, which have been written by God in the hearts of all, by being disposed to obey God and to lead a virtuous and correct life, can, by the power of divine light and grace, attain eternal life. For God, who sees, examines, and knows completely the minds and souls, the thoughts and qualities of all, will not permit, in his infinite goodness and mercy, anyone who is not guilty of a voluntary fault to suffer eternal punishment.[91]

Explicit and Implicit Desire for Baptism: The Letter of the Holy Office to Archbishop Cushing of 1949

In those who are invincibly ignorant of the truth of Christian faith,

---

[89] De Lugo, *De virtute fidei divinae*, disp. 18, no. 25 (Lyon, 1646), 496, translated in Sullivan, *Salvation Outside the Church?*, 97.

[90] Pius IX, *Singulari Quadam*, in Denzinger, *Sources of Catholic Dogma*, trans. Roy Deferrari, 13th ed., §1647.

[91] Pius IX, *Quanto Conficiamur Moerore* (DS, 2866). For the context of these two texts by Pius IX, see Sullivan, *Salvation Outside the Church?*, 112–19.

the desire for Baptism would be implicit rather than explicit. In his encyclical on the Church *Mystici Corporis Christi* from 1943, Pius XII mentions an "unconscious desire" for membership in the Church, which implies a desire for Baptism. He acknowledges that such a desire gives one "a relationship with the Mystical Body" with its power of salvation, but also highlights the uncertainty of this state in which one lacks many divine aids, such as the sacraments and sacramental grace. He invites those

> who do not belong to the visible Body of the Catholic Church ... to seek to withdraw from that state in which they cannot be sure of their salvation. For even though by an unconscious desire and longing they have a certain relationship with the Mystical Body of the Redeemer, they still remain deprived of those many heavenly gifts and helps which can only be enjoyed in the Catholic Church.[92]

More clarification of this "unconscious desire" was given in an important letter of the Holy Office (predecessor of the Congregation for the Doctrine of the Faith) from 1949, approved by Pius XII, to the Bishop of Boston. A priest of that diocese, Fr. Leonard Feeney, S.J., held a rigorist view on the matter, denying the possibility of salvation through an implicit desire for Baptism on the basis of the axiom that there is "no salvation outside of the Church."[93] The Holy Office affirmed the possibility of salvation for those outside the Church who have invincible ignorance and a true and efficacious desire to follow God's will for their salvation. Such a desire would implicitly include a desire to enter the Church through Baptism if they knew it was the ark of salvation.

The Letter defines this implicit salvific desire as follows:

> However, this desire need not always be explicit, as it is in catechumens; but when a person is involved in invincible ignorance God accepts also an implicit desire, so called because it is included in that good disposition of soul whereby a person wishes his will to be conformed to the will of God.[94]

---

[92] Pius XII, *Mystici Corporis Christi*, §103 (DS, 3821).

[93] For context, see Sullivan, *Salvation Outside the Church?*, 135–40.

[94] Holy Office, Letter of Aug 8, 1949 to the Archbishop of Boston (DS, 3870).

Here it is clear how the implicit desire for Baptism is included in an explicit desire to be conformed to God's will.

The Letter adds that an implicit (or explicit) desire for Baptism must be accompanied by some crucial conditions without which it cannot be fruitful in anticipating the grace of Baptism:

> Nor must it be thought that any kind of desire of entering the Church suffices for one to be saved. It is necessary that the desire by which one is related to the Church be animated by perfect charity. The implicit desire can produce no effect unless a person has supernatural faith.[95]

The document here quotes Hebrews 11:6, which points to the necessity of an act of faith and hope: "Without faith it is impossible to please him. For whoever would draw near to God must believe that he exists and that he rewards those who seek him." The habit of supernatural faith does not refer to the full knowledge of what God has revealed but to the disposition to assent firmly to God's Revelation on account of His authority and truth. One can have this disposition of faith without having been exposed to the fullness of Revelation. The faith that God "rewards those who seek Him" also implies the habit of hope. The necessity of "perfect charity" means that the contrition for sin that accompanies the desire for salvation must be perfect—motivated by love for God—rather than imperfect, which is motivated only by shame or fear of hell.

In summary, this Letter from the Holy Office stipulates various conditions for a desire for Baptism to gain its salvific effect. There must be invincible ignorance, which excludes religious indifferentism or grave negligence; there must be the sincere desire to do the will of God as known by conscience; there must be supernatural faith, hope, and charity (made possible by actual grace); and there must be contrition for grave sins.

Vatican II and Post-Conciliar Magisterium on Baptism of Desire and the Necessity of Baptism

The most authoritative statement of the Magisterium on the possibil-

---

[95] Holy Office, Letter of Aug 8, 1949 to the Archbishop of Boston (DS, 3872). On the necessity of faith for salvation according to the Catholic theological tradition, see Lombardi, *The Salvation of the Unbeliever*, 26–99.

ity of implicit desire for Baptism is found in *Lumen Gentium*, §§14–16. *Lumen Gentium*, §14 explains how Catholics should understand the principle, *extra ecclesiam nulla salus*:

> Basing itself upon Sacred Scripture and Tradition, [this sacred synod] teaches that the Church, now sojourning on earth as an exile, is necessary for salvation. Christ, present to us in His Body, which is the Church, is the one Mediator and the unique way of salvation. In explicit terms He Himself affirmed the necessity of faith and baptism and thereby affirmed also the necessity of the Church, for through baptism as through a door men enter the Church. *Whosoever*, therefore, *knowing that the Catholic Church was made necessary by Christ, would refuse to enter or to remain in it, could not be saved.*[96]

All men are called to the Church, and all salvation comes from the redemptive sacrifice of Christ made present to us in the Church through her sacraments. Not all unbelievers, however, have the possibility of knowing that the "Church was made necessary by Christ," and thus their ignorance would not be culpable, and they could still be saved. Those, on the other hand, who are aware of the obligation but still refuse to enter, through causes such as prejudice, fear of worldly disadvantage or suffering, or indifference, have blocked the door to salvation. In other words, *Lumen Gentium*, §14 teaches that the dogma, "no salvation outside the Church," must be understood to refer only to those who are not invincibly ignorant of her necessity and still obstinately choose not to enter the Church through Baptism.

Lumen Gentium, §16 speaks of the possibility of salvation for those who are invincibly ignorant:

> Those also can attain to salvation who through no fault of their own do not know the Gospel of Christ or His Church, yet sincerely seek God and moved by grace strive by their deeds to do His will as it is known to them through the dictates of conscience. Nor does Divine Providence deny the helps necessary for salvation to those who, without blame on their part, have not yet arrived at an explicit knowledge of God and with His grace strive to live a good life.

---

[96] My italics. See also Pius IX, *Quanto Conficiamur Moerore* (DS, 2867).

People who are in invincible ignorance, like everyone else, can only be saved through the aid of God's grace. This grace would allow them to make an act of desire that is animated by faith, hope, and love. Invincible ignorance, being something purely negative, is not sufficient for salvation. There must be, through the aid of grace, an implicit desire for Baptism and the Church enfolded within a sincere seeking for God and His will as made known "through the dictates of conscience." Although *Lumen Gentium*, §16 does not state this explicitly, seeking the will of God should be understood to contain this implicit desire for Baptism and for the Church, and contrition for grave sins of which they are aware in conscience.

Even though people who do not know the Gospel through no fault of their own can still be saved through grace and an upright conscience, *Lumen Gentium*, §16 suggests that such salvation is very difficult, for "often men, deceived by the Evil One, have become vain in their reasonings and have exchanged the truth of God for a lie, serving the creature rather than the Creator." Others, "living and dying in this world without God, are exposed to final despair."[97] Therefore, the missionary activity of the Church is always a pressing obligation of charity. *Lumen Gentium*, §17 enumerates the indispensable benefits worked by missionaries:

> For the Church is compelled by the Holy Spirit to do her part that God's plan may be fully realized, whereby He has constituted Christ as the source of salvation for the whole world. By the proclamation of the Gospel she prepares her hearers to receive and profess the faith. She gives them the dispositions necessary for baptism, snatches them from the slavery of error and of idols and incorporates them in Christ so that through charity they may grow up into full maturity in Christ. Through her work, whatever good is in the minds and hearts of men, whatever good lies latent in the religious practices and cultures of diverse peoples, is not only saved from destruction but is also cleansed, raised up and perfected unto the glory of God, the confusion of the devil and the happiness of man. The obligation of spreading the faith is imposed on every disciple

---

[97] See the illuminating treatment of *LG*, §16 in Ralph Martin, *Will Many Be Saved?: What Vatican II Actually Teaches and Its Implications for the New Evangelization* (Grand Rapids, MI: Wm. B. Eerdmans, 2012).

of Christ, according to his state.

Even though following an erring conscience through invincible ignorance excuses one from culpability, it is still a tragic state of affairs,
for it blocks the achievement of the full good that could have been
achieved if one had not been ignorant. Such persons are not able to
know the full truth about Christ, His Church, and the price of our
Redemption, and to attain to the full sacramental channels of grace so
as to renew all things in Christ.

Gaudium et Spes, §22 also treats the theme of an implicit desire
for Baptism and union with Christ. After speaking of the centrality of
Christ, the Pastoral Constitution goes on to state:

> All this holds true not only for Christians, but for all men of
> good will in whose hearts grace works in an unseen way. For,
> since Christ died for all men, and since the ultimate vocation
> of man is in fact one, and divine, we ought to believe that
> the Holy Spirit in a manner known only to God offers to
> every man the possibility of being associated with this paschal
> mystery.

The conciliar text does not spell out how the Holy Spirit offers to
every man this possibility of salvation in Christ's Paschal mystery. In
the light of the development of doctrine on this issue, we can infer that
actual grace, which is offered in a sufficient way to all men, invites and
makes possible (but does not necessarily bring about)[98] a response of
desire for union with God and of repentance for grave sin. This desire
aroused by grace includes an implicit desire for Baptism that anticipates, through the divine mercy, Baptism's principal effects, which are
the infusion of sanctifying grace and charity, by which one dies to sin
and rises to new life in Christ.

The number of people who are saved in this way is "known only
to God," as stated in the Credo of the People of God, promulgated by
St. Paul VI in 1968:

> We believe that the Church is necessary for salvation, because

---

[98] God's prevenient or operative grace makes possible a free cooperation in that
divine initiative. See Feingold, "God's Movement of the Soul through Operative and Cooperative Grace," in *Thomism and Predestination*, 166–91.

Christ, who is the sole mediator and way of salvation, renders Himself present for us in His body which is the Church. But the divine design of salvation embraces all men, and those who without fault on their part do not know the Gospel of Christ and His Church, but seek God sincerely, and under the influence of grace endeavor to do His will as recognized through the promptings of their conscience, they, in a number known only to God, can obtain salvation. [99]

Baptism of desire is also briefly mentioned in the *Code of Canon Law*, canon 849, which states that Baptism is "the gateway to the sacraments and necessary for salvation by actual reception or at least by desire."

In *Redemptoris Missio*, John Paul II touches on implicit Baptism of desire, stressing God's universal salvific will:

The universality of salvation means that it is granted not only to those who explicitly believe in Christ and have entered the Church. Since salvation is offered to all, it must be made concretely available to all. But it is clear that today, as in the past, many people do not have an opportunity to come to know or accept the gospel revelation or to enter the Church. The social and cultural conditions in which they live do not permit this, and frequently they have been brought up in other religious traditions. For such people salvation in Christ is accessible by virtue of a grace which, while having a mysterious relationship to the Church, does not make them formally part of the Church but enlightens them in a way which is accommodated to their spiritual and material situation. This grace comes from Christ; it is the result of his Sacrifice and is communicated by the Holy Spirit. It enables each person to attain salvation through his or her free cooperation.[100]

John Paul II then goes on to quote the text from *Gaudium et Spes*, §22, given above. He also emphasizes that the possibility of salvation

---

[99] Paul VI, Credo of the People of God *Solemni hac Liturgia* (June 30, 1968), §23. See also Pius XII, *Mystici Corporis Christi*, §103 (DS, 3821).

[100] John Paul II, Encyclical on the Permanent Validity of the Church's Missionary Mandate *Redemptoris Missio* (Dec 7, 1990), §10.

through Baptism of desire does not lessen the urgency of the Church's mission to evangelize the nations, because every man has a right to know the truth about Christ, who died for every man:

> Newness of life in him is the "Good News" for men and women of every age: all are called to it and destined for it. Indeed, all people are searching for it, albeit at times in a confused way, and have a right to know the value of this gift and to approach it freely. The Church, and every individual Christian within her, may not keep hidden or monopolize this newness and richness which has been received from God's bounty in order to be communicated to all mankind.[101]

The *Catechism of the Catholic Church* treats the issue of the Baptism of desire in §§1257–1261. The explicit desire of catechumens is explained in §1259: "For *catechumens* who die before their Baptism, their explicit desire to receive it, together with repentance for their sins, and charity, assures them the salvation that they were not able to receive through the sacrament." The Second Vatican Council's Decree on Missionary Activity, *Ad Gentes*, states that catechumens "are joined to the Church, they are already of the household of Christ, and not seldom they are already leading a life of faith, hope, and charity."[102] To live the life of the theological virtues presupposes sanctifying grace, which they can receive through their desire for Baptism.

The more difficult case of implicit desire in those who are invincibly ignorant of the necessity of Baptism is discussed in §1260. After citing *Lumen Gentium*, §16, it states:

> Every man who is ignorant of the Gospel of Christ and of his Church, but seeks the truth and does the will of God in accordance with his understanding of it, can be saved. It may be supposed that such persons would have *desired Baptism explicitly* if they had known its necessity.

---

[101] John Paul II, *Redemptoris Missio*, §11.

[102] Second Vatican Council, Decree on the Mission Activity of the Church, *Ad Gentes* (Dec 7, 1965), §14. This is quoted in *CCC*, §1249. See CIC, can. 206, §1: "Catechumens, that is, those who ask by explicit choice under the influence of the Holy Spirit to be incorporated into the Church, are joined to it in a special way. By this same desire, just as by the life of faith, hope, and charity which they lead, they are united with the Church which already cherishes them as its own."

Spiritual Communion

Baptism is not the only sacrament whose principal effect can be received without receiving the sacrament. The Church teaches that the effects of grace of the Eucharist and increased union with the Lord can be obtained not only from sacramental reception of Holy Communion but also from a fervent desire to receive the sacrament. This is usually referred to as spiritual communion, which involves receiving the effect of the grace of Holy Communion even though one cannot receive sacramentally but only in desire.

The importance of this question comes from the fact that Jesus speaks in very strong terms about the necessity of Holy Communion for salvation in John 6:53–54: "Truly, truly, I say to you, unless you eat the flesh of the Son of man and drink his blood, you have no life in you; he who eats my flesh and drinks my blood has eternal life." If the Eucharist is necessary for salvation and for spiritual nourishment, there must be some means by which the grace of the sacrament can still be received by those who, because of inculpable ignorance or other causes, are unable to receive the Eucharist sacramentally. As in the case of Baptism, this grace is made available through desire for the sacrament working through faith, hope, and charity.

St. Augustine

We have seen above in chapter 7 on sacramental character that St. Augustine distinguished the sacrament from its effect of grace: "The sacrament is one thing, the efficacy of the sacrament another."[103] The notion of spiritual communion is contained in germ in this Augustinian distinction between reception of the reality of grace communicated by the sacrament, which is the communion of the Mystical Body, and mere reception of the sacrament without its spiritual fruit due to the lack of proper dispositions. Unworthy communion is receiving the sacrament without its corresponding reality of grace or communion with Christ and the Church.[104] Those who receive unworthily receive both

---

[103] Augustine, Tractate 26.11.2 on John 6:49, in *Tractates on the Gospel of John 11–27*, 268.

[104] See Augustine, Tractate 26.15.3 on John 6:55, in *Tractates on the Gospel of John 11–27*, 273: "The sacrament of this reality, that is, of the unity of the body and blood of Christ, is provided at the Lord's table, in some places daily, in other places with certain intervals of days; and it is taken from the Lord's table: for

the sacramental sign and the *res et sacramentum*, which is the Real Presence of Christ's Body and Blood, but fail to receive its spiritual effect, which is salvific communion. St. Augustine refers to this as eating sacramentally but not spiritually. Those who receive worthily receive both the sacrament and its spiritual effect, which is communion with Christ and His Mystical Body, and thus receive both sacramentally and spiritually. He exhorts the faithful: "See to it, therefore, brothers; eat the heavenly bread spiritually."[105]

Thus some receive sacramentally and not spiritually, and others both. Is it possible to receive spiritually and not sacramentally, which would be a spiritual communion? St. Augustine answers affirmatively by citing 1 Corinthians 10:3–4. Speaking of the Israelites in the Exodus, St. Paul says that "all ate the same supernatural food and all drank the same supernatural drink. For they drank from the supernatural Rock which followed them, and the Rock was Christ." St. Augustine concludes that the just among the Israelites received Christ spiritually (through their faith, hope, and charity): "Because they understood the visible food spiritually, they hungered spiritually, they tasted spiritually, that they might be filled spiritually."[106] St. Augustine, therefore, speaks of three kinds of reception of the Eucharist: sacramentally alone (unworthy and thus unfruitful communion), both sacramentally and spiritually (fruitful sacramental reception), and spiritually alone (which corresponds to our spiritual communion).

Peter Lombard commented on this text of St. Augustine in his *Sentences*,[107] which gave this distinction of three kinds of reception of the Eucharist an important place in scholastic discussions on the Eucharist.

St. Thomas Aquinas on Spiritual Communion

St. Thomas, following St. Augustine, holds that Jesus's words on the necessity of eating His Body and drinking His Blood so as to have

---

some, for life, for some, for destruction. But the reality of which it is the sacrament is for every man for life, for no man for destruction, whoever shall have been a sharer in it."

[105] Augustine, Tractate 26.11.2 on John 6:49, in *Tractates on the Gospel of John 11–27*, 268.

[106] Augustine, Tractate 26.11.1 on John 6:49, in *Tractates on the Gospel of John 11–27*, 268.

[107] Peter Lombard, Sentences, bk. 4, dist. 9.

spiritual life are to be understood as eating "spiritually," but not necessarily sacramentally.[108] In order to have eternal life, we must receive the
essential effect of the Eucharist, its *res tantum*, which is communion
with Christ.

He treats spiritual communion in an article in which he asks
whether reception of the Eucharist is necessary for salvation, as implied
by the strong words of John 6:54. He answers by distinguishing the
sacramental sign from the reality communicated by the sacrament (*res*).
The reality communicated by the sacrament is ecclesial life in Christ,
the communion of the mystical Body, which is necessary for salvation.
This communion can be had, however, not only through reception of
the sacrament but also through desire for it. Thus reception of the
Eucharist, at least by desire, is necessary for salvation:

> Two things have to be considered in this sacrament, namely,
> the sacrament itself, and what is contained in it. . . . The
> reality [*res*] of the sacrament is the unity of the mystical body,
> without which there can be no salvation; for there is no enter-
> ing into salvation outside the Church, just as in the time of
> the deluge there was none outside the Ark, which denotes the
> Church, according to 1 Peter 3:20-21. And it has been said
> above (q. 68, a. 2), that *before receiving a sacrament, the reality
> of the sacrament can be had through the very desire of receiving the
> sacrament. Accordingly, before actual reception of this sacrament, a
> man can obtain salvation through the desire of receiving it,* just as
> he can before Baptism through the desire of Baptism.[109]

St. Thomas then goes on to distinguish the necessity of the Eucharist from that of Baptism. The latter is necessary as the gateway to and
birth of the entire spiritual life. The Eucharist is necessary as the consummation of union with Christ and His Mystical Body, to which all
the other sacraments are intrinsically ordered:

> Yet there is a difference in two respects. First of all, because
> Baptism is the beginning of the spiritual life, and the door of the
> sacraments; whereas the Eucharist is, as it were, the consum-

---

[108] *ST* III, q. 65, a. 4, ad 2. St. Thomas is drawing here on Augustine, Tractate 26
on John 6:41–59 (PL 35:1614).
[109] *ST* III, q. 73, a. 3 (my italics).

mation of the spiritual life, and the end of all the sacraments, as was observed above (q. 63, a. 6): for by the sanctification of all the sacraments preparation is made for receiving or consecrating the Eucharist. Consequently, *the reception of Baptism is necessary for starting the spiritual life, while the receiving of the Eucharist is required for its consummation; by partaking not indeed actually, but in desire*, as an end is possessed in desire and intention.[110]

In the first millennium, children ordinarily received First Communion immediately after their Baptism.[111] By the time of St. Thomas, that custom had become less common in the West. In order to explain the legitimacy of the separation of Communion from Baptism, St. Thomas argues that reception of Baptism, even in infants, generates a desire for the Eucharist by which they receive the reality of the sacrament. For this reason, St. Thomas holds that the reception of Baptism in infants accomplishes in them an ordering to the Eucharist by which they receive its reality of grace in advance. This should not be understood as a conscious or elicited act of desire in infants (as it would be in adults) but rather as an habitual inclination of grace brought about by the grace of Baptism.

A personal desire for Baptism, on the other hand, requires the age of reason, by which one can cooperate with grace so as to order oneself to God as one's end.[112] Thus St. Thomas held that baptized infants have a desire for the Eucharist in virtue of Baptism, whereas unbaptized infants do not have a desire for any of the sacraments simply in virtue of human nature. This desire can be formulated only by a person at the age of reason and with the aid of grace. For this reason St. Thomas concluded that infants have a greater need to receive the sacrament of Baptism than the Eucharist even though they need the grace (*res*) of the Eucharist as well as Baptism:

> Another difference is because by Baptism a man is ordained to the Eucharist, and therefore from the fact of children being baptized, they are destined by the Church to the Eucharist; and just as they believe through the Church's faith, so they

---

[110] *ST* III, q. 73, a. 3 (my italics).

[111] See Newman, *An Essay on the Development of Christian Doctrine*, 133.

[112] See *ST* I-II, q. 89, a. 6.

desire the Eucharist through the Church's intention, and, as a result, receive its reality. But they are not disposed for Baptism by any previous sacrament, and consequently before receiving Baptism, in no way have they Baptism in desire; but adults alone have. Consequently, they cannot have the reality of the sacrament without receiving the sacrament itself. Therefore this sacrament is not necessary for salvation in the same way as Baptism is.[113]

St. Thomas returns to this theme in *ST* III, q. 79, a. 1, ad 1, in which he is treating the grace given by the Eucharist. An objection argues that the Eucharist does not give grace because initial grace is given by Baptism and its growth by Confirmation. Thus there does not seem to be any necessity for an additional sacrament to give grace. He responds by making the strong affirmation, in harmony with John 6:54, that no one has grace except through the Eucharist, whether received sacramentally or by desire:

> This sacrament has of itself the power of bestowing grace; nor does anyone possess grace before receiving this sacrament except from some desire thereof; from his own desire, as in the case of the adult; or from the Church's desire in the case of children, as stated above (q. 73, a. 3). Hence it is due to the efficacy of its power, that even from desire thereof a man procures grace whereby he is enabled to lead the spiritual life.

St. Thomas explains that desire for the Eucharist, or spiritual communion, can be in those who know about the sacrament but cannot receive it at that time, but also in those who do not directly know about it. Thus the Israelites received the effect of Communion in desire through receiving the types that prefigured it:

> The effect of the sacrament can be secured by every man if he receive it in desire, though not in reality. Consequently, just as some are baptized with the Baptism of desire, through their desire of baptism, before being baptized in the Baptism of water; so likewise some eat this sacrament spiritually before they receive it sacramentally. Now this happens in two ways.

---

[113] *ST* III, q. 73, a. 3.

First of all, from desire of receiving the sacrament itself, and thus are said to be baptized, and to eat spiritually, and not sacramentally, they who desire to receive these sacraments since they have been instituted. Secondly, by a figure: thus the Apostle says (1 Corinthians 10:2), that the fathers of old were "baptized in the cloud and in the sea," and that "they did eat . . . spiritual food, and . . . drank . . . spiritual drink." Nevertheless sacramental eating is not useless, because the actual receiving of the sacrament produces more fully the effect of the sacrament than does the desire thereof.[114]

Thus, as in the case of desire for Baptism, we can speak both of explicit as well as implicit spiritual communion.

The Council of Trent to the Present

The Council of Trent clearly teaches the common doctrine that some of the effects of Holy Communion can be gained by devout desire for it. It adopts the threefold distinction made by St. Augustine and St. Thomas between unfruitful sacramental reception, fruitful spiritual non-sacramental reception, and fruitful sacramental reception:

As regards the use, our Fathers have correctly and appropriately distinguished three ways of receiving this holy Sacrament. They teach that some receive it only *sacramentally* because they are sinners. Others receive it only *spiritually*; they are the ones who, receiving in desire the heavenly bread put before them, with a living faith "working through love" [Gal 5:6], experience its fruit and benefit from it. The third group receive it both sacramentally and spiritually; they are the ones who examine and prepare themselves beforehand to approach this divine table, clothed in the wedding garment.[115]

Nevertheless, Trent recommends that the faithful "frequently" receive, not just spiritually, but also sacramentally,[116] and exhorts the faithful

---

[114] *ST* III, q. 80, a. 1, ad 3.
[115] Council of Trent, Decree on the Sacrament of the Eucharist (session 13), ch. 8 (DS, 1648).
[116] Council of Trent, Decree on the Sacrament of the Eucharist (session 13), ch. 8

when they attend Mass "to communicate not only by a spiritual communion but also by a sacramental one, so that they may obtain more abundant fruit from this most holy sacrifice."[117]

St. Teresa of Avila earnestly recommends the practice of spiritual communion to her sisters in *The Way of Perfection*:

> When you do not receive Communion, daughters, but hear Mass, you can make a spiritual communion. Spiritual communion is highly beneficial; through it you can recollect yourselves in the same way after Mass, for the love of this Lord is thereby deeply impressed on the soul. . . . It is like approaching a fire; even though the fire may be a large one, it will not be able to warm you well if you turn away and hide your hands. . . . But it is something else if we desire to approach Him. If the soul is disposed (I mean, if it wants to get warm), and if it remains there for a while, it will stay warm for many hours.[118]

Pope Pius XII praises the practice of spiritual communion in *Mediator Dei*, §117:

> She wishes in the first place that Christians—especially when they cannot easily receive holy communion—should do so at least by desire, so that with renewed faith, reverence, humility and complete trust in the goodness of the divine Redeemer, they may be united to Him in the spirit of the most ardent charity.

John Paul II extolled the value of spiritual communion in *Ecclesia de Eucharistia*:

> The Eucharist thus appears as the culmination of all the sacraments in perfecting our communion with God the Father

---

(DS, 1649).

[117] See Council of Trent, Doctrine and Canons on the Sacrifice of the Mass (session 22), ch. 6 (DS, 1747).

[118] Teresa of Avila, *The Way of Perfection*, 35.1, in *The Collected Works of St. Teresa of Avila*, vol. 2, trans. Otilio Rodriguez, O.C.D. and Kieran Kavanaugh, O.C.D. (Washington, DC: ICS Publications, 2000), 174–75.

by identification with his only-begotten Son through the working of the Holy Spirit. With discerning faith a distinguished writer of the Byzantine tradition voiced this truth: in the Eucharist "unlike any other sacrament, the mystery [of communion] is so perfect that it brings us to the heights of every good thing: here is the ultimate goal of every human desire, because here we attain God and God joins himself to us in the most perfect union."[119] Precisely for this reason it is good to *cultivate in our hearts a constant desire for the sacrament of the Eucharist*. This was the origin of the practice of "spiritual communion," which has happily been established in the Church for centuries and recommended by saints who were masters of the spiritual life.[120]

He goes on to quote the text of St. Teresa of Avila on spiritual communion from *The Way of Perfection*. Cultivating a "constant desire" for the Eucharist both nourishes the soul in the present and strengthens the fruitfulness of subsequent reception of sacramental Communion by increasing our habitual disposition of hunger and thirst for the sacrament.

When the effects of the sacraments are received through desire for the sacrament, the *res et sacramentum* is never received. Thus those who are justified by desire for Baptism do not receive baptismal character. Similarly, Christ's Body and Blood, which is the *reality and sign* of the Eucharist, is not made present and received in a spiritual communion. Only the *res tantum*, the effects of Christ's grace, are received. This means that there is a very significant difference between a spiritual and a sacramental communion. Only the latter involves receiving the whole of Christ's humanity into our bodies, where He abides until the digestive process corrupts the sacramental species, at which point the Real Presence ceases.

Protestants who do not have a valid Eucharist do not receive Christ sacramentally in Holy Communion, which means that they are not receiving His Body and Blood into their bodies. They can be receiving some of the graces that are the effect of Communion, however, by an explicit desire to receive Him, as long as they are in a state of grace and seek to grow in union.

---

[119] Nicolas Cabasilas, *Life in Christ*, IV, 10.
[120] John Paul II, *Ecclesia de Eucharistia*, §34 (italics original).

As in the case of desire for Baptism, there are conditions for receiving the grace of the sacrament without the sacrament itself. Since the Eucharist is a "sacrament of the living," one must be in a state of grace and desire to be united with the Lord through charity. Those in a state of mortal sin can certainly have a profitable desire for Holy Communion, which should help to lead them to repentance. Without repentance leading to an act of perfect contrition, however, sanctifying grace and the spiritual effects of Communion cannot yet be received. Spiritual communion, therefore, in those aware of mortal sin, presupposes the desire for Penance and perfect contrition.[121]

Like Baptism, some of the effects of grace of this sacrament can be received through implicit as well as explicit desire. This would have been the case in the desire of the people of Israel for intimate union with God, and today of Jews, Muslims, and others who have Baptism of desire and wish to be intimately united with God.

Desire for the Sacrament of Penance

The sacrament of Penance also admits an anticipation of its proper sacramental effect of the forgiveness of sins through a desire to receive the sacrament accompanied by an act of perfect contrition. As in the case of Baptism, there has been a long development of this doctrine.

Desire for Penance in the Practice of the Early Church

The doctrine that a desire for sacramental Reconciliation can anticipate the effect of the sacrament seems to be implicit in the practice of the early Church that limited public penance to one time only. Those who fell into grave sin a second time after completing public penance were not permitted to receive public penance again or to be reconciled with the Church, although they might receive viaticum in danger of death. St. Augustine explains the practice of the Church

---

[121] See Feingold, *The Eucharist*, 530–31; Benoît-Dominique de La Soujeole, O.P., "Communion sacramentelle et communion spirituelle," *Nova et Vetera* (French) 86 (2011): 147–53; Paul Jerome Keller, "Is Spiritual Communion for Everyone?" *Nova et Vetera* (English) 12, no. 3 (2014): 631–55; John Corbett et al., "Recent Proposals for the Pastoral Care of the Divorced and Remarried: A Theological Assessment," *Nova et Vetera* (English) 12, no. 3 (2014): 616–17.

in his day of denying public penance a second time, but also gives grounds to hope for the sinner's salvation:

> Vice, however, sometimes makes such inroads among men that, even after they have done penance and have been readmitted to the Sacrament of the altar, they commit the same or more grievous sins. . . . And, although that same opportunity of penance is not again granted them in the Church, God does not forget to exercise His patience toward them. . . . It may, therefore, be a careful and useful enactment that the opportunity of that very humble penance be granted only once in the Church, lest that remedy, by becoming common, be less helpful to sick souls, for it is now more effective by being more respected. Yet, who would dare to say to God: "Why do you pardon this man a second time when he has been caught again in the snare of sin after his first penance?"[122]

If God secretly pardons such a person who was not allowed to be sacramentally reconciled again in public penance, it seems clear that this effect should be attributed to the person's contrition and desire for the sacrament, even though St. Augustine does not spell this out. This implies that the contrition and desire of such a person who is not eligible for public penance can still be efficacious in attaining the principal effect of the sacrament of Penance, which is the forgiveness of grave sins.

In treating the situation of those who repent in danger of death, St. Leo the Great likewise implies that God's pardon will follow on their interior repentance, even if they have no opportunity for works of penance:

> But satisfaction must not be ruled out or absolution denied to those who in time of necessity or in the moment of pressing danger beg for the protection of penance followed by absolution. For we cannot put limitations on the mercy of God or fix limits to times. With Him there is no delaying of pardon when the conversion is genuine, as the Spirit of God says through the Prophet: 'If being converted you lament,

---

[122] Augustine, Letter 153 to Macedonius, in *Letters: Volume III (131–164)*, trans. Parsons, 284–85.

you will be saved' [Isa 30:15].[123]

Theologians of the Twelfth
and Thirteenth Centuries

One of the first scholastic theologians, Peter Abelard (1079–1142), defended the thesis that contrition with the intention of confessing wins the forgiveness of sins. Drawing on the typology of the raising of Lazarus, which Augustine had used to illustrate the sacrament of Penance,[124] Abelard wrote:

> The Lord calls Lazarus when he inspires the sinner with the cry of salutary repentance. In this cry, indeed, the dead man comes to life, since the death of the soul, which is sin, by its means is gone. In fact, "in whatever hour the sinner shall lament his sin he will be saved" [Ezek 33:14]. . . . And so, whoever is prepared now to confess and to undertake satisfaction is immediately reconciled to God in virtue of this resolve; so much so, that if he is prevented for whatever cause from carrying out this resolve, he should in no way despair of his salvation, since there no longer remains in him what he wills to be removed by so many desires.[125]

Abelard's emphasis on the efficacy of interior contrition ignited a lively controversy in the following century. Although he has the merit of emphasizing the doctrine of Penance by desire, he lacked the distinction between perfect and imperfect contrition, for, as later theologians make clear, anticipation of the effect of justification can only be accomplished by a desire for Penance that is animated by perfect contrition, which is motivated by love for God. Furthermore, Abelard

[123] Leo the Great, Letter 108 to Bishop Theodore, dated AD 452, in *Letters*, trans. E. Hunt, FC 34 (New York: Fathers of the Church, 1957), 192.

[124] See Augustine, Tractate 49.24 on John 11:44 in *Tractates on the Gospel of John 28–54*, trans. J. W. Rettig, FC 88 (Washington, DC: Catholic University of America Press, 1993), 257.

[125] Peter Abelard, Sermon 8, in P. F. Palmer, *Sources of Christian Theology*, vol. 2, *Sacraments and Forgiveness; History and Doctrinal Development of Penance, Extreme Unction and Indulgences* (Westminster, MD: Newman Press, 1960), 186.

does not explain what priestly absolution adds to contrition.

Peter Lombard further develops the position of Abelard in his *Sentences*. After citing authorities for and against, he determines the question:

> What to be held? Surely, that sins are blotted out by contrition and humility of heart, even without confession by the mouth and payment of outward punishment. For from the moment when one proposes, with compunction of mind, that one will confess, God remits; because there is present confession of the heart, although not of the mouth, by which the soul is cleansed inwardly from the spot and contagion of the sin committed, and the debt of eternal death is released.[126]

But lest this doctrine lead to the neglect of sacramental confession, Peter Lombard stresses that the intention to sacramentally confess when this is possible is essential to true contrition:

> For just as inward penance is enjoined upon us, so also are outward satisfaction and confession by the mouth, if they are possible; and so he is not truly penitent, who does not have the intention to confess.... And so it is necessary for a penitent to confess, if he has the time; and yet, before there is confession by the mouth, if there is the intention in the heart, remission is granted to him.[127]

St. Thomas follows Peter Lombard on the power of perfect contrition to anticipate the effect of sacramental Penance. He explicitly compares this desire for Penance with that for Baptism: "And so for the remission of both actual and original fault, a sacrament of the Church is required, whether actually received or at least in desire, when an emergency, not contempt, excludes the sacrament."[128] In speaking about

---

[126] Peter Lombard, *Sentences*, bk. 4, d. 17, ch. 1.11, trans. Silano, p. 96.

[127] Lombard, *Sentences*, bk. 4, d. 17, ch. 1.13, trans. Silano, p. 97.

[128] Thomas Aquinas, *In IV Sent.*, d. 17, q. 3, a. 1, qla. 1, trans. Mortensen, 8:318. See also ad 1: "But for the infusion of grace to be obtained, sacraments of grace are ordained, before the reception of which, either actually or in intention, a person cannot obtain grace, as is seen in the case of baptism. And it is similar with confession." The same teaching is present in *In IV Sent.*, d. 17, q. 3, a. 3, qla. 1, ad 2, trans. Mortensen, 8:333, in which he explains that the sacrament

how interior contrition leads to justification, St. Thomas explains that this act of contrition is moved by actual grace and has to be accompanied by faith in God's mercy and charity by which one sorrows for the sin.[129] Before the institution of the sacrament of Penance, contrition coupled with faith and charity would have gained the forgiveness of sins.[130]

The Council of Trent and Subsequent Magisterium on Desire for Penance

The doctrine of the scholastics on the efficacy of desire for Penance was taken up by the Council of Trent:

> Although it sometimes happens that this contrition is perfect through charity and reconciles man to God before this sacrament is actually received, this reconciliation, nevertheless, is not to be ascribed to contrition itself without the desire of the sacrament, a desire that is included in it.[131]

For those who are invincibly ignorant about the sacrament of Penance, the act of perfect contrition and the desire to do fitting penance implicitly contain the desire for the sacrament and are sufficient to gain the

---

of Baptism is more necessary than Penance, because those who need Penance are at the age of reason and can attain the salvific effect of Penance through an act of contrition and desire for the sacrament: "Baptism is more a sacrament of necessity than the sacrament of penance, both as to confession and absolution. For sometimes baptism could not be omitted without risking eternal salvation, as is seen in children, who do not yet have the use of reason. But it is not so with confession and absolution, which only pertain to adults, in whom contrition with the intention of confessing and the desire for absolution suffices for freeing them from eternal death."

[129] See *ST* III, q. 85, a. 5; *ST* III q. 86, a. 6, ad 1.

[130] See *ST* III, q. 86, a. 6, sed contra: "Now forgiveness of sin can come from God without the sacrament of Penance, but not without the virtue of penance, as stated above (q. 84, a. 5, ad 3; q. 85, a. 2); so that, even before the sacraments of the New Law were instituted, God pardoned the sins of the penitent."

[131] Council of Trent, Doctrine on the Sacrament of Penance (session 14), ch. 4 (DS, 1677). See also Pius V, Bull *Ex omnibus afflictionibus* (DS, 1971), which condemns the following proposition of Michael Baius: "Through contrition even when joined with perfect charity and with the desire to receive the sacrament, guilt is not remitted without the actual reception of the sacrament, except in case of necessity, or of martyrdom."

proper effect of the sacrament, which is the forgiveness of sins.

Contrition is said to be perfect when, through the aid of actual grace, it is motivated by love for God above all things. When sorrow for sin is motivated only by fear of punishment in hell or by the shame of sin, it is said to be imperfect contrition, which is also called "attrition." Imperfect contrition is a supernatural gift of God, despite its imperfection. It stems from faith and a movement of actual grace. Imperfect contrition is sufficient to receive the sacrament of Penance, but of itself it does not obtain the forgiveness of sins as does an act of perfect contrition, as the Council of Trent makes clear: "Though without the sacrament of penance it [imperfect contrition] cannot of itself lead the sinner to justification, it nevertheless disposes him to obtain the grace of God in the sacrament of penance."[132]

The doctrine of Trent is taken up by the *Catechism of the Catholic Church*, §1452:

> When it arises from a love by which God is loved above all else, contrition is called "perfect" (contrition of charity). Such contrition remits venial sins; it also obtains forgiveness of mortal sins if it includes the firm resolution to have recourse to sacramental confession as soon as possible.

The fact that an act of perfect contrition anticipates the forgiveness of sins is the foundation for canon 916 of the *Code of Canon Law*:

> A person who is conscious of grave sin is not to celebrate Mass or receive the body of the Lord without previous sacramental confession unless there is a grave reason and there is no opportunity to confess; in this case the person is to remember the obligation to make an act of perfect contrition which includes the resolution of confessing as soon as possible.

The act of perfect contrition with the intention of confessing when possible anticipates the effect of the sacrament of Penance so that justification takes place and the state of sanctifying grace is restored,[133] and

---

[132] Council of Trent, Doctrine on the Sacrament of Penance (session 14), ch. 4 (DS, 1677).

[133] See Fagan, "Sacramental Spirituality," in *Sacraments: The Gestures of Christ*, ed. O'Callaghan, 159: "In the case of the sinner who intends to go to confession,

thus no sacrilege is committed in receiving Holy Communion when there is a grave reason to do so.

In *Reconciliatio et Paenitentia,* John Paul acknowledges that the forgiveness of mortal sins can be anticipated by contrition and desire, for God and His mercy are not bound to the sacramental sign. At the same time he stresses that the sacrament of Penance is the primary and ordinary way through which post-baptismal mortal sins are to be healed by His redemptive mercy, which it would be folly for a Christian to disregard:

> For a Christian the sacrament of penance is the primary way of obtaining forgiveness and the remission of serious sin committed after baptism. Certainly the Savior and his salvific action are not so bound to a sacramental sign as to be unable in any period or area of the history of salvation to work outside and above the sacraments. But in the school of faith we learn that the same Savior desired and provided that the simple and precious sacraments of faith would ordinarily be the effective means through which his redemptive power passes and operates. It would therefore be foolish, as well as presumptuous, to wish arbitrarily to disregard the means of grace and salvation which the Lord has provided and, in the specific case, to claim to receive forgiveness while doing without the sacrament which was instituted by Christ precisely for forgiveness.[134]

DESIRE FOR CONFIRMATION

What has been said above about Baptism would seem to apply equally to Confirmation. The major difference is that the effect of Baptism—justification—is absolutely necessary for salvation, whereas that is not the case for Confirmation. The effect of Confirmation, however, is necessary for full sanctification and active cooperation with Christ's mission. For sanctification presupposes that one grow to spiritual maturity and act in docility to the inspirations of the Holy Spirit in giving witness to Christ in the Christian life and in sharing Christ's prophetic, kingly, and priestly mission, which is the proper effect of

---

the sorrow he has for his sins and the desire to be forgiven enable him to benefit from the sacrament of penance long before he confesses to the priest."

[134] John Paul II, *Reconciliatio et Paenitentia,* §31, no. 1.

Confirmation. Sanctification also requires the gift of fortitude and other gifts of the Spirit necessary to "fight the good fight of the faith" (1 Tim 6:12) in a world marked by sin and concupiscence. Thus those who are not yet able to receive it should desire Confirmation, at least implicitly. It is reasonable to hold that God will grant an anticipation of the essential effects of the sacrament, although without imprinting character, to those who sincerely desire it, are in a state of grace (through sacramental Baptism or Baptism of desire), and make an act of faith, hope, and charity. St. Thomas thus argues that desire for Confirmation can anticipate the effects of Confirmation:

> The divine power is not confined to the sacraments. Hence man can receive spiritual strength to confess the Faith of Christ publicly, without receiving the sacrament of Confirmation, just as he can also receive remission of sins without Baptism. Yet, just as none receive the effect of Baptism without the desire of Baptism; so none receive the effect of Confirmation, without the desire of Confirmation. And man can have this even before receiving Baptism.[135]

That the essential effect of Confirmation can be received by desire is important also for ecumenical considerations. Protestants either do not recognize the sacrament at all or, in the case of Anglicans, are not able to validly confer it for lack of valid Holy Orders. But it is unreasonable to hold that no Protestants receive the effect of this sacrament, which is to grow towards spiritual maturity and to have the gifts of the Spirit to engage in spiritual combat. Nevertheless, although these effects can be received by desire, they are more abundantly provided, other things being equal, by sacramental reception.[136]

Those who reach the age of reason can have a personal desire for the sacrament of Confirmation, whether explicit or implicit. An implicit desire can be present also in those who do not know about the sacrament itself. This would be a desire for the reality conferred by the sacrament (*res*), which is the gift of the Spirit, His animating presence, inspirations, and His strength.

What about children before the age of reason who are baptized but

---

[135] *ST* III, q. 72, a. 6, ad 1.

[136] St. Thomas states this principle with regard to Baptism and the Eucharist; see *ST* III, q. 69, a. 4, ad 2; q. 79, a. 1, ad 1; q. 80, a. 1, ad 3.

not confirmed? Although Baptism and Chrismation are almost always received together in the Eastern churches (except in an emergency Baptism), they became detached in the Latin rite because celebration of Confirmation was reserved for the bishop, who was not ordinarily present at infant Baptisms. When Confirmation is not received immediately after Baptism, as in the Eastern rites, but delayed until the age of reason or adolescence, can we suppose that the grace of Confirmation is given through desire, even in babies?

It seems reasonable to extend the argument of St. Thomas in *ST* III, q. 79, a. 1, ad 1, from the Eucharist to Confirmation. There, as we have seen, he holds that baptized babies, even before they receive Communion, receive the grace of Communion through desire because Baptism is ordered by its nature to the Eucharist. If that is the case with regard to the Eucharist, it is reasonable to hold that the same happens with regard to Confirmation, for Baptism is intrinsically ordered to Confirmation, which in turn is ordered to the Eucharist. If the two sacraments are related as that of spiritual birth to spiritual growth and activity, how could the former not be ordered to the latter?

For this reason, the delaying of Confirmation (like Communion) for infants and children does not pose a grave danger to the salvation of the child. Nevertheless, that does not make it right to overly delay reception of the sacrament significantly beyond the age of reason, according to the principle given by St. Thomas that more grace is given by sacramental reception than through desire for the sacrament that anticipates its effects. Sacramental reception also imprints the character of Confirmation, which lasts in eternity as a deeper configuration with Christ as prophet, priest, and king. For this reason the *Catechism of the Catholic Church*, §1307 states that "in danger of death children should be confirmed even if they have not yet attained the age of discretion," and every priest has the faculty to confirm in danger of death according to canon 883 of the *Code of Canon Law*.

Sacramental reception of Confirmation will give an increase in sanctifying grace and all that flows from it, as well as the series of sacramental graces ordered to deeper participation in Christ's threefold mission against the pressures of a hostile world. These sacramental graces will also greatly aid deeper participation in the Eucharist, both in participating in the sacrifice through offering oneself with Christ and in receiving Holy Communion.

If the grace of the three sacraments of Christian initiation is always given together in germ, it makes sense for the reception of the three sacraments to also be joined, as they are in the Eastern rites and in the Latin rite for adults in the RCIA; at least they should be more closely connected, unless a necessity stands in the way.[137]

DESIRE FOR ANOINTING OF THE SICK

What about the sacrament of Anointing of the Sick? Could those who are seriously ill and in danger of death receive an anticipatory effect of the sacrament through desire for it? It would seem that something analogous with Confirmation would apply here although I am not aware of any magisterial text that explicitly affirms this hypothesis. In order to receive the graces proper to this sacrament through desire, one would have to be in a state of grace (with perfect contrition for mortal sins not yet sacramentally forgiven) and with the desire, explicit or implicit, to conform one's sufferings to those of Christ, offering them for the good of others. This desire would contain within it an implicit act of faith, hope, and charity. Nevertheless, other things being equal, it should be held that more grace would be given to those who actually receive the sacrament compared to those who only desire it.

Many Catholics delay too long before requesting the sacrament, and this was especially true in earlier times, and it is comforting to know that a desire for the sacrament by someone in a state of grace would anticipate some of the effects of the sacrament. For Protestants who do not recognize Anointing of the Sick as a sacrament, it seems that they also could receive the graces proper to this sacrament by a desire to unite their sufferings with Christ and to be strengthened by His grace in serious illness. Nevertheless, it is tragic that there would be no visible and sacramental manifestation of this configuration with Christ in His sufferings, nor the greater divine aids given by actual reception of the sacrament.

Similarly, for non-Christians who have been justified through Baptism of desire, there can be a yearning to prepare for death according to the will of God through a deeper purging from sin and strengthening from God. A desire to unite their sufferings to those of Christ, whom they tragically do not know, would be implicit in this yearning, moved secretly by grace inspiring some act of faith, hope, and charity. It seems that such a desire could draw forth some of the

---

[137] See Benedict XVI, *Sacramentum Caritatis*, §17 (discussed above on p. 80); Finnegan, *Confirmation at an Impasse*, 392–93.

graces proper to this sacrament.

Desire for the Graces to Sanctify Matrimony by Those with a Valid but Non-Sacramental Marriage

Can the doctrine on desire for the sacraments be applied to Matrimony? That is, can a desire animated by actual grace and the proper dispositions (an act of faith, hope, charity, and contrition) anticipate the graces that are proper to the sacrament of Matrimony?

As always in this matter, one must distinguish the *res et sacramentum* from the reality of grace. Desire for the sacraments never brings about the *res et sacramentum*, which always requires valid realization of the sacramental sign. Thus one can never contract the matrimonial bond by desire, for this requires the public exchange of mutual consent and constitutes a public state in society and the Church.

Nevertheless, it seems reasonable to think that some sacramental graces of Matrimony—actual graces and gifts of docility ordered towards mutual self-donation[138]—could be received through desire by couples who have a valid but non-sacramental marriage, in that one or both are not baptized. Such a desire would presuppose that they have desire for Baptism (implicit or explicit) and a holy desire to sanctify their marriage so that they could love with a participation of the divine love and be an image of that love in society.

This consideration applies in a particular way to marriage in the Old Covenant, which prefigured Christian Matrimony. Surely the holy spouses of the Old Testament received many graces, merited by Christ on Calvary, to sanctify their marriages and overcome the obstacles to the full gift of self called for by the married state. Similar considerations apply to all non-Christian married people who have true implicit desire for Baptism and desire the grace of God to perfect and sanctify their conjugal and parental love.

IMPORTANCE OF THE DOCTRINE OF SACRAMENTAL GRACE THROUGH DESIRE

The doctrine that the grace of the sacraments can also be received

---

[138] See Pius XI, *Casti Connubii*, §40, analyzed above on pp. 354–55.

through a graced desire for them accompanied by perfect contrition, applies both to Catholics who are temporarily unable to receive some sacraments and to those who are in varying degrees outside the visible Church. Through cooperating with actual grace that is denied to none, all those who come to the age of reason can explicitly or implicitly desire Baptism, Penance, the Eucharist, Confirmation, and Anointing. If their desire is accompanied by faith, hope, charity, and perfect contrition, they can receive the essential effects of those sacraments, although not in the fullness that actual reception of the sacraments would give.

The seven petitions of the "Our Father" express desire for the sacraments. As the prayer given to the Church by Jesus Himself, it is fitting that the Our Father would express the fundamental desires for sacramental grace that He wishes to give to the faithful through the sacramental economy. At the center of the prayer is the desire for the Eucharist, expressed in the petition that the Lord grant us our daily bread.[139] Although this petition also includes our temporal needs in general, it is especially directed to spiritual nourishment given by the Bread of Life. This is followed by the desire for Penance by which our sins may be forgiven. The prayer for the coming of the Kingdom implies a desire for Baptism and Confirmation, for Baptism is the gate by which we enter His Kingdom, and Confirmation strengthens the faithful to build up that Kingdom. The desire that the Lord's will be done in our lives on earth also implies a reference to Confirmation, through which the Holy Spirit is given to enable us to act through divine inspirations and have God's law written on the heart. The prayer for aid in temptation also corresponds to a desire for Confirmation by which the faithful are strengthened with the gift of fortitude. The grace of Anointing of the Sick in times of illness is implied in the final petition to be liberated from all evil.[140]

---

[139] See *CCC*, §2835: "The specifically Christian sense of this fourth petition concerns the Bread of Life." While commenting on this verse of the Our Father in *The Way of Perfection*, ch. 35, St. Teresa of Avila speaks about the great value of spiritual communion.

[140] See *CCC*, §2854: "When we ask to be delivered from the Evil One, we pray as well to be freed from all evils, present, past, and future, of which he is the author or instigator. In this final petition, the Church brings before the Father all the distress of the world. Along with deliverance from the evils that overwhelm humanity, she implores the precious gift of peace and the grace of perseverance in expectation of Christ's return."

We can think of desire for the sacraments as operative in concentric circles of relationship with the Church. The power of sacramental desire to anticipate graces from God is greatest within the visible Church itself and among the Eastern Orthodox, where the desire, especially for the Eucharist and Penance, is explicit. Next, it can be present among Protestants in an explicit form if they recognize those sacraments or in an implicit way if they do not. Next, this desire would be present in Jews whose worship, sacramental rites, and prayers are directed to the salvation to be brought by the Messiah. This desire for Baptism and the other sacraments would be a mixture of explicit and implicit aspects. Finally, it can be present only implicitly in those who do not accept Judeo-Christian revelation.

Desire for the Sacraments among Protestants

It follows that Protestants in a state of grace can receive some of the effects of the sacraments that are not valid in their ecclesial communities. Moved by actual grace, they can have a desire for the forgiveness of post-baptismal grave sins, which, in reality, is an implicit desire for the sacrament of Penance even if they do not recognize it as a sacrament in the proper sense. If they repent for such sins out of love for God (perfect contrition), they will gain the essential effect of the sacrament of Penance, which is the forgiveness of those sins and the restoration of sanctifying grace.

Similarly Protestants, moved by grace, desire to be intimately united with Jesus. Even if they reject the Real Presence of Christ in the Eucharist they can still desire the ultimate reality (*res tantum*) of this sacrament, which is communion with Christ and with His Mystical Body. If this desire is accompanied by charity and perfect contrition, it will nourish the state of sanctifying grace already present through Baptism and the desire for Penance.

Protestants also desire to be strengthened with the Spirit and His seven gifts (Isa 11:1–2) to be witnesses of Christ, which is an implicit desire for Confirmation. The charismatic movement in the Protestant world is a testimony to the power of desire for the sacramental gift of the Spirit.[141] They also desire an aid of grace in the trial of severe illness.

---

[141] See, for example, James D. G. Dunn, *Baptism in the Holy Spirit: A Re-examination of the New Testament Teaching on the Gift of the Spirit in Relation to Pentecostalism Today* (Naperville, IL: A. R. Allenson, 1970); Raniero Canta-

If they are rightly disposed by perfect contrition and charity, these desires will draw upon them, in varying degrees, the graces proper to Confirmation and Anointing of the Sick. It seems reasonable to hold that their Baptism strengthens an implicit desire to the other sacraments to which Baptism orders them, as St. Thomas held with regard to baptized infants in relation to the Eucharist. For this reason, as well as through their explicit faith in the Gospel and its promises, they are obviously in a far more favorable situation than non-Christians with regard to desire for the sacraments. Nevertheless, it remains a great tragedy that the Reformation, through the denial of the sacrament of Holy Orders, resulted in the loss of the five sacraments that require a priestly minister for validity (all except Baptism and Matrimony).

Desire for the Sacraments among Non-Christians

This doctrine that the unbaptized may receive the grace of the sacraments through an implicit desire moved by actual grace is of great importance for understanding two key theological principles: God's universal salvific will and the principle that all salvation comes through Christ and the Church. This doctrine concerns billions of human beings who, through no grave fault of their own, have not had the opportunity to receive Baptism or the other sacraments. Without this doctrine it would be impossible to uphold both God's universal salvific will and the necessity of Christ and the Church for salvation.

The biblical text that speaks most clearly of God's universal salvific will also specifies that Christ is the one Mediator between God and men: "God our Saviour, who desires all men to be saved and to come to the knowledge of the truth. For there is one God, and there is one mediator between God and men, the man Christ Jesus, who gave himself as a ransom for all" (1 Tim 2:3–6). This one mediation of Christ was realized once and for all in His Paschal mystery, but has to be applied to all men in all times and places. On Calvary He merited the graces that are applied to mankind throughout human history after the Fall. The sacraments are the ordinary means by which that grace won on Calvary is applied to human beings in the Church.

---

lamessa, *Sober Intoxication of the Spirit: Filled with the Fullness of God*, trans. Marsha Daigle-Williamson (Cincinnati, OH: Servant Books, 2005); Peter Hocken, *Azusa, Rome, and Zion: Pentecostal Faith, Catholic Reform, and Jewish Roots* (Eugene, OR: Pickwick Publications, 2016).

The Church has the beauty of being catholic, or universal in time and space, embracing all cultures, languages, and peoples, in response to Jesus's missionary mandate: "Go into all the world and preach the gospel to the whole creation" (Mark 16:15). Over the centuries, this immense mission is slowly and progressively realized so that a large part of mankind has been able to come into sacramental contact with Jesus Christ and His grace through the sacraments.

But despite the Church's missionary efforts, a greater part of mankind has remained outside the Church's visible boundaries and thus outside the reach of her sacraments. Even among Protestants, Christ touches Christians sacramentally solely through Baptism and Matrimony, whereas the other sacraments are only received through desire. Among non-Christians no sacrament of the New Covenant is received. But the immense and inexhaustible grace-giving power of the sacraments is not rendered void by the fact that the Church's missionary mandate is never complete. The power mediated by the sacraments overflows their boundaries so that all those who truly seek, repenting and believing according to their possibilities, find. Sacramental grace given in response to desire, whether explicit or implicit, makes it possible for Christ and His Church to be a universal mediator of grace, despite the fact that not all human beings know of the Church, her motives of credibility, and her sacraments.

Although the graces given through the sacramental system, in their richness and variety, are also available to those who, through no grave fault of their own, are outside the Church, it remains tragic that much of mankind receives sacramental grace only through yearning, without knowing the object of that yearning and without the directness and fullness of grace and truth present in the sacraments. Jesus alludes to this when He says in Matthew 13:17: "Truly, I say to you, many prophets and righteous men longed to see what you see, and did not see it, and to hear what you hear, and did not hear it." Their longing was surely not without salvific effect, but more blessed are those who encounter Christ sacramentally than those unable to encounter Him in that way, though they long for it from afar.

As St. Thomas specifies, even if their effect can be received in part through desire alone, it is not in vain to receive the sacraments.[142] First

---

[142] With regard to the Eucharist, see *ST* III, q. 80, a. 1, ad 3: "The actual receiving of the sacrament produces more fully the effect of the sacrament than does the desire thereof, as stated above of Baptism (q. 69, a. 4, ad 2)."

of all, because the sacraments visibly mediate the grace of God in a way suitable to our nature and to the Incarnation. Secondly, because the sacraments imprint indelible character or other *res et sacramentum* (in Matrimony, Penance, and Anointing of the Sick) that remains within us as an instrumental cause of grace that has been received interiorly.[143] Only those who have received the sacraments have been interiorly configured to Christ in an abiding way according to the difference of the sacraments, and have thus received a new identity in Christ, a new ecclesial mission, and an interior spiritual power to share in Christ's prophetic, priestly, and kingly mission. Third, because, other things being equal (such as the dispositions of desire, faith, hope, charity, and repentance), those who receive the sacraments receive a fuller effect of grace than those who receive only spiritually through desire. Finally, only those who are inside the Church can receive Christ Himself, present in His humanity as well as His divinity, in the Eucharist.

The fullness of grace comes when the sacraments are received with a disposition of yearning and a progressive cooperation with the sacramental graces of each day. Here the Gospel principle applies: "For to every one who has will more be given, and he will have abundance" (Matt 25:29).

Study Questions

1. (a) Explain the Church's teaching on Baptism of desire. (b) Trace the development of the Church's teaching on Baptism of desire. (c) Explain the distinction between explicit and implicit desire. (d) Explain the notion of invincible ignorance as it applies to Baptism of desire. (e) What are some of the most important magisterial documents that speak of Baptism of desire? (f) What dispositions are necessary in the subject to receive the essential effects of Baptism of desire?

2. (a) In what other sacraments can the essential effect be received through desire for the sacrament? (b) What disposition of the subject is necessary to receive the essential effect of Penance through desire? Explain briefly the historical development of this doctrine. (c) What disposition of the subject is necessary to receive the essential effect of Communion through desire? (d) Is

---

[143] See Nicolas, *Synthèse dogmatique: de la Trinité à la Trinité*, 788–89.

it reasonable to think that one can receive the essential effects of Confirmation and Anointing of the Sick through desire?

3. Explain the theological significance of the doctrine that some of the effects of the sacraments can be anticipated by desire with the right dispositions. What theological principles does it shed light on?

SUGGESTIONS FOR FURTHER READING

Holy Office. Letter to the Archbishop of Boston, August 8, 1949. DS, 3866–73.

John Paul II. Encyclical on the Permanent Validity of the Church's Missionary Mandate *Redemptoris Missio*. December 7, 1990. §§5–12, 46.

Martin, Ralph. *Will Many Be Saved?: What Vatican II Actually Teaches and Its Implications for the New Evangelization*. Grand Rapids, MI: Eerdmans, 2012.

Morali, Ilaria. "Religions and Salvation," and "The Early Modern Period." In *Catholic Engagement with World Religions: A Comprehensive Study*. Edited by Karl Joseph Becker and Ilaria Morali. Maryknoll, NY: Orbis Books, 2010. Pp. 54–90.

Nutt, Roger. *General Principles of Sacramental Theology*. Washington, DC: Catholic University of America Press, 2017. Pp. 88–96.

Sullivan, Francis A. *Salvation Outside the Church: Tracing the History of the Catholic Response*. Eugene, OR: Wipf & Stock, 2002.

Vatican II. Dogmatic Constitution on the Church *Lumen Gentium*. §§14–16.

CHAPTER SIXTEEN

The Desire of the Church for the Salvation of Infants Who Die without Baptism

In the preceding chapter, we have seen that the universal salvific will of God extends beyond the limits of the visible Church and her sacramental system and makes it possible for those who rightly desire salvation to receive the salvific effect of the sacraments without receiving the sacramental sign. But reception of grace through personal prayer and desire for the sacraments and their effect of salvation presupposes that one is at the age of reason by which one could personally direct oneself to one's due end through desire. What of those who are yet incapable of a personal act of rational desire and prayer and who die without Baptism? Is the universal salvific will of God rendered void in their regard? Can the desires of their parents and the Church be of avail for them?

At the risk of oversimplifying, the dominant answers given to this question by theologians over the centuries can be reduced to three. One solution, which could be called the Augustinian, speaks of the souls of those dying without Baptism before the age of reason as enduring sorrow for what they have lost, even though this penalty is the "lightest."[1] This position was dominant in the West from Augus-

---

[1] See Augustine, *Against Julian* 5.11.44, trans. M. A. Schumacher, FC 35 (Washington, DC: Catholic University of America Press, 1957), 286: "Who can doubt that non-baptized infants, having only original sin and no burden of personal sins, will suffer the lightest condemnation of all? I cannot define the amount and kind of their punishment, but I dare not say it were better for them never to have existed than to exist there"; *Enchiridion* 23.93, in *NPNF*1, 3:267: "And, of course, the mildest punishment of all will fall upon those who have added no

tine to Aquinas and continued to be defended in differing degrees by theologians such as St. Robert Bellarmine,[2] the Jansenists, and theologians of the Augustinian school of the eighteenth century.[3]

A second dominant solution, generally referred to as the theory of "limbo," is that represented by St. Thomas, which holds that those who die without Baptism before the age of reason enjoy a perpetual state of natural happiness, but without supernatural beatitude. Although perpetually deprived of the vision of God, they do not suffer on that account, but "they will rejoice in the fact that they participate greatly in the divine goodness in their natural perfections."[4] Far more optimistic than the Augustinian position, this theory was dominant among theologians until the middle of the twentieth century, but it was never formally taught or imposed by the Magisterium, which allowed for theological debate with the Augustinian position.[5]

The seed of a third position was proposed in the early sixteenth century by Cardinal Cajetan, who put forward the hypothesis that the faith and desire of the parents for Baptism could supply for the lack both of the sacrament and of the personal desire for it on the part of their children not yet capable of it. This seed developed into a third broad position in the twentieth century, drawing in different ways on Cajetan's proposal, and based firmly on God's universal salvific will. It is briefly summarized in the *Catechism of the Catholic Church*, §1261:

> As regards children who have died without Baptism, the Church can only entrust them to the mercy of God, as she does in her funeral rites for them. Indeed, the great mercy of God who desires that all men should be saved, and Jesus' tenderness toward children which caused him to say: "Let the

---

actual sin, to the original sin they brought with them"; *The Punishment and Forgiveness of Sins and the Baptism of Little Ones* 1.16.21, in *Answer to the Pelagians*, trans. Roland J. Teske, WSA I/23 (Hyde Park, NY, New City Press, 1997), 45: "One can correctly say that little ones who leave the body without baptism will be under the mildest condemnation of all."

[2] See Robert Bellarmine, *De amissione gratiae*, bk. 6, chs. 2–7, in *Opera omnia*, 5:455–73; see ITC, "The Hope of Salvation for Infants" (Apr 19, 2007), §26, p. 367.

[3] See George J. Dyer, *Limbo: Unsettled Question* (New York: Sheed & Ward, 1964), 68–90.

[4] Thomas Aquinas, *In II Sent.*, d. 33, q. 2, a. 2.

[5] See ITC, "The Hope of Salvation for Infants," §26, p. 368.

children come to me, do not hinder them," allow us to hope that there is a way of salvation for children who have died without Baptism.[6]

The Augustinian position has long been abandoned. The Thomistic position of limbo, although no longer held by most contemporary theologians, remains an open thesis,[7] and it is important to understand its theological foundation and the arguments of fittingness for and against it, which shall be examined below.

The question is important for obvious practical and theoretical reasons. First of all, it concerns the final beatitude of perhaps billions of human beings who have died before the age of reason without Baptism. How many Catholic mothers have agonized over the fate of their children who died by miscarriage and thus without the possibility of Baptism! And how many babies are deprived of the possibility of Baptism through abortion! The question is also of supreme theoretical importance because it concerns the necessity of coming into some kind of relation with the sacramental order established by Christ and the distinction between the natural and the supernatural orders.[8] First we shall set forth the Thomistic teaching on limbo and its foundations, examine its difficulties, and then set forth arguments in favor of the position of the *Catechism of the Catholic Church*, §1261.[9]

THE THOMISTIC DOCTRINE OF LIMBO

Limbo is a term used to designate the terminal state of those who die with original sin but without any personal sin, in which they would be

---

[6] See also *CCC*, §1283: "With respect to children who have died without Baptism, the liturgy of the Church invites us to trust in God's mercy and to pray for their salvation"; John Paul II, *Evangelium Vitae* (Mar 25, 1995), §99.

[7] See ITC, "The Hope of Salvation for Infants," §41, p. 374, which speaks of the theory of limbo as remaining a "possible theological opinion."

[8] On the importance of the problem, see George J. Dyer, "The Unbaptized Infant in Eternity," *Chicago Studies* 2 (1963): 141–53, at 141.

[9] For an earlier version of the content of this chapter, see Lawrence Feingold, "Maritain's Eschatological Reverie and the Fittingness of Limbo," in *The Things That Matter: Essays Inspired by the Later Work of Jacques Maritain*, ed. Heidi M. Giebel (Washington, DC: Catholic University of America Press in partnership with the American Maritain Association, 2018), 3–23.

excluded from heaven but not subject to the pains of hell.[10] It has been postulated to clarify what such a state would entail. In more precise terms, it designates a state in which there is the penalty of loss of the beatific vision (*poena damni*) on account of original sin, but because of the lack of personal sin there would be no pain of sense or spirit.

The term "limbo" comes from the Latin "*limbus*" which means hem or border. The word was coined to refer to the upper border of hell. It is part of "hell" in the broad sense of the word, which designates any state after death entailing exclusion from the beatific vision. There are two distinct states that have been spoken of as limbo: the limbo of the patriarchs who died in the grace of God before Good Friday,[11] and the limbo of the children who died without receiving the forgiveness of original sin.

The traditional doctrine of limbo, as understood, for example, by St. Thomas Aquinas and the Thomistic school, is a complex whole composed of various theses that have different degrees of certainty. In what follows, I will distinguish five theses that together structure the Thomistic conception. Of these, the first two require an assent of faith, but the other three are open questions. By far the most problematic is the last, which holds that a natural happiness is possible in this economy of salvation.

1. The Penalty of Original Sin Is the Loss of the Beatific Vision

First of all, it is *de fide* that those who die with original sin, even though without personal sin, cannot attain to the beatific vision. As seen above, the forgiveness of original sin is an indispensable means for salvation. Innocent III declared:

> We say that two kinds of sin must be distinguished, original and actual: original, which is contracted without consent; and actual, which is committed with consent. Thus original sin, which is contracted without consent is remitted without

---

[10] See George J. Dyer, "Limbo: A Theological Evaluation," *Theological Studies* 19 (1958): 32–49, at 32: "As the Scholastics envision it, limbo embraces two ideas: the exclusion of infants from heaven and their exemption from the pains of hell."

[11] The event in which Jesus releases these souls from the limbo of the just to bring them to heaven is traditionally called "the harrowing of hell."

consent through the power of the sacrament [of baptism]; but actual sin, which is committed with consent, is by no means remitted without consent. . . . The punishment of original sin is the deprivation of the vision of God, but the punishment of actual sin is the torment of eternal hell.[12]

This text is very rich. It specifies the proper penalty of original sin, which is the deprivation of the beatific vision. It also specifies that since original sin is incurred without our consent, it is fitting that it can be taken away without consent. Thus the forgiveness of original sin can and should be received before the age of reason. It is fitting therefore that God provide a generous means by which original sin can be taken away. Before the promulgation of Baptism, circumcision was an occasion for this cleansing.

The Second Council of Lyons, in 1274 stated: "As for the souls of those who die in mortal sin or with original sin only, they go down immediately to hell, to be punished, however, with different punishments."[13] The Council would have understood the second category to apply to those who die before the age of reason, whose original sin was not forgiven through Baptism or in any other way, such as through circumcision under the Old Covenant or through the faith of their parents. This teaching should be interpreted in the light of the earlier teaching of Innocent III. Here the word "hell" is being used in the broad sense to include any state deprived of the vision of God.

This text was repeated with a slight addition by Pope John XXII in 1321: "The souls, however, of those who die in mortal sin or with original sin only descend immediately into hell; to be punished, though, with different pains and in different places,"[14] and was taken up again by the Council of Florence.[15]

---

[12] Innocent III, *Maiores Ecclesiae causas*, (DS, 780). See also ITC, "The Hope of Salvation for Infants," §83, p. 392: "There is no question of denying Innocent's teaching that those who die in original sin are deprived of the beatific vision [DS, 780]. What we may ask and are asking is whether infants who die without baptism necessarily die in original sin, without a divine remedy." See also Peter Gumpel, S.J., "Unbaptized Infants: May They Be Saved?" *The Downside Review* 72 (1954): 345.

[13] Council of Lyons II, Profession of Faith of Emperor Michael Paleologus (DS, 858).

[14] John XXII, Letter to the Armenians *"Nequaquam sine dolore*, (Nov 21, 1321; DS, 926).

[15] Council of Florence, Bull of Union with the Greeks *Laetentur caeli* (July 6,

2. Since Its Promulgation, Baptism Is the One and Only Ordinary Means for the Forgiveness of Original Sin; Its Lack Can Be Supplied by a Desire for Baptism or Baptism of Blood

In this economy of salvation, Baptism is the one and only ordinary means established by Christ by which original sin is forgiven. This is based on the clear words of Jesus in John 3:5: "Truly, truly, I say to you, unless one is born of water and the Spirit, he cannot enter the kingdom of God."

The necessity of Baptism for the forgiveness of original sin was a key issue in the Pelagian controversy, and thus we find the necessity of infant Baptism taught in the third canon of the Synod of Carthage of 418: "If anyone says that the Lord said: 'in my Father's house there are many rooms' [Jn 14:2], in such a way that it is understood that in the kingdom of heaven there is some place in the middle or elsewhere where little children may live blessedly even if they have gone forth from this world without baptism, without which they cannot enter into the kingdom of heaven, which is everlasting life, let him be anathema."[16] St. Augustine,[17] and others who followed him such as St. Fulgentius,[18] understood the necessity of Baptism to mean that infants

---

1439; DS, 1306): "As for the souls of those who die in actual mortal sin or with original sin only, they go down immediately to hell, to be punished, however, with different punishments."

[16] Fifteenth Synod of Carthage (418; DS, 224). This canon was not included in the Indiculus and Epistula Tractoria of Pope Zosimus in which he expressed his approval of other canons of this Synod. Thus there is no clear evidence that this particular canon received papal approval. See Denzinger, *Enchiridion Symbolorum*, 43rd ed., p. 82; Otto Wermelinger, *Rom und Pelagius: die theologische Position der römischen Bischöfe im pelagianischen Streit in den Jahren 411-432* (Stuttgart: Anton Hiersemann, 1975), 166–79.

[17] See Augustine, *The Nature and Origin of the Soul* 3.9.12, in *Answer to the Pelagians*, trans. Roland J. Teske, WSA, 1/23 (Hyde Park, NY: New City Press, 1997), 522: "If you want to be Catholic, do not believe or say or teach that infants who die before they are baptized 'can attain pardon of their original sins.'"

[18] Fulgentius, *To Peter on the Faith* 27.70, in *Fulgentius: Selected Works*, trans. Eno, 100: "Hold most firmly and never doubt that, not only adults with the use of reason but also children who either begin to live in the womb of their mothers and who die there or, already born from their mothers, pass from this world without the Sacrament of Holy Baptism, which is given in the name of the Father and of the Son and of the Holy Spirit, must be punished with the endless penalty of eternal fire. Even if they have no sin from their own actions, still, by their

who died without Baptism after the promulgation of the Gospel would not be saved.

The most important magisterial teaching on this subject is from the Council of Trent. The necessity of Baptism (including Baptism of desire) is treated in the Decree on Justification. Speaking of justification, which is defined as the "transition from the state in which a man is born a son of the first Adam to the state of grace and adoption as sons of God," the Decree states: "After the promulgation of the gospel, this transition cannot take place without the bath of regeneration or the desire for it, as it is written: 'Unless one is reborn of water and the Spirit, he cannot enter the kingdom of God.'"[19] The same doctrine is stated in canon 5 on Baptism: "If anyone shall say that baptism is optional, that is, not necessary for salvation: let him be anathema."[20]

A century earlier, the Council of Florence treated this question:

> With regard to children, since the danger of death is often present and the only remedy available to them is the sacrament of baptism by which they are snatched away from the dominion of the devil and adopted as children of God, she admonishes that sacred baptism is not to be deferred for forty or eighty days. . . , but it should be conferred as soon as it conveniently can; and if there is imminent danger of death, the child should be baptized straightaway without any delay, even by a layman or woman in the form of the Church, if there is no priest.[21]

The *Catechism of the Council of Trent* also gives an important witness on this subject:

---

carnal conception and birth, they have contracted the damnation of Original Sin." Peter Lombard quotes this in his *Sentences*, bk. 4, ch. 4.12, trans. Silano, 24, attributing it to St. Augustine, before which he says: "Nor is someone else's faith so useful to a child as his own faith is to an adult. For the faith of the Church is not sufficient for children without the sacrament. If they should die without baptism, even as they are being brought to baptism, they will be damned, as is proved by many testimonies of the Saints."

[19] Council of Trent, Decree on Justification (session 6), ch. 4 (DS, 1524).

[20] Council of Trent, Decree on the Sacraments, (session 7), can. 5 on Baptism (DS, 1618).

[21] Council of Florence, *Cantate Domino* (DS, 1349).

The law of Baptism applies to all mankind without exception. Unless they are reborn through the grace of Baptism—no matter whether they were born of believing or of unbelieving parents—they are in fact born to eternal misery and loss. . . . If, then, through the sin of Adam children inherit the stain of original sin, is it not even more cogent to conclude that through Christ the Lord they can receive sanctifying grace which will enable them to live forever? But without Baptism this grace and this life are impossible. . . . For infants there is no other way of attaining salvation but by sacramental Baptism.[22]

Although this catechism is not an act of the papal Magisterium, it is an important witness of Tradition and reflects the consensus of theologians in the sixteenth century. That Baptism is the only ordinary means for the forgiveness of original sin is also witnessed by the *Catechism of the Catholic Church*, §1257: "The Church does not know of any means other than Baptism that assures entry into eternal beatitude."

As seen in the definition of Trent, although Baptism is necessary, it is not always necessary to actually receive the outward sacramental sign. The forgiveness of original sin is also given by a sincere desire for Baptism (explicit or implicit) or by the Baptism of blood (being killed for Christ), as seen in the previous chapter.

Nevertheless, although Baptism of blood can be received also by infants, even in the womb, a *personal* act of desire for Baptism presupposes the use of reason, which would not be possible for those who do not reach the age of reason. Pius XII, in an important Address to Italian midwives in 1951, stated that Baptism of desire, understood as a personal act of desire, is impossible for infants:

What we have said up to now concerns the protection and care of life on the natural plane, but it is much more applicable to the supernatural life the child receives when it is baptized. Under the present economy there is no other way of giving this life to the child who is still without the use of reason. In any case, the state of grace at the moment of death is absolutely necessary for salvation; without it, no one can attain to supernatural happiness, the beatific vision of God. In the case of a grown-up person, an act of love may suffice for

---

[22] *CCT*, part 2, ch. 1, §§31–34, pp. 178–80.

obtaining sanctifying grace and making up for the lack of Baptism. To the child still unborn or the child just born this path is not open. If, then, you consider that charity to one's neighbor means helping him when necessary, that this obligation is all the more serious and urgent when the good to be wrought or the evil to be avoided is greater and when the needy person is less capable of helping and saving himself, then it is easy to understand the great importance of seeing that Baptism is given to a child deprived completely of the use of reason, in grave danger or certain of dying.[23]

3. It Is Not Fitting That There Be Suffering after Death for Those Who Die without Personal Sin

St. Thomas Aquinas adds two further points that define the Thomistic conception of limbo in opposition to the less optimistic position of the Augustinian tradition, which held that those who died without Baptism before the age of reason would suffer the mildest penalty. Following and building upon Peter Lombard,[24] he holds that there will be *no penalty of suffering* after this life, whether spiritual or sensible, for those who die with only original sin and no personal sin. This is based on the understanding of original sin, proposed by St. Anselm, as essentially the privation of sanctifying grace and all other supernatural gifts.[25] The proportionate penalty for the privation of sanctifying grace is the privation of supernatural happiness but not the loss of natural happiness and other gifts proportionate to human nature. An endless suffering, no matter how light, could not be a proportionate penalty

---

[23] Pius XII, Address to Italian Midwives (Oct 29, 1951), in *The Major Addresses of Pope Pius XII*, ed. Vincent Yzermans, vol. 1: *Selected Addresses* (St. Paul: North Central Publishing, 1961), 165. Italian original in *AAS* 43 (1951): 841. On the interpretation of this text, see George J. Dyer, *Limbo: Unsettled Question*, 153–57.

[24] See Peter Lombard, *Sentences*, bk. 2, d. 33, no. 5 (PL 192:730, my translation): "The children will be damned with no other penalty than the perpetual lack of the vision of God, and will not be touched by material fire or the worm of conscience."

[25] St. Anselm has the merit of introducing this way of understanding original sin. However, he did not apply this insight with respect to its consequences for the fate of infants dying without baptism. See Richard Weberberger, O.S.B., "Limbus puerorum. Zur Entstehung eines theologischen Begriffes," *Recherches de théologie ancienne et médiévale* 35 (1968): 84–87.

for a person without grave and unrepented personal sin. Thus it is fitting that those who die with only original sin should suffer a penalty that is the privation of the vision of God, due to their lack of sanctifying grace, but nothing more. Since there was no personal sin, there should be no personal suffering as a consequence, no matter how light, but only the "lack of what nature was powerless to provide."[26] Indeed, they should enjoy all "perfections and goods that stem from the principles of human nature," comprising a happiness proper to innocence.

This generates a very difficult theological problem. How could those in limbo not suffer an interior sorrow on account of the loss of the beatific vision? The solution to this question requires two steps. First, one must distinguish clearly between the natural and the supernatural orders, and delineate a natural happiness that could exist independently of the supernatural happiness consisting in the beatific vision. Secondly, one must show that a natural happiness is possible in this economy of salvation, in which man has been elevated to a supernatural end, fallen with Adam in original sin, and redeemed in Christ.

4. A Purely Natural Happiness Is Possible

St. Thomas's position presupposes that a purely natural happiness is possible for human beings after death. Such happiness would be proportionate to our nature and consist in the loving contemplation of God as known through His creation. St. Thomas affirms in many texts that happiness or beatitude for a rational creature can be of two kinds: natural and supernatural.[27] For example, in *De virtutibus*, q. 1, a. 10, he writes: "It should be considered that there is a twofold good for man; one which is proportional to his nature, and another which exceeds the capacity of his nature." Likewise, in *De veritate*, q. 27, a. 2, he writes:

---

[26] Thomas Aquinas, *In II Sent.*, d. 33, q. 2, a. 1 (my translation): "As they had no guilt through their action, they should have no penalty through their suffering, but only that consisting in the lack of what nature was powerless to provide. But in other perfections and goods that stem from the principles of human nature, those damned on account of original sin should suffer no loss."

[27] See the discussion of this Thomistic thesis in Feingold, *The Natural Desire to See God*, 230–50; Bernard Mulcahy, *Aquinas's Notion of Pure Nature and the Christian Integralism of Henri de Lubac: Not Everything Is Grace* (New York: Peter Lang, 2011); Steven A. Long, *Natura Pura: On the Recovery of Nature in the Doctrine of Grace* (New York: Fordham University Press, 2010).

Man by his nature is proportioned to a *certain end for which he has a natural appetite*, and which he can work to achieve by his natural powers. This end is a certain contemplation of the divine attributes, in the measure in which this is possible for man through his natural powers; and in this end even the philosophers placed the final happiness of man.

But there is another end to which man is prepared by God which exceeds the proportionality of human nature. This end is eternal life which consists in the vision of God in His essence, an end which exceeds the proportionality of any created nature, being connatural only to God alone.[28]

According to the Thomistic view, this natural happiness proportionate to human nature will be the lot of the infants who die before the age of reason without Baptism.

Compared with supernatural beatitude, of course, this hypothetical natural happiness would indeed be imperfect, for it would fail to satisfy the natural desire to see God. St. Thomas, however, holds that such happiness would be proportionate to the limitations of human nature and would satisfy its proportionate natural desires. In other words, St. Thomas holds that rational creatures are intrinsically open to two final ends: (a) a *proportionate but imperfect* eternal happiness after this life consisting in the contemplation of God in social harmony (and with resurrected bodies) but without the vision of God; and (b) a *disproportionate supernatural perfect* happiness consisting in the vision of God.[29] It is up to the gratuitous love of God to determine which of these ends to realize, and He has, in fact, created mankind for a supernatural end.

The Magisterium has affirmed the possibility of a purely natural end for "intellectual beings" in Pius XII's encyclical *Humani Generis*:

---

[28] My translation and italics. See also *ST* I, q. 62, a. 1, where St. Thomas writes: "Now there is a twofold ultimate perfection of rational or of intellectual nature. The first is one which it can procure of its own natural power; and this is in a measure called beatitude or happiness. Hence Aristotle (*Ethic.* x.) says that man's ultimate happiness consists in his most perfect contemplation, whereby in this life he can behold the best intelligible object; and that is God. Above this happiness there is still another, which we look forward to in the future, whereby we shall see God as He is. This is beyond the nature of every created intellect."

[29] See Feingold, *The Natural Desire to See God*, 1–3, 435–41; Lawrence Feingold, "The Natural Desire to See God, the Twofold End of Man, and Henri de Lubac," *Josephinum Journal of Theology* 18, no. 1 (Winter/Spring 2011): 112–32.

"Others destroy the gratuity of the supernatural order, since God, they say, cannot create intellectual beings without ordering and calling them to the beatific vision."[30] One cannot deny the possibility of a "state of pure nature" for a rational creature without undermining the gratuitousness of the supernatural order.

Opposition to the Thomistic Position

The greatest disagreements over the doctrine of limbo throughout the centuries have concerned the absence of suffering and the possibility of a natural happiness for human beings. St. Thomas vigorously defended these two points, whereas they were denied by the Augustinian school, by the Jansenists, and by others influenced by the Jansenist heresy. The Augustinian school was represented principally by H. Noris (1631–1704), F. Bellelli (1675–1742), and J. L. Berti (1696–1766).[31] These theologians, following St. Augustine, held that unbaptized babies who die before the age of reason are properly in hell, where they must experience some suffering, although the lightest. This position is linked with the denial of the possibility of a purely natural happiness. Part of the reason for this stems from their interpretation of the natural desire to see God as innate.[32] Like the Jansenists, they held that without the beatific vision, the soul would necessarily be essentially frustrated and suffer from its loss, which would make the state of limbo impossible.[33] The Holy See never condemned the Augustinian position, thus leaving as an open question the existence of limbo, understood as the

---

[30] Pius XII, Encyclical *Humani Generis* (Aug 12, 1950), §26 (DS, 3891).

[31] For the position of Noris and Berti with regard to limbo, see George Dyer, "Limbo: A Theological Evaluation," *Theological Studies* 19 (1958): 32–49; Dyer, *Limbo: Unsettled Question,* 72–85.

[32] For the position of Noris, Bellelli, and Berti, denying the possibility of a state of pure nature or a natural happiness, see F. Litt, *La question des rapports entre la nature et la grâce de Baius au Synode de Pistoie,* doctoral dissertation in theology, PUG (Fontaine l'Évêque, 1934), 75–102; J. M. Mejía, "La hipótesis de la naturaleza pura," *Ciencia y fe* 2 (1955): 58–90; M. Wrede, *Die Möglichkeit des Status Naturae Purae im Lichte der kirchlich verurteilten Sätze des Bajus vom Urstand* (Limburg, 1953), 24–28, 49–51; Feingold, *The Natural Desire to See God,* 292.

[33] See Dyer, "Limbo: A Theological Evaluation," 32: "As the Scholastics envision it, limbo embraces two ideas: the exclusion of infants from heaven and their exemption from the pains of hell." The Augustinians denied the second point. See Dyer, *Limbo: Unsettled Question,* 74.

state of exclusion from the beatific vision but without any suffering.[34] The Augustinian and Jansenist rejection of limbo ceased to have a significant following in the nineteenth and twentieth centuries.

Today, almost all contemporary theologians would agree that there should be no eternal suffering for infants who die without personal sin and without Baptism. Many, however, would reject the very possibility of a purely natural happiness for man short of the beatific vision, rejecting the possibility of a "state of pure nature."[35] If the possibility of a natural beatitude is excluded, then the doctrine of limbo no longer makes sense and would appear to be impossible. This is one important reason, I think, that many contemporary theologians reject it.[36]

However, it is one thing to admit the possibility of a natural happiness for an abstract rational creature, or in some other order of creation, as in the hypothetical state of pure nature, and quite another to admit that possibility in *this* supernatural economy of salvation in which mankind has been elevated to a supernatural end and has

---

[34] See the conclusion of Dyer, "Limbo: A Theological Evaluation," 48: "From the sixteenth to the nineteenth century limbo was, as we saw, an open question—debatable and debated. In the nineteenth century the controversy died, and limbo won a common, although uncertain, acceptance among theologians. In our own century we found that theologians were at once unanimous in accepting limbo and at variance in evaluating it."

[35] I have argued in *The Natural Desire to See God According to St. Thomas*, 424–26, 435–41, that there are important reasons for holding the possibility, although certainly not the fittingness, that God could have created mankind in a state in which we would not have been elevated to the supernatural order.

[36] See Charles Cardinal Journet, *La volonté divine salvifique sur les petits enfants* (Bruges: Desclée de Brouwer, 1958), 181–85. See also Henri De Lubac, *The Mystery of the Supernatural*, trans. Rosemary Sheed (New York: Herder and Herder, 1998), 54: "The 'desire to see God' cannot be permanently frustrated without an essential suffering. . . . And consequently—at least in appearance—a good and just God could hardly frustrate me, unless I, through my own fault, turn away from him by choice." Nevertheless, de Lubac's position seems to presuppose that man has already been elevated to the supernatural order, on account of which an absolute desire to see God has been imprinted on every concrete human being. Drawing on this idea, Karl Rahner proposes the thesis that a "supernatural existential" exists in a person prior to Baptism that orients every human being immediately to the beatific vision and gives rise to an innate desire to see God, which likewise rules out the possibility of any natural happiness and thus any possibility of limbo. This supernatural existential, however, is also proper to this supernatural economy of salvation. See Karl Rahner, "Concerning the Relationship Between Nature and Grace," 297–317, esp. 312–13. For a discussion of the differences between de Lubac and Rahner on this point, see Feingold, *The Natural Desire to See God*, 329–39.

received a new Head and King. The principal difficulty with the Thomistic solution is not the affirmation of the abstract possibility of a state of connatural human happiness short of the beatific vision, but in explaining how there can be a state of natural happiness in *this* salvific economy in which mankind has been elevated to a supernatural end.[37] Thus I agree with St. Thomas on the abstract possibility of a connatural end for human beings, but still hold that his solution is very problematic in this supernatural economy of salvation, as will be explained in the following section.

5. St. Thomas's Two Attempts to Explain How a Purely Natural Happiness without Suffering Could Be Possible in This Economy of Salvation

We have seen that there should be no penalty of suffering for souls who leave this life without any personal sin, but those who die with original sin cannot see God. The great difficulty of the Thomistic position is to show how these two theses can go together in *this* economy of salvation. This is by far the most problematic aspect of the question of limbo. St. Thomas deals with this question in only two articles, one at the beginning of his career (*In II Sent.*, d. 33, q. 2, a. 2) and the other from his maturity (*De malo*, q. 5, a. 3). In both cases, St. Thomas vigorously defends the thesis that there is no interior suffering or sorrow in this state, but for different reasons.

Early Hypothesis in the Commentary on the Sentences: Those in Limbo Know What They Are Missing

To explain how the souls in limbo do not experience interior sorrow, it must first be asked whether they know what they have lost. St. Thomas tried both possibilities.[38] In the earlier treatment, *In II Sent.*, d. 33, q.

---

[37] See Edmond Boissard, *Réflexions sur le sort des enfants morts sans baptême* (Paris: Éditions de la Source, 1974), 136–38; ITC, "The Hope of Salvation for Infants," §95, pp. 396–97: "Though a purely natural order is conceivable, no human life is actually lived in such an order. The actual order is supernatural; channels of grace are open from the very beginning of each human life. All are born with that humanity which was assumed by Christ himself, and all live in some kind of relation to him, with different degrees of explicitness (cf. *LG* §16) and acceptance, at every moment."

[38] For an excellent analysis of both solutions of St. Thomas and the develop-

2, a. 2, he considers three opinions put forth on this question by his predecessors. The first opinion says that they do not know what they have lost and therefore do not grieve over it. St. Thomas here argues that this is improbable because a separated soul should have perfect knowledge of all that is open to natural reason "and much more." The second opinion, which follows the Augustinian tradition, is that the separated souls know God and what they have lost through original sin, and they experience some sorrow, which, however, is mitigated by the fact that they know that they did not lose heaven through their own fault. St. Thomas also rejects this view as improbable because if it is admitted that they experience some sorrow over the lack of the beatific vision, this suffering cannot be a "light" suffering, given that it involves the loss of the infinite good with no hope of recovery.

The third opinion, to which St. Thomas subscribes, is a kind of synthesis of the first two. It is similar to the second in admitting knowledge of what has been lost through original sin, but it differs in holding that all interior sorrow is excluded, as in the first view. This third opinion supposes that souls of the children in limbo will know the fundamental outline of salvation history and that they would thus know what they lost, but they do not grieve over it because, since they are no longer in a state of trial, their wills permanently abide in conformity with the divine will, from which they never voluntarily deviated.[39] In this state they cannot rebel against the divine plan nor grieve over the fact that it results in their being deprived of the beatific vision, for they will recognize that the vision is immeasurably above their own nature:

---

ment of his thought on this matter, see Serge-Thomas Bonino, "The Theory of Limbo and the Mystery of the Supernatural in St. Thomas Aquinas," in *Surnaturel: A Controversy at the Heart of Twentieth-Century Thomistic Thought*, ed. Bonino, trans. Robert Williams (Ave Maria, FL: Sapientia Press of Ave Maria University, 2009), 117–54. See also Christopher Beiting, "The Idea of Limbo in Thomas Aquinas," *The Thomist* 62 (1998): 237–44; Bertrand Gaullier, *L'état des enfants morts sans baptême d'après saint Thomas d'Aquin* (Paris: Lethielleux, 1961).

[39] This type of solution, using the notion of wise resignation, was defended by St. Bonaventure in II *Sent.*, d. 33, q. 3, a. 2, ad 2 (797b), and by St. Albert in *Quaestio de Poena*, a. 1. This position was maintained earlier by William of Auvergne, who introduces the example that reasonable people do not suffer over not being king because they know that it is not due to them. See Richard Weberberger, O.S.B., "Limbus puerorum. Zur Entstehung eines theologischen Begriffes," *Recherches de théologie ancienne et médiévale* 35 (1968): 131.

It should be realized that if someone lacks that which exceeds his proportionality, he will not be afflicted, if he follows right reason. He will only be afflicted if he lacks that to which in some way he was proportioned. No wise man is afflicted that he cannot fly like a bird, or that he is not king or emperor, since such things are not due to him. He would be afflicted, however, if he were deprived of something which in some way he had an aptitude to possess. Therefore I say that every man having the use of free will was proportioned to achieving eternal life, because he could prepare himself for grace, by which he would be able to merit eternal life. Therefore, if he fails to achieve this he will have a maximum sorrow for having lost something that could have been his. However, the children [who died before the age of reason without Baptism] were never proportioned to having eternal life, because this was not due them from the principles of their nature since it exceeds all the powers of nature, nor could they accomplish personal acts by which they could have attained so great a good. Therefore, they will not sorrow at all because they lack the vision of God; rather, they will rejoice in the fact that they participate greatly in the divine goodness in their natural perfections.[40]

In his response to the fifth objection in this article, Aquinas says that the souls in limbo should not be considered to be deprived of beatitude because of a perpetual separation from God,[41] for he indicates that there are two grades of union (and thus of beatitude) with God: through natural goods and through glory. The souls in limbo are deprived of the union with God through glory, but they are still united with Him through a "participation in natural goods," in which they rejoice in a natural knowledge and love of God.

---

[40] Thomas Aquinas, *In II Sent.*, d. 33, q. 2, a. 2.

[41] Thomas Aquinas, *In II Sent.*, d. 33, q. 2, a. 2, ad 5: "Although the unbaptized children are separated from God with regard to that union which is through glory, they are nevertheless not wholly separated from Him. On the contrary, they are united to Him through a participation in natural goods, and thus they will also be able to rejoice in Him through natural knowledge and love."

Problems with Aquinas's Earlier Hypothesis: "Faith" in Limbo without Hope and Charity?

This early solution has some major difficulties because it involves a strange mixture of natural and supernatural elements. This solution presupposes that in limbo there will be a supernatural knowledge of salvation history and of Jesus as Redeemer.[42] This knowledge would seem to involve supernatural faith because it would involve holding truths whose evidence remains unseen, for they are excluded from the vision of God. According to this hypothesis, they would be assenting to mysteries that transcend the power of human reason, which cannot be done without the aid of grace.

Although, according to this hypothesis, the souls in limbo would have supernatural knowledge without the beatific vision (and thus seemingly through a kind of faith), they certainly would not have the theological virtue of hope, possessed by the faithful in the Church militant or in Purgatory, or previously in the "limbo of the Fathers," referred to also as the bosom of Abraham, because they would know that there is no hope of them attaining to the beatific vision. It would certainly be odd and unfitting for souls in limbo eternally to have faith in God's plan of salvation history but without any hope of ever having vision of what they believe.

Likewise, the souls in limbo, according to this hypothesis, would lack supernatural love for God although they would love Him naturally as the Creator of every good. But if the souls in limbo know that Jesus died for them on the Cross and has loved them in a mad and superabundant way, how could their love for Him fittingly remain on a purely natural level?

In other words, if one assumes that the children in limbo have knowledge of what they have lost, there follows not only the problem of how they are not envious. A more difficult problem, to my mind, not addressed by St. Thomas, is how God could fittingly will to give them some supernatural knowledge without giving them supernatural grace, charity, or the beatific vision. He would be giving them the power to know *truths worthy of the deepest adoration but without giving them the power to love them accordingly.* How would this be for God's

---

[42] On the grave difficulties of admitting this supernatural knowledge in limbo, see Edmond Boissard, *Réflexions sur le sort des enfants morts sans baptême* (Paris: Éditions de la Source, 1974).

greater glory? This hypothesis admits two elements of the supernatural order—supernatural knowledge and the perpetual conformity of the will with that of God—into the natural happiness of the persons in limbo while at the same time denying the most essential elements of the supernatural order, which are sanctifying grace, charity, glory, and ultimately the vision of God.

A secondary problem is that St. Thomas argues that there will be no envy in limbo by proposing a perpetual conformity of the free will of those in limbo with the divine will. But it is not clear by what means this perpetual conformity would come about. In the case of the blessed in heaven, this conformity is explained by the beatific vision, for all who see God face to face can never prefer some other finite good to Him and His plan. But in limbo they will not see God and will lack both grace and glory.[43]

Later Hypothesis from De Malo*: Those in Limbo Do Not Know What They Are Missing*

It is not surprising that the mature St. Thomas sought a different hypothesis to explain the absence of suffering in the souls in limbo, one that would avoid the problem of mixing the natural and supernatural levels. In the later work, *De malo*, q. 5, a. 3, St. Thomas explains the lack of sorrow of the souls in limbo by a more nuanced version of the opinion ascribing ignorance to the children that he had rejected as improbable in his commentary on the *Sentences*. He does this by distinguishing more carefully between natural and supernatural knowledge,[44] affirming a perfect knowledge of the natural order for the souls in limbo, while denying *all knowledge* of the supernatural order:

---

[43] The souls in purgatory are confirmed in good, but in their case, that is possible through the power of grace.

[44] See Bonino, "The Theory of Limbo," 143: "With this article, the originality of St. Thomas on the question of limbo comes to light. . . . He holds—and he alone—that the infant who dies unbaptized knows *nothing* about true beatitude. He does not know therefore of what he is deprived (nor, *a fortiori*, why) and in consequence experiences no suffering. On the contrary, he rejoices in what he believes to be his ultimate happiness. To my knowledge, the prior theological tradition had never plumbed this possibility; perhaps because it had not sufficiently highlighted the transcendence of faith compared with all natural knowledge, even the most perfect."

We say that the children's souls indeed do not lack the natural knowledge that the separated soul by its nature deserves. And the separated souls lack the supernatural knowledge that faith implants in us in this life. . . . It belongs to natural cognition that the soul know that it is created for happiness, and that happiness consists of attainment of the perfect good. But that the perfect good for which human beings have been created is the glory that the saints possess is beyond natural knowledge. And so the Apostle says in 1 Cor 2:9 that "the eye has not seen, nor the ear heard, nor has it entered into the heart of human beings, what things God has prepared for those who love him," and then (v. 10) adds: "And God has revealed them to us through his Spirit." And this revelation indeed belongs to faith. And so the children's souls do not know that they are deprived of such a good, and they accordingly do not grieve. But those souls possess without anguish what they have by natural knowledge.[45]

This solution is clearly more consistent than the first solution. It depicts the state of limbo as a purely natural state in which knowledge of the natural order is perfected,[46] but all knowledge of the supernatural order is absent, and thus those in limbo have no supernatural faith, hope, or charity, whereas they have a perfect knowledge of natural theology and a natural love of God above all things.

Problems with the Later Hypothesis

Although this solution is elegant and clear, it is problematic because it presupposes that the souls in limbo are entirely ignorant of the true shape of human history, which, in fact, is salvation history. It seems

---

[45] Thomas Aquinas, *De malo*, q. 5, a. 3, in *On Evil*, trans. Richard Regan (Oxford: Oxford University Press, 2003), 241.

[46] Aquinas, *De malo*, q. 5, a. 3, in Regan, 240: "It is natural for separated souls to be more rather than less endowed with knowledge than souls in the present life." St. Thomas and others who follow this position would also hold that those in limbo will have a bodily existence (in resurrected bodies after the general resurrection) like that in Eden. Thus they would have natural and preternatural gifts (immortality, integrity, immunity from suffering, infused natural knowledge) but without supernatural gifts, such as sanctifying grace, faith, hope, and charity. See Journet, *La volonté divine salvifique sur les petits enfants*, 169.

that a key element of natural happiness for human beings is a true understanding of our own identity, origin, place, and mission in human society and history, and in God's plan. We know that orphans suffer from a lack of knowledge of their biological parents. We all have a proportionate natural desire to understand our place in the world and in society and history. This later solution of St. Thomas does not provide for such knowledge to be possessed by these children, for human history and destiny cannot be understood without knowledge of the supernatural order. It seems that such a proportionate natural desire to know one's true origins, family history, and proper destiny could not remain unfulfilled in a state of natural happiness. Parents of children who died before Baptism (as in a miscarriage), for example, are rightly distressed by the thought that those children may never be united to them or know them, through no fault of their own.

In other words, the purely natural state that St. Thomas is suggesting as the state of souls in limbo is not at all equivalent to the well-known hypothesis of a "state of pure nature." For in a "state of pure nature," human beings would rightly understand themselves as living in a purely natural order with its own proper history and development, in which their family history would be situated. This would not be the case, however, for the unbaptized children in St. Thomas's solution in *De malo*, q. 5, a. 3. In this hypothesis the inhabitants of limbo would be living in a supernatural economy with a supernatural history of salvation, of which they would be entirely ignorant, and thus they would be mistaken about who they are and unable to understand their own history or even know their parents. That would not be the case at all in a hypothetical "state of pure nature." Thus one could, without inconsistency, maintain that God could have made human beings without elevating them to the supernatural order[47] and yet maintain that a purely natural state for human beings in this concrete order, as in the hypothesis of limbo, would not be fitting.

I am presupposing here that the notion of natural happiness implies the fulfillment of all natural desire that is *proportionate* to human nature. Supernatural beatitude includes the fulfillment of all natural desire, even that which is disproportionate to human nature,

---

[47] See Pius XII, *Humani Generis*, §26: "Others destroy the gratuity of the supernatural order, since God, they say, cannot create intellectual beings without ordering and calling them to the beatific vision."

such as the natural desire to see God.[48] Knowledge of one's own identity and place in the divine plan, however, would seem to be proportionate to a rational being, who poses the questions: Who am I? What is the meaning of history? For what end did God create human beings? What is the happiness for which we were made? What are the ordinary means to attain that end?

Even though Christ, the Church, and the sacraments are supernatural realities, knowledge of them is indispensable in order to answer these most basic questions that ought to be posed by all those who come to the age of reason. Therefore, the fulfillment of the natural desire to know the answers to these questions ought to be fulfilled in order for natural happiness to exist in a terminal state.

Christ became man and died for the unbaptized children, as for everyone else, and He established the sacraments as the ordinary means for their salvation.[49] It seems that it would be unfitting for them never to know this fact essential to who they really are in the divine plan. They are members of humanity that has been gratuitously elevated to a supernatural end and persons for whom Christ died. The earlier solution of St. Thomas is better in this regard, I think, because it supposes that the unbaptized children would know the true shape of human history, their place in it, and why they are not united with the blessed in seeing God.[50]

---

[48] See *ST* I-II, q. 3, a. 8.

[49] See the condemnation of the fifth proposition of Cornelius Jansenius (DS, 2005): "It is Semipelagian to say that Christ died or shed His blood for all men without exception."

[50] In the middle of the twentieth century, Jacques Maritain made an interesting attempt to defend the traditional Thomistic doctrine of limbo in its most optimistic form by following the logic of St. Thomas's earlier treatment, even though he leaves open the possibility of the later solution. See Jacques Maritain, "Beginning with a Reverie," in *Untrammeled Approaches*, trans. Bernard Doering (Notre Dame, IN: University of Notre Dame Press, 1997), 3–26. For the date of this essay, see *Untrammeled Approaches*, 3n1, which states that thirty copies of this essay were distributed in 1939 and again in 1961 before finally being published in 1973, the year of Maritain's death. See 16–17: "They are not envious, and having themselves everything to which their nature as such can lay claim, they rejoice rather in the happiness of the elect, supposing that they are aware of the existence of these elect. . . . For if not they, at least their happier, blessed, sisters have profited from the redemption which this fall brought about. And they are happy that their sisters are blessed, and they admire and love Jesus, with a natural love—just as they love Beauty and Goodness. And the holy angels—who can cross the chaos, and who like stars illumine

It seems that both of St. Thomas's opposing solutions to this question fail to eliminate grave difficulties that stem from the mixing of the natural and supernatural orders. If they have only knowledge of the natural order, as in the later solution of *De malo*, then they would not be able to understand their own fundamental history, which in fact is supernatural. They would also find themselves eternally excluded from the society of those to whom they are naturally bound by ties of birth and would never know the cause for that exclusion. If, on the other hand, they are granted supernatural knowledge, as in St. Thomas's earlier solution, how could they receive that without supernatural faith, and how could they fittingly lack supernatural love?

St. Thomas therefore does not seem to have been successful in elucidating how there can be a true and fitting natural happiness for the souls who die with original sin in this economy of salvation.

Reasons for Hope for the Salvation of Infants Who Die without Baptism

God Is Not Bound by the Sacraments

Another principle central to this question is that it is theologically certain that God can grant the effect of Baptism without a person receiving the sacrament or, in the case of an infant, even personally desiring it. It is traditionally held that St. John the Baptist received the forgiveness of original sin while still in the womb,[51] when Mary came to visit St. Elizabeth.[52]

---

the night of Limbo—tell them the stories of Paradise." For an evaluation of Maritain's proposal, see Feingold, "Maritain's Eschatological Reverie," 3–23. Maritain's position was followed by his friend Charles Journet in *La volonté divine salvifique sur les petits enfants*, esp. 41–42. On the general tendency of the commentators of St. Thomas to follow Aquinas's earlier solution, see Bonino, "The Theory of Limbo," 149–53.

[51] See Luke 1:15: "He will be filled with the Holy Spirit, even from his mother's womb."

[52] See Augustine, *Questions on the Heptateuch* 3.84, in *Writings on the Old Testament*, trans. Joseph Lienhard and Sean Doyle (Hyde Park, NY: New City Press, 2016) 260: "From this [the examples of Moses, John the Baptist, and the good thief] one gathers that invisible sanctification was present to some and benefited them even without visible sacraments." See also Hugh of St. Victor, *On the Sacraments of the Christian Faith* 1.9.5, trans. Deferrari, 161: "Now God can

St. Thomas admits this possibility of an extraordinary intervention of God to forgive original sin in the womb in an article in the
Summa on the impossibility of Baptism for a fetus still in the womb:

> Children while in the mother's womb have not yet come forth
> into the world to live among other men. Consequently they
> cannot be subject to the action of man, so as to receive the
> sacrament, at the hands of man, unto salvation. They can,
> however, be subject to the action of God, in Whose sight they
> live, so as, by a kind of privilege, to receive the grace of sanc-
> tification; as was the case with those who were sanctified in
> the womb.[53]

Although there are no ordinary means other than sacramental
Baptism that can be applied by human action for infants to receive
the forgiveness of original sin and the infusion of sanctifying grace,
all must hold the possibility that God can act mercifully outside the
sacraments.[54] Fetuses in the womb in danger of death cannot be aided
by any sacramental action, but they are open to directly receiving
God's saving action. Nevertheless, while acknowledging the abstract
possibility of such a divine intervention, St. Thomas and his contemporaries assumed that this kind of extraordinary intervention was
limited to rare cases, such as Mary's Immaculate Conception, St. John
the Baptist, and the prophet Jeremiah (Jer 1:5).

---

save man without these [sacraments], who can bestow upon man His virtue and
sanctification and salvation in whatever way He wills. For by that spirit with
which He teaches man without word, He can also justify without sacrament if
he wills, since the virtue of God is not subject to elements from necessity, even
if the grace of God be given according to dispensation through sacraments.
Hence it is that we read that certain ones even without sacraments of this
kind were justified and, we believe, were saved, just as it is read that Jeremias
was sanctified in the womb and it is prophesied that John the Baptist was to
be filled with the Holy Ghost from his mother's womb and those who as just
under the natural law pleased God."

[53] *ST* III, q. 68, a. 11, ad 1.

[54] See Peter Lombard, *Sentences*, bk. 4, d. 1, ch. 5; *Summa sententiarum*, tract. 5, ch.
6 (PL 176:133D); Bonaventure, *Breviloquium* 6.1.5. See also Charles-Vincent
Héris, "Le salut des enfants morts sans baptême," *La Maison-Dieu* 10 (1947),
86–105, at 89–90, 105; L. Renwart, S.J., "Le Baptême des enfants et les limbes,"
Nouvelle revue théologique 80 (May 1958): 449–67, at 467; Albert Michel, *Enfants
morts sans baptême, certitudes et hypothèses* (Paris: Téqui, 1954), 24.

St. Thomas's teaching on the privilege of sanctification in the womb was anticipated by Guerric de Saint-Quentin (d. 1245), the first Dominican to have a teaching chair at the University of Paris. Referring to remedies for original sin, he distinguishes between a remedy for original sin by way of law and by way of privilege. The latter is outside of the general law and can operate where the law cannot be fulfilled:

> There are two kinds of remedies, one by way of Law and another by way of privilege. The way of privilege is the remedy of sanctification in the womb, and this belongs to few and thus occurs by an invisible action. The remedy that is by way of Law was circumcision in its time, and Baptism and Penance in our time. This happens in a manifest way by bodily action. But this remedy cannot be given to infants existing in the womb because they are still hidden. Therefore they cannot be given the remedy that is by way of Law. But the remedy that is by way of secret privilege is given, and God can give this to whom He wills, when He wills, and as He wills.[55]

The sacraments are willed by God to serve as instrumental causes in the infusion of sanctifying grace and the other supernatural gifts that flow from grace. It is fitting for human nature and in harmony with the Incarnation that grace be granted to us through sensible signs established by God. Thus the sacraments are necessary for man both by fittingness and by the divine law establishing their necessity as ordinary means. God, however, has no need of sacraments in order to infuse grace and can always work outside of the sacramental order. John Paul II, in *Reconciliatio et Paenitentia*, writes: "Certainly the Savior and his salvific action are not so bound to a sacramental sign as to be unable in any period or area of the history of salvation to work outside and above the sacraments."[56] The *Catechism of the Catholic Church* emphasizes this: "*God has bound salvation to the sacrament of*

---

[55] Guerric de Saint-Quentin, *Quæstiones de quolibet*, q. 4, a. 2, secundo, critical edition by Walter H. Principe (Toronto: Pontifical Institute of Medieval Studies, 2002), 245–46; quoted in Jean Pateau, *Le salut des enfants morts sans baptême: d'après saint Thomas d'Aquin, où est Abel, mon frère?* (Paris; Perpignan: Artège-Lethielleux, 2017), 42–43. See Michel, *Enfants morts sans baptême*, 52–53.

[56] John Paul II, *Reconciliatio et Paenitentia*, §31, no. 1.

Baptism, but he himself is not bound by his sacraments."[57]

Every human being, including the unborn child at any stage of development, is *capax Dei* on account of being made in the image of God. All babies have a specific *obediential potency* proper to the rational creature[58] to obey God if He chooses to elevate them and calls them: "Friend, go up higher" (Luke 14:10). We can hope therefore that God, by extra-sacramental means, will give sanctifying grace to infants before they die without Baptism, such that they will not die with original sin and thus will not be deprived of the vision of God for eternity. Even if this does not occur through Baptism of blood because they were not killed for Christ, or through their own act of desire for Baptism because they are not yet able to make a personal act, it is reasonable to hope that it would be granted by God, not through any human act, but in response to the desire of the Church, expressing the desire of Christ who died for those children.

Vatican II and Post-Conciliar Teaching on Hope for Infants Who Die without Baptism

The Second Vatican Council did not directly address the thesis of limbo, but the teaching of *Gaudium et Spes*, §22 has profound implications for this question:

> Since Christ died for all men, and since the ultimate vocation of man is in fact one, and divine, we ought to believe that the Holy Spirit in a manner known only to God offers to every man the possibility of being associated with this paschal mystery.

In the previous chapter we have analyzed the importance of this conciliar text for the question of Baptism of desire for those who attain the age of reason. The text, however, speaks universally of "every man," and is not limited to those who attain the age of reason. Thus we must hold that the Holy Spirit also makes it possible for infants or the unborn who die without Baptism before the dawning of reason to be associated with the Paschal mystery and the grace Christ has merited. This belief provides a solid foundation for the hope that God's mercy

---

[57] *CCC*, §1257 (italics original).
[58] See Feingold, *The Natural Desire to See God*, 112–19.

will make those who die without Baptism and without the ability to personally desire it, partakers of the grace of being configured to the Paschal mystery.

Four years after the Council, prayers were included in the *Ordo Exsequiarum* (Order of Christian Funerals) for the Roman Rite for babies dying without Baptism whose parents intended to have the child baptized. These prayers entrust the child to the mercy and "loving embrace" of the Lord, and also mention the faith and desire of the parents and the Christian community. In the prayer of Final Commendation in the *Order of Christian Funerals* for a child who died before Baptism, the minister prays: "Let us commend this child to the Lord's merciful keeping; and let us pray with all our hearts for N. and N. Even as they grieve at the loss of their child, they entrust him (her) to the loving embrace of God."[59] In the rite of Committal for an unbaptized baby, the minister prays that God enfold the unbaptized child with eternal life:

> Lord God, ever caring and gentle, we commit to your love this little one (N), who brought joy to our lives for so short a time. Enfold him (her) in eternal life. We pray for his (her) parents who are saddened by the loss of their child. . . . May they all meet one day in the joy and peace of your Kingdom.[60]

The concluding prayer prays that the unbaptized child find a place in God's Kingdom:

> God of mercy, in the mystery of your wisdom you have drawn this child N. to yourself. In the midst of our pain and sorrow, we acknowledge you as Lord of the living and the dead and we search for our peace in your will. In these final moments we stand together in prayer, believing in your compassion and generous love. Deliver this child N. out of death and grant him/her a place in your kingdom of peace.[61]

---

[59] *Order of Christian Funerals: The Roman Ritual Revised by Decree of the Second Vatican Ecumenical Council and Published by Authority of Pope Paul VI* (Chicago: Liturgy Training Publications, 2018), Final Commendation, §320C, p. 176.

[60] *Order of Christian Funerals*, Rite of Committal, §322B, p. 188.

[61] *Order of Christian Funerals*, Rite of Committal, §325C, p. 190.

The faith of the parents is mentioned in the opening prayer at the Vigil and Funeral Mass for a child who died before Baptism: "O God, searcher of hearts and most loving consoler, who know the faith of these parents, grant that, as they mourn their child, now departed from this life, they may be assured that he (she) has been entrusted to your divine compassion."[62]

Canon 1183 of the 1983 *Code of Canon Law* ratified this practice, permitting the celebration of ecclesiastical funerals for unbaptized babies whose parents intended to baptize them.[63]

In harmony with the prayers of the *Ordo Exsequiarum*, the *Catechism of the Catholic Church*, §1261 affirms that because of God's universal salvific will, and because Jesus asked that the little children come to Him, it is possible to hope that there is a "way of salvation" for those who die before the age of reason without Baptism. This possibility of hope is mentioned again in the *Catechism of the Catholic Church*, §1283: "With respect to children who have died without Baptism, the liturgy of the Church invites us to trust in God's mercy and to pray for their salvation."

In §1257, the *Catechism* affirms that the Church knows of no means other than Baptism to assure entrance into Heaven. Baptism is the ordinary means established by God for the forgiveness of original sin, to which He has "bound salvation." Adults can attain the effect of the sacrament through an upright personal desire for it, but this would not be available to infants. The paragraph ends, however, with the italicized sentence: "*God has bound salvation to the sacrament of Baptism, but he himself is not bound by his sacraments.*" God can cause the infusion of grace in an infant outside of the sacrament of Baptism.

In the encyclical *Evangelium Vitae*, §99 of 1995, St. John Paul II applied the teaching of the *Catechism of the Catholic Church*, §1261 to the tragic case of aborted children, speaking of "sure hope" of their salvation: "I would now like to say a special word to women who have had an abortion. . . . To the same Father and his mercy you can with sure hope entrust your child."[64]

---

[62] *Order of Christian Funerals*, Vigil for a Deceased Child, §254C, p. 146.

[63] CIC, can. 1183, §2: "The local ordinary can permit children whom the parents intended to baptize but who died before baptism to be given ecclesiastical funerals."

[64] John Paul II, *Evangelium Vitae*, §99. This text (taken from the Vatican website) is the correct translation of the official Latin version. A commonly used English translation, instead of alluding to the possibility of hope ("you are able

On April 20, 2007, the International Theological Commission produced a document on the question of limbo, *The Hope of Salvation for Infants Who Die Without Being Baptized*. This is not a magisterial document but simply the consultation of eminent theologians. It does not seek to break new ground but to reflect on the theological foundations for the hope for unbaptized babies expressed in the *Catechism of the Catholic Church*, §1261, in the funeral rites for infants who have died without Baptism, and in *Evangelium Vitae*, §99. This ITC document states:

> Our conclusion is that the many factors that we have considered above give serious theological and liturgical grounds for hope that unbaptised infants who die will be saved and enjoy the beatific vision. We emphasise that these are reasons for prayerful *hope*, rather than grounds for sure knowledge. There is much that has not been revealed to us (cf. Jn 16:12). We live by faith and hope in the God of mercy and love who had been revealed to us in Christ, and the Spirit moves us to pray in constant thankfulness and joy (1 Thess 5:18).[65]

The Necessity of Baptism as the Sole Ordinary Means, and God's Extraordinary Action

Christ instituted the sacraments—and Baptism in particular—to be the sole *ordinary channels by which we obtain sanctifying grace* in the New Covenant. We have seen that the sacrament of Baptism is the sole ordinary means to receive the indispensable means, which is sanctifying grace. That is, *the effect* of Baptism is indispensable for salvation, but not the *sacrament itself*, because God can accomplish the effect

---

to entrust with hope your infant to the same Father and His mercy"), states: "You will come to understand that nothing is definitively lost and you will also be able to ask forgiveness from your child, who is now living in the Lord." This however, does not represent the official text, which is always the Latin text, regardless of what language such documents were originally written in. See Francis A. Sullivan, "The Development of Doctrine About Infants Who Die Unbaptized," *Theological Studies* 72 (2011): 11–14.

[65] ITC, "The Hope of Salvation for Infants," §102, p. 400 (italics original). For a good summary of the principal arguments and conclusions of this document, see Gavin D'Costa, *Christianity and World Religions: Disputed Questions in the Theology of Religions* (Oxford: Blackwell, 2009), 196–98.

of the sacrament without making use of the sacrament, by directly infusing grace.[66] As mentioned above, God does this in Baptism of desire and Baptism of blood. He could do it for infants who are not martyred, whenever He wills.

It is fitting that God anticipate the effect of the sacrament when He is beseeched by an act of faith, hope, and charity. This is the foundation for Baptism of desire. It is also fitting that He anticipate the effect when someone is killed for His name's sake, and this is the basis for Baptism of blood. Why then would it not be fitting for God to anticipate the effect of the sacrament when He is beseeched with faith, hope, and charity, not by the person himself if he or she is incapable, but by the community to whom these persons are entrusted by God, and by the universal Church, for they come into this world utterly dependent on others?

Although all must grant this possibility of God's extraordinary action on behalf of unbaptized babies, the extension of this action can be understood in very different ways. Should we think of this as a rare privilege, limited to Mary, John the Baptist, and a few others like Jeremiah,[67] or are there theological foundations for hope that this group has, analogously, an extension that is much broader, or even universal, to include all those who die before the age of reason?

God has not directly revealed the answer to this question.[68] Why this "gap" in Revelation? God has revealed to His Church the sacramental actions that she is obliged to administer. But with regard to unbaptized infants, we are speaking precisely about cases in which the sacramental order cannot be applied, either in fact or through personal desire. Thus we are dealing with cases that escape the possibility of

---

[66] Many theologians have taught that Baptism is necessary for those before the age of reason by a *relative* but not absolute *necessity of means*. See chapter 15 above, pp. 555–60 and ITC, "The Hope of Salvation for Infants," §10, p. 360; Albert Michel, *Enfants morts sans baptême, certitudes et hypothèses* (Paris: Téqui, 1954), 4–5; Goupil, *Les sacraments* (Paris, 1926), 1:106.

[67] See Jer 1:5: "Before I formed you in the womb I knew you, and before you were born I consecrated you."

[68] See ITC, "The Hope of Salvation for Infants," §79, p. 390: "It must be clearly acknowledged that the Church does not have sure knowledge about the salvation of unbaptised infants who die. She knows and celebrates the glory of the Holy Innocents, but the destiny of the generality of infants who die without baptism has not been revealed to us, and the Church teaches and judges only with regard to what has been revealed. What we do positively know of God, Christ and the Church gives us grounds to hope for their salvation."

human cooperation except through the desire of the Church, leaving the action to God Himself. It is not necessary for the Church to know with certainty what lies outside her possible sphere of action.

The theological tradition until the twentieth century has generally presupposed that such extraordinary interventions of God are few in number. The prayers of the *Ordo Exsequiarum*, the *Catechism of the Catholic Church*, and *Evangelium Vitae*, §99, on the contrary, invite us to hope for a much larger or even universal extension of this divine intervention. Reasons for hoping in this more extended merciful action of God include God's universal salvific will and Christ's universal kingship. An additional factor is the intrinsic difficulty of the Thomistic solution in maintaining the possibility of a natural happiness in this supernatural economy, as shown above.

The Role of the Desire of Parents and the Church for the Salvation of Infants Not Able to Receive Baptism

Salvation of Babies through the Faith of Their Parents before the Promulgation of Baptism

It was the common teaching of medieval scholastics that God provided a remedy for original sin also for babies dying before the age of reason before the promulgation of the Gospel.[69] Innocent III wrote: "Indeed, it is unthinkable that all the little children, of whom so great a multitude dies every day, should perish without the merciful God, who wishes no one to perish, having provided them also with some means of salvation."[70]

St. Thomas, like his contemporaries, was very concerned to defend the universal salvific will of God with respect to children who died

---

[69] See, for example, Augustine, *On Marriage and Concupiscence* 2.11.24, in *NPNF*1, 5:292; Gregory the Great, *Morals on the Book of Job* 4.3, trans. Parker, 179: "But that which the water of Baptism avails for with us, this either faith alone did of old in behalf of infants, or, for those of riper years, the virtue of sacrifice, or, for all that came of the stock of Abraham, the mystery of circumcision"; Bede, Homily 11, bk. 1, On the Octave Day of Christmas; Bernard, *Ad Hugonem de sancto Victore, Epistula seu Tractatus de Baptismo* (Letter to Hugh of St. Victor on Baptism), PL 182:1033–34; Peter Lombard, *Sentences*, bk. 4, d. 1, ch. 8.

[70] Innocent III, *Maiores Ecclesiae causas* (DS, 780).

before the promulgation of the Gospel. As seen in chapter 14, he argues that the children of Israel received sanctifying grace on the eighth day when the boys were circumcised.[71] He even poses the question of a child who died before being circumcised on the eighth day and mentions the opinion of Hugh of St. Victor, according to which such a child would be saved by the faith of the parents, as in the time before the institution of circumcision.[72]

What about the Gentile babies? Following an established theological tradition,[73] St. Thomas held, as seen above, that the grace of God would have been given to remit original sin prior to Abraham and to those outside of Israel. He thinks it probable that this would have been occasioned by the prayers of parents for their children, according to whatever rite was traditional in their culture:

> Just as before the institution of circumcision, faith in Christ to come justified both children and adults, so, too, after its institution. But before, there was no need of a sign expressive of this faith; because as yet believers had not begun to be united together apart from unbelievers for the worship of one God. It is probable, however, that parents who were believers offered up some prayers to God for their children, especially if these were in any danger. Or bestowed some blessing on them, as a "seal of faith"; just as the adults offered prayers and sacrifices for themselves.[74]

If the grace of justification was given gratuitously and liberally even to pagan infants before the promulgation of the Gospel, it seems reasonable to think that in the Christian era God would still will to give it generously and gratuitously to those who are not able to receive

---

[71] See *ST* III, q. 70, a. 4.

[72] Thomas Aquinas, *In IV Sent.*, d. 1, q. 2, a. 3, qla. 1, ad 4. He cites Hugh of St. Victor, *On the Sacraments of the Christian Faith* 1.12.3.

[73] See chapter 14 above, pp. 514–15; Gregory the Great, *Morals on the Book of Job* 4.3; Bede, Homily 11, bk. 1, On the Octave Day of Christmas; Hugh of St. Victor, *On the Sacraments of the Christian Faith* 1.12.2; Peter Lombard, *Sentences*, bk. 4, d. 1, ch. 8, trans. Silano, p. 7: "As for those who lived before circumcision, children were justified by the faith of their parents, and parents by the power of sacrifices, namely, the power which they perceived spiritually in those sacrifices."

[74] *ST* III, q. 70, a. 4, ad 2.

Baptism. The promulgation of the Gospel should not limit the avail-ability of the infusion of sanctifying grace, but, if anything, enlarge it.

St. Thomas does not directly address this point. Instead he assumed, following St. Augustine,[75] Fulgentius,[76] Peter Lombard,[77] and the great majority of the theologians of his time,[78] that after the Gospel's promulgation we cannot hope in general for the salvation of infants who die unbaptized,[79] even though before that promulga-tion such salvation could have been possible through the faith of the parents without any particular rite. Why has the promulgation of the Gospel restricted the power of the faith of parents to join their dying children, born or unborn, to the Savior? If there was hope for the pagan infants snatched away by death before the age of reason, why does that hope not continue under the Gospel, and why would it not still continue in those vast regions where the Gospel has not yet been sufficiently promulgated?

As seen above, St. Thomas assumed, with the theologians of his time, that by the end of the apostolic age, and certainly in his own day, the Gospel was sufficiently promulgated in the whole world.[80] Today we are far more aware of the wide extent of invincible igno-rance. For this reason, the *Catechism of the Catholic Church*, §1257 says that Baptism "is necessary for salvation for those to whom the Gospel has been proclaimed and who have had the possibility of asking for this sacrament." That which is necessary by a necessity of precept and not by an indispensable necessity of means should only be binding on those who know about it and are able to receive it.

---

[75] Augustine, *The Nature and Origin of the Soul* 3.9.12.

[76] Fulgentius, *To Peter on the Faith* 27.70.

[77] Peter Lombard, bk. 4, ch. 4, no. 12, trans. Silano, 24: "Nor is someone else's faith so useful to a child as his own faith is to an adult. For the faith of the Church is not sufficient for children without the sacrament. If they should die without baptism, even as they are being brought to baptism, they will be damned, as is proved by many testimonies of the Saints."

[78] Two interesting exceptions to this in the twelfth century are Petrus of Poitiers and an anonymous commentary on the fourth book of the Sentences conserved in the Bamberg library; see Weberberger, "Limbus puerorum," 114–17.

[79] See *ST* III, a. 68, a. 3.

[80] See, for example, Hugh of St. Victor, *On the Sacraments of the Christian Faith* 2.6.5, trans. Deferrari, 292. On this topic, see Ángel Santos Hernández, S.J., *Los niños del mundo pagano* (Santander: Sal Terrae, 1960).

Cardinal Cajetan's Proposal Concerning Parental Desire for Baptism

From the fourteenth to the early sixteenth century, a few eminent theologians spoke of the hope that God might act by way of privilege and mercy in those who die before the age of reason without Baptism. Jean Gerson (1363–1429), chancellor of the University of Paris, emphasized hope for the children who die unbaptized before the age of reason, and recommended that parents pray for the salvation of their unborn children:

> Therefore pregnant women and also their husbands, on their own and through others, ought to diligently pour forth their prayers to God and to the guardian angels on behalf of the child in the womb. They ought to fly to the refuge of the other saints, both men and women, so that the unborn infant, if it should happen to die before reaching the grace of the waters of baptism, might mercifully be consecrated by the high priest, our Lord Jesus, with an anticipatory baptism of the Holy Spirit. For who knows whether God hears, indeed who cannot devoutly hope that he will never scorn the prayers of the humble who place their hope in him? . . . But, short of a revelation, there is not, I think, any certainty about it.[81]

In the beginning of the sixteenth century, Cardinal Cajetan sought to apply the reasoning of St. Thomas's articles on the salvation of Gentile babies before the promulgation of the Gospel also to similar cases after the promulgation of the Gospel in Christian societies. He considers the case of Christian parents who desire to baptize their children but are unable to do so because of a child's sudden death before or after birth. He argues that it would be contrary to the mercy of God and the glory of the Gospel if means of salvation were less available after its promulgation than before. But if one accepts St. Thomas's thesis that original sin could have been forgiven to Gentile

---

[81] Jean Gerson, Sermon *De nativitate Virginis Mariae*, 2nd consideration, in *Opera omnia* (Antwerp, 1706), 3:1350. English translation by Clarence H. Miller in *Collected Works of Erasmus*, vol. 77, *Controversies Hyperaspistes 2*, ed. Charles Trinkaus (Toronto: University of Toronto Press, 2000), 745. See Michel, *Enfants morts sans baptême*, 53; Peter Gumpel, "Unbaptized Infants: May They Be Saved?" *The Downside Review* 72 (1954): 354.

babies by means of any rite or prayer through the faith and desire of the parents, then it seems that the means of salvation in the New Covenant have been limited rather than enlarged with respect to infants who die in the womb or after birth but before Baptism. Cajetan writes:

> It does not appear irrational to say that in the case of necessity it seems to be sufficient for the salvation of the child that baptism be in the desire of the parents, especially with some exterior sign. . . . I argue from this. The simple[82] faith of the ancient fathers was not of greater power among them than it is among us. And for this reason it could not aid more, in the case of urgent necessity than now. But then, when the proper remedy for the salvation of the child was lacking, the simple faith of the parents was sufficient for the salvation of the child. Therefore now also, when the proper remedy for the child, which is baptism, is lacking, the simple faith of the parents, offering their child to God, is sufficient for his salvation. . . . As uncircumcised children then, on account of the impossibility of circumcision, so now unbaptized children can be saved in the faith of their parents.[83]

Cajetan extends this reasoning to explicitly include babies who die in their mother's womb:

> They can be saved, I say, through the sacrament of Baptism received not in fact, but in the desire of the parents, with some blessing of the child or offering of him to God, with the invocation of the Trinity. I am moved to this through two reasons. The first is that it is reasonable that the divine mercy provide a remedy of salvation for man in any natural state, so that there is no state in which one could allege that it is impossible for him to find a remedy for salvation. The state of one dying in the womb would be without remedy if the faith of the parents could not aid them. . . . Second, from the fact that they are capable of Baptism of blood. If an infant were killed

---

[82] The Latin here is "sola fides," by which he means the faith of the parents independently of an external ritual or sacrament.

[83] Thomas Cardinal Cajetan, Commentary on *ST* III, q. 68, a. 2, in *Sancti Thomae Aquinatis Opera omnia*, Leonine ed., 12:93–94 (my translation).

on account of Christ in the womb he or she would be a martyr, no less than the Holy Innocents. It is reasonable to think that the faith of the parents, desiring, can lead their children to what bodily suffering would obtain for them.[84]

Cajetan's position is in harmony with several key theological principles. First of all, it takes seriously the universal salvific will of God, assuming that God would provide an effective means of salvation to a large class of human beings who otherwise would be lost through no fault of their own.[85] This is in harmony with St. Thomas's views on the salvation of Gentile babies dying prematurely. It also follows the development of doctrine in the Church, in which God's universal salvific will has been taught with increasing clarity against those who have tried to restrict it, such as the Jansenists, who held that Christ died only for the elect[86] and denied that sufficient grace is given to those not predestined.[87] Finally, it is in harmony with the text from *Gaudium et Spes*, §22 quoted above, that the Holy Spirit accords to all men "the possibility of being associated with this paschal mystery."

Numerous texts of Scripture show that God truly wills the salvation of all men. In 1 Timothy 2:1–4, St. Paul tells Timothy that prayers should "be made for all men, for kings and all who are in high positions, that we may lead a quiet and peaceable life, godly and respectful in every way. This is good, and it is acceptable in the sight of God our Savior, who desires all men to be saved and to come to the knowledge

---

[84] Cajetan, Commentary on *ST* III, q. 68, a. 11, 12:104 (my translation). This reasoning has been developed in an interesting way by E. Boudes, "Réflexion sur la solidarité des hommes avec le Christ," *Nouvelle revue théologique* 71 (1949): 589–604. Cajetan's text is referred to by the ITC, "The Hope of Salvation for Infants," §83, 400n115.

[85] See Bruno Webb, "Unbaptized Infants and the Quasi-Sacrament of Death," *The Downside Review* 71 (1953): 243–57, at 245: "If this be true [the universal salvific will as taught in Scripture], then the *fact* that infants dying without sacramental baptism are offered the grace of redemption and so its fruition in the Vision of God, follows necessarily."

[86] See Innocent X, *Cum occasione* (DS, 2005), which condemned the following proposition of Cornelius Jansen: "To say that Christ died or shed His blood for all men, is Semipelagianism."

[87] See Innocent X, *Cum occasione* (DS, 2001), which condemned the following proposition of Cornelius Jansen: "Some of God's commandments cannot be observed by just men with the strength they have in the present state, even if they wish and strive to observe them; nor do they have the grace that would make their observance possible."

of the truth." St. Paul then goes on to explain more fully this universal salvific will and its relation to Christ's mediation and sacrificial
death of atonement: "For there is one God, and there is one mediator
between God and men, the man Christ Jesus, who gave himself as a
ransom for all, the testimony to which was borne at the proper time"
(1 Tim 2:5–6).

Secondly, Cajetan's position respects the condition of infants who
are completely dependent on others for supplying their needs. It is
fitting therefore that their salvation should come to them through
the mediation of society, and in particular through the family and the
Church, to whom they are entrusted by God. St. Thomas uses this
principle to defend the fittingness of infant Baptism:

> The spiritual regeneration effected by Baptism is somewhat
> like carnal birth, in this respect, that as the child while in the
> mother's womb receives nourishment not independently, but
> through the nourishment of its mother, so also children before
> the use of reason, being as it were in the womb of their mother
> the Church, receive salvation not by their own act, but by the
> act of the Church.[88]

Cajetan's hypothesis was generally rejected by most theologians
until the twentieth century. There was debate about condemning his
hypothesis at the Council of Trent. The hypothesis was defended by
the Master General of the Dominicans and by Seripando, General of
the Augustinian Order, and it was not condemned.[89] Nevertheless, his
hypothesis gained no adherents for four centuries, until it began to
gain an important following in the middle of the twentieth century.[90]

Interestingly, Cajetan's proposal is in harmony with the liturgical prayers in the funeral rites for children who have died without
Baptism, introduced in the Latin rite in 1969, which, as seen above,
expressly mention the faith of the parents entrusting their child to the

---

[88] *ST* III, q. 68, a. 9, ad 1.

[89] For the discussion of the theologians at the Council of Trent on Cajetan's proposal, see Dyer, *Limbo: Unsettled Question*, 140–47.

[90] Cajetan's proposal was taken up vigorously by Charles-Vincent Héris, "Le salut
des enfants morts sans baptême," *La Maison-Dieu* 10 (1947): 86–105, and by E.
Boudes, "Réflexion sur la solidarité des hommes avec le Christ," *Nouvelle revue
théologique* 71 (1949): 589–604, who extended the desire from the parents to the
Church.

mercy of the Lord.[91] Thus it seems fair to say that Cajetan's hypothesis, after long opposition, has been vindicated by the development of the life of the Church in her liturgical practice.

Extension of Cajetan's Proposal

Cajetan limited his hypothesis to the children of believers. It seems, however, that the principles that he uses, which are (a) the natural dependence of children on their parents and caretakers, and (b) God's universal salvific will, should be more broadly applied.[92] Since the Church also plays a mediatorial role with respect to children, analogous to the parents but universal in scope, it is not unreasonable to extend Cajetan's hypothesis to all infants dying before Baptism. For all infants are equally dependent on others for their salvation, and ultimately on the Church. It would therefore not be unreasonable to think that the Church's desire that all men be saved could serve as a means of mediation on behalf of all who die before the age of reason. Speaking of baptized babies whose parents are unbelievers, St. Augustine says that they are offered for Baptism not only by their parents but "by the whole company of the saints and believers":

> Surely, the little ones are offered for the reception of the spiritual grace, not so much by those in whose arms they are carried—although they are offered by them if they are good and faithful—as by the whole company of the saints and believers. We rightly understand that they are offered by all who consent to the offering, and by whose holy and indivisible charity they are helped to share in the outpouring of the Holy Spirit. Mother Church who is in the saints does this wholly, because she wholly brings forth all and each.[93]

Since the faith of the Church, and not just of the parents, is operative in every infant Baptism, it seems to follow that the faith of the Church, and not just of the parents, could be operative also in desiring

---

[91] See *Order of Christian Funerals*, Vigil for a Deceased Child, §254C, p. 146, quoted above.

[92] See Boissard, *Réflexions sur le sort des enfants morts sans baptême*, 139–40.

[93] Augustine, Letter 98 to Boniface (408), in *Letters, Volume II (83–130)*, trans. Parsons, 134.

Baptism for all infants unable to receive the sacrament at the point of death. We have seen that Innocent III taught that "original sin, which is contracted without consent is remitted without consent through the power of the sacrament [of baptism]; but actual sin, which is committed with consent, is by no means remitted without consent."[94] It is clear that no one can make an act of contrition for anyone else. This is because personal sin formally consists in a disordered consent, which persists until the person formally retracts it in the act of contrition or repentance. Original sin, however, is received without consent, and there seems to be no intrinsic reason why it cannot be removed by God without personal consent through the faith-filled prayer of the Church when the sacramental means is impossible because of sudden death. The prayer of the Church is especially powerful when she prays for all men in the Sacrifice of the Mass, uniting her petition to the sacrifice of her Lord.[95]

The document of the International Theological Commission on this question has a profound reflection on this role of the prayer of the Church in mediating this desire. Since infants are baptized not in their own faith but in the faith of the Church, it seems reasonable to hope that unbaptized infants can be saved not through their own personal desire, but through that of the Church, expressed above all in the Eucharistic liturgy:

> If an unbaptised infant is incapable of a *votum baptismi*, then by the same bonds of communion the Church might be able to intercede for the infant and express a *votum baptismi* on his or her behalf that is effective before God. Moreover, the Church effectively does express in her liturgy just such a *votum* by the very charity towards all that is renewed in her in every celebration of the Eucharist.[96]

The document then states that the teaching of Jesus on the necessity of Baptism and the Eucharist should be interpreted to mean that "no-one is saved without some relation to Baptism and Eucharist, and therefore to the Church which is defined by these sacraments." The text continues:

---

[94] Innocent III, *Maiores Ecclesiae causas* (DS, 780).
[95] See E. Boudes, "Réflexion sur la solidarité des hommes avec le Christ," *Nouvelle revue théologique* 71 (1949): 589–604, at 602–3.
[96] ITC, "The Hope of Salvation for Infants," §98, p. 398

All salvation has some relation to Baptism, Eucharist and the Church. The principle that there is "no salvation outside the Church" means that there is no salvation which is not from Christ and ecclesial by its very nature. Likewise, the scriptural teaching that "without faith it is impossible to please [God]" (Heb 11:6) indicates the intrinsic role of the Church, the communion of faith, in the work of salvation. It is especially in the liturgy of the Church that this role becomes manifest, as the Church prays and intercedes for all, including unbaptised infants who die.[97]

Some theologians have proposed a different way by which God might extend to the infants "the possibility of being associated with this paschal mystery" (*Gaudium et Spes*, §22). The hypothesis has been put forth that God gives to the unbaptized infants a choice to opt for salvation at the moment of death.[98] This would be in accordance with the principle given in *Gaudium et Spes*, §22. Nevertheless, I hold that such a position should be rejected as improbable because it seems unfitting to human nature. Such a choice, without any human experience that it could be based on, would be without foundation. Such a choice is proper to the angels, for they are created with their intellects full, and thus they choose based on a fullness of natural knowledge.

Human infants, on the contrary, come into being totally dependent first on their mother and then, after birth, on their family and society. This natural dependence is a key part of human nature. For this reason it seems that it would be more fitting for God to respect this aspect of our nature by which the little ones are entrusted to the care of others

---

[97] ITC, "The Hope of Salvation for Infants," §99, pp. 398–99.

[98] A position of this kind has been defended, among others, by Heinrich Klee (1800–1840), M. Laurenge, and Palémon Glorieux. See E. J. Fortman, S.J., *Everlasting Life After Death* (New York: Alba House, 1976), 150–56, for a discussion and defense of this view. Laurenge's position is the most problematic because he puts this decision right *after* death instead of at the moment of death, as in the view of Glorieux. See M. Laurenge, "Esquisse d'une étude sur le sort des enfants morts sans baptéme," *L'Année Théologique Augustinienne* 12 (1952): 145–85; Palémon Glorieux, "In hora mortis," *Mélanges de Science Religieuse* 6 (1949): 185–216; summarized in "The Moment of Death," *Theology Digest* 10 (1962): 94–96. Laurenge's position is analyzed and criticized by Journet in *La volonté divine salvifique sur les petits enfants*, 126–27, and by Dyer in *Limbo: Unsettled Question*, 122–26. The position of Glorieux is discussed by Dyer in 117–22, and by Lombardi in *The Salvation of the Unbeliever*, 248–64.

for their natural life. Why would He not allow them to be entrusted to the Church for their salvation? Normally this is accomplished through the sacrament of Baptism. But where this is impossible, it seems fitting that their salvation come to them through the Church's desire that they receive the fruit of Baptism, even though she could not make them sharers in the sacramental sign.

Arguments of Fittingness for and Against the Hope of Salvation for Those Who Die Unbaptized before the Age of Reason

Maritain's Argument for Limbo Based on the Hierarchy of Creation

In an interesting essay on limbo, Jacques Maritain defended the existence of the limbo of the children as occupying a key place in the hierarchy of creation, as the summit of the natural order. He held that without limbo, an important degree of being would never be realized. There would exist no purely natural happiness as a terminal state in which the natural order in its pure state would be brought to the highest point that it is capable of:

> What is more exciting for a philosopher, and more instructive, than this fact that the state of pure nature at the best of its own order is the same as that in which, when the flesh has risen ... the souls of the children who have died without baptism will be found! It is doubtless for this reason and because in this way *all the degrees of being* will find their fulfillment, that I feel so attached to the notion of Limbo.[99]

He ends his reflection with a similar thought:

> Oh, little children who have died without baptism, rejected though you have never done evil, you are not an accident in the divine economy, a peculiar case from which the theologians, pressed on all sides, extricate themselves as they can, an

---

[99] Maritain, *Untrammeled Approaches*, 16 (my italics).

insignificant parenthesis. Your role is great, and your destiny well determined and very significant. You are the first fruits of natural felicity, of nature divinely restored.[100]

Maritain's position is based on a principle governing creation, that goodness is diffusive of itself.[101] It seems that God maximizes the manifestation of His goodness in creation by realizing many different and complementary levels of goodness rather than limiting Himself just to the higher forms alone, such as angels. We could call it the principle of the maximization of goodness by creating goodness on a multiplicity of levels. Given this principle, wouldn't it be more fitting for God to create a world in which goodness is multiplied not only by persons enjoying supernatural beatitude but also by some who enjoy only natural beatitude? In other words, wouldn't it be a better world if there were a limbo in addition to heaven?

Some years ago I was defending a position similar to Maritain's concerning the place of limbo in the hierarchy of creation and a student challenged it by asking me if I would be willing to volunteer to make the sacrifice to occupy that position in the hierarchy of creation. Of course no one would or should volunteer for such a destiny.[102] Nor could one volunteer one's children! Precisely for this reason Jesus has so urgently commanded Baptism. When put in those existential terms, it becomes clear that the divine glory is not more magnified by having many souls occupy the terminal position of natural rather than supernatural beatitude.

I would argue that the hierarchy of creation with its distinct levels of being is not lost even if the state of limbo does not exist. Natural happiness is *included* within supernatural happiness, and thus it will be present for eternity glorifying God by representing a certain level of participation of the divine goodness. The fact that it does not exist in a pure state, but only as a part of a larger whole in supernatural beatitude, does not take anything away from its ability to glorify God by filling out a level of being that is at the midpoint of the created order.

---

[100] Maritain, *Untrammeled Approaches*, 17.

[101] See Pseudo-Dionysius, *Divine Names*, bk. 4.

[102] One could, on the other hand, volunteer to have natural misfortunes, such as persecutions, short life, physical handicaps, etc. (as St. Ignatius teaches in his Principle and Foundation), because, as Jesus tells us, all of these could lead to a more perfect supernatural life of grace.

Other forms of complementarity do not work in this way. It is good that there are males and females because each represents a complementary way of being human, and they cannot be fittingly combined in one person. It is good that people have different abilities and belong to different cultures; they should not all be absorbed in one person or culture. Natural and supernatural beatitude, however, are both immensely perfected when they exist together in the same subject. Supernatural beatitude presupposes the possession of natural happiness as grace presupposes nature and perfects it.

Gratuitousness Argument

Another argument in favor of the traditional Thomistic view of limbo is that it better demonstrates the gratuitousness of our supernatural end. I would answer that the gratuitousness of grace is not endangered by the fact that there is no terminal state of purely natural happiness in this concrete economy of salvation. What guarantees the double gratuitousness of the supernatural order is solely the fact that God *could* have created us in a purely natural state without elevation to the supernatural order.[103] The actual realization of such a state is not necessary for supernatural beatitude to be doubly gratuitous.

Is the Necessity of Baptism Undermined without Limbo?

The most important argument in favor of limbo is that this thesis clearly manifests the necessity and grandeur of Baptism. The objection is made that theories promoting the hope of salvation for all who die unbaptized before the age of reason undermine the necessity of Baptism and of the sacramental system.[104] If unbaptized babies can be saved, does Baptism really matter?

This objection can be answered, I think, by considering that the distinction between baptized and unbaptized infants is not done away with by the hope affirmed in the *Catechism of the Catholic Church*,

---

[103] See Pius XII, *Humani Generis*, §26.

[104] See, for example, Journet, *La volonté divine salvifique sur les petits enfants*, 11, 135; J. McCarthy, "The Fate of Unbaptized Infants – A Recent View," *Irish Ecclesiastical Record* 74 (1950, II): 436–43, at 441–42. This objection is posed and responded to by Boissard, in *Réflexions sur le sort des enfants morts sans baptême*, 134–36.

§1261. Baptism offers a certainty of salvation for infants through the title of justice, on the basis of God's own fidelity to His covenantal obligations. For those who die before the age of reason without Baptism, that title of covenantal justice is not present. But there is still the sure hope for God's superabundant mercy.

It is undoubtedly better for the infant to be baptized and thus inserted into the New Covenant with its immense privileges. Through Baptism he is made a member of the visible Church, receives grace and thus justification through that title, and becomes an heir of heaven, marked by an indelible sacramental character that will glorify Christ for eternity. The Church, called to be universal, is also glorified through the increase of holy members in her visible ranks. Christ is also glorified in visibly manifesting His salvation through Baptism.

Even though salvation is always supremely gratuitous, the means of salvation are *due*, in virtue of God's own utterly gratuitous covenant, to those received into the covenant through Baptism who place no obstacle of mortal sin. These means are *not due* in that sense to infants who died without being received by Baptism into the New Covenant. However, the fact that they are not due does not mean that God cannot give them through His mercy by infusing sanctifying grace before death. Furthermore, the baptized baby is brought into the communion of the Church in a way more fitting for a human being, using sensible sacramental signs that are proportionate to our bodily and social nature, and to the Incarnation of Christ.

A similar objection is that this would confuse the ordinary and extraordinary means. That would be the case if one assumed that God is obligated by justice to give supernatural grace and glory to all. This confusion can be avoided, however, as long as the distinction between the title of God's mercy and God's covenantal justice are clearly distinguished. Whereas the extraordinary path is the fruit of mercy, the ordinary path is better because it manifests both mercy and justice.

To call something an ordinary means does not mean that it is used more frequently than extraordinary means. It could well be the reverse. The distinction here is not a question of numbers but of the nature of covenantal justice and extra-covenantal mercy. Only sacramental Baptism gives the sacramental character of membership in the Church militant so that the baptized baby who dies before the age of reason will have an eternal glory lacking to the unbaptized but sanctified baby.[105] Both will give glory to God, but in two complementary ways: the one magnifying His covenantal justice and the other His superabundant mercy.

A comparison of the burial rites for baptized and unbaptized babies in the current Roman Rite brings out this fundamental difference between the title of covenantal justice for the baptized and our hope in the mercy of God for the unbaptized. First, only if the baby has been baptized is the coffin sprinkled with holy water. The minister then says: "In the waters of baptism N. died with Christ and rose with him to new life. May he/she now share with him eternal glory." If the baby is not baptized, the minister says: "My brothers and sisters, the Lord is a faithful God who created us all after his own image. All things are of his making, all creation awaits the day of salvation. We now must entrust the soul of N. to the abundant mercy of God, that our beloved child may find a home in his Kingdom."[106] Only if the baby is baptized is a funeral pall placed on the coffin, for it represents the new garment of baptismal grace, and the body is incensed at the commendation. In the prayers for baptized children, the fact of Baptism and the assurance it brings is emphasized. In the prayers for unbaptized babies, as seen above, the child is entrusted to the care and mercy of God, and the faith of the parents and community is mentioned.

The dignity and glory of the sacramental system is not magnified by the rigorist idea that no grace is given without actual reception of the sacraments, for God is glorified above all by His mercy. Rather, the dignity of the sacraments of the New Covenant comes from the fact that these sacraments alone are direct instrumental causes of grace through which Christ's salvific humanity, the conjoined instrument of the divinity, touches the recipient. The sacraments alone are direct instruments of grace *ex opere operato*.

Prior to the New Covenant there were no direct instruments of grace, but grace was given to humanity through the foreseen merits of Christ on Calvary. As seen in chapter 14 above, the sacramental rites of Israel should be understood not as instrumental causes of grace like the sacraments of the New Covenant, but as occasions in which God granted grace through the faith and desire of His people. The hope that God gives grace to infants on the occasion of their imminent death would not denigrate the special dignity of the sacraments that

---

[105] See *ST* III, q. 68, a. 1, ad 3.

[106] *Order of Christian Funerals*, Vigil for a Deceased Child, 249A and B, p. 144.

work *ex opere operato*. Here there would be no instrumental causality, but another instance of God mercifully granting grace through the merits of Christ and through the intercession of His Church, who desires that the fruits of the Passion be extended to all.

God's Universal Salvific Will

The position of the *Catechism of the Catholic Church*, §1261 is favored by the development of the Church's understanding of the full import of God's universal salvific will. God wills "all men to be saved and come to the knowledge of the truth," according to 1 Timothy 2:4. God's universal salvific will is not a mere metaphor but implies action on God's part to make the means of salvation, merited for *all* men by Christ on the Cross,[107] actually available to all.

The universal salvific will, defined against Calvinism,[108] Michael Baius,[109] and the Jansenist heresy in the seventeenth century,[110] was affirmed numerous times in the Second Vatican Council. Perhaps the clearest statement, as seen above, is in *Gaudium et Spes*, §22.[111] After speaking about how Christ reveals man to himself and has united Himself in a certain manner with every human being, and has died

---

[107] See Synod of Quiercy (853), ch. 4 (DS, 624): "Just as there is not, nor has been, nor will be any man whose nature has not been assumed by Christ Jesus our Lord, so also there is not, nor has been, nor will be any man for whom he has not suffered"; *Gaudium et Spes*, §22.

[108] See Council of Trent, Decree on Justification (session 6), ch. 11 (DS, 1536). See chapter 15 above, p. 579.

[109] See Pius V, *Ex omnibus afflictionibus* (DS, 1954).

[110] See Innocent X, *Cum occasione* (DS, 2001).

[111] Other relevant conciliar texts are *Gaudium et Spes*, §19; *LG*, §§15–16; *Nostra Aetate* (Oct 28, 1965), §1; Declaration on Religious Freedom *Dignitatis Humanae* (Dec 7, 1965), §11; *Ad Gentes*, §7. See ITC, "The Hope of Salvation for Infants," §81, pp. 390–91; Sullivan, "The Development of Doctrine About Infants Who Die Unbaptized," 6: "One can ask whether Vatican II made any contribution to the discussion of this question. In my opinion, it did make an important contribution by insisting so strongly on the universality of the salvific will of God. The basic difficulty with the traditional doctrine about limbo is that Christian salvation is eternal life in the enjoyment of the beatific vision of God, from which infants in limbo are excluded through no fault of their own. This raises the question about the sense in which it can be said that God wills their salvation. While Vatican II did not address this problem, it did insist, more strongly than any previous council had done, that the salvific will of God is truly universal."

for all, the Council concludes that "we ought to believe that the Holy Spirit in a manner known only to God offers to every man the possibility of being associated with this paschal mystery."

The ordinary means by which this is made available to all is Baptism. Baptism of blood is available to those who are killed for hatred of Christ and thus conformed to His death; Baptism of desire, through a personal act, is available to all who arrive at the age of reason and choose to cooperate with the prevenient action of God's actual grace calling them to acts of faith, hope, and charity. However, what about people who die before the age of reason and without the possibility of receiving sacramental Baptism? How has God's universal salvific will made possible the salvation of the great number who die in the womb by miscarriage or abortion? How has He offered them sufficient grace? The biggest problem with the traditional theory of limbo is that it does not leave open an effective means of salvation that can be applied to these human beings in their concrete circumstances.

And if it is made open to them and they can pose no obstacle through a contrary and rebellious will (as in those damned for unrepented mortal sin), then why should one doubt that God's mercy, under that glorious title, will bring them to salvation by infusing sanctifying grace before they die?[112]

An analogy can be taken from the apostolic blessing given at the point of death. The Church, from her treasury of merits, offers to all the faithful who have prayed during their life a plenary indulgence if they are in a state of grace and have contrition for their sins. This is given even if no priest is available to impart the apostolic blessing. The Norms for Indulgences states:

---

[112] See Adrian Hastings, "The Salvation of Unbaptized Infants," *The Downside Review* 77 (1959): 172–78, at 178: "It is of faith that Christ died for all men, and 'all men' includes unbaptized infants. As a consequence, though all men are not saved, all men do receive sufficient grace to be saved. . . . But if unbaptized infants receive sufficient grace for salvation, it would be contradictory to say that they cannot receive baptism by desire, given that that is the only way whereby they can be saved. Either they do not receive sufficient grace for salvation or they can be baptized by desire; and if they do not receive sufficient grace, how can it be true that Christ died for all men? . . . For my part I feel convinced that if any man—and that includes an unbaptized infant—does not enter heaven, as Christ died that he should, it is not because that man is a son of Adam but uniquely because he personally has refused to be a brother with Christ."

If a priest is unavailable, Holy Mother Church benevolently grants to the Christian faithful, who are duly disposed, a plenary indulgence to be acquired at the point of death, provided they have been in the habit of reciting some prayers during their lifetime; in such a case, the Church supplies for the three conditions ordinarily required for a plenary indulgence.[113]

If the Church takes care that nothing is left undone for the faithful at the point of death, it is reasonable to think that God would not fail to withhold what He alone can give, imparting sanctifying grace to unbaptized infants at the point of death, through the merits of Christ and out of His love for those who are conformed to Him by their innocence, their littleness, and their suffering, and for whom His Church prays.[114]

In conclusion, what would seem more fitting to our limited theological imagination: a creation in which some rational creatures enjoy natural but not supernatural happiness, because they died without Baptism before the age of reason and thus lacked a title of justice to receive salvation, or one in which the mercy of God supplied what His justice need not supply, giving supernatural beatitude to such children by the title of mercy?

Although the foundation of hope in the salvation of unbaptized babies who die before the age of reason is God's mercy and not His sacramental system based on His covenantal justice, God's mercy is indeed a solid foundation for "sure hope," in the words of St. John Paul II.[115] For His covenantal justice and the glorious power of His sacraments are based ultimately on His gratuitous and overflowing mercy, as St. Thomas recognized.[116] Furthermore, although these human

---

[113] Apostolic Penitentiary, *Manual of Indulgences: Norms and Grants* (Washington, DC: United States Conference of Catholic Bishops, 2006), 54.

[114] See E. Boudes, "Réflexion sur la solidarité des hommes avec le Christ," *Nouvelle revue théologique* 71 (1949): 589–604, at 602.

[115] John Paul II, *Evangelium Vitae*, §99. The ITC, "The Hope of Salvation for Infants," §103, p. 400, concludes with an affirmation of "strong grounds for hope": "As we want to reaffirm in conclusion, they provide strong grounds for hope that God will save infants when we have not been able to do for them what we would have wished to do, namely, to baptize them into the faith and life of the Church."

[116] See *ST* I, q. 21, a. 4: "Now the work of divine justice always presupposes the work of mercy; and is founded thereupon. For nothing is due to creatures,

beings were neither able to receive Baptism and the other sacraments nor even to desire them personally, they have a connection with the sacraments through the desire of the Church on their behalf that God extend to them the grace of Baptism, although they could not receive the sacrament.

STUDY QUESTIONS

1. What is the teaching of the *Catechism of the Catholic Church* on the destiny of infants who die without Baptism?
2. What is suggested by the prayers for the funeral Mass for baptized and unbaptized babies?
3. What is the teaching of St. Thomas Aquinas on the question of limbo? (a) Does St. Thomas hold that the souls in limbo experience any type of sorrow or suffering? (b) What are the two hypotheses he proposes, in his early period and in his maturity, to explain their condition? (c) What are the difficulties in each hypothesis?
4. What must be held with regard to infants who die without Baptism, and what is open to free discussion of theologians?
5. What is the role of the desire of parents in the salvation of unbaptized infants dying before the age of reason?
6. What did Cardinal Cajetan propose with regard to the salvation of the unbaptized who die before the age of reason, including in their mother's womb? What arguments support his position?
7. Explain the relevance of God's universal salvific will, and the

---

except for something pre-existing in them, or foreknown. Again, if this is due to a creature, it must be due on account of something that precedes. And since we cannot go on to infinity, we must come to something that depends only on the goodness of the divine will—which is the ultimate end. We may say, for instance, that to possess hands is due to man on account of his rational soul; and his rational soul is due to him that he may be man; and his being man is on account of the divine goodness. So in every work of God, viewed at its primary source, there appears mercy. In all that follows, the power of mercy remains, and works indeed with even greater force; as the influence of the first cause is more intense than that of second causes. For this reason does God out of the abundance of His goodness bestow upon creatures what is due to them more bountifully than is proportionate to their deserts: since less would suffice for preserving the order of justice than what the divine goodness confers; because between creatures and God's goodness there can be no proportion."

development of doctrine in this regard, to this question of the destiny of the unbaptized who die before the age of reason.

8. How should one present this issue to a family grieving over a miscarriage or the death of an unbaptized infant?

Suggestions for Further Reading

Alviar, J. Jose. "El destino de los niños que mueren sin baptismo. Comentario al documento de la Comisión Teológica Internacional." *Scripta Theologica* 41, no. 3 (2009): 711–43.

Bonino, Serge-Thomas, O.P. "The Theory of Limbo and the Mystery of the Supernatural in St. Thomas Aquinas." In *Surnaturel: A Controversy at the Heart of Twentieth-Century Thomistic Thought.* Edited by Bonino, translated by Robert Williams. Ave Maria, FL: Sapientia Press of Ave Maria Univeristy, 2009. Pp. 117–54.

Boudes, E. "Réflexion sur la solidarité des hommes avec le Christ." *Nouvelle revue théologique* 71 (1949): 589–604.

Catechism of the Catholic Church. §§1257, 1261, 1283.

Dyer, George J. "Limbo: A Theological Evaluation." *Theological Studies* 19 (1958): 32–49.

_____. *Limbo: Unsettled Question.* New York: Sheed & Ward, 1964.

Fortman, E. J., S.J. *Everlasting Life After Death.* New York: Alba House, 1976. Pp. 143–56.

Hastings, Adrian. "The Salvation of Unbaptized Infants." *The Downside Review* 77 (1959): 172–78.

International Theological Commission, "The Hope of Salvation for Infants Who Die without Being Baptised," 2007. In International Theological Commission, *Texts and Documents, 1986–2007.* San Francisco: Ignatius Press, 2009. Pp. 353–400.

John Paul II. *Evangelium Vitae.* March 25, 1995. §99.

Maritain, Jacques. *Untrammeled Approaches.* Translated by Bernard Doering. Notre Dame, IN: University of Notre Dame Press, 1997, 11–17.

Sullivan, Francis A. "The Development of Doctrine About Infants Who Die Unbaptized." *Theological Studies* 72 (2011): 3–14.

Webb, Bruno. "Unbaptized Infants and the Quasi-Sacrament of Death." *The Downside Review* 71 (Summer 1953): 243–57.

Conclusion

1. Sacraments and the Development of Doctrine

The Church's teaching on the seven sacraments and the sacramental system provides many striking examples of the organic development of doctrine over the centuries. Since public Revelation has concluded with the death of the Apostles, the development of doctrine in the life of the Church is always an unfolding of the seeds of Revelation present from the beginning.[1] The Second Vatican Council, in *Dei Verbum*, §8, calls attention to the development of doctrine:

> This tradition which comes from the Apostles develops in the Church with the help of the Holy Spirit. For there is a growth in the understanding of the realities and the words which have been handed down. This happens through the contemplation and study made by believers, who treasure these things in their hearts (see Luke 2:19, 51) through a penetrating understanding of the spiritual realities which they experience, and through the preaching of those who have received through Episcopal succession the sure gift of truth. For as the centuries succeed one another, the Church constantly moves forward toward the fullness of divine truth until the words of God reach their complete fulfillment in her.

Another fruitful cause of development of doctrine is the need of the Church to defend her faith and worship from heresies and distortions

---

[1] On the topic of development of doctrine, see the classic work by John Henry Newman, *An Essay on the Development of Christian Doctrine*. On development of doctrine with regard to sacramental theology, see Van Roo, *The Christian Sacrament*, 24–26.

that force her theologians to reflect more deeply on revealed truths and their implications.

The development of doctrine is compared in *Dei Verbum* with Luke's description of Mary's contemplation of the mystery of the Incarnation. After the visit of the shepherds in Luke 2:19, we are told that "Mary kept all these things, pondering them in her heart." After the finding of the child Jesus in the Temple in Luke 2:51 we are told again that Mary "kept all these things in her heart." Over the centuries the Church has contemplated the seeds of divine Revelation concerning the sacraments in the prayer of the faithful, in the development of the Church's liturgical life, and in the defense of the faith against heresies and challenges from secular culture.

In the case of the sacraments, the primacy of divine Revelation is safeguarded by the dogma that Jesus personally instituted the sacraments, as seen in chapter 4. All seven sacraments have structured the life of the Church since Pentecost. However, while Jesus instituted them with an essential nucleus that remains constant, He also allowed great space for His Church to develop all that surrounds this central nucleus and to reflect on the meaning, fittingness, and fruitfulness of the sacraments.

The liturgical life of the Church and her theological reflection are distinct, although both organically develop through the life of the Church. Theological reflection, as a reflexive operation, follows on the development of liturgical practice and thus can lag behind it. In its meditation on the sacraments, theology considers the Church's rich liturgical practice[2] in the light of theological principles of various kinds, such as the centrality and fittingness of the Incarnation, original sin and its effects, the necessity of Baptism and the Church, and the universal salvific will of God.

Theological reflection seeks to define, distinguish, and order, as well as to refute heretical understandings and practices. Thus with regard to the sacraments there was the task to define them, distinguish them from those of the Old Covenant and from sacramentals, number them, analyze their order and hierarchy, explain their fittingness and

---

[2] See Van Roo, *The Christian Sacrament*, 24: "The theology of the Christian sacrament illustrates strikingly the degree to which Church teaching and theological understanding must reckon with the witness of the living tradition of the Christian community through the centuries. We cannot erect a theology of the Christian sacraments . . . upon the basis of New Testament witness alone."

multiplicity, their institution by Christ, their component levels (sacramental sign, invisible reality and sign, and the reality of grace and communion), their signification, their causality, the differing permanence of their effects, their necessity, and the possibility of their effects being granted through desire for them. These have been the principal topics investigated in this book. It should not be surprising, therefore, that this theological reflection on the sacraments has slowly and gradually matured over the centuries.

Definition and Number of the Sacraments

Even with regard to something as basic as the definition of the sacraments, there has been a long and rich development. We have seen a key role played by St. Augustine, Hugh of St. Victor, Peter Lombard, and St. Thomas Aquinas. The definition given by the theologians of the twelfth century highlighting the efficacy of the sacraments to cause the grace that they signify enabled the Church to determine that seven sacraments fit that definition. Although the Church has always had exactly seven sacraments, it is surprising that theologians before the twelfth century neither had a proper definition nor had determined their number. An alternative definition by Luther and Calvin prompted the Protestant view that there are only two sacraments.

A good definition of sacrament also distinguishes the essential elements of a sacrament. The sacraments of the New Covenant are (a) sacred signs of human sanctification, (b) instituted by Christ, (c) entrusted to the Church, (d) that cause the grace that they represent. Sacraments are in the genus of sacred signs, which situates them firmly in human culture. But like Christ, they have properties that are both human and divine. Because they are His words, spoken through the mediation of a minister, they have the power to accomplish what they signify.

The Three Levels of the Sacraments

One of the most important developments in sacramental theology is the distinction between three levels of the sacraments: (a) the outward sacramental sign, which causes two invisible effects: (b) the reality and sign (*res et sacramentum*) and (c) the reality of grace and communion with God and the Church.

Chapters 7 and 8 traced various stages of the development of this doctrine. The intermediate level of reality and sign was first grasped with regard to Baptism and Holy Orders through the liturgical tradition of the non-repeatability of both consecrations. The Donatist controversy led St. Augustine to articulate the existence of an abiding effect of Baptism and ordination distinct from grace, which came to be called sacramental character.

A second stage of the development was the response to the heresy of Berengarius. This was the immediate catalyst for the theologians of the twelfth century to elaborate the three levels of the sacraments, for the Real Presence of Christ in the Eucharist is the prime example of the intermediate level of *reality and sign* (*res et sacramentum*).

The *reality and sign* was then extended to the other sacraments and has come to be a key component of the Church's understanding of the sacramental system. It is a reality that is either directly Christ's humanity, which occurs only in the Eucharist, or a configuration to Christ, as in the other sacraments. Configuration to Christ means membership in His Body and participation in His threefold mission, and thus the *reality and sign* has both a Christological and an ecclesiological focus. We have seen that this reality and sign has three intimately connected aspects: it gives (a) Christian and ecclesial identity; (b) an ecclesial mission proper to that sacrament; and (c) spiritual power ordered to the progressive realization of that mission.

The *res et sacramentum* of Matrimony is the marital bond, elevated and consecrated by insertion into Christ so as to be an efficacious sign of Christ's spousal union with the Church. I have argued that the *res et sacramentum* of Penance should be understood as a configuration to Christ's work of satisfaction for sin, and that of Anointing of the Sick as a configuration with Christ's redemptive suffering, so as to consecrate serious illness and unleash its redemptive power on behalf of the Church.

The abiding nature of the intermediate level, especially in sacramental character and in Matrimony, also enables us to understand how the sacraments can continue to grant sacramental graces over time and how they can come back to life if mortal sin has rendered them unfruitful. This distinction of three levels in the sacraments, therefore, is crucial for understanding the great importance of the dispositions of the recipient over time in receiving sacramental grace. Although all who receive a sacrament validly receive the *reality and sign* that abides (such as sacramental character or the matrimonial bond), not all receive the grace of the sacrament, for one can pose the obstacle of unrepentance, and of those who receive its grace, each one receives according to his disposition of desire. Since the reality and sign abides, it provides an abiding foundation for the sacramental graces proper to that sacrament over time, always in accordance with the changing dispositions of the recipient.

Sacramental Grace

The teaching on sacramental grace has experienced no less development. It is a reality proclaimed in the New Testament and in the teaching of the Fathers. The fact that there are seven sacraments and not just one implies that the sacraments give different graces according to their particular purpose and place in the sacramental system. Determining precisely what is proper to the grace of each sacrament, however, has proven to be a difficult task. The great theologians of the thirteenth century, such as St. Thomas, affirmed the existence of distinct graces and "divine aids" but left the question rather vague. Cajetan interpreted St. Thomas's reference to "divine aid" to refer to actual graces that help the recipient to accomplish the mission of the sacrament, and this has gradually become common doctrine. John of St. Thomas proposed that sacramental grace includes not only actual grace but also a particular modality of sanctifying grace and the gifts of the Holy Spirit. I think this is also correct, and I have argued that these distinct habitual gifts proper to each sacrament involve a particular docility with regard to the actual graces proper to the mission of that sacrament. This means that sacramental grace not only involves actual graces, but also strengthens particular gifts of the Holy Spirit that aid the faithful to be habitually attentive and receptive to the actual graces ordered to realizing the ecclesial mission of that sacrament and the particular configuration to Christ that it confers.

Sacramental Causality

Development of doctrine is beautifully manifested in theological reflection on the great and central question of the causality exercised by the sacraments. The Gospels, as in the Bread of Life discourse and Jesus's nocturnal discussion with Nicodemus, powerfully witness to the efficacy of Baptism and the Eucharist. The Church has lived with the consciousness of sacramental causality and efficacy from the beginning of her public life at Pentecost. This causality, however, poses great difficulties to theological reflection. It is one thing to assert the efficacy of the sacramental signs in infusing the grace that they represent. It is another to give some account of how sensible and material realities can be causes of the supernatural and invisible reality of grace.

It is in this question that St. Thomas Aquinas's contribution has been particularly significant. Although several Fathers and medieval theologians used the analogy of instruments of various kinds to illuminate the role of the sacraments in the giving of grace, it was St. Thomas who first applied in a coherent way a theory of instrumental causality and gave an account of how the sensible sacraments can be true causes of a reality that immeasurably transcends them. They can give what they do not have of themselves because they are instruments used by Christ.

It is proper to an instrument to work above its own nature, bringing about an effect on the level of the principal agent. In this case, the principal agent is the Trinity, who works through the humanity of Christ and His Paschal mystery (the conjoined instrument), who then works through sacramental ministers, who work through the sacramental signs to produce the effect of sanctification through the Spirit's action in configuring the faithful to Christ.

Although St. Thomas defends sacramental instrumental causality from his early commentary on the *Sentences*, one of the most significant developments in his own theology was a simplification of this teaching. In his early works he held that the outward sacramental sign was the instrumental cause only of the reality and sign (*res et sacramentum*), which was the proximate disposition for the reception of grace. The sacrament thus was not directly the cause of grace, but the cause of a disposition for grace. In his mature works he simplifies his thesis, holding that as the sacramental sign is the instrumental cause of the abiding *res et sacramentum*, the latter is the instrumental cause of the imparting of grace, as long as there is no obstacle. The sacrament can have this kind of causality because the outward sign is performed by a minister through whom Christ's humanity is acting, and His divinity is at work through His humanity. St. Thomas thus outlines a chain of instrumental causes directed by the principal cause, God, who imparts grace through His humanity, through the minister, through the matter and form of the sacramental sign, and through the sacramental character or *res et sacramentum*, which is an abiding sacramental sign imprinted by Christ that is efficacious to bring about the grace that it signifies. The *res et sacramentum* can be thought of as a kind of abiding word that enables Christ's word to continue to *resound* and call down graces for as long as the *res et sacramentum* lasts.

One of the great merits of this theory is that it manifests more than other theories the intimate connection between the Incarnation and the sacraments, and it assigns a clearer role to Christ's humanity at work in sacramental action. The hypostatic union is the key link in the causal chain connecting the divine power with Christ's human actions that instituted the sacraments and continue to speak in them through the human minister acting in His person. Thus we should hear the words of absolution and consecration as being spoken by Christ through the lips of His ministers.

This elegant and harmonious solution did not immediately attract a following. On the contrary, even the disciples of St. Thomas generally followed his earlier rather than his mature view, which only became the dominant position of the Thomistic school through the commentary of Cardinal Cajetan in the sixteenth century.[3] Although extremely influential and fecund in theology, the Magisterium has not formally adopted St. Thomas's mature theory of instrumental causality, allowing freedom to different theological schools to continue to debate the mode of efficacy of the sacraments.[4]

Sacraments of the Old Covenant

The question of the causal efficacy of the sacraments of the New Covenant naturally raises the question of the causality of the sacraments of the Old Covenant. Numerous scriptural texts imply a difference in the efficacy of the sacraments of the New Covenant from those of the Old. The messianic expectations of prophecies of Jeremiah 31:31–33 and Ezekiel 36:24–27 imply that the New Covenant will write the Law of God on the heart and wash away sins in a new manner. John the Baptist announces the efficacy of Christ's Baptism compared with his own: "I baptize you with water for repentance, but he who is coming after me is mightier than I, . . . he will baptize you with the Holy Spirit and with fire" (Matt 3:11). St. Paul speaks of the Old Testament rites

---

3   See Lynch, "The Sacraments as Causes of Sanctification," 809–12.

4   See La Soujeole, "The Sacraments and the Development of Doctrine," in *OHST*, 592: "Even if St. Thomas's elaboration of the relationship between sign and cause through recourse to instrumentality has not been officially 'canonized,' one should nonetheless note that magisterial statements seem to refer to it implicitly."

as "weak and beggarly" (Gal 4:9), and Hebrews 10:1 says that "the law has but a shadow of the good things to come instead of the true form of these realities." The difference in efficacy has been taught by the Councils of Florence and Trent.[5]

At the same time it was recognized that the grace of Christ was not absent from the saints of the Old Covenant and their forms of sacred worship, which were commanded by God Himself. Thus a theological problem was posed. How can we explain the difference in the sacramental efficacy of the two covenants without denying the holiness of the Old Covenant, on the one hand, or minimizing the significance of the Incarnation and Passion of Christ, on the other?

To my mind, the doctrine of St. Thomas gives the most profound answer to this question by intimately fusing Christological and sacramental doctrine and by introducing the notion of instrumental causality by which Christ acts in the sacraments through His theandric power. The Incarnation stands between the two sacramental systems of the Old and New Covenants. Through the Incarnation, Christ's humanity can be understood to act as the living, free, and supremely holy instrument of His divinity, so that the actions of His humanity can have a divinizing grace-giving power to communicate the grace that His words signify.

There has also been a non-linear and torturous development with regard to the vexed question of the status of the sacramental rites of the Old Covenant after the promulgation of the Gospel, and whether it can be licit for Christians to participate in them. At first we see the Apostles and the first generation of Christians in Israel continuing to frequent the Temple and observe the ceremonial law of Moses together with the "breaking [of] bread" (Acts 2:46) in their houses, which is Luke's way of speaking of the Eucharist. But already at the beginning of the second century things changed and we find the Apostolic Fathers, such as St. Ignatius of Antioch, speaking against Christian participation in the Old Testament ceremonial law.[6] There was a painful parting of the ways, to the point that it was regarded as mortally sinful for Christians to participate in the ceremonial rites of the Old Covenant.

---

[5] Council of Florence, *Exsultate Deo* (DS, 1310); Council of Trent, Decree on the Sacraments (session 7), can. 2 (DS, 1602).

[6] See Ignatius of Antioch, Letter to the Magnesians 8–10, in *The Apostolic Fathers*, trans. Holmes, 207–09.

St. Augustine understood this change to have occurred when the Gospel was fully promulgated, which he identified with the end of the apostolic age.[7] St. Thomas and the Council of Florence follow this view that observance of the rites of the Old Law after the promulgation of the Gospel would involve a sin against faith by signifying that Christ has not yet come.

We have seen reasons for questioning this view. First, we can ask whether the Gospel has indeed been fully promulgated. Is not this a task that will go on to the parousia? In many ways the situation of Western society today has come to resemble the situation of the apostolic age more than the centuries of Christendom. In this new ecclesial context, the observance of certain aspects of the Old Covenant can take on a new light. Such observance need not signify that Christ has not yet come, but can perform other purposes, such as manifesting typology, showing respect for Jewish worship of the Old Covenant that has "never been revoked,"[8] providing a way to preserve Jewish identity in Hebrew Catholics, and serving as a devotion to the humanity of Christ.

Grace of the Sacraments Received through Desire

The organic development of doctrine with regard to the sacraments is most striking, perhaps, with regard to the doctrine of Baptism of desire, and the analogous role of desire, moved by actual grace and informed by perfect contrition, to anticipate the principal effect of Penance, the Eucharist, and probably Confirmation and Anointing of the Sick. The effect of this desire is the infusion or increase of sanctifying grace and all that follows upon it, including the forgiveness of original and mortal sin.

We see this doctrine emerging in St. Ambrose and St. Augustine with regard to Baptism. It is then taken up by the theologians of the twelfth century such as Hugh of St. Victor and Peter Lombard, who extend it to Penance and the Eucharist. St. Thomas Aquinas explores it more deeply and extends it also to Confirmation.

---

[7] See Augustine, Letter 82 to St. Jerome of AD 405, in *Letters*, vol. 1 (1–82), 401–4.

[8] See Second Vatican Council, *Nostra Aetate*, §4; Pope Francis, *Evangelii Gaudium*, §247: "We hold the Jewish people in special regard because their covenant with God has never been revoked, for 'the gifts and the call of God are irrevocable' (Rom 11:29)."

A key step in this reflection was the distinction between the three levels of the sacraments in the twelfth century, which made it possible for the theologians of the thirteenth century, such as St. Thomas, to speak of the *res tantum* being realized without the sacramental sign or the *res et sacramentum*. This also shows the limitations of sacramental grace received through desire for the sacraments, for although it anticipates the central effect of grace, it does not grant sacramental character or the *res et sacramentum* of the other sacraments.

Another step in the development of this doctrine was the gradual acquisition of a more realistic understanding of invincible or inculpable ignorance. In the context of the Christian culture of the Middle Ages (Christendom), it was generally assumed that the Gospel had been sufficiently promulgated in the world of their day such that invincible ignorance would be very rare. This assumption was challenged by the discovery of the Americas, and the doctrine of invincible ignorance began to be explained by the Magisterium in the mid-nineteenth century.[9]

Based on this broader notion of invincible ignorance, coupled with the strong notion of God's universal salvific will defined in the Jansenist controversy, *Lumen Gentium*, §16 teaches that it is possible to be saved through an implicit desire for Baptism: "Those also can attain to salvation who through no fault of their own do not know the Gospel of Christ or His Church, yet sincerely seek God and moved by grace strive by their deeds to do His will as it is known to them through the dictates of conscience." *Gaudium et Spes*, §22 makes a still stronger statement: "We ought to believe that the Holy Spirit in a manner known only to God offers to every man the possibility of being associated with this paschal mystery."

The elements of the doctrine of *Lumen Gentium*, §16 have been operative in the Church for centuries, but it took a long time for the principles to come together to develop their implications. This teaching has huge ramifications for understanding the ultimate fate of the large part of humanity outside of the visible confines of the Catholic Church through no grave fault of their own.

---

[9]   See Pius IX, *Quanto Conficiamur Moerore* (DS, 2866), and *Singulari Quadam*.

Development of Doctrine on Hope for Those Who Die Unbaptized before the Age of Reason

One consequence of this strong statement of God's universal salvific will is its implications for those who have died before the age of reason without Baptism. If God makes it possible for every human being of whatever race, age, or condition to be associated with the Paschal mystery and with the grace that it has merited for us, this must also be true for the great number who die before the age of reason without Baptism. But since Baptism is the only means communicated to us to introduce a person into the life of Christ and His Church, what should we think of the eternal destiny of those who died without it through no fault of their own before awakening to the life of reason and free self-determination through which they might personally desire Baptism in an act of faith, hope, and love?

The solution to this problem must keep in mind the following six theological principles: the existence of original sin; the absolute necessity of receiving sanctifying grace for salvation; the institution of Baptism as the unique ordinary means given to mankind for the forgiveness of original sin and the infusion of sanctifying grace; the fact that while God *"has bound salvation to the sacrament of Baptism,"* He Himself *"is not bound by his sacraments"*;[10] the existence of Baptism of blood and desire; and finally, God's universal salvific will. It should not be surprising, therefore, that this should have proven to be among the most difficult problems of sacramental theology, and which thus has required a long period of gestation.

We have seen three principal positions with regard to this question: the Augustinian position that holds that infants who die without Baptism incur the lightest condemnation; the Thomistic position of limbo which posits that they enjoy a natural happiness without suffering and without the beatific vision; and the position represented by the *Catechism of the Catholic Church*, §1261, which allows "us to hope that there is a way of salvation for children who have died without Baptism."

As with regard to the question of Baptism of desire, increasing reflection on the immeasurable gifts given through the sacraments has grown together with an increasing awareness of the universality of God's saving will. Since God can anticipate the granting of sacra-

---

[10] *CCC*, §1257.

mental graces to a person through his or her desire for the sacraments (which God Himself arouses through actual graces with which we must cooperate), it is more than reasonable to hope that He would anticipate those graces also to those who are most needy and weak who cannot desire for themselves but are dependent on the intercession of the Church on their behalf. John Paul II, in *Evangelium Vitae*, §99, speaking to mothers of aborted children, spoke not simply of hope, but of "sure hope."[11] It is "sure" because it rests on the solid foundation of the love and mercy of God, the same love that is the foundation of the sacramental system to which these infants were tragically unable to find direct access.

2. Fostering a Sacramental Spirituality

The development of doctrine on the sacraments is an excellent example of how the seed of the Gospel, landing on good soil in the Church, bears much fruit over time. The hundredfold harvest concerns, above all, the fruits of grace of the sacraments in countless lives. It also includes, as part of the Church's life, an increased awareness of her treasures.

This increase, however, is accompanied by the growth of an opposite phenomenon in the world. As the Church grows and develops her doctrine, attitudes contrary to the Gospel also grow and spread. Modern Western culture is increasingly marked by a "disenchanted,"[12] anti-sacramental worldview, which can take many different or even opposite forms, from materialism on the one hand to varieties of dualism or neo-gnosticism on the other. Modern man has great difficulty seeing the value of sacred signs in general, and still greater difficulty in believing their power to do what they represent and to mediate spiritual gifts.

The New Evangelization, therefore, must foster a rediscovery of the sacramental principle and awe before the sacramental mystery. At the conclusion of this work, I hope that the reader may be more struck by wonder before the mysteries of salvation contained in the

---

[11] John Paul II, *Evangelium Vitae*, §99: "I would now like to say a special word to women who have had an abortion. . . . To the same Father and his mercy you can with sure hope entrust your child."

[12] See Max Weber, "Science as a Vocation," in *From Max Weber*, 139.

sacraments. Veiled by the most humble realities—such as water, olive oil, bread, wine, the laying on of hands, and human words—the sacraments communicate a sharing in the divine nature, give or increase faith, hope, and charity, and wipe away sins. In addition to giving created gifts of grace, the Holy Spirit is sent and given through the sacraments.

St. Ignatius of Antioch spoke of the Eucharist as a "medicine of immortality." Although preeminently true of the Eucharist, this could be said of all the sacraments, each in its own way. Theology can name the different gifts given by the sacraments, but we cannot grasp what we are saying, for they are above our minds and hearts. Just as all grace was merited by Christ, we should hold that in God's plan, all grace that is given to human beings has a connection to the sacraments—and thus to the Church—for it comes through the sacraments or through desire for them.[13] Even prevenient actual graces have a sacramental source in that they are showered on the world through the Sacrifice of the Mass.

Sacramental Spirituality

Catholics often speak of different forms of Catholic spirituality associated with great saints and religious orders, such as Benedictine, Franciscan, Carmelite, and Ignatian. "Spirituality" in this sense indicates a particular way of living out one's spiritual life or relationship with God that gives a particular focus and emphasis to certain means of sanctification. It seems that a great pastoral task of the present day is to foster a sacramental spirituality. For all Christians, this would be built on the sacraments of initiation and Penance. For the married, it would also include the sacrament of Matrimony; the ordained are called to live a spirituality of Holy Orders; and those who are seriously ill are called to a spirituality of redemptive suffering built on the consecration of Anointing of the Sick.

Sacraments and Faith

A sacramental spirituality must live by faith, for the sacraments high-

---

[13] See Fagan, "Sacramental Spirituality," in *Sacraments: The Gestures of Christ*, ed. O'Callaghan, 157; Nicolas, *Synthèse dogmatique: de la Trinité à la Trinité*, 789; Nicolas, "La grâce sacramentelle," 525–38.

light the contrast between what is seen by the senses and what is believed to be present and operative under the veil of the most ordinary realities that compose the matter and form of the sacraments. A sacramental spirituality involves an intimate awareness that the time of the Church in which we have lived for two thousand years is a time of exile from the Lord's visible presence extending from the Lord's Ascension[14] to His Second Coming. A sacramental spirituality thus involves an intimate awareness that the Lord, in ascending from the world to the right hand of the Father with His visible and sensible presence, continues, through the sacramental liturgy, to be most intimately present in this world that He has visibly left. St. Leo states this beautifully: "What was to be seen of our Redeemer has passed over into the Sacraments."[15]

Every sacramental celebration involves actions greater than any natural change. Through the sacraments, the divine breaks into the created order, initiating and increasing our participation in the divine life. Every infant Baptism, although a brief and simple ceremony, involves the adoption of a human being as a son or daughter of God. Every Baptism cancels the essential penalty of original sin and restores an unthinkable inheritance: eternal life with God and His saints. Confirmation gives us the mission to be pliable and docile instruments of the Holy Spirit's activity and to be transformed as the Apostles were at Pentecost. Every Confirmation renews the miracle of Pentecost,[16] but it takes the eyes of faith to see it. The merit of faith in the celebration of the sacraments reaches its summit in the Eucharist, in which all of our senses are deceived except hearing Christ's words of power.[17]

A sacramental spirituality, therefore, is both humble and magnanimous at the same time. It is humble because it is a remedy that is simple and universally available. Billions have been baptized. Pride

---

[14] For a reflection on the theological significance of the Ascension, see Douglas Farrow, *Ascension Theology* (London: T&T Clark, 2011).

[15] Leo the Great, Sermon 74.2, in *Sermons*, 326.

[16] See Paul VI, *Divinae Consortium Naturae*: "From that time on the apostles, in fulfillment of Christ's will, imparted to the newly baptized by the laying on of hands the gift of the Spirit that completes the grace of Baptism. . . . The imposition of hands is rightly recognized by the Catholic tradition as the origin of the sacrament of Confirmation, which in a certain way perpetuates the grace of Pentecost in the Church."

[17] See Thomas Aquinas, *Adoro Te Devote*, trans. Caswall, in Cantalamessa, *This Is My Body*, 13: "Sight, touch, and taste in Thee are each deceived; the ear alone most safely is believed."

desires exclusivity in privilege, but the sacramental system is maximally open and costs nothing. The very fact that the grace of the sacraments can be obtained by an upright desire for it, even an implicit desire, further excludes any corporate pride that seeks to boast of an exclusive gift.

The intensity of the faith that accompanies reception of the sacraments, together with repentance and loving desire, determines the intensity of the sacramental grace that is received.[18] This faith and desire is very often aided precisely by the recognition of weakness and the need for forgiveness and divine mercy. Thus the sacramental system by its nature brings out the Gospel principle that "the last will be first, and the first last" (Matt 20:16). Even as we recognize our lowliness, however, faith also believes that the sacraments open us up to divine sonship and divinization, which is easy to say but impossible to conceive, for "no eye has seen, nor ear heard, nor the heart of man conceived, what God has prepared for those who love Him" (1 Cor 2:9).

Sacraments and the Trinity

Faith in the sacraments is exercised with regard to the three Persons of the Trinity. The sacraments give the faithful, first and foremost, an encounter with Jesus Christ in His humanity, who instituted the sacraments, merited the grace they give, and works through them to touch and breathe[19] upon us today. He works through the sacraments to configure us to Himself, stamping us with His image, calling us to participate in His mission and to offer ourselves with Him in the Eucharist.

The Incarnate Word, however, is never encountered without the other two Persons of the Trinity. Since the Spirit proceeds from the Father and the Son as their mutual love, the Son's task, working through the sacraments, is to communicate to us the Spirit, through whom "God's love has been poured into our hearts" (Rom 5:5). The Spirit's task is to configure the faithful to the incarnate Son through sacramental grace, progressively realizing in the faithful the image of Christ, that they might become an *alter Christus*. Since Christ's entire life is lived in intimate filial relationship to His Father, the Spirit's work of configuring us to Christ necessarily means establishing the

---

[18] See Bl. Columba Marmion, *Christ, the Life of the Soul*, 190–91.
[19] See John 20:22.

faithful in the same filial relationship with the Father, as sons in the Son, through the gift of Baptism. As St. Paul says in Romans 8:14–17:

> For all who are led by the Spirit of God are sons of God. For you did not receive the spirit of slavery to fall back into fear, but you have received the spirit of sonship. When we cry, "Abba! Father!" it is the Spirit himself bearing witness with our spirit that we are children of God, and if children, then heirs, heirs of God and fellow heirs with Christ.

The sacramental life, therefore, is marked by a twofold order. The Father sends the Son in the Incarnation, which is the foundation of the sacramental order. The Son sends the Spirit, visibly at Pentecost but invisibly through the sacraments. Here the order reverses. The mission of the Spirit communicated to the faithful is to configure them to the Son, thus ordering them to the Father in filial love and union. Therefore liturgical prayer, mirroring the sacramental life and the movement of *exitus* and *reditus*, is directed to the Person of the Father, through the Son, in the Holy Spirit whom He has given to us.

Spirituality of Baptism and Confirmation

Instead of speaking of a spirituality of Baptism or Confirmation taken individually, it seems better to foster a spirituality based on awareness of one's Baptism and Confirmation taken together as complementary sacraments of Christian initiation, both intrinsically ordered to the Eucharist, the source and summit of the Church's life. A spirituality of Baptism and Confirmation should be marked by the awareness that we have been inserted into Christ's death and Resurrection. Insertion into His death means that we are configured to the ascetical battle against sin. Insertion into His Resurrection configures us to living the divine life of faith, hope, and charity. Bl. Columba Marmion states this eloquently:

> *The Christian life is nothing other than the progressive and con-tinued development, the application in practice, throughout the whole of our human existence, of the twofold initial act put into us in seed form at baptism, of the twofold super-natural result of 'death' and of 'life' produced by this sacrament.* In that is to be

found the whole programme of Christianity.[20]

Secondly, this spirituality involves intimate awareness of our divine filiation. Once again, this encompasses the whole of the Christian life, for nothing should remain unaffected by the fact that we have been made sons or daughters of such a Father. On this account, the spirituality of Baptism and Confirmation is one of thanksgiving, joy, and filial confidence in the awareness that we have been inserted into Christ, made a son of the Father in Him, and made an heir to His heavenly inheritance, and that He has given us His Spirit as the pledge of that inheritance. Bl. Marmion says:

> Gratitude is the first feeling that baptismal grace should cause to arise in us. Joy is the second. We ought never to think of our baptism without a deep feeling of inner exhilaration. On the day of our baptism we were born, in principle, to eternal bliss. . . . Having entered into the family of God, we have the right to share in the inheritance of the only Son. . . . Finally and above all, we should yield up our souls to great *confidence*. In our dealings with our Heavenly Father we should remember that we are His children.[21]

This supernatural confidence engendered by the sacraments of Christian initiation also involves an awareness that this identity in Christ has been stamped indelibly on us, and this stamp is an abiding source of the dynamic series of graces we need to live out this calling. The stamp on our soul marks it with Christ and His word of power that continues to call down His Spirit to be our interior Teacher and Paraclete.

Third, the spirituality of Baptism and Confirmation involves awareness of our reception of a prophetic, kingly, and priestly mission that is a share in Christ's own prophetic, kingly, and priestly mission, and as such, orients us out of ourselves to God, the Church, and the world. Every healthy person seeks a mission that focuses our existence. At Baptism, and in a deeper way in Confirmation, we have received a mission that exceeds any other mission conceivable.[22]

---

[20] Marmion, *Christ, the Life of the Soul*, 211 (emphasis original).

[21] Marmion, *Christ, the Life of the Soul*, 214.

[22] See Pecknold and Laborde, "Confirmation," in *OHST*, 498: "There is nothing

St. Ignatius of Loyola has a famous meditation on this calling given
to all Christians through the sacraments of initiation. He imagines a
saintly earthly king inviting his subjects to go on a crusade to conquer the
enemies of Christ and defend Christendom. All magnanimous Christian knights would offer themselves to this service. This is an analogy for
a greater, more magnanimous enterprise: Christ the King is calling us
to serve Him in His universal battle against His enemies which are sin,
the devil, and the temptations of the world. Every Christian soldier—as
we all become through the character of Confirmation—ought to offer
himself to the battle and imitate the conduct of Christ, the head of our
militia. St. Ignatius also invites us to make special offerings of humility and poverty in imitation of Christ:

> If such a summons of an earthly king to his subjects deserves
> our attention, how much more worthy of consideration is
> Christ our Lord, the Eternal King, before whom is assembled
> the whole world. To all His summons goes forth, and to each
> one in particular He addresses the words: "It is my will to
> conquer the whole world and all enemies, and thus to enter
> into the glory of my Father. Therefore, whoever wishes to join
> me in this enterprise, must be willing to labor with me, that by
> following me in suffering, he may follow me in glory.
>
> Second Point. Consider that all persons who have judg-
> ment and reason will offer themselves entirely for this work.
>
> Third Point. Those who wish to give greater proof of their
> love, and to distinguish themselves in whatever concerns the
> service of the eternal King and the Lord of all, will not only
> offer themselves entirely for the work, but will act against
> their sensuality and carnal and worldly love, and make offer-
> ings of greater value and of more importance.[23]

---

more important for young Catholics than to see the sacrament of confirmation
not as a diploma, but as a deputizing to proclaim the Gospel. . . . If the new
evangelization is to be truly effective in our lifetimes, then we will see the first
fruits of the church's renewed evangelical mission precisely through the door
of the sacrament of confirmation." See also Afanasiev, *The Church of the Holy
Spirit*, 3: "We are not aware of how extraordinary and audacious the idea of the
priestly ministry of all members of the Church is."

[23] St. Ignatius, *Spiritual Exercises*, §§95–97, in *The Spiritual Exercises of St. Ignatius: Based on Studies in the Language of the Autograph*, trans. Louis J. Puhl
(Chicago: Loyola Press, 1951), 44–45.

The spirituality of Baptism and Confirmation is a spirit of magnanimity and discernment. This meditation from the *Spiritual Exercises* offers an image of the virtue of magnanimity and its central importance in the spiritual life. It also points to the need of the gift of discernment to see where I am called to serve the King of kings. Magnanimity has to be coupled with Christian prudence, spiritual direction, and the gift of the Holy Spirit called counsel. Magnanimity asks for charisms, and the gift of counsel discerns the beautiful way of serving God to which we are actually called.

The Baptismal Call to Holiness and to Consecrate Earthly Realities

Although Baptism and Confirmation are received only once in Christian initiation, their abiding character means that we can call upon the grace of Baptism and Confirmation in all the events of everyday life. Baptism and Confirmation never cease to be active in configuring us further to Christ's death and Resurrection and to the Spirit's power to lead us to act in a supernatural way. Thus the spirituality of Baptism and Confirmation involves an awareness of the sacramental mystery in all the events of ordinary life. This has been referred to by Jean-Pierre de Caussade, S.J. as the "sacrament of the present moment."[24]

The Incarnation has implanted a divine dimension into all human labor and all the mundane dimensions of human life. Especially in His hidden life in Nazareth, Jesus sanctified the daily realities of family life, work, communal worship, meals, and recreation. "For by His Incarnation the Son of God has united Himself in some fashion with

---

[24] Jean-Pierre de Caussade, *Abandonment to Divine Providence*, trans. Algar Thorold, ed. John Joyce (Rockford, IL: TAN Books, 1987). See, for example, p. 35: "What happens at each moment bears the imprint of the will of God and of his adorable name.... How just, then, to bless it, to treat it as a sacrament which hallows by its own power souls which place no obstacle to its action!" See also p. 5, speaking of the hidden life of the Holy Family: "What is the sacrament of each of their sacred moments? What treasures of grace are contained in each of these moments underneath the commonplace appearance of the events that fill them? Outwardly these events are no different from those which happen to everyone, but the interior invisible element discerned by faith is nothing less than God himself performing great works. O bread of angels, heavenly manna, the pearl of the Gospel, the sacrament of the present moment! You present God in such lowly forms as the manger, the hay and straw!" This work has also been published under the title, *The Sacrament of the Present Moment*.

every man. He worked with human hands, He thought with a human mind, acted by human choice and loved with a human heart."[25]

Since Baptism and Confirmation configure the faithful to Christ and give them a participation in His mission, it follows that the baptized and confirmed faithful are called to sanctify ordinary life—centering on work, family, worship, and friendship—and consecrate it to the Father as Jesus did, discovering that divine dimension inserted into it by the fact that Christ took them up. Baptism and Confirmation, through the sacramental graces they bestow, give the faithful the spiritual power to attain holiness in the ordinary realities of life.[26]

Eucharistic Focus of Baptism and Confirmation

Since Baptism and Confirmation, like the other sacraments, are ordered to the Eucharist, the spirituality of Baptism and Confirmation is fundamentally a Eucharistic spirituality. The consecration of earthly realities that is the specific mission of the lay faithful is accomplished by living them in a holy way through charity and sacramental grace. This consecration culminates, however, through the offering of those realities of ordinary life through, with, and in Christ to the Father in the Sacrifice of the Mass, as stated in *Lumen Gentium*, §34:

> For all their works, prayers and apostolic endeavors, their ordinary married and family life, their daily occupations, their physical and mental relaxation, if carried out in the Spirit, and even the hardships of life, if patiently borne—all these become "spiritual sacrifices acceptable to God through Jesus Christ" [1 Pt 2:5]. Together with the offering of the Lord's body, they are most fittingly offered in the celebration of the Eucharist. Thus, as those everywhere who adore in holy activity, the laity consecrate the world itself to God.

The faithful have the glorious mission, given by incorporation into

---

[25] *Gaudium et Spes*, §22.

[26] See *LG*, §31, speaking of the vocation of the laity: "Led by the spirit of the Gospel they may work for the sanctification of the world from within as a leaven. In this way they may make Christ known to others, especially by the testimony of a life resplendent in faith, hope and charity. Therefore, since they are tightly bound up in all types of temporal affairs it is their special task to order and to throw light upon these affairs."

Christ and His Mystical Body through Baptism and Confirmation, of offering the Paschal mystery of God the Son to God the Father, and of inserting all of their Christian life, all people, and all created realities into the offering. The strength for this offering comes from being frequently nourished by a renewed gift of the fire of the Spirit in Holy Communion.[27]

Spirituality of Penance

Unlike that of Baptism and Confirmation, the spirituality of Penance involves frequent reception of the sacrament, by which we renew again and again the resolve to die to sin and make satisfaction for it, living in a spirit of renewed reconciliation with God and the Church.

To live the spirit of Penance is to have an intimate awareness of sin and its power to destroy relationships with God and neighbor, and of the need to join with Christ in doing satisfaction for it. St. John Paul II speaks about the "sense of sin" in *Reconciliatio et Paenitentia*, §18. He begins by defining it as a "fine sensitivity and an acute perception of the seeds of death contained in sin, as well as a sensitivity and an acuteness of perception for identifying them in the thousand guises under which sin shows itself." This awareness of sin should not be understood merely in the sense of an abstract intellectual understanding of sin. Rather, we are speaking of a knowledge of sin that is a gift of the Holy Spirit, coming from friendship with Christ crucified for sin.

A spirituality of Penance combines the supernatural sense of sin with the desire to make satisfaction for sin in union with Christ so as to restore the extrinsic glory of the Father that has been offended and obscured before men by sin. The spirit of Penance is expressed in various petitions of the Our Father. Above all it is motivated by the desire to sanctify the Father's name, to do His will, and to have our sins forgiven as we forgive our neighbor. Forgiveness of our neighbor is thus a key part of the spirit of Penance.

As in the case of Baptism and Confirmation, a spirituality founded on the sacrament of Penance involves a spirit of joy and thanksgiving for the great gift of reconciliation and the restoration of the divine life. It is part of the paradox of the Christian life that a sacrament whose matter includes sorrow over sin, brings about deep consolation and joy.

---

[27] See John Paul II, *Ecclesia de Eucharistia*, §17; Feingold, *The Eucharist*, 514–16.

John Paul II speaks of this joy:

> Contrition and conversion are even more a drawing near to the holiness of God, a rediscovery of one's true identity, which has been upset and disturbed by sin, a liberation in the very depth of self and thus a regaining of lost joy, the joy of being saved, which the majority of people in our time are no longer capable of experiencing.[28]

An inexhaustible biblical figure for the spirituality of Penance is the prodigal son (Luke 15:11–52).[29] Everyone who receives the sacrament of Penance is called to relive the experience of the prodigal son in his reconciliation with his father, in "his return to the truth about himself,"[30] and the recovery of "the joy of being saved." Together with this joy comes an obligation of the heart to generously seek to make satisfaction, above all through the occasions of daily life,[31] for one's sin and those of the human family divided by sin.

Spirituality of Anointing

The sacrament of Anointing of the Sick does not confer a permanent ecclesial status, for one hopes that the serious illness that is the occasion for the sacrament can be cured. Nevertheless, it does give a particular mission of redemptive suffering on behalf of the Church during the time of that illness.[32] Reception of the sacrament of Anointing thus gives a particular configuration with Christ in His Passion, a

---

[28] John Paul II, *Reconciliatio et Paenitentia*, §31, no. 3.

[29] See John Paul II, Encyclical *Dives in Misericordia* (Nov 30, 1980), §§5–6; *Reconciliatio et Paenitentia*, §§5–6; Henri J. M. Nouwen, *Return of the Prodigal Son: Story of Homecoming* (New York: Doubleday, 1992).

[30] John Paul II, *Dives in Misericordia*, §6.

[31] The spirituality of Penance thus goes intimately together with the "sacrament of the present moment," discussed above with regard to the spirituality of Baptism and Confirmation.

[32] See *CCC*, §1522: "An *ecclesial grace*. The sick who receive this sacrament, 'by freely uniting themselves to the passion and death of Christ,' 'contribute to the good of the People of God.' By celebrating this sacrament the Church, in the communion of saints, intercedes for the benefit of the sick person, and he, for his part, though the grace of this sacrament, contributes to the sanctification of the Church and to the good of all men for whom the Church suffers and offers herself through Christ to God the Father."

corresponding ecclesial mission, and the power of grace to accomplish it. Those who receive this sacrament are consecrated in their illness and called to redeem suffering by offering it for their own purification from sin and for the whole Body of Christ.[33] A key biblical text for the spirituality of those who have received this sacrament is given in Colossians 1:24: "Now I rejoice in my sufferings for your sake, and in my flesh I complete what is lacking in Christ's afflictions for the sake of his body, that is, the church."

Anointing of the Sick, therefore, like the Eucharist and the other sacraments, has an ascending and a descending dimension. It involves a reception of grace, the descending aspect, but this grace is ordered to the offering of that suffering, in union with the Eucharistic Sacrifice, in an ascending oblation on behalf of the sick person and for the good of the whole Church.

Spirituality of Marriage

Marriage is elevated into a sacrament by insertion into Christ. When an unbaptized married couple receives Baptism together, as my wife and I did, their marriage becomes sacramental through the simple reception of Baptism. This illuminates the foundational role of Baptism and the interconnection of the sacraments. Matrimony presupposes the mission and graces of Baptism and Confirmation and gives to that general mission a new focus, which is to be living icons of Christ's spousal love for His Church, for whom He shed His blood.

The sacrament of Matrimony also has a profoundly Eucharistic dimension, just as the Eucharist is itself a nuptial mystery. As St. John Paul II wrote: "The Eucharist is the sacrament of our redemption. It is the sacrament of the Bridegroom and of the Bride."[34] In *Sacramentum Caritatis*, Benedict XVI writes:

> "The entire Christian life bears the mark of the spousal love
> of Christ and the Church. Already Baptism, the entry into the
> People of God, is a nuptial mystery; it is so to speak the nuptial

---

[33] See *CCC*, §1521: "By the grace of this sacrament the sick person receives the strength and the gift of uniting himself more closely to Christ's Passion: in a certain way he is consecrated to bear fruit by configuration to the Savior's redemptive Passion. Suffering, a consequence of original sin, acquires a new meaning; it becomes a participation in the saving work of Jesus."

[34] John Paul II, *Mulieris Dignitatem*, §26.

bath which precedes the wedding feast, the Eucharist."[35] The Eucharist inexhaustibly strengthens the indissoluble unity and love of every Christian marriage. By the power of the sacrament, the marriage bond is intrinsically linked to the eucharistic unity of Christ the Bridegroom and his Bride, the Church (cf. Eph 5:31–32). The mutual consent that husband and wife exchange in Christ, which establishes them as a community of life and love, also has a eucharistic dimension. Indeed, in the theology of Saint Paul, conjugal love is a sacramental sign of Christ's love for his Church, a love culminating in the Cross, the expression of his "marriage" with humanity and at the same time the origin and heart of the Eucharist.[36]

Spirituality of Priestly Character

By Holy Orders, the priest is inserted into the spousal mystery of Christ and the Church. Priestly character gives him the power and mission to act in the Person of the Bridegroom, above all in realizing the Eucharistic Sacrifice on behalf of His Bride, the Church. As seen above in chapter 6, this is the reason why male gender is part of the sacramental sign of Holy Orders.

The spirituality of the priesthood is outlined in Hebrews 5:1–10:

> Every high priest chosen from among men is appointed to act on behalf of men in relation to God, to offer gifts and sacrifices for sins. He can deal gently with the ignorant and wayward, since he himself is beset with weakness. Because of this he is bound to offer sacrifice for his own sins as well as for those of the people. And one does not take the honor upon himself, but he is called by God, just as Aaron was. So also Christ did not exalt himself to be made a high priest, but was appointed by him who said to him, "You are my Son, today I have begotten you."

Priesthood is essentially ordered to the offering of sacrifice and the exercise of mediation between God and human society.[37] All priestly

---

[35] *CCC*, §1617.

[36] Benedict XVI, *Sacramentum Caritatis*, §27.

[37] On the connection of priesthood with mediation and sacrifice, see Congar, *Lay*

spirituality is sacrificial and intercessory. As Christ was both priest and Victim, so must be every priest in the New Covenant. As Christ put Himself in solidarity with those for whom He exercises His priesthood—all mankind—so must the priest.

Christ in His humanity is the one perfect priest, who, by virtue of the hypostatic union, stands perfectly between and is perfectly united to the two parties who need to be reconciled: God and man. Only Christ can be the perfect priest, for He alone has the hypostatic union, which cannot be shared with others. But priestly character mysteriously configures the recipient to Christ so that Christ can act through him.[38]

Priestly spirituality is founded upon an awareness of being constituted, by an additional title distinct from Baptism and Confirmation, as an *alter Christus*, which means that the priest must lose himself in pastoral charity so that Christ can be encountered in him by others. Benedict XVI spoke of this in a General Audience on the Year for Priests:

> For the priest, then, being the "voice" of the Word is not merely a functional aspect. On the contrary, it implies a substantial "losing of himself" in Christ, participating with his whole being in the mystery of Christ's death and Resurrection: his understanding, his freedom, his will and the offering of his body as a living sacrifice (cf. Rom 12: 1–2). . . . As an *alter Christus*, the priest is profoundly united to the Word of the Father who, in becoming incarnate took the form of a servant, he became a servant (Phil 2: 5–11). The priest is

---

People in the Church, 152–55. On priestly spirituality, see John Paul II, *Pastores Dabo Vobis*, §§19–33; Jean-Pierre Torrell, *A Priestly People: Baptismal Priesthood and Priestly Ministry*, 186–95; C. Marmion, *Christ: The Ideal of the Priest*, trans. Matthew Dillon (San Francisco: Ignatius Press, 2005); Garrigou-Lagrange, *The Priest in Union with Christ*; André Feuillet, *The Priesthood of Christ and His Ministers*, trans. Matthew J. O'Connell (Garden City, NY: Doubleday, 1975); Galot, *Theology of the Priesthood*; Dermot Power, *A Spiritual Theology of the Priesthood: The Mystery of Christ and the Mission of the Priest* (Washington, DC: Catholic University of America Press, 1998); David L. Toups, *Reclaiming Our Priestly Character* (Omaha, NB: Institute for Priestly Formation, IPF Publications, 2008), 133–95.

[38] See *SCG* IV, ch. 74, no. 2 (quoted above on 262n95); and Scheeben, *Mysteries of Christianity*, 586–87, in which Scheeben argues that sacramental character has an analogical relationship with the hypostatic union in Christ.

a servant of Christ, in the sense that his existence, configured to Christ ontologically, acquires an essentially relational
character: he is *in* Christ, *for* Christ and *with* Christ, at the
service of humankind. Because he belongs to Christ, the priest
is radically at the service of all people: he is the minister of
their salvation, their happiness and their authentic liberation,
developing, in this gradual assumption of Christ's will, in
prayer, in "being heart to heart" with him.[39]

Like every sacrament, but in a supreme degree, Holy Orders
requires the exercise of the complementary virtues of humility and
magnanimity. The priestly office of mediation in the person of Christ
the Head involves a greater dignity than any other earthly station.
Hence there is a greater need for humility in the recipient. Hebrews
5:2 stresses that the priest is "beset with weakness" precisely so that
he can be experientially aware of his solidarity with "the ignorant and
the wayward." Awareness of his own human weakness and its immense
disproportion with the office conferred is essential to the priest. For
this reason, "no one takes the honor upon himself" but must be called,
and the vocation must be discerned by the Church.

But humility also recognizes that God's sacramental grace is more
powerful than human weakness, and thus humility makes possible true
magnanimity. As Hebrews 5:5 indicates, priestly spirituality involves a
unique participation in Christ's sonship and, through administration
of the sacraments, in His life-giving spiritual paternity.

The Curé of Ars, in his *Little Catechism*, describes the dignity of
the priesthood and the irreplaceable mission of the priest in the distribution of sacramental graces:

> Go to confession to the Blessed Virgin, or to an angel; will
> they absolve you? No. Will they give you the Body and Blood
> of Our Lord? No. The Holy Virgin cannot make her Divine
> Son descend into the Host. You might have two hundred
> angels there, but they could not absolve you. A priest, however
> simple he may be, can do it; he can say to you, "Go in peace;
> I pardon you." Oh, how great is a priest! The priest will not
> understand the greatness of his office till he is in Heaven. If he

---

[39] Benedict XVI, General Audience, June 24, 2009; see also John Paul II, *Pastores Dabo Vobis*, §23.

understood it on earth, he would die, not of fear, but of love. The other benefits of God would be of no avail to us without the priest. What would be the use of a house full of gold, if you had nobody to open you the door! The priest has the key of the heavenly treasures; it is he who opens the door; he is the steward of the good God, the distributor of His wealth.[40] . . . The priesthood is the love of the Heart of Jesus. When you see the priest, think of Our Lord Jesus Christ.[41]

Eucharistic Spirituality

Since the Eucharist is the source and summit of the Christian life, sacramental spirituality must center on the Eucharist, the queen of the sacraments. Everything said about the spirituality of the other sacraments is ordered to the Eucharist and finds its fulfillment there. The Christian life that begins in Baptism through entering into Christ's death and Resurrection is entirely ordered to a union with Christ that is consummated and sacramentally nourished in every Eucharistic Communion, and to a sacrificial gift of self to the Father with and in Christ.[42]

The Eucharist brings together an alternation of descending and ascending movements from heaven to earth and from earth to heaven. This ought to mark all Christian spirituality, which is symbolized by Jacob's ladder in Genesis 28:12–13:

> And he dreamed that there was a ladder set up on the earth, and the top of it reached to heaven; and behold, the angels of God were ascending and descending on it! And behold, the LORD stood above it and said, "I am the LORD, the God of Abraham your father and the God of Isaac.

---

[40] John Vianney, *The Little Catechism of the Curé of Ars* (Rockford, IL: TAN Books, 1987), 34.

[41] Vianney, *The Little Catechism of the Curé of Ars*, 36.

[42] See La Soujeole, "The Sacraments and the Development of Doctrine," *OHST*, 596: "If sacramentality in the strict sense occurs in the seven sacraments, it does so in an analogical fashion. There is a great difference here between the Eucharist and the other six sacraments. These latter have their finality in the Eucharist. These six sacraments sanctify people so that they may glorify God by the gift of their lives, a gift that attains its perfection in being united to the sacrifice of Christ."

The Eucharist is like Jacob's ladder but better, because the Lord Himself descends and ascends on it. God takes the initiative by descending first. He descends to us in the liturgy of the Word, and we ascend to Him in the prayer of the faithful and in the spiritual movement of the Offertory. A far greater descent then occurs in the Eucharistic Prayer in which the Word made flesh in Mary's womb becomes present on the altar under the species of bread and wine. Through transubstantiation He becomes present in His entire human reality, but in a way suited to our pilgrimage of faith.

He becomes present as the Victim of Calvary, present in His Body and Blood under the species of bread and wine which are separately consecrated to sacramentally represent His bloody immolation on Calvary in which His Blood was physically separated from His Body in His Passion. This is the supreme self-emptying.

Immediately after the realization of the sacrifice, however, the movement reverses. Christ, made present on the altar, offers Himself to the Father, and the Church offers Him through the hands and prayers of the priest, who prays: "We offer you in thanksgiving this holy and living sacrifice."[43] Or: "Therefore, as we celebrate the memorial of his Death and Resurrection, we offer you, Lord, the Bread of life and the Chalice of salvation, giving thanks that you have held us worthy to be in your presence and minister to you."[44]

Just as the consecration represents a supreme descending movement, so the offering of the Victim made in the anamnesis is a corresponding ascending movement. In offering the Victim to the Father, the faithful are to join in the offering by spiritually offering Christ to the Father together with their own Christian lives. *Lumen Gentium*, §11, in a justly famous text, says: "Taking part in the Eucharistic Sacrifice, which is the fount and apex of the whole Christian life, they offer the Divine Victim to God, and offer themselves along with It."

Although frequently cited with regard to "source and summit," this text is less understood by the faithful with regard to their twofold participation in the offering, which is to co-offer Christ to His Father, and to offer themselves with Christ to the Father. It is primarily in this way that all earthly and human realities (except sin, but including repentance for it) are consecrated to the Lord and become a priestly

---

43 Third Eucharistic Prayer, *The Roman Missal*, 3rd ed., 653.
44 First Eucharistic Prayer, *The Roman Missal*, 3rd ed., 648.

offering, which gains infinitely in dignity and drama by being joined to the offering of the Son of God. As Bl. Marmion states: "We ought to be united with Christ in His immolation, to offer ourselves with Him. Then He takes us with Him, He immolates us with Himself, He bears us before His Father 'with an odor of sweetness.' It is *we ourselves* that we ought to offer with Jesus Christ."[45]

Eucharistic spirituality therefore involves the whole of life. It cannot be a mere liturgical or cultic spirituality, because the offering has to include the entire Christian life, including everything that is done in the kingly office of service to neighbor and the common good, as well as our prophetic office of giving Christian witness. But where do we find the spiritual strength and nourishment to live life in such a way that it can be offered with Christ? This could seem to be the supreme hubris.

Christ Himself provides the nourishment in the final descending movement: Holy Communion. This descent is deeper still, because He is not content to remain on the altar or in the tabernacle. He descends into our humanity, being received totally by us under the sacred species of bread and wine. But instead of turning Him into ourselves, as we do other food, He progressively transforms us into Himself through nourishing us with divine charity, according to our dispositions of hunger and thirst for Him, and thereby unites us in deeper communion with the other actual and potential members of His Mystical Body.[46]

With regard to Holy Communion, Marmion writes:

> Christ Jesus gives Himself to us, but after having died for us. He gives Himself as food, but after having offered Himself as Victim. In the Eucharist, Victim and food are sacrifice and sacrament—two inseparable features. And this is why that habitual disposition of making a total gift of oneself is so important. Christ gives Himself to us in the measure that we give ourselves to Him, to His Father, to our brethren who are the members of His mystical body.[47]

Taking the Lord into our bodies is the supreme sign of spousal union, which the Eucharist nourishes day by day. He gives Himself

---

[45] Marmion, *Christ, the Life of the Soul*, 354.

[46] See Augustine, *Confessions* 7.10.16.

[47] Marmion, *Christ, the Life of the Soul*, 374–75.

totally to us so that we learn to give ourselves back to Him in thanksgiving and in living in charity such that we can offer our life to Him in the next Mass more fully than in the one before.

Mary, the Model of the Sacramental Life

Mary, because of her unique relationship with the divine Persons and through her perfect sacramental receptivity and self-gift, is the supreme model of the sacramental life of the Church. Although she could not receive the sacraments of healing that presuppose the presence of sin, nor the forgiveness of original sin through Baptism, nor Holy Orders, she is the supreme model for participation in the Eucharistic Sacrifice and reception of Holy Communion,[48] as St. John Paul II points out in *Ecclesia de Eucharistia*, §56:

> The body given up for us and made present under sacramental signs was the same body which she had conceived in her womb! For Mary, receiving the Eucharist must have somehow meant welcoming once more into her womb that heart which had beat in unison with hers and reliving what she had experienced at the foot of the Cross.

What Mary received in her Immaculate Conception—sanctifying grace—is received by the faithful in Baptism and strengthened by every sacrament received with the right dispositions. What Mary received into her body at the Annunciation—the Word Incarnate— was received by her and is received by all of the faithful in Holy Communion. Although the dispositions of perfect faith, hope, and love with which she received Him are not fully shared by us, let us ask her intercession so that we may receive her Son's life through the sacraments ever more deeply.

STUDY QUESTIONS

1. (a) What are some of the factors leading to development of Catholic doctrine? (b) How can there be significant developments of doctrine with regard to the sacraments if they have all

---

[48] See Feingold, *The Eucharist*, 29–31, 422–23.

existed since Pentecost? (c) What are some of the ways in which doctrine has developed with regard to the sacraments?

2. (a) What does it mean to foster a sacramental spirituality? (b) Why is this important for the spiritual life and pastoral practice? (c) Describe some of the key elements of a sacramental spirituality for each of the seven sacraments.

Suggestions for Further Reading

Fagan, Sean. "Sacramental Spirituality." In *Sacraments: The Gestures of Christ*. Edited by Denis O'Callaghan. New York: Sheed & Ward, 1964. Pp. 153–73.

Marmion, Columba. *Christ, the Life of the Soul*. Translated by Alan Bancroft. Bethesda, MD: Zaccheus Press, 2005. Pp. 190–271; 329–88.

Newman, John Henry. *An Essay on the Development of Christian Doctrine*. Foreword by Ian Ker. Notre Dame, IN: University of Notre Dame Press, 1989.

Nutt, Roger W. *General Principles of Sacramental Theology*. Washington, DC: Catholic University of America Press, 2017. Pp. 185–92.

O'Neill, Colman E. *Meeting Christ in the Sacraments*. Revised edition, revised by Romanus Cessario. Staten Island, NY: St. Paul's, 1991. Pp. 293–307.

❧ Select Bibliography

Magisterial Texts

Conciliar Documents

Council of Florence. Bull of Union with the Armenians *Exsultate Deo*. November 22, 1439.

_____. Bull of Union with the Copts and the Ethiopians *Cantate Domino*, Decree for the Jacobites. February 4, 1442.

Council of Trent. Decree Concerning Original Sin. Session 5, June 17, 1546.

_____. Decree on Justification. Session 6, January 13, 1547.

_____. Decree on the Sacraments. Session 7, March 3, 1547.

_____. Decree Concerning the Most Holy Sacrament of the Eucharist. Session 13, October 11, 1551.

_____. Doctrine and Canons on the Sacrament of Penance and Extreme Unction. Session 14, November 25, 1551.

_____. Doctrine of Communion under Both Kinds and the Communion of Little Children. Session 21, July 16, 1562.

_____. Doctrine Concerning the Sacrifice of the Mass. Session 22, September 17, 1562.

_____. Decree Concerning the Sacrament of Orders. Session 23, July 15, 1563.

_____. Doctrine and Canons on the Sacrament of Marriage. Decree *Tametsi*. Session 24, November 11, 1563.

_____. Decree Concerning Purgatory. Session 25, December 4, 1563.

Vatican I. Dogmatic Constitution on the Catholic Faith *Dei Filius*. April 24, 1870.

_____. Dogmatic Constitution on the Church of Christ *Pastor Aeternus.* July 18, 1870.

Second Vatican Council. Constitution on the Sacred Liturgy, *Sacrosanctum Concilium.* December 4, 1963.

_____. Dogmatic Constitution on the Church *Lumen Gentium.* November 21, 1964.

_____. Declaration on the Relation of the Church to Non-Christian Religions *Nostra Aetate.* October 28, 1965.

_____. Dogmatic Constitution on Divine Revelation *Dei Verbum.* November 18, 1965.

_____. Decree on the Mission Activity of the Church *Ad Gentes.* December 7, 1965.

_____. Declaration on Religious Freedom *Dignitatis Humanae.* December 7, 1965.

_____. Decree on the Ministry and Life of Priests *Presbyterorum Ordinis.* December 7, 1965.

_____. Pastoral Constitution on the Church in the Modern World *Gaudium et Spes.* December 7, 1965.

Papal Documents

Innocent I. Letter to Bishop Decentius of Gubbio. March 19, 416. DS, 216.

Leo the Great. Letter 168 to all the Bishops of Campania *Magna indignatione.* March 6, 459. DS, 323.

Innocent II. Letter to the Bishop of Cremona *Apostolicam sedem.* DS, 741.

Innocent III. Letter to Archbishop Humbert of Arles *Maiores Ecclesiae causas.* 1201. DS, 781.

_____. Letter to Bishop Berthold of Metz *Debitum pastoralis officii.* August 28, 1206. DS, 788.

John XXII. Letter to the Armenians *Nequaquam sine dolore.* November 21, 1321. DS, 926.

Benedict XIV. Encyclical on the Euchologian *Ex quo primum.* March 1, 1756. In *The Papal Encyclicals 1740–1878.* Edited by Claudia Carlen. Wilmington, NC: McGrath Publishing, 1981.

Pius IX. Encyclical *Singulari Quadam.* 1854.

_____. Encyclical on the Promotion of False Doctrines *Quanto Conficiamur Moerore.* August 10, 1863. DS, 2866.

Leo XIII. Apostolic Letter on the Nullity of Anglican Orders *Apostol-*

icae Curae. September 13, 1896.

_____. Encyclical on the Holy Spirit *Divinum Illud Munus.* May 9, 1897.

Pius X. Decree on Frequent and Daily Reception of Holy Communion *Sacra Tridentina.* December 20, 1905.

Pius XI. Encyclical on Christian Marriage *Casti Connubii.* December 31, 1930.

Pius XII. Encyclical on the Mystical Body of Christ *Mystici Corporis Christi.* June 29, 1943.

_____. Encyclical on the Sacred Liturgy *Mediator Dei.* November 20, 1947.

_____. Apostolic Constitution *Sacramentum Ordinis.* November 30, 1947.

_____. Encyclical *Humani Generis.* August 12, 1950.

Paul VI. Encyclical on the Eucharist *Mysterium Fidei.* September 3, 1965.

_____. Apostolic Letter motu proprio *Sacrum Diaconatus Ordinem.* June 18, 1967.

_____. Apostolic Constitution Approving New Rites for the Ordination of Deacons, Priests, and Bishops *Pontificalis Romani Recognitio.* June 18, 1968.

_____. Apostolic Letter on the Credo of the People of God *Solemni hac Liturgia.* June 30, 1968.

_____. Apostolic Constitution on the Sacrament of Confirmation *Divinae Consortium Naturae.* August 15, 1971.

_____. *Ordo Confirmationis.* 1971.

_____. Apostolic Constitution *Sacram Unctionem Infirmorum.* November 30, 1972.

John Paul II. Discourse to Representatives of the Jewish People in Mainz. November 17, 1980.

_____. Encyclical *Dives in Misericordia.* November 30, 1980.

_____. Apostolic Exhortation on the Role of the Christian Family in the Modern World *Familiaris Consortio.* November 22, 1981.

_____. Post-Synodal Apostolic Exhortation on Reconciliation and Penance in the Mission of the Church Today *Reconciliatio et Paenitentia.* December 2, 1984.

_____. *Man and Woman He Created Them: A Theology of the Body.* Translated by Michael Waldstein. Boston, MA: Pauline Books & Media, 2006. (Catecheses delivered 1979–1984.)

_____. Address to Representatives of the Jewish Organizations of the

United States on September 11, 1987.

_____. Apostolic Letter On the Dignity and Vocation of Women *Mulieris Dignitatem*. August 15, 1988.

_____. Post-Synodal Apostolic Exhortation *Christifideles Laici*. December 30, 1988.

_____. Encyclical on the Permanent Validity of the Church's Missionary Mandate *Redemptoris Missio*. December 7, 1990.

_____. Post-Synodal Apostolic Exhortation on the Formation of Priests in the Circumstances of the Present Day *Pastores Dabo Vobis*. March 15, 1992.

_____. Apostolic Letter on Priestly Ordination *Ordinatio Sacerdotalis*. May 22, 1994. DS, 4980–4983.

_____. Encyclical Letter on the Eucharist in Its Relationship to the Church *Ecclesia de Eucharistia*. April 17, 2003.

Benedict XVI. Post-Synodal Apostolic Exhortation on the Eucharist as the Source and Summit of the Church's Life and Mission *Sacramentum Caritatis*. February 22, 2007.

Francis. Encyclical *Lumen Fidei*. June 29, 2013.

_____. Apostolic Exhortation on the Proclamation of the Gospel in Today's World *Evangelii Gaudium (The Joy of the Gospel)*. November 24, 2013.

_____. General Audience on the Sacrament of Penance. February 19, 2014.

_____. Address to Participants in a Course on the Internal Forum Organized by the Apostolic Penitentiary. March 12, 2015.

_____. Post-Synodal Apostolic Exhortation on Love in the Family *Amoris Laetitia*. March 19, 2016.

Other Magisterial Texts and Collections

Roman Catechism. Translated by Robert I. Bradley and Eugene Kevane. Boston: St. Paul Editions, 1985.

Holy Office. Decree *Lamentabili*. July 3, 1907.

_____. Letter to the Archbishop of Boston. August 8, 1949. DS, 3866–3873.

_____. Response of December 28, 1949 on the Intention of the Minister of Baptism. DS, 3874.

Missale Romanum: Ex Decreto SS. Concilii Tridentini Restitutum Summorum Pontificum Cura Recognitum. Vatican City: Typis Polyglottis Vaticanis, 1962.

Ordo Exsequiarum: Rituale Romanum Ex Decreto Sacrosancti Oecumenici

Concilii Vaticani II Instauratum. Rome: Typis Polyglottis Vaticanis, 1969. English edition: *Order of Christian Funerals: The Roman Ritual Revised by Decree of the Second Vatican Ecumenical Council and Published by Authority of Pope Paul VI.* Chicago: Liturgy Training Publications, 2018.

Sacred Congregation for the Doctrine of the Faith. Declaration on the Question of the Admission of Women to Priestly Ministry *Inter Insigniores.* October 15, 1976. DS, 4590–4606.

―――. Instruction on Infant Baptism *Pastoralis Actio.* October 20, 1980.

Commission for Religious Relations with the Jews. Notes on the Correct Way to Present the Jews and Judaism in Preaching and Catechesis in the Roman Catholic Church. June 24, 1985.

International Commission on English in the Liturgy. *The Rites of the Catholic Church as Revised by the Second Vatican Ecumenical Council.* 2 vols. Collegeville, MN: Liturgical Press, 1990–1991.

Congregation for the Doctrine of the Faith. Doctrinal Commentary on the Concluding Formula of the *Professio Fidei.* June 29, 1998.

Catechism of the Catholic Church. 2nd edition. Washington, DC: United States Catholic Conference, 2000.

Congregation for the Doctrine of the Faith. Declaration on the Unicity and Salvific Universality of Jesus Christ and the Church *Dominus Jesus.* August 6, 2000.

Compendium of the Catechism of the Catholic Church. Washington, DC: United States Catholic Conference, 2006.

Pontificium Consilium pro Laicis. *Rediscovering Confirmation.* Vatican City: Pontifical Council for the Laity, 2000.

Pontifical Council for Promoting Christian Unity. Guidelines for Admission to the Eucharist between the Chaldean Church and the Assyrian Church of the East. July 20, 2001.

Pontifical Biblical Commission. *The Jewish People and Their Sacred Scriptures in the Christian Bible.* Vatican City: Libreria Editrice Vaticana, 2002.

Rites of Ordination of a Bishop, of Priests, and of Deacons. 2nd typical edition. Washington, DC: United States Conference of Catholic Bishops, 2003.

Congregation for the Doctrine of the Faith. Note on the Minister of the Sacrament of the Anointing of the Sick, with commentary. February 11, 2005.

―――. Responses to Questions Proposed on the Validity of Baptism.

February 1, 2008. With Commentary by Antonio Miralles posted on the Vatican website.

Apostolic Penitentiary. *Manual of Indulgences: Norms and Grants.* Washington, DC: United States Conference of Catholic Bishops, 2006.

Roman Missal. 3rd typical edition. Washington, DC: United States Conference of Catholic Bishops, 2011.

Denzinger, Heinrich. *Enchiridion Symbolorum: Compendium of Creeds, Definitions, and Declarations on Matters of Faith and Morals.* 43rd edition. Edited by Peter Hünermann. English edition edited by Robert Fastiggi and Anne Englund Nash. San Francisco: Ignatius Press, 2012.

Congregation for Divine Worship and the Discipline of the Sacraments. *The Roman Pontifical.* Vatican City: Vox Clara Committee, 2012.

Commission for Religious Relations with the Jews. "The Gifts and the Calling of God Are Irrevocable" (Rom 11:29): A Reflection on Theological Questions Pertaining to Catholic–Jewish Relations on the Occasion of the 50th Anniversary of *Nostra Aetate.* December 10, 2015.

Congregation for the Doctrine of the Faith. Responses to Questions Proposed on the Validity of Baptism Conferred with the Formula "We baptize you in the name of the Father and of the Son and of the Holy Spirit." August 6, 2020.

_____. Doctrinal Note on the Modification of the Sacramental Formula of Baptism. August 6, 2020.

Patristic Sources

Ambrose. *De obitu Valentiniani.* In *Ambrose of Milan: Political Letters and Speeches*, 374–78. Translated by J. H. W. G. Liebeschuetz. Liverpool: Liverpool University Press, 2005.

_____. *De sacramentis.* In Edward Yarnold, S.J. *The Awe-Inspiring Rites of Initiation: The Origins of the R.C.I.A*, 98–159. 2nd edition. Collegeville, MN: Liturgical Press, 1994.

Athanasius. *The Letters of Saint Athanasius Concerning the Holy Spirit.* Translated by C. R. B. Shapland. London: The Epworth Press, 1951.

Augustine. *Against Julian.* Translated by M. A. Schumacher. FC 35.

Washington, DC: Catholic University of America Press, 1957.

_____. *Baptism*. In *The Donatist Controversy I*. Translated by Maureen Tilley and Boniface Ramsey. WSA I/21. Hyde Park, NY: New City Press, 2019.

_____. *The City of God, Books VIII–XVI*. Translated by G. G. Walsh and G. Monahan. FC 14. Washington, DC: Catholic University of America Press, 1952.

_____. *Commentary on the Lord's Sermon on the Mount with Seventeen Related Sermons*. Translated by Denis J. Kavanagh. FC 11. Washington, DC: Catholic University of America Press, 1951.

_____. *Expositions of the Psalms 73–98*. Translated by Maria Boulding. WSA III/18. Hyde Park, NY: New City Press, 2002.

_____. *The Good of Marriage*. Translated by C. T. Wilcox. In *Treatises on Marriage and Other Subjects*. FC 27. Washington, DC: Catholic University of America Press, 1955.

_____. *Letters: Volume I (1–82)*. Translated by Wilfrid Parsons. FC 12. Washington, DC: Catholic University of America Press, 1951.

_____. *Letters: Volume II (83–130)*. Translated by Wilfrid Parsons. FC 18. Washington, DC: Catholic University of America Press, 1953.

_____. *Letters: Volume III (131–164)*. Translated by Wilfrid Parsons. FC 20. Washington, DC: Catholic University of America Press, 1953.

_____. *Marriage and Desire*. In *Answer to the Pelagians II*. Translated by Roland J. Teske. WSA I/24. Hyde Park, NY: New City Press, 1998.

_____. *Newly Discovered Sermons*. Translated by Edmund Hill. WSA III/11. Hyde Park, NY: New City Press, 1997.

_____. *On Christian Doctrine*. Translated by J. F. Shaw. *NPNF*1, vol. 2.

_____. *The Punishment and Forgiveness of Sins and the Baptism of Little Ones*. In *Answer to the Pelagians*, 18–137. Translated by Roland J. Teske. WSA I/23. Hyde Park, NY: New City Press, 1997.

_____. *Reply to Faustus the Manichaean*. Translated by Richard Stothert. *NPNF*1, vol. 4.

_____. *Sermons (184–229Z) on the Liturgical Seasons*. Translated by Edmund Hill. WSA III/6. New Rochelle, NY: New City Press, 1993.

_____. *Sermons (230–272B)*. Translated by Edmund Hill. WSA III/7. New Rochelle, NY: New City Press, 1993.

_____. *Sermons on the New Testament*. Translated by Edmund Hill. WSA III/4. Brooklyn, NY: New City Press, 1992.

_____. *St. Augustine on the Psalms.* Vol. 1. *Psalms 1–29.* Translated by Scholastica Hebgin and Felicitas Corrigan. ACW 29. New York; Mahwah, NJ: Paulist Press, 1960.

_____. *Tractates on the Gospel of John 1–10.* Translated by J. W. Rettig. FC 78. Washington, DC: Catholic University of America Press, 1988.

_____. *Tractates on the Gospel of John 11–27.* Translated by J. W. Rettig. FC 79. Washington, DC: Catholic University of America Press, 1988.

_____. *Tractates on the Gospel of John 28–54.* Translated by J. W. Rettig. FC 88. Washington, DC: Catholic University of America Press, 1993.

_____. *Tractates on the Gospel of John 55–111.* Translated by J. W. Rettig. FC 90. Washington, DC: Catholic University of America Press, 1994.

_____. *Tractates on the Gospel of John 112–24; Tractates on the First Epistle of John.* Translated by J. W. Rettig. FC 92. Washington, DC: Catholic University of America Press, 1995.

Bede. *Homilies on the Gospels Book One: Advent to Lent.* Translated by Lawrence T. Martin. Collegeville, MN: Cistercian Publications, 2008.

Chrysostom, John. *Homilies on Genesis 18–45.* Translated by R. C. Hill. FC 82. Washington, DC: Catholic University of America Press, 1990.

_____. *Saint Chrysostom: Homilies on the Epistles of Paul to the Corinthians. NPNF*1, vol. 12.

_____. *Commentary on Saint John the Apostle and Evangelist: Homilies 1–47.* Translated by Sister Thomas Aquinas Goggin. FC 33. Washington, DC: Catholic University of America Press, 1957.

_____. *Commentary on Saint John the Apostle and Evangelist: Homilies 48–88.* Translated by Sister Thomas Aquinas Goggin. FC 41. Washington, DC: Catholic University of America Press, 1959.

Cyprian of Carthage. *The Letters of St. Cyprian of Carthage,* vol. 4, *Letters 67–82.* Translated by G. W. Clarke. ACW 47. New York; Mahwah, NJ: Newman Press, 1989.

Cyril of Alexandria. *Commentary on John.* Translated by David R. Maxwell. Edited by Joel C. Elowsky. 2 vols. Ancient Christian Texts. Downers Grove, IL: InterVarsity Press, 2013–2015.

Cyril of Jerusalem. *Lectures on the Christian Sacraments.* Edited by F. L. Cross. Crestwood, NY: St. Vladimir's Seminary Press, 1977.

_____. *The Works of Saint Cyril of Jerusalem.* Translated by L. P. McCauley and A. A. Stephenson. 2 vols. FC 61, 64. Washington, DC: The Catholic University of America Press, 1969–70.

_____. *Mystagogic Catecheses.* In Edward Yarnold, S.J. *The Awe-Inspiring Rites of Initiation: The Origins of the R.C.I.A,* 67–97. 2nd edition. Collegeville, MN: Liturgical Press, 1994.

Damascene, John. *An Exact Exposition of the Orthodox Faith.* In *Writings.* Translated by F. H. Chase Jr. FC 37. Washington, DC: Catholic University of America Press, 1958.

Fulgentius. *To Peter on the Faith.* In *Fulgentius: Selected Works.* Translated by R. B. Eno. FC 95. Washington, DC: Catholic University of America Press, 1997.

Gregory the Great. *Morals on the Book of Job.* Translated by John Henry Parker. Vol. 1. London, 1844.

Hippolytus. *On the Apostolic Tradition: An English Version with Introduction and Commentary.* Translated by Alistair Stewart-Sykes. Crestwood, NY: St. Vladimir's Seminary Press, 2001.

Holmes, Michael W., translator. *The Apostolic Fathers: Greek Texts and English Translations.* 3rd edition. Grand Rapids, MI: Baker Academic, 2007.

Irenaeus. *Against Heresies.* Translated by Alexander Roberts and William Rambaut. In *The Ante-Nicene Fathers* 1. Peabody, MA: Hendrickson, 1994.

Isidore of Seville, *De ecclesiasticis officiis.* Translated by T. L. Knoebel. ACW 61. New York; Mahwah, NJ: The Newman Press, 2008.

_____. *The Etymologies of Isidore of Seville.* Trans. Stephen A. Barney. Cambridge: Cambridge University Press, 2006.

Jerome. *St. Jerome's Commentaries on Galatians, Titus, and Philemon.* Translated by Thomas P. Scheck. Notre Dame, IN: University of Notre Dame Press, 2010.

Johnson, L. J., editor. *Worship in the Early Church: An Anthology of Historical Sources.* Collegeville, MN: Liturgical Press, 2009.

Justin Martyr. *St. Justin Martyr: The First and Second Apologies.* New York; Mahwah, NJ: Paulist Press, 1997.

Leo the Great. *Letters.* Translated by E. Hunt. FC 34. New York: Fathers of the Church, 1957.

_____. *Sermons.* Translated by J. P. Freeland and A. J. Conway. FC 93. Washington, DC: Catholic University of America Press, 1996.

Melito of Sardis. *Sermon "On the Passover."* Translated by Richard C. White. Lexington, KY: Lexington Theological Seminary Library,

1976.

Pseudo-Dionysius. *The Complete Works.* Translated by Colm Luibhéid. Classics of Western Spirituality. New York; Mahwah, NJ: Paulist Press, 1987.

Quodvultdeus of Carthage. *The Creedal Homilies.* Translated and edited by Thomas Macy Finn. ACW 60. New York: The Newman Press, 2004.

Tertullian. *Adversus Marcionem.* Translated and edited by Ernest Evans. 2 vols. Oxford: Clarendon Press, 1972.

_____. *De Baptismo.* In *Worship in the Early Church: An Anthology of Historical Sources,* edited by L. J. Johnson, 1:119–32. Collegeville, MN: Liturgical Press, 2009.

_____. *De resurrectione carnis.* Translated by Ernest Evans. *Tertullian's Treatise on the Resurrection.* London: SPCK, 1960.

Yarnold, Edward, S.J. *The Awe-Inspiring Rites of Initiation: The Origins of the R.C.I.A.* 2nd edition. Collegeville, MN: Liturgical Press, 1994.

Medieval, Reformation, and Renaissance Sources

Albert the Great. *Commentarii in libros Sententiarum.* Edited by Augustus Borgnet. In *Opera omnia,* vol. 29. *In IV Sent., d. 1–22.* Paris: Vivès, 1894.

Alexander of Hales. *Glossa in quatuor libros Sententiarum Petri Lombardi.* Vol. 4. Quaracchi, Florence: Editiones Collegii S. Bonaventurae, 1957.

_____. *Summa Theologica.* Edited by Bernard Klumper. 4 vols. Rome: Ad Claras Aquas, 1924–1948.

Alger of Liège. *De Sacramentis Corporis et Sanguinis Dominici.* In *Patrologiae Cursus Completus: Series Latina,* 180:739–834. Edited by J. P. Migne. Paris: Garnier and J. P. Migne, 1855.

Aquinas, Thomas. *Commentary on Aristotle's Metaphysics.* Translated by John P. Rowan. Notre Dame, IN: Dumb Ox Books, 1995.

_____. *Commentary on Aristotle's Physics.* Translated by Richard J. Blackwell, Richard J. Spath, and W. Edmund Thirkel. Notre Dame, IN: Dumb Ox Books, 1999.

_____. *Commentary on the Epistle to the Hebrews.* Translated by F. R. Larcher. Lander, WY: Aquinas Institute for the Study of Sacred

Doctrine, 2012.

_____. *Commentary on the Gospel of John: Chapters 1–8.* Translated by Fabian R. Larcher. Vol. 35 of Latin/English Edition of the Works of St. Thomas Aquinas. Lander, WY: Aquinas Institute for the Study of Sacred Doctrine, 2013.

_____. *Commentary on the Gospel of Matthew: Chapters 13–28.* Translated by Jeremy Holmes. Vol. 34 of Latin/English Edition of the Works of St. Thomas Aquinas. Lander, WY: Aquinas Institute for the Study of Sacred Doctrine, 2013.

_____. *Commentary on the Letter of Saint Paul to the Romans.* Translated by F. R. Larcher. Lander, WY: Aquinas Institute for the Study of Sacred Doctrine, 2012.

_____. *Commentary on the Sentences, Book IV.* Translated by Beth Mortensen. Vols. 7–10 of Latin/English Edition of the Works of St. Thomas Aquinas. Green Bay, WI: Aquinas Institute, 2017.

_____. *De articulis fidei et ecclesiae sacramentis ad archiepiscopum Panormitanum.* In *Opuscula Theologica.* Vol. 1, *De re dogmatica et morali,* edited by Raymund Verardo, 147–51. Turin and Rome: Marietti, 1954. English translation: St. Thomas Aquinas. *God's Greatest Gifts: Commentaries on the Commandments and the Sacraments,* translated by J. B. Collins, 83–100. Manchester, NH: Sophia Press, 1992.

_____. *Disputed Questions on Virtue: Quaestio disputata de virtutibus in communi and Quaestio disputata de virtutibus cardinalibus.* Translated by Ralph McInerny. South Bend, IN: St. Augustine's Press, 1999.

_____. *On Evil.* Translated by Richard Regan. Oxford: Oxford University Press, 2003.

_____. *On Love and Charity: Readings from the Commentary on the Sentences of Peter Lombard.* Translated by Peter A. Kwasniewski, Thomas Bolin, and Joseph Bolin. Washington, DC: Catholic University of America Press, 2008.

_____. *Summa contra gentiles.* Translated by Anton Pegis, James Anderson, Vernon Bourke, and Charles O'Neil. 4 vols. Notre Dame, IN: University of Notre Dame Press, 1975.

_____. *Summa theologiae.* 2nd edition. Translated by Fathers of the English Dominican Province. London: Burns, Oates, & Washbourne, 1920–1932.

_____. *Truth [De veritate].* Translated by Robert W. Mulligan, James V. McGlynn, and Robert W. Schmidt. 3 vols. Chicago: Henry

Regnery, 1952–1954.

The Babylonian Talmud: A Translation and Commentary. Edited and translated by Jacob Neusner. Peabody, MA: Hendrickson Publishers, 2011.

Bañez, Domingo. *Comentarios inéditos a la tercera parte de Santo Tomas.* Vol. 2, *De Sacramentis: QQ. 60–90.* Edited by Vincente Beltran de Heredia. Biblioteca de Teólogos Españoles 19. Salamanca: 1953.

Bellarmine, Robert. *De controversiis christianae fidei. De Sacramentis in genere. De sacramento Ordinis. De amissione gratiae.* In *Opera omnia.* Edited by Justinus Fèvre. Vols. 3–5. Paris: Vivès, 1870–1873.

Bonaventure. *Breviloquium.* Translated by Dominic V. Monti, O.F.M. St. Bonaventure, NY: The Franciscan Institute, 2005.

_____. *Commentary on the Sentences: Sacraments.* Translated by Wayne Hellmann, Timothy R. Lecroy, and Luke Davis Townsend. St. Bonaventure, NY: The Franciscan Institute, 2016.

Cabasilas, Nicholas. *The Life in Christ.* Translated by Carmino J. deCatanzaro. Crestwood, NY: St. Vladimir's Seminary Press, 1974.

Caietanus de Vio, Thomas Card. Commentary on *Summa theologiae,* tertia pars. In *Sancti Thomae Aquinatis Opera omnia.* Leonine edition, vol. 12. Rome: Typographia poliglotta S. C. de Propaganda Fide, 1906.

Calvin, John. *Institutes of the Christian Religion.* Translated by Henry Beveridge. Peabody, MA: Hendrickson Publishers, 2008.

Capreolus, Johannis. *Defensiones Theologiae Divi Thomae Aquinatis.* Edited by Ceslai Paban and Thomae Pègues. Vol. 6. Tours: Alfred Cattier, 1906.

Hugh of St. Victor. *On the Sacraments of the Christian Faith.* Translated by Roy J. Deferrari. Cambridge, MA: Mediaeval Academy of America, 1951.

John of St. Thomas. *Cursus Theologicus.* Vol. 9. Paris: Vivès, 1886.

Luther, Martin. *Address to the Christian Nobility of the German Nation.* In *Luther's Works,* vol. 44, *The Christian in Society I.* Edited by James Atkinson. Philadelphia: Fortress Press, 1966.

_____. *The Babylonian Captivity of the Church.* In *Luther's Works,* vol. 36. *Word and Sacrament II,* 3–126. Translated by A. T. W. Steinhäuser. Philadelphia: Muhlenberg Press, 1959.

Paschasius Radbertus. *De Corpore et Sanguine Domini: Cum Appendice Epistola ad Fredugardum.* Edited by Bedae Paulus. Corpus Christianorum, Continuatio Mediaevalis 16. Turnhout, BE: Brepols,

1969.

Peter Lombard. *The Sentences. Book 4: On the Doctrine of Signs.* Translated by Giulio Silano. Mediaeval Sources in Translation 48. Toronto: Pontifical Institute of Mediaeval Studies, 2010.

Rabanus Maurus. *De clericorum institutione libri tres.* Edited by Aloisius Knoepfler. Munich: Lentner, 1900.

Salmanticenses. *Cursus Theologicus.* Vol. 17. *De sacramentis in communi.* Paris, Palmé, 1881.

Suárez, Franciscus. *Opera omnia.* Vol. 20. *Commentaria ac Disputationes in Tertiam Partem D. Thomae. De Sacramentis in genere.* Paris: Vivès, 1866.

Sylvester de Ferrara, Francis. Commentary on *Summa contra Gentiles* IV. In *Sancti Thomae Aquinatis Opera omnia.* Leonine edition. Vol. 15. Rome, 1926.

Teresa of Avila. *The Collected Works of St. Teresa of Avila.* Translated by Kieran Kavanaugh and Otilio Rodriguez. 3 vols. Washington, DC: ICS Publications, 1980–1987.

Secondary Sources

Adams, Marilyn McCord. *Some Later Medieval Theories of the Eucharist: Thomas Aquinas, Gilles of Rome, Duns Scotus, and William Ockham.* Oxford: Oxford University Press, 2012.

Afanasiev, Nicholas. *The Church of the Holy Spirit.* Translated by Vitaly Permiakov. Notre Dame, IN: University of Notre Dame Press, 2007.

Akinwale, Anthony O.P. "Reconciliation." In *The Oxford Handbook of Sacramental Theology,* edited by Hans Boersma and Matthew Levering, 545–57. Oxford; New York: Oxford University Press, 2015.

Allen, Michael. "Sacraments in the Reformed and Anglican Reformation." In *The Oxford Handbook of Sacramental Theology,* edited by Hans Boersma and Matthew Levering, 283–97. Oxford; New York: Oxford University Press, 2015.

Allevi, Luigi. "I misteri pagani e i sacramenti christiani." In *Problemi e orientamenti di teologia dommatica,* edited by the Pontificia Facoltà Teologica di Milano, vol. 2, 751–74. Milan: C. Marzorati, 1957.

Alviar, J. Jose. "El destino de los niños que mueren sin baptismo. Comentario al documento de la Comisión Teológica Internacional." *Scripta Theologica* 41, no. 3 (2009): 711–43.

Ambrose, Glenn P. *The Theology of Louis-Marie Chauvet: Overcoming Onto-Theology with the Sacramental Tradition.* Burlington, VT: Ashgate, 2012.

Anciaux, Paul, O.S.B. "The Ecclesial Dimension of Penance." In *The Mystery of Sin and Forgiveness*, edited by Michael Taylor, 155–165. Staten Island, NY: Alba House, 1971.

_____. *The Sacrament of Penance.* Tenbury Wells, Worcester: Challoner Publications, 1962.

Anderson, Gary A. *Sin: A History.* New Haven, CT: Yale University Press, 2009.

Anderson, Gary A., and Jon D. Levenson, editors. *The Call of Abraham: Essays on the Election of Israel in Honor of Jon D. Levenson.* Notre Dame, IN: University of Notre Dame Press, 2013.

Appleyard, J. A. "How Does a Sacrament 'Cause by Signifying'?" *Science et Esprit* 23 [1971]: 167–200.

Aquila, Samuel. "The Sacrament of Confirmation." 2011 Hillenbrand Lecture at the Liturgical Institute in Mundelein. Available online at http://www.catholicculture.org/culture/library/view.cfm?recnum=9670. Accessed on May 11, 2020.

Argenlieu B.-T. d'. "La Doctrine du caractère sacramentel dans la Somme." *Revue Thomiste* 34 (1929): 289–302.

Arnau-García, Ramón. *Tratado general de los sacramentos.* Madrid: Biblioteca de autores cristianos, 2001.

Ashley, Benedict. "Gender and the Priesthood of Christ: A Theological Reflection." *The Thomist* 57 (1993): 343–79.

Audet, Lionel. "Notre Participation au Sacerdoce du Christ." *Laval Théologique et Philosophique* 1 (1945), 9–46, 257–301.

Auer, Johann. *A General Doctrine of the Sacraments and the Mystery of the Eucharist.* Translated by Erasmo Leiva-Merikakis and Hugh M. Riley. Vol. 6 of *Dogmatic Theology.* Johann Auer and Joseph Ratzinger. Washington, DC: Catholic University of America Press, 1995.

Aumann, Jordan. *Spiritual Theology.* London; New York: Continuum, 2006.

Avvakumon, Yury P. "Sacramental Ritual in Middle and Later Byzantine Theology: Ninth–Fifteenth Centuries. In *The Oxford Handbook of Sacramental Theology*, edited by Hans Boersma and Matthew Levering, 249–66. Oxford; New York: Oxford University Press, 2015.

Barth, Karl. *The Teaching of the Church Regarding Baptism.* Translated by Ernest A. Payne. London: SCM Press, 1948.

Barton, John M. T. *Penance and Absolution*. London: Burns & Oates, 1961.

Becker, Karl Joseph. "Le don de la confirmation." *La Maison-Dieu* 168 (1986): 15–32.

Becker, Karl Joseph, and Ilaria Morali, editors. *Catholic Engagement with World Religions: A Comprehensive Study*. Maryknoll, NY: Orbis Books, 2010.

Beiting, Christopher. "The Idea of Limbo in Thomas Aquinas." *The Thomist* 62 (1998): 237–44.

Bellini, Alberto. "I Sacramenti in genere, il Battesimo e la Cresima." In *Il Protestantesimo ieri e oggi*, edited by Antonio Piolanti, 987–1089. Rome: Libreria Editrice religiosa F. Ferrari, 1958.

Bergoglio, Jorge Mario (Pope Francis). *The Name of God Is Mercy: A Conversation with Andrea Tornielli*. Translated by Oonagh Stransky. New York: Random House, 2016.

Berrouard, M.-F. "Le Tractatus 80, 3 in Iohannis Evangelium de saint Augustin: La parole, le sacrement et la foi." *Revues des études augustiniennes* 33 (1987): 235–54.

Biagi, Ruggero, *La causalità dell'umanità di Cristo e dei Sacramenti nella "Summa theologiae" di san Tommaso d'Aquino*. Bologna: Edizioni Studio Domenicano, 1985.

Billot, Ludovicus. *De Ecclesiae Sacramentis: Commentarius in Tertiam Partem S. Thomae*. Vol. 1, 7th edition. Rome: Apud aedes universitatis Gregorianae, 1931.

Bittremieux, J. "L'institution des sacrements d'après Alexandre de Halès." *Ephemerides Theologicae Lovanienses* 9 (1932): 234–51.

Blankenhorn, Bernard. "The Instrumental Causality of the Sacraments: Thomas Aquinas and Louis-Marie Chauvet." *Nova et Vetera* (English) 4, no. 2 (2006): 255–94.

———. "The Place of Romans 6 in Aquinas's Doctrine of Sacramental Causality: A Balance of History and Metaphysics." In *Ressourcement Thomism: Sacred Doctrine, the Sacraments, and the Moral Life: Essays in Honor of Romanus Cessario, O.P.*, edited by R. Hütter and M. Levering, 136–49. Washington, DC: Catholic University of America Press, 2010.

Blessing, Claus Ulrich. *Sacramenta in quibus principaliter salus constat: Taufe, Firmung und Eucharistie bei Hugo von St. Viktor*. Vienna: LIT, 2017.

Boersma, Hans, and Matthew Levering. *The Oxford Handbook of Sac-*

ramental Theology. Oxford; New York: Oxford University Press, 2015.

Boguslawski, Steven C. *Thomas Aquinas on the Jews: Insights into His Commentary on Romans 9–11*. New York; Mahwah, NJ: Paulist Press, 2008.

Boissard, Edmond. *Réflexions sur le sort des enfants morts sans baptême*. Paris: Éditions de la Source, 1974.

Bonino, Serge-Thomas, O.P. "The Theory of Limbo and the Mystery of the Supernatural in St. Thomas Aquinas." In *Surnaturel: A Controversy at the Heart of Twentieth-Century Thomistic Thought*, edited by Bonino, translated by Robert Williams, 117–54. Ave Maria, FL: Sapientia Press of Ave Maria University, 2009.

Boudes, E. "Réflexion sur la solidarité des hommes avec le Christ." *Nouvelle revue théologique* 71 (1949): 589–604.

Bouëssé, Humbert. "La causalité efficiente instrumentale de l'humanité du Christ et des sacrements chrétiens." *Revue Thomiste* 39 (83) (1934): 370–93.

_____. *Doctrina Sacra IV. Le Sauveur du Monde, 4. L'Economie sacramentaire*. Paris: Chambéry-Leysse, 1951.

Bouteneff, Peter. "Sacraments: Mystery of Union: Elements in an Orthodox Sacramental Theology." In *The Gestures of God: Explorations in Sacramentality*, edited by Geoffrey Rowell and Christine Hall, 91–108. London; New York: Continuum, 2004.

Bouyer, Louis. *Christian Initiation*. Translated by Joseph R. Foster. New York: Macmillan, 1960.

_____. *The Christian Mystery: From Pagan Myth to Christian Mysticism*. Translated by Illtyd Trethowan. Petersham, MA: Saint Bede's, 1990.

_____. *Rite and Man*. Notre Dame, IN: University of Notre Dame Press, 1963.

_____. "The Sacramental System." In *Sacraments: The Gestures of Christ*, edited by Denis O'Callaghan, 45–55. New York: Sheed & Ward, 1964.

_____. *The Spirit and Forms of Protestantism*. Translated by A. V. Littledale. Princeton, NJ: Scepter, 2001.

_____. "Word and Sacrament." In *Sacraments: The Gestures of Christ*, edited by Denis O'Callaghan, 139–52. New York: Sheed & Ward, 1964.

_____. *The Word, Church and Sacraments in Protestantism and Catholicism*. Translated by A. V. Littledale. San Francisco: Ignatius Press, 2004.

Brazzarola, Bruno. *La natura della grazia sacramentale nella dottrina di San Tommaso*. Grottaferrata, 1941.

Brennan, Robert Edward, O.P. *The Seven Horns of the Lamb: A Study of the Gifts Based on Saint Thomas Aquinas*. Milwaukee, WI: Bruce, 1966.

Bro, Bernard. *The Spirituality of the Sacraments: Doctrine and Practice for Today*. Translated by Theodore Dubois. New York: Sheed & Ward, 1968.

Brown, David. "A Sacramental World: Why It Matters." In *The Oxford Handbook of Sacramental Theology*, edited by Hans Boersma and Matthew Levering, 603–14. Oxford; New York: Oxford University Press, 2015.

Buccellati, Giorgio. "Sacramentality and Culture." *Communio* 30/4 (2003): 532–80.

Burke, Cormac. *The Theology of Marriage: Personalism, Doctrine, and Canon Law*. Washington, DC: Catholic University of America Press, 2015.

Burke, Patrick. *Reinterpreting Rahner: A Critical Study of His Major Themes*. New York: Fordham University Press, 2002.

Burke, Raymond, Card. "An Interview with Archbishop Raymond L. Burke for the Occasion of the AHC Conference of October 1–3, 2010," by David Moss. In *You Shall Be My Witnesses: Hebrew Catholics and the Mission of the Church*, 34–41. St. Louis, MO: Association of Hebrew Catholics, 2010.

Cabié, Robert, Jean Evenou, and Pierre-Marie Gy. *The Sacraments*. London: Geoffrey Chapman, 1988.

Camelot, Tommaso. "Il Battesimo e la Cresima nella teologia contemporanea." In *Problemi e orientamenti di teologia dommatica*, edited by the Pontificia Facoltà Teologica di Milano, vol. 2, 795–821. Milan: C. Marzorati, 1957.

———. "Sacramentum, Notes de théologie sacramentaire augustinienne." *Revue Thomiste* 57 (1957): 429–49.

Cantalamessa, Raniero. *Sober Intoxication of the Spirit: Filled with the Fullness of God*. Translated by Marsha Daigle-Williamson. Cincinnati, OH: Servant Books, 2005.

———. *This Is My Body: Eucharistic Reflections Inspired by* Adoro Te Devote *and* Ave Verum. Boston: Pauline Books & Media, 2005.

Cappello, Felix M., S.J. *Tractatus Canonico-Moralis de Sacramentis*. 5 vols. Taurini: Marietti, 1943–1950.

Caprioli, A. "Alle origini della 'definizione' di sacramento: da Berengario a Pier Lombardo," *La Scuola cattolica* 102 (1974): 718–43.

Cary, Phillip. *The Meaning of Protestant Theology: Luther, Augustine, and the Gospel That Gives Us Christ*. Grand Rapids, MI: Baker Academic, 2019.

_____. "Why Luther Is Not Quite Protestant: The Logic of Faith in a Sacramental Promise." *Pro Ecclesia* 14, no. 4 (Fall 2005): 447–86.

Casel, Odo. *The Mystery of Christian Worship*. Edited by Burkhard Neunheuser. New York: Crossroad, 1999.

Catão, Bernard. *Salut et rédemption chez S. Thomas d'Aquin: l'acte sauveur du Christ*. Paris: Aubier, 1965.

Cessario, Romanus, O.P. "Sacramental Causality: Da capo!" *Nova et Vetera* (English) 11, no. 2 (2013): 307–316.

Chauvet, Louis-Marie. *The Sacraments: The Word of God at the Mercy of the Body*. Collegeville, MN: Liturgical Press, 2001.

_____. *Symbol and Sacrament*. Collegeville, MN: Liturgical Press, 1995.

Chavasse, Antoine. *Etude sur l'onction des infirmes dans l'Église latine du IIIe au XIe siècle* Lyon: Facultés Catholiques de Lyon, 1942.

Chenu, M.-D. "Pour une anthropologie sacramentelle." *La Maison-Dieu* 119 (1974): 85–100.

Christian, Robert. "Midway between Baptism and Holy Orders: Saint Thomas' Contribution to a Contemporary Understanding of Confirmation." *Angelicum* 69 (1992): 157–73.

Ciappi, Aloisius M. *De Sacramentis in Communi: Commentarius in Tertiam Partem S. Thomae (qq. LX–LXV)*. Pontificium Institutum Internationale Angelicum. Turin: R. Berruti, 1957.

Clarke, W. Norris, S.J. *The Creative Retrieval of Saint Thomas Aquinas: Essays in Thomistic Philosophy, New and Old*. New York: Fordham University Press, 2009.

Coffey, David. "The Whole Rahner on the Supernatural Existential." *Theological Studies* 65 (2004): 95–118.

Colish, Marcia L. *Faith, Fiction, and Force in Medieval Baptismal Debates*. Washington, DC: Catholic University of America Press, 2014.

_____. *Peter Lombard*. 2 vols. Leiden: E.J. Brill, 1994.

Cole, Basil, O.P. "Is Limbo Ready to Be Abolished? Limbo Revisited." *Nova et Vetera* (English) 6, no. 2 (2008): 403–18.

Colombo, Giuseppe. "Dove va la teologia sacramentaria?" *La Scuola Cattolica* 102 (1974): 673–717.

Congar, Yves M.-J. *I Believe in the Holy Spirit*. Translated by David Smith. New York: Crossroad, 1997.

_____. "The Idea of the Church in St. Thomas Aquinas." *The Thomist* 1 (1939): 331–59.

_____. *Lay People in the Church: A Study for a Theology of Laity.* Westminster: Newman Press, 1965.

Coolman, Boyd Taylor. "The Christo-Pneumatic-Ecclesial Character of Twelfth-Century Sacramental Theology." In *The Oxford Handbook of Sacramental Theology*, edited by Hans Boersma and Matthew Levering, 201–17. Oxford; New York: Oxford University Press, 2015.

_____. *The Theology of Hugh of St. Victor: An Interpretation.* New York: Cambridge University Press, 2010.

Courtenay, William. "The King and the Leaden Coin: The Economic Background of 'sine qua non' Causality." *Traditio* 29 (1972): 185–209.

_____. "Sacrament, Symbol and Causality in Bernard of Clairvaux." In *Bernard of Clairvaux: Studies Presented to Dom Jean Leclercq*, edited by Basil Pennington, 111–22. Cistercian Studies Series 23. Washington, DC: Cistercian Publications, 1973.

Couturier, C. "'Sacramentum' et 'mysterium' dans l'œuvre de saint Augustin." In Études augustiniennes, edited by H. Rondet and others, 161–332. Théologie 28. Paris: Aubier, 1953.

Cross, Richard. *Duns Scotus.* Oxford; New York: Oxford University Press, 1999.

Crowley, Charles B. "The Role of Sacramental Grace in the Christian Life." *The Thomist* 2 (1940): 519–45.

Crowley, Paul. "*Instrumentum Divinitatis* in Thomas Aquinas: Recovering the Divinity of Christ." *Theological Studies* 52 (1991): 451–75.

Cunningham, Francis L. B. *The Indwelling of the Trinity: A Historical-Doctrinal Study of the Theory of St. Thomas Aquinas.* Dubuque, IA: The Priory Press, 1955.

Daniélou, Jean. *The Bible and the Liturgy.* Notre Dame, IN: University of Notre Dame Press, 1956.

_____. *L'entrée dans l'histoire du Salut: Baptême et Confirmation.* Paris: Éditions du Cerf, 1967.

_____. *From Shadows to Reality: Studies in the Biblical Typology of the Fathers.* Translated by Dom Wulstan Hibberd. Westminster, MD: The Newman Press, 1960.

_____. *The Theology of Jewish Christianity.* Translated and edited by John A. Baker. London: Darton, Longman & Todd, 1964.

D'Costa, Gavin. *Catholic Doctrines on Jews After the Second Vatican Council*. Oxford: Oxford University Press, 2019.

_____. *Christianity and World Religions: Disputed Questions in the Theology of Religions*. Oxford: Blackwell, 2009.

_____. "Israel, Jewish Christians, Messianic Christians, and the Catholic Church." *The Hebrew Catholic* 103 (Spring 2018): 14–15.

_____. "The Mystery of Israel: Jews, Hebrew Catholics, Messianic Judaism, the Catholic Church, and the Mosaic Ceremonial Laws." *Nova et Vetera* (English) 16, no. 3 (2018): 939–77.

_____. *Vatican II: Catholic Doctrines on Jews and Muslims*. Oxford: Oxford University Press, 2016.

De Aldama, Joseph A., Severino Gonzalez, Francis A. P. Sola, and Joseph F. Sagües. *Sacrae Theologiae Summa*. Vol. 4A, *On the Sacraments in General; On Baptism, Confirmation, Eucharist, Penance and Anointing*. 3rd edition. Translated by Kenneth Baker. Keep the Faith, 2015.

De Baciocchi, J. "Présence eucharistique et transsubstantiation." *Irénikon* 32 (1959): 139–61.

_____. *La vie sacramentaire de l'église*. Paris: Éditions du Cerf, 1959.

De Baets, M. "Quelle question le concile de Trente a entendu trancher touchant l'institution des sacrements par le Christ." *Revue Thomiste* 14 (1906): 31–47.

De Caussade, Jean-Pierre, S.J. *Abandonment to Divine Providence*. Translated by Algar Thorold. Edited by John Joyce. Rockford, IL: TAN Books, 1987.

De Margerie, Bertrand, S.J. *An Introduction to the History of Exegesis*. Vol. 1, *The Greek Fathers*. Translated by Leonard Maluf. Petersham, MA: Saint Bede's Publications, 1993.

Denis, E. "Les sacrements dans la vie de l'Eglise." *La Maison-Dieu* 93 (1968): 39–59.

De Vooght, P., O.S.B. "A propos de la causalité du sacrement de pénitence. Théologie thomiste et Théologie tout court." *Ephemerides Theologicae Lovanienses* 7 (1930): 663–75.

Dillenschneider, Clement, C.Ss.R. *The Dynamic Power of Our Sacraments*. Translated by M. Renelle. St. Louis, MO: B. Herder, 1966.

DiNoia, Augustine, O.P. and Joseph Fox, O.P. "Priestly Dimensions of the Sacrament of the Anointing of the Sick." *The Priest* 62 (August 2006): 10–13.

Dix, Gregory. *The Shape of the Liturgy*. Westminster, London: Dacre Press, 1945.

_____. *The Theology of Confirmation in Relation to Baptism.* Westminster: Dacre Press, 1948.

Donahue, John M. "Sacramental Character: The State of the Question." *The Thomist* 31 (1967): 445–64.

Dondaine, Hyacinthe-François, O.P. "La définition des sacrements dans la *Somme théologique.*" *Revue des Sciences Philosophiques et Théologiques* 31 (1947): 214–28.

_____. "A propos d'Avicenne et de S. Thomas: De la causalité dispositive à la causalité instrumentale." *Revue thomiste* 51 (1951): 441–53.

Doronzo, Emmanuel. *De Baptismo et Confirmatione.* Milwaukee, WI: Bruce, 1946.

_____. *De Extrema Unctione.* 2 vols. Milwaukee, WI: Bruce, 1954–55.

_____. *De Ordine.* 2 vols. Milwaukee, WI: Bruce, 1959.

_____. *De Poenitentia.* 4 vols. Milwaukee, WI: Bruce, 1949–1953.

_____. *De Sacramentis in genere.* Milwaukee, WI: Bruce, 1946.

Dumont, C., S.J. "La réconciliation avec l'Église et la nécessité de l'aveu sacramentel." *Nouvelle Revue Théologique* 81 (1959): 577–97.

Dunn, James D. G. *Baptism in the Holy Spirit: A Re-examination of the New Testament Teaching on the Gift of the Spirit in Relation to Pentecostalism Today.* Naperville, IL: A. R. Allenson, 1970.

Dupuis, J., and J. Neuner. *The Christian Faith in the Doctrinal Documents of the Catholic Church.* 7th edition. New York: Alba House, 2001.

Dyer, George J. "Limbo: A Theological Evaluation." *Theological Studies* 19 (1958): 32–49.

_____. *Limbo: Unsettled Question.* New York: Sheed & Ward, 1964.

_____. "The Unbaptized Infant in Eternity." *Chicago Studies* 2 (1963): 141–53.

Egan, James, O.P. "A Contemporary Approach to Sacramental Grace." In *Readings in Sacramental Theology,* edited by C. S. Sullivan, 124–43. Englewood Cliffs, NJ: Prentice-Hall, 1964.

Eisenberg, Ronald L. *The JPS Guide to Jewish Traditions.* Philadelphia: The Jewish Publication Society, 2004.

Elberti, Arturo S.J. "Witness of Christ in the Spirit." In *Rediscovering Confirmation.* Edited by the Pontificum Concilium pro Laicis. Vatican City, 2000.

Emery, Gilles. "The Ecclesial Fruit of the Eucharist in St. Thomas Aquinas." Translated by Therese C. Scarpelli. *Nova et Vetera* (English) 2, no. 1 (2004): 43–60.

_____. "Reconciliation with the Church and Interior Penance: The Contribution of Thomas Aquinas on the Question of the *Res et Sacramentum* of Penance." Translated by Robert E. Williams. *Nova et Vetera* (English) 1, no. 2 (2003): 283–302.

Ernst, Cornelius. "Acts of Christ: Signs of Faith." In *Sacraments: The Gestures of Christ*, edited by Denis O'Callaghan, 56–75. New York: Sheed & Ward, 1964.

Everett, Lawrence P. *The Nature of Sacramental Grace*. Washington, DC: Catholic University of America Press, 1948.

Fagan, Sean. "Sacramental Spirituality." In *Sacraments: The Gestures of Christ*, edited by Denis O'Callaghan, 153–73. New York: Sheed & Ward, 1964.

Fagerberg, David W. *Consecrating the World: On Mundane Liturgical Theology*. Kettering, OH: Angelico Press, 2016.

_____. "Divine Liturgy, Divine Love." *Letter & Spirit* 3 (2007): 95–112.

_____. "Liturgy and Divinization." In *Called to Be the Children of God: The Catholic Theology of Human Deification*, edited by David Vincent Meconi and Carl Olson, 274–83. San Francisco: Ignatius Press, 2016.

_____. "Liturgy, Signs, and Sacraments." In *The Oxford Handbook of Sacramental Theology*, edited by Hans Boersma and Matthew Levering, 455–65. Oxford; New York: Oxford University Press, 2015.

_____. *On Liturgical Asceticism*. Washington, DC: Catholic University of America Press, 2013.

_____. "The Sacraments as Actions of the Mystical Body." *Communio* 39/4 (2012): 554–68.

_____. *Theologia Prima: What Is Liturgical Theology?* 2nd edition. Chicago: Hillenbrand Books, 2004.

_____. *What Is Liturgical Theology?: A Study in Methodology*. Collegeville: Liturgical Press, 1992.

Farrow, Douglas. *Ascension Theology*. London: T&T Clark, 2011.

_____. "Jew and Gentile in the Church Today." *Nova et Vetera* (English) 16, no. 3 (2018): 979–93.

_____. *Theological Negotiations: Proposals in Soteriology and Anthropology*. Grand Rapids, MI: Baker Academic, 2018.

Fastiggi, Robert. *The Sacrament of Reconciliation: An Anthropological and Scriptural Understanding*. Chicago: Hillenbrand Books, 2017.

Feingold, Lawrence. *The Eucharist: Mystery of Presence, Sacrifice, and Communion*. Steubenville, OH: Emmaus Academic, 2018.

_____. *Faith Comes from What Is Heard: An Introduction to Fundamental*

Theology. Steubenville, OH: Emmaus Academic, 2016.

_____. "God's Movement of the Soul through Operative and Cooperative Grace." In *Thomism and Predestination: Principles and Disputations*, edited by Steven A. Long, Roger W. Nutt, and Thomas Joseph White, 166–91. Washington, DC: Catholic University of America Press, 2017.

_____. "Maritain's Eschatological Reverie and the Fittingness of Limbo." In *The Things That Matter: Essays Inspired by the Later Work of Jacques Maritain*, edited by Heidi M. Giebel, 3–23. Washington, DC: Catholic University of America Press in partnership with the American Maritain Association, 2018.

_____. *The Mystery of Israel and the Church*. Vol. 1, *Figure and Fulfillment*. St. Louis, MO: Miriam Press, 2010.

_____. *The Mystery of Israel and the Church*. Vol. 2, *Things New and Old*. St. Louis, MO: Miriam Press, 2010.

_____. *The Mystery of Israel and the Church*. Vol. 3, *The Messianic Kingdom of Israel*. St. Louis, MO: Miriam Press, 2010.

_____. *The Natural Desire to See God According to St. Thomas Aquinas and His Interpreters*. Ave Maria, FL: Sapientia Press of Ave Maria University, 2010.

_____. "The Natural Desire to See God, the Twofold End of Man, and Henri de Lubac." *Josephinum Journal of Theology* 18, no. 1 (Winter/Spring 2011): 112–32.

_____. "The Word Breathes Forth Love: The Psychological Analogy for the Trinity." *Nova et Vetera* (English) 17, no. 2 (Spring 2019): 501–32.

Feliziani, Alfonso. "La Causalità dei Sacramenti in Domenico Soto." *Angelicum* 16 (1939): 148–94.

Ferguson, Everett. *Baptism in the Early Church: History, Theology, and Liturgy in the First Five Centuries*. Grand Rapids, MI: William B. Eerdmans, 2009.

_____. "Sacraments in the Pre-Nicene Period." In *The Oxford Handbook of Sacramental Theology*, edited by Hans Boersma and Matthew Levering, 125–39. Oxford; New York: Oxford University Press, 2015.

Feuillet, André. *The Priesthood of Christ and His Ministers*. Translated by Matthew J. O'Connell. Garden City, NY: Doubleday, 1975.

Finn, Thomas. "The Sacramental World in the *Sentences* of Peter Lombard." *Theological Studies* 69 (2008): 557–82.

Finnegan, Eugene M. *Confirmation at an Impasse: The Historical*

Origins of the Sacrament of Confirmation. Linus Publications, 2008.

Fisher, J.D.C. *Christian Initiation: Baptism in the Medieval West. A Study in the Disintegration of the Primitive Rite of Initiation.* London: SPCK, 1965.

_____. *Christian Initiation: The Reformation Period: Some Early Reformed Rites of Baptism and Confirmation and Other Contemporary Documents.* Chicago: Hillenbrand Books, 2007.

_____. *Confirmation: Then and Now.* London: SPCK, 1978.

Fortman, E. J., S.J. *Everlasting Life After Death.* New York: Alba House, 1976.

Fransen, Peter. "Erwägungen über das Firmalter." *Zeitschrift Für Katholische Theologie* 84, no. 4 (1962): 401–26.

Friedman, Elias. *Jewish Identity.* New York: Miriam Press, 1987.

Gaillard, Jean, O.S.B. "La Théologie des mystères." *Revue thomiste* 57 (1957): 510–51.

Gallagher, John F. *Significando causant: A Study of Sacramental Efficiency.* Fribourg, CH: University Press, 1965.

Galot, Jean, S.J. *La nature du caractère sacramentel: étude de théologie médiévale.* Bruges: Desclée de Brouwer, 1956.

_____. "La salvezza dei bambini morti senza battesimo." *La civiltà cattolica* 122 (1971) 228–40.

_____. *Theology of the Priesthood.* Translated by Roger Balducelli. San Francisco: Ignatius Press, 1984.

Galtier, Paul. *Sin and Penance.* Translated by B. Wall. St. Louis, MO: Herder, 1932.

_____. *De paenitentia: Tractatus dogmatico-historicus.* Rome: Apud Aedes Universitatis Gregorianae, 1956.

Ganoczy, Alexandre. *An Introduction to Catholic Sacramental Theology.* Translated by William Thomas. New York; Ramsey, NJ: Paulist Press, 1984.

_____. "Théologie sacramentaire. Bilan d'une double décennie." *Recherches de Sciences Religieuses* 91 (2003): 223–58.

Gardeil, Ambroise, O.P. *The Holy Spirit in Christian Life.* St. Louis, MO: Herder, 1954.

Garland, Peter. *The Definition of Sacrament According to Saint Thomas.* Ottawa: University of Ottawa Press, 1959.

Garrigou-Lagrange, Réginald. *Christian Perfection and Contemplation: According to St. Thomas Aquinas and St. John of the Cross.* Translated by Timothea Doyle. Rockford, IL: TAN Books, 2003.

_____. *Grace: Commentary on the Summa Theologica of St. Thomas,*

Ia IIae, Q. 109–114. Translated by Dominican Nuns of Corpus Christi Monastery, Menlo Park, CA. St. Louis, MO: B. Herder, 1952.

_____. *The Priest in Union with Christ.* Translated by G. W. Shelton. Westminster, MD: Newman Press, 1952.

_____. *The Three Ages of the Interior Life: Prelude of Eternal Life.* 2 vols. Translated by Timothea Doyle. Rockford, IL: Tan Books, 1989.

Gaullier, Bertrand. *L'état des enfants morts sans baptême d'après saint Thomas d'Aquin.* Paris: Lethielleux, 1961.

Gavin, Frank. *The Jewish Antecedents of the Christian Sacraments.* New York: Ktav, 1969.

Gervais, P., S.J. "La célébration du mystère chrétien." *Nouvelle Revue Théologique* 115 (1993): 496–515.

Ghellinck, J. de, Émile de Backer, Jean B. Poukens, and G Lebacqz. *Pour L'histoire Du Mot "sacramentum."* Louvain: "Spicilegium sacrum lovaniense," 1924.

Gierens, M. *De causalitate sacramentorum: seu de modo explicandi efficientiam sacramentorum novae legis. Textus scholasticorum principaliorum.* Rome: Apud Aedes Pont. Universitatis Gregorianae, 1935.

_____. "Zur Lehre des hl. Thomas über die Kausalität der Sakramente." *Scholastik* 9 (1934): 321–45.

Gillis, James R. *The Effects of the Sacrament of Confirmation.* Dissertation at the Angelicum. Washington, DC, 1940.

Ginhoven Rey, Christopher van. *Instruments of the Divinity: Providence and Praxis in the Foundation of the Society of Jesus.* Leiden: Brill, 2013.

Giraudo, Cesare, S.J. "La genesi anaforica del racconto istituzionale alla luce dell'anafora di Addai e Mari: tra storia delle forme e liturgia comparata." In *The Anaphoral Genesis of the Institution Narrative in Light of the Anaphora of Addai and Mari: Acts of the International Liturgy Congress, Rome 25-26 October 2011,* edited by Cesare Giraudo, 425–53. Rome: Edizioni Orientalia Christiana, 2013.

Glorieux, Palémon. "Endurcissement final et graces dernieres." *Nouvelle Revue Theologique* 59 (1932): 865–92.

_____. "In hora mortis." *Mélanges de Science Religieuse* 6 (1949): 185–216; summarized in "The Moment of Death." *Theology Digest* 10 (1962): 94–96.

Gomez, E., O.P. "La causalidad de los Sacramentos de la ley nueva según Santo Tomás." *Divus Thomas* (Piacenza) 40 (1937): 56–68.

Granados, José. "The Liturgy: Presence of a New Body, Source of a Fulfilled Time." *Communio* 39/4 (2012): 529–53.

Gray, Tim. *Sacraments in Scripture*. Steubenville, OH: Emmaus Road Publishing, 2001.

Gregory, Brad S. *The Unintended Reformation: How a Religious Revolution Secularized Society*. Cambridge, MA: Harvard University Press, 2012.

Guardini, R. *Sacred Signs*. London; New York: Sheed & Ward, 1931.

——. *The Spirit of the Liturgy*. London; New York: Sheed & Ward, 1935.

Gumpel, Peter. "Unbaptized Infants: May They Be Saved?" *The Downside Review* 72 (1954): 342–458.

Gy, Pierre-Marie, O.P. "Divergences de théologie sacramentaire autour de S. Thomas." In *Ordo sapientiae et amoris: Image et message de Saint Thomas D'Aquin à travers les récentes études historiques, herméneutiques et doctrinales*, edited by Carlos-Josaphat Pinto de Oliveira, O.P., 425–33. Fribourg, CH: Editions Universitaires Fribourg Suisse, 1993.

——. "Penance and Reconciliation." In *The Church at Prayer*. Vol. 3, *The Sacraments*, edited by A. G. Martimort, 101–15. Translated by Matthew J. O'Connell. Collegeville, MN: Liturgical Press, 1988.

Haffner, Paul. *The Sacramental Mystery*. Trowbridge, UK, 1999.

Haring, N. "Berengar's Definitions of *Sacramentum* and Their Influence on Medieval Sacramentology." *Mediaeval Studies* 10 (1948): 109–46.

——. "St. Augustine's Use of the Word *Character*." *Mediaeval Studies* 14 (1952): 79–97.

——. "A Study of the Sacramentology of Alger of Liege." *Mediaeval Studies* 20 (1958): 41–78.

Hastings, Adrian. "The Salvation of Unbaptized Infants." *The Downside Review* 77 (1959): 172–78.

Haynal, A., O.P. "De Reviviscentia Sacramentorum fictione recedente." *Angelicum* (1927): 51–80; 203–23; 382–405.

Hayward, Robert. "The Jewish Roots of Christian Liturgy." In *T&T Clark Companion to Liturgy*, edited by Alcuin Reid, 23–42. London: Bloomsbury T&T Clark, 2016.

Hellmann, J. A. Wayne. "Bonaventure: On the Institution of the Sacraments." In *A Companion to Bonaventure*, edited by Jay M. Hammond, J. A. Wayne Hellmann, and Jared Goff, 333–57.

Leiden/Boston: Brill, 2014.

Henquinet, P. J. M. "De causalitate Sacramentorum iuxta codicem autographum S. Bonaventurae." *Antonianum* 8 (1933): 377–424.

Héris, Charles-Vincent. "Le salut des enfants morts sans baptême." *La Maison-Dieu* 10 (1947), 86–105.

Hocedez, E. "La conception augustinienne du sacrement dans le tractatus 80 in Ioannem." *Recherches de science religieuse* 10 (1919): 1–29.

Hocken, Peter. *Azusa, Rome, and Zion: Pentecostal Faith, Catholic Reform, and Jewish Roots*. Eugene, OR: Pickwick Publications, 2016.

Hödl, Ludwig. "Sacramentum und res: Zeichen und Bezeichnetes. Eine begriffsgeschichtliche Arbeit zum frühscholastischen Eucharistietraktat." *Scholastik* 38 (1963): 161–82.

Hofer, Andrew, O.P., editor. *Divinization: Becoming Icons of Christ through the Liturgy*. Chicago; Mundelein, IL: Hillenbrand Books, 2015.

Holtz, F. "La valeur sotériologique de la Résurrection du Christ selon saint Thomas." *Ephemerides Theologicae Lovanienses* 29 (1953): 609–45.

Hugon, Edouard. *La causalité instrumentale en théologie*. Paris: Pierre Téqui, 1907.

_____. *Tractatus Dogmatici*. Vol. 4, *De sacramentis in communi; De Eucharistia; De novissimis*. Paris: Lethielleux, 1920.

Hürth, Francis. "Constitutio Apostolica de Sacris Ordinibus, Textus et Commentarius cum Appendice." *Periodica de re morali, canonica, liturgica* 37 (1948): 1–56.

Hütter, Reinhard and Matthew Levering, editors. *Ressourcement Thomism: Sacred Doctrine, the Sacraments, and the Moral Life*. Washington, DC: Catholic University of America Press, 2010.

Ibáñez, Ángel García. *L'Eucaristia, Dono e Mistero: Trattato storico-dogmatico sul mistero eucaristico*. Rome: Edizioni Università della Santa Croce, 2008.

Illanes, J. L. "La sacramentalidad y sus presupuestos. Contribución al planteamiento de la teología sacramentaria." *Scripta Theologica* 8 (1976): 607–59.

_____. "Los sacramentos en la misión pastoral de la Iglesia." *Scripta Theologica* 10 (1978): 987–1009.

International Theological Commission. *From the Diakonia of Christ to the Diakonia of the Apostles: Historico-Theological Research Docu-*

ment. Chicago; Mundelein, IL: Hillenbrand Books, 2003.

_____. "The Hope of Salvation for Infants Who Die without Being Baptised," 2007. In International Theological Commission, *Texts and Documents, 1986–2007*, 353–400. San Francisco: Ignatius Press, 2009.

_____. "The Reciprocity between Faith and Sacraments in the Sacramental Economy," March 3, 2020.

Irwin, Kevin W. *The Sacraments: Historical Foundations and Liturgical Theology*. New York; Mahwah, NJ: Paulist Press, 2016.

Iturrioz, Daniel. "La definición del Concilio de Trento sobre la causalidad de los sacramentos." *Estudios eclesiásticos* 24 (1950): 291–340.

Jeremias, Joachim. *The Eucharistic Words of Jesus*. Translated by Norman Perrin from the 3rd German edition. Philadelphia: Fortress Press, 1977.

Johnson, Lawrence J. *Worship in the Early Church: An Anthology of Historical Sources*. 4 vols. Collegeville, MN: Liturgical Press, 2009.

Johnson, Maxwell. *The Rites of Christian Initiation: Their Evolution and Interpretation*. Collegeville, MN: Liturgical Press, 2007.

Johnson, Maxwell, editor. *Sacraments and Worship: The Sources of Christian Theology*. Louisville, KY: Westminster John Knox Press, 2012.

Jones, Cheslyn, Geoffrey Wainwright, and Edward Yarnold, editors. *The Study of Liturgy*. New York: Oxford University Press, 1978.

Joret, D. "L'Efficacité sacramentelle." *Vie spirituelle* 15 (1926–1927): 122–48.

Jounel, P. "Ordinations." In *The Church at Prayer*. Vol. 3, *The Sacraments*, edited by A. G. Martimort, 139–79. Translated by Matthew J. O'Connell. Collegeville, MN: Liturgical Press, 1988.

Jourjon, Maurice. "Quatre conseils pour un bon usage des Pères en sacramentaire." *La Maison-Dieu* 119 (1974): 74–84.

Journet, Charles. *The Church of the Word Incarnate: An Essay in Speculative Theology*. Vol. 1, *The Apostolic Hierarchy*. Translated by A. H. C. Downes. London and New York: Sheed & Ward, 1955.

_____. "L'économie de la loi mosaïque." *Revue Thomiste* 63 (1963): 5–36, 193–224; 515–47.

_____. "Le mystère de la sacramentalité." *Nova et Vetera* (1974): 161–214.

_____. "Le mystère de l'Église selon Vatican II." *Revue Thomiste* 65 (1965): 5–51.

_____. *Theology of the Church*. Translated by Victor Szczurek. San Francisco: Ignatius Press, 2004.

_____. *La volonté divine salvifique sur les petits enfants*. Bruges: Desclée de Brouwer, 1958.

Kandler, Karl-Hermann. "Luther and Lutherans on Confession, the 'Forgotten Sacrament.'" *Lutheran Quarterly* 31 (2017): 50–63.

Kappes, Christiaan. "A New Narrative for the Reception of Seven Sacraments into Orthodoxy: Peter Lombard's *Sentences* in Nicholas Cabasilas and Symeon of Thessalonica and the Utilization of John Duns Scotus by the Holy *Synaxis*." *Nova et Vetera* (English) 15, no. 2 (2017): 465–501.

Kasper, Walter Cardinal. *Mercy: The Essence of the Gospel and the Key to Christian Life*. Translated by William Madges. New York; Mahwah, NJ: Paulist Press, 2013.

Kasten, Horst. *Taufe und Rechtfertigung bei Thomas von Aquin und Martin Luther*. Munich: Christian Kaiser, 1970.

Kasza, John C. "Anointing of the Sick." In *The Oxford Handbook of Sacramental Theology*, edited by Hans Boersma and Matthew Levering, 558–71. Oxford; New York: Oxford University Press, 2015.

_____. *Understanding Sacramental Healing: Anointing and Viaticum*. Chicago: Hillenbrand Books, 2007.

Keating, Daniel. *Deification and Grace*. Naples, FL: Sapientia Press of Ave Maria University, 2007.

_____. "Deification in the Greek Fathers." In *Called to Be the Children of God: The Catholic Theology of Human Deification*, 40–58. Edited by David Vincent Meconi and Carl Olson. San Francisco: Ignatius Press, 2016.

Kereszty, Roch. "Real Presence, Manifold Presence: Christ and the Church's Eucharist." *Antiphon* 6, no. 3 (2001): 23–36.

King, R. F. "The Origin and Evolution of a Sacramental Formula: *Sacramentum Tantum, Res et Sacramentum, Res Tantum*." *The Thomist* 31 (1967): 21–82.

Kinzer, Mark. *Jerusalem Crucified, Jerusalem Risen: The Resurrected Messiah, the Jewish People, and the Land of Promise*. Eugene, OR: Cascade Books, 2018.

_____. *Post-Missionary Messianic Judaism: Redefining Christian Engagement with the Jewish People*. Grand Rapids, MI: Brazos Press, 2005.

_____. *Searching Her Own Mystery: Nostra Aetate, the Jewish People, and the Identity of the Church*. Eugene, OR: Cascade Books, 2015.

Kizhakkeparampil, Isaac. *The Invocation of the Holy Spirit as Constitutive of the Sacraments according to Cardinal Yves Congar*. Rome: Gregorian University Press, 1995.

Korošak, Bruno J. *The Holy Spirit and the Sacraments: Theological Essay.* Nova Gorica: Branko, 2005.

Kreeft, Peter. *Christianity for Modern Pagans: Pascal's Pensées Edited, Outlined and Explained.* San Francisco: Ignatius Press, 1993.

Labourdette, Michel M. *Le péché original et les origines de l'homme.* Paris: Alsatia, 1953.

Ladaria, Luis, S.J. "The Question of the Validity of Baptism Conferred in the Church of Jesus Christ of Latter-Day Saints." *L'Osservatore Romano* English Edition, August 1, 2001, p. 4.

Lampe, G. W. H. *The Seal of the Spirit: A Study of the Doctrine of Baptism and Confirmation in the New Testament and the Fathers.* London: Longmans, Green, 1951.

Lampen, Willibrord, O.F.M. "De causalitate sacramentorum iuxta S. Bonaventuram. *Antonianum* 7 (1932): 77–86.

_____. *De causalitate sacramentorum iuxta scholam franciscanam.* Bonn: Hanstein, 1931.

Landgraf, Artur Michael. *Dogmengeschichte der Frühscholastik.* 4 vols. Regensburg: Friedrich Pustet, 1952–1956.

Lane, Thomas. "The Jewish Temple Is Transfigured in Christ and the Temple Liturgies Are Transfigured in the Sacraments." *Antiphon* 19, no. 1 (2015): 14–28.

Lang, David P. *Why Matter Matters: Philosophical and Scriptural Reflections on the Sacraments.* Huntington, IN: Our Sunday Visitor, 2002.

Langevin, Dominic M., O.P. *From Passion to Paschal Mystery: A Recent Magisterial Development Concerning the Christological Foundation of the Sacraments.* Fribourg, CH: Academic Press Fribourg, 2015.

La Soujeole, Benoit-Dominique de, O.P. "The Sacraments and the Development of Doctrine." Translated by Dominic M. Langevin. In *The Oxford Handbook of Sacramental Theology*, edited by Hans Boersma and Matthew Levering, 590–601. Oxford; New York: Oxford University Press, 2015.

_____. "The Economy of Salvation: Entitative Sacramentality and Operative Sacramentality." *The Thomist* 75 (2011): 537–53.

_____. "The Importance of the Definition of Sacraments as Signs." In *Ressourcement Thomism: Sacred Doctrine, the Sacraments, and the Moral Life*, 127–35. Edited by Reinhard Hütter and Matthew Levering. Washington, DC: Catholic University of America Press, 2010.

Laitreille, Jean. "L'adulte chrétien, ou l'effet du sacrement de confirmation chez saint Thomas d'Aquin." *Revue Thomiste* 57 (1957): 5–28.

Laurenge, M. "Esquisse d'une étude sur le sort des enfants morts sans baptéme." *L'Année Théologique Augustinienne* 12 (1952): 145–85.

Lavaud, M.-Benoit. "Saint Thomas et la causalité physique instrumentale de la sainte humanité et des sacraments." *Revue thomiste* 32 (1927): 292–316, 405–22.

Lawler, Michael G. *Symbol and Sacrament: A Contemporary Sacramental Theology*. Omaha, NE: Creighton University Press, 1995.

Leclercq, Jacques. *The Interior Life*. Translated by Fergus Murphy. New York: P. J. Kenedy & Sons, 1961.

Lécuyer, Joseph. "La causalité efficiente des mystères du Christ selon saint Thomas." *Doctor communis* 6 (1953): 91–120.

_____. "Les étapes de l'enseignement thomiste sur l'épiscopat." *Revue Thomiste* 57 (1957): 29–52.

_____. *Le sacerdoce dans le mystère du Christ*. Paris: Éditions du Cerf, 1957.

_____. *What Is a Priest?* Translated by Lancelot C. Sheppard. New York: Hawthorn Books, 1959.

Leeming, Bernard. *Principles of Sacramental Theology*. 2nd edition. London: Longmans; Westminster, MD: Newman Press, 1960.

_____. "Recent Trends in Sacramental Theology." *Irish Theological Quarterly* 23 (1956): 195–217.

Lefler, Nathan. "Sign, Cause, and Person in St. Thomas's Sacramental Theology: Further Considerations." *Nova et Vetera* 4/2 (2006): 381–404.

Le Guillou, M.-J. "La sacramentalité de l'Eglise." *La Maison-Dieu* 93 (1968): 9–38.

Lennan, Richard. *The Ecclesiology of Karl Rahner*. Oxford: Clarendon Press, 1995.

Lennerz, H., S.J. *De sacramentis novae legis in genere*. 3rd edition. Rome: Gregorian University Press, 1950.

_____. *De Sacramento Ordinis*. 2nd edition. Rome: Apud aedes universitatis Gregorianae, 1953.

_____. "Salva Illorum Substantia." *Gregorianum* 3 (1922): 385–419; 524–57.

Levering, Matthew. *Christ and the Catholic Priesthood: Ecclesial Hierarchy and the Pattern of the Trinity*. Chicago: Hillenbrand Books, 2010.

_____. "Christ the Priest: An Exploration of *Summa Theologiae*, III, Question 22." *The Thomist* 71 (2007): 379–417.

_____. *Christ's Fulfillment of Torah and Temple: Salvation According to Thomas Aquinas*. Notre Dame, IN: University of Notre Dame Press, 2002.

_____. *Jewish-Christian Dialogue and the Life of Wisdom: Engagements with the Theology of Michael Novak*. New York: Continuum, 2010.

Levering, Matthew, and Michael Dauphinais, editors. *Rediscovering Aquinas and the Sacraments: Studies in Sacramental Theology*. Chicago: Hillenbrand Books, 2009.

Lienhard, Joseph, S.J. "*Sacramentum* and the Eucharist in St. Augustine." *The Thomist* 77 (2013): 173–92.

Litt, F. *La question des rapports entre la nature et la grâce de Baius au Synode de Pistoie*. Doctoral dissertation in theology, PUG. Fontaine l'Évêque, 1934.

Little, Joyce A. "The New Evangelization and Gender: The Remystification of the Body." *Communio* 21 (Winter, 1994): 776–99.

Lohfink, Norbert. *The Covenant Never Revoked: Biblical Reflections on Christian-Jewish Dialogue*. Translated by John J. Scullion, S.J. New York; Mahwah, NJ: Paulist Press, 1991.

Loisy, Alfred. *The Gospel and the Church*. Translated by Christopher Home. New York: Charles Scribner's Sons, 1909.

Lombardi, Riccardo. *The Salvation of the Unbeliever*. London: Burns & Oates, 1956.

Long, Steven A. "The Efficacy of God's Sacramental Presence." *Nova et Vetera* (English) 7, no. 4 (2009): 869–76.

_____. *Natura Pura: On the Recovery of Nature in the Doctrine of Grace*. New York: Fordham University Press, 2010.

Luczynski, I., O.P. "Essai d'interprétation de la théorie de S. Thomas sur la causalité des sacrements." *Divus Thomas* (Piacenza) 64 (1961): 70–83.

Luijten, Eric. *Sacramental Forgiveness as a Gift of God: Thomas Aquinas on the Sacrament of Penance*. Leuven: Peeters, 2003.

Luscombe, D. E. *The School of Peter Abelard: The Influence of Abelard's Thought in the Early Scholastic Period*. Cambridge: Cambridge University Press, 2008.

Luykx, Bonifaas, O.Praem. "Confirmation in Relation to the Eucharist." In *Readings in Sacramental Theology*, edited by C. S. Sullivan, 187–209. Englewood Cliffs, NJ: Prentice-Hall, 1964.

Lynch, Kilian F. "The Doctrine of Alexander of Hales on the Nature of Sacramental Grace." *Franciscan Studies* 19 (1959): 334–83.

_____. "The Sacramental Grace of Confirmation in Thirteenth-Century Theology." *Franciscan Studies* 22 (1962): 172–300.

Lynch, Reginald M., O.P. "Cajetan's Harp: Sacraments and the Life of Grace in Light of Perfective Instrumentality." *The Thomist* 78 (2014): 65–106.

———. "Domingo Bañez on Moral and Physical Causality: Christic Merit and Sacramental Realism." *Angelicum* 91, no. 1 (2014): 105–25.

———. *The Cleansing of the Heart: The Sacraments as Instrumental Causes in the Thomistic Tradition.* Washington, DC: Catholic University of America Press, 2017.

———. "The Sacraments as Causes of Sanctification." *Nova et Vetera* (English) 12, no. 3 (2014): 791–836.

Lynn, William D. *Christ's Redemptive Merit: The Nature of Its Causality according to St. Thomas.* Rome: Gregorian University Press, 1962.

Macdonald, A. J. *Berengar and the Reform of Sacramental Doctrine.* London, New York: Longmans, Green, 1930.

Maltha, A., O.P. "De causalitate intentionali sacramentorum animadversiones quaedam." *Angelicum* 15 (1938): 337–66.

Mansini, Guy, O.S.B. "Episcopal Munera and the Character of Episcopal Orders." *The Thomist* 66 (2002): 369–94.

———. "On Affirming a Dominical Intention of a Male Priesthood." *The Thomist* 61 (1997): 301–16.

———. "Sacerdotal Character at the Second Vatican Council." *The Thomist* 66 (2003): 539–77.

———. *The Word Has Dwelt Among Us: Explorations in Theology.* San Francisco: Ignatius Press, 2008.

Marin-Sola, F., O.P. "Proponitur nova solutio ad conciliandam causalitatem physicam sacramentorum cum eorum reviviscentia." *Divus Thomas* (Fribourg) 3 (1925): 49–63.

Maritain, Jacques. "Sign and Symbol." In *Redeeming the Time*, 191–224, 268–76. Translated by Harry Lorin Binsse. London: G. Bles, The Centenary Press, 1943.

———. *Three Reformers: Luther, Descartes, Rousseau.* New York: Scribner's, 1929.

———. *Untrammeled Approaches.* Translated by Bernard Doering. Notre Dame, IN: University of Notre Dame Press, 1997.

Marmion, Columba, O.S.B. *Christ: The Ideal of the Priest.* Translated by Matthew Dillon. San Francisco: Ignatius Press, 2005.

———. *Christ, the Life of the Soul.* Translated by Alan Bancroft. Bethesda, MD: Zaccheus Press, 2005.

Marsh, Thomas. "The Sacramental Character." In *Sacraments: The*

Gestures of Christ, edited by Denis O'Callaghan, 109–38. New York: Sheed & Ward, 1964.

Marshall, Bruce D. "Christ and Israel: An Unsolved Problem in Catholic Theology." In *The Call of Abraham: Essays on the Election of Israel in Honor of Jon D. Levenson*, edited by Gary A. Anderson and Jon D. Levenson, 330–50. Notre Dame, IN: University of Notre Dame Press, 2013.

_____. "Elder Brothers: John Paul II's Teaching on the Jewish People as a Question to the Church." In *John Paul II and the Jewish People: A Jewish-Christian Dialogue*, edited by David Dalin and Matthew Levering, 113–29. Lanham, MD: Rowman & Littlefield, 2008.

_____. "Postscript and Prospect." *Nova et Vetera* (English) 7, no. 2 (2009): 523–24.

_____. "Quasi in Figura: A Brief Reflection on Jewish Election, after Thomas Aquinas." *Nova et Vetera* (English) 7, no. 2 (2009): 477–84.

_____. "Religion and Election: Aquinas on Natural Law, Judaism, and Salvation in Christ." *Nova et Vetera* (English) 14, no. 1 (2016): 61–125.

Martelet, Gustave. *The Risen Christ and the Eucharistic World*. Translated by René Hague. New York: Seabury Press, 1976.

Martimort, Aimé Georges, editor. *The Church at Prayer*. Vol. 3, *The Sacraments*. New edition. Translated by Matthew J. O'Connell. Collegeville, MN: Liturgical Press, 1988.

_____. "Prayer for the Sick and Sacramental Anointing." In *The Church at Prayer*. Vol. 3, *The Sacraments*. edited by A. G. Martimort, 117–137. Translated by Matthew J. O'Connell. Collegeville, MN: Liturgical Press, 1988.

_____. *The Signs of the New Covenant*. Collegeville, MN: Liturgical Press, 1963.

Martin, Francis. "Election, Covenant, and Law." *Nova et Vetera* (English) 4, no. 4 (2006): 857–90.

Martin, Ralph. "The Post-Christendom Sacramental Crisis: The Wisdom of Thomas Aquinas." *Nova et Vetera* (English) 11, no. 1 (2013): 57–75.

_____. *Will Many Be Saved?: What Vatican II Actually Teaches and Its Implications for the New Evangelization*. Grand Rapids, MI: Eerdmans, 2012.

Martinez, Luis M. *The Sanctifier*. Translated by Sr. M. Aquinas. Boston: Pauline Books & Media, 2003.

Martos, Joseph. *Doors to the Sacred: A Historical Introduction to Sac-*

raments in the Catholic Church. Revised edition. Ligouri, MO: Ligouri/Triumph, 2001.

Masterson, Robert Reginald. "Sacramental Graces: Modes of Sanctifying Grace." *The Thomist* 18 (1955): 311–72.

———. "The Sacramental Grace of Penance." In *Proceedings of the XIII Annual Convention of the Catholic Theological Society of America*, 17–47. St. Paul, MN: 1958. Online at https://ejournals.bc.edu/index.php/ctsa/article/view/2457/2086, accessed May 12, 2020.

Matthijs, Mannes M. *De aeternitate Sacerdotii Christi et de unitate Sacrificii crucis et altaris.* Rome: Pontificia Studiorum Universitas a S.Thoma Aq. in Urbe, 1963.

———. "'Mysteriengegenwart' secundum S. Thomam." *Angelicum* 34 (1957): 393–99.

Mattox, Mickey L. "Sacraments in the Lutheran Reformation." In *The Oxford Handbook of Sacramental Theology*, edited by Hans Boersma and Matthew Levering, 269–82. Oxford; New York: Oxford University Press, 2015.

McAuliffe, Clarence, S.J. *De sacramentis in genere.* St. Louis, MO: B. Herder, 1960.

———. "Penance and Reconciliation with the Church." *Theological Studies* 26.1 (1965): 1–39.

———. *Sacramental Theology: A Textbook for Advanced Students.* St. Louis, MO: B. Herder, 1961.

McCord Adams, Marilyn. "Powerless Causes: The Case of Sacramental Causality." In *Thinking about Causes: From Greek Philosophy to Modern Physics*, edited by Peter Machamer and Gereon Wolters, 47–76. Pittsburgh: University of Pittsburgh Press, 2007.

———. "Essential Orders and Sacramental Causality." In Proceedings of the Quadruple Congress on John Duns Scotus, edited by Mary Beth Ingham and Oleg Bychov, Part 1: 191–205. St. Bonaventure, NY: Franciscan Institute Publications, 2010.

McDonnell, Kilian, and George T. Montague. *Christian Initiation and Baptism in the Holy Spirit: Evidence from the First Eight Centuries.* Collegeville, MN: Liturgical press, 1991.

McGuckin, John Anthony. *The Orthodox Church: An Introduction to Its History, Doctrine, and Spiritual Culture.* Malden, MA; Oxford: Blackwell, 2008.

McHenry, Stephen P. *Three Significant Moments in the Theological Development of the Sacramental Character of Orders: Its Origin, Standardization, and New Direction in Augustine, Aquinas, and*

Congar. Doctoral Thesis in Theology at Fordham University, 1983.

McNamara, Kevin. "The Church, Sacrament of Christ." In *Sacraments: The Gestures of Christ*, edited by Denis O'Callaghan, 76–90. New York: Sheed & Ward, 1964.

McNicholl, A. J., O.P. "Sacramental Signification." *The Thomist* 10 (1947): 334–48.

McShane, Philip. "On the Causality of the Sacraments." *Theological Studies* 24.3 (1963): 423–36.

Mejía, J. M. "La hipótesis de la naturaleza pura." *Ciencia y fe* 2 (1955): 58–90.

Mersch, Émile. *Theology of the Mystical Body*. Translated by C. Vollert. St. Louis, MO: Herder, 1951.

Meyendorff, Paul. *The Anointing of the Sick*. Crestwood, NY: St. Vladimir's Seminary Press, 2009.

Michel, Albert. *Enfants morts sans baptême, certitudes et hypothèses*. Paris: Téqui, 1954.

_____. "Sacrements." *Dictionnaire de théologie catholique*. Edited by A. Vacant, E. Mangenot, and E. Amann. 14:485–644.

Millare, Roland. "The Nominalist Justification for Luther's Sacramental Theology." *Antiphon* 17, no. 2 (2013): 168–90.

Miller, Monica Migliorino. *Sexuality and Authority in the Catholic Church*. London; Toronto: Associated University Presses; Scranton, PA: University of Scranton Press, 1995.

Miralles, Antonio. *Ecclesia et sacramenta: raccolta di studi*. Edited by Rafael Díaz Dorronsoro and Ángel García Ibáñez. Siena: Cantagalli, 2011.

_____. "La noción de sacramento en Santo Tomás." In *Veritas et Sapientia. En el VII Centenario de Santo Tomás de Aquino*, edited by J. J. Rodríguez Rosado and P. Rodríguez García, 375–92. Pamplona: EUNSA, 1975.

_____. *Los sacramentos cristianos: curso de sacramentaria fundamental*. Madrid: Ediciones Palabra, 2006. Also available in Italian: *I sacramenti cristiani: trattato generale*. 2nd edition. Rome: Apollinare studi, 2008.

Mitchell, Leonel L. *Baptismal Anointing*. London: SPCK, 1966.

Mitzka, F. "Das Wirken der Menschheit Christi zu unserem Heil nach dem hl. Thomas v. Aquin." *Zeitschrift für Katholische Theologie* 69 (1947): 189–208.

Miyakawa, Toshiyuki. "The Ecclesial Meaning of the 'Res et Sacramentum.'" *The Thomist* 31 (1967): 381–444.

_____. "St. Thomas Aquinas on the Relation between *Res et Sacramentum* and *Res Tantum.*" *Euntes Docete* 18 (1965): 61–108.

Mohrmann, Christine. "*Sacramentum* chez les plus anciens textes chrétiens." *Harvard Theological Review* 47 (1954): 141–52.

Moloney, Raymond. *The Eucharist.* Collegeville, MN: Liturgical Press, 1995.

Mork, Wulstan, O.S.B. *Led by the Spirit: A Primer of Sacramental Theology.* Milwaukee, WI: Bruce, 1965.

Morrow, Maria C. "Reconnecting Sacrament and Virtue: Penance in Thomas's *Summa Theologiae.*" *New Blackfriars* 91 (2010): 304–20.

Mosebach, Martin. *The Heresy of Formlessness: The Roman Liturgy and Its Enemy.* Translated by Graham Harrison. San Francisco: Ignatius Press, 2006.

Mudd, Joseph C. *Eucharist as Meaning: Critical Metaphysics and Contemporary Sacramental Theology.* Collegeville, MN: Liturgical Press, 2014.

Mulcahy, Bernard. *Aquinas's Notion of Pure Nature and the Christian Integralism of Henri de Lubac: Not Everything Is Grace.* New York: Peter Lang 2011.

Müller, Gerhard Ludwig. *Priesthood and Diaconate: The Recipient of the Sacrament of Holy Orders from the Perspective of Creation Theology and Christology.* Translated by Michael J. Miller. San Francisco: Ignatius Press, 2002.

Murphy, Francesca Aran. "Christ, the Trinity, and the Sacraments." In *The Oxford Handbook of Sacramental Theology*, edited by Hans Boersma and Matthew Levering, 616–60. Oxford; New York: Oxford University Press, 2015.

Mussone, Davide. *L'Eucaristia nel Codice di Diritto Canonico: Commento ai cann. 897–958.* Città del Vaticano: Libreria Editrice Vaticana, 2002.

Natalini, Valentino. *De natura gratiae sacramentalis iuxta S. Bonaventuram.* Rome: Pontificium Athenaeum Antonianum, 1961.

Nellas, Panayiotis. *Deification in Christ: Orthodox Perspectives on the Nature of the Human Person.* Translated by Norman Russell. Crestwood, NY: St. Vladimir's Seminary Press, 1987.

Neunheuser, Burkhard. *Baptism and Confirmation.* Translated by John Jay Hughes. New York: Herder and Herder, 1964.

Neveut, E., "La Grâce sacramentelle." *Divus Thomas* (Piacenza) 38 (1935): 249–85.

Newman, John Henry. *An Essay on the Development of Christian Doc-

trine. 6th edition. Notre Dame, IN: University of Notre Dame Press, 1989.

_____. *Lectures on the Doctrine of Justification.* 3rd edition. London: Longmans, Green, 1908.

_____. *The Present Position of Catholics in England.* New York: The America Press, 1942.

Nicolas, Jean-Hervé, O.P. "La causalité des sacrements." *Revue thomiste* 62 (1962): 517–70.

_____. "La grâce sacramentelle." *Revue thomiste* 61 (1961): 165–92; 522–38.

_____. *The Mystery of God's Grace.* London: Bloomsbury, 1960.

_____. "Réactualisation des mystères rédempteurs dans et par les Sacrements." *Revue thomiste* 58 (1958): 20–54.

_____. *Synthèse dogmatique: de la Trinité à la Trinité.* Fribourg, CH: Editions Universitaires, 1985.

Novak, David. *Talking with Christians: Musings of a Jewish Theologian.* Grand Rapids, MI: Eerdmans, 2005.

Nutt, Roger. "Configuration to Christ the Priest: Aquinas on Sacramental Character." *Angelicum* 85 (2008): 697–713.

_____. "From Within the Mediation of Christ: The Place of Christ in the Christian Moral and Sacramental Life According to St. Thomas Aquinas." *Nova et Vetera* (English) 5, no. 4 (2007): 817–41.

_____. *General Principles of Sacramental Theology.* Washington, DC: Catholic University of America Press, 2017.

_____. "On Analogy, the Incarnation, and the Sacraments of the Church: Considerations from the *Tertia pars* of the *Summa theologiae*," *Nova et Vetera* (English) 12, no. 3 (2014): 989–1004.

O'Callaghan, Denis, editor. *Sacraments: The Gestures of Christ.* New York: Sheed & Ward, 1964.

O'Connell, Robert J., S.J. "When Saintly Fathers Feuded: The Correspondence between Augustine and Jerome." *Thought* 54 (1979): 344–64.

O'Doherty, Michael Kevin. *The Scholastic Teaching on the Sacrament of Confirmation.* Washington, DC: Catholic University of America Press, 1949.

O'Dwyer, Michael. *Confirmation: A Study in the Development of Sacramental Theology.* New York: Benziger Brothers, 1915.

O'Neil, A. "La Causalité sacramentelle d'après le Docteur subtil." *Etudes franciscaines* 30 (1913): 141–55.

O'Neill, Colman E., O.P. "The Instrumentality of the Sacramental

Character. An Interpretation of *Summa Theologiae*, III, q. 63, a. 2."
Irish Theological Quarterly 25 (1958): 262–68.

_____. *Meeting Christ in the Sacraments*. Revised edition, revised by
Romanus Cessario. Staten Island, NY: St. Paul's, 1991.

_____. "The Mysteries of Christ and the Sacraments." *The Thomist* 25
(1962): 1–53.

_____. "The Role of the Recipient and Sacramental Signification." *The
Thomist* 21 (1958): 257–301; 508–40.

_____. *Sacramental Realism: A General Theory of the Sacraments*. Wilm-
ington, DE: M. Glazier, 1983.

_____. "St. Thomas on the Membership of the Church," *The Thomist*
27 (1963): 88–140.

Ordeig, Manuel J. "Significación y causalidad sacramental según Santo
Tomás de Aquino." *Scripta Theologica* 13 (1981): 63–114.

Osborne, Kenan B., O.F.M. *Sacramental Theology Fifty Years after
Vatican II*. Hobe Sound, FL: Lectio Publishing, 2014.

Ouellet, Marc Cardinal. *Mystery and Sacrament of Love: A Theology
of Marriage and the Family for the New Evangelization*. Grand
Rapids, MI: Eerdmans, 2015.

Palmer, Paul F. *Sources of Christian Theology*. Vol. 2, *Sacraments and
Forgiveness; History and Doctrinal Development of Penance, Extreme
Unction and Indulgences*. Westminster, MD: Newman Press, 1960.

_____. "The Theology of the *Res et Sacramentum* with Particular
Emphasis on Its Application to Penance." *Proceedings of the XIV
Annual Convention of the Catholic Theological Society of America*,
120–41. New York, 1960.

_____. "The Theology of the *Res et Sacramentum*." In *Readings in Sac-
ramental Theology*, edited by C. S. Sullivan, 104–23. Englewood
Cliffs, NJ: Prentice-Hall, 1964.

Pásztori-Kupán, István. *Theodoret of Cyrus*. London; New York: Routledge, 2006.

Pateau, Jean. *Le salut des enfants morts sans baptême: d'après saint Thomas
d'Aquin, où est Abel, mon frère?* Paris; Perpignan: Artège-Lethielleux, 2017.

Payne, John B. *Erasmus: His Theology of the Sacraments*. Atlanta: M.E.
Bratcher, 1970.

Pecknold, Chad C. and Lucas Laborde, S.S.J. "Confirmation." In *The
Oxford Handbook of Sacramental Theology*, 487–99. Edited by Hans
Boersma and Matthew Levering. Oxford; New York: Oxford Uni-
versity Press, 2015.

Pègues, T. O.P. "De la causalité des sacrements d'après le R. P. Billot." *Revue thomiste* 11 (1903): 689–708.

_____. "Si les sacrements sont causes perfectives de la grâce." *Revue thomiste* 12 (1904): 339–56.

Perrier, Emmanuel, O.P. "The Election of Israel Today: Supersessionism, Post-supersessionism, and Fulfillment." *Nova et Vetera* (English) 7, no. 2 (2009): 485–504.

Perrin, Bertrand-Marie. *L'institution des Sacrements dans le Commentaire des Sentences de Saint Thomas.* Paris: Parole et silence, 2008.

Perrin, Nicholas. "Sacraments and Sacramentality in the New Testament." In *The Oxford Handbook of Sacramental Theology*, edited by Hans Boersma and Matthew Levering, 52–66. Oxford: Oxford University Press, 2015.

Pesch, Christianus. *De Sacramentis*, pars 1: *De Sacramentis in genere. De Baptismo. De Confirmatione. De Eucharistia.* Freiburg in Breisgau: B. Herder, 1914.

Phelan, Owen M. "Horizontal and Vertical Theologies: 'Sacraments' in the Works of Paschasius Radbertus and Ratramnus of Corbie." *Harvard Theological Review* 103:3 (2010): 271–89.

Philips, Gérard. *L'Église et son mystère au deuxième concile du Vatican: Histoire, texte et commentaire de la constitution "Lumen Gentium."* Paris: Desclée, 1968.

Piault, Bernard. *What Is a Sacrament?* Translated by A. Manson. Twentieth-Century Encyclopedia of Catholicism 49. New York: Hawthorn Books, 1963.

Pilon, Mark A. *Magnum Mysterium: The Sacrament of Matrimony.* Staten Island, NY: St. Pauls, 2010.

Piolanti, Antonio, editor. *Il Protestantesimo ieri e oggi.* Rome: Libreria Editrice Religiosa F. Ferrari, 1958.

Pitre, Brant. *Jesus and the Jewish Roots of the Eucharist: Unlocking the Secrets of the Last Supper.* New York: Doubleday Religion, 2011.

Pohle, Joseph. *The Sacraments: A Dogmatic Treatise.* Vol. 1, *The Sacraments in General. Baptism. Confirmation.* 2nd edition. Translated by Arthur Preuss. St. Louis, MO; London: B. Herder, 1917.

Poschmann, Bernhard. "Die innere Struktur des Bußsakraments." *Münchener Theologische Zeitschrift* 1 (1950): 12–30.

_____. "'Mysteriengegenwart' im Licht des hl. Thomas." *Theologische Quartalschrift* 116 (1935): 53–116.

_____. *Penance and the Anointing of the Sick.* Translated by Francis Courtney. New York: Herder and Herder, 1964.

Pourrat, P. *Theology of the Sacraments: A Study in Positive Theology.* St. Louis, MO; B. Herder, 1910.

Power, Dermot. *A Spiritual Theology of the Priesthood: The Mystery of Christ and the Mission of the Priest.* Washington, DC: Catholic University of America Press, 1998.

Poyer, A. "A propos de 'salva illorum substantia.'" *Divus Thomas* (Piacenza) 30 (1953): 39–66.

Quasten, Johannes. *Patrology.* 4 vols. Westminster, MD: Newman Press, 1950–1986.

Rahner, Hugo. *Our Lady and the Church.* Bethesda, MD: Zaccheus Press, 2004.

Rahner, Karl. *The Church and the Sacraments.* 3rd edition. Translated by W. J. O'Hara. New York: Herder and Herder, 1963. The German original is: *Kirche und Sakramente.* Freiburg in Breisgau: Herder, 1961.

———. "Concerning the Relationship Between Nature and Grace." In *Theological Investigations.* Vol. 1, 297–317. Translated by Cornelius Ernst. Baltimore: Helicon Press, 1961.

———. "Forgotten Truths Concerning the Sacrament of Penance." In *Theological Investigations.* Vol. 2, *Man in the Church*, 135–74. Translated by Karl-H. Kruger. Baltimore: Helicon, 1963.

———. "Introductory Observations on Thomas Aquinas' Theology of the Sacraments in General." In *Theological Investigations.* Vol. 14, *Ecclesiology, Questions in the Church, The Church in the World*, 149–60. Translated by David Bourke. New York: Seabury Press, 1976.

———. "Kirche und Sakramente." *Geist und Leben* 28 (1955): 434–53.

———. *Meditations on the Sacraments.* New York: Seabury Press, 1977.

———. "Nature and Grace." In *Theological Investigations.* Vol. 4, *More Recent Writings*, 165–88. Translated by Kevin Smyth. Baltimore: Helicon Press, 1966.

———. "On the Theology of Worship." In *Theological Investigations.* Vol. 19, *Faith and Ministry*, 141–49. Translated by Edward Quinn. New York: Crossroad, 1983.

———. "The Person in the Sacramental Event." In *Theological Investigations.* Vol. 14, *Ecclesiology, Questions in the Church, The Church in the World*, 161–84. Translated by David Bourke. New York: Seabury Press, 1976.

———. "Personal and Sacramental Piety." In *Theological Investigations.* Vol. 2, *Man in the Church*, 109–33. Translated by Karl-H. Kruger.

Baltimore: Helicon Press, 1963.

_____. "Secular Life and the Sacraments: A Copernican Revolution." *The Tablet* (March 6,1971): 236–38, and (March 13, 1971): 267–68.

_____. *Theology of Pastoral Action.* Translated by W. J. O'Hara. New York: Herder and Herder, 1968.

_____. "The Theology of the Symbol." In *Theological Investigations.* Vol. 4, *More Recent Writings*, 221–52. Translated by Kevin Smyth. Baltimore: Helicon, 1966.

_____. "What Is a Sacrament?" In *Theological Investigations.* Vol. 14, *Ecclesiology, Questions in the Church, The Church in the World*, 135–48. Translated by David Bourke. New York: Seabury Press, 1976.

_____. "The Word and the Eucharist." In *Theological Investigations.* Vol. 4, *More Recent Writings*, 253–286. Translated by Kevin Smyth. Baltimore: Helicon, 1966.

Rambaldi, Giuseppe. *L'oggetto dell'intenzione sacramentale nei teologi dei secoli XVI e XVII.* Rome: Apud Aedes Universitatis Gregorianae, 1944.

Ratzinger, Joseph. *Behold the Pierced One: An Approach to a Spiritual Christology.* Translated by Graham Harrison. San Francisco: Ignatius Press, 1986.

_____. *The Spirit of the Liturgy.* Translated by John Saward. San Francisco, Ignatius Press, 2000.

_____. *Theology of the Liturgy: The Sacramental Foundation of Christian Existence.* Vol. 11 in *Collected Works.* Edited by Michael Miller. Translated by John Saward, Kenneth Baker, Henry Taylor, et al. San Francisco: Ignatius Press, 2014.

Reid, Alcuin, editor. *T&T Clark Companion to Liturgy.* London: Bloomsbury T&T Clark, 2016.

Remy, P. "La Causalité des sacrements d'après saint Bonaventure." *Etudes franciscaines* 42 (1930): 324–39.

Reynolds, Philip J. "Efficient Causality and Instrumentality in Thomas Aquinas's Theology of the Sacraments." In *Essays in Medieval Philosophy and Theology in Memory of Walter H. Principe, O.S.B.*, edited by James R. Ginther and Carl N. Still, 67–84. Burlington, VT: Ashgate, 2005.

Ricciardelli, R. M. "De Causalitate Sacramentorum iuxta S. Thomam et R. P. Billot." *Divus Thomas* (Piacenza) (1904): 525–42.

Richard, J. "La Causalité instrumentale: physique, morale, intentionnelle." *Revue néo-scolastique* 16 (1909): 4–31; 260–69.

Riley, Hugh. *Christian Initiation: A Comparative Study of the Interpretation of the Baptismal Liturgy in the Mystagogical Writings of Cyril of Jerusalem, John Chrysostom, Theodore of Mopsuestia, and Ambrose of Milan.* Washington, DC: Catholic University of America Press, 1974.

Rogers, Elizabeth Frances. *Peter Lombard and the Sacramental System.* New York: Columbia University, 1917.

Roguet, A.-M. *The Sacraments: Signs of Life.* London: Blackfriars, 1954.

Root, Michael. "Luther and Calvin on the Role of Faith in the Sacraments: A Catholic Analysis." *Nova et Vetera* (English) 15, no. 4 (2017): 1065–84.

Röper, Anita. *The Anonymous Christian.* Translated by Joseph Donceel. New York: Sheed & Ward, 1966.

Rosemann, Philipp W. *Peter Lombard.* Oxford: Oxford University Press, 2004.

_____. *The Story of a Great Medieval Book: Peter Lombard's* Sentences. Peterborough, Ont.; Orchard Park, NY: Broadview Press, 2007.

Rosier-Catach, Irène. "Signes sacramentels et signes magiques; Guillaume d'Auvergne et la théorie du pacte." In *Autour de Guillaume d'Auvergne (1249)*, edited by F. Morenzoni and Jean-Yves Tilliette, 93–116. Turnhout, BE: Brepols, 2005.

Rowell, Geoffrey and Christine Hall, editors. *The Gestures of God: Explorations in Sacramentality.* London; New York: Continuum, 2004.

Roza, Devin. *Fulfilled in Christ: The Sacraments: A Guide to Symbols and Types in the Bible and Tradition.* Steubenville, OH: Emmaus Academic, 2015.

Rudolph, David, and Joel Willitts, editors. *Introduction to Messianic Judaism: Its Ecclesial Context and Biblical Foundations.* Grand Rapids, MI: Zondervan, 2013.

Ruether, Rosemary Radford. *Faith and Fratricide: The Theological Roots of Anti-Semitism.* Eugene, OR: Wipf & Stock, 1996.

Salaville, S. "Épiclèse eucharistique." In *Dictionnaire de théologie catholique.* Vol. 5, edited by Alfred Vacant and Eugène Mangenot, 247–65. Paris: Letouzey et Ané, 1913.

Sanders, E. P. *Judaism: Practice and Belief 63 BCE–66 CE.* London: SCM Press, 1992.

Santogrossi, Ansgar. "Anaphoras without Institution Narrative: Historical and Dogmatic Considerations." *Nova et Vetera* (English) 10, no. 1 (2012): 27–59.

Schanz, John P. *The Sacraments of Life and Worship*. Milwaukee, WI: Bruce, 1966.

Scheeben, Matthias Joseph. *The Mysteries of Christianity*. Translated by Cyril Vollert. St. Louis, MO: B. Herder, 1951.

Scheffczyk, Leo. *The Specific Saving Effect Proper to the Sacrament of Penance*. Rome: International Community "The Work of Christ," 1996.

Schenk, Richard, O.P. "Views of the Two Covenants in Medieval Theology." *Nova et Vetera* (English) 4, no. 4 (Fall 2006): 891–916.

Schillebeeckx, E., O.P. *Christ the Sacrament of the Encounter with God*. New York: Sheed & Ward, 1963.

———. *The Eucharist*. Translated by N. D. Smith. New York: Sheed & Ward, 1968.

———. *Marriage: Human Reality and Saving Mystery*. Translated by N. D. Smith. London: Sheed & Ward, 1965.

Schleck, Charles A. "On Sacramental Grace." *Revue de L'Université d'Ottawa* 24 (1954): 227–51.

———. "The Sacramental Chracter of Baptism and Worship." In *Readings in Sacramental Theology*, edited by C. S. Sullivan, 165–86. Englewood Cliffs, NJ: Prentice-Hall, 1964.

———. *The Sacrament of Matrimony: A Dogmatic Study*. Milwaukee, WI: Bruce, 1964.

———. "St. Thomas on the Nature of Sacramental Grace." *The Thomist* 18 (1955): 1–30; 242–78.

Schmaus, Michael. *Dogma*, vol. 5. *The Church as Sacrament*. Translated by Mary Lederer. Kansas City: Sheed & Ward, 1975.

Schmemann, Alexander. *Introduction to Liturgical Theology*. Translated by Asheleigh E. Moorhouse. London; Portland, ME : American Orthodox, 1966.

———. *For the Life of the World: Sacraments and Orthodoxy*. Crestwood, NY: St. Vladimir's Seminary Press, 1973.

———. *Liturgy and Tradition: Theological Reflections of Alexander Schmemann*. Edited by Thomas Fisch. Crestwood, NY: St. Vladimir's Seminary Press, 1990.

———. *Of Water and the Spirit: A Liturgical Study of Baptism*. Crestwood, NY: St. Vladimir's Seminary Press, 1974.

Schönborn, Christoph Cardinal. *Living the Catechism of the Catholic Church: The Sacraments*. San Francisco: Ignatius Press, 2000.

Schoonenberg, Piet. "Presence and Eucharistic Presence." *Cross Currents* 17 (1967): 39–54.

Semmelroth, Otto. *Church and Sacrament.* Translated by Emily Schossberger. Notre Dame, IN: Fides Publishers, 1965.

Sepe, Crescenzo. *La Dimensione trinitaria del carattere sacramentale.* Rome: Lateran University, 1969.

Shea, George. "A Survey of the Theology of Sacramental Grace." *Proceedings of the CTSA* (1953): 81–130.

Sheedy, Charles. *The Eucharistic Controversy of the Eleventh Century Against the Background of Pre-Scholastic Theology.* Washington, DC: Catholic University of America Press, 1947.

Sheen, Fulton. *These Are the Sacraments.* New York: Hawthorn Books, 1962.

Simonin, H. D. "La notion d'intention dans l'oeuvre de S. Thomas d'Aquin." *Revue des Sciences Philosophiques et Théologiques* 19 (1930): 445–63.

Simonin, H. D. and G. Meersseman, editors. *De sacramentorum efficientia apud theologos Ord. Praed.* Fasc. 1, 1229–76. Rome: *Angelicum,* 1936.

Sirilla, Michael G. *The Ideal Bishop: St. Thomas Aquinas's Commentaries on the Pastoral Epistles.* Washington, DC: Catholic University of America Press, 2017.

Slesinski, Robert F. *A Primer on Church and Eucharist: Eastern Perspectives.* Fairfax, VA: Eastern Christian Publications, 2007.

Socias, James. *The Sacraments: Source of Our Life in Christ.* Downers Grove, IL: Midwest Theological Forum, 2009.

Solère, Jean-Luc. "Scotus versus Aquinas on Instrumental Causality." In *Oxford Studies in Medieval Philosophy*, vol. 7, edited by Robert Pasnau, 147–85. Oxford: Oxford University Press, 2019.

Soulen, R. Kendall. *The God of Israel and Christian Theology.* Minneapolis: Fortress Press, 1996.

——. "Replacement Theology." In *A Dictionary of Jewish-Christian Relations*, edited by Edward Kessler and Neil Wenborn, 375–76. Cambridge: Cambridge University Press, 2008.

——. "'They Are Israelites: The Priority of the Present Tense for Jewish-Christian Relations." In *Between Gospel and Election: Explorations in the Interpretation of Romans 9-11*, edited by Florian Wilk and J. Ross Wagner, 497–504. Tübingen, Ger.: Mohr Siebeck, 2010.

Spacil, Theophilus, S.J. *Doctrina theologiae orientis separati: de sac-*

ramentis in genere. Rome: Pontificium Institutum Orientalium Studiorum, 1937.

———. *Doctrina theologiae orientis separati: de SS. Eucharistia.* 2 vols. Rome: Pontificium Institutum Orientalium Studiorum, 1929.

Spicq, C. "Les Sacrements sont cause instrumentale perfective de la grâce." *Divus Thomas* (Piacenza) 32 (1929): 337–56.

Stein, Edith. *Essays on Woman.* Translated by Freda Mary Oben. Washington, DC: ICS Publications, 1987.

Struyf, F. "La nouvelle Théorie de R. P. Billot sur les sacrements." *Revue augustinienne* 6 (1905): 35–53.

Stufler, J. "Bermerkungen zur Lehre des hl. Thomas über die 'virtus instrumentalis.'" *Zeitschrift für Katholische Theologie* 42 (1918): 719–62.

Sullivan, Francis A. "The Development of Doctrine About Infants Who Die Unbaptized." *Theological Studies* 72 (2011): 3–14.

———. *Salvation Outside the Church: Tracing the History of the Catholic Response.* Eugene, OR: Wipf & Stock, 2002.

Sweeney, Conor. *Sacramental Presence after Heidegger: Ontotheology, Sacraments, and a Mother's Smile.* Eugene, OR: Cascade Books, 2015.

Tanquerey, Adolphe. *The Spiritual Life: A Treatise on Ascetical and Mystical Theology.* 2nd edition. Translated by Herman Branderis. Rockford, IL: TAN Books, 2000.

Tapie, Matthew A. *Aquinas on Israel and the Church: The Question of Supersessionism in the Theology of Thomas Aquinas.* Eugene, OR: Pickwick Publications, 2016.

Tappeiner, Daniel A. "Sacramental Causality in Aquinas and Rahner: Some Critical Thoughts." *Scottish Journal of Theology* 28 (1975): 243–57.

Taymans d'Eypernon, François, S.J. *The Blessed Trinity and the Sacraments.* Westminster, MD: Newman Press, 1961.

Teixidor, A. "De Causalitate Sacramentorum." *Gregorianum* (1927): 76–100.

Thornton, L. S. *Confirmation: Its Place in the Baptismal Mystery.* London: Dacre Press, 1954.

Thurian, Max. *Consecration of the Layman: New Approaches to the Sacrament of Confirmation.* Translated by W. J. Kerrigan with Foreword by Frank B. Norris. Baltimore: Helicon, 1963.

———. *Confession.* Translated by Edwin Hudson. London: Mowbray, 1985.

Tillard, J. M. R. "Le nuove prospettivi della teologia sacramentaria." *Sacra Doctrina* 45 (1967): 37–58.

Toups, David L. *Reclaiming Our Priestly Character*. Omaha, NB: Institute for Priestly Formation, IPF Publications, 2008.

Torrell, Jean-Pierre. "La causalité salvifique de la résurrection du Christ selon saint Thomas." *Revue Thomiste* 96 (1996): 179–208.

_____. *A Priestly People: Baptismal Priesthood and Priestly Ministry.* Translated by Peter Heinegg. New York; Mahwah, NJ: Paulist Press, 2013.

_____. *Saint Thomas Aquinas.* Volume 2. *Spiritual Master.* Translated by Robert Royal. Washington, DC: Catholic University of America Press, 2003.

Trigg, Jonathan. "Luther on Baptism and Penance." In *The Oxford Handbook of Martin Luther's Theology*, edited by Robert Kolb, Irene Dingel, and L'ubomír Batka, 310–21. Oxford: Oxford University Press, 2014.

Tschipke, Theophil. *Die Menschheit Christi als Heilsorgan der Gottheit: Unter Besonderer Berücksichtigung der Lehre des Heiligen Thomas von Aquin.* Freiburger Theologische Studien 55. Freiburg in Breisgau: Herder, 1940. French translation: *L'humanité du Christ comme instrument de salut de la divinité.* Translated by Philibert Secrétan. Fribourg, CH: Academic Press Fribourg, 2003.

Turner, Paul. *Ages of Initiation: The First Two Christian Millennia.* Collegeville, MN: Liturgical Press, 2000.

_____. "Benedict XVI and the Sequence of the Sacraments of Initiation." *Worship* 82/2 (2008): 132–40.

_____. *Confirmation: The Baby in Solomon's Court.* Revised edition. Chicago: Hillenbrand Books, 2006.

_____. *Sources of Confirmation from the Fathers through the Reformers.* Collegeville: Liturgical Press, 1993.

Tuyaerts, M., O.P. "Utrum S. Thomas causalitatem sacramentorum respectu gratiae mere dispositivam umquam docuerit." *Angelicum* 8 (1931): 149–86.

Unterleidner, A. "La causalité des sacrements." *Revue augustinienne* 6 (1905): 353–68; 465–88; 9 (1907): 216–23; 16 (1910): 409–40; 17 (1910): 25–57.

_____. "L'effet immédiat des Sacrements." *Revue augustinienne* 12 (1908): 186–94; 343–45; 454–56.

Vagaggini, Cyprian. "'Per unctionem chrismatis in fronte, quae fit manus impositione': Una curiosa affermazione dell'*Ordo Confirmationis* del 1971 sulla materia prossima essenziale della Confermazione." In *Mysterion: nella celebrazione del Mistero di Cristo la vita della Chiesa: Miscellanea liturgica in occasione dei 70 anni dell'Abate Salvatore Marsili.* Turin: Elle di Ci, 1981, pp. 363–439.

———. *Theological Dimensions of the Liturgy.* Translated by Leonard J. Doyle and W. A. Jurgens. Collegeville, MN: Liturgical Press, 1976.

Vaillancourt, Mark G. "Sacramental Theology from Gottshalk to Lanfranc." In *The Oxford Handbook of Sacramental Theology*, edited by Hans Boersma and Matthew Levering, 187–200. Oxford; New York: Oxford University Press, 2015.

Van Den Eynde, Damien. *Les définitions des sacrements pendant la première période de la théologique scholastique (1050–1240).* Rome: Antonianum, 1950.

———. "Stephen Langton und Hugh of St. Cher on the Causality of the Sacraments." *Franciscan Studies* 11 (1951): 141–55.

———. "The Theory of the Composition of the Sacraments in Early Scholasticism (1125–1240)." *Franciscan Studies* 11 (1951): 1–20; 117–44; 12 (1952): 1–26.

Van Meegeren, D. *De causalitate instrumentali humanitatis Christi iuxta D. Thomae doctrinam expositio exegetica.* Venlo, Ger.: NVN Venlosche Courant, 1940.

Van Roo, William A., S.J. *The Christian Sacrament.* Rome: Editrice Pontificia Università Gregoriana, 1992.

———. *De Sacramentis in genere.* Rome: Apud Aedes Universitatis Gregorianae, 1957.

———. "Infants Dying without Baptism: A Survey of Recent Literature and Determination of the State of the Question," *Gregorianum* 35 (1954): 406–73.

———. *The Mystery.* Rome: Gregorian University Press, 1971.

———. "Reflections on Karl Rahner's *Kirche und Sakramente.*" *Gregorianum* 44 (1963): 465–500.

———. "The Resurrection of Christ. Instrumental Cause of Grace." *Gregorianum* 39 (1958): 271–84.

Van Slyke, Daniel G. "Confirmation: A Sacrament in Search of a Theology?" *New Blackfriars* 92/1041 (September 2011): 521–51.

———. *Liturgy 101: Sacraments and Sacramentals.* Ligouri, MO: Ligouri Publications, 2010.

Vass, George. *The Sacrament of the Future: An Evaluation of Karl Rahner's Concept of the Sacraments and the End of Time.* Leominster,

UK: Gracewing, 2005.

Vianney, John. *The Little Catechism of the Curé of Ars*. Rockford, IL: TAN Books, 1987.

Vollert, Cyril, S.J. "The Church and the Sacraments." In *Readings in Sacramental Theology*, edited by C. S. Sullivan, 89–103. Englewood Cliffs, NJ: Prentice-Hall, 1964.

Von Hildebrand, Alice. *The Privilege of Being a Woman*. Ann Arbor, MI: Sapientia Press, 2002.

Von Hildebrand, Dietrich. *Man and Woman: Love and the Meaning of Intimacy*. Manchester, NH: Sophia Institute Press, 1992.

_____. *Marriage*. London: Longmans, Green and Co., 1956.

Vorgrimler, Herbert. *Sacramental Theology*. Translated by Linda Maloney. Collegeville, MN: Liturgical Press, 1992.

Walsh, Liam G., O.P. "The Divine and the Human in St. Thomas's Theology of Sacraments." In *Ordo sapientiae et amoris: Image et message de Saint Thomas D'Aquin à travers les récentes études historiques, herméneutiques et doctrinales*, edited by Carlos-Josaphat Pinto de Oliveira, 321–52. Fribourg, CH: Editions Universitaires Fribourg Suisse, 1993.

_____. "Sacraments." In *The Theology of Thomas Aquinas*, edited by Rik van Nieuwenhove and Joseph Wawrykow, 327–67. Notre Dame, IN: University of Notre Dame Press, 2005.

_____. *Sacraments of Initiation: A Theology of Life, Word, and Rite*. 2nd edition. Chicago: Hillenbrand Books, 2011.

Walsh, Milton. *Witness of the Saints: Patristic Readings in the Liturgy of the Hours*. San Francisco: Ignatius Press, 2012.

Ware, Timothy. *The Orthodox Church*. London; New York: Penguin Books, 1997.

Wawrykow, Joseph. "The Sacraments in Thirteenth-Century Theology." In *The Oxford Handbook of Sacramental Theology*, edited by Hans Boersma and Matthew Levering, 218–33. Oxford; New York: Oxford University Press, 2015.

Webb, Bruno. "Unbaptized Infants and the Quasi-Sacrament of Death." *The Downside Review* 71 (Summer 1953): 243–57.

Weinandy, Thomas G. "The Human Acts of Christ and the Acts That Are the Sacraments." In *Ressourcement Thomism: Sacred Doctrine, the Sacraments, and the Moral Life*, edited by Reinhard Hütter and Matthew Levering, 150–68. Washington, DC: Catholic University of America Press, 2010.

Welch, Lawrence J. *The Presence of Christ in the Church: Explorations in*

Theology. Ave Maria, FL: Sapientia Press of Ave Maria University, 2012.

Whitaker, E. C. "The History of the Baptismal Formula." *Journal of Ecclesiastical History* 16 (1965): 1–12.

Whitaker, E. C., editor. *Documents of the Baptismal Liturgy*. 3rd edition. Edited by Maxwell Johnson. Collegeville, MN: Pueblo, 2003.

White, James F. *The Sacraments in Protestant Practice and Faith*. Nashville: Abingdon Press, 1999.

White, Thomas Joseph. "Sacraments and Philosophy." In *The Oxford Handbook of Sacramental Theology*, edited by Hans Boersma and Matthew Levering, 575–89. Oxford; New York: Oxford University Press, 2015.

Wilkin, Vincent, S.J. *From Limbo to Heaven: An Essay on the Economy of Redemption*. New York: Sheed & Ward, 1961.

Wojtyla, Karol. *The Way to Christ: Spiritual Exercises*. New York: Harper & Row, 1984.

Wood, Jacob W. *Speaking the Love of God: An Introduction to the Sacraments*. Steubenville, OH: Emmaus Road Publishing, 2016.

Wood, Susan. "The Sacramentality of Episcopal Consecration." *Theological Studies* 51 (1990): 479–96.

Wrede, M. *Die Möglichkeit des Status Naturae Purae im Lichte der kirchlich verurteilten Sätze des Bajus vom Urstand*. Limburg: Druckerei der Pallottiner, 1953.

Wyschogrod, Michael. *Abraham's Promise: Judaism and Jewish-Christian Relations*. Grand Rapids: MI: William B. Eerdmans, 2004.

_____. "A Jewish Reading of St. Thomas Aquinas." In *Understanding Scripture: Explorations of Jewish and Christian Traditions of Interpretation*, edited by Clemens Thoma and Michael Wyschogrod, 125–40. New York; Mahwah, NJ: Paulist Press, 1987.

_____. *The Body of Faith: Judaism As Corporeal Election*. New York: Seabury Press, 1983.

Xiberta, Bartolomé M. *Clavis ecclesiae: de ordine absolutionis sacramentalis ad reconciliationem cum Ecclesia*. Barcelona: Apud Sectionem Sancti Paciani Facultatis Theologiae, 1974.

Yarnold, Edward, S.J. *The Awe-Inspiring Rites of Initiation: The Origins of the R.C.I.A.* 2nd edition. Collegeville, MN: Liturgical Press, 1994.

Ysebaert, J. *Greek Baptismal Terminology: Its Origins and Early Development*. Nijmegen: Dekker & Van de Vegt, 1962.

Zheltov, Michael, "The Moment of Eucharistic Consecration in Byzantine Thought." In *Issues in Eucharistic Praying in East and West: Essays in Liturgical and Theological Analysis*, edited by Maxwell Johnson, 263–306. Collegeville, MN: Liturgical Press, 2010.

Zizioulas, John D. *The Eucharistic Communion and the World*. Edited by Luke Ben Tallon. New York; London: T&T Clark, 2011.

Index of Subjects and Names

A

Abel, 462, 479

Abelard, 601–2

Abraham, 89, 141, 229, 462, 479, 505, 510nn22–24, 513n36, 514n37, 535, 542n100, 567, 569n47, 633, 646n69, 693

absolution, 23, 25–26, 73n21, 84, 103, 152, 166–68, 180n17, 197, 214, 215n85, 215n87, 264, 288–91, 294, 298–99, 302, 378n84, 385, 392, 437, 600, 602, 603n128, 673

actual grace

cooperation with, 289, 337, 339, 508, 610, 662, 678

and desire for the sacraments, xlv, 508, 552, 573, 585, 588, 603–4, 609–12, 662, 675, 678–79

and gifts of the Holy Spirit, 333–35, 352–53

as sacramental grace, xlii, 28, 252, 256, 285, 294, 298, 300, 303, 307–8, 347–49, 352–60, 364, 367–68, 371–72, 375–78, 576, 609, 671, 679

and sanctifying grace, 312–16, 319, 552

Adam, xxxv, 20, 100, 106, 118–19, 185–86, 198, 296, 332n48, 337, 479, 623–24, 626, 662n112

Addai and Mari, Anaphora of, 160n77, 161–62

Ad Tuendam Fidem (John Paul II), 217n93

Afanasiev, Nicholas, 260, 684n22

age of reason, 81, 137n7, 152, 167, 176, 182, 182n21, 185, 188, 211, 302, 337, 373, 381–82, 513, 578–79, 594, 603n128, 606–7, 610

dying before without Baptism, xlv, 617–665, 677–78

Akinwale, Anthony, 24n49

Albert the Great (saint), 9, 275

on causality of sacraments, xliii, 410, 413–16, 432n29, 433–34

on character, 247–48

on intention, 178

on limbo, 631n39

on *res et sacramentum* of Penance, 296n55

on sacramental grace, 345, 349–52

on sacramentality of episcopate, 266n110

Alexander of Hales, xliii, 49, 410, 413–16, 432n29, 433–34

Alexander VIII, 180n18

Alger of Liège, 41n12

alter Christus, 681, 691–92

Ambrose (saint)

on Baptism of blood, 562–63

on Baptism of desire, 562–63,
571, 574, 675
on efficacy of Christ's words
in the sacraments, 160n78,
395–97
on institution of Anointing of
the Sick, 105
origin of phrase, *ex opere operato*,
397
on Real Presence, 160n78
on Trinitarian form of Baptism,
156n61, 158
amendment, firm purpose of, 188,
338, 381, 383, 385n100, 555n11
analogy, 19, 92, 297, 313–14
between character and printed
words, 441
of Confirmation and supernatural movement, 78–81
between creation of the soul and
infusion of grace, 432–35,
438
of human and divine words,
442–43
of instrumental causality,
422–29, 495, 672
of matter and form to the sacraments, 134–38
between natural and supernatural order, 318–20, 329, 341,
365, 493
of proportionality, 139, 318–20
between *res et sacramentum* and
character, 295
between sacramental sign and
effect of grace, 48–49, 63,
138–40
between sacraments and lead
coin, 409–10, 416, 420
between sacraments and medi-

cine vials, 406–7, 410, 436
between sacraments and miracles of Christ, 381, 429–31,
436–37, 496
between sacraments and seven
needs of our natural life,
74–78, 81, 125
between sacraments of Old and
New Covenant, 51, 56–59,
523–24
anamnesis, 160n80, 694
angelism, 11–12
Anglican Orders, 63, 138, 169–70,
172, 179, 606
Anointing of the Sick
and age of reason, 188, 373
completes Penance, 88, 215, 372,
503
conditional administration, 187
desire for, 560, 608–12, 615, 675
ecclesial mission of, 285–87, 303,
374
fittingness of, 75, 82, 84, 87–90,
148
and forgiveness of sins, 344, 373,
393
fruitfulness of, 251, 344, 384
form of, 110, 168–69
habitual intention for, 184
institution of, 104–5, 112
licitly administered to
non-Catholics, 204–5
minister of, 215–17, 264
and redemptive suffering, 87,
220, 284–87, 303, 374, 441,
670, 679, 688–89
res et sacramentum of, 283–87,
295, 297, 300, 303, 304, 353,
359, 441, 670
reviviscence of, 251, 483–84

sacramental grace of, 372–75,
608, 688–89
sacramentality of, 71
spirituality of, 679, 688–89
subject of, 188–89, 384
Apostles, xxxii, 6, 8, 37n1, 39, 99,
102–5, 112–13, 120, 122, 124,
127, 156–57, 164–65, 196n41,
199–200, 206, 208–10, 213n82,
236, 256–57, 362, 380, 391, 401,
467, 503n10, 517n47, 522n58,
525–26, 527n67, 533–34, 546,
667, 674, 680
Apostolicae Curae (Leo XIII), 63, 138,
169–70, 172, 179
apostolic blessing, 662–63
apostolic Tradition, 99, 167, 200, 203,
236, 241
Apostolic Tradition, 158, 162, 164
Appleyard, J. A., 482n71
Aquila, Samuel, 81n38, 363n48
Aquinas, Thomas (saint), xxxviii–xl
on Anointing of the Sick, 283,
287, 373n73, 373n75,
374n76, 503–4
on Baptism and Confirmation,
75, 78, 83, 93n68, 256–57,
360, 363nn49–50, 484n75,
503–4
on causality of the sacraments,
xliii, 406, 412, 414–15,
419–455, 476, 481, 483,
492n95–96, 494–96, 506–7,
520, 672–74
on character, 241–51
on charity, 317–26
on circumcision, 510–15
on conjoined and extrinsic
instruments, 426–29, 453
on definition of sacrament,

49–59
on desire for sacraments, 571–72,
592–96, 602–3, 606–7
on dispositions for sacraments,
356n35, 384, 484n75
on episcopate, 264n99, 266,
266–67n110
on the Eucharist, 75, 83, 91n61,
93n68, 277, 278, 284n26,
366–67
on *ex opere operato*, 57, 471,
473–74
on fittingness of the sacramental economy, 8, 11n20, 13,
20–21
on fittingness of the seven sacraments, 74–78, 81–83, 125
on the gifts of the Holy Spirit,
334–35, 352
on grace, 310, 313–20
on Holy Orders, 76, 83, 93n68,
264n99, 265n103, 265n105,
266–67, 379n86, 380n88
on Incarnation and the sacraments, xlin26, xliii, 8–9, 419,
426–31, 437–38, 444–54,
494–96, 506–7, 556, 672–74
on the indwelling, 329n44,
330–31
on instrumental causality, 55–56,
412, 414n51, 422–55,
672–73 (*see also* instrumental cause)
on intention, 179, 183n22
on invincible ignorance, 580, 648
on justification, 337–39, 489
on limbo, 620–40
on Matrimony, 93n68, 136, 153,
503
on Mosaic Law, threefold divi-

sion of, 501–2

on mysteries of Christ's life,
444–55, 480–81

on obediential potency, 311–12

on Old vs. New Covenant sacraments, 55–59, 506–9

on Old Testament sacraments,
xlv, 34n69, 49–51, 55–59,
462, 501–4, 506–7, 510–15,
520, 674

on participation in Christ's
priesthood, 244–46, 249,
264n99, 266n110

on participation in Old Covenant sacraments by
Christians, 526–28, 530,
533–40, 543, 675

on Penance, 24n47, 75, 83,
93n68, 136, 151, 152n50,
288–91, 295, 297–99,
372n71, 437n41

on *res et sacramentum*, 275, 277,
278, 280, 284n26

on sacramental grace, xlii, 344n3,
345–48, 351, 355, 366, 671

on sacramentals, 54n54, 520–21

on sacramental sign signifying
past, present, and future,
29–34

on sin and its consequences,
283n21, 369n64, 370n66

on supernatural virtues, 321–28

ascending and descending aspects
of the sacraments, 65, 92, 689,
693–94

Ascension, xxxi, xxxiv, 8, 15, 64, 101,
104, 419, 427–28, 445, 448–50,
680

Athanasius (saint), 231

Augustine (saint)

on Baptism, 135, 176n2, 183–84,
653

on Baptism of blood, 561,
571n51

on Baptism of desire, 562,
564–66, 570–71, 574, 675

on character, 19, 225–226,
231–33, 235–41, 251, 670

on circumcision, 45, 509–10,
525n64

on Confirmation, 70, 144

on cooperative grace, 315n10

on definition of sacrament, 41,
44–49, 52–53, 59, 120, 483,
669

against Donatists, 226, 231,
235–41, 401, 458, 471, 670

on ecclesial symbolism of
Eucharistic bread and wine,
147, 278n10

on efficacy of the sacraments,
400–2, 421, 458–59

on the Eucharist, 225, 591–92,
593n108, 596, 695n46

on faith in recipient of sacraments, 135, 382

on fittingness of sacraments, 19

on grace of the sacraments, 46,
226

on Holy Orders, 238–40

on infants who die without
Baptism, 617–18, 622–23,
628, 648

on infant Baptism in the faith of
the Church, 653

on intention, 176n2, 177,
183–84

on interior teacher, 365–66

on Matrimony, 71

on matter and form of the sacra-

ments, 135, 137
on number of sacraments, 69–71
on Old Covenant sacraments,
45–46, 52
on participation in Old Covenant sacraments by
Christians, 522n58, 524–28,
530, 539, 541, 675
on Penance, 599–601
that sacraments make the
Church, 97, 120
on sacraments as visible words,
61n72
on sanctification of infants
before the promulgation of
Baptism, 638n52, 646n69
on seal or brand, 231–32
on sufficient grace, 579
on three levels of the sacraments,
225–26, 241
on unfruitful sacramental reception, 225, 238–40, 302n59,
383n97, 384, 570, 574,
591–92
Aumann, Jordan, 549n1, 551n3

B

Báñez, Domingo, 481
Baptism
birth of supernatural life, xxxvi,
33, 75–78, 125, 255, 392,
421, 607
character of, xli, 231, 243, 246,
253, 255–56, 268–69, 280,
382n94, 384, 451, 576, 598
desire for (*see* Baptism of desire)
and eternal life, 32, 43, 566, 577,
680
fittingness of, 75–78
and forgiveness of original sin,

xxxv, 83, 142, 359, 489, 554,
622–24, 640, 643, 677, 680,
696
of infants, 26n53, 176, 461n9,
575, 578, 607, 622, 652–54,
680
infants who die without, xlv,
617–64, 677–78
institution of, 7, 100–1
and maternity of the Church,
89–90
matter of, 140–42
Mormon, 185–86
necessity of, 553, 558–60, 566,
622–25, 644
ordered to the Eucharist, 64, 80,
91, 93, 212 261, 607, 682,
686–87, 689–90, 693
in prophecy, 5
subject of, 187
minister of, 207
sacramental grace of, 359–61
spirituality of, 682–87
and threefold mission of Christ,
256, 258–59, 683
reviviscence of, 239, 384, 483
signifying Christ's death and
resurrection, 30n61, 32–33,
140–41, 157n63, 186,
237n35, 360, 392–93
Trinitarian dimension of, 17,
87–88, 142, 155–56, 230,
247, 268–70, 682, 687
Trinitarian form of, 109, 155–59,
170–71, 400
unfruitful, 237–38, 302n59,
383–84, 570, 574
validity of, 109
and visibility of the Church, 19,
64

Baptism of blood, 560–63, 566, 568, 570–74, 622, 624, 641, 645, 650, 662, 677

Baptism of Christ, 17, 100–1

Baptism of desire, xlv, 331, 348, 450n66, 553n7, 561–90, 594–96, 598–99, 606, 608–11, 614, 622–624, 641, 645, 662, 675–77

Barth, Karl, 466

Basil (saint), 156n61

beatific vision, 198, 627–28, 644
  loss of as penalty for original sin, 620–21, 624, 626, 661n111
  and perfect human happiness, 628–38, 677

Becker, Karl Joseph, 361n44

Bede, 510, 567, 646, 647

Beiting, Christopher, 631n38

Bellarmine, Robert, 153n53
  on episcopal character, 266–68
  on fate of infants dying without Baptism, 617–18
  on physical causality of the sacraments, 436n40, 481–82

Benedict XIV, 153–54, 531–32, 546

Benedict XVI
  on Matrimony and faith, 181n20
  on order of sacraments to the Eucharist, 80–81, 261n93, 689–90
  on priest as *alter Christus*, 691–92
  on sacraments of initiation, 608n137

Berengarius, 273, 274n2, 403, 670

Bernard of Clairvaux, xliii, 406, 409, 494

Biel, Gabriel, 409

Billot, Ludovicus, 479n55, 485n79, 494n101

bishop. *See* episcopate

Blankenhorn, Bernard, xliv, 426, 431, 434, 438, 492

blood and water from Christ's side, xxxv–xxxvi, 69, 74, 89, 118–19, 124

Body and Blood of Christ
  and bread and wine, 146–47
  caused by the words of consecration, 55n58, 392–403, 437
  conversion into, 159–61, 398, 402, 437, 489–91, 496
  instrumental cause of grace, 289, 358, 394, 437–38, 441
  priestly offering of, 102, 170, 692
  real presence of, 43, 159–61, 284, 302, 592, 694
  received spiritually, 592–93
  res et sacramentum in Eucharist, xli, xliv, 273–79, 284, 289, 295, 300–2, 353, 358, 367, 414n52, 592, 598
  and sacraments of Old Covenant, 505, 544
  as sacrifice, 159–61, 451
  spiritual nourishment, 4, 6–7, 34, 195, 277–78, 395, 398, 402–3, 421

Body of Christ. *See* Mystical Body

Boissard, Edmond, 630, 633, 653, 658

Bonaventure (saint)
  on causality of sacraments, xliii, 406, 409–11, 413, 419, 462
  on definition of sacrament, 48n36
  on fittingness of sacraments, 10, 21
  on institution of the sacraments,

112
  on intention, 176n4
  on limbo, 631n39
  on minister of sacraments,
    176n4
  on *res et sacramentum*, 247–48,
    266, 275
  on sacramental grace, 345,
    349–52
  on sacramentality of episcopate,
    266n110
Bonino, Serge-Thomas, 630–31n38,
  634n44, 638n50, 663n114
Boudes, E., 651n84, 652n90, 654n95
Bouyer, Louis
  on Confirmation, 144–45
  on the Eucharist as heart of
    the sacramental system,
    xxxiiin4, 92–93
  on Holy Orders, 217n95
  on sacraments as visible divine
    words, 61n74, 466–68
bread, 7–8, 32, 43, 72, 79, 86, 92, 109,
  111, 135, 139, 145–47, 150, 151,
  159–61, 172, 177, 225, 274–78,
  289, 300, 396–98, 402, 436, 437,
  462, 464, 467, 551, 610, 679, 694,
  695
Bread of Life, xxxv, 6, 80, 94, 227,
  382, 392–93, 394n3, 396,
  489–91, 496, 550, 592, 596, 610,
  671, 674, 685n24
Brennan, Robert, 334n50
Bultmann, Rudolph, 12n24
Burke, Cormac, 182n20
Burke, Raymond, 544n103

C

Cabasilas, Nicholas, xxxiv, 79, 90–91,
  93n66, 212n77, 361n44, 598

Cajetan, Thomas
  on children who die in the
    womb, 650–51
  on desire of parents for unbap-
    tized infants, 618, 649–53
  on sacramental causality, xliii,
    432, 481, 494n102, 673
  on sacramental grace as actual
    graces, xlii, 347–48, 352,
    671
Calvary, xxxvi, xxxvii, 24, 32–35, 61,
  74, 84, 91, 126, 146, 159, 208,
  381, 408, 427, 471, 508, 512, 555,
  609, 612, 660, 694
Calvin, John
  on efficacy of the sacraments,
    61–62, 463–65
  on causality *ex opere operato*,
    460n6, 463–65
  on rejection of sacramental
    character, 253
  on the definition of sacrament,
    60–61
  on Holy Orders, 218
  on invisibility of the Church, 20,
    218
  on number of sacraments, 73
  on sacraments nourishing faith,
    382n93
  on sacraments of the Old and
    New Covenants, 59, 465
  on sufficient grace and universal
    salvific will, 578
Cantate Domino (Council of Florence), 522n56, 529–545, 577–78,
  623
capax Dei, 53, 436, 453, 641
Cappello, Felix, 153n53, 154n54,
  267n112, 283n23
Capreolus, Johannis, 432n29

Cary, Phillip, 12n23, 60n66, 73n21,
    382n93, 462n11
Casel, Odo, xxxin1, 38n2, 39n6, 40n8
Casti Connubii (Pius XI), 348n13,
    354–57, 376, 609n138
Catechism of the Catholic Church, xl, 99
    on Anointing of the Sick, 105,
        148, 215n86, 286, 344n1,
        374n78, 503n11, 688n32,
        689n33
    on Baptism of blood and desire,
        560–61, 590
    on Baptism's necessity, 207, 553,
        558–60, 624
    on character, 254, 265, 270–71
    on Confirmation, 79n34,
        107n22, 143, 209–13,
        234–35, 362n47, 607
    on definition of sacrament, 63
    on disposition, 474n45
    on efficacy *ex opere operato*, 469,
        472
    on the Eucharist, 160n80, 161,
        610n139
    on fittingness of sacraments,
        xxxiii, xxxviii, 15, 65, 77–78
    on gifts of the Holy Spirit, 333,
        334n49
    on grace, 313, 345, 347n11
    on Holy Orders, 262n94, 263,
        265, 428n19
    on infants who die without
        Baptism, xlv–xlvi, 618–19,
        624, 640–41, 643–44, 646,
        648, 658–59, 661, 677
    on institution of the sacraments,
        99, 105
    on justification, 339n59, 367
    on Matrimony, 281n18
    on minister of sacraments, 181,

        210, 213
    on Old Covenant never revoked,
        517
    on Paschal mystery, 33n66
    on Penance, 103n13, 167n101,
        293n49, 367, 369n63, 604
    on *res et sacramentum*, 286
    on symbolism of sacraments,
        143, 148
    on virtues, 320n19, 321n21,
        323–24
Catechism of the Council of Trent, xl,
    116
    on Anointing of the Sick, 105,
        189n30
    on Baptism of desire, 578
    on character, 255
    on Christ's institution of the
        sacraments, 105, 116
    on definition of sacrament,
        62–63
    on disposition of repentance,
        383
    on efficacy of sacraments, 90n57,
        459, 471
    on fittingness of sacraments, 13,
        19, 21, 24, 25n52, 32
    on matter and form of sacra-
        ments, 137, 156–57
    on ministers, 134n2
    on necessity of sacraments,
        90n57, 623–24
    on Old Testament sacraments,
        505
    on threefold temporal dimen-
        sion of sacraments, 32
cause
    broad sense, 404n28, 415
    dispositive, *res et sacramentum* as,
        xliii, 410, 413–15, 433–34,

437, 481n64, 494n102, 672
efficient, xliv, 35, 116, 125, 126,
 133n1, 149, 278–79n11,
 280, 313–15, 339, 340n60,
 376, 404–6, 411–16,
 419–55, 464, 476–78,
 480–85, 488–89, 491–96,
 507–9, 513, 518
exemplar, 398, 446–49, 452,
 454–55, 582
final, 339–40, 404, 445n57, 477,
 507
formal, 313–15, 339–41, 404,
 446, 512
instrumental (*see* instrumental
 cause)
material, 404, 414–15, 476
meritorious (*see* merit)
moral, xliv, 432, 475–82, 485,
 494, 497
and occasion (*see* occasion)
physical, xliv, 412, 419, 475–78,
 481–83, 485, 497
ceremonial law of the Old Covenant
 abrogation of, 518, 520, 532
 Aquinas on, 49–51, 501–4,
  506–7, 674
 Augustine and Jerome on,
  524–26, 530, 675
 observance by Christians,
  521–41, 545, 674–75
character, sacramental
 abiding, 80, 229–32, 238–40,
  243, 246, 249–54, 259,
  265n105, 270, 273
 Aquinas on, 241–51
 Augustine on, 225–226, 231–32,
  235–41, 670
 of Baptism, 231, 243, 246, 253,
  255–56, 268–69, 280,

382n94, 384, 451, 576, 598,
 683
Biblical foundation of, 226–29
of bishop, 263–68
Christian identity given by, xli,
 226–35, 242–44, 247–49,
 253, 255–56, 270, 276, 285,
 295, 358, 488, 614, 683
of Confirmation, 253–62
of deacon, 263–66
distinct from grace, 381, 670
Eucharistic focus, 261
indelible, 82, 249–52, 254
instrumental cause of grace (*see
 under* instrumental cause)
as invisible word of power (*see*
 words of power)
and kingly mission, 258–59, 358
magisterial teaching on, 252–59,
 261–68
mission given by (*see under*
 mission)
ontological reality of, 246–49,
 253–54
and participation in Christ's
 priesthood, 233, 244–45,
 260–61, 358
Patristic doctrine of, 229–41
priestly (*see* priestly character)
and prophetic mission, 358
Protestant denial of, 253–54
as spiritual power, 245–49, 255
synonymous with seal, 226–35
Trent on, 253–54
Trinitarian dimension of, 247,
 268–70
and visibility of the Church,
 254–55
charisms, 86, 259–60, 377, 685
charity

act of possible through actual
grace, 552, 585, 662
as agape, 324
and Baptism of desire, xlv, 574,
585, 588, 590, 624, 645, 662
and circumcision, 512–13
common effect of the sacraments, 343, 353, 371n68
condition of salutary desire,
427n17, 552, 560, 574, 585,
590, 591, 592, 606, 608–12,
662
definition of, 324
and desire of the Church for the
salvation of all, 645, 653–54
disposition for sacramental grace,
352, 357, 386
distinct from sanctifying grace
and the Holy Spirit, 317–19
and divine filiation, 332–33
and docility to God's inspirations, 336, 352–53, 355–56
double commandment of, 4, 327
elevates love of friendship,
323–25
Eucharist as sacrament of, 83, 92
flows from sanctifying grace,
307, 321, 325
form of the supernatural virtues,
324
and forgiveness of sins, 337–39,
367
and gifts of the Holy Spirit,
333–36, 371n68
given through sacraments, xxxiii,
xlii, 5, 7, 96, 226, 325, 343,
549n1, 552, 679, 682
and grace, 310, 313, 314nn9–10,
317–20

as grace of Matrimony, 375–77
incompatible with mortal sin,
325
and indwelling of the Trinity,
328–31
and justification, 337–41
and kingly mission, 258–59
and limbo, 633–35
love of friendship for God,
323–25
and merit, 516, 549n1, 551–52
necessary for salvation, 555, 558
nourished by the Eucharist, 84,
86, 92, 96, 277–78, 358,
366–67, 695–96
orders the will to our supernatural end, 321–23
offering of common priesthood,
261, 686
pastoral, 268, 378–79, 475, 587,
691
and perfect contrition, 325–26,
339, 381, 585, 603–4
perfects the will, 321
queen of the virtues, 92
restored by Penance, 290
and spiritual communion, 597,
599
supernatural inclination, 319–20
unitive power, 324
and unity of the Church, 96, 147,
156n59, 237, 239n40, 274,
276–78, 296n55, 367
and venial sin, 385
Chauvet, Louise-Marie, xliv, 58n64,
434n34, 491–93
Chavasse, Antoine, 71n12, 216n91
chisel, 56, 314, 423, 429, 444, 472,
506, 508, 513

chrism, 69n1, 70n9, 77n29, 79,
107–8n22, 110, 113, 137,
142–45, 147, 162, 163, 211n72,
212, 219, 259, 284n26, 361n44,
363, 397–98
Chrismation, 47, 69–70, 79 142–45,
607
Christ
acting through the sacraments,
xxxi–xxxvii, xliii–xlv, 3, 8–9,
15–17, 26, 55, 59, 64–65, 85,
114, 419, 426–31, 437–38,
444–54, 468, 469, 471–74,
484–85, 494–96, 507–9, 556,
672–74, 680
as Bridegroom, xli, 88, 89, 118,
120, 195–203, 219, 268, 279,
281, 303, 441, 689–90
death of (*see* death of Christ)
and fittingness of the sacraments,
15–16, 614, 640, 659
heart of, xxxin1, 261, 277, 371,
693
humanity of, xxxi, xxxviii, xliii,
xlv, 3–4, 8–9, 15–16, 18, 91,
114–15, 116, 126, 206, 277,
279, 367n59, 391, 425–31,
436–38, 441–43, 448, 452,
453–54, 469, 477–78, 480,
484n74, 487, 494, 507–9,
534, 542, 556, 598, 660, 670,
672–75, 681, 691
instituted the sacraments,
99–127
miracles of (*see* miracles of
Christ)
in the person of (*see under* priest)
touches us in the sacraments,
3–4, 15, 42, 64, 114, 399,
419, 428, 430–31, 452, 455,

472n39, 487–88, 496, 507,
509, 536, 681
words of power of (*see* words of
power)
Christian identity given by sacraments, xli, 17, 156, 226–32,
242–44, 247–49, 255–56, 270,
276, 285–86, 294–98, 253, 358,
488, 614, 670, 683
Christendom, 538, 569, 675, 676, 684
Chrysostom, John (saint)
on Anointing of the Sick, 105
on Baptism and chrismation,
118, 142, 143–44n26,
158–59, 162, 233–34,
399–400
on efficacy of the sacraments,
196, 219n99, 399–400
on the Eucharist, 118, 160n78,
196, 400
on fittingness of sacramental
economy, 13
on participation in Christ's
threefold mission, 233–34
Church
as Bride of Christ, xli, xliv, 20,
33–34, 71, 88–89, 93, 105–6,
120, 125, 135, 152, 175,
195–201, 203–4, 279, 285,
297, 303, 359, 376–77, 393,
503, 689–90
built up by sacraments, xxxiii,
xxxix, 4, 9, 18, 38, 64, 76,
85–87, 97, 104, 114, 117–21,
124–25, 213, 237, 274–79,
454
as Marian and Petrine, 203–4
Mother of the faithful, 77n29,
89–90, 97, 117–20, 203, 652
as sacrament of unity, 94–97

as universal sacrament of salvation, 94–97, 613

as visible and invisible, 17–20, 64, 218

See also Mystical Body

circumcision

of Christ, 229

and Council of Florence, 529–31

efficacy of, 509–15

entrance into the Covenant, 514

figure of baptismal character, 229

and forgiveness of original sin, xlv, 509–15

and giving of sanctifying grace and charity, 511–13

and necessity of precept, 557

not efficacious *ex opere operato*, 504–6, 510–11, 513

observance by Christians, 525n64, 530–31

sacrament of the Old Covenant, 45, 502, 513

Clarke, Norris, 11n19

Clement of Alexandria, xxxivn8, 230

Code of Canon Law

on act of perfect contrition, 604

on Anointing forgiving sins, 373

on ceremonial rites of the Old Covenant, 531

on desire for Baptism, 589, 590n102

on ecclesial dimension of sacraments, 64–65

on funerals for unbaptized babies, 643

on licitness of sacraments, 301n58

on matter of the sacraments, 147, 148

on minister of sacraments, 207, 208, 209nn65–66, 210, 211nn73–74, 212, 214, 216, 217, 385n102, 429n20, 607

on recipient of sacraments, 184, 187, 204, 385, 607

on sacramental character of bishop, 267–68

on validity of sacraments, 109, 110n27, 111n31, 146, 154, 181

Coffey, David, 486n83

Colish, Marcia, 48n38

common priesthood. *See under* priesthood

Compendium of the Catechism of the Catholic Church, 63n81

complementarity of man and woman, xli, 111, 189–95, 219, 658

concupiscence, xxxv, 20, 83, 142, 512, 606

condescension, divine, 15, 61n71, 543, 567

conditional administration of the sacraments, 187

confession

desire for, 331, 385n102, 483–84, 599–605

frequent, 81, 168, 298

matter of Penance, 151–52, 166n99, 167–68, 220, 288–89

validity of, 188

of venial sin, 294, 298

See also Penance

configuration to Christ

by Anointing of the Sick, 33, 220, 284–87, 303, 374n78, 375, 441, 608, 670, 688

by Baptism and Confirmation,

144–45, 219, 230, 303, 364,
607, 682, 685–86
by character or *res et sacra-*
mentum, 33, 90, 219, 231,
235n30, 246, 249, 265,
268–69, 285, 302–3, 346,
349n14, 351, 353, 358,
267n110, 431, 438, 441, 451,
576, 614, 670, 681
by desire, 573, 608
by Holy Orders, 206–8, 265, 268,
269, 380, 303, 378, 691–92
by martyrdom, 572
by Matrimony, 303, 441
by mercy of God, 642
and mysteries of Christ's life,
447–52
by Penance, 220, 295–99, 303,
368, 370, 371n68, 441, 670
and sacramental grace, 351, 353,
358
Confirmation
character of, 246, 253–62,
265n105, 269, 606–7,
683–84
completes Baptism, 6, 79, 213,
213n82, 361, 372, 503,
680n16
desire for, 605–8
fittingness of, 75–81
form of, 162–63
growth to maturity 75–81
and the Holy Spirit (*see* Holy
Spirit)
institution of, 103–4
matter of, 142–45
minister of, 209–13
mission to build up the Church,
85, 104, 213, 256–57,
363n47, 610

mission to consecrate the world,
257
no Old Testament counterpart,
503
ordered to the Eucharist, 64,
80–81, 91, 93, 212, 261, 363,
607–8, 682, 686–87
as Pentecost sacramentally continued, 6, 34, 256, 680n16
reviviscence of, 483
sacramental grace of, 361–66
spirituality of, 682–87
and spiritual movement, 78–81
subject of, 80–81, 184, 187,
211–13
and threefold mission of Christ,
84, 85, 95, 213, 246, 256–61,
269, 303, 364, 605–7, 683
Trinitarian dimension of, 162,
269, 687
Congar, Yves M.-J., 245n55, 257n85,
258n88, 690–1n37
consecration
Anointing of the Sick as, 88,
284–87, 670, 679, 689
anticipating Baptism, 645n67,
649
character or *res et sacramentum* as,
47n33, 50, 235n30, 242, 247,
249, 265, 284–85, 395, 670
of chrism, 69n1, 143, 211
Confirmation as, 144, 213n82
of the Eucharist, 47n33, 84,
93n68, 102, 135, 146, 154,
155n58, 160, 170, 196–97,
219, 396–97, 422n7, 458,
489–91, 594, 673, 694
Holy Orders as, 77n29, 164–65,
177, 207–9, 219
of Israel by Old Covenant sacra-

ments, 45, 502–3

Matrimony as, 285, 670

of the world, 249, 257, 685–86, 694

consolation, 23, 25, 148, 284n24, 331, 371–72, 385–86, 687–88

contrition

condition for fruitfulness of sacraments, 381, 383–86, 474

deepening of, 290, 367–68

and desire for sacraments, xlv, 25n50, 560, 570, 585, 587, 599–605, 608–12, 675

imperfect, 339, 344, 373

and joy, 688

matter of Penance, 103, 151–52, 167–8, 188, 220, 287–90, 296, 302, 384

necessary for salvation, 554, 654

perfect, 290, 325–6, 331, 337–39, 368, 381, 483, 585, 599, 603–4

Coolman, Boyd Taylor, 117n43, 274n2

cooperative grace, 314–15, 357, 588n98

Cornelius, 560, 574, 576, 581

Cornelius (Pope), 177

counsel, gift of, 333, 336, 362, 368, 379, 685

Courtenay, William, 408n37, 409n38

Couturier, C., 41n11

covenantal causality, 408, 421n4, 494

covenantal justice, 659–60, 663

creation, 10–11, 14, 17n33, 52, 100, 106, 109, 133, 139–42, 186, 200, 259, 294, 308–11, 332, 369, 377, 411n44, 466, 489, 626, 629, 656–58, 660, 663

ex nihilo and infusion of grace,

432–37, 453

Credo of the People of God (Paul VI), 588–89

culture, xxxvii, xl, 3, 14, 53, 89, 95–96, 109, 113, 133, 148, 200, 230, 514, 587, 613, 647, 658, 668, 669, 676, 678

Cyprian (saint), 43–44, 95, 235–38, 239n40, 292, 562, 564

Cyril of Alexandria (saint), 227n9, 402–3

Cyril of Jerusalem (saint), 143–44n26, 158, 162–63, 229, 233, 363–64, 397–99

D

Damascene, John (saint)

on blood and water from Christ's side, xxxvin19

on causal efficacy of Baptism, 403

on Christ's Baptism, 100

on Christ's humanity as instrument of divinity, 426, 430

on disposition for fruitful reception, 383n97

on grace of the Eucharist, 366–67

on one Baptism, 237

on Trinitarian form of Baptism, 157n63

Daniélou, Jean, 35n71, 522n59, 542n98

David, 5, 144, 233n24, 504

D'Costa, Gavin, 516n45, 518n50, 531nn74–75, 532n77, 537n87, 538n90, 539n92, 644n65

deacon. *See* diaconate

de Aldama, Joseph, 181n18, 349n14

death

and Anointing of the Sick, 82,
286, 373–74, 503n11, 608,
688n32
and Baptism of blood and desire,
561, 563, 566, 570–75, 662
of Christ, 28, 30n61, 31–33,
50, 87n50, 115n38, 119,
146n32, 166, 237n35, 303,
363n47, 427, 445, 447–52,
694
configuration to Christ's
through Baptism, 393,
450–51, 682, 685, 693
consequence of original sin, xxxv,
xxxvi, 142
danger of, 181, 184, 188–89,
204, 211, 215, 429n20, 578,
599–600, 607, 608, 623, 639
destroyed by Christ, 6, 33n66,
142, 285n28, 403, 449
doubt about, 187
and Matrimony, 82, 83, 280–81,
300, 354
moment of, 655, 662–63
mystical, 299n56, 447–52, 691
necessity of grace at, 369, 624,
659, 663
offering of, 374
preparation for, 75, 82, 84, 88,
373, 429n20, 608
seeds of in sin, 371n69, 687
to sin, xxxiv, 28, 33, 91, 337n54,
361n43, 447–52, 455, 481,
496, 572
and symbolism of Baptism,
30n61, 32–33, 91, 139–41,
157n63, 186, 237n35, 360,
392–93, 403, 450–51
of unbaptized infants, xlv–xlvi,
617–64, 677–78

De Baciocchi, J., 489n90
De Caussade, Jean-Pierre, 27, 685
definition of sacrament, xl, 38, 42–65,
72–73, 133, 406–7, 421n3, 669
Dei Verbum, 37n1, 99n2, 322,
424–25n12, 667–68
Descartes, Rene, 11
desire for sacramental grace
for Anointing of the Sick, 560,
608, 610, 612
for Baptism, xlv, 561–90, 624,
641–43, 645, 662, 675
of the Church, xlv, 641, 653–56,
678
conditions for, 427n17, 552, 560,
574, 584–92, 606, 608–12,
662
for Confirmation, 560, 605–8,
610
as disposition for fruitfulness,
357, 365, 386, 598, 614, 671
for the Eucharist, 591–99
grace given through, xxxviii, xliv,
xlv, 4, 549–615, 624, 675–76
implicit or explicit, xlv, 551,
553n7, 556, 565, 566n38,
567, 569, 583–90, 595–96,
598–99, 606–14, 624, 676,
681
of Israel, xlv, 513, 515, 595, 599,
611
of Matrimony, 553n7, 609
outside the Church, 611–14
of parents and the Church
for infants dying without
Baptism, xlv–xlvi, xlv,
641–43, 649–56, 678
for Penance, 599–605, 610–11
personal, 594, 606, 618, 643, 645,
654

possible through actual grace,
552, 662
in prayer, 550–51, 610
of Protestants, 598, 606, 608,
611–12
development of doctrine
Dei Verbum on, 37n1, 99n2,
667–68
on the sacraments, 37, 69, 99,
588, 651, 667–78
devotion, 72, 216n92, 385, 474–75,
491, 502, 521, 528, 541n97, 543,
568, 575
to humanity of Christ, 542–43,
544n103, 675
interior as *res et sacramentum* of
Anointing, 283, 287
diaconate
character of, 264–66
configured to Christ the Servant,
265, 380
mission of, 265
prefigured by Levites, 102
sacramental grace of, 265, 380
service of the altar and charity,
264, 266
DiNoia, Augustine, 284n24, 286n30
disciplinary precept, 531
disposition for fruitfulness, xxxix,
8, 61, 84, 225, 238, 340, 352,
356–57, 365, 386, 474, 598, 614,
671, 695
Dives in Misericordia (John Paul II),
688nn29–30
Divinae Consortium Naturae (Paul
VI), 6, 77, 110n28, 163nn90–91,
362, 395n5, 503n10, 680n16
divine condescension, 15, 543, 567
Donatism, 226, 231, 235, 238, 240,

271, 274, 384, 401, 458, 471, 670
Dondaine, Hyacinthe-François,
52n49, 58n64
Doronzo, Emmanuel, 266n109,
267n112, 459n3
dowry, sacraments as, xxxvin10, 96,
119
dual covenant theory, 520
Dumont, C., 291n44
Dunn, James D. G., 611n141
Durandus, 40
Dyer, George J., 618n3, 619n8,
620n10, 625n23, 628n31,
628n33, 629n34, 652n89,
655n98

E

Eastern Orthodox, xxxiv, 73, 79–80,
80n36, 90–91, 93n66, 161, 204,
212n77, 259–60, 361n44, 598,
611
Ecclesia de Eucharistia (John Paul
II), 86n46, 92n64, 205, 597–98,
687n27, 696
Elijah, 233n24, 396
Emery, Gilles, 86n45, 278n9, 289n35,
291nn39–40, 291nn42–43, 295
Enlightenment, xxxvii, 10
Ephesus, 8n11, 209
epiclesis, 143, 160–61, 165, 355
episcopate
character of, 266–68
fullness of Holy Orders, 264,
268
and the Holy Spirit, 269–70
institution of, 102
mission of ecclesial headship,
268
prefigured by High Priest, 102,

164

  sacramental grace of, 269, 380

  sacramentality of, 266–68

Ernst, Cornelius, 127n65

eternal life, xxxin1, 6–7, 26, 30, 32,
  43, 77, 148, 227, 242n49, 295,
  318n18, 319, 321n21, 323,
  337n54, 339–40, 369n63, 382,
  392, 394, 451, 486n81, 512n33,
  550, 551n4, 565n36, 566, 577,
  583, 591, 593, 627, 632, 642,
  661n111, 680

Eucharist

  ascending and descending
    dimensions, 92, 689, 693

  breaking of bread, 674

  and Christ's Paschal Mystery,
    451, 687, 693

  desire for, 560, 591–99, 610–12,
    613n142, 675

  ecclesial effect of, 86, 146–47,
    276–79, 295, 367, 393, 593

  efficacy of, 396–98, 400, 402,
    431, 437, 496, 671

  and eternal life, 6–7, 77, 227,
    392, 394, 451, 550, 591,593
    679

  and faith, 92, 381–82, 680

  fittingness of, 75–80

  form of, 135, 159–62, 394,
    396–98, 400, 402

  frequent communion, 81

  fruitfulness of, 287, 385, 592,
    598

  and glorification of God, 92

  as heart of Mystical Body,
    xxxiiin4, 92, 101, 279, 509

  and holiness, 84

  institution of, 100–2, 328

  and instrumental causality, 431,

437, 441

  as Jacob's ladder, 693–94

  matter of, 109, 111, 145–47,
    284n26

  necessity of, 549–50, 591,
    593–95

  and New Covenant, 88–89, 509

  and offering of the Church, 4,
    93, 258–59, 261, 681, 687,
    693, 694–96

  and Penance, 93, 292–95, 299,
    367

  prefigured, 502–3, 509, 544

  priestly minister of, 102, 118,
    196–204, 207–8, 217, 219,
    264, 400, 458

  and Protestants, 204–5, 598,
    611–12

  queen of sacramental system, 92,
    302, 693

  recipient of, 204–5, 344, 385

  remedy against sin, 83, 367

  res et sacramentum of, 273–79,
    284, 295, 300–2, 353, 358,
    367, 441, 598, 670

  sacramental grace of, 358,
    366–67, 385–86, 431

  sacrament of charity, 83–84, 92,
    358, 366–67

  as sacrifice, 84–86, 88–89, 102,
    118, 146, 198, 207–8, 480,
    695

  source and summit, 64, 80–81,
    86, 90–94, 431, 593–94,
    597–98, 682, 686–87,
    693–94

  spiritual communion, 591–99,
    610–11

  spirituality of, 686–87, 693–96

  as spiritual nourishment, 75–80,

90–91, 96, 139, 146, 225,
    358, 421, 591
substantial conversion, 396–98,
    400, 402, 489–91, 496
substantial presence of Christ,
    84, 88–90, 126, 220, 274–79,
    284, 303, 358, 394, 396–98,
    431, 509, 614
summit of Christian initiation,
    212, 261n93, 594, 607, 682,
    686
as union with Christ, 84, 120,
    279, 366, 593, 597–98
as wedding banquet, 198–201,
    366, 689–90
Euchologion, 163n89, 531, 531n76
Eusebius, 177
Evangelii Gaudium (Francis), 517,
    675n8
Evangelium Vitae (John Paul II),
    619n6, 643–44, 646, 663, 678
Eve, xxxvi, 20, 97, 106, 118–19, 199,
    337, 479
Everett, Lawrence P., 69n2, 347n10,
    348n12, 349n15, 350nn18–20,
    351n21, 351nn23–25
ex opere operantis, 356n35, 458, 472,
    473n41, 475, 506n16, 508, 549n1
ex opere operato, 457–76
    CCC on, 472
    Christological foundation,
        57n63, 397, 472, 504–9, 660
    and dispositions of the recipient,
        356n35, 357, 474–75
    efficacy, 55, 343, 397, 549n1
    and instrumental causality,
        504–9, 660–61
    meaning of, 55, 397, 458,
        467–68, 469n30, 506n16
    not dependent on the holiness

of the minister, 237, 401,
    458, 472
Old Covenant sacraments not,
    57, 504–15
Protestant rejection of, 459–66,
    470, 495, 518
Trent on, xliv, 468–72
Exodus, 34, 35, 133, 544, 592
explicit desire, xlv, 184, 564–55, 569,
    573, 575–76, 579–80, 583–85,
    590, 596, 598, 599, 606–10, 613,
    614, 624
Ex quo primum (Benedict XIV),
    531–33
Exsultate Deo (Council of Florence),
    xxxix –xl, xlv, 73, 109n26, 136,
    150, 152, 160, 166n97, 180n16,
    252–53, 280n15, 457, 470, 479,
    505–6, 544, 674
extrinsicism, sacramental, 408, 494

F

Fagan, Sean, 381n91, 552n6,
    604n133, 679n13
Fagerberg, David, xxxin1, 17n33,
    78n31
faith
    of the Church and parents
        for infants, 26n53, 176,
        618, 623n18, 642–43, 645,
        647–55, 660
    and desire for sacraments, xlv,
        585, 587, 591–92, 596,
        603–4, 606, 608–10, 612,
        645, 662, 677
    as disposition for sacramental
        grace, 46, 381–82, 681, 696
    increased by sacraments, xlii, 26,
        60–62, 66, 76, 96, 679
    and justification, 338–40

in limbo, 633–35, 638

meritorious in the sacraments, 91–92, 680

necessity of, 26, 42, 381–83, 554–55, 585–87

and sacramental economy, xxxi, xxxiii, xxxvii, 16, 26–28, 381–83, 679–81, 694

sacramental structure of, 27

as theological virtue, 318–22

Fall, the. *See* original sin

Familiaris Consortio (John Paul II), 181n20, 191n33, 280n16, 282

Farrow, Douglas, 519nn50–51, 520n52, 530n72, 531n74, 533n79, 540n95, 541n97, 545n108, 680n14

fear of the Lord, gift of, 333, 360, 362, 368, 371, 379

Ferguson, Everett, 140n15, 141n18, 157n64, 158n66, 381n90

Feuillet, André, 691n37

Fieschi, Sinibaldo (Innocent IV), 178n10

filiation, divine, xlii, 17, 80, 156, 307, 332–33, 341, 362n47, 379, 681–83, 692

Finn, Thomas, xxxvin10, xxxixn19, 163n87

Finnegan, Eugene M., 70n7, 162n84, 162– 63n87, 163nn89–90, 608n137

Fisher, J.D.C., 163n87, 461n9

fittingness

argument of, 74

of bishop as minister of Confirmation, 212–13

of Eastern practice for sacraments of initiation, 211–12

of grace and supernatural gifts,

312–28

of Incarnation, 556

of infant Baptism, 652

of institution of the sacraments by Christ, 114–21, 124

of limbo, 619, 656–64

of male priesthood, 195–201

of matter of the sacraments, 138–53

of Penance, 22–26

of sacraments, xxxviii, xl, 3–35, 556, 640, 668

of sacraments for the Church, 17–20, 83–90, 556

of sacraments for faith, 26–28

of sacraments for human nature, 10–15, 20–26, 556

of sacraments because of the Incarnation, 10, 15–17, 556

of sacramental character, 242–46, 249–52

of the sacramental economy, 9–35

of seven sacraments, 74–90, 125, 139, 363

of supernatural end, 629n35

of Thomistic theory of sacramental causality, 496

of typology, 28–29

Florence, Council of, xxxix, xlv, 109n26

on causal efficacy of the sacraments, 457–58, 465, 470, 478, 501, 505–6

on intention in the minister, 180

on matter and form of sacraments, 136, 150–51, 160, 166n97, 169n109, 280n15

on necessity of Baptism, 577, 621, 623

on Old and New Covenant sacraments, 457–58, 462, 479, 501, 505–6, 544n105, 674

on Old Testament sacraments after promulgation of the Gospel, 522n56, 529–33, 537–39, 675

on sacramental character, 252–53

on the seven sacraments, 72–73

form, sacramental, 134–38, 149, 153–72, 269, 300, 437

formal cause

of justification, 339–41

sanctifying grace as, 313–16

fortitude, 83, 322n25, 328, 333, 335, 362–64, 368, 375, 606, 610

Fortman, E. J., 655n98

Fox, Joseph, 284n24, 286n30

Francis (pope), 22, 24–25, 27, 371–72, 517, 675n8

Franciscan school, 406, 408n36, 414

Francisco de Vitoria, 478, 581–82

Friedman, Elias, 542nn98–99

fruitfulness of sacraments, 26n53, 118, 182, 203, 225, 226, 237, 238, 287, 300–2, 356n35, 381–86, 461, 474–75, 598, 668

Fulgentius of Ruspe (saint), 566, 570, 577, 622–23, 648

funeral liturgy for unbaptized infants, 618, 642–44, 652, 653n91, 660

G

Gallagher, John F., 57n63, 239n40, 408n36, 409n40, 411n46, 412n47, 434n34, 436n40, 469n30, 476nn47–48, 477n50, 479n55, 481n62, 484n74,

485n77

Galot, Jean, 231n20, 241n47, 247n63, 249n70, 267n113, 691n37

Galtier, Paul, 293n50

Garland, Peter, 56n59, 58n65

Garrigou-Lagrange, Reginald, 326n40, 334n50, 335n53, 357n37, 378n84, 549n1, 692n37

Gaudium et Spes, 95–96, 156n59, 281, 285, 376–77, 685–86

and Baptism of desire, 578n74, 588–90, 676

and infants who die without Baptism, 641, 651, 655, 661

Gaullier, Bertrand, 631n38

Gavin, Frank, 7nn7–8, 141n18

gender

as condition for subject in Matrimony, xli, 110, 189–95, 219–20

in Holy Orders, xli, 110, 195–203, 219–20, 690

Gerson, Jean, 649

gifts of the Holy Spirit. *See under* Holy Spirit

Giraudo, Cesare, 160n77

Glorieux, Palémon, 655n98

Gnostic, 10, 533n79

Good Samaritan, xxxiv–xxxv, 148, 230

grace

actual (*see* actual grace)

all connected to sacraments, 552, 556–57, 679

given through sacraments (*see* sacramental grace)

gratuitous, 308–10, 313, 320n20, 325n38, 327, 348n12, 486, 627, 658, 659, 663 merited by Christ (*see* merit)

sanctifying (*see* sanctifying grace)

state of, 229, 273, 296, 317, 325,
326n39, 327, 330, 332, 336,
339, 343, 349, 356–57, 372,
385, 521, 549, 551, 558,
598–99, 606, 608, 611, 623,
624, 662

Gregory, Brad S., xxxviin15

Gregory Nazianzen (saint), 100

Gregory the Great (saint), 105,
268n116, 510, 567, 646n69,
647n73

Gumpel, Peter, 621n12, 649n81

Gy, Pierre-Marie, 166n100,
167nn101–2, 167n104

H

happiness, natural, 327–28, 617–18,
620, 625–38, 646, 656–58, 677

Haring, N., 226n4, 231n19

Hastings, Adrian, 662n112

Hayward, Robert, 7n7

Hebrew Catholics, 519n51, 523, 526,
539, 541–45, 675

Heidegger, Martin, 492–93

Héris, Charles-Vincent, 639n54,
652n90

hierarchy of creation, 10–11, 656–58

Hippolytus, 158n67, 158n70, 162,
164

Hocken, Peter, 612n141

holiness
call to, 31n63, 42, 359–60,
685–86
of the Church, 20, 83–85, 119
and dispositions of sacramental
recipients, 356, 384n98
and frequent confession, 168
lack of in sacramental minister,

401, 458, 460, 469, 472–74

Mary as model of, 203

of Matrimony, 281–82, 375–77

of the Old Covenant, 674

of the priesthood, 165, 378–80,
474–75

from the sacraments, 20, 34,
47n3150n42, 53–59, 63,
83–87, 116, 144n26, 237,
356

Holy Orders
acting in the person of Christ
(*see under* priest)
administering the sacraments,
206–7, 246, 249–50, 255,
265n105, 269
character of, xli, 187, 206–7,
238–41, 243, 246, 248,
252–54, 260–70
and common priesthood, 84–85,
203, 260–62
configures to Christ (*see under*
configuration to Christ)
and ecclesial headship, 118, 125,
196–99, 203, 262–63
fittingness of, 75–78, 82–85,
87–90, 125, 206–7
form of, 164–65, 169–70
and gifts of the Holy Spirit, 269,
378–80
and Holy Spirit, 269–70
and humility and magnanimity,
692
indelible, 82, 250, 265
institution of, 7, 102, 113
invalidity of Anglican, 138,
169–70
and maternity of the Church, 90
matter of, 148–51
minister of, 208–9

and New Covenant, 89

no reception by desire, xlv,
552–53

Old Testament prefiguration,
113, 503

ordered to the Eucharist, 64,
84–85, 93, 118, 196, 208,
261–64, 690–91

participation in Christ's priesthood, 261–63

and pastoral charity, 268,
378–79, 475, 587, 691

Protestant rejection of, 217–18,
253

reviviscence of, 251

sacramental grace of, 85, 250,
265n105, 377–80

sanctifying the Church, 84–85,
203–4, 218, 246, 250,
692–93

spirituality of, 690–93

and spiritual paternity, 269, 379,
692

spiritual power given by, 196,
246, 248, 250

three grades of, 113, 263–68

Trent on, 74, 102, 253–54

Trinitarian dimension, 165,
269–70

unfruitful reception of, 238–39,
251, 483–84

and unity of the Church, 83, 85,
87, 379

and visibility of the Church, 19,
218, 243

Holy Spirit

configuring the faithful to
Christ, 17, 145, 269–70,
672, 681–82

and Confirmation, 6, 70, 79–81,

82n39, 86, 95, 103–4, 110,
117, 212, 256–58, 260, 269,
328, 361, 363, 503n10, 606,
611, 680n16

gifts of, xlii, 5, 84, 143, 269, 307,
312, 319, 333–36, 343, 345,
352–55, 359–65, 368, 371,
375–80, 464n17, 512, 606,
671, 680, 687

given through the sacraments,
xxxviii–xxxix, 17, 116–17,
165, 269–70, 343, 679,
681–82

indwelling of (*see* indwelling)

inspirations of, xlii, 28, 79, 81,
269, 333, 336, 352–53, 355,
358, 361, 363–64, 367–68,
605–6, 610

power of in sacraments, 31,
63–65, 87–88, 145, 161, 165,
402, 458, 465, 469, 572, 574,
673, 676

working in desire for sacraments,
572–74, 588–89

hope

and desire for sacraments,
427n17, 552, 560, 573, 585,
587, 590–92, 606, 608–10,
662

disposition for sacramental grace,
300, 381, 386, 614, 696

ecclesial, 18, 86

for infants dying without
Baptism, xlvi, 619, 641,
643–49, 654, 658–60, 663,
677–78

and justification, 337–41, 555

in limbo, 633, 635

nourished by sacraments, xxxiii,
xlii, 373–74, 376, 377n82,

679, 682

in Old Covenant sacraments, xlv,
465, 507–8, 513, 516, 520,
529–31, 543

and prophetic mission of laity,
259, 686n26

as theological virtue, 82n40, 307,
312, 319, 321–23, 337, 343

Hugh of St. Victor, xxxix

on causality of the sacraments,
48, 406–7, 411, 465

definition of sacrament, 48–50,
71–72, 669

on desire for sacraments, 567n42,
568–69, 675

on fittingness of sacraments, 21

on the indwelling, 331

on institution of sacraments, 112

on intention, 177

on necessity of the sacraments,
559, 567, 638–39n52,
646n69, 647, 648

on sacraments of Old Testament,
510

on three levels in the sacraments,
274–75

Hugon, Edouard, 476n47, 477n51

Humanae Vitae (Paul VI), 190,
281–82

Humani Generis (Pius XII), 627–28,
636n47, 658n103

humility

Christ as model of, 446, 543

fostered by the sacraments,
xxxviii, 21, 26

and Holy Orders, 692

and magnanimity of sacramental life, xxxviii, 4, 27, 679,
680–81, 684, 692

supernatural, 328

Hürth, Francis, 111n32

hypostatic union, xliii, 3, 426–27, 441,
445, 480, 673, 691

I

Ibáñez, Ángel García, 490n90

identity. *See* Christian identity

Ignatius of Antioch (saint), 8, 394,
451, 522n60, 674, 679

ignorance. *See* invincible ignorance

immersion, 7, 135, 138, 140–42, 172,
360, 392–93, 395n5, 399–400,
451

implicit desire, xlv, 551, 553n7, 556,
565–67, 569, 575–76, 579–80,
583–90, 595–96, 599, 606, 608,
609, 611–14, 624, 676, 681

implicit institution of the sacraments,
96n74, 122–28

Incarnation

acting through the sacraments,
xxxi–xxxiii, xliii, xlv, 3, 8,
10, 15–16, 39, 114, 116,
206, 426, 452n71, 453, 459,
507–9, 518, 521, 673, 674,
682

Mary's contemplation of, 668

necessity of, 555–56

preparation for, 523

indwelling of the Trinity, xlii, 126,
145, 307, 317, 328–31, 333, 343,
362, 368, 512

infallible teaching, 201–3

infants

Baptism of, 26n53, 176, 461n9,
575, 578, 607, 622, 652–54,
680

dying without Baptism, xlv–xlvi,
617–64, 677–78

Innocent I, 71, 216n91

Innocent II, 570–71

Innocent III, 252, 275–76, 279,
    458–59, 509, 554, 571, 620–21,
    646, 654

in persona Christi. See under priest

inspirations. *See under* Holy Spirit

institution of sacraments by Christ,
    99–127
    fittingness of, 114–21
    generic or specific, 106–13, 123
    implicit, 122–28
    Scripture on, 99–106

instrumental cause
    chain of, 289, 427–31, 437–38,
        453, 477–78, 672–73
    character or *res et sacramentum* as,
        xliii, 250–51, 265, 270, 274,
        277, 286, 289, 299, 349n14,
        353, 358, 478, 614, 672
    Christ's humanity as, 18, 91n61,
        426–31, 453, 477, 480,
        506–9, 672, 674
    Church as, 18, 95–97
    conjoined, 426–29, 438, 447–48,
        452n71, 453, 455, 480,
        506–9, 545–46, 660, 672
    minister as, 57n63, 176, 206–7,
        217, 246, 262–63, 472–74
    sacraments as, xxxviii, xliii,
        55–56, 100, 115, 161, 217,
        340n60, 348, 394, 414n51,
        115, 422–55, 466, 471,
        475–77, 482–83, 492n96,
        494–95, 513–14, 572, 672

intention
    actual, 182–83
    to do what the Church does,
        136, 176, 178–82, 183n22,
        185–86, 207, 469, 471, 473
    habitual, 183–84

liturgical, 533–36, 540–45
    of the minister and subject,
        175–84, 301
    in Mormon Baptism, 185–86
    necessity for validity, 301, 383,
        400
    in participation in Old Cov-
        enant sacraments by
        Christians, 527–28, 533–35,
        540–45
    virtual, 182–83

intentional causality, 479n55, 485n79,
    494n101

Inter Insigniores, 196n41, 197,
    199–201

International Theological Commis-
    sion, 557, 644, 654

invincible ignorance, xlv, 238, 515–16,
    521n54, 537–38, 553, 580–90,
    648, 676

Irenaeus (saint), xxxivn8, 135, 230

Isidore of Seville (saint), 9, 46–47,
    70–71, 115

J

Jacob's ladder, 693–94

Jansenism, 578, 618, 628–29, 637n49,
    651, 661, 676

Jeremiah, 559, 639n52

Jeremias, Joachim, 159n76

Jerome (saint), 38–39, 266, 266n107,
    524–26, 530, 537n86, 541n96,
    546, 675n7

Jerusalem, Council of, 522, 531–33,
    537–38

Jewish Christians. *See* Hebrew
    Catholics

Jewish identity, 541–42, 675

Jewish roots of sacraments, 4–7,
    45, 57–59, 104, 113, 139–41,

143–46, 149, 501–15, 541,
543–45, 675
John of St. Thomas, xliin27, 347n10,
349–52, 481–82, 671
John Paul II (saint)
on administration of sacraments
to non-Catholics, 205
on Anointing of the Sick, 374
on Church as sacrament, 97
on Eucharist, 86n46, 92n64,
200–1, 208n63, 689
on grace outside the sacraments,
560n25, 589–90, 605, 640
on holiness of minister, 475
on hope for children who die
without Baptism, 619n6,
643, 663, 678
on Jewish-Christian dialogue,
516–17
on laity, 258–59
on male priesthood, 200–3,
217n93
on marriage of baptized non-believers, 181n20
on Mary, 696
on maternity, 193–94
on Matrimony, 190–91, 280n16,
282–3, 377n83
on Old Covenant not revoked,
516–17
on Penance, 22n45, 293n49, 294,
368, 371n69, 687–88
on priesthood, 379–80, 691n37,
692n39
on sacrament and mystery, 42
on sense of sin, 371n69, 687
on spiritual communion, 597–98
on universal salvific will of God,
589–90
John the Baptist, 7, 101, 106, 116–17,

392, 401, 559, 560, 638, 639, 645,
673
Jounel, P., 165n93
Journet, Charles, 40n9, 90n56,
111n32, 150n47, 267n112,
426n15, 629n36, 635n46,
638n50, 655n98, 658n104
joy of reconciliation, 23, 25, 687–88
justification
through Christ, 91n61, 339–41,
431, 530
through desire for the sacraments, 331–32, 567, 576–79,
647–48
through faith, hope, and charity,
338–41
of Israel, 505–15, 520
through penance, 293–94, 331,
338–39, 367, 601–5
Protestant views of, 60n66, 180,
340, 459–62, 464–65
through the sacraments, 91n61,
280, 289, 308, 331–32,
339, 413n49, 431, 434n33,
476, 489, 493, 507n18,
530, 551n14, 552–55, 576,
578–79, 605, 623, 647, 659
Trent on, 336–41, 459, 578–79,
623
Justin Martyr (saint), 8, 394

K

Kappes, Christiaan, 73n20
Kasper, Walter, 22n45
Kasza, John C., 215n87
Kereszty, Roch, 490n90
King, R. F., 274n2
kingly and prophetic mission, 95, 213,
233–34, 245–46, 258–59, 263,
303, 364, 605, 614, 683, 695

Kinzer, Mark, 522n60, 525n62, 537n85, 545n108
Kizhakkeparampil, Isaac, 257n85
Klee, Heinrich, 655n98
knowledge, gift of, 333, 336, 362, 364–65, 368, 371, 379, 687
Kreeft, Peter, 11n21

L

Laborde, Lucas, 220n100, 683n22
Ladaria, Luis, 185–86
laity, 95, 243, 257–59, 686
La Soujeole, Benoit-Dominique de, 41n9, 49n41, 56n60, 57n62, 92n64, 337n54, 428n19, 599n121, 673n4, 693n42
Lamentabili, 121–23
Landgraf, Artur Michael, 510n25, 511nn30–31
Lang, David, P., 143, 148
Last Supper, 32, 102–3, 121, 159, 161, 199, 206, 328, 365, 400
Laurenge, M., 655n98
laying on of hands, 6, 43, 70n3, 72, 73–74n23, 104, 107, 110, 113, 121, 122n53, 135–39, 145, 148–51, 162, 164–65, 197, 206, 209n68, 210, 218, 266, 267–68, 284, 292, 380, 393, 401, 503n10, 679, 680n16
Leclercq, Jacques, 409n38, 543n101
Lécuyer, Joseph, 267n110, 380
Leeming, Bernard, 64n82, 107n21, 111n32, 112n34, 112n35, 121n52, 178n10, 179nn11–12, 226n4, 230n15, 238n38, 244n53, 253n79, 291n44, 284n29, 413n48, 469n30, 479n55, 509n21
Lennerz, H., 111n32, 150n47,

178n10
Leo the Great (saint), 31, 167n103, 360, 429n21, 600–01, 680
Leo XIII
    on the definition of sacrament, 63
    on the invalidity of Anglican Orders, 63, 138, 169–70, 172, 179–80
Levering, Matthew, xxxin1, 261n93, 262n95, 519nn50–51, 541n97, 545n108
licitness of sacraments, 204, 209, 237, 301–2
Lienhard, Joseph, xxxivn8, 40n8, 41n11, 638n52
limbo, 618–38, 677
    and hierarchy of creation, 656–58
    as open question, 619, 628–29, 645
    problems with, 633–38
    Thomas Aquinas on, 619–38
Litt, F., 628n32
liturgy, sacramental
    active participation in, 363
    of Anointing of the Sick, 147–48, 168–69, 284
    of Baptism, 8, 140–41, 155–59, 212
    of Christian initiation, 212, 234n26, 399
    Christ present through, xxxiii, 680
    of Confirmation, 142–45, 162–63, 209–13, 228
    diaconate of, 266
    definition of, 17n33
    development of, 154–69
    ecclesial dimension of, 64n82,

95, 114, 120n49
Eucharistic, 8, 95, 102, 145–47,
   159–62, 654, 694
ex opere operantis, 475
expresses sacramental efficacy,
   480
and faith, 27
heavenly, 78n31
history of, 107, 112
of Holy Orders, 148–51, 164–65
and the Holy Spirit, 355
and intention, 533–36, 540–45
interceding for all, 654–55
Jewish, 113, 140, 501–45,
   673–75
mutable and immutable elements, 107–14, 154–71
of the Old and New Covenant,
   457–58, 517–45, 673–75
ordered to the Eucharist, 94
and Paschal mystery, 545
of Penance, 151–52, 166–68
reform of, 155
reverence and fruitfulness,
   474–75
threefold temporal dimension,
   31–35
Trinitarian dimension, 17n33,
   682 (*see also* Trinitarian
   dimension of sacraments)
of the Word, 534
Loisy, Alfred, 121
Lombard, Peter
   on causality of sacraments, 49,
      406–8, 411, 412, 422
   on character, 241
   on charity and the Holy Spirit,
      317
   on children dying unbaptized,
      623n18, 625, 648

on circumcision, 510–11,
   513–14, 514n37
definition of sacrament, 46, 49,
   52, 57n62, 58–59, 69, 72,
   406, 669
on desire for the sacraments, 570,
   592, 602, 675
on the Eucharist, 90n59, 275,
   592
on fittingness of the sacraments,
   21n42
on God not bound by the sacraments, 559–60, 639n54
on intention, 177–78
on justification before the sacraments, 567n42, 646n69,
   693n73
on parable of the Good Samaritan, xxxv
on *res et sacramentum* of Penance,
   288, 290
on sacrament as efficacious sign,
   49
on sacraments as extensions of
   Christ's humanity, 114n37
on sacraments as remedies for
   sin, xxxv
on sacramentality of episcopate,
   266, 266n108
Sentences, importance of, xxxix
on seven sacraments, 72
on three levels of the sacraments,
   275
Lombardi, Riccardo, 554n9, 555n12,
   585n95, 655n98
Long, Steven A., 315n11, 626n27
love. *See* charity
love of desire, 322–24
love of friendship, 322–26
Lubac, Henri de, 279n13, 292,

626n27, 627n29, 629n36

Lumen Fidei (Pope Francis), 27

Lumen Gentium, xl

    on Baptism of desire, 585–88, 590, 676, 694

    on character, 255–56

    on Church as sacrament, 18, 40, 95–97

    on common and ministerial priesthood, 261

    on Confirmation, 210, 256–58, 361

    ecclesial dimension of the sacraments, 64, 85–87, 293

    on the Eucharist, 86, 299n56, 694

    on Holy Orders, 261–68

    on laity, 257–58, 686

    on Penance, 293

Luscombe, D. E., 48n38

Luther, Martin

    on definition of sacrament, 59–61, 73, 669

    on efficacy of the sacraments, 59–61, 460–62

    on faith's role in sacraments, 382n93, 460–62

    on Holy Orders, 217–18

    on intention in the minister, 180

    on number of sacraments, 73, 669

    on Penance, 73

    on sacramental character, 253

    on sacraments of the Old and New Covenants, 461–62, 465

    on sacraments as visible signs of God's promise, 60, 73

    on sacraments as visible words of God, 61, 466

    on the visibility of the Church, 20

Lynch, Reginald M., xliiin28, xliiin30, 240n43, 409n39, 411n46, 421n5, 434n34, 435n35, 436n40, 469n28, 476n47, 478nn53–54, 481n63, 673n3

M

magnanimity, 364, 680–81, 684–85, 692

Mansini, Guy, 268n115

Maritain, Jacques, 11n22, 619n9, 637–38n50, 656–57

Marmion, Columba, 360n40, 681n18, 682–83, 691n37, 695

marriage. *See* Matrimony

Marsh, Thomas, 235n30, 245n55

Marshall, Bruce, 518n48, 534n80, 539n93, 542n100

Martelet, Gustave, 45n27

Martimort, Aimé Georges, 165n93, 166n100

Martin, Ralph, 356n35, 587n97

Martinez, Luis M., 334n50

Mary Magdalene, 199

Mary

    contemplation of, 668

    and the Eucharist, 33, 694, 696

    Immaculate Conception, 337, 560, 645, 696

    as model for receiving sacraments, 696

    model and mother of the Church, 203

    not chosen as Apostle, 199

    and Visitation, 638

Masterson, Robert Reginald, 371n67

masterworks, sacraments as, xxxiii, xxxviii, 59, 65, 523, 540 materialism, xxxvii, 11–12, 678

Matrimony

canonical form of, 110–11, 207

as consecration, 281–82, 285

desire for sacramental grace of,
553n7, 609

and domestic church, 87n51,
376–77

ecclesial mission of, 64, 90,
281–82, 375–77

elevation of natural bond, 136,
152, 281, 297, 303, 670

Eucharistic dimension of, 64, 93,
690

and faith, 181

fittingness of, 76–77, 83–90

fruitfulness of, 344, 386

gender complementarity in, xli,
111, 175, 189–95, 219

icon of Christ and the Church,
33, 71, 88, 105–6, 219, 297,
303, 503, 670

indissoluble, 71, 106, 190–91,
300, 503

institution of, 105–6, 136, 152

matter and form of, 135–36,
151–54, 280

ministers of, 154, 181, 184n25,
189, 207, 219, 429n20

monogamous, 191

mystical with Christ, 198, 204

procreative dimension of,
190–95

res et sacramentum of, 280–83,
287n31, 295, 297, 300, 303,
353, 441, 484, 614, 670

reviviscence of, 251, 483–84

as sacrament, 71–74, 105–6, 190,
218, 376, 503

sacramental grace of, 84, 348n13,

354–57, 375–77, 670

sanctification of, 77n29, 84, 106,
376–77

spirituality of, 679, 689–90

total gift of self, 190–92

matter, sacramental, xli, 104, 107–13,
121, 128, 131–154, 164, 166,
169n112, 172, 179, 180n16, 188,
197, 220, 284–85, 287, 289–90,
296, 301, 302, 385, 393, 428, 437,
471, 484–85, 672, 680

McAuliffe, Clarence, 107n21, 292n46

McGuckin, John Anthony, 259–60

McNamara, Kevin, 96n74

Mediator Dei (Pius XII), xxxvi, 146,
196, 207, 219n99, 256, 263,
299n56, 367, 597

Mejía, J. M., 628n32

Melchior Cano, 476, 478–80, 494

Melito of Sardis, 523–24, 117n41

mercy, xlv–xlvi, 25, 33, 87n49, 166,
168–69, 220, 293, 299, 338,
339n59, 371, 372n71, 374, 427,
434n33, 550, 552, 563, 583, 588,
600, 603, 605, 618–19, 641–44,
649–50, 652–53, 659–60,
662–64, 678, 681

merit

of Christ and His Passion, xxxvii,
23–24, 35, 53–55, 57, 64, 89,
91, 106n19, 114, 116, 126,
332, 339–41, 376, 408, 425,
426n15, 427–28, 445–46,
448–49, 452, 454–55, 474,
479, 508, 512, 555, 609, 612,
641, 660–61, 663, 677, 679,
681

ex opere operantis, 216n92, 472,
508

of faith, 44n20, 92, 391, 680

through grace, 285, 307, 319,
321n21, 352, 516, 521, 549,
551–52, 561n27, 568, 632

and moral causality, 476–79

not of minister, 58n63, 460, 467,
469n30, 472

and Old Covenant worship, 505,
516, 521

opposed to gratuitous, 308n1,
309, 566

treasury of, 662

messianic Judaism, 525n62, 530n72,
545, 545nn106–8

microcosm, man as, 10–11

mikveh, 140–41

Michel, Albert, 639n54, 640n55,
645n66, 649n81

minister, xli, 23–24, 57–58n63, 134,
136–38, 159, 175–85, 206–8,
218, 219–21, 232, 236–37,
245–46, 273, 382n94, 392,
397–402, 427–29, 438, 441n49,
442, 458–459, 467–69, 471–75,
478, 491, 492n96, 496–97,
508–9, 612, 669, 672–73

of Anointing of the Sick,
215–217

of Baptism, 171, 407–8, 571

of Confirmation, 209–213

of the Eucharist, 208

of Holy Orders, 208–9,
262– 63n95, 264–65n99,
266n106, 691–92

of Penance, 24–25, 213–15,
290n36, 292, 301, 407–8

miracles of Christ, xxxii–xxxiii, 381,
394, 426, 429–31, 435–37, 441,
443, 454, 483, 496

Miralles, Antonio, 40n7, 43n14,
43n19, 65n83, 107n21, 121n52,

124n59, 170n115, 249n70,
284n24, 355n32, 466n24,
476n47, 479n55, 493n99

mission

of Anointing of the Sick, xlii,
285–87, 374, 688–69

of Baptism, 255–56, 259,
261–62, 268–69, 359–60,
451, 576, 683–87, 689

of Christ, participation in, 84,
88, 213, 233, 246, 256–61,
364, 576, 605–7, 614, 681,
683, 686

of the Church, 80, 95, 361, 559,
590, 613

of Confirmation, 84, 88, 213,
256–62, 268–69, 361–64,
605–7, 680, 683–87

of the Eucharist, 366–67

given by character or *res et sacramentum*, xli–xlii, 226, 230,
232–34, 242, 244–45, 249,
252, 255, 265n105, 270–71,
302–3, 307, 353, 356,
358–59, 488, 556, 614, 670

given by the sacraments, 77, 82,
346

of Holy Orders, 261–69, 377–80,
690–92

of Matrimony, 191–95, 281–82,
375–77, 689

of Penance, xlii, 295–99, 368,
371

and sacramental grace, xlii,
117, 307–8, 349, 352–55,
358–59, 671

missionary mandate, 155, 361–62,
365, 613

mode of the recipient, received
according to, xl–xli, 12, 352, 357,

386, 474

Modernism, 121–23

Mohrmann, Christine, 40n8

moral causality of the sacraments,
    432, 475–80, 482, 485, 494, 497

Morali, Ilaria, 559n19

mortal sin, 283n21, 300, 302, 312,
    325, 331, 343–44, 348–49,
    355–57, 368–69, 373n73,
    383–85, 581, 599, 621–22, 659,
    662, 670
    in Christian observance of cere-
        monial law, 526–46
    forgiveness of, 5n2, 22, 81–83,
        188, 336–39, 359, 367–68,
        463, 489, 512n35, 554–55,
        604–5, 608, 675
    in minister, 458–59, 497
    matrimonial bond persists with,
        280
    and *res et sacramentum* of
        Penance, 298
    sacramental character persists
        with, 239–40, 248, 251

Mosaic Law
    Apostles' observance of, 524–26,
        534–35, 541, 674
    baptism in, 140
    Christ source of grace in, 479
    Council of Florence on, 529–33
    divided into moral, ceremonial,
        and judicial precepts, 501–2
    from God, 113, 526
    never revoked, 515–46, 675
    and New Covenant sacraments,
        113, 140, 503
    See also Old Covenant
        sacraments

Moses, 104, 143–44n27, 149, 264n99,
    506, 520, 521, 526n65, 534, 535,

540, 563, 638n52

Mt. Sinai, 34, 104, 502, 557

Müller, Gerhard Ludwig, 190n31,
    196n38

Mulieris Dignitatem (John Paul II),
    193–94, 200, 201, 689

munera, threefold of Christ, 84–85,
    95, 213, 233–34, 246, 256–61,
    268n115, 364, 605–6, 614, 681,
    683

Munificentissimus Deus (Pius XII),
    202n53

Mussone, Davide, 385n101

mysteries of Christ's life, 445–55, 542

mysterion, 38–42, 69–70

Mysterium Fidei (Paul VI), 126n63,
    472n39, 490–91

mystery
    of Christ and the Church, 8, 19,
        38–42, 175, 227, 281–83,
        393, 690
    of the Eucharist, 490–91, 598,
        689
    of grace given by the sacraments,
        274, 325
    Matrimony as, 87n51, 105–6,
        194, 198
    nuptial, 175, 199–200, 375, 377,
        689–90
    of participation in Christ's
        mission, 258n89
    Paul on, 38–42
    and sacrament, 8, 16, 38–42, 44,
        47, 127, 228
    sacramental, 678, 685
    of sacramental causality, 459,
        678

Mystical Body
    built up by sacraments, xxxiii, 4,
        17–19, 64–65, 76, 92, 161,

296n55, 481, 487

Christ head of, 302n61, 360, 446, 487

membership in, 232, 255–56, 687

and priesthood, 196, 263, 266n110

relation to through desire, 579, 584

unity of as effect of the Eucharist, 275, 277, 279, 591–93, 611, 695

See also Church

Mystici Corporis Christi (Pius XII), 579, 584, 589n99

N

natural desire, 627–28, 636–37

Nazirite vow, 526, 534

necessity

of grace, 549, 554

grades of, 552–60

of means, 553–58, 645n66, 648

of precept, 557–58, 560, 648

of sacraments (*see* ordinary means)

Nellas, Panayiotis, xxxivn7

New Covenant and the sacraments, xxxiii, xxxv, xxxviiii, 3–9, 16, 30, 35, 55, 87–89, 506–9, 523, 540, 673–74

Newman, John Henry (saint), 23, 561n27, 594n111, 667n1

Nicolas, Jean-Hervé, xlvn33, 52n48, 290n38, 292n44, 344n2, 345n4, 346n7, 350n19, 358n38, 552n6, 553n7, 614n143, 679n13

Novak, David, 519n50

Nutt, Roger, 107n21, 249n70, 315n11

O

obediential potency, 310–12, 435–36, 454, 488–89, 641

occasion, opposed to cause, xliii, xlv, 58, 60, 404–6, 408, 413, 420, 432, 453, 461, 479, 505, 508–11, 513–16, 518–21, 647, 660

occasionalism, sacramental, xliii, 404–6, 408–13, 419–21, 432, 453, 461, 470, 477, 478, 494, 518

O'Connell, Robert J., 524–25n62

O'Dwyer, Michael, n505

oil, olive, xxxviii, 113, 142, 147–48, 233, 284, 679

Old Covenant never revoked, 515–21, 675

Old Covenant sacraments

Aquinas on, xlv, 49–51, 55–59, 501–4, 506–7, 510–15, 520, 674

causality of, xliv–xlv, 57–58, 457–58, 462, 465, 504–15, 673–74

as figures of Christ and the sacraments, xlv, 35, 45, 57, 113, 140–41, 501–5, 520–29, 534–35, 541

Hebrew Catholic observance of, 533–45, 674–75

holiness of, 479, 526, 674

after promulgation of the Gospel, xlv, 515–45, 674–75

signs of justifying faith, 505, 507n18, 520

threefold temporal dimension of, 34–35

as worship, 502, 520, 529–46, 557

omnipotence, 115–16, 133, 311, 322n25, 391, 425, 437, 443, 466,

471, 491, 554, 673
O'Neill, Colman E., 57n61, 552n6
operative grace, 314–15, 357, 588n98
Ordeig, Manuel J., 56n58
ordinary life, sanctification of,
    27–28, 96, 257–60, 376, 379n85,
    685–86
ordinary means, sacraments as, 116,
    218, 307, 310, 325, 332, 336,
    549, 551, 553, 557–60, 605, 612,
    622–24, 637, 639–40, 643, 644,
    659, 662, 677
ordinary minister
    of Baptism, 181, 218, 429n20
    of Confirmation, 209–13
Ordinatio Sacerdotalis (John Paul II),
    111n30, 201–3
Origen, xxxiv
original sin
    consequences of, xxxv, 20, 142,
        286, 337, 373, 374n78, 668
    forgiveness of through
        Baptism, xxxv, 83, 359, 489,
            554, 622–24, 640, 643, 677,
            680, 696
        Baptism of blood, 572, 624
        Baptism of desire, 570–71,
            572, 624
        circumcision, xlv, 509–14, 640
        desire of the Church, 653–56
        desire of the parents, 649–53
        faith before promulgation of
            Baptism, 514 567, 638,
            646–49
        God's mercy, 641–46
        special privilege, 638–40, 649
    as privation of sanctifying grace,
        336–37, 511, 554, 625
    punishment of, 554, 617–23,
        625–26, 630–31, 638

Orthodox. *See* Eastern Orthodox
Ouellet, Marc Cardinal, 38n2

P

paintbrush, 314, 423, 439, 440, 465,
    472
Palmer, Paul F. 166n99, 167nn101–2,
    168n106, 244n53, 284n24,
    291n44, 296n55, 371n67,
    601n125
participation
    in attaining our supernatural
        end, 307
    in building up the Church, 85,
        145, 361–62
    in Christ, 86, 277, 278n8, 282,
        302n61, 393
    in Christ's anointing, 143–45
    in Christ's death, 299n56, 685,
        691
    in Christ's headship, 262–63
    in Christ's paschal mystery (*see*
        paschal mystery)
    in Christ's paternity, 120, 692
    in Christ's priesthood, 65,
        242n48, 244–50, 254–57,
        260–62, 358, 694–95
    in Christ's redemptive suffering,
        88, 286, 374n78, 679
    in Christ's sonship, 87, 692
    in Christ's threefold mission, 84,
        85, 95, 213, 233–34, 245–46,
        254–61, 263, 269, 303, 358,
        364, 605–7, 614, 670, 681,
        683, 686–87, 695
    in divine goodness, 310, 330n46,
        618, 632, 657
    in divine life, 3, 17n33, 18, 146,
        307, 309, 404, 493, 680
    in divine love, 317n13, 325n38,

553n7, 609

in divine nature (*see* sanctifying grace)

in heavenly glory, 31, 33

in liturgy, 363

in power of Holy Orders, 264

of sacraments in efficient causality, 402, 413, 432–33, 438, 476, 479, 493–96

Paschal Lamb, 7, 57, 502, 503n8, 528n68

Paschal Mystery

as exemplar and efficient causes of sanctification, 35, 450–52

and liturgical calendar, 545

offered in the Mass, 687

operative in the sacraments, xxxi, 3, 10, 16, 29–35, 50, 54, 64, 97, 114–15, 447, 450–52, 455, 478, 612, 672, 676–77, 693

participation in, 8, 140, 186, 286, 360, 393, 450–52, 455, 588, 641–42, 651, 655, 662, 685, 691, 693

prefigured in Old Covenant, 479, 520, 523, 535, 544

transcends time, 29, 33, 452, 455

type of Christian life, 28

Paschasius Radbertus, 47, 70

Passion of Christ

merit of (*see* merit)

source of the sacraments, xxxvi–vii, 451–2

See also Paschal mystery

Passover, 7, 34, 45, 146, 502, 521, 523–24, 539n93, 541, 543–44, 546

Pastor Aeternus, 202nn52–53

Pastores Dabo Vobis (John Paul II),

379–80, 475, 691n37, 692n39

Paucis abhinc (Benedict XIV), 153–54

Paul (saint)

on Baptism, 32–33, 140, 237, 392–93, 450–51, 572

on charity and the Holy Spirit, 317, 328, 332–33, 336

on Christ as exemplar, 29n60, 446

and Confirmation, 104, 210, 393

on divine filiation, 17, 156, 682

on efficacy of the sacraments, 392–93, 450–51, 466, 471

on the Eucharist, 31–32, 86, 147, 220, 393

on Holy Orders, 149, 380, 393

on matter and form, 135

on Matrimony signifying Christ and the Church, 105–6, 175, 198, 375, 393

on merit, 551

on mystery, 38–39

on Old Covenant rites, 457, 505, 510, 526, 534–35, 541n96, 545n108, 673–74

on Old Covenant not revoked, 516

on sacraments signifying past, present, and future, 31–32

on sacramental sealing, 227–29

on typology of sacraments, 592

union with Christ, 299n56, 475

on universal salvific will, 651–52

Paul VI (saint)

on Anointing of the Sick, 105, 148, 169

on Baptism of desire, 588–89

on character of diaconate, 265

on Confirmation, 6, 110, 163, 362, 503n10, 680n16

on fittingness of sacraments of initiation, 77

on form of Holy Orders, 164–65

on Matrimony, 281–82

on Real Presence, 126n63, 490–91

on sacraments as actions of Christ, 472n39

on total gift of self in marriage, 190–91

on transubstantiation and transignification, 491

Pecknold, Chad C., 220n100, 683n22

Penance

    desire for, 331, 385n102, 483–84, 599–605

    ecclesial dimension of, 166, 291–99, 303

    fittingness of, 22–26, 75–77, 81, 83–84, 87–90, 93

    form of, 166–68

    frequent, 81, 168, 298

    history of, 166–68, 291–94

    institution of, 103

    justification through, 331

    matter of, 151–52

    minister of, 213–15

    res et sacramentum of, xlii, 278, 287–99, 372, 670

    and reviviscence of sacraments, 483

    sacramental grace of, 367–72

    Trinitarian dimension of, 166

    valid reception of, 302, 384–85, 483

    virtue of, 136, 151, 289n35, 297, 338, 371, 603n130

Pentecost, 6–8, 34, 37, 70n7, 95, 103–4, 106, 256, 257n85, 361–2, 401, 668, 671, 680, 682, 696–97

Perrier, Emmanuel, 519n50, 519–20n51

Perrin, Bertrand-Marie, 140n13, 422n6

person of Christ. *See under* priest

Pesch, Christianus, 514n38

Peter (Apostle), 5–6, 88, 104, 203, 209, 231n17, 260, 316, 361n44, 382, 383, 393, 401, 504, 581

Peter Abelard, 601–2

Peter of Aquila, 412–13

physical causality, xliv, 475–78, 481–82, 497

Piault, Bernard, 178n9

piety, gift of, 360, 377, 379

Pilon, Mark A., 281n17

Pitre, Brant, 146n34

Pius IX, 202, 516, 538, 583, 586, 676

Pius X (saint), 121

Pius XI, 354–56

Pius XII

    on baptismal character, 256

    on Baptism of desire, 579, 584, 589n99, 624–25

    on Christ's Passion as source of sacraments, xxxvi

    on definition of sacrament, 63

    on the Eucharist, 146n32, 299n56, 367n60, 597

    on fittingness of sacraments, 76

    on gratuitousness of supernatural order, 627–28, 636n47, 658n103

    on Holy Orders, 149–51, 164n93, 196, 206–7, 219n99, 263

    on institution of sacraments by Christ, 99n1, 109

    on Matrimony, 154n55

    on substance of the sacraments,

109

Poschmann, Bernhard, 167n101, 291, 292n45

Pourrat, P., 136n5

Power, Dermot, 691n37

power

  of Christ in sacraments (*see under* Christ)

  divine, xliii, xlv, 8–9, 15, 33, 46–47, 115–16, 133, 156n61, 262, 316, 344n3, 394, 426–31, 439, 447, 450n67, 452, 454, 473, 477, 480, 484, 489, 507, 606, 673

  redemptive, 33, 87

  words of (*see* words of power)

power, spiritual

  of Baptism, 100–1, 255, 392, 686

  character as, 245–49, 265n105, 270, 441n49

  given by character, xli, 234, 242, 245–49, 252, 255, 257, 303, 488, 496, 515, 614, 686

  given by Holy Orders, 76n27, 85, 196, 208, 241n46, 263n95, 264n99, 267n110, 269, 273, 438, 488–89

  given by *res et sacramentum*, 285, 287, 295, 298–99, 302–3, 670

  instrumental, 441n49, 442n50

  of sacraments, xliii, 3, 33, 46–47, 55, 61, 63, 95–96, 442, 461

power of the keys, 213–15, 289n35

prayer

  and common priesthood, 260–61, 361–63

  as desire for sacramental grace, 22, 550–51

  and disposition for sacramental grace, 378

  and domestic church, 376–77

  as expression of desire for God, 550–51

  and the gifts of the Holy Spirit, 260, 361–63

  grace given through, 550–51

  necessity of, 555

  "Our Father," 610, 687

  and penance, 370

  and priestly character, 263

  in sacramental form and liturgy, 135, 138 160–66, 169, 362–63, 393, 394, 396

  Trinitarian dimension of, 681–82

Presbyterorum Ordinis, 93–94, 196n40, 262, 264n102, 378, 379n85, 474–75

present moment, sacrament of, 27–28, 685–86

priest

  as *alter Christus*, 691–92

  and Christ as Bridegroom, xli, 196–201, 219, 303, 690

  and Christ's headship, 84, 87, 89, 125, 148–49, 196, 206, 208, 261–64, 303, 379, 428, 692

  dignity of, 692–93

  and holiness, 474–75, 691–92

  and humility and magnanimity, 692

  living instrument of Christ, 176, 206–7, 428, 438

  minister of Anointing of the Sick, 215–17

  minister of the Eucharist, 208

  minister of Penance, 213–15, 692

  person of Christ, acting in,

25, 34, 84, 89, 160, 171,
196–201, 207–8, 215, 217,
219, 261–64, 265n105, 303,
397, 428, 471, 690, 692
priesthood
of Christ, 82, 89, 244, 247, 250,
261, 429
common or royal, 84–85, 145,
220, 233–34, 244–46,
256–62, 299, 362–63,
684n22, 686–87, 693–95
Hebrews on, 208, 429, 690
male, xli, 110, 111n31, 175,
195–204, 219, 690
ministerial distinct from
common, 260–63, 691
permanent, 82
and sacrifice, 34, 76n27, 89, 102,
118, 170, 196, 208, 690–91
spirituality of, 690–93
and spiritual paternity, 269, 379,
692
priestly character, 196, 208, 213, 218,
260–64, 269, 428, 438, 488,
690–93
promulgation of the Gospel
means of salvation before, 565,
567–69, 621, 646–49
and necessity of Baptism,
332n48, 578, 623
and observance of the ceremonial Law, xlv, 501, 525–30,
532–33, 537–40, 674–75
prophecy, 5, 89, 260, 280n16, 424,
525n64
Protestant Reformation
on character, 253
on Confirmation, 361, 606, 611
on definition of sacrament,
59–62, 495, 669
and desire for sacramental grace,
598, 606, 608, 611–12
on efficacy of the sacraments,
xliii, 12, 55, 59–62, 459–70,
495, 518
on Holy Orders, 169–70,
217–18, 253, 612
on justification, 60n66, 180, 340,
459–62, 464–65
on number of sacraments, 60,
73–74, 669
on Old and New Covenant sacraments, 518, 461–62, 465
on Penance, 23, 73
and rejection of sacramentality,
xxxvii, 10, 12
on the role of faith in sacramental reception, 382n93
on sacraments as visible divine
words, 61, 62n74, 466–68
on the visibility of the Church,
20, 218
prudence, 83, 187, 269, 327, 335,
352n29, 368, 378–79, 685
Pseudo-Dionysius, xlin26, 13, 69, 94,
267n110, 430n23, 657n101
pure nature, state of, 628–29, 636,
656
Purgatory, 369n63, 633
purification, 100, 218, 285, 369n63,
374, 399, 403, 503, 505, 509–10,
557, 689

Q

Quanto Conficiamur Moerere (Pius
XI), 516n42, 538n91, 583,
586n96, 676n9
Quodvultdeus of Carthage, xxxvin10,
118–19

R

Rabanus Maurus, 71

Rahner, Hugo, xxxvin11

Rahner, Karl

on causality of sacraments,
xliv, 126, 133n1, 278n11,
443n52, 482–89, 495–96

on Church as fundamental sacrament, 96–97n74, 454n74

critique of Thomistic theory,
482–85

on the Eucharist, 278–79, 489

on implicit institution of the
sacraments, 122–27

on intrinsic symbol, sacrament
as, xliv, 96n74, 485–89,
495–96

res et sacramentum as ecclesial,
278–79, 292

on *res et sacramentum* of Penance,
291–92

Ratzinger, Joseph

on the *res tantum* of the Eucharist, 279n13

on Church as bride and mother,
120n49

on *ex opere operato*, 472n39,
476n47, 506n16

on fittingness of sacramental
symbolism xxxviin14,
12n24, 14

on mystery, 38n2

on sacraments and typology,
28–29

on transignification, 489n90

reality and sign. *See res et
sacramentum*

Real Presence. *See* Eucharist: substantial presence of Christ

recapitulation, 29, 233

Reconciliatio et Paenitentia (John Paul
II), 22n45, 97, 293n49, 294, 368,
371n69, 374, 560n25, 605, 640,
687–88

Reconciliation, sacrament of. *See*
Penance

reconciliation

with the Church, 23, 97, 103,
291–95, 296n55, 299, 303,
367, 687

with God, 23–24, 89, 95, 97,
103, 294, 296–97, 374, 603,
687–88

Redemptoris Missio (John Paul II),
589–90

Reformation. *See* Protestant

reparation for sin, 296–99, 368–69

repentance

condition for Baptism of desire,
427n17, 573–74, 578, 588,
590

condition for spiritual communion, 599

elevated as matter for Penance,
136, 237

grace of merited on Calvary, 479

John's baptism of, 116, 673

and justification, 338–39, 600,
654

lack of, 8, 46, 117, 239, 250–51,
284, 287, 343–86, 514, 570,
671

necessary for fruitfulness, 302,
381, 383, 438, 558n18, 681

necessary for validity of Penance,
302

possible by actual grace, 588

as *res et sacramentum*, 288–90,
437n41

and reviviscence, 239, 251, 273,

287, 483
sacramental graces of ongoing,
298, 368
as spiritual offering, 299, 694
res et sacramentum, 273–303
abiding, 273, 279, 280–82,
286–87, 291, 297, 299,
349n14, 353, 355, 358–59,
386, 670–73
analogy with character, 285–87,
295–98, 303, 670
of Anointing of the Sick,
283–87, 295, 297, 300, 303,
304, 353, 359, 441, 670
Christological and ecclesial
dimension of, 278–79,
280–83, 284–87, 291–99,
302–3, 358–59, 670
effect distinct from grace, 273,
280, 287
as efficacious imprinted word,
358, 673
of the Eucharist, 273–79
of Matrimony, 280–83, 670
meaning of, 274–76
mission given by (*see* mission)
of Penance, 278, 287–99, 372,
670
and sacramental grace, 299,
349n14, 353, 355, 357–59
and validity, 301–2
res tantum, 161, 252, 274–80, 283,
290, 292n46, 293, 295, 301, 307,
354, 437, 552, 554, 559, 572, 593,
598, 611, 676
Resurrection of Christ, 101, 104, 166,
363n47, 509n20, 530n72
and Baptism, 140, 142n22, 360,
392–93, 557n17, 572, 573,
685, 693

efficient instrumental cause,
28, 427–28, 445, 447–55,
480–81
exemplar cause, 140, 446–51
participation in, xxxiii–xxxiv,
31–35, 114, 140–41, 186,
286, 360, 392–93, 503n11,
557n17, 572, 573, 682–83,
685, 691, 693
Revelation, 40–42, 61, 109, 126–27,
156, 157n62, 269, 311n6, 312,
321, 322, 329, 391–92, 419,
424–25, 493–94, 496, 536, 579,
585, 589, 611, 635, 645, 667–68
reverence, 44, 108, 187, 360, 377, 379,
474, 521, 534, 537, 541, 575, 597
reviviscence, 239, 251, 483–84, 670
Rogers, Elizabeth Frances, xxxixn19
Roman Catechism. *See Catechism of
the Council of Trent*
Roman Pontifical, 163, 164n93, 165
Root, Michael, 463n12
Rosier-Catach, Irène, 409n39
royal priesthood. *See* priesthood:
common
Rudolph, David, 545nn106–7
Ruether, Rosemary Radford, 520n53

S

Sacram Unctionem Infirmorum (Paul
VI), 105
sacraments of the living and dead,
343–44
sacramentals, 46–47, 54–55, 69,
71–73, 265n103, 520–21, 543,
545, 669
sacramental economy, 3–10, 15–16,
35, 64, 90, 197, 428, 530, 610
sacramental grace, 343–86, 671
as actual graces, 347–49, 352–57,

359–60, 364, 671 (*see also*
    actual grace: sacramental
    grace as)
of Anointing of the Sick,
    372–75, 608, 688–89
of Baptism, 359–61
of Confirmation, 361–66
dispositions for (*see* disposition
    for fruitfulness)
of the Eucharist, 366–67
and the gifts of the Holy Spirit,
    xlii, 352–55, 358–59,
    364–65, 671
of Holy Orders, 377–80
of Matrimony, 354, 375–77, 609
as modality of habitual grace,
    349–54
of Penance, 367–72
and the *res et sacramentum*,
    357–59
sacramentality, 14, 22–26, 28–29, 41,
    57, 80n36, 97–98, 106, 220n100,
    265n103, 266n110, 267n112,
    293n42, 693n42
Sacramentum Caritatis (Benedict
    XVI), 80–81, 261n93, 608n137,
    689–90
Sacramentum Ordinis (Pius XII), 63,
    99n1, 109, 149–51, 164n93
sacramentum tantum, 275–76, 280,
    288
sacrifice
    of Calvary, xxxvi, 10, 16, 28–29,
        88–89, 92, 91, 93, 122n53,
        145–46, 159, 161, 478–81,
        509, 533, 555, 586, 589, 654,
        693–94
    of the lay faithful, 220, 233–34,
        257–59, 299n56, 328,
        362–63, 451, 510n22,

514n37, 646n69, 686–87,
    693–95
of the Mass, 19, 77n29, 95, 102,
    118, 170, 196, 200–1, 207–8,
    220, 245, 255, 258–59,
    261–63, 299, 362–63, 378,
    400, 451, 480–81, 509, 533,
    586, 596–97, 607, 654, 679,
    686–87, 689–91, 694–95,
    696
of the Old Covenant, 479,
    502–3, 515, 526, 529, 533,
    647
Sacrosanctum Concilium, 95, 154n57,
    155, 171
Salaville, S., 161n81
Salmanticenses, 482
salvation history, xxxiv, 29n60, 31, 33,
    35, 59, 133, 138, 141, 143, 146,
    539, 541, 556, 631, 633, 635
Samaria, 8, 104, 209
sanctification. *See* holiness
sanctifying grace
    and Baptism of desire or blood,
        572, 579, 588–90, 625, 641,
        645, 648, 675
    and Baptism as sole ordinary
        means, 557, 639, 641,
        644–45, 659, 662–63, 677
    and Christ's Resurrection, 449,
        451
    and circumcision, 510–14, 567,
        646–48
    common effect of the sacra-
        ments, xlii, 54, 64, 85, 120,
        195, 307–8, 336, 339–40,
        343–45, 353–54, 359,
        488–89, 557, 640, 696
    and divine filiation, 332
    fittingness of, 310–20, 347

and forgiveness of sins, 4, 239, 336–37, 511, 555

as formal cause, 313–315

and gifts of the Spirit, 333, 336

increase of, 336, 343–44, 354, 368, 385, 576, 607, 611

and indwelling, 328, 330–31

for infants who die without Baptism, 659, 662, 663

and instrumental causality, 433, 437, 449, 454, 489, 508

lost through original and mortal sin, xxxv, 251–52, 273, 300, 336–37, 355, 624–26

nature of, 248, 300, 312–19

necessary for salvation, 552–55, 558, 644, 677

and need for faith and repentance, 382–83, 599

obediential potency for, 310, 312, 435–36, 454, 488–89, 641

as participation in divine nature, 116, 313–14, 316, 319, 325, 391

as *res tantum*, 288, 307–8, 572

restored by Penance, 239, 288, 300, 337, 367, 604, 611

and sacramental grace, 344–45, 347–55, 358n38, 371n68, 376, 671

and supernatural virtues, 307, 317–28, 590

Sanders, E. P., 140nn15–17

Santogrossi, Ansgar, 161n81

Sarah, 479

Scheeben, Matthias

    on character, 302n61, 691n38

    on Church as visible and invisible, 17n34

    on Incarnation as archetype for sacraments, 16n32

    on instrumental causality of Christ's humanity, 480–81

    on moral and physical causality, 482

    on *res et sacramentum*, 285n28, 484n74

    on sacrament and mystery, 40–41

    on sacraments as heart and arteries of the Church, xxxiii

Schillebeeckx, Edward, xxxin1, 31n64, 55n57, 292n44, 489–90, 507n17, 515n41

Schleck, Charles A., 153n53

Schmemann, Alexander, 80n36

Schoonenberg, Piet, 489–90

Scotus, Duns, xliii, 275, 409, 411–12, 414n51, 479, 485, 494

seal, 163, 226–35, 238, 242, 244, 248, 249, 252, 270, 409, 415, 515

    circumcision as, 415, 465, 505, 513n36, 515

Second Council of Lyons, 72, 621

Second Vatican Council

    on Baptism, 171, 255–56

    on Church as sacrament, 18–19, 40, 94–98, 156n59

    on Confirmation, 210, 256–58

    on desire for Baptism, 578–79n74, 585–90, 676

    on development of doctrine, 37n1, 99, 667–68

    on ecclesial dimension of sacraments, 64–65, 293

    on *extra ecclesia nulla salus*, 586–88, 651, 655, 676

    on Eucharistic sacrifice, 86, 694

    on faith, 322

on grace of the sacraments, 361, 378

on holiness of minister, 474–75

on Holy Orders, 261–68

on infallibility, 202

on inspiration, 424n12

on limbo, 641–42

on Matrimony, 281, 285, 376–77

on Old Covenant, 516–17, 675

on participation of the laity in threefold mission of Christ, 258

on reform of the liturgy, 154n57

on sacraments ordered to the Eucharist, 93–94, 686–87

on universal salvific will, 578n74, 588, 641, 661–62

Semmelroth, Otto, 472n41

Sepe, Crescenzo, 228n12

seven sacraments, xlii, 9, 48, 69–97, 99, 106–7, 109, 139, 217n95, 344, 346n8, 348, 355, 363, 669, 671, 693n42

Shavuot, 34

Shea, George, 346n7, 348nn12–13

sign, sacramental, 41–65

and creation, 14, 33, 133, 139–42, 200

four elements of, 134, 175

as genus in the definition of sacrament, 52, 483

symbolism of (*see* symbolism)

simplicity of the sacraments, xxxviii, 26, 156, 605, 679–81

sin

mortal (*see* mortal sin)

original (*see* original sin)

sense of, 22n45, 368, 371, 687

venial, 81, 83, 294, 298, 343, 367–68, 370, 373n73,

374n76, 395, 604

Singulari Quadam (Pius XI), 583

Sirilla, Michael G., 267n110, 380n88

Slesinski, Robert F., 93n66

sonship. *See* filiation

Soulen, R. Kendall, 519n50

sower, parable of, 386

Spacil, Theophilus, 73n20, 161n81

spiritual communion, 591–99, 610n139

spirituality, sacramental, 678–96

Stein, Edith, 193n35

subject of the sacraments

dispositions of (*see* disposition for fruitfulness)

of Holy Orders, 110, 175, 195–204, 219

intention in, 175–86

of Matrimony, 111, 189–95

necessary conditions in, 175–205, 219–20

non-Catholic, 204–5

sufficient grace, 578–79, 651, 662

Sukkoth, 34

Sullivan, Francis, 558n18, 566n38, 569n48, 581nn81–86, 583n89, 583n91, 584n93, 644n64, 661n111

Summa Sententiarum, 48–49, 407n33, 559, 639n54

superabundance, xxxvii, xl, 39, 633, 659–60

supernatural end, 302n61, 307, 316, 319–21, 323, 326–27, 333, 335, 347, 486, 626–27, 629–30, 637, 658

supernatural existential, 486, 495, 629n36

supersessionism, 517–21, 539

Sylvester of Ferrara, 432n29

symbol, 3, 14, 19n37, 45n27, 52–53,
    483–85
    intrinsic, xliv, 96n74, 278n11,
        485–89, 495
symbolism, sacramental
    and analogy, 138
    of Baptism, 140–42, 229
    of bread and wine, 145–47
    and causality, 133, 140, 483, 485,
        490–93, 495–96
    of Confirmation, 142–45
    and creation, 14, 133, 139–42,
        200, 556
    and culture and religion, 3, 14,
        53, 133, 148, 669
    of gender complementarity, 175,
        189–95, 219
    of laying on of hands in ordina-
        tion, 148–51
    loss of sensitivity to, xxxvii, 678
    of male gender for priesthood,
        175, 195–201, 219
    of matter and form, 133–71
    not merely conventional, 138–39,
        139n11, 196n41
    of oil for Anointing of the Sick,
        147–48
    and salvation history, 31, 133,
        138, 141, 143, 146, 556
    signifying the Paschal mystery,
        35, 133, 139, 451–52, 455
    signifying past, present, and
        future, 29–35
    signifying sacramental grace, 345
    of subject and minister, 175,
        190–201, 206–20

T

Tanquerey, Adolphe, 348n13

Tapie, Matthew A., 518n48, 528n68
Taymans d'Eypernon, François,
    xliiin29
Temple, 91, 140, 144–45, 213n82,
    220, 329n43, 330, 330–31n46,
    331, 526, 668, 674
Tertullian, 42–43, 69–70, 119,
    145n29, 394–395, 416, 422,
    422n5, 561n27
tevilah, 140–41
Toups, David, 691n37
Theodoret of Cyrus, xxxvi, 9n16
Torah, 34, 523, 541n97
Torrell, Jean-Pierre, 144n27, 449n63,
    452nn70–71, 691n37
transignification, 278–79n11, 489–91
transubstantiation, xli–xlii, 41–42,
    159, 161, 197, 262, 278–79n11,
    289, 422n7, 437, 489–91, 496,
    694
Trent, Council of, xl, 37
    on Anointing of the Sick, xxxii–
        xxxiiin3, 105, 147, 215–16,
        372n72, 374
    on Baptism of desire, 577–78
    on Baptism's necessity, 623–24,
        652
    on character, 253–54
    on Church's power over the
        sacraments, 108, 121n51
    on definition of sacrament, 62
    on the Eucharist, 33n67, 91n62,
        367n59, 385n103, 491,
        596–97
    on Holy Orders, 74, 102,
        150n47, 170n113, 253–54,
        459
    on institution of the sacraments,
        99, 102, 103, 105, 106–7,

109, 112, 121–22
on intention, 175, 180
on justification, 289n34, 332n48,
    337–40, 516n43, 530n72,
    544n105, 551nn4–5, 554n9,
    555n12, 578–79, 623
on Matrimony, 106nn18–19,
    110, 376
on minister of Confirmation,
    210
on Penance, 152n49, 166n97,
    167n103, 214, 296, 303n63,
    370, 603–4
on sacramental efficacy *ex opere
    operato*, xliv, 62, 461n8, 459,
    464–65, 468–72, 475–76,
    488n88, 494n100, 495
on sacraments of the Old and
    New Law, 458, 479, 501,
    505–6, 521n55, 544n105,
    674
on seven sacraments, 74
on threefold temporal dimen-
    sion of sacrament, 32
on universal salvific will, 579,
    661
Trigg, Jonathan, 460n7
Trinity, 40–41, 95, 117, 203, 230, 332,
    672
Trinitarian dimension of sacra-
    ments, xxxviii, 3, 17, 87–88,
    142, 155–56, 166, 228n12, 230,
    235n30, 247, 268–70, 681–82
Trinitarian form of sacraments, 70,
    135, 156–59, 162, 165, 170–71,
    185–86, 230, 396
Turner, Paul, 212n78
typology
    of blood and water from Christ's
        pierced side, xxxv–xxxvi,

118
and fittingness of sacramental
    system, 28–29
Christ as type of the Christian
    life, 450–52
of Good Samaritan, xxxiv–xxxv
of the sacraments, xlv, 35, 45, 57,
    141, 143, 501–5, 520–29,
    534–35, 541

U

understanding, gift of, 5, 333, 336,
    362, 364–65, 379
unfruitful sacramental reception,
    237–38, 301–2, 356n35, 383–85,
    570, 574, 592, 596, 670
universal salvific will of God, 550,
    579, 589, 612–13, 617–18, 643,
    646, 651–53, 661–64, 668,
    676–77

V

Vagaggini, Cyprian, 16, 31n63, 64n82,
    108n22
Valentinian II (emperor), 562–63,
    574–75
validity of sacraments, 109–13, 128,
    148n40, 150–51, 154–56, 161,
    169–72, 176–89, 195, 207–11,
    214–16, 225, 235–38, 241,
    251, 273, 287, 294, 301–2, 304,
    381–86, 401, 458, 471, 474, 571,
    612
Van Den Eynde, Damien, 422n7
Van Roo, William A., 38n2, 40n8,
    44–45n25, 58n65, 107n21,
    111n32, 112n33, 124n59,
    127n65, 381n90, 667n1, 668n2
Vass, George, 97n75, 125n62, 486n81
Vatican I, 202n52–53, 322

Vatican II. *See* Second Vatican
Council
Verbeke, G., 11n19
Vianney, John (saint), 692–93
virtue
analogy with seven sacraments,
82–83, 363, 373
and connaturality, 320
given by the sacraments, 72,
90n59, 141, 358n39,
366–67, 375, 379, 552
infused, 326–28, 363–64, 379,
685
of penance (*see under* Penance)
of religion, 287n31
theological, 82–83, 307, 316, 319,
321–27, 332–33, 335, 368,
512, 521, 553–55, 558, 590
visible word, sacrament as, 61, 135,
466–68
Vollert, Cyril, 96n74, 291n44
Von Hildebrand, Alice, 193n35
Von Hildebrand, Dietrich, 192n34,
193n35, 194–95n37
Vorgrimler, Herbert, 31n63

W

Waldensians, 458
Walsh, Liam G., 80n36, 492nn95–96
Walsh, Milton, xxxvin12
water
in Baptism, 43, 61n72, 100,
109, 119, 135–42, 146n31,
157, 159, 172, 206n58, 243,
256, 284n26, 289n35, 360,
382, 392–93, 395, 399–400,
402–3, 421, 434n33
from Christ's side, xxxin1, xxxv
–xxxviii, xliv, 69, 74, 89,
118–19, 124

figure of Baptism, 5, 144n26
living, 115
Webb, Bruno, 651n85
Weber, Max, xxxviin16, 678n12
White, James F., xxxviin15, 60n67,
60n69
White, Thomas Joseph, 65n83,
315n11, 413nn49–50, 476n49,
479n56
William of Auxerre, on intention,
178n10, 244n53
wine, xxxviii, 6, 92, 109, 111, 135,
138–39, 145–47, 150–51,
159–61, 172
wisdom, gift of, 5, 333, 336, 351n25,
362, 364–65, 375, 379–80
women in the Church, Marian
dimension of the Church,
189–203, 514n37, 696
Word of God, xlivn31, 135, 203,
417n47, 424, 442, 443, 466–68,
492n95
words of power, sacraments as, xxxviii,
xli, 16, 25, 26, 59, 61, 114, 391,
398, 437, 454, 468, 483–85, 496,
673, 680
Wrede, M., 628n32
Wyschogrod, Michael, 535n81,
536–37

X

Xiberta, Bartolomé, 291, 293n48

Y

Yarnold, Edward, xxxixn18, 143n26,
158nn68–72, 159n74, 160n78,
162n87, 233n23, 396nn7–9,
397n10, 398n12, 398n14,
399n15,
Ysebaert, J., 149n42, 227n7

Z

Zheltov, Michael, 161n81
Zizioulas, John D., 80n36, 212n75
Zwingli, Ulrich, 60–61, 253, 460–61,
    518

Scripture Index

Genesis
2:24, 106n18, 190
3:15, 203, 374
3:20, 89, 97
28:12–13, 693

Exodus
14:1–32, 503n11
19:5–6, 502
19:6, 243
29:1–7, 233n24, 503n7
40:12–13, 144n26

Leviticus
8:6–12, 233n24, 503n7, 564n34
14:1–32, 503n11
15:1–33, 140n14
21:15, 564n34, 574

Numbers
11:17, 264
19:11–22, 140n14
19:22, 236n31
27:20–23, 149n41

Deuteronomy
34:9, 149n41

1 Samuel
16:12–13, 233n24

1 Kings
1:38–39, 144n26
18:36–38, 396
19:16, 233n24

Job
510n22, 646n69, 647n73
567
21:14, 580n79

Psalms
4:6, 248
18:5, 569n46
19:1, 52
21:31, 231n20
24:7, xxxiii
26, 144n27
39:13, 183n22
51:17, 5
74:13, 100n4
87:3–7, 89n55
104:15, 146
104:30, 311n5
109:4: 250
118:19, xxxiv
118:72, 512n35
143:10: 335

Wisdom
8:1, 13, 320n20
11:24, 310

797

Isaiah

1:6, 148
1:16–18, 5n3
4:4, 573
11:1–2, 611
11:2, 377n83
11:2–3, xlii, 79, 333, 334
25:6–8, 6
30:15, 600–1
43:18–19, 35n73
50:5, 335
55:10–11, 466, 451n68

Jeremiah

1:5, 559, 639, 645
4:4, 229
23:5–8, 35n73
31:31–33, 673
31:33: 88, 104,
31:31–34, 4–5
31:34, 365

Ezekiel

9:4, 145
33:14, 601
36:24–27, 5, 88, 104, 673,

Zechariah

13:1, 5
Malachi
1:11, 6n6

Matthew

3:11, 116, 673
3:16–17, 17
7:7–11, 551, 552
8:3, 466
8:9, xxxiii
9:5–8, xxxii
10:1, xxxii

10:42, 551
16:19, 206n58, 292
18:18, 292n46
19:3–9, 106
19:10, 375
20:16, 681
21:22, 551n3
25:15, 13
25:29, 357, 386, 614
25:34–46, 555
26:20–29, 102
28:19, 101, 135, 155–58

Mark

1:8, 392
1:15, 383
1:25–26, xxxii
1:27, xxxii
1:40–42, xxxii,
2:5, 25, 391
2:19, 398
4:25, 301n57, 474
6:12–13, xxxii, 104–5
10:2–12, 106
14:17–25, 102
14:24, 134
16:15–16, 95, 207, 613

Luke

1:15, 638n51
2:19, 37n1, 667, 668
2:51, 37n1, 667, 668
3:22, 143
6:19, 9, 114
7:28, 117n42
9:31, 544n104
10:25–37, xxxivn8
10:34, 148
14:10, 641
15:11–52, 688

22:14–20, 88, 102, 159, 206
23:42, 550
23:43, 550
24:49, 75n26

John

1:14, 9
1:31, 116
1:33, 392, 401
3:1–6, 101, 549–50
3:5–6, 392, 399, 400nn17 and 19, 402–3, 421, 566, 568
3:16, 198n44
3:22–26, 101n9
3:22–4:3, 101
4:1–3, 101
6, 102, 139, 464
6:27, 227, 235
6:29, 382
6:41–59, 225n1, 593
6:49, 591, 592
6:51, 277, 392
6:53–54, 550, 591
6:54, 75n26, 593, 595
6:55, 591
6:55–57, 421
6:56, 147n35
6:68–69, 26, 382
7:39, 104
9:31, 472n40
10:10, 312
11:44, 601
14, 329
14–16, 103–4
14:2, 622
14:13, 551n3
14:15–26, 328, 331
14:16–17, 103n14, 365
14:21, 331
14:26, 103n14, 353

15:3, 61n72, 135n3, 382n95
15:5, 312
15:7, 551n3
15:13, 574
15:26–17, 103n14
16:7, 104
16:7–15, 103–4
16:12, 644
16:24, 551n3
17:11, 380–81
17:21–22, 156n59, 380–81
19:34, 118n44
20:21, 207
20:22–23, 103, 117, 196n42, 292n46, 391, 392, 681

Acts

1:4–8, 103, 104
1:13–14, 257
2:15–21, 504
2:16, 5–6, 88, 260
2:17–18, 6
2:38, 6, 383, 156, 383
2:42, 8
2:46, 8, 674
3:1, 525
6:1–6, 8, 102, 110
8, 213n82
8:12–17, 8, 104, 156, 361
8:14–18, 209, 393
8:17–19, 107, 110
10:14, 525
10:44–48, 574
10:45, 538
10:48, 156
11:2, 538
13:3, 149
15, 532
15:1–29, 522, 537–38
16:3, 526

17:28, 79
18:18, 526
19:2–7, 8, 104, 107, 156, 209, 210,
    237, 393, 401
21:20–26, 526, 534, 541
21:24–27, 525

Romans

2:25, 510
3:2, 511n30
3:3, 516
3:22, 382n94
3:24, 338
4:4, 308n1
4:9–12, 510, 505, 510–11, 465,
    513n36, 538
5:5, 317, 328, 340, 337n55, 341,
    352n29, 681
5:10, 340n60
6:2–11, 28, 32, 33, 140, 186, 237n35,
    360, 392, 450, 572, 157n63, 449,
    450n66,
6:12, 259
7, 8
8:14–17, 17, 156, 333, 335, 682
8:24, 337n55, 555n13
8:26–27, 336
9–11, 519n50
10:13, 550
11:29, 516, 517, 518n48, 675n8
12:1–2, 220, 233, 259, 691
16:26, 322

1 Corinthians

1:13–15, 237
1:18–2:2, 375n79
1:27, 379n85
2:9, 233, 321, 635, 681
3:6–7, 471
3:9, 213n82

3:16–17, 329n43
4:1, 108, 134n2
6:11, 340n60
6:19, 329n43
10:1–4, 45
10:2, 596
10:3–4, 592
10:5, 46
10:16–17, 86, 147, 393, 147n36
11:23–25, 88, 102
11:26, 31–32
12:11, 340
12:13, 117
15:54, 449

2 Corinthians

1:20, 228
1:21–22, 144n26, 227–28, 233–35,
    340
3:2-3, 213n82
5:14, 358n39, 367
6:16, 329n43
8:9, 446n60
13:10, 263n95, 438

Galatians

457
2:12, 538
2:20, 475
3:27, 157n61, 383
4:4, 542
4:6–7, 156, 332–33
4:9, 505, 674
5:6, 596

Ephesians

1:9–12, 29n60, 38–39, 42
1:13–14, 228, 235, 340n60
3:2–10, 39
4:1–8, 86,

4:4–6, 237
4:23, 340
4:30, 228, 235
5:25–27, 34, 393, 106, 175, 198
5:25–33, 88, 119, 135, 375–76, 446
5:31–32, 105–6, 393, 375, 690
6:11–12, 255

Philippians
1:6, 315n10
2:5–11, 446, 691
3:14, 360–61
4:7, 371
4:13, 364

Colossians
1:24, 296n55, 446–47, 689
2:11–13, 186, 229, 503n8
3:1–3, 449
4:11, 538

1 Thessalonians
2:13, 466
4:3–5, 377n83
5:18, 644

1 Timothy
2:1–4, 550, 651, 661
2:3–6, 612, 652
4:4, 522n57
4:10, 296n54
4:14–16, 149, 380
6:12, 606

2 Timothy
1:6, 149, 380, 393
1:14, 329n43
2:11, 234
2:13, 516
4:8, 551

Titus
1:5, 266n107
3:4–7, 75n36, 117n41

Hebrews
1:3, 226, 227n9, 244
2:17, 9
4:12, 8, 466
5:1, 134, 208
5:1–10, 690, 692
7:19, 504
7:23–26, 429
7:27, 76n27
9:13–14, 505
10:1, 674
10:14, 452n70
11:6, 339, 382, 555n12, 585, 655

1 Peter
3:15, 493
3:20–21, 593

2 Peter
1:3–4, 231n17, 307, 316, 319

1 John
70n6
2:2, 296n54
2:27, 365, 366n55
4:10, 198n44
4:16, 329n43
5:14–15, 551n3

Revelation
7:3, 145
7:14, 572
9:4, 145
12:1, 203
14:1, 145
18:7, 370n64